I0303634

A PLAIN INTRODUCTION TO THE CRITICISM OF THE NEW TESTAMENT

FOR THE USE OF BIBLICAL STUDENTS

VOLUME I

FREDERICK HENRY AMBROSE SCRIVENER

DEDICATION

[IN THE THIRD EDITION]

TO HIS GRACE

EDWARD, LORD ARCHBISHOP OF CANTERBURY.

MY LORD ARCHBISHOP,

Nearly forty years ago, under encouragement from your venerated predecessor Archbishop Howley, and with the friendly help of his Librarian Dr. Maitland, I entered upon the work of collating manuscripts of the Greek New Testament by examining the copies brought from the East by Professor Carlyle, and purchased for the Lambeth Library in 1805. I was soon called away from this employment—*ἑκὼν ἀέκοντί γε θυμῷ*—to less congenial duties in that remote county, wherein long after it was your Grace's happy privilege to refresh the spirits of Churchmen and Churchwomen, by giving them pious work to do, and an example in the doing of it. What I have since been able to accomplish in the pursuits of sacred criticism, although very much less than I once anticipated, has proved, I would fain hope, not without its use to those who love Holy Scripture, and the studies which help to the understanding of the same.

Among the scholars whose sympathy cheered and aided my Biblical labours from time to time, I have had the honour of including your Grace; yet it would be at once unseemly and fallacious to assume from that circumstance, that the principles of textual criticism which I have consistently advocated have approved themselves to your judgement. All that I can look for or desire in this respect is that I may seem to you to have stated my case fairly and temperately, in earnest controversy with opponents far my superiors in learning and dialectic power, and for whom, in spite of literary differences, I entertain deep respect and true regard.

My Lord, you have been called by Divine Providence to the first place in our Communion, and have entered upon your great office attended by the applauses, the hopeful wishes, and the hearty prayers of the whole Church. May it please God to endow you richly with the Christian gifts as well of wisdom as of courage: for indeed the highest minister of the Church of England, no less than the humblest, will need courage in the coming time, now that faith is waxing cold and adversaries are many.

I am, my Lord Archbishop,

Your obliged and faithful servant,

F. H. A. SCRIVENER.

HENDON VICARAGE,
Whitsuntide, 1883.

PREFACE TO FOURTH EDITION.

At the time of the lamented death of Dr. Scrivener a new edition of his standard work was called for, and it was supposed that the great Master of Textual Criticism had himself made sufficient corrections and additions for the purpose in the margin of his copy. When the publishers committed to me the task of preparation, I was fully aware of the absolute necessity of going far beyond the materials placed at my disposal, if the book were to be really useful as being abreast of the very great progress accomplished in the last ten years. But it was not till I had laboured with absolute loyalty for some months that I discovered from my own observation, and from the advice of some of the first textual critics, how much alteration must at once be made.

Dr. Scrivener evidently prepared the Third Edition under great disadvantage. He had a parish of more than 5,500 inhabitants upon his hands, with the necessity of making provision for increase in the population. The result was that after adding 125 pages to his book he had an attack of paralysis, and so it is not surprising that his work was not wholly conducted upon the high level of his previous publications. The book has also laboured under another and greater disadvantage of too rapid, though unavoidable, growth. The 506 pages of the First Edition have been successively expanded into 626 pages in the Second, 751 in the Third, and 874 in the Fourth; while the framework originally adopted, consisting only of nine chapters, was manifestly inadequate to the mass of material ultimately gathered. It has therefore been found necessary, as the work proceeded, to do violence, amidst much delicate embarrassment, to feelings of loyalty to the author forbidding alteration. The chief changes that have been made are as follows :—

The first intention of keeping the materials within the compass of one volume has been abandoned, and it has been divided into two volumes, with an increase of chapters in each.

Instead of 2,094 manuscripts, as reckoned in the third edition under the six classes, no less than 3,791 have been recorded in this edition, being an increase of 236 beyond the 3,555 of Dr. Gregory, without counting the numerous vacant places which have been filled up.

Most of the accounts of ancient versions have been rewritten by distinguished scholars, who are leaders in their several departments.

The early part of Volume I has been enriched from the admirable book on 'Greek and Latin Palaeography,' by Mr. E. Maunde Thompson, who with great kindness placed the proof-sheets at my disposal before publication.

Changes have been made in the headlines, the indexes, and in the printing, and sometimes in the arrangement, which will, I trust, enable the reader to find his way more easily about the treatise.

And many corrections suggested by eminent scholars have been introduced in different places all through the work.

A most pleasing duty now is to tender my best thanks to the Right Reverend the Lord Bishop of Salisbury and the Rev. H. J. White, M.A., for the rewriting of the chapter on Latin Versions by the latter under Dr. John Wordsworth's supervision, with help from M. Samuel Berger; to the Rev. G. H. Gwilliam, B.D., Fellow of Hertford College, now editing the Peshitto for the University of Oxford, for the improvement of the passages upon the Peshitto and the Curetonian; the Rev. H. Deane, B.D., for additions to the treatment of the Harkleian; and the Rev. Dr. Waller, Principal of St. John's Hall, Highbury, for the results of a collation of the Peshitto and Curetonian; to the Rev. A. C. Headlam, M.A., Fellow of All Souls College, for a revision of the long chapter upon Egyptian Versions; to F. C. Conybeare, Esq., M.A., late Fellow of University College, for rewriting the sections on the Armenian and Georgian Versions; to Professor Margoliouth, M.A., Fellow of New College, for rewriting the sections on the Arabic and Ethiopic Versions; to the Rev. Ll. J. M. Bebb, M.A., Fellow of Brasenose College, for rewriting the section upon the Slavonic Version; to Dr. James W. Bright, Assistant-Professor in the Johns Hopkins University, for rewriting the section on the Anglo-Saxon Version, through Mr. White's kind offices; to E. Maunde Thompson, Esq., D.C.L., LL.D., F.S.A., &c., for kindness already mentioned, and other help, and to G. F. Warner, Esq., M.A., of the Manuscript Department of the British Museum, for correction of some of the notices of cursive MSS. belonging to the Museum, and for other assistance; to J. Rendel Harris, Esq., M.A., Fellow of Clare College and Reader in Palaeology in the University of Cambridge, for much help of a varied nature; to Professor Isaac H. Hall, Ph.D., of New York City, for sending and placing at my disposal many of his publications; to the lamented Professor Bensly, for writing me a letter upon the Syriac Versions; to the Rev. Nicholas Pocock, M.A., of Clifton, for some results of a collation of F and G of St. Paul; to Professor Bernard, D.D., Trinity College, Dublin, for a paper of suggestions; to the Rev. Walter Slater, M.A., for preparing Index II in Vol. I; and to several other kind friends, for assistance of various kinds freely given. The generosity of scholars in communicating out of their stores of learning is a most pleasing feature in the study of the present day. Whatever may be my own shortcomings—and I fear that they have been enhanced by limitations of time and space, and through the effects of ill-health and sorrow—the contributions enumerated cannot but render the present edition of Dr. Scrivener's great work eminently useful to students.

EDWARD MILLER.

9, Bradmore Road, Oxford,
January 17, 1894.

CONTENTS.

CHAPTER VI.

CHAPTER VII.

CHAPTER VIII.

CHAPTER IX.

CHAPTER X.

CHAPTER XI.

CHAPTER XII.

CHAPTER XIII.

CHAPTER XIV.

DESCRIPTION OF THE CONTENTS OF THE LITHOGRAPHED PLATES[1].

PLATE I . . . . *opposite page* 29

1. (1) Alphabet from the Rosetta Stone [B.C. 196], a specimen of capitals.
2. (2) Alphabet from Cod. Sinaiticus } specimens of uncials.
3. (3) Alphabet from Cod. Alexandrinus } specimens of uncials.

PLATE II 32

1. (4) Alphabet from the Cotton Fragment (Evan. N) and Titus C. xv [vi],
2. (5) And from Cod. Nitriensis (Evan. R, Brit. Mus. Add. 17,211).

PLATE III 34

1. (6) Alphabet from Cod. Dublinensis (Evan. Z).
2. (7) From Brit. Mus. Harl. 5598 (Evst. 150), [A.D. 995].
3. (8) From Brit. Mus. Burney 19 (Evan. 569).
   Note that above *psi* in 2 stands the cross-like form of that letter as found in Apoc. B [viii].

PLATE IV 90

1. (9) Extract from Hyperides' Oration for Lycophron, col. 15, l. 23, &c. (Ὑπερίδου Λόγοι, ed. Babington, 1858). Dating between B.C. 100 to A.D. 100, on Egyptian papyrus, in a cursive or running hand. *λυντασ τινα των πο|λιτων αδικως δεο|μαι υμων και ετωι | και αντιβολωι κε|λευσαι καμε καλεσαι|τους συνερουντασ* >. *See* pp. 44, 51.
2. (10) Extract from Philodemus *περὶ κακιῶν* (*Herculanensium voluminum quae supersunt*, fol., Tom. 3, Col. xx. ll. 6–15). *See* pp. 30, 33. *οντως πολυμαθεστατον προσ|αγορευομενον οιεται παντα | δυνασθαι γινωσκειν και ποι|ειν ουχ οιον εαυτον οσ ενιοισ|ουδεν τι φωραται κατεχων | και ου συνορων οτι πολλα δει|ται τριβης αν και απο τησ αυ|τησ γινηται μεθοδου καθα|περ τα τησ ποιητικησ μερη και | διοτι περι τουσ πολυμαθεισ|*.

[1] Unfortunately, it did not occur to us till after the work was nearly all in type to transfer the Lithographed Plates to places opposite the pages which they chiefly illustrate, and that in consequence a few expressions in the text ought to be altered. The advantage of this arrangement appears to be so great as to overbalance the slight inaccuracies alluded to, which cannot now be removed. The plates and their references will, it is hoped, be found easily from the explanations here given.

3. (11[a]) Cod. Friderico-August. [iv], 2 Sam. vii. 10, 11, Septuagint: *σεαυτον καθωσ αρ|χησ και αφ ημερω̄ | ων εταξα κριτασ | επι τον λαον μου | ισ̄λ και εταπινω|σα απαντασ τους | εχθρουσ σου και | αυξησω σε και οι |.*

4. (11[b]) Cod. Sinaiticus, ℵ [iv], Luke xxiv. 33–4: *τη ωρα ϋπεστρε|ψαν εισ ϊερουσα|λημ*[1] *και ευρον η|θροισμενουσ τουσ | ενδεκα και τουσ | συν αυτοισ λεγο|.*

5. (11[c]) Cod. Sin., 1 Tim. iii. 16, *το τησ ευσεβειασ | μυστηριον οσ ε* with a recent correction. *See* II. 391. There are no capital letters in this Plate.

1. (12) Cod. Alexandrinus, A [v], Gen. i. 1–2, Septuagint. These four lines are in bright red, with breathings and accents[2]. Henceforth capital letters begin to appear. *Ἐν ἀρχῇ ἐπόιησεν ὁ θσ̄ τὸν ὀυ|ρανὸν και τὴν γῆν ἡ δὲ γῆ ἦν α'ό|ρατοσ κὰι ἀκατασκεύαστοσ· | και σκότοσ ἐπάνω τῆσ αβύσσου. |*

2. (13) Cod. Alex., Acts xx. 28, in common ink. *See* II. 37. *Προσεχετε εαυτοισ και παντι τω | ποιμνιω· εν ω ϋμασ το πν̄α το | αγιον εθετο επισκοπουσ· | ποιμαινειν την εκκλησιαν | του κῡ ην περιεποιησατο δια | του αιματος του ιδιου· |*

3. (14) Cod. Cotton., Titus C. xv, Evan. N, with Ammonian section and Eusebian canon in the margin. John xv. 20: *του λογου ου | εγω ειπον ὑ|μιν· ουκ εστιν | δουλοσ μιζω̄ | του κῡ αυτου.*

1. (15) Cod. Burney 21 [A.D. 1292], Evan. 571. *See* p. 257. John xxi. 17–18: *πρόβατά μου· ἀμὴν ἀμὴν λέγω σοι· | ὅτε ἦσ νεώτεροσ, ἐζώννυεσ ἐ|αυτὸν· καὶ περιεπάτησ ὅπου ἤθε|λεσ· ὅταν δε γηράσησ, ἐκτενεῖσ|*

2. (16) Cod. Arundel 547, Evst. 257 [ix or x]. *See* p. 345. The open work indicates stops and musical notes in red. John viii. 13–14: *Αυτω δι φαρισᾶι | οι + σὺ περὶ σὲαυτε̃υ | μαρτυρεῖσ ἡ μαρ|τυρία σου ὀυκ ἔσ|τιν ἀληθήσ + ἀπε|*

3. (17) Cod. Nitriensis, R of the Gospels, a palimpsest [vi]. Luke v. 26: *ξαζον τον θν | και επλησθη|σαν φοβου λε|γοντεσ οτι|.*

1. (18) Cod. Dublin., Z of the Gospels, a palimpsest [vi] from Barrett. Matt. xx. 33–4: *ανοιγωσιν οι οφθαλ|μοι ημων | Cπλαγχνισθεισ δε ο ισ̄ | ηψατο των ομματω̄ | αυτων και ευθεωσ|.*

2. (19) Cod. Cyprius, K of the Gospels [ix], John vi. 52–3: *'Εμάχοντο ὀῦν προσ ἀλλήλουσ δι ϊουδαῖοι λε|γοντεσ· πῶσ δύναται ὀῦτοσ ἡμῖν τὴν σάρ|κα δοῦναι φαγεῖν· ἐῖπεν ὀῦν ἀυτοῖσ ὁ ισ̄· α|.* It has the Ammonian section in the margin (*ξς*=66), and a flourish in the place of the Eusebian canon. *See* p. 137.

[1] In later manuscripts Proper Names are often distinguished by a horizontal line placed over them, but no such examples occur in these Plates.

[2] The reader will observe throughout these specimens that the breathings and accents are usually attached to the *first* vowel of a diphthong.

PLATE VIII 105

(20) Cod. Vaticanus, B of the Gospels, Acts and Epistles [iv], taken from Burgon's photograph of the whole page. Mark xvi. 3–8 : μῖν τὸν λίθον ἐκ τῆς | θύρασ τοῦ μνημέῖου | κὰι ἀναβλέψασαι θεω|ροῦσιν ὅτι ἀνακεκύ|λισται ὁ λιθοσ ἦν γὰρ | μέγασ σφόδρα κὰι ἐλ|θοῦσαι ἐισ τὸ μνημεῖ|ον ἔιδον νεανίσκον | καθήμενον ἐν τοῖσ | δεξιοῖσ περιβεβλημέ|νον στολὴν λευκὴν | κὰι ἐξεθαμβήθησαν | ὁ δὲ λέγει ἀυτᾶισ μὴ | ἐκθαμβεῖσθε ῖν̄ ζητει|τε τὸν ναζαρηνὸν τὸ | ἐσταυρωμένον ἠγέρ|θη ὀυκ ἔ'στιν ὧδε ἴδε | ὁ τόποσ ὅπου ἔθηκᾶ | ἀυτὸν ἀλλα ὑπάγετε | ἔιπατε τοῖσ μαθηταῖσ | ἀυτοῦ κὰι τῷ πέτρῳ | ὅτι προάγει ὑμᾶς ἐισ | τὴν γαλιλάιαν ἐκεῖ ἀυ|τὸν ὄψεσθε καθὼσ ἔι|πεν ὑμῖν κὰι ἐξελθοῦ|σαι ἔφυγον ἀπὸ τοῦ | μνημέιου ἔιχεν γὰρ | ἀυτὰσ τρόμοσ κὰι ἔκ|στασισ κὰι ὀυδενὶ ὀυ|δὲν ἔιπον ἐφοβοῦν|το γάρ : Here again, as in Plate IV, no capital letters appear. What follows on the Plate is by a later hand.

PLATE IX 137

1. (21) Cod. Par. Nat. Gr. 62, Evan. L of the Gospels [viii], as also 3 (23) below, are from photographs given by Dean Burgon : *see* pp. 133–4. In the first column stands Mark xvi. 8 with its Ammonian section (σλγ 233) and Eusebian canon (β = 2) : Καὶ ἐξελθουσαι ἐ|φυγον ἀπο τοῦ | μνημειου + ἐι|χεν δὲ αὐτας τρο|μοσ καὶ εκστασεισ· | καὶ ουδενι οὐδεν | εἰπον + ἐφοβουν|το γάρ' + In the second column, after the strange note transcribed by us (II. 388), εστην δε και | ταῦτα φερο|μενα μετα το | ἐφοβουντο | γαρ + | Ἀναστὰσ δὲ πρωῒ | πρωτη σαββατϭ + (ver. 9) *Xi* much resembles that in Plate XI, No. 27.

2. (22) Cod. Nanianus, Evan. U, retraced after Tregelles. Burgon (*Guardian*, Oct. 29, 1873) considers this facsimile unworthy of the original writing, which is 'even, precise, and beautiful.' Mark v. 18 : Βάντοσ αυτου | ἐισ τὸ πλοῖο | παρεκάλει ἀυ|τὸν ὁ δαιμο|νισθεισ ἵνα. The Ammonian section ($\overline{\mu\eta}$ = 48) is in the margin with the Eusebian canon (B, in error for H) underneath. The ν on the other side is by a much later hand. *See* p. 149.

3. (23) Cod. Basil. of the Gospels, Evan. 1 [x ?]. *See* p. 190. Luke i. 1, 2 (the title : ἐυαγγέ[λιον] κατὰ λουκᾶν : being under an elegant arcade) : Ἐπειδήπερ πολλοὶ ἐπεχείρησαν ἀνατάξασθαι | διήγησιν περὶ τῶν πεπληροφορημένων | ἐν ἡμῖν πραγματων . καθὼς παρέδοσαν ἡμῖ | οἱ ἀπαρχῆσ αὐτόπται καὶ ὑπηρεται γενόμενοι |. The numeral in the margin must indicate the Ammonian section, not the larger κεφάλαιον (*see* p. 57).

PLATE X 121

1. (24) Cod. Ephraemi, C, a palimpsest [v], from Tischendorf's facsimile. The upper writing [xii ?] is τοῦ τὴν πληθῦν τῶν | ἐμῶν ἁμαρτημά || σομαι· οἶδα ὅτι μετὰ | τὴν γνῶσιν ἥμαρτον. Translated from St. Ephraem the Syrian. The earlier text is 1 Tim. iii. 15–16 : ωμα τησ αληθείασ· | Και ομολογουμενωσ μέγα ἐστιν το τησ ἐυσεβειασ μυ|'στηριον· $\overline{\theta\sigma}$ ἐφανερωθη εν σαρκι· εδικαιωθη ἐν πνῖ. For the accents, &c., *see* p. 123.

2. (25) Cod. Laud. 35, E of the Acts [vi], Latin *and* Greek, in a sort of stichometry. Acts xx. 28 : regere | ecclesiam | domini || *ποιμενειν* | *την εκκλησιαν* | *του κυ.* Below are specimens of six letters taken from other parts of the manuscript. *See* p. 169.

3. (26) Matt. i. 1–3, Greek and Latin, from the Complutensian Polyglott, A.D. 1514. *See* II. 176.

PLATE XI 131

1. (27) Cod. Basil., Evan. E [vii], from a photograph given by Dean Burgon, Mark i. 5–6 : *Προσ αὐτὸν. πᾶσα ἡ ἰουδαία* | *χωρα. και οἱ ἱεροσολυμῖται·* | *και ἐβαπτιζοντο παντεσ,* | *ἐν τῶ ἰορδάνη ποταμῶ ὑ|π' ἀυτοῦ . ἐξομολογόυμε|νοι τὰσ ἁμαρτίασ αυτῶν·* | *Ηῦ δε ὁ ἰωάννησ ενδεδυμένοσ.* The harmonizing references will be found underneath, and some stops in the text (*see* p. 48). The next two specimens are retraced after Tregelles.

2. (28) Cod. Boreeli, Evan. F [viii–x], Mark x. 13 (Ammonian section *only*, $\overline{\rho\varsigma}$ = 106) : *Καὶ προσέφερον* | *αὐτῶ παιδία* | *ἵν' ἅψηται ἀυ|τῶν· δι δὲ μαθη|τὰι ἐπετίμων* |.

3. (29) Cod. Harleian. 5684, Evan. G [x], Matt. v. 30–1 : *βληθη· εισ γεεν|ναν· τε τῆσ λε.* | *'Ερρηθη δέ· "Οτι ὅσ* | *αν ἀπολυση την* | *γυνάικα ἀυτοῦ·* | *αρ (ἀρχὴ)* stands in the margin of the new Lesson.

4. (30) Cod. Bodleian., Λ of the Gospels [x or ix], in *sloping* uncials, Luke xviii. 26, 27, and 30 : *σαντεσ· κὰι Τίσ,* | *δύναται σωθῆναι·* | *ὁ δὲ ισ. ἐῖπεν·* || *τοῦτω· κὰι ἐν* | *τῶ ἀιῶνι τῶ ἐρ|χομένω ζωὴν* |. *See* p. 160.

PLATE XII 134

1. (31) Cod. Wolfii B, Evan. H [ix], John i. 38–40 : *τοὺσ ἀκολουθοῦντασ λέγει ἀυτοῖσ + τί ζη|τεῖτε + δι δε . ἐῖπον ἀυτῶ + ραββεί· ὃ λέγε|ται ἑρμηνευόμενον διδάσκαλε ποῦ μέ|νεισ + λέγει ἀυτοῖσ + ἔρχεσθε και ἴδετε + ἦλ|.* Retraced after Tregelles : in the original the dark marks seen in our facsimile are no doubt red musical notes.

2. (32) Cod. Campianus, Evan. M [ix], from a photograph of Burgon's. John vii. 53—viii. 2 : *Καὶ ἐπορέυθησαν ἕκα|στοσ : ἐις τὸν ὄικον* | *ἀυτοῦ· ισ δὲ ἐπορεῦ|θη ἐισ τὸ ὄροσ τῶν ἐ|λαιῶν . ὄρθρου δὲ πά|.* Observe the asterisk set against the passage.

3. (33) Cod. Emman. Coll. Cantab., Act. 53, Paul. 30 [xii]. *See* p. 288. This minute and elegant specimen, beginning Rom. v. 21, *χυ τοῦ κυ ἡμων·* and ending vi. 7, *δεδικαίωται ἀ*, is left to exercise the reader's skill.

4. (34) Cod. Ruber., Paul. M [x]. *See* p. 184. 2 Cor. i. 3–5 : *παρακλήσεωσ· ὁ παρακαλῶν* | *ἡμᾶσ ἐπὶ πάση Τῆι θλίψει· ἐισ τὸ* | *δύνασθαι ἡμᾶσ παρακαλεῖν* | *τοὺς ἐν πάση θλίψει διὰ τῆς πα|ρακλήσεωσ ἧσ παρεκαλούμε|θα ἀυτοὶ ὑπὸ τοῦ θυ. ὅτι καθῶσ* |.

5. (35) Cod. Bodleian., Evan. Γ of the Gospels [ix]. *See* p. 155. Mark viii. 33 : *πιστραφεὶσ καὶ ἰδὼν τουσ μα|θητὰσ ἀυτοῦ. ἐπετίμησεν τῶ* | *πέτρω λέγων. ὕπαγε ὀπίσω μ**ο*** |.

PLATE XIII 343

1. (36) Parham. 18, Evst. 234 [A.D. 980], Luke ix. 34: *γοντοσ ἐγένετο νε|φέλη κὰι ἐπεσκίασεν | ἀυτοὺσ ἐφοβήθησά|.* Annexed are six letters taken from other parts of the manuscript.

2. (37) Cod. Burney 22, Evst. 259 [A.D. 1319]. The Scripture text is Mark vii. 30: *βεβλημέν ον ἐ|πὶ τὴν κλίνην ϗ | τὸ δαιμόνιον ἐξε|λή-λυθῶσ* :—The subscription which follows is given at length in p. 43, note 3.

3. (38) Cod. Monacensis, Evan. X [ix], retraced after Tregelles. *See* p. 152. Luke vii. 25–6: *τίοισ ἠμφιεσμένον· ἴδου δι | ἐν ἵματισμώ ἐνδοξω και τρυ|φῆ ὑπάρχοντεσ ἐν τοισ βασιλεί | οισ εισὶν· ἀλλα τί ἐξεληλυθα |.*

4. (39) Cod. Par. Nat. Gr. 14, or Evan. 33: from a photograph of Burgon's. *See* p. 195. Luke i. 8–11: *ξει τῆς ἐφημερίασ ἀυτοῦ ἔναντι τοῦ $\overline{κυ}$ κατὰ τὸ ἔθοσ τῆς ἱερατείασ. ἔλαχεν τοῦ θυμιᾶ|σαι εἰσελθὼν εἰς τὸν ναὸν τοῦ $\overline{κυ}$. κὰι πᾶν τὸ πλῆθοσ ἦν περ λαοῦ προσευχόμενον ἔξω τῆ | ὥρα τοῦ θυμιάματοσ. ὤφθη δε ἀυτῶ ἄγγελος $\overline{κυ}$ ἑστὼσ ἐκδεξιὼν τοῦ θυσιαστηρίου, τοῦ θυ|.*

5. (40) Cod. Leicestrensis, Evan. 69, Paul. 37 [xiv]. *See* p. 202. 1 Tim. iii. 16: *τῆς εὐσεβε(?)ίας μυστήριον· ὁ θὸ ἐφανερώθη ἐν σαρ|κί· ἐδικαιώθη ἐν πνεύματι· ὤφθη ἀγγέλοις· | ἐκηρύχθη ἐν ἔθνεσιν· ἐπιςεύθη ἐν κόσμω· ἀνελή—.*

PLATE XIV. Contains specimens of open leaves of the two chief bilingual manuscripts 124

1. (41) Cod. Claromontanus or Paul. D (1 Cor. xiii. 5–8), p. 173.

2. (42) Cod. Bezae or Evan. and Act. D (John xxi. 19–23), p. 124. Observe the stichometry, the breathings, &c., of the Pauline facsimile (which we owe to Dean Burgon's kindness). These codices, so remarkably akin as well in their literary history as in their style of writing and date (vi or v), will easily be deciphered by the student.

3. (43) Cod. Rossanensis or Evan. Σ (p. 163), is one of the most interesting, as it is amongst the latest of our discoveries. Our passage is Matt. vi. 13, 14: *πονηρου οτι | σου εστιν η βα|σιλεια και η δυ|ναμισ και η δο|ξα εισ τουσ αιω|νασ αμην. | Єαν γαρ αφητε | τοισ $\overline{ανοισ}$ τα | παραπτωματα |.* In the margin below the capital Є is the Ammonian section *μδ* (44) and the Eusebian canon *ϛ* (66): *ανοισ* is an abbreviation for *ἀνθρώποις*. All is written in silver on fine purple vellum.

PLATE XV 166

Cod. Beratinus or Evan. Φ, Matt. xxvi. 19–20: *ως συνεταξεν | αυτοις ΐς και ητοιμασαν το | πασχα· | Οψιας δε γενομενης ανε|κειτο μετα των | δωδεκα μαθη|των· και αισθι|.* Observe the reference given for the paragraph to the Ammonian section and Eusebian canon on the left: *σοθ* = 279, *δ* = 4. The MS. is written in two columns, and the initial letters of each line are exhibited on the right, with *Am.* and *Eus.*, *σπα* = 279, and *β* = 2; which as in the other case are in a different hand.

ADDENDA ET CORRIGENDA.

Pages 1-224, *passim*, for reasons given in Vol. II. 96 note, *for* Memphitic *read* Bohairic; *for* Thebaic *read* Sahidic.

P. 7, l. 25, *for* Chapter XI *read* Chapter XII.

P. 14, l. 20, *for* Chapter X *read* Chapter XI.

P. 87, l. 19, *for* Synaxaria *read* Menologies.

P. 119, ll. 11 and 12 from bottom, *for* 93 *read* 94; *for* Memoranda in our Addenda *read* ingenious argument in n. 1.

P. 149, T[f] Horner, *add* now in the Bodleian at Oxford.

P. 214, l. 8 from bottom, *for* 464 *read* iv. 64.

P. 224, Evan. 250, l. 3, *for* p. 144 *read* p. 150.

P. 226, Evan. 274, l. 2 from end, *for* Chapter IX *read* Chapter XII.

P. 255, l. 6 from bottom, *for* Bibl. Gr. L. *read* Bibl. Gr. d.

P. 335, l. 1, *for* 41 *read* 4.

P. 343, l. 12, *for* Ev. 1 (2) *read* Ev. 1 (1).

INTRODUCTION

TO

THE CRITICISM OF THE TEXT OF THE NEW TESTAMENT.

CHAPTER I.

PRELIMINARY CONSIDERATIONS.

1. WHEN God was pleased to make known to man His purpose of redeeming us through the death of His Son, He employed for this end the general laws, and worked according to the ordinary course of His Providential government, so far as they were available for the furtherance of His merciful design. A revelation from heaven, in its very notion, implies supernatural interposition; yet neither in the first promulgation nor in the subsequent propagation of Christ's religion, can we mark any *waste* of miracles. So far as they were needed for the assurance of honest seekers after truth, they were freely resorted to: whensoever the principles which move mankind in the affairs of common life were adequate to the exigences of the case, more unusual and (as we might have thought) more powerful means of producing conviction were withheld, as at once superfluous and ineffectual. Those who heard not Moses and the prophets would scarcely be persuaded, though one rose from the dead.

2. As it was with respect to the *evidences* of our faith, so also with regard to the volume of Scripture. God willed that His Church should enjoy the benefit of His written word, at once as a rule of doctrine and as a guide unto holy living. For

this cause He so enlightened the minds of the Apostles and Evangelists by His Spirit, that they recorded what He had imprinted on their hearts or brought to their remembrance, without the risk of error in anything essential to the verity of the Gospel. But this main point once secured, the rest was left, in a great measure, to themselves. The style, the tone, the language, perhaps the special occasion of writing, seem to have depended much on the taste and judgement of the several penmen. Thus in St. Paul's Epistles we note the profound thinker, the great scholar, the consummate orator: St. John pours forth the simple utterings of his gentle, untutored, affectionate soul: in St. Peter's speeches and letters may be traced the impetuous earnestness of his noble yet not faultless character. Their individual tempers and faculties and intellectual habits are clearly discernible, even while they are speaking to us in the power and by the inspiration of the Holy Ghost.

3. Now this self-same parsimony in the employment of miracles which we observe with reference to Christian evidences and to the inspiration of Scripture, we might look for beforehand, from the analogy of divine things, when we proceed to consider the methods by which Scripture has been preserved and handed down to us. God *might*, if He would, have stamped His revealed will visibly on the heavens, that all should read it there: He *might* have so completely filled the minds of His servants the Prophets and Evangelists, that they should have become mere passive instruments in the promulgation of His counsel, and the writings they have delivered to us have borne no traces whatever of their individual characters: but for certain causes which we can perceive, and doubtless for others beyond the reach of our capacities, He has chosen to do neither the one nor the other. And so again with the subject we propose to discuss in the present work, namely, the relation our existing text of the New Testament bears to that which originally came from the hands of the sacred penmen. Their autographs *might* have been preserved in the Church as the perfect standards by which all accidental variations of the numberless copies scattered throughout the world should be corrected to the end of time: but we know that these autographs perished utterly in the very infancy of Christian history. Or if it be too much to expect that the autographs of the inspired writers should escape the fate which has over-

taken that of every other known relique of ancient literature, God *might* have so guided the hand or fixed the devout attention both of copyists during the long space of fourteen hundred years before the invention of printing, and of compositors and printers of the Bible for the last four centuries, that no jot or tittle should have been changed of all that was written therein. Such a course of Providential arrangement we must confess to be quite possible, but it could have been brought about and maintained by nothing short of a continuous, unceasing miracle;—by making fallible men (nay, many such in every generation) for one purpose absolutely infallible. If the complete identity of all copies of Holy Scripture prove to be a fact, we must of course receive it as such, and refer it to its sole Author: yet we may confidently pronounce beforehand, that such a fact could not have been reasonably anticipated, and is not at all agreeable to the general tenour of God's dealings with us.

4. No one who has taken the trouble to examine any two editions of the Greek New Testament needs be told that this supposed complete resemblance in various copies of the holy books is not founded on fact. Even several impressions derived from the same standard edition, and professing to exhibit a text positively the same, differ from their archetype and from each other, in errors of the press which no amount of care or diligence has yet been able to get rid of. If we extend our researches to the manuscript copies of Scripture or of its versions which abound in every great library in Christendom, we see in the very best of them variations which we must at once impute to the fault of the scribe, together with many others of a graver and more perplexing nature, regarding which we can form no probable judgement, without calling to our aid the resources of critical learning. The more numerous and venerable the documents within our reach, the more extensive is the view we obtain of the variations (or VARIOUS READINGS as they are called) that prevail in manuscripts. If the number of these variations was rightly computed at thirty thousand in Mill's time, a century and a half ago, they must at present amount to at least fourfold that quantity.

5. As the New Testament far surpasses all other remains of antiquity in value and interest, so are the copies of it yet existing in manuscript and dating from the fourth century of our

era downwards, far more numerous than those of the most celebrated writers of Greece or Rome. Such as have been already discovered and set down in catalogues are hardly fewer than three thousand six hundred, and more must still linger unknown in the monastic libraries of the East. On the other hand, manuscripts of the most illustrious classic poets and philosophers are far rarer and comparatively modern. We have no complete copy of Homer himself prior to the thirteenth century, though some considerable fragments have been recently brought to light which may plausibly be assigned to the fifth century; while more than one work of high and deserved repute has been preserved to our times only in a single copy. Now the experience we gain from a critical examination of the few classical manuscripts that survive should make us thankful for the quality and abundance of those of the New Testament. These last present us with a vast and almost inexhaustible supply of materials for tracing the history, and upholding (at least within certain limits) the purity of the sacred text: every copy, if used diligently and with judgement, will contribute somewhat to these ends. So far is the copiousness of our stores from causing doubt or perplexity to the genuine student of Holy Scripture, that it leads him to recognize the more fully its general integrity in the midst of partial variation. What would the thoughtful reader of Aeschylus give for the like guidance through the obscurities which vex his patience, and mar his enjoyment of that sublime poet?

6. In regard to modern works, it is fortunate that the art of printing has wellnigh superseded the use of *verbal* or (as it has been termed) *Textual* criticism. When a book once issues from the press, its author's words are for the most part fixed, beyond all danger of change; graven as with an iron pen upon the rock for ever. Yet even in modern times, as in the case of Barrow's posthumous works and Pepys's Diary and Lord Clarendon's History of the Rebellion, it has been occasionally found necessary to correct or enlarge the early editions, from the original autographs, where they have been preserved. The text of some of our older English writers (Beaumont and Fletcher's plays are a notable instance) would doubtless have been much improved by the same process, had it been possible; but the criticism of Shakespeare's dramas is perhaps the most delicate and difficult problem in the whole history of literature

since that great genius was so strangely contemptuous of the praise of posterity, that even of the few plays that were published in his lifetime the text seems but a gathering from the scraps of their respective parts which had been negligently copied out for the use of the actors.

7. The design of the science of TEXTUAL CRITICISM, as applied to the Greek New Testament, will now be readily understood. By collecting and comparing and weighing the variations of the text to which we have access, it aims at bringing back that text, so far as may be, to the condition in which it stood in the sacred autographs; at removing all spurious additions, if such be found in our present printed copies; at restoring whatsoever may have been lost or corrupted or accidentally changed in the lapse of eighteen hundred years. We need spend no time in proving the value of such a science, if it affords us a fair prospect of appreciable results, resting on grounds of satisfactory evidence. Those who believe the study of the Scriptures to be alike their duty and privilege, will surely grudge no pains when called upon to separate the pure gold of God's word from the dross which has mingled with it through the accretions of so many centuries. Though the criticism of the sacred volume is inferior to its right interpretation in point of dignity and practical results, yet it must take precedence in order of time: for how can we reasonably proceed to investigate the sense of holy writ, till we have done our utmost to ascertain its precise language?

8. The importance of the study of Textual criticism is sometimes freely admitted by those who deem its successful cultivation difficult, or its conclusions precarious; the rather as Biblical scholars of deserved repute are constantly putting forth their several recensions of the text, differing not a little from each other. Now on this point it is right to speak clearly and decidedly. There is certainly nothing in the nature of critical science which ought to be thought hard or abstruse, or even remarkably dry and repulsive. It is conversant with varied, curious, and interesting researches, which have given a certain serious pleasure to many intelligent minds; it patiently gathers and arranges those facts of *external* evidence on which alone it ventures to construct a revised text, and applies them according to rules or canons of *internal* evidence, whether suggested by

experience, or resting for their proof on the plain dictates of common sense. The more industry is brought to these studies, the greater the store of materials accumulated, so much the more fruitful and trustworthy the results have usually proved; although beyond question the true application even of the simplest principles calls for discretion, keenness of intellect, innate tact ripened by constant use, a sound and impartial judgement. No man ever attained eminence in this, or in any other worthy accomplishment, without much labour and some natural aptitude for the pursuit; but the criticism of the Greek Testament is a field in whose culture the humblest student may contribute a little that shall be really serviceable; few branches of theology are able to promise, even to those who seek but a moderate acquaintance with it, so early and abundant reward for their pains.

9. Nor can Textual criticism be reasonably disparaged as tending to precarious conclusions, or helping to unsettle the text of Scripture. Even putting the matter on the lowest ground, critics have not *created* the variations they have discovered in manuscripts or versions. They have only taught us how to look ascertained phaenomena in the face, and try to account for them; they would fain lead us to estimate the relative value of various readings, to decide upon their respective worth, and thus at length to eliminate them. While we confess that much remains to be done in this department of Biblical learning, we are yet bound to say that, chiefly by the exertions of scholars of the last and present generations, the debateable ground is gradually becoming narrower, not a few strong controversies have been decided beyond the possibility of reversal, and while new facts are daily coming to light, critics of very opposite sympathies are learning to agree better as to the right mode of classifying and applying them. But even were the progress of the science less hopeful than we believe it to be, one great truth is admitted on all hands;—the almost complete freedom of Holy Scripture from the bare suspicion of wilful corruption; the absolute identity of the testimony of every known copy in respect to doctrine, and spirit, and the main drift of every argument and every narrative through the entire volume of Inspiration. On a point of such vital moment I am glad to cite the well-known and powerful statement of the great

Bentley, at once the profoundest and the most daring of English critics: 'The real text of the sacred writers does not now (since the originals have been so long lost) lie in any MS. or edition, but is dispersed in them all. 'Tis competently exact indeed in the worst MS. now extant; nor is one article of faith or moral precept either perverted or lost in them; choose as awkwardly as you will, choose the worst by design, out of the whole lump of readings.' And again: 'Make your 30,000 [variations] as many more, if numbers of copies can ever reach that sum: all the better to a knowing and a serious reader, who is thereby more richly furnished to select what he sees genuine. But even put them into the hands of a knave or a fool, and yet with the most sinistrous and absurd choice, he shall not extinguish the light of any one chapter, nor so disguise Christianity, but that every feature of it will still be the same[1].' Thus hath God's Providence kept from harm the treasure of His written word, so far as is needful for the quiet assurance of His church and people.

10. It is now time for us to afford to the uninitiated reader some general notion of the nature and extent of the various readings met with in manuscripts and versions of the Greek Testament. We shall try to reduce them under a few distinct heads, reserving all formal discussion of their respective characters and of the authenticity of the texts we cite for the next volume (Chapter XI).

(1) To begin with variations of the gravest kind. In two, though happily in only two instances, the genuineness of whole passages of considerable extent, which are read in our printed copies of the New Testament, has been brought into question. These are the weighty and characteristic paragraphs Mark xvi. 9–20 and John vii. 53—viii. 11. We shall hereafter defend these passages, the first without the slightest misgiving, the second with certain reservations, as entitled to be regarded authentic portions of the Gospels in which they stand.

(2) Akin to these omissions are several considerable interpolations, which, though they have never obtained a place in the printed text, nor been approved by any critical editor, are

[1] 'Remarks upon a late Discourse of Free Thinking by Phileleutherus Lipsiensis,' Part i, Section 32.

supported by authority too respectable to be set aside without some inquiry. One of the longest and best attested of these paragraphs has been appended to Matt. xx. 28, and has been largely borrowed from other passages in the Gospels (see below, class 9). It appears in several forms, slightly varying from each other, and is represented as follows in a document as old as the fifth century:

'But you, seek ye that from little things ye may become great, and not from great things may become little. Whenever ye are invited to the house of a supper, be not sitting down in the honoured place, lest should come he that is more honoured than thou, and to thee the Lord of the supper should say, Come near below, and thou be ashamed in the eyes of the guests. But if thou sit down in the little place, and he that is less than thee should come, and to thee the Lord of the supper shall say, Come near, and come up and sit down, thou also shalt have more glory in the eyes of the guests[1].'

We subjoin another paragraph, inserted after Luke vi. 4 in only a single copy, the celebrated Codex Bezae, now at Cambridge: 'On the same day he beheld a certain man working on the sabbath, and said unto him, Man, blessed art thou if thou knowest what thou doest; but if thou knowest not, thou art cursed and a transgressor of the law.'

(3) A shorter passage or mere clause, whether inserted or not in our printed books, may have appeared originally in the form of a marginal note, and from the margin have crept into the text, through the wrong judgement or mere oversight of the scribe. Such we have reason to think is the history of 1 John v. 7, the verse relating to the Three Heavenly Witnesses, once so earnestly maintained, but now generally given up as spurious. Thus too Acts viii. 37 may have been derived from some Church Ordinal: the last clause of Rom. viii. 1 (μὴ κατὰ σάρκα περιπατοῦσιν, ἀλλὰ κατὰ πνεῦμα) is perhaps like a gloss on τοῖς ἐν Χριστῷ Ἰησοῦ: εἰκῇ in Matt. v. 22[2] and ἀναξίως in 1 Cor. xi. 29 might have been inserted to modify statements that seemed too strong: τῇ ἀληθείᾳ

[1] I cite from the late Canon Cureton's over-literal translation in his 'Remains of a very antient recension of the four Gospels in Syriac,' in the Preface to which (pp. xxxv–xxxviii) is an elaborate discussion of the evidence for this passage.

[2] But see Dean Burgon's 'The Revision Revised,' pp. 358–361.

μὴ πείθεσθαι Gal. iii. 1 is precisely such an addition as would help to round an abrupt sentence (compare Gal. v. 7). Some critics would account in this way for the adoption of the doxology Matt. vi. 13; of the section relating to the bloody sweat Luke xxii. 43, 44; and of that remarkable verse, John v. 4: but we may well hesitate before we assent to their views.

(4) Or a genuine clause is lost by means of what is technically called Homoeoteleuton (ὁμοιοτέλευτον), when the clause ends in the same word as closed the preceding sentence, and the transcriber's eye has wandered from the one to the other, to the entire omission of the whole passage lying between them. This source of error (though too freely appealed to by Meyer and some other commentators hardly less eminent than he) is familiar to all who are engaged in copying writing, and is far more serious than might be supposed prior to experience. In 1 John ii. 23 ὁ ὁμολογῶν τὸν υἱὸν καὶ τὸν πατέρα ἔχει is omitted in many manuscripts, because τὸν πατέρα ἔχει had ended the preceding clause: it is not found in our commonly received Greek text, and even in the Authorized English version is printed in italics. The whole verse Luke xvii. 36, were it less slenderly supported, might possibly have been early lost through the same cause, since vv. 34, 35, 36 all end in ἀφεθήσεται. A safer example is Luke xviii. 39, which a few copies omit for this reason only. Thus perhaps we might defend in Matt. x. 23 the addition after φεύγετε εἰς τὴν ἄλλην of κἂν ἐν τῇ ἑτέρᾳ διώκωσιν ὑμᾶς, φεύγετε εἰς τὴν ἄλλην (ἑτέραν being substituted for the first ἄλλην), the eye having passed from the first φεύγετε εἰς τήν to the second. The same effect is produced, though less frequently, when two or more sentences *begin* with the same words, as in Matt. xxiii. 14, 15, 16 (each of which commences with οὐαὶ ὑμῖν), one of the verses being left out in some manuscripts.

(5) Numerous variations occur in the order of words, the sense being slightly or not at all affected; on which account this species of various readings was at first much neglected by collators. Examples abound everywhere: e.g. τὶ μέρος or μέρος τι Luke xi. 36; ὀνόματι Ἀνανίαν or Ἀνανίαν ὀνόματι Acts ix. 12; ψυχρὸς οὔτε ζεστός or ζεστὸς οὔτε ψυχρός Apoc. iii. 16. The order of the sacred names Ἰησοῦς Χριστός is perpetually changed, especially in St. Paul's Epistles.

(6) Sometimes the scribe has mistaken one word for another, which differs from it only in one or two letters. This happens chiefly in cases when the *uncial* or capital letters in which the oldest manuscripts are written resemble each other, except in some fine stroke which may have decayed through age. Hence in Mark v. 14 we find ΑΝΗΓΓΕΙΛΑΝ or ΑΠΗΓΓΕΙΛΑΝ; in Luke xvi. 20 ΗΛΚΩΜΕΝΟC or ΕΙΛΚΩΜΕΝΟC; so we read Δαυίδ or Δαβίδ indifferently, as, in the later or *cursive* character, β and υ have nearly the same shape. Akin to these errors of the eye are such transpositions as ΕΛΑΒΟΝ for ΕΒΑΛΟΝ or ΕΒΑΛΛΟΝ, Mark xiv. 65: omissions or insertions of the same or similar letters, as ΕΜΑCCΩΝΤΟ or ΕΜΑCΩΝΤΟ Apoc. xvi. 10: ΑΓΑΛΛΙΑCΘΗΝΑΙ or ΑΓΑΛΛΙΑΘΗΝΑΙ John v. 35: and the dropping or repetition of the same or a similar syllable, as ΕΚΒΑΛΛΟΝΤΑΔΑΙΜΟΝΙΑ or ΕΚΒΑΛΛΟΝΤΑΤΑΔΑΙΜΟΝΙΑ Luke ix. 49; ΟΥΔΕΔΕΔΟΞΑCΤΑΙ or ΟΥΔΕΔΟΞΑCΤΑΙ 2 Cor. iii. 10; ΑΠΑΞΕΞΕΔΕΧΕΤΟ or ΑΠΕΞΕΔΕΧΕΤΟ 1 Pet. iii. 20. It is easy to see how the ancient practice of writing uncial letters without leaving a space between the words must have increased the risk of such variations as the foregoing.

(7) Another source of error is described by some critics as proceeding *ex ore dictantis*, in consequence of the scribe writing from dictation, without having a copy before him. One is not, however, very willing to believe that manuscripts of the better class were executed on so slovenly and careless a plan. It seems more simple to account for the *itacisms* [1] or confusion of certain vowels and diphthongs having nearly the same sound, which exist more or less in manuscripts of every age, by assuming that a vicious pronunciation gradually led to a loose mode of orthography adapted to it. Certain it is that itacisms are much more plentiful in the original subscriptions and marginal notes of the writers of mediaeval books, than in the text which they copied from older documents. Itacisms prevailed the most extensively from the eighth to the twelfth century, but not by any means during that period exclusively:—indeed, they are found frequently in the oldest existing manuscripts. In the most ancient manuscripts the principal changes are between ι and ει, αι and ε,

[1] The word ἠτακισμός or ἰτακισμός is said to have been first used by Cassiodorus (A. D. 468-560?). See Migne, Patr. Lat. t. 70, col. 1128.

though others occur: in later times η ι and ει, η οι and υ, even ο and ω, η and ε, are used almost promiscuously. Hence it arises that a very large portion of the various readings brought together by collators are of this description, and although in the vast majority of instances they serve but to illustrate the character of the manuscripts which exhibit them, or the fashion of the age in which they were written, they sometimes affect the grammatical form (e.g. ἔγειρε or ἔγειραι Mark iii. 3; Acts iii. 6; *passim*: ἴδετε or εἴδετε Phil. i. 30), or the construction (e.g. ἰάσωμαι or ἰάσομαι Matt. xiii. 15: οὐ μὴ τιμήσῃ or οὐ μὴ τιμήσει Matt. xv. 5: ἵνα καυθήσωμαι or ἵνα καυθήσομαι 1 Cor. xiii. 3, compare 1 Pet. iii. 1), or even the sense (e.g. ἑταίροις or ἑτέροις Matt. xi. 16: μετὰ διωγμῶν or, as in a few copies, μετὰ διωγμόν Mark x. 30: καυχᾶσθαι δὴ οὐ συμφέρει or καυχᾶσθαι δεῖ· οὐ συμφέρει 2 Cor. xii. 1: ὅτι χρηστὸς ὁ Κύριος or ὅτι χριστὸς ὁ Κύριος 1 Pet. ii. 3). To this cause we may refer the perpetual interchange of ἡμεῖς and ὑμεῖς, with their oblique cases, throughout the whole Greek Testament: e.g. in the single epistle of 1 Peter, ch. i. 3; 12; ii. 21 *bis*; iii. 18; 21; v. 10. Hence we must pay the less regard to the reading ἡμέτερον Luke xvi. 12, though found in two or three of our chief authorities: in Acts xvii. 28 τῶν καθ' ἡμᾶς, the reading of the great Codex Vaticanus and a few late copies, is plainly absurd. On the other hand, a few cases occur wherein that which at first sight seems a mere *itacism*, when once understood, affords an excellent sense, e.g. καθαρίζων Mark iii. 19, and may be really the true form.

(8) Introductory clauses or Proper Names are frequently interpolated at the commencement of Church-lessons (περικοπαί), whether from the margin of ordinary manuscripts of the Greek Testament (where they are usually placed for the convenience of the reader), or from the Lectionaries or proper Service Books, especially those of the Gospels (Evangelistaria). Thus in our English Book of Common Prayer the name of Jesus is introduced into the Gospels for the 14th, 16th, 17th, and 18th Sundays after Trinity; and whole clauses into those for the 3rd and 4th Sundays after Easter, and the 6th and 24th after Trinity[1]. To this cause may be due the prefix εἶπε δὲ ὁ Κύριος Luke

[1] To this list of examples from the Book of Common Prayer, Dean Burgon ('The last twelve verses of St. Mark's Gospel Vindicated' p. 215) adds the Gospels

vii. 31; *καὶ στραφεὶς πρὸς τοὺς μαθητὰς εἶπε* Luke x. 22; and such appellations as *ἀδελφοί* or *τέκνον Τιμόθεε* (after *σὺ δέ* in 2 Tim. iv. 5) in some copies of the Epistles. The inserted prefix in Greek Lectionaries is sometimes rather long, as in the lesson for the Liturgy on Sept. 14 (John xix. 6–35). Hence the frequent interpolation (e.g. Matt. iv. 18; viii. 5; xiv. 22) or changed position (John i. 44) of *Ἰησοῦς*. A peculiarity of style in 1, 2 Thess. is kept out of sight by the addition of *Χριστός* in the common text of 1 Thess. ii. 19; iii. 13: 2 Thess. i. 8, 12.

(9) A more extensive and perplexing species of various readings arises from bringing into the text of one of the three earlier Evangelists expressions or whole sentences which of right belong not to him, but to one or both the others[1]. This natural tendency to assimilate the several Gospels must have been aggravated by the laudable efforts of Biblical scholars (beginning with Tatian's *Διὰ τεσσάρων* in the second century) to construct a satisfactory Harmony of them all. Some of these variations also may possibly have been mere marginal notes in the first instance. As examples of this class we will name *εἰς μετάνοιαν* interpolated from Luke v. 32 into Mark ii. 17: the prophetic citation Matt. xxvii. 35 *ἵνα πληρωθῇ κ. τ. λ.* to the end of the verse, unquestionably borrowed from John xix. 24, although the fourth Gospel seldom lends itself to corruptions of this kind. Mark xiii. 14 *τὸ ῥηθὲν ὑπὸ Δανιὴλ τοῦ προφήτου*, is probably taken from Matt. xxiv. 15: Luke v. 38 *καὶ ἀμφότεροι συντηροῦνται* from Matt. ix. 17 (where *ἀμφότεροι* is the true reading): the whole verse Mark xv. 28 seems spurious, being received from Luke xxii. 37. Even in the same book we observe an anxiety to harmonize two separate narratives of the same event, as in Acts ix. 5, 6 compared with xxvi. 14, 15.

(10) In like manner transcribers sometimes quote passages from the Old Testament more fully than the writers of the New Testament had judged necessary for their purpose. Thus *ἐγγίζει*

for Quinquagesima, 2nd Sunday after Easter, 9th, 12th, and 22nd after Trinity, Whitsunday, Ascension Day, SS. Philip and James, All Saints.

[1] Dean Alford (see his critical notes on Luke ix. 56; xxiii. 17) is reasonably unwilling to admit this source of corruption, where the language of the several Evangelists bears no close resemblance throughout the whole of the parallel passages.

μοι . . . τῷ στόματι αὐτῶν καί Matt. xv. 8: ἰάσασθαι τοὺς συντετριμμένους τὴν καρδίαν Luke iv. 18: αὐτοῦ ἀκούσεσθε Acts vii. 37: οὐ ψευδομαρτυρήσεις Rom. xiii. 9: ἢ βολίδι κατατοξευθήσεται Heb. xii. 20, and (less certainly) καὶ κατέστησας αὐτὸν ἐπὶ τὰ ἔργα τῶν χειρῶν σου Heb. ii. 7, are all open to suspicion as being genuine portions of the Old Testament text, but not also of the New. In Acts xiii. 33, the Codex Bezae at Cambridge stands almost alone in adding Ps. ii. 8 to that portion of the previous verse which was unquestionably cited by St. Paul.

(11) Synonymous words are often interchanged, and so form various readings, the sense undergoing some slight and refined modification, or else being quite unaltered. Thus ἔφη should be preferred to εἶπεν Matt. xxii. 37, where εἶπεν of the common text is supported only by two known manuscripts, that at Leicester, and one used by Erasmus. So also ὀμμάτων is put for ὀφθαλμῶν Matt. ix. 29 by the Codex Bezae. In Matt. xxv. 16 the evidence is almost evenly balanced between ἐποίησεν and ἐκέρδησεν (cf. ver. 17). Where simple verbs are interchanged with their compounds (e.g. μετρηθήσεται with ἀντιμετρηθήσεται Matt. vii. 2; ἐτέλεσεν with συνετέλεσεν *ibid.* ver. 28; καίεται with κατακαίεται xiii. 40), or different tenses of the same verb (e.g. εἰληφώς with λαβών Acts xiv. 24; ἀνθέστηκε with ἀντέστη 2 Tim. iv. 15), there is usually some *internal* reason why one should be chosen rather than the other, if the *external* evidence on the other side does not greatly preponderate. When one of two terms is employed in a sense peculiar to the New Testament dialect, the easier synonym may be suspected of having originated in a gloss or marginal interpretation. Hence *caeteris paribus* we should adopt δικαιοσύνην rather than ἐλεημοσύνην in Matt. vi. 1; ἐσκυλμένοι rather than ἐκλελυμένοι ix. 36; ἀθῷον rather than δίκαιον xxvii. 4.

(12) An irregular, obscure, or incomplete construction will often be *explained* or *supplied* in the margin by words that are subsequently brought into the text. Of this character is ἐμέμψαντο Mark vii. 2; δέξασθαι ἡμᾶς 2 Cor. viii. 4; γράφω xiii. 2; προσλαβοῦ Philem. 12 (compare ver. 17), and perhaps δῆλον 1 Tim. vi. 7. More considerable is the change in Acts viii. 7, where the true reading πολλοὶ...φωνῇ μεγάλῃ ἐξήρχοντο, if translated with grammatical rigour, affords an almost impossible sense. Or an elegant Greek idiom may be transformed into simpler language,

as in Acts xvi. 3 ᾔδεισαν γὰρ πάντες ὅτι Ἕλλην ὁ πατὴρ αὐτοῦ ὑπῆρχεν for ᾔδεισαν γὰρ ἅπαντες τὸν πατέρα αὐτοῦ ὅτι Ἕλλην ὑπῆρχεν: similarly, τυγχάνοντα is omitted by many in Luke x. 30; compare also Acts xviii. 26 *fin.*; xix. 8, 34 *init.* The classical μέν has often been inserted against the best evidence: e.g. Acts v. 23: xix. 4, 15; 1 Cor. xii. 20; 2 Cor. iv. 12; Heb. vi. 16. On the other hand a Hebraism may be softened by transcribers, as in Matt. xxi. 23, where for ἐλθόντι αὐτῷ many copies prefer the easier ἐλθόντος αὐτοῦ before προσῆλθεν αὐτῷ διδάσκοντι, and in Matt. xv. 5; Mark vii. 12 (to which perhaps we may add Luke v. 35), where καί is dropped in some copies to facilitate the sense. Hence καὶ οἱ ἄνθρωποι may be upheld before οἱ ποιμένες in Luke ii. 15. This perpetual correction of harsh, ungrammatical, or Oriental constructions characterizes the printed text of the Apocalypse and the recent manuscripts on which it is founded (e.g. τὴν γυναῖκα Ἰεζαβὴλ τὴν λέγουσαν ii. 20, for ἡ λέγουσα).

(13) Hence too arises the habit of changing ancient dialectic forms into those in vogue in the transcriber's age. The whole subject will be more fitly discussed at length hereafter (vol. ii. c. ǂ.); we will here merely note a few peculiarities of this kind adopted by some recent critics from the oldest manuscripts, but which have gradually though not entirely disappeared in copies of lower date. Thus in recent critical editions Καφαρναούμ, Μαθθαῖος, τέσσερες, ἔνατος are substituted for Καπερναούμ, Ματθαῖος, τέσσαρες, ἔννατος of the common text; οὕτως (not οὕτω) is used even before a consonant; ἤλθαμεν, ἤλθατε, ἦλθαν, γενάμενος are preferred to ἤλθομεν, ἤλθετε, ἦλθον, γενόμενος: ἐκαθερίσθη, συνζητεῖν, λήμψομαι to ἐκαθαρίσθη, συζητεῖν, λήψομαι: and ν ἐφελκυστικόν (as it is called) is appended to the usual third persons of verbs, even though a consonant follow. On the other hand the more Attic περιπεπατήκει ought not to be converted into περιεπεπατήκει in Acts xiv. 8.

(14) Trifling variations in spelling, though very proper to be noted by a faithful collator, are obviously of little consequence. Such is the choice between καὶ ἐγώ and κἀγώ, ἐάν and ἄν, εὐθέως and εὐθύς, Μωυσῆς and Μωσῆς, or even between πράττουσι and πράσσουσι, between εὐδόκησα, εὐκαίρουν and ηὐδόκησα, ηὐκαίρουν. To this head may be referred the question whether ἀλλά[1], γε, δέ,

[1] The oldest manuscripts seem to elide the final syllable of ἀλλά before nouns, but not before verbs: e.g. John vi. 32, 39. The common text, therefore, seems

τε, μετά, παρά &c. should have their final vowel elided or not when the next word begins with a vowel.

(15) A large portion of our various readings arises from the omission or insertion of such words as cause little appreciable difference in the sense. To this class belong the pronouns αὐτοῦ, αὐτῷ, αὐτῶν, αὐτοῖς, the particles οὖν, δέ, τε, and the interchange of οὐδέ and οὔτε, as also of καί and δέ at the opening of a sentence.

(16) Manuscripts greatly fluctuate in adding and rejecting the Greek article, and the sense is often seriously influenced by these variations, though they seem so minute. In Mark ii. 26 ἐπὶ Ἀβιάθαρ ἀρχιερέως 'in the time that Abiathar was high priest' would be historically incorrect, while ἐπὶ Ἀβιάθαρ τοῦ ἀρχιερέως 'in the days of Abiathar the high priest' is suitable enough. The article will often impart vividness and reality to an expression, where its presence is not indispensable: e. g. Luke xii. 54 τὴν νεφέλην (if τήν be authentic, as looks probable) is the peculiar cloud spoken of in 1 Kings xviii. 44 as portending rain. Bishop Middleton's monograph ('Doctrine of the Greek Article applied to the Criticism and Illustration of the New Testament'), though apparently little known to certain of our most highly esteemed Biblical scholars, even if its philological groundwork be thought a little precarious, must always be regarded as the text-book on this interesting subject, and is a lasting monument of intellectual acuteness and exact learning.

(17) Not a few various readings may be imputed to the peculiarities of the style of writing adopted in the oldest manuscripts. Thus ΠΡΟϹΤЄΤΑΓΜЄΝΟΥϹΚΑΙΡΟΥϹ Acts xvii. 26 may be divided into two words or three; ΚΑΙΤΑΠΑΝΤΑ ibid. ver. 25, by a slight change, has degenerated into κατὰ πάντα. The habitual abridgement of such words as Θεός or Κύριος sometimes leads to a corruption of the text. Hence possibly comes the grave variation ΟϹ for $\overline{\Theta C}$ 1 Tim. iii. 16, and the singular reading τῷ καιρῷ δουλεύοντες Rom. xii. 11, where the true word Κυρίῳ was first shortened into $\overline{\text{KPΩ}}$[1], and then read as ĶPω,

wrong in Rom. i. 21; iv. 20; v. 14; viii. 15; 1 Cor. i. 17; vi. 11; ix. 27; xiv. 34; 1 Pet. ii. 25; Jude 9. Yet to this rule there are many exceptions, e. g. Gal. iv. 7 ἀλλὰ υἱός is found in nearly all good authorities.

[1] Tischendorf indeed (Nov. Test. 1871), from a suggestion of Granville Penn

Κ being employed to indicate KAI in very early times[1]. Or a large initial letter, which the scribe usually reserved for a subsequent review, may have been altogether neglected: whence we have τι for Οτι before στενή Matt. vii. 14. Or —, placed over a letter (especially at the end of a line and word) to denote ν, may have been lost sight of; e.g. λίθον μέγα Matt. xxvii. 60 in several copies, for ΜΕΓᾹ. The use of the symbol ⳁ, which in the Herculanean rolls and now and then in Codex Sinaiticus stands for προ and προσ indifferently, may have produced that remarkable confusion of the two prepositions when compounded with verbs which we notice in Matt. xxvi. 39; Mark xiv. 35; Acts xii. 6; xvii. 5, 26; xx. 5, 13; xxii. 25. It will be seen hereafter that as the earliest manuscripts have few marks of punctuation, breathing or accent, these points (often far from indifferent) must be left in a great measure to an editor's taste and judgement.

(18) Slips of the pen, whereby words are manifestly lost or repeated, mis-spelt or half-finished, though of no interest to the critic, must yet be noted by a faithful collator, as they will occasionally throw light on the history of some particular copy in connexion with others, and always indicate the degree of care or skill employed by the scribe, and consequently the weight due to his general testimony.

The great mass of various readings we have hitherto attempted to classify (to our *first* and *second* heads we will recur presently) are manifestly due to mere inadvertence or human frailty, and certainly cannot be imputed to any deliberate intention of transcribers to tamper with the text of Scripture. We must give a different account of a few passages (we are glad they are only a few) which yet remain to be noticed.

(19) The copyist may be tempted to forsake his proper

in loc., says, 'ΚΥΡΙω omnino scribi solet $\overline{\text{Kω}}$,' and this no doubt is the usual form, even in manuscripts which have $\overline{χρω}$ $\overline{ιηυ}$, as well as $\overline{χω}$ $\overline{ιυ}$, for χριστῷ Ἰησοῦ. Yet the Codex Augiensis (Paul. F) has $\overline{κρν}$ in 1 Cor. ix. 1.

[1] Especially, yet not always, at the end of a line. Και in καιρός is actually thus written in Cod. Sinaiticus (א), 1 Macc. ix. 7; xv. 33; Matt. xxi. 34; Rom. iii. 26; Heb. xi. 11; Apoc. xi. 18. So Cod. Sarravianus of the fourth century in Deut. ix. 20, Cod. Rossanensis of the sixth (but only twice in the text), the Zurich Psalter of the seventh century is Ps. xcvii. 11; cvi. 3; cxvi. 5, and the Bodleian Genesis (ch. vi. 13) of about a century later. Similarly, καινήν is written κνην in Cod. B. 2 John 5.

function for that of a reviser, or critical corrector. He may simply omit what he does not understand (e.g. *δευτεροπρώτῳ* Luke vi. 1; *τὸ μαρτύριον* 1 Tim. ii. 6), or may attempt to get over a difficulty by inversions and other changes. Thus the *μυστήριον* spoken of by St. Paul 1 Cor. xv. 51, which rightly stands in the received text *πάντες μὲν οὐ κοιμηθησόμεθα, πάντες δὲ ἀλλαγησόμεθα*, was easily varied into *πάντες κοιμηθησόμεθα, οὐ π. δὲ ἀλ.*, as if in mere perplexity. From this source must arise the omission in a few manuscripts of *υἱοῦ Βαραχίου* in Matt. xxiii. 35; of *Ἱερεμίου* in Matt. xxvii. 9; the insertion of *ἄλλου ἐκ* before *θυσιαστηρίου* in Apoc. xvi. 7; perhaps the substitution of *τοῖς προφήταις* for *Ἠσαΐᾳ τῷ προφήτῃ* in Mark i. 2, of *οὔπω ἀναβαίνω* for *οὐκ ἀναβαίνω* in John vii. 8, and certainly of *τρίτη* for *ἕκτη* in John xix. 14. The variations between *Γεργεσηνῶν* and *Γαδαρηνῶν* Matt. viii. 28, and between *Βηθαβαρᾶ* and *Βηθανίᾳ* John i. 28, have been attributed, we hope and believe unjustly, to the misplaced conjectures of Origen.

Some would impute such readings as *ἔχωμεν* for *ἔχομεν* Rom. v. 1; *φορέσωμεν* for *φορέσομεν* 1 Cor. xv. 49, to a desire on the part of copyists to *improve* an assertion into an ethical exhortation, especially in the Apostolical Epistles; but it is at once safer and more simple to regard them with Bishop Chr. Wordsworth (N. T. 1 Cor. xv. 49) as instances of *itacism*: see class (7) above.

(20) Finally, whatever conclusion we arrive at respecting the true reading in the following passages, the discrepancy could hardly have arisen except from doctrinal preconceptions. Matt. xix. 17 *Τί με λέγεις ἀγαθόν; οὐδεὶς ἀγαθὸς εἰ μὴ εἷς, ὁ Θεός·* or *Τί με ἐρωτᾷς περὶ τοῦ ἀγαθοῦ; εἷς ἐστὶν ὁ ἀγαθός*: John i. 18 *ὁ μονογενὴς υἱός* or *μονογενὴς Θεός*: Acts xvi. 7 *τὸ πνεῦμα* with or without the addition of *Ἰησοῦ*: Acts xx. 28 *τὴν ἐκκλησίαν τοῦ Θεοῦ* or *τὴν ἐκκλησίαν τοῦ Κυρίου*: perhaps also Jude ver. 4 *δεσπότην* with or without *Θεόν*. I do not mention Mark xiii. 32 *οὐδὲ ὁ υἱός*, as there is hardly any authority for its rejection now extant; nor Luke ii. 22, where *τοῦ καθαρισμοῦ αὐτῆς* of the Complutensian Polyglott and most of our common editions is supported by almost no evidence whatever.

11. It is very possible that some scattered readings cannot be reduced to any of the above-named classes, but enough has

been said to afford the student a general notion of the nature and extent of the subject[1]. It may be reasonably thought that a portion of these variations, and those among the most considerable, had their origin in a cause which must have operated at least as much in ancient as in modern times, the changes gradually introduced after publication by the authors themselves into the various copies yet within their reach. Such revised copies would circulate independently of those issued previously, and now beyond the writer's control; and thus becoming the parents of a new family of copies, would originate and keep up diversities from the first edition, without any fault on the part of transcribers[2]. It is thus perhaps we may best account for the omission or insertion of whole paragraphs or verses in manuscripts of a certain class [see above (1), (2), (3)]; or, in cases where the work was in much request, for those minute touches and trifling improvements in words, in construction, in tone, or in the mere colouring of the style [(5), (11), (12)], which few authors can help attempting, when engaged on revising their favourite compositions. Even in the Old Testa-

[1] My departed friend, Dr. Tregelles, to whose persevering labours in sacred criticism I am anxious, once for all, to express my deepest obligations, ranged various readings under three general heads:—*substitutions; additions; omissions.* Mr. C. E. Hammond, in his scholarlike little work, 'Outlines of Textual Criticism applied to the N. T., 1876, 2nd edition,' divides their possible sources into Unconscious or unintentional errors, (1) of *sight;* (2) of *hearing;* (3) of *memory:* and those that are Conscious or intentional, viz. (4) incorporation of marginal glosses; (5) corrections of harsh or unusual forms of words, or expressions; (6) alterations in the text to produce supposed harmony with another passage, to complete a quotation, or to clear up a presumed difficulty; (7) Liturgical insertions. While he enumerates (8) alterations for dogmatic reasons, he adds that 'there appears to be no strong ground for the suggestion' that any such exist (Hammond, p. 17). Professor Roberts ('Words of the New Testament' by Drs. Milligan and Roberts, 1873) comprehends several of the foregoing divisions under one head: 'Again and again has a word or phrase been slipped in by the transcriber which had no existence in his copy, but which was due to the working of his own mind on the subject before him.' His examples are ἔρχεται inserted in Matt. xxv. 6; ἰδοῦσα in Luke i. 29; ὑπὲρ ἡμῶν in Rom. viii. 26 (Part I. Chap. I. pp. 5, 6).

[2] This source of variations, though not easily discriminated from others, must have suggested itself to many minds, and is well touched upon by the late Isaac Taylor in his 'History of the Transmission of Antient Books to modern times,' 1827, p. 24. So Dr. Hort, when perplexed by some of the textual problems which he fails to solve, throws out as an hypothesis not in itself without plausibility, the notion of 'a first and a second edition of the Gospels, both conceivably apostolic' (Gr. Test. Introduction, p. 177).

ment, the song of David in 2 Sam. xxii is evidently an early draft of the more finished composition, Ps. xviii. Traces of the writer's *curae secundae* may possibly be found in John v. 3, 4; vii. 53—viii. 11; xiii. 26; Acts xx. 4, 15; xxiv. 6–8. To this list some critics feel disposed to add portions of Luke xxi—xxiv.

12. The fullest critical edition of the Greek Testament hitherto published contains but a comparatively small portion of the whole mass of variations already known; as a rule, the editors neglect, and rightly neglect, mere errors of transcription. Such things must be recorded for several reasons, but neither they, nor real various readings that are slenderly supported, can produce any effect in the task of amending or restoring the sacred text. Those who wish to see for themselves how far the common printed editions of what is called the 'textus receptus' differ from the judgement of the most recent critics, may refer if they please to the small Greek Testament published in the series of 'Cambridge Greek and Latin Texts [1],' which exhibits in a thicker type all words and clauses wherein Robert Stephen's edition of 1550 (which is taken as a convenient standard) differs from the other chief modifications of the *textus receptus* (viz. Beza's 1565 and Elzevir's 1624), as also from the revised texts of Lachmann 1842–50, of Tischendorf 1865–72, of Tregelles 1857–72, of the Revisers of the English New Testament (1881), and of Westcott and Hort (1881). The student will thus be enabled to estimate for himself the limits within which the text of the Greek Testament may be regarded as still open to discussion, and to take a general survey of the questions on which the theologian is bound to form an intelligent opinion.

13. The work that lies before us naturally divides itself into three distinct parts.

I. A description of the sources from which various readings are derived (or of their EXTERNAL EVIDENCE), comprising

(*a*) Manuscripts of the Greek New Testament or of portions thereof.

(*b*) Ancient versions of the New Testament in various languages.

[1] 'Novum Testamentum Textûs Stephanici A.D. 1550 . . . curante F. H. A. Scrivener.' Cantabr. 1877 (Editio Major, 1887).

(*c*) Citations from the Greek Testament or its versions made by early ecclesiastical writers, especially by the Fathers of the Christian Church.

(*d*) Early printed or later critical editions of the Greek Testament.

II. A discussion of the principles on which external evidence should be applied to the recension of the sacred volume, embracing

(*a*) The laws of INTERNAL EVIDENCE, and the limits of their legitimate use.

(*b*) The history of the text and of the principal schemes which have been proposed for restoring it to its primitive state, including recent views of Comparative Criticism.

(*c*) Considerations derived from the peculiar character and grammatical form of the dialect of the Greek Testament.

III. The application of the foregoing materials and principles to the investigation of the true reading in the chief passages of the New Testament, on which authorities are at variance.

In this edition, as has already been explained in the preface, it has been found necessary to dividé the treatise into two volumes, which will contain respectively—

I. First Volume :—Ancient Manuscripts.

II. Second Volume:—Versions, Citations, Editions, Principles, and Selected Passages.

It will be found desirable to read the following pages in the order wherein they stand, although the chief part of Chapters VII–XIV of the first volume and some portions elsewhere (indicated by being printed like them in smaller type) are obviously intended chiefly for reference, or for less searching examination.

CHAPTER II.

GENERAL CHARACTER OF THE GREEK MANUSCRIPTS OF THE NEW TESTAMENT.

AS the extant Greek manuscripts of the New Testament supply both the most copious and the purest sources of Textual Criticism, we propose to present to the reader some account of their peculiarities in regard to material, form, style of writing, date and contents, before we enter into details respecting individual copies, under the several subdivisions to which it is usual to refer them.

1. The subject of the present section has been systematically discussed in the 'Palaeographia Graeca' (Paris, 1708, folio) of Bernard de Montfaucon [1655–1741[1]], the most illustrious member of the learned Society of the Benedictines of St. Maur. This truly great work, although its materials are rather too exclusively drawn from manuscripts deposited in French libraries, and its many illustrative facsimiles are somewhat rudely engraved, still maintains a high authority on all points relating to Greek manuscripts, even after more recent discoveries, especially among the papyri of Egypt and Herculaneum, have necessarily modified not a few of its statements. The four splendid volumes of M. J. B. Silvestre's 'Paléographie Universelle' (Paris, 1839–41, &c. folio) afford us no less than 300 plates of the Greek writing of various ages, sumptuously executed; though the accompanying letter-press descriptions, by F. and A. Champollion Fils, seem in this branch of the subject a little disappointing; nor are the valuable notes appended to his translation of their work by Sir Frederick Madden (London, 2 vols. 1850, 8vo) sufficiently numerous or elaborate to supply the Champollions' defects. Much, however, may also be learnt from the 'Hercu-

[1] In this manner we propose to indicate the dates of the birth and death of the person whose name immediately precedes.

lanensium voluminum quae supersunt' (Naples, 10 tom. 1793–1850, fol.); from Mr. Babington's three volumes of papyrus fragments of Hyperides, respectively published in 1850, 1853 and 1858; and especially from the Prolegomena to Tischendorf's editions of the Codices Ephraemi (1843), Friderico-Augustanus (1846), Claromontanus (1852), Sinaiticus (1862), Vaticanus (1867), and those other like publications (e.g. Monumenta sacra inedita 1846–1870, and Anecdota sacra et profana 1855) which have rendered his name perhaps the very highest among scholars in this department of sacred literature. What I have been able to add from my own observation, has been gathered from the study of Biblical manuscripts now in England. To these sources of information may now be added Professor Wattenbach's 'Anleitung zur griechischen Palaeographie' second edition, Leipsic, 1877, Gardthausen's 'Griechische Palaeographie,' Leipsic, 1879; Dr. C. R. Gregory's 'Prolegomena' to the eighth edition of Tischendorf, and especially the publication of 'The Palaeographical Society Greek Testament, Parts I and II, Leipsic, 1884, 1891, 'Facsimiles of Manuscripts and Inscriptions' edited by E. A. Bond and E. M. Thompson, Parts I–XII, London, 1873–82, and a Manual on 'Greek and Latin Palaeography' from the hands of Mr. E. Maunde Thompson, of which the proof-sheets have been most kindly placed by the accomplished author at the disposal of the editor of this work, and have furnished to this chapter many elements of enrichment. It may be added, that since manuscripts have been photographed, all other facsimiles have been put in the shade: and in this edition references as a rule will be given only to photographed copies.

2. The *materials* on which writing has been impressed at different periods and stages of civilization are the following:— Leaves, bark, especially of the lime (*liber*), linen, clay and pottery, wall-spaces, metals, lead, bronze, wood, waxen and other tablets, papyrus, skins, parchment and vellum, and from an early date amongst the Chinese, and in the West after the capture of Samarcand by the Arabs in A.D. 704, paper manufactured from fibrous substances[1]. The most ancient manuscripts of the New Testament now existing are composed of vellum or parchment (*membrana*), the term vellum being

[1] 'Greek and Latin Palaeography,' Chaps. II, III.

strictly applied to the delicate skins of very young calves, and parchment to the integuments of sheep and goats, though the terms are as a rule employed convertibly. The word parchment seems to be a corruption of *charta pergamena*, a name first given to skins prepared by some improved process for Eumenes, king of Pergamum, about B. C. 150. In judging of the date of a manuscript on skins, attention must be paid to the quality of the material, the oldest being almost invariably written on the thinnest and whitest vellum that could be procured; while manuscripts of later ages, being usually composed of parchment, are thick, discoloured, and coarsely grained. Thus the Codex Sinaiticus of the fourth century is made of the finest skins of antelopes, the leaves being so large, that a single animal would furnish only two (Tischendorf, Cod. Frid.-August. Prolegomena, § 1). Its contemporary, the far-famed Codex Vaticanus, challenges universal admiration for the beauty of its vellum: every visitor at the British Museum can observe the excellence of that of the Codex Alexandrinus of the fifth century: that of the Codex Claromontanus of the sixth century is even more remarkable: the material of those purple-dyed fragments of the Gospels which Tischendorf denominates N, also of the sixth century, is so subtle and delicate, that some persons have mistaken the leaves preserved in England (Brit. Mus. Cotton, Titus C xv) for Egyptian papyrus. Paper made of cotton[1] (*charta bombycina*, called also *charta Damascena* from its place of manufacture) may have been fabricated in the ninth[2] or tenth century, and linen paper (*charta* proper) as early as 1242 A. D.; but they were seldom used for Biblical manuscripts sooner than the thirteenth, and had not entirely displaced parchment at the era of the invention of printing, about A. D. 1450. Lost portions of parchment or vellum manuscripts are often supplied in paper by some later hand;

[1] 'Recent investigations have thrown doubts on the accuracy of this view; and a careful analysis of many samples has proved that, although cotton was occasionally used, no paper that has been examined is entirely made of that substance, hemp or flax being the more usual material.' Maunde Thompson, p. 44.

[2] Tischendorf (Notitia Codicis Sinaitici, p. 54) carried to St. Petersburg a fragment of a Lectionary which cannot well be assigned to a later date than the ninth century, among whose parchment leaves are inserted two of cotton paper, manifestly written on by the original scribe.

but the Codex Leicestrensis of the fourteenth century is composed of a mixture of inferior vellum and worse paper, regularly arranged in the proportion of two parchment to three paper leaves, recurring alternately throughout the whole volume. Like it, in the mixture of parchment and paper, are codd. 233 and Brit. Mus. Harl. 3,161—the latter however not being a New Testament MS.

3. Although parchment was in occasional, if not familiar, use at the period when the New Testament was written (*τὰ βιβλία, μάλιστα τὰς μεμβράνας* 2 Tim. iv. 13), yet the more perishable papyrus of Egypt was chiefly employed for ordinary purposes. This vegetable production had been used for literary purposes from the earliest times. 'Papyrus rolls are represented on the sculptured walls of Egyptian temples.' The oldest roll now extant is the papyrus Prisse at Paris, which dates from 2500 B.C., or even earlier, unless those which have been lately discovered by Mr. Flinders Petrie reach as far, or even farther, back [1]. The ordinary name applied in Greek to this material was *χάρτης* (2 John 12), though Herodotus terms it *βύβλος* (ii. 100, v. 58), and in Latin *charta* (2 Esdr. xv. 2; Tobit vii. 14—Old Latin Version). Papyrus was in those days esteemed more highly than skins: for Herodotus expressly states that the Ionians had been compelled to have recourse to goats and sheep for lack of byblus or papyrus; and Eumenes was driven to prepare parchment because the Alexandrians were too jealous to supply him with the material which he coveted [2]. Indeed, papyrus was used far beyond the borders of Egypt, and was plentiful in Rome under the Empire, being in fact the common material among the Romans during that period: and as many of the manuscripts of the New Testament must have been written upon so perishable a substance in the earliest centuries since the Christian era, this probably is one of the reasons why we possess no considerable copies from before the second quarter of the fourth century. Only a few fragments of the New Testament on papyrus remain. We find a minute, if not a very clear description of the mode of preparing the papyrus for the scribe in the works of the elder Pliny (Hist. Nat. xiii. 11, 12). The plant grew in Egypt, also

1 'Ten Years Digging in Egypt,' pp. 120, &c.
2 'Greek and Latin Palaeography,' p. 35; Pliny, Nat. Hist. xiii. 11.

in Syria, and on the Niger and the Euphrates. Mainly under Christian influence it was supplanted by parchment and vellum, which had superior claims to durability, and its manufacture ceased altogether on the conquest of Egypt by the Mohammedans (A.D. 638).

4. Parchment is said to have been introduced at Rome not long after its employment by Attalus. Nevertheless, if it had been in constant and ordinary use under the first Emperors, we can hardly suppose that specimens of secular writing would have failed to come down to us. Its increased growth and prevalence about synchronize with the rise of Constantinopolitan influence. It may readily be imagined that vellum (especially that fine sort by praiseworthy custom required for copies of Holy Scripture) could never have been otherwise than scarce and dear. Hence arose, at a very early period of the Christian era, the practice and almost the necessity of erasing ancient writing from skins, in order to make room for works in which the living generation felt more interest, especially when clean vellum failed the scribe towards the end of his task. This process of destruction, however, was seldom so fully carried out, but that the strokes of the elder hand might still be traced, more or less completely, under the more modern writing. Such manuscripts are called *codices rescripti* or palimpsests (παλίμψηστα[1]), and several of the most precious monuments of sacred learning are of this description. The Codex Ephraemi at Paris contains large fragments both of the Old and New Testament under the later Greek works of St. Ephraem the Syrian: and the Codex Nitriensis, more recently disinterred from a monastery in the Egyptian desert and brought to the British Museum, comprises a portion of St. Luke's Gospel, nearly obliterated, and covered over by a Syriac treatise of Severus of Antioch against Grammaticus, comparatively of no value whatever. It will be easily believed that the collating or transcribing of palimpsests has cost much toil and patience to those whose loving zeal has led them to the attempt: and after all the true readings will be sometimes (not often) rather uncertain,

[1] 'Nam, quod in palimpsesto, laudo equidem parcimoniam.' Cicero, Ad Diversos, vii. 18, though of a waxen tablet. Maunde Thompson, p. 75.

even though chemical mixtures (of which 'the most harmless is probably hydrosulphuret of ammonia') have recently been applied with much success to restore the faded lines and letters of these venerable records.

5. We need say but little of a practice which St. Jerome[1] and others speak of as prevalent towards the end of the fourth century, that of dyeing the vellum purple, and of stamping rather than writing the letters in silver and gold. The Cotton fragment of the Gospels, mentioned above (p. 23), is one of the few remaining copies of this kind, as are the newly discovered Codex Rossanensis and the Codex Beratinus, and it is not unlikely that the great Dublin palimpsest of St. Matthew owes its present wretched discoloration to some such dye. But, as Davidson sensibly observes, 'the value of a manuscript does not depend on such things' (Biblical Criticism, vol. ii. p. 264). We care for them only as they serve to indicate the reverence paid to the Scriptures by men of old. The style, however, of the pictures, illustrations, arabesques and initial ornaments that prevail in later copies from the eighth century downwards, whose colours and gilding are sometimes as fresh and bright as if laid on but yesterday[2], will not only interest the student by tending to throw light on mediaeval art and habits and modes of thought, but will often fix the date of the books which contain them with a precision otherwise quite beyond our reach.

6. The ink found upon ancient manuscripts is of various colours[3]. Black ink, the ordinary writing fluid of centuries (μέλαν, *atramentum*, &c.) differs in tint at various periods and in different countries. In early MSS. it is either pure black or slightly brown; in the Middle Ages it varies a good deal according to age and locality. In Italy and Southern Europe it is generally blacker than in the North, in France and Flanders

[1] 'Habeant qui volunt veteres libros, vel in membranis purpureis auro argentoque descriptos.' Praef. in Job. 'Inficiuntur membranae colore purpureo, aurum liquescit in litteras.' Epist. ad Eustochium.

[2] Miniatures are found even as early as in the Cod. Rossanensis (Σ) at the beginning of the sixth century.

[3] This paragraph which has been rewritten, has been abridged from Mr. Maunde Thompson's 'Greek and Latin Palaeography,' pp. 50–52, to which readers are referred for verification and amplification.

it is generally darker than in England; a Spanish MS. of the fourteenth or fifteenth century may usually be recognized by the peculiar blackness of the ink. Deterioration is observable in the course of time. The ink of the fifteenth century particularly is often of a faded grey colour. Inks of green, yellow, and other colours, are also found, but generally only for ornamental purposes. Red, either in the form of a pigment or fluid ink, is of very ancient and common use, being seen even in early Egyptian papyri. Gold was also used as a writing fluid at a very early period. Purple-stained vellum MSS. were usually written upon in gold or silver letters, and ordinary white vellum MSS. were also written in gold, particularly in the ninth and tenth centuries, in the reigns of the Carlovingian kings. Gold writing *as a practice* died out in the thirteenth century: and writing in silver appears to have ceased contemporaneously with the disuse of stained vellum. The ancients used the liquid of cuttle-fish. Pliny mentions soot and gum as the ingredients of writing-ink. Other later authors add gall-apples: metallic infusions at an early period, and vitriol in the Middle Ages were also employed.

7. While papyrus remained in common use, the chief instrument employed was a reed (κάλαμος 3 John ver. 13, *canna*), such as are common in the East at present: a few existing manuscripts (e.g. the Codd. Leicestrensis and Lambeth 1350) appear to have been thus written. Yet the firmness and regularity of the strokes, which often remain impressed on the vellum or paper after the ink has utterly gone, seem to prove that in the great majority of cases the *stilus* made of iron, bronze, or other metal, or ivory or bone, sharp at one end to scratch the letters, and furnished with a knob or flat head at the other for purposes of erasure, had not gone wholly out of use. We must add to our list of writing materials a bodkin or needle (*acus*), by means of which and a ruler the blank leaf was carefully divided, generally on the outer side of the skin, into columns and lines, whose regularity much enhances the beauty of our best copies. The vestiges of such points and marks may yet be seen deeply indented on the surface of nearly all manuscripts, those on one side of each leaf being usually sufficiently visible to guide the scribe when he came to write on the reverse. The quill pen

probably came into use with vellum, for which it is obviously suited. The first notices of it occur in a story respecting Theodoric the Ostrogoth, and in a passage of Isidore's 'Origines'[1] (vi. 13).

8. Little need be said respecting the *form* of manuscripts, which in this particular (*codices*) much resemble printed books. A few are in large folio; the greater part in small folio or quarto, the prevailing shape being a quarto (*quaternio* or quire) whose height but little exceeds its breadth; some are in octavo, a not inconsiderable number smaller still: and quires of three sheets or six leaves, and five sheets or ten leaves (Cod. Vaticanus), are to be met with. In some copies the sheets have marks in the lower margin of their first or last pages, like the *signatures* of a modern volume, the folio at intervals of two, the quarto at intervals of four leaves, as in the Codex Bezae of the Gospels and Acts (D), and the Codex Augiensis of St. Paul's Epistles (F). Not to speak at present of those manuscripts which have a Latin translation in a column parallel to the Greek, as the Codex Bezae, the Codex Laudianus of the Acts, and the Codices Claromontanus and Augiensis of St. Paul, many copies of every age have two Greek columns on each page; of these the Codex Alexandrinus is the oldest: the Codex Vaticanus has three columns on a page, the Codex Sinaiticus four. The unique arrangement[2] of these last two has been urged as an argument

[1] 'Greek and Latin Palaeography,' p. 49.

[2] Besides the Cod. Sinaiticus, the beautiful Psalter purchased by the National Library from the Didot sale at Paris has four columns (Mr. J. Rendel Harris), and besides the Cod. Vaticanus, the Vatican Dio Cassius, the Milan fragment of Genesis, two copies of the Samaritan Pentateuch at Nablous described by Tischendorf (Cod. Frid.-Aug. Proleg. § 11), the last part of Cod. Monacensis 208 (Evan, 429), and two Hebrew MSS. Cod. Mon. Heb. 422, and Cod. Reg. Heb. 17, are arranged in *three* columns. Tischendorf has more recently discovered a similar arrangement in two palimpsest leaves of Wisdom and Ecclesiasticus from which he gives extracts (Not. Cod. Sinait. p. 49); in a Latin fragment of the Pentateuch, the same as the Ashburnham manuscript below, seen by him at Lyons in 1843; in a Greek Evangelistarium of the eighth century, and a Patristic manuscript at Patmos of the ninth (ibid. p. 10); so that the argument drawn from the *triple* columns must not be pressed too far. He adds also a Turin copy of the Minor Prophets in Greek (Pasinus, Catalogue, 1749), and a Nitrian Syriac codex in the British Museum 'quem circa finem quarti saeculi scriptum esse subscriptio testatur' (Monum. sacra inedita, vol. i, Proleg. p. xxxi). To this not slender list Mr. E. Maunde Thompson enables us to annex B. M. Addit. 24142, a Flemish Latin Bible of the eleventh century. The late Lord Ashburnham in 1868

(1)

Α Β Γ Δ Ε Ζ Η Θ Ι Κ Λ Μ Ν Ξ Ο Π Ρ Σ Τ Υ Φ

Χ Ψ Ω.

(2)

Α Β Γ Δ Ε Ζ Η Θ Ι Κ Λ Μ Ν Ξ Ο Π Ρ C Τ Υ Φ Χ Ψ ω ΗΝ

(3)

Α Β Γ Δ Ε Ζ Η Θ Ι Κ Λ Μ Ν ξ Ο Π Ρ C Τ Υ Φ Χ Ψ ω.

for their higher antiquity, as if they were designed to imitate *rolled* books, whose several skins or leaves were fastened together lengthwise, so that their contents always appeared in parallel columns; they were kept in scrolls which were unrolled at one end for reading, and when read rolled up at the other. This fashion prevails in the papyrus fragments yet remaining, and in the most venerated copies of the Old Testament preserved in Jewish synagogues.

9. We now approach a more important question, the *style* of writing adopted in manuscripts, and the shapes of the several letters. These varied widely in different ages, and form the simplest and surest criteria for approximating to the date of the documents themselves. Greek characters are properly divided into 'majuscules' and 'minuscules,' or by a subdivision of the former, into Capitals, which are generally of a square kind, fitted for inscriptions on stones like E; Uncials, or large letters[1], and a modification of Capitals, with a free introduction of curves, and better suited for writing, like Є; and Cursives, or small letters, adapted for the running hand. *Uncial* manuscripts were written in what have frequently been regarded as capital letters, formed separately, having no connexion with each other, and (in the earlier specimens) without any space between the words, the marks of punctuation being few: the *cursive* or running hand comprising letters more easily and rapidly made, those in the same word being usually joined together, with a complete system of punctuation not widely removed from that of printed books. Speaking generally, and limiting our statement to Greek manuscripts of the New Testament, Uncial letters or the Literary or Book-hand prevailed from the fourth to the tenth, or (in the case of liturgical books) as late as the eleventh century; Cursive letters were employed as early as the ninth or tenth century, and continued in use until the invention of

printed his Old Latin fragments of Leviticus and Numbers, also in three columns, with a facsimile page; and the famous Utrecht Psalter, assigned by some to the sixth century, by others to the ninth or tenth, is written with three columns on a page.

[1] 'Uncialibus, ut vulgo aiunt, literis, onera magis exarata, quam codices,' Hieronymi Praef. in Job. From this passage the term *uncial* seems to be derived, *uncia* (an inch) referring to the size of the characters. Yet the conjectural reading '*initialibus*' will most approve itself to those who are familiar with the small Latin writing of the Middle Ages, in which *i* is undotted, and *c* much like *t*.

printing superseded the humble labours of the scribe. But cursive writing existed before the Christian era: and it seems impossible to suppose that so very convenient a form of penmanship could have fallen into abeyance in ordinary life, although few documents have come down to us to demonstrate the truth of this supposition.

Besides the broad and palpable distinction between uncial and cursive letters, persons who have had much experience in the study of manuscripts are able to distinguish those of either class from one another in respect of style and character; so that the period at which each was written can be determined within certain inconsiderable limits. After the tenth century many manuscripts bear dates, and such become standards to which we can refer others resembling them which are undated. But since the earliest dated Biblical manuscript yet discovered (Cursive Evan. 481, see below Chap. VII) bears the date May 7, A.D. 835, we must resort to other means for estimating the age of more venerable, and therefore more important, copies. By studying the style and shape of the letters on Greek inscriptions, Montfaucon was led to conclude that the more simple, upright, and regular the form of uncial letters; the less flourish or ornament they exhibit; the nearer their breadth is equal to their height; so much the more ancient they ought to be considered. These results have been signally confirmed by the subsequent discovery of Greek papyri in Egyptian tombs especially in the third century before the Christian era; and yet further from numerous fragments of Philodemus, of Epicurus, and other philosophers, which were buried in the ruins of Herculaneum in A.D. 79 ('Fragmenta Herculanensia,' Walter Scott). The evidence of these papyri, indeed, is even more weighty than that of inscriptions, inasmuch as workers in stone, as has been remarked, were often compelled to prefer straight lines, as better adapted to the hardness of their material, where writings on papyrus or vellum would naturally flow into curves.

10. While we freely grant that a certain tact, the fruit of study and minute observation, can alone make us capable of forming a trustworthy opinion on the age of manuscripts; it is worth while to point out the *principles* on which a true

judgement must be grounded, and to submit to the reader a few leading facts, which his own research may hereafter enable him to apply and to extend.

The first three plates at the beginning of this volume represent the Greek alphabet, as found in the seven following monuments:

(1) The celebrated Rosetta stone, discovered near that place during the French occupation of Egypt in 1799, and now in the British Museum. This most important inscription, which in the hands of Young and Champollion has proved the key to the mysteries of Egyptian hieroglyphics, records events of no intrinsic consequence that occurred B.C. 196, in the reign of Ptolemy V Epiphanes. It is written in the three several forms of hieroglyphics, of the demotic or common characters of the country, and of Greek Capitals, which last may represent the *lapidary* style of the second century before our era. The words are undivided, without breathings, accents, or marks of punctuation, and the uncial letters (excepting Ⲷ for *zeta*) approach very nearly to our modern capital type. In shape they are simple, perhaps a little rude; rather square than oblong: and as the carver on this hard black stone was obliged to avoid curve lines whenever he could, the forms of E, Ξ and Σ differ considerably from the specimens we shall produce from documents described on soft materials. Plate I. No. (1).

(2) The Codex Friderico-Augustanus of the fourth century, published in lithographed facsimile in 1846, contains on forty-three leaves fragments of the Septuagint version, chiefly from 1 Chronicles and Jeremiah, with Nehemiah and Esther complete, in oblong folio, with four columns on each page. The plates are so carefully executed that the very form of the ancient letters and the colour of the ink are represented to us by Tischendorf, who discovered it in the East. In 1859 the same indefatigable scholar brought to Europe the remainder of this manuscript, which seems as old as the fourth century, anterior (as he thinks) to the Codex Vaticanus itself, and published it in 1862, in facsimile type cast for the purpose, 4 tom., with twenty pages lithographed or photographed, at the expense of the Emperor Alexander II of Russia, to whom the original had been presented. This book, which Tischendorf calls Codex Sinaiticus, contains, besides much more of the Septuagint, *the whole New Testament*

with Barnabas' Epistle and a part of Hermas' Shepherd annexed. As a kind of *avant-courier* to his great work he had previously put forth a tract entitled 'Notitia Editionis Codicis Bibliorum Sinaitici Auspiciis Imperatoris Alexandri II susceptae' (Leipsic, 1860). Of this most valuable manuscript a complete account will be given in the opening of the fourth chapter, under the appellation of *Aleph* (א), assigned to it by Tischendorf, in the exercise of his right as its discoverer. Plate I. No. 2.

(3) Codex Alexandrinus of the fifth century (A). Plate I.
(Plate II.) (4) Codex Purpureus Cotton.: N of the Gospels (of the sixth century)
(Plate II.) (5) Codex Nitriensis Rescriptus, R of the Gospels (of the sixth century)
(Plate III.) (6) Codex Dublinensis Rescriptus, Z of the Gospels (of the sixth century)
(Plate III.) (7) Evangelistarium Harleian. 5598, *dated* A.D. 995.

The leading features of these manuscripts will be described in the fourth and fifth chapters. At present we wish to compare them with each other for the purpose of tracing, as closely as we may, the different styles and fashions of uncial letters which prevailed from the fourth to the tenth or eleventh century of the Christian era. The varying appearance of cursive manuscripts cannot so well be seen by exhibiting their alphabets, for since each letter is for the most part joined to the others in the same word, *connected* passages alone will afford us a correct notion of their character and general features. For the moment we are considering the uncials only.

If the Rosetta stone, by its necessary avoiding of curve lines, gives only a notion of the manner adopted on stone and not in common writing, it resembles our earliest uncials at least in one respect, that the letters, being as broad as they are high, are all capable of being included within circumscribed squares. Indeed, yet earlier inscriptions are found almost totally destitute of curves, even O and Θ being represented by simple squares, with or without a bisecting horizontal line (see *theta*, p. 35)[1].

[1] The Cotton fragment of the book of Genesis of the fifth century, whose poor shrivelled remains from the fire of 1731 are still preserved in the British Museum, while in common with all other *manuscripts* it exhibits the round shapes of O and Θ, substitutes a lozenge ◇ for the circle in *phi*, after the older fashion (Φ). *Phi* often has much the same shape in Codex Bezae; e.g. Matt. xiii. 26, Fol. 42 *b*, l. 13, and once in Codex Z (Matt. xxi. 26, Plate xlviii).

Plate II.

(4)

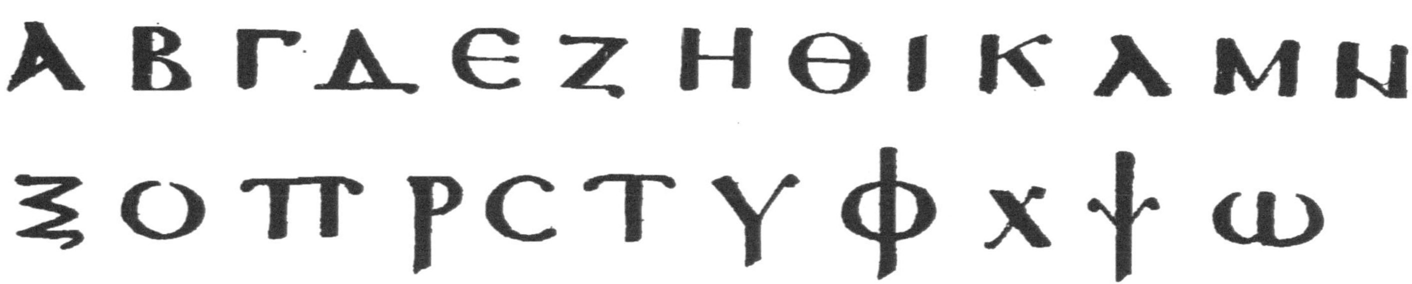

(5)

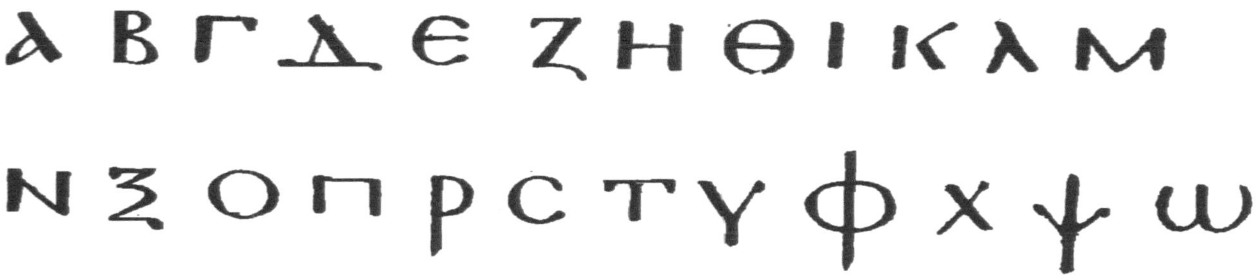

The Herculanean papyri, however (a specimen of which we have given in Plate iv. No. 10), are much better suited than inscriptions can be for comparison with our earliest copies of Scripture[1]. Nothing can well be conceived more elegant than these simply-formed graceful little letters (somewhat diminished in size perhaps by the effects of heat) running across the volume, thirty-nine lines in a column, without capitals or breaks between the words. There are scarcely any stops, no breathings, accents, or marks of any kind; only that >, < or ▷ are now and then found at the end of a line, to fill up the space, or to join a word or syllable with what follows. A very few abbreviations occur, such as $\overset{\rho}{\pi}$ in the first line of our specimen, taken from Philodemus *περὶ κακιῶν* (Hercul. Volum. Tom. iii. Col. xx. ll. 6–15), the very manuscript to which Tischendorf compared his Cod. Friderico-Augustanus (Proleg. § 11). The papyri, buried for so many ages from A. D. 79 downwards, may probably be a century older still, since Philodemus the Epicurean was the contemporary and almost the friend of Cicero[2]. Hence from three to four hundred years must have elapsed betwixt the date of the Herculanean rolls and that of our earliest Biblical manuscripts. Yet the fashion of writing changed but little during the interval, far less in every respect than in the four centuries which next followed, wherein the plain, firm, upright and square uncials were giving place to the compressed, oblong, ornamented, or even sloping forms which predominate from the seventh or eighth century downwards. While advising the reader to exercise his skill on facsimiles of *entire passages*, especially in contrasting the lines from Philodemus (No. 10) with those from the oldest uncials of the New Testament (Nos. 11–14; 17; 18; 20; 24); we purpose to examine the several alphabets (Nos. 1–7) letter by letter, pointing out to the student those variations in shape which palaeographers have judged the safest criteria of their relative ages. *Alpha*, *delta*, *theta*, *xi*, *pi*, *omega*, are among the best tests for this purpose.

Alpha is not often found in its present familiar shape, except in

[1] Our facsimile is borrowed from the Neapolitan volumes, but Plate 57 in the Paléographie Universelle *φιλοδημου περι μουσικη* has the advantage of *colours* for giving a lively idea of the present charred appearance of these papyri.

[2] Cicero de Finibus, Lib. ii. c. 35. The same person is apparently meant in Orat. in Pisonem, cc. 28, 29.

inscriptions, where the cross line is sometimes broken into an angle with the vertex downwards (A). Even on the Rosetta stone the left limb leans against the upper part of the right limb, but does not form an angle with its extremity, while the cross line, springing not far from the bottom of the left limb, *ascends* to meet the right about half way down. Modifications of this form may be seen in the Herculanean rolls, only that the cross line more nearly approaches the horizontal, and sometimes is almost entirely so. The Cod. Frid.-August.[1] does not vary much from this form, but the three generating lines are often somewhat curved. In other books, while the right limb is quite straight, the left and cross line form a kind of loop or curve, as is very observable in the Nitrian fragment R, and often in Codd. Alex., Ephraemi, Bezae, the newly discovered Rossanensis, and in the Vatican more frequently still, in all which *alpha* often approximates to the shape of our English *a*. *And this curve may be regarded as a proof of antiquity;* indeed Tischendorf (Proleg. Cod. Sin. p. xxx, 1863) considers it almost peculiar to the papyri and the Coptic character. Cod. N (which is more recent than those named above) makes the two lines on the left form a sharp angle, as do the Cotton fragment of Genesis (see p. 32, note 1) and Cod. Claromontanus, Plate xiv. No. 41, only that the lines which contain the angle in this last are very fine. In later times, as the letters grew tall and narrow, the modern type of A became more marked, as in the first letter of Arundel 547 (No. 16), of about the tenth century, though the form and thickness seen in the Cod. Claromontanus continued much in vogue to the last. Yet *alpha* even in Cod. Claromontanus and Cotton Genesis occasionally passes from the angle into the loop, though not so often as in Cod. A and its companions. Cod. Borgianus (T), early in the fifth century, exaggerated this loop into a large ellipse, if Giorgi's facsimile may be trusted. In Cod. Laudianus E of the Acts and Cureton's palimpsest Homer too the loop is very decided, the Greek and Latin *a* in Laud. (No. 25) being alike. Mark also its form in the papyrus scrawl No. 9 (from one of the orations of Hyperides edited by Mr. Babington), which *may* be as old as the Rosetta stone. The angular shape adopted in Cod. Z (Nos. 6, 18) is unsightly enough, and (I believe) unique.

Beta varies less than *Alpha*. Originally it consisted of a tall perpendicular line, on the right side of which four straight lines are so placed as to form two triangles, whereof the vertical line comprises the bases, while a small portion of that vertical line entirely separates the triangles (B). This ungraceful figure was modified very early, even in inscriptions. On the Rosetta stone (No. 1) the triangles are rounded off into semicircles, and the lower end of the vertical curved. Yet the shape in manuscripts is not quite so elegant. The lower curve is usually the larger, and the curves rarely touch each other.

[1] We prefer citing Cod. Frid.-August., because our examples have been actually taken from its exquisitely lithographed pages; but the facsimile of part of a page from Luke xxiv represented in Tischendorf's Cod. Sinaiticus, from which we have borrowed six lines (No. 11 b), will be seen to resemble exactly the portion published in 1846.

(6)

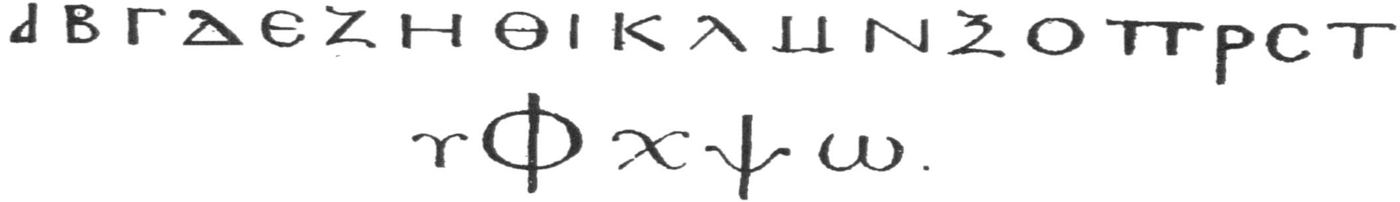

(7)

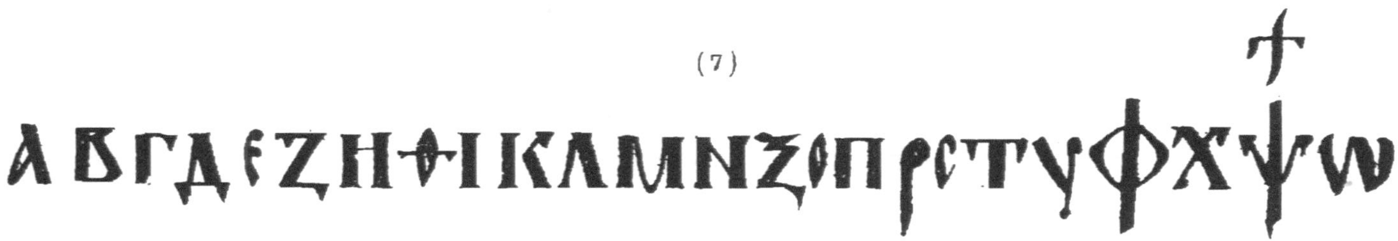

(8)

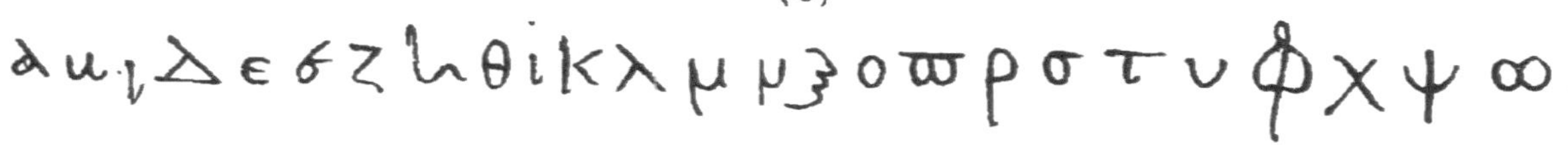

Such are Codd. ANRZ, Rossanensis (sometimes), and the Cotton Genesis. In the Herculanean rolls the letter comes near the common cursive β; in some others (as Cod. Rossanensis at times) its shape is quite like the modern B. When oblong letters became common, the top (e.g. in Cod. Bezae) and bottom extremities of the curve ran into straight lines, by way of return into the primitive shape (see No. 36, *dated* A.D. 980). In the very early papyrus fragment of Hyperides it looks like the English R standing on a base (No. 9, l. 4). But this specimen rather belongs to the semi-cursive hand of common life, than to that of books.

Gamma in its simplest form consists of two lines of equal thickness, the shorter so placed upon the longer, which is vertical, as to make one right angle with it on the right side. Thus we find it in the Rosetta stone, the papyrus of Hyperides, the Herculanean rolls, and very often in Cod. A. The next step was to make the horizontal line very thin, and to strengthen its extremity by a point, or knob, as in Codd. Ephraemi (No. 24), RZ: or the point was thus strengthened without thinning the line, e.g. Codd. Vatican., Rossanensis, N and most later copies, such as Harl. 5598 (No. 7) or its contemporary Parham 18 (No. 36). In Cod. Bezae (No. 42) *gamma* much resembles the Latin r.

Delta should be closely scrutinized. Its most ancient shape is an equilateral triangle, the sides being all of the same thickness (Δ). Cod. Claromontanus, though of the sixth century, is in this instance as simple as any: the Herculanean rolls, Codd. Vatican., Sinait., and the very old copy of the Pentateuch at Paris (Colbert) or 'Cod. Sarravianus' and Leyden, much resemble it, only that sometimes the Herculanean sides are slightly curved, and the right descending stroke of Cod. Vatican. is thickened. In Cod. A begins a tendency to prolong the base on one or both sides, and to strengthen one or both ends by points. We see a little more of this in Cod. Rossanensis and in the palimpsest Homer of the fifth century, published by Cureton. The habit increases and gradually becomes confirmed in Codd. Ephraemi (No. 24), the Vatican Dio Cassius of the fifth or sixth century, in Cod. R, and particularly in N and E of the Acts (Nos. 4, 14, 25). In the oblong later uncials it becomes quite elaborate, e.g. Cod. B of the Apocalypse, or Nos. 7, 21, 36. On the Rosetta stone and in the Cod. Bezae the right side is produced beyond the triangle, and is produced and slightly curved in Hyperides, curved and strongly pointed in Cod. Z.

Epsilon has its angular form on the Rosetta marble and other inscriptions in stone; in the oldest manuscripts it consists as an uncial of a semicircle, from whose centre to the right of it a horizontal radius is drawn to the concave circumference. Thus it appears in the Herculanean rolls (only that here the radius is usually broken off before it meets the circle), in Codd. Frid.-August., Vatican., the two Paris Pentateuchs (Colbert-Leyden fifth century, Coislin. sixth) and the Cotton Genesis. In Cod. Alex. a slight trace is found of the more recent practice of strengthening each of the three extremities with knobs, but only the radius at times in Cod. Rossanensis. The custom increases in Codd. Ephraemi, Bezae, and still more in Codd. NRZ, wherein the curve becomes greater than a semicircle. In Hyperides (and in a slighter degree in Cod. Claromon. No. 41) the shape almost resembles the Latin *e*. The form of this and the other round letters was afterwards much affected in the narrow oblong uncials: see Nos. 7, 16, 36.

Zeta on the Rosetta stone maintains its old form (Ɪ), which is indeed but the next letter reversed. In manuscripts it receives its usual modern shape (Z), the ends being pointed decidedly, slightly, or not at all, much after the manner described for *epsilon*. In old copies the lower horizontal line is a trifle curved (Cod. R, No. 5), or even both the extreme lines (Cod. Z, No. 6, and Cod. Augiensis of St. Paul). In such late books as Parham 18 (A.D. 980, facsim. No. 36) *Zeta* is so large as to run far below the line, ending in a kind of tail.

Eta does not depart from its normal shape (H) except that in Cod. Ephraemi (No. 24) and some narrow and late uncials (e.g. Nos. 7, 36) the cross line is often more than half way up the letter. In a few later uncials the cross line passes *outside* the two perpendiculars, as in the Cod. Augiensis, twenty-six times on the photographed page of Scrivener's edition.

Theta deserves close attention. In some early inscriptions it is found as a square, bisected horizontally (⊟). On the Rosetta stone and most others (but only in such monuments) it is a circle, with a strong central *point*. On the Herculanean rolls the central point is spread into a short horizontal line, yet not reaching the circumference (No. 10, l. 8). Thence in our uncials from the fourth to the sixth century the line becomes a horizontal diameter to a true circle (Codd. Vatican., Sinait., Codd. ANRZ, Ephraemi, Claromont., Rossanensis, and Cureton's Homer). In the seventh century the diameter began to pass out of the circle on both sides: thence the circle came to be compressed into an ellipse (sometimes very narrow), and the ends of the minor axis to be ornamented with knobs, as in Cod. B of the Apocalypse (eighth century), Cod. Augiensis (ninth century), LX of the Gospels, after the manner of the tenth century (Nos. 7, 16, 21, 36, 38).

Iota would need no remark but for the custom of placing over it and *upsilon*, when they commence a syllable, either a very short straight line, or one or two dots. After the papyrus rolls no copy is quite without them, from the Codex Alexandrinus, the Cotton Genesis and Paris-Leyden Pentateuch, Cod. Z and the Isaiah included in it, to the more recent cursives; although in some manuscripts they are much rarer than in others. By far the most usual practice is to put two points, but Cod. Ephraemi, in its *New* Testament portion, stands nearly alone with the Cotton Genesis (ch. xviii. 9) in exhibiting the straight line; Cod. Alexandrinus in the Old Testament, but not in the New, frequently resembles Codd. Ephraemi and the Cotton

Genesis in placing a straight line over *iota*, and more rarely over *upsilon*, instead of the single or double dots; Cod. Sinaiticus employs two points or a straight line (as in Z's Isaiah) promiscuously over both vowels, and in Wake 12, a cursive of the eleventh century, the former frequently pass into the latter in writing. Codd. Borgianus (T) and Claromont. have but one point; Codd. N and Rossanensis have two for *iota*, one for *upsilon*.

Kappa deserves notice chiefly because the vertex of the angle formed by the two inclined lines very frequently does not meet the perpendicular line, but falls short of it a little to the right: we observe this in Codd. ANR, Ephraemi, Rossanensis, and later books. The copies that have strong points at the end of *epsilon* &c. (e.g. Codd. NR and AZ partly) have the same at the extremity of the thin or upper limb of *Kappa*. In Cod. D a fine horizontal stroke runs a little to the left from the bottom of the vertical line. Compare also the initial letter in Cod. M, No. 32.

Lambda much resembles *alpha*, but is less complicated. All our models (except Harl. 5598, No. 7), from the Rosetta stone downwards, have the right limb longer than the left, which thus leans against its side, but the length of the projection varies even in the same passage (e.g. No. 10). In most copies later than the Herculanean rolls and Cod. Sinaiticus the shorter line is much the thinner, and the longer slightly curved. In Cod. Z (Nos. 6, 18) the projection is curved elegantly at the end, as we saw in *delta*.

Mu varies as much as most letters. Its normal shape, resembling the English M, is retained in the Rosetta stone and most inscriptions, but at an early period there was a tendency to make the letter broader, and not to bring the re-entering or middle angle so low as in English (e.g. Codd. Vaticanus and Sinaiticus). In Cod. Ephraemi this central angle is sometimes a little rounded: in Codd. Alex. and Parham 18 the lines forming the angle do not always spring from the top of the vertical lines: in Arund. 547 (No. 16) they spring almost from their foot, forming a thick inelegant loop below the line, the letter being rather narrow: Harl. 5598 (No. 7) somewhat resembles this last, only that the loop is higher up. In the Herculanean rolls (and to a less extent in the Cotton Genesis) the two outer lines cease to be perpendicular, and lean outwards until the letter looks much like an inverted W (No. 10). In the papyrus Hyperides (No. 9) these outer lines are low curves, and the central lines rise in a kind of flourish above them. *Mu* assumes this shape also in Cod. T, and at the end of a line even in Codd. Vaticanus and Sinaiticus. This form is so much exaggerated in some examples, that by discarding the outer curves we obtain the shape seen in Cod. Z (Nos. 6, 18) and one or two others (e.g. Paul M in Harl. 5613, No. 34), almost exactly resembling an inverted *pi*. So also in the Isaiah of Cod. Z, only that the left side and base line were made by one stroke of the pen.

Nu is easier, the only change (besides the universal transition from the square to the oblong in the later uncials) being that in a few cases the thin cross line does not pass from the top of the left to the bottom of the right vertical line as in English (N), but only from about half-way or two-thirds down the left vertical in the Cotton Genesis, Codd. A, Rossanensis, Harl. 5598 (No. 7), and others; in Codd. ℵNR Parham 18 it often neither springs from the top of one, nor reaches the foot of the other (Nos. 4, 5, 11 b, 12, 36); while in Cod. Claromont. (No. 41) it is here and there not far from horizontal. In a few *cursives* (e.g. 440 Evan. at Cambridge, and Tischendorf's lo^ti^ or 61 of the Acts), H and N almost interchange their shapes: so in Evan. 66 and Wake 34 at the end of a line only.

Xi in the Rosetta stone and Herculanean rolls consists of three parallel straight lines, the middle one being the shortest, as in modern printed Greek: but all our Biblical manuscripts exhibit modifications of the small printed ξ, such as must be closely inspected, but cannot easily be described. In the Cotton Genesis this *xi* is narrow and smaller than its fellows, much like an old English ȝ resting on a horizontal base which curves downwards: while in late uncials, as B of the Apocalypse, Cod. Augiensis (l. 13 Scrivener's *photographed page*), and especially in Parham 18 (No. 36), the letter and its flourished finial are continued far below the line. For the rest we must refer to our facsimile alphabets, &c. The figures in Cod. Frid.-August. (Nos. 2, 11 a, ll. 3, 8) look particularly awkward, nor does the shape in Cod. Rossanensis much differ from these. In Cod. E, the Zurich Psalter of the seventh century, and Mr. W. White's fragment W^d^, *xi* is the common Z with a large horizontal line over it, strengthened by knobs at each end.

Omicron is unchanged, excepting that in the latest uncials (No. 16, 36) the circle is mostly compressed, like *theta*, into a very eccentric ellipse.

Pi requires attention. Its original shape was doubtless two vertical straight lines joined at top by another horizontal, thinner perhaps but not much shorter than they. Thus we meet with it on the Rosetta stone, Codd. R, Vatican., Sinaiticus, Ephraemi, Claromontanus, Laud. of the Acts, the two Pentateuchs, Cureton's Homer, and sometimes Cod. A (No. 12). The fine horizontal line is, however, slightly produced on both sides in such early documents as the papyri of Hyperides and Herculaneum, and in the Cotton Genesis, as well as in Cod. A occasionally[1]. Both extremities of this line are fortified by strong points in Codd. N and Rossanensis, and mostly in Cod. A, but the left side only in Cod. Z, and this in Cod. Bezae occasionally becomes a sort of hooked curve. The later oblong *pi* was usually very plain, with thick vertical lines and a very fine horizontal, in Arund. 547 (No. 16) not at all produced; in Harl. 5598 (No. 7) slightly produced on both sides; in Parham 18 (No. 36) produced only on the right.

Rho is otherwise simple, but in all our authorities except inscriptions is produced below the line of writing, least perhaps in the papyri and

[1] Cod. A is found in the simpler form in the Old Testament, but mostly with the horizontal line produced in the New.

Cod. Claromont., considerably in Codd. AX (Nos. 12, 38), most in Parham 18 (No. 36): Codd. N, Rossanensis, and many later copies have the lower extremity boldly *bevelled.* The form is P rather than P in Codd. ℵA. In Cod. D a horizontal stroke, longer and thicker than in *kappa*, runs to the left from the bottom of the vertical line.

Sigma retains its angular shape (C or Σ) only on inscriptions, as the Rosetta, and that long after the square shapes of *omicron* and *theta* were discarded. The uncial or semicircular form, however, arose early, and to this letter must be applied all that was said of *epsilon* as regards terminal points (a knob at the lower extremity occurs even in Cod. ℵ, e.g. Acts ii. 31), and its cramped shape in later ages.

Tau in its oldest form consists of two straight lines of like thickness, the horizontal being bisected by the lower and vertical one. As early as in Cod. Sinaiticus the horizontal line is made thin, and strengthened on the left side *only* by a point or small knob (Nos. 3, 11): thus we find it in Cod. Laud. of the Acts sometimes. In Cod. Alex. *both* ends are slightly pointed, in Codd. Ephraemi, Rossanensis, and others much more. In Cod. Bezae the horizontal is curved and flourished; in the late uncials the vertical is very thick, the horizontal fine, and the ends formed into heavy triangles (e.g. No. 16).

Upsilon on the Rosetta stone and Herculanean rolls is like our Y, all the strokes being of equal thickness and not running below the line: nor do they in Hyperides or in Codd. XZ and Augiensis, which have the upper lines neatly curved (Nos. 6, 9, 18, 38). The right limb of many of the rest is sometimes, but not always curved; the vertical line in Codd. Vatican. and Sinaiticus drops slightly below the line; in Codd. A, Ephraemi, Cotton Genesis, Cureton's Homer, Laud. of the Acts and Rossanensis somewhat more; in others (as Codd. Bezae NR) considerably. In the subscription to St. Matthew's Gospel, which may be by a somewhat later hand, a horizontal line crosses the vertical a little below the curved lines in Cod. Rossanensis. In later uncials (Nos. 7, 36) it becomes a long or awkward Y, or even degenerates into a long V (No. 16); or, in copies written by Latin scribes, into Y reversed. We have described under *iota* the custom of placing dots, &c. over *upsilon.* But in Tischendorf's Leipzig II. (fragments from Numbers to Judges of the seventh or eighth century) *upsilon* receives two dots, *iota* only one. Once in Cod. Z (Matt. xxi. 5) and oftener in its Isaiah a convex semicircle, like a circumflex, stands over *upsilon.*

Phi is a remarkable letter. In most copies it is the largest in the alphabet, quite disproportionately large in Codd. ZL (Paris 62) and others, and to some extent in Codd. AR, Ephraemi, Rossanensis, and Claromont. The circle (which in the Cotton Genesis is *sometimes* still a lozenge, see above, p. 32, note 1), though large and in some copies even too broad (e.g. No. 18), is usually in the line of the other letters, the vertical line being produced *far* upwards (Cod. Augiens. and Nos. 16, 41), or downwards (No. 10), or both (No. 36). On the Rosetta stone the circle is very small and the straight line short.

Chi is a simple transverse cross (X) and never goes above or below the line. The limb that inclines from left to right is in the uncial form for the most part thick, the other thin (with final points according to the practice stated for *epsilon*), and this limb or both (as in Cod. Z) a little curved.

Psi is a rare but trying letter. Its oldest form resembled an English V with a straight line running up bisecting its interior angle. On the Rosetta stone it had already changed into its present form (Ψ), the curve being a small semicircle, the vertical rising above the other letters and falling a little below the line. In the Cotton Genesis *psi* is rather taller than the rest, but the vertical line does not rise above the level of the circle. In Codd. ANR and Rossanensis the under line is prolonged: in R the two limbs are straight lines making an angle of about 45° with the vertical, while oftentimes in Hyperides and Cod. Augiensis (Scrivener's *photograph*, ll. 18, 23) they curve *downwards*; the limbs in N and R being strongly (slightly in Rossanensis) pointed at the ends, and the bottom of the vertical bevelled as usual. In Cod. B of the Apocalypse, in Evan. OW^{d}Ξ, and even in Hyperides, the limbs (strongly pointed) fall into a straight line, and the figure becomes a large cross (No. 7). In Evan. 66 the vertical is crossed above the semicircle by a minute horizontal line.

Omega took the form Ω, even when *omicron* and *theta* were square; thus it appears on the Rosetta stone, but in the Hyperides and Herculaneum rolls it is a single curve, much like the w of English writing, only that the central part is sometimes only a low double curve (No. 10, l. 6). In the Cotton Genesis, Codd. Vatican., Sinaiticus, Alex., Ephraemi, Bezae, Claromont., Nitriens., Rossanensis, there is little difference in shape, though sometimes Cod. Vatican. comes near the Herculanean rolls, and Cod. Alex. next to it: elsewhere their strokes (especially those in the centre) are fuller and more laboured. Yet in Cod. N it is often but a plain semicircle, bisected by a perpendicular radius, with the ends of the curve bent inwards (No. 14, l. 2). In the late uncials (Nos. 7, 16) it almost degenerates into an ungraceful W, while in Cod. Augiensis (*photograph*, l. 18) the first limb is occasionally a complete circle.

These details might be indefinitely added to by references to other codices and monuments of antiquity, but we have employed most of the principal copies of the Greek Testament, and have indicated to the student the chief points to which his attention should be drawn. Three leading principles have perhaps been sufficiently established by the foregoing examples:

First, that the uncials used in writing differ from the capitals cut in stone by the curved shapes which the writing hand naturally adopts[1].

Secondly, that the upright uncials of square dimensions

[1] See Maunde Thompson's 'Greek and Latin Palaeography.'

are more ancient than those which are narrow, oblong, or *leaning*[1].

Thirdly, that the simpler and less elaborate the style of writing, the more remote is its probable date.

Copies of a later age occasionally aim at imitating the fashion of an earlier period, or possibly the style of the older book from which their text is drawn. But this anachronism of fashion may be detected, as well by other circumstances we are soon to mention, as from the air of constraint which pervades the whole manuscript: the rather as the scribe will now and then fall into the more familiar manner of his contemporaries; especially when writing those small letters which our Biblical manuscripts of all dates (even the most venerable) perpetually crowd into the ends of lines, in order to save space.

11. We do not intend to dwell much on the cursive handwriting. No books of the Greek Scriptures earlier than the ninth century in this style are now extant[2], though it was prevalent long before in the intercourse of business or common life. The papyri of Hyperides (e. g. No. 9) and the Herculanean rolls, in a few places, show that the process had then commenced, for the letters of each word are often joined, and their shapes prove that swiftness of execution was more aimed at than distinctness. This is seen even more clearly in a petition to Ptolemy Philometor (B. C. 164) represented in the 'Paléographie Universelle' (No. 56). The same great work contains (No. 66) two really cursive charters of the Emperors

[1] Codd. B of Apocalypse, Θ^{a} Λ (No. 30) of the Gospels, and Silvestre's No. 68, all of about the eighth century, slope more or less to the right; Cod. Γ (No. 35) of the ninth century, a very little to the left. Tischendorf assigns to the seventh century the fragments comprising Leipzig II. (see p. 39), though they lean much to the right (Monum. sacra ined. tom. i, pp. xxx–xxxiv, 141–176), and those of Isaiah (ibid. pp. xxxvi, xxxvii, 187–199).

[2] The earliest cursive Biblical manuscript formerly alleged, i.e. Evan. 14, on examination proves to have no inscription whatever. 'On folio 392, in a comparatively modern hand, is rather uncouthly written *ἐγράφη νικηφόρου βασιλεύοντος* A. Z. What the initials A. Z. stand for I do not know.' (Dean Burgon, *Guardian*, Jan. 15, 1873.) The claim of priority for Cod. 14 being thus disposed of (though it must be noted that Dr. C. R. Gregory refers it without doubt to the tenth century), we may note that Cod. 429 of the Gospels is dated 978, Cod. 148 of the Acts 984, Cod. 5^{pe} 994, and Λ, written partly in cursives, and partly in uncials is of the ninth century. But the date May 7, 835 A. D. is plainly visible on Cod. 481, which is therefore indisputably the earliest.

Maurice (A. D. 600) and Heraclius (A. D. 616). Other instances of early cursive writing may be found in two Deeds of Sale, A. D. 616, and 599, a Manumission in 355, an Official Deed in 233, a Deed of Sale in 154, in Aristotle on the Constitution of Athens, about 100, in a Farm Account in 78–79, in a Receipt in A. D. 20, in the Casati contract in B. C. 114, in a Letter on Egyptian Contracts in 146, a Treasury Circular in 170, in a Steward's letter of the third century B.C., in various documents of the same century lying in the British Museum, at Paris, Berlin, Leyden, and elsewhere, of which the oldest, being amongst the papyri discovered by Dr. Flinders Petrie at Gurob is referred to B. C. 268, and the Leyden papyrus to 260[1]. Yet the earliest books of a later age known to be written in cursive letters are Cod. 481 (Scholz 461, dated A. D. 835) the Bodleian Euclid (dated A. D. 888) and the twenty-four dialogues of Plato in the same Library (dated A. D. 895)[2]. There is reason to believe, from the comparatively unformed character of the writing in them all, that Burney 19 in the British Museum (from which we have extracted the alphabet No. 8, Plate iii), and the minute, beautiful and important Codex 1 of the Gospels at Basle (of which see a facsimile No. 23), are but little later than the Oxford books, and may be referred to the tenth century. Books copied after the cursive hand had become regularly formed, in the eleventh,

[1] See Maunde Thompson, Greek and Latin Palaeology, chap. x. pp. 130, &c., and chap. viii. pp. 107, &c; Notices et Extracts des MSS. de la Bibliothèque Imperiale, Paris, plate xxiv. no. 21, pl. xlviii. no. 21 *ter*, xlvi. no. 69, *e*, xxi. no. 17, xiii. no. 5, xl. no. 62, xviii. 2, pl. xliv; Cat. Gr. Papyri in Brit. Mus. Palaeograph. Soc. ii. pl. 143, 144, Mahaffy, Petrie Papyri, pl. xiv, xxix. &c. (Cunningham Memoirs of R. Irish Academy).

[2] At the end of the Euclid we read *εγραφη χειρι στεφανου κληρικου μηνι σεπτεμβριωι ινδ. ζ ετει κοσμου ϛ̄τ̄ ϟ̄ ζ εκτησαμην αρεθας πατρευς την παρουσαν βιβλιον*: of the Plato, *εγραφη χειρι ιω καλλιγραφου · ευτυχως αρεθη διακονωι πατρει · νομισματων βυζαντϊεων δεκα και τριων · μηνι νοεμβριωι ινδικτιωνος ι̅δ̅ · ετει κοσμου ϛ̅υ̅δ̅ βασιλειας λεοντος του φιλοχ̅υ̅ νιου βασιλειου του αειμνιστου.* It should be stated that these very curious books, both written by monks, and indeed *all the dated manuscripts of the Greek Testament we have seen* except Canonici 34 in the Bodleian (which reckons from the Christian era, A.D. 1515–6), calculate from the Greek era of the Creation, September 1, B.C. 5508. To obtain the year A.D., therefore, from January 1 to August 31 in any year, subtract 5508 from the given year; from September 1 to December 31 subtract 5509. The indiction which usually accompanies this date is a useful check in case of any corruption or want of legibility in the letters employed as numerals. Both dates are given in Evan. 558, viz. A. M. 6938, and A. D. 1430.

twelfth and thirteenth centuries, are hard to be distinguished by the mere handwriting, though they are often dated, or their age fixed by the material (see p. 23), or the style of their illuminations. Colbert. 2844, or 33 of the Gospels (facsim. No. 39), is attributed to the eleventh century, and Burney 21 (No. 15)[1], is dated A.D. 1292, and afford good examples of their respective dates. *Beta* (l. 1 letter 4), *when joined to other letters*, is barely distinguishable from *upsilon*[2]; *nu* is even nearer to *mu*; the tall forms of *eta* and *epsilon* are very graceful, the whole style elegant and, after a little practice, easily read. Burney 22 (facsimile No. 37) is dated about the same time, A.D. 1319, and the four Biblical lines much resemble Burney 21[3]. In the fourteenth century a careless style came into fashion, of which Cod. Leicestrensis (No. 40) is an exaggerated instance, and during this century and the next our manuscripts, though not devoid of a certain beauty of appearance, are too full of arbitrary and elaborate contractions to be conveniently read. The formidable list of abbreviations and ligatures represented in Donaldson's Greek Grammar (p. 20, third edition)[4] originated at this period in the perverse ingenuity of the Greek emigrants in the West of Europe, who subsisted by their skill as copyists;

[1] The writer of Burney 21 (r^scr) A.D. 1292 (Evan. 571), *ὁ ταπεινος Θεοδωρος ἁγιωπετριτης ταχα και καλλιγραφος* as he calls himself (that is, as I once supposed, monk of the Convent of Sancta Petra at Constantinople, short-hand and fair writer), was the scribe of at least *five* more copies of Scripture now extant: Birch's Havn. 1, A.D. 1278 (Evan. 284); Evan. 90, A.D. 1298; Evan. 543, A.D. 1295; Scholz's Evan. 412, A.D. 1301; Evan. 74, *undated*. To this list Franz Delitzsch (1813–1890) (Zeitschr. f. luth. Theol. 1863, ii, Abhandlungen, pp. 217, 218) adds from Matthaei, Synaxarion in Mosc. Syn. Typograph. xxvi. A.D. 1295, and recognizes *Hagios Petros*, the country of Theodoros, as a town in the Morea, on the borders of Arcadia, from whose school students have attended his own lectures at Erlangen.

[2] Hence in the later uncials, some of which must therefore have been copied from earlier cursives, B and Υ (which might seem to have no resemblance) are sometimes confounded: e.g. in Parham 18 (A.D. 980), *υ* for *β*, Luke vi. 34; *β* for *υ*, John x. 1, especially where *β* begins or ends a line: e.g. Evan. 59, John vii. 35. Evan. 59 has *β* for *υ* very often, yet there is no extra trace that it was copied from an uncial.

[3] The full signature not easily deciphered is *ἐτελειώθη τὸ παρὸν ἅγιον εὐαγγέλιον κατὰ τὴν κ̄ζ τοῦ ἰαννουαρίου μηνὸς τῆς* [?] *ω̄ κ̄ ζ ἐγχρονίας.* Presuming that ϛ̄ is suppressed before ω̄ κ̄ ζ this is 6827 of the Greeks, A.D. 1319.

[4] Compare also Buttmann's Greek Grammar (Robinson's translation) p. 467; Bast in (Schaefer's Gregorius Corinthius) tabb. ad fin.; Gardthausen, Palaeographie, p. 248, &c.

and these pretty puzzles (for such they now are to many a fair classical scholar), by being introduced into early printed books[1], have largely helped to withdraw them from use in modern times.

12. We have now to describe the practice of Biblical manuscripts as regards the insertion of ι forming a diphthong with the long vowels *eta* and *omega*, also with *alpha* long, whether by being *ascript*, i. e. written by their side, or *subscript*, i. e. written under them. In the earliest inscriptions and in the papyri of Thebes ι *ascript* (the *iota* not smaller than other letters) is invariably found. In the petition to Ptolemy Philometor (*above*, p. 41) it occurs four times in the first line, three times in the third: in the fragments of Hyperides it is perpetually though not always read, even where (especially with verbs) it has no rightful place, e. g. ετωι και αντιβολωι (facsimile No. 9, ll. 3, 4) for αἰτῶ καὶ ἀντιβολῶ. A little before the Christian era it began to grow obsolete, probably from its being lost in pronunciation. In the Herculanean Philodemus (the possible limits of whose date are from B. C. 50 to A. D. 79) as in Evann. 556, 604 (Matt. ii. 12, 13), it is often dropped, though more usually written. In Codd. Vaticanus and Sinaiticus it is probably not found, and from this period it almost disappears from Biblical uncials[2]; in Cureton's Homer, of the fifth or perhaps of the sixth century, ι *ascript* is sometimes neglected, but usually inserted; sometimes also ι is placed *above* H or Ω, an arrangement neither neat nor convenient. With the cursive character ι *ascript* came in again, as may be seen from the subscriptions in the Bodleian Euclid and Plato (p. 42, note 1). The *semicursive* fragment of St. Paul's Epistles in red letters (M of St. Paul, Plate xii No. 34), used for the binding of Harleian 5613, contains ι *ascript* twice, but I have tried in vain to verify Griesbach's statement (Symbol. Crit. ii. p. 166) that it has ι *subscript* 'bis tantum aut ter.' I can find no such instance in

[1] Thus the type cast for the Royal Printing Office at Paris, and used by Robert Stephen, is said to have been modelled on the style of the calligrapher Angelus Vergecius, from whose skill arose the expression 'he writes like an angel.' Codd. 296 of the Gospels, 124 of the Acts, 151 of St. Paul are in his hand.

[2] Yet Tischendorf (N.T. 1859, Proleg. p. cxxxiii) cites ηιδισαν from Cod. Bezae (Mark i. 34), ξυλωι (Luke xxiii. 31) from Cod. Cyprius, ωι from Cod. U (Matt. xxv. 15) and Cod. Λ (Luke vii. 4). Add Cod. Bezae πατρωιου Acts xxii. 3, Scrivener's edition, Introd. p. xix. Bentley's nephew speaks of ι *ascript* as in the first hand of Cod. B, but he seems to have been mistaken.

these leaves. The cursive manuscripts, speaking generally, either entirely omit both forms, or, if they give either, far more often neglect than insert them. Cod. 1 of the Gospels exhibits the *ascript* ι. Of forty-three codices now in England which have been examined with a view to this matter, twelve have no vestige of either fashion, fifteen represent the *ascript* use, nine the *subscript* exclusively, while the few that remain exhibit both indifferently[1]. The earliest cursive copy ascertained to exhibit ι *subscript* is Matthaei's r (Apoc. 50[2] [x]), and after that the Cod. Ephesius (Evan. 71), dated A.D. 1160. The *subscript* ι came much into vogue during the fifteenth century, and thus was adopted in printed books.

13. Breathings (*spiritus*) and accents[2] were not applied systematically to Greek Texts before the seventh century. But a practice prevailed in that and the succeeding century of inserting them in older manuscripts, where they were absent *primâ manu*. That such was done in many instances (e.g. in Codd. Vatican. and Coislin. 202 or H of St. Paul) appears clearly from the fact that the passages which the scribe who retouched the old letters for any cause left unaltered, are destitute of these marks, though they appear in all other places. Cod. ℵ exhibits breathings, apparently by the original scribe, in Tobit vi. 9; Gal. v. 21 only. The case of Cod. Alexandrinus is less easy. Though the rest of the book has neither breathings (except a few here and there) nor accents, the first four lines of *each* column of the book of Genesis (see facsimile No. 12), which are written in red, are fully furnished with them. These marks Baber, who edited the Old Testament portion of Cod. A, pronounced to be by a second hand (Notae, p. 1); Sir Frederick Madden, a more competent judge, declares them the work of the original scribe (Madden's Silvestre, Vol. i. p. 194, note), and after repeated examination we know not how to dissent from his view[3]. So too in the Sarravian Pentateuch of the fifth century

[1] In B-C iii. 10 (*dated* 1430), the whole manuscript being written by the same hand, we have ι *ascript* twenty-five times up to Luke i. 75, then on the same page ι *subscript* in Luke i. 77 and eighty-five times afterwards: the two usages are nowhere mixed. In Evan. 558, *subscript* and *ascript* are mixed in the same page, Luc. i. 75, 77.

[2] The invention of breathings, accents, and stops is attributed to Aristophanes of Byzantium, 260 B.C.

[3] See below vol. ii. c. ix. 9. note, end. Dr. Scrivener appears not to have formed a positive opinion, which indeed in some of these cases is hardly possible.

we read ΤΟΝΎΝ (Lev. xi. 7) by the first hand. The Cureton palimpsest of Homer also has them, though they are occasionally obliterated, and some few are evidently inserted by a corrector; the case is nearly so with the Milan Homer edited by Mai; and the same must be stated of the Vienna Dioscorides (Silvestre, No. 62), whose date is fixed by internal evidence to about A.D. 500. In the papyrus fragment of the Psalms, now in the British Museum, the accents are very accurate, and the work of the original scribe. These facts, and others like these, may make us hesitate to adopt the notion generally received among scholars on the authority of Montfaucon (Palaeogr. Graec. p. 33), that breathings and accents were not introduced *primâ manu* before the seventh or eighth century; although up to that period, no doubt, they were placed very incorrectly, and often omitted altogether. The breathings are much the more ancient and important of the two. The *spiritus lenis* indeed may be a mere invention of the Alexandrian grammarians of the second or third century before Christ, but the *spiritus asper* is in fact the substitute for a real letter (H) which appears on the oldest inscriptions; its original shape being the first half of the H (⊢), of which the second half was subsequently adopted for the *lenis* (⊣). This form is sometimes found in manuscripts of about the eleventh century (e.g. Lebanon, B. M. Addit. 11300 or k^{scr}, and usually in Lambeth 1178 or d^{scr}) ed. of 1550, but even in the Cod. Alexandrinus the comma and inverted comma are several times substituted to represent the *lenis* and *asper* respectively (facsimile No. 12): and at a later period this last was the ordinary, though not quite the invariable, mode of expressing the breathings. Aristophanes of Byzantium (keeper of the famous Library at Alexandria under Ptolemy Euergetes, about B.C. 240), though probably not the inventor of the Greek accents, was the first to arrange them in a system. Accentuation must have been a welcome aid to those who employed Greek as a learned, though not as their vernacular tongue, and is so convenient and suggestive that no modern scholar can afford to dispense with its familiar use: yet not being, like the rough breathing, an essential portion of the language, it was but slowly brought into general vogue. It would seem that in Augustine's age [354–430] the distinction between the smooth and rough breathing in the manuscripts was just such a point as a careful reader would mark, a hasty one overlook[1]. Hence it is not surprising that though these marks are entirely absent both from the Theban and Herculanean papyri, a few breathings are apparently by the first hand in Cod. Borgianus or T (Tischendorf, N. T. 1859, Proleg. p. cxxxi). One rough breathing is just visible in that early palimpsest of St. John's Gospel, I^b or N^b. Such as appear, together with some accents, in the Coislin Octateuch of the sixth or seventh century, may not the less be *primâ manu* because many pages are destitute of them; those of Cod. Claromontanus, which were once deemed original, are now pronounced by its editor Tischendorf to be a later addition. Cod. N, the purple fragment so often spoken of already, exhibits *primâ manu* over certain vowels a kind of smooth breathing or slight acute accent, sometimes little larger than a point, but inserted on no intelligible principle, so far as we can see, and far oftener omitted entirely. All copies of Scripture which have not been specified, down to the end of the seventh century, are quite destitute of breathings and accents. An important manuscript of the eighth or ninth century, Cod. L or Paris 62 of the Gospels, has them for the most part, but not always; though often in the wrong place, and at times in utter defiance of all grammatical rules. Cod. B of the Apocalypse, however, though of the same age, has breathings and accents as constantly and correctly as most. Codices of the ninth century, with the exception of three written in the West of Europe (Codd. Augiensis or Paul F, Sangallensis or Δ of the Gospels, and Boernerianus or Paul G, which will be particularly described afterwards), are all accompanied with these marks in full, though often set down without any precise rule, so far as our experience has enabled us to observe. The uncial Evangelistaria (e.g. Arundel 547; Parham 18; Harleian 5598), especially, are much addicted to prefixing the *spiritus asper* improperly; chiefly, perhaps, to words beginning with H, so that documents of that age are but slender authorities on such points. Of the cursives the general tendency is to be more and more accurate as regards the accentua-

[1] He is speaking (Quaestion. super Genes. clxii) of the difference between *ῥάβδου αὐτοῦ* and *ῥάβδου αὑτοῦ*, Gen. xlvii. 31. 'Fallit enim eos verbum Graecum, quod eisdem literis scribitur, sive *ejus*, sive *suae*: sed accentus [he must mean the breathings] dispares sunt, et ab eis, qui ista noverunt, in codicibus non contemnuntur' (Opera, Tom. iv. p. 53, ed. 1586, Lugdun.); adding that 'suae' *might* be expressed by ἑαυτοῦ.

tion, the later the date: but this is only a general rule, as some that are early are as careful, and certain of the latest as negligent, as can well be imagined. All of them are partial to placing accents or breathings over both parts of a word compounded with a preposition (e.g. ἐπὶσυνάξαι), and on the other hand often drop them between a preposition and its case (e.g. ἐπάροτρου).

14. The punctuation in early times was very simple. In the papyri of Hyperides there are no stops at all, in the Herculanean rolls exceeding few: Codd. Sinaiticus and Vaticanus (the latter very rarely by the first hand) have a single point here and there on a level with the top of the letters, and occasionally a very small break in the continuous uncials, with or (as always in Cod. I[b] of the sixth century) without the point, to denote a pause in the sense. Codd. A N have the same point a little oftener; in Codd. C W[a] (Paris 314) Z and the Cotton Genesis the single point stands indiscriminately at the head, middle, or foot of the letters, while in E (Basil. A. N. iii. 12) of the Gospels and B of the Apocalypse, as in Cod. Marchalianus of the Prophets (sixth or seventh century), this change in the position of the point indicates a full-stop, half stop, or comma respectively. In Cod. L, of the same date as Codd. E and B (Apoc.), besides the full point we have the comma (::.) and semicolon (::), with a cross also for a stop. In Codd. Y Θ[a] (of about the eighth century) the single point has its various powers as in Cod. E, &c., but besides this are double, treble, and in Cod. Y quadruple, points with different powers. In late uncials, especially Evangelistaria, the chief stop is a cross, often in red (e.g. Arund. 547); while in Harleian 5598 ⁝ seems to be the note of interrogation[1]. When the continuous writing came to be broken up into separate words (of which Cod. Augiensis in the ninth century affords one of the earliest examples) the single point was intended to be placed after the last letter of each word, on a level with the middle of the letters. But even in this copy it is often omitted in parts, and in Codd. ΔG, written on the same plan, more frequently still. Our statements refer only to the Greek portions of these

[1] In the Gale Evangelistarium (Trin. Coll. Camb. O. 4. 22) the interrogative clause is set between two such marks in red. Hence it seems not so much a stop as a vocal note. In the Armenian and Spanish languages the note of interrogation is set before the interrogative clause, and very conveniently too.

copies; the Latin semicolon (;) and the note of interrogation (?) occur in their Latin versions. The Greek interrogation (;) first occurs about the ninth century, and (,) used as a stop a little later. The Bodleian Genesis of this date, or a little earlier, uses (,) also as an interrogative: so in later times B–C. iii. 5 [xii], and Evan. 556 [xii]. In the earliest cursives the system of punctuation is much the same as that of printed books: the English colon (:) not being much used, but the upper single point in its stead[1]. In a few cursives (e. g. Gonville or 59 of the Gospels), this upper point, set in a larger space, stands also for a full stop: indeed (·) is the only stop found in Tischendorf's lo[ti] or 61 of the Acts (Brit. Mus. Add. 20,003): while (;) and (·) are often confused in 440 of the Gospels (Cantab. Mm. 6. 9). The English comma, placed above a letter, is used for the apostrophus, which occurs in the very oldest uncials, especially at the end of proper names, or to separate compounds (e. g. *απ' ορφανισθεντες* in Cod. Clarom.), or when the word ends in *ξ* or *ρ* (e. g. *σαρξ'* in Cod. B, *θυγατηρ'* in Codd. Sinait. and A, *χειρ'* in Cod. A, *ὥσπερ'* in the Dioscorides, A.D. 500), or even to divide syllables (e. g. *συριγ'γας* in Cod. Frid.-August., *πολ'λα, κατεστραμ'μενη, αναγ'γελι* in Cod. Sinaiticus). In Cod. Z it is found only after *αλλ* and *μεθ*, but in Z's Isaiah it indicates other elisions (e. g. *επ*). This mark is more rare in Cod. Ephraemi than in some others, but is used more or less by all, and is found after *εξ*, or *ουχ*, and a few like words, even in the most recent cursives. In Cod. Bezae and others it assumes the shape of > rather than that of a comma.

15. Abbreviated words are perhaps least met with in Cod. Vatican., but even it has $\overline{θσ}$, $\overline{κσ}$, $\overline{ισ}$, $\overline{χσ}$, $\overline{πνα}$ for *θεός, κύριος, ἰησοῦς, χριστός, πνεῦμα*, &c. and their cases. The Cotton Genesis has $\overline{θου}$ ch. i. 27 by a later hand, but *θεου* ch. xli. 38. Besides these Codd. Sinaiticus, Alex., Ephraemi and the rest supply $\overline{ανοσ}$, $\overline{ουνοσ}$, $\overline{πηρ}$ ($\overline{πρ}$ Cod. Sarrav. Num. xii. 14, &c., $\overline{πτηρ}$ Cod.

[1] The earliest known example of the use of two dots occurs in the Artemisia papyrus at Vienna (Maunde Thompson, p. 69), and other early instances are found in a letter of Dionysius to Ptolemy about B.C. 160, published by the French Institute, 1865, in 'Papyrus grecs du Musée du Louvre,' &c. tom. xviii. 2e ptie, pl. xxxiv, pap. 49, and in fragments of the Phaedo of Plato discovered at Gurob. The same double points are also occasionally set in the larger spaces of Codd. Sinaiticus, Sarravianus, and Bezae, but in the last-named copy for the most part in a later hand.

Rossanensis), μηρ, ιλημ or ιηλμ or ιλμ or ιημ (ιελμ Cod. Sarrav.), ιηλ or ισλ or ισηλ, δαδ, and some of them σηρ for σωτήρ, υσ for υἱός, παρ^θ^νος for παρθένος (Bodleian Genesis), σρσ for σταυρός: Cod. L has πνεᵛ, and Cod. Vatican. in the *Old* Testament ανος and προ occasionally, ισλ and ιλημ or ιλμ often[1]; Evan. 604 has σηρ for σωτήρ, and ἐθν for ἐθνῶν[2]. Cod. Bezae always writes at length ανθρωπος, μητηρ, υἱος, σωτηρ, οὐρανος, δαυειδ, ἰσραηλ, ἱερουσαλημ; but abridges the sacred names into χρσ, ιησ[3] &c. and their cases, as very frequently, but by no means invariably, do the kindred Codd. Augiens., Sangall., and Boerner. Cod. Z seldom abridges, and all copies often set υἱος in full. A few dots sometimes supply the place of the line denoting abbreviation (e. g. θσ Cotton Genesis, ανοσ Colbert. Pentateuch). A straight line over the last letter of a line, sometimes over any vowel, indicates N (or also M in the Latin of Codd. Bezae and Claromont.) in all the Biblical uncials, but is placed only over numerals in the Herculanean rolls: κ, τ, and less often θ for καί (see p. 16, note 1), -ται, -θαι are met with in Cod. Sinaiticus and all later except Cod. Z: ȣ for ου chiefly in Codd. L, Augiensis, B of the Apocalypse, and the more recent uncials. Such *compendia scribendi* as ΠΡ in the Herculanean rolls (above p. 33) occur mostly at the end of lines: that form, with ΜᵒΥ (No. 11 a, l. 4), and a few more even in the Cod. Sinaiticus; in Cod. Sarrav. Μ̊ stands for both μου and μοι; in Cureton's Homer we have Πˢ for πους, Cˢ for -σας and such like. In later books they are more numerous and complicated, particularly in cursive writing. The terminations ° for ος, ‾ for ν, ˋ or ˵ for ου, " for αις, ~ for ων or ω or ως, ˢ for ης, ᵛ for ου are familiar; besides others, peculiar to one or a few copies, e. g. τγ for ττ in Burney 19, and Burdett-Coutts i. 4, h for αυ, b for ερ, ‾ for α, ⁊ for αρ in the Emmanuel College copy of the Epistles (Paul 30, No. 33), and : for α, (or ᵒ for αν, ✓ for ας in Parham 17 of the Apocalypse. Other more rare abridgements are ˢˢ for εις in Wake 12, ✓ (Burdett-Coutts I. 4) or < or ᵃ for εν, ·· for ι and ö for εσ (B–C. iii. 37), ·;· for εσ and ⁊ for σε and ⸗ for τησ (B–C.

[1] Abbot, ubi supra.

[2] Hoskier, Cod. 604, p. xiii.

[3] Even Codex Sinaiticus has ιηυ and ιυ in consecutive lines (Apoc. xxii. 20, 21), and χρυ Rom. vii. 4.

ii. 26), ⲧ for ται and ϛ for ωσ (B–C. iii. 42), ∧ for ην (B–C. iii. 10), ϋ for ισ and ȣ or ʒ for ουν (B–C. iii. 41), Ӓ for ιν or ἐστι, ᵅ for αν, ᵖ or ᵈ for οις, ᵕ for ας, ˥ or ᵔ for οις, ᵀ for τε or -τες or την or του, ″ for ειν, ϵ̀ for ους or ως (Gale O. iv. 22). The mark > is not only met with in the Herculanean rolls, but in the Hyperides (facsimile 9, l. 6), in Codd. Vaticanus and Sinaiticus, the two Pentateuchs, Codd. Augiensis, Sangall. and Boernerianus, and seems merely designed to fill up vacant space, like the flourishes in a legal instrument [1].

16. Capital letters of a larger size than the rest at the beginning of clauses, &c. are freely met with in all documents excepting in the oldest papyri, the Herculanean rolls, Codd. Vaticanus, Sinaiticus, the Colbert Pentateuch, Isaiah in Cod. Z, and one or two fragments besides [2]. Their absence is a proof of high antiquity. Yet even in Codd. Vaticanus, Sinaiticus, and Sarravianus, which is the other part of the Colbert Pentateuch (in the first most frequently in the earlier portions of the Old Testament), the initial letter stands a little outside the line of writing after a break in the sense, whether the preceding line had been quite filled up or not. Such breaks occur more regularly in Codex Bezae, as will appear when we come to describe it [3]. Smaller capitals occur in the middle of lines in Codd. Bezae and Marchalianus, of the sixth and seventh centuries respectively. Moreover, all copies of whatever date are apt to crowd small

[1] See below p. 64, note 4.

[2] 'Fragmenta pauca evangelii Johannis palimpsesta Londinensia [Evan. I^b or N^b]. In ceteris haec fere tria: Dionis Cassii fragmenta Vaticana—vix enim qui in his videntur speciem majorum litterarum habere revera differunt—item fragmenta palimpsesta [Phaëthontis] Euripidis Claromontana et fragmenta Menandri Porphiriana' (Tischendorf, Cod. Vatic. Proleg. p. xviii, 1867).

[3] The English word *paragraph* is derived from the παραγραφαί, which are often straight lines, placed in the margin to indicate a pause in the sense. Professor Abbot, ubi supra, p. 195, alleges not a few instances where these dashes are thus employed. A specimen is given in Scrivener's Cod. Sinaiticus, facsimile 3: see his Cod. Sin., Introduction, p. xl and note. Thus also they appear in Cod. Sarravianus (Tischendorf, Mon. sacra ined. vol. iii. pp. xiv, xx). In Cod Bezae Γ is set in the margin forty-nine times by a later hand, and must be designed for the same purpose, though the mark sometimes occurs where we should hardly look for it (Scrivener, Cod. Bezae, Introduction, p. xxviii and note). In Cod. Marchalianus the dash stands over the capital at the beginning of a line, or over the first letter where there is no capital. Lastly, in Codd. Vatic. and Sinait. ┌ is sometimes set in the middle of a line to indicate a paragraph break, followed by ↲ in the margin of the next line.

letters into the end of a line to save room, and if these small letters preserve the form of the larger, it is reasonable to conclude that the scribe is writing in a natural hand, not an assumed one, and the argument for the antiquity of such a document, derived from the shape of its letters, thus becomes all the stronger. The continuous form of writing separate words must have prevailed in manuscripts long after it was obsolete in common life: Cod. Claromont., whose text is continuous even in its Latin version, divides the words in the inscriptions and subscriptions to the several books.

17. The stichometry of the sacred books has next to be considered. The Greeks and Romans measured the contents of their MSS. by lines, not only in poetry, but also artificially in prose for a standard line of fifteen or sixteen syllables, called by the earliest writers ἔπος, afterwards στίχος[1]. Not only do Athanasius [d. 373], Gregory Nyssen [d. 396], Epiphanius [d. 403], and Chrysostom [d. 407] inform us that in their time the Book of Psalms was already divided into στίχοι, while Jerome [d. 420?] testifies the same for the prophecies of Isaiah; but Origen also [d. 254] speaks of the second and third Epistles of St. John as both of them not exceeding one hundred στίχοι, of St. Paul's Epistles as consisting of few, St. John's first Epistle as of very few (Euseb. Hist. Eccles. vi. 25, cited by Tischendorf, Cod. Sinait., Proleg. p. xxi, note 2, 1863). Even the apocryphal letter of our Lord to Abgarus is described as ὀλιγοστίχου μέν, πολυδυνάμου δὲ ἐπιστολῆς (Euseb. H. E. i. 13): while Eustathius of Antioch in the fourth century reckoned 135 στίχοι between John viii. 59 and x. 41. More general is the use of the word in Ephraem the Syrian [d. 378], Ὅταν δὲ ἀναγινώσκῃς, ἐπιμελῶς καὶ ἐμπόνως ἀναγίνωσκε, ἐν πολλῇ καταστάσει διερχόμενος τὸν στίχον (tom. iii. 101). As regards the

[1] Many other examples of the use of στίχοι and *versus* in this sense will be found in that admirable monument of exact learning, now so little read, Prideaux Connections, An. 446. Stichometry can be traced back to nearly a century before Callimachus, who (B.C. 260) has been credited with the invention (Palaeography, p. 79). The term στίχοι, like the Latin *versus*, originally referring whether to rows of trees, or to the oars in the trireme (Virg. Aen. v. 119), would naturally come to be applied to lines of poetry, and in this sense it is used by Pindar (ἐπέων στίχες Pyth. iv. 100) and also by Theocritus (γράψον καὶ τόδε γράμμα, τό σοι στίχοισι χαράξω Idyl. xxiii. 46), if the common reading be correct.

Psalms, we may see their arrangement for ourselves in Codd. Vaticanus and Sinaiticus, wherein, according to the true principles of Hebrew poetry, the verses do not correspond in metre or quantity of syllables, but in the parallelism or relationship subsisting between the several members of the same sentence or stanza[1]. Such στίχοι were therefore not 'space-lines,' but 'sense-lines.' It seems to have occurred to Euthalius, a deacon of Alexandria, as it did long afterwards to Bishop Jebb when he wrote his 'Sacred Literature,' that a large portion of the New Testament might be divided into στίχοι on the same principles: and that even where that distribution should prove but artificial, it would guide the public reader in the management of his voice, and remove the necessity for an elaborate system of punctuation. Such, therefore, we conceive to be the use and design of stichometry, as applied to the Greek Testament by Euthalius[2], whose edition of the Acts and Epistles was published A.D. 490. Who distributed the στίχοι of the Gospels (which are in truth better suited for such a process than the Epistles) does not appear. Although but few manuscripts now exist that are written στοιχηδόν or στιχηρῶς (a plan which consumed too much vellum to become general), we read in many copies, added usually to the subscription at the foot of each of the books of the New Testament, a calculation of the number of στίχοι it contained, the numbers being sufficiently unlike to show that the arrangement was not the same in all codices, yet near enough to prove that they were divided on the same principle[3]. In the few documents written στιχηρῶς that survive, the length of the clauses is very unequal; some (e.g. Cod. Bezae, *see* the description below

[1] That we have rightly understood Epiphanius' notion of the στίχοι is evident from his own language respecting Psalm cxli. 1, wherein he prefers the addition made by the Septuagint to the second clause, because by so doing its authors ἀχώλωτον ἐποίησαν τὸν στίχον: so that the passage should run 'O Lord, I cry unto Thee, make haste unto me || Give ear to the voice of my request,' τῆς δεήσεώς μου to complete the rhythm. This whole subject is admirably worked out in Suicer, Thesaur. Eccles. tom. ii. pp. 1025–37.

[2] In the Epistles of St. Paul, Euthalius seems to have followed a Syrian writer. Gregory, Prolegomena, p. 118; Zacagnius, Collectanea Monumentorum Veterum Ecclesiae, Rome, A.D. 1698, pp. 404, 409.

[3] At the end of 2 Thess., in a hand which Tischendorf states to be very ancient, but not that of the original scribe, the Codex Sinaiticus has στιχων ρπ [180; the usual number is 106]: at the end of Rom., 1 Cor., 1 Thess., and the Catholic Epistles, there is no such note; but in all the other Pauline Epistles the στίχοι are numbered.

and the facsimile, No. 42) containing as much in a line as might be conveniently read aloud in a breath, others (e.g. Cod. Laud. of the Acts, Plate x. No. 25) having only one or two words in a line. The Cod. Claromontanus (facsim. No. 41) in this respect lies between those extremes, and the fourth great example of this class (Cod. Coislin. 202, H of St. Paul), of the sixth century, has one of its few surviving pages (of sixteen lines each) arranged *literatim* as follows (1 Cor. x. 22, &c.): εσμεν | παντα μοι εξεστι | αλλ ου παντα συμφερει | παντα μοι εξεστιν | αλλ ου παντα οικοδομει | μηδεισ το εαυτου ζη | (*ob necessitatem spatii*) τειτω | αλλα το του ετερου | παν το εν μακελλω πω | (*ob necessitatem*) λουμενον | εσθιετε μηδεν ανα | κρινωντες δια την | συνειδησιν | του γαρ κ̅υ̅ η γη και το πλη | ρωμα αυτης. Other manuscripts written στιχηρῶς are Matthaei's V of the eighth century (though with verses like ours more than with ordinary στίχοι), Bengel's Uffenbach 3 of St. John (Evan. 101), Alter's Forlos. 29 (36 of the Apocalypse), and, as it would seem, the Cod. Sangallensis Δ. In Cod. Claromontanus there are scarcely any stops (the middle point being chiefly reserved to follow abridgements or numerals), the stichometry being of itself an elaborate scheme of punctuation; but the longer στίχοι of Cod. Bezae are often divided by a single point.

18. In using manuscripts of the Greek Testament, we must carefully note whether a reading is *primâ manu* (*) or by some subsequent corrector (**). It will often happen that these last are utterly valueless, having been inserted even from printed copies by a modern owner (like some marginal variations of the Cod. Leicestrensis)[1], and such as these really ought not to have been extracted by collators at all; while others by the second hand are almost as weighty, for age and goodness, as the text itself. All these points are explained by critical editors for each document separately; in fact to discriminate the different corrections in regard to their antiquity and importance is often the most difficult portion of such editor's task (e.g. in Codd. Bezae and Claromontanus), and one on which he often feels it hard to satisfy his own judgement. Corrections by the original scribe, or

[1] So the margin of Gale's Evan. 66 contains readings cited by Mill and his followers, which a hand of the sixteenth century took, some of them from the Leicester manuscript, others from early editions.

by a contemporary reviser, where they can be satisfactorily distinguished, must be regarded as a portion of the testimony of the manuscript itself, inasmuch as every carefully prepared copy was reviewed and compared (*ἀντεβλήθη*), if not by the writer himself, by a skilful person appointed for the task (*ὁ διορθῶν*, *ὁ διορθωτής*), whose duty it was to amend manifest errors, sometimes also to insert ornamental capitals in places which had been reserved for them; in later times (and as some believe at a very early period) to set in stops, breathings and accents; in copies destined for ecclesiastical use to arrange the musical notes that were to guide the intonation of the reader. Notices of this kind of revision are sometimes met with at the end of the best manuscripts. Such is the note in Cod. H of St. Paul: *εγραψα και εξεθεμην προσ το εν Καισαρια αντιγραφον τησ βιβλιοθηκησ του αγιου Παμφιλου*, the same library of the Martyr Pamphilus to which the scribe of the Cod. Frid.-August. resorted for his model[1]; and that in Birch's most valuable Urbino-Vatican. 2 (157 of the Gospels), written for the Emperor John II (1118–1143), wherein at the end of the first Gospel we read *κατὰ Ματθαῖον ἐγράφη καὶ ἀντεβλήθη ἐκ τῶν ἐν ἱεροσολύμοις παλαιῶν ἀντιγράφων τῶν ἐν ἁγίῳ ὄρει* [Athos] *ἀποκειμένων*: similar subscriptions are appended to the other Gospels. See also Evan. Λ. 20, 164, 262, 300, 376; Act. 15, 83, in the list of manuscripts below.

[1] The following subscription to the book of Ezra (and a very similar one follows Esther) in the Cod. Frid.-August. (fol. 13. 1), though in a hand of the seventh century, will show the care bestowed on the most ancient copies of the Septuagint: *Αντεβληθη προσ παλαιωτατον λιαν αντιγραφον δεδιορθωμενον χειρι του αγιου μαρτυροσ Παμφιλου· ὁπερ αντιγραφον προσ τω τελει υποσημειωσισ τισ ἰδιοχειροσ αυτου ὑπεκειτο εχουσα ουτωσ· μετεληµφθη και διορθωθη προσ τα εξαπλα ωριγενουσ· Αντωνινοσ αντεβαλεν· Παμφιλοσ διορθωσα.* Tregelles suggests that the work of the *διορθωτὴς* or *corrector* was probably of a critical character, the office of the *ἀντιβάλλων* or *comparer* being rather to eliminate mere clerical errors (Treg. Horne's Introd., vol. iv. p. 85). Compare Tischendorf, Cod. Sinait. Proleg. p. xxii.

CHAPTER III.

DIVISIONS OF THE TEXT, AND OTHER PARTICULARS.

WE have next to give some account of ancient divisions of the text, as found in manuscripts of the New Testament; and these must be carefully noted by the student, since few copies are without one or more of them.

1. So far as we know at present, the oldest sections still extant are those of the Codex Vaticanus. These seem to have been formed for the purpose of reference, and a new one always commences where there is some break in the sense. Many, however, at least in the Gospels, consist of but one of our modern verses, and they are so unequal in length as to be rather inconvenient for actual use. In the four Gospels only the marginal numerals are in red, St. Matthew containing 170 of these divisions, St. Mark 62, St. Luke 152, St. John 80. In the Acts of the Apostles are two sets of sections, thirty-six longer and in an older hand, sixty-nine smaller and more recent[1]. Each of these also begins after a break in the sense, but they are quite independent of each other, as a larger section will sometimes commence in the middle of a smaller, the latter being in no wise a subdivision of the former. Thus the greater Γ opens Acts ii. 1, in the middle of the lesser β, which extends from Acts i. 15 to ii. 4. The first forty-two of the lesser chapters, down to Acts xv. 40, are found also with slight variations in the margin of Codex Sinaiticus, written by a very old hand. As in most manuscripts, so in Codex Vaticanus, the Catholic Epistles follow the Acts, and in them also and in St. Paul's Epistles there are two sets of sections, only that in the Epistles the older sections are the more numerous. The Pauline Epistles are reckoned throughout as one book in the

[1] 'Simile aliquid invenitur in codice Arabico epp. Pauli anno 892, p. Chr., quem ex oriente Petropolin pertulimus.' Tischendorf, Cod. Vat. Proleg. p. xxx, n. 8.

elder notation, with however this remarkable peculiarity, that though in the Cod. Vatican. itself the Epistle to the Hebrews stands next after the second to the Thessalonians, *and on the same leaf with it*, the sections are arranged as if it stood between the Epistles to the Galatians and Ephesians. For whereas that to the Galatians ends with § 58, that to the Ephesians begins with § 70, and the numbers proceed regularly down to § 93, with which the second to the Thessalonians ends. The Epistle to the Hebrews which then follows opens with § 59; the last section extant (§ 64) begins at Heb. ix. 11, and the manuscript ends abruptly at καθα ver. 14. It plainly appears, then, that the sections of the Codex Vaticanus must have been copied from some yet older document, in which the Epistle to the Hebrews preceded that to the Ephesians. It will be found hereafter (vol. ii) that in the Thebaic version the Epistle to the Hebrews preceded that to the Galatians, instead of following it, as here. For a list of the more modern divisions in the Epistles, see the Table given below. The Vatican sections of the Gospels have also been discovered by Tregelles in one other copy, the palimpsest Codex Zacynthius of St. Luke (Ξ), which he published in 1861.

2. Hardly less ancient, and indeed ascribed by some to Tatian the Harmonist, the disciple of Justin Martyr, is the division of the Gospels into larger chapters or κεφάλαια *majora*[1]. It may be noticed that in none of the four Gospels does the first chapter stand at its commencement. In St. Matthew chapter A begins at chap. ii. verse 1, and has for its title περὶ τῶν μάγων: in St. Mark at chap. i. ver. 23 περὶ τοῦ δαιμονιζομένου: in St. Luke at chap. ii. ver. 1 περὶ τῆς ἀπογραφῆς: in St. John at chap. ii. ver. 1 περὶ τοῦ ἐν Κανᾶ γάμου. Mill accounts for this circumstance by supposing that in the first copies the titles at the head of each Gospel were reserved till last for more splendid illumination, and were thus eventually forgotten (Proleg. N. T. § 355); Griesbach holds, that the general inscriptions of each Gospel, Κατὰ Ματθαῖον, Κατὰ Μάρκον, &c., were regarded as the special titles of the first chapters also. On either supposition, however, it would

[1] Lat. *breves*, or τίτλοι: but τίτλος means properly the brief summary of the contents of a κεφάλαιον placed at the top or bottom of a page, or with the κεφάλαια in a table to each Gospel. The κεφ. *minora* = Ammonian Sections.

be hard to explain how what was really the second chapter came to be *numbered* as the first; and it is worth notice that the same arrangement takes place in the *κεφάλαια* (though these are of a later date) of all the other books of the New Testament except the Acts, 2 Corinth., Ephes., 1 Thess., Hebrews, James, 1 and 2 Peter, 1 John, and the Apocalypse: e.g. the first chapter of the Epistle to the Romans opens ch. i. ver. 18 *Πρῶτον μετὰ τὸ προοίμιον, περὶ κρίσεως τῆς κατὰ ἐθνῶν τῶν οὐ φυλασσόντων τὰ φυσικά.* But the fact is that this arrangement, strange as it may seem, is conformable to the practice of the times when these divisions were finally settled. Both in the Institutes and in the Digest of Justinian the first paragraph is always cited as pr. (i.e. *principium*, *προοίμιον*, *Preface*), and what we should regard as the second paragraph is numbered as the first, and so on throughout the whole work[1].

The *τίτλοι* in St. Matthew amount to sixty-eight, in St. Mark to forty-eight, in St. Luke to eighty-three, in St. John to eighteen. This mode of division, although not met with in the Vatican and Sinaitic manuscripts, is found in the Codices Alexandrinus and Ephraemi of the fifth century, and in the Codex Nitriensis of the sixth, each of which has tables of the *τίτλοι* prefixed to the several Gospels: but the Codices Alexandrinus, Rossanensis, and Dublinensis of St. Matthew, and that portion of the purple Cotton fragment which is in the Vatican, exhibit them in their usual position, at the top and bottom of the pages. Thus it appears that they were too generally diffused in the fifth century not to have originated at an earlier period; although we must concede that the *κεφάλαιον* spoken of by Clement of Alexandria (Stromat. i) when quoting Dan. xii. 12, or by Athanasius (contra Arium) on Act. ii, and the *Capitulum* mentioned by Tertullian (ad Uxorem ii. 2) in reference to 1 Cor. vii. 12, contain no certain allusions to any specific divisions of the sacred text, but only to the particular paragraphs or passages in which their citations stand. Except that the contrary habit has grown inveterate[2], it were much to be desired that the term *τίτλοι* should be applied to these longer

[1] This full explanation of a seeming difficulty was communicated to me independently by Mr. F. W. Pennefather of Dublin, and Mr. G. A. King of Oxford.

[2] And this too in spite of the lexicographer Suidas: *Τίτλος διαφέρει κεφαλαίου· καὶ ὁ μὲν Ματθαῖος τίτλους ἔχει ξη', κεφάλαια δὲ τνε'.* And of Suicer, s. v.

divisions, at least in the Gospels; but since usage has affixed the term κεφάλαια to the larger chapters and sections to the smaller, and τίτλοι only to the subjects or headings of the former, it would be useless to follow any other system of names.

3. The Ammonian Sections were not constructed, like the Vatican divisions and the τίτλοι, for the purpose of easy reference, or distributed like them according to the breaks in the sense, but for a wholly different purpose. So far as we can ascertain, the design of Tatian's Harmony was simply to present to Christian readers a single connected history of our Lord, by taking from the four Evangelists indifferently whatsoever best suited his purpose[1]. As this plan could scarcely be executed without *omitting* some portions of the sacred text, it is not surprising that Tatian, possibly without any evil intention, should have incurred the grave charge of mutilating Holy Scripture[2]. A more scholar-like and useful attempt was subsequently made by Ammonius of Alexandria, early in the third century [A.D. 220], who, by the side of St. Matthew's Gospel, which he selected as his standard, arranged in parallel columns, as it would seem, the corresponding passages of the other three Evangelists, so as to exhibit them all at once to the reader's eye; St. Matthew in his proper order, the rest as the necessity of abiding by St. Matthew's order prescribed. This is the account given by the celebrated Eusebius, Bishop of Caesarea, the Church

[1] Ὁ Τατιανός, συνάφειάν τινα καὶ συναγωγὴν οὐκ οἶδ' ὅπως τῶν εὐαγγελίων συνθείς, τὸ διὰ τεσσάρων τοῦτο προσωνόμασεν· ὃ καὶ παρά τισιν εἰσέτι νῦν φέρεται. Euseb. Hist. Eccl. iv. 29.

[2] Ambros. in Prooem. Luc. seems to aim at Tatian when he says 'Plerique etiam ex quatuor Evangelii libris in unum ea quae venenatis putaverunt assertionibus convenientia referserunt.' Eusebius H. E. iv. 29 charges him on report with *improving* not the Gospels, but the Epistles: τοῦ δὲ ἀποστόλου φασὶ τολμῆσαί τινας αὐτὸν μεταφράσαι φωνάς, ὡς ἐπιδιορθούμενον αὐτῶν τὴν τῆς φράσεως σύνταξιν. Dr. Westcott's verdict is rather less favourable than might have been anticipated: 'The heretical character of the Diatessaron was not evident on the surface of it, and consisted rather of faults of defect than of erroneous teaching' (History of the Canon, p. 354). From the Armenian version of Ephraem the Syrian's Exposition of Tatian's Harmony, printed in 1836, translated in 1841 by Aucher of the Melchitarist Monastery at Venice, but buried until it was published with notes by Moesinger in 1876, a flood of light is thrown upon this question, and it is now clear 'that Tatian habitually abridged the language of the passages which he combined' (Hort, Gk. Test. Introduction, p. 283), and that apparently in perfect good faith.

historian, who in the fourth century, in his letter to Carpianus, described his own most ingenious system of Harmony, as founded on, or at least as suggested by, the labours of Ammonius [1]. It has been generally thought that the *κεφάλαια*, of which St. Matthew contains 355, St. Mark 236 [2], St. Luke 342, St. John 232, in all 1165, were made by Ammonius for the purpose of his work, and they have commonly received the name of the Ammonian sections: but this opinion was called in question by Bp. Lloyd (Nov. Test. Oxon. 1827, Monitum, pp. viii–xi), who strongly urges that, in his Epistle to Carpianus, Eusebius not only refrains from ascribing these numerical divisions to Ammonius (whose labours in this particular, as once seemed the case with Tatian's, must in that case be deemed to have perished utterly), but he almost implies that they had their origin at the same time with his own ten canons, with which they are so intimately connected [3]. That they were essential to Eusebius' scheme is plain enough; their place in Ammonius' parallel Harmony is not easily understood, unless indeed (what is nowhere stated, but rather the contrary) he did not set the passages from the other Gospels at full length by the side of St. Matthew's, but only these numerical references to them [4].

[1] *Ἀμμώνιος μὲν ὁ Ἀλεξανδρεύς, πολλήν, ὡς εἰκός, φιλοπονίαν καὶ σπουδὴν εἰσαγηοχώς, τὸ διὰ τεσσάρων ἡμῖν καταλέλοιπεν εὐαγγέλιον, τῷ κατὰ Ματθαῖον τὰς ὁμοφώνους τῶν λαιπῶν εὐαγγελιστῶν περικοπὰς παραθείς, ὡς ἐξ ἀνάγκης συμβῆναι τὸν τῆς ἀκολουθίας εἱρμὸν τῶν τριῶν διαφθαρῆναι, ὅσον ἐπὶ τῷ ὕφει τῆς ἀναγνώσεως. Ἵνα δὲ σωζομένου καὶ τοῦ τῶν λοιπῶν δι' ὅλου σώματός τε καὶ εἱρμοῦ, εἰδέναι ἔχοις τοὺς οἰκείους ἑκάστου εὐαγγελιστοῦ τόπους, ἐν οἷς κατὰ τῶν αὐτῶν ἠνέχθησαν φιλαλήθως εἰπεῖν, ἐκ τοῦ πονήματος τοῦ προειρημέναυ ἀνδρὸς εἰληφὼς ἀφορμάς* (‘taking the hint from Ammonius’ as Dean Burgon rightly understands the expression), *καθ' ἑτέραν μέθοδον κανόνας δέκα τὸν ἀριθμὸν διεχάραξά σοι τοὺς ὑποτεταγμένους.* Epist. ad Carpian. initio. I have thankfully availed myself on this subject of Burgon's elaborate studies in The Last Twelve Verses of St. Mark, pp. 125–132; 295–312.

[2] This is the number given for St. Mark by Suidas and Stephen. It is an uncertain point: thirty-four manuscripts givo 233, reckoning only to xvi. 8; while thirty-six give 341. See Burgon Twelve Last Verses, p. 311.

[3] I subjoin Eusebius' own words (Epist. ad Carpian.) from which no one would infer that the *sections* were not his, as well as the *canons*. *Αὕτη μὲν οὖν ἡ τῶν ὑποτεταγμένων κανόνων ὑπόθεσις· ἡ δὲ σαφὴς αὐτῶν διήγησις, ἔστιν ἥδε. Ἐφ' ἑκάστῳ τῶν τεσσάρων εὐαγγελίων ἀριθμός τις πρόκειται κατὰ μέρος, ἀρχόμενος ἀπὸ τοῦ πρώτου, εἶτα δευτέρου, καὶ τρίτου, καὶ καθεξῆς προϊὼν δι' ὅλου μέχρι τοῦ τέλους τοῦ βιβλίου* [the sections]. *Καθ' ἕκαστον δὲ ἀριθμὸν ὑποσημείωσις διὰ κινναβάρεως πρόκειται* [the canons], *δηλοῦσα ἐν ποίῳ τῶν δέκα κανόνων κείμενος ὁ ἀριθμὸς τυγχάνει.*

[4] Something of this kind, however, must be the plan adopted in Codex E (see Plate xi. No. 27) of the Gospels, as described by Tregelles, who himself collated it. ‘[It has] the Ammonian sections; but instead of the Eusebian

There is, however, one ground for hesitation before we ascribe the sections, as well as the canons, to Eusebius; namely, that not a few ancient manuscripts (e.g. Codd. FHY) contain the former, while they omit the latter. Of palimpsests indeed it might be said with reason, that the rough process which so nearly obliterated the ink of the older writing, would completely remove the coloured paint (κιννάβαρις, *vermilion*, prescribed by Eusebius, though blue or green is occasionally found) in which the canons were invariably noted; hence we need not wonder at their absence from the Codices Ephraemi, Nitriensis (R), Dublinensis (Z), Codd. IW^b of Tischendorf, and the Wolfenbüttel fragments (PQ), in all which the sections are yet legible in ink. The Codex Sinaiticus contains both; but Tischendorf decidedly pronounces them to be in a later hand. In the Codex Bezae too, as well as the Codex Cyprius (K), even the Ammonian sections, without the canons, are by later hands, though the latter has prefixed the list or table of the canons. Of the oldest copies the Cod. Alex. (A), Tischendorf's Codd. W^{a}Θ, the Cotton frag. (N), and Codd. Beratinus and Rossanensis alone contain both the sections and the canons. Even in more modern cursive books the latter are often deficient, though the former are present. This peculiarity we have observed in Burney 23, in the British Museum, of the twelfth century, although the Epistle to Carpianus stands at the beginning; in a rather remarkable copy of about the twelfth century, in the Cambridge University Library (Mm. 6. 9, Scholz Evan. 440), in which, however, the table of canons but not the Epistle to Carpianus precedes; in the Gonville and Caius Gospels of the twelfth century (Evan. 59), and in a manuscript of about the thirteenth century at Trinity

canons there is a kind of harmony of the Gospels noted at the foot of each page, by a reference to the parallel sections of the other Evangelists.' Horne's Introd. vol. iv. p. 200. Yet the canons *also* stand in the margin of this copy under the so-called Ammonian sections: only the *table* of Eusebian canons is wanting. The same kind of harmony at the foot of the page appears in Cod. W^d at Trinity College, Cambridge, but in this latter the sections in the margin are not accompanied by the canons. Tischendorf states that the same arrangement prevails in the small fragment T^b at St. Petersburg; Dean Burgon adds to the list Codd. M. 262, 264 at Paris, and conceives that this method of harmonizing, which he regards as far simpler than the tedious and cumbersome process of resorting to the Eusebian canons (ubi supra, p. 304), was in principle, though not in details, derived to the Greek Church from early Syriac copies of the Gospels, some of which still survive (p. 306).

College, Cambridge (B. x. 17)[1]. These facts certainly seem to indicate that in the judgement of critics and transcribers, whatever that judgement may be deemed worth, the Ammonian sections had a previous existence to the Eusebian canons, as well as served for an independent purpose[2].

In his letter to Carpianus, their inventor clearly yet briefly describes the purpose of his canons, ten in number. The first contains a list of seventy-one places in which all the four Evangelists have a narrative, discourse, or saying in common: the second of 111 places in which the three Matthew, Mark, Luke agree: the third of twenty-two places common to Matthew, Luke, John: the fourth of twenty-six passages common to Matthew, Mark, John: the fifth of eighty-two places in which the two Matthew, Luke coincide: the sixth of forty-seven places wherein Matthew, Mark agree: the seventh of seven places common to Matthew and John: the eighth of fourteen places common to Luke and Mark: the ninth of twenty-one places in which Luke and John agree: the tenth of sixty-two passages of Matthew, twenty-one of Mark, seventy-one of Luke, and ninety-seven of John which have no parallels, but are peculiar to a single Evangelist. Under each of the 1165 so-named Ammonian sections, in its proper place in the margin of a manuscript, is put in coloured ink the number of that Eusebian canon to which it refers. On looking for that section in the proper table or canon, there will also be found the parallel place or places in the other Gospels, each indicated by its proper numeral, and so

[1] To this list of manuscripts of the Gospels which have the Ammonian sections without the Eusebian canons add Codd. 38, 54, 60, 68, 117; Brit. Mus. Addit. 16184, 18211, 19389; Milan Ambros. M. 48 *sup.*; E. 63 *sup.*; Burdett-Coutts I. 4; II. 18; 26[2]; III. 9. Now that attention has been specially directed to the matter, it is remarkable how many copies have the Ammonian sections without the corresponding Eusebian canons under them, sometimes even when (as in Codd. 572, 595, 597) the letter to Carpianus and the Eusebian tables stand at the beginning of the volume. To the list here given must now be added Codd. O, Υ, 185, 187, 190, 193, 194, 207, 209, 214, 217, 367, 406, 409, 410, 414, 418, 419, 456, 457, 494, 497, 501, 503, 504, 506, 508, 518, 544, 548, 550, 555, 558, 559, 564, 573, 575, 584, 586, 591, 592, 601, 602, 620: in all seventy-one manuscripts.

[2] No doubt they do serve, in the manuscripts which contain them and omit the canons, for marks of reference, like in kind to our modern chapters and verses; but in consequence of their having been constructed for a wholly different purpose, they are so unequal in length (as Burgon sees very clearly, pp. 297, 303), that they answer that end as ill as any the most arbitrary divisions of the text well could do.

readily searched out. A single example will serve to explain our meaning. In the facsimile of the Cotton fragment (Plate v. No. 14), in the margin of the passage (John xv. 20) we see $\frac{\overline{\text{PΛΘ}}}{\Gamma}$, where PΛΘ (139) is the proper section of St. John, Γ (3) the number of the canon. On searching the third Eusebian table we read MT. ϟ, Λ. $\overline{\nu\eta}$, ΙΩ. $\overline{\rho\lambda\theta}$, and thus we learn that the first clause of John xv. 20 is parallel in sense to the ninetieth (ϟ) section of St. Matthew (x. 24), and to the fifty-eighth ($\overline{\nu\eta}$) of St. Luke (vi. 40). The advantage of such a system of parallels to the exact study of the Gospels is too evident to need insisting on.

4. The Acts of the Apostles and the Epistles are also divided into *chapters* (κεφάλαια), in design precisely the same as the κεφάλαια or τίτλοι of the Gospels, and nearly like them in length. Since there is no trace of these chapters in the two great Codices Alexandrinus and Ephraemi, of the fifth century (which yet exhibit the τίτλοι, the sections, and one of them the canons), it seems reasonable to assume that they are of later date. They are sometimes connected with the name of Euthalius, deacon of Alexandria, afterwards Bishop of Sulci [1], whom we have already spoken of as the reputed author of Scriptural stichometry (*above*, p. 53). We learn, however, from Euthalius' own Prologue to his edition of St. Paul's Epistles (A. D. 458,) that the 'summary of the chapters' (and consequently the numbers of the chapters themselves) was taken from the work of 'one of our wisest and pious fathers [2],' i. e. some Bishop that he does not wish to particularize, whom Mill (Proleg. N. T. § 907) conjectures to be Theodore of Mopsuestia, who lay under the censure of the Church. Soon after [3] the publication of St. Paul's Epistles, on

[1] Sulci in Sardinia is the only Bishop's see of the name I can find in Carol. a Sancto Paulo's Geographia Sacra (1703), or in Bingham's Antiquities, Bk. ix. Chapp. II, VII. Horne and even Tregelles speak of Sulca in Egypt, but I have searched in vain for any such town or see. Euthalius is called Bishop of Sulce both in Wake 12 (infra, note 4), and in the title to his works as edited by L. A. Zacagni (Collectanea Monument. Veter. Eccles. Graec. ac Latin., Rom. 1698, p. 402). But one of Zacagni's manuscripts reads Σούλκης once, and he guesses Ψέλχη near Syene, which appears in no list of Episcopal sees.

[2] Καθ' ἑκάστην ἐπιστολὴν προτάξομεν τὴν τῶν κεφαλαίων ἔκθεσιν, ἑνὶ τῶν σοφωτάτων τινὶ καὶ φιλοχρίστων πατέρων ἡμῶν πεπονημένην.

[3] Αὐτίκα δῆτα is his own expression.

the suggestion of one Athanasius, then a priest and afterwards Patriarch of Alexandria, Euthalius put forth a similar edition of the Acts and Catholic Epistles[1], also divided into chapters, with a summary of contents at the head of each chapter. Even these he is thought to have derived (at least in the Acts) from the manuscript of Pamphilus the Martyr [d. 308], to whom the same order of chapters is ascribed in a document published by Montfaucon (Bibliotheca Coislin. p. 78); the rather as Euthalius fairly professes to have compared his book in the Acts and Catholic Epistles 'with the copies in the library at Caesarea' which once belonged to 'Eusebius the friend of Pamphilus[2].' The Apocalypse still remains. It was divided, about the end of the fifth century, by Andreas, Archbishop of the Cappadocian Caesarea, into twenty-four *paragraphs* (λόγοι), corresponding to the number of the elders about the throne (Apoc. iv. 4); each paragraph being subdivided into three *chapters* (κεφάλαια)[3]. The summaries which Andreas wrote of his seventy-two chapters are still reprinted in Mill's and other large editions of the Greek Testament.

5. To Euthalius has been also referred a division of the Acts into sixteen lessons (*ἀναγνώσεις*) and of the Pauline Epistles into thirty-one (see table on p. 68); but these lessons are quite different from the much shorter ones adopted by the Greek Church. He is also said to have numbered in each Epistle of St. Paul the quotations from the Old Testament[4], which are

[1] E.g. in Wake 12, of the eleventh century, at Christ Church, the title at the head of the list of chapters in the Acts is as follows: Εὐθαλίου ἐπισκόπου Ϲουλκῆς ἔκθεσις κεφαλαίων τῶν Πράξεων σταλῆσα (-εῖσα) πρὸς Ἀθανάσιον ἐπίσκοπον Ἀλεξανδρείας.

[2] In Wake 12 certain of the longer *κεφάλαια* are subdivided into *μερικαὶ ὑποδιαιρέσεις* in the Acts, 1 Peter, 1 John, Romans, 1, 2 Corinthians, Colossians, 2 Thessalonians, 1 Timothy, Hebrews only. For a similar subdivision in the Gospels, see Evan. 443 in the list of cursive MSS. given below.

[3] *Διὰ τὴν τριμερῆ τῶν εἴκοσι τεσσάρων πρεσβυτέρων ὑπόστασιν, σώματος καὶ ψυχῆς καὶ πνεύματος.* See Matthaei, N. T. Gr. et Lat. vii. 276, note 4.

[4] Many manuscripts indicate passages of the Old Testament cited in the New by placing > (as in Codd. Vatican. W[d], &c., but in Sinait. more rarely), or ⋧, or some such mark in the margin before every line. Our quotation-marks are probably derived from this sign, the angle being rounded into a curve. Compare the use of " in the margin of the Greek Testament of Colinaeus, 1534, and Stephen's editions of 1546, -49, -50, &c. Evan. 348 and others have ※. In Codd. Bezae, as will appear hereafter, the words cited are merely thrown a letter or two back in each line.

still noted in many of our manuscripts, and is the first known to have used that reckoning of the *στίχοι* which was formerly annexed we know not when to the Gospels and Epistles, as well as to the Acts. Besides the division of the text into *στίχοι* or *lines* (*above*, p. 52) we find in the Gospels alone another division into *ῥήματα* or *ῥήσεις* 'sentences,' differing but little from the *στίχοι* in number. Of these last the precise numbers vary in different copies, though not considerably: whether that variation arose from the circumstance that ancient numbers were represented by letters and so easily became corrupted, or from a different mode of arranging the *στίχοι* and *ῥήματα* adopted by the various scribes.

6. It is proper to state that the *subscriptions* (*ὑπογραφαί*) appended to St. Paul's Epistles in many manuscripts, and retained even in the Authorized English version of the New Testament, are also said to be the composition of Euthalius. In the best copies they are somewhat shorter in form, but in any shape they do no credit to the care or skill of their author, whoever he may be. 'Six of these subscriptions,' writes Paley in that masterpiece of acute reasoning, the Horae Paulinae, 'are false or improbable;' that is, they are either absolutely contradicted by the contents of the epistle [1 Cor., Galat., 1 Tim.], or are difficult to be reconciled with them [1, 2 Thess., Tit.].

The *subscriptions* to the Gospels have not, we believe, been assigned to any particular author, and being seldom found in printed copies of the Greek Testament or in modern versions, are little known to the general reader. In the earliest manuscripts the subscriptions, as well as the *titles* of the books, were of the simplest character. *Κατὰ Μαθθαῖον, κατὰ Μάρκον*, &c. is all that the Codd. Vaticanus and Sinaiticus have, whether at the beginning or the end. *Εὐαγγέλιον κατὰ Ματθαῖον* is the subscription to the first Gospel in the Codex Alexandrinus; *εὐαγγέλιον κατὰ Μάρκον* is placed at the beginning of the second Gospel in the same manuscript, and the self-same words at the end of it by Codices Alex. and Ephraemi: in the Codex Bezae (in which St. John stands second in order) we merely read *εὐαγγέλιον κατὰ Μαθθαῖον ἐτελέσθη, ἄρχεται εὐαγγέλιον κατὰ Ἰωάννην*. The same is the case throughout the New Testament. After a while the titles become more elaborate, and the subscriptions afford more information, the truth of which it would hardly be safe to vouch for. The earliest worth notice are found in the Codex Cyprius (K) of the eighth or ninth century, which, together with those of several other copies, are given in Scholz's Prolegomena N. T. vol. i. pp. xxix, xxx. *ad fin. Matthaei*: Τὸ κατὰ Ματθαῖον εὐαγγέλιον ἐξεδόθη ὑπ' αὐτοῦ ἐν ἱεροσολύμοις μετὰ χρόνους η̄ [ὀκτὼ] τῆς τοῦ Χριστοῦ ἀναλήψεως. *Ad fin. Marci*: Τὸ κατὰ Μάρκον εὐαγγέλιον ἐξεδόθη μετὰ χρόνους δέκα τῆς τοῦ Χριστοῦ ἀναλήψεως. Those to the other two Gospels exactly resemble St. Mark's, that of St. Luke however being dated fifteen, that of St. John thirty-two years after our Lord's Ascension, periods in all probability far too early to be correct.

7. The foreign matter so often inserted in later manuscripts has more value for the antiquarian than for the critic. That splendid copy of the Gospels Lambeth 1178, of the tenth or eleventh century, contains more such than is often found, set off by fine illuminations. At the end of each of the first three Gospels (but not of the fourth) are several pages relating to them extracted from Cosmas Indicopleustes, who made the voyage which procured him his cognomen about A.D. 522; also some iambic verses of no great excellence, as may well be supposed. In golden letters we read: *ad fin. Matth.* ἰστέον ὅτι τὸ κατὰ Ματθαῖον εὐαγγέλιον ἑβραΐδι διαλέκτωι γραφὲν ὑπ' αὐτοῦ· ἐν ἱερουσαλὴμ ἐξεδόθη· ἑρμηνεύθη δὲ ὑπὸ ἰωάννου· ἐξηγεῖται δὲ τὴν κατὰ ἄνθρωπον τοῦ χ̄ῡ γένεσιν, καί ἐστιν ἀνθρωπόμορφον τοῦτο τὸ εὐαγγέλιον. The last clause alludes to Apoc. iv. 7, wherein the four living creatures were currently believed to be typical of the four Gospels[1]. *Ad fin. Marc.* ἰστέον ὅτι τὸ κατὰ Μάρκον εὐαγγέλιον ὑπηγορεύθη ὑπὸ Πέτρου ἐν ῥώμηι· ἐποιήσατο δὲ τὴν ἀρχὴν ἀπὸ τοῦ προφητικοῦ λόγου τοῦ ἐξ ὕψους ἐπιόντος τοῦ Ἡσαΐου· τὴν πτερωτικὴν εἰκόνα τοῦ εὐαγγελίου δεικνύς. *Ad fin. Luc.* ἰστέον ὅτι τὸ κατὰ Λουκᾶν εὐαγγέλιον ὑπηγορεύθη ὑπὸ Παύλου ἐν ῥώμηι· ἅτε δὲ ἱερατικοῦ χαρακτῆρος ὑπάρχοντος

[1] The whole mystery is thus unfolded (apparently by Cosmas) in Lamb. 1178, p. 159: Καὶ γὰρ τὰ χερουβὶμ τετραπρόσωπα· καὶ τὰ πρόσωπα αὐτῶν εἰκόνες τῆς πραγματείας τοῦ υἱοῦ τοῦ θεοῦ· τὸ γὰρ ὅμοιον λέοντι, τὸ ἔμπρακτον καὶ βασιλικὸν καὶ ἡγεμονικὸν [John i. 1–3] χαρακτηρίζει· τὸ δὲ ὅμοιον μόσχωι, τὴν ἱερουργικὴν καὶ ἱερατικὴν [Luke i. 8] ἐμφανίζει· τὸ δὲ ἀνθρωποειδές, τὴν σάρκωσιν [Matt. i. 18] διαγράφει. τὸ δὲ ὅμοιον ἀετῶι, τὴν ἐπιφοίτησιν τοῦ ἁγίου πνεύματος [Mark i. 2] ἐμφανίζει. More usually the lion is regarded as the emblem of St. Mark, the eagle of St. John.

ἀπὸ Ζαχαρίου τοῦ ἱερέως θυμιῶντος ἤρξατο. The reader will desire no more of this.

8. The oldest manuscript known to be accompanied by a *catena* (or continuous commentary by different authors) is the palimpsest Codex Zacynthius (Ξ of Tregelles), an uncial of the eighth century. Such books are not common, but there is a very full commentary in minute letters, surrounding the large text in a noble copy of the Gospels, of the twelfth century, which belonged to the late Sir Thomas Phillipps (Middle Hill 13975, since removed to Cheltenham), yet uncollated; another of St. Paul's Epistles (No. 27) belongs to the University Library at Cambridge (Ff. 1. 30). The Apocalypse is often attended with the exposition of Andreas (p. 64), or of Arethas, also Archbishop of the Cappadocian Caesarea in the tenth century, or (what is more usual) with a sort of epitome of the two (e.g. Parham No. 17), above, below, and in the margin beside the text, in much smaller characters. In *cursive* manuscripts only the subject (ὑπόθεσις), especially that written by Oecumenius in the tenth century, sometimes stands as a *Prologue* before each book, but not so often before the Gospels or Apocalypse as the Acts and Epistles. Before the Acts we occasionally meet with Euthalius' Chronology of St. Paul's Travels, or another Ἀποδημία Παύλου. The Leicester manuscript contains between the Pauline Epistles and the Acts (1) An Exposition of the Creed and statement of the errors condemned by the seven general Councils, ending with the second at Nice. (2) Lives of the Apostles, followed by an exact description of the limits of the five Patriarchates. The Christ Church copy Wake 12 also has after the Apocalypse some seven or eight pages of a Treatise Περὶ τῶν ἁγίων καὶ οἰκουμενικῶν ζ̄ συνόδων, including some notice περὶ τοπικῶν συνόδων. Similar treatises may be more frequent in manuscripts of the Greek Testament than we are at present aware of.

9. We have not thought it needful to insert in this place either a list of the τίτλοι of the Gospels, or of the κεφάλαια of the rest of the New Testament, or the tables of the Eusebian canons, inasmuch as they are all accessible in such ordinary books as Stephen's Greek Testament 1550 and Mill's of 1707, 1710. The Eusebian canons are given in Bishop Lloyd's Oxford

TABLE OF ANCIENT AND MODERN DIVISIONS OF THE NEW TESTAMENT.

	Vatican MS. older sections	Vatican MS. later sections	τίτλοι	κεφάλαια Ammon	στίχοι	ῥήματα	Modern chapters	Modern verses
Matthew ...	170	—	68	355	2560	2522	28	1071
Mark	62	—	48	236	1616	1675	16	678
Luke	152	—	83	342	2740	3803	24	1151
John	80	—	18	232[1]	2024	1938	21	880 A. V. 879
			Euthal. κεφ λ.			ἀναγνώσματα		
Acts	36	69	40	N.B. The στίχοι of the Acts and of all the Epistles except Hebr. are taken from the Codex Passionei (G or L), an uncial of the ninth century.	2524	16	28	1007 A. V. 1008
James.........	9	5	6		242	[ἀναγνώσματα of Matt. 116, Mark 71, Luke 114, John 67, in Wake 25, Mutin. [5] ii. A. 5].	5	108
1 Peter	8	3	8		236		5	105
2 Peter	desunt	2	4		154		3	61
1 John	14	3	7		274		5	105
2 John	1	2	2		30		1	13
3 John	2	desunt	3		32		1	15 A. V. 14
Jude	2	desunt	4		68		1	25
Romans	93 sections in Rom. 1, 2 Corinth. Gal. Eph. Coloss. 1, 2 Thess. to Hebr. ix. 14.	8	19		920	5	16	433
1 Corinth. ...		} 19	9		870	5	16	437
2 Corinth. ...			11		590	4	13	256 A. V. 257
Galat.		3	12		293	2	6	149
Ephes.		3	10		312	2	6	155
Philipp.		2	7		208	2	4	104
Coloss.		3	10		208	2	4	95
1 Thess.		2	7		193	1	5	89
2 Thess.		2	6		106	1	3	47
1 Tim.		—	18		230	1	6	113
2 Tim.		—	9		172	1	4	83
Titus		—	6		98 (97, Mill)	1	3	46
Philem.		—	2		38	1	1	25
Hebrews ...		5 to ch. ix. 11.	22		703	3	13	303
Apocalypse..	24 λόγοι, 72 κεφάλαια, 1800 στίχοι.						22	405 A. V. 404

[1] The Ammonian κεφάλαια in the Gospels vary from the normal number in many copies, especially in SS. Matthew and Mark, but not considerably. The ἀναγνώσματα of the Gospels set down in column seven are also given in Mendham, Evan. 562. See p. 75, note 1.

Greek Test. of 1827 &c. and in Tischendorf's of 1859. We exhibit, however, for the sake of comparison, a tabular view of 'Ancient and Modern Divisions of the New Testament.' The numbers of the *ῥήματα* and *στίχοι* in the Gospels are derived from the most approved sources, but a synopsis of the variations of manuscripts in this respect has been drawn up by Scholz, Prolegomena N. T. vol. i. Cap. v, pp. xxviii, xxix[1]. A computation of their number, as also of that of the *ἀναγνώσματα*, is often given in the subscription at the end of a book.

10. On the divisions into chapters and verses prevailing in our modern Bibles we need not dwell long. For many centuries the Latin Church used the Greek *τίτλοι* (which they called *breves*) with the Euthalian *κεφάλαια*, and some of their copies even retained the calculation by *στίχοι*: but about A.D. 1248 Cardinal Hugo de Sancto Caro, while preparing a Concordance, or index of declinable words, for the *whole Bible*, divided it into its present chapters, subdividing them in turn into several parts by placing the letters A, B, C, D &c. in the margin, at equal distances from each other, as we still see in many old printed books, e.g. Stephen's N. T. of 1550. Cardinal Hugo's divisions, unless indeed he merely adopted them from Lanfranc or some other scholar, such as was very probably Stephen Langton the celebrated Archbishop of Canterbury, soon took possession of copies of the Latin Vulgate; they gradually obtained a place in later Greek manuscripts, especially those written in the West of Europe, and are found in the earliest printed and all later editions of the Greek Testament, though still unknown to the Eastern Church. They certainly possess no strong claim on our preference, although they cannot now be superseded. The chapters are inconveniently and capriciously unequal in length; occasionally too they are distributed with much lack of judge-

[1] The numbers of the Gospel *στίχοι* in our Table are taken from the uncial copies Codd. GS and twenty-seven cursives named by Scholz: those of the *ῥήματα* from Codd. 9, 13, 124 and seven others. In the *ῥήματα* he cites no other variation than that Cod. 339 has 2822 for St. Matthew: but Mill states that Cod. 48 (Bodl. 7) has 1676 for Mark, 2507 for Luke (Proleg. N. T. § 1429). In Cod. 56 (Lincoln Coll.) the *ἀναγνώσματα* of St. Matthew are 127, of St. Mark 74, of St. Luke 130 (Mill).

In the *στίχοι*, a few straggling manuscripts fluctuate between 3397? and 1474 for Matthew; 2006 and 1000 for Mark; 3827 and 2000 for Luke; 2300 and 1300 for John. But the great mass of authorities stand as we have represented.

ment. Thus Matt. xv. 39 belongs to ch. xvi, and perhaps ch. xix. 30 to ch. xx; Mark ix. 1 properly appertains to the preceding chapter; Luke xxi. 1-4 had better be united with ch. xx, as in Mark xii. 41-44; Acts v might as well commence with Acts iv. 32; Acts viii. 1 (or at least its first clause) should not have been separated from ch. vii; Acts xxi concludes with strange abruptness. Bp. Terrot (on Ernesti's Institutes, vol. ii. p. 21) rightly affixes 1 Cor. iv. 1-5 to ch. iii. Add that 1 Cor. xi. 1 belongs to ch. x; 2 Cor. iv. 18 and vi. 18 to ch. v and ch. vii respectively: Col. iv. 1 must clearly go with ch. iii.

In commendation of the modern verses still less can be said. As they are stated to have been constructed after the model of the ancient στίχοι (called '*versus*' in the Latin manuscripts), we have placed in the Table the exact number of each for every book in the New Testament. Of the στίχοι we reckon 19241 in all, of the modern verses 7959[1], so that on the average (for we have seen that the manuscript variations in the number of στίχοι are but inconsiderable) we may calculate about five στίχοι to every two modern verses. The fact is that some such division is simply indispensable to every accurate reader of Scripture; and Cardinal Hugo's divisions by letters of the alphabet, as well as those adopted by Sanctes Pagninus in his Latin version of the whole Bible (1528), having proved inconveniently large, Robert Stephen, the justly celebrated printer and editor of the Greek Testament, undertook to form a system of verse-divisions, taking for his model the short verses into which the Hebrew Bible had already been divided, as it would seem by Rabbi Nathan, in the preceding century. We are told by Henry Stephen (Praef. Concordantiae) that his father Robert executed this design on a journey from Paris to Lyons '*inter equitandum*[2];' that is, we

[1] Our English version divides 2 Cor. xiii. 12 of the Greek into two, and unites John i. 38, 39 of the Greek. The English and Greek verses begin differently in Luke i. 73, 74; vii. 18, 19. Acts ix. 28, 29; xi. 25, 26; xiii. 32, 33; xix. 40, 41; xxiv. 2, 3. 2 Cor. ii. 12, 13; v. 14, 15; xi. 8, 9. Eph. i. 10, 11; iii. 17, 18. Phil. iii. 13, 14. 1 Thess. ii. 11, 12. Heb. vii. 20, 21; x. 22, 23. 1 Jo. ii. 13, 14. 3 Jo. 14, 15. Apoc. xii. 18 or xiii. 1; xviii. 16, 17. In a few of these places editions of the Greek vary a little. The whole subject of the verses is discussed in Dr. Ezra Abbot's tract 'De Editionibus Novi Testamenti Graece in versuum quos dicunt distinctione inter se discrepantibus' 1882, included in the Prolegomena for Tischendorf's N. T., eighth edition, pp. 167, &c.

[2] 'I think it would have been better done on one's knees in the closet,' is

presume, while resting at the inns on the road. Certain it is that, although every such division must be in some measure arbitrary, a very little care would have spared us many of the disadvantages attending that which Robert Stephen first published at Geneva in his Greek Testament of 1551, from which it was introduced into the text of the Genevan English Testament of 1557, into Beza's Greek Testament of 1565, and thence into subsequent editions. It is now too late to correct the errors of the verse-divisions, but they can be neutralized, at least in a great degree, by the plan adopted by modern critics, of banishing both the verses and the chapters into the margin, and breaking the text into paragraphs, better suited to the sense. The *pericopae* or sections of Bengel[1] (whose labours will be described in their proper place) have been received with general approbation, and adopted, with some modification, by several recent editors. Much pains were bestowed on their arrangement of the paragraphs by the Revisers of the English version of 1881.

11. We now come to the *contents* of manuscripts of the Greek Testament, and must distinguish regular copies of the sacred volume or of parts of it from Lectionaries, or Church-lesson books, containing only extracts, arranged in the order of Divine Service daily throughout the year. The latter we will consider presently: with regard to the former it is right to bear in mind, that comparatively few copies of the whole New Testament remain; the usual practice being to write the four Gospels in one volume, the Acts and Epistles in another: manuscripts of the Apocalypse, which was little used for public worship, being much rarer than those of the other books. Occasionally the Gospels, Acts, and Epistles form a single volume; sometimes the Apocalypse is added to other books; as to the Pauline Epistles in Lambeth 1186, or even to the Gospels, in a later hand (e.g. Cambridge University Libr. Dd. 9. 69: Gospels No. 60, *dated* A.D. 1297). The Apocalypse, being a short work, is often

Mr. Kelly's quaint and not unfair comment (Lectures on the Minor Prophets, p. 324), unless, as is not unlikely, he copied what was done before.

[1] Novum Testamentum Graecum. Edente Jo. Alberto Bengelio. Tubingae 1734. 4to. The practice of the oldest Greek manuscripts in regard to paragraphs has been stated above (p. 49, note 2), and will be further explained in the next section under our descriptions of Codd. ℵBD.

found bound up in volumes containing very miscellaneous matter (e. g. Vatican. 2066 or B; Brit. Mus. Harleian. 5678, No. 31; and Oxon. Barocc. 48, No. 28). The Codex Sinaiticus of Tischendorf is the more precious, in that it happily exhibits the whole New Testament complete: so would also the Codices Alexandrinus and Ephraemi, but that they are sadly mutilated: no other uncial copies have this advantage, and very few cursives. In England only ~~five~~ such are known, the great Codex Leicestrensis, which is imperfect at the beginning and end; Butler 2 (Evan. 201) Additional 11837, dated A.D. 1357, and (Evan. 584) Additional 17469, both in the British Museum; Canonici 34 (Evan. 488) in the Bodleian, dated A.D. 1515-16. Additional MS. 28815 (Evan. 603, and Paul 266, and Apoc. 89) in the British Museum and B-C. II. 4 at Sir Roger Cholmely's School, Highgate, are separated portions of one complete copy. The Apocalypse in the well-known Codex Montfortianus at Dublin is usually considered to be by a later hand. Besides these Scholz enumerates only nineteen foreign copies of the whole New Testament[1]; making but twenty-four in all, as far as was then known, out of the vast mass of extant documents.

12. Whether copies contain the whole or a part of the sacred volume, the general *order* of the books is the following: Gospels, Acts, Catholic Epistles, Pauline Epistles, Apocalypse. A solitary manuscript of the fifteenth century (Venet. 10, Evan. 209) places the Gospels between the Pauline Epistles and the Apocalypse[2]; in the Codices Sinaiticus, Leicestrensis, Fabri (Evan. 90), and Montfortianus, as in the Bodleian Canonici 34, the copy in the King's Library Brit. Mus. (Act. 20), and the

[1] Coislin. 199 (Evan. 35); Vatic. 2080 (Evan. 175); Palat. Vat. 171 (Evan. 149); Lambec. 1 at Vienna (Evan. 218); Vatic. 1160 (Evan. 141); Venet. 5 (Evan. 205); its alleged duplicate Venet. 10 (Evan. 209); Matthaei k (Evan. 241); Moscow Synod. 380 (Evan. 242); Paris, Reg. 47 (Evan. 18); Reg. 61 (Evan. 263); Vat. Ottob. 66 (Evan. 386); Vat. Ottob. 381 (Evan. 390); Taurin. 302 (Evan. 339); S. Saba, 10 and 20 (Evan. 462 and 466); Laurent. 53 (Evan. 367); Vallicel. F. 17 (Evan. 394); Phillipps 7682 (Evan. 531); perhaps Scholz ought to have added Venet. 6 (Evan. 206) which he states to contain the whole New Testament, Proleg. N. T. vol. i. p. lxxii. In Evan. 180 all except the Gospels are by a later hand. Add (Evan. 622) also copies at Poictiers, Ferrara, and Toledo. Lagarde (Genesis, pp. 7, 8) describes another copy at Zittau, collated by Matthaei in 1801-2, apparently unpublished.

[2] I presume that the same order is found in Evan. 393, whereof Scholz states 'sec. xvi. continet epist. cath. paul. ev.' Proleg. N. T. vol. i. p. xc.

Complutensian edition (1514), the Pauline Epistles precede the Acts. The Pauline Epistles stand between the Acts and the Catholic Epistles in Phillipps 1284, Evan. 527; Parham 71. 6, Evan. 534; Upsal, Sparfwenfeldt 42, Acts 68; Paris Reg. 102 A, Acts 119; Reg. 103 A, Acts 120. In Oxford Bodl. Miscell. 74 the order is Acts, Cath. Epp., Apocalypse, Paul. Epp., but an earlier hand wrote from 3 John onwards. In Evan. 51 Dr. C. R. Gregory points out minute indications that the scribe, not the binder, set the Gospels last. In the Memphitic and Thebaic the Acts follow the Catholic Epistles (*see* below, vol. ii, chap. iii). The Codex Basiliensis (No. 4 of the Epistles), Acts Cod. 134, Brit. Mus. Addl. 19388, Lambeth 1182, 1183, and Burdett-Coutts III. 1, have the Pauline Epistles immediately after the Acts and before the Catholic Epistles, as in our present Bibles. Scholz's Evan. 368 stands thus, St. John's Gospel, Apocalypse, then all the Epistles; in Havniens. 1 (Cod. 234 of the Gospels, A.D. 1278) the order appears to be Acts, Paul. Ep., Cath. Ep., Gospels; in Ambros. Z 34 *sup.* at Milan, Dean Burgon testifies that the Catholic and Pauline Epistles are followed by the Gospels; in Basil. B. VI. 27 or Cod. 1, the Gospels have been bound after the Acts and Epistles; while in Evan. 175 the Apocalypse stands between the Acts and Catholic Epistles; in Evan. 51 the binder has set the Gospels last: these, however, are mere accidental exceptions to the prevailing rule[1]. The four Gospels are almost invariably found in their familiar order, although in the Codex Bezae (as we partly saw above, p. 65) they stand Matthew, John, Luke, Mark[2]; in the Codex Monacensis (X) John, Luke,

[1] Hartwell Horne in the second volume of his Introduction tells us that in some of the few manuscripts which contain the whole of the New Testament the books are arranged thus: Gospels, Acts, Catholic Epistles, Apocalypse, Pauline Epistles (p. 92, ed. 1834). This statement may be true of some of the foreign MSS. named in p. 69 note, but of the English it can refer to none, although Wake 34 at Christ Church commences with the Acts and Catholic Epistles, followed by the Apocalypse beginning on the same page as Jude ends, and the Pauline Epistles on the same page as the Apocalypse ends. The Gospels, which come last, may have been misplaced by an early binder.

[2] This is the true *Western* order (Scrivener, Cod. Bezae, Introd. p. xxx and note), and will be found in the copies of the Old Latin a_1, a_2, *b*, *e*, f_1, ff_2, *i*, *n*, *q*, *r* to be described in vol. ii, and in the Gothic version. In Burdett-Coutts II. 7, p. 4, also, prefixed to the Gospels, we read the following rubric-title to certain verses of Gregory Nazianzen: $\overline{\chi\upsilon}$ *θαύματα· παρὰ ματθαίω ἰωάννη τὲ καὶ λουκᾶ καὶ μάρκω· κ.τ.λ.*

Mark, Matthew (but two leaves of Matthew *also* stand before John), also in the Latin *k*; in Cod. 90 (Fabri) John, Luke, Matthew, Mark; in Cod. 399 at Turin John, Luke, Matthew, an arrangement which Dr. Hort refers to the Commentary of Titus of Bostra on St. Luke which accompanies it; in the Curetonian Syriac version Matthew, Mark, John, Luke. In the Pauline Epistles that to the Hebrews immediately follows the second to the Thessalonians in the four great Codices Vaticanus, Sinaiticus, Alexandrinus, and Ephraemi[1]: in the copy from which the Cod. Vatican. was taken the Hebrews followed the Galatians (*above*, p. 57). The Codex Claromontanus, the document next in importance to these four, sets the Colossians appropriately enough next to its kindred and contemporaneous Epistle to the Ephesians, but postpones that to the Hebrews to Philemon, as in our present Bibles: an arrangement which at first, no doubt, originated in the early scruples prevailing in the Western Church, with respect to the authorship and canonical authority of that divine epistle.

13. We must now describe the *Lectionaries* or Service-books of the Greek Church, in which the portions of Scripture publicly read throughout the year are set down in chronological order, without regard to their actual places in the sacred volume. In length and general arrangement they resemble not so much the Lessons as the Epistles and Gospels in our English Book of Common Prayer, only that every day in the year has its own proper portion, and the numerous Saints' days independent services of their own. These Lectionaries consist either of lessons from the Gospels, and are then called *Evangelistaria* or *Evangeliaria* (εὐαγγελιστάρια)[2]; or from the Acts and Epistles, termed *Praxapostolos* (πραξαπόστολος) or *Apostolos*[3]: the general name of Lectionary is often, though incorrectly, confined to the latter class. A few books called ἀποστολοευαγγέλια have lessons

[1] Tischendorf cites the following copies in which the Epistle to the Hebrews stands in the same order as in Codd. ℵABC, 'H [Coislin. 202], 17, 23, 47, 57, 71, 73 aliique.' Add 77, 80, 166, 189, 196, 264, 265, 266 (Burdett-Coutts II. 4). So in Zoega's Thebaic version. Epiphanius (adv. Haer. i. 42) says: ἄλλα δὲ ἀντίγραφα ἔχει τὴν πρὸς ἑβραίους δεκάτην, πρὸ τῶν δύο τῶν πρὸς Τιμόθεον καὶ Τίτον. So Paul 166, 281, and also Bp. Lightfoot's MSS. of the Memphitic except 7 and 16. In the Thebaic it follows 2 Cor. See below.

[2] They are also termed Εὐαγγέλια—evidently a popular, as well as a misleading name.

[3] Suicer, s. v.

taken both from the Gospels and the Apostolic writings. In *Euchologies*, or Books of Offices, wherein both the *Apostolos* and the *Gospels* are found, the former always precede in each Office, just as the Epistle precedes the Gospel in the Service-books of Western Christendom. The peculiar arrangement of Lectionaries renders them very unfit for the hasty, partial, cursory collation which has befallen too many manuscripts of the other class, and this circumstance, joined with the irksomeness of using Service-books never familiar to the habits even of scholars in this part of Europe, has caused these documents to be so little consulted, that the contents of the very best and oldest among them have until recently been little known. Matthaei, of whose elaborate and important edition of the Greek Testament (12 tom. Riga 1782–88) we shall give an account hereafter, has done excellent service in this department; two of his best copies, the uncials B and H (Nos. 47, 50), being Evangelistaria. The present writer also has collated three noble uncials of the same rank, Arundel 547 being of the ninth century, Parham 18 bearing date A.D. 980, Harleian 5598, A.D. 995. Not a few other uncial Lectionaries remain quite neglected, for though none of them perhaps are older than the eighth century, the ancient character was retained for these costly and splendid Service-books till about the eleventh century (Montfaucon, Palaeogr. Graec. p. 260), before which time the cursive hand was generally used in other Biblical manuscripts. There is, of course, no place in a Lectionary for divisions by *κεφάλαια*, for the so-called Ammonian sections, or for the canons of Eusebius.

The division of the New Testament into Church-lessons was, however, of far more remote antiquity than the employment of separate volumes to contain them. Towards the end of the fourth century, that golden age of Patristic theology, Chrysostom recognizes some stated order of the lessons as familiar to all his hearers, for he exhorts them to peruse and mark beforehand the passages (*περικοπαί* [1]) of the Gospels which were to be publicly read to them the ensuing Sunday or Saturday [2]. All the infor-

[1] This was the word for a lection or lesson, and Suicer tells us that *ἀνάγνωσις* and *ἀνάγνωσμα* were employed as equivalents. But in modern textual criticism, *ἀναγνώσματα* is used to signify the marks indicating lections, which are found in the margin or at the head or foot of pages, or the computation of their number which is often appended at the end of a book. See pp. 68, note 1, 69.

[2] Chrysost. in Joan. Hom. x *κατὰ μίαν σαββάτων ἢ καὶ κατὰ σάββατον*. Traces

mation we can gather favours the notion that there was no great difference between the calendar of Church-lessons in earlier and later stages. Not only do they correspond in all cases where such agreement is natural, as in the proper services for the great feasts and fasts, but in such purely arbitrary arrangements as the reading of the book of Genesis, instead of the Gospels, on the week days of Lent; of the Acts all the time between Easter and Pentecost[1]; and the selection of St. Matthew's history of the Passion alone at the Liturgy on Good Friday[2]. The earliest formal *Menologium*, or Table of proper lessons, now extant is prefixed to the Codex Cyprius (K) of the eighth or ninth century; another is found in the Codex Campianus (M), which is perhaps a little later; they are more frequently found than the contrary in later manuscripts of every kind; while there are comparatively few copies that have not been accommodated to ecclesiastical use either by their original scribe or a later hand, by means of noting the proper days for each lesson (often in red ink) at the top or bottom or in the margin of the several pages. Not only in the margin, but even in the text itself are perpetually interpolated, mostly in vermilion or red ink, the beginning (ἀρχή or αρˣ) and ending (τέλος or τεˡ) of each lesson, and the several words to be inserted or substituted in order to suit the purpose of public reading; from which source (as we have stated above, p. 11) various readings have almost unavoidably sprung: e.g. in Acts iii. 11 τοῦ ἰαθέντος χωλοῦ of the Lectionaries ultimately displaced αὐτοῦ from the text itself.

of these Church-lessons occur in manuscripts as early as the fifth and sixth centuries. Thus Cod. Alexandrinus reads Rom. xvi. 25–27 not only in its proper place, but also at the end of ch. xiv where the Lectionaries place it (see p. 84). Codex Bezae prefixes to Luke xvi. 19 εἶπεν δὲ καὶ ἑτέραν παραβολήν, the proper introduction to the Gospel for the 5th Sunday in St. Luke. To John xiv. 1 the same manuscript prefixes καὶ εἶπεν τοῖς μαθηταῖς αὐτοῦ, as does our English Prayer Book in the Gospel for May 1. Even τέλος or τὸ τέλος, which follows ἀπέχει in Mark xiv. 41 in tho same manuscript and other authorities, probably has the same origin.

[1] See the passages from Augustine Tract. VI. in Joan.; and Chrysost. Hom. VII ad Antioch.; Hom. LXIII, XLVII in Act. in Bingham's Antiquities, Book XIV, Chap. III. Sect. 3. Chrysostom even calls the arrangement τῶν πατέρων ὁ νόμος. The strong passage cited from Cyril of Jerusalem by Dean Burgon (Last Twelve Verses of St. Mark, p. 195) shows the confirmed practice as already settled in A.D. 348.

[2] August. Serm. CXLIII de Tempore. The few verses Luke xxiii. 39–43, John xix. 31–37 are merely wrought into one narrative with Matt. xxvii, each in its proper place. See p. 85.

Verlag der J. C. Hinrichs'schen Buchhandlung in Leipzig.

Urtext und Übersetzungen der Bibel

in übersichtlicher Darstellung.

Sonderabdruck der Artikel

Bibeltext und Bibelübersetzungen

aus der dritten Auflage der

Realencyklopädie für protestantische Theologie und Kirche.

1897. 15 Bogen. 3 Mark.

Die wissenschaftliche Forschung der letzten Jahrzehnte hat sich mit Vorliebe der Frage nach der Überlieferung und Gestaltung des Textes der heiligen Schrift und nach der Entstehung und dem Wert der alten Bibelübersetzungen zugewandt. Doch fehlt es in der deutschen Litteratur an einem Werke, das die gesicherten Ergebnisse der neueren Untersuchungen zusammenfassend darstellte. Die Verlagshandlung glaubt deshalb den Dank vieler zu erwerben, indem sie die von hervorragenden Fachmännern bearbeiteten Artikel über den Bibeltext und die Bibelübersetzungen aus der dritten Auflage der Realencyklopädie für protestantische Theologie und Kirche gesondert veröffentlicht und dadurch weiteren Kreisen zugänglich macht.

Käufern dieses Sonderabdrucks, die sich zur Anschaffung der Realencyklopädie selbst (3. Aufl.) entschließen, werden bei Benutzung des vorn beigefügten Verlangzettels 2 Mark, bei Rücksendung des Heftes selbst der volle Betrag von 3 Mark gutgebracht.

We purpose to annex to this Chapter a table of lessons throughout the year, according to the use laid down in Synaxaria, Menologies, and Lectionaries, as well to enable the student to compare the proper lessons of the Greek Church with our own, as to facilitate reference to the manuscripts themselves, which are now placed almost out of the reach of the inexperienced. On comparing the manner in which the terms are used by different scribes and authors, we conceive that *Synaxarion* (συναξάριον) is, like Eclogadion, a name used for a table of daily lessons for the year beginning at Easter, and that these have varied but slightly in the course of many ages throughout the whole Eastern Church; that tables of Saints' day lessons, called *Menologies*, (μηνολόγιον), distributed in order of the months from September (when the new year and the indiction began) to August, differed widely from each other, both in respect to the lessons read and the days kept holy [1]. While the great feasts remained entirely the same, different generations and provinces and even dioceses had their favourite worthies, whose memory they specially cherished; so that the character of the menology (which sometimes forms a larger, sometimes but a small portion of a Lectionary) will often guide us to the country and district in which the volume itself was written. The Parham Evangelistarium 18 affords us a conspicuous example of this fact: coming from a region of which we know but little (Ciscissa in Cappadocia Prima), its menology in many particulars but little resembles those usually met with [2].

14. It only remains to say a few words about the *notation* adopted to indicate the several classes of manuscripts of the Greek Testament. These classes are six in number; that con-

[1] Besides this special meaning, Synaxarion was also employed in a general sense for any catalogue of Church-lessons, both for daily use and for Saints' days.

[2] This was naturally even more the case in countries where the Liturgy was not in Greek. Thus in the 'Calendar of the Coptic Church' translated from the Arabic by Dr. S. C. Malan (1873), the only Feast-days identical with those given below (pp. 87–89) are Sept. 14; Oct. 8; Nov. 8, 13, 14, 17, 25, 30; Dec. 20, 24, 25, 29; Jan. 1, 6 (the Lord's Baptism), 22; Feb. 2, 24; March 25; April 25; May 2; June 19, 24, 29; July 22; Aug. 6, 25. Elsewhere the day is altered, even if the festival be the same; e.g. St. Thomas' Day is Oct. 6 with the Greeks, Oct. 23 with the Copts; St. Luke's Day (Oct. 18), and the Beheading of the Baptist (Aug. 29), are kept by the Copts a day later than by the Greeks, since Aug. 29 is their New Year's Day.

taining the Gospels (*Evangelia* or *Evan.*), or the Acts and Catholic Epistles (*Act.* and *Cath.*), or the Pauline Epistles (*Paul.*), or the Apocalypse (*Apoc.*), or Lectionaries of the Gospels (*Evangelistaria* or *Evst.*), or those of the Acts and Epistles (*Apostolos* or *Apost.*). When one manuscript (as often happens) belongs to more than one of these classes, its distinct parts are numbered separately, so that a copy of the whole New Testament will appear in four lists, and be reckoned four times over. All critics are agreed in distinguishing the documents written in the uncial character by capital letters; the custom having originated in the accidental circumstance that the Codex Alexandrinus was designated as Cod. A in the lower margin of Walton's Polyglott. Lectionaries in uncial letters are not marked by capitals, but by Arabic numerals, like cursive manuscripts of all classes [1]. Of course no system can escape some attendant evils. Even the catalogue of the later manuscripts is often upon its first appearance full of mis-statements, of repetitions and loose descriptions, which must be remedied and supplied in subsequent examination, so far as opportunity is granted from time to time. In describing the uncials (as we purpose to do in the two next chapters) our course is tolerably plain; but the lists that comprise the last eight chapters of this volume, and which respectively detail the cursive manuscripts and the Lectionaries of the Greek Testament, must be regarded only as an approximation to what such an enumeration ought to be, though much pains and time have been spent upon them: the comparatively few copies which seem to be sufficiently known are distinguished by an asterisk from their less fortunate kindred.

For indeed the only method of grappling with the perplexity produced by the large additions of manuscripts, especially of the cursive character, which constant discovery has effected during late years, is to enumerate arithmetically those which have been supplied from time to time, as was done in the last edition of this work, carefully noting if they have been examined by a competent judge or especially if they have been properly collated. In the Appendix of the third edition, the late Dean Burgon continued his work in this direction by adding a list of some

[1] This system was introduced by Wetstein (N. T. 1751-52). Mill used to cite copies by abridgements of their names, e.g. Alex. Cant. Mont. &c.

three hundred and seventy-four cursives, besides the others with which he had previously increased the number before known. That list, as was stated in the Postcript to the Preface, awaited an examination and collation by competent persons. Such an examination has been made in many instances by Dr. C. R. Gregory, who also, whether fired by Dean Burgon's example as shown in his published letters in the *Guardian* or not, has in his turn added with most commendable diligence in research a very large number of MSS. previously unknown. Some more have been added in this edition, but much work is still required of scholars, before this mass of materials can be used with effect by Textual students.

APPENDIX TO CHAPTER III.

SYNAXARION AND ECLOGADION OF THE GOSPELS AND APOSTOLIC WRITINGS DAILY THROUGHOUT THE YEAR.

[Gathered chiefly from Evangelist. Arund. 547, Parham 18, Harl. 5598, Burney 22, Gale O. 4. 22, Christ's Coll. Camb. F. 1. 8, compared with the Liturgical notes in Wake 12, and those by later hands in Cod. Bezae (D). Use has been made also of Apostolos B–C. III. 24, B–C. III. 53, and the Euchology, or Book of Offices, B–C. III. 42.]

Ἐκ τοῦ κατὰ Ἰωάννην [Arundel 547]

Τῇ ἁγίᾳ καὶ μεγάλῃ κυριακῇ τοῦ πάσχα.

Easter-day	John i. 1–17.	Acts i. 1–8.
2nd day of Easter week (τῆς διακινησίμου)	18–28.	12–26.
3rd	Luke xxiv. 12–35.	ii. 14–21
4th	John i. 35–52.	38–43.
5th	iii. 1–15.	iii. 1–8.
6th (παρασκευῇ)	ii. 12–22.	ii. 12–36.
7th (σαββάτῳ)	iii. 22–33.	iii. 11–16.

Ἀντίπασχα or 1st Sunday after Easter (τοῦ Θωμᾶ, B–C. III. 42)	xx. 19–31.	v. 12–20.
2nd day of 2nd week	ii. 1–11.	iii. 19–26.
3rd	iii. 16–21.	iv. 1–10.
4th	v. 17–24.	13–22.
5th	24–30.	23–31.
6th (παρασκευῇ)	v. 30—vi. 2.	v. 1–11.
7th (σαββάτῳ)	vi. 14–27.	21–32.

Κυριακῇ γ′ or 2nd after Easter (τῶν μυροφόρων, B–C. III. 42)	Mark xv. 43—xvi. 8.	vi. 1–7.
2nd day of 3rd week	John iv. 46–54.	8—vii. 60.
3rd	vi. 27–33.	viii. 5–17.
4th (6th, Gale)	48–54.	18–25.
5th	40–44.	26–39.
6th (παρασκευῇ) (4th, Gale)	35–39.	40—ix. 19.
7th (σαββάτῳ)	xv. 17—xvi. 1.	19–31.

Κυριακῇ δ′ or 3rd Sunday after Easter (τοῦ παραλύτου sic, B–C. III. 42)	John v. 1–15.	Acts ix. 32–42.
2nd day of 4th week	vi. 56–69.	x. 1–16.
3rd	vii. 1–13.	21–33.
4th (τῆς μεσοπεντηκοστῆς, B–C. III. 42)	14–30.	xiv. 6–18.
5th	viii. 12–20.	x. 34–43.
6th (παρασκευῇ)	21–30.	44—xi. 10.
7th (σαββάτῳ)	31–42.	xii. 1–11.

Κυριακῇ ε′ or 4th Sunday after Easter (τῆς σαμαρείτιδος)	iv. 5–42.	xi. 19–30.
2nd day of 5th week	viii. 42–51.	xii. 12–17.
3rd	51–59.	25—xiii. 12.
4th	vi. 5–14.	xiii. 13–24.
5th	ix. 39—x. 9.	xiv. 20–27 (–xv. 4, B–C. III. 24).
6th (παρασκευῇ)	x. 17–28.	xv. 5–12.
7th (σαββάτῳ)	27–38.	35–41.

Κυριακῇ ϛ′ or 5th Sunday after Easter (τοῦ τυφλοῦ)	ix. 1–38.	xvi. 16–34.
2nd day of 6th week	xi. 47–54.	xvii. 1–9.
3rd	xii. 19–36.	19–27.
4th	36–47.	xviii. 22–28.

5th 'Αναλήψεως, Ascension Day		
Matins,	Mark xvi. 9–20.	
Liturgy,	Luke xxiv. 36–53.	Acts i. 1–12.
6th (παρασκευῇ)	John xiv. 1–10 (11, Gale, Wake 12).	xix. 1–8.
7th (σαββάτῳ)	10–21 (om. 18–20, Gale).	xx. 7–12.

Κυριακῇ ζ' or 6th Sunday after Easter τῶν ἁγίων τιη πατέρων ἐν Νικαίᾳ.	xvii. 1–13.	16–38.
2nd day of 7th week	xiv. 27—xv. 7.	xxi. 8–14.
3rd	xvi. 2–13.	26–32.
4th	15–23.	xxiii. 1–11.
5th	23–33.	xxv. 13–19.
6th (παρασκευῇ)	xvii. 18–26.	xxvii. 1–xxviii. 1.
7th (σαββάτῳ)	xxi. 14–25.	xxviii. 1–31.

Κυριακῇ τῆς πεντηκοστῆς Whitsunday		
Matins,	xx. 19–23.	
Liturgy,	vii. 37—viii. 12[1].	ii. 1–11.

'Εκ τοῦ κατὰ Ματθαῖον.

2nd day of 1st week Τῇ ἐπαύριον τῆς πεντηκοστῆς.	Matt. xviii. 10–20.	Eph. v. 8–19.
3rd	iv. 25—v. 11.	
4th	20–30.	
5th	31–41.	
6th (παρασκευῇ)	vii. 9–18.	
7th (σαββάτῳ)	v. 42–48.	Rom. i. 7–12.
Κυριακῇ α' τῶν ἁγίων πάντων	x. 32–33; 37–38; xix. 37–30;	Heb. xi. 33–xii. 2.
2nd day of 2nd week	vi. 31–34; vii. 9–14.	Rom. ii. 1–6.
3rd	vii. 15–21.	13, 17–27.
4th	11–23.	28—iii. 4.
5th	viii. 23–27.	iii. 4–9.
6th (παρασκευῇ)	ix. 14–17.	9–18.
7th (σαββάτῳ)	vii. 1–8.	iii. 19–26.
Κυριακῇ β'	Matt. iv. 18–23.	Rom. ii. 10–16.
2nd day of 3rd week	ix. 36—x. 8.	iv. 4–8.
3rd	9–15.	8–12.
4th	16–22.	13–17.
5th	23–31.	18–25.
6th (παρασκευῇ)	32–36; xi. 1.	v. 12–14.
7th (σαββάτῳ)	vii. 24—viii. 4.	iii. 28—iv. 3.
Κυριακῇ γ'	vi. 22–23.	v. 1–10.
2nd day of 4th week	xi. 2–15.	15–17.
3rd	16–20.	17–21.
4th	20–26.	vii. 1. . . .
5th	27–30.	
6th (παρασκευῇ)	xii. 1–8.	
7th (σαββάτῳ)	viii. 14–23 (om. 19–22, Gale).	vi. 11–17.
Κυριακῇ δ'	viii. 5–13.	vi. 18–23.
2nd day of 5th week	xii. 9–13.	vii. 19–viii. 3.
3rd	14–16; 22–30.	viii. 2–9.
4th	38–45.	8–14.
5th	xii. 46—xiii. 3.	22–27.
6th (παρασκευῇ)	3–12.	ix. 6–13.
7th (σαββάτῳ)	ix. 9–13.	viii. 14–21.
Κυριακῇ ε'	viii. 28—ix. 1.	x. 1–10.
2nd day of 6th week	xiii. 10–23.	ix. 13–19.
3rd	24–30.	17–28.
4th	31–36.	29–33.
5th	36–43.	ix. 33; x. 12–17.
6th (παρασκευῇ)	44–54.	x. 15—xi. 2.
7th (σαββάτῳ)	ix. 18–26.	ix. 1–5.
Κυριακῇ ς'	ix. 1–8.	xii. 6–14.
2nd day of 7th week	xiii. 54–58.	xi. 2–6.
3rd	xiv. 1–13.	7–12.
4th	xiv. 35—xv. 11.	13–20.
5th	12–21.	19–24.
6th (παρασκευῇ)	29–31.	25–28.
7th (σαββάτῳ)	x. 37–xi. 1.	xii. 1–3.

[1] The *pericope adulterae* John vii. 53—viii. 11 is omitted in all the copies we know on the feast of Pentecost. Whenever read it was on some Saint's Day (*vid. infra*, p. 87, *notes* 2, 3).

Κυριακῇ ζ′ Matt. ix. 27–35. Rom. xv. 1–7.
2nd day of 8th week xvi. 1–6. xi. 29–36.
3rd 6–12. xii. 14–21.
4th 20–24. xiv. 10–18.
5th 24–28. xv. 8–12.
6th (παρασκευῇ) xvii. 10–18. 13–16.
7th (σαββάτῳ) xii. 30–37. xiii. 1–10.

Κυριακῇ η′ xiv. 14–22. 1 Cor. i. 10–18.
2nd day of 9th week xviii. 1–11. Rom. xv. 17–25.
3rd xviii. 18–20 (al. 22); xix. 1–2; 13–15. 26–29.
4th xx. 1–16. xvi. 17–20.
5th 17–28. 1 Cor. ii. 10–15.
6th (παρασκευῇ) xxi. 12–14; 17–20. 16—iii. 8.
7th (σαββάτῳ) xv. 32–39. Rom. xiv. 6–9.

Κυριακῇ θ′ xiv. 22–34. 1 Cor. iii. 9–17.
2nd day of 10th week xxi. 18–22. 18–23.
3rd 23–27. iv. 5–8.
4th 28–32. v. 9–13.
5th 43–46. vi. 1–6.
6th (παρασκευῇ) xxii. 23–33. 7–11.
7th (σαββάτῳ) xvii. 24—xviii. 1. Rom. xv. 30–33.

Κυριακῇ ι′ xvii. 14–23. 1 Cor. iv. 9–16.
2nd day of 11th week xxiii. 13–22. vi. 20–vii. 7.
3rd 23–28. vii. 7–15.
4th 29–39.
5th xxiv. 13 (14, Wake 12; 15 Cod. Bezae) –28.
6th (παρασκευῇ) 27–35 (33 Sch. and Matt.); 42–51. —vii. 35.
7th (σαββάτῳ) xix. 3–12. i. 3–9.

Κυριακῇ ια′ xviii. 23–35. ix. 2–12.

Ἐκ τοῦ κατὰ Μάρκον.

2nd day of 12th week Mark i. 9–15. vii. 37—viii. 3.
3rd 16–22. viii. 4–7.
4th 23–28. ix. 13–18.
5th 29–35. x. 2–10.
6th (παρασκευῇ) ii. 18–22. 10–15.
7th (σαββάτῳ) Matt. xx. 29–34. i. 26–29.

Κυριακῇ ιβ′ Matt. xix. 16–26. 1 Cor. xv. 1–11.
2nd day of 13th week Mark iii. 6–12. x. 14–23.
3rd 13–21. 31—xi. 3.
4th 20–27. xi. 4–12.
5th 28–35. 13–23.
6th (παρασκευῇ) iv. 1–9. 31. xii. 6.
7th (σαββάτῳ) Matt. xxii. 15–22. ii. 6–9.

Κυριακῇ ιγ′ Matt. xxi. 33–42. 1 Cor. xvi. 13–24.
2nd day of 14th week Mark iv. 10–23. xii. 12–18.
3rd 24–34. 18–26.
4th 35–41. xiii. 8—xiv. 1.
5th v. 1–20 (al. 17). xiv. 1–12.
6th (παρασκευῇ) v. 22–24; 35–vi. 1. 12–20.
7th (σαββάτῳ) Matt. xxiii. 1–12. iv. 1–5.

Κυριακῇ ιδ′ Matt. xxii. 2–14. 2 Cor. i. 21—ii. 4.
2nd day of 15th week Mark v. 24–34. 1 Cor. xiv. 26–33.
3rd vi. 1–7. 33–40.
4th 7–13. xv. 12–20.
5th 30–45. 29–34.
6th (παρασκευῇ) 45–53. 34–40.
7th (σαββάτῳ) Matt. xxiv. 1–13 (om. 10–12, Gale). iv. 7—v. 5.

Κυριακῇ ιε′ Matt. xxii. 35–40. 2 Cor. iv. 6–11 (15, B-C. III. 24).
2nd day of 16th week Mark vi. 54 (al. 56) —vii. 8. 1 Cor. xvi. 3–13.
3rd 5–16. 2 Cor. i. 1–7.
4th 14–24. 12–20.
5th 24–30. ii. 4–15.

6th (παρασκευῇ) viii. 1–10.
7th (σαββάτῳ)
Matt. xxiv. 34–37; 42–44.

15—iii. 3.
1 Cor. x. 23–28.

[Κυριακῇ ιϛ′ (16th) Matt. xxv. 14–30 (29, Gale). 2 Cor. vi. 1–10[1].
σαββάτῳ ιζ′ (17th) Matt. xxv. 1–13.
Κυριακῇ ιζ′ (17th) Matt. xv. 21–28].

Ἀρχὴ τῆς ἰνδικτοῦ τοῦ νέου ἔτους, ἤγουν τοῦ εὐαγγελιστοῦ λουκᾶ [Arund. 547, Parham 18].

Ἐκ τοῦ κατὰ Λουκᾶν [Christ's Coll. F. 1. 8].

2nd day of 1st week Luke iii. 19–22.
3rd 23—iv. 1.
4th 1–15.
5th 16–22.
6th (παρασκευῇ) 22–30.
7th (σαββάτῳ) 31–36.

Κυριακῇ α′ v. 1–11.
2nd day of 2nd week iv. 38–44.
3rd v. 12–16.
4th 33–39.
5th vi. 12–16 (al. 19).
6th (παρασκευῇ) 17–23.
7th σαββάτῳ). v. 17–26.

Κυριακῇ β′ v. 31–36.
2nd day of 3rd week 24–30.
3rd 37–45.
4th vi. 46—vii. 1.
5th vii. 17–30.
6th (παρασκευῇ) 31–35.
7th (σαββάτῳ) v. 27–32.

Κυριακῇ γ′ vii. 11–16.
2nd day of 4th week 36–50.
3rd vii. 1–3.
4th 22–25.
5th ix. 7–11.
6th (παρασκευῇ) 12–18.
7th (σαββάτῳ) vi. 1–10.

Κυριακῇ δ′ Luke viii. 5–8, 9–15.
2nd day of 5th week ix. 18–22.
3rd 23–27.
4th 43–50.
5th 49–56.
6th (παρασκευῇ) v. 1–15.
7th (σαββάτῳ) vii. 1–10.

Κυριακῇ ε′ xvi. 19–31.
2nd day of 6th week x. 22–24.
3rd xi. 1–10 (Mt.).
4th 9–13.
5th 14–23.
6th (παρασκευῇ) 23–26.
7th (σαββάτῳ) viii. 16–21.

Κυριακῇ ϛ′ viii. 27 (26, Gale) –35; 38–39.
2nd day of 7th week xi. 29–33.
3rd 34–41.
4th 42–46.
5th 47—xii. 1.
6th (παρασκευῇ) xii. 2–12.
7th (σαββάτῳ) ix. 1–6.

Κυριακῇ ζ′ viii. 41–56.
2nd day of 8th week xii. 13–15; 22–31.
3rd xii. 42–48.
4th 48–59.
5th xiii. 1–9.
6th (παρασκευῇ) 31–35.
7th (σαββάτῳ) ix. 37–43.

Κυριακῇ η′ x. 25–37.
2nd day of 9th week xiv. 12–51.
3rd Luke xiv. 25–35.
4th xv. 1–10.
5th xvi. 1–9.
6th (παρασκευῇ) xvi. 15–18; xvii. 1–4.
7th (σαββάτῳ) ix. 57–62.

Κυριακῇ θ′ xii. 16–21.
2nd day of 10th week xvii. 20–25.
3rd xvii. 26–37; xviii. 18.
4th xviii. 15–17; 26–30.
5th 31–34.
6th (παρασκευῇ) xix. 12–28.
7th (σαββάτῳ) x. 19–21.

Κυριακῇ ι′ xiii. 10–17.
2nd day of 11th week xix. 37–44.
3rd 45–48.
4th xx. 1–8.
5th 9–18.
6th (παρασκευῇ) 19–26.
7th (σαββάτῳ) xii. 32–40.

Κυριακῇ ια′ xiv. 16–24.
2nd day of 12th week xx. 27–44.
3rd xxi. 12–19.
4th xxi. 5–8; 10–11; 20–24.
5th xxi. 28–33.
6th (παρασκευῇ) xxi. 37—xxii. 8.
7th (σαββάτῳ) xiii. 19–29.

Κυριακῇ ιβ′ xvii. 12–19.
2nd day of 13th week Mark viii. 11–21.
3rd 22–26.
4th 30–34.
5th ix. 10–16.

[1] Lessons for the week in B-C. III. 24 are (2) 2 Cor. iii. 4–12. (3) iv. 1–6. (4) 11–18. (5) v. 10–15. (6) 15–21.

6th (παρασκευῇ) Mark ix. 33–41.
7th (σαββάτῳ) Luke xiv. 1–11.

Κυριακῇ ιγ′ Luke xviii. 18–27.
2nd day of 14th week Mark ix. 42.—x. 1.
3rd x. 2–11.
4th 11–16.
5th 17–27.
6th (παρασκευῇ) 24–32.
7th (σαββάτῳ) Luke xvi. 10–15.

Κυριακῇ ιδ′ Luke xviii. 35–43.

[2nd day of 15th week Mark x. 46–52.
3rd xi. 11–23.
4th 22–26.
5th 27–33.
6th (παρασκευῇ) xii. 1–12.
7th (σαββάτῳ) Luke xvii. 3–10.

Κυριακῇ ιε′ Luke xix. 1–10.
2nd day of 16th week Mark xii. 13–17.
3rd 18–27.
4th 28–34.
5th 38–44.
6th (παρασκευῇ) xiii. 1–9.

7th (σαββάτῳ) Luke xviii. 1–8.

Κυριακῇ ιϛ′ (*of the Publican*) Luke xviii. 9–14].
Apost. 2 Tim. iii. 10–15 (B–C. III. 42).
2nd day of 17th week Mark xiii. 9–13.
3rd 14–23.
4th 24–31.
5th xiii. 31—xiv. 2.
6th (παρασκευῇ) xiv. 3–9.
7th (σαββάτῳ) Luke xx. 46—xxi. 4.

Κυριακῇ ιζ′ (*of the Canaanitess*) Matt. xv. 21–28.

σαββάτῳ πρὸ τῆς ἀποκρέω, Luke xv. 1–10.

Κυριακῇ πρὸ τῆς ἀποκρέω (*of the Prodigal*) Luke xv. 11–32. 1 Thess. v. 14–23 (1 Cor. vi. 12–20, B–C. III. 42).
2nd day of the week *of the Carnival* Mark xi. 1–11. 2 Tim. iii. 1–10.
3rd xiv. 10–42. iii. 14–iv. 5.
4th 43—xv. 1. iv. 9–18.
5th xv. 1–15. Tit. i. 5–12.
6th (παρασκευῇ) xv. 20; 22; 25; 33–41. Tit. i. 15–ii. 10.
7th (σαββάτῳ) Luke xxi. 8–9; 25–27; 33–36; 1 Cor. vi. 12–20 (2 Tim. ii. 11–19, B–C. III. 24).

Κυριακῇ τῆς ἀποκρέω Matt. xxv. 31–46. 1 Cor. viii. 8—ix. 2 (1 Cor. vi. 12–20, B–C. III. 24).
2nd day of the week *of the cheese-eater* Luke xix. 29–40; xxii. 7–8; 39. Heb. iv. 1–13.
3rd xxii. 39—xxiii. 1. Heb. v. 12–vi. 8.
4th *deest.*
5th xxiii 1–33; 44–56. Heb. xxii. 14–27.
6th (παρασκευῇ) *deest.*
7th (σαββάτῳ) Matt. vi. 1–13. Rom. xiv. 19–23; xvi. 25–27.

Κυριακῇ τῆς τυροφάγου Matt. vi. 14–21. Rom. xiii. 11—xiv. 4.

Παννυχὶς τῆς ἁγίας νηστείας.
Vigil of Lent (Parh., Christ's) Matt. vii. 7–11.

Τῶν νηστειῶν (Lent).

σαββάτῳ α′ Mark ii. 23—iii. 5. Heb. i. 1–12.
Κυριακῇ α′ John i. 44–52. Heb. xi. 24–40.
σαββάτῳ β′ Mark i. 35–44. iii. 12–14.
Κυριακῇ β′ ii. 1–12. i. 10—ii. 3.
σαββάτῳ γ′ 14–17. x. 32–37.
Κυριακῇ γ′ viii. 34—ix 1. iv. 14—v. 6.
σαββάτῳ δ′ vii. 31–37. vi. 9–12.
Κυριακῇ δ′ ix. 17–31. 13–20.
σαββάτῳ ε′ viii. 27–31. ix. 24–28.
Κυριακῇ ε′ x. 32–45. 11–14.
σαββάτῳ ϛ′ (*of Lazarus*) John xi. 1–45. xii. 28—xiii. 8.

Κυριακῇ ϛ′ τῶν Βαΐων, Matins, Matt. xxi. 1–11; 15–17 [εἰς τὴν λιτήν, Mark x. 46—xi. 11, Burney 22]. Liturgy, John xii. 1–18. Phil. iv. 4–9.

Τῇ ἁγίᾳ μεγάλῃ (Holy Week).

2nd { Matins, Matt. xxi. 18–43.
Liturgy, xxiv. 3–35.

3rd { Matins, xxii. 15—xxiv. 2.
Liturgy, xxiv. 36—xxvi. 2.

4th { Matins, John (xi. 47–53 (al. 56) Gale) xii. 17 (al. 19)–47 (al. 50).
Liturgy, Matt. xxvi. 6–16.

5th { Matins, Luke xxii. 1–36 (39, Gale).
Liturgy, Matt. xxvi. 1–20.

Εὐαγγέλιον τοῦ νιπτῆρος, John xiii. 3–10.
μετὰ τὸ νίψασθαι 12–17[1];
Matt. xxvi. 21–39; Luke xxii. 43, 44; Matt. xxvi. 40—xxvii. 2. 1 Cor. xi. 23–32.

Εὐαγγέλια τῶν ἁγίων πάθων ιυ̅ χυ̅ (Twelve Gospels of the Passions).

(1) John xiii. 31—xviii. 1. (2) John xviii. 1–28. (3) Matt. xxvi. 57–75. (4) John xviii. 28—xix. 16. (5) Matt. xxvii. 3–32. (6) Mark xv. 16–32. (7) Matt. xxvii. 33–54. (8) Luke xxiii. 32–49. (9) John xix. 25–37. (10) Mark xv. 43–47. (11) John xix. 38–42. (12) Matt. xxvii. 62–66.

Εὐαγγέλια τῶν ὡρῶν τῆς ἁγίας παραμονῆς (Night-watches of Vigil of Good Friday).

Hour (1) Matt. xxvii. 1–56. (3) Mark xv. 1–41. (6) Luke xxii. 66—xxiii. 49. (9) John xix. 16 (al. 23 or xviii. 28)–37.

Τῇ ἁγίᾳ παρασκευῇ (Good Friday) εἰς τὴν λειτουργίαν (ἑσπέρας, B-C. III. 42).

Matt. xxvii. 1–38; Luke xxiii. 39–43; Matt. xxvii. 39–54; John xix. 31–37; Matt. xxvii. 55–61. 1 Cor. i. 18—ii. 2.

Τῷ ἁγίῳ καὶ μεγάλῳ σαββάτῳ (Easter Even).

Matins, Matt. xxvii. 62–66. 1 Cor. v. 6–8 (Gal. iii. 13, 14, B-C. III. 24).
Evensong, Matt. xxviii. 1–20. Rom. vi. 3–11 (λειτουργ. Matt. xxviii. 1–20, ἑσπέρας Rom. vi. 3–11, B-C. III. 42).

Εὐαγγέλια ἀναστάσιμα ἑωθινά (*vid.* Suicer Thes. Eccles. I. 1229), eleven Gospels, used in turn, one every Sunday at Matins, beginning with All Saints' Day (B-C. III. 42). In some Evst. these are found at the end of the book.

(1) Matt. xxviii. 16–20. (2) Mark xvi. 1–8. (3) *ib.* 9–20. (4) Luke xxiv. 1–12. (5) *ib.* 12–35. (6) *ib.* 36–53. (7) John xx. 1–10. (8) *ib.* 11–18. (9) *ib.* 19–31. (10) John xxi. 1–14. (11) *ib.* 15–25.

We have now traced the daily service of the Greek Church, as derived from the Gospels, throughout the whole year, from Easter Day to Easter Even, only that in Lent the lessons from the 2nd to the 6th days inclusive in each week are taken from the book of Genesis. The reader will observe that from Easter to Pentecost St. John and the Acts are read for seven weeks, or eight Sundays. The first Sunday after Pentecost is the Greek All Saints' Day, their Trinity Sunday being virtually kept a fortnight earlier; but from the Monday next after the day of Pentecost (Whit-Monday) St. Matthew is used continuously every day for eleven weeks and as many Sundays. For six weeks more, St. Matthew is appointed for the Saturday and Sunday lessons, St. Mark for the other days of the week. But inasmuch as St. Luke was to be taken up with the new year, the year of the

1 In B-C. III. 42 all the Gospels for this day run into each other without break, e.g. John xiii. 3–17 being read *uno tenore*. Just so in the same manuscript stands the mixed lesson for Good Friday evening.

indiction [Arund. 547], which in *this* case must be September 24 [1], if all the lessons in Matthew and Mark were not read out by this time (which, unless Easter was very early, would not be the case), they were at once broken off, and (after proper lessons had been employed for the Sunday before and the Saturday and Sunday which followed [2] the feast of the Elevation of the Cross, Sept. 14) the lessons from St. Luke (seventeen weeks and sixteen Sundays in all) were taken up and read on as far as was necessary: only that the 17th Sunday of St. Matthew (called from the subject of its Gospel *the Canaanitess*) was always resumed on the Sunday preceding that before the Carnival (πρὸ τῆς ἀποκρέω), which is also named from its Gospel that of *the Prodigal*, and answers to the Latin *Septuagesima*. Then follow the Sunday of the Carnival (ἀποκρέω) or *Sexagesima*, that of *the Cheese-eater* (τυροφάγου) or *Quinquagesima*, and the six Sundays in Lent. The whole number of Sunday Gospels in the year (even reckoning the two interpolated about September 14) is thus only fifty-three, *the Canaanitess* coming twice over: but in the Menology or Catalogue of immoveable feasts will be found proper lessons for three Saturdays and Sundays about Christmas and Epiphany, which could either be substituted for, or added to the ordinary Gospels for the year, according as the distance from Easter in one year to Easter in the next exceeded or fell short of fifty-two weeks. The system of lessons from the Acts and Epistles is much simpler than that of the Gospels: it exhibits fifty-two Sundays in the year, without any of the complicated arrangements of the other scheme. Since the Epistles from the Saturday of the 16th week after Pentecost to the Sunday of the Prodigal could not be set (like the rest) by the side of their corresponding Gospels, they are given separately in the following table [3].

Κυριακῇ ιϛ′	2 Cor. vi. 1-10.	Κυριακῇ κα′	Gal. ii. 16-20.
σαββάτῳ ιζ′	1 Cor. xiv. 20-25.	σαββάτῳ κβ′	2 Cor. v. 1-10 (1-4 in B-C. III. 24).
Κυριακῇ ιζ′	2 Cor. vi. 16—viii. 1.	Κυριακῇ κβ′	Gal. vi. 11-18.
σαββάτῳ ιη′	1 Cor. xv. 39-45.	σαββάτῳ κγ′	2 Cor. viii. 1-5.
Κυριακῇ ιη′	2 Cor. ix. 6-11.	Κυριακῇ κγ′	Eph. ii. 4-10.
σαββάτῳ ιθ′	1 Cor. xv. 58—xvi. 3.	σαββάτῳ κδ′	2 Cor. xi. 1-6.
Κυριακῇ ιθ′	2 Cor. xi. 31—xii. 9.	Κυριακῇ κδ′	Eph. ii. 14-22.
σαββάτῳ κ′	2 Cor. i. 8-11.	σαββάτῳ κε′	Gal. i. 3-10.
Κυριακῇ κ′	Gal. i. 11-19.	Κυριακῇ κε′	Eph. iv. 1-7.
σαββάτῳ κα′	2 Cor. iii. 12-18.		

[1] The more usual indiction, which dates from Sept. 1, is manifestly excluded by the following rubric (Burney, 22, p. 191, and in other copies): Δέον γινώσκειν ὅτι ἄρχεται ὁ Λουκᾶς ἀναγινώσκεσθαι ἀπὰ τῆς Κυριακῆς μετὰ τὴν ὕψωσιν· τότε γὰρ καὶ ἡ ἰσυμερία [i. e. ἰσημερία] γίνεται, ὃ καλεῖται νέον ἔτος. Ἢ ὅτι ἀπὸ τὰς [τῆς] κγ′ τοῦ σεπτεμβρίου ἁ Λουκᾶς ἀναγινώσκεται.

[2] The lesson for the Sunday after Sept. 14 is the same as that for the 3rd Sunday in Lent.

[3] The ordinary lessons for week days stand thus in B-C. III. 24. Week ιϛ′. (2) 2 Cor. iii. 4-12. (3) iv. 1-6. (4) 11-18. (5) v. 10-15. (6) 15-21. ιζ′. (2) vi. 11-16. (3) vii. 1-11. (4) 10-16. (5) viii. 7-11. (6) 10-21. ιη′. (2) viii. 20—ix. 1. (3) ix. 1-5. (4) 12—x. 5. (5) 4-12. (6) 13-18. ιθ′. (2) xi. 5-9. (3) 10-18. (4) xii. 10-14. (5) 14-19. (6) 19—xiii. 1. κ′. (2) xiii. 2-7. (3) 7-11. (4) Gal. i. 18—ii. 5. (5) ii. 6-16. (6) ii. 20—iii. 7. κα′. (2) iii. 15-22. (3) 28—iv. 5. (4) iv. 9-14. (5) 13-26. (6) 28—v. 6. κβ′. (2) v. 4-14. (3) 14-21. (4) vi. 2-10. (5) Eph. i. 9-17. (6) 16-23. κγ′. (2) ii. 18—iii. 5. (3) 5-12. (4) 13-21. (5) iv. 12-16. (6) 17-25. κδ′. (2) v. 18-26. (3) 25-31. (4) 28—vi. 6. (5) 7-11. (6) 17-21. κε′. (2) Phil. i. 2. *Hiat codex usque ad* λ′. (1) 1 Thess. i. 6-10. (3) 9—ii. 4. (4) 4-8. (5) 9-14. (6) 14-20. λα′. (2) iii. 1-8. (3) 6-11. (4) 11—iv. 6. (5) 7-11. (6) 17—v. 5. λβ′. (2) v. 4-11. (3) 11-15. (4) 15-23. (5) 2 Thess. i. 1-5. (6) 11—ii. 5. λγ′. (2) ii. 13—iii. 5. (3) 3-9. (4) 10-18. (5) 1 Tim. i. 1-8. (6) 8-14. λδ′. (2) 1 Tim. ii. 5-15. (3) iii. 1-13. (4) iv. 4-9. (5) 14—v. 10. (6) 17—vi. 2. λε′. (2) vi. 2-11. (3) 17-21. (4) 2 Tim. i. 8-14. (5) 14—ii. 2. (6) 22-26.

σαββάτῳ κϛʹ	Gal. iii. 8–12.	Κυριακῇ λαʹ	2 Tim. i. 3–9.
Κυριακῇ κϛʹ	Eph. v. 8–19.	σαββάτῳ λβʹ	Col. ii. 8–12.
σαββάτῳ κζʹ	Gal. v. 22—vi. 2.	Κυριακῇ λβʹ	1 Tim. vi. 11–16.
Κυριακῇ κζʹ	Eph. vi. 10–17.	σαββάτῳ λγʹ	1 Tim. ii. 1–7.
σαββάτῳ κηʹ	Col. i. 9–18.	Κυριακῇ λγʹ	as Κυρ. λαʹ. (2 Tim. i. 3–9 in B-C. III. 24).
Κυριακῇ κηʹ	2 Cor. ii. 14—iii. 3.		
σαββάτῳ κθʹ	Eph. ii. 11–13.	σαββάτῳ λδʹ	1 Tim. iii. 13—iv. 5.
Κυριακῇ κθʹ	Col. iii. 4–11.	Κυριακῇ λδʹ	2 Tim. iii. 10–15.
σαββάτῳ λʹ	Eph. v. 1–8.	σαββάτῳ λεʹ	1 Tim. iv. 9–15.
Κυριακῇ λʹ	Col. iii. 12–16.	Κυριακῇ λεʹ	2 Tim. ii. 1–10.
σαββάτῳ λαʹ	Col. i. 2–6.	σαββάτῳ λϛʹ	2 Tim. ii. 11–19.

ON THE MENOLOGY, OR CALENDAR OF IMMOVEABLE FESTIVALS AND SAINTS' DAYS.

We cannot in this place enter very fully into this portion of the contents of Lectionaries, inasmuch as, for reasons wo have assigned above, the investigation would be both tedious and difficult. All the great feast-days, however, as well as the commemorations of the Apostles and of a few other Saints, occur alike in all the books, and ought not to be omitted here. We commence with the month of September (the opening of the year at Constantinople), as do all the Lectionaries and ~~Synaxaria~~ we have seen [1].

Sept. 1. Simeon Stylites, Luke iv. 16–22; Col. iii. 12–16 (1 Tim. ii. 1–7, B-C. III. 53).

2. John the Faster, Matt. v. 14–10 (Wake 12). (John xv. 1–11, Parham 18.)

8. Birthday of the Virgin, Θεοτόκος, Matins, Luke i. 39–49, 56 (B-C. III. 24 and 42). Liturgy, Luke x. 38–42; xi. 27, 28; Phil. ii. 5–11.

Κυριακῇ πρὸ τῆς ὑψώσεως, John iii. 13–17; Gal. vi. 11–18.

14. Elevation of the Cross, Matins, John xii. 28–36. Liturgy, John xix. 6–35 (diff. in K and some others); 1 Cor. i. 18–24.

σαββάτῳ μετὰ τὴν ὕψωσιν, John viii. 21–30; 1 Cor. i. 26–29.
Κυριακῇ μετὰ τὴν ὕψωσιν, Mark viii. 34—ix. 1; Gal. ii. 16–20.

18. Theodora [2], John viii. 3–11 (Parham).

24. Thecla, Matt. xxv. 1–13; 2 Tim. i. 8–9.

Oct. 3. Dionysius the Areopagite, Matt. xiii. 45–54; Acts xvii. 16 (19, Cod. Bezae)—34 (16–23, 30, B-C, III. 24) (diff. in K).

6. Thomas the Apostle, John xx. 19–31; 1 Cor. iv. 9–16.

8. Pelagia, John viii. 3–11 [3].

9. James son of Alphaeus, Matt. x. 1–7, 14, 15.

18. Luke the Evangelist, Luke x. 16–21; Col. iv. 5–9, 14, 18.

23. James, ὁ ἀδελφόθεος, Mark vi. 1–7; James i. 1–12.

Nov. 8. Michael and Archangels, Matins, Matt. xviii. 10–20. Liturgy, Luke x. 16–21; Heb. ii. 2–10.

13. Chrysostom, Matins, John x. 1–9.

1 In the *Menology*, even Arund. 547 has μηνὶ σεπτεμβρίῳ ᾱ· ἀρχὴ τῆς ἰνδίκτου. So Burn. 22 nearly.

2 *Theodoria* in Codex Cyprius (*see* p. 73), with the cognate lesson, Luke vii. 36–50, which lesson is read in Gale for Sept. 16, Euphemia and in Evst. 261 (B.M. Addit. 11,840). In Burdett-Coutts II. 7, John viii. 3–11 is used εἰς μετανοοῦντας: B-C. II. 30 adds καὶ γυναικῶν.

3 So Cod. Cyprius, but the Christ's Coll. Evst. removes Pelagia to Aug. 31, and reads John viii. 1–11.

Liturgy, John x. 9–16 ; Heb.vii. 26—viii. 2.

Nov. 14. Philip the Apostle, John i. 44–55 ; Acts viii. 26–39.

16. Matthew the Apostle, Matt. ix. 9–13 ; 1 Cor. iv. 9–16.

17. Gregory Thaumaturgus, Matt. x. 1–10 (Wake 12) ; 1 Cor. xii. 7, 8, 10, 11.

25. Clement of Rome, John xv. 17—xvi. 1 ; Phil. iii. 20—iv. 3.

30. Andrew the Apostle, John i. 35–52 ; 1 Cor. iv. 9–16.

Dec. 20. Ignatius, ὁ θεόφορος, Mark ix. 33–41 ; Heb. iv. 14—v. 6 (Rom. viii. 28–39, B-C. III. 24).

Saturday before Christmas, Matt. xiii. 31–58 (Luke xiii. 19–29, Gale) ; Gal. iii. 8–12.

Sunday before Christmas, Matt. i. 1–25 ; Heb. xi. 9–16 (9, 10, 32–40, B-C. III. 24).

24. Christmas Eve, Luke ii. 1–20 ; Heb. i. 1–12. Προεόρτια, 1 Pet. ii. 10 (B-C. III. 24).

25. Christmas Day, Matins, Matt. i. 18–25. Liturgy, Matt. ii. 1–12 ; Gal. iv. 4–7.

26. εἰς τὴν σύναξιν τῆς θεοτόκου, Matt. ii. 13–23 ; Heb. ii. 11–18.

27. Stephen [1], Matt. xxi. 33–42 (Gale) ; Acts vi. 1–7.

Saturday after Christmas, Matt. xii. 15–21 ; 1 Tim. vi. 11–16.

Sunday after Christmas, Mark i. 1–8 ; Gal. i. 11–19. The same Lessons for

29. Innocents (Gale).

Saturday πρὸ τῶν φώτων, Matt. iii. 1–6 ; 1 Tim. iii. 13—iv. 5.

Sunday πρὸ τῶν φώτων, Mark i. 1–8 ; 1 Tim. iii. 13—iv. 5 (2 Tim. iv. 5–8, B-C. III. 24).

Jan. 1. Circumcision, Luke ii. 20, 21, 40–52 ; 1 Cor. xiii. 12—xiv. 5.

5. Vigil of θεοφανία, Luke iii. 1–18 ; 1 Cor. ix. 19—x. 4.

6. θεοφανία (Epiphany) { Matins, Mark i. 9–11. Liturgy, Matt. iii. 13–17. } { Titus ii. 11–14 (B-C. III. 42 adds iii. 4–7). }

7. John, ὁ πρόδρομος, John i. 29–34.

Saturday μετὰ τὰ φῶτα, Matt. iv. 1–11 ; Eph. vi. 10–17.

Sunday μετὰ τὰ φῶτα, Matt. iv. 12–17 ; Eph. iv. 7–13.

16. Peter *ad Vincula*, John xxi. 15–19 (B-C. III. 42).

22. Timothy, Matt. x. 32, 33, 37, 38 ; xix. 27–30 ; 2 Tim. i. 3–9.

Feb. 2. Presentation of Christ, Matins, Luke ii. 25–32. Liturgy, Luke ii. 22–40 ; Heb. vii. 7–17.

3. Simeon ὁ θεοδόχος and Anna, Luke ii. 25–38 ; Heb. ix. 11–14.

23. Polycarp, John xii. 24–36,

24. Finding of the Head of John the Baptist { Matins, Luke vii. 18–29 (17–30, B-C. III. 42). Liturgy, Matt. xi. 5–14 ; 2 Cor. iv. 6–11. }

March 24. Vigil of Annunciation, Luke i. 39–56 (Gale).

25. Annunciation, Luke i. 24–38 ; Heb. ii. 11–18.

April 23. St. George, Matins, Mark xiii. 9–13. Liturgy, Acts xii. 1–11 (Cod. Bezae) [2].

25. (Oct. 19, B-C. III. 24). Mark the Evangelist, Mark vi. 7–13 ; Col. iv. 5, 10, 11, 18.

30. James, son of Zebedee, Matt. x. 1–7, 14, 15.

May 2. Athanasius, Matt. v. 14–19 ; Heb. iv. 14.—v. 6.

8. (Sept. 26, B-C. III. 42). John, ὁ θεόλογος, John xix. 25–27 ; xxi. 24, 25 ; 1 John i. 1–7 (iv. 12–19, B-C. III. 42).

21. Helena, Luke iv. 22, &c., Evst. 298.

26. Jude the Apostle, John xiv. 21–24.

[1] The Proto-martyr Stephen is commemorated on August 2 in Evst. 3 (Wheeler 3).

[2] The same Saint is commemorated in the fragment of a Golden Evangelistarium seen at Sinai by the Rev. E. M. Young in 1864, and in B-C. III. 42 as μεγαλόμαρτυς ὁ τροπαιοφόρος ; which (Evst. 286) is described in its place below.

June 11. Bartholomew and Barnabas the Apostles, Mark vi. 7-13; Acts xi. 19-30.

19. Jude, brother of the Lord, Mark vi. 7-13, or εὐαγγέλιον ἀποστολικόν (Matt. x. 1-8? June 30).

24. Birth of John the Baptist, Luke i. 1-25; 57-80; Rom. xiii. 11—xiv. 4.

29. Peter and Paul the Apostles, Matins, John xxi. 15-31. Liturgy, Matt. xvi. 13-19; 2 Cor. xi. 21—xii. 9.

30. The Twelve Apostles, Matt. x. 1-8.

July 20. Elijah, Luke iv. 22, &c., Evst. 229.

22. Mary Magdalene, ἡ μυροφόρος, Mark xvi. 9-20; 2 Tim. ii. 1-10.

Aug. 1. τῶν ἁγίων μακκαβαίων, Matt. x. 16, &c., Evst. 228 and others.

Aug. 6. Transfiguration { Matins, Luke ix. 29-36 or Mark ix. 2-9. Liturgy, Matt. xvii. 1-9; 2 Pet. i. 10-19.

15. Assumption of the Virgin, Luke x. 38-42 (Gale, Codex Bezae).

20. Thaddaeus the Apostle, Matt. x. 16-22; 1 Cor. iv. 9-16.

25. Titus, Matt. v. 14-19 (Gale); 2 Tim. ii. 1-10.

29. Beheading of John the Baptist, Matins, Matt. xiv. 1-13. Liturgy, Mark vi. 14-30; Acts xiii. 25-32 (39, B-C. III. 24).

Εἰς τὰ ἐγκαίνια, Dedication, John x. 22 (17, Gale)—28 (Gale, Cod. Bezae); 2 Cor. v. 15-21; Heb. ix. 1-7.

At Cambridge (Univ. Libr. II. 28. 8) is a rare volume containing the Greek Gospel Church-Lessons, Θεῖον καὶ ἱερὸν εὐαγγέλιον, Venice, 1615-24, once belonging to Bishop Hacket: also the Apostolos of a smaller size. Another edition appeared in 1851, also at Venice.

For a comparison of the Greek with the Coptic Calendar, see p. 77, note 2. For the Menology in the Jerusalem Syriac Lectionary, see Vol. II, Chap. I.

CHAPTER IV.

THE LARGER UNCIAL MANUSCRIPTS OF THE GREEK TESTAMENT.

WE proceed to describe in detail the uncial manuscripts of the Greek Testament, arranged separately as copies of the Gospels, of the Acts and Catholic Epistles, of the Pauline Epistles, and of the Apocalypse. They are usually indicated by the capital letters of the English and Greek alphabets, and stand on the list not in the order of their relative value or antiquity, but mainly as they were applied from time to time to the purposes of Textual criticism.

Manuscripts of the Gospels.

א (*Aleph*). CODEX SINAITICUS, now at St. Petersburg, the justly celebrated copy which sometime ago for a quarter of a century attracted general attention in the learned world. Tischendorf (Notitia Ed. Cod. Sinaitici, pp. 5, 6) when travelling in 1844 under the patronage of his own sovereign, King Frederick Augustus of Saxony, picked out of a basket full of papers destined to light the oven of the Convent of St. Catherine on Mount Sinai, the forty-three leaves of the Septuagint which he published in 1846 as the Codex Friderico-Augustanus (*see* p. 32). These, of course, he easily got for the asking, but finding that further portions of the same codex (e. g. the whole of Isaiah and 1, 4 Maccabees) were extant, he rescued them from their probable fate, by enlightening the brotherhood as to their value. He was permitted to copy one page of what yet remained, containing the end of Isaiah and the beginning of Jeremiah, which he afterwards published in the first volume of his 'Monumenta Sacra Inedita' (1855), pp. xxx. and 213–16; and he departed in the full hope that he should be allowed to purchase the whole. But he had taught the monks a sharp lesson, and neither then, nor

(9)

λυνγαστιναπωντιο
λιπωνδαικωυσδεο
μανυλλιωνκαιετωι
καιαντιβολωικε
λεγεσαιιουλιεκαιλεγω
τουσσυνεργουντας

(10)

ΟΝΤΩϹΠΟΛΥΜΑΘΕϹΤΑΤΟΝΠΡ
ΑΓΟΡΕΥΟΜΕΝΟΝΟΙΕΤΑΙΠΑΝΤΑ
ΔΥΝΑϹΘΑΙΓΙΝΩϹΚΕΙΝΚΑΙΠΟΙ
ΕΙΝΟΥΧΟΙΟΝΕΑΥΤΟΝ ΟϹΕΝΙΟΙϹ
ΟΥΔΕΝΤΙΦΩΡΑΤΑΙ ΚΑΤΕΧΩΝ
ΚΑΙΟΥϹΥΝΟΡΩΝΟΤΙΠΟΛΛΑΔΕΙ
ΤΑΙΤΡΙΒΗϹΑΝΚΑΙΑΠΟΤΗϹΑΥ
ΤΗϹΓΙΝΗΤΑΙΜΕΘΟΔΟΥΚΑΘΑ
ΠΕΡΤΑΤΗϹΠΟΙΗΤΙΚΗϹΜΕΡΗ ΚΑΙ
ΔΙΟΤΙΠΕΡΙΤΟΥϹΠΟΛΥΜΑΘΕΙϹ

(11 a)

ϹΕΑΥΤΟΝ ΚΑΘΩϹΑΡ
ΧΗϹΚΑΙΑΦΗΜΕΡΩ
ΩΝΕΤΑΞΑΚΡΙΤΑϹ
ΕΠΙΤΟΝΛΑΟΝΜΟΥ
ΙϹΛΚΑΙΕΤΑΠΙΝΩ
ϹΑΑΠΑΝΤΑϹΤΟΥϹ
ΕΧΘΡΟΥϹϹΟΥΚΑΙ
ΑΥΞΗϹΩϹΕΚΑΙΟΙ

(11 b)

ΤΗΩΡΑΥΠΕϹΤΡΕ
ΨΑΝΕΙϹΙΕΡΟΥϹΑ
ΛΗΜΚΑΙΕΥΡΟΝΗ
ΘΡΟΙϹΜΕΝΟΥϹΤΟΥϹ
ΕΝΔΕΚΑΚΑΙΤΟΥϹ
ϹΥΝΑΥΤΟΙϹΛΕΓΟ

(11 c)

ΤΟΤΗϹΕΥϹΕΒΕΙΑϹ
ΜΥϹΤΗΡΙΟΝ ΘϹ ΟϹΕ

on his subsequent visit in 1853, could he gain any tidings of the leaves he had left behind;—he even seems to have concluded that they had been carried into Europe by some richer or more fortunate collector. At the beginning of 1859, after the care of the seventh edition of his N.T. was happily over, he went for a third time into the East, under the well-deserved patronage of the Emperor of Russia, the great protector of the Oriental Church; and the treasure which had been twice withdrawn from him as a private traveller, was now, on the occasion of some chance conversation, spontaneously put into the hands of one sent from the champion and benefactor of the oppressed Church. Tischendorf touchingly describes his surprise, his joy, his midnight studies over the priceless volume ('*quippe dormire nefas videbatur*') on that memorable 4th of February, 1859. The rest was easy; he was allowed to copy his prize at Cairo, and ultimately to bring it to Europe, as a tribute of duty and gratitude to the Emperor Alexander II. To that monarch's wise munificence both the larger edition (1862), and the smaller of the New Testament only (1863), are mainly due.

The Codex Sinaiticus is 13½ inches in length by 14⅞ inches high, and consists of 346½ leaves of the same beautiful vellum as the Cod. Friderico-Augustanus which is really a part of it whereof 199 contain portions of the Septuagint version, 147½ the whole New Testament, Barnabas' Epistle, and a considerable fragment of Hermas' Shepherd. It has subsequently appeared that the Russian Archimandrite (afterwards Bishop) Porphyry had brought with him from Sinai in 1845 some pieces of Genesis xxiii, xxiv, and of Numbers v, vi, and vii, which had been applied long before to the binding of other books[1]. Each page comprises four columns (*see* p. 27), with forty-eight lines in each column, of those continuous, noble, simple uncials (*compare* Plate IV. 11 a *with* 11 b). The poetical books of the Old Testament,

[1] These fragments were published by Tischendorf in his Appendix Codd. cel. Sin. Vat. Alex. 1867. They consist of Gen. xxiii. 19—xxiv. 4; 5–8; 10–14; 17, 18; 25–27; 30–33; 36–41; 43–46; Num. v. 26–30; vi. 5, 6, 11, 12, 17, 18; 22–27; vii. 4, 5, 12, 13; 15–26. Another leaf of the same manuscript, containing Lev. xxii. 3—xxiii. 22, was also found at Sinai by Dr. H. Brügsch Bey, of Göttingen, and published by him in his Neue Bruchstücke des Codex Sinaiticus aufgefunden in der Bibliothek des Sinai Klosters, 1875, but is not, after all, part of Cod. ℵ. Another morsel, containing Gen. xxiv. 9, 10, and 41–43, now at St. Petersburg, really belongs to it.

however, being written in στίχοι, admit of only two columns on a page (*above*, p. 52). 'In the Catholic Epistles the scribe has frequently contented himself with a column of forty-seven lines[1].' The order of the sacred books is remarkable, though by no means unprecedented. St. Paul's Epistles precede the Acts, and amongst them, that to the Hebrews follows 2 Thess., standing on the same page with it (p. 74). Although this manuscript has hitherto been inspected by few Englishmen (Tregelles, however, and Dean Stanley were among the number), yet its general aspect has grown familiar to us by the means of photographs of its most important pages taken for the use of private scholars[2], as well as from the facsimiles contained in Tischendorf's several editions. Breathings and accents there are none except in Tobit vi. 9, and Gal. v. 21, as has been already mentioned: the apostrophus and the single point for punctuation are entirely absent for pages together, yet occasionally are rather thickly studded, not only in places where a later hand has been unusually busy (e.g. Isaiah i. 1—iii. 2, two pages), but in some others (e.g. in 2 Cor. xii. 20 there are eight stops). Even words very usually abridged (except θσ̄, κσ̄, ισ̄, χσ̄, πνα̅ which are constant) are here written in full though the practice varies, πατηρ, υιος, ουρανος, ανθρωπος, δαυειδ: we find ϊσραηλ', ισλ̅, or ιηλ̅: ϊερουσαληµ', ιηµ̅, ιλµ̅, ιηλµ̅'. Tischendorf considers the two points over *iota* and *upsilon* (which are sometimes wanting) as seldom from the first hand: the mark >, besides its rather rare marginal use in citations (*see* p. 64, note 4), we notice in the text oftener in the Old Testament than in the New. Words are divided at the end of a line: thus K in OΥK, and X in OΥX are separated[3]. Small

[1] J. Rendel Harris, New Testament Autographs, Baltimore (without date), an original and ingenious contribution to textual criticism; as is the Origin of the Leicester Codex (1887) Camb. Synd. by the same author, Fellow of Clare College, and Reader in Palaeography at Cambridge. Curious results in Bradshaw's spirit. Identity of hand with Caius Psalter.

[2] Abbot, Comparative Antiquity of the Sinaitic and Vatican Manuscripts, p. 195. Dean Burgon surrendered the position maintained in The Last Twelve Verses of St. Mark.

[3] It has been suggested that this strange mode of division originated in the reluctance of scribes to begin a new line with any combination of letters which could not commence a Greek word, and to end a line with any letter which is not a vowel, or a liquid, or σ, or γ before another consonant, except in the case of Proper Names (Journal of Sacred Literature, April 1863, p. 8). Certainly the general practice in Cod. ℵ bears out the rule thus laid down, though a few

letters, of the most perfect shape, freely occur in all places, especially at the end of lines, where the—*superscript* (*see* p. 50) is almost always made to represent N (e.g. seventeen times in Mark i. 1–35). Other *compendia scribendi* are K for και, and HN written as in Plate I. No. 2[1]. Numerals are represented by letters, with a straight line placed over them, e.g. $\bar{\mu}$ Mark i. 13[1]. Although there are no capitals, the initial letter of a line which begins a paragraph generally (not always) stands out from the rank of the rest, as in the Old Testament portion of Cod. Vaticanus, and less frequently in the New, after the fashion of certain earlier pieces on papyrus. The titles and subscriptions of the several books are as short as possible (*see* p. 65). The τίτλοι or κεφάλαια *majora* are absent; the margin contains the so-called Ammonian sections and Eusebian canons, but Tischendorf is positive that neither they nor such notes as στιχων $\overline{\rho\pi}$ (*see* p. 53, note 3) appended to 2 Thessalonians, are by the original scribe, although they may possibly be due to a contemporary hand. From the number of ὁμοιοτέλευτα and other errors, one cannot affirm that it is very carefully written. Its itacisms are of the oldest type, and those not constant; chiefly ι for ει, and δε and ε, and much more rarely η and υ and οι interchanged. The grammatical forms commonly termed Alexandrian occur, pretty much as in other manuscripts of the earliest date. The whole manuscript is disfigured by corrections, a few by the original scribe, or by the usual comparer or διορθώτης (*see* p. 55); very many by an ancient and elegant hand of the sixth century (ℵ^a), whose emendations are of great importance; some again by a hand but little later (ℵ^b); far the greatest number by a scholar of the seventh century (ℵ^c), who often cancels the changes introduced by ℵ^a; others by as many as eight several later writers, whose varying styles Tischendorf has carefully discriminated and illustrated by facsimiles[2].

instances to the contrary occur here and there (Scrivener, Collation of Cod. Sinaiticus, Introd. p. xiv, note). Hort refers it to a grammatical rule not to end a line with οὐκ or οὐχ, or a consonant preceding an elided vowel, as ἀπ', οὐδ'. New Testament in Greek, p. 315.

[1] But MH NH, for μη, νη occur even in the Septuagint Cod. Sarravianus, also of the fourth century, in which copy numerals are quite constantly expressed by letters.

[2] Tischendorf, however, describes ℵ^a as 'et formis et atramento primam

The foregoing considerations were bringing even cautious students to a general conviction that Cod. א, if not, as its enthusiastic discoverer had announced, 'omnium antiquissimus' in the absolute sense of the words, was yet but little lower in date than the Vatican manuscript itself, and a veritable relic of the middle of the fourth century—the presence in its margin of the sections and canons of Eusebius [d. 340?], by a hand nearly if not quite contemporaneous, seems to preclude the notion of higher antiquity [1]—when Constantine Simonides, a Greek of

manum tantum non adaequans,' and its writer has been regarded by some as little inferior in value to the first scribe. Thus Dr. Hort (Introd. p. 271), calling him the 'corrector' proper, states that he 'made use of an excellent exemplar, and the readings which he occasionally uses take high rank as authority.' Hort considers $א^b$ as mixed, $א^c$ as still more so.

[1] I am indebted for the following Memoranda on Cod. א to the kindness of the Dean of Derry and Raphoe.

i. It is demonstrable that the Eusebian Sections and Canons on the margin are contemporaneous with the text. For they are wanting from leaves 10 and 15. Now these leaves are conjugate; and they have been (on other grounds) noted by Tischendorf as written not by the scribe of the body of the N. T., but by one of his colleagues ('D') who wrote part of the O. T. and acted as Diorthota of the N. T. It thus appears that, after the marginal numbers had been inserted, the sheet containing leaves 10 and 15 was cancelled, and rewritten by a contemporary hand. The numbers must therefore have been written before the MS. was completed and issued.

ii. The exemplar whence these numbers were derived, differed considerably from that which the text follows. For, in some cases, the sectional numbers indicate the presence of passages which are absent from the text. E. g. St. Matt. xvi. 2, 3, which is sect. 162, is wanting; and 162 is assigned to ver. 4, while the wrong canon (5 for 6) betrays the presence in the canonizer's exemplar of the passage omitted by the scribe. The same is true of St. Mark xv. 28 (in which case the scribe is 'D').

iii. The scribe who wrote the text was unacquainted with the Eusebian sections. For the beginning of a section is not marked, as in A and most subsequent MSS., by a division of the text and a larger letter. On the contrary the text is divided into paragraphs quite independent of the Eusebian divisions, which often begin in the middle of a line, and are marked merely by two dots (:) in vermilion, inserted no doubt by the rubricator as he entered the numbers in the margin. The fact that the numbers of the sections as well as of the canons (not as in other MSS. of the Canons only) are in vermilion, points the same way.

iv. From the above it follows, (1) That while Cod. א proves the absence from its exemplar of certain passages, its margin proves the presence of some of them in a contemporaneous exemplar; (2) that while on the one hand the Eusebian numbers, coeval with the text, show that the MS. cannot be dated before the time of Eusebius, on the other hand the form of the text, inasmuch as it is not arranged so as to suit them, and as it differs from the text implied in them, marks for it a date little, if at all, after his time—certainly many years earlier than A.

v. As regards the omission of the verses of St. Mark xvi. 9–20, it is not correct to

Syme, who had just edited a few papyrus fragments of the New Testament alleged to have been written in the first century of the Christian era, suddenly astonished the learned world in 1862 by claiming to be himself the scribe who had penned this manuscript in the monastery of Panteleemon on Mount Athos, as recently as in the years 1839 and 1840. The writer of these pages must refer to the Introduction to his Collation of the Codex Sinaiticus (pp. lx—lxxii, 2nd edition, 1867) for a statement of the reasons which have been universally accepted as conclusive, why the manuscript which Simonides may very well have written under the circumstances he has described neither was nor possibly could be that venerable document. The discussion of the whole question, however, though painful enough in some aspects, was the means of directing attention to certain peculiarities of Cod. א which might otherwise have been overlooked. While engaged in demonstrating that it could not have been transcribed from a Moscow-printed Bible, as was 'Cod. Simoneidos' (to borrow the designation employed by its author), critics came to perceive that either this copy or its immediate prototype must have been derived from a papyrus *exemplar*, and that probably of Egyptian origin (Collation, &c. pp. viii*; xiv; lxviii), a confirmation of the impression conveyed to the reader by a first glance at the eight narrow columns of each open leaf (p. 28). The claim of Simonides to be the sole writer of a book which must have consisted when complete of about 730 leaves, or 1460 pages of very large size (Collation, &c. p. xxxii), and that too within the compass of eight or ten months[1] (he inscribed on

assert that Cod. א betrays no sign of consciousness of their existence. For the last line of ver. 8, containing only the letters ΤΟΓΑΡ, has the rest of the space (more than half the width of the column) filled up with a minute and elaborate 'arabesque' executed with the pen in ink and vermilion, nothing like which occurs anywhere else in the whole MS. (O. T. or N. T.), such spaces being elsewhere invariably left blank. By this careful filling up of the blank, the scribe (who here is the diorthota 'D'), distinctly shows that the omission is not a case of 'non-interpolation,' but of deliberate excision. John Gwynn, May 21, 1883.

[1] He would have written about 20,000 separate uncial letters every day. Compare the performance of that veritable Briareus, Nicodemus ὁ ξένος, who transcribed the Octateuch (in cursive characters certainly) now at Ferrara (Holmes, Cod. 107), beginning his task on the 8th of June, and finishing it the 15th of July, A. D. 1334, 'working very hard'—as he must have done indeed (Burgon, *Guardian*, Jan. 29, 1873).

his finished work, as he tells us, the words Σιμωνίδου τὸ ὅλον ἔργον), made it important to scrutinize the grounds of Tischendorf's judgement that four several scribes had been engaged upon it, one of whom, as he afterwards came to persuade himself, was the writer of its rival, Codex Vaticanus[1]. Such an investigation, so far as it depends only on the handwriting, can scarcely be carried out satisfactorily without actual examination of the manuscript itself, which is unfortunately not easily within the reach of those who could use it independently; but it is at all events quite plain, as well from internal considerations as from minute peculiarities in the writing, such as the frequent use of the apostrophus and of the mark > (*see above*, p. 50) on some sheets and their complete absence from others (Collation, &c. pp. xvi–xviii; xxxii; xxxvii), that at least two, and probably more, persons have been employed on the several parts of the volume[2].

It is indeed a strange coincidence, although unquestionably it can be nothing more, that Simonides should have brought to the West from Mount Athos some years before one genuine fragment of the Shepherd of Hermas in Greek, and the transcript of a second (both of which materially aided Tischendorf in editing the remains of that Apostolic Father), when taken in connexion with the fact that the worth of Codex Sinaiticus is vastly enhanced by its exhibiting next to the Apocalypse, and on the same page with its conclusion, the only complete extant copy, besides the one discovered by Bryennios in 1875, of the Epistle of Barnabas in Greek, followed by a considerable portion of this

[1] This opinion, first put forth by Tischendorf in his N. T. Vaticanum 1867, Proleg. pp. xxi–xxiii, was minutely discussed in the course of a review of that book in the *Christian Remembrancer*, October 1867, by the writer of these pages. Although Dr. Hort labours to show that no critical inferences ought to be drawn from this identity of the scribe of Cod. B with the writer of six conjugate leaves of Cod. ℵ (being three pairs in three distinct quires, one of them containing the conclusion of St. Mark's Gospel), he is constrained to admit that 'the fact appears to be sufficiently established by concurrent peculiarities in the form of one letter, punctuation, avoidance of contractions, and some points of orthography' (Introduction, p. 213). The internal evidence indeed, though relating to minute matters, is cumulative and irresistible, and does not seem to have been noticed by Tischendorf, who drew his conclusions from the handwriting only.

[2] Prothero (Memoir of H. Bradshaw, pp. 92–118) reprints a letter of Bradshaw from *Guardian*, Jan. 28, 1863, worth studying :—'Simonides died hard, and to the very end was supported by a few dupes of his ingenious mendacity.' (p. 99.)

self-same Shepherd of Hermas, much of which, as well as of Barnabas, was previously known to us only in the Old Latin translation. Both these works are included in the list of books of the New Testament contained in the great Codex Claromontanus D of St. Paul's Epistles, to be described hereafter, Barnabas standing there in an order sufficiently remarkable; and their presence, like that of the Epistles of Clement at the end of Codex Alexandrinus (p. 99), brings us back to a time when the Church had not yet laid aside the primitive custom of reading publicly in the congregation certain venerated writings which have never been regarded exactly in the same light as Holy Scripture itself. Between the end of Barnabas and the opening of the Shepherd are lost the last six leaves of a quaternion (which usually consists of eight) numbered 91 at its head in a fairly ancient hand. The limited space would not suffice for the insertion of Clement's genuine Epistle, since the head of the next quaternion is numbered 92, but might suit one of the other uncanonical books on the list in Cod. Claromontanus, viz. the Acts of Paul and the Revelation of Peter.

With regard to the deeply interesting question as to the critical character of Cod. א, although it strongly supports the Codex Vaticanus in many characteristic readings, yet it cannot be said to give its exclusive adherence to any of the witnesses hitherto examined. It so lends its grave authority, now to one and now to another, as to convince us more than ever of the futility of seeking to derive the genuine text of the New Testament from any one copy, however ancient and, on the whole, trustworthy, when evidence of a wide and varied character is at hand.

A. Codex Alexandrinus in the British Museum, where the open volume of the New Testament is publicly shown in the Manuscript room. It was placed in that Library on its formation in 1753, having previously belonged to the king's private collection from the year 1628, when Cyril Lucar, Patriarch of Constantinople (whose crude attempts to reform the Eastern Church on the model of Geneva ultimately provoked the untoward Synod of Bethlehem in 1672 [1]), sent this most precious

[1] A more favourable estimate of the ecclesiastical policy of Cyril (who was murdered by order of the Sultan in 1638, aet. 80) is maintained by Dr. Th. Smith, 'Collectanea de Cyrillo Lucario, Patriarcha Constantinopolitano,' London 1707.

document by our Ambassador in Turkey, Sir Thomas Roe, as a truly royal gift to Charles I. An Arabic inscription, several centuries old, at the back of the Table of Contents on the first leaf of the manuscript, and translated into Latin in another hand, which Mr. W. Aldis Wright recognizes as Bentley's (Academy, April 17, 1875), states that it was written by the hand of Thecla the Martyr[1]. A recent Latin note on the first page of the first of two fly-leaves declares that it was given to the Patriarchal Chamber in the year of the Martyrs, 814 [A.D. 1098]. Another, and apparently the earliest inscription, in an obscure Moorish-Arabic scrawl, set at the foot of the first page of Genesis, was thus translated for Baber by Professor Nicoll of Oxford, 'Dicatus est Cellae Patriarchae in urbe munitâ Alexandriâ. Qui eum ex eâ extraxerit sit anathematizatus, vi avulsus. Athanasius humilis' (Cod. Alex. V. T., Prolegomena, p. xxvi, note 92). That the book was brought from Alexandria by Cyril (who had been Patriarch of that see from 1602 to 1621) need not be disputed, although Wetstein, on the doubtful authority of Matthew Muttis of Cyprus, Cyril's deacon, concludes that he procured it from Mount Athos. In the volume itself the Patriarch has written and subscribed the following words: 'Liber iste scripturae sacrae N. et V. Testamenti, prout ex traditione habemus, est scriptus manu Theclae, nobilis foeminae Aegyptiae, ante mile [sic] et trecentos annos circiter, paulò post Concilium Nicenum. Nomen Theclae in fine libri erat exaratum, sed extincto Christianismo in Aegypto a Mahometanis, et libri unà Christianorum in similem sunt reducti conditionem. Extinctum ergo est Theclae nomen et laceratum, sed memoria et traditio recens observat.' Cyril seems to lean wholly on the Arabic inscription on the first leaf of the volume: independent testimony he would appear to have received none.

This celebrated manuscript, the earliest of first-rate importance applied by scholars to the criticism of the text, and yielding in value to but one or two at the utmost, is now bound in four volumes, whereof three contain the Septuagint version of

[1] I.e. 'Memorant hunc Librum scriptū fuisse ma-nu Theclae Martyris.' On the page over against Cyril's note the same hand writes 'videantur literae ejusdē Cyrill: Lucar: ad Georgium Episco Cant' [Abbot]; *Harl:* 823, 2. quae extant in Clementis Epistolis ad Corinthios editionis Colomesii Lond. 1687 8° page 354 &c.'

(12)

ΕΝΑΡΧΗΙ ΕΠΟΙΗϹΕΝΟΘΕΟϹΤΟΝΟΥ
ΡΑΝΟΝΚΑΙΤΗΝΓΗΝ ΗΔΕΓΗΗΝΑΟ
ΡΑΤΟϹΚΑΙΑΚΑΤΑϹΚΕΥΑϹΤΟϹ·
ΚΑΙϹΚΟΤΟϹΕΠΑΝΩΤΗϹΑΒΥϹϹΟΥ·

(13)

ΠΡΟϹΕΧΕΤΕΕΑΥΤΟΙϹΚΑΙΠΑΝΤΙΤΩ
ΠΟΙΜΝΙΩΕΝΩΥΜΑϹΤΟΠΝΑΤΟ
ΑΓΙΟΝΕΘΕΤΟΕΠΙϹΚΟΠΟΥϹ·
ΠΟΙΜΑΙΝΕΙΝΤΗΝΕΚΚΛΗϹΙΑΝ
ΤΟΥΚΥΗΝΠΕΡΙΕΠΟΙΗϹΑΤΟΔΙΑ
ΤΟΥΑΙΜΑΤΟϹΤΟΥΙΔΙΟΥ·

(14)

ΡΛΘ Γ ΤΟΥΛΟΓΟΥΟΥ
ΕΓΩΕΙΠΟΝΥ
ΜΙΝΟΥΚΕϹΤΙΝ
ΔΟΥΛΟϹΜΙΖΩ
ΤΟΥΚΥΑΥΤΟΥ

the Old Testament almost complete[1], the fourth volume the New Testament with several lamentable defects. In St. Matthew's Gospel some twenty-five leaves are wanting up to ch. xxv. 6 ἐξέρχεσθε, from John vi. 50 ἵνα to viii. 52 καὶ σύ[2] two leaves are lost, and three leaves from 2 Cor. iv. 13 ἐπίστευσα to xii. 6 ἐξ ἐμοῦ. All the other books of the New Testament are here entire, the Catholic Epistles following the Acts, that to the Hebrews standing before the Pastoral Epistles (*see above*, p. 74). After the Apocalypse we find what was till very recently the only known extant copy of the first or genuine Epistle of Clement of Rome, and a small fragment of a second of suspected authenticity, both in the same hand as the latter part of the New Testament. It would appear also that these two Epistles of Clement were designed to form a part of the volume of Scripture, for in the Table of Contents exhibited on the first leaf of the manuscript under the head H KAINH ΔΙΑΘΗΚΗ, they are represented as immediately following the Apocalypse: next is given the number of books, OMOΥ BIBΛΙΑ, the numerals being now illegible; and after this, as if distinct from Scripture, the eighteen Psalms of Solomon. Such uncanonical works (ἰδιωτικοὶ ψαλμοὶ . . . ἀκανόνιστα βιβλία) were forbidden to be read in churches by the 59th canon of the Council of Laodicea (A.D. 363?); whose 60th canon, which seems to have been added a little later, enumerates the books of the N.T. in the precise order seen in Cod. A, only that the Apocalypse and Clement's Epistles do not stand on the list.

This manuscript is in quarto, $12\frac{3}{4}$ inches high and $10\frac{1}{4}$ broad, and consists of 773 leaves (of which 639 contain the Old Testament), each page being divided into two columns of fifty or fifty-one lines each, having about twenty letters or upwards in a line. These letters are written continuously in uncial charac-

[1] Not to mention a few casual *lacunae* here and there, especially in the early leaves of the manuscript, the lower part of one leaf has been cut out, so that Gen. xiv. 14–17; xv. 1–5; 16–20; xvi. 6–9 are wanting. The leaf containing 1 Sam. xii. 20—xiv. 9, and the nine leaves containing Ps. l. 20—lxxx. 10 (Engl.) are lost.

[2] Yet we may be sure that these two leaves did not contain the Pericope Adulterae, John vii. 53—viii. 11. Taking the Elzevir N. T. of 1624, which is printed without breaks for the verses, we count 286 lines of the Elzevir for the two leaves of Cod. A preceding its defect, 288 lines for the two which follow it; but 317 lines for the two missing leaves. Deduct the thirty lines containing John vii. 53—viii. 11, and the result for the lost leaves is 287.

ters, without any space between the words, the uncials being of an elegant yet simple form, in a firm and uniform hand, though in some places larger than in others. Specimens of both styles may be seen in our facsimiles (Plate v, Nos. 12, 13)[1], the first, Gen. i. 1, 2, being written in vermilion, the second, Acts xx. 28, in the once black, but now yellowish-brown ink of the body of the Codex. The punctuation, which no later hand has meddled with, consists merely of a point placed at the end of a sentence, usually on a level with the top of the preceding letter, but not always; and a vacant space follows the point at the end of a paragraph, the space being proportioned to the break in the sense. Capital letters of various sizes abound at the beginning of books and sections, not painted as in later copies, but written by the original scribe in common ink. As these capitals stand entirely outside the column in the margin (excepting in such rare cases as Gen. i. 1), if the section begins in the middle of a line, the capital is necessarily postponed till the beginning of the next line, whose first letter is always the capital, even though it be in the middle of a word (*see* p. 51). Vermilion is freely used in the initial lines of books, and has stood the test of time much better than the black ink: the first four lines of each column on the first page of Genesis are in this colour, accompanied with the only breathings and accents in the manuscript (*see above*, pp. 45, 46). The first line of St. Mark, the first three of St. Luke, the first verse of St. John, the opening of the Acts down to *δι*, and so on for other books, are in vermilion. At the end of each book are neat and unique ornaments in the ink of the first hand: see especially those at the end of St. Mark and the Acts. As we have before stated this codex is the earliest which has the *κεφάλαια* proper, the so-called Ammonian sections, and the Eusebian canons complete. Lists of the *κεφάλαια* precede each Gospel, except the first, where they are lost. Their titles stand or have stood at the top of the pages, but the binder has often ruthlessly cut them short, and committed other yet more serious mutilation at the edges. The

[1] An excellent facsimile of A is given in the Facsimiles of the Palaeographical Society, Plate 106; others in Woide's New Testament from this MS. (1786), and in Baber's Old Test. (1816). Two specimens from the first Epistle of Clement are exhibited in Jacobson's Patres Apostolici, vol. i. p. 110, 1838 (1863); and one in Cassell's Bible Dict. vol. i. p. 49.

places at which they begin are indicated throughout, and their numbers are moreover set in the margin of Luke and John. The sections and Eusebian canons are conspicuous in the margin, and at the beginning of each of these sections a capital letter is found. The rest of the New Testament has no division into *κεφάλαια*, as was usual in later times, but paragraphs and capitals occur as the sense requires.

The palaeographic reasons for assigning this manuscript to the beginning or middle of the fifth century (the date now very generally acquiesced in, though it may be referred even to the end of the fourth century, and is certainly not much later) depend in part on the general style of the writing, which is at once firm, elegant and simple; partly on the formation of certain letters, in which respect it holds a middle place between copies of the fourth and sixth centuries. The reader will recall what we have already said (pp. 33–40) as to the shape of *alpha*, *delta*, *epsilon*, *pi*, *sigma*, *phi*, and *omega* in the Codex Alexandrinus. Woide, who edited the New Testament, believes that two hands were employed in that volume, changing in the page containing 1 Cor. v—vii, the vellum of the latter portion being thinner and the ink more thick, so that it has peeled off or eaten through the vellum in many places. This, however, is a point on which those who know manuscripts best will most hesitate to speak decidedly[1].

The external arguments for fixing the date are less weighty, but all point to the same conclusion. On the evidence for its being written by St. Thecla, indeed, no one has cared to lay much stress, though some have thought that the scribe might belong to a monastery dedicated to that holy martyr[2], whether

[1] Notice especially what Tregelles says of the Codex Augiensis (Tregelles' Horne's Introd. vol. iv. p. 198), where the difference of hand in the leaves removed from their proper place is much more striking than any change in Cod. Alexandrinus. Yet even in that case it is likely that one scribe only was engaged. It should be stated, however, that Mr. E. Maunde Thompson, who edits the autotype edition, believes that the hand changed at the beginning of St. Luke, and altered again at 1 Cor. x. 8. His reasons appear to us precarious and insufficient, and he seems to cut away the ground from under him when he admits (Praef. p. 9) that 'sufficient uniformity is maintained to make it difficult to decide the exact place where a new hand begins.'

[2] Tischendorf, Septuagint, Proleg. p. lxv, cites with some approval Grabe's references (Proleg. Cap. i. pp. 9–12) to Gregory Nazianzen [d. 389], three of whose Epistles are written to a holy virgin of that name (of course not the

the contemporary of St. Paul be meant, or her namesake who suffered in the second year of Diocletian, A.D. 286 (Eusebius de Martyr. Palaestin. c. iii). Tregelles explains the origin of the Arabic inscription, on which Cyril's statement appears to rest, by remarking that the New Testament in our manuscript at present commences with Matt. xxv. 6, this lesson (Matt. xxv. 1–13) *being that appointed by the Greek Church for the festival of St. Thecla* (see above, Menology, p. 87, Sept. 24). Thus the Egyptian who wrote this Arabic note, observing the name of Thecla in the now mutilated upper margin of the Codex, where such rubrical notes are commonly placed by later hands, may have hastily concluded that she wrote the book, and so perplexed our Biblical critics. It seems a fatal objection to this shrewd conjecture, as Mr. E. Maunde Thompson points out, that the Arabic numeration of the leaf, set in the *verso* of the lower margin, itself posterior in date to the Arabic note relating to Thecla, is 26[1]; so that the twenty-five leaves now lost must have been still extant when that note was written.

Other more trustworthy reasons for assigning Cod. A to the fifth century may be summed up very briefly. The presence of the canons of Eusebius [A.D. 268–340?], and of the epistle to Marcellinus by the great Athanasius, Patriarch of Alexandria [300?–373], standing before the Psalms, place a limit in one direction, while the absence of the Euthalian divisions of the Acts and Epistles (*see above*, p. 64), which came into vogue very soon after A.D. 458, and the shortness of the ὑπογραφαί (*above*, p. 65), appear tolerably decisive against a later date than A.D. 450. The insertion of the Epistles of Clement, like that of the treatises of Barnabas and Hermas in the Cod. Sinaiticus (p. 92), recalls us to a period when the canon of Scripture was in some particulars a little unsettled, that is, about the age of the Councils of Laodicea (363?) and of Carthage (397). Other arguments have been urged both for an earlier and a later date, but they scarcely deserve discussion. Wetstein's objection to the name Θεοτόκος as

martyr), to whose παρθενών at Seleucia he betook himself, the better to carry out his very sincere *nolo episcopari* on the death of his father Gregory, Bishop of Nazianzus: Πρῶτον μὲν ἦλθον εἰς Σελεύκειαν φυγὰς | Τὸν παρθενῶνα τῆς ἀοιδίμου κόρης | Θέκλας· κ.τ.λ. 'De vitâ suâ.'

[1] The last Arabic numeral in the Old Testament is 641, the first in the New Testament 667.

applied to the Blessed Virgin in the title to her song, added to the Psalms, is quite groundless: that appellation was given to her by both the Gregories in the middle of the fourth century (*vid.* Suicer, Thesaur. Eccles. i. p. 1387), as habitually as it was a century after: nor should we insist much on the contrary upon Woide's or Schulz's persuasion that the *τρισάγιον* (*ἅγιος ὁ θεός, ἅγιος ἰσχυρός, ἅγιος ἀθάνατος*) would have been found in the *ὕμνος ἑωθινός* after the Psalms, had the manuscript been written as late as the fifth century.

Partial and inaccurate collations of the New Testament portion of this manuscript were made by Patrick Young, Librarian to Charles I[1], who first published from it the Epistles of Clement in 1633: then by Alexander Huish, Prebendary of Wells, for Walton's Polyglott, and by some others[2]. The Old Testament portion was edited in 1707–20, after a not very happy plan, but with learned Prolegomena and notes, by the Prussian J. E. Grabe, the second and third of his four volumes being posthumous.

In 1786, Charles Godfrey Woide, preacher at the Dutch Chapel Royal and Assistant Librarian in the British Museum, a distinguished Coptic scholar [d. 1790], published, by the aid of 456 subscribers, a noble folio edition of the New Testament from this manuscript, with valuable Prolegomena, a copy of the text which, so far as it has been tested, has been found reasonably accurate, together with notes on the changes made in the codex by later hands, and a minute collation of its readings with the common text as presented in Kuster's edition of Mill's N. T. (1710). In this last point Woide has not been taken as a model by subsequent editors of manuscripts, much to the inconvenience of the student. In 1816–28 the Old Testament portion of the

[1] Very interesting is Whitelock's notice of a design which was never carried out, under the date of March 13, 1645. 'The Assembly of Divines desired by some of their brethren, sent to the House [of Commons] that Mr. Patrick Young might be encouraged in the printing of the Greek Testament much expected and desired by the learned, especially beyond seas; and an ordinance was read for printing and publishing the Old Testament of the Septuagint translation, wherein Mr. Young had formerly taken pains and had in his hand, as library keeper at St. James's, an original *Teeta* [sic] Bible of that translation' (Memorials, p. 197, ed. 1732).

[2] 'MS^{m} Alexand^{m} accuratissime ipse contuli, A. D. 1716. Rich: Bentleius.' Trin. Coll. Camb. B. xvii. 9, in a copy of Fell's Greek Testament, 1675, which contains his collation. Ellis, Bentleii Critica Sacra, p. xxviii.

Codex Alexandrinus was published in three folio volumes at the national expense, by the Rev. Henry Hervey Baber, also of the British Museum, the Prolegomena to whose magnificent work are very inferior to Woide's, but contain some additional information. Both these performances, and many others like them which we shall have to describe, are printed in an uncial type, bearing some general resemblance to that of their respective originals, but which must not be supposed to convey any adequate notion of their actual appearance. Such quasi-facsimiles (for they are nothing more), while they add to the cost of the book, seem to answer no useful purpose whatever; and, if taken by an incautious reader for more than they profess to be, will seriously mislead him. In 1860 Mr. B. H. Cowper put forth an octavo edition of the New Testament pages in common type, but burdened with modern breathings and accents, the lacunae of the manuscript being unwisely supplied by means of Kuster's edition of Mill, and the original paragraphs departed from, wheresoever they were judged to be inconvenient. These obvious faults are the more to be regretted, inasmuch as Mr. Cowper has not shrunk from the labour of revising Woide's edition by a comparison with the Codex itself, thus giving to his book a distinctive value of its own. An admirable autotype facsimile of the New Testament was published in 1879, and afterwards of the Old Testament, by Mr. E. Maunde Thompson, then the Principal Keeper of Manuscripts, now the Principal Librarian, of the British Museum.

The Codex Alexandrinus has been judged to be carelessly written; many errors of transcription no doubt exist, but not so many as in some copies (e.g. Cod. ℵ), nor more than in others (as Cod. B). None other than the ordinary abridgements are found in it (*see* pp. 49–50): numerals are not expressed by letters except in Apoc. vii. 4; xxi. 17: ι and υ have usually the dots over them at the beginning of a syllable. Of itacisms it may be doubted whether it contains more than others of the same date: the interchange of ι and ει, η and ι, ε αι, are the most frequent; but these mutations are too common to prove anything touching the country of the manuscript. Its external history renders it very likely that it was written at Alexandria, that great manufactory of correct and elegant copies, while Egypt was yet a Christian land: but such forms as λήμψομαι,

ΜΙΝΤΟΝΛΙΘΟΝΕΚΤΗϹ
ΘΥΡΑϹΤΟΥΜΝΗΜΕΙΟΥ
ΚΑΙΑΝΑΒΛΕΨΑϹΑΙΘΕΩ
ΡΟΥϹΙΝΟΤΙΑΝΑΚΕΚΥ
ΛΙϹΤΑΙΟΛΙΘΟϹΗΝΓΑΡ
ΜΕΓΑϹϹΦΟΔΡΑΚΑΙΕΛ
ΘΟΥϹΑΙΕΙϹΤΟΜΝΗΜΕΙ
ΟΝΕΙΔΟΝΝΕΑΝΙϹΚΟΝ
ΚΑΘΗΜΕΝΟΝΕΝΤΟΙϹ
ΔΕΞΙΟΙϹΠΕΡΙΒΕΒΛΗΜΕ
ΝΟΝϹΤΟΛΗΝΛΕΥΚΗΝ
ΚΑΙΕΞΕΘΑΜΒΗΘΗϹΑΝ
ΟΔΕΛΕΓΕΙΑΥΤΑΙϹΜΗ
ΕΚΘΑΜΒΕΙϹΘΕΙΝΖΗΤΕΙ
ΤΕΤΟΝΝΑΖΑΡΗΝΟΝΤΟΝ
ΕϹΤΑΥΡΩΜΕΝΟΝΗΓΕΡ
ΘΗΟΥΚΕϹΤΙΝΩΔΕΙΔΕ
ΟΤΟΠΟϹΟΠΟΥΕΘΗΚΑΝ
ΑΥΤΟΝΑΛΛΑΥΠΑΓΕΤΕ
ΕΙΠΑΤΕΤΟΙϹΜΑΘΗΤΑΙϹ
ΑΥΤΟΥΚΑΙΤΩΠΕΤΡΩ
ΟΤΙΠΡΟΑΓΕΙΥΜΑϹΕΙϹ
ΤΗΝΓΑΛΙΛΑΙΑΝΕΚΕΙΑΥ
ΤΟΝΟΨΕϹΘΕΚΑΘΩϹΕΙ
ΠΕΝΥΜΙΝΚΑΙΕΞΕΛΘΟΥ
ϹΑΙΕΦΥΓΟΝΑΠΟΤΟΥ
ΜΝΗΜΕΙΟΥΕΙΧΕΝΓΑΡ
ΑΥΤΑϹΤΡΟΜΟϹΚΑΙΕΚ
ϹΤΑϹΙϹΚΑΙΟΥΔΕΝΙΟΥ
ΔΕΝΕΙΠΟΝΕΦΟΒΟΥΝ
ΤΟΓΑΡ:

ΚΑΤΑ
ΜΑΡΚΟΝ

ἐλάβαμεν, ἦλθαν, ἔνατος, ἐκαθερίσθη, and others named by Woide, are peculiar to no single nation, but are found repeatedly in Greek-Latin codices which unquestionably originated in Western Europe. This manuscript is of the very greatest importance to the critic, inasmuch as it exhibits (especially in the Gospels) a text more nearly approaching that found in later copies than is read in others of its high antiquity, although some of its errors are portentous enough, e.g. θῡ for ιῡ in John xix. 40. This topic, however, will be discussed at length in another place, and we shall elsewhere consider the testimony Codex A bears in the celebrated passage 1 Tim. iii. 16.

B. CODEX VATICANUS 1209 is probably the oldest large vellum manuscript in existence, and is the glory of the great Vatican Library at Rome. To this legitimate source of deep interest must be added the almost romantic curiosity which was once excited by the jealous watchfulness of its official guardians. But now that an acquaintance with it has been placed within the reach of scholars through the magnificent autotype edition issued by the authorities of the Vatican, it may be hoped that all such mystic glamour will soon be left with the past. This book seems to have been brought into the Vatican Library shortly after its establishment by Pope Nicolas V in 1448, but nothing is known of its previous history[1]. It is entered in the earliest catalogue of that Library, made in 1475. Since the missing portions at the end of the New Testament are believed to have been supplied in the fifteenth century from a manuscript belonging to Cardinal Bessarion, we may be allowed to conjecture, if we please, that this learned Greek brought the Codex into the west of Europe. It was taken to Paris by Napoleon I, where it was studied by Hug in 1809. Although this book has not even yet been as thoroughly collated, or rendered as available as it might be to the critical student, its general character and appearance are sufficiently well known. It is a quarto volume, arranged in quires of five sheets or ten leaves each, like Codex Marchalianus of the Prophets written in the sixth or seventh century and Cod. Rossanensis of

[1] See Bibliothèque du Vatican au Xme siècle, par Eugène Müntz et Paul Fabre, Paris, Thorn. 824 Lat., 400 Gr.

the Gospels to be described hereafter, not of four or three sheets as Cod. ℵ, the ancient, perhaps the original, numbering of the quires being often found in the margin. The New Testament fills 142 out of its 759 thin and delicate vellum leaves, said to be made of the skins of antelopes: it is bound in red morocco, being 10½ inches high, 10 broad, 4½ thick. It once contained the whole Bible in Greek, the Old Testament of the Septuagint version (a tolerably fair representation of which was exhibited in the Roman edition as early as 1587[1]), except the books of the Maccabees and the Prayer of Manasses. The first forty-six chapters of Genesis (the manuscript begins at *πολιν*, Gen. xlvi. 28) and Psalms cv—cxxxvii, also the books of the Maccabees, are wanting. The New Testament is complete down to Heb. ix. 14 *καθα*: the rest of the Epistle to the Hebrews (the Catholic Epistles had followed the Acts, *see* p. 74), and the Apocalypse, being written in the later hand alluded to above. The peculiar arrangement of three columns on a page, or six on the opened leaf of the volume, is described by eye-witnesses as very striking: in the poetical books of the Old Testament (since they are written *στιχηρῶς*) only two columns fill a page. Our facsimile (Plate viii, No. 20) comprises Mark xvi. 3 *μιν του λιθου* to the end of verse 8, where the Gospel ends abruptly; both the arabesque ornament and the subscription KATA MAPKON being in a later hand (for M *see* p. 37). All who have inspected the Codex are loud in their praises of the fine thin vellum, the clear and elegant hand of the first penman, the simplicity of the whole style of the work: capital letters, so frequent in the Codex Alexandrinus, were totally wanting in this document for some centuries. In several of these particulars our manuscript resembles the Herculanean rolls, and thus asserts a just claim to high antiquity, which the absence of the divisions into *κεφάλαια*, of the sections and canons, and the substitution in their room of another scheme of chapters of its own (described above, p. 56), beyond question

[1] The 'Epistle' of Cardinal Carafa to Sixtus V, and the Preface to the Reader by the actual editor Peter Morinus, both of which Tischendorf reprints in full (Septuagint, Proleg. pp. xxi—xxvii), display an amount of critical skill and discernment quite beyond their age, and in strange contrast with the signal mismanagement in regard to the revision of the Latin Vulgate version under the auspices of the same Pope.

tend very powerfully to confirm. Each column contains ordinarily forty-two lines[1], each line from sixteen to eighteen letters, of a size somewhat less than in Cod. A, much less than in Cod. ℵ (though they all vary a little in this respect), with no intervals between words, a space of the breadth of half a letter being left at the end of a sentence, and a little more at the conclusion of a paragraph; the first letter of the new sentence occasionally standing a little out of the line (*see* pp. 51, 93). It has been doubted whether any of the stops are *primâ manu*, and (contrary to the judgement of Birch and others) the breathings and accents are now universally allowed to have been added by a later hand. This hand, referred by some to the eighth century (although Tischendorf, with Dr. Hort's approval, assigns it to the tenth or eleventh[2]), retraced, with as much care as such an operation would permit, the faint lines of the original writing (the ink whereof was perhaps never quite black), the remains of which can even now be seen by a keen-sighted reader by the side of the thicker and more modern strokes; and, anxious at the same time to represent a critical revision of the text, the writer left untouched such words or letters as he wished to reject. In these last places, *where no breathings or accents and scarcely any stops*[3] *have ever been detected*, we have an opportunity of seeing the manuscript in its primitive condition, before it had been tampered with by the later scribe. There are occasional breaks in the continuity of the writing, every

[1] In Pentateuch, Joshua, Judges, Ruth, and 1 Kings i. 1—xix. 11, there are forty-four lines in a column; and in 2 Paralip. x. 16—xxvi. 13, there are forty lines in a column.

[2] The writer of the Preface to the sixth volume of the Roman edition of 1881 (apparently Fabiani), is jubilant over his discovery of the name of this retracer ('eruditissimi et patientissimi viri,' as he is pleased to call him, p. xviii) in the person of Clement the Monk, who has written his name twice in the book in a scrawl of the fifteenth century. But mere resemblance in the ink is but a lame proof of identity, and Fabiani recognizes some other correctors, whom he designates as B[1], posterior to the mischievous 'instaurator.'

[3] Hug says *none*, but Tischendorf (Cod. Frid.-Aug. Proleg. p. 9) himself detected two in a part that the second scribe had left untouched; and not a very few elsewhere (N. T. Vatican. Proleg. pp. xx, xxi, 1867); though a break often occurs with no stop by either hand. In the much contested passage Rom. ix. 5, Dr. Vance Smith ('Revised Texts and Margins,' p. 34, note*), while confidently claiming the stop after *σαρκα* in Cod. A as *primâ manu*, and noticing the space after the word in Cod. Ephraemi (C), admits that 'in the Vatican the originality of the stops may be doubtful.' In the judgement of Fabiani, 'vix aliqua primo exscriptori tribuenda' (Praef. N. T. Vat. 1881, p. xviii).

descent in the genealogies of our Lord (Matt. i, Luke iii[1]), each of the beatitudes (Matt. v), of the parables in Matt. xiii, and the salutations of Rom. xvi, forming a separate paragraph; but such a case will oftentimes not occur for several consecutive pages. The writer's plan was to proceed regularly with a book until it was finished: then to break off from the column he was writing, and to begin the next book on the very next column. Thus only *one* column perfectly blank is found in the whole New Testament[2], that which follows ἐφοβοῦντο γάρ in Mark xvi. 8: and since Cod. B is the only one yet known, except Cod. א, that actually omits the last twelve verses of that Gospel, by leaving such a space the scribe has intimated that he was fully aware of their existence, or even found them in the copy from which he wrote. The capital letters at the beginning of each book are likewise due to the corrector, who sometimes erased, sometimes merely touched slightly, the original initial letter, which (as in the Herculanean rolls) is no larger than any other. The *paragraph* marks (usually straight lines, but sometimes Γ[3]) are seen quite frequently in some parts; whether from the first hand is very doubtful. The note of citation >[3] is perpetual, not occasional as in Cod. א. Fewer abridgements than usual occur in this venerable copy[3]. The formation of *delta, pi, chi*; the loop-like curve on the left side of *alpha*; the absence of points at the extremities of *sigma* or *epsilon*; the length and size of *rho, upsilon, phi*, all point to the FOURTH century as the date of this manuscript. The smaller letters so often found at the end of lines preserve

[1] The publication of the Roman edition (1868–81) enables us to add (Abbot, *ubi supra*, p. 193) that the blessings of the twelve patriarchs in Gen. xlix are in separate paragraphs numbered from A to IB, that the twenty-two names of the unclean birds Deut. xiv. 12–18, twenty-five kings in Josh. xii. 10–22, eleven dukes in 1 Chr. i. 51–54, each stand in a separate line. In Cod. א, especially in the New Testament, this arrangement στιχηρῶς is much more frequent than in Cod. B, although the practice is in some measure common to both.

[2] The Roman edition (1868–81) also makes known to us that in the Old Testament two columns are left blank between Nehemiah and the Psalms, which could not have been otherwise, inasmuch as the Psalms are written στιχηρῶς with but two columns on a page. Between Tobit and Hosea (which book stands first of the Prophetical writings) a column is very naturally left blank, and two columns at the end of Daniel, with whose prophecy the Old Testament concludes. But these peculiarities obviously bear no analogy to the case of the end of St. Mark's Gospel.

[3] See above, pp. 49–51.

the same firm and simple character as the rest; of the use of the apostrophus, so frequent in Codd. ℵ, A and some others, Tischendorf enumerates ten instances in the New Testament (N. T. Vatican. Proleg. p. xxi), whereof four are represented in the Roman edition of 1868, with two more which Tischendorf considers as simple points (Acts vii. 13, 14).

Tischendorf says truly enough that something like a history might be written of the futile attempts to collate Cod. B, and a very unprofitable history it would be. The manuscript is first distinctly heard of (for it does not appear to have been used for the Complutensian Polyglott[1]) through Sepulveda, to whose correspondence with Erasmus attention has been seasonably recalled by Tregelles. Writing in 1533, he says, 'Est enim Graecum exemplar antiquissimum in Bibliothecâ Vaticanâ, in quo diligentissimè et accuratissimè literis majusculis conscriptum utrumque Testamentum continetur longè diversum a vulgatis exemplaribus': and, after noticing as a weighty proof of excellence its agreement with the Latin version (multum convenit cum vetere nostrâ translatione) against the common Greek text (vulgatam Graecorum editionem), he furnishes Erasmus with 365 readings as a convincing argument in support of his statements. It would probably be from this list that in his Annotations to the Acts, published in 1535, Erasmus cites the reading καῦδα, ch. xxvii. 16 ('quidam admonent' is the expression he uses), from a Greek codex in the Pontifical Library, since for this reading Cod. B is the only known *Greek* witness, except a corrector of Cod. ℵ. It seems, however, that he had obtained some account of this manuscript from the Papal Librarian Paul Bombasius as early as 1521 (*see* Wetstein's Proleg. N. T., vol. i. p. 23). Lucas Brugensis, who published his Notationes in S. Biblia in 1580, and his Commentary on the Four Gospels (dedicated to Cardinal Bellarmine) in 1606, made known some twenty extracts from Cod. B taken by Werner of Nimeguen; that most imperfect collection being the only source from which Mill and even Wetstein had any acquaintance with the contents of this first-rate document.

[1] The writer of the Preface to the Roman edition (vol. vi. Praef. p. 9, 1881) vainly struggles to maintain the opposite view, because the Cardinal, in his Preface to the Complutensian N. T., speaks about 'adhibitis Vaticanis libris,' as if there was but one there.

More indeed might have been gleaned from the Barberini readings gathered in or about 1625 (of which we shall speak in the next section), but their real value and character were not known in the lifetime of Wetstein. In 1698 Lorenzo Alexander Zacagni, Librarian of the Vatican, in his Preface to the Collectanea Monumentorum Veterum Eccles., describes Cod. B, and especially its peculiar division into sections, in a passage cited by Mill (Proleg. § 1480). In 1669 indeed the first real collation of the manuscript with the Aldine edition (1518) had been attempted by Bartolocci, then Librarian of the Vatican; from some accident, however, it was never published, though a transcript under the feigned name of Giulio a Sta. Anastasia yet remains in the Imperial Library of Paris (MSS. Gr. Supplem. 53), where it was first discovered and used by Scholz in 1819, and subsequently by Tischendorf and Muralt, the latter of whom (apparently on but slender grounds) regards it as the best hitherto made; others have declared it to be very imperfect, and quite inferior to those of Bentley and Birch. The collation which bears Bentley's name (Trin. Coll. B. xvii. 3, in Cephalaeus' N. T. 1524) was procured about 1720 by his money and the labour of the Abbate Mico, for the purpose of his projected Greek Testament. When he had found out its defects, by means of an examination of the original by his nephew Thomas Bentley in 1726, our great critic engaged the Abbate Rulotta in 1729 for forty scudi (Bentley's Correspondence, p. 706) to revise Mico's sheets, and especially to note the changes made by the second hand. Rulotta's papers came to light in 1855 among the Bentley manuscripts in the Library of Trinity College, Cambridge (B. xvii. 20), and have lately proved of signal value[1]; Mico's were published in 1799 at Oxford, by Henry Ford, Lord Almoner's Reader in Arabic there (1783–1813), together with some Thebaic fragments of the New Testament, in a volume which (since it was chiefly drawn from Woide's posthumous papers) he was pleased to call an Appendix to the Codex Alexandrinus. A fourth collation of the Vatican MS. was made about 1780 by Andrew Birch of Copenhagen, and is included in the notes to the first volume of his Greek Testament 1788, or published separately in three volumes which

[1] Rulotta's labours are now printed in Bentleii Critica Sacra by Mr. A. A. Ellis, 1862, pp. 121–154.

were issued successively 1798 (Acts, Cath. Epp., Paul.), 1800 (Apoc.), and 1801 (Evans). Birch's collation does not extend to the Gospels of St. Luke and St. John, and on the whole is less full and exact than Mico's. In 1810, however, when, with the other best treasures of the Vatican, Codex B was at Paris, the celebrated critic J. L. Hug sent forth his treatise 'de Antiquitate Vaticani Codicis Commentatio,' and though even he did not perceive the need of a new and full collation when he examined it in 1809, he has the merit of first placing it in the paramount rank it still holds as one of the oldest and most venerable of extant monuments of sacred antiquity. His conclusion respecting its date, that it is not later than the middle of the fourth century, has been acquiesced in with little opposition, though Tischendorf declares rather pithily that he holds this belief 'non propter Hugium sed cum Hugio' (Cod. Ephraem. Proleg. p. 19). Some of his reasons, no doubt, are weak enough[1]; but the strength of his position depends on an accumulation of minute particulars, against which there seems nothing to set up which would suggest a lower period. On its return to Rome, this volume was no longer available for the free use and reference of critics. In 1843 Tischendorf, after long and anxious expectation during a visit to Rome that lasted some months, obtained a sight of it for two days of three hours each[2]. In 1844 Edward de Muralt was admitted to the higher privilege of three days or nine hours' enjoyment of this treasure, and on the strength of the favour published an edition of the New Testament, *ad fidem codicis principis Vaticani*, in 1846. Tregelles, who went to Rome in 1845 for the special purpose of consulting it, was treated even worse. He had forearmed himself (as he fondly imagined) with recommendatory letters from Cardinal Wiseman, and was often

[1] Thus the correspondence of Codex B with what St. Basil (c. Eunom. ii. 19) states he found in the middle of the fourth century, *ἐν τοῖς παλαιοῖς τῶν ἀντιγράφων*, in Eph. i. 1, viz. *τοῖς οὖσιν* without *ἐν Ἐφέσῳ*, though now read only in this and the Sinaitic manuscript *primâ manu*, and in one cursive copy (Cod. 67) *secundâ manu*, seems in itself of but little weight. Another point that has been raised is the position of the Epistle to the Hebrews. But this argument can apply only to the elder document from which the Vatican MS. was taken, and wherein this book unquestionably followed that to the Galatians. In Cod. B it *always* stood in its present place, after 2 Thess., as in the Codices cited p. 74, note.

[2] Besides the twenty-five readings Tischendorf observed himself, Cardinal Mai supplied him with thirty-four more for his N. T. of 1849. His seventh edition of 1859 was enriched by 230 other readings furnished by Albert Dressel in 1855.

allowed to *see* the manuscript, but hindered from transcribing any of its readings[1].

What the Papal authorities would not entrust to others, they had at least the merit of attempting and at length accomplishing themselves. As early as 1836 Bishop Wiseman announced in his Lectures on the Connection between Science and Revelation, vol. ii. pp. 187–191, that Cardinal Mai, whose services to classical and ecclesiastical literature were renowned throughout Europe, was engaged on an edition of the Codex Vaticanus, commenced under the immediate sanction of Pope Leo XII (1823–29). As years passed by and no such work appeared, adverse reports and evil surmises began to take the place of hope, although the Cardinal often spoke of his work as already finished, only that he desired to write full Prolegomena before it should appear. In September 1854 he died, honoured and ripe in years; and at length, when no more seemed to be looked for in that quarter, five quarto volumes issued from the Roman press in 1857, the New Testament comprising the fifth volume, with a slight and meagre preface by the Cardinal, and a letter to the reader by 'Carolus Vercellone, Sodalis Barnabites,' which told in a few frank manly words how little accuracy we had to expect in a work, by the publication of which he still persuaded himself he was decorating Mai's memory 'novâ usque gloriâ atque splendidiore coronâ' (tom. i. p. iii). The cause of that long delay now required no explanation. In fact so long as Mai lived the edition never would have appeared; for though he had not patience or special skill enough to accomplish his task well, he was too good a scholar not to know that he had done it very ill. The text is broken up into paragraphs, the numbers of the modern chapters and verses being placed in the margin; the peculiar divisions of the Codex Vaticanus (*see* p. 56) sometimes omitted, sometimes tampered with. The Greek type employed is not an imitation of the uncials in the manuscript (of which circumstance we do not complain), but has modern stops, breathings, accents, *ι subscript*, &c., as if the venerable document were written yesterday. As regards the orthography

[1] 'They would not let me open it,' he adds, 'without searching my pocket, and depriving me of pen, ink, and paper... If I looked at a passage too long the two *prelati* would snatch the book out from my hand.' Tregelles, Lecture on the Historic Evidence of the N. T., p. 84.

it is partially, and only partially, modernized; clauses or whole passages omitted in the manuscript are supplied from other sources, although the fact is duly notified[1]; sometimes the readings of the first hand are put in the margin, while those of the second stand in the text, sometimes the contrary: in a word, the plan of the work exhibits all the faults such a performance well can have. Nor is the execution at all less objectionable. Although the five volumes were ten years in printing (1828–38), Mai devoted to their superintendence only his scanty spare hours, and even then worked so carelessly that after cancelling a hundred pages for their incurable want of exactness, he was reduced to the shift of making *manual* corrections with moveable types, and projected huge tables of errata, which Vercellone has in some measure tried to supply. When once it is stated that the type was set up from the common Elzevir or from some other printed Greek Testament, the readings of the Codex itself being inserted as corrections, and the whole revised by means of an assistant who read the proof-sheets to the Cardinal while he inspected the manuscript; no one will look for accuracy from a method which could not possibly lead to it. Accordingly, when Mai's text came to be compared with the collations of Bartolocci, of Mico, of Rulotta, and of Birch, or with the scattered readings which had been extracted by others, it was soon discovered that while this edition added very considerably to our knowledge of the Codex Vaticanus, and often enabled us to form a decision on its readings when the others were at variance; it was in its turn convicted by them of so many errors, oversights, and inconsistencies, that its single evidence could never be used with confidence, especially when it agreed with the commonly received Greek text. Immediately after the appearance of Mai's expensive quartos, an octavo reprint of the New Testament was struck off at Leipsic for certain London booksellers, which proved but a hasty, slovenly, unscholarlike performance, and was put aside in 1859 by a cheap Roman edition in octavo, prepared, as was the quarto, by Mai, prefaced by another graceful and sensible epistle of Vercellone[2]. This

[1] The great gap in the Pauline Epistles is filled up from Vatic. 1761 (Act. 158, Paul. 192) of the eleventh century.

[2] Other editions of the Vatican N. T. appeared at Ratisbon; at Leyden (1860) by A. Kuenen and C. G. Cobet, with a masterly Preface by the latter; and at

last edition was undertaken by the Cardinal, after sad experience had taught him the defects of his larger work, and he took good care to avoid some of the worst of them: the readings of the second hand are usually, though not always, banished to the margin, their number on the whole is increased, gross errors are corrected, omissions supplied, and the Vatican chapters are given faithfully and in full. But Mai's whole procedure in this matter is so truly unfortunate, that in a person whose fame was less solidly grounded, we should impute it to mere helpless incapacity[1]. Not only did he split up the paragraphs of his quarto into the modern chapters and verses (in itself a most undesirable change, *see above*, p. 70), but by omitting some things and altering others, he introduced almost as many errors as he removed. When Dean Burgon was permitted to examine the Codex for an hour and a half in 1860, on consulting it for sixteen passages out of hundreds wherein the two are utterly at variance, he discovered that the quarto was right in seven of them, the octavo in nine: as if Mai were determined that neither of his editions should supersede the use of the other. Dean Alford also collated numerous passages in 1861[2], and his secretary Mr. Cure in 1862, especially with reference to the several correcting hands: 'in errorem quidem et ipse haud raro inductus,' is Tischendorf's verdict on his labours. Thus critics of every shade of opinion became unanimous on one point, that

Berlin (1862) by Philip Buttmann, furnished with an Appendix containing the varying results of no less than nine collations, eight of which we have described in the text, the ninth being derived from Lachmann's Greek Testament (1842, 1850), whose readings were all obtained second-hand. Tischendorf does not much commend the accuracy of Buttmann's work.

[1] 'Angelus Mai, quamquam, ut in proverbio est, *ἐν τυφλῶν πόλει γλαμυρὸς βασιλεύων*, non is erat cui tanta res rectè mandari posset:' Kuenen and Cobet, N. T. Vat. Praef. p. 1. Tischendorf too, in his over querulous Responsa ad Calumnias Romanas &c., 1870, p. 11, is not more than just in alleging 'Angelum Maium in editionibus suis Codicis Vaticani alienissimum se praebuisse ab omni subtiliore rei palaeographicae scientiâ, ac tantum non ignarum earum legum ad quas is codex in usum criticum edendus esset.' The defence set up for Mai in the Preface to the Roman volume of 1881, was that he intended to produce only a new edition of the 'authentic' Septuagint of 1586–7, chiefly for the use of Greek-speaking Catholics.

[2] The Dean himself on Feb. 20, 1861, and for four subsequent days, 'went twice over the doubtful passages and facsimilized most of the important various readings,' in spite of much opposition from the Librarian, who 'insisted that our order from Antonelli, although it ran "per verificare," to verify passages, only extended to seeing the Codex, not to using it.' (Life by his Widow, pp. 310, 315.)

a new edition of the Codex Vaticanus was as imperatively needed as ever; one which should preserve with accuracy all that the first hand has written (transcriptural errors included), should note in every instance the corrections made by the second hand, and, wherever any one of the previous collators might be found in error, should expressly state the true reading.

It would have been a grievous reproach had no efforts been made to supply so great and acknowledged a want. Early in 1866, Tischendorf again visited Rome, and when admitted into the presence of Pope Pius IX, boldly sought permission to edit at his own cost such an edition of Cod. B as he had already published of Cod. א. The request was denied by his Holiness, who obscurely hinted his intention of carrying out the same design on his own account. Tischendorf, however, obtained permission to use the manuscript so far as to consult it in such parts of the New Testament as presented any special difficulty, or respecting which previous collators were at variance. He commenced his task February 28, and in the course of it could not refrain from copying at length twenty pages of the great Codex—nineteen from the New Testament, and one from the Old. This licence was not unnaturally regarded as a breach of his contract, so that, after he had used the manuscript for eight days, it was abruptly withdrawn from him on March 12. An appeal to the generosity of Vercellone, who had been entrusted with the care of the forthcoming edition, procured for him the sight of this coveted treasure for six days longer between March 20 and 26, the Italian being always present on these latter occasions, and receiving instruction for the preparation of his own work by watching the processes of a master hand. Thus fourteen days of three hours each, used zealously and skilfully, enabled Tischendorf to put forth an edition of Cod. B far superior to any that preceded it[1]. The Prolegomena are full of matter from which we have drawn freely in the foregoing description, the text is in cursive type, the nineteen pages which cost him so dearly being arranged in their proper lines, the remainder according to columns. Much that ought to have been noted was doubtless passed over by Tischendorf for mere pressure of time; but he takes great

[1] 'Novum Testamentum Vaticanum post Angeli Maii aliorumque imperfectos labores ex ipso codice edidit Ae. F. C. Tischendorf.' Lipsiae, 4to, 1867.

pains to distinguish the readings of the original writer or his διορθωτής (*see* p. 55)[1], both of whom supplied words or letters here and there in the margin or between the lines[2], from the corrections of a second yet ancient scribe (B^2), and those of the person (B^3) who retraced the faded writing at a later period[3]. One notion, taken up by Tischendorf in the course of his collation in 1866, was received at first with general incredulity by other scholars. He has pronounced a decided opinion, not only that Codd. ℵ and B are documents of the same age, but that the scribe who wrote the latter is one of the four [D] to whose diligence we owe the former. That there should be a general similarity in the style of the two great codices is probable enough, although the letters in Cod. ℵ are about half as large again as those of its fellow, but such as are aware of the difficulty of arriving at a safe conclusion as to identity of penmanship after close and repeated comparison of one document with another, will hardly attach much weight to the impression of any person, however large his experience, who has nothing but memory to trust to. Tregelles, who has also seen both copies, states that Cod. ℵ looks much the fresher and clearer of the two. Yet the reasons alleged above, which are quite independent of the appearance of the handwriting, leave scarcely a doubt that Tischendorf's judgement was correct.

The Roman edition, projected by Vercellone and Cozza

[1] To his hand Tischendorf assigns seven readings, Matt. xiii. 52; xiv. 5; xvi. 4; xxii. 10; xxvii. 4. Luke iii. 1 (*bis*), 7. 'For some six centuries after it was written B appears to have undergone no changes in its text except from the hand of the "corrector," the "second hand"' (Hort, Introd. p. 270). What then of B^2?

[2] It must surely be to these, the earliest scribes, that Cobet refers when he uses language that would not be at all applicable to the case of B^2 or B^3: 'In Vaticano duorum librorum veterum testimonia continentur, et nihilo plus in primâ manu quam in secundâ inest auctoritatis ac fidei. Utriusque unaquaeque lectio ex se ipsâ spectanda ponderandaque est, et si hoc ages, modo hanc modo illam animadvertes esse potiorem. Hoc autem in primis firmiter tenendum est, non esse secundae manûs lectiones correctoris alicujus suspiciones aut conjecturas, sive illae sunt acutiores sive leviores, sed quidquid a secundâ manu correctum, mutatum, deletum esse Maius referat, id omne haud secus atque id quod prior manus dederit, perantiqui cujusdam Codicis fide nixum esse.' (N. T. Vat. Praef. p. xxvi.)

[3] It may be mere oversight that in Matt. xxvii. 4 he does not say in 1867 of what hand the marginal δικαιον is: in his eighth edition (1865) he adjudges it to B^2. In Matt. xxiv. 23 πιστευητε and ver. 32 εκφύη he gives to B^3 in 1867 what he had assigned to B^2 in 1865. The Roman Commentary gives no light in the other places, but assigns πιστεύητε to B^2, B^3.

under the auspices of Pius IX, was designed to consist of six volumes, four containing the Old Testament, one the New, another being devoted to the notes and discrimination of corrections by later hands. The New Testament appeared in 1868[1], a second volume in 1869, containing the text from Genesis to Joshua; three more have since completed the Old Testament (1870, 1871, 1872). The learned, genial, and modest Vercellone (b. 1814) died early in 1869, so that the later volumes bear on their title-page the mournful inscription 'Carolum Vercellone excepit Caietanus Sergio Sodalis Barnabites' as Cozza's associate. These editors fared but ill whether as Biblical critics or as general scholars, under the rough handling of Tischendorf, whom the wiser policy of Vercellone had kept in good humour, but whose powers his successors greatly undervalued. There seems, however, to be no great cause, in spite of their adversary's minute diligence in fault-finding (Appendix N. T. Vatic. 1869, p. xi, &c.)[2], for doubting their general correctness, although they persist in placing on the page with the rest of their text readings which are known or credibly stated to be of decidedly later date, in spite of the incongruousness of the mixture of what was original with matter plainly adscititious[3]. Thus in the Roman edition *αδελφων μου των* Matt. xxv. 40, imputed by Tischendorf to B^2 and B^3, stands in the margin just in the same way as *ο γαμος* Matt. xxii. 10, which he refers to the first hand. But this is only one instance of a lack of judgement which deforms every page of their performance: e.g. Matt. xix. 12; xxiii. 26; 37; xxv. 16; xxvii. 12; 13; 45; xxviii. 15; Acts xv. 1: all which places exhibit, undistinguished from emendations of the original scribe or his 'corrector,' readings

[1] 'Bibliorum Sacrorum Graecus Codex Vaticanus, Auspice Pio IX Pontifice Maximo, collatis studiis Caroli Vercellone Sodalis Barnabitae, et Josephi Cozza Monachi Basiliani editus. Romae typis et impensis S. Congregationis de Propaganda Fide,' square folio, 1868.

[2] The feeble rejoinder of the Roman editors was followed up in 1870 by Tischendorf's Responsa ad Calumnias Romanas, &c., the tone of which pamphlet we cannot highly praise.

[3] This practice is plainly confessed to in the Preface to the volume of 1881 (p. xvi) without any consciousness of the fatal mistake which it involves: 'Facies libri Vaticani repraesentata est [ut] ea primum omnia apparerent, quae a priore codicis notario profecta adhuc manifesto perspiciuntur, tum ea tantum a posterioribus sive emendatoribus, sive instauratoribus commutata addorentur, quae sine scripturae confusione legi possent.'

in the margin or between the lines which Tischendorf asserts to belong mostly to B^3, a few to B^2.[1]

At length, after baffling delays only too readily accounted for by the public calamities of the Papal state, the concluding volume of this sumptuous and important work was published late in 1881. Sergius had now retired through failing eyesight, and his place was taken by 'Henricus Canonicus Fabiani,' Cozza (who is now Abbot of the Grotta Ferrata at Tusculum near Frascati, the chief seat of the monks of the Greek order of St. Basil) still holding the second place. From the laudatory tone in which the latter is spoken of (p. xiv), it would seem that the Preface was written by his new colleague, who acknowledges the help of U. Ubaldi and the Basilian monk Ant. Rocchi, all three 'adjutoribus et administris miratis equidem se tantis viris adjutores et successores datos' (p. xv). This Preface consists of twenty-two pages, and contains almost nothing that is interesting to the critic, much that displays superficial and newly-acquired acquaintance with the whole subject. Fabiani assigns the end of the fourth century as the date of the manuscript, regarding it as only a few years older than the Sinaitic copy [2], whose discovery he

[1] In 1 Cor. vii. 29 Vercellone joins ἐστιν and το closely, but Tischendorf leaves a space between them, with a middle point, which he expressly states to be *primâ manu*. Again, in ver. 34 Vercellone joins μεμερισται with the following και. Tischendorf in 1867 (but not in his last edition of the N. T.) interposes a point and space. In these *minutiae* Vercellone, who was not working against time, may be presumed to be the more accurate of the two. The editors of the sixth volume have no note at either place. Tischendorf detects an error of Vercellone, ειτε for ειχε Heb. ix. 1, but this has been corrected by the hand in some copies of the Roman volume, as also in the Commentary.

[2] His reasons for regarding the Sinaitic manuscript as the younger (*see* p. 89, note 2) are valid enough so far as they go (Praef. p. vi): its initial letters stand out more from the line of the writing; abridgements of words are fewer and less simple; it contains the Ammonian sections and Eusebian canons instead of the antiquated divisions of its rival, and the text is broken up into smaller paragraphs. Tregelles, who had seen both copies, used to plead the fresher appearance of the Sinaitic, contrasted with the worn look of the Vatican MS.; but then its extensive hiatus proves that the latter had been less carefully preserved.

Eusebius sent to Constantine's new city (Euseb. Vit. Const. Lib. iv) πεντήκοντα σωμάτια ἐν διφθέραις (c. 36)...ἐν πολυτελῶς ἠσκημένοις τεύχεσι τρισσὰ καὶ τετρασσά (c. 37): on which last words Valesius notes, 'Codices enim membranacei ferè per quaterniones digerebantur, hoc est quatuor folia simul compacta, ut terniones tria sunt folia simul compacta. Et quaterniones quidem sedecim habebant paginas, terniones vero duodenas.' But now that we have come to know that Cod. B is arranged in quires of five sheets (*see* p. 105), that manuscript will hardly answer to the description τρισσὰ καὶ τετρασσά (*see* p. 27, note 1)

hails without a vestige of ungenerous jealousy: 'Quorum tale est demum par, ut potius liber Vaticanus gaudere debeat quod tam sui similem invenerit fratrem, quam expavescere quod aemulum' (p. viii). Since that time a splendid edition has been issued of the New Testament in 1889, and the Old in 1890, under the care of the Abbate Cozza-Luzi, in which the whole is beautifully exhibited in photograph: so that all students can now examine for themselves the readings and characteristics of this celebrated manuscript with all but the advantage which is given in an examination of the original vellum itself (Novum Testamentum e Codd. Vat. 1209, &c. Rom. 1889, 4to): and gratitude is due from all textual scholars to the authorities of the Vatican.

Those who agree the most unreservedly respecting the age of the Codex Vaticanus, vary widely in their estimate of its critical value. By some it has been held in such undue esteem that its readings, if probable in themselves, and supported (or even though not supported) by two or three other copies and versions, have been accepted in preference to the united testimony of all

as Cod. ℵ does. Indeed Canon Cook (Revised Version, &c., p. 162) objects to Valesius' explanation altogethor, on the ground that his sense would rather require τριπλόα καὶ τετραπλόα, and that the rare words τρισσά ('three by three') and τετρασσά ('four by four') exactly describe the arrangement of three columns on a page in Cod. B, and four on a page in Cod. ℵ. The Canon has since observed that the same view is maintained by O. von Gebhardt ('Bibel-text' in Herzog's Real-Encyklopädie, Leipsic 1878, second edition). On the other hand Archdeacon Palmer, in an obliging communication made to me, comparing the words πεντήκοντα σωμάτια ἐν διφθέραις ἐγκατασκεύοις (c. 36) with ἐν πολυτελῶς ἠσκημένοις τεύχεσιν τρισσὰ καὶ τετρασσὰ διαπεμψάντων ἡμῶν, and interpreting Eusebius' compliance (c. 37) by means of Constantine's directions (c. 36), is inclined to refer τρισσὰ καὶ τετρασσά to σωμάτια, as if it were 'we sent abroad the collections [of writings] in richly adorned cases, three or four in a case.' It will probably be thought that the expression is on the whole too obscure to be depended on for any controversial purposes. It is safer to argue that if the sections and canons extant in Cod. ℵ be by a contemporary hand (*see* p. 93, and Dean Gwynn's *Memoranda* in our *Addenda* for that page), that circumstance, the great antiquity of the manuscript considered, will confirm the probability of Eusebius' connexion with it. Eusebius agrees also with ℵ in omitting ἡ πύλη, Matt. vii. 13, and knew of copies, not however the best or with his approval, which inserted ἡσαΐου before τοῦ προφήτου in Matt. xiii. 35: ℵ being the only uncial which exhibits that reading. So again Eusebius after Origen maintains the impossible number ἑκατὸν ἑξήκοντα of ℵ and a few others in Luke xxiv. 13. Dr. C. R. Gregory, Prolegomena, pp. 347, 348, inclines to the belief that B and ℵ were among the fifty MSS. sent by Eusebius to Constantine about A.D. 331–2. Canon Cook's entire argument (Revised Version of the First Three Gospels (1882), pp. 160–165) should be consulted.

authorities besides: while others, admitting the interest due to age, have spoken of its text as one of the most vicious extant. Without anticipating what must be discussed hereafter we may say at once, that, while we accord to Cod. B at least as much weight as to any single document in existence, we ought never to forget that it is but one out of many, several of them being nearly (and one quite) as old, and in other respects not less worthy of confidence than itself. One marked feature, characteristic of this copy, is the great number of its omissions, which has induced Dr. Dobbin to speak of it as presenting 'an abbreviated text of the New Testament:' and certainly the facts he states on this point are startling enough [1]. He calculates that Codex B leaves out words or whole clauses no less than 330 times in Matthew, 365 in Mark, 439 in Luke, 357 in John, 384 in the Acts, 681 in the surviving Epistles; or 2,556 times in all. That no small proportion of these are mere oversights of the scribe seems evident from the circumstance that this same scribe has repeatedly written words and clauses *twice over*, a class of mistakes which Mai and the collators have seldom thought fit to notice, inasmuch as the false addition has not been retraced by the second hand, but which by no means enhances our estimate of the care employed in copying this venerable record of primitive Christianity [2]. Hug and others have referred the origin of Codex B to Egypt, but (unlike in this respect to Codex A) its history does not confirm their conjecture, and the argument derived from orthography or grammatical forms, is now well understood to be but slight and ambiguous [3]. Dr. Hort, on no very substantial

[1] Dublin University Magazine, Nov. 1859, p. 620. Even Bishop Lightfoot, a strong and consistent admirer of the manuscript, speaks of its 'impatience of apparently superfluous words' (Epistle to the Colossians, p. 316). Dr. Hort (Introduction, p. 235) pleads that such facts 'have no bearing on either the merits or the demerits of the scribe of B, except as regards the absolutely singular readings of B,' whereas multitudes of these omissions are found in other good documents.

[2] Dean Burgon cites four specimens of such repetitions: Matt. xxi. 4, five words written twice over; ib. xxvi. 56–7, six words; Luke i. 37, three words or one line; John xvii. 18, six words. These, however, are but a few out of many. Nor is Tischendorf's judgement at variance with our own. Speaking of some supposed or possible gross *errata* of the recent Roman edition, he puts in the significant proviso 'tamen haec quoque satis cum universâ scripturae Vaticanae vitiositate conveniunt' (Appendix N. T. Vaticani, 1869, p. xvii).

[3] The latest Roman editors incline to an Egyptian origin, rather than one suggested in Magna Graecia, but the only fresh reason they allege can have very slight weight, namely, that two of the damaged leaves have been repaired by

(24)

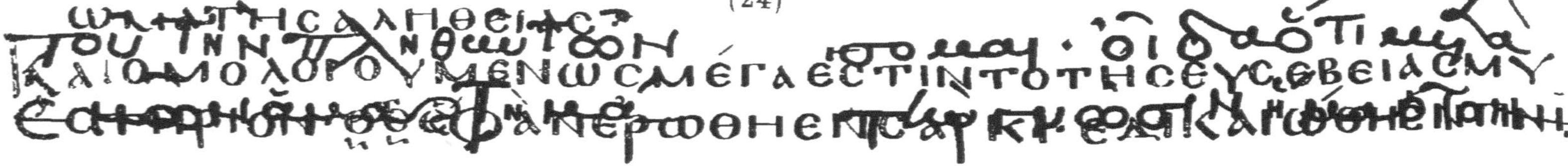

(25)

RECEKE
ECCLESIAM
DOMINI

B Θ Φ

ΠΟΙΜΕΝΕΙΝ
ΤΗΝΕΚΚΛΗΣΙΑΝ
ΤΟΥΚΥ

Δ Ξ Ψ

(26)

/Το[a] κατά[b] ματθαίομ[c] άγιομ[d] ευαγγέλιομ. Cap. I.

ίβλος[b] γενέσεως[c] ιησού[d] χρισ=
τού[e] υιού[f] δαυίδ[g] υιού[h] αβραάμ.
[i] αβραάμ[k] εγέμμησε/τομ[l] ισαάκ.[m] ι=
σαάκ[n] δε[o] εγέμμησε/τομ[p] ιακώβ.[q] ια=
κώβ[r] δε[s] εγέμμησε/τομ[t] ιουδαμ,
[u] και/τους[x] αδελφούς[y] αυτού.[z] ιούδας[a] δε[b] εγεμ=
μησε/τομ[c] φαρές[d] και/τομ[e] ζαρά[f] εκ/της[g] θάμαρ.

[b] Euangelium[a] scdm[b] Mattheu. Cap. j.

Jber[b] gñatiõis[c] iesu[d] chri
sti[e] filij[f] dauid[g] filij[h] abraã.
[i] Abraã[k] genuit[l] ysaac.[m] J
saac[n] aũt[o] genuit[p] iacob.[q] Ja
cob[r] aũt[s] genuit[t] iudam:
[u] et[x] fratres[y] eius.[z] Judas[a] autem[b] genuit
[c] phares[d] et[e] zaram[f] de[g] thamar.

grounds, is 'inclined to surmise that B and ℵ were both written in the West, probably at Rome' (Introduction, pp. 265–7).

C. CODEX EPHRAEMI, No. 9, in the Royal Library of Paris, is a most valuable palimpsest containing portions of the Septuagint version of the Old Testament on sixty-four leaves, and fragments of every part of the New on 145 leaves, amounting on the whole to less than two-thirds of the volume [1]. This manuscript seems to have been brought from the East by Andrew John Lascar [d. 1535], a learned Greek patronized by Lorenzo de' Medici; it once belonged to Cardinal Nicolas Ridolphi of that family, was brought into France by Queen Catherine de' Medici of evil memory, and so passed into the Royal Library at Paris [2]. The ancient writing is barely legible, having been almost removed about the twelfth century to receive some Greek works of St. Ephraem, the great Syrian Father [299–378]. A chemical preparation applied at the instance of Fleck in 1834, though it revived much that was before illegible, has defaced the vellum with stains of various colours, from green and blue to black and brown. The older writing was first noticed by Peter Allix

pieces of papyrus. The learned Ceriani of Milan believes that Cod. B was written in Italy, Cod. ℵ in Palestine or Syria (Quarterly Review, April, 1882, p. 355). The supposed Eusebian origin of both has been already stated.

[1] As this manuscript is of first-rate importance it is necessary to subjoin a full list of the passages it contains, that it may not be cited *e silentio* for what it does not exhibit: Matt. i. 2—v. 15; vii. 5—xvii. 26; xviii. 28—xxii. 20; xxiii. 17—xxiv. 10; xxiv. 45—xxv. 30; xxvi. 22—xxvii. 11; xxvii. 47—xxviii. 14: Mark i. 17—vi. 31; viii. 5—xii. 29; xiii. 19—xvi. 20: Luke i. 2—ii. 5; ii. 42—iii. 21; iv. 25—vi. 4; vi. 37—vii. 16 or 17; viii. 28—xii. 3; xix. 42—xx. 27; xxi. 21—xxii. 19; xxiii. 25—xxiv. 7; xxiv. 46–53: John i. 1–41; iii. 33—v. 16; vi. 38—vii. 3; viii. 34—ix. 11; xi. 8–46; xiii. 8—xiv. 7; xvi. 21—xviii. 36; xx. 26—xxi. 25: Acts i. 2—iv. 3; v. 35—x. 42; xiii. 1—xvi. 36; xx. 10—xxi. 30; xxii. 21—xxiii. 18; xxiv. 15—xxvi. 19; xxvii. 16—xxviii. 4: James i. 1—iv. 2: 1 Pet. i. 2—iv. 6: 2 Pet. i. 1—1 John iv. 2: 3 John 3–15: Jude 3–25: Rom. i. 1—ii. 5; iii. 21—ix. 6; x. 15—xi. 31; xiii. 10—1 Cor. vii. 18; ix. 6—xiii. 8; xv. 40—2 Cor. x. 8: Gal. i. 20—vi. 18: Eph. ii. 18—iv. 17: Phil. i. 22—iii. 5: Col. i. 1—1 Thess. ii. 9: Heb. ii 4—vii. 26; ix. 15—x. 24; xii. 15—xiii. 25: 1 Tim. iii. 9—v. 20; vi. 21—Philem. 25: Apoc. i. 2—iii. 19; v. 14—vii. 14; vii. 17—viii. 4; ix. 17—x. 10; xi. 3—xvi. 13; xviii. 2—xix. 5. Of all the books only 2 John and 2 Thess. are entirely lost; about thirty-seven chapters of the Gospels, ten of the Acts, forty-two of the Epistles, eight of the Apocalypse have perished. The order of the books is indicated, p. 74.

[2] The following Medicean manuscripts seem to have come into the Royal Library by the same means; Evan. 16, 19, 42, 317. Act. 12, 126. Paul. 164. It appears therefore that Cod. C was not one of the manuscripts bought of Marshal Strozzi (Pattison, Life of Is. Casaubon, p. 202), which were only 800 out of the 4,500 which belonged to the Queen (ibid. p. 204).

nearly two centuries ago; various readings extracted from it were communicated by Boivin to Kuster, who published them (under the notation of Paris 9) in his edition of Mill's N.T., 1710. A complete collation of the New Testament was first made in 1716 by Wetstein, then very young, for Bentley's projected edition, for which labour (as he records the fact himself) he paid Wetstein £50. This collation Wetstein of course used for his own Greek Testament of 1751–2, and though several persons subsequently examined the manuscript, and so became aware that more might be gathered from it, it was not until 1843 that Tischendorf brought out at Leipsic his full and noble edition of the New Testament portion; the Old Testament he published in 1845. Although Tischendorf complains of the typographical errors made in his absence in the former of these two volumes, and has corrected them in the other, they probably comprise by far the most masterly production of this nature up to that date published; it is said too that none but those who have seen Codex C can appreciate the difficulty of deciphering some parts of it [1], in fact, whatever is not patent at first sight. The Prolegomena are especially valuable; the uncial type does not aim at being an imitation, but the facsimile faithfully represents the original, even to the present colour of the ink. In shape Codex C is about the size of Cod. A, but not quite so tall; its vellum is hardly so fine as that of Cod. A and a few others, yet sufficiently good. In this copy there is but one column in a page, which contains from forty to forty-six lines (usually forty-one), the characters being a little larger than those of either A or B, and somewhat more elaborate [2]. Thus the points at the ends of *sigma*, *epsilon*, and especially of the horizontal line of *tau*, are more decided than in Codex A; *delta*, though not so fully formed as in later books, is less simple than in A, the strokes being of less equal thickness, and the base more

[1] Bp. Chr. Wordsworth (N. T. Part iv. p. 159) reminds us of Wetstein's statement (Bentley's Correspondence, p. 501) that it had cost him two hours to read one page; so that his £50 were not so easily earned, after all. This collation is preserved in Trinity College Library, B. xvii. 7, 9.

[2] Dr. Hort, with his ever ready acuteness, draws certain inferences to be discussed hereafter from the fact that a displacement in the leaves of the exemplar wherefrom the Apocalypse in Cod. C was copied, which the scribe of C did not notice, proves it to have been a book of nearly 120 small leaves, and accordingly that it 'formed a volume either to itself or without considerable additions' (Introduction, p. 268).

ornamented. On the other hand, *alpha* and *pi* are nearer the model of Codex B. *Iota* and *upsilon*, which in Cod. A and many other copies have two dots over them when they commence a syllable, and are sometimes found with one dot, have here a small straight line in their place (*see* p. 36). There are no breathings or accents by the first hand: the apostrophus is found but rarely, chiefly with Proper names, as $\overline{\delta\alpha\delta}$'. The uncial writing is continuous; the punctuation of Cod. C, like that of A and B, consisting only of a single point, mostly but not always put level with the top of the preceding letter; wherever such a point was employed, a space of one letter broad was usually left vacant: these points are most common in the later books of the N.T. The *κεφάλαια* are not placed in the upper margin of the page as in Cod. A, but a list of their *τίτλοι* preceded each Gospel: the so-called Ammonian sections stand in the margin, but not at present the Eusebian canons; though, since lines of the text written in vermilion have been thoroughly washed out, the canons (for which that colour was commonly employed) may easily have shared the same fate (*see* p. 61). There is no trace of chapters in the Acts, Epistles, or Apocalypse, and both the titles and subscriptions to the various books are very simple. Capital letters are used quite as freely as in Cod. A, both at the commencement of the (Ammonian) sections, and in many other places. All these circumstances taken together indicate for Cod. C as early a date as the fifth century, though there is no sufficient cause for deeming it at all older than Cod. A. Alexandria has been assigned as its native country, for the very insufficient reasons stated when we were describing A and B. It is carefully transcribed, and of its great critical value there is no doubt; its text seems to stand nearly midway between A and B, somewhat inclining to the latter. Two correctors have been very busily at work on Cod. C, greatly to the perplexity of the critical collator: they are respectively indicated by Tischendorf as C**, C***. The earliest, or the second hand, may have been of the sixth century, and his corrections are for some cause regarded by Dr. Hort as almost equally valuable for critical purposes with the manuscript itself: the second corrector, or the third hand, is perhaps of the ninth century, and he revised such portions as were adapted to ecclesiastical use, inserting many accents, the *rough* breathing, and some vocal notes. By him or more probably by a fourth hand (who did not change the text, but added some liturgical directions in the margin) small crosses were interpolated as stops, agreeably to the fashion of their times.

D OF THE GOSPELS AND ACTS, CODEX BEZAE GRAECO-LATINUS, belongs to the University Library at Cambridge, where the open volume is conspicuously exhibited to visitors in the New Building (Nn. II. 41). It was presented to the University in 1581 by Theodore Beza, for whom and his master Calvin the heads of that learned body then cherished a veneration which already boded ill for the peace of the English Church [1]. Between the Gospels (whose order was spoken of above, pp. 72–4) and the Acts, the Catholic Epistles once stood, of which only a few verses remain in the Latin translation (3 John ver. 11–15), followed by the words 'epistulae Johannis III explicit, incipit actus apostolorum,' as if St. Jude's Epistle were displaced or wanting. There are not a few hiatus both in the Greek and Latin texts [2]. The contents of this remarkable document were partially made known by numerous extracts from it, under the designation of β′, in the margin of Robert Stephen's Greek Testament of 1550, whose account of it is that it was collated for him in Italy by his friends (τὸ δὲ β′ ἐστὶ τὸ ἐν Ἰταλίᾳ ὑπὸ τῶν ἡμετέρων ἀντιβληθὲν φίλων. Epistle to the Reader) [3]. It is not very easy to reconcile this statement with Beza's account pre-

[1] Very remarkable is the language of the University in returning thanks for the gift: 'Nam hoc scito, post unicae scripturae sacratissimam cognitionem, nullos unquam ex omni memoriâ temporum scriptores extitisse, quos memorabili viro Johanni Calvino tibique praeferamus.' Scrivener's Codex Bezae, Introd. p. vi.

[2] Matt. i. 1–20; vi. 20—ix. 2; xxvii. 2–12: John i. 16—iii. 26: Acts viii. 29—x. 14; xxi. 2–10; 15–18 (though Ussher, Mill, Wetstein and Dickinson cite several readings from these verses, which must have been extant in their time); xxii. 10–20; 29—xxviii. 31 in the *Greek:* Matt. i. 1–11; vi. 8—viii. 27; xxvi. 65—xxvii. 1: John i. 1—iii. 16: Acts viii. 20—x. 4; xx. 31—xxi. 2; 7–10; xxii. 2–10; xxii. 20—xxviii. 31 in the *Latin.* The original writing has perished in the following, which are supplied by a scribe of not earlier than the ninth century: Matt. iii. 7–16: Mark xvi. 15–20: John xviii. 14—xx. 13 in the *Greek:* Matt. ii. 21—iii. 7: Mark xvi. 6–20: John xviii. 2—xx. 1 in the *Latin.* A fragment, containing a few words of Matt. xxvi. 65–67 (Latin) and xxvii. 2 (Greek), (Fol. 96, Scrivener), was overlooked by Kipling.

[3] It is surprising that any one should have questioned the identity of Cod. D with Stephen's β′. No other manuscript has been discovered which agrees with β′ in the many singular readings and arbitrary additions in support of which it is cited by Stephen. That he omitted so many more than he inserted is no argument against their identity, since we know that he did the same in the

(41)

ΟΥΚΑCΧΗΜΟΝΕΙ
ΟΥΖΗΤΕΙΤΑΕΑΥΤΗC
ΟΥΠΑΡΟΞΥΝΕΤΑΙ
ΟΥΛΟΓΙΖΕΤΑΙΤΟΚΑΚΟΝ
ΟΥΧΑΙΡΕΙΕΠΙΤΗΑΔΙΚΙΑ
CΥΓΧΑΙΡΕΙΔΕΤΗΑΛΗΘΕΙΑ
ΠΑΝΤΑCΤΕΓΕΙ
ΠΑΝΤΑΠΙCΤΕΥΕΙ
ΠΑΝΤΑΕΛΠΙΖΕΙ
ΠΑΝΤΑΥΠΟΜΕΝΕΙ
ΗΑΓΑΠΗ
ΟΥΔΕΠΟΤΕΕΚΠΙΠΤΕΙ +

ΚΑΤ ΙΩΑΝ

(42)

ΗΜΕΝΩΝΠΟΙΩΘΑΝΑΤΩΔΟΞΑCΕΙΤΟΝΘΝ
ΚΑΙΤΟΥΤΟΕΙΠΩΝΛΕΓΕΙΑΥΤΩΑΚΟΛΟΥΘΕΙΜΟΙ
ΕΠΙCΤΡΑΦΕΙCΔΕΟΠΕΤΡΟCΒΛΕΠΕΙΤΟΝΜΑΘΗΤΗΝ
ΟΝΗΓΑΠΑΙΗC ΑΚΟΛΟΥΘΟΥΝΤΑ
ΟCΚΑΙΑΝΕΠΕCΕΝΕΝΤΩΔΕΙΠΝΩ
ΕΠΙΤΟCΤΗΘΟCΑΥΤΟΥ ΚΑΙΕΙΠΕΝΑΥΤΩ
ΚΕ ΤΙCΕCΤΙΝΟΠΑΡΑΔΙΔΩΝCΕ
ΤΟΥΤΟΝΟΥΝΕΙΔΩΝΟΠΕΤΡΟCΛΕΓΕΙΑΥΤΩΙΗΥ·
ΚΕ ΟΥΤΟCΔΕΤΙ · ΛΕΓΕΙΑΥΤΩΟΙΗC
ΕΑΝΑΥΤΟΝΘΕΛΩΜΕΝΕΙΝΟΥΤΩC
ΕΩCΕΡΧΟΜΑΙΤΙΠΡΟCCΕ CΥΜΟΙΑΚΟΛΟΥΘΕΙ
ΕΞΗΛΘΕΝΟΥΝΟΥΤΟCΟΛΟΓΟCΕΙCΤΟΥC

NONAMBITIOSAEST
NONQUAERITQUAESUASUNT
NONINRITATUR
NONCOGITATMALUM
NONGAUDETSUPERINIQUITATEM
CONGAUDETAUTEMUERITATI
OMNIASUFFERIT
OMNIACREDIT
OMNIASPERAT
OMNIASUSTENET
CARITAS
NUMQUAMEXCIDET

SEC. IOHAN.

(43)

ΠΟΝΗΡΟΥΟΤΙ
ϹΟΥΕϹΤΙΝΗΒΑ
ϹΙΛΕΙΑΚΑΙΗΔΥ
ΝΑΜΙϹΚΑΙΗΔΟ
ΞΑΕΙϹΤΟΥϹΑΙΩ
ΝΑϹΑΜΗΝ·
ΕΑΝΓΑΡΑΦΗΤΕ
Mt 6 ΤΟΙϹΑΝΟΙϹΤΑ
ΠΑΡΑΠΤΩΜΑΤΑ

SIGNIFICANSQUAMORTEHONORIFICABITDM
HOCCUMDIXISSETDICITILLISEQUEREME
CONUERSUSAUTEMPETRUSUIDETDISCIPULUM
QUEMDILIGEBATIHSSEQUENTEM
QUIETRECUBUITINCENA
SUPERPECTUSEIUS ETDIXITILLI
DMEQUISESTQUITRADIDITTE
HUNCERGOUIDENSPETRUSDICITADIHM
DMEHICAUTEMQUID· DICITILLIIHS
SIEUMUOLOSICMANERE
USQUEDUMUENIOQUIDADTETUMESEQUERE
EXIUITERGOHICUERBUS APUTFRATRES

fixed to the manuscript and still extant in his own cramped handwriting, wherein he alleges that he obtained the volume in 1562 from the monastery of St. Irenaeus at Lyons ('oriente ibi civili bello'), where it had long lain buried ('postquam ibi in pulvere diu jacuisset'). This great city, it must be remembered, was sacked in that very year by the infamous Des Adrets, whom it suited to espouse for a while the cause of the Huguenots; and we can hardly doubt that some one who had shared in the plunder of the abbey[1] conveyed this portion of it to Beza, whose influence at that juncture was paramount among the French Reformed[2].

case of his α′ (the Complutensian Polyglott) and η′ (Codex L, Paris 62). The great inaccuracy of Stephen's *margin* (the text is much better revised) is so visible from these and other well-ascertained instances that no one ought to wonder if β′ is alleged occasionally (not often) for readings which D does not contain. On a careful analysis of all the variations imputed to β′ by Stephen, they will be found to amount to 389 in the parts written in the original hand, whereof 309 are alleged quite correctly, forty-seven a little loosely, while in eight instances corrected readings are regarded in error as from the original scribe. Of the twenty-five places which remain, all but three had been previously discovered in other copies used by Stephen, so that β′ in their case has been substituted by mistake for some other numeral. One of the three remaining has recently been accounted for by Mr. A. A. Vansittart, who has found καὶ περισσευθήσεται added to δοθήσεται αὐτῷ (Luke viii. 18 from Matt. xiii. 12) in Stephen's θ′ or Coislin 200 at Paris (No. 38, of the Gospels). I do not find β′ cited by Stephen after Acts xx. 24, except indeed in Rom. iii. 10 (with α′), in manifest error, just as in the Apocalypse xix. 14 ε′ (No. 6 of the Gospels), which does not contain this book, is cited instead of ιε′; or as ια′ is quoted in xiii. 4, *but not elsewhere in the Apocalypse*, undoubtedly in the place of ιϛ′; or as ιϛ′, which had broken off at xvii. 8, reappears instead of ιε′ in xx. 3. In the various places named in the last note, wherein the Greek of Cod. D is lost, β′ is cited only at Matt. xxvii. 3, beyond question instead of η′; and for *part* of the reading in Acts ix. 31, δ′ (to which the whole rightly belongs) being alleged for the other part. In John xix. 6, indeed, where the original Greek is missing, β′ is cited, but it is for a reading actually extant in the modern hand which has there supplied Codex D's defects.

[1] 'Ils s'emparèrent des portes et de tous les lieux forts . . . non pas sans leur impiétés et barbaries accoutumées envers les choses saintes' (Mézeray, Hist. de France, tom. iii. p. 87, 1685). Accordingly, travellers are shown to this day the bones of unclean animals which the Huguenots, in wanton mockery, then mingled with the presumed remains of St. Irenaeus and tho martyrs of Lyons.

[2] One cannot understand why Wetstein (N. T. Proleg. vol. i, 30) should have supposed that Beza *prevaricated* as to the means whereby he procured his manuscript. He was not the man to be at all ashamed of spoiling the Philistines, and the bare mention of Lyons in connexion with the year 1562 would have been abundantly intelligible scarce twenty years afterwards. It is however remarkable that in the last edition of his Annotations (1598) he nowhere calls it Codex Lugdunensis, but *Claromontanus* (notes on Luke xix. 26; Acts xx. 3); for, though it might be natural that Beza, at eighty years of age and after the

Beza in his editions of the Greek Testament published in 1582, 1589, and 1598, made some occasional references to the readings of his manuscript. Archbishop Whitgift borrowed it from Cambridge in 1583, and caused a poor transcript to be made of its Greek text, which he bequeathed to Trinity College (whereof he had been Master), in whose Library it still remains (B. x. 3).

Patrick Young, of whom we have heard in connexion with Cod. A (p. 103 and note 1), sent extracts from Cod. D to the brothers Dupuy at Paris, through whom they reached Morinus and Steph. Curcellaeus. An unusually full collation was made for Walton's Polyglott (Tom. vi, Num. xvi, 1657) by pious Archbishop Ussher, who devoted to these studies the doleful leisure of his latter years. Mill collated and Wetstein transcribed (1716) this document for their great editions of the Greek Testament, but they both did their work carelessly; and though Bentley was allowed to keep it at home for seven years, his notices of its readings, as represented by Mr. Ellis (Bentleii Critica Sacra, pp. 2–26), or preserved in Stephen's N.T. of 1549 (Trin. Coll. B. xvii. 4), were put to no practical use. The best collation by far was made about 1732 by John Dickinson of St. John's College for John Jackson of Leicester, with whose other books it came into Jesus College Library (O. θ. 2), where it has lain neglected. But a manuscript replete as this is with variations from the sacred text beyond all other example could be adequately represented only by being published in full; a design entrusted by the University of Cambridge to Dr. Thomas Kipling, Senior Wrangler in 1768 and afterwards Dean of Peterborough [d. 1822], whose 'Codex Theodori Bezae Cantabrigiensis' 1793, 2 vols. fol. (in type imitating the original handwriting much more closely than in Cod. A and the rest), is a not unfaithful transcript of the text[1],

lapse of so long a time, should confound the Lyons copy with his own Codex Claromontanus of St. Paul's Epistles (D); yet the only way in which we can account for the Codex Bezae being collated in *Italy* for Stephen, is by adopting Wetstein's suggestion that it was the actual copy ('antiquissimum codicem Graecum') taken to the Council of Trent in 1546 by William a Prato, Bishop of *Clermont* in Auvergne, to confirm the Latin reading in John xxi. 22 '*sic* eum volo,' which D alone may seem to do. Some learned man (*ὑπὸ τῶν ἡμετέρων φίλων* does not well suit his son Henry) might have sent to Robert Stephen from Tren the readings of a manuscript to which attention had been thus specially directed.

[1] Not more than eighty-three typographical errors have been detected in

though the Prolegomena too plainly testify to the editor's pitiable ignorance of sacred criticism, while his habit of placing the readings of the several later hands (very loosely distinguished from each other) in the text, and those of the first hand in the notes (a defect we have also noted in the Roman editions of Cod. B), renders his volumes very inconvenient for use. Let Kipling be praised for the care and exact diligence his work evinces, but Herbert Marsh [1757–1839] was of all Cambridge men of that period the only one known to be competent for such a task. In 1864 the present writer was aided by the Syndics of the Cambridge Press in publishing an edition of Codex Bezae in common type, illustrated by a copious Introduction and critical notes, to which work the reader is referred for fuller information respecting this manuscript.

The Codex Bezae is a quarto volume 10 inches high by 8 broad, with one column on a page, the Greek text and its Latin version being parallel, the Greek on the left, or *verso* of each leaf, and the Latin on the right, opposite to it, on the *recto* of the next. Notwithstanding the Alexandrian forms that abound in it as much as in any other copy, and which have been held by some to prove the Egyptian origin of Codd. ABC, the fact of its having a Latin version sufficiently attests its Western origin. The vellum is not quite equal in fineness to that of a few others. There are thirty-three lines in every page, and these of unequal length, as this manuscript is arranged in *στίχοι*, being the earliest in date that is so (*see* p. 53). The Latin is placed in the same line and as nearly as possible in the same order as the corresponding Greek. It has not the larger *κεφάλαια* or Eusebian canons, but only the so-called Ammonian sections, often incorrectly placed, and obviously in a later hand of about the ninth century. The original absence of these divisions is no proof that the book was not at first intended for ecclesiastical use (as some have stated), inasmuch as the sections and canons were constructed for a very different purpose (*see above*, pp. 59–63), but is another argument for its being copied in the West, perhaps not far from the place where it rested so long. Other proofs of its Occidental, perhaps of its Gallican origin, especially that derived from the style of the Latin version, are

Kipling throughout his difficult task, whereof sixteen are in his Annotations, &c.

collected in Scrivener's edition (Introd. pp. xxxi, xl—xlv). The characters are of the same size as in C, larger on the whole than in AB, but betray a later age than any of those, although the Latin as well as the Greek is written continuously, excepting that in the titles and subscriptions of the several books (as in Codd. DH of St. Paul) the words are separated. This copy has paragraph divisions of unequal length peculiar to itself[1]. They are indicated by placing the initial letter out in the margin, that letter being usually of the same size with the rest, though sometimes a little larger. Cod. D appears to be the earliest which exhibits larger letters after a pause in the middle of a line; but these are not very frequent. Instances of each case may be noticed in our facsimile (No. 42), wherein the shapes of *kappa*, *rho* and *phi*, as indicated before (pp. 32, note 1, 37, 39), are very observable. The Greek and Latin writing on the opposite pages are much like each other in appearance, the Latin letters being round and flowing, not square as in codices a little earlier in date, such as the Medicean and Vatican fragments of Virgil. This manuscript has been corrected, first by the original penman with a light stroke made by a pen nearly empty; after him by not less than eight or nine different revisers, some nearly coeval with the Codex itself, others not many centuries old. The changes they have made, especially when they employed a knife to scrape away the primitive reading, render too many places almost illegible. The first scribe often used a sponge to wash out his error before the ink was well dried in (*see* p. 27). In addition to the single point about three-fourths of the height of a letter up, which often subdivides the στίχοι in both languages (facsimile, No. 42, l. 9) the coarse late hand which inserted the Ammonian sections placed double dots (:) after the numerals, and often inserted similar points in the text, before or over the first letter of a section. Each member of the genealogy in Luke iii forms a separate στίχος, as in Cod. B: quotations are indicated by throwing the commencement of the lines which contain them, both Greek and Latin, about an inch back or less

[1] In St. Luke 136 (143 Lat.): in what remains of St. Matthew 583 (590 Lat.), of St. Mark 148, of St. John 165 (168 Lat.), of the Acts 285. The later παραγραφαί, indicated by ʃ (*see* p. 51, note 3), though forty-five out of the forty-nine are firmly and neatly made, and often resemble in colour the ink of the original scribe, can be shown to be full four centuries later (Scrivener, Cod. Bezae, Introd. p. xxviii).

(e.g. Matt. xxvi. 31; Mark i. 2, 3; Acts ii. 34, 35; iv. 25, 26). The first three lines of each book, in both languages, were written in bright red ink, which was also employed in the alternate lines of the subscriptions, and in other slight ornaments. The traces of the scribe's needle and lines (*see* p. 27) are very visible, the margin ample, and the volume on the whole in good keeping, though its first extant page (Latin) is much decayed, and it is stained in parts by some chemical mixture that has been applied to it. The portions supplied by a later hand are of course in the uncial Greek and cursive Latin characters usual at the dates assigned to them. The liturgical notes in the margin of the Saturday and Sunday lessons (*αυναγνοσμα* is the form often used) are in thick letters, of a yet later date than the Ammonian sections. A few others for the great Feasts and Fast days occur; and, in a hand of about the twelfth century, lessons for the Festivals of St. George and St. Dionysius, the patron saints of England and France, as may be seen in the table of Menology.

The vellum employed for Codex Bezae is arranged in quires of four sheets (or eight leaves) each even throughout[1], the numeral signatures of which are set *primâ manu* so low down in the margin at the foot of the last page of each, that they are mostly cut off, in whole or partly, by the binder. Assuming that it ended with the Acts of the Apostles, it originally consisted of upwards of sixty-four (probably of sixty-seven) quires, of which the first, forty-fourth, and sixty-fourth, have each lost some leaves, the thirty-fourth is entire though containing but six leaves, while those signed Γ (3), IΔ (14), KB (22), ME (45), down to NB (52), NZ (57), and all after ΞΔ (64), are wholly wanting. The result is that out of the 534 leaves it originally contained, only 406 now survive, about twelve of them being more or less mutilated. It is not easy to surmise what may have been written on the sixty-seven leaves that intervened between MΔ 5 and NΓ 1; the gap ends with 3 John ver. 11

[1] Bradshaw (Prothero's Memoirs, p. 97) in a letter to the *Guardian*, Jan. 28, 1863, writes thus:—'I saw Cod. ℵ at Leipsig *per* Tischendorf. I had been curious to know whether it was written in even quaternions throughout, like the Cod. Bezae, or in a series of fasciculi, each ending with a quire of varying size, like the Cod. Alexandrinus, and I found the latter to be the case. This, by-the-bye, is sufficient to prove'—why, is not quite clear—'that it cannot be the volume which Dr. Simonides speaks of having written at Mount Athos.'

(Greek), but the space is apparently too great for the Catholic Epistles alone, even though we suppose that Jude was inserted (as appears in some catalogues) otherwise than in the last place. The leaves added by later hands are nine in number. The Greek portion of the supplement to St. John (xviii. 14—xx. 13) much resembles in text the style of the original manuscript, and is often supported by Codd. ℵAB(C). The Latin of this portion is taken from the Vulgate version.

The internal character of the Codex Bezae is a most difficult and indeed an almost inexhaustible theme. No known manuscript contains so many bold and extensive interpolations (six hundred, it is said, in the Acts alone), countenanced, where they are not absolutely unsupported, chiefly by the Old Latin and the Curetonian version: its own parallel Latin translation is too servilely accommodated to the Greek text to be regarded as an independent authority, save where the corresponding Greek is lost.

This passage was penned by Dr. Scrivener before the publication of the highly ingenious treatise by Mr. Rendel Harris, entitled 'A Study of the Codex Bezae' (1891), being the beginning of the second volume of the Cambridge 'Texts and Studies.' Mr. Harris from curious internal evidence, such as the existence in the text of a vitiated rendering of a verse of Homer which bears signs of having been retranslated from a Latin translation, infers that the Greek has been made up from the Latin, and traces the latter to the second century. He shows its affinity with the text of Irenaeus, and discovers traces in it of Montanism. He opens up many points of interest for any one who would examine this 'singular Codex': but injustice must not be done to the fertile author by supposing that in what is evidently 'a Study' he concludes that he has settled all the numerous questions which he broaches. No one however can really investigate the Codex Bezae without studying this work, which will be found both instructive in the highest degree and amusing.

Plate XI.

ΠΡΟCΑΥΤΟΝ. ΠΑCΑΗ ΙΟΥΔΑΙΑ
ΧΩΡΑ. ΚΑΙΟΙΙΕΡΟCΟΛΥΜΙΤΑΙ·
ΚΑΙΕΒΑΠΤΙΖΟΝΤΟΠΑΝΤΕC.
ΕΝΤΩΙΟΡΔΑΝΗΠΟΤΑΜΩΥ
ΠΑΥΤΟΥ. ΕΞΟΜΟΛΟΓΟΥΜΕ
ΝΟΙΤΑCΑΜΑΡΤΙΑCΑΥΤΩΝ·
ΗΝΔΕΟΙΩΑΝΝΗCΕΝΔΕΔΥΜΕΝΟC

(26)

ΚΑΙΠΡΟCΕΦΕΡΟΝ
ΑΥΤΩΠΑΙΔΙΑ
ΙΝΑΑΨΗΤΑΙΑΥ
ΤΩΝ· ΟΙΔΕΜΑΘΗ
ΤΑΙΕΠΕΤΙΜΩΝ

(29)

ΒΛΗΘΗ· ΕΙCΓΕΕΝ
ΝΑΝ· ΤΕΤΗCΛ
ΕΡΡΗΘΗΔΕ· ΟΤΙΟC
ΑΝΑΠΟΛΥCΗΤΗΝ
ΓΥΝΑΙΚΑΑΥΤΟΥ·

(30)

σαντες· καὶ τίς
δύναται σωθῆναι·
ὁ δὲ εἶς εἶπεν·

τούτῳ· καὶ ἐν
τῷ αἰῶνι τῷ ἐρ
χομένῳ ζωὴν

CHAPTER V.

UNCIAL MANUSCRIPTS OF THE GOSPELS.

OF the manuscripts hitherto described, Codd. ℵABC for their presumed critical value, Cod. D for its numberless and strange deviations from other authorities, and all five for their high antiquity, demanded a full description. Of those which follow many contain but a few fragments of the Gospels, and others are so recent in date that they hardly exceed in importance some of the best cursive copies (e.g. FGHS)[1]. None of these need detain us long.

E. Codex Basiliensis (B vi. 21, now A. N. iii. 12) (κεφ. τ., κεφ., *Am.*, *Eus.* at foot of the pages) contains the four Gospels, excepting Luke iii. 4–15; xxiv. 47–53, and was written about the middle of the eighth century, unless (with Dean Burgon) we refer it to the seventh. It measures 9 × 6½ inches, and contains 318 folios. There are 247 folios *verso*, and 71 *recto*[2]. Three leaves (160, 207, 214) on which are Luke i. 69—ii. 4; xii. 58—xiii. 12; xv. 8–20 are in a cursive and later hand, above the obliterated fragments of a homily as old as the main body of the manuscript. There is a 'liber praedicatorum' on the first folio. This copy is one of the most notable of the later uncials, and might well have been published at length. It was given to a religious house in Basle by Cardinal John de Ragusio, who was sent on a mission to the Greeks by the Council of Basle (1431), and probably brought it from Constantinople. Erasmus much overlooked it for later books when preparing his Greek Testament at Basle; indeed it was not brought into the Public Library there before 1559. A collation was sent to Mill by John Battier, Greek Professor at Basle: Mill named it B. I, and truly declared it to

[1] Yet Φ (Beratinus) and Σ (Rossanensis) contain St. Matthew and St. Mark, and are probably a little older than D.

[2] H. C. Hoskier, Collation of Cod. 604, &c. Appendix F. Mr. Hoskier saw the MS. on May 18, 1886.

be 'probatae fidei et bonae notae.' Bengel (who obtained a few extracts from it) calls it Basil. *α*: but its first real collator was Wetstein, whose native town it adorns. Since his time, Tischendorf in 1843, Professor Müller of Basle and Tregelles in 1846, have independently collated it throughout. Judging from the specimen sent to him, Mill (N. T. Proleg. § 1118) thought the hand much like that of Cod. A; the uncial letters (though not so regular or neat) are firm, round, and simple: indeed 'the penmanship is exceedingly tasteful and delicate throughout. The employment of green, blue, and vermilion in the capitals I do not remember to have met with elsewhere' (Burgon, *Guardian*, Jan. 29, 1873). There is but one column of about twenty-four lines on the page; it has breathings and accents pretty uniformly, and not ill placed; otherwise, from the shape of most of the letters (e.g. *pi*, facsimile No. 27, lines 1, 3), it might be judged of earlier date: observe, however, the oblong form of *omicron* where the space is crowded in the last line of the facsimile, when the older scribes would have retained the circular shape and made the letter very small (*see* facsimile No. 11 b. l. 6): *delta* also and *xi* betray a less ancient scribe. The single stop in Cod. E, as was stated above (p. 48), changes its place according to the variation of its power, as in other copies of about the same age. The capitals at the beginning of sections stand out in the margin as in Codd. AC. The lists of the larger κεφάλαια together with the numbers of the sections in the margin and the Eusebian canons beneath them, as well as harmonizing references to the other Gospels at the foot of the page, names of Feast days with their Proper lessons, and other liturgical notices, have been inserted (as some think, but erroneously in Burgon's judgement) by a later hand. Under the text (Mark i. 5, 6) are placed the harmonizing references, in the order (varying in each Gospel) Mark, Luke, John, Matthew. Iω (John) furnishes no parallel on this page. The first section (α) of Mρ (Mark i. 1, 2) corresponds to the seventieth (ο) of Λο (Luke vii. 27), and to the 103rd (ργ) of M (Matt. xi. 10). Again the second (β) of Mark (i. 3) is parallel to the seventh (ϛ) of Luke (iii. 3), and to the eighth (η) of Matt. (iii. 3). The passage given in our facsimile (No. 27) is part of the third (γ) of Mark (i. 4–6), and answers to nothing in Luke, but to the ninth (θ) of Matt. (iii. 4–6). See p. 60, note 4. The value of this codex, as supplying materials for criticism, is considerable. It approaches more nearly than some others of its date to the text now commonly received, and is an excellent witness for it. The asterisk is much used to indicate disputed passages: e.g. Matt. xvi. 2, 3: Luke xxii. 43, 44; xxiii. 34: John viii. 2-11. (For the fragments attached to this Codex, *see* Apoc. 15.)

F. CODEX BOREELI, now in the Public Library at Utrecht, once belonged to John Boreel [d. 1629], Dutch ambassador at the court of King James I. Wetstein obtained some readings from it in 1730, as far as Luke xi, but stated that he knew not where it then was. In 1830 Professor Heringa of Utrecht discovered it in private hands at Arnheim, and procured it for his University Library, where in 1850 Tregelles found it, though with some difficulty, the leaves being torn and all loose in a box, and he then made a facsimile; Tischendorf had looked through it in 1841. In 1843, after Heringa's death, H. E. Vinke published that scholar's 'Disputatio de Codice Boreeliano,' which includes a full and exact collation of the text. Cod. F contains the Four Gospels with many defects, some of which have been caused since the collation was made which Wetstein published: hence the codex must still sometimes be cited on his authority as F^w. In fact there are but 204 leaves and a few fragments remaining, written with two columns of about nineteen lines each on the page, in a tall, oblong, upright form; it was referred by Mr. H. Deane in 1876 to the eighth, by Tischendorf to the ninth, by Tregelles to the tenth century. In St. Luke there are no less than twenty-four gaps: in Wetstein's collation it began at Matt. vii. 6, but now at Matt. ix. 1. Other hiatus are Matt. xii. 1-44; xiii. 55—xiv. 9; xv. 20-31; xx. 18—xxi. 5: Mark i. 43—ii. 8; ii. 23—iii. 5; xi. 6-26; xiv. 54—xv. 5; xv. 39—xvi. 19: John iii. 5-14; iv. 23-38; v. 18-38; vi. 39-63; vii. 28—viii. 10; x. 32—xi. 3; xi. 40—xii. 3; xii. 14-25: it ends at John xiii. 34. Few manuscripts have fallen into such unworthy hands. The Eusebian canons are wanting, the sections standing without them in the margin. Thus in Mark x. 13 (*see* facsimile No. 28) the section *ρϛ* (106) has not under it the proper canon *β* (2). The letters *delta*, *epsilon*, *theta*, *omicron*, and especially the cross-like *psi* (*see* p. 40), are of the most recent uncial form, *phi* is large and bevelled at both ends; the breathings and accents are fully and not incorrectly given.

F[a]. CODEX COISLIN. I is that great copy of the Septuagint Octateuch, the glory of the Coislin Library, first made known by Montfaucon (Biblioth. Coislin., 1715), and illustrated by a facsimile in Silvestre's Paléogr. Univ. No. 65. It contains 227 leaves in two columns, 13 inches by 9: the fine massive uncials of the sixth or seventh century are much like Cod. A's in general appearance. In the margin *primâ manu* Wetstein found Acts ix. 24, 25, and so inserted this as Cod. F in his list of MSS. of the Acts. In 1842 Tischendorf observed nineteen other passages of the New Testament, which he published in his Monumenta sacra inedita (1846, p. 400, &c.) with a facsimile. The texts are Matt. v. 48; xii. 48; xxvii. 25: Luke i. 42; ii. 24; xxiii. 21: John v. 35; vi. 53, 55: Acts iv. 33, 34; ix. 24, 25; x. 13, 15; xxii. 22: 1 Cor. vii. 39; xi. 29: 1 Cor. iii. 13; ix. 7; xi. 33: Gal. iv. 21, 22: Col. ii. 16, 17; Heb. x. 26.

G. COD. HARLEIAN. 5684 or WOLFII A, H. COD. WOLFII B. } These two copies were brought from the East by Andrew Erasmus Seidel, purchased by La Croze, and by him presented to J. C. Wolff, who published loose extracts from them both in his 'Anecdota Graeca' (vol. iii. 1723), and barbarously mutilated them in 1721 in order to send pieces to Bentley, among whose papers in Trinity College Library (B. XVII. 20) Tregelles found the fragments in 1845 (Account of the Printed Text, p. 160). Subsequently Cod. G came with the rest of the Harleian collection into the British Museum; Cod. H, which had long been missing, was brought to light in the Public Library of Hamburg, through Petersen the Librarian, in 1838. Codd. GH have now been thoroughly collated both by Tischendorf and Tregelles. Cod. G appears to be of the tenth, Cod. H of the ninth century, and is stated to be of higher critical value. Besides the mutilated fragments at Trinity College (Matt. v. 29–31; 39–43 of Cod. G; Luke i. 3–6; 13–15 of Cod. H), many parts of both have perished: viz. in Cod. G 372 verses; Matt. i. 1—vi. 6; vii. 25—viii. 9; viii. 23—ix. 2; xxviii. 18—Mark i. 13; xiv. 19–25: Luke i. 1–13; v. 4—vii. 3; viii. 46—ix. 5; xii. 27–41; xxiv. 41–53: John xviii.

(31.)

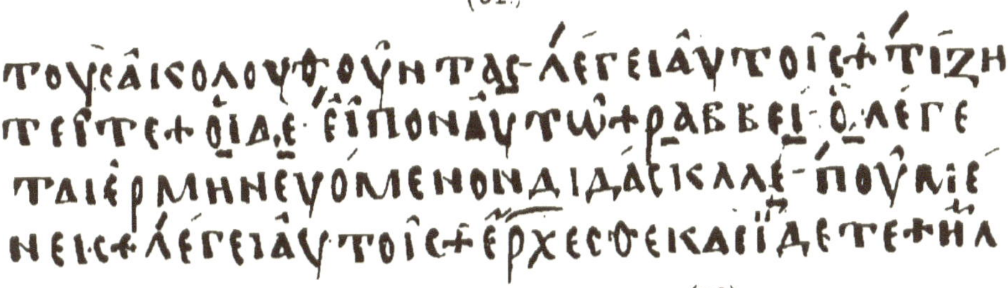

(32.)

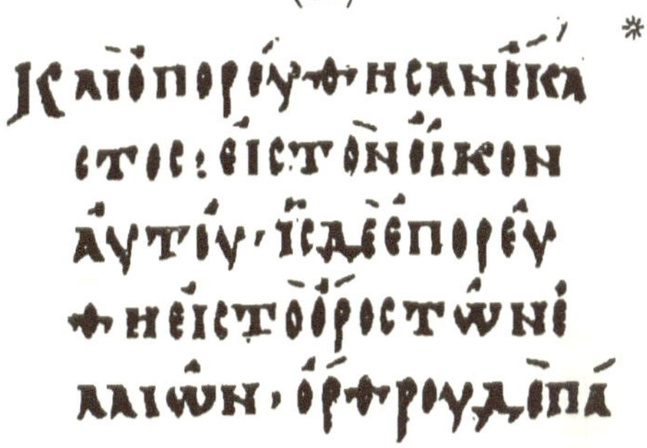

(33)

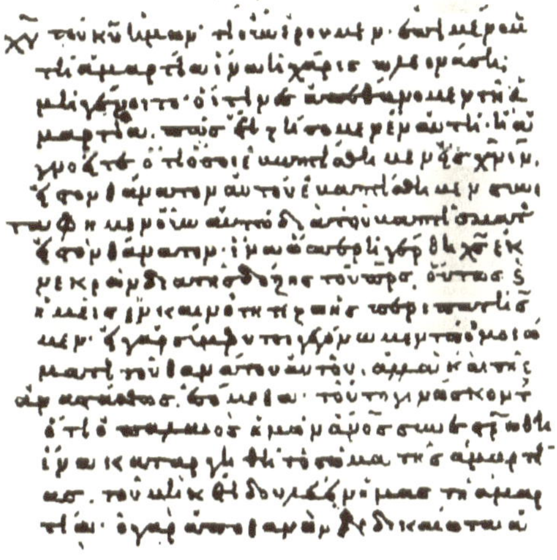

(34)

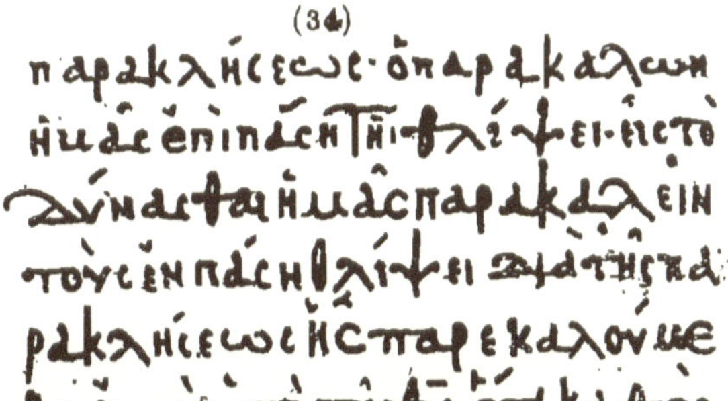

(35)

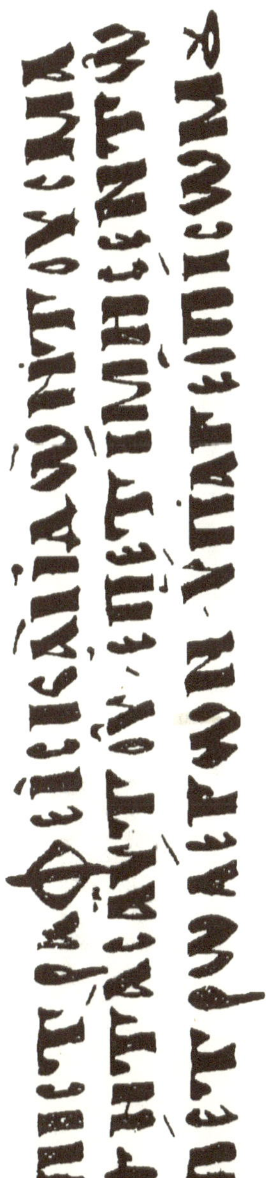

5-19; xix. 4-27 (of which one later hand supplies Matt. xxviii. 18—Mark i. 8: John xviii. 5-19; another Luke xii. 27-41): in Cod. H 679 verses; Matt. i. 1—xv. 30; xxv. 33—xxvi. 3; Mark i. 32—ii. 4; xv. 44—xvi. 14; Luke v. 18-32; vi. 8-22; x. 2-19: John ix. 30—x. 25; xviii. 2-18; xx. 12-25. Cod. G has some Church notes in the margin; Cod. H the sections without the Eusebian canons; G however has both sections and canons; its τίτλοι and larger κεφάλαια are in red (those of St. John being lost), and the Church notes seem *primâ manu*. Each member of the genealogy in Luke iii forms a separate line. Both G and H are written in a somewhat rude style, with breathings and accents rather irregularly placed, as was the fashion of their times; G in two columns of twenty-two lines each on a page, H in one column of twenty-three lines. In each the latest form of the uncial letters is very manifest (e.g. *delta, theta*), but G is the neater of the two. In G the single point, in H a kind of Maltese cross, are the prevailing marks of punctuation. Our facsimiles (Nos. 29 of G, 31 of H) are due to Tregelles; that of G he took from the fragment at Trinity College. Inasmuch as beside Matt. v. 30, 31 in Cod. G ΑΡ with × above (ἀρχή) is conspicuous in the margin, and ΤЄ̂ ΤΗ̄C Λ̄ε (τέλος τῆς λέξεως) stands in the text itself, good scholars may be excused for having mistaken it for a scrap of some Evangelistarium.

I. Cod. Tischendorfian. II at St. Petersburg, consists of palimpsest fragments found by Tischendorf in 1853 'in the dust of an Eastern library,' i.e. in the Convent of St. Saba near the Red Sea, and published in his new series of 'Monumenta sacra inedita,' vol. i, 1855. On the twenty-eight vellum leaves (eight of them on four double leaves) Georgian writing covers the partially obliterated Greek, which is for the most part very hard to read. They compose portions of no less than seven different manuscripts; the first two, of the fifth century, are as old as Codd. AC (the first having scarcely any capital letters and those very slightly larger than the rest); the third fragment seems of the sixth century, nearly of the date of Cod. N (p. 139), about as old as Cod. P (*see* p. 143); the fourth scarcely less ancient: all four, like other palimpsests, have the pseudo-Ammonian sections without the Eusebian canons (*see* p. 61). Of the

Gospels we have 190 verses: viz. (*Frag.* 1 or I_a) John xi. 50—xii. 9; xv. 12—xvi. 2; xix. 11–24: (*Frag.* 2 or I_b) Matt. xiv. 13–16; 19–23; xxiv. 37—xxv. 1; xxv. 32–45; xxvi. 31–45: Mark ix. 14–22; xiv. 58–70: (*Frag.* 3 or I_c) Matt. xvii. 22—xviii. 3; xviii. 11–19; xix. 5–14: Luke xviii. 14–25: John iv. 52—v. 8; xx. 17–26: (*Frag.* 4 or I_d) Luke vii. 39–49; xxiv. 10–19. The fifth fragment (I_e), containing portions of the Acts and of St. Paul's Epistles (1 Cor. xv. 53—xvi. 9: Tit. i. 1–13: Acts xxviii. 8–17) is as old as the third, if not as the first. The sixth and seventh fragments are of the seventh century: viz. (*Frag.* 6 or I_f, *of two leaves*) Acts ii. 6–17; xxvi. 7–18: (*Frag.* 7 or I_g, *of one leaf*) Acts xiii. 39–46. In all seven are 255 verses. All except *Frag.* 6 are in two columns of from twenty-nine to eighteen lines each, and unaccentuated; *Frag.* 6 has but one column on a page, with some accents. The first five fragments, so far as they extend, must be placed in the highest rank as critical authorities. The first, as cited in Tischendorf's eighth edition of his Greek Testament, agrees with Cod. A thirty-four times, four times with Cod. B, and twenty-three times with the two united; it stands alone eleven times. The text of the second and third is more mixed though they incline more to favour Codd. ℵB; not, however, so decidedly as the first does Cod. A. Tischendorf gives us six facsimiles of them in the 'Monumenta sacra inedita,' Nova Collect. vol. i (1885), a seventh in 'Anecdota sacra et profana,' 1855. From the same Armenian book, as Tischendorf thinks (and he was very likely to *know*), are taken the three palimpsest leaves of 2 and 3 Kings, and the six of Isaiah published by him in the same volume of the 'Monumenta.'

I^b. See N^b, below.

K. Cod. Cyprius, or No. 63 of the Royal Library at Paris, shares only with Codd. ℵBMSU the advantage of being a *complete* uncial copy of the Four Gospels. It was brought into the Colbert Library from Cyprus in 1673; Mill inserted its readings from Simon; it was re-examined by Scholz, whose inaccuracies (especially those committed when collating Cod. K for his 'Curae Criticae in Historiam textûs Evangeliorum,' Heidelberg, 1820) have been strongly denounced by later editors, and it must be feared with too good reason. The indepen-

(21)

ΚΑΙ ΕΞΕΛΘΟΥϹΑΙ Ε
ΦΥΓΟΝ ΑΠΟ ΤΟΥ
ΜΝΗΜΕΙΟΥ· ΕΙ
ΧΕΝ ΔΕ ΑΥΤΑϹ ΤΡΟ
ΜΟϹ ΚΑΙ ΕΚϹΤΑϹΙϹ·
ΚΑΙ ΟΥΔΕΝΙ ΟΥΔΕΝ
ΕΙΠΟΝ· ΕΦΟΒΟΥΝ
ΤΟ ΓΑΡ·

ΕϹΤΗΝ ΔΕ ΚΑΙ
ΤΑΥΤΑ ΦΕΡΟ
ΜΕΝΑ ΜΕΤΑ ΤΟ
ΕΦΟΒΟΥΝΤΟ
ΓΑΡ·

ΑΝΑϹΤΑϹ ΔΕ ΠΡΩΙ
ΠΡΩΤΗ ϹΑΒΒΑΤΟΥ·

(22)

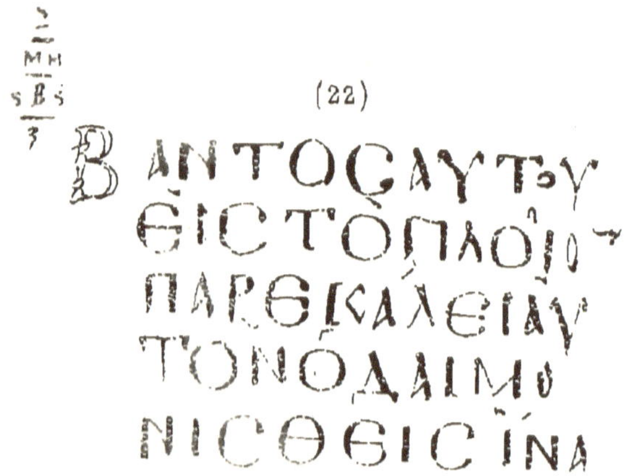

ΒΑΝΤΟϹ ΑΥΤΟΥ
ΕΙϹ ΤΟ ΠΛΟΙΟΝ
ΠΑΡΕΚΑΛΕΙ ΑΥ
ΤΟΝ Ο ΔΑΙΜΟ
ΝΙϹΘΕΙϹ ΙΝΑ

(23)

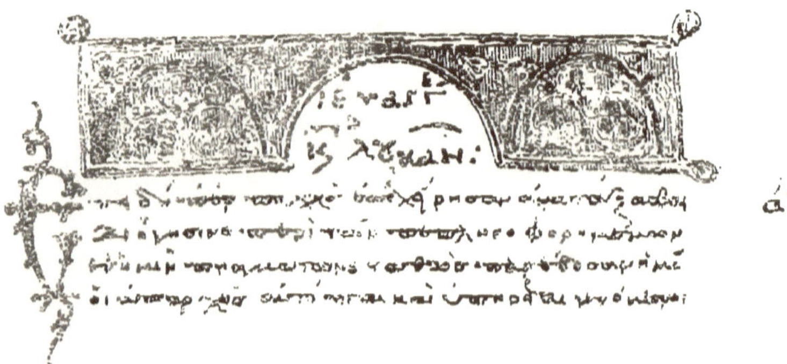

dent collations of Tischendorf and Tregelles have now done all that can be needed for this copy. It is an oblong quarto, in compressed uncials, of about the middle of the ninth century at the latest, having one column of about twenty-one lines on each page, but the handwriting is irregular and varies much in size. A single point being often found where the sense does not require it, this codex has been thought to have been copied from an older one arranged in στίχοι; the ends of each στίχος may have been indicated in this manner by the scribe. The subscriptions, τίτλοι, the sections, and indices of the κεφάλαια of the last three Gospels are believed to be the work of a later hand: the Eusebian canons are absent. The breathings and accents are *primâ manu*, but often omitted or incorrectly placed. Itacisms and permutations of consonants are very frequent, and the text is of an unusual and interesting character. Scholz regards the directions for the Church lessons, even the ἀρχαί and τέλη in the margin at the beginning and end of lessons, as by the original scribe. He transcribes at length the ἐκλογάδιον τῶν δ' εὐαγγελιστῶν and the fragments of a menology prefixed to Cod. K (N. T. vol. i, pp. 455–493), of which tables it affords the earliest specimen. The second hand writes at the end προσδέξηται αὐτὴν [τὴν δέλτον] ἡ παναγία θεοτόκος καὶ ὁ ἅγιος εὐτύχιος. The style of this copy will be seen from our facsimile (No. 19) taken from John vi. 52, 53: the number of the section (ξϛ') or 66 stands in the margin, but the ordinary place of the Eusebian canon (ι or 10) under it is filled by a simple flourish. The stop in l. 1 after λεγοντεσ illustrates the unusual punctuation of this copy, as may that after ὁ $\overline{\iota\sigma}$ in l. 3.

L. Cod. Regius, No. 62 in the Royal Library at Paris, is by far the most remarkable document of its age and class. It contains the Four Gospels, except the following passages, Matt. iv. 22—v. 14; xxviii. 17–20: Mark x. 16–30; xv. 2–20: John xxi. 15–25. It was written in about the eighth century and consists of 257 leaves quarto, of thick vellum, 9 inches high by 6½ broad, with two columns of twenty-five lines each on a page, regularly marked, as we so often see, by the *stilus* and ruler (p. 27). This is doubtless Stephen's η', though he cites it erroneously in Acts xxiv. 7 bis; xxv. 14; xxvii. 1; xxviii. 11: it was even then in the Royal Library, although 'Roberto Stephano' is marked in the volume. Wetstein collated Cod. L but loosely; Griesbach, who set a very high value on it, studied it with peculiar care; Tischendorf published it in full in his 'Monumenta sacra inedita,' 1846. It is but carelessly written, and abounds with errors of the ignorant scribe, who was more probably an Egyptian than a native Greek. The breathings and accents are often deficient, often added wrongly, and placed throughout without rule or propriety. The apostrophus also is common, and frequently out of place; the points for stops are quite irregular, as we have elsewhere stated (p. 48). Capitals occur plentifully, often painted and in questionable taste (see facsimile No. 21, column 2), and there is a tendency throughout to inelegant ornament. This codex is in bad condition through damp, the ink brown or pale, the uncial letters of a debased oblong shape: *phi* is enormously large and sometimes quite angular; other letters are such as might be looked for from its date, and are neither neat nor remarkably clear. The lessons for Sundays, festivals, &c. and the ἀρχαί and τέλη are marked everywhere in the margin, especially in St. Matthew; there are also many corrections and important critical notes (e.g. Mark xvi. 8) in the text or margin, apparently *primâ manu*. Our facsimile is taken from a photograph of its most important page, Mark xvi. 8, 9, with part of the note cited at length below. Before each Gospel are indices of the κεφάλαια, now imperfect: we find also the τίτλοι at the head and occasionally at the foot of the several pages; the numbers of the κεφάλαια (usually pointed out by the sign of the cross), the sections and Eusebian canons stand in the inner margin [1], often ill put, as if only half understood. The critical weight of this copy may best be discussed hereafter; it will here suffice barely to mention its strong resemblance to Cod. B (less, however, in St. John's Gospel than elsewhere), to the citations of Origen [186–253], and to the margin of the Harkleian Syriac version [A.D. 616]. Cod. L abounds in what are termed Alexandrian forms, beyond any other copy of its date.

M. Cod. Campianus, No. 48 in the Royal Library at Paris,

[1] In our facsimile (No. 21), over against the beginning of Mark xvi. 8, is set the number of the section (CΛΓ or 233), above the corresponding Eusebian canon (B or 2).

contains the Four Gospels complete in a small quarto form, written in very elegant and minute uncials of the end of the ninth century, with two columns of twenty-four lines each on a page. The Abbé François de Camps gave it to Louis XIV, Jan. 1, 1707. This document is Kuster's 2 (1710); it was collated by Wetstein, Scholz, and Tregelles; transcribed in 1841 by Tischendorf. Its synaxarion and menology have been published by Scholz in the same place as those of Cod. K, and obviously with great carelessness. Ἀναγνώσματα, i.e. notes of the Church Lessons, abound in the margin (Tischendorf thinks them *primâ manu*) in a very small hand, like in style to the Oxford Plato (Clarke 39, *above*, p. 42). We find too Hippolytus' Chronology of the Gospels, Eusebius' letter to Carpianus with his canons, and some Arabic scrawl on the last leaf, of which the name of Jerusalem alone has been read, a note in Slavonic, and others in a contemporaneous cursive hand. Dean Burgon also observed at the foot of the several pages the same kind of harmony as we described for Cod. E. It has breathings, accents pretty fairly given, and a musical notation in red, so frequent in Church manuscripts of the age. Its readings are very good; itacisms and ν ἐφελκυστικόν are frequent. Tischendorf compares the form of its uncials to those of Cod. V; which, judging from the facsimile given by Matthaei, we should deem somewhat less beautiful. From our facsimile (No. 32) it will be seen that the round letters are much narrowed, the later form of *delta* and *theta* quite decided, while *alpha* and *pi* might look earlier. Our specimen (John vii. 53—viii. 2) represents the celebrated Pericope adulterae in one of its earliest forms.

N. Codex Purpureus. Only twelve leaves of this beautiful copy were till recently believed to survive, and some former possessor must have divided them in order to obtain a better price from several purchasers than from one. Four leaves are now in the British Museum (Cotton, Titus C. xv), six in the Vatican (No. 3785), two at Vienna (Lambec. 2), at the end of a fragment of Genesis in a different hand. The London fragments (Matt. xxvi. 57–65; xxvii. 26–34: John xiv. 2–10; xv. 15–22) were collated by Wetstein on his first visit to England in 1715, and marked in his Greek Testament by the letter J: Scrivener transcribed them in 1845, and announced that they contained fifty-seven various readings, of which Wetstein had given but five. The Vienna fragment (Luke xxiv. 13–21; 39–49) had long been known by the descriptions of Lambecius: Wetstein had called it N; Treschow in 1773 and Alter in 1787 had given imperfect collations of it. Scholz first noticed the Vatican leaves (Matt. xix. 6–13; xx. 6–22; xx. 29—xxi. 19), denoted them by Γ, and used some readings extracted by Gaetano Marini. It was reserved for Tischendorf (Monumenta sacra inedita, 1846) to publish them all in full, and to determine by actual inspection that they were portions of the same manuscript, of the date of about the end of the sixth century. Besides these twelve leaves John Sakkelion the Librarian saw in or about 1864 at the Monastery of St. John in Patmos thirty-three other leaves containing portions of St. Mark's Gospel (ch. vi. 53—xv. 23) [1], whose readings were communicated to Tischendorf, and are included in his eighth edition of the N. T. The others were probably stolen from the same place. This book is written on the thinnest vellum (*see* pp. 23, 25), dyed purple, and the silver letters (which have turned quite black) were impressed in some way upon it, but are too varied in shape, and at the end of the lines in size, to admit the supposition of moveable type being used, as some have thought to be the case in the Codex Argenteus of the Gothic Gospels. The abridgements $\overline{\Theta C}$, $\overline{XC}$, &c. are in gold; and some changes have been made by an ancient second hand. The so-called Ammonian sections and the Eusebian canons are faithfully given (*see* p. 59), and the Vatican portion has the forty-first, forty-sixth, and forty-seventh *τίτλοι* of St. Matthew at the head of the pages. Each page has two columns of sixteen lines, and the letters (about ten or twelve in a line) are firm, uniform, bold, and unornamented, though not quite so much so as in a few older documents; their lower extremities are bevelled. Their size is at least four times that of the letters in Cod. A, the punctuation quite as simple, being a single point (and that usually neglected) level with the top of the letter (see our facsimile, Plate v, No. 14,

[1] Dr. Hort more exactly reckons that these leaves apparently contain Mark vi. 53—vii. 4; vii. 21—viii. 32; ix. 1—x. 43; xi. 7—xii. 19; xiv. 25—xv. 22 (*Addenda and Corrigenda* to Tregelles's N. T., p. 1019), adding that Tischendorf had access also to a few verses preserved in the collections of the Russian Bishop Porphyry. They are published in Duchesne's 'Archives des Missions scientifiques et littéraires' (Paris, 1877), 3e sér. tom. iii. pp. 386–419.

l. 3), and there is no space left between words even after stops. A few letters stand out as capitals at the beginning of lines; of the breathings and accents, if such they be, we have spoken above (p. 47). Letters diminished at the end of a line do not lose their ancient shape, as in many later books: *compendia scribendi* are rare, yet ⊢⊣ stands for N at the end of a line no less than twenty-nine times in the London leaves alone, but ⲭ for αι only once. I at the beginning of a syllable has two dots over it, Υ but one. We have discussed above (pp. 32–39) the shape of the alphabet in N (for by that single letter Tischendorf denotes it), and compared it with others of nearly the same date; *alpha, omega, lambda* look more ancient than *delta* or *xi* (*see* Plate ii. No. 4). It exhibits strong Alexandrian forms, e. g. παραλήμψομε, ειχοσαν (the latter condemned *secundâ manu*), and not a few such itacisms as the changes of ι and ει, αι and ε.

Cod. N^b (I^b of Tischendorf's N. T., eighth edition), Musei Britannici (Addit. 17136), is a 12mo volume containing the hymns of Severus in Syriac, and is one of the books brought thither from the Nitrian desert. It is a palimpsest, with a second Syriac work written below the first, and, under both, *four* leaves (117, 118, 127, 128) contain fragments of seventeen verses of St. John (xiii. 16; 17; 19; 20; 23; 24; 26; 27; xvi. 7; 8; 9) although only one word—περί—is preserved; 12; 13; 15; 16; 18; 19). These Tischendorf (and Tregelles about the same time) deciphered with great difficulty, as every one who has examined the manuscript would anticipate, and published in the second volume of his new collection of 'Monumenta sacra inedita.' Each page contained two columns. We meet with the sections without the Eusebian canons, the earliest form of uncial characters, no capital letters (*see* p. 51, note 2), and only the simplest kind of punctuation, although one rough breathing is legible. Tischendorf hesitates whether he shall assign the fragment to the fourth or fifth century. It agrees with Cod. A five or six times, with Cod. B five, with the two together six, and is against them both thrice.

O. No less than nine small fragments have borne this mark. O of Wetstein was given by Anselmo Banduri to Montfaucon, and contains only Luke xviii. 11–14: *this* Tischendorf discards as taken from an Evangelistarium (of the tenth century, as he judges from the writing) chiefly because it wants the number of the section at ver. 14. In its room he puts for Cod. O Moscow Synod. 120 (Matthaei, 15), a few leaves of about the ninth century (containing the fifteen verses, John i. 1, 3, 4; xx. 10–13; 15–17; 20–24, with some scholia), which had been used for binding a copy of Chrysostom's Homilies on Genesis, brought from the monastery of Dionysius at Mount Athos, and published in Matthaei's Greek Testament with a facsimile (*see* ix. 257 &c., and facsimile in tom. xii). Further portions of this fragment were seen at Athos in 1864 by Mr. Philip E. Pusey. Tregelles has also appended it to his edition of Cod. Ξ. In this fragment we find the cross-like *psi*, the interrogative ; (John xx. 13), and the comma (ib. ver. 12). Alford's Frag. Ath. b=Tisch. W^e—p. 145—and Frag. Ath. a are probably parts of O. The next five comprise N. T. hymns.

Cod. O^a. *Magnificat* and *Benedictus* in Greek uncials of the eighth or ninth century, in a Latin book at Wolfenbüttel, is published by Tischendorf, Anecdota sacr. et prof. 1855; as is also O^b, which contains these two and *Nunc Dimittis*, of the ninth century, and is at Oxford, Bodleian, Misc. Gr. 5, ff. 313–4[1]. O^c. *Magnificat* in the Verona Psalter of the sixth century (the Greek being written in Latin letters), published by Bianchini (Vindiciae Canon. Script. 1740). O^d, O^e, both contain the three hymns, O^d in the great purple and silver Zurich Psalter of the seventh century (Tischendorf, Monum. sacra inedita, tom. iv, 1869)[2]; O^e of the ninth century at St. Gall (Cod. 17), partly written in Greek, partly in Latin. O^f, also of the ninth century, is described by Tischendorf (N. T., eighth edition) once as 'Noroff. Petrop.,' once as 'Mosquensis.' O^g (IX) in the Arsenal Library at Paris (MS. Gr. 2), containing, besides the Psalms and Canticle of the Old Testament, the *Magnificat*, *Benedictus*, and *Nunc Dimittis*, besides the *Lord's Prayer*, the *Sanctus* and other such pieces. O^h. Taurinensis Reg. B. vii.

[1] These songs, with thirteen others from the Old Testament and Apocrypha, though *partially* written in uncial letters, are included in a volume of Psalms and Hymns, whose prevailing character is early cursive.

[2] From Tischendorf's copy of O^d Dr. Caspar René Gregory has gathered readings in Heb. v. 8—vi. 10, and sent them to Dr. Hort.

30 (viii or ix), $5\frac{3}{4} \times 4$, ff. 303 (20)[1]. Psalter with Luke i. 46–55; ii. 29–31. See Gregory, Prolegomena, p. 441.

P. CODEX GUELPHERBYTANUS A. }
Q. .... B. } These are two palimpsests, discovered by F. A. Knittel, Archdeacon of Wolfenbüttel, in the Ducal Library of that city, which (together with some fragments of Ulphilas' Gothic version) lie under the more modern writings of Isidore of Seville. He published the whole in 1762[2], so far at least as he could read them, though Tregelles believed more might be deciphered, and Tischendorf, with his unconquerable energy, collating them both in 1854, was able to re-edit them more accurately, Cod. Q in the third volume (1860) and Cod. P in the sixth (1869) of his Monumenta sacra inedita. The volume (called the Codex Carolinus) seems to have been once at Bobbio, and has been traced from Weissenburg to Mayence and Prague, till it was bought by a Duke of Brunswick in 1689. Codex P contains, on forty-three or forty-four leaves, thirty-one fragments of 518 verses, taken from all the four Evangelists[3]; Codex Q, on thirteen leaves, twelve fragments of 247 verses from SS. Luke and John[4]; but all can be traced only with great difficulty. A few portions, once written in vermilion, have quite departed, but Tischendorf has made material additions to Knittel's labours, both in extent and accuracy. He assigns P to the sixth, Q to the fifth century. Both are written in two columns, the uncials being bold, round or square, those of Q not a little the smaller. The letters in P, however, are sometimes compressed at the end of a line. The capitals in P are large and frequent, and both have the sections without the canons of

[1] I.e., twenty lines on a page, according to the form used in this edition.

[2] They had been previously described in a tract 'Jac. Frid. Heusinger, de quatuor Evan. Cod. Graec. quem antiqua manu membrana scriptum Guelferbytana bibliotheca servat.' Guelf. 1752.

[3] Codex P contains Matt. i. 11–21; iii. 13—iv. 19; x. 7–19; x. 42—xi. 11; xiii. 40–50; xiv. 15—xv. 3; xv. 29–39: Mark i. 1–11; iii. 5–17; xiv. 13–24; 48–61; xv. 12–37; Luke i. 1–13; ii. 9–20; vi. 21–42; vii. 32—viii. 2; viii. 31–50; ix. 26–36; x. 36—xi. 4; xii. 34–45; xiv. 14–25; xv. 13—xvi. 22; xviii. 13–39; xx. 21—xxi. 3; xxii. 3–16; xxiii. 20–33; 45–56; xxiv. 1, 14–37: John i. 29–41; ii. 13–25; xxi. 1–11.

[4] Codex Q contains Luke iv. 34—v. 4; vi. 10–26; xii. 6–43; xv. 14–31; xvii. 34—xviii. 15; xviii. 34—xix. 11; xix. 47—xx. 17; xx. 34—xxi. 8; xxii. 27–46; xxiii. 30–49: John xii. 3–20; xiv. 3–22.

Eusebius (*see* p. 59). The table of τίτλοι found in the volume is written in oblong uncials of a lower date, as Knittel thought, possibly without good reason. Itacisms, what are termed Alexandrian forms, and the usual contractions ($\overline{\text{IC}}$, $\overline{\text{XC}}$, $\overline{\text{KC}}$, $\overline{\Theta\text{C}}$, $\overline{\Upsilon\text{C}}$, $\overline{\Pi\text{HP}}$, $\overline{\Pi\text{NA}}$, $\overline{\text{I}\Lambda\text{HM}}$, $\overline{\text{ANOC}}$, $\overline{\Delta\text{A}\Delta}$, $\overset{\text{ȣ}}{\text{M}}$) occur in both copies. Breathings also are seen here and there in Q. From Tischendorf's beautiful facsimiles of Codd. PQ we observe that while *delta* is far more elaborate in P than in Q, the precise contrary is the case with *pi*. *Epsilon* and *sigma* in P have strong points at all the extremities; *nu* in each is of the ancient form exhibited in Codd. אNR (*see* p. 37); while in P *alpha* resembles in shape that of our alphabet in Plate ii. No. 5, *eta* that in Plate iii. No. 7. As regards their text we observe that in the first hundred verses of St. Luke which are contained in both copies, wherein P is cited for various readings 216 times, and Q 182 times, P stands alone fourteen times, Q not once. P agrees with other manuscripts against AB twenty-one times, Q nineteen: P agrees with AB united fifty times, Q also fifty: P sides with B against A twenty-nine times, Q thirty-eight: but P accords with A against B in 102 places, Q in seventy-five.

R. This letter, like some that precede, has been used to represent different books by various editors, a practice the inconvenience of which is very manifest. (1) R of Griesbach and Scholz is a fragment of one quarto leaf containing John i. 38–50, at Tübingen, with musical notes, which from its thick vellum, from the want of the sections and Eusebian canons, and the general resemblance of its uncials to those of late Service Books, Tischendorf pronounces to be an Evangelistarium, and puts in its room (2) in his N.T. of 1849, fourteen leaves of a palimpsest in the Royal Library of Naples (Borbon. ii. C. 15) of the eighth century, under a *Typicum* (see Suicer, Thes. Eccles. tom. ii. p. 1335), or Ritual of the Greek Church, of the fourteenth century. These are fragments from the first three Evangelists, in oblong uncials, leaning to the right. Tischendorf, by chemical applications, was able in 1843 to read one page, in two columns of twenty-five lines each (Mark xiv. 32–39)[1], and saw the sections in the margin; the Eusebian canons he thinks have been washed out (*see* p. 59): but

[1] Published in the Jahrbücher (Vienna) d. Lit. 1847.

(15)

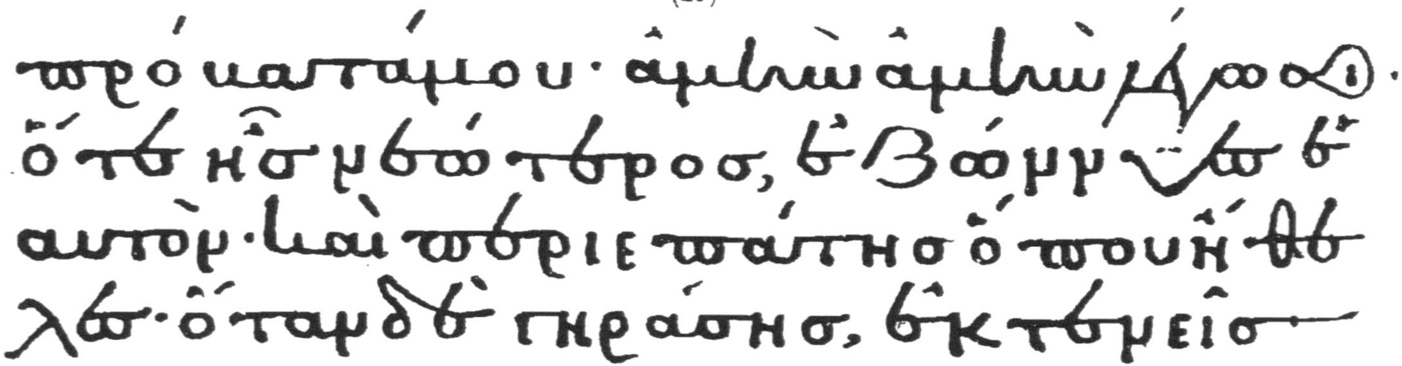

(16)

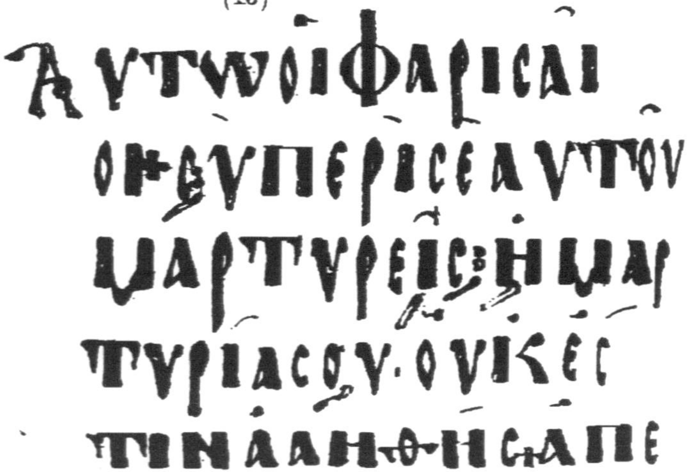

(17)

in 1859 he calls this fragment W^b, reserving the letter R for (3) CODEX NITRIENSIS, Brit. Museum, Additional 17211, the very important palimpsest containing on forty-eight (53) leaves about 516 verses of St. Luke in twenty-five fragments[1], under the black, broad Syriac writing, being a treatise of Severus of Antioch against Johannes Grammaticus, of the eighth or ninth century. There are two columns of about twenty-five lines each on a page; for their boldness and simplicity the letters may be referred to the end of the sixth century; we have given a facsimile of the manuscript (which cannot be read in parts but with the utmost difficulty), and an alphabet collected from it (Nos. 5, 17). In size and shape the letters are much like those of Codd. INP, only that they are somewhat irregular and straggling: the punctuation is effected by a single point almost level with the top of the letters, as in Cod. N. The pseudo-Ammonian sections are there without the Eusebian canons, and the first two leaves are devoted to the τίτλοι of St. Luke. This most important palimpsest is one of the 550 manuscripts brought to England, about 1847, from the Syrian convent of S. Mary Deipara, in the Nitrian Desert, seventy miles N.W. of Cairo. When examined at the British Museum by the late Canon Cureton, then one of the Librarians, he discovered in the same volume, and published in 1851 (with six pages in facsimile), a palimpsest of 4000 lines of Homer's Iliad not in the same hand as St. Luke, but quite as ancient. The fragments of St. Luke were independently transcribed, with most laudable patience, both by Tregelles in 1854, and by Tischendorf in 1855, who afterwards re-examined the places wherein he differed from Tregelles (e.g. chh. viii. 5; xviii. 7, 10), and discovered by the aid of Dr. Wright a few more fragments of chh. vi–viii. Tischendorf published an edition of Cod. R in his 'Monumenta sacra inedita,' vol. ii, with a facsimile: the amended readings, together with the newly-discovered variations in chh. vi. 31–36, 39, vii. 44, 46, 47, are inserted in the eighth edition of his Greek Testament. In this palimpsest as at present bound

[1] Codex R contains Luke i. 1–13; i. 69—ii. 4; 16–27; iv. 38—v. 5; v. 25—vi. 8; 18–36, 39; vi. 49—vii. 22; 44, 46, 47; viii. 5–15; viii. 25—ix. 1; ix. 12–43; x. 3–16; xi. 5–27; xii. 4–15; 40–52; xiii. 26—xiv. 1; xiv. 12—xv. 1; xv. 13—xvi. 16; xvii. 21—xviii. 10; xviii. 22—xx. 20; xx. 33–47; xxi. 12—xxii. 15; 42–56; xxii. 71—xxiii. 11; xxiii. 38–51. A second hand has supplied ch. xv. 19–21.

up in the Museum the fragments of St. Luke end on f. 48, and the rest of the Greek in the volume is in later, smaller, sloping uncials, and contains propositions from the tenth and thirteenth books of Euclid. On the critical character of the readings of this precious fragment we shall make some comments below.

S. Codex Vaticanus 354 contains the four Gospels entire, and is amongst the earliest dated manuscripts of the Greek Testament (p. 41, note 2). This is a folio of 234 leaves, written in large oblong or compressed uncials: the Epistle to Carpianus and Eusebian canons are prefixed, and it contains many later corrections (e.g. Luke viii. 15) and marginal notes (e.g. Matt. xxvii. 16, 17). Luke xxii. 43, 44; John v. 4; vii. 53—viii. 11 are obelized. At the end we read *ἐγράφει ἡ τιμία δέλτος αὕτη διὰ χειρὸς ἐμοῦ Μιχαὴλ μοναχοῦ ἁμὰρτωλοῦ μηνὶ μαρτίω α′. ἡμέρα ϵ′, ὥρα ϛ′, ἔτους ϛυνζ. ινδ. ζ′*: i. e. A.D. 949. 'Codicem bis diligenter contulimus,' says Birch: but collators in his day (1781–3) seldom noticed orthographical forms or stated where the readings *agree* with the received text, so that a more thorough examination was still required. Tregelles only inspected it, but Tischendorf, when at Rome in 1866, carefully re-examined it, and has inserted many of its readings in his eighth edition and its supplementary leaves. He states that Birch's facsimile (consisting of the obelized John v. 4) is coarsely executed, while Bianchini's is too elegant; he made another for himself.

T. Codex Borgianus I, now in the Propaganda at Rome (*see below*, Evan. 180), contains thirteen or more quarto leaves of SS. Luke and John, with a Thebaic or Sahidic version at their side, but on the opposite and left page. Each page consists of two columns: a single point indicates a break in the sense, but there are no other divisions. The fragment contains Luke xxii. 20—xxiii. 20; John vi. 28–67; vii. 6—viii. 31 (179 verses, since John vii. 53—viii. 11 are wanting). The portion containing St. John, both in Greek and Egyptian, was carefully edited at Rome in 1789 by A. A. Giorgi, an Augustinian Eremite; his facsimile, however (ch. vii. 35), seems somewhat rough, though Tischendorf (who has inspected the codex) says that its uncials look as if written by a Copt, from their resemblance to Coptic letters[1]: the shapes of *alpha* and *iota* are specially noticeable. Birch had previously collated the Greek text. Notwithstanding the occasional presence of the rough and smooth breathing in this copy (p. 47)[2], Giorgi refers it to the fourth century, Tischendorf to the fifth. The Greek fragment of St. Luke was first collated by Mr. Bradley H. Alford, and inserted by his brother, Dean Alford, in the fourth edition of his Greek Testament, vol. i (1859). Dr. Tregelles had drawn Mr. Alford's attention to it, from a hint thrown out by Zoega, in p. 184 of his 'Catalogus codd. Copt. MSS. qui in Museo Borgiano Velitris adservantur.' Romae, 1810.

T[a] or T[woi] is used by Tischendorf to indicate a few leaves in Greek and Thebaic, which once belonged to Woide, and were published with his other Thebaic fragments in Ford's Appendix to the Codex Alexandrinus, Oxon. 1799. They contain Luke xii. 15—xiii. 32; John viii. 33–42 (eighty-five verses). From the second fragment it plainly appears (what the similarity of the facsimiles had suggested to Tregelles) that T and T[a] are parts of the same manuscript, for the page of T[a] which contains John viii. 33 in Greek exhibits on its reverse the Thebaic version of John viii. 23–32, of which T affords us only the Greek text. This fact was first noted by Tischendorf (N.T. 1859), who adds that the Coptic scribe blundered much over the Greek: e.g. *βαβουσα* Luke xiii. 21; so *δεκαι* for *δεκα και*, ver. 16. He transcribed T and T[woi] (as well as T[b], T[c], T[d], which we proceed to describe), for publication in the ninth volume of his 'Monumenta sacra inedita' (1870), but owing to his death they never appeared. But Bp. Lightfoot gives reasons (*see below*, vol. ii.

[1] For the Coptic style of the letters Tischendorf compares a double palimpsest leaf in the British Museum, containing 1 Kings viii. 58—ix. 1, which he assigns to the fifth century, although the capital letters stand out a little, and are slightly larger than the rest (Monum. sacr. ined. vol. ii. Proleg. p. xliv). But both Dr. Wright and Mr. E. Maunde Thompson, from their great experience in this style of writing, have come to suspect that it is usually somewhat less ancient than from other indications might be supposed.

[2] Tischendorf found breathings also in the palimpsest Numbers (Monum. sac. ined. *ubi supra*, p. xxv).

c. 2) for thinking that this fragment was not originally a portion of T.

T^b at St. Petersburg much resembles the preceding in the Coptic-like style of writing, but is not earlier than the sixth century. It contains on six octavo leaves John i. 25–42; ii. 9—iv. 50, spaces left in the text answering the purpose of stops. T^b has a harmony of the Gospels at the foot of the page.

T^c is a fragment of about twenty-one verses between Matt. xiv. 19 and xv. 8, also of the sixth century, and at St. Petersburg, in the collection of Bishop Porphyry. Its text in the twenty-nine places cited by Tischendorf in his eighth edition accords with Cod. א twenty-four times, with Cod. B twenty times, with Codd. C and D sixteen times each, with Cod. 33 nine times. Cod. A is wanting here. Compared with these primary authorities severally, it agrees with א alone once, with 33 alone twice, with אB united against the rest four times: so that its critical character is very decided.

T^d is a fragment of a Lectionary, Greek and Sahidic, of about the seventh century, found by Tischendorf in 1866 among the Borgian manuscripts at Rome. It contains Matt. xvi. 13–20; Mark i. 3–8, xii. 35–37; John xix. 23–27; xx. 30–31: twenty-four verses only. This fragment and the next have been brought into this place, rather than inserted in the list of Evangelistaria, because they both contained fragments of the Thebaic version.

T^e is a fragment of St. Matthew at Cambridge (Univ. Libr. Addit. 1875). Dr. Hort communicated its readings to Dr. C. R. Gregory, for his Prolegomena to the eighth edition of Tischendorf's N. T. It is 'a tiny morsel' of an uncial Lectionary of the sixth century, containing only Matt. iii. 13–16, the parallel column probably in the Thebaic version having perished. It was brought, among other Coptic fragments, from Upper Egypt by Mr. Greville Chester. Dr. Hort kindly enables me to add to his description of T^e (Addenda to Tregelles' N. T. p. 1070) that this 'tiny morsel' is irregular in shape, frequently less than four inches in width and height, the uncial Greek letters being three-eighths of an inch high. There seem to have been two columns of either eight or more probably of twenty-four lines each on a page, but no Coptic portions survive. 'If of twenty-four lines the fragment might belong to the inner column of a bilingual MS. with the two languages in parallel columns, or to the outer column of a wholly Greek MS. or of a bilingual MS. with the section in the two languages consecutively, as in Mr. Horner's Graeco-Thebaic fragment (Evst. 299: *see* p. 398). In the latter case it might belong to the inner column of a wholly Greek MS. or of a bilingual MS. with the section in two consecutive languages. The size of the letters renders it improbable, however, that the columns were of eight lines only.' (Hort.)

T^f Horner. See below under Thebaic or Sahidic MSS. at the end.

T^g Cairo, Cod. Papadopulus Kerameus [vi or vii], $9\frac{1}{2} \times 8\frac{1}{4}$, ff. 3 (27), two cols., written in letters like Coptic. Matt. xx. 3–32; xxii. 4–16. Facsimile by the Abbate Cozza-Luzi in 'N.T. e Cod. Vat. 1209 nativi textus Graeci primo omnium phototypice representatum'—Danesio, Rome, 1889. See Gregory, Prolegomena, p. 450.

U. Codex Nanianus I, so called from a former possessor, is now in the Library of St. Mark, Venice (I. viii). It contains the four Gospels entire, carefully and luxuriously written in two columns of twenty-one lines each on the quarto page, scarcely before the tenth century, although the 'letters are in general an imitation of those used before the introduction of compressed uncials; but they do not belong to the age when full and round writing was customary or natural, so that the stiffness and want of ease is manifest' (Tregelles' Horne, p. 202). It has *Carp.*, *Eus. t.*, κεφ. *t.*, τίτλ., κεφ., *pict.*, with much gold ornament. Thus while the small ο in l. 1 of our facsimile (No. 22) is in the oldest style, the oblong *omicrons* creep in at the end of lines 2 and 4. Münter sent some extracts from this copy to Birch, who used them for his edition, and states that the book contains the Eusebian canons. Accordingly in Mark

v. 18, B (in error for H) stands under the proper section $\overline{\mu\eta}$ (48). Tischendorf in 1843 and Tregelles in 1846 collated Cod. U thoroughly and independently, and compared their work at Leipsic for the purpose of mutual correction.

V. Codex Mosquensis, of the Holy Synod, is known almost[1] exclusively from Matthaei's Greek Testament: he states, no doubt most truly, that he collated it 'bis diligentissimè,' and gives a facsimile of it, assigning it to the eighth century. Judging from Matthaei's plate, it is hard to say why others have dated it in the ninth. It contained in 1779, when first collated, the Four Gospels in 8vo with the sections and Eusebian canons, in uncial letters down to John vii. 39, *ουπω γαρ ην*, and from that point in cursive letters of the thirteenth century, Matt. v. 44—vi. 12; ix. 18—x. 1 being lost: when re-collated but four years later Matt. xxii. 44—xxiii. 35; John xxi. 10–25 had disappeared. Matthaei tells us that the manuscript is written in a kind of stichometry by a diligent scribe: its resemblance to Cod. M has been already mentioned. The cursive portion is Matthaei's V, Scholz's Evan. 250.

W^a. Cod. Reg. Paris 314 consists of but two leaves at the end of another book, containing Luke ix. 34–47; x. 12–22 (twenty-three verses). Its date is about the eighth century; the uncial letters are firmly written, *delta* and *theta* being of the ordinary oblong shape of that period. Accents and breathings are usually put; all the stops are expressed by a single point, whose position makes no difference in its power. This copy was adapted to Church use, but is not an Evangelistarium, inasmuch as it exhibits the sections and Eusebian canons[2], and *τίτλοι* twice at the head of the page. This fragment was brought to light by Scholz, and published by Tischendorf, Monumenta sacra inedita, 1846.

[1] I say *almost*, for Bengel's description makes it plain that this is the Moscow manuscript from which F. C. Gross sent him the extracts that Wetstein copied and numbered Evan. 87. Bengel, however, states that the cursive portion from John vii onwards bears the date of 6508 or A. D. 1000. Scholz was the first to notice this identity (*see* Evan. 250).

[2] Notwithstanding, the Eusebian canons have been washed out of W^b, a strong confirmation of what was conjectured above, p. 61.

W^b. Tischendorf considers the fragment at Naples he had formerly numbered R (2) as another portion of the same copy, and therefore indicates it in his seventh edition of the N.T. (1859) as W^b. It has seventy-nine leaves, of which the fourteen last are palimpsest, is written in two columns, with twenty-five lines in each page; has the Ammonian sections and lections, and contains Matt. xix. 14–28; xx. 23—xxi. 2; xxvi. 52—xxvii. 1; Mark xiii. 21—xiv. 67; Luke iii. 1—iv. 20. (Prolegomena to Tischendorf, p. 395.)

W^c is assigned by Tischendorf to three leaves containing Mark ii. 8–16; Luke i. 20–32; 64–79 (thirty-five verses), which have been washed to make a palimpsest, and the writing erased in parts by a knife. There are also some traces of a Latin version, but all these were used up to bind other books in the library of St. Gall. They are of the eighth century, or the ninth according to Tischendorf, edd. 7 and 8, and have appeared in vol. iii of 'Monumenta sacra inedita,' with a facsimile, whose style closely resembles that of Cod. Δ, and its kindred FG of St. Paul's Epistles.

W^d was discovered in 1857 by Mr. W. White, sub-librarian of Trinity College, Cambridge, in the College Library, and was afterwards observed and arranged by Mr. H. Bradshaw, University Librarian, its slips (about twenty-seven in number) having been worked into the binding of a volume of Gregory Nazianzen: they are now carefully arranged under glass (B. viii. 5). They comprise portions of four leaves, severally containing Mark vii. 3–4; 6–8; 30–36; 36—viii. 4; 4–10; 11–16; ix. 2; 7–9, in uncial letters of the ninth century, if not rather earlier, slightly leaning to the right. The sections are set in the margin without the Eusebian canons, with a table of harmony at the foot of each page of twenty-four lines. The τίτλοι are in red at the top and bottom of the pages, their corresponding numerals in the margin. The breathings and accents are often very faint: lessons and musical notes, crosses, &c. are in red, and sometimes cover the original stops. In text it much resembles Codd. ℵBDLΔ: one reading (Mark vii. 33) appears to be unique. Dr. Scrivener has included it in a volume of fresh collations of manuscripts and editions which is shortly to appear under the accomplished editorship of Mr. J. Rendel Harris.

W^e is a fragment containing John iv. 7–14, in three leaves, found by the Very Rev. G. W. Kitchin, Dean of Winchester, in Christ Church Library, when Tischendorf was at Oxford in 1865. It much resembles O at Moscow, and, like it, had a commentary annexed, to which there are numeral references set before each verse.

W^f is a palimpsest fragment of St. Matt. xxv. 31–36, and vi. 1–18 (containing the doxology in the Lord's Prayer), of about the ninth century, underlying Wake 13 at Christ Church, Oxford (Acts 192, Paul. 246), discovered by the late Mr. A. A. Vansittart (Journal of Philology, vol. ii. no. 4, p. 241, note 1).

X. CODEX MONACENSIS, in the University Library at Munich (No. $\frac{1}{26}$), is a valuable folio manuscript of the end of the ninth or early in the tenth century, containing the Four Gospels (in the order described above, with serious omissions[1], and a commentary (chiefly from Chrysostom) surrounding and interspersed with the text of all but St. Mark, in early cursive letters, not unlike (in Tischendorf's judgement) the celebrated Oxford Plato dated 895. The very elegant uncials of Cod. X 'are small and upright; though some of them are compressed, they seem as if they were *partial* imitations of those used in very early copies' (Tregelles' Horne, p. 195). Each page has two columns of about forty-five lines each. There are no divisions by κεφάλαια or sections, nor notes to serve for ecclesiastical use. From a memorandum we find that it came from Rome to Ingoldstadt, as a present from Gerard Vossius [1577–1649]; from Ingoldstadt it was taken to Landshut in 1803, thence to Munich in 1827. When it was at Ingoldstadt Griesbach obtained some extracts from it through Dobrowsky; Scholz first collated it, but in his usual unhappy way; Tischendorf in 1844, Tregelles in 1846. Dean Burgon examined it in 1872.

[1] Codex X contains Matt. vi. 6, 10, 11; vii. 1—ix. 20; ix. 34—xi. 24; xii. 9—xvi. 28; xvii. 14—xviii. 25; xix. 22—xxi. 13; 28—xxii. 22; xxiii. 27—xxiv. 2; 23–35; xxv. 1–30; xxvi. 69—xxvii. 12; Mark vi. 47—Luke i. 37; ii. 19—iii. 38; iv. 21—x. 37; xi. 1—xviii. 43; xx. 46—John ii. 22; vii. 1—xiii. 5; xiii. 20—xv. 25; xvi. 23—xxi. 25. The hiatus in John ii. 22—vii. 1 is supplied on paper in a hand of the twelfth century; Mark xiv. 61–64; xiv. 72—xv. 4; xv. 33—xvi. 6 are illegible in parts, and xvi. 6–8 have perished. Matt. v. 45 survives only in the commentary.

(18)

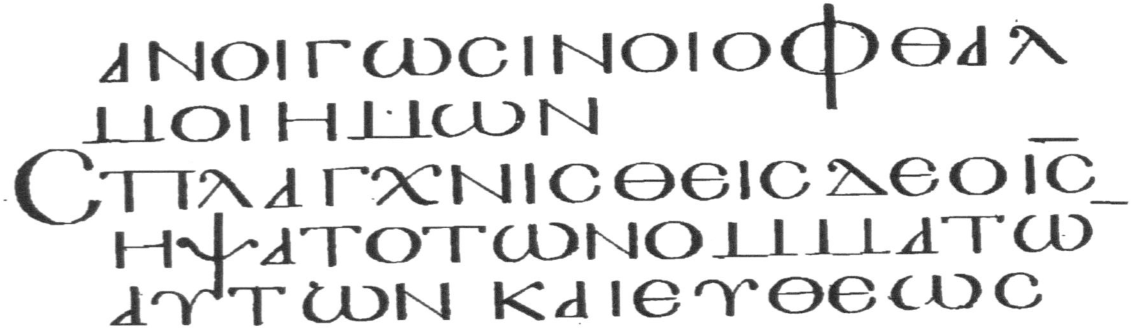
ΑΝΟΙΓΩϹΙΝΟΙΟΦΘΑΛ
ΜΟΙΗΜΩΝ
ϹΠΛΑΓΧΝΙϹΘΕΙϹΔΕΟΙϹ
ΗΨΑΤΟΤΩΝΟΜΜΑΤΩ
ΑΥΤΩΝ ΚΑΙΕΥΘΕΩϹ

(19)

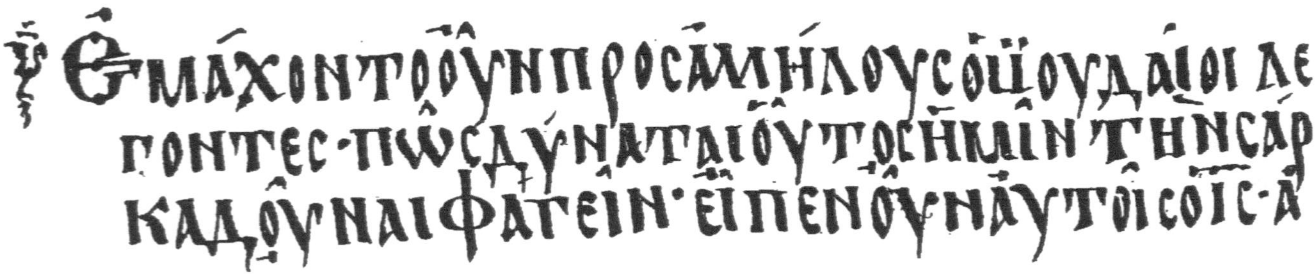
ΕΜΑΧΟΝΤΟΟΥΝΠΡΟϹΑΛΛΗΛΟΥϹΟΙΙΟΥΔΑΙΟΙ ΛΕ
ΓΟΝΤΕϹ·ΠΩϹΔΥΝΑΤΑΙΟΥΤΟϹΗΜΙΝ ΤΗΝϹΑΡ
ΚΑΔΟΥΝΑΙΦΑΓΕΙΝ·ΕΙΠΕΝΟΥΝΑΥΤΟΙϹΟΙϹ·Α

Y. Codex Barberini 225 at Rome (in the Library founded by Cardinal Barberini in the seventeenth century) contains on six large leaves the 137 verses John xvi. 3—xix. 41, of about the eighth century. Tischendorf obtained access to it in 1843 for a few hours, after some difficulty with the Prince Barberini, and published it in his first instalment of 'Monumenta sacra inedita,' 1846. Scholz had first noticed, and loosely collated it. A later hand has coarsely retraced the letters, but the ancient writing is plain and good. Accents and breathings are most often neglected or placed wrongly: κ̨ θ̨ π̨ are frequent at the end of lines. For punctuation one, two, three or even four points are employed, the power of the single point varying as in Codd. E Θᵃ and B of the Apocalypse. The pseudo-Ammonian sections are without the Eusebian canons: and such forms as λήμψεται xvi. 14, λήμψεσθε ver. 24 occur. These few uncial leaves are prefixed to a cursive copy of the Gospels with Theophylact's commentary (Evan. 392): the text is mixed, and lies about midway between that of Cod. A and Cod. B.

Z. Codex Dublinensis rescriptus, one of the chief palimpsests extant, contains 295 verses of St. Matthew's Gospel in twenty-two fragments [1]. It is of a small quarto size, originally 10½ inches by 8, now reduced to 8¼ inches by 6, once containing 120 leaves arranged in quaternions, of which the first that remains bears the *signature* 13 (IΓ): fourteen sheets or double leaves and four single leaves being all that survive. It was discovered in 1787 by Dr. John Barrett, Senior Fellow of Trinity College, Dublin, under some cursive writing of the tenth century or later, consisting of Chrysostom de Sacerdotio, extracts from Epiphanius, &c. In the same volume are portions of Isaiah (eight leaves) and of Gregory Nazianzen, in erased uncial letters, the latter not so ancient as the fragment of St. Matthew. All the thirty-two leaves of this Gospel that remain were engraved in copper-plate facsimile [2] at the expense of Trinity College, and

[1] Codex Z contains Matt. i. 17—ii. 6; ii. 13-20; iv. 4-13; v. 45—vi. 15; vii. 16—viii. 6; x. 40—xi. 18; xii. 43—xiii. 11; 57—xiv. 19; xv. 13-23; xvii. 9-17; 26—xviii. 6; xix. 4-12; 21-28; xx. 7—xxi. 8; 23-30; xxii. 16-25; 37—xxiii. 3; 15-23; xxiv. 15-25; xxv. 1-11; xxvi. 21-29; 62-71.

[2] Not in moveable type, as a critic in the *Saturday Review* (Aug. 20, 1881) seems to suppose.

published by Barrett in 1801, furnished with Prolegomena, and the contents of each facsimile plate in modern Greek characters, on the opposite page. The facsimiles are not very accurate, and the form of the letters is stated to be less free and symmetrical than in the original: yet from these plates (for the want of a better guide) our alphabet (No. 6) and specimen (No. 18) have been taken. The Greek type on the opposite page was not very well revised, and a comparison with the copper-plate will occasionally convict it of errors, which have been animadverted upon more severely than was quite necessary. The Prolegomena were encumbered with a discussion of our Lord's genealogies quite foreign to the subject, and the tone of scholarship is not very high; but Barrett's judgement on the manuscript is correct in the main, and his conclusion, that it is as old as the sixth century, has been generally received. Tregelles in 1853 was permitted to apply a chemical mixture to the vellum, which was already miserably discoloured, apparently from the purple dye: he was thus enabled to add a little (about 200 letters) to what Barrett had read long since [1], but he found that in most places which that editor had left blank, the vellum had been cut away or lost: it would no doubt have been better for Barrett to have stated, in each particular case, why he had been unable to give the text of the passage. A far better edition of the manuscript, including the fragment of Isaiah, and a newly-discovered leaf of the Latin Codex Palatinus (*e*), with Prolegomena and two plates of real facsimiles, was published in 1880 by T. K. Abbott, B.D., Professor of Biblical Greek in the University of Dublin. He has read 400 letters hitherto deemed illegible, and is inclined to assign the fifth century as the date of the Codex. Codex Z, like many others, and for the same orthographical reasons, has been referred to Alexandria as its native country. It is written with a single column on each page of twenty-one or twenty-three lines [2]. The so-named Ammonian sections are given, but not the

[1] Mr. E. H. Hansell prints in red these additional readings thus fresh brought to light in the Appendix to his 'Texts of the oldest existing manuscripts of the New Testament,' Oxford, 1864.

[2] 'Barrett's edition shows that of the sixty-four pages of the MS. fifty had originally twenty-one lines to the page, and fourteen had twenty-three.' Dr. Ezra Abbot.

Eusebian canons: the τίτλοι are written at the top of the pages by a later hand according to Porter and Abbott, though this may be questioned (Gebhardt and Harnack's 'Texte,' &c., I. iv. p. xxiii ff., 1883), their numbers being set in the margin. The writing is continuous, the *single* point either rarely found or quite washed out: the abbreviations are very few, and there are no breathings or accents. Like Cod. B, this manuscript indicates citations by > in the margin, and it represents N by —, but only at the end of a word and line. A space, proportionate to the occasion, is usually left when there is a break in the sense, and capitals extend into the margin when a new section begins. The letters are in a plain, steady, beautiful hand: they yield in elegance to none, and are never compressed at the end of a line. The shape of *alpha* (which varies a good deal), and especially that of *mu*, is very peculiar: *phi* is inordinately large: *delta* has an upper curve which is not usual: the same curves appear also in *zeta*, *lambda*, and *chi*. The characters are less in size than in N, about equal to those in R, much greater than in AB. In regard to the text, it agrees much with Codd. ℵBD: with Cod. A it has only twenty-three verses in common: yet in them A and Z vary fourteen times. Mr. Abbott adds that while ℵBZ stand together ten times against other uncials, BZ are never alone, but ℵZ against B often. It is freer than either of them from transcriptural errors. Codd. ℵBCZ combine less often than ℵBDZ. On examining Cod. Z throughout twenty-six pages, he finds it alone thirteen times, differing from ℵ thirty times, from B forty-four times, from Stephen's text ninety-five times. Thus it approaches nearer to ℵ than to B.

Γ. Codex Tischendorfian. IV was brought by Tischendorf from an 'eastern monastery' (he usually describes the locality of his manuscripts in such like general terms), and was bought of him for the Bodleian Library (Misc. Gr. 313) in 1855. It consists of 158 leaves, 12 inches × 9¼, with one column (of twenty-four not very straight or regular lines) on a page, in uncials of the ninth century, leaning slightly back, but otherwise much resembling Cod. K in style (facsimile No. 35).

St. Luke's Gospel is complete; the last ten leaves are hurt by damp, though still legible. In St. Mark only 105 verses are wanting (iii. 35—vi. 20); about 531 verses of the other Gospels survive[1]. Tischendorf, and Tregelles by his leave, have independently collated this copy, of which Tischendorf gives a facsimile in his 'Anecdota sacra et profana,' 1855. Some of its peculiar readings are very notable, and few uncials of its date deserve that more careful study, which it has hardly yet received. In 1859 Tischendorf, on his return from his third Eastern journey, took to St. Petersburg ninety-nine additional leaves of this self-same manuscript, doubtless procured from the same place as he had obtained the Bodleian portion six years before (Notitia Cod. Sinait. p. 53). This copy of the Gospels, though unfortunately in two distant libraries, is now nearly perfect[2], and at the end of St. John's Gospel, in the more recently discovered portion, we find an inscription which seems to fix the date: *ετελειωθη ἡ δέλτος αὔτη μηνι νοεμβριω κ͞ζ, ινδ. η̄, ἡμερα ε̄, ωρα β̄*. Tischendorf, by the aid of Ant. Pilgrami's 'Calendarium chronologum medii potissimum aevi monumentis accommodatum,' Vienn. 1781, pp. vii, 11, 105, states that the only year between A. D. 800 and 950, on which the Indiction was eight, and Nov. 27 fell on a Thursday, was 844[3]. In the Oxford sheets we find tables of *κεφάλαια* before the Gospels of SS. Matthew and Luke; the *τίτλοι* at the heading of the pages; their numbers *rubro* neatly set in the margin; capitals in red at the commencement of these chapters; the *ἀρχαὶ καὶ τέλη* of lections; the sections and Eusebian canons in their usual places, and some liturgical directions. Over the original breathings and accents some late scrawler has in many places put others, in a very careless fashion.

Δ. Codex Sangallensis, was first inspected by Gerbert (1773), named by Scholz (N. T. 1830), and made fully known

[1] These are Matt. vi. 16–29; vii. 26—viii. 27; xii. 18—xiv. 15; xx. 25—xxi. 19; xxii. 25—xxiii. 13; John vi. 14—viii. 3; xv. 24—xix. 6.

[2] In the St. Petersburg portion are all the rest of St. John, and Matt. i. 1—v. 31; ix. 6—xii. 18; xiv. 15—xx. 25; xxiii. 13—xxviii. 20; or all St. Matthew except 115 verses.

[3] Dr. Gregory, Tisch. Prolegomena, p. 401, quotes Gardthausen, Griechische Palaeogr., Lipsiae, 1879, pp. 159, 344, as assigning A. D. 979 as the date.

to us by the admirable edition in lithographed facsimile of every page, by H. Ch. M. Rettig [1799–1836], published at Zurich, 1836 [1], with copious and satisfactory Prolegomena. It is preserved and was probably transcribed a thousand years since in the great monastery of St. Gall in the north-east of Switzerland (Stifts bibliothek, 48). It is rudely written on 197 leaves of coarse vellum quarto, 8⅞ inches by 7⅛ in size, with from twenty to twenty-six (usually twenty-one) lines on each page, in a very peculiar hand, with an interlinear Latin version, and contains the four Gospels complete except John xix. 17–35. Before St. Matthew's Gospel are placed Prologues, Latin verses, the Eusebian canons in Roman letters, tables of the *κεφάλαια* both in Greek and Latin, &c. Rettig thinks he has traced several different scribes and inks employed on it, which might happen easily enough in the Scriptorium of a monastery; but, if so, their style of writing is very nearly the same, and they doubtless copied from the same archetype, about the same time. He has produced more convincing arguments to show that Cod. Δ is part of the same book as the Codex Boernerianus, G of St. Paul's Epistles. Not only do they exactly resemble each other in their whole arrangement and appearance, but marginal notes by the first hand are found in each, of precisely the same character. Thus the predestinarian doctrines of the heretic Godeschalk [d. 866] are pointed out for refutation at the hard texts, Luke xiii. 24; John xii. 40 in Δ, and six times in G [2]. St. Mark's Gospel represents a text different from that of the other

[1] The edition was posthumous, and has prefixed to it a touching 'Life' of two pages in length, by his brother and pupil, dwelling especially on Rettig's happy change in his later days from rationalism to a higher and spiritual life.

[2] Viz. Rom. iii. 5; 1 Cor. ii. 8; 1 Tim. ii. 4; iv. 10; vi. 4; 2 Tim. ii. 15. Equally strong are the notices of Aganon, who is cited eight times in Δ, about sixteen in G. This personage was Bishop of Chartres, and a severe disciplinarian, who died A.D. 941; a fact which does not hinder our assigning Cod. Δ to the ninth century, as Rettig states that all notices of him are by a later hand. There is the less need of multiplying proofs of this kind, as Tregelles has observed, a circumstance which demonstrates to a certainty the identity of Cod. Δ and G. When he was at Dresden he found in Cod. G twelve leaves of later writing in precisely the same hand as several that are lithographed by Rettig, because they were attached to Cod. Δ. 'Thus,' he says, 'these MSS. once formed ONE BOOK; and when separated, some of the superfluous leaves with additional writing attached to the former part, and some to the latter' (Tregelles' Horne's Introd. vol. iv. p. 197).

Evangelists, and the Latin version (which is clearly *primâ manu*) seems a mixture of the Vulgate with the older Italic, so altered and accommodated to the Greek as to be of little critical value. The penmen seem to have known but little Greek, and to have copied from a manuscript written continuously, for the divisions between the words are sometimes absurdly wrong. There are scarcely any breathings or accents, except about the opening of St. Mark, and once an aspirate to ἑπτα; what we do find are often falsely given; and a dot is set in most places regularly at the end of every *Greek* word. The letters have but little tendency to the oblong shape, but *delta* and *theta* are decidedly of the latest uncial type. Here, as in Paul. Cod. G, the mark >>> is much used to fill up vacant spaces. The text from which Δ was copied seems to have been arranged in στίχοι, for almost every line has at least one Greek capital letter, grotesquely ornamental in colours[1]. We transcribe three lines, taken almost at random, from pp. 80–1 (Matt. xx. 13–15), in order to explain our meaning:

dixit uni eor̄ amice non ĩjusto tibi n̄n̄e
ειπεν · μοναδι · αυτων · Εταιρε · ουκ · αδικω · σε · Ουχι

ex denario convenisti mecū tolle tuū et vade
δηναριου συνεφωνησασ · μοι · Αρον · το · σον και υπαγε

volo autē huic novissimo dare sicut et tibi antā non li
Θελω δε τουτω τω εσχατω δουναι ωσ και · σοι · Η · ουκ εξ

It will be observed that, while in Cod. Δ a line begins at any place, even in the middle of a word; if the capital letters be assumed to commence the lines, the text divides itself into regular στίχοι. See above, pp. 52–54. Here are also the τίτλοι, the sections and canons. The letters Ν and Π, Ζ and Ξ, Τ and Θ, Ρ and the Latin R are perpetually confounded. Facsimiles of Luke i. 1–9 may be seen in Pal. Soc. xi. 179. As in the kindred Codd. Augiensis and Boernerianus the Latin f is much like r. Tregelles has noted ι ascript in Cod. Δ, but this is rare. There is no question that this document was written by Latin (most probably by Irish) monks, in the west of Europe, during the ninth century (or the tenth, Pal. Soc.). *See below*, Paul. Cod. G.

[1] The portion of this manuscript contained in Paul. G was divided into στίχοι on the same principle by Hug (Introduction, vol. i. p. 283, Wait's translation).

Θ^a. Codex Tischendorfian. I was brought from the East by Tischendorf in 1845, published by him in his 'Monumenta sacra inedita,' 1846, with a few supplements in vol. ii of his new collection (1857), and deposited in the University Library at Leipsic. It consists of but four leaves (all imperfect) quarto, of very thin vellum, almost too brittle to be touched, so that each leaf is kept separately in glass. It contains about forty-two verses; viz. Matt. xii. 17–19; 23–25; xiii. 46–55 (in mere shreds); xiv. 8–29; xv. 4–14, with the greater *κεφάλαια* in red; the sections and Eusebian canons stand in the inner margin. A few breathings are *primâ manu*, and many accents by two later correctors. The stops (which are rather numerous) resemble those of Cod. Y, only that four points are not found in Θ^a. Tischendorf places its date towards the end of the seventh century, assigning Mount Sinai or lower Egypt for its country. The uncials (especially ЄΘOC) are somewhat oblong, leaning to the right (*see* p. 41 note), but the writing is elegant and uniform; *delta* keeps its ancient shape, and the diameter of *theta* does not extend beyond the curve. In regard to the text, it much resembles ℵB, and stands alone with them in ch. xiv. 12 (*αὐτόν*).

Seven other small fragments, of which four and part of another are from the manuscripts of Bishop Porphyry at St. Petersburg, were intended to be included in Tischendorf's ninth volume of 'Monumenta sacra inedita' (1870), but owing to Tischendorf's death they never appeared. That active critic had brought two (Θ^b, ^d) and part of another (Θ^c) from the East, and deposited them in the Library at St. Petersburg. They are described by him as follows:

Θ^b, six leaves in large 8vo, of the sixth or seventh century, torn piecemeal for binding and hard to decipher, contains Matt. xxii. 16—xxiii. 13; Mark iv. 24–35; v. 14–23.

Θ^c, one folio leaf, of the sixth century, much like Cod. N, contains Matt. xxi. 19–24. Another leaf contains John xviii. 29–35.

Θ^d, half a leaf in two columns, of the seventh or eighth century, with accents by a later hand, contains Luke xi. 37–41; 42–45.

Θ^e, containing fragments of Matt. xxvi. 2–4; 7–9: Θ^f, of Matt. xxvi. 59–70; xxvii. 44–56; Mark i. 34—ii. 12 (not continuously throughout): Θ^g, of John vi. 13, 14; 22–24; are all of about the sixth century.

Θ^h, consisting of three leaves, in Greek and Arabic of the ninth or tenth centuries, contains imperfect portions of Matt. xiv. 6–13; xxv. 9–16; 41—xxvi. 1.

Λ. Codex Tischendorfian. III[1], whose history, so far as we know it, exactly resembles that of Cod. Γ, and like it is now in the Bodleian (Auct. T. Infra I. 1). It contains 157 leaves, written in two columns of twenty-three lines each, in small, oblong, clumsy, sloping uncials of the eighth or rather of the ninth century (*see* p. 41, note 1, and facsimile No. 30). It has the Gospels of St. Luke and St. John complete, with the subscription to St. Mark, each Gospel being preceded by tables of *κεφάλαια*, with the *τίτλοι* at the heads of the pages; the numbers of the *κεφάλαια*, of the sections, and of the Eusebian canons (these last *rubro*) being set in the margin. There are also scholia interspersed, of some critical value; a portion being in uncial characters. This copy also was described (with a facsimile) by Tischendorf, Anecdota sacra et profana, 1855, and collated by himself and Tregelles. Its text is said to vary greatly from that common in the later uncials, and to be very like Scholz's 262 (Paris 53). For *ι ascriptum* see p. 44, note 2.

Here again the history of this manuscript curiously coincides with that of Cod. Γ. In his Notitia Cod. Sinaitici, p. 58, Tischendorf describes an early cursive copy of St. Matthew and St. Mark (*the subscription to the latter being wanting*), which he took to St. Petersburg in 1859, so exactly corresponding in general appearance with Cod. Λ (although that be written in uncial characters), as well as in the style and character of the marginal scholia, which are often in small uncials, that he pronounces them part of the same codex. Very possibly he *might* have added that he procured the two from the same source: at any rate the subscription to St. Matthew at St. Petersburg precisely resembles the other three subscriptions at Oxford, and

[1] Λ (1) is really an Evangelistary. See Evst. 493.

those in Paris 53 (Scholz's 262)[1], with which Tischendorf had previously compared Cod. Λ (N. T. Proleg. p. clxxvii, seventh edition). These cursive leaves are preceded by Eusebius' Epistle to Carpianus, his table of canons, and a table of the κεφάλαια of St. Matthew. The τίτλοι in uncials head the pages, and their numbers stand in the margin.

From the marginal scholia Tischendorf cites the following notices of the Jewish Gospel, or that according to the Hebrews, which certainly have their value as helping to inform us respecting its nature: Matt. iv. 5 *το ιουδαικον ουκ εχει εις την αγιαν πολιν αλλ εν ιλημ.* xvi. 17 *Βαριωνα· το ιουδαικον υιε ιωαννου.* xviii. 22 *το ιουδαικον εξης εχει μετα το ἑβδομηκοντακις ἑπτα· και γαρ εν τοις προφηταις μετα το χρισθηναι αυτους εν πνι ἁγιω εὑρισκετω* (*sic*) *εν αυτοις λογος ἁμαρτιας*:—an addition which Jerome (contra Pelag. III) expressly cites from the Gospel of the Nazarenes. xxvi. 47 *το ιουδαικον· και ηρνησατο και ωμοσεν και κατηρασατο.* It is plain that this whole matter requires careful discussion, but at present it would seem that the first half of Cod. Λ was written in cursive, the second in uncial letters; if not by the same person, yet on the same plan and at the same place.

Ξ. Codex Zacynthius is a palimpsest in the Library of the British and Foreign Bible Society in London, which, under a cursive Evangelistarium written on coarse vellum in or about the thirteenth century, contains large portions (342 verses) of St. Luke, down to ch. xi. 33[2], in full well-formed uncials, but surrounded by and often interwoven with large extracts from the Fathers, in a hand so cramped and, as regards the round letters (ЄΘOC), so oblong, that it cannot be earlier than the eighth century, although some such compressed forms occur in Cod. P of the sixth (*see* p. 144). The general absence of accents and breathings also would favour an earlier date. As the

[1] The subscription to St. Matthew stands in *both*: *ευαγγελιον κατα ματθαιον. εγραφη και αντεβληθη εκ των* [*sic*] *ἱεροσολυμοις παλαιων αντιγραφων· των εν τω ἁγιω ορει αποκειμενων· εν στιχοις βφιδ· κεφφ. τνε.* Very similar subscriptions occur in Codd. 20, 215, 300, 376, 428, 573.

[2] Cod. Ξ contains Luke i. 1–9; 19–23; 27, 28; 30–32; 36–66; 77—ii. 19; 21, 22; 33–39; iii. 5–8; 11–20; iv. 1, 2; 6–20; 32–43; v. 17–36; vi. 21—vii. 6; 11–37; 39–47; viii. 4–21; 25–35; 43–50; ix. 1–28; 32, 33; 35; 41—x. 18; 21–40; xi. 1, 2; 3, 4; 24–30; 31; 32, 33.

arrangement of the matter makes it certain that the commentary is contemporaneous, Cod. Ξ must be regarded as the earliest known, indeed as the only uncial, copy furnished with a catena. This volume, which once belonged to 'Il Principe Comuto, Zante,' and is marked as Μνημόσυνον σεβάσματος τοῦ Ἱππέος Ἀντωνίου Κόμητος 1820, was presented to the Bible Society in 1821 by General Macaulay, who brought it from Zante. Mr. Knolleke, one of the Secretaries, seems first to have noticed the older writing, and on the discovery being communicated to Tregelles in 1858 by Dr. Paul de Lagarde of Berlin, with characteristic eagerness that critic examined, deciphered, and published the Scripture text, together with the Moscow fragment O, in 1861: he doubted whether the small Patristic writing could all be read without chemical restoration. Besides the usual τίτλοι above the text and other notations of sections, and numbers running up from 1 to 100 which refer to the catena, this copy is remarkable for possessing also the division into chapters, hitherto as has been stated deemed unique in Cod. B. To this notation is commonly prefixed *psi*, formed like a cross, in the fashion of the eighth century. The ancient volume must have been a large folio (14 inches by 11), of which eighty-six leaves and three half-leaves survive: of course very hard to read. Of the ecclesiastical writers cited by name Chrysostom, Origen, and Cyril are the best known. In text it generally favours the B and ℵ and their company. In the 564 places wherein Tischendorf cites it in his eighth edition, it supports Cod. L in full three cases out of four, and those the most characteristic. It stands alone only fourteen times, and with Cod. L or others against the five great uncials only thirty times. In regard to these five, Cod. Ξ sides plainly with Cod. B in preference to Cod. A, following B alone seven times, BL twenty-four times, but ℵ thirteen times, A fifteen times, C (which is often defective) five times, D fourteen times, with none of these unsupported except with ℵ once. Their combinations in agreement with Ξ are curious and complicated, but lead to the same result. This copy is with ℵB six times, with ℵBL fifty-five; with ℵBC twenty, but with ℵBD as many as fifty-four times, with ℵBCD thirty-eight times; with BCD thrice, with BC six times, with BD thirteen. It combines with ℵA ten times, with AC fifteen, with AD eleven, with ℵAC sixteen, with ACD twelve, with ℵAD six, with ℵACD twelve. Thus Cod. Ξ favours B against A 226 times, A against B ninety-seven. Combinations of its readings opposed to both A and B are ℵC six, ℵD eight, CD two, ℵCD three. In the other passages it favours ABC against ℵD eleven times, ABCD against ℵ eight times, ℵABC against D eighteen times, ℵABD against C, or where C is defective, thirty-nine times, and is expressly cited twenty-seven times as standing with ℵABCD against later copies. The character of the variations of Cod. Ξ from the Received text may be judged of by the estimate made by some scholar, that forty-seven of them are transpositions in the order of the words, 201 are substitutions of one word for another, 118 are omissions, while the additions do not exceed twenty-four (*Christian Remembrancer*, January, 1862). The cursive Evangelistarium written over the uncial is noticed below, and bears the mark 200*.

Π. CODEX PETROPOLITANUS consists of 350 vellum leaves in small quarto, and contains the Gospels complete except Matt. iii. 12—iv. 18; xix. 12—xx. 3; John viii. 6–39; seventy-seven verses. A century since it belonged to Parodus, a noble Greek of Smyrna, and its last possessor was persuaded by Tischendorf, in 1859, to present it to the Emperor of Russia. Tischendorf states that it is of the age of the later uncials (meaning the ninth century), but of higher critical importance than most of them, and much like Cod. K in its rarer readings. There are many marginal and other corrections by a later hand, and John v. 4; viii. 3–6 are obelized. In the table of κεφάλαια before St. Mark, there is a gap after λϛ: Mark xvi. 18–20; John xxi. 22–25 are in a later hand. At the end of St. Mark, the last section inserted is σλδ by the side of ἀναστὰς δέ ver. 9, with η under it for the Eusebian canon. Tischendorf first used its readings for his Synopsis Evangelica 1864, then for the eighth edition of his Greek Testament 1865, &c. This manuscript in the great majority of instances sides with the later uncials (whether supported by Cod. A or not) against Codd. ℵBCD united.

Σ. COD. ROSSANENSIS, like Cod. N described above, is a manuscript written on thin vellum leaves stained purple, in silver letters, the first three lines of each Gospel being in gold. Like

Cod. D it probably dates from the sixth century, if not a little sooner, and is the earliest known copy of Scripture which is adorned with miniatures in watercolours, seventeen in number, very interesting and in good preservation. The illustrated Dioscorides at Vienna bears about the same date. Attention was called to the book by Cesare Malpica in 1846, but it was not seen by any one who cared to use it before March, 1879, when Oscar von Gebhardt of Göttingen and Adolf Harnack of Giessen, in their search for codices of Hippolytus, of Dionysius of Alexandria, and of Cyril of Jerusalem, described by Cardinal Sirlet in 1582, found it in the Archbishop's Library at Rossano, a small city in Calabria, and published an account of it in 1880 in a sumptuous form, far more satisfactory to the artist than to the Biblical critic. Their volume is illustrated by two facsimile leaves, of one of which a reduction may be seen in our Plate xiv, No. 43. A copy of the manuscripts was published at Leipsic in 1883 with an Introduction by Oscar von Gebhardt, the Text being edited by Adolf Harnack [1]. The page we have exhibited gives the earliest MS. authority, except Φ, for the doxology in the Lord's Prayer, Matt. vi. 13. The manuscript is in quarto, 13½ inches high by 10¼ broad, and now contains only the Gospels of St. Matthew and St. Mark on 188 leaves of two columns each, there being twenty lines in each column of very regular writing, and from nine to twelve letters in each line. It ends abruptly at Mark xvi. 14, and the last ten leaves have suffered from damp; otherwise the writing (especially on the inner or smooth side of the vellum) is in good preservation, and the colours of the paintings wonderfully fresh. The binding is of strong black leather, about 200 years old. As in Cod. B, the sheets are ranged in quinions, the *signatures* in silver by the original scribe standing at the lower border of each quire on the right, and the pages being marked in the upper border in modern black ink. In Cod. Σ there is no separation between the words, it has no breathings or accents. Capital letters stand outside the columns, being about twice the size of the rest, and the smaller letters at the end of lines are not compressed, as we

[1] Texte und Untersuchungen zur Geschichte der altchristlichen Literatur, 1. Bd. 4: Hft., 1883, Leipsig. Also see *Church Quarterly*, Jan. 1884. Prof. Sanday in Studia Biblica, i. p. 111. 'Would delight the heart of the Dean of Chichester.' *Athenaeum*, No. 302, Sept. 19, 1885.

find them even in Cod. P (*see* pp. 144, 163). The letters are round and square, and, as was abundantly seen above (pp. 33–40), belong to the older type of writing. The punctuation is very simple: the full stop occurs half up the letter. There are few erasures, but transcriptural errors are mostly corrected in silver letters by the original scribe. To St. Matthew's Gospel is prefixed Eusebius' Epistle to Carpianus and his Tables of Canons, both imperfect; also lists of the κεφάλαια *majora* and τίτλοι in the upper margins of the several leaves, with a subscription to the first Gospel (Ευαγγελιον κατα ματθαιον). This supplementary matter is written somewhat smaller, but (as the editors judge) by the same hand as the text, although the letters are somewhat more recent in general appearance, and ι *ascriptum* occurs, as it never does in the body of the manuscript: ϛ also is only twice abridged in the text, but often in the smaller writing. In the margin of the Greek text the Ammonian sections stand in minute characters over the numbers of the Eusebian canons. The text agrees but slightly with ℵ or B, and rather with the main body of uncials and cursives, which it favours in about a proportion of three to one. With the cognate purple manuscript Cod. N it accords so wonderfully, that although one of them cannot have been copied directly from the other, they must have been drawn directly or indirectly from the same source. Strong proofs of the affinity between N and Σ are Matt. xix. 7 ἡμῖν added to ἐνετείλατο: xxi. 8 ἐκ (for ἀπό): Mark vi. 53 ἐκεῖ added to προσω(ο in Σ)ρμισθησαν: vii. 1 οἱ prefixed to ἐλθόντες: *ibid.* 29 ὁ ισ̄ added to εἶπεν αὐτῇ: viii. 3 ἐγλυθήσονται: *ibid.* 13 καταλιπών for ἀφείς: *ibid.* 18 οὔπω νοεῖτε for καὶ οὐ μνημονεύετε: ix. 3 λευκᾶναι οὕτως: x. 5 ἐπέτρεψεν for ἔγραψεν: xiv. 36 πλήν before ἀλλ': xv. 21 omit παράγοντα: in all which places the two manuscripts are either virtually or entirely alone. Generally speaking, the Codex Rossanensis follows the Traditional Text, but not invariably. We find here the usual itacisms, as ει for ι, αι for ε, η for ει and ι, ου for ω, and vice versa; even ο for ω, which is rarer in very ancient copies. The so-called Alexandrian forms ἤλθατε, ἐλθάτω, ἴδαμεν, ἴδαν for verbs, τρίχαν and νύκταν for nouns, ἐκαθερίσθη, λήμψομαι, δεκατέσσερες, τεσσεράκοντα, it has in common with all copies approaching it in age.

Υ. Codex Blenheimius. Brit. Mus. Additional 31919,

formerly Blenheim 3. D. 13, purchased at Puttick's from the Sunderland sale in April, 1882. Under a Menaeum (*see* our Evst. 282) for the twenty-eight days of February [A.D. 1431], $12\frac{7}{8} \times 8\frac{1}{8}$, containing 108 leaves, Professors T. K. Abbott and J. P. Mahaffy of Trinity College, Dublin, discovered at Blenheim in May, 1881, *palimpsest* fragments of the Gospels of the eighth century, being seventeen passages scattered over thirty-three of the leaves: viz. Matt. i. 1–14; v. 3–19; xii. 27–41; xxiii. 5—xxv. 30; 43—xxvi. 26; 50—xxvii. 17. Mark i. 1–42; ii. 21—v. 1; 29—vi. 22; x. 50—xi. 13. Luke xvi. 21—xvii. 3; 19–37; xix. 15–31. John ii. 18—iii. 5; iv. 23–37; v. 35—vi. 2: in all 484 verses. In 1883, Dr. Gregory discovered two more leaves, making thirty-six in all, with a reduction of the passages to sixteen by filling up an hiatus, and giving a total of 497 verses. It is probable that writing lies under all the 108 leaves. It exhibits *Am.* (not *Eus.*) in gold, ἀρχαί and τέλη, but is very hard to read, and has not yet been collated. Of less account are palimpsest pieces of the eleventh century on some of the leaves, containing Matt. xi. 13, &c.; Luke i. 64, &c.; ii. 25–34, and a later cursive patch (fol. 23) containing Mark vi. 14–20.

Φ. Codex Beratinus. This symbol was taken by Herr Oscar von Gebhardt to denote the imaginary parent of Cursives 13, 69, 124, 346, of which the similarity has been traced by the late W. H. Ferrar and Dr. T. K. Abbott in 'A Collection of Four Important MSS.' (1877). But it is now permanently affixed to an Uncial MS. seen by M. Pierre Batiffol on the instigation of Prof. Duchesne in 1875 at Berat or Belgrade in Albania. This manuscript had been previously described by Mgr. Anthymus Alexoudi, Orthodox Metropolitan of Belgrade, in an account of his diocese published in 1868 in Corfu. According to M. Batiffol, it is a purple manuscript, written in silver letters on vellum, an *édition de grande luxe*, and therefore open to the charge brought by St. Jerome in his Prolegomena to Job against the great adornment of manuscripts, as being far from constituting an index of accuracy. It contains 190 unpaged leaves in quaternions, firmly sewn together, having two columns in a page of seventeen lines each, and from eight to twelve words in a line. The leaves are in size about $12\frac{1}{4}$ inches by $10\frac{1}{2}$, and

Plate XV.

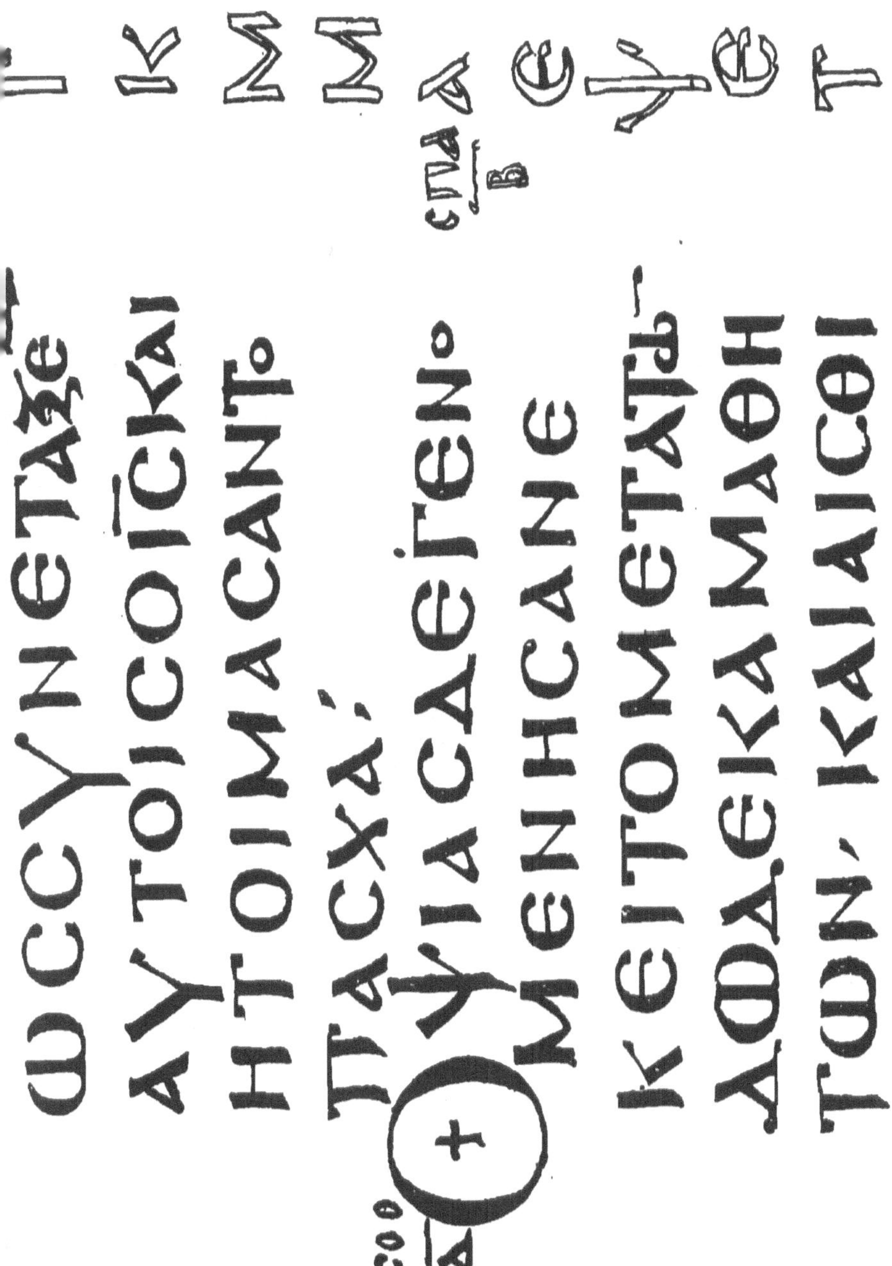

CODEX PURPUREUS Φ

the columns measure $8\frac{1}{4}$ inches high by rather more than $4\frac{1}{4}$ broad. The pages have the *κεφάλαια* marked at the top, and the sections and canons in writing of the eighth century at the side. The letters are in silver, very regular, and clearly written. None are in gold, except the title and the first line in St. Mark, and the words Πατήρ, Ἰησοῦς, and some others in the first six folios. There is no ornamentation, but the first letters of paragraphs are twice as large as the other letters. The letters have no decoration, except a cross in the middle of the initial O's. The writing is continuous in full line without stichometry. Quotations from the Old Testament are marked with a kind of inverted comma. There are no breathings, or accents. Punctuation is made only with the single comma or double comma, consisting of a point slightly elongated much like a modern written comma, and placed at about mid-height, or else with a vacant space, or by passing to the next line. The apostrophe is not always used to mark elisions, but is generally put after P final. Abbreviations are of the most ancient kind. The character of the letters may be seen in the specimen given above, No. 43. Altogether, the Codex Beratinus (Φ) may probably be placed at the end of the fifth century, a little before the Dioscorides (506 A. D.), and before the Codex Rossanensis.

As to the character of the text, it inclines to the large body of Uncials and Cursives, and is rarely found with Bℵ and Z of St. Matthew or Δ of St. Mark. A specimen examination of fifty passages at the beginning of St. Matthew gives forty-four instances in which it agrees with the larger body of Uncials and Cursives, six when it passes over to the other side, whilst in thirty-eight it agrees with Σ. In the same passages, Σ agrees thirty-eight times with the larger body, and twelve times with ℵ or B. Like Σ it contains the doxology in Matt. vi. 13.

Codex Φ has gone through many vicissitudes. It has perhaps been at Patmos, where it may have been mutilated by some of the Crusaders, and at Antioch. It contains only St. Matthew and St. Mark; a note says that the disappearance of St. Luke and St. John is due to the Franks of Champagne. The first six folios are in a bad state, so that the text as we have it does not begin till St. Matt. vi. 3 *η αριστερα σου κ.τ.λ.* Hiatus occurs Matt. vii. 26—viii. 7, in xviii. 23—xix. 3, and in Mark xiv. 62–fin. So that Cod. Φ presents no direct evidence—only the testimony to the general character of its companions derived from its own character and general coincidence—upon the last twelve verses of St. Mark. Part of folio 112, at the end of St. Matthew, is blank, and folios 113, 114, contain the *κεφάλαια* of St. Mark.

It was handsomely bound in 1805 in wood covered with chased silver. See le Mss Grecs &c, par Pierre Batiffol, Paris 1886

Ψ. In the Monastery of Laura at Mount Athos [viii or ix], $8\frac{1}{4} \times 6$, ff. 261 (31), *κεφ. t.*, *Am.*, *Eus.*, *lect.* Mark ix. 5–end; Luke, John, Acts, 1, 2 Peter, James, 1, 2, 3 John, Romans, Hebrews viii. 13; ix. 19–end. Inserts the supplement of L to St. Mark before the last twelve verses, and the lectionary *τέλος* after *ἐφοβοῦντο γάρ*. See Gregory, Prolegomena, p. 445.

Ω. In the Monastery of Dionysius at Athos [viii or ix], $8\frac{3}{4} \times 6\frac{1}{2}$, ff. 289 (22), two columns. Whole four Gospels. Gregory, p. 446.

ב. In the Monastery of St. Andrew at Athos [ix or x], $8 \times 6\frac{1}{4}$, ff. 152 (37). The four Gospels. Gregory, p. 446.

CHAPTER VI.

UNCIAL MANUSCRIPTS OF THE ACTS AND CATHOLIC EPISTLES, OF ST. PAUL'S EPISTLES, AND OF THE APOCALYPSE.

I. *Manuscripts of the Acts and Catholic Epistles.*

ℵ. Cod. Sinaiticus. B. Cod. Vaticanus.
A. Cod. Alexandrinus. C. Cod. Ephraemi.
D. Codex Bezae.

E. Codex Laudianus 35 is one of the most precious treasures preserved in the Bodleian at Oxford. It is a Latin-Greek copy, with two columns on a page, the Latin version holding the post of honour on the left, and is written in very short *στίχοι*, consisting of from one to three words each, the Latin words always standing opposite to the corresponding Greek. This peculiar arrangement points decisively to the West of Europe as its country, notwithstanding the abundance of Alexandrian forms has led some to refer it to Egypt. The very large, bold, thick, rude uncials, without break in the words and without accents, lead us up to the end of the sixth century as its date. The Latin is not of Jerome's or the Vulgate version, but is made to correspond closely with the Greek, even in its interpolations and rarest various readings. The contrary supposition that the Greek portion of this codex *Latinised*, or had been altered to coincide with the Latin, is inconsistent with the facts of the case. This manuscript contains only the Acts of the Apostles (from ch. xxvi. 29 *παυλος* to ch. xxviii. 26 *λέγον* being lost), and exhibits a remarkable modification of the text, of which we shall speak in Chapter VII. That the book was once in Sardinia, appears from an edict of Flavius Pancratius, *συν θεω απο επαρχων δουξ σαρδινιας*, appended (as also is the Apostles' Creed in Latin, and some other foreign matter) in a later hand: Imperial governors ruled in that island with the title of *dux* from the reign of Justinian, A.D. 534 to A.D. 749. It was probably among the Greek volumes brought into England by the fellow-countryman of St. Paul, Theodore of Tarsus [1], 'the grand old man' as he has been called by one of kindred spirit to his own (Dean Hook, Lives of the Archbishops of Canterbury, vol. i. p. 150), who came to England as Primate at the age of sixty-six, A.D. 668, and died in 690. At all events, Mill (N. T. Proleg. §§ 1022–6) [2] has rendered it all but certain, that the Venerable Bede [d. 735] had this very codex before him when he wrote his 'Expositio Retractata' of the Acts [3], and Woide (Notitia Cod. Alex., p. 156, &c.) has since alleged six additional instances of agreement between them. The manuscript, however, must have been complete when Bede used it, for he cites in the Latin ch. xxvii. 5; xxviii. 2. Tischendorf (Proleg. p. xv) adds ch. xxvii. 1, 7, 14, 15, 16, 17: but these last instances are somewhat uncertain. This manuscript, with many others, was presented to the University of Oxford in the year 1636, by its munificent Chancellor, Archbishop Laud. Thomas Hearne, the celebrated antiquary, published a full edition of it in 1715, which is now very scarce, and was long known to be far from accurate. Sabatier in 1751 gave the Latin of it taken from Hearne. Tischendorf has published a new edition, from two separate collations made by himself in 1854 and 1865, in the ninth volume by way of Appendix to his 'Monumenta sacra inedita,' 1870. It is also found in vol. ii of Hansell's edition of the Ancient Texts, published at the Clarendon Press in 1864. Cod. E

[1] Dean Gywnn of Raphoe is so good as to remind me that among the other proper names enumerated by Wetstein and Semler as written on the reverse of the last leaf of this manuscript, ΘΕΩΔΟΡΟC stands by itself in a hand which may be as old as the seventh century. Common as the name is, the fact is interesting and suggestive. For the orthography compare *κωλονια* Acts xvi. 12 in Cod. E.

[2] It is probable that Mill got this from 'Nouvelles Observations sur le Texte et les Versions du Nouveau Testament,' par R. Simon, Paris, 1695.

[3] I see no force in Tischendorf's objection, that if Theodore had brought Cod. E to England, Bede would have used it before he came to write his 'Expositio Retractata.'

has been stated to have capital letters at the commencement of each of the Euthalian sections, but as the capitals occur at other places where the sense is broken but slightly (e.g. ch. xvii. 20), this circumstance does not prove that those sections were known to the scribe. It is in size 10¼ inches by 8½, and consists of 227 leaves of twenty-three, twenty-four, twenty-five, or twenty-six lines each; about fifteen leaves are lost: the vellum is rather coarse in quality, and the ink in many places very faint. There seem to be no stops nor breathings, except an aspirate over initial *upsilon* (ῦ or ὑ, sometimes ῡ or ϋ) almost invariably. The shape of *xi* is more complicated than usual (see our facsimile, No. 25); the other letters (e.g. *delta* or *psi*) are such as were common in the sixth or early in the seventh century. There are also many changes by a later uncial hand. Mr. Hansell (Ancient Texts, Oxford, 1864), as well as Tischendorf, exhibits one whole page in zinco-photography.

F^a. Cod. Coislin. I.

G. Tischendorf, in his eighth edition of the N. T., assigns this letter (formerly appropriated to Cod. L) to one octavo leaf of the seventh century, now at St. Petersburg, written in thick uncials without accents, torn from the wooden cover of a Syriac book, and containing Acts ii. 45—iii. 8. It has a few rare and valuable readings. Dr. Hort (Supplement to Tregelles, p. 1021) cites it as G^a.

G^b. Vaticanus Romanus 9671 [iv?] fol., ff. 5 (22), palimpsest. *See* Gregory, Prolegomena, p. 414.

H. Cod. Mutinensis [cxcvi] ii. G. 3, of the Acts, in the Grand Ducal Library at Modena, is an uncial copy of about the ninth century, defective in Acts i. 1—v. 28; ix. 39—x. 19; xiii. 36—xiv. 3, all supplied by a cursive hand [h], 'in my judgement . . . scarcely later' (Burgon), and in xxvii. 4—xxviii. 31 (written in uncials of about the eleventh century). The Epistles are in cursive letters of the twelfth century, indicated in the Catholic Epistles by h, in the Pauline by 179. Scholz first collated it loosely, as usual; then Tischendorf in 1843,

Tregelles in 1846, afterwards comparing their collations for mutual correction.

I. COD. PETROPOLIT. or TISCHENDORFIAN. II.

K. COD. MOSQUENSIS, S. Synodi No. 98, is Matthaei's g, and came from the monastery of St. Dionysius on Mount Athos. It contains the Catholic Epistles entire, but not the Acts; and the Pauline Epistles are defective only in Rom. x. 18—1 Cor. vi. 13; 1 Cor. viii. 7–11. Matthaei alone has collated this document, and judging from his facsimile (Cath. Epp. 1782) it seems to belong to the ninth century. This copy is Scholz's Act. 102, Paul. 117. It is not so thoroughly known but that it is often necessary to cite its readings *ex silentio.*

L (formerly G). COD. BIBLIOTH. ANGELICAE A. 2. 15, belonging to the Augustinian monks at Rome, formerly 'Cardinalis Passionei,' contains the Acts from ch. viii. 10, *μισ του θεου* to the end, the Catholic Epistles complete, and the Pauline down to Heb. xiii. 10, *οὐκ ἔχουσιν*, of a date not earlier than the middle of the ninth century. It was collated in part by Bianchini and Birch, in full by Scholz (1820, J. Paul) and by F. F. Fleck (1833). Tischendorf in 1843, Tregelles in 1845, collated it independently, and subsequently compared their papers, as they have done in several other instances.

M of Gregory (G^b), fol., ff. 5 (22), palimpsest, containing fragments of Acts xvi—xviii of the eighth or ninth century, was published by Cozza (Sacr. Bibl. Vetust. Frag. iii: Rome, 1877). It was transferred to the Vatican (No. 9671) from the Greek convent of Grotta Ferrata.

P. COD. PORPHYRIANUS is a palimpsest containing the Acts, all the Epistles, the Apocalypse, and a few fragments of 4 Maccabees, of the ninth century, found by Tischendorf in 1862 at St. Petersburg in the possession of the Archimandrite (now Bishop) Porphyry, who allowed him to take it to Leipsic to decipher. He has published it at length in his 'Monumenta sacra inedita,' vol. v, vi, whence Tregelles derived its readings for the Pauline Epistles and the Apocalypse. In the latter book it is especially useful, and generally confirms Codd. AC, though it is often with

Cod. ℵ, sometimes against all the rest. It has the ἀρχ and τέ of Church lessons in the margin, and is defective (besides a few words or letters lost here and there) in Acts i. 1—ii. 15; 1 John iii. 20—v. 1; Jude 4–15; Rom. ii. 16—iii. 5; viii. 33—ix. 11; xi. 22—xii. 1; 1 Cor. vii. 16, 17; xii. 23—xiii. 5; xiv. 23–39; 2 Cor. ii. 14, 15; Col. iii. 16—iv. 8; 1 Thess. iii. 5—iv. 17; Apoc. xvi. 13—xvii. 1; xx. 1–9; xxii. 6–21. Moreover James ii. 12–21; 2 Pet. i. 20—ii. 5 are barely legible. Mr. Hammond (Outlines of Textual Criticism) has taken from Tischendorf's fifth volume a neat facsimile of it in Acts iv. 10–15, comprising uncials of the latest form, leaning to the right, lying under cursive writing (Heb. vii. 17–25), some four centuries more recent. Dr. Hort (Supplement to Tregelles, p. xxx) states that in the Acts the text of Cod. P is almost exclusively of a very late type, but that it contains a much larger though varying proportion of various readings elsewhere, except in 1 Peter. The upper or later writing in this manuscript is, for once, available for critical purposes, since it consists of fragments of the labours of Euthalius (*see* p. 64), and is cited by Tischendorf under the notation of Euthal.[cod.]

S. From the monastery of Laura at Mount Athos [viii or ix], 11 × 8½, ff. 120 (30), Acts, Cath. Rom. 1 Cor. i. 1—v. 8; xiii. 8—xvi. 24; 2 Cor. i. 1—xi. 23; Eph. iv. 20—vi. 20. *See* Gregory, p. 447.

ב. Rom. Vat. Gr. 2061, formerly Basil 100, before Patiriensis 27 [v], palimpsest, ff. 21 out of 316. Fragments of Acts, Cath., and Paul. Came from the monastery of St. Mary of Patirium, a suburb of Rossana in Calabria. Discovered by M. Pierre Batiffol, the investigator of Cod. Φ. *See* Gregory, p. 447.

II. *Manuscripts of the Pauline Epistles.*

ℵ. Cod. Sinaiticus
A. Cod. Alexandrinus.
B. Cod. Vaticanus.
C. Cod. Ephraemi.

D. Cod. Claromontanus, No. 107 of the Royal Library at Paris, is a Greek-Latin copy of St. Paul's Epistles, one of the most ancient and important in existence. Like the Cod. Ephraemi in the same Library it has been fortunate in such an editor as Tischendorf, who published it in 1852 with complete Prolegomena, and a facsimile traced by Tregelles. This noble volume is in small quarto, written on 533 leaves of the thinnest and finest vellum: indeed its extraordinary delicacy has caused the writing at the back of every page to be rather too visible on the other side. The words, both Greek and Latin, are written continuously (except the Latin titles and subscriptions), but in a stichometrical form (*see* p. 52): the Greek, as in Cod. Bezae, stands on the left or first page of the opened book, not on the right, as in the Cod. Laudianus. Each page has but one column of about twenty-one lines, so that in this copy, as in the Codex Bezae, the Greek and Latin are in parallel lines, but on separate pages. The ink is dark and clear, and otherwise the book is in good condition. It contains all St. Paul's Epistles (the Hebrews after Philemon), except Rom. i. 1–7; 27–30, both Greek and Latin: Rom. i. 24–27 in the Latin is supplied in a later but very old hand, as also are Rom. i. 27–30 and 1 Cor. xiv. 13–22 in the Greek: the Latin of 1 Cor. xiv. 8–18; Heb. xiii. 21–23 is lost. The Epistle to the Hebrews has been erroneously imputed by some to a later scribe, inasmuch as it is not included in the list of the sacred books and in the number of their στίχοι or *versus*, which stand immediately *before* the Hebrews in this codex[1]: but the same list overlooks the Epistle to the Philippians, which has never been doubted to be St. Paul's: in this manuscript, however, the Epistle to the Colossians precedes that to the Philippians. Our earliest notice of it is derived from the Preface to Beza's third edition of the N. T. (Feb. 20, 1582): he there describes it as of equal antiquity with his copy of the Gospels (D), and states that it had been found 'in Claromontano apud Bellovacos coenobio,' at Clermont near Beauvais. Although Beza sometimes through inadvertence calls his codex of the Gospels Claromontanus, there seems no reason for disputing with Wetstein the correctness of his account (*see*

[1] The names and order of the books of the New Testament in this most curious and venerable list stand thus: Matthew, John, Mark, Luke, Romans, 1, 2 Corinth., Galat., E*f*es., 1, 2 Tim., Tit., Colos., *Filimon*, 1, 2 Pet., James, 1, 2, 3 John, Jude, Barnabas' Ep., John's Revelation, Act. Apost., Pastor [Hermas], Actus Paul., Revelatio Petri.

p. 125, note 2), though it throws no light on the manuscript's early history. From Beza it passed into the possession of Claude Dupuy, Councillor of Paris, probably on Beza's death [1605]: thence to his sons Jacques and Pierre Dupuy: before the death of Jacques (who was the King's Librarian) in 1656, it had been bought by Louis XIV for the Royal Library at Paris. In 1707, John Aymont, an apostate priest, stole thirty-five leaves; one, which he disposed of in Holland, was restored in 1720 by its possessor Stosch; the rest were sold to that great collector, Harley, Earl of Oxford, but sent back in 1729 by his son, who had learnt their shameful story. Beza made some, but not a considerable, use of this document; it was amongst the authorities consulted for Walton's Polyglott; Wetstein collated it twice in early life (1715–16); Tregelles examined it in 1849, and compared his results with the then unpublished transcript of Tischendorf, which proved on its appearance (1852) the most difficult, as well as one of the most important, of his critical works; so hard it had been found at times to determine satisfactorily the original readings of a manuscript which had been corrected by *nine* different hands, ancient and modern. The date of the codex is doubtless the sixth century, in the middle or towards the end of it. The Latin letters, especially *d*, are the latest in form (facsimile No. 41, 1 Cor. xiii. 5–8), and are much like those in the Cod. Bezae (No. 42), which in many points Cod. Claromontanus strongly resembles. Leaves 162, 163 are palimpsest, and contain part of the Phaethon, a lost play of Euripides. We have already noticed many of its peculiarities (pp. 33–40), and need not here repeat them. *Delta* and *pi* look more ancient even than in Cod. A: the uncials are simple, square, regular and beautiful, of about the size of those in Codd. CD, and larger than in Cod. B. The stichometry forbids our assigning it to a period earlier than the end of the fifth century while other circumstances connected with the Latin version tend to put it a little lower still. The apostrophus is frequent, but there are few stops or abridgements; no breathings or accents are *primâ manu.* Initial letters, placed at the beginning of books or sections, are plain, and not much larger than the rest. The comparative correctness of the Greek text, and its Alexandrian forms, have caused certain critics to refer us as usual to Egypt for its country: the Latin text is more faulty, and shows comparative ignorance of the language: yet of what use a Latin version could be except in Africa or western Europe it were hard to imagine. This Latin is more independent of the Greek, and less altered from it than in Codd. Bezae or Laudian., wherein it has little critical value: that of Cod. Claromont. better represents the African type of the Old Latin. Of the corrections, a few were made by the original scribe when revising; a hand of the seventh century went through the whole (D**); two others follow; then in sharp black uncials of the ninth or tenth century another made more than two thousand critical changes in the text, and added stops and all the breathings and accents (D***); another D^{**}_{**} (among other changes) added to the Latin subscriptions. D^b supplied Rom. i. 27–30 very early; D^c, a later hand, 1 Cor. xiv. 13–22. Tischendorf distinguishes several others besides these.

E. Cod. Sangermanensis is another Greek-Latin manuscript and takes its name from the Abbey of St. Germain des Prez near Paris. Towards the end of the last century the Abbey (which at the Revolution had been turned into a saltpetre manufactory) was burnt down, and many of its books were lost. In 1805 Matthaei found this copy, as might almost have been anticipated, at St. Petersburg, where it is now deposited. The volume is a large quarto, the Latin and Greek in parallel columns on the same page, the Greek standing on the left; its uncials are coarse, large, and thick, not unlike those in Cod. E of the Acts, but of later shape, with breathings and accents *primâ manu*, of about the tenth, or late in the ninth, century[1]. It was used for the Oxford New Testament of 1675: Mill obtained some extracts from it, and noted its obvious connexion with Cod. Claromontanus: Wetstein thoroughly collated it; and not only he but Sabatier and Griesbach perceived that it was, at least in the Greek, nothing better than a mere transcript of Cod. Claromontanus, made by some ignorant person later than the corrector indicated by D^{**}_{**}. Muralt's endeavours to shake this conclusion have not satisfied

[1] Facsimiles of this manuscript are given by Semler in his edition of Wetstein's Prolegomena (1764, Nos. 8, 9). Bianchini's estimate of its age (Evangeliarium Quadruplex, tom. ii. fol. 591, 2), as of the seventh century, is certainly too high.

better judges; indeed the facts are too numerous and too plain to be resisted. Thus, while in Rom. iv. 25 Cod. D reads *δικαιωσιν* (accentuated *δικαίωσιν* by D***), in which D*** changes *ν* into *νην*, the writer of Cod. E adopts *δικαίωσινην* with its monstrous accent: in 1 Cor. xv. 5 Cod. D reads *μετα ταυτα τοις ενδεκα*, D*** *εἶτα τοῖς δώδεκα* (again observe the accents), out of which Cod. E makes up *μετα ταυεῖτα τοῖς δώενδεκα*. In Gal. iv. 31 Cod. D has *διο*, which is changed by D*** into *ἄρα*: Cod. E mixes up the two into *διᾶραο*. Compare Tischendorf's notes on Eph. ii. 19; Heb. x. 17, 33, and Dr. Hort's longer specimen, Rom. xv. 31–3 (Introd. p. 254). The Latin version also is borrowed from Cod. D, but is more mixed, and may be of some critical use: the Greek is manifestly worthless, and should long since have been removed from the list of authorities. This copy is defective, Rom. viii. 21–33; ix. 15–25; 1 Tim. i. 1—vi. 15; Heb. xii. 8—xiii. 25.

F[a]. COD. COISLIN. I.

F. COD. AUGIENSIS in the Library of Trinity College, Cambridge (B. xvii. 1), is another Greek-Latin manuscript on 136 leaves of good vellum 4to (the *signatures* proving that seven more are lost, *see* p. 28), 9 inches by $7\frac{1}{4}$, with the two languages in parallel columns of twenty-eight lines on each page, the Greek being always inside, the Latin next the edge of the book. It is called from the monastery of Augia Dives or Major (Reichenau, or *rich meadow*), on a fertile island in the lower part of Lake Constance, to which it long appertained, and where it may even have been written, a thousand years since. By notices at the beginning and end we can trace it through the hands of G. M. Wepfer of Schaffhausen and of L. Ch. Mieg, who covered many of its pages with Latin notes wretchedly scrawled, but allowed Wetstein to examine it. In 1718 Bentley was induced by Wetstein to buy it at Heidelberg for 250 Dutch florins, and both he and Wetstein collated the Greek portion, the latter carelessly, but Bentley somewhat more fully in the margin of a Greek Testament (Oxon. 1675) still preserved in Trinity College (B. xvii. 8). Tischendorf in 1842, Tregelles in 1845, re-examined the book (which had been placed where it now is on the death of Bentley's nephew in 1787), and drew attention to the Latin version: in 1859 Scrivener published an edition of the Codex in common type, with Prolegomena and a photograph of one page (1 Tim. iii. 14—iv. 5)[1]. The Epistles of St. Paul are defective in Rom. i. 1—iii. 19; and the Greek only in 1 Cor. iii. 8–16; vi. 7–14; Col. ii. 1–8; Philem. 21–25; in which four places the Latin stands in its own column with no Greek over against it. In the Epistle to the Hebrews, the Greek being quite lost, the Latin occupies both columns: this Epistle alone has an Argument, almost verbatim the same as we read in the great Cod. Amiatinus of the Vulgate. At the end of the Epistle, and on the same page (fol. 139, *verso*), commences a kind of Postscript (having little connexion with the sacred text), the larger portion of which is met with under the title of Dicta Abbatis Pinophi, in the works of Rabanus Maurus, Archbishop of Mayence, who died in A.D. 856; from which circumstance the Cod. Augiensis has been referred to the ninth century. Palaeographical arguments also would lead us to the same conclusion. The Latin version (a modification of the Vulgate in its purest form, though somewhat tampered with in parts to make it suit the Greek text[2]) is written in the cursive minuscule character common in the age of Charlemagne. The Greek must have been taken from an archetype with the words continuously written; for not only are they miserably ill divided by the unlearned German[3] scribe, but his design (not always acted upon) was to put a single middle point at the end of each word. The Latin is exquisitely written, the Greek uncials are neat, but evidently the work of an unpractised hand, which soon changes from weariness. The shapes of *eta*, *theta*, *pi*, and other testing letters are such as we might have expected from the date; some others have an older look. Contrary to the more ancient custom, capitals, small but numerous, occur in the *middle* of the lines in both languages. Of the ordinary breathings[4] and accents there are no traces. Here and there we meet with a straight line, inclined between the horizontal and the acute accent, placed over an initial vowel, usually when it should be aspirated, but not always (e.g. ἴδιον 1 Cor. vi. 18).

[1] Facsimile of 1 Tim. vi. 19—2 Tim. i. 5 is given in Pal. Soc. Pt. ix (1879), Pl. 127.

[2] So 1 Cor. xii. 2. For ἄφωνα, Vulg. *muta*, Cod. Aug. ἄμορφα. Rom. viii. 26. For ἀσθενείαις, Vulg. *infirmitatem orationis nostrae*, Cod. Aug. τῆς δεήσεως, cf. 1 Cor. vii. 11. Infinitives for Imperatives.

[3] He betrays his nationality by placing 'waltet' *primâ manu* over the first εξουσειαζει, 1 Cor. vii. 4.

[4] In 1 Tim. iv. 2 the Latin h is inserted *secundâ manu* before υποκρισι.

Over ι and υ double or single points, or a comma, are frequently placed, especially if they begin a syllable; and occasionally a large comma or kind of circumflex over ι, ει, and some other vowels and diphthongs. The arrangement of the Greek forbids punctuation there; in the Latin we find the single middle point as a colon or after an abridgement, the semicolon (;) sometimes, the note of interrogation (?) when needed. Besides the universal forms of abridgement (*see* p. 49), ϗ and ȣ are frequent in the Greek, but no others: in the Latin the abbreviations are numerous, and some of them unusual: Scrivener (Cod. Augiensis Proleg. pp. xxxi–ii) has drawn up a list of them. This copy abounds as much as any with real variations from the common text, and with numberless errors of the pen, itacisms of vowels, and permutations of consonants. It exhibits many corrections, a few *primâ manu*, some unfortunately very recent, but by far the greater number in a hand almost contemporary with the manuscript, which has also inserted over the Greek, in 106 places, Latin renderings differing from those in the parallel column, but which in eighty-six of these 106 instances agree with the Latin of the sister manuscript.

G. COD. BOERNERIANUS, so called from a former possessor, but now in the Royal Library at Dresden. In the sixteenth century it belonged to Paul Junius of Leyden: it was bought dear at the book-sale of Peter Francius, Professor at Amsterdam, in 1705, by C. F. Boerner, a Professor at Leipsic, who lent it to Kuster to enrich his edition of Mill (1710), and subsequently to Bentley. The latter so earnestly wished to purchase it as a companion to Cod. F, that though he received it in 1719, it could not be recovered from him for five years, during which he was constantly offering high sums for it[1]: a copy, but not in Bentley's hand, had been already made (Trin. Coll. B. xvii. 2). Cod. G was published in full by Matthaei in 1791, in common type, with two facsimile

[1] Boerner's son tells the tale thirty years afterwards with amusing querulousness in his Catalogus Bibl. Boern. Lips. 1754, p. 6, cited by Matthaei Cod. Boern. p. xviii. But there must have been some misunderstanding on both sides, for it appears from a manuscript note in his copy of the Oxford N. T. of 1675 (Trin. Coll. B. xvii. 8), that Bentley considered Cod. G his own property; since after describing Cod. F before the Epistle to the Romans as his own, and as commencing at Rom. iii. 19, he adds 'Variae lectiones ex altero *nostro* MSto, ejusdem veteris exemplaris apographo.'

pages (1 Cor. ii. 9—iii. 3; 1 Tim. i. 1–10), and his edition is believed to be very accurate; Anger, Tischendorf, Tregelles, Böttiger and others who have examined it have only expressly indicated three errors[1]. Rettig has abundantly proved that, as it is exactly of the same size, so it once formed part of the same volume with Cod. Δ (*see* p. 157 and note): they must date towards the end of the ninth century, and may very possibly have been written in the monastery of St. Gall (where Δ still remains) by some of the Irish monks who flocked to those parts. That Cod. G has been in such hands appears from some very curious Irish lines at the foot of one of Matthaei's plates (fol. 23), which, after having long perplexed learned men, have at length been translated for Dr. Reeves, the eminent Celtic scholar[2]. All that we have said respecting the form of Cod. Δ applies to this portion of it: the Latin version (a specimen of the Old Latin, but as in Codd. Bezae and Laudianus much changed to suit the Greek) is cursive and interlinear; the Greek uncials coarse and peculiar; the punctuation chiefly a stop at the end of the words, which have no breathings nor accents. Its affinity to the Cod. Augiensis has no parallel in this branch of literature. Scrivener has noted all the differences between them at the foot of each page in his

[1] viz. *ημας* for *υμας*, Rom. xvi. 17; *μετρους* for *μερους*, Eph. iv. 16; *εσκοτισμενος* for *-μενοι*, iv. 18. Add to these *στωμα* for *σωμα*, 1 Cor. ix. 27, as cited by Bentley (Ellis, Critica Sacra, p. 36).

[2] By John O'Donovan, Editor of Irish Annals. I have been favoured with corrections by the late Dr. Todd, of Trinity College, Dublin, and recently by the Rev. Robert King of Ballymena, whose version I have ventured to adopt.

Téicht do róim [téicht do róim]	To come to Rome, to come to Rome,
Mór saido becic torbai	Much of trouble, little of profit,
Inri chondaigi hifoss	The thing thou seekest here,
Manimbera latt ni fog bai	If thou bring not with thee, thou findest not.
Mór báis mór baile	Great folly, great madness,
Mór coll ceille mór mire	Great ruin of sense, great insanity,
Olais airchenn teicht dóecaib	Since thou hast set out for death,
Beith fó étoil maic Maire.	That thou shouldest be in disobedience to the Son of Mary.

The second stanza intimates that as the pilgrimage to Rome is at the risk of life, it is folly not to be at peace with Christ before we set out. The opening words 'To come to Rome' imply that the verses were written there by some disappointed pilgrim. Since the handwriting resembles that of the interlinear Latin, Mr. King suggests that both may have been the work of the Scottish Bishop Marcus, or of his nephew Moengal (Rettig, Cod. Δ, Prolegomena, p. xx), who called at St. Gall on their return from Rome, whence Marcus went homewards, leaving his books and Moengal behind him.

edition of Cod. F: they amount to but 1,982 places, whereof 578 are mere blunders of the scribe, 967 changes of vowels or itacisms, 166 interchanges of consonants, seventy-one grammatical or orthographical forms; the remaining 200 are real various readings, thirty-two of them relating to the article. While in Cod. F (whose first seven leaves are lost) the text commences at Rom. iii. 19, *μω· λεγει*, this portion is found complete in Cod. G, except Rom. i. 1–5; ii. 16–25. All the other lacunae of Cod. F occur also in Cod. G, which ends at Philem. 20 ἐν $\overline{χρω}$: there is no Latin version to supply these gaps in Cod. G, but a blank space is always left, sufficient to contain what is missing. At the end of Philemon G writes Προσ (ad) λαουδακησασ[1] (laudicenses) *αρχεται* (incipit) *επιστολη* (epistola), but neither that writing nor the Epistle to the Hebrews follows. It seems tolerably plain that one of these manuscripts was not copied immediately from the other, for while they often accord even in the strangest errors of the pen that men unskilled in Greek could fall into, their division of the Greek words, though equally false and absurd, is often quite different: it results therefore that they are independent transcripts of the same venerable archetype (probably stichometrical and some centuries older than themselves) which was written without any division between the words[2]. From the form of the letters

[1] Here *αου* standing to represent *au* shows that the Greek is derived from the Latin, not *vice versâ*.

[2] That Cod. G cannot have been taken from Cod. F appears both from matters connected with their respective Latin versions, and because F contains no trace of the vacant lines left in G at the end of Rom. xiv to receive ch. xvi. 25–27. But Dr. Hort (Journal of Philology, vol. iii. No. 5, pp. 67, 68 note) has come to think that F is a mere transcript of G, the scribe of the former being by far the more ignorant of the two. He meets our argument to the contrary stated above in the text, by alleging that in respect to the division of words F is free from no outrageous portent found in G, while it has to answer for many of its own. But (to take our examples from one open leaf) if the writer of F were so helplessly ignorant as Dr. Hort represents, how could he have set right G's error in 1 Tim. iv. 7, reading *και · γραωδεις* for G's *και αιγραωδεις*? Again, if F had before him an undivided manuscript, one can easily account for such monsters as in 1 Tim. iv. 2 *και · καυτη ριασ μενων·* F (*photographed page*), but no one could possibly have so written with G's *κεκαυτηριασμενων* before him. That the two copies were compared together in after times seems evident from the fact stated in p. 179, that Latin renderings from G stand in eighty-six places above the Greek of F. It was at the same time perhaps that some ill-divided words in F were corrected by means of a loop from the Greek of G: e.g. 2 Cor. i. 3 *οικτιρμων* G, *οικ ◡ τιρμων* F; ii. 14 *θριαμβευοντι* G, *θριαμ ◡ βευοντι* F; iv. 9 *ενκαταλιμπαννομενοι* G, *εν · καταλιμπαν ◡ νομενοι* F; ver. 15 *πλεονασασα* G, *πλεονα ◡ σασα* F. 'Mr. Hort's

and other circumstances Cod. F may be deemed somewhat but not much the older; its corrector *secundâ manu* evidently had both the Greek and the Latin of Cod. G before him, and Rabanus, in whose works the Dicta Pinophi are preserved (p. 178), was the great antagonist of Godeschalk, on whom the annotator of Codd. ΔG bears so hard. Cod. G is in 4to, of ninety-nine leaves, with twenty-one lines in each. The line indicating breathing (if such be its use, *see* p. 178) and the mark > employed to fill up spaces (p. 51), more frequent in it than in F.

Since Dr. Scrivener wrote the above, a very valuable little treatise—a 'specimen primum'—has been given to the learned world by Herr P. Corssen [1], and a most clear and carefully argued paper has been sent to the editor by the Rev. Nicholas Pocock of Clifton. Both Herr Corssen and Mr. Pocock agree in showing that F was not derived from G, nor G from F, but that they come from the same original. Both agree, again, that the Greek version is derived, at least in large measure, from the Latin, as in such instances as the following, which are supplied by Mr. Pocock, who holds, and appears to prove, that F and G were copied from an interlinear manuscript: *ut sciatis*, *ινα οιδαται* (F, G), 1 Thess. iii. 3; *sicut cancer ut serpat*, *ως γαγγρα, ινα νομηνεξει* (G), 2 Tim. ii. 17, F having the same reading, only dividing the last word; Gal. iv. 3 *eramus autem servientes*, *ημεθα δε δουλωμενοι* (F, G). Herr Corssen considers that a Latin was the scribe of the original, that it was written in Italy, and that it was better than the Claromontanus (D), to which it had affinities, this last having an amended text with corrections from the Greek. The original of all three he supposes to date from not before the fifth century. But in some of these last suppositions we are getting upon the ocean of conjecture.

view, that F was copied directly from G' (writes Bishop Lightfoot very gently, Journal of Philology, vol. iii. No. 6, p. 210, note), 'deserves consideration, and may prove true, though his arguments do not seem quite conclusive.' Lightfoot elsewhere pronounces that 'the divergent phenomena of the two Latin texts' seem unfavourable to Dr. Hort's hypothesis (Ep. to Coloss. p. 355, note 2). But the latter still adheres to it with characteristic firmness: 'we believe F to be as certainly in its Greek text a transcript of G [as E is of D]; if not, it is an inferior copy of the same immediate exemplar' (Introd. p. 150). Yet why 'inferior'?

[1] Epistularum Paulinarum codd. Gr. et Lat. scriptas Augiensem Boernerianum Claromontanum examinavit, &c. Petrus Corssen, H. Fienche Kiliensis, 1889.

H. COD. COISLIN. 202 is a very precious fragment, of which twelve leaves are in the Imperial Library at Paris; nine are in the monastery or laura of St. Athanasius at Mount Athos, and have been edited by M. Duchesne in the 'Archives des missions scientifiques et littéraires' (1876); two more are at Moscow, and have been described by Matthaei (D. Pauli Epp. ad Hebr. et Col. Riga, 1784, p. 58); some others are in the Antonian Library of St. Petersburg (three); some more in the Imperial Library as described by Muralt (two), or in that of Bishop Porphyry (one), or at Turin (two). The leaves at Paris contain 1 Cor. x. 22–29; xi. 9–16; 1 Tim. iii. 7–13; Tit. i. 1–3; 15—ii. 5; iii. 13–15; Heb. ii. 11–16; iii. 13–18; iv. 12–15. At Mount Athos are 2 Cor. x. 18—xi. 6; xi. 12—xii. 2; Gal. i. 1–4; ii. 4–17; iv. 30—v. 5. At Moscow, Heb. x. 1–7; 32–38. At St. Petersburg, 2 Cor. iv. 2–7; 1 Thess. ii. 9–13; iv. 5–11 (Antonian; Gal. i. 4–10; ii. 9–14 (Imperial). In the Library of Bishop Porphyry, Col. iii. 4–11; and at Turin, 1 Tim. vi. 9–13; 2 Tim. ii. 1–9. They are in quarto, with large square uncials of about sixteen lines on a page, and date from the sixth century. Breathings and accents are added by a later hand, which retouched this copy (*see* Silvestre, Paléographie Universelle, Nos. 63, 64). These leaves, which comprise one of our best authorities for stichometrical writing, were used in A.D. 1218 to bind some other manuscripts on Mount Athos, and thence came into the library of Coislin, Bishop of Metz. Montfaucon has published Cod. H in his 'Bibliotheca Coisliniana,' but Tischendorf, who transcribed it, projected a fuller and more accurate edition. He observed at Paris in 1865 an additional passage, 2 Cor. iv. 4–6 (Monum. sacr. ined. vol. ix. p. xiv, note), and cites Cod. H in his eighth edition on 1 Tim. vi. 19; Heb. x. 1–6; 34–38. The subscriptions, which appear due to Euthalius of Sulci[1], written in vermilion, are not retouched, and consequently have neither breathings nor accents. Besides arguments to the Epistles, we copy the following final subscription from Tischendorf (N. T. 1859, p. clxxxix): *ἔγραψα καὶ ἐξεθέμην κατὰ δύναμιν στειχηρὸν· τόδε τὸ τεύχος παύλου τοῦ ἀποστόλου πρὸς ἐγγραμμὸν καὶ εὐκατάλημπτον ἀνάγνωσιν. τῶν καθ' ἥμας ἀδελφῶν· παρῶν ἀπάντων τολμης συγγνώμην αἰτῶ. εὐχὴ τῆ ὑπὲρ ἐμῶν· τὴν*

[1] *See* p. 63, note 1.

συνπεριφορὰν κομιζόμενος· ἀντεβλήθη δὲ ἡ βίβλος· πρὸς τὸ ἐν καισαρία ἀντίγραφον τῆς βιβλιοθήκης τοῦ ἁγίου παμφίλου χειρὶ γεγραμμένον αὐτοῦ (*see* p. 55, note 1). From this subscription we may conclude with Dr. Field (Proleg. in Hexapla Origenis, p. xcix) that the noble Library at Caesarea was still safe in the sixth century, though it may have perished A.D. 638, when that city was taken by the Saracens.

I. COD. TISCHENDORFIAN. II, at St. Petersburg. Add also two large leaves of the sixth century, elegantly written, without breathings or accents, containing 2 Cor. i. 20—ii. 12. Described by Tischendorf, Notitia Cod. Sin. Append. p. 50, cited as O in his eighth edition of the N. T.

K. COD. MOSQUENSIS.

L. COD. ANGELICUS at Rome.

M. CODEX RUBER is peculiar for the beautifully bright red colour of the ink [1], the elegance of the small uncial characters, and the excellency and critical value of the text. Two folio leaves, containing Heb. i. 1—iv. 3; xii. 20—xiii. 25, once belonged to Uffenbach, then to J. C. Wolff, who bequeathed them to the Public Library (Johanneum) of Hamburg (*see* Cod. H of the Gospels. To the same manuscript pertain fragments of two leaves used in binding Cod. Harleian. 5613 in the British Museum, and seen at once by Griesbach, who first collated them (Symbol. Crit. vol. ii. p. 164, &c.), to be portions of the Hamburg fragment [2]. Each page in both contains two columns, of forty-five lines in the Hamburg, of thirty-eight in the London leaves. The latter comprise 1 Cor. xv. 52—2 Cor. i. 15; x. 13—xii. 5; reckoning both fragments, 196 verses in all. Tischendorf has since found one leaf more. Henke in 1800 edited the Hamburg portion, Tregelles collated it twice, and Tischendorf in 1855 published the text of both in full in his 'Anecdota Sacra et Profana,' but corrected in the second edition, 1861 (Praef. xvi),

[1] Scholz describes Codd. 196, 362, 366 of the Gospels as also written in red ink. See too Evan. 254.

[2] Dr. C. R. Gregory has read a few words more of this MS. Griesbach and Scholz number the London part as 64, the Hamburg part as 53.

five mistakes in his printed text. The letters are a little unusual in form, perhaps about the tenth century in date; but though sometimes joined in the same word, can hardly be called *semicursive*. Our facsimile (Plate xii, No. 34) is from the London fragment: the graceful, though peculiar, shapes both of *alpha* and *mu* (*see* p. 37, ter) closely resemble those in some writing of about the same age, added to the venerable Leyden Octateuch, on a page published in facsimile by Tischendorf (Monum. sacr. ined. vol. iii). Accents and breathings are given pretty correctly and constantly: *iota* ascript occurs three times (2 Cor. i. 1; 4; Heb. xiii. 21)[1]; only ten *itacisms* occur, and ν ἐφελκυστικόν (as it is called) is rare. The usual stop is the single point in its three positions, with a change in power, as in Cod. E of the Gospels. The interrogative (;) occurs once (Heb. iii. 17), and > is often repeated to fill up space, or, in a smaller size, to mark quotations. After the name of each of the Epistles (2 Cor. and Heb.) in their titles we read εκτεθεισα ὡς εν πινακι, which Tischendorf thus explains; that whereas it was customary to prefix an argument to each Epistle, these words, originally employed to introduce the argument, were retained even when the argument was omitted. Henke's account of the expression looks a little less forced, that this manuscript was set forth ὡς εν πινακι, that is, in vermilion, after the pattern of Imperial letters patent.

N. (O[d] Hort.) Two leaves of the ninth century at St. Petersburg, containing Gal. v. 14—vi. 2; Heb. v. 8—vi. 10.

O. (N[c] Tisch.) FRAGMENTA MOSQUENSIA used as early as A.D. 975 in binding a volume of Gregory Nazianzen now at Moscow (S. Synodi 61). Matthaei describes them on Heb. x. 1: they contain only the twelve verses Heb. x. 1–3; 3–7; 32–34; 35–38. These very ancient leaves may possibly be as old as the sixth century, for their letters resemble in shape those in Cod. H

[1] Griesbach (Symbol. Critic. vol. ii. p. 166) says that in the Harleian fragment 'Iota bis tantum aut ter subscribitur, semel postscribitur, plerumque omittitur,' overlooking the second ascript. Scrivener repeats this statement about ι subscript (Cod. Augiens. Introd. p. lxxii), believing he had verified it: but Tischendorf cannot see the subscripts, nor can Scrivener on again consulting Harl. 5613 for the purpose. Tregelles too says, 'I have not seen a *sub*scribed iota in any uncial document' (Printed Text, p. 158, note).

which the later hand has so coarsely renewed; but they are more probably a little later.

O[a]. One unpublished double leaf brought by Tischendorf to St. Petersburg from the East, of the sixth century, containing 2 Cor. i. 20—ii. 12.

O[b] of the same date, at Moscow, contains Eph. iv. 1–18.

P. Cod. Porphyrianus.

Q. Tischendorf also discovered in 1862 at St. Petersburg five or six leaves of St. Paul, written on papyrus of the fifth century. From the extreme brittleness of the leaves only portions can be read. He cites them at 1 Cor. vi. 13, 14; vii. 3, 13, 14. These also Porphyry brought from the East. It contains 1 Cor. i. 17–20; vi. 13–15; 16–18; vii. 3, 4, 10, 11, 12–14, with defects. This is the only papyrus manuscript of the New Testament written with uncials.

R. Cod. Cryptoferratensis Z. β. 1. is a palimpsest fragment of the end of the seventh or the eighth century, cited by Caspar René Gregory as first used by Tischendorf. It is one leaf, containing 2 Cor. xi. 9-19. Edited by Cozza, and published amongst other old fragments at Rome in 1867 with facsimile (Greg., p. 435).

S. From Laura of Athos.

T. Paris, Louvre, Egyptian Museum, 7332 [iv–vi], $5\frac{3}{4} \times 4$, two small fragments, 1 Tim. vi. 3; iii. 15, 16. *See* Gregory, p. 441, who, however, unconsciously classes it as an Evan.

ב. Rom. Vat. Gr. 2061.

III. *Manuscripts of the Apocalypse.*

א. Cod. Sinaiticus.

A. Cod. Alexandrinus.

B. Cod. Vaticanus 2066 (formerly 105 in the Library of the Basilian monks in the city) was judiciously substituted by Wetstein for the modern portion of the great Vatican MS., collated by Mico, and published in 1796 by Ford in his 'Appendix' to Codex Alexandrinus, as also in 1868 by Vercellone and Cozza[1]. It is an uncial copy of about the end of the eighth century, and the volume also contains in the same hand Homilies of Basil the Great and of Gregory of Nyssa, &c. It was first known from a notice (by Vitali) and facsimile in Bianchini's Evangeliarium Quadruplex (1749), part i. vol. ii. p. 524 (facs. p. 505, tab. iv): Wetstein was promised a collation of it by Cardinal Quirini, who seems to have met with unexpected hindrances, as the papers only arrived after the text of the New Testament was printed, and then proved very loose and defective. When Tischendorf was at Rome in 1843, though forbidden to collate it afresh (in consequence, as we now know, of its having been already printed in Mai's then unpublished volumes of the Codex Vaticanus), he was permitted to make a facsimile of a few verses, and while thus employed he so far contrived to elude the watchful custodian, as to compare the whole manuscript with a modern Greek Testament. The result was given in his Monumenta sacra inedita (1846), pp. 407–432, with a good facsimile; but (as was natural under the unpromising circumstances—'*arrepta potius quam lecta*' is his own confession) Tregelles in 1845 was able to observe several points which he had overlooked, and more have come to light since Mai's edition has appeared. In 1866, however, Tischendorf was allowed to transcribe this document at leisure, and re-published it in full in his Appendix N. T. Vaticani, 1869, pp. 1–20.

This Codex is now known to contain the whole of the Apocalypse, a fact which the poor collation that Wetstein managed to procure had rendered doubtful. It is rather an octavo than a folio or quarto; the uncials being of a peculiar kind, simple and unornamented, leaning a little to the right (*see* p. 41, note): they hold a sort of middle place between square and oblong characters. The shape of *beta* is peculiar, the two loops to the right nowhere touching each other, and *psi* has degenerated into

[1] Tregelles, wishing to reserve the letter B for the great Codex Vaticanus 1209, called this copy first L (N. T. Part iv. p. iii), and afterwards Q (N. T. Part vi. p. i). Surely Mr. Vansittart was right (Journal of Philology, vol. ii. No. 3, p. 41) in protesting against a change so needless and inconvenient; nor has Tischendorf adopted it in his eighth edition of the N. T.

the form of a cross (*see* Plate iii, No. 7): *delta*, *theta*, *xi* are also of the latest uncial fashion. The breathings and accents are *primâ manu*, and pretty correct; the rule of the grammarians respecting the change of power of the single point in punctuation according to its change of position is now regularly observed. The scarcity of old copies of the Apocalypse renders this uncial of some importance, and it often confirms the readings of the older codices ℵAC, though on the whole it resembles them considerably less than does Cod. P, and agrees in preference with the later or more ordinary cursives.

C. Codex Ephraemi.

P. Codex Porphyrianus.

Note. Of the three large uncials which contain the Apocalypse, ℵA are complete, but C has lost 171 verses out of 405. In the 286 places wherein the three are available, and Lachmann, Tregelles, and Tischendorf, one or all, depart from the Received text, ℵAC agree fifty-two times, ℵA seventeen, ℵC twenty-six, AC eighty-two, and this last combination supplies the best readings: ℵ stands alone twenty-three times, A fifty-nine, C twenty-seven. When C has failed us ℵA agree fifty-two times and differ eighty-eight.

CHAPTER VII.

CURSIVE MANUSCRIPTS OF THE GOSPELS.

Part I.

THE later manuscripts of the Greek Testament, written in cursive characters from the tenth down to the fifteenth century or later, are too numerous to be minutely described in an elementary work like the present. We shall therefore speak of them with all possible brevity, dwelling only on a few which present points of especial interest, and employing certain abbreviations, a list of which we subjoin for the reader's convenience[1].

Abbreviations used in the following Catalogue.

Act. MS. of Acts and Catholic Epistles.
Am. Ammonian Sections (so-called) in the margin of MSS.
Apoc. MS. of the Apocalypse.
Apost. MS. of Apostolos.
'*Αναγν.* '*Αναγνώσματα* or *ἀναγνώσεις*, *readings* or *lections*: here marks of the lections in the margin or at the head or foot of pages, or the computation of them at the end of the book.
Argent. Written in silver letters, either capitals or all.
'*Αρχή* and *τέλος*, see *Lect.*
Aur. Written in gold letters, either capitals (*l. l.*) or all.
Carp. Epistle to Carpianus.
Chart. Written on paper.
Chart. by itself = linen paper.
Chart. b. = *bombycina*, or cotton paper.
Cols. Columns. When the MS. is written only in one, no notice is given.
Coll. Collated.
Curs. Cursive MSS.
Eus. Eusebian Canons standing in the margin under Ammonian Sections.

[1] Very many corrections have been made in the following Catalogue as well from investigations of my own as from information kindly furnished to me by Mr. H. Bradshaw, University Librarian at Cambridge, by Professor Hort, by Mr. A. A. Vansittart, late Fellow of Trinity College there [d. 1882], by Mr. W. Kelly, and especially by Dean Burgon, to whom the present edition is more deeply indebted than it would be possible to acknowledge in detail. His series of Letters addressed to me in the *Guardian* newspaper (1873) contains but a part of the help he has afforded towards the preparation of this and the second edition. Ed. iii.

Eus. t. Tables of so-called Eusebian Canons prefixed to the Gospels.
Euthal. κεφ. Euthalian *κεφάλαια* found in Acts and Epistles.
Evan. Evangelia.
Evst. Evangelistaria.
Ff. *Folia*, or leaves. The figures in brackets immediately appended denote the number of lines on a page.
Harm. Harmony, sometimes given with *κεφ. t.*
Insp. Inspected.
Κεφ. Letters in the margin denoting the *κεφάλαια majora.*
Κεφ. *t.* Tables of *κεφ.* prefixed to each book.
Lect. Notices of proper lessons for feasts, &c., in the margin, or above, or below, or interspersed with the text. Often marked with *ἀρχή* and *τέλος* at beginning and end.
Membr. On vellum.
Men. A menology, or calendar, of Saints' Days at the beginning or end of a book.
Mus. Musical notes, especially in Evangelistaria.
Mut. That the copy is mutilated.
Orn. Ornamented.
Paul. MS. of St. Paul's Epistles.
Pict. Illuminated with pictures.
Prol. Contains a prologue or *ὑπόθεσις.*
'Ρήμ. Where the *ῥήματα*, or phrases are numbered.
Syn. A synaxarion, or calendar, of daily lessons—also called *eclogadion.*
Στίχ. Where the *στίχοι*, or lines, are numbered.
Subscr. Subscriptions (*ὑπογραφαί*) at the end of books.
Τίτλ. Titles of *κεφ.* at the head or foot of the pages.
Vers. Greek or Latin metrical verses at beginning or end of books.
Unc. Uncial MS.

The other Abbreviations will be evident upon perusing this work. Where *Chart.* is not printed, the MS. is written on vellum. The Latin numeral within square brackets denotes the date of the book, whether fixed by a subscription in the book itself, or approximated by other means, e. g. [xiii] indicates a book of the thirteenth century. The Arabic numerals within ordinary brackets denote the number of lines on a page. Thus 297 (38) = 297 leaves and thirty-eight lines in a page. The names within parentheses indicate the *collators* or *inspectors* of each manuscript, and if it has been satisfactorily examined, an asterisk is prefixed to the number by which it is known. If the copy contain other portions of the New Testament, its notation in those portions is always given. Measurements where given are in inches [1].

(1) *Manuscripts of the Gospels.*

*1. (Act. 1, Paul. 1.) Basiliensis A. N. iv. 2 at Basle [x, Burgon xii or xiii], $7\frac{3}{8} \times 4\frac{1}{2}$, ff. 297 (38); *prol., pict., τίτλ., syn., ἀναγν.* in Acts and Epp. by later hand. Hebrews last in Paul. Gospels bound up last of all. Among the illuminations were what have been said to be pictures of the Emperor Leo the Wise [886–911] and his son Constantine Porphyrogenitus, but all the beautiful miniatures were stolen prior to 1860–2, except one before St. John's Gospel. Its later history is the same as that of Cod. E of the Gospels: it was known to Erasmus; it was borrowed by Reuchlin, a few extracts given by Bengel

[1] For the Authorities chiefly consulted in the list of Cursive Manuscripts given in this edition, see Appendix A to this volume; and for a list of Facsimiles, see Appendix B.

(Bas. γ), collated by Wetstein, and recently in the Gospels by C. L. Roth and Tregelles, who have compared their results. Our facsimile (No. 23) gives an excellent notion of the elegant and minute style of writing, which is fully furnished with breathings, accents, and ι ascript. The initial letters are gilt, and on the first page of each Gospel the full point is a large gilt ball. In the Gospels the text adheres frequently to the uncials Codd. ℵB, BL and such cursives as 118, 131, and especially 209 (Insp. by Burgon, Hoskier, Greg.).

2. Basil. A. N. iv. 1 [xv or earlier], 7¾ × 6, ff. 248 (20), *subscr.*, *κεφ. t.*, *κεφ.* (not John), *τίτλ.*, *Am.*, is the inferior manuscript chiefly used by Erasmus for his first edition of the N. T. (1516), with press corrections by his hand, and barbarously scored with red chalk to suit his pages. The monks at Basle had bought it for two Rhenish florins (Bengel, Wetstein, Burgon, Hoskier, Greg.).

3. (Act. 3, Paul. 3.) Cod. Corsendonck. [xii], 4to, 9¾ × 7, ff. 451 (24), *Carp.*, *Eus. t.*, *κεφ. t.*, *prol.*, *pict.*, *κεφ.*, *τίτλ.*, *Am.*, *Eus.*, *syn.*, once belonging to a convent at Corsendonck near Turnhout, now in the Imperial Library at Vienna (Forlos. 15, Kollar. 5). It was lent to Erasmus for his second edition in 1519, as he testifies on the first leaf (Alter). It had been collated before Alter by J. Walker for Bentley, when in 'the Dominican Library, Brussels.' This collation is unpublished (Trin. Coll. B. xvii. 34): Ellis, Bentleii Critica Sacra, p. xxix (Greg.).

4. Cod. Regius 84 [xii], 7¼ × 5¾, ff. 212 (27), *κεφ. t.*, *κεφ.*, *τίτλ.*, *Am.*, *Eus.*, *lect.*, *syn.*, *men.*, *subscr.*, *στίχ.*, in the Royal Library at Paris (designated RI by Tischendorf), was rightly recognized by Le Long as Robert Stephen's γʹ (*see* Chap. V). Mill notices its affinity to the Latin versions and the Complutensian edition (N. T. Prol. § 1161); *mut.* in Matt. ii. 9–20; John i. 49—iii. 11; forty-nine verses. It is clumsily written and contains *syn.* from some Fathers (Scholz, Greg.).

5. (Act. 5, Paul. 5.) Paris, National (Library), Greek 106 [xii or later], is Stephen's δʹ: 8¼ × 6⅛, ff. 348 (28), *prob.*, *κεφ. t.*, *κεφ.*, *τίτλ.*, *Am.*, *Eus.* Carefully written and full of flourishes (Wetstein, Scholz, Greg.).

6. (Act. 6, Paul. 6.) Par. Nat. Gr. 112 [xi or later], is Stephen's εʹ; in text it much resembles Codd. 4, 5, and 75. 12mo, 5½ × 4⅛, ff. 235, *prol.*, *κεφ. t.*, *κεφ.*, *τίτλ.*, *Am.*, *syn.* with St. Chrysostom's Liturgy, *men.* (Wetstein, Griesbach, Scholz). This exquisite manuscript is written in characters so small, that some pages require a glass to read them. Scholz collated Matt., Mark i—iv, John vii, viii (Greg.).

7. Par. Nat. Gr. 71 [xi], is Stephen's ϛʹ. 8 × 6¼, ff. 186 (29), *prol.*, *syn.*, *Carp.*, *Eus. t.*, *pict.*, *τίτλ.* with metrical paraphrase, *Am.*, *Eus.*, *men.*, very full *lect.* In style not unlike Cod. 4, but neater (Wetst., Scholz, Abbé Martin, Greg.).

8. Par. Nat. Gr. 49 [xi], 11¼ × 8½, ff. 199 (22), two columns, proved by Mr. Vansittart to be Stephen's ζʹ[1]: beautifully written in two columns

[1] Stephen's margin cites ζʹ eighty-four times in the Gospels, usually in company with several others, but alone in Mark vi. 20; xiv. 15; Luke i. 37. Since Evan. 18 or Reg. 47 contains the whole N. T., and Stephen cites ζʹ in the Acts

on the page. *Carp.*, *Eus. t.*, *prol.*, *pict.*, *κεφ.*, *τίτλ.*, *lect.*, *men.*, *Am.*, *Eus.*, *syn.* (Wetst., Scholz, Greg.).

9. Par. Nat. Gr. 83 [A.D. 1167, when 'Manuel Porphyrogenitus was ruler of Constantinople, Amauri of Jerusalem, William II of Sicily': this note (derived from Wetstein) is now nearly obliterated], $9\frac{1}{4} \times 6\frac{3}{4}$, ff. 298(20), is probably Stephen's *ιβ'*. *Carp.*, *Eus. t.*, *pict.*, *κεφ.*, *τίτλ.*, *Am.*, *syn.*, *mut.*, *men.*, *subscr.*, *στίχ.* (first leaf of St. John). It once belonged to Peter Stella. The style is rather barbarous, and ornamentation peculiar (Kuster's Paris 3, Scholz, Greg.).

10. Par. Nat. Gr. 91 [xiii or later], $7\frac{1}{2} \times 5\frac{7}{8}$, ff. 275 (24), given in 1439 to a library of Canons Regular at Verona by Dorotheus Archbishop of Mitylene, when he came to the Council of Florence. Scholz tells us that it was 'antea Joannis Huraultii Boistallerii.' Griesbach mistook this copy for Reg. 95, olim $\frac{2865}{3}$, which is Kuster's Paris 1 and Wetstein's Cod. 10, being Cod. 285 of Scholz and our own list (Burgon, *Guardian*, Jan. 15, 1873). *Carp.*, *Eus. t.*, *pict.*, *κεφ.*, *τίτλ.*, *Am.*, *Eus.*, *lect.*, *syn.*, *men.* (Griesbach, Scholz, Greg.).

11. Par. Nat. Gr. 121–2 [xii or earlier], in two small volumes, $6\frac{3}{8} \times 3\frac{5}{8}$, neatly written, ff. 230 and 274 (16), *Eus. t.*, *κεφ.*, *τίτλ.*, *Am.*, *Eus.* It also once belonged to ~~Teller~~ (Kuster's Paris 4, Scholz, Greg.).

12. Par. Nat. Gr. 230 [xi], $10\frac{3}{8} \times 8\frac{1}{8}$, 294 (21), *prol.*, *pict.*, *Eus. t.*, *κεφ. t.*, *κεφ.*, *τίτλ.*, with a commentary, that on St. Mark being Victor's of Antioch (Greg.).

13. Par. Nat. Gr. 50 [xii], $9\frac{1}{4} \times 7\frac{1}{2}$, ff. 170 (29), *κεφ. t.*, *κεφ.*, *τίτλ.*, *Am.* *lect.*, *syn.*, *men.*, *subscr.*, *στίχ.*, is Kuster's Paris 6, who says that it supplied him with more various readings than all the rest of his Paris manuscripts put together. This, like Codd. 10, 11, once belonged to Teller: it is not correctly written. *Syn.*, *mut.* in Matt. i. 1—ii. 20; xxvi. 33–53; xxvii. 26—xxviii. 10; Mark i. 20–45; John xxi. 3–25; 163 verses (Kuster, Wetstein, Griesbach, Begtrup in 1797). This manuscript was collated in 1868 by Professor W. H. Ferrar, Fellow of Trinity College, Dublin [d. 1871], who regarded Codd. 13, 69, 124, 346 as transcripts of one archetype, which he proposed to restore by comparing the four copies together. His design was carried out by Professor T. K. Abbott, Fellow and Tutor of Trinity College. For facsimiles of them all, &c., *see* 'Collation of Four Important Manuscripts of the Gospels,' &c. Dublin, 1877 (Greg.).

14. Par. Nat. Gr. 70 [xii or xiii, Greg. x], $6\frac{7}{8} \times 4\frac{5}{8}$, ff. 392 (17), once Cardinal Mazarin's; was Kuster's Paris 7. A facsimile of this beautiful copy, with round conjoined minuscule letters, regular breathings and

once (ch. xvii. 5), in the Catholic Epistles seven times, in the Pauline twenty-seven, in the Apocalypse never; Reg. 47 has been suggested to have been Stephen's ζ', rather than Cod. 8 or Reg. 49. On testing the two with Steph. ζ' in eight places, Mr. Vansittart found that they both agreed with it in five (Matt. xx. 12; Mark vi. 20; x. 52; Luke vi. 37; John vi. 58), but that in the remaining three (Mark xii. 31; Luke i. 37; John x. 32) Reg. 49 agreed with ζ', while Reg. 47 did not.

accents, is given in the 'Paléographie Universelle,' No. 78, and in Montfaucon, Pal. Gr., p. 282. *Mut.* Matt. i. 1-9; iii. 16—iv. 9. Κεφ. *t.*, *pict.*, Paschal Canon, *Carp.*, *Eus. t.*, κεφ. *t.*, κεφ., τίτλ., *Am.*, *Eus.* (Kuster, Scholz).

15. Par. Nat. Gr. 64 [x], 7¼ × 5⅝, ff. 225 (23), *Carp.*, *prol.*, κεφ. *t.*, κεφ., τίτλ., *Am.*, *lect.*, *men.*, is Kuster's Paris 8. *Eus. t.*, *syn.*, *pict.* very superb: the first three pages are written in gold, with exquisite miniatures, four on p. 2, four on p. 3, Burgon. (Kuster, Scholz, Greg.)

16. Par. Nat. Gr. 54, formerly 1881 [xiv], 12⅜ × 10, ff.?, 2 cols., *Eus. t.* (Latin), *pict.*, κεφ., τίτλ., *Am.* (Matt. and Mark), *lect.*, *subscr.*; once belonged to the Medici; it has a Latin version in parts; *mut.* Mark xvi. 6-20. *Eus. t.*, *syn.*, *pict.* (Wetstein, Scholz). This gorgeous and 'right royal' copy was never quite finished, but is unique in respect of being written in four colours, vermilion, lake, blue, and black, according to the character of the contents (Burgon, Greg.).

17. Par. Nat. Gr. 55 [xvi], 11¾ × 8¼, ff. 353 (25), 2 cols., has the Latin Vulgate version: it was neatly written, not by George Hermonymus the Spartan (but see Greg.), as Wetstein guesses, but by a Western professional scribe, Burgon. It once belonged to Cardinal Bourbon. *Syn.*, *pict.* very elegant, *lect.* (Wetstein, Griesbach, Scholz).

18. (Act. 113, Paul. 132, Apoc. 51.) Par. Nat. Gr. 47, formerly 2241 [A.D. 1364], 11½ × 8⅜, ff. 444 (23), *prol.*, κεφ. *t.*, κεφ., *lect.*, ἀναγν., *subscr.*, στίχ., *syn.*, *men.*; bought in 1687, and written at Constantinople. It is one of the few copies of the whole New Testament (*see* p. 72, note), and was given by Nicephorus Cannabetes to the monastery τοῦ ζωοδότου χριστοῦ ἐν τῷ τοῦ Μυζιθρᾶ (Misitra) τῆς Λακεδαίμονος κάστρῳ. Two *syn.* between the Pauline Epistles and the Apocalypse, psalms, hymns (Scholz, Greg., Reiche).

19. Par. Nat. Gr. 189, formerly 1880 [xii], 12½ × 9¼, ff. 387, κεφ. *t.*, κεφ., τίτλ., *Am.*, *Eus.*, *subscr.*, Wetstein's 1869, once belonged to the Medici, *pict.*, with Victor's commentary on St. Mark, a catena to St. John, and scholia to the other Gospels. In marvellous condition, with much gold ornamentation (Scholz, Greg.).

20. Par. Nat. Gr. 188, formerly 1883 [xii], 13⅛ × 9⅛, a splendid folio, ff. 274, κεφ. *t.*, κεφ., τίτλ., *Am.*, *Eus.*, *lect.*, *subscr.*, στίχ.—all by second hand (Greg.), brought from the East in 1669. It is beautifully written, and contains catenae, Victor's commentary on St. Mark, and other treatises enumerated by Scholz, who collated most of it. At the end of SS. Mark, Luke, and John 'dicitur etiam hoc evangelium ex accuratis codicibus esse exscriptum, nec non collatum' (Scholz). A second (or perhaps the original) hand has been busy here to assimilate the text to that of Codd. 215, 300, or to some common model. In Cod. 215 the foregoing subscription is appended to all the Four Gospels, and the other contents correspond exactly (Burgon, Last Twelve Verses of St. Mark, pp. 119, 279). See on Evann. Λ, 428. Collated by W. F. Rose.

21. Par. Nat. Gr. 68, formerly 2860 [x], 9 × 7⅛, ff. 203, 2 cols., *pict.*, κεφ., τίτλ., *Am.*, *men.*, with *syn.* on paper in a later hand (Scholz, Greg.).

22. Par. Nat. Gr. 72, once Colbert. 2467 [xi], 10¼ × 7½, ff. 232 (22),

contains remarkable readings. John xiv. 22—xvi. 27. Fully collated by the Rev. W. F. Rose (*see* Evan. 563). It begins Matt. ii. 2, six leaves containing Matt. v. 25—viii. 4 being misplaced before it. Κεφ. *t.*, τίτλ., κεφ., *Am.*, *Eus.* partial, *subscr.* No *lect.*, ἀρχ., or *mut.* Matt. iv. 20—v. 25; τέλ. p. m. A beautiful copy, singularly free from itacisms and errors from homœoteleuton, and very carefully accentuated, with slight illuminated headings to the Gospels, which I recently had the pleasure of inspecting (Wetstein, Scholz, Scriv., Greg.).

23. Par. Nat. Gr. 77, Colbert. 3947 [xi], 9 × 7¼, 4to, ff. 230, κεφ. *t.*, κεφ., τίτλ., *Am.*, *lect.*, with the Latin Vulgate version down to Luke iv. 18. *Mut.* Matt. i. 1–17; Luke xxiv. 46—John ii. 20; xxi. 24, 25; ninety-six verses (Scholz).

24. Par. Nat. Gr. 178, Colbert. 4112 [xi, Greg. x], 10¼ × 5⅞, ff. 240, with a commentary (Victor's on St. Mark), *prol.*, κεφ. *t.*, κεφ., τίτλ., *Am.*, *Eus.*, and also *syn.*, but in a later hand. *Mut.* Matt. xxvii. 20—Mark iv. 22; 186 verses (Griesb., Scholz). See Burgon, *ubi supra*, p. 228. Used in Cramer's Cat. on St. Mark, 1840 (Greg.).

25. Par. Nat. Gr. 191, Colbert. 2259 [x, Greg. xi], 11¾ × 9⅛, ff. 292, with Victor's commentary on St. Mark, and scholia, κεφ. *t.*, κεφ., τίτλ., *lect.* (partial). 'Grandly written,' but very imperfect, wanting about 715 verses, viz. Matt. xxiii. 1—xxv. 42; Mark i. 1—vii. 36; Luke viii. 31–41; ix. 44–54; x. 39—xi. 4; John xiii. 19?—xxi. 25 (Griesbach, Scholz, Greg., Martin).

26. Par. Nat. Gr. 78, Colbert. 4078 [xi], 9½ × 7¼, ff. 179 (27), neatly and correctly written by Paul a priest. *Carp.*, *Eus. t.*, κεφ. *t.*, τίτλ., *Am.*, *lect.*, *syn.*, *men.* (Wetstein, Scholz, Greg.).

27. Par. Nat. Gr. 115, Colbert. 6043 [xi, Greg. x], 6¼ × 4¾, ff. 460 (19), is Mill's Colb. 1. That critic procured Larroque's collation of Codd. 27–33 (a very imperfect one) for his edition of the New Testament. From John xviii. 3 the text is supplied, cotton *chart.* [xiv]. κεφ. *t.*, *pict.*, κεφ., τίτλ., *Am.*, *Eus.* (*syn.*, *men.* later), *syn.*, *pict.* Extensively altered by a later hand (Wetstein, Scholz, Greg.).

28. Par. Nat. Gr. 379, Colbert. 4705 [xi], 9⅛ × 7⅛, ff. 292 (19), is Mill's Colb. 2, most carelessly written by an ignorant scribe; it often resembles Cod. D, but has many unique readings and interpolations, with 'many relics of a very ancient text hereabouts' (Hort on Mark vi. 43, Introd. p. 242). Κεφ. *t.* (inaccurate), κεφ., τίτλ., *Am.*, *Eus.*, *subscr.* (*lect.* later), *syn.* *Mut.* in 334 verses, viz. Matt. vii. 17—ix. 12; xiv. 33—xvi. 10; xxvi. 70—xxvii. 48; Luke xx. 19—xxii. 46; John xii. 40—xiii. 1; xv. 24—xvi. 12; xviii. 16–28; xx. 20—xxi. 5; 18–25 (Scholz, Greg.).

29. Par. Nat. Gr. 89, Colbert. 6066 [xii, Greg. x], 7⅝ × 5½, ff. 169, is Mill's Colb. 3, correctly written by a Latin scribe, with very many peculiar corrections by a later hand. Lost leaves in the three later Gospels are supplied [xv]. Scholia, *Eus. t.*, *prol.*, κεφ., τίτλ., *Am.*, *Eus.*, *subscr.*, *syn.*, *men.* *Mut.* Matt. i—xv. Mill compares its text with that of Cod. 71 (Scholz, Greg.).

30. Par. Nat. Gr. 100, Colbert. 4444 [xvi, Greg. xv], 8⅞ × 5⅞, *chart.*,

ff. 313 (18), *κεφ.* (Gr. and Lat.), *τίτλ.*, is Mill's Colb. 4, containing all the Gospels, by the writer of Cod. 70. In text it much resembles Cod. 17 (Scholz, Greg.).

31. Par. Nat. Gr. 94, Colbert. 6083 [xiii], $7\frac{1}{8} \times 5\frac{1}{2}$, ff. 188, *pict.*, *κεφ. t.*, *κεφ.*, *τίτλ.*, is also Mill's Colb. 4, but contains all the Gospels with prayers. This copy has many erasures (Scholz, Greg.).

32. Par. Nat. Gr. 116, Colbert. 6511 [xii], $5\frac{3}{4} \times 4\frac{1}{4}$, ff. 244 (21), *prol.*, *κεφ. t.*, *κεφ.*, *τίτλ.*, *Am.* (*lect.* and *ἀναγν.* later), is Mill's Colb. 5. It begins Matt. x. 22. *Mut.* Matt. xxiv. 15–30; Luke xxii. 35—John iv. 20 (Scholz). Mill misrepresented the contents of Codd. 30–32, through supposing that they contained no more than the small portions which were collated for his use.

*33. (Act. 13, Paul 17.) Par. Nat. Gr. 14, Colbert. 2844 [xi, Greg. ix or x], fol., $14\frac{3}{4} \times 9\frac{3}{4}$, ff. 143 (52), *κεφ.*, *τίτλ.*, is Mill's Colb. 8, containing some of the Prophets and all the New Testament, except Mark ix. 31—xi. 11; xiii. 11—xiv. 60; Luke xxi. 38—xxiii. 26; and the Apocalypse. In text it resembles Codd. BDL more than any other cursive manuscript. After Larroque, Wetstein, Griesbach, Begtrup, and Scholz, it was most laboriously collated by Tregelles in 1850. There are fifty-two long lines in each page, in a fine round hand, the accents being sometimes neglected, and *eta* unusually like our English letter h. The ends of the leaves are much damaged, and greatly misplaced by the binder; so that the Gospels now stand last, though on comparing the style of handwriting (which undergoes a *gradual* change throughout the volume) at their beginning and end with that in the Prophets which stand first, and that in the Epistles which should follow them, it is plain that they originally occupied their usual place. The ink too, by reason of the damp, has often left its proper page blank, so that the writing can only be read *set off* on the opposite page, especially in the Acts. Hence it is no wonder that Tregelles should say that of all the manuscripts he has collated 'none has ever been so wearisome to the eyes, and exhaustive of every faculty of attention.' (Account of the Printed Text, p. 162.)

The next eight copies, like Cod. H of St. Paul, belonged to that noble collection made by the Chancellor Seguier, and on his death in 1672 bequeathed to Coislin, Bishop of Metz. Montfaucon has described them in his 'Bibliotheca Coisliniana,' fol. 1715, and all were slightly collated by Wetstein and Scholz.

34. Par. Nat. Coislin. 195, formerly 306 [xi, Greg. x], $11\frac{1}{4} \times 7\frac{1}{2}$, ff. 469 (22), *Carp.*, *Eus. t.*, *prol.*, *pict.*, *κεφ.*, *τίτλ.*, *Am.*, *subscr.*, *στίχ.*; 'a grand folio, splendidly written and in splendid condition' (Burgon), from Mount Athos, has a catena (Victor's commentary on St. Mark) resembling that of Cod. 194. Fresh as from the artist's hand.

35. (Act. 14, Paul. 18, Apoc. 17.) Par. Nat. Coislin. 199, formerly 44 [xi], $7\frac{3}{8} \times 5\frac{1}{2}$, ff. 328 (27), *κεφ. t.*, *lect.*, *ἀναγν.*, *syn.*, *men.*, *subscr.*, *στίχ.*, contains the whole New Testament (*see* p. 72, note), with many corrections.

36. Par. Nat. Coislin. 20, formerly 26 [xi, Greg. x], $11\frac{1}{2} \times 8\frac{3}{8}$, ff. 509 (19), *Carp.*, *Eus. t.*, *κεφ. t.*, *prol.*, *pict.*, *κεφ.*, *τίτλ.*, *Am.*, *Eus. t.*, *prol.*, with a commentary (Victor's on St. Mark), from the *laura* [i. e. convent, Suicer, Thes. Eccles. tom. ii. 205] of St. Athanasius in Mount Athos, very sumptuous.

37. Par. Nat. Coislin. 21, formerly 238 [xii], $12\frac{1}{8} \times 9\frac{1}{2}$, ff. 357, *Eus. t.*, *κεφ. t.*, *prol.*, *pict.*, *κεφ.*, *τίτλ.*, *Am.*, *Eus.*, with short scholia, Victor's commentary on St. Mark, *Eus. t.*, *syn.*, *prol.*, *pict.* (Montfaucon).

38. (Act. 19, Paul. 23.) Par. Nat. Coislin. 200, formerly 500 [xiii], $6\frac{7}{8} \times 5\frac{3}{8}$, ff 300 (30), copied for the Emperor Michael Palaeologus [1259–1282], and by him sent to St. Louis [d. 1270], containing all the N. T. except St. Paul's Epistles, has been rightly judged by Wetstein to be Stephen's θ′ [1]. *Pict.*, *κεφ.*, *τίτλ.*, *Am.* (not *Eus.*), *mut.* 143 verses; Matt. xiv. 15—xv. 30; xx. 14—xxi. 27; Mark xii. 3—xiii. 4. A facsimile of this beautiful book is given in the 'Paléographie Univers.,' No. 84 (collated by Wetstein). Burgon has also a photograph of it, and, like Wetstein and Silvestre, notices that it was Ex Bibl. Pattr. Cadomensium [Caen] Soc. Jesu, 1640.

39. Par. Nat. Coislin. 23, formerly 315 [xi], $13\frac{1}{8} \times 10\frac{1}{4}$, ff. 288, *κεφ. t.* (*see* Greg.), *κεφ.*, *τίτλ.*, *Am.*, *subscr.*, *στίχ.*, written at Constantinople with many abbreviations εἰς τὰ πατριαρχεῖον, ἐπὶ Σεργίου [II] τοῦ πατριάρχου, and in 1218 conveyed to the convent of St. Athanasius on Mount Athos. With a commentary (Victor's on St. Mark, from the same original as that in Cod. 34). Not *written by* Sergius, as Scholz says (Burgon).

40. Par. Nat. Coislin. 22, formerly 375 [xi], $11\frac{3}{4} \times 8\frac{1}{2}$, ff. 312, *Carp.*, *Eus. t.*, *prol.*, *κεφ. t.*, *κεφ.*, *τίτλ.*, *Am.*, *Eus.*, once belonged to the monastery of St. Nicholas σταυρονικήτας, with a commentary (Victor's on St. Mark) and *Eus. t.* Ends at John xx. 25.

41. Par. Nat. Coislin. 24, formerly 241 [xi], 4to, $12 \times 9\frac{1}{2}$, ff. 224 (32), *κεφ. t.* (Mark), *κεφ.*, *τίτλ.*, *lect.*, *subscr.*, *στίχ.*, contains SS. Matthew and Mark with a commentary (Victor's on St. Mark).

42. Cod. Medicaeus exhibits many readings of the same class as Codd. 1, 13, 33, but its authority has the less weight, since it has disappeared under circumstances somewhat suspicious. Edward Bernard communicated to Mill these readings, which he had found in the hand of Peter Pithaeus, a former owner, in the margin of Stephen's N. T. of 1550: they professed to be extracted from an 'exemplar Regium Medicaeum' (which may be supposed to mean that portion of the King's Library which Catherine de' Medici brought to France: above, p. 117, note 3), and were inserted under the title of *Med.* in Mill's great work, though he remarked their resemblance to the text of Cod. K (N. T., Proleg. § 1462). The braggart Denis Amelotte [1606–78] professes to

[1] Stephen includes his θ′ among the copies that αὐτοὶ πανταχόθεν συνηθροίσαμεν, which might suit the case of Coislin. 200, as St. Louis would have brought or sent it to France. Mr. Vansittart tested Cod. 38 in Matt. xxvi. 45; Luke viii. 18; xix. 26; James v. 5; 2 Pet. ii. 18, and found it agree in all with Stephen's θ′. What of ἀγγελία, 1 John i. 5? In Luke viii. 18 that most careless editor misprints β′ when he means θ′. See above, p. 124, note 3.

have used the manuscript about the middle of the seventeenth century, and states that it was in a college at Troyes; but Scholz could find it neither in that city nor elsewhere.

43. (Act. 54, Paul. 130.) Par. Biblioth. Armament. 8409, 8410, formerly Gr. 4 [xi], in two volumes; the first containing the Gospels with *Eus. t.*, the second the Acts and Epistles, $8\frac{1}{8} \times 6\frac{3}{8}$, ff. 199 (23) and 190 (25), *Carp.*, *Eus. t.*, *prol.*, *κεφ. t.*, *κεφ.*, *τίτλ.*, *Am.*, *Eus.*, *subscr.* (*lect.* and *ἀναγν.* later, *see* Greg.). Perhaps written at Ephesus; given by P. de Berzi in 1661 to the Oratory of San Maglorian (Amelotte, Simon, Scholz).

44. Lond. British Museum, Add. 4949 [xi], $12 \times 9\frac{1}{4}$, ff. 259 (21), *syn.*, *men.*, *pict.*, *κεφ.*, *τίτλ.*, *Am.*, *Eus.*, *lect.* (*ἀρχή* and *τέλος* later), *subscr.* and *στίχ.* in John, brought from Mount Athos by Caesar de Missy [1703–75], George III's French chaplain, who spent his life in collecting materials for an edition of the N. T. His collation, most imperfectly given by Wetstein, is still preserved with the manuscript (Bloomfield, 1860).

45. Oxford Bodleian Barocc. 31 [xii or xiii], $7\frac{1}{4} \times 5\frac{1}{4}$, ff. 399 (20), is Mill's Bodl. 1, a very neat copy, with *Eus. t.*, *κεφ. t.*, *κεφ.*, *τίτλ.* (occasional), *Am.*, *Eus.*, *lect.* (here and there), *subscr.*, *στίχ.* *Mut.* Mark ii. 5–15 (Mill, Griesbach).

46. Oxf. Bodl. Barocc. 29 [xi], Mill's Bodl. 2, $7\frac{1}{4} \times 5$, ff. 342 (18), with *τὸ νομικὸν* and *τὸ κυριακὸν πάσχα*, *Carp.*, *Eus. t.*, *κεφ. t.*, *pict.*, *κεφ.*, *τίτλ.*, *Am.*, *Eus.*, *lect.*, *syn.*, *men.*, *vers.*, *subscr.*, *στίχ.*, *ἀναγν.* Preliminary matter in later hand (Mill, Griesbach).

47. Oxf. Bodl. Gr. Misc. 9 [xv], $4\frac{3}{4} \times 3\frac{1}{4}$, ff. 554 (30), *prol.*, *κεφ. t.*, *κεφ.*, *τίτλ.*, *subscr.*, *στίχ.* (Mark), *vers.* (Polyglott, Mill, Greg.), in a vile hand, *κεφ. t.*, and much foreign matter, is Mill's Bodl. 6 and Bodl. 1 of Walton's Polyglott (Polyglott, Mill).

48. Oxf. Bodl. Misc. Gr., formerly 2044 (Mill's Bodl. 5) [xii], $11\frac{1}{8} \times 8\frac{3}{4}$, ff. 145 (50), 2 cols., *pict.*, *Eus. t.*, *κεφ.*, *subscr.*, *ῥήμ.*, *στίχ.*, scholia in a later hand (Mill).

49. Oxf. Bodl. Roe 1, formerly 247 [xi], $5\frac{3}{4} \times 4\frac{1}{8}$, ff. 223 (26), ll. rubr., is also Mill's Roe 1, brought by Sir T. Roe from Turkey about 1628; it has *Eus. t.*, *κεφ. t.*, *κεφ.*, *τιτλ.*, *Am.*, some *Eus.*, *lect.*, *subscr.*, *στίχ.* (Luke) (Mill).

50. Oxf. Bodl. Laud. Gr. 33, formerly D. 122 [xi], $11 \times 8\frac{3}{4}$, ff. 241, *prol.* (Mark), *κεφ. t.*, *pict.*, *κεφ.*, *τίτλ.*, *Am.*, some *Eus.*, *στίχ.*, is Mill's Laud. 1 (*see* p. 170), surrounded by a catena (Victor's or Cyril's of Alexandria in St. Mark), and attended with other matter. *Mut.* Matt. i. 1—ix. 35; xii. 3–23; xvii. 12–24; xxv. 20–32; John v. 29–end; and Mark xiv. 40—xvi. 20 is by a later hand. It contains many unusual readings (Mill, Griesbach).

51. (Act. 32, Paul. 38.) Oxf. Bodl. Laud. Gr. 31, formerly C. 63 [xiii], $11\frac{3}{4} \times 8\frac{3}{4}$, ff. 325 (28), 2 cols., Mill's Laud. 2, whose resemblance to the Complutensian text is pointed out by him (N. T., Proleg. § 1437), though, judging from his own collation of Cod. 51, his statement 'per omnia penè respondet' is rather too strong. *Prol.*, *κεφ. t.*, *κεφ.*, *τίτλ.*, *Am.* (not Eus.), *lect.*, *syn.*, *men.*, *subscr.* The *present* order of the

contents (*see* p. 72) is Act., Paul., Cath., Evangelia (Mill, Griesbach): but it ought to be collated afresh. This is Bentley's γ in the unpublished margin of B. xvii. 5 at Trin. Coll., Cambridge. He calls it a quarto, 400 years old. *Mut.* 2 Pet. iii. 2–17; Matt. xviii. 12–35; Mark ii. 8—iii. 4 (*see* Codd. 54, 60, 113, 440, 507, 508, Acts 23, Apoc. 28, Evst. 5).

52. Oxf. Bodl. Laud. Gr. 3, formerly C. 28 [dated A.D. 1286], 6½ × 5, ff. 158 (27), elegant, written by *νικητας ὁ μαυρωνης*, is Mill's Laud. 5, with *Pict.*, *prol.*, *κεφ. t.*, *κεφ.*, *τίτλ.*, *Am.*, *Eus.*, *lect.*, *subscr.*, *mut.* in initio (Mill, Griesbach).

53. Oxf. Bodl. Seld. supr. 28, formerly 3416 [xiv], 6 × 4¾, ff. 140, is Mill's Seld. 1, who pronounces it much like Stephen's γ′ (Cod. 4), having *prol.*, *κεφ. t.*, *κεφ.*, *τίτλ.*, *subscr.*, *ἀναγν.*, beautifully written (Mill, Griesbach).

54. Oxf. Bodl. Seld. supr. 29 (Coxe 54), formerly 3417, Mill's Seld. 2[1] [dated A.D. 1338], 4to, 6⅝ × 4¾, ff. 230 (sic), *Syn.*, *men.*, *Eus. t.*, *κεφ. t.*, *τίτλ.*, *Am.*, *lect.*, *vers.* (Mill). This is Bentley's κ (*see* Cod. 51). *See under* 58.

55. Oxf. Bodl. Seld. supr. 6 (Coxe 5), formerly 3394, Mill's Seld. 3 [xiii], 4to, 7½ × 5½, ff. 349 (21), containing also Judges vi. 1–24 (Grabe, Prol. V. T., tom. i. cap. iii. § 6), has *prol.* in Matt., *κεφ. t.*, *pict.*, *κεφ.*, *lect.*, *syn.*, *men.*, *ἀναγν.*, *subscr.*, *στίχ.* (Mill).

56. Oxf. Lincoln Coll. II (Gr.) 18 [xv or xvi], 4to, 8⅛ × 5⅝, ff. 232 (24), *chart.*, was presented about 1502, by Edmund Audley, Bishop of Salisbury: *prol.* (Mark, Luke), *κεφ. t.*, *κεφ.*, some *τίτλ.*, *ἀναγν.*, *vers.*, titles to Gospels, *subscr.*, *στίχ.* (John). Walton gives some various readings, but confounds it with Act. 33, Paul. 39, speaking of them as if one 'vetustissimum exemplar.' It has been inspected by Dobbin, Scrivener, and Mill, but so loosely that the late Rev. R. C. Pascoe, Fellow of Exeter College, detected thirty-four omissions for thirty-one citations (one of them being an error) in four chapters.

57. (Act. 35, Paul. 41.) Oxf. Magdalen Coll., Greek 9 [xii, opening], 9 × 7½, ff. 291 (25), *aur.* beautiful, in a small and beautiful hand, with abbreviations. *Mut.* Mark i. 1–11, and at end. Psalms and Hymns follow the Epistles. It has *κεφ. t.*, *κεφ.*, *τίτλ.* (*lect.* in red, *vers.* later). Collated twice by Dr. Hammond, the great commentator, whose papers seem to have been used for Walton's Polyglott (Magd. 1): also examined by Dobbin (Mill).

58. Oxf. New Coll. 68 [xv], 7¾ × 5¼, ff. 342 (20), is Walton and Mill's N. 1. This, like Codd. 56–7, has been accurately examined by Dr. Dobbin, for the purpose of his 'Collation of the Codex Montfortianus' (London, 1854), with whose readings Codd. 56, 58 have been compared in 1922 places. He has undoubtedly proved the close connexion

[1] 'Textus ipse distinctus est in clausulas majores, seu Paragraphos; ad initium notatos singulos literâ majusculâ miniatâ,' Mill (N. T. Proleg. § 1445). Yet since Burgon testifies that its text 'is not broken up into Paragraphs after all,' Mill can only intend to designate in a roundabout way the presence of the larger chapters (p. 55) with their appropriate capitals.

subsisting between the three manuscripts (which had been observed by Mill, N. T. Proleg. § 1388), though he may not have quite demonstrated that they must be direct transcripts from each other. *Prol.*, κεφ. *t.*, κεφ. (partially), τίτλ., *Am.* (partial), ἀναγν. (partial), *syn.*, *subscr.* (Mark), *vers.*, with scholia. The writing is very careless, and those are in error who follow Walton in stating that it contains the Acts and Epistles (Walton's Polyglott, Mill, Dobbin). Mr. C. Forster rightly asks for photographs and a thorough re-collation of Codd. 56, 58, 61, 'to throw light upon their direct relationship, or non-relationship to each other' ('A New Plea for the Three Heavenly Witnesses,' 1867, p. 139). Dr. C. R. Gregory has expressed the opinion that Codd. 47, 56, 58 are in the same hand, and one of them copied from Cod. 54.

*59. Cambridge, Gonville and Caius Coll. 403 [xii], 8 × 6, ff. 238 (23), an important copy, 'textu notabili,' as Tischendorf states (much like D, 61, 71), but carelessly written, and exhibiting no less than eighty-one omissions by ὁμοιοτέλευτον (*see* p. 9). It was very poorly examined for Walton's Polyglott, better though defectively by Mill, seen by Wetstein in 1716, minutely collated by Scrivener in 1860. It once belonged to the House of Friars Minor at Oxford, from whence Richard Brynkley borrowed it and took it to the Grey Friars at Cambridge, whence it went to Thomas Hatcher, who gave it to the College in 1867 (J. Rendel Harris, The origin of the Leicester Codex, 1887). It has τίτλ., κεφ., *Am.* (but not *Eus.*), and exhibits (many and rare *compendia scribendi*.

60. (Apoc. 10.) Camb. University Library, Dd. ix. 69 [A.D. 1297], 8 × 6, ff. 324 = 293 + 1 + 30 (24), but the Apocalypse is later, and has a few scholia from Arethas about it. This copy is Mill's Moore 1[1], and is still badly known. *Carp.*, *Eus. t.*, κεφ. *t.*, *pict.*, κεφ., τίτλ., *lect.* (later), *Am.* without *Eus.*, *subscr.*, and it is an elegant copy (Mill). The Gospels appear to have been written in the East, the Apocalypse in the West of Europe. This is Bentley's ε (*see* Cod. 51).

*61. (Act. 34, Paul. 40, Apoc. 92.) Codex Montfortianus at Trinity College, Dublin, G. 97 [xv or xvi], $6\frac{1}{4} \times 4\frac{3}{4}$, ff. 445 (21), *chart.*, so celebrated in the controversy respecting I John v. 7. Its last collator, Dr. Orlando Dobbin (*see* on Cod. 58), has discussed in his Introduction every point of interest connected with it. It contains the whole New Testament, apparently the work of three or four successive scribes, paper leaves, only one of them—that on which I John v. 7 stands—being glazed[2],

[1] On the death of Dr. John Moore, Bishop of Ely (whose honesty as a book-collector is impeached, on no fair grounds, by Tew in Bridge's 'Northamptonshire,' vol. ii. p. 45, Oxon. 1791), in 1714, George I was induced to buy his books and manuscripts for the Library at Cambridge, amounting to 30,000 volumes, in acknowledgement of the attachment of the University to the House of Hanover. Every one remembers the epigram which this royal gift provoked. *See* 'Cap and Gown,' p. 15.

[2] 'We often hear,' said a witty and most reverend Irish Prelate, 'that the text of the Three Heavenly Witnesses is a *gloss*; and any one that will go into the College Library may see as much for himself.' It was a little bold in Mr. Charles Forster ('A New Plea,' &c., pp. 119, 120, 139), whose zeal in defence of what he held to be the truth I heartily revere, to urge the authority of Dr. Adam Clarke for assigning this manuscript to the thirteenth century, the rather since almost in the same breath, he stigmatizes the Wesleyan minister

as if to protect it from harm. This manuscript was first heard of between the publication of Erasmus' second (1519) and third (1522) editions of his N. T., and after he had publicly declared, in answer to objectors, that if any *Greek* manuscript could be found containing the passage, he would insert it in his revision of the text; a promise which he fulfilled in 1522. Erasmus describes his authority as 'Codex Britannicus,' 'apud Anglos repertus,' and there is the fullest reason to believe that the Cod. Montfortianus is the copy referred to (*see* Vol. II. Chap. XI). Its earliest known owner was Froy[1], a Franciscan friar, then Thomas Clement [fl. 1569], then William Chark [fl. 1582], then Thomas Montfort, D.D. of Cambridge, from whom it derives its name, then Archbishop Ussher, who caused the collation to be made which appears in Walton's Polyglott (Matt. i. 1—Acts xxii. 29; Rom. i), and presented the manuscript to Trinity College. Dr. Barrett appended to his edition of Cod. Z a full collation of the parts left untouched by his predecessors; but since the work of Ussher's friends was known to be very defective, Dobbin has re-collated the whole of that portion which Barrett left unexamined, comparing the readings throughout with Codd. 56, 58 of the Gospels, and Cod. 33 of the Acts. This copy has *prol.*, *κεφ. t.*, *κεφ.*, *τίτλ.*, *Am.*, *Eus.*, *subscr.*, *στίχ.*, besides which the division by the Latin chapters in St. Mark is employed, a sure proof—if any were needed—of the modern date of the manuscript. There are many corrections by a more recent hand, erasures by the pen, &c. It has been supposed that the Gospels were first written; then the Acts and Epistles (transcribed, in Dobbin's judgement, from Cod. 33, Acts); the Apocalypse last; having been added about 1580, as Tregelles and Dr. Dobbin think, from Cod. 69, when they were both in Chark's possession. The text, however, of the Apocalypse is not quite the same in the two codices, nor would it be easy, without seeing them together, to verify Dobbin's conjecture, that the titles to the sacred books, in pale red ink, were added by the same person in both manuscripts. In the margin of this copy, as of Cod. 69, are inserted many readings in Chark's handwriting, even the misprint of Erasmus, ἐμαῖς for ἐν αἶς, Apoc. ii. 13.

62. Walton's *Goog.*, which was brought from the East, and once belonged to Dr. Henry Googe, Fellow of Trinity College. The collations of Codd. D, 59, 61, 62 made for the London Polyglott were given in 1667 to Emmanuel College, where they yet remain. *Goog.* was identified with the Cambridge Kk. v. 35 by Bp. Marsh, who was a little careless in this kind of work.

62[2]. Camb. Univ. Lib. Kk. v. 35 [xv], $9\frac{1}{4} \times 5\frac{3}{4}$, ff. 403 (14), *chart.*, *κεφ.*, (*κεφ.* Lat.), *τίτλ.*, *subscr.*, *vers.* Mr. Bradshaw has pointed out that Kk. v. 35 is a mere transcript by George Hermonymus from Cod. 70 also

for a 'self-taught philomath' (p. 122). Dr. Clarke tells us fairly the grounds on which he arrived at his strange conclusion (Observations on the Text of the Three Divine Witnesses, Manchester, 1805, pp. 8–10), and marvellously unsound they are. But what avails authority, *quum res ipsa per se clamat?* The facsimile made for Dr. Clarke nearly seventy years ago has been copied in Horne's Introduction and twenty other books, and leaves no sort of doubt about the date of Codex Montfortianus.

[1] This Froy or Roy is believed by Mr. Rendel Harris (Origin of Cod. Leic., p. 48) to be the forger of Cod. 61.

in his handwriting, and hastily copied from it, errors of the pen and all. It has no *men.*, *lect.*, as *Goog.* had, but the ordinary κεφάλαια and *Latin* chapters. Again, *Goog.*, as Walton says, 'ex Oriente advectus est,' and must have been in England before 1657; whereas Bp. Moore got Kk. v. 35 from France in 1706, with other books from the collection of J. B. Hantin, the numismatist.

63. Cod. Ussher 1, Trin. Coll. Dublin, A. i. 8, formerly D. 20 [x], fol., with a commentary, $12\frac{3}{8} \times 9\frac{1}{2}$, ff. 237 (18–24), *prol.*, *κεφ. t.*, *pict.*, *κεφ.*, *τίτλ.*, *Am.*, *Eus.* (*lect.*, *later.*), *subscr.* Henry Dodwell made a few extracts for Bishop Fell's N. T. of 1675; Richard Bulkeley loosely collated it for Mill, Dr. Dobbin in 1855 examined St. Matthew, and the Rev. John Twycross, of the Charter House, re-collated the whole manuscript in 1858. The last leaf, containing John xxi. 25, is lost; but (*see* Scrivener, Cod. Sin., Introd., p. lix, note, and an admirable paper by Dr. Gwynn in *Hermathena*, xix, 1893, p. 368) it originally contained the verse and witnesses to it. Dr. C. R. Gregory has noticed in Cod. 63 a mutilated double leaf of an Evangelistarium in two columns [ix or x], containing part of ὥρα γ'.

64. Bute, formerly Ussher 2. This MS. belonged, like the preceding, to the illustrious Primate of Ireland, but has been missing from Trin. Coll. Library in Dublin ever since 1742, or, as Dr. C. R. Gregory thinks on the authority of Dr. T. K. Abbott, 1702. It was collated, like Cod. 63, by Dodwell for Fell, by Bulkeley for Mill. It once belonged to Dr. Thomas Goad, and was very neatly, though incorrectly, written in octavo. As the Emmanuel College copy of the Epistles (Act. 53, Paul. 30) never contained the Gospels, for which it is perpetually cited in Walton's Polyglott as *Em.*, the strong resemblance subsisting between *Usser.* 2 and *Em.* led Mill to suspect that they were in fact the same copy. The result of an examination of Walton's with Mill's collations is that they are in numberless instances cited together in support of readings, in company with other manuscripts; often with a very few or even alone (e. g. Matt. vi. 22; viii. 11; xii. 41; Mark ii. 2; iv. 1; ix. 10; 25; Luke iv. 32; viii. 27; John i. 21; iv. 24; v. 7; 20; 36; vii. 10; xvi. 19; xxi. 1). That *Usser.* 2 and *Em.* are sometimes alleged separately is easily accounted for by the inveterate want of accuracy exhibited by all early collators. But all doubt is at an end since Dean Burgon in 1880 found this celebrated copy in the library of the Marquis of Bute, and has traced the curious history of its rovings. From Dr. Goad (d. 1638) it came into the keeping of Primate Ussher, by whose hand the modern chapters seem to have been written in the margin. Then towards the end of the seventeenth century (as his signature proves) it belonged to one John Jones: a later hand puts in the date Saturday, May 25, 1728. It has also the book plate of John Earl of Moira (d. 1793). Then we trace it to James Verschoyle, afterwards Bishop of Killala from 1793 to 1834, thence to the Earls of Huntingdon for two generations, when it was purchased at the Donnington Park sale by Lord Bute. Without doubt this is the long lost Cod. 64, the *Usser.* 2 and *Em.* of Mill: it was recognized at once by the reading in John viii. 8. Dean Burgon describes it as [xii or xiii] now in two volumes, bound in red morocco about 150 years since. It has 440 leaves, $4\frac{3}{8}$ inches by $3\frac{2}{5}$ in size. *Carp.*,

Eus. t., *κεφ. t.*, *τίτλ.*, *κεφ.*, *Am.* (gilt), *Eus.* (carmine), *lect.*, ἀρχαί and τέλη. At the end are fourteen leaves of *syn.* Though beautifully written, it has no *pict.* or elaborate headings. Previous collators had done their work very poorly, as we have reason to know. Out of about sixty variations in Mark i—v, Mill has recorded only twenty-six. Over each proper name of a *person* stands a little waved stroke: cf. Evan. 530. (Collated for Burgon.)

65. Lond. Brit. Mus. Harleian 5776 [xiii], 9 × 7, ff. 309 (22), is Mill's Cov. 1, brought from the East in 1677 with four other manuscripts of the Greek Testament by Dr. John Covell [1637–1722], once English Chaplain at Constantinople, then Chaplain to Queen Mary at the Hague, afterwards Master of Christ's College, Cambridge. *Carp.*, *Eus. t.*, *κεφ. t.*, *κεφ.*, *τίτλ.*, *Am.*, *Eus.*, *στίχ.*, *subscr.* (Mill). This book was presented to Covell in 1674 by Daniel, Bishop of Proconnesus. The last verse is supplied by a late hand, the concluding leaf being lost, as in Cod. 63.

*66. Camb. Trin. Coll. O. viii. 3, Cod. Galei Londinensis [xii], 8¾ × 6, *chart.*, ff. 282 (21), *pict.*, *syn.*, *men.*, *Carp.* ten blank pages, *κεφ.*, no *τίτλ.*, *lect.*, *Am.*, *Eus.*, *subscr.* (later), *ἀναγν.*, *κεφ. t.*, *στίχ.*, once belonged to Th. Gale [1636–1702], High Master of St. Paul's School, Dean of York (1697), with some scholia in the margin by a recent hand, and other changes in the text by one much earlier. Known to (Mill), but for a time lost sight of. Collated by Scrivener, 1862. Inserted in the great printed Catalogue of Manuscripts, Oxford, 1697.

67. Oxf. Bodl. Misc. Gr. 76 [x or xi], 9 × 7, ff. 202 (20), 2 cols., is Mill's Hunt. 2, brought from the East by Dr. Robert Huntington, Chaplain at Aleppo, Provost of Trinity College, Dublin, and afterwards Bishop of Raphoe [d. 1701]. *Mut.* John vi. 64—xxi. 25. *Eus. t.*, *pict.*, *κεφ. t.*, *κεφ.*, *τίτλ.*, *Am.*, *Eus.*, *lect.*, *subscr.* On f. 3, the Athanasian Creed is on *rect.* on gold ground (Mill).

68. Oxf. Lincoln Coll. (Evst. 199) II. Gr. 17 [xii], 8 × 5, ff. 29 (23), *Carp.*, *Eus. t.*, *κεφ. t.*, *orn.*, *κεφ.*, *τίτλ.* (gold), *Am.*, *lect.*, *στίχ.*, besides *syn.*, *men.*, and verses at the end of each Gospel by Theodulos Hieromonachus, is Mill's Wheel. 1, brought from Zante in 1676, with two other copies, by George Wheeler, Canon of Durham. Between the Gospels of SS. Luke and John are small fragments of two leaves of a beautiful Evangelistarium [ix ?], with red musical notes (Mill, Scr.).

*69. (Act. 31, Paul. 37, Apoc. 14.) Codex Leicestrensis [xiv Harris; end of xv], 14½ × 10⅝, ff. 213 (38), like Codd. 206 and 233, and Brit. Mus. Harl. 3161; rapidly written on 83 leaves of vellum and 130 of paper, the vellum being outside the quinion at beginning and end, and three paper leaves within (*see* p. 24), apparently with a reed (*see* p. 27), is now in the library of the Town Council of Leicester. It contains the whole New Testament, except Matt. i. 1—xviii. 15; Acts x. 45—xiv. 17; Jude 7–25; Apoc. xviii. 7—xxii. 21, but with fragments down to xix. 10. The original order was Paul., Acts, Cath. Epp., Apoc., Gospels last and missing when the MS. came into Chark's hands. Written in the strange hand which our facsimile exhibits (No. 40), *epsilon* being recumbent and almost like *alpha*, and with accents placed over the succeeding consonant instead of the vowel[1]. The words Ειμι Ιλερμου Χαρκου at the top of the first page, in the same beautiful hand that wrote many (too many) marginal notes, prove that this codex once belonged to the William Chark, mentioned under Cod. 61 (p. 201) who got it from Brynkley, who probably got it like the Caius MS. (Evan. 59) from the Convent of Grey Friars at Cambridge. In 1641 (Wetstein states 1669) Thomas Hayne, M.A., of Trussington, in that county, gave this MS. with his other books to the Leicester Library. Mill was permitted to use it at Oxford, and collated it there in 1671. A collation also made by John Jackson and William Tiffin was lent to Wetstein through Caesar de Missy and Th. Gee, a Presbyterian minister of But Close, Leicester. Tregelles re-collated it in 1852 for his edition of the Greek Testament, and Scrivener very minutely in 1855; the latter published his results, with a full description of the book itself, in the Appendix to his 'Codex Augiensis.' No manuscript of its age has a text so remarkable as this, less however in the Acts than in the Gospels. Though none of the ordinary divisions into sections, and scarcely any liturgical marks, occur throughout, there is evidently a close connexion between Cod. 69 and the Church Service-books, as well in the interpolations of proper names, particles of time, or whole passages (e.g. Luke xxii. 43, 44 placed after Matt. xxvi. 39) which are common to both, as especially in the titles of the Gospels: ἐκ τοῦ κατὰ μάρκον εὐαγγέλιον (*sic*), &c., being in the very language of the Lectionaries[2]. Codd. 178, 443 have the same peculiarity. Tables of κεφάλαια stand before the three later Gospels, with very unusual variations; for which, as well as for the foreign matter inserted and other peculiarities of Cod. 69, consult Scrivener's Cod. Augiensis (Introd. pp. xl–xlvii). See also Mr. J. Rendel Harris, Origin of the Leicester Codex, 1887.

70. Camb. Univ. Lib. Ll. ii. 13 [xv], $11\frac{1}{4} \times 7\frac{1}{4}$, ff. 186 (23), *orn.*, τίτλ. in margin, κεφ. Lat., *vers.*, was written, like Codd. 30, 62[2], 287, by G. Hermonymus the Spartan (who settled at Paris, 1472, and became the Greek teacher of Budaeus and Reuchlin), for ~~William Bodet~~; there are marginal corrections by Budaeus, from whose letter to Bp. Tonstall we may fix the date about A. D. 1491–4. It once belonged to Bunckle of London, then to Bp. Moore. Like Cod. 62[2] it has the Latin chapters (Mill).

*71. Lambeth 528 [A. D. 1100], $6\frac{1}{2} \times 4\frac{3}{4}$, ff. 265 (26), is Mill's *Eph.* and Scrivener's g. This elegant copy, which once belonged to an Archbishop of Ephesus, was brought to England in 1675 by Philip Traheron, English Chaplain at Smyrna. Traheron made a careful collation of his manuscript, of which both the rough copy (B. M., Burney 24) and a fair one (Lambeth 528 b) survive. This last Scrivener in

[1] Another facsimile (Luke xxi. 36—John viii. 6) is given by Abbott in his 'Collation of Four Important Manuscripts' (*see* Cod. 13). In all four the *pericope adulterae* follows Luke xxi. 38.

[2] See the style of the Evangelistaria, as cited above, pp. 80–83; Matthaei's uncials BH and Birch's 178 of the Gospels, described below. So B.-C. ii. 13, to be described hereafter, reads in St. Matthew only ἀρχ' ἐκ τοῦ κατὰ ματθαῖον ἁγίου εὐαγγελίου. Compare also Codd. 211, 261, 357, and B.-C. iii. 5 in SS. Matthew and Mark.

1845 compared with the original, and revised, especially in regard to later corrections, of which there are many. Mill used Traheron's collation very carelessly. *Carp.*, *Eus. t.*, *κεφ. t.* [xv], *κεφ.*, *τίτλ.*, *Am.*, *Eus.*, *lect.* This copy presents a text full of interest, and much superior to that of the mass of manuscripts of its age. *See* Cod. 29.

72. Brit. Mus. Harleian. 5647 [xi], large 4to, 10×8, ff. 268 (22, 24), an elegant copy, with a catena on St. Matthew, *κεφ. t.*, *pict.*, *κεφ.*, *τίτλ.*, *lect.*, *Am.*, *Eus.*, *subscr.*, *στίχ.* (Mark), various readings in the ample margin. Lent by T. Johnson to (Wetstein).

73. Christ Church, Oxford, Wake 26 [xi], 4to, $9\frac{7}{8} \times 8\frac{1}{8}$, ff. 291, *κεφ. t.*, *Eus. t.*, *vers.*, *κεφ.*, *Am.*, *Eus.*, *τίτλ.*, *pict.*, few *lect.* It is marked 'Ex dono Mauri Cordati Principis Hungaro-Walachiae, A° 1724.' This and Cod. 74 were once Archbishop Wake's, and were collated for Wetstein by (Jo. Walker, *Wake MS.* 35)[1].

74. Christ Church, Oxford, Wake 20 [xiii], 8×6, ff. 204, written by Theodore (*see* p. 42, note 8). *Mut.* Matt. i. 1–14; v. 29—vi. 1; thirty-two verses. It came in 1727 from the Monastery of Παντοκράτωρ, on Mount Athos. *Carp.*, *Eus. t.*, *κεφ. t.*, *syn.*, *men.*, *κεφ.*, *τίτλ.*, *Am.*, *Eus.*, *lect.*, *subscr.*, *vers.*

75. Cod. Genevensis 19 [xi], $9 \times 6\frac{1}{2}$, ff. 500 (19), *Carp.*, *Eus. t.*, *prol.*, *κεφ. t.*, *Am.*, *τίτλ.*, *Eus.*, *lect.*, *pict.*, *men.* In text it much resembles that of Cod. 6. Seen in 1714 by Wetstein, examined by Scholz (collated Matt. i—vi, John vii, viii), collated (Matt. i—xviii, Mark i—v) by Cellérier, a Professor at Geneva, whose collation (Matt. i—xviii) is corrected and supplemented with Matt. xix—end by H. C. Hoskier, though his visit to the MS. was unfortunately short. The first diorthota made corrections and additions as regards breathings and stops. Other corrections made not much later (Hoskier, Collation of 604, App. G).

76. (Act. 43, Paul. 49.) Cod. Caesar-Vindobonensis, Nessel. 300, Lambec. 28 [xi–xiii], $7\frac{1}{2} \times 5\frac{3}{8}$, ff. 358 (27), *prol.*, *κεφ. t.*, *κεφ.*, *τίτλ.*, *Am.*, *lect.*, *syn.*, *men.*, *pict.* This copy (the only one known to read *αὐτῆς* with the Complutensian and other editions in Luke ii. 22) is erroneously called an uncial by Mill (Gerhard à Mastricht 1690; Ashe 1691; F. K. Alter 1786) (Greg.).

77. Caesar-Vindobon. Nessel. 154, Lambec. 29 [xi], $9\frac{1}{4} \times 8$, ff. 300 (21), very neat; with a commentary (Victor's on St. Mark), *Carp.*, *Eus. t.*, *prol.*, *κεφ. t.*, *κεφ.*, *τίτλ.*, *Am.*, *Eus.* (*lect.* and *syn.* by a later hand). It once belonged to Matthias Corvinus, the great king of Hungary (1458–90). Collated in 'Tentamen descriptionis codicum,' &c. 1773 by (Treschow, and also by Alter) (Greg.).

[1] Of the 183 manuscript volumes bequeathed by William Wake, Archbishop of Canterbury [1657–1737] to Christ Church (of which he had been a Canon), no less than twenty-eight contain portions of the Greek Testament. They are all described in this list from a comparison of Dean Gaisford's MS. Catalogue (1837) with the books themselves, to which Bp. Jacobson's kindness gave me access in 1861. Corrected by E. M., to whom similar kindness has been shown. See also 'Account of some MSS. at Christ Church, Oxford,' by the Rev. Charles H. Hoole, Student.

78. Cod. Nicolae Jancovich de Vadass, now in Hungary [xii], 9⅛ × 5¾, ff. 293 (22), *Eus. t.*, κεφ. *t.*, τίτλ., κεφ., *lect.*, *syn.*, *pict.* It was once in the library of king Matthias Corvinus: on the sack of Buda by the Turks in 1527, his noble collection of 50,000 volumes was scattered, and about 1686 this book fell into the hands of S. B., then of J. G., Carpzov of Leipsic, at whose sale it was purchased and brought back to its former country. A previous possessor, in the seventeenth century, was Γεώργιος δεσμοφύλαξ Ναυπλίου. (Collated by C. F. Boerner for Kuster, and 'in usum' of Scholz.)

79. Leyden, Bibl. Univ. 74 [xv], Latin version older, 6½ × 4¾, ff. 208 (26–28), 2 cols., κεφ., *lect.*, ἀναγν. (all partial). *Mut.* Matt. i. 1—xiv. 13. Brought by Georg. Douze from Constantinople in 1597, consulted by Gomar in 1644 (Greg.).

80. Paris, Lesoeuf [xii], 9⅛ × 6⅜, ff. 309 (23), *prol.*, κεφ. *t.*, κεφ. (also Lat. cent. xv), τίτλ. This MS. belonged to J. G. Graevius, and was collated by Bynaeus in 1691: then it passed into the hands of J. Van der Hagen, who showed it to Wetstein in 1739: afterwards it was bought by Ambrose Didot at a sale, and sold to Mons. Lesoeuf, where Dr. C. R. Gregory saw it. (*See* Proleg. to Tisch. ed. viii. p. 485.)

81. Oxf. Bodl. Misc. Gr. 323, Auct. T. Infr. i. 5 [xiii], 7 × 5, ff. 182. Κεφ., τίτλ., some *Am.* Bought in 1883 from Mr. William Ward who brought it from Ephesus. Contains Matt. xix. 15—xxi. 19; 31–41; xxii. 7—xxviii. 20; Mark i. 9—iii. 18; 35—xv. 15; 32—xvi. 14; Luke i. 18—ii. 19; iii. 7—iv. 40; v. 8—xxii. 5; 36—xxiii. 10; John viii. 4—xxi. 18. This place has been hitherto occupied by Greek MSS. cited in a Correctorium Bibliorum Latinorum of the thirteenth century[1]. Dr. Hort appropriates this numeral to Muralt's 2^{pe}. (Evan. 473.)

82. Oxf. Bodl. MS. Bibl. Gr. e. 1. Some fragments: (1) John iii. 23; (2) 26, 27; (3) 2 Cor. xi. 3: Chart. (1, 2) [xiii], (3) [vi or vii] uncials and minuscules intermixed, and some Coptic and Arabic words.

In this place other fragments have been placed till now. Seven unknown Greek manuscripts of St. John, three of St. Matthew and (apparently) of the other Gospels, cited in Laurentius Valla's 'Annotationes in N.T., ex diversorum utriusque linguae, Graecae et Latinae, codicum collatione,' written about 1440, edited by Erasmus, Paris 1505. His copies seem modern, and have probably been used by later critics. The whole subject, however, is very carefully examined in the Rev. A. T. Russell's 'Memoirs of the life and works of Bp. Andrewes,' pp. 282-310. Hort's Cod. 82 is Burgon's Venet. xii, to be described hereafter.

[1] These formal revisions of the Latin Bible were mainly two, one made by the University of Paris with the sanction of the Archbishop of Sens about 1230, and a rival one undertaken by the Mendicant Orders, through Cardinal Hugo de St. Caro (*see* above, p. 69), and adopted by their general Chapter held at Paris in 1256. A previous revision had been made by Cardinal Nicolaus and the Cistercian Abbot Stephanus in 1150. A manuscript of that of 1256 was used by Lucas Brugensis and Simon (Wetstein, N. T. Prol. vol. i. p. 85). Canon Westcott calls attention to a *Correctorium* in the British Museum, King's Library, 1 A. viii.

83. Cod. Monacensis 518 [xi], $8\frac{1}{2} \times 6\frac{1}{2}$, ff. 321 (20), beautifully written, *prol.*, *κεφ. t.*, *κεφ.*, *lect.*, *ἀναγν.*, *syn.*, *men.*, *subscr.*, *στίχ.*, in the Royal Library at Munich, whither it was brought from Augsburg (Bengel's August. 1, Scholz, Greg.).

84. Monacensis 568 [xii], $6\frac{5}{8} \times 5\frac{1}{8}$, ff. 65, *κεφ.*, *τίτλ.*, *Am.* (not *Eus.*), *lect.* both in the text and margin, contains SS. Matthew and Mark. *Mut.* Matt. i. 18—xiii. 10; xiii. 27–42; xiv. 3—xviii. 25; xix. 9–21; xxii. 4—Mark vii. 13 (Burgon, Greg.).

85. Monacensis 569 [xiii], $5\frac{1}{2} \times 3\frac{3}{4}$, ff. 30, *κεφ.*, *lect.* in vermilion, *τίτλ.*, *Am.* (not *Eus.*), contains only Matt. viii. 15—ix. 17; xvi. 12—xvii. 20; xxiv. 26–45; xxvi. 25–54; Mark vi. 13—ix. 45; Luke iii. 12—vi. 44; John ix. 11—xii. 5; xix. 6–24; xx. 23—xxi. 9 (Bengel's August. 3, Scholz).

86. Posoniensis Lycaei Aug. [x], $9\frac{1}{2} \times 7\frac{1}{8}$, ff. 280, *prol.*, *Eus. t.*, *pict.*, *syn.* Once at Buda, but it had been bought in 1183 at Constantinople for the Emperor Alexius II Comnenus (Bengel, Endlicher). It was brought by Rayger, a doctor of medicine, from Italy, where it had been carried, to Pressburg, to his brother-in-law Gleichgross, who was a pastor in that place, amongst whose books it was sold to the library of the Lycaeum in Pressburg. (*See* Gregory, Proleg. p. 486.)

87. Trevirensis [xii], fol., contains St. John's Gospel with a catena, published at length by Cordier at Antwerp. It once belonged to the eminent philosopher and mathematician, Cardinal Nicolas of Cusa, on the Moselle, near Trèves [1401–64: *see* Cod. 129 Evan., and Cod. 59 Acts]; previously at the monastery of Petra or of the Fore-runner of Constantinople[1] (Scholz). Wetstein's 87 is our 250.

88. Codex of the Gospels, 4to, on vellum, cited as ancient and correct by Joachim Camerarius (who collated it) in his Annotations to the New Testament, 1642. It resembles in text Codd. 63, 72, 80.

*89. Gottingensis Cod. Theol. 53 [1006], fol., ff. 172, *Carp.*, *Eus. t.*, *κεφ. t.*, *κεφ.*, *Eust.*, *lect.*, with corrections. Collated by A. G. Gehl in 1729 (?), and by Matthaei (No. 20) in 1786–7.

90. (Act. 47, Paul. 14.) Cod. Jac. Fabri, a Dominican of Deventer, now in the library of the church of the Remonstrants at Amsterdam, 186 [xvi, but copied from a manuscript written by Theodore and dated 1293], 4to, *chart.*, 2 vols., *κεφ.* (Lat.), *lect.*, *syn.* The Gospels stand John, Luke, Matthew, Mark (*see* p. 70); the Pauline Epistles precede the Acts; and Jude is written twice, from different copies. This codex (which has belonged to Abr. Hinckelmann of Hamburg, and to Wolff) was collated by Wetstein. Faber [1472—living in 1515] had also compared it with another 'very ancient' vellum manuscript of the Gospels presented by Sixtus IV (1471–84) to Jo. Wessel of Groningen, but which was then at Zvolle. As might be expected, this

[1] On fol. 4 we read *ἡ βίβλος αὕτη* (*ἧδε* 178) *τῆς μονῆς τοῦ Προδρόμου* | *τῆς κειμένης ἔγγιστα τῆς Ἀε[αι]τίου* | *ἀρχαϊκὴ δὲ τῇ μονῇ κλῆσις Πέτρα.* Compare Cod. 178 and Montfauc., Palaeogr. Graeca, pp. 39, 110, 305.

copy much resembles Cod. 74. See Delitzsch, Handschr. Funde, ii. pp. 54–57.

91. Perronianus [x], of which extracts were sent by Montfaucon to Mill, had been Cardinal Perron's [d. 1618], and before him had belonged to 'S. Taurini monasterium Ebroicense' (Evreux). Hort suggests, and Gregory favours the suggestion, that this is the same as Evan. 299 (Cod. Par. Reg. 177), which came from Evreux.

92. Faeschii 1 (Act. 49) [xiv or xv]
94. Faeschii 2 [xvi or xvii]
The former, $10\frac{1}{4} \times 8$, ff. 141, *κεφ. t.*, *τίτλ.*, *pict.*, contains St. Mark with Victor's commentary on vellum, and scholia on the Catholic Epistles, with the authors' names, Didymus, Origen, Cyril, &c., and is referred by Gregory to the tenth century; the latter, $8\frac{1}{2} \times 5\frac{1}{2}$, ff. 172 (22), SS. Mark and Luke, with Victor's commentary on St. Mark, that of Titus of Bostra on St. Luke, on paper [xv or xvi, Greg.]. Both belonged to Andrew Faesch, of Basle, and were collated by Wetstein. Dean Burgon found them both at Basle (O. ii. 27 and O. ii. 23).

93. Graevii [1632–1703] of the Gospels, cited by Vossius on the Genealogy, Luke iii, but not known (Cod. 80 ? Greg.).

95. Oxf. Lincoln Coll. II. Gr. 16 [xii or earlier], $10\frac{1}{2} \times 8$, ff. 110 (20), is Mill's Wheeler 2[1]. It contains SS. Luke and John with commentary, *mut.* Luke i. 1—xi. 2; John vii. 2–17; xx. 31—xxi. 10. With full scholia neatly written in the margin, *κεφ.*, *Am.* (later), *syn.*, *men.* (Mill, Professor Nicoll).

96. Bodl. Misc. Gr. 8 (Auct. D. 5. 1) [xv], $5\frac{3}{8} \times 3\frac{3}{4}$, ff. 62 (18), *chart.*, is Walton's and Mill's Trit., with many rare readings, containing St. John with a commentary, beautifully written by Jo. Trithemius, Abbot of Spanheim [d. 1516]. Received from Abraham Scultet by Geo. Hackwell, 1607 (Walton's Polyglott, Mill, Griesbach).

97. Hirsaugiensis [1500, by Nicolas, a monk of Hirschau in Bavaria], 12mo, ff. 71, on vellum, containing St. John, seems but a copy of 96. Collated by Maius, and the collation given in J. D. Michaelis, Orientalische und exegetische Bibliothek, ii. p. 243, &c. (Greg., Bengel[2], Maius, Schulz).

98. Oxf. Bodl. E. D. Clarke 5 [xii], $8\frac{1}{2} \times 6$, ff. 222 (25), *pict.*, *κεφ. t.*, *κεφ.*, *τίτλ.*, *Am.*, *lect.*, *subscr.*, *στίχ.*, brought by Clarke from the East. It was collated in a few places for Scholz, who substituted it here for Cod. R (*see* p. 139) of Griesbach.

99. Lipsiensis, Bibliothec. Paul. [xvi], $8\frac{1}{4} \times 7\frac{1}{8}$, ff. 22 (22, 23), Matthaei's 18, contains Matt. iv. 8—v. 27; vi. 2—xv. 30; Luke i. 1–13; *Carp.*, *κεφ. t.*, *κεφ.*, *τίτλ.*, *Am.*, *Eus.*, *lect.*, *syn.* (Matthaei, Greg.). Wetstein's 99 is our 155.

[1] Noted 'Ex libris Georgii Wheleri Westmonasteriensis perigrinatione ejus Constantinopolitanâ collect. Anno Domini 1676.' See Evan. 68; Evst. 3.

[2] Cod. 101 better suits Bengel's description of Uffen. 3 than 97: they are written on different materials, and the description of their respective texts will not let us suspect them to be the same. Wetstein never cites Cod. 101, but the addition of τὸν θεόν at the end of John viii. 27, the reading of the margin of Uffen. 3, has been erroneously ascribed in the critical editions to 97, not to 101.

100. Paul. ~~L. B.~~ de Eubeswald [x], 4to, $9\frac{1}{4} \times 7\frac{1}{8}$, ff. 374, *κεφ.*, *τίτλ.*, *Am.*, *Eus.*, *lect.* (*syn.*, *men.*, *ἀναγν.* later), vellum, *mut.* John xxi. 25; *pict.*, *κεφ. t.*, *Eus. t.*, and in a later hand many corrections with scholia, *chart.* J. C. Wagenseil used it in Hungary for John viii. 6. Now in the University of Pesth, but in the fifteenth century belonging to Bp. Jo. Pannonius. Edited at Pesth in 1860 'cum interpretatione Hungaria' by S. Markfi.

101. Uffenbach. 3 [xvi], 12mo, *chart.*, St. John *στιχήρης*. So near the Basle (that is, we suppose, Erasmus') edition, that Bengel scarcely ever cites it. With two others (Paul. M. and Acts 45) it was lent by Z. C. Uffenbach, Consul of Frankfort-on-the-Main, to Wetstein in 1717, and afterwards to Bengel. (Gregory would omit it.)

102. Bibliothecae Medicae, an unknown manuscript with many rare readings, extracted by Wetstein at Amsterdam for Matt. xxiv—Mark viii. 1, from the margin of a copy of Plantin's N. T. 1591, in the library of J. Le Long. Canon Westcott is convinced that the manuscript from which these readings were derived is none other than Cod. B itself, and Dr. Gregory agrees with him. In St. Matthew's Gospel he finds the two authorities agree seventy times and differ only five times, always in a manner to be easily accounted for: in St. Mark they agree in eighty-four out of the eighty-five citations, the remaining one (ch. ii. 22) being hardly an exception. Westcott, New Test., Smith's 'Dictionary of the Bible.' Hort's Cod. 102 is w^{scr} (Evan. 507), to be described hereafter.

103. Regius 196 [xi], fol., once Cardinal Mazarin's, seems the same manuscript as that from which Emericus Bigot gave extracts for Curcellaeus' N. T. 1658 (Scholz). Burgon supposes some mistake here, as he finds Reg. 196 to be a copy of Theophylact's commentary on SS. Matthew and Mark, written over an older manuscript [viii or ix]. Perhaps the same as 14 or 278 (Greg.).

104. Hieronymi Vignerii [x], from which also Bigot extracted readings, which Wetstein obtained through J. Drieberg in 1744, and published. Perhaps 697 (Greg.).

105. (Act. 48, Paul. 24.) Cod. Ebnerianus, Bodl. Misc. Gr. 136, a beautiful copy [xii], $8 \times 6\frac{1}{4}$, ff. 426 (27), formerly belonging to Jerome Ebner von Eschenbach of Nuremberg. *Pict.*, *Carp.*, *Eus. t.*, *κεφ. t.*, *τίτλ.*, *κεφ.*, *Am.* (not *Eus.*), *subscr.*, *στίχ.*, the Nicene Creed, all in gold: with *lect.* throughout and *syn.*, *men.* prefixed by Joasaph, a calligraphist, A.D. 1391, who also added John viii. 3–11 at the end of that Gospel. Facsimile in Horne's Introduction, and in Tregelles' Horne, p. 220 (Schoenleben 1738, Rev. H. O. Coxe, by whom the collation was lent before 1845 to the Rev. R. J. F. Thomas, Vicar of Yeovil [d. 1873], together with one of Canon. Graec. 110 of the Acts and Epistles, both of which are mislaid).

106. Winchelsea [x], with many important readings, often resembling the Harkleian Syriac: not now in the Earl of Winchelsea's Library (Jackson collated it for Wetstein in 1748).

107. Bodl. E. D. Clarke 6 [xiv and later], $8\frac{1}{2} \times 6\frac{3}{4}$, ff. 351, *κεφ. t.*, *pict.*,

κεφ., τίτλ., containing the Gospels in different hands. (Like 98, 111, 112, *partially* collated for Scholz.) Griesbach's 107 is also 201.

108. Vindobonensis Caesarei, Suppl. Gr. 2, formerly Kollar. 4 [xi], $12\frac{3}{8} \times 9\frac{1}{4}$, ff. 426, 2 vols. With a commentary (Victor's on St. Mark: Burgon, Last Twelve Verses, &c., p. 288), *Carp.*, *Eus. t.*, *prol.*, *κεφ. t.*, *pict.*, *κεφ.*, *τίτλ.*, *Am.*, *Eus.*, *subscr.*, *στίχ.* It seems to have been written at Constantinople, and formerly belonged to Parrhasius, then to the convent of St. John de Carbonaria at Naples (Treschow, Alter, Birch, Scholz).

109. Brit. Mus. Addit. 5117 [A.D. 1326], $7\frac{1}{4} \times 5\frac{3}{4}$, ff. 225 (24–30), ll. rubr., *Carp.*, *prol.*, *κεφ. t.*, *Eus. t.*, *syn.*, *men.*, *lect.*, *Am.*, *τίτλ.*, *subscr.*, *στίχ.*, Mead. 1, then Askew (5115 is Act. 22, and 5116 is Paul. 75, these two in the same hand; different from that employed in the Gospels).

110[1]. Brit. Mus. Addit. 19,386 [xiv], 11 × 8, ff. 267 (?), *Carp.*, *Eus. t.* (faded), *κεφ. t.*, *prol.*, *κεφ.*, *τίτλ.*, *lect.*, *syn.*, with a dial of the year. Four Gospels with commentary by Theophylact. Purchased from Constantine Simonides in 1853. (Greg. 1260.)

111[2]. Bodl. Clarke 7 [xii], $8\frac{1}{4} \times 6$, ff. 181 (31), *κεφ. t.* (*mut.* Matt.),

[1] Cod. Ravianus, Bibl. Reg. Berolinensis [xvi], 4to, 2 vols., on parchment, once belonging to Jo. Rav. of Upsal, has been examined by Wetstein, Griesbach, and by G. G. Pappelbaum in 1796. It contains the whole New Testament, and has attracted attention because it has the disputed words in 1 John v. 7, 8. It is now, however, admitted by all to be a mere transcript of the N. T. in the Complutensian Polyglott with variations from Erasmus or Stephen, and as such has no independent authority.

[2] (Wetstein.) THE VELESIAN READINGS. The Jesuit de la Cerda in his 'Adversaria Sacra,' cap. xci (Lyons, 1626), a collection of various readings, written in vermilion in the margin of a *Greek* Testament (which from its misprint in 1 Pet. iii. 11 we know to be R. Stephen's of 1550) by Petro Faxardo, Marquis of Velez, a Spaniard, who had taken them from sixteen manuscripts, eight of which were in the king's library, in the Escurial. It is never stated what codices or how many support each variation. De la Cerda had received the readings from Mariana, the great Jesuit historian of Spain, then lately dead, and appears to have inadvertently added to Mariana's account of their origin, that the sixteen manuscripts were in Greek. These Velesian readings, though suspected from the first even by Mariana by reason of their strange resemblance to the Latin Vulgate and the manuscripts of the Old Latin, were repeated as critical authorities in Walton's Polyglott, 1657, and (contrary to his own better judgement) were retained by Mill in 1707. Wetstein, however (N. T. Proleg. vol. i. pp. 59–61), and after him Michaelis and Bp. Marsh, have abundantly proved that the various readings must have been collected by Velez from *Latin* manuscripts, and by him translated into Greek, very foolishly perhaps, but not of necessity with a fraudulent design. Certainly, any little weight the Velesian readings may have, must be referred to the Latin, not to the Greek text. Among the various proofs of their Latin origin urged by Wetstein and others, the following establish the fact beyond the possibility of doubt:

	Greek Text.	Vulgate Text.	Vulgate various reading.	Velesian reading.
Mark viii. 38	ἐπαισχυνθῇ	confusus fuerit	confessus fuerit	ὁμολογήσῃ
Heb. xii. 18	κεκαυμένῳ	accensibilem	accessibilem	προσίτῳ
— xiii. 2	ἔλαθον	latuerunt	placuerunt	ἤρεσαν
James v. 6	κατεδικάσατε	addixistis	adduxistis	ἠγάγετε
Apoc. xix. 6	ὄχλου	turbae	tubae	σάλπιγγος
— xxi. 12	ἀγγέλους	angelos	angelos	γωνίας

κεφ., *τίτλ.*, *Am.*, *vers.*, *subscr.*, *στίχ.* *Mut.* John xvi. 27—xvii. 15; xx. 25–end, and

112[1]. Bodl. Clarke 10 [xi], 5½ × 4¼, ff. 167 (33), *Carp.*, *Eus. t.*, *prol.*, *pict.*, *syn.*, *men.*, *κεφ. t.*, *κεφ.*, *τίτλ.*, *lect.*, with commencement and large letters in gold, having both *Am.* and *Eus.*, in Matt. i—Mark ii, in the same line (a very rare arrangement; *see* Codd. 192, 198, 212, and Wake 21 *below*), a very beautiful copy. These two, very partially collated for Scholz, were substituted by him and Tischensdorf for collations whose history is not a little curious.

113. Brit. Mus. Harleian. 1810 [xi], 8 × 7¼, ff. 270 (26), *prol.*, *syn.* (later), *Carp.*, *Eus. t.*, *κεφ. t.*, *pict.*, *κεφ.*, *τίτλ.*, *Am.*, *Eus.*, *lect.* (Griesbach, Bloomfield). Apparently this is Bentley's *θ* 'membr. 4to 600 annorum,' collated by him in the margin of Trin. Coll. B. xvii. 5 (*see* Cod. 51). Its readings are of more than usual interest, as are those of

114. Brit. Mus. Harl. 5540 [x], 5¼ × 4¼, ff. 280 (20) (facsimile in a Greek Testament, published in 1837 by Taylor, London), very elegant, with more recent marginal notes and Matt. xxviii. 19—Mark i. 12 in a later hand. *Mut.* Matt. xvii. 4–18; xxvi. 59–73 (Griesbach, Bloomfield). *Carp.*, *τίτλ.*, *κεφ.*, *Am.* (not *Eus.*), *κεφ. t.* (Luke, John). *See* Canon Westcott's article, 'New Test.,' in Smith's 'Dictionary of the Bible.'

115. Brit. Mus. Harl. 5559 [xii], 6¾ × 5¾, ff. 271 (19), *κεφ.*, some *τίτλ.*, *Am.*, frequently *Eus.*[2], once Bernard Mould's (Smyrna, 1724), with an unusual text. *Mut.* Matt. i. 1—viii. 10; Mark v. 23–36; Luke i. 78—ii. 9; vi. 4–15; John xi. 2—xxi. 25 (Griesbach, Bloomfield). A few more words of John xi survive.

116. Brit. Mus. Harl. 5567 [xii], 6¼ × 5, ff. 300 (23), *Syn.*, *Eus. t.*, *κεφ. t.*, *κεφ.*, *τίτλ.*, *Am.*, *lect.*, *subscr.*, *ἀναγν.*, *στίχ.*, *men.*, of some value.

[1] (Wetstein.) THE BARBERINI READINGS must also be banished from our list of critical authorities, though for a different reason. The collection of various readings from twenty-two manuscripts (ten of the Gospels, eight of the Acts and Epistles, and four of the Apocalypse), seen by Isaac Vossius in 1642 in the Barberini Library at Rome, was made about 1625, and first published in 1673 by Peter Possinus (Poussines), a Jesuit, at the end of a catena of St. Mark. He alleged that the collations were made by John M. Caryophilus [d. 1635], a Cretan, while preparing an edition of the Greek Testament, under the patronage of Paul V [d. 1621] and Urban VIII [d. 1644]. As the Barberini readings often favour the Latin version, they fell into the same suspicion as the Velesian: Wetstein especially (N. T. Proleg. vol. i. pp. 61, 62), after pressing against them some objections more ingenious than solid, declares 'lis haec non aliter quam ipsis libris Romae inventis et productis, *quod nunquam credo fiet*, solvi potest.' The very papers Wetstein thus called for were discovered by Birch (Barberini Lib. 209) more than thirty years later, and besides them Caryophilus' petition for the loan of six manuscripts from the Vatican (Codd. BS, 127, 129, 141, 144), which he doubtless obtained and used. The good faith of the collator being thus happily vindicated, we have only to identify his eleven [Cod. 141 of the Gospels being also Act. 75, Paul. 86, Apoc. 40. Another of his manuscripts was Act. 73, Paul. 80] remaining codices, most of them probably being in that very Library, and may then dismiss the Barberini readings as having done their work, and been fairly superseded.

[2] In Codd. 115 and 202 *Eus.* is usually, in Codd. 116, 117, 417, 422, and B. M. Addit. 15,581 but rarely, written under *Am.*: these copies therefore were probably never quite finished. See p. 62, and note 1.

It belonged in 1649 to Athanasius a Greek monk, then to Bernard Mould (Griesbach, Bloomfield).

117. (Apost. 6.) Brit. Mus. Harl. 5731 [xv], 8 × 6, ff. 202 (28), carelessly written, once belonged to Bentley. *Mut.* Matt. i. 1–18: *pict.*, *prol.*, *Eus. t.*, *κεφ. t.*, *κεφ.*, *τίτλ.*, *lect.*, *Am.*, *syn.*, fragments of a Lectionary on the last twenty leaves (Griesbach, Bloomfield).

*118. Oxf. Bodl. Misc. Gr. 13 [xiii], 7¾ × 5¼, ff. 257, an important palimpsest (with the Gospels *uppermost*) once the property of Archbishop Marsh of Armagh [d. 1713]. *Eus. t.*, *κεφ. t.*, *τίτλ.*, *lect.*, *Am.*, *Eus.*, *στίχ.*, *ῥήμ.* (*syn.*, *men.* later), and some of the Psalms on paper. Later hands also supplied Matt. i. 1—vi. 2; Luke xiii. 35—xiv. 20; xviii. 8—xix. 9; John xvi. 25—xxi. 25. Well collated by (Griesbach).

119. Paris Nat. Gr. 85 [xii], 9 × 6⅜, ff. 237 (23), formerly Teller's of Rheims, is Kuster's Paris 5 (Griesbach, Gregory), *prol.*, *κεφ. t.*, *κεφ.*, *τίτλ.*, *Am.*, *lect.*, *subscr.*, *στίχ.*, *pict.*

120. Par. Nat. Suppl. Gr. 185 [xiii], 7½ × 5⅜, ff. 177, *κεφ.*, *τίτλ.*, *Am.*, formerly belonged to St. Victor's on the Walls, and seems to be Stephen's *ιδ'*, whose text (1550) and Colinaeus' (1534) it closely resembles. St. Mark is wanting (Griesbach).

121. Par. St. Geneviève, A. O. 34 [Sept. 1284, Indiction 12], 7⅞ × 6, ff. 241, *κεφ. t.*, *κεφ.*, *τίτλ.*, *Am.*, *lect.*, *syn.*, *men.* *Mut.* Matt. v. 21—viii. 24 (Griesbach).

122. (Act. 177, Paul. 219.) Lugdunensis-Batavorum Bibl. publ. Gr. 74 A [xii], 7⅛ × 5½, ff. 222, *Eus. t.*, *κεφ. t.*, *κεφ.*, *τίτλ.*, *Am.*, *Eus.*, *lect.*, *vers.*, *στίχ.*, *men.*, once Meerman's[1] 116. *Mut.* Acts i. 1–14; xxi. 14—xxii. 28; 1 John iv. 20—Jude 25; Rom. i. 1—vii. 13; 1 Cor. ii. 7—xiv. 23 (J. Dermout, Collectanea Critica in N. T., 1825). Griesbach's 122 is also 97. See Cod. 435.

123. Vindobon. Caesar, Nessel. 240, formerly 30 [xi], 4to, 8⅛ × 6, ff. 328 (18), brought from Constantinople about 1562 by the Imperial Ambassador to the Porte, Ogier de Busbeck; *Carp.*, *Eus. t.*, *prol.*, *κεφ. t.*, *pict.*, *κεφ.*, *τίτλ.*, *Am.*, *subscr.*, corrections by another hand (Treschow, Alter, Birch).

*124. Vind. Caes. Ness. 188, formerly 31 [xii], 4to, 8½ × 7⅛, ff. 180 (25), *Carp.*, *Eus. t.*, *harm.*, *κεφ. t.*, *κεφ.*, *τίτλ.*, *Am.*, *Eus.*, *syn.*, *men.*, an eclectic copy, with corrections by the first hand (Mark ii. 14; Luke iii. 1, &c.). This manuscript was written in Calabria, where it belonged to a certain Leo, and was brought to Vienna probably in 1564. It resembles the Harkleian Syriac, Old Latin, Codd. DL. i. 13, and especially 69 (Treschow, Alter, Birch). Collated by Dr. Em. Hoffmann for Professor Ferrar where Alter and Birch disagree. *See* Cod. 13, for Abbott's recent edition.

125. Vind. Caes. Suppl. G. 50, formerly Kollar. 6 [x], 8¾ × 6⅞, ff. 306 (23), *κεφ. t.*, *κεφ.*, *τίτλ.*, *Am.*, *Eus.*, *pict.* (*lect.*, *subscr.*, *στίχ.*, *vers.* later), with many corrections in the margin and between the lines (Treschow, Alter, Birch).

[1] Meerman's other manuscript of the N. T., sold at his sale in 1824, is No. 562.

126. Guelpherbytanus xvi. 6, Aug. Quarto [xi], 8¼ × 6⅛, ff. 219 (26), carelessly written, *Eus. t.*, *κεφ. t.*, *prol.*, *pict.*, with *lect.*, *syn.* in a later hand, and some quite modern corrections. Matt. xxviii. 18–20 is cruciform, capitals often occur in the middle of words, and the text is of an unusual character. Inspected by (Heusinger 1752, Knittel, Tischendorf).

N.B. Codd. 127–181, all at Rome, were inspected, and a few (127, 131, 157) really collated by Birch, about 1782. Of 153 Scholz collated the greater part, and small portions of 138–44; 146–52; 154–57; 159–60; 162; 164–71; 173–75; 177–80.

127. Rom. Vatican. Gr. 349 [xi], 12⅜ × 9⅝, ff. 370 (16), ll. rubr., *Carp.*, *Eus. t.*, *prol.*, *κεφ. t.*, *κεφ.*, *τίτλ.*, *Am.*, *lect.*, a neatly written and important copy, with a few later corrections (e. g. Matt. xxvii. 49).

128. Rom. Vat. Gr. 356 [xi Birch, xiii or xiv Greg.], 12½ × 9⅝, ff. 370 (18), ll. rubr., *prol.*, *κεφ. t.* with harmony, *κεφ.*, *τίτλ.*, *subscr.*, *στίχ.* (p. 69, note).

129. Rom. Vat. Gr. 358 [xii], 11¼ × 8⅞, ff. 355, ll. rubr., *Carp.* (with addition), *Eus. t.*, *prol.*, *κεφ. t.*, *κεφ.*, *τίτλ.*, *Am.*, *Eus.*, *syn.*, *men.*, *pict.*, with scholia, Victor's commentary on St. Mark, and a note on John vii. 53, such as we read in Cod. 145 and others. Bought at Constantinople in 1438 by Nicolas de Cuza, Eastern Legate to the Council of Ferrara (*see* Cod. 87).

130. Rom. Vat. Gr. 359 [xiii Birch, xv or xvi Greg.], 11⅛ × 8¼, *chart.*, ff. 229 (26), ll. rubr., *κεφ.* lat., a curious copy, with the Greek and Latin in parallel columns, and the Latin chapters.

131. (Act. 70, Paul. 77.) Rom. Vat. Gr. 360 [xi Birch, xiv or xv Greg.], 9¼ × 7, ff. 233 (37), 2 cols., contains the whole New Testament except the Apoc. (Birch), with many remarkable variations, and a text somewhat like that of Aldus' Greek Testament (1518). The manuscript was given to Sixtus V [1585–90] for the Vatican by 'Aldus Manuccius Paulli F. Aldi.' The Epistle to the Hebrews stands before 1 Tim. *Carp.*, *Eus. t.*, *κεφ. t.*, of an unusual arrangement (viz. Matt. 74, Mark 46, Luke 57). *Am.*, *syn.*, *men.*, *subscr.*, *στίχ.* (*lect.* with *init.* later). This copy contains many itacisms, and corrections *primâ manu*.

132. Rom. Vat. Gr. 361 [xi Birch, xii or xiii Greg.], 10⅝ × 6¼, ff. 289 (20), *Eus. t.*, *prol.*, *κεφ. t.*, *κεφ.*, *Am.*, *Eus.*, *subscr.*, *pict. in aur.*, *lect.* (later).

133. (Act. 71, Paul. 78.) Rom. Vat. Gr. 363 [xi ?], 7⅞ × 6⅜, ff. 332 (29), *prol.*, *κεφ. t.*, *κεφ.*, *τίτλ.*, *Am.*, *lect.*, *subscr.*, *syn.*, *men.*, *pict.*, Euthalian prologues.

134. Rom. Vat. Gr. 364 [xi or xii], 4to, elegant, 8½ × 6⅛, ff. 297 (20), *Carp.*, *Eus. t.*, *κεφ. t.*, *κεφ.*, *τίτλ.*, *Am.*, *Eus.*, *syn.*, *men.*, *pict.*, titles in gold.

135. Rom. Vat. Gr. 365 [xi ?], 9⅝ × 7⅞, *κεφ. t.*, *pict.* The first 26 of its 174 leaves are later and *chart.*

136. Rom. Vat. Gr. 665 [xiii], 9¾ × 6¾, ff. 235 (32), on cotton paper;

contains SS. Matthew and Mark with Euthymius' commentary. *Mut.* Mark xv. 1–end.

137. Rom. Vat. Gr. 756 [xi or xii], $11\frac{1}{4} \times 8\frac{1}{2}$, ff. 300 (19), *κεφ. t.*, *κεφ.*, *τίτλ.*, *Am.*, *syn.*, *men.*, *pict.*, with a commentary (Victor's on St. Mark). At the end we read *κσ φραγκισκος ακκιδας ευγενης κολασσευς . . . ρωμη ηγαγε το παρον βιβλιον ετει απο αδαμ ζφο* [A. D. 1583], *μηνι ιουλιῳ, ινδ. ια.*

138. Rom. Vat. Gr. 757 [xii], $11\frac{3}{4} \times 9\frac{1}{8}$, ff. 380 (37), *κεφ. t.*, with commentary from Origen, &c., and that of Victor on St. Mark, mixed up with the text, both in a slovenly hand (Burgon). Comp. Cod. 374.

139. Rom. Vat. Gr. 758 [dated 1173 by a somewhat later hand (Greg.)], $14\frac{3}{4} \times 10\frac{7}{8}$, ff. 233, contains SS. Luke and John with a commentary.

140. Rom. Vat. Gr. 1158 [xii], $9\frac{1}{4} \times 6\frac{3}{4}$, ff. 408 (22), 2 cols., beautifully written, and given by the Queen of Cyprus to Innocent VII (1404–6). *Eus. t.*, *κεφ.*, *τίτλ.*, *Am.*, *Eus.*, *pict.* In Luke i. 64 it supports the Complutensian reading, *καὶ ἡ γλῶσσα αὐτοῦ διηρθρώθη.*

141. (Act. 75, Paul. 86, Apoc. 40.) Rom. Vat. Gr. 1160 [xiii], 2 vols., $9\frac{1}{4} \times 6\frac{1}{2}$, ff. 400 (26), *prol.*, *κεφ. t.*, *κεφ.*, *τίτλ.*, *lect.*, *ἀναγν.*, *syn.*, *men.*, *subscr.*, *στίχ.*, *pict.*, *Euthal.*, contains the whole New Testament, *syn.*, *pict.* The leaves are arranged in quaternions, but separately numbered for each volume (Birch).

142. (Act. 76, Paul. 87.) Rom. Vat. Gr. 1210 [xi], $4\frac{3}{4} \times 3\frac{1}{4}$, ff. 324 (30), very neat, *κεφ. t.* at end, *κεφ.*, *τίτλ.*, *subscr.*, *pict.*, *Euthal.* (*syn.*, *men.*, A. D. 1447), containing also the Psalms. There are many marginal readings in another ancient hand.

143. Rom. Vat. Gr. 1229 [xi], $12\frac{1}{2} \times 9\frac{3}{4}$, ff. 275 (24), *κεφ. t.*, *κεφ.*, *τίτλ.*, *Am.*, *Eus.*, *pict.*, with a marginal commentary (Victor's on St. Mark). On the first leaf is read *της ορθης πιστεως πιστῳ οικονομῳ και φυλακι Παυλῳ τετάρτῳ* [1555—59].

144. Rom. Vat. Gr. 1254 [xi], $6\frac{1}{8} \times 4\frac{5}{8}$, ff. 267, *Eus. t.*, *κεφ. t.*, *κεφ.*, *τίτλ.*, *Am.*, *lect.*

145. Rom. Vat. Gr. 1548 [xi Greg., xiii Birch], $7 \times 5\frac{1}{8}$, ff. 161 (17), *prol.*, *κεφ. t.*, *κεφ.*, *τίτλ.*, *Am.*, *Eus.*, *lect.*, contains SS. Luke and John. *Mut.* Luke iv. 15—v. 36; John i. 1–26. A later hand has written Luke xvii—xxi, and made many corrections.

146. Rom. Palatino-Vatican. 5[1] [xii], $12\frac{1}{8} \times 9\frac{1}{8}$, ff. 265 (13), *κεφ. t.*, Mark, *Am.*, *Eus.*, contains SS. Matt. and Mark with a commentary (Victor's on St. Mark?).

147. Rom. Pal.-Vat. 89 [xi Birch, xiv Greg.], $6\frac{1}{2} \times 5\frac{1}{8}$, ff. 351 (20), *prol.*, *κεφ. t.*, *κεφ.*, *τίτλ.*, *syn.*, *men.*, *subscr.*, *στίχ.*

148. Rom. Pal.-Vat. 136 [xi Greg., xiii Birch], $7\frac{1}{2} \times 4\frac{1}{8}$, ff. 153, *κεφ. t.*, *κεφ.*, *τίτλ.*, *Am.*, *Eus.*, *syn.*, with some scholia and unusual readings.

[1] A collection presented to Urban VIII (1623–44) by Maximilian, Elector of Bavaria, from the spoils of the unhappy Elector Palatine, titular king of Bohemia.

149. (Act. 77, Paul. 88, Apoc. 25.) Rom. Pal.-Vat. 171 [xiv or xv], fol., ff. 179, *prol.* in Cath. and Paul., *lect.*, contains the whole New Testament (*see* p. 69, note).

150. Rom. Pal.-Vat. 189 [xi or xii], $4\frac{1}{2} \times 3\frac{3}{8}$, ff. 331 (23), *Eus. t.*, *prol.*, *κεφ. t.*, *Am.*, *Eus.*, *lect.*, *syn.*, *men.*, *subscr.*, *στίχ.*, *pict.*

151. Rom. Pal.-Vat. 220 [x or xi], $9\frac{5}{8} \times 7$, ff. 224 (28), ll. black and gold, *Carp.*, *Eus. t.*, *κεφ. t.*, *κεφ.*, *τίτλ.*, *Am.*, *pict.*, scholia in the margin, and some rare readings (e. g. John xix. 14). The sheets are in twenty-one quaternions. After St. Matthew stands εκλογη εν συντομω εκ των συντεθεντων ὑπο Ευσεβιου προς Στεφανον λ.

152. Rom. Pal.-Vat. 227 [xiii], $8\frac{1}{2} \times 6\frac{1}{4}$, ff. 308 (20), *κεφ. t.*, *κεφ.*, *τίτλ.*, *pict.*

153. Rom. Pal.-Vat. 229 [xiii], 4to, $8\frac{1}{4} \times 5\frac{3}{8}$, ff. 266 (25), ll. rubr., *chart.*, *prol.*, *κεφ. t.*, *κεφ.*, *τίτλ.*, *Am.*, *lect.*, *men.*, *subscr.* (full), *στίχ.*

154. Rom. Alexandrino-Vatican. vel Christinae 28 [dated April 14, 1442], written in Italy on cotton paper, $10\frac{3}{8} \times 8\frac{1}{8}$, ff. 355 (40), ll. rubr., *κεφ.*, *Am.* (*lect.*, *syn.*, *men.*, and date later, true date xiii, Greg.), with Theophylact's commentary. This and the two next were given by Christina, Queen of Sweden, to Card. Azzolini, and bought from him by Alexander VIII (1689–91).

155. Rom. Alex.-Vat. 79 [xi ? Birch, xiv Scholz], $6 \times 4\frac{3}{8}$, ff. 306 (20), *κεφ.*, *τίτλ.*, *Am.*, *syn.*, *subscr.*, *στίχ.*, with some lessons from St. Paul prefixed. Given by Andrew Rivet to Rutgersius, Swedish Ambassador to the United Provinces. This copy is Wetstein's 99, the codex Rutgersii cited by Dan. Heinsius in his Exercitat. sacr. in Evangel.

156. Rom. Alex.-Vat. 189 [xii], $4\frac{3}{4} \times 4$, ff. 244 (23), *κεφ. t.*, *κεφ.*, *τίτλ.*, *Am.*; 'ex bibliothecâ Goldasti' is on the first page.

157. Rom. Urbino-Vat. 2 [~~xii~~], $7\frac{3}{8} \times 5\frac{1}{4}$, ff. 325 (22), *Carp.*, *prol.*, *Eus. t.*, *κεφ. t.*, *κεφ.*, *τίτλ.*, *lect.*, *subscr.*, *pict.* It belonged to the Ducal Library at Urbino, and was brought to Rome by Clement VII (1523–34). It is very beautifully written (Birch, N. T. 1788, gives a facsimile), certain chronicles and rich ornaments in vermilion and gold. On fol. 19 we read underneath two figures respectively Ιωαννης εν χω τω θω πιστος βασιλευς πορφυρογεννητος και αυτοκρατωρ ῥωμαιων, ὁ Κομνηνος, and Αλεξιος εν χω τω θω πιστος βασιλευς πορφυρογεννητος ὁ Κομνηνος. The Emperor John II the Handsome succeeded his father, the great Alexius, A. D. 1118. This MS. is remarkable for its eclectic text, which is said by Zahn to approach sometimes that of Marcion (Geschichte d. N. T. Kanons, i. 456, note 2, and 457, note 1). It is often in agreement with Codd. BDL, 69, 106, and especially with 1.

158. Cod. Pii II, Rom. Vat. 55 [xi], $3\frac{1}{2} \times 3$, ff. 235 (20), *κεφ. t.*, *κεφ.*, *τίτλ.*, *Am.*, *Eus.*, *lect.* (partial), and readings in the margin, *primâ manu.* This copy was given to the Library by Pius II (1458–64).

159. Rom. Barberinianus ~~164,~~ formerly 8 [xi], $10\frac{3}{8} \times 8\frac{1}{8}$, ff. 203 (23), 2 cols., *κεφ. t.*, *κεφ.*, *τίτλ.*, *Am.*, *Eus.*, *lect.*, *subscr.* (*Carp.*, *Eus. t.*, *κεφ. t.* Matt., *syn.*, *men.* xvi), in the Barberini Library, at Rome,

founded above two centuries since by the Cardinal, Francis II, of that name.

160. Rom. Barb. iv. 27, formerly 9 [dated 1123], $8\frac{7}{8} \times 7\frac{1}{8}$, ff. 216, *κεφ. t.*, *κεφ.*, *τίτλ.*, *Am.*, *lect.*, *syn.*, *men.*, *subscr.*

161. Rom. Barb. iii. 17, formerly 10 [x or xi], $8 \times 6\frac{1}{2}$, ff. 203 (24), 2 cols., *κεφ. t.*, *κεφ.*, *τίτλ.*, *Am.*, *Eus.* (*lect.* later), ending at John xvi. 4. This copy follows the Latin version both in its text (John iii. 6) and marginal scholia (John vii. 29). Various readings are often thus noted in its margin.

162. Rom. Barb. iv. 31, formerly 11 [dated May 13, 1153 (ϛχξά), Indict. 1], $9\frac{1}{4} \times 6\frac{3}{4}$, written by one Manuel: ff. 248 (23), *Carp.*, *Eus. t.*, *κεφ.*, *τίτλ.*, *Am.*, *pict.*, *subscr.*

163. Rom. Barb. v. 16, formerly 12 [xi], $11\frac{1}{8} \times 8$, ff. 173 (33), 2 cols., *Eus. t.*, *κεφ. t.*, *κεφ.*, *Am.*, *Eus.*, *lect.*, *syn.*, *men.*, *subscr.*, *pict.*, written in Syria. Scholz says it contains only the portions of the Gospels read in Church-lessons, but Birch the four Gospels, with the numbers of *ῥήματα* and *στίχοι* to the first three Gospels.

164. Rom. Barb. iii. 38, formerly 13 [dated Oct. 1039], $6\frac{7}{8} \times 5\frac{3}{8}$, ff. 214 (27), *Carp.*, *Eus. t.*, *κεφ. t.*, *κεφ.*, *τίτλ.*, *Am.*, *Eus.*, *lect.*, *subscr.*, *pict.* (*syn.*, *men.* later), and the numbers of *στίχοι*. The subscription states that it was written by Leo, a priest and calligrapher, and bought in 1168 by Bartholomew, who compared it with ancient Jerusalem manuscripts on the sacred mount.

165. Rom. Barb. v. 37, formerly 14 [dated 1291], $11\frac{7}{8} \times 8$, ff. 215, 2 cols., *Carp.*, *Eus. t.*, *κεφ. t.*, *κεφ.*, *τίτλ.*, *Am.*, *Eus.*, *syn.*, with the Latin Vulgate version. Written for one Archbishop Paul, and given to the Library by Eugenia, daughter of Jo. Pontanus.

166. Rom. Barb. iii. 131, formerly 115 [xiii], 4to, $8\frac{3}{8} \times 6\frac{1}{2}$, ff. 75 (27), *κεφ.*, *τίτλ.*, *Am.*, *Eus.*, *lect.*, containing only SS. Luke ix. 33—xxiv. 24 and John.

167. Rom. Barb. iii. 6, formerly 208 [xiii], $4\frac{7}{8} \times 3\frac{1}{4}$, ff. 264 (25), *κεφ. t.*, *κεφ.*, *τίτλ.*, *pict.* (later).

168. Rom. Barb. vi. 9, formerly 211 [xiii], $13\frac{3}{8} \times 8\frac{5}{8}$, ff. 217, 2 cols., *κεφ. t.*, *κεφ.*, *τίτλ.*, *Am.*, *Eus.* (Mark *subscr.*, *στίχ.*).

169. Rom. Vallicellianus B. 133 [xi], $4\frac{3}{4} \times 4$, ff. 249 (19), *prol.*, *κεφ. t.*, *κεφ.*, *τίτλ.*, *Am.*, *Eus.*, *subscr.*, *syn.*, *men.*, *pict.*, once the property of Achilles Statius, as also was Cod. 171. This codex and the next three are in the Library of St. Maria in Vallicella at Rome, and belong to the Fathers of the Oratory of St. Philippo Neri.

170. Rom. Vallicell. C. 61 [xiii–xv], $8\frac{1}{2} \times 6\frac{1}{4}$, ff. 277 (23), *prol.*, *κεφ. t.* *κεφ.*, *τίτλ.*, *Am.*, *Eus.*, *lect.*, *ἀναγν.*, *subscr.*, *στίχ.* (occasionally in later hand). The end of St. Luke and most of St. John is in a later hand.

171. Rom. Vallicell. C. 73 [xiv, Montfaucon xi], $5\frac{3}{4} \times 4\frac{1}{4}$, ff. 253 (20), *prol.*, *κεφ. t.*, *κεφ.*, *τίτλ.*, *Am.*, *Eus.*, *lect.*, *subscr.*

172. Rom. Vallicell. F. 90 [xii], 4to, ff. 217, now only contains the

Pentateuch, but from Bianchini, I. ii. pp. 529–30, we infer that the Gospels were once there.

173. Rom. Vat. Gr. 1983, formerly Basil. 22, ending John xiii. 1, seems to have been written in Asia Minor [xi Birch and Burgon, xii or xiii Greg.], $7\frac{7}{8} \times 5\frac{1}{4}$, ff. 155 (20), 2 cols., *Carp.*, *Eus. t.*, κεφ. *t.*, κεφ., τίτλ., *Am.*, *lect.*, *men.*, *subscr.*; ῥήμ., στίχ. as in Codd. 163, 164, 167. This codex, and the next four, were brought from the Library of the Basilian monks.

174. Rom. Vat. Gr. 2002, formerly Basil. 41 [dated second hour of Sept. 7, A. D. 1052], $9\frac{3}{4} \times 7\frac{1}{2}$, ff. 132 (30), 2 cols., κεφ. *t.*, κεφ., τίτλ., *Am.*, *Eus.*, *lect.*, *subscr.*, στίχ. *Mut.* Matt. i. 1—ii. 1; John i. 1–27; ending John viii. 47. Written by the monk Constantine 'tabernis habitante,' 'cum praeesset praefecturae Georgilas dux Calabriae' (Scholz).

175. (Act. 41, Paul. 194, Apoc. 20.) Rom. Vat. Gr. 2080, formerly Basil. 119 [x–xii], $8 \times 5\frac{3}{4}$, ff. 247, *subscr.*, contains the whole New Testament, beginning Mtt. iv. 17, with scholia to the Acts, between which and the Catholic Epistles stands the Apocalypse. There are some marginal corrections *primâ manu* (e.g. Luke xxiv. 13). The Pauline Epistles have Euthalius' subscriptions. Also inspected by Bianchini.

176. Rom. Vat. Gr. 2113, formerly Basil. 152 [x or xi], $8\frac{1}{4} \times 5\frac{3}{4}$, ff. 77, ll. coloured, John ii. 1, κεφ., τίτλ., *Am.*, *lect.* Begins Matt. x. 13, ends John ii. 1.

177. Rom. Vat. Gr.? formerly Basil. 163 [xi], 8vo, *mut.* John i. 1–29. Dr. Gregory thinks that it is 2115, his Evan. 870.

178. Rom. Angelicus A. 1. 5 [xii], $14\frac{7}{8} \times 11\frac{5}{8}$, ff. 272 (23), 2 cols., *Eus. t.*, κεφ., τίτλ. with harmony, *Am.*, *mut.* Jo. xxi. 17–25. Arranged in quaternions, and the titles to the Gospels resemble those in Cod. 69. Codd. 178–9 belong to the Angelica convent of Augustinian Eremites at Rome. It has on the first leaf the same subscription as we gave under Cod. 87, and which Birch and Scholz misunderstand.

179. Rom. Angelic. A. 4. 11 [xii], $7\frac{3}{4} \times 6\frac{1}{2}$, ff. 248 (22), *Eus. t.*, κεφ. *t.*, κεφ., τίτλ., *Am.*, *Eus.*, *lect.* (*syn.*, *men.*, xv or xvi, *chart.*). The last five leaves (214–18) and two others (23, 30) are *chart.*, and in a later hand.

180. (Act. 82, Paul. 92, Apoc. 44.) Rom. Propagandae L. vi. 19, formerly 251, before Borgiae 2 [Gospels xi, Greg. xiv], $8\frac{1}{8} \times 5\frac{1}{4}$, ff. ? κεφ. *t.*, κεφ., τίτλ., *Am.*, *Eus.*, *lect.* (*syn.*, *men.*, xv *chart.*); the Gospels were written by one Andreas: the rest of the New Testament and some apocryphal books by one John, November, 1284 [1]. This manuscript, with Cod. T and Evst. 37, belonged to the Velitrant Museum of 'Praesul Steph. Borgia, Collegii Urbani de Propaganda Fide a secretis.'

181. Cod. Francisci Xavier, Cardinal. de Zelada [xi], fol., ff. 596, with scholia in the margin. This manuscript (from which Birch took

[1] Or rather A. D. 1274. According to Engelbreth the letters stand ψτψπβ, which can only mean A. M. 6782 (see p. 42, note 2).

extracts) is now missing. Compare Birch, N. T., Proleg. p. lviii; Burgon, Last Twelve Verses &c., pp. 284, 288.

Codd. 182–198, all in that noble Library at Florence, founded by Cosmo de' Medici [d. 1464], increased by his grandson Lorenzo [d. 1492], were very slightly examined by Birch, and subsequently by Scholz. Dean Burgon has described his own researches at Florence in the *Guardian* for August 20 and 27, 1873, from which I have thankfully corrected the statements made in my first edition respecting all the manuscripts there. They have been examined since then more leisurely by Dr. Gregory, from whose careful account some particulars have been added in this edition (*see* Greg., Prolegomena (ii), pp. 505–509).

182. Flor. Laurentianus Plut. vi. 11 [xii], $10 \times 7\frac{1}{8}$, ff. 226 (24), *κεφ. t.*, *κεφ.*, *τίτλ.* to St. John only, *subscr.* (in Luke). The titles of the Gospels in lake, forming a kind of imitation of ropework.

183. Flor. Laur. vi. 14 [xiv, xii Greg.], $6\frac{1}{2} \times 5\frac{1}{8}$, ff. 349 (19), *Eus. t.*, *κεφ. t.*, *κεφ.*, *τίτλ.*, *Am.*, *Eus.* in gold; and in a later hand, *capp. Lat.*, *ἀναγν.*, *lect.*, *syn.*, *men.*, at the end of which is *τέλος σὺν Θεῷ ἁγίῳ τοῦ μηνολογίου, ἀμήν· αυιη′*, i.e. A.D. 1418. This mode of reckoning is very rare (*see* p. 42, note 2), and tempted Scholz to read *ϛυιη′* of the Greek era, i.e. A.D. 910.

184. Flor. Laur. vi. 15 [xiii], $11\frac{1}{4} \times 5\frac{1}{2}$, ff. 72 (49), 2 cols., *Carp.*, *prol.*, *κεφ. t.*, *Am.*, *Eus.*, *lect.* Left in an unfinished state.

185. Flor. Laur. vi. 16 [xii], $14 \times 6\frac{3}{4}$, ff. 341 (21), *prol.*, *κεφ. t.*, *κεφ.*, *τίτλ.*, *Am.*, *lect.*, *ἀναγν.*, *subscr.*, *στίχ.* The summary of the Synaxarion is subscribed Πόνος Βασιλείου, καὶ Θῦ λόγου λόγοι (Burgon).

186. Flor. Laur. vi. 18 [xi], fol., $11\frac{1}{8} \times 8\frac{1}{2}$, ff. 260 (20), *Carp.*, *Eus. t.*, *prol.*, *κεφ. t.*, *κεφ.*, *τίτλ.*, *Am.*, *Eus.*, *syn.*, *men.*, *pict.* (Matt.), commentary (Victor's on St. Mark); written by Leontius, a calligrapher. Burgon cites Bandini's Catal. i. 130–3, where the elaborate *syn.* are given in full.

187. Flor. Laur. vi. 23 [xii], $7\frac{7}{8} \times 6\frac{1}{4}$, ff. 212 (25), *pict.* very rich and numerous. *Carp.*, *Eus. t.*, *κεφ. t.*, *τίτλ.*, *Am.* (not *Eus.*), all in gold. A peculiar kind of asterisk occurs very frequently in the text and margin, the purpose of which is not clear.

188. Flor. Laur. vi. 25 [xi], $6 \times 4\frac{1}{2}$, ff. 228 (26), *syn.* and *men.* full and beautiful. *Prol.*, *κεφ. t.*, *κεφ.*, *τίτλ.*, *Am.*, *Eus.*, *lect.*, *subscr.*, *στίχ.*

189. (Act. 141, Paul. 239.) Flor. Laur. vi. 27 [xii], $4\frac{1}{2} \times 3\frac{7}{8}$, ff. 452 (24), *κεφ. t.*, *κεφ.*, *lect.*, *ἀναγν.*, *Euthal.* in Cath. and Paul., minute and beautifully written, *mut.* from John xix. 38.

190. Flor. Laur. vi. 28 [July, 1285, Ind. 13], 8vo, $5\frac{5}{8} \times 4\frac{3}{8}$, ff. 439 (17), *prol.*, *κεφ. t.*, *κεφ.*, *τίτλ.*, *Am.*, *lect.*, *pict.*

191. Flor. Laur. vi. 29 [xiii], $5\frac{1}{8} \times 3\frac{3}{4}$, ff. 180 (27), *prol.*, *κεφ.* Lat., *subscr.*, with *στίχοι* numbered: *ἀναγνώσματα* marked in a more recent hand.

192. Flor. Laur. vi. 30 [xiii], $4\frac{3}{4} \times 3\frac{1}{2}$, ff. 200 (28), *prol.*, *κεφ. t.*, *κεφ.*,

τίτλ., *lect.*, *subscr.*, *Am.* and *Eus.* in one line, the latter later (*see* Cod. 112): ἀρχὴ of *lect.*, never τέλος.

193. Flor. Laur. vi. 32 [xi], 8vo, 6¼ × 5, ff. 165 (27), *Carp.*, *Eus. t.*, *pict.*, κεφ., *Am.* (not *Eus.*), (ἀναγν., *lect.* in later hand).

194. Flor. Laur. vi. 33 [xi], 11¾ × 9¾, ff. 263 (22), *pict.*, and a marginal catena (Victor's on St. Mark) resembling that of Cod. 34: e.g. on Luke xxiv. 13. Κεφ., *Am.* (not *Eus.*), *subscr.*, στίχ., *pict.* Begins Matt. iii. 7.

195. Flor. Laur. vi. 34 [xi], 10⅞ × 8⅝, ff. 277 (25), once belonged to the Cistercian convent of S. Salvator de Septimo. *Prol.* (the same as in Cod. 186 but briefer, attributed to Eusebius), *syn.*, and a commentary (Victor's on St. Mark). The date of the year is lost, but the month (May) and indiction (8) remain. Κεφ. *t.*, κεφ., τίτλ., *Am.*, *Eus.*, *syn.*, *men.*

196. Flor. Laur. viii. 12 [xii], 9¾ × 7¼, ff. 369 (44), *prol.*, κεφ. *t.* (all together at the beginning), κεφ., τίτλ., the text in red letters (*see* p. 184, note 1), *pict.*, with a catena in black. Given by (a son of Cosmo de' Medici) in 1473 to the Convent of St. Mark at Florence.

197. (Act. 90.) Flor. Laur. viii. 14 [xi], fol., 11¾ × 9¼, ff. 154 (29), *prol.*, κεφ. *t.*, κεφ., τίτλ., contains the Epistle of St. James with a marginal gloss: also portions of SS. Matthew and Mark, with Chrysostom's commentary on St. Matthew, and Victor's on St. Mark, all imperfect.

198. Flor. Laur. Ædil. 221 [xiii], 4to, 9¾ × 6⅝, ff. 171 (29), *chart.*, *Carp.*, *Eus. t.*, κεφ. *t.*, *Am.*, *Eus.*, *lect.*, *subscr.*: from the library 'Aedilium Flor. Ecc.' Here again *Am.* and *Eus.* are in the same line (*see* Cod. 112): the ἀναγνώσματα also are numbered.

Codd. 199–203 were inspected, rather than collated, by Birch at Florence before 1788; the first two in the Benedictine library of St. Maria; the others in that of St. Mark, belonging to the Dominican Friars. Scholz could not find any of them, but 201 is Wetstein's 107, Scrivener's m; 202 is now in the British Museum, Addit. 14,774. The other two Burgon found in the Laurentian Library, whither they came at the suppression of monasteries in 1810. They were examined afterwards by Gregory.

199. Flor. Laur. Conv. Sopp. 160, formerly Badia 99 or S. Mariae 67 [xii], 5⅝ × 4¾, ff. 229 (25), *Eus. t.*, κεφ. *t.* with *harm.*, κεφ., τίτλ., *subscr.*, *pict.*, *lect.*, with iambic verses and various scholia. The στίχοι are numbered and, besides *Am.*, *Eus.*, there exists in parts a Harmony at the foot of the pages, such as is described in p. 58, note 2.

200. Flor. Laur. Conv. Sopp. 159, formerly Badia 69 or S. Mariae 66 [x], 8¾ × 6⅞, ff. 229 (25), *pict.*, *Carp.*, *Eus. t.*, κεφ. *t.*, *Am.*, all in gold: *Eus.* in red, κεφ., τίτλ., with fragments of Gregory of Nyssa against the Arians (*syn.* and *men.* xiv). There are many scholia in vermilion scattered throughout the book. Codd. 199, 200 were presented to St. Maria's by Antonia Corbinelli [d. 1423]: the latter from St. Justina's, another Benedictine house.

*201. (Act. 91, Paul. 104, Apoc. 94.) Lond. Brit. Mus. Addit. 11,837, formerly Praedicator. S. Marci 701 [Oct. 7, 1357, Ind. 11], $13\frac{1}{2} \times 11$, ff. 492 (22), is m^{scr}. in the Gospels, p^{scr}. in Act., Paul., and b^{scr}. in Apoc. This splendid copy was purchased for the British Museum from the heirs of Dr. Samuel Butler, Bishop of Lichfield. It contains the whole New Testament; was first cited by Wetstein (107) from notices by Jo. Lamy, in his 'de Eruditione Apostolorum,' Florence, 1738; glanced at by Birch, and stated by Scholz (N. T. vol. ii. pp. xii, xxviii) to have been cursorily collated by himself: how that is possible can hardly be understood, as he elsewhere professes his ignorance whither the manuscript had gone (N. T. vol. i. p. lxxii). Scrivener collated the whole volume. There are many changes by a later hand, also *syn.*, *κεφ. t.*, *κεφ.*, *τίτλ.*, *Am.*, some *Eus.*, *lect.*, *prol.*, *ἀναγν.*, *subscr.*, *στίχ.*, *vers.*, and some foreign matter.

202. Brit. Mus. Addit. 14,774, formerly Praed. S. Marci 705 [xii], 10×8, ff. 278 (21), *κεφ. t.* (in red and gold), *orn.*, *κεφ.*, *τίτλ.*, *Am.*, *Eus.* (the last often omitted), *lect.*, *subscr.*, *στίχ.*, *men.*, *syn.* This splendid copy cost the Museum £84 (Bloomfield).

203. Flor. Bibl. Nat. Convent. i. 10, 7, formerly Praed. S. Marci 707 [xv], $8\frac{5}{8} \times 5\frac{3}{4}$, *chart.*, is really in modern Greek. Birch cites it for John vii. 53, but it ought to be expunged from the list.

204. (Act. 92, Paul. 105.) [xi or xiii] Bologna, Bibl. Univ. 2775, formerly Bononiensis Canonicor. Regular. St. Salvador. 640. After the suppression of the house in 1867, it was moved to its present place. $7\frac{3}{4} \times 5\frac{3}{8}$, ff. 443 (25). *Syn.*, *κεφ.*, *ἀναγνώσματα* numbered (without *Am.*, *Carp.*), *lect.*, *pict.* (Birch, Scholz, corrected by Burgon). Also *τίτλ.*, *men.*, *subscr.*, *στίχ.*

Codd. 205–215, 217 in the Ducal palace at Venice, were slightly examined by Birch in 1783, carefully by Burgon in 1872, and by Gregory in 1886.

205. (Act. 93, Paul. 106, Apoc. 88.) Venice, Mark 5 [xv], large fol., $15\frac{1}{2} \times 11$, ff. 441 (55, 56), *prol.* (Cath., Paul.), *κεφ. t.*, *κεφ.* (Gr. and Lat.), *τίτλ.*, *subscr.*, contains both Testaments, with many peculiar readings. It was written for Cardinal Bessarion (apparently by John Rhosus his librarian), the donor of all these books. This is Dean Holmes' No. 68 in the Septuagint, and contains a note in the Cardinal's hand: *τόπος μκ. Ἡ θεία γραφὴ παλαιά τε καὶ νέα πᾶσα· κτῆμα Βησσαρίωνος Καρδηνάλεως Ἐπισκόπου Οαβίνων τοῦ* (*sic*) *καὶ Νικαίας.* By *τόπος μκ* Holmes understands the class mark of the volume in Bessarion's Library. W. F. Rinck considers it in the *Gospels* a copy of Cod. 209 ('Lucubratio Critica in Act. Apost. Epp. C. et P.,' Basileae, 1830). Burgon, who fully admits their wonderful similarity in respect to the text, judges that Cod. 205, which is much more modern than Cod. 209, was transcribed from the same *uncial* archetype.

206. (Act. 94, Paul. 107, Apoc. 101.) Ven. Mark 6 [xv or xvi], $15 \times 10\frac{5}{8}$, ff. 431, like Codd. 69 and 233, is partly on parchment, partly on paper. It contains both Testaments, but is not numbered for the Apocalypse. A mere duplicate of Cod. 205, as Holmes saw clearly: it is his No. 122.

207. Ven. Mark 8 [xi or xii], $10\frac{7}{8} \times 8\frac{3}{8}$, ff. 267 (22), 2 cols., *Carp.*,

prol., *pict.*, *κεφ. t.*, *τίτλ.*, *κεφ.*, *Am.* (not *Eus.*) in gold, *syn.*, *men.*, *mut.* in Matt. i. 1–13; Mark i. 1–11, for the sake of the gorgeous illuminations. Written in two columns. Once owned by A. F. R.

208. Ven. Mark 9 [xi or xii], 7⅞ × 5¾, ff. 239 (23), *Carp.*, *Eus. t.*, *κεφ. t.*, *κεφ.*, *τίτλ.*, *Am.*, *Eus.*, of some value.

209. (Act. 95, Paul. 108, Apoc. 46.) Ven. Mark 10 [xi, xiv Greg.], 7¾ × 4¾, ff. 411 (27), of the whole New Testament, once Bessarion's, who had it with him at the Council of Florence, 1439. There are numerous minute marginal notes in vermilion, obviously *primâ manu.* In its delicate style of writing this copy greatly resembles Cod. 1 (facsimile No. 23). *Κεφ. t.*, *τίτλ.*, *κεφ.*, *Am.* (not *Eus.*), also the modern chapters in the margin. *Prol.* to Epistles, *lect.*, but not much in the Gospels, before each of which stands a blank leaf, as if for *pict.* A good collation of Codd. 205 and 209 is needed; Birch did little, Engelbreth gave him some readings, and Fleck has published part of a collation by Heimbach. Rinck collated Apoc. i–iii. In the Gospels they are very like Codd. B, 1. The Apocalypse is in a later hand, somewhat resembling that of Cod. 205, and has *prol.* For the unusual order of the books, *see* above, p. 72.

210. Ven. Mark 27 [xi or xii], a noble fol., 14 × 11⅞, ff. 372, with a catena (Victor's commentary on St. Mark). *Mut.* Matt. i. 1—ii. 18, from the same cause as in Cod. 207. Rich blue and gold illuminations, and pictures of SS. Mark and Luke. *Τίτλ.*, *κεφ.*, *pict.*

211. Ven. Mark 539 [xii], fol., 11½ × 9½, ff. 280 (29–26), 2 cols., *mut.* Luke i. 1—ii. 32; John i. 1—iv. 2, with an Arabic version in the right-hand column of each page. *Κεφ. t.*, *Am.*, *Eus.* (irregularly inserted), *lect.*, *syn.*, *men.*, *subscr.*, *ῥῆμ.*, *στίχ.*

Burgon cites Zanetti, Graeca D. Marc. Bibl. Codd. MSS., Venet. 1740, p. 291, for the enumeration of the five Patriarchates (*see* above, p. 67), and other curious matter appended to St. John. The heading of the second Gospel is εὐαγγέλιον ἐκ τοῦ κατὰ Μάρκον.

212. Ven. Mark 540 [xi or xii], 6⅞ × 5, ff. 273 (23), the first page in gold, with *pict.* and most elaborate illuminations. Much *mut.*, twenty leaves being supplied in a modern hand. *Carp.*, *Eus. t.*, *κεφ.*, *vers.*, *τίτλ.*, *lect.*, *Am.* with *Eus.* in a line with them (*see* Cod. 112), a little later, carried only to the end of St. Mark.

213. Ven. Mark 542 [xi], 8vo, 8⅜ × 6¼, ff. 356 (18), *mut.* John xviii. 40—xxi. 25. *Eus. t.*, *τίτλ.*, *κεφ.* (*Am.*, *Eus.* most irregularly inserted), few *ἀρχαί* and *τέλη*, *ἀναγν.*, heroic verses as colophons to the Gospels. Large full stops are found in impossible places.

214. Ven. Mark 543 [xiv], 8vo, 9¾ × 6¼, ff. 227 (27), *chart.*, *argent.*, *prol.*, *κεφ. t.* with *harm.*, *κεφ.*, *Am.* (not *Eus.*), *ἀναγν.*, *lect.*, *syn.*, *men.*, *subscr.*, *vers.*

215. Ven. Mark 544 [xi], fol., 12¾ × 9½, ff. 271 (24), *Carp.*, *Eus. t.*, *κεφ. t.* with *harm.*, *τίτλ.*, *κεφ.*, *Am.*, *Eus.*, *lect.*, *syn.*, *pict.* (later). This copy is a duplicate of Codd. 20, 300, as well in its text as in the subscriptions and commentary, being without any of the later corrections

seen in Cod. 20. The commentary on St. John is Chrysostom's, those on the other Gospels the same as in Cod. 300 (Burgon).

216. Codex Canonici, brought by him from Corcyra, written in a small character [no date assigned], never was at St. Mark's, as Scholz alleges: Griesbach inserted it in his list through a misunderstanding of Birch's meaning. It is probably one of those now at Oxford, to be described hereafter (*see* Codd. 489, 490).

217. Ven. Mark, Gr. i. 3, given in 1478 by Peter de Montagnana to the monastery of St. John in Viridario, at Padua (viii. A.) [xii or xiii], $8\frac{1}{8} \times 6\frac{1}{8}$, ff. 306 (21), in fine condition. *Carp.*, *Eus. t.*, *κεφ. t.*, *τίτλ.*, *κεφ.*, *Am.* (not *Eus.*), full *syn.*, few *lect.*, *prol.*, *vers.*

Codd. 218–225 are in the Imperial Library at Vienna. Alter and Birch collated them about the same time, the latter but cursorily, and Gregory examined them in 1887.

*218. (Act. 65, Paul. 57, Apoc. 33.) Vindobon. Caesar, Nessel. 23, formerly 1 [xiii], fol., $12\frac{1}{2} \times 8\frac{3}{4}$, ff. 623 (49, 50), 2 cols., *κεφ. t.*, *κεφ.*, *τίτλ.*, *Am.*, *subscr.*, Euthal. in Acts, Cath., Paul., contains both Testaments. *Mut.* Apoc. xiii. 5—xiv. 8; xv. 7—xvii. 2; xviii. 10—xix. 15; ending at xx. 7 λυθήσεται. This important copy, containing many peculiar readings, was described by Treschow, and comprises the text of Alter's inconvenient, though fairly accurate N. T. 1786–7, to be described in Vol. II. Like Cod. 123 it was brought from Constantinople by De Busbeck.

219. Vind. Caes. Ness. 321, formerly 32 [xiii], $6\frac{1}{4} \times 4\frac{3}{4}$, ff. 232 (21), *κεφ. t.*, *κεφ.*, *τίτλ.*, *Am.*, *Eus.*, *subscr.*

220. Vind. Caes. Ness. 337, formerly 33 [xiv], 12mo, $3\frac{7}{8} \times 2\frac{5}{8}$, ff. 303 (22), in very small letters, *κεφ.*, *τίτλ.*, *Am.*, *lect.*, *syn.*

221. Vind. Caes. Ness. 117, formerly 38 [x or xi], $11 \times 7\frac{5}{8}$, ff. 251 (41–43), with commentaries (Chrysostom on Matt., John; Victor on Mark, Titus of Bostra on Luke), to which the *fragments* of text here given are accommodated.

222. Vind. Caes. Ness. 180, formerly 39 [xiv], $8\frac{1}{2} \times 6$, ff. 346 (32), on cotton paper, *mut.* Contains *fragments* of the Gospels, with a commentary (Victor's on St. Mark). This and the last were brought from Constantinople by De Busbeck.

223. Vind. Caes. 301, formerly 40 [xiv, Greg. x], $7 \times 5\frac{1}{2}$, ff. 115 (32), contains fragments of SS. Matthew, Luke, and John, with a catena. Codd. 221–3 must be cited cautiously: Alter appears to have made no systematic use of them.

224. Vind. Caes. Suppl. Gr. 97, formerly Kollar. 8 [xii], $5\frac{1}{2} \times 4\frac{5}{8}$, ff. 97 (19), *κεφ. t.*, *κεφ.*, *τίτλ.*, *Am.*, *lect.*, *syn.*, *men.*, *subscr.*, only contains St. Matthew. This copy came from Naples.

225. Vind. Caes. Suppl. Gr. 102, formerly Kollar. 9 [dated ϛψ' or A.D. 1192], $5\frac{3}{8} \times 3\frac{7}{8}$, ff. 171 (29), *pict.*, *lect.*, *ἀναγν.*, *syn.*, *men.*

Codd. 226–233 are in the Escurial, described by D. G. Moldenhawer, who collated them about 1783, loosely enough, for Birch's edition. In 1870 the Librarian, José Fernandez Montana (in order to correct Haenel's errors) sent to Mr. Wm. Kelly, who obligingly communicated it to me, a complete catalogue of the four copies of the Greek Bible, and of nineteen of the New Testament 'neither more or less,' then at the Escurial, with their present class-marks. I do not recognize, either in his list or in that subjoined, the 'Codex Aureus containing the Four Gospels in letters of gold, a work of the early part of the eleventh century,' spoken of in the *Globe* newspaper of Oct. 3, 1872, on occasion of the fire at the Escurial on Oct. 2, which however did not touch the manuscripts. Perhaps that Codex is in Latin, unless it be Evst. 40. *See* also Emmanuel Miller, Cat. des MSS. Gr. de la Bibl. de l'Escurial, Paris, A.D. 1848.

226. (Act. 108, Paul. 228.) Cod. Escurialensis χ. iv. 17 [xi], 8vo, ff. ?, on the finest vellum, richly ornamented, in a small, round, very neat hand. *Eus. t.*, *κεφ. t.*, *lect.*, *pict.*, *τίτλ.*, *κεφ.*, *Am.*, *Eus.* Many corrections were made by a later hand, but the original text is valuable, and the readings sometimes unique. Fairly collated.

227. Escurial. χ. iii. 15 [xiii], 4to, ff. 158, *prol.*, *κεφ. t.*, *Am.*, *pict.* A later hand, which dates from 1308, has been very busy in making corrections.

228. (Act. 109, Paul. 229.) Escurial. χ. iv. 12 [xiv, Montana xvi], 8vo, ff. ?, *chart.* Once belonged to Nicolas Nathanael of Crete, then to Andreas Damarius of Epidaurus, a calligrapher. *Eus. t.*, *syn.*[1]

229. Escurial. χ. iv. 21 [dated 1140], 8vo, ff. 296, written by Basil Argyropolus, a notary. *Mut.* Mark xvi. 15–20; John i. 1–11. *Pict.*, *lect.*; the latter by a hand of about the fourteenth century, which retraced much of the discoloured ink, and corrected in the margin (since mutilated by the binder) very many important readings of the first hand, which often resemble those of ADK. i. 72. This copy must be mislaid, as it is not in Montana's list.

230. Escurial. φ (Montana ψ).[2] iii. 5 [dated Oct. 29, 1013, with the wrong Indiction, 11 for 12: Montana's date is 1014, and the error is probably not his: *see* p. 42, note 2], 4to, ff. 218, written by Luke a monk and priest, with double *syn.*[3], *Carp.*, *κεφ. t.*, *subscr.*, *ῥήμ.*, *στίχ.*: *see* p. 67, note. An interesting copy, deemed by Moldenhawer worthy of closer examination.

231. Escurial. φ (Montana ψ).[2] iii. 6 [xii], 4to, ff. 181, *lect.*, *Eus. t.* torn, *κεφ. t.*, a picture 'quae Marcum mentitur,' *subscr.*, *στίχ.*, *syn.*, *men.* There are some marginal glosses by a later hand (which obelizes John vii. 53 *seq.*), and a Latin version above parts of St. Matthew.

232. Escurial. φ (Montana ψ).[2] iii. 7 [xiii: dated ~~1292~~ 1302, Montana], 4to, ff. 288, very elegant but otherwise a poor copy. Double *syn.*, *τίτλοι* in the margin of SS. Matthew and Luke, but elsewhere kept apart.

233. Escurial. Υ. ii. 8 [xi ?, Montana xiii], ff. 279, like Codd. 69 and 206, is partly of parchment, partly paper, in bad condition, and once

[1] Thus, at least, I understand Moldenhawer's description, 'Evangeliis et Actis λέξεις subjiciuntur dudum in vulgus notae.'

[2] Others F.

[3] By double *syn.* Moldenhawer may be supposed to mean here and in Cod. 232 both *syn.* and *men.*

belonged to Matthew Dandolo, a Venetian noble. It has a catena, and by reason of ligatures, &c. (*see* p. 43), is hard to read. *Prol.*, *κεφ. t.*, *Eus. t.* (apart), *vers.*, *ῥήμ.*, *στίχ.*

234. (Act. 57, Paul. 72.) Cod. Havniensis reg. theol. 1322, formerly 1 [dated 1278], 10 × 7$\frac{1}{8}$, ff. 315 (35), 2 cols., one of the several copies written by Theodore (*see* p. 43, note 1). This copy and Cod. 235 are now in the Royal Library at Copenhagen, but were bought at Venice by F. Rostgaard in 1699. The order of the books in Cod. 234 is described p. 73. *Carp.*, *Eus. t.*, *lect.*, *syn.*, *men.*, with many corrections. (C. G. Hensler, 1784.)

235. Havniens. reg. theol. 1323, formerly 2 [dated 1314], 4to, ff. 279, *chart.*, written by the *ἱερομόναχος* Philotheus, though very incorrectly; the text agrees much with Codd. DK. i. 33 and the Harkleian Syriac. *Κεφ. t.*, *lect.*; the words are often ill divided and the stops misplaced (Hensler).

236[1]. London, J. Bevan Braithwaite 3 [xi], 6½ × 4$\frac{3}{8}$, ff. 256 (20), 7 *chart.*, *syn.*, *men.*, *Eus. t.*, *Am.*, *κεφ.*, some *τίτλ.*, some *lect.*, *κεφ. t.* *Mut.* at beginning and at end after John ix. 28. Beautifully written. Bought at Athens in 1889. Collated by W. C. Braithwaite.

Codd. 237–259 are nearly all Moscow manuscripts, and were thoroughly collated by C. F. Matthaei, for his N. T., to be described in Vol. II. These Russian codices were for the most part brought from the twenty-two monasteries of Mount Athos by the monk Arsenius, on the suggestion of the Patriarch Nico, in the reign of Michael, son of Alexius (1645–76), and placed in the Library of the Holy Synod, at Moscow.

*237. Mosc. S. Synod 42 [x], fol., ff. 288, Matthaei's d, from Philotheus (a monastery), *pict.*, with scholia, and Victor's commentary on St. Mark.

*238. Mosc. Syn. 48 (Mt. e) [xi], fol., ff. 355, *Eus. t.* (*mut.*), *κεφ. t.*, *pict.*, with a catena and scholia; contains only SS. Matthew and Mark, but is of good quality. This copy formed the basis of Matthaei's edition of Victor's commentary on St. Mark, 1775 (Burgon).

*239. Mosc. Syn. 47 (Mt. g) [xi], fol., ff. 277, *Eus. t.*, *κεφ. t.* (Luke, John), contains Mark xvi. 2–8; Luke; John to xxi. 23, with scholia.

*240. Mosc. Syn. 49 (Mt. i) [xii], fol., ff. 410, *κεφ. t.*, once belonging to Philotheus, then to Dionysius (monasteries) on Athos, with the commentary of Euthymius Zigabenus. *Mut.* Mark viii. 12–34; xiv. 17–54; Luke xv. 32—xvi. 8.

*241. Mosc. (Act. 104, Paul. 120, Apoc. 47) Dresdensis Reg. A. 172 (Tregelles), once Matthaei's (k) [xi], 4to, 8$\frac{7}{8}$ × 6$\frac{3}{4}$, ff. 356 (31), *prol.*, *κεφ. t.*, *κεφ.*, *τίτλ.*, *syn*, *men.* (Gregory); Epp. *prol.*, *κεφ. t.*, the whole N. T. (p. 69, note), beautifully written, with rare readings. Bought by Alexius for fifty-two *aspri* at the siege of Constantinople (A.D. 1453), after-

[1] Readings extracted by Griesbach (Symb. Crit. i. pp. 247–304) from the margin of a copy of Mill's Greek Testament in the Bodleian, in his own or Thomas Hearne's handwriting, were placed here, but are omitted. Scrivener (Cod. Augiensis, Introd. p. xxxvi) has shown that they were derived from Evan. 440.

wards given by Pachomius to a monastery at Athos, and thence called δοχειαρίου.

*242. Mosc. (Act. 105, Paul. 121, Apoc. 48) Syn. 380 (Mt. 1) [xii], 8vo, ff. 510, the whole N. T., with Psalms, ᾠδαί, *prol.*, *pict.*, *Am.*

243. Mosc. Cod. Typographei S. Syn. 13 (Mt. m) [xiv], fol., *chart.*, ff. 224, from the Iberian monastery on Athos, contains SS. Matthew and Luke with Theophylact's commentary.

*244. Mosc. Typograph. 1 (Mt. n) [xii], fol., ff. 274, *pict.*, with Euthymius Zigabenus' commentary.

*245. Mosc. Syn. 265, 278, formerly (Greg.) (Mt. o) [dated 1199], 4to, ff. 246, from the famous monastery of Batopedion, written by John, a priest.

*246. Mosc. Syn. 261 (Mt. p) [xiv], 4to, *chart.*, ff. 189, *syn.*, *κεφ. t.*, with marginal various readings. *Mut.* Matt. xii. 41—xiii. 55; John xvii. 24—xviii. 20.

*247. Mosc. Syn. 373 (Mt. q) [xii], 8vo, ff. 223, *syn.*, *men.*, *κεφ. t.*, *κεφ.*, *Am.*, *Eus.*, *lect.*, *prol.*, from Philotheus.

*248. Mosc. Syn. 264 (Mt. r) [dated 1275], 4to, ff. 260 (8 *chart.* + 252), *κεφ. t.* (*chart.*), *Eus.*, *lect.*, written by Meletius a Beraean for Cyrus Alypius, οἰκόνομος of St. George's monastery, in the reign of Michael Palaeologus (1259–82).

*249. Mosc. Syn. 94 (Mt. s) [xi], fol., ff. 809 (more likely 309 as Greg.), from Παντοκράτωρ monastery (as Cod. 74). Contains St. John with a catena.

*250. Mosc. Syn. in a box (Mt. v) [xiii], small 8vo, ff. 225, *Carp.*, *Eus. t.*, *κεφ. t.*, *Am.*, *Eus.*, *syn.*, is the cursive portion of Cod V (*see* p. 144, and note), John vii. 39—xxi. 25. It is also Wetstein's Cod. 87.

*251. Mosc. Tabularii Caesarei (Mt. x) [xi], 4to, ff. 270, *Carp.*, *Eus. t.*, *pict.*, *Am.*, presented to a monastery in A. D. 1400.

*252. Dresd. Reg. A. 145 (Tregelles), once Matthaei's (z) [xi], $8\frac{5}{8} \times 7$, ff. 123 (31), *κεφ. t.*, *κεφ.*, *τίτλ.*, *Am.*, *Eus.*, *lect.*, *ἀναγν.* (Greg.), with corrections and double readings (as from another copy), but *primâ manu.*

*253. Mosc. of Nicephorus Archbishop of Cherson 'et Slabinii' (Slaviansk ?)[1], formerly belonged to the monastery of St. Michael at Jerusalem (Mt. 10) [xi], fol., ff. 248, *prol.*, *κεφ. t.*, *Am.*, *Eus.*, with scholia, Victor's commentary on St. Mark, and rare readings, much resembling those of Cod. 259.

*254. Dresd. A. 100 (Matthaei 11) (Tregelles) [xi], $11\frac{5}{8} \times 9\frac{1}{8}$, ff. 247 (24), *κεφ. t.*, *κεφ.*, *Am.*, *Eus.*, *pict.*, from the monastery of St. Athanasius. Contains SS. Luke and John with scholia.

[1] Holmes, Praefatio ad Pentateuchum, describes his Cod. 32 as 'e Codicibus Eugenii, olim Archiepiscopi Slabinii et Chersonis.' Nicephorus also is named by Holmes as the editor of a Catena on the Octateuch and the four books of Kings from the Constantinopolitan manuscripts (Leipzig, 1772-3), and is described as 'primo Hieromonachus, et postea Archiepiscopus Slabiniensis et Chersonensis, sedem Astracani habens' (*ubi supra*, cap. iv).

*255. Mosc. Syn. 139 (Mt. 12) [xiii], fol., ff. 299 *chart.* + 9, once 'Dionysii monachi rhetoris *et amicorum*.' Commentaries of Chrysostom and others (ἐξηγητικαὶ ἐκλογαί), with fragments of the text interspersed.

*256. Mosc. Typogr. Syn. 3 (Mt. 14) [ix?], fol., ff. 147, scholia on SS. Mark and Luke, with portions of the text. The commentary on St. Mark is *ascribed* to Victor, but in this copy and the preceding the scholia are but few in number (Burgon).

*257. Mosc. Syn. 120 (Mt. 15) is Evan. O, described above.

*258. Dresd. Reg. A. 123 (Tregelles), (Mt. 17) [xiii], $8\frac{1}{2} \times 6\frac{1}{2}$, ff. 126, barbarously written; *pict.*, *lect.*, *syn.*

*259. Mosc. Syn. 45 (Mt. a) [xi], fol., ff. 263, *Carp.*, *Eus. t.*, *prol.*, *κεφ. t.*, *Am.*, *Eus.*, *syn.*, *men.*, from the Iberian monastery, with a commentary (Victor's on St. Mark). This is one of Matthaei's best manuscripts. His other twenty-two copies contain portions of Chrysostom, and therefore come under the head of Patristic Quotations.

Codd. 260–469 were added to the list by Scholz: the very few he professes to have collated thoroughly will be distinguished by an asterisk.

260. Paris National. Gr. 51 [xiii], $12 \times 8\frac{3}{4}$, ff. 241 (24), *prol.*, *argent.*, *κεφ. t.*, *κεφ.*, *τίτλ.*, *Am.*, *Eus.*, *pict.*, once (like Cod. 309) 'domini du Fresne'; correctly written.

261. Par. Nat. Gr. 52 [xiv], $11 \times 8\frac{7}{8}$, ff. 175, *κεφ. t.*, *τίτλ.*, *κεφ.*, *Am.*, *lect.*, *ἀναγν.* (*subscr.*, *στίχ.* later), once at the monastery of the Forerunner at Constantinople. *Mut.* Luke xxiv. 39–53. Matt. i. 1—xi. 1 supplied [xiv] *chart.*

*262. Par. Nat. Gr. 53 [x], $12\frac{3}{4} \times 9\frac{7}{8}$, ff. 212 (27), 2 cols., *κεφ. t.*, *κεφ.*, some *τίτλ.* (*Am.*, *Eus.*, *harm.* at bottom of page, except in Luke, John, where too *Am.* is later), *subscr.*, with rare readings, like those of Evan. Λ and Evann. 300, 376, 428.

263. (Act. 117, Paul. 137.) Par. Nat. Gr. 61 [xiii], $8\frac{1}{4} \times 6\frac{1}{8}$, ff. 294 (28, 29), *κεφ. t.*, *κεφ.*, *τίτλ.*, *Am.*, *lect.*, *subscr.*, *στίχ.* Probably from Asia Minor. It once belonged to Jo. Hurault Boistaller, as did Codd. 301, 306, 314.

264. Par. Nat. Gr. 65 [xiii], 4to, $8 \times 5\frac{5}{8}$, ff. 287 (20), *κεφ. t.*, *τίτλ.*, *κεφ.*, *Am.*, *Eus.*, *harm.*, *subscr.*, *στίχ.*, *syn.*, with what have been called Coptic-like letters, but brought from the East in 1718 by Paul Lucas. The leaves are misplaced in binding, as are those of Cod. 272. At the foot of every page is a harmony like those in Codd. E, W[d]. *See* p. 58, note 2 (Burgon).

Of these copies, 265–270, Burgon states that the grand 4to Cod. 265 seems to contain an important text, 270 a peculiar text, though less beautiful externally than 266, 267, 269. Cod. 268 in double columns has *Eus. t.* very superb, but *pict.* of Evangelists only sketched in ink. Cod. 269, once belonging to Henry IV (in which the last leaf of St. Luke is missing), is in its ancient binding, and is full of very uncommon representations of Gospel incidents.

265. Par. Nat. Gr. 66 [x], $9\frac{7}{8} \times 7\frac{1}{2}$, ff. 372, *κεφ. t.*, *τίτλ.*, *κεφ.*, *Am.*, *Eus.*, once belonged to Philibert de la Mare.

266. Par. Nat. Gr. 67 [x], $9\frac{1}{2} \times 6\frac{1}{2}$, ff. 282 (23), *κεφ. t.*, *τίτλ.*, *κεφ.*, *Am.*, *lect.*, *subscr.*, *vers.*, *syn.*, *men.*

267. Par. Nat. Gr. 69 [x], $8 \times 6\frac{1}{8}$, ff. 396 (19), *prol.*, *κεφ. t.*, *Am.*, *Eus.* in same line, *lect.*, *ἀναγν.*, *subscr.*, *στίχ.* *Mut.* Matt. i. 1–8; Mark i. 1–7; Luke i. 1–8; xxiv. 50—John i. 12.

268. Par. Nat. Gr. 73 [xii], $9\frac{3}{4} \times 7\frac{3}{4}$, ff. 217 (25), 2 cols., *Carp.*, *Eus. t.*, *κεφ. t.*, *κεφ.*, *τίτλ.*, *Am.*, *Eus.*, *lect.*, *syn.*, *men.*, *pict.*

269. Par. Nat. Gr. 74 [xi], $9\frac{1}{4} \times 7\frac{3}{4}$, ff. 215 (28), *prol.*, *κεφ. t.*, *κεφ.*, *τίτλ.*, *Am.*, *vers.*, *pict.*, *Eus. t.* (later).

270. Par. Nat. Gr. 75 [xi], $7\frac{1}{4} \times 5\frac{1}{4}$, ff. 346 (19), *κεφ.*, *τίτλ.*, *Am.*, *Eus.*, *pict.*, *syn.*, *men.*, with a mixed text.

271. Par. Nat. Gr. Suppl. Gr. 75 [xii], 8vo, $7\frac{3}{8} \times 5\frac{1}{4}$, ff. 252 (22), 2 cols., *Carp.*, *Eus. t.*, *κεφ. t.*, *τίτλ.*, *κεφ.*, *Am.*, *Eus.*, *pict.*

272. Brit. Mus. Addit. 15,581 [xii], $5\frac{1}{2} \times 4\frac{3}{4}$, ff. 218 (21), *κεφ. t.*, *κεφ.*, few *τίτλ.*, *Am.*, *Eus.* (mostly omitted). Once Melchisedek Thevenot's. Gregory traces it through the Paris Nat. Library and Th. Rodd to the Brit. Museum, which purchased it.

273. Par. Nat. Gr. 79, 4to, $8\frac{5}{8} \times 6\frac{1}{4}$, ff. 201 (29–31), *Carp.*, *Eus. t.*, *κεφ. t.* with *harm.*, *κεφ.*, *τίτλ.*, *Am.*, *Eus.*, *syn.*, *men.*, *subscr.*, *vers.*, and *syn.*, *men.* again in the later hand, on vellum [xii], but partly on cotton paper [xiv], contains also some scholia, extracts from Severianus' commentary, annals of the Gospels, a list of the Gospel parables, with a mixed text.

274. Par. Nat. Gr. Suppl. Gr. 79 [x], $9\frac{3}{8} \times 6\frac{1}{2}$, ff. 232 (26), *κεφ.*, *τίτλ.*, *Am.*, *lect.*, *syn.*, *men.*, once belonged to Maximus Panagiotes, *protocanon* of the Church at Callipolis (there were many places of this name: but *see* Evan. 346). *Mut.* (but supplied in a later hand) Mark i. 1–17; vi. 21–54; John i. 1–20; iii. 18—iv. 1; vii. 23–42; ix. 10–27; xviii. 12–29. Dean Burgon had a photograph of this manuscript, which he regarded as a specimen of the transition period between uncial and cursive writing. The subscription, resembling that of Cod. L, set in the margin of Cod. 274, he judges to look as old as that of L: *see* Chapter IX, Mark xvi. 9–20.

275. Par. Nat. Gr. 80 [xi], $10\frac{1}{8} \times 8\frac{1}{8}$, ff. 230 (24), *prol.*, *argent.*, *κεφ. t.*, *κεφ.*, *τίτλ.*, *Am.*, *Eus.*, antea Memmianus.

276. Par. Nat. Gr. 81 [A.D. 1092], $7\frac{7}{8} \times 5\frac{3}{4}$, ff. 307, *Eus. t.*, *κεφ. t.*, *κεφ.*, *τίτλ.*, *Am.*, *Eus.*, *lect.*, *pict.*, *vers.*, written by Nicephorus of the monastery Meletius.

277. Par. Nat. Gr. 81 A [xi], $6\frac{3}{4} \times 5\frac{3}{8}$, ff. 261, *Carp.*, *Eus. t.*, *κεφ. t.*, *κεφ.*, *τίτλ.*, *lect.*, *Am.*, *Eus.*, *subscr.*, *στίχ.* (*ἀναγν.*, *syn.*, *men.*, *pict.* later).

278. Par. Nat. Gr. 82 [xii, Greg. A.D. 1072], $8 \times 5\frac{7}{8}$, ff. 305 (21), *Carp.*, *Eus. t.*, *κεφ.*, *τίτλ.*, *lect.*, *Am.*, *Eus.*, *syn.*, *men.*, *vers.*, *pict.*, once Mazarin's, with Armenian inscriptions. Matt. xiii. 43—xvii. 5 is in a later hand.

279. Par. Nat. Gr. 86 [xii], $7 \times 5\frac{3}{8}$, ff. 250, *Eus. t.*, κεφ. *t.*, κεφ., τίτλ., *lect.*, *Am.*, *Eus.*, *syn.*; this copy and Cod. 294 were brought from Patmos and given to Louis XIV in 1686 by Joseph Georgirenus, Archbishop of Samos.

280. Par. Nat. Gr. 87 [xii], $7\frac{3}{8} \times 5\frac{1}{2}$, ff. 177 (25, 26), κεφ. *t.*, κεφ., τίτλ., *Am.*, *Eus.*, *syn.*, *subscr.*, στίχ. *Mut.* Mark viii. 3—xv. 36.

281. Par. Nat. Gr. 88 [xii], $8\frac{3}{8} \times 6\frac{1}{8}$, ff. 249 (22, 23), *Eus. t.*, κεφ., τίτλ., *Am.*, *subscr.* (*lect.* later). *Mut.* Matt. xxviii. 11–20; Luke i. 1–9. Given to the Monastery 'Deiparae Hieracis' by the eremite monk Meletius.

282. Par. Nat. Gr. 90 [A.D. 1176], 7×5, ff. 150 (33), 2 cols., *argent.*, κεφ. *t.*, κεφ., τίτλ., *lect.*, *subscr.* (*Am.* later).

283. Par. Nat. Gr. 92 [xiv], $7\frac{1}{2} \times 5$, ff. 159 (32), κεφ., τίτλ.

284. Par. Nat. Gr. 93 [xiii], $7\frac{5}{8} \times 5\frac{7}{8}$, ff. 254 (22), *Carp.*, *Eus. t.*, *argent.*, κεφ. *t.*, κεφ., τίτλ., some *lect.*, *Am.*, *Eus.*, *subscr.*, *pict.* Once Teller's of Rheims and Peter Stella's.

285. Par. Nat. Gr. 95, olim $\frac{2865}{3}$ [xiv], $7\frac{3}{4} \times 5\frac{3}{8}$, ff. 246 (22), κεφ. *t.*, κεφ., *subscr.*, *pict.*, once Teller's (58): given by Augustin Justinian to Jo. Maria of Catana. This codex is Kuster's Paris 1 and Wetstein's 10. *See* Evan. 10.

286. Par. Nat. Gr. 96 [April 12, 1432, Indiction 10], $8\frac{1}{2} \times 5\frac{1}{2}$, by the monk Calistus, with the Paschal canon for the years 1432–1502. Ff. 264 (21), *chart.*, *Carp.*, κεφ. *t.*, κεφ., τίτλ., *Am.*, *Eus.*

287. Par. Nat. Gr. 98 [A.D. 1478], $9\frac{3}{8} \times 5\frac{1}{2}$, *chart.*, ff. 322 (18), κεφ., τίτλ., *Am.*, *pict.* Written by Hermonymus (*see* Evan. 70), with a most interesting personal memorandum by its original owner D. Chambellan, and a portrait of his betrothed, 1479. Burgon, *Guardian*, Jan. 22, 1873.

288. According to Dr. C. R. Gregory, the following three fragments are parts of the same MS.—

(1) Oxf. Bodl. Canon. Gr. 33 (Scriv. Ed. iii. Evan. 487), St. Matthew; once belonged to Antony Dizomaeus.

(2) Par. Nat. Gr. 99, once German Brixius'. St. Luke.

(3) Par. Institut. III in Quarto (Scriv. Ed. iii. Evan. 471), St. John. On the first page is written 'C. Emmerei Sanguntiniani, emptus 40 assibus.' M. Tardieu, the librarian, informed Dean Burgon that it came from the City Library, to which it was bequeathed by 'M. Morrian, procureur du roi et de la ville de Paris.'

[xv], $9\frac{1}{2} \times 6\frac{1}{4}$, *chart.*, ff. 90+93+67 (18), κεφ. (Gr. et Lat.), τίτλ. (κεφ. Lat. only in Luke): written by George Hermonymus. (F. Madan from Omont, Bulletin de la société de l'histoire, Paris, tome xii, 1885, and Gregory.)

289. Par. Nat. Gr. 100 A [A.D. Feb. 15, 1625], *chart.*, ff. 336, *capp. Lat.*, written by Lucas ἀρχιθύτης.

290. Par. Nat. Suppl. Gr. 108 a [xiii], $8\frac{5}{8} \times 5\frac{3}{4}$, *chart.*, ff. 259 (22), *argent.*, κεφ. *t.* with *harm.*, κεφ., *lect.*, ἀναγν., *syn.*, *subscr.*, στίχ., *vers.*, from the Sorbonne.

291. Par. Nat. Gr. 113 [xii], $8\frac{5}{8} \times 5\frac{1}{8}$, ff. 290 (20), *prol.*, *argent.*, κεφ. *t.*, κεφ., τίτλ., *lect.*, ἀναγν., belonged to one Nicolas.

292. Par. Nat. Gr. 114 [xi], $7\frac{1}{4} \times 4\frac{3}{8}$, ff. 290, κεφ., τίτλ., *Am.*, *Eus.*, *lect.*, *syn.* (later), *pict.* *Mut.* Matt. i. 1—vii. 14; John xix. 14—xxi. 25.

293. Par. Nat. Gr. 117 [Nov. 1262], $5\frac{3}{8} \times 3\frac{1}{8}$, ff. 340 (20), *prol.*, *argent.*, κεφ. *t.*, κεφ., τίτλ., *Am.*, *syn.*, *subscr.*, στίχ., *pict.*, written by Manuel for Blasius a monk.

294. Par. Nat. Gr. 118 [A.D. 1291], ff. 238, κεφ., τίτλ., *Am.*, *Eus.*, *lect.*, *pict.* *Mut.* Matt. i. 18—xii. 25. *See* Evan. 279.

295. Par. Nat. Gr. 120 [xiii], $4\frac{1}{2} \times 2\frac{3}{4}$, ff. 239, κεφ. *t.*, κεφ., τίτλ. *Mut.* Matt. i. 1–11.

296. (Act. 124, Paul. 49, Apoc. 57.) Par. Nat. Gr. 123 and 124 [xvi], $4\frac{7}{8} \times 3\frac{1}{2}$, ff. 257 and 303 (20), *capp. Lat.*, written by Angelus Vergecius (*see* p. 44, note 1).

297. Par. Nat. Suppl. Gr. 140 [xii], $5\frac{3}{8} \times 3\frac{1}{2}$, ff. 196, κεφ. *t.*, some *Am.*, *lect.*, *syn.*, *men.*

298. Par. Nat. Suppl. Gr. 175 [xii], $7\frac{1}{2} \times 5\frac{1}{2}$, ff. 222 (27), κεφ. *t.*, κεφ., τίτλ., *Am.*, *lect.*, ἀναγν., *syn.*, *men.*, from the Jesuits' Public Library, Lyons.

*299. Par. Nat. Gr. 177 [xi], $10\frac{7}{8} \times 8\frac{1}{4}$, ff. 328 (24), *Carp.*, *Eus. t.*, *prol.*, κεφ. *t.*, κεφ., τίτλ., *Am.*, *Eus.*, *subscr.*, *pict.*, an accurately written copy with a mixed text, Victor's commentary on St. Mark, and scholia which seem to have been written in Syria by a partisan of Theodore of Mopsuestia: and other fragments.

*300. Par. Nat. Gr. 186 [xi], $13 \times 9\frac{1}{8}$, ff. 209 (36), *Eus. t.*, κεφ. *t.*, κεφ., τίτλ., *Am.*, *Eus.*, more roughly written than the sister-copy, Evan. 20, 'olim Fonte-Blandensis' (Fontainbleau), contains the first three Gospels, with subscriptions like that of Cod. 262. Contains catena, 'πάρεργα de locis selectis,' and in the outer margin commentaries in a later hand, Chrysostom's on St. Matthew, Victor's or Cyril's of Alexandria on St. Mark (Evann. 20, 300 mention both names), and that of Titus of Bostra on St. Luke. *See* Evan. 428, and especially Evan. 215. Collated by Scholz and W. F. Rose.

301. Par. Nat. Gr. 187 [xi], $13\frac{3}{8} \times 10\frac{1}{2}$, ff. 221 (22), κεφ. *t.*, *Am.*, *subscr.*, στίχ., once Boistallet's, a mixed text with a catena (Victor on St. Mark).

302. Par. Nat. Gr. 193 [xvi], *chart.*, ff. 172, once Mazarin's: contains fragments of SS. Matthew and Luke with a commentary. Poor.

303. Par. Nat. Gr. 194 A [xi], $11\frac{1}{2} \times 9\frac{1}{8}$, ff. 321 (33), *syn.* (later), contains vellum fragments of John i–iv; and on cotton paper, dated 1255, Theophylact's commentary, and some iambic verses written by Nicander, a monk.

304. Par. Nat. Gr. 194 [xiii], $10\frac{7}{8} \times 8\frac{1}{2}$, ff. 242 (31–33), once Teller's; contains SS. Matthew and Mark with a catena, that of St. Mark possibly a modification of Victor's (Burgon).

305. Par. Nat. Gr. 195 [xiii], $12\frac{1}{4} \times 9$, *chart.*, ff. 261 (51, 54), *κεφ. t.* all together, *κεφ.*, *τίτλ.* (*Am.*, *lect.* later), once Mazarin's. Burgon states that this copy contains nothing but the commentary of Euthymius Zigabenus.

306. Par. Nat. Gr. 197 [xii], 11×8, ff. 559 (25), *mut.* John xxi. 1–8, 24, 25, once Boistaller's, contains SS. Matthew and John with Theophylact's commentary.

307. Par. Nat. Gr. 199 [xi], $11\frac{3}{8} \times 8\frac{3}{4}$, ff. 306 (30), *mut.*, contains only Chrysostom's Homilies on SS. Matthew and John (Burgon).

308. Par. Nat. Gr. 200 [xii], $11 \times 8\frac{7}{8}$, ff. 187 (27), once Mazarin's; *mut.*, contains the same as Cod. 307.

309. Par. Nat. Gr. 201 [x–xii], $10\frac{1}{4} \times 7\frac{3}{4}$, ff. 303 (37), 'very peculiar in its style and beautifully written,' *pict.*, once Du Fresne's, has SS. Matthew and John with Chrysostom's commentary, Luke with that of Titus of Bostra, Mark with Victor's. 'This is not properly a text of the Gospel: but parts of the text (*κείμενον*) interwoven with the commentary (*ἑρμήνεια*)' (Burgon, Last Twelve Verses, pp. 282, 287).

310. Par. Nat. Gr. 202 [xi], $12\frac{1}{8} \times 8\frac{1}{8}$, ff. 378 (27), has St. Matthew with a catena, once Colbert's (as also were Evann. 267, 273, 279, 281–3, 286–8, 291, 294, 296, 315, 318–9). Formerly given to St. Saba's monastery by its Provost Arsenius.

311. Par. Nat. Gr. 203 [xii], $14 \times 11\frac{1}{2}$, ff. 357 (28), once Mazarin's; this also has St. Matthew with a catena.

312. Par. Nat. Gr. 206 [A.D. 1308], $10\frac{1}{4} \times 8$, ff. 87 (30), Victor's commentary without the text, like that in Cod. 20, which (and Cod. 300) it closely resembles (Burgon, *ibid.* p. 279, note).

313. Par. Nat. Gr. 208 [xiv or xv], $12 \times 8\frac{1}{4}$, *chart.*, ff. 460, *mut.*, once Mazarin's; contains St. Luke with a catena.

314. Par. Nat. Gr. 209 [x–xii], 11×8, ff. 349 (32), once Boistaller's, contains St. John with a remarkable catena (quite different from that published by Cramer), with the names of the several authors (Burgon).

315. Par. Nat. Gr. 210 [xiii], $10\frac{7}{8} \times 7\frac{3}{8}$, ff. 156, has the same contents as Cod. 314. *Mut.* John i. 1–21; xiv. 25—xv. 16; xxi. 22–25.

316. Par. Nat. Gr. 211 [xii], $13\frac{3}{8} \times 8\frac{5}{8}$, *chart.*, ff. 129 (33), *κεφ.*, *τίτλ.*, brought from Constantinople. Contains SS. John and Luke with a commentary.

317. Par. Nat. Gr. 212 [xii], $12\frac{3}{4} \times 9\frac{1}{4}$, ff. 352 (29), 'olim Medicaeus' (*see* p. 121, note 2), contains John x. 9—xxi. 25 with a catena.

318. Par. Nat. Gr. 213 [xiv], $13\frac{3}{8} \times 9\frac{3}{8}$, ff. 16, 2 cols., has John vii. 1—xxi. 25 with a commentary.

319. Par. Nat. Gr. 231 [xii], $8\frac{1}{4} \times 6\frac{1}{4}$, ff. 203 (33), with a commentary, *mut.*

320. Par. Nat. Gr. 232 [xi], $9 \times 7\frac{1}{4}$, ff. 392 (21), *κεφ. t.*, *κεφ.*, *τίτλ.*, has St. Luke with a commentary.

321, 322 are Evst. 101 and 14 (Burgon, Greg.). Instead of these—

321. Brit. Mus. Addit. 34,107 [xi–xii], 5¼ × 4¼, ff. 213 (21-24), *mut.* at beginning (five leaves); κεφ., κεφ. *t.*, *Am.* Very minute. Purchased of H. L. Dupuis, Esq., in 1891.

322. Brit. Mus. Addit. 34,108 [xiii], 8½ × 6½, ff. 175 (28), (148 *membr.* + 17 *chart.*), *Carp.*, *Eus. t.*, *prol.*, κεφ. *t.*, κεφ., τίτλ., *lect.*, *Am.*, *Eus.*, *subscr.*, στίχ., *syn.* Seventeen leaves of paper are added at the end containing Luke iv. 3—viii. 19, *syn.*, *men.* [xv]. The writing is clear and firm, injured in part. Belonged to monastery of Ῥενδήνη: purchased of H. L. Dupuis in 1891.

323. Par. Nat. Suppl. Gr. 118 [xv or xvi], 8¼ × 5⅝, *chart.*, ff. 94, contains Matt. vi, vii, and a Greek version of some Arabic fables.

324. (Evst. 97, Apost. 32.) Par. Nat. Gr. 376 [xiii or xiv], 7⅜ × 5, ff. 315 (29), *Carp.*, *Eus. t.*, κεφ. *t.*, κεφ., τίτλ., *Am.*, *Eus.*, *lect.* (*syn.*, *men.* later), once Mazarin's, together with lessons from the Acts, Epistles, and Gospels, contains also Gospels complete (on cotton paper), and a list of Emperors from Constantine to Manuel Porphyrogenitus (A.D. 1143).

325. Instead of 325 (Ed. 3), which is Evst. 99—

Brit. Mus. Addit. 32,341 [xi], 7¾ × 6, ff. 222 (23), *prol.*, κεφ. *t.*, κεφ., τίτλ., *lect.*, *Am.*, *Eus.*, *subscr.*, *syn.* *Mut.* Matt. vi. 56—vii. 17; Luke xi. 17–32; xxiv. 26—John i. 22; end of *syn.* worn and faded. Purchased of the Rev. G. J. Chester in 1884.

326. Par. Nat. Gr. 378 [xiv], *chart.*, ff. 255, contains commentaries (ἑρμηνεία) on certain ecclesiastical lessons or texts (τὸ κείμενον). This is not a manuscript of the Gospels, properly so called.

327 and 328 are Evst. 99 and 100 (Burg. Greg.). Instead—

327. London, J. Bevan Braithwaite 1 [xii], 8 × 7, ff. 98 (21), τίτλ., κεφ., *Am.*, *Eus.*, *subscr.*, *prol.*, κεφ. *t.* *Mut.* beg. and end. Contains St. Mark and St. Luke. Bought at Athens in 1884 with the next. (Collated, as also the next, by W. C. Braithwaite.) (Greg. 531.)

328. J. Bevan Braithwaite 2 [xiii–xiv], 4⅜ × 3, 2 vols., ff. 97 + 113 = 210 (29), *lect.*, τίτλ., κεφ. *Mut.* Matt. i. 1–12. Well written. (Greg. 573.)

329. Par. Nat. Coisl. Gr. 19 [xi], 12¾ × 9¼, ff. 321 (25), κεφ. *t.* (John), *subscr.* (Luke), στίχ. (Luke, John), with a commentary (Victor's on St. Mark). Described (as is also Cod. 331) by Montfaucon.

330. (Act. 132, Paul. 131.) Formerly Petrop. Muralt. 101–xi. 1, 2, 330. (8 pe.) Coislin. 196 [xi], 9 × 7, ff. 289 (30), *Eus. t.*, *prol.* κεφ. *t.*, κεφ., *Am.*, *Eus.*, *men.*, *subscr.*, *Euthal.*, *subscr.* (Paul.), from Athanasius at Athos.

331. Par. Nat. Coisl. Gr. 197 [x–xii], 9½ × 7, ff. 275 (20), *Carp.*, *Eus. t.*, *prol.*, κεφ. *t.*, κεφ., τίτλ., *Am.*, *Eus.*, *lect.*, once Hector D'Ailli's, Bishop of Toul.

332. Taurinensis Univ. C. ii. 4 (20) [xi], at Turin, 12⅛ × 9⅛, ff. 304 (33), κεφ. *t.*, κεφ., τίτλ., *pict.*, with a commentary (Victor's on St. Mark). Bound in A.D. 1258. Burgon cites Pasinus' Catalogue, P. i. p. 91.

333. Taurin. B. i. 9 (4) [A.D. 1214], 13⅝ × 10¼, ff. 377, *chart.*, once belonged to Arsenius, Abp. of Monembasia in the Morea, then to Gabriel, metropolitan of Philadelphia; SS. Matthew and John with Nicetas' catena.

334. Taurin. B. iii. 8 (43) [xiv], $11\frac{1}{4}\times 8\frac{1}{2}$, ff. 267, SS. Matthew and Mark with a commentary; *prol.*, *κεφ. t.*, *κεφ.*, *τίτλ.*

335. Taurin. B. iii. 2 (44) [xvi], *chart.*, $11\frac{1}{2}\times 8\frac{1}{8}$, ff. 110 (29), *prol.*, *argent.*, *στίχ.* (Matt.).

336. Taurin. B. ii. 17 (101) [xvi], *chart.*, $11\frac{3}{4}\times 8\frac{3}{8}$, ff. 191 +, St. Luke with a catena.

337. Taurin. B. iii. 25 (52) [xii], $11\frac{1}{2}\times 8\frac{7}{8}$, ff. 114 (28), 2 cols., parts of St. Matthew with a commentary.

338. Taurin. B. vii. 33 (335) [xii], $5\frac{1}{2}\times 4\frac{1}{4}$, ff. 362 (18), *Carp.*, *Eus. t.*, *κεφ. t.*, *κεφ.*, *τίτλ.*, *Am.*, *Eus.*, *pict.*

339. (Act. 135, Paul. 170, Apoc. 83.) Taurin. B. v. 8 (302) [xiii], $8\frac{1}{2}\times 6\frac{1}{8}$, ff. 200, 2 cols., *Carp.*, *Eus. t.*, *κεφ. t.*, *κεφ.*, *τίτλ.*, *Am.*, *Eus.*, *syn.*, *men.*, *Euthal.* (Act., Cath., Paul.), and other matter [1].

340. Taurin. B. vii. 16 (344) [xiv], $5\frac{3}{4}\times 4\frac{1}{8}$, ff. 243 (21), *κεφ. t.* (*κεφ.*, *τίτλ.*, *Am.*, *lect.* later), with later corrections.

341. Taurin. B. vii. 14 (350) [dated 1296], $6\times 4\frac{3}{4}$, ff. 268 (24), *Carp.*, *κεφ. t.*, *lect.* Written by Nicetas Mauron, a reader.

342. Taurin. B. v. 24 (149) [xiii], $8\times 6\frac{1}{8}$, ff. 300 (21), *Carp.*, *Eus. t.*, *κεφ. t.*, *κεφ.*, *τίτλ.*, *Am.*, *Eus.*, *pict.*

343. Mediolani Ambrosianus H. 13 Sup. [xi or xii], $7\times 4\frac{3}{4}$, ff. 263, *Carp.*, *Eus. t.*, *κεφ. t.*, *κεφ.*, *τίτλ.*, *Am.*, *Eus.*, *lect.* (later), *pict.* Written by Antony, a priest, on Sunday, Sept. 1, of the third Indiction, which in the twelfth century, might be A.D. 1140 or 1185. Seen by Burgon.

344. Med. Ambros. G. 16 Sup. [x–xii], $6\frac{3}{8}\times 4\frac{3}{4}$, ff. 327 (19), *Carp.* (later), *κεφ. t.*, *κεφ.*, *τίτλ.*, *Am.* (*lect.*, *syn.* later), *subscr.* *Mut.* John xxi. 12–25. But Luke xiii. 21—xvi. 23; xxi. 12[?]; xxii. 12–23; xxiii. 45—John xxi. 25 are [xiv] *chart.* First page of St. Matthew, and several of the early pages of St. Luke, have been re-written over the original text. (Burgon.)

345. Med. Ambros. 17 Sup. [xi or xii], $5\frac{3}{4}\times 4\frac{1}{2}$, ff. 375 (15), 2 cols., *κεφ.*, *τίτλ.*, *Am.*, *Eus.*, *lect.*, *subscr.*, *ῥήμ.*, *στίχ.*, *vers.*, *pict.* (John), (*syn.*, *men.* later). *Mut.* Matt. i. 1–11.

*346. Med. Ambros. S. 23 Sup. [xii], $8\frac{3}{4}\times 6\frac{1}{2}$, ff. 168, *κεφ. t.*, *κεφ.*, *τίτλ.*, *Am.*, *lect.*, *subscr.*, *ῥήμ.*, *στίχ.*, *syn.*, *men.*, carelessly written, with very unusual readings [2]. *Mut.* John iii. 26—vii. 52. Bought in 1606 at Gallipoli. Collated by Ceriani for Professor Ferrar, by Burgon and Rose from Luke xxi. 37 . . . . xxiv. 53. Last of Abbott's four (*see* Evan. 13). He gives a facsimile of Luke xi. 49–51.

347. Med. Ambros. 35 Sup. [xii], $9\times 6\frac{1}{2}$, ff. 245 (15), 2 cols., *Carp.*,

[1] Written in three several and minute hands (Hort):—A for the Gospels, the Epistle of Pilate and its Answer, and a treatise on the genealogy of the Virgin; B for the Apocalypse and a Synaxarion; C the Acts, Cath. Paul. (Hebrews last), and Lives of the Apostles, followed on the same page by the Psalter by B, so that Apoc. and *syn.* probably stood last.

[2] This manuscript appears to be the only Greek witness for the Old Latin and Curetonian Syriac variation Matt. i. 16 *ἰωσὴφ ᾧ μνηστευθῆσα παρθένος μαριὰμ ἐγέννησεν ιν̅ τὸν λεγόμενον χν̅.* But then it was written in Italy, as Ceriani judges.

κεφ. t., *vers.*, *κεφ.*, *τίτλ.*, *Am.*, *Eus.*, *lect.*, correctly written by Constantine Chrysographus.

348. Med. Ambros. B. 56 Sup. [Dec. 29, 1022], $7\frac{3}{4} \times 5\frac{7}{8}$, ff. 187, 2 cols., *Carp.*, *Eus. t.*, *prol.*, *κεφ.*, *τίτλ.*, *Am.*, *Eus.*, *lect.*, *syn.*, *men.*, once 'J. V. Pinelli.' Citations from the O. T. are asterisked. Burgon had a photograph.

349. Med. Ambros. F. 61 Sup. [1322], *chart.*, $8\frac{7}{8} \times 5\frac{7}{8}$, ff. 399, *κεφ.*, *τίτλ.*, *Am.*, *subscr.*, *syn.*, *men.*, *vers.*, bought at Corfu.

350. Med. Ambros. B. 62 Sup. [xi], $7\frac{7}{8} \times 6\frac{1}{4}$, ff. 305 (21), *κεφ.*, *τίτλ.*, *Am.*, *lect.*, *pict.* (*syn.*, *men.* later). The first four leaves [xvi], *chart.* *Mut.* John xxi. 9–25.

351. Med. Ambros. B. 70 Sup. [xi or xii], $8\frac{1}{2} \times 6$, ff. 268 (22), *Carp.*, *Eus. t.*, *κεφ. t.*, *Am.*, *Eus.*, *subscr.*, with a Latin version [xv] here and there written above the text 'school-boy fashion.' Burgon.

352. Med. Ambros. B. 93 Sup. [xii], $9\frac{3}{4} \times 7\frac{3}{8}$, ff. 219 (20), *κεφ.*, *τίτλ.*, *Am.* (later), brought from Calabria, 1607. *Mut.* Matt. i. 1–17; Mark i. 1–15; xvi. 13–20; Luke i. 1–7; xxiv. 43–53; John i. 1–10; xxi. 3–25. *Lect.* in margin, and the faded ink retouched [xiv].

353. Med. Ambros. M. 93 Sup. [xiii], $11\frac{1}{8} \times 6\frac{1}{8}$, ff. 194 (23), *κεφ.*, *τίτλ.*, *Am.*, *Eus.*, *lect.* (in latter parts, later), with the same commentary as Evan. 181. *Mut.* John xxi. 24, 25.

354. Venetiis Marcianus 29 [xi], ff. $9\frac{3}{8} \times 6\frac{1}{4}$, ff. 442 (22), Matt. with Theophylact; ch. xxviii is wanting. Written in a very large hand, and bought at Constantinople in 1419 (Burgon, *Guardian*, Oct. 29, 1873).

355. Ven. Marc. 541 [xi ?], $6\frac{1}{2} \times 4\frac{7}{8}$, ff. 410 (18), *Carp.*, *Eus. t.*, *κεφ. t.*, *κεφ.*, *τίτλ.*, *Am.*, *Eus.*, *lect.* (later), *syn.* (later still), a sumptuous and peculiar copy.

356. Ven. Marc. 545 [xvi], *chart.*, $8\frac{7}{8} \times 6\frac{1}{4}$, ff. 176 (21), with Titus of Bostra's catena on St. Luke. A note runs thus: Ἀντωνίου τοῦ Ἀγγελίου καὶ χρήσει καὶ κτήσει, pro quo solvit librario qui descripserat HS. cxxvi. l. Δ'. 3.

357. Ven. Marc. 28 [xi], $12\frac{1}{2} \times 8\frac{1}{2}$, ff. 281 (35), *κεφ. t.* (rather later), *κεφ.*, *τίτλ.*, *lect.*, SS. Luke and John with a catena. The titles resemble those of Evan. 69.

358. Mutinensis ii. A. 9 [xiv], $6 \times 4\frac{7}{8}$, ff. ?, *κεφ. t.*, *κεφ.*, *τίτλ.*, *Am.*, *Eus.*, *lect.* (later), *subscr.*, at Modena, in a small hand with rude illuminations.

359. Mutin. [242], iii. B. 16 [xiv], $7\frac{1}{4} \times 4\frac{7}{8}$, ff. ?, with slight decorations, on brownish paper, having scribe's name on last page. *Carp.*, *Eus. t.*, *prol.*, *κεφ. t.*, *κεφ.*, *τίτλ.*, *Am.*, *Eus.* (later), *lect.*, *syn.*, *men.*

360. Parmae reg. 2319 [xi], $7\frac{3}{8} \times 6\frac{1}{8}$, ff. ?, *κεφ. t.*, *κεφ.*, *τίτλ.*, *Am.*, *Eus.*, *lect.* (later), *vers.*, *pict.* (*syn.*, *men.* later still), with an uuusual text, in double columns, collated by De Rossi, who once possessed this codex and

361. Parmae reg. 1821 [xiii], $4\frac{1}{4} \times 3\frac{1}{8}$, ff. ?, *κεφ. t.* with *harm.*, *lect.*,

ἀναγν., *subscr.*, *στίχ.*, *syn.*, *men.*, faded. *Mut.* Luke viii. 14—xi. 20. Fully described (as also Cod. 360) in De Rossi's printed Catalogue.

362. Florentiae Laurentianus Conv. Soppr. 176, formerly Cod. Biblioth. S. Mariae No. 74 [xiii], 13⅛ × 9¼, ff. 314 (32), Luke vi. 29—xii. 10, with a fuller catena than Cramer's, citing the names of Greek expositors. Text in vermilion, commentary in black (Burgon). Described, like Evann. 201, 370, by Jo. Lamy, 'De eruditione Apostolorum,' Florent. 1738, p. 239.

363. (Act. 144, Paul. 180.) Flor. Laur. vi. 13 [xiii], a beautiful small 4to, 8¼ × 5⅝, ff. 306 (32), *argent.*, *κεφ. t.* with *harm.*, *lect.*, *ἀναγν.*, *subscr.*, *στίχ.*, *vers.*; *Euthal.* (Paul., Cath.).

364. Flor. Laur. vi. 24 [xiii, Greg. x], 8vo, 5⅜ × 4, ff. 224 (20), *ἀναγν.* (*κεφ.*, *τίτλ.*, *Am.*, *Eus.* only in Matt., *lect.* later), (*syn.*, *men.* xv), the style of the characters rather peculiar, without the usual breaks between the Gospels; some leaves at the beginning and end [xiv].

365. (Act. 145, Paul. 181.) Flor. Laur. vi. 36 [xiii], 4to, 7½ × 5⅜, ff. 358 (33), *Eus. t.*, *κεφ.*, *τίτλ.*, *Am.*, *vers.*, *pict.*, contains also the Psalms. Scholz collated it in select passages. *See* Gregory, who saw it.

366. Flor. Laur. Conv. Soppr. 171 (St. Maria's No. 20), [xii], a grand fol., 11½ × 8⅞, ff. 323 (31), *κεφ.*, *τίτλ.*, with *harm.*, St. Matthew in vermilion with catena in black. *Mut.* ch. i. 1—ii.16, with many later marginal notes. Entirely dissimilar in style from Cod. 362.

367. (Act. 146, Paul. 182, Apoc. 23.) Flor. Laur. Conv. Soppr. 53 (St. Maria's No. 6 [dated 26 Decembr. 1332], 4to, *chart.*, 9¾ × 7, ff. 349 (32), *prol.*, *κεφ. t.*, *κεφ.*, *τίτλ.*, *Am.*, *lect.*, *subscr.*, *vers.*, *στίχ.*, *syn.*, *men.*, written by one Mark. Bought in 1482 for three aurei by the Benedictines of St. Maria (Burgon).

368. (Act. 150, Apoc. 84.) Flor. Riccardianus 84, in the Libreria Riccardi, 'olim Cosmae Oricellarii *et amicorum*' (Evan. 255) [xv], 8vo, *chart.*, 6⅛ × 4⅛, ff. 124 (21), contains St. John's Gospel, the Apocalypse, the Epistles and lessons from them, with Plato's Epistles, carelessly written.

369. Flor. Ricc. 90 [xii or xiv], 4to, 5⅜ × 4¼, ff. 23 + (25), *κεφ.*, *τίτλ.*, *Am.*, *Eus.*, *lect.*, contains Mark vi. 25—ix. 45; x. 17—xvi. 9, with part of a Greek Grammar and 'Avieni Fabulae.' The text is much rubricated.

370. Flor. Ricc. 5 [xiv], fol., *chart.*, 10⅞ × 7¾, ff. 424, *κεφ.*, *τίτλ.*, *Am.*, *lect.*, with Theophylact's commentary. *Mut.* Matt. i. 1—iv. 17; John xvi. 29—xxi. 25. Described by Lamy, *see* Evan. 362.

371. Rom. Vatican. Gr. 1159 [x], 4to, 8 × 6½, ff. 315 (21), *Eus. t.*, *κεφ. t.*, *κεφ.*, *τίτλ.*, *Am.*, *Eus.*, *pict.*

372. Rom. Vat. Gr. 1161 [xv], 4to, 9½ × 6½, ff. 199 (30), *capp. Lat.*, ends John iii. 1. Beautifully written.

373. Rom. Vat. Gr. 1423 [xv], fol., *chart.*, 16⅛ × 11, ff. 221 (46), *Am.*, *subscr.*, *στίχ.*, 'olim Cardinalis Sirleti,' with a catena, *mut.* in fine. G. Sirlet [1514–85] became Librarian of the Vatican 1573.

374. Rom. Vat. Gr. 1445 [xii], fol., $11\frac{1}{2} \times 8\frac{3}{8}$, ff. 173 (45), *pict.* (κεφ. *t.*, κεφ., τίτλ. later), with a commentary ascribed to Peter of Laodicea, who is also named on the fly-leaf of Cod. 138. Burgon, however, says, 'This is simply a mistake. No such work exists: and the commentary on the second Evangelist is that of Victor,' *ubi supra*, p. 286. In 1221 one John procured it from Theodosiopolis; there were at least five cities of that name, three of them in Asia Minor.

375. Rom. Vat. Gr. 1533 [xii], $6\frac{3}{4} \times 5\frac{1}{2}$, ff. 199 (26), 2 cols., *Eus. t.*, κεφ. *t.*, κεφ., τίτλ., *Am.*, *Eus.*, *pict.*

376. Rom. Vat. Gr. 1539 [xi], $4\frac{1}{4} \times 3$, ff. 185 (28), κεφ. *t.*, κεφ., τίτλ., *Am.*, *subscr.*, given by Francis Accidas. With subscriptions resembling those of Codd. Λ, 262, 300 (*see* pp. 160, 161, and note).

377. Rom. Vat. Gr. 1618 [xv], *chart.*, $12 \times 8\frac{1}{4}$, ff. 339 (30), St. Matthew with a catena, the other Gospels with questions and answers.

378. Rom. Vat. Gr. 1658 [xiv], $12\frac{1}{8} \times 8\frac{5}{8}$, ff.?, portions from St. Matthew with Chrysostom's Homilies, and from the prophets.

379. Rom. Vat. Gr. 1769 [xv], *chart.*, $11\frac{5}{8} \times 8$, ff. 437 (27), κεφ. *t.*, κεφ., τίτλ., with a commentary.

380. Rom. Vat. Gr. 2139 [xv], *chart.*, $9\frac{1}{8} \times 6$, ff. 202 (23), *Carp.*, *Eus. t.*, *prol.*, κεφ. *t.* (*capp. Lat.*), *Am.*, *Eus.*, *subscr.*

381. Rom. Palatino-Vat. Gr. 20 [xiv], *chart.*, $12\frac{1}{4} \times 9\frac{7}{8}$, ff. 226 (33), St. Luke with a catena.

382. Rom. Vat. Gr. 2070 [xiii], $8\frac{1}{2} \times 7\frac{1}{4}$, ff. 167 (24), 2 cols., κεφ. *t.*, κεφ., τίτλ., *Am.*, *lect.*, *subscr.*, στίχ.; 'olim Basil.,' carelessly written, fragments of SS. John and Luke are placed by the binder before SS. Matthew and Mark. Much is lost.

383, 384, 385 are all Collegii Romani [xvi], 4to, *chart.*, with a commentary.

386. (Act. 151, Paul. 199, Apoc. 70: *see* p. 72, note.) Rom. Vat. Ottobon. 66 [xv], $11\frac{1}{2} \times 8\frac{3}{8}$, ff. 393 (24), *Eus. t.*, κεφ. *t.*, *lect.*, ἀναγν., *subscr.*, στίχ., *syn.*, *men.*, *Euthal.* (Cath., Paul.), once 'Jo. Angeli ducis ab Altamps,' as also Codd. 388, 389, 390, Paul. 202.

387. Rom. Vat. Ottob. 204 [xii], $8\frac{1}{2} \times 6\frac{1}{2}$, ff. 298 (21), *lect.*, *subscr.*, στίχ.

388. Rom. Vat. Ottob. 212 [xii], $8\frac{3}{8} \times 6\frac{1}{4}$, ff. 315 (21), *argent.*, κεφ. *t.*, κεφ., τίτλ., *Am.*, *Eus.*, *lect.*, ἀναγν., *subscr.*, στίχ., *pict.*, *syn.*, *men.*, once belonged to Alexius and Theodora.

389. Rom. Vat. Ottob. 297 [xi], $6\frac{3}{4} \times 5\frac{3}{8}$, ff. 192 (23), *Eus. t.*, κεφ. *t.*, κεφ., τίτλ. with *harm.*, *Am.*, *Eus.*, *subscr.*, στίχ.

390. (Act. 164, Paul. 203.) Rom. Vat. Ottob. 381 [dated 1282], 4to, $8\frac{5}{8} \times 6$, ff. 336 (29), *Carp.*, *Eus. t.*, *prol.*, κεφ. *t.*, κεφ., τίτλ., *Am.*, *Eus.*, *lect.*, *subscr.*, *vers.*, *syn.*, *men.*; *Euthal.* (Paul.), with scholia, was in a church at Scio A.D. 1359.

391. Rom. Vat. Ottob. 432 [xi, April 13, Indiction 8], $11\frac{3}{8} \times 9\frac{1}{8}$, ff.

232 (17), *Carp.*, *prol.*, *κεφ. t.*, *κεφ.*, *τίτλ.*, *Am.*, *Eus.*, with a commentary. Given to Benedict XIII (1724–30) by Abachum Andriani, an abbot of Athos. Matt. i. 1–8; Luke i; John vii. 53—viii. 11 were written [xv].

392. Rom. Barberin. v. 17, formerly 225, is the cursive portion of Evan. Y [xii], 11¼ × 8, ff. (391 – 8 =) 383 (36), *κεφ.*, *τίτλ.*, with Theophylact's commentary.

393. (Act. 167, Paul. 185.) Rom. Vallicell. E. 22 [xvi], *chart.*, 10½ × 6⅞, ff. 222 (34), *κεφ.*, *τίτλ.* (*lect.* later).

394. (Act. 170, Paul. 186.) Rom. Vallicell. F. 17 [July 4, 1330, Indict. 13], *chart.*, 9¼ × 6¼, ff. 344 (29), *argent.*, *κεφ. t.*, *lect.*, *ἀναγν.*, *syn.*, *men.*, written by Michael, a priest.

395. Rom. Casanatensis G. iv. 1 [xii], 11 × 8¼, ff. ?, *κεφ. t.*, *τίτλ.*, *Am.*, *Eus.*, *pict.*, with marginal corrections, bought about 1765.

396. Rom. Chisianus R. iv. 6 [xii], 8¾ × 6½, ff. 115 (27), *argent.*, *κεφ. t.*, *κεφ.*, *τίτλ.*, *Am.*, *Eus.*, begins Matt. xxiii. 27.

397. Rom. Vallicell. E. 40 [xv], 9⅝ × 8¼, ff. 295 (10), St. John with a catena (described by Bianchini).

398. Taurin. Univ. C. ii. 5 [xiii, or xvi in Pasinus' Catalogue], select passages with a catena, 12⅛ × 8½, *chart.*, ff. 310 (30), 2 cols.

399. Taurin. C. ii. 14 [xv, or xvi in Pasinus' Cat.], *chart.*, 11⅝ × 8, ff. 404 (22), *prol.*, *κεφ. t.*, *vers.*, commentary, sometimes without the text. Found by Dr. Hort to contain SS. John, Luke (with Titus of Bostra's commentary), Matthew, *hoc ordine.* *See* p. 73.

400. (Act. 181, Paul. 200.) Berolinensis Reg. A. Duodec. 10, Diezii [xv], 5 × 3¾, ff. 249 (14–16), *Euthal.*, *mut.*, damaged by fire and water, contains Matt. xii. 29—xiii. 2: and the Acts and Epistles, except Acts i. 11—ii. 11; Rom. i. 1–27; 1 Cor. xiv. 12—xv. 46; 2 Cor. i. 1–8; v. 4–19; 1 Tim. iv. 1—Heb. i. 9. This copy belonged to Henry Benzil, Archbishop of Upsal, then to Laurence Benzelstierna, Bishop of Arosen: it was described by C. Aurivill (1802), collated by G. T. Pappelbaum (1815).

401. Neapolit. Bibl. Nat. II. Aa. 3 [xi or xii], 8⅛ × 6⅛, ff. 113 (23), *κεφ. t.*, *κεφ.*, *τίτλ.*, *Am.*, *vers.* (later), contains Matthew, Mark vi. 1—xvi. 20, Luke, John i. 1—xii. 1.

402. Neapol. Nat. II. Aa. 5 [xiv or xv], 6¼ × 4½, ff. 253 (24), *κεφ. t.*, *lect.*, *ἀναγν.*, *subscr.*, *στίχ.*, *pict.*

403. Neapol. Nat. II. Aa. 4 [xii or xiii], *chart.*, 7 × 4⅞, ff. 212 (22), *argent.*, *κεφ. t.*, *Am.*, *lect.*, *men.* Contains Matt. xii. 23—xix. 12; 28—xxviii. 20; Mark; Luke i. 1—v. 21; 36—xxiv. 53; John i. 1—xviii. 36.

404. Neapol. 'Abbatis Scotti' [xi], 8vo, *prol.* Not known.

The manuscripts once belonging to the Nani family, which include Evan. U, were catalogued by J. A. Mingarelli ('Graeci codices manu scripti apud Nanios Patricios Venetos asservati,' Bononiae, 1784), and, being now at St. Mark's, were inspected by Burgon.

405. Venet. Marc. i. 10, 'olim Nan. 3, antea monasterii SS. Cosmae et Damiani urbis Prusiensis,' i.e. Brusa or Prusa [xi], $8\frac{1}{8} \times 7$, ff. 228 (22), *Carp.*, *Eus. t.*, *κεφ. t.*, *τίτλ.*, *κεφ.*, *Am.*, *Eus.*, *lect.*, *subscr.*, the leaves utterly disarranged by the binder. (Wiedmann and J. G. J. Braun collated portions of 405–417 for Scholz.)

406. Ven. Marc. i. 10, Nan. 4 [xi], $6\frac{5}{8} \times 5\frac{7}{8}$, ff. 297 (18), *κεφ. t.*, *κεφ.*, *τίτλ.*, *Am.* (not *Eus.*), few *lect.* *Mut.* Mark iv. 41—v. 14; Luke iii. 16—iv. 4.

407. Ven. Marc. i. 12, Nan. 5 [xi], $6 \times 5\frac{1}{8}$, ff. 87 (21), contains Luke v. 30—John ix. 2. *Κεφ. t.*, *κεφ.*, *τίτλ.*, *Am.*, *lect.*, *pict.*, *στίχοι βω̄* at the end of St. Luke, *subscr.*, *vers.*

408. Ven. Marc. i. 14, Nan. 7 [xii], $9\frac{1}{4} \times 5\frac{1}{8}$, ff. 261 (22), once belonged to St. John Chrysostom's monastery, by the Jordan, as stated in a note of the original scribe. *Carp.*, *Eus. t.*, *κεφ. t.*, *κεφ.*, *τίτλ.*, *Am.*, *Eus.*, few *lect.*, *στίχ.*, *subscr.*, *vers.*, *pict.*, full stops very numerous in the text. Matt. i. 1–13 and *syn.* later.

409. Ven. Marc. i. 15, Nan. 8 [xii or xiv], $8\frac{1}{4} \times 5\frac{3}{4}$, ff. 210 (28), the writing and *pict.* very rough, the stops being mostly red crosses. *Carp.*, *Eus. t.*, *prol.*, *κεφ. t.*, *τίτλ.*, *κεφ.*, *Am.* (not *Eus.*), *lect.*, *vers.*, *subscr.*, *στίχ.*, *syn.*, *men.*, foreign matter by Cosmas, &c. (*see* p. 66).

410. Ven. Marc. i. 17, Nan. 10 [xiii or xiv], $9\frac{1}{4} \times 6\frac{3}{4}$, *chart.*, ff. 212, written by one Joasaph a monk, *Carp.*, *Eus. t.*, *prol.* [xiii] on parchment, *κεφ. t.* on paper. *Κεφ.*, *τίτλ.*, *Am.* (not *Eus.*), *lect.*, *prol.*, *vers.*, *subscr.*, *στίχ.*, *syn.*, *men.*

411. Ven. Marc. i. 18, Nan. 11 [x or xi], $6\frac{1}{2} \times 4\frac{7}{8}$, ff. 375 (20), very beautifully written in upright characters. *Carp.*, *Eus. t.*, *prol.*, matter by Cosmas (*see* p. 66), *κεφ. t.*, *τίτλ.*, *κεφ.*, *Am.*, *Eus.*, *lect.*, *syn.*, *men.*, *vers.* *Pict.* torn out.

412. Ven. Marc. i. 19, Nan. 12 [1301], $7 \times 5\frac{1}{4}$, ff. 327 (22), written by Theodore (*see* p. 43, note 1). *Carp.*, *Eus. t.*, *prol.*, *κεφ. t.*, *τίτλ.*, *κεφ.*, *Am.*, *Eus.*, *lect.*, *syn.*, *men.*, *στίχ.*, *vers.* In text it much resembles Scrivener's q and r by the same hand, without being identical with either.

413. Ven. Marc. i. 20, Nan. 13 [1302, Indiction 15], $8\frac{3}{4} \times 6\frac{3}{4}$, ff. 270 (24), once belonged to St. Catherine's monastery on Sinai, where Cod. א was found, and is elegantly written by one Theodosius *ῥακενδύτης*. *Carp.*, *Eus. t.*, *prol.*, *κεφ. t.*, *τίτλ.*, *κεφ.*, *Am.*, *Eus.*, rude *pict.*, *lect.*, *subscr.*, *στίχ.*, *syn.*, *men.*

414. Ven. Marc. i. 21, Nan. 14 [xiv], $9\frac{1}{4} \times 6\frac{1}{2}$, ff. 225 (26), *κεφ.*, *τίτλ.*, *Am.*, *lect.*, *subscr.*, *syn.*, *men.*, written by Philip, a monk.

415. Ven. Marc. i. 22, Nan. 15 [dated January, 1356], $7\frac{1}{4} \times 5\frac{1}{4}$, ff. ?, *syn.*, *men.*, rude *pict.*, *κεφ. t.*, *κεφ.*, *τίτλ.*, *ἀναγν.*, *subscr.*

416. Ven. Marc. i. 24, Nan. 17 [xiv], $7\frac{3}{4} \times 5\frac{7}{8}$, ff. 225 (22), very roughly written, begins Matt. xxv. 36, ends John xviii. 7. *Mut.* Matt. xxvi. 17—xxvii. 17; 35—Mark ii. 27. *Κεφ. t.* (*κεφ.*, *τίτλ.* later), *Am.*, *Eus.*, *lect.* (later), *ἀναγν*, with changes by different hands.

417. Ven. Marc. i. 25, Nan. 18 [xii–xiv], $9\frac{1}{8} \times 5\frac{7}{8}$, ff. 112 (27, 26), begins Matt. v. 44, ends Luke vi. 9. Κεφ., τίτλ., *Am.*, *Eus.*, *lect.* (later), *subscr.*

418. Ven. Marc. i. 28, Nan. 21 [xv], *chart.*, $8\frac{3}{4} \times 6\frac{1}{4}$, ff. 110 (17), 2 cols., contains SS. Matthew and Mark, down to ch. xiii. 32, unfinished, in two columns. Κεφ. *t.* with *harm.*, κεφ., τίτλ., *Am.* (not *Eus.*), *lect.*, many red crosses for stops.

419. Ven. Marc. i. 60, formerly at St. Michael's, Venice, 'prope Murianum,' 241 [xi or xii], $7\frac{5}{8} \times 6$, ff. 260 (22), ends John xxi. 7 (described by J. B. Mittarelli, Venice, 1779). *Mut.* John viii. 44—xi. 32, supplied by a later hand. Κεφ. *t.*, τίτλ., κεφ., *Am.* (not *Eus.*), *lect.*, with red musical notes.

420. Messanensis Univ. 18 (Schulz's 237) [xiv], $6\frac{7}{8} \times 4\frac{7}{8}$, ff. 127 (22), *Carp.*, *Eus. t.*, *prol.* (πρόγραμμα), κεφ. *t.*, κεφ., τίτλ. with *harm.*, also *harm.* at bottom of the page, *Am.*, *Eus.*, *subscr.*, στίχ., *vers.*, *pict.*, by different hands, with readings from other copies (inspected by Munter, as was Cod. 421).

421. (Act. 176, Paul. 218.) Syracusanus (Schulz's 238) [xii]?, once Landolini's; *prol.*, *Eus. t.* Dr. Gregory could not find it.

422. Monacensis Reg. 210, at Munich [xi or later], $9\frac{1}{4} \times 6\frac{1}{2}$, ff. 256 (28), 2 cols., *Carp.*, *prol.*, κεφ. *t.*, τίτλ., κεφ., *Am.*, *Eus.* (partially), *lect.* (later), *subscr.*, στίχ., *syn.*, *men.*, roughly written in two columns by the monk Joseph, but St. John in a somewhat more recent hand; described by Ignatius Hardt and Dean Burgon. It abounds with itacisms and strange blunders, and other tokens of great ignorance on the part of the scribe.

423. Mon. Reg. 36 [1556], *chart.*, $13\frac{3}{8} \times 9\frac{1}{4}$, ff. 465 (30), contains St. Matthew with Nicetas' catena. Marked Τόμος A and superbly bound, as in Cod. 432 The same scribe wrote Codd. 424, 425, 432 (Burgon).

424. Mon. Reg. 83 [xvi], *chart.*, $13\frac{3}{8} \times 8\frac{3}{4}$, ff. 399, contains St. Luke with the commentary of Titus of Bostra and others.

425. Mon. Reg. 37 [xvi] *chart.*, $13\frac{3}{8} \times 9\frac{1}{4}$, ff. 576 (30), second volume of 423, contains St. John with a very full catena of Nicetas. Marked Τόμος B.

426. Mon. Reg. 473, once Augsburg 9 [xiv], $9\frac{3}{4} \times 6\frac{3}{4}$, *chart.*, ff. 208 (26), κεφ. *t.*, contains Luke vi. 17—xi. 26 with Nicetas' catena, the second of four volumes (δεύτερον τῶν τεσσάρων τεῦχος τῶν εἰς τὸ κατὰ Λουκᾶν ἅγιον εὐαγγέλιον κατὰ συναγωγὴν ἐξηγήσεων).

427. Mon. Reg. 465, Augsburg 10 [xii or xiii], $10\frac{5}{8} \times 8\frac{1}{8}$, ff. 140 (34), *Am.*, *lect.* (ῥήμ., στίχ. Luke), written by one Maurus, contains SS. Luke and Mark with Theophylact's (and Victor's ?) commentary.

428. Mon. Reg. 381, Augsburg 11 [xiii], $12\frac{5}{8} \times 9\frac{1}{4}$, *chart.*, ff. 335 (33), with rude pictures of the Evangelists on a vellum leaf. Its subscriptions are like those of Evann. Λ, 262, &c. The commentary is Theophylact's.

429. Mon. Reg. 208 [xii or xiii], a superb 4to, $10\frac{7}{8} \times 9\frac{5}{8}$, ff. 234 (35),

2 cols., written by John, a priest and 'ἔκδικος magnae ecclesiae,' contains Luke i. 1—ii. 39 with a catena, questions and answers from SS. Matthew and John, with the text. Burgon declares that the date June 20, A.D. 978, Indiction 6, which we took from Scholz (*see* above, p. 41, note 2), is that of the manuscript this was copied from, not of Cod. 429 itself. In that case we have another early dated cursive the less. Gregory, Prolegomena, p. 449, inclines to the placing of this MS. amongst the uncials.

430. Mon. Reg. 437 [xi], $11\frac{5}{8} \times 8\frac{5}{8}$, ff. 354 (24), contains John i–viii with the catena of Nicetas, metropolitan of Heraclia Serrarum in Macedonia, now *Xevosna.* Martin Crusius of Tübingen procured it from Leontius, a Cyprian monk, in 1590, and sent it to the Library at Augsburg.

431. (Act. 180, Paul. 238.) Molsheimensis [xii], *Eus. t.*, *prol.* with many unusual readings, was brought to Strasburg from the Jesuits' College at Molsheim in Alsace. Extracts were made from it by the Jesuit Hermann Goldhagen (N. T. Mogunt. 1753), and it was collated by Arendt, 1833. 'Periit a. 1870,' Gregory.

432. Mon. Reg. 99 [xvi], *chart.*, $13\frac{1}{2} \times 8\frac{7}{8}$, ff. 572 (30), contains St. Mark with the commentary of Victor of Antioch, being the same copy as Peltanus used for his Latin edition of that work, Ingolstad, 1580.

433. Berolinensis Reg. MS. 4to, 12 (kn) (Schulz's 239) [xi or xii], $8 \times 5\frac{3}{4}$, ff. 80 (24), *κεφ. t.*, *κεφ.*, *τίτλ.*, *Am.*, *Eus.*, *lect.*, brought from the East by W. Ern. de Knobelsdorf, with a mixed text and many errors in very minute letters. It contains Matt. i. 1–21; vi. 12–32; xxii. 25—xxviii. 20; Mark i. 1—v. 29; ix. 21—xiii. 12; Luke viii. 27—John ix. 21; xx. 15—xxi. 25. (G. T. Pappelbaum, 1824.)

434. Vindobon. Caes. 71, formerly 42 [xiv], $11\frac{3}{4} \times 7\frac{3}{4}$, ff. 424 (29), contains St. Luke with a catena. Like Codd. 218, &c., bought at Constantinople by De Busbeck.

435. Lugd.-Bat. Bibl. Univ. Gronovii 137 (Schulz's 245) [x], $8\frac{5}{8} \times 6\frac{1}{8}$, ff. 284 (24), *pict.* *Mut.* Matt. i. 20—ii. 13; xxii. 4–9 (John x. 14—xxi. 25 in a rather later hand). It has a somewhat unusual text (collated, as was also Evan. 122, by J. Dermout, Collectanea Critica in N. T., 1825).

436. Meerman. 117 [A.D. 1322], ff. 277. Dr. Gregory has traced this MS. to No. 54 in the library of the Jesuit College at Clermont, then to Meerman, then to Payne a London bookseller, who bought it in 1824. It is not known now. For the MS. once in Dean Burgon's possession but in the Bodleian Library, *see* Evan. 562.

437. Petropol. Caes. [xi], like Cod. E of the Pauline Epistles, one leaf of the Colbert Pentateuch, and some other manuscripts, has found its way from the Coislin library and the Abbey of St. Germain des Prés near Paris, to St. Petersburg. It was written by Michael Cerularius, Patriarch of Constantinople, and noticed by Matthaei (N. T. iii. p. 99, 2nd ed.). Not in Muralt's List.

438. Brit. Mus. Addit. 5111, 5112 (Askew 621) [A. D. 1189], 10 × 7, ff. 211 and 241 (18), *Carp.*, *Eus. t.*, *κεφ. t.*, *pict.*, *κεφ.*, *τίτλ.*, *Am.*, *Eus.* (no *subscr.*). It was written by Gregory a monk, and is in two volumes, containing severally Matt. and Mark, Luke and John.

439. Brit. Mus. Addit. 5107 (Askew 622) [dated April, 1159, Ind. 7], $12\frac{1}{4} \times 9\frac{1}{2}$, ff. 219 (23), 2 cols., written by the monk Nepho, at Athos, *Carp.*, *Eus. t.*, *κεφ. t.*, *pict.*, *τίτλ.*, *κεφ.*, *Am.*, *Eus.* (Bloomfield).

440. (Act. 111, Paul. 221.) Camb. Univ. Libr. Mm. vi. 9 [xii], $7 \times 5\frac{1}{2}$, ff. 288 (28), *Eus. t.*, *κεφ.*, *τίτλ.*, *lect.*, *Am.*, *syn.* (later); *prol.* (Cath. and Paul.), *subscr.* (Paul.). From this copy Griesbach's readings in Cod. 236 were derived. Described below under Scrivener's v before Evan. 507.

441, 442, at Cambridge, must be removed from Scholz's list; they are *printed* editions with manuscript notes. Cod. 441 is Act. 110, Paul. 222; Cod. 442 is Act. 152, Paul. 223.

443. Camb. Univ. Libr. Nn. ii. 36, once Askew 624 [xii], $11 \times 8\frac{1}{4}$, ff. 235 (24), 2 cols, *Carp.*, *Eus. t.*, *κεφ. t.*, *τίτλ.*, *Am.*, *Eus.*, some *lect.* (later), *syn.*, *men.*, *prol.* The *κεφάλαια* proper are subdivided in this copy, e.g. the 19th of St. Matthew, into no less than thirteen parts (*see* p. 64, note 2). For the titles of the Gospels, *see* Evan. 69. Evan. 443 was bought for the University Library in 1775 for £20, at the celebrated book-sale of Anthony Askew [1722–74], the learned physician who projected an edition of Aeschylus. See Marsh on Michaelis, vol. ii. pp. 661–2.

444. (Act. 153, Paul. 240.) Brit. Mus. Harl. 5796 [xv], $10\frac{1}{4} \times 7\frac{1}{2}$, ff. 324 (26–29), *κεφ. t.*, *τίτλ.*, *lect.*, *ἀναγν.*, *subscr.*, *στίχ.*, *syn.*, *men.*, neatly written, sold in 1537 'aspris 500:[1]' bought at Smyrna in 1722 by Bernard Mould.

445. Brit. Mus. Harl. 5736 [A.D. 1506], *chart.*, $8\frac{1}{4} \times 6$, ff. 194 (24), *κεφ.*, *τίτλ.*, *Am.*, *lect.*, in the hand 'Antonii cujusdam eparchi,' once (like Apoc. 31) in the Jesuits' College, Agen, on the Garonne.

446. Brit. Mus. Harl. 5777 [xv], 9 × 6, ff. 228 or 231 (25), *κεφ.*, *τίτλ.*, *Am.*, *lect.*, *κεφ. t.* (not Matt.), *subscr.* (Luke), *syn.*, *men.* *Mut.* Matt. i. 1–17; Mark i. 7–9; Luke i. 1–18; John i. 1–22, by a person who mischievously cut out the ornaments. It is clearly but unskilfully written, and Covell states on the outer leaf that it seems a copy from his manuscript, noted above as Evan. 65. This codex is Cov. 5 (Bloomfield).

447. Brit. Mus. Harl. 5784 [xv], $7\frac{1}{4} \times 5\frac{3}{4}$, ff. 329 (21), *Eus. t.*, *prol.*, *κεφ. t.*, *orn.*, *κεφ.*, *τίτλ.*, *lect.*, *subscr.*, *στίχ.*, *prol.* (Paul.); well written, and much like

448. Brit. Mus. Harl. 5790 [dated Rome, April 25, 1478], $12\frac{1}{4} \times 8\frac{1}{2}$, ff. 299 (22), *κεφ. t.*, *pict.*, *κεφ.*, *τίτλ.* in margin, *subscr.*, beautifully written by John Rhosus of Crete a priest for Francis Gonzaga Cardinal of S. Maria Nuova: belonged to Giovanni Pietro Arrivabene.

449. Brit. Mus. Addit. 4950–1 [xiii], $5 \times 3\frac{1}{2}$, 2 vols., ff. 146 and 171,

[1] The asper or asprum was a mediaeval Greek silver coin (derived from ἄσπρος, *albus*); we may infer its value from a passage cited by Ducange from Vincentius Bellovac. xxx. 75 'quindecim drachmas seu asperos.'

(23), *prol.*, *κεφ. t.*, *pict.*, *κεφ.*, *τίτλ.*, *lect.*, *Am.*, *Eus.*, *men.*, *syn.*, clearly and carefully written; once Caesar de Missy's (*see* Evan. 44).

Out of this whole mass of 190 manuscripts, Scholz collated five entire (262, 299, 300, 301, 346), eleven in the greater part (260, 270, 271, 277, 284, 285, 298, 324, 353, 382, 428), many in a few places, and not a few seem to have been left by him untouched. His list of Oriental manuscripts (Evann. 450–469), as it is given in the first volume of his Greek Testament (Proleg. pp. xcvi–xcvii)[1], has been withdrawn from the catalogue of cursive copies of the Gospels, in deference to the wish of the Dean of Chichester (Letter iii addressed to myself in the *Guardian* newspaper, July 5, 1882). It must be confessed indeed that Scholz's account of what he had seen in the East about 1823 cannot be easily reconciled with the description of the Rev. H. O. Coxe of the Bodleian Library thirty-five years later ('Report to Her Majesty's Government of the Greek Manuscripts yet remaining in the Libraries of the Levant, 1858'); that most of the books which Scholz catalogued at St. Saba on the Dead Sea were removed before 1875, as Mr. F. W. Pennefather informs us, to the Great Greek Convent of the Cross at Jerusalem; and that at least four of them were brought to Parham in Sussex from St. Saba in 1834 by the late Lord de la Zouche. Instead of Scholz's seven (450–6), Coxe saw fourteen copies of the Gospels at Jerusalem; twenty of the Gospels (besides a noble palimpsest of the Orestes and Phoenissae) at St. Saba after the four had been subtracted, instead of Scholz's ten (457–466); at Patmos five instead of Scholz's three (467–469). In spite of one's respect for the memory of that zealous and worthy labourer, M. A. Scholz, with whom I had a personal conference regarding our common studies in 1845, I cannot help acquiescing in Dean Burgon's decision, though not, perhaps, without some natural reluctance.

[1] 450. Great Gr. Monastery at Jerusalem 1 [July 1, 1043], 8vo, *syn.*, *Eus. t.*, first three Gospels with an Arabic version, neatly written by a reader, Euphemius. This appears to be Coxe's 6, 4to, St. Luke only.

451. Jerusalem 2 [xii], 8vo. 452. Jerusalem 3 [xiv], 8vo.
453. Jerusalem 4 [xiv], 8vo. 454. Jerusalem 5 [xiv], 8vo.
455. Jerusalem 6 [xiv], 4to, with a commentary.
456. Jerusalem 7 [xiii], 4to, St. Matthew with a commentary, neatly written. *Perhaps* Coxe's 43 [xi], in gold *uncial* letters.
457. St. Saba 2 [xiii], 4to, *syn.*, *men.*, is Act. 186, Paul. 234.
458. St. Saba 3 [dated 1272, Indiction 15], 16mo.
459. St. Saba 7 [xii], 8vo. 460. St. Saba 8 [xii], 8vo.
461. *See* Evan. 481.
462. St. Saba 10 [xiv], 4to, is also Act. 187, Paul. 235, Apoc. 86.
463. St. Saba 11 [xiv], 4to, *chart.* 464. St. Saba 12 [xi], 4to.
465. St. Saba 19 [xiii], 8vo.
466. St. Saba 20 [xiii], 8vo, is Act. 189, Paul. 237, Apoc. 86^2 or 89. Also 'from a monastery in the island of Patmos.'
467. [xi], 4to. 468. [xii], 8vo, with a commentary. 469. [xiv], 4to.

CHAPTER VIII.

CURSIVE MANUSCRIPTS OF THE GOSPELS.

Part II.

WE have already intimated that Tischendorf has chosen to make no addition to the numerical list of cursive manuscripts furnished by Scholz, preferring to indicate the fresh materials which have since come to light by another notation, derived from the names of the collators or the places where they are deposited. As this plan has proved in practice very inconvenient, it is no wonder that Dean Burgon, after casting away Scholz's numbers from 450 to 469, on account of their evident inaccuracy, which has since then received definite proof, should have assigned numerals to the cursives unknown to Scholz from 450 to 737, still excluding, as far as was then possible, those whose location or character was uncertain. Burgon's method, as laid down in his Letters in the *Guardian* for July 5, 12, 19, 26, 1882, having the priority of publication, and being arranged with regard to the places where the manuscripts are deposited rather than to their actual collators, may as well be adopted as any other that might be made. The only important point to be secured is that all scholars should employ the SAME NUMBERS when speaking of the SAME MANUSCRIPTS.

It is greatly to be regretted that Dr. C. R. Gregory, even upon advice tendered by other critics, if such was the case, should have neglected the important principle laid down in the preceding sentence, and in Part II of his very valuable Prolegomena to Tischendorf's eighth edition, published seven years after the third edition of this work, should have helped to make confusion worse confounded in this large and increasing field. But it is not my object to assail one who has done this study very great service, but only to point out an inconvenience which I shall endeavour to minimize as far as I can. It is clear that Dr. Scrivener's order, being the first out, and having been followed since then in quotations in books, and notably by the late learned Abbé Martin, cannot be allowed to drop. I have therefore followed it in the succeeding pages. But it has been my object to bring together the two lists as soon as possible after the close of Dr. Scrivener's, and the end of the supplementary lists of Dean Burgon and the Abbé Martin, and to follow, as far as the case will admit, the lead of Dr. Gregory, where he has every right to prescribe the series of numbers. Unfortunately, this course is not always open, because when the time has arrived it is found that some MSS. have been already forestalled, and others are in arrear.

It should be added, that the number of the MSS. as standing in Dr. Gregory's list, where it varies from the present, is given at the end of the account of each manuscript; and reversely a table is added at the end of this volume of the varying numbers in this list which answer to the numbers in Dr. Gregory's list.

We begin with the following twenty Italian manuscripts, added to our previous list of cursive copies of the Gospels by Burgon in Letters addressed to Dr. Scrivener and inserted in the *Guardian* of Jan. 29 and Feb. 5, 1873.

450. Ferrara, Univ. 119, NA. 4 [xiv], 8vo, ff. ?, *κεφ. t.* (Lat. later), *Am.*, *lect.*, *syn.*, *men.* (Lat. *syn.* later). (Greg. 581.)

451. (Act. 194, Paul. 222, Apoc. 102.) Ferr. Univ. 187, 188, NA. 7 [A. D. 1334], $6\frac{3}{4} \times 4\frac{3}{4}$, *chart.*, ff. ?, *capp.* Lat., containing the whole New Testament: the only divisions recognized are those of the modern chapters in vermilion. (Greg. 582.)

452. Parma, Reg. 5 [xi or xii], $13\frac{1}{2} \times 9\frac{1}{2}$, ff. 284 (21), *Carp.*, *Eus. t.*, *argent.*, *κεφ. t.*, *κεφ.*, *τίτλ.*, *Am.*, *Eus.*, *lect.*, *pict.*, *syn.*, *men.*, once belonging to the Bonvisi family, then transferred to the Public Library at Lucca. As superb a copy as any known, the illuminations gorgeous, the first page of the Gospel and other portions in gold, with a 'luxurious prodigality' of miniatures. (Greg. 583.)

453. Parma, Reg. 95 [xi, or older], $7\frac{3}{8} \times 5\frac{1}{8}$, ff. 318. *κεφ. t.*, *κεφ.*, *τίτλ.*, *Am.*, *Eus.*, *lect.*, *subscr.*, very tastefully decorated. *Mut.* Matt. i. 1–20. *Lect.* and marginal corrections by the first hand in vermilion. (Greg. 584.)

454. Modena, Bibl. Estensis ii. A. 1 [xi or xii], a beautiful copy, $7\frac{1}{2} \times 4\frac{1}{2}$, ff. ?, *syn.* at beginning and end, *κεφ. t.*, *κεφ.*, *τίτλ.*, *Am.*, *Eus.*, superb *pict.*, *men.*, with slight marginal corrections of the text. (Greg. 585.)

455. Mod. Bibl. Est. ii. A. 5 [xiv], $6\frac{1}{2} \times 4\frac{7}{8}$, ff. 239 (20), *argent.*, κεφ *t.*, κεφ., *lect.*, ἀναγν., *subscr.*, στίχ., *vers.*, *syn.*, *men.*, small and neat, without *pict.* or illuminations. (Greg. 586.)

Here also is a late copy of Victor of Antioch's commentary on St. Mark.

456. Milan, in the great Ambrosian Library, M. 48 sup., $8\frac{3}{4} \times 7\frac{3}{8}$, ff. 183, *prol.*, *argent.*, κεφ. *t.*, κεφ., τίτλ., *Am.*, *pict.*, beautifully written, *pict.* almost obliterated. *Am.* (not *Eus.*). The last leaf more recent. (Greg. 587.)

457. Milan, Ambros. E. 63 sup. [May, 1321, Indiction 4], $8\frac{1}{2} \times 5\frac{7}{8}$, ff. 221, *Eus. t.*, *prol.*, κεφ. *t.*, κεφ., τίτλ., *Am.*, *Eus.*, *lect.*, ἀναγν., *subscr.*, *pict.* *Mut.* Luke xxiv. 5—John i. 8, and the early part of John v. *Am.* (not *Eus.*), *lect.*, *pict.* (Greg. 588.)

458, 459, 460. For these Dr. Gregory inserts Milan, Ambr. A. 178 sup., Parmae Reg. 15, Rom. Corsin. 41. G. 16, but without explanation. *See* below, Evann. 830, 831, 837.

458. Milan, Ambros. D. 161 inf. [xvi], transcribed from an original in the Vatican, *chart.* St. Mark's Gospel with Victor of Antioch's commentary.

459. Milan, Ambros. D. 282 inf., transcribed by John Sancta Maura, a one-eyed Cyprian, aged 74, June 9, 1612: *chart.*, with a catena.

460. Milan, Ambros. D. 298 inf., transcribed by the same, fol., *chart.* These two codices purport to be commentaries of Peter of Laodicea on St. John and St. Mark respectively: but 'such titles are quite misleading.' *See* Burgon, Letter to *Guardian*, Feb. 5, 1873.

461. (Act. 197, Paul. 223.) Milan, Ambros. Z. 34 sup. [xiii or xiv], *chart.*, $6\frac{1}{2} \times 4\frac{3}{4}$, ff. 295 (31), κεφ. *t.*, κεφ., τίτλ., *Am.*, *syn.*, *men.*, *subscr.*, ῥῆμ., στίχ., *vers.*, with *pict.* on vellum not belonging to it. The order of its contents is Catholic Epp., Pauline Epp., *syn.*, Gospels. (Greg. 592.)

462. Venice, Ven. Marc. i. 58 [xiii], $9\frac{3}{4} \times 7$, ff. 153 (22), κεφ. *t.*, κεφ., τίτλ., *Am.*, *lect.*, wrongly called an Evangelistarium in the Supplementary Catalogue, contains only Mark i. 44—Luke xxiv. 53; John i. 15—xi. 13. (Greg. 593.)

463. Instead of Ven. i. xxxix. 8, 7, or Nan. 27, which appears to be a commentary—Ven. Marc. ii. 7 [xiv], $12\frac{3}{4} \times 9\frac{7}{8}$, ff. 430 (31), κεφ. *t.* (John), κεφ., τίτλ., with Euthymius Zigabenus' commentary. (Greg. 600.)

464. Ven. Marc. i. 59 [xii, Greg. xiii], $6\frac{1}{2} \times 4\frac{7}{8}$, κεφ. *t.*, κεφ., τίτλ. (*lect.*, *subscr.*, στίχ. later), with very remarkable readings. Burgon collated sixteen chapters in the several Gospels. (Greg. 597.)

465. Ven. Marc. i. 57 [xi or xii], $11\frac{5}{8} \times 8\frac{1}{4}$, ff. 228 (29), κεφ. *t.*, κεφ., τίτλ., ends Mark xii. 18, with Theophylact's commentary. (Greg. 596.)

466. Ven. Marc. 494 [xv, Greg. xiii], $16\frac{3}{4} \times 11\frac{1}{4}$, *chart.*, ff. 320 (50), 2 cols., full of various Patristic matter. (Greg. 598.)

467. Ven. Marc. 495 [xv], $16 \times 11\frac{1}{4}$, *chart.*, ff. 437 (42), κεφ. *t.*, κεφ., τίτλ., *Am.*, *lect.*, *vers.*, described by Zanetti, p. 259, with a commentary (Victor's on St. Mark). (Greg. 599.)

We do not include Ven. Marc. i. 61, which is a mere catena on Matt. i—ix, or an unnumbered catena of St. Luke in the same Library, or Ven. M. 1, an uncial copy of the Old Testament [ix?], at the end of which are found *Carp.*, *Eus. t.* of unique fullness, as if the Gospels were to follow.

468. Ven. Marc. 56 [xvi], fol., *chart.*, $11\frac{3}{8} \times 7\frac{7}{8}$, ff. ?, *κεφ. t.* (John), *capp. Lat.*, *Am.*, *lect.*, *syn.*, wrongly set down by Scholz as Evst. 143, contains the Gospels, beginning Matt. v. 44. It was once 'S. Michaelis Venet. prope Muriannum,' and is described in Mittarelli's Catalogue of that Library, p. 1099. (Greg. 595.)

469. Quaritch i. [xi–xii], $10\frac{1}{4} \times 7\frac{1}{2}$, ff. ? (19), *prol.*, *κεφ. t.*, *κεφ.*, *τίτλ.*, *Am.*, *Eus.*, headings. *Mut.* at beginning and at beginning of St. Luke and end of St. John. Beautifully written in gold letters. (E. M., March 18, 1893.)

470. Ven. s. Lazarus 1531 [xiii, Greg. xiv], $10 \times 7\frac{3}{4}$, ff. 234 (?), *κεφ. t.*, *prol.* (John), *lect.*, *ἀναγν.* (later), *subscr.*, *στίχ.*, is a fragment of the Gospels containing Matt. i. 22—Luke xxiii. 15; 33–48. (Greg. 594.)

471. Quaritch ii. [xi], $5\frac{7}{8} \times 4\frac{3}{4}$, ff. ? (25), *Carp.*, *Eus. t.*, *κεφ. t.*, *κεφ.*, *τίτλ.*, *Am.*, *Eus.*, *lect.*, *subscr.*, *στίχ.*, *ἀναγν.* *Mut.* here and there: beautifully written, and otherwise complete. Belonged to the Hon. Frederic North. (E. M., March 18, 1893.)

472. (Act. 235, Paul. 276, Apoc. 103.) Poictiers [xvi], small folio, *chart.*, of the whole New Testament, as described to Burgon by M. Dartige, the librarian there. Two librarians named Cavou successfully robbed the library, and probably sold miniatures and pictures. (H. C. Hoskier.) G. Haenel (Catal. Librorum MSS. Lips. 1830) names this and another of the whole N. T. at Arras [xv], 8vo, but of the latter the librarian, M. Wicquot, knows nothing.

Edward de Muralt, in his N. T. 'ad fidem codicis principis Vaticani,' 1848 (p. 111), inserts a collation of eleven manuscripts (five of the Gospels, one Psalter with hymns, five Lectionaries), chiefly at St. Petersburg. He also describes them in his Preface (pp. lv–lvii), and in the Catalogue of Greek Manuscripts in the Imperial Library there. The copies of the Gospels are—

473. 2pe, 81 Hort (Petrop. vi. 470) [ix–x Hort], $8\frac{1}{8} \times 5\frac{1}{8}$, ff. 405 (18, 19), *Am.*, *Eus. t.*, *pict.*, *κεφ. t.*, *κεφ.*, *τίτλ.* (in silver uncials), *subscr.*, a purple MS. with golden letters, very beautiful, said to have been written by the Empress Theodora. *Mut.* John xi. 26–48; xiii. 2–23. St. Mark of this MS. was edited by J. Belsheim with facsimile in 1885 (Jacob Dybwad, Christiania). Highly valued by some critics. (Greg. 565.)

474. 4pe, Petrop. 98. Formerly Pogodini 472 [xii or xiii], ff. 194 (23, 24), *Eus. t.*, *κεφ. t.*, *Am.*, *Eus.*, *lect.*, *pict.* (Greg. 571.)

475. 7pe, Petrop. ix. 3. 471 [A.D. 1062], $9\frac{7}{8} \times 7\frac{1}{8}$, ff. 357 (12), *Eus. t.*, *κεφ. t.*, *κεφ.*, *τίτλ.*, *στίχ.*, *pict.*, *lect.*, *syn.*, *men.*, with Victor's Commentary on St. Mark. (Greg. 569.)

476. 8pe, Petrop. Muralt. 105 [xii or xiii], $7 \times 4\frac{7}{8}$, ff. 225 (27), *κεφ. t.*, *pict.* Brought by Titoff from Turkey.

477. 11pe, Petrop. 118 (Q. v. 1, 15) [xv], 7 × 5⅝, ff. 384, *Eus. t.*, *pict.*, *syn.*, *men.*, written for Demetrius Palaeologus.

478[1]. tisch.[1] Leipzig, Univ. Libr. Tisch. iv. [x], 6¾ × 5¼, ff. 360 (21), *Carp.*, *Eus. t.*, *prol.*, *κεφ.*, *Am.*, *Eus.*, *lect.*, *men.*, *subscr.*, *vers.* Brought by Tischendorf from the East (Tisch., Anecdota sacra et profana, pp. 20–29). (Greg. 564.)

479. tisch.[2] Petrop. Muralt. 97 [xii], 7⅞ × 6⅛, ff. 191. *Mut.* Matt. i. 1–16; 30; John xvi. 20—xx. 25. (Tisch., Notitia Cod. Sinait., p. 60.) (Greg. 570.)

480. tisch.[3] Petrop. Muralt. 99 [xii], 7⅜ × 4⅞, ff. 19 (12), Matt. viii. 3—ix. 50. (Tisch., Notitia Cod. Sinait., p. 64.) (Greg. 572.)

481. Petrop. (Scholz's 461, St. Saba 9) [May 7, 835, Indiction 13], 6⅛ × 3⅞, ff. 344 (19), *κεφ.*, *τίτλ.*, *lect.* The date, being the earliest known of a Greek N. T. MS., is plainly visible in a photographed facsimile in 'Exempla Codicum Graecorum literis minusculis scriptorum' (fol., Heidelberg, 1878), Tab. 1, by Wattenbach and von Velsen. This precious treasure was the property of Porphyry Uspensky, Bp. of Kiew, but is now at St. Petersburg. (*See* Greg. 461.)

The five following are in the Bodleian Library, and for the most part uncollated:—

482. Oxf. Bodl. Cromwell 15 [xi], 8½ × 6¼, ff. 216 (24), exquisitely written, with textual corrections in the margin. *Carp.*, *Eus. t.*, *prol.*, *κεφ. t.*, *τίτλ.*, *κεφ.*, *Am.*, *Eus.*, *lect.* (few in later hand). *Mut.* Mark xvi. 17 (ταῦτα)–end; John xix. 29–end. This copy and the next in order came in 1727 from Παντοκράτωρ on Athos. (Greg. 527.)

483. Oxf. Bodl. Crom. 16 [xi], 8 × 6, ff. 354 (20), fairly written. The Gospels are followed by the Proper Lessons for the Holy Week. *Pict.*, *Carp.*, *Eus. t.*, *κεφ. t.*, *Am.*, *Eus.*, *syn.* (later), ἀρχαί and τέλη. Collated in 1749 by Th. Mangey, Prebendary of Durham, the editor of Philo [1684–1755]. 'It is well worth proper examination' (E. B. Nicholson, Bodley's Librarian). (Greg. 528.)

484. Oxf. Bodl. Misc. Gr. 17, Auct. D. Infra 2, 21 [xi], 5½ × 4, ff. 363 (20), *prol.*, *κεφ. t.*, *κεφ.*, *τίτλ.*, *Am.*, *lect.*, *subscr.*, *syn.*, *men.*, in text said to resemble Cod. 71, once Humphrey Wanley's [1672–1726], bought in 1776 by Sam. Smalbroke, fifty-four years Canon Residentiary of Lichfield, was presented by him on his eightieth birthday, June 4, 1800. (Greg. 529.)

485. Oxf. Bodl. Misc. Gr. 141, Rawl. G. 3 [xi], 6 × 4¼, ff. 303 (20), with some foreign matter, has *κεφ. t.*, *κεφ.*, *τίτλ.*, *Am.*, a few *Eus.*, ἀρχαί and τέλη, *subscr.* *Mut.* John xxi. 3–24. (Greg. 430.)

486. Oxf. Bodl. Misc. Gr. 293, Auct. T. V. 34 [xii or xiii], 7¼ × 5¼, ff. 213 (27), *orn.*, *τίτλ.*, *κεφ.*, *lect.*, *Am.*, *subscr.* (except in Luke), ἀναγν., στίχ., *κεφ. t.* (Luke). Of a very unusual style. (Greg. 706.)

To this list we must add the five following copies from the collection

[1] The Psalter 5pe (Petrop. ix. 1) [994], containing the hymns, Luke i. 46–55; 68–79; ii. 29–32, is like our Evan. 612, which see.

of the Abbot M. Aloy. Canonici, purchased at Venice in 1817 for the Bodleian Library by Dr. Bandinel, who secured 2045 out of the total number of 3550 manuscripts.

487. Oxf. Bodl. Canon. Gr. 33. Part of Evan. 288, which see.

488. Oxf. Bodl. Canon. Gr. 34 (Act. 211, Paul. 249, Apoc. 98) [A.D. 1515, 1516], 9 × 6¼, *chart.*, ff. 319 (25), *capp. Lat.*, written by Michael Damascenus the Cretan for John Francis Picus of Mirandola, contains the whole N. T., the Apocalypse alone being yet collated (k[scr]): *mut.* Apoc. ii. 11–23. It has Œcumenius' and Euthalius' *prol.* (Greg. 522.)

489. Oxf. Bodl. Canon. Gr. 36 [xi], 10 × 7½, ff. 270 (22), κεφ. *t.*, *syn.*, *men.*, *pict.*, τίτλ., κεφ., *Am.*, *Eus.*, *lect.*, ἀναγν., Gospels: olim Georg. Phlebaris. (Greg. 523.)

490. Oxf. Bodl. Canon. Gr. 112 [xii], 5½ × 4½, ff. 186 (21 &c.), *pict.*, *Carp.*, κεφ. *t.*, κεφ., τίτλ., *Am.*, *Eus.*, *lect.*, *syn.*, *men.*, Gospels well written. (Greg. 524.)

491. Oxf. Bodl. Canon. Gr. 122 Cod. Sclavonicus [A.D. 1429], 12½ × 9, ff. 312 (20), 2 cols., *pict.*, *prol.*, *syn.*, *men.*, κεφ. *t.*, κεφ., τίτλ., *lect.*, *subscr.*, στίχ., Gospels in Sclavonian with a Greek version later, written in Moldavia by Gabriel, a monk. (Greg. 525.)

*492. Oxf. Ch. Ch. Wake[1] 12 (Act. 193, Paul. 277, Apoc. 26) Cod. Dionysii (who wrote it) [xi], 12 × 9½, ff. 240 (36), 2 cols., was also noted by Scholz, on Gaisford's information, Evangelistarium 181, Apostol. 57: but this is an error, as the Gospels are contained at full length and in their proper order, with unusually full liturgical matter, *pict.*, *Carp.*, *Eus. t.*, *prol.*, κεφ. *t.*, κεφ., τίτλ., *Am.*, *Eus.*, *lect.*, στίχ., ἀναγν., *vers.* (*syn.*, *men.* with synopsis). The Acts, Catholic and Pauline Epistles (Œcumenius' *prol.*, κεφ., scholia) follow them, and last of all comes the Apocalypse. *Mut.* Luke xvi. 26–30; xvii. 5–8; xxiv. 22–24; John i. 1—vii. 39; viii. 31—ix. 11; x. 10—xi. 54; xii. 36—xiii. 27; Acts i. 1—vii. 49; x. 19—xiv. 10; xv. 15—xvi. 11; xviii. 1—xxi. 25; xxiii. 18—James iii. 17; 1 Cor. xii. 11—xv. 12; xvi. 13–15; 2 Cor. xiii. 4, 5; Gal. v. 16—vi. 18 (partly); 2 Tim. iii. 10, 11; Tit. iii. 5–7; the illuminations also being often wantonly cut out. This copy contains much foreign matter besides; its contents were carefully tabulated by J. Walker; it was thoroughly collated by Scrivener in 1864. (Greg. 606.)

493. Oxf. Ch. Ch. Wake 21 [xi], 11 × 8¼, ff. 221 (26), 2 cols., *Carp.* (later), *Eus. t.*, *prol.* (later), κεφ. *t.*, τίτλ., κεφ., *lect.* (partly later), ῥήμ., στίχ., *syn.*, brought from Παντοκράτωρ on Athos, 1727. The scribe's name, Abraham Teudatus, a Patrician (Montfaucon, Palaeo. Gr., p. 46), is written cruciform after *Eus. t.* (Greg. 507.)

494. Oxf. Ch. Ch. Wake 22 [xiii], 10 × 8, ff. 160 (24, 27), κεφ. *t.*,

[1] In addition to Evann. 73, 74, Gaisford in 1837 catalogued, and Scrivener in 1861 inspected, these fourteen copies of the Gospels in the collection of Archbishop Wake, now at Christ Church, Oxford. They were brought from Constantinople about 1731, and have now been described in the Rev. G. W. Kitchin's Catalogue of the Manuscripts in Christ Church Library (4to, 1867).

τίτλ., *κεφ.*, *lect.*, *subscr.*, *ἀναγν.*, in a wretched hand and bad condition, begins Matt. i. 23, ends John xix. 31. Also *mut.* Matt. v. 26—vi. 23; Luke xxiv. 9–28; John iii. 14—iv. 1; xv. 9—xvi. 6. (Greg. 508.)

495. Oxf. Ch. Ch. Wake 24 [xi], 11¾ × 8¾, ff. 229 (24), from Παντοκράτωρ in 1727. *Eus. t.*, *prol.*, *κεφ. t.*, *pict.*, *τίτλ.*, *κεφ.*, *Am.*, *Eus.* in gold. One leaf (John xix. 13–29), and another containing John xxi. 24, 25, are in duplicate at the beginning, *primâ manu.* (Greg. 509.) This copy (as Wake remarks) is in the same style, but less free than

496. Oxf. Ch. Ch. Wake 25 [x or xi], 10⅝ × 8¼, ff. 292 (22), *κεφ. t.*, *pict.*, *κεφ.*, *lect.*, *τίτλ.*, some *Eus.*, *ἀναγν.*, *subscr.*, *στίχ.*, *syn.*, *men.*, *pict.* (in red ink, nearly faded). (Greg. 510.)

497. Oxf. Ch. Ch. Wake. 27, *chart.* [xiii], 9½ × 6¼, ff. 337 (20), *pict.* (Matt.), *κεφ.*, *τίτλ.*, *lect.*, *κεφ. t.*, *prol.* (Luke), *subscr.* (Mark). *Mut.* at beginning. Matt. xviii. 9—Mark xiv. 13; Luke vii. 4—John xxi. 13 are [xiii], the rest supplied [xv]. (Greg. 511.)

498. Oxf. Ch. Ch. Wake 28 [xiii], 9 × 6¾, ff. 210 (24), *κεφ. t.*, some *τίτλ.*, *κεφ.*, *syn.*, *men.*, *lect.*, much of this *rubro*, *vers.*, *subscr.*, *στίχ.*, *ἀναγν.* Subscribed θῦ το δωρον και γρηγοριου πονος. (Greg. 512.)

499. Oxf. Ch. Ch. Wake 29 [ϛχ[1]λθ or A.D. 1131, Indict. 9], 7¾ × 6¼, ff. 162–4, *chart.* in later hand (25), *κεφ. t.*, *κεφ.*, *τίτλ.*, *Am.*, *Eus.*, *lect.*, *vers.*, *subscr.*, *στίχ.* After some later fragments (Matt. i. 12—v. 3, and other matter) on paper, the older copy begins Matt. v. 29. (Greg. 513.)

500. Oxf. Ch. Ch. Wake 30 [xii], 7½ × 5½, ff. 226 (23), *Eus. t.*, *prol.*, *κεφ. t.* (almost illegible), *κεφ.*, *τίτλ.*, *lect.* in red, almost obliterated from damp; ending John xx. 18, neatly written, but in ill condition. (Greg. 514.)

501. Oxf. Ch. Ch. Wake 31 [xi], 7 × 5½, ff. 127 (34), small, in a very elegant and minute hand. *Pict.*, *κεφ. t.*, some *τίτλ.* (in gold), *κεφ.*, *Am.*, (no *Eus.*), *lect.* full, some *στίχ.*, *mut.* (Greg. 515.)

502. Oxf. Ch. Ch. Wake 32 [x or xi], 7¼ × 5½, ff. 287 (23), small, elegant, and with much gold ornament. *Pict.*, *κεφ. t.*, *κεφ.*, some *τίτλ.*, *Am.*, *lect.*, some *στίχ.* *Mut.* in places. (Greg. 516.)

*503 (Act. 190, Paul. 244, Apoc. 27.) Oxf. Ch. Ch. Wake 34 [xi or xii], 10 × 8, ff. 201 (31, 29). This remarkable copy begins with the *ὑπόθεσις* to 2 Peter, the second leaf contains Acts xvii. 24—xviii. 13 misplaced, then follow the five later Catholic Epistles (*mut.* 1 John iii. 19—iv. 9) with *ὑποθέσεις*: then the Apocalypse on the same page as Jude ends, and the *ὑπόθεσις* to the Romans on the same page as the Apocalypse ends, and then the Pauline Epistles (*mut.* Heb. vii. 26—ix. 28). All the Epistles have *prol.*, *κεφ. t.*, and Œcumenius' smaller (not the Euthalian) *κεφ.*, with much *lect.* *primâ manu*, and *syn.* later. Last, but seemingly misplaced by an early binder, follow the Gospels, *κεφ. t.*, *κεφ.*, *τίτλ.*, *Am.*, *lect.*, *subscr.* *Mut.* Mark xvi. 2–17; Luke ii. 15–47; vi. 42—John xxi. 25, and in other places. This copy is Scholz's Act. 190, Paul.

[1] The letter χ is quite illegible, but the Indiction 9 belongs only to A.D. 831, 1131, 1431, while the style of the manuscript leaves no doubt which to choose.

244, Apoc. 27, but unnumbered in the Gospels. Collated fully by Scrivener in 1863. (Greg. 517.)

504. Oxf. Ch. Ch. Wake 36 [xii], 6 × 5, ff. 249–6 *chart.* (23), κεφ. *t.*, κεφ., τίτλ., *Am.*, *lect.*, *prol.* (Luke), *pict.* (Luke, John), *syn.*, *men.* (Greg. 518.)

505. Oxf. Ch. Ch. Wake 39 [xiii], 5¼ × 4¼, ff. 308 (17 &c.), κεφ., some τίτλ., a poor copy, in several hands. (Greg. 567.)

506. Oxf. Ch. Ch. Wake. 40 [xii], 4½ × 3⅜, ff. 218 (22, 23), a beautiful little copy. *Syn.*, *men.*, κεφ. *t.*, *lect.* in the faintest red, but no other divisions. (Greg. 520.)[1]

F. H. A. Scrivener has published the following in his 'Collation of Greek Manuscripts of the Holy Gospels, 1853,' and 'Codex Augiensis' (Appendix), 1859.

*v^{scr}, or cant^{scr}. of Tischendorf. *See* Evan. 440 (Act. 111, Paul. 221 of Scholz; Evan. 236, Act. and Paul. 61 of Griesbach; Act. and Paul. o^{scr}), in a minute hand, with many unusual readings, especially in the Epistles, from Bp. Moore's Library. *Men.* 'Υποθέσεις Oecumenii to the Catholic and first eight Pauline Epistles: beautifully written with many contractions. This is Bentley's o (*see* Evan. 51).

*507. w^{scr}. (Act. 224, Paul. 260.) Camb. Trin. Coll. B. x. 16 [dated A.D. 1316], *chart.*, 7¼ × 5, ff. 363 (28, 29), was inelegantly written by a monk James on Mount Sinai. *Prol.*, κεφ. *t.*, *Am.*, *Eus.*, κεφ., *lect.*, *subscr.*, ἀναγν., *vers.*, *syn.*, *men.*; also ὑποθέσεις, *lect.*, *syn.*, *men.* to Epistles; and much extraneous matter[2]. *See* Evan. 570. This is Bentley's τ (Evan. 51), and, like i^{scr} which follows, came to him from Παντοκράτωρ. Hort makes it his Cod. 102. (Greg. 489.)

*508. i^{scr}. Camb. Trin. Coll. B. x. 17 [xiii], 8½ × 6, ff. 317 (20), from

[1] Of these manuscripts Thomas Mangey (Evan. 483) states on the fly-leaves that he collated Nos. 12, 25, 28, 34 in 1749. Caspar Wetstein collated the Apocalypse in Nos. 12 and 34 for his relative's great edition; while in the margin of No. 35, a 4to Greek Testament printed at Geneva (1620), is inserted a most laborious collation (preceded by a full description) of eight of the Wake manuscripts with ~~Wetstein's~~ N. T. of 1711, having this title prefixed to them, 'Hae Variae lectiones ex MSS. notatae sunt manu et opera Johannis Walkeri, A. 1732.' John Walker, most of whose labours seem never yet to have been used, although they were known to Berriman in 1741 (Critical Dissertation on 1 Tim. iii. 16, pp. 102–4), was Fellow of Trinity College, Cambridge, where so many of his critical materials accumulated for the illustrious Bentley are deposited. Walker d. 1741, Archdeacon of Hereford, after Bentley's will, six months before him. The codd. in Trinity College were bought from Bentley's heirs (not from Richard Bentley) when Wordsworth was Master (1820–41), and so were not in Bentley's hands when Walker died. Old Latin Biblical Texts, xxiv–vi. Of his eight codices, we find on investigation that Walker's C is Wake 26; Walker's 1 is Wake 20 (collations of these two, sent by Walker to Wetstein, comprise Codd. 73, 74, described above); Walker's B is Wake 21; Walker's D is Wake 24, both of Gospels; Walker's E is Wake 18, his H is Wake 19, both Evangelistaria; Walker's q is Wake 12, of which Caspar Wetstein afterwards examined the Apocalypse (Cod. 26); Walker's W is Wake 38 of the Acts and Epistles, or Scholz's Act. 191, Paul. 245.

[2] Bentley specifies 'argumenta inedita Cosmae Indicopleustae in 4 Evangelia, et versus iambici fortasse Jacobi Calligraphi: argumenta incerti ad Actus: prologus ineditus et argumenta Oecumenii ad Epistolas omnes.'

Athos, bequeathed to Trinity College by Bentley. Κεφ. *t.*, τίτλ., κεφ., *Am.* (not *Eus.*), *lect.*, and (on paper) are ὑπόθεσις to St. Matthew and *syn.* This is Bentley's δ, who dates it 'annorum 700' [xi], and adds 'nuper in monasterio Pantocratoris in monte Atho, nunc *meus*.' (Greg. 477.)

*j^scr. Evan. N.

*509. a^scr. London, Lambeth 1175 [xi], $11\frac{7}{8} \times 9\frac{3}{4}$, ff. 220, five leaves bound up with it (23–35), 2 cols. (23, 24), 2 cols., κεφ. *t.*, κεφ., τίτλ., *Am.*, *Eus.*, *lect.*, *subscr.* *Mut.* Matt. i. 1–13; once at Constantinople, but brought (together with the next five) from the Greek Archipelago by J. D. Carlyle, Professor of Arabic at Cambridge [d. 1804]. (Greg. 470.)

*510. b^scr. Lond. Lamb. 1176 [xii], $7\frac{3}{4} \times 6$, ff. 209 (24), *Carp.*, *Eus. t.*, *syn.*, *pict.*, κεφ. *t.* (*chart.*), *men.*, τίτλ., κεφ., *subscr.*, *proll.* at end, very elegant. A copy 'eximiae notae,' but with many corrections by a later hand, and some foreign matter. (Greg. 471.)

*511. c^scr. Lond. Lamb. 1177 [xi–xii], $7\frac{1}{2} \times 5\frac{5}{8}$, ff. 210 (17 &c.), τίτλ., *Am.*, *lect.*, κεφ. *t.* (Luke, John), *subscr.*, στίχ., *syn.*, for valuable readings by far the most important at Lambeth, shamefully ill written, torn and much mutilated[1]. (Greg. 472.)

*512. d^scr. Lond. Lamb. 1178 [xi or xiv], $11\frac{3}{8} \times 9\frac{1}{4}$, ff. 302 (23), *Syn.*, *lect.*, τίτλ., κεφ., *Am.*, *Eus.*, *prol.*, κεφ. *t.*, *orn.*, *subscr.*, *men.*, in a fine hand, splendidly illuminated, and with much curious matter in the subscriptions. *Mut.* Matt. i. 1–8. A noble-looking copy. (Greg. 473.)

*513. e^scr. Lond. Lamb. 1179 [x or later], $8\frac{3}{4} \times 6\frac{3}{4}$, ff. 176 (24), 2 cols., τίτλ., κεφ., *lect.*, *Am.*, *Eus.*, *subscr.*, κεφ. *t.*, neatly written but in wretched condition, beginning Matt. xiii. 53, ending John xiii. 8. Also *mut.* Matt. xvi. 28—xvii. 18; xxiv. 39—xxv. 9; xxvi. 71—xxvii. 14; Mark viii. 32—ix. 9; John xi. 8–30. Carlyle brought it from Trinity Monastery, Chalké. (Greg. 474.)

514. *v*^scr. Constantinople, Library of Patriarch of Jerusalem, restored from Lambeth in 1817, where it was No. 1180 [xiv], ff. 246, *chart.*, τίτλ., *Am.*, *Eus.*, *lect.*, with important variations: collated by Dr. Charles Burney in Mark i. 1—iv. 16; John vii. 53—viii. 11 (Lambeth 1223). (Greg. 488.)

*515. f^scr. Lond. Lamb. 1192 [xiii], $8 \times 6\frac{1}{2}$, ff. 472–6, *chart.* (22), *lect.*, τίτλ., κεφ., *Am.*, *Eus.*, κεφ. *t.*, *pict.*; from Syria, beautifully written, but tampered with by a later hand. *Mut.* John xvi. 8–22, and a later hand [xv] has supplied Mark iii. 6–21; Luke xii. 48—xiii. 2; John xviii. 27—xxi. 25; at the beginning stand some texts, περὶ ἀνεξικακίας. Re-examined by Bloomfield. About Luke xix, xx its readings agree much with those of Evan. Δ, and those of the oldest uncials. (Greg. 475.)

(g^scr is Lamb. 528 and Evan. 71, described above.)

516. u^scr. Constantin. Libr. Patr. of Jerus., C. 4 of Archdeacon Todd's Lambeth Catalogue, was a copy of the Gospels, in the Carlyle

[1] Matt. iv. 1—vii. 6; xx. 21—xxi. 12; Luke iv. 29—v. 1; 17–33; xvi. 24—xvii. 13; xx. 19–41; John vi. 51—viii. 2; xii. 20–40; xiv. 27—xv. 13; xvii. 6—xviii. 2; 37—xix. 14.

collection, restored with six others to the Patriarch of Jerusalem [1]. The collation of SS. Matthew and Mark by the Rev. G. Bennet is at Lambeth (1255, No. 25). (Greg. 487.)

*517. t[scr]. Lond. Lamb. 1350 [xiv], $8\frac{1}{2} \times 5\frac{3}{4}$, ff. 51 (20), St. John on paper, written with a reed, appended to a copy of John Damascene 'De Fide Orthodoxa:' has ὑπόθεσις or *prol.*, κεφ., and a few rubrical directions; carelessly written, and inscribed 'T. Wagstaffe ex dono D. Barthol. Cassano e sacerdotibus ecclesiae Graecae, Oct. 20, 1732.' (Greg. 486.)

518. Lond. Sion College Library, A. 32. 1 (Ev. 1. (3)), [xi], $11 \times 8\frac{3}{8}$, ff. 152 (24), a beautiful fragment, miserably injured by damp and past neglect, consisting of 153 leaves preserved in a box, was given by 'Mr. Edward Payne, a tenant in Sion College, as were also Evst. 227, 228, and perhaps Evst. 229.' The capitals, stops, and τίτλοι are in gold, κεφ., *Am.* (no *Eus.*) in red. Full *lect.*, ἀρχαί and τέλη in red. It begins at Matt. x. 17, ends at John ix. 14. St. Mark's Gospel only has *κεφ. t.* Mark i. 1–13; Luke i. 1–13; John i. 1–17 have been taken away for the sake of the illuminations, and much of the text is illegible. (Greg. 559.)

519. Edinburgh, University Library, A. C. 25 [xi], 8vo, ff. 198, *κεφ. t.*, *κεφ.*, *τίτλ.*, *Am.*, *Eus.*, *lect.*, *subscr.*, *pict.*, in bad condition, presented in 1650 by Sir John Chiesley. (Greg. 563.)

520. Glasgow, Hunterian Museum, V. vii. 2 [xii], 4to, ff. 367, *Carp.*, *Eus. t.*, *κεφ. t.*, *κεφ.*, *τίτλ.*, *Am.*, *Eus.*, *syn.*, *men.*, *pict.* (Greg. 560.)

521. Glasg. Hunt. Mus. Q. 7, 10 [xi], 4to, ff. 291, *prol.*, *κεφ. t.*, *κεφ.*, *τίτλ.*, *Am.*, *subscr.* Both these were once Caesar de Missy's (*see* Evan. 44). (Greg. 561.)

522. Glasg. Hunt. Mus. S. 8, 141 [xv], 4to, ff. 78, *κεφ.*, *Lat.* Codd. 519–22 were first announced by Haenel (*see* under Evan. 472). (Greg. 562.)

523. Lond., Mr. White, formerly Blenheim 3. B. 14 [xiii, Greg. xiv], $7\frac{1}{2} \times 6\frac{1}{4}$, ff. 170 (22), *prol.*, *κεφ. t.*, *κεφ.*, *τίτλ.*, *Am.*, *Eus.*, *lect.*, *ἀναγν.*, *syn.*, *men.*: like Apost. 52, once belonging to the Metropolitan Church of Heraclea on the Propontis, and presented in 1738 to Charles, Duke of Marlborough, *amoris et observantiae ergo* by Thomas Payne, Archdeacon of Brecon, once our Chaplain at Constantinople: a bright, clean copy, written in very black ink, with vermilion ornamentation, and barbarous *pict.* (Greg. 701.)

Mr. Bradshaw indicated in the 'Transactions of the Royal Society of Literature,' vol. ii. p. 355, two copies of the Gospels belonging to the Earl of Leicester at Holkham, to be described with facsimiles in the Catalogue of the Library there. They were examined by Dean Burgon, who thus reported of them:—

[1] In Mr. Coxe's 'Report to Her Majesty's Government,' we find an account (which illness compelled him to give at second hand) of several copies of the Gospels and one palimpsest Evangelistarium, all dated [xii], still remaining in this Prelate's Library.

524. Holkham 3 [xiii], $8\frac{3}{4}\times 6\frac{1}{8}$, of 183 leaves, four being misplaced. It is beautifully written in twenty-seven long lines on a page. *Eus. t.*, τίτλ., *Am.* (not *Eus.*), imperfectly given: no *lect.* (κεφ., *subscr.*, *pict.*). Besides five pictures of the Evangelists and gorgeous headings to the Gospels are seventeen representations of Scripture subjects, some damaged. This 'superb MS. of extraordinary interest' in the style of its writing closely resembles Evan. 38. (Greg. 557.)

525. Holkham 4 [xiii or earlier], $8\frac{1}{2}\times 6\frac{1}{3}$, ff. 352 (20), finely written, but quite different in style from Cod. 524. Τίτλ. in gold, *lect.*, ἀρχαί and τέλη in vermilion, κεφ., στίχ. numbered. (Κεφ. *t.*, *Am.*, ἀναγν., *subscr.*, στίχ., *pict.*) (Greg. 558.)

Eight copies of the Gospels, brought together by the late Sir Thomas Phillipps, Bart., at Middle Hill, Worcestershire, are now the property of Mr. Fitzroy Fenwick, and, with the rest of this unrivalled private collection of manuscripts, are now at Thirlestaine House, Cheltenham, where Burgon examined them in 1880, and Hoskier in 1886, who quotes (Cod. 604, App. E), some of the readings. Scrivener had used some of them at Middle Hill in 1856.

526. Phillipps 13,975 [xii], $12\frac{1}{2}\times 9\frac{1}{2}$, ff. 196, once Lord Strangford's 464, a grand copy, the text being surrounded with a commentary (abounding, as usual, in contractions) in very minute letters. That on St. Mark is Victor's. *Pict.* of SS. Mark and Luke, beautiful illuminations for headings of the Gospels. Κεφ., τίτλ., *Am.*, *Eus.* in gold, *pict.* (*syn.*, *men.* at end). (Greg. 556.)

527. Phillipps 1284 (Act. 200, Paul. 281) [xii], $7\frac{2}{3}\times 5\frac{1}{4}$, ff. 344 (28), from the library of Mr. Lammens of Ghent, a rough specimen, contains the Gospels, Acts, and Epistles, the Pauline preceding the Catholic. *Mut.* Matt. ix. 36—x. 22; Mark i. 21–45, and the first page of St. John. The writing varies; that from Acts to 1 Thess. is more delicate, and looks older. No *Am.*, *Eus.* Much *lect.* in vermilion, ἀρχαί and τέλη. Τίτλ., κεφ. *t.*, ἀναγν., *subscr.*, *syn.*, and sparse *men.* (Greg. 676.)

528. Phillipps 2387 [xiii], $6\frac{1}{4}\times 4\frac{1}{2}$, ff. 222 (25), bought of Thorpe for thirty guineas: rough, but interesting. One leaf only of *Eus. t.* Wantonly *mut.* in headings of the Gospels, and in Mark i. 1–19; Luke i. 1–18; John i. 1–23. Κεφ., τίτλ., *Am.* (not *Eus.*), ἀρχαί and τέλη later, *syn.*, *men.* (xvii) at the beginning, and much marginal *lect.* by a modern hand.

529. Phillipps 3886 [xi or xii], $10\frac{1}{2}\times 8\frac{1}{3}$, ff. 326 (20), a beautiful copy, bought (as were Evann. 530, 532, 533) by Payne at Lord Guildford's sale. *Eus. t.*, *Carp.*, *pict.*, κεφ. *t.*, τίτλ., *Am.*, *Eus.* (*lect.*, ἀρχ., τέλη, ἀναγν. later). (Greg. 678.)

530. Phillipps 3887 [xii], $8\frac{1}{4}\times 6$, ff. 240 (25, 26), the first four lines in SS. Matt., Mark, Luke being of gold, with *pict.* of the four Evangelists and nineteen others, *Eus. t.*, *Am.* incomplete and irregular (no *Eus.*). No *lect.*, but marginal critical notes. As in Evan. 64, a line (~) is set over Proper Names of persons in the Genealogies (*see* at end of Evan. 64). (Greg. 679.)

531. (Acts 199, Paul. 231, Apoc. 104.) Phillipps 7682 [xi], $6\frac{5}{8}\times 5$, ff. 190 (41 or 50), 2 cols. (two scribes, Hoskier; several, Greg.), the hands

so minute as to require a magnifying glass, contains the whole New Testament, also from Lord Guildford's (871), being, like Evann. 532 and 583, to be described below, from the Hon. F. North's collection (319). The ink is a dull brown, the ornaments in blue, vermilion, and carmine. *Carp.*, *Eus. t.*, *prol.*, κεφ. *t.*, κεφ. (Gr. and Lat.), τίτλ., *Am.*, few *Eus.*, *lect.*, *subscr.* There are many important corrections in the margin, and 18½ pages from Epiphanius at the end. This copy has every appearance of having been made from a very ancient codex: observe the arrangement of the Beatitudes in Matt. v in single lines, as also the genealogy in Luke iii. (Greg. 680.)

532. Phillipps 7712, North 184 (*see* Evan. 529), [xiii], 7½ × 5½, ff. ?, in a large hand and very black ink, the first page being in gold, with many gold balls for stops. There is much preliminary matter, *Eus. t.* (two sets in different hands), *pict.* (*Carp.*, *prol.* later), κεφ., τίτλ., *Am.*, *lect.* (later), *syn.*, *men.*, *subscr.*, στίχ. The text is corrected throughout by an ancient scribe, in a hand bright, clear, and small. (Greg. 681.)

533. Phillipps 7757 [xi], 6 × 4½, ff. ?, an exquisite little manuscript, with accessories in lake, vermilion, and blue. *See* Evan. 529. *Prol.*, *Carp.*, *Eus. t.*, κεφ. *t.*, κεφ., τίτλ., *Am.*, *Eus.*, *subscr.*, vers.

Haenel is mistaken in supposing that a Greek Evangelistarium is included in this grand and unique collection.

The Parham copies of the New Testament are described in a 'Catalogue of materials for writing, early writings on tablets and stones, rolled and other Manuscripts and Oriental Manuscript books in the library of Robert Curzon (Lord de la Zouche of Harynworth, 1870–73) at Parham,' fol., 1849. This accomplished person collected them in the course of his visits to Eastern Monasteries from 1834 to 1837, and permitted me in 1855 to collate thoroughly three of them, and to inspect the rest. They were all examined by Dean Burgon, to whom his son, the present Lord de la Zouche, had given free access to them. The codices of the Gospels are eight in number.

534. (Act. 215, Paul. 233.) Parham lxxi. 6 [xi], 9 × 6½, ff. 348 (41), contains the Gospels, Acts, and Epistles, the Pauline preceding the Catholic, and was brought in 1837 from Caracalla on Athos. *Prol.*, κεφ. *t.*, τίτλ., *Am.*, *lect.* (ἀρχ. and τέλ.), ἀναγν., *subscr.*, στίχ., *vers.*, *syn.*, *men.* The usual arabesque ornaments are in red. (Greg. 547.)

535. Parh. lxxi. 7 [xi, Greg. x], 6⅓ × 4½, ff. 167 (26), brought from St. Saba in 1834. *Pict.*, κεφ. *t.*, illuminated headings, τίτλ., *Am.* (not *Eus.*). *Mut.* John xvi. 27—xix. 40. There is a musical notation on the first four leaves, and the first nine lines of St. John are in gold. (Greg. 548.)

536. Parh. lxxiii. 8 [xi], 4to, 11 × 9, ff. 198, brought from Xenophon on Athos 1837. The text is surrounded by a commentary, that on St. Mark being Victor's. *Prol.*, κεφ. *t.*, κεφ., τίτλ., *lect.* (ἀρχ. and τέλ.), *subscr.*, *syn.*, *men.* (Greg. 549.)

537. Parh. lxxiv. 9 [xi, Greg. xii], 10¼ × 7¾, ff. 219 (28), brought from Caracalla 1837, in its old black binding. *Carp.*, *prol.* (later), κεφ. *t.*, κεφ., τίτλ., *Am.*, *lect.* (ἀρχ. and τέλ.), *subscr.*, στίχ., *syn.*, *men.* With faded red arabesques (no *pict.*) and lake headings to the Gospels, the

writing being large and spread. There are marginal notes here and there. (Greg. 550.)

538. Parh. lxxv. 10 [xii], 4to, ff. 233 (22, 23), from Caracalla, also in its old black binding. There are rude *pict.* of the four Evangelists, and barbarous headings to the Gospels. Κεφ. *t.*, κεφ., τίτλ., *Am.*, few *Eus.*, *lect.*, *subscr.*, στίχ., *vers.* (*syn.*, *men.* later). The number of *Am.*, κεφ. varies from what is usual. (Greg. 551.)

539. Parh. lxxvi. 11 [xii], 4to, ff. 252 (27), κεφ. *t.* (Luke), κεφ., τίτλ., *Am.*, ἀρχ. and τέλ., brought from St. Saba in 1834. Rough illuminations. It contains some rare and even unique readings. (Greg. 552.)

540. Parh. lxxvii. 12 [xiii], 8½ × 6, ff. 304 (21), brought from St. Saba in 1834. Externally uninteresting, with decorations in faded lake, κεφ. *t.*, κεφ., τίτλ., *subscr.*, στίχ. (Greg. 553.)

541. Parh. lxxviii. 13 [A.D. 1272], 5¾ × 4½, ff. 230 (21). A facsimile is given in the Catalogue. This 'singularly rough little object' was bought at St. Saba in 1834 for ten dollars. Κεφ., τίτλ., *lect.* (Greg. 554.)

*542. l^scr^. (Act. 188, Paul. 258.) Wordsworth [xiii], 4to, ff. 231, was bought in 1837 by Dr. Christopher Wordsworth, Bishop of Lincoln, and bears a stamp 'Bibliotheca Suchtelen' (Russian Ambassador at Stockholm). Κεφ. *t.*, τίτλ., *Am.*, *lect.*, *syn.*, *men.*, *prol.* or ὑποθέσεις are prefixed to the Epistles, and scholia of Chrysostom, &c. set in the margin. (Greg. 479.)

*543. q^scr^. (Act. 187, Paul. 257.) Theodori, from the name of the scribe [A.D. 1295], 8vo, ff. 360, passed from Caesar de Missy into the Duke of Sussex's library: in 1845 it belonged to the late Wm. Pickering, the much-respected bookseller: its present locality is unknown. *Syn.*, *Carp.*, *Eus. t.*, κεφ. *t.*, κεφ., *Am.*, *lect.*, ὑποθέσεις or *prol.*, and *syn.* before Act. and all Epp., Euthalius περὶ χρόνων, *men.* after St. Jude; it has many later changes made in the text. (Greg. 483.)

544. Ashburnham 204 [xiii], 4to, ff. 104, 'a piteous fragment,' brought from Greece by the Earl of Aberdeen, and bought at his sale. It contains only Matt. xxv. 32–5, 40, 41—xxviii. 20; Mark i. 4—xv. 47 (but defective throughout); Luke i. 1—xxiv. 48; John i. 1—ii. 4: about Luke vi a different hand was employed. There is no heading to St. Luke's Gospel, but a blank space is left, so that perhaps the MS. was never finished. Κεφ. *t.*, κεφ., τίτλ., *Am.*, *Eus.* (partially). (Greg. 671.)

The Baroness Burdett-Coutts imported in 1870–2 from Janina in Epirus upwards of one hundred manuscripts, chiefly Greek and theological, among which are sixteen copies of the Gospels or parts of them, three of the Acts, two of the Catholic, and three of St. Paul's Epistles, one of the Apocalypse, sixteen Evangelistaria and five Praxapostoli. Those marked I and II are deposited in the Library of Sir Roger Cholmely's School, Highgate; those marked III are in the Baroness's possession. The copies of the Gospels are—

*545. B.-C. I. 3 [xii], 7⅜ × 5⅝, ff. ? *Mut.* John x. 1—xii. 10; xv. 24—xxi. 25. *Carp.*, *Eus. t.*, κεφ. *t.*, τίτλ., κεφ., *Am.*, *Eus.*, *pict.*, *lect.*, *vers.* (Greg. 532.)

*546. B.-C. I. 4 [xii], 6¾ × 5⅜, ff. ?, a fine copy. *Mut.* Matt. i. 1—ix. 13, with gilded illuminations. *Syn.*, *κεφ. t.*, *τίτλ.*, *Am.* (not *Eus.*), *lect.*, iambic verses. (Greg. 533.)

*547. B.-C. I. 7 [xiii], 6 × 4, ff. 267 (22), *chart.* *Mut.* Luke. i. 26–42; xx. 16—xxi. 24. *Syn.*, *men.*, *pict.*, *κεφ. t.*, *τίτλ.*, *lect.* (not *Am.*, *Eus.*). After the subscription to St. John follow the numerals ξ θ ϙ π. It has on the cover a curious metal tablet adorned with figures and a superscription. (Greg. 534.)

*548. B.-C. I. 9 [xii], 7 × 5, ff. 125 (18), SS. Matthew and Mark only. *Mut.* Matt. xi. 28—xiii. 34; xviii. 13—xxi. 15; 33—xxii. 10; xxiv. 46—xxv. 21; Mark iii. 11—v. 31; ix. 18—xii. 6; 34–44; ends with πανταχοῦ Mark xvi. 20. *Syn.*, *lect.*, *κεφ.*, *τίτλ.*, *Am.*, *Eus.* (Greg. 535.)

*549. B.-C. II. 7 [xii or xiii], 5 × 3, ff. 172 (26–31), a very curious volume in ancient binding with two metal plates on the covers much resembling that of B-C. I. 7, contains the Four Gospels and the Acts, breaking off at ch. xxvi. 24 μαίνῃ παῦλε; the writing being unusually full of abbreviations, and the margin gradually contracting, as if vellum was becoming scarce. The last five pages are in another, though contemporary hand. Seven pages containing Gregory Nazianzen's heroic verses on the Lord's genealogy, and others on His miracles and parables, partly in red, precede *κεφ. t.* to St. Matthew; other such verses of Gregory precede SS. Mark and Luke, and follow St. John, and *κεφ. t.* stand before SS. Luke and John. There are *τίτλ.*, *κεφ.* (no *lect.*; and *Am.*, *Eus.*, only in the open leaf containing Luke xii): in the Gospels there is a *prol.*, and no chapter divisions in the Acts, but a few capitals in red. Pretty illuminations precede each book. (Greg. 536.)

*550. B.-C. II. 13 [xii], 7 × 5, ff. 143 (29), with poor arabesque ornamentation, complete. *Lect.*, a few *τίτλ.* by a later hand, as is also much of *Am.*, *Eus.*, which are only partially inserted. (Greg. 537.)

*551. B.-C. II. 16 [xiii], 6⅞ × 4⅞, ff. ? *Mut.* Matt. i. 1–17; Luke i. 1–17; John i. 1–46. *Lect.*, *κεφ. t.* (defective), *τίτλ.*, *κεφ.*, *Am.*, *Eus.*, *pict.* (Greg. 539.)

*552. B.-C. II. 18 [xii], 6 × 4⅝, ff. ?, very neat. The first leaf forms part of a Lectionary: on the second the Gospels begin with Matt. xiii. 7. *Mut.* John i. 1–15. *Κεφ. t.*, *τίτλ.*, *κεφ.*, *Am.* (not *Eus.*), *men.* at the end, *lect.* in abundance, *pict.* of St. Mark washed out: arabesques at the head of each book. (Greg. 538.)

*553 & *554. B.-C. II. 26[1] and 26[2] are two fragments of the Gospels, whereof 26[1] comprises 27 leaves of St. Mark (19–21), covered with vile modern scribbling (ch. iii. 21—iv. 13; 37—vii. 29; viii. 15–27; ix. 9—x. 5; 29—xii. 32) [xiii], 7½ × 5½, neat, with *τίτλ.*, *Am.*, *Eus.*, *lect.*; and 26[2] consists of 48 leaves [xiv], 8½ × 5½, containing Matt. xviii. 32—xxiv. 10; xxvi. 28—xxviii. 20; Mark i. 16—xiii. 9; xiv. 9–27, with *κεφ. t.*, *τίτλ.*, *Am.* (*Eus.* only partially), *lect.* There are many abridgements in the writing. Dated, perhaps by the first hand, A.D. 1323. (Greg. 540, 541.)

*555. B.-C. III. 4 [xiii], 7 × 5, ff. 264 (24), *prol.*, *κεφ. t.*, *τίτλ.*, *κεφ.*, *Am.*, *Eus.*, *lect.*, *pict.* of the four Evangelists, *syn.* incomplete at the end.

Some leaves are misplaced in St. Matthew. *Mut.* John xix. 25—xxi. 2. (Greg. 542.)

*556. B.-C. III. 5 [xii], 11 × 8½, ff. 183 (26), 2 cols., *κεφ. t.*, *lect.*, *syn.*, *men.*, *prol.*, *κεφ.*, *τίτλ.*, *Am.*, *Eus.* *Mut.* Matt. xii. 11—xiii. 10; Mark viii. 4–28; Luke xv. 20—xvi. 9; John ii. 22—iv. 6; 53—v. 43; xi. 21–47, one leaf lost in each case, and one (John i. 51—ii. 22) misplaced in binding. This copy has John vii. 53—viii. 11 after Luke xxi. 38, like Ferrar's four, with which its text much agrees, and the titles to SS. Matthew and Mark only run εὐαγγέλιον ἐκ τοῦ κατὰ M ... (Greg. 543.)

*557. B.-C. III. 9 [xiii], 5½ × 3½, ff. 256 (22), *κεφ. t.* to the last three Gospels, *τίτλ.*, *κεφ.*, *Am.* (not *Eus.*), *pict.* of SS. Matthew, Mark, and John. This copy is remarkably free from *lect.* Neatly written, but four considerable passages in St. Luke are omitted, the text running on *uno tenore.* (Greg. 544.)

*558. B.-C. III. 10 [dated A. D. 1430], 8 × 5½, ff. 374 (+16+34) (16), *chart.*, *pict.* of the four Evangelists, of the Saviour, and of the Virgin and Child. *Carp.*, *Eus. t.*, *κεφ. t.*, *prol.*, *Am.*, *Eus.*, *lect.*, *vers.* The leaves are much misplaced in binding. (Greg. 545.)

*559. B.-C. III. 41 [xii or xiii], 6½ × 4½, ff. 275 (22). *Mut.* at beginning and end (John xviii. 30–end) and about Matt. xii. 16. *Κεφ. t.*, *τίτλ.*, *pict.*, in a bad condition. (Greg. 546.)

The next two were purchased in 1876 of Quaritch for £120 and £50 respectively by Mr. Jonathan Peckover, and now belong to Miss Algerina Peckover, of Bank House, Wisbech. Burgon examined them, and J. R. Harris since then.

560. (Act. 222, Paul. 278.) Algerina Peckover (1) [xi], small 4to, ff. 239 (33), contains the Gospels, Acts, and Epistles in their usual Greek order, 'an exquisite specimen, in a somewhat minute character.' It begins with a picture of St. Matthew, the lost preliminary matter being prefixed *chart.* by a later hand. *Pict.*, *τίτλ.*, *κεφ.*, *Am.*, *Eus.*, *lect.* (*ἀρχ.* and *τέλ.*), *subscr.*, *στίχ.*, *vers.*, *syn.*, *men.* On the last leaf is written in uncial letters: ὡς ἡδὺς τοῖς πλέουσιν ὁ εὔδιος λιμήν· | οὕτως καὶ τοῖς γράφουσιν ὁ ἔσχατος στίχος. ἰωαννικίου μοναχοῦ. (Greg. 712.)

561. Algerina Peckover (2), [xi or a little later], 7⅝ × 5¾, ff. 356 (16), with 17 (3+14) uncial palimpsest leaves at the beginning and end, containing Lessons from the Epistles to be described hereafter (Apost. 43). *Carp.*, *prol.* (later), *κεφ. t.*, *pict.*, *κεφ.*, *τίτλ.*, *Am.*, *Eus.*, *lect.* (*ἀρχ.* and *τέλ.*), *subscr.*, *syn.*, *men.* (later). *Mut.* Matt. xxvii. 43, 44; John vii. 53—viii. 11; x. 27—xi. 14 (2 ff.); xi. 29–42 (1 f.). Marg. notes, Matt. v. 14; xvi. 15. One of the Ferrar group. *See* J. R. Harris, Codex Algerina Peckover (Journal of Exegetical Society). (Greg. 713.)

*562. Oxf. Bodl. MS. Bibl. Gr. e. 1. Mendham [xiv], 9½ × 7, ff. 270 [sic] (20), *κεφ. t.*, *κεφ.*, *τίτλ.*, *lect.*, *subscr.*, *στίχ.*, *ἀναγν.*, *vers.*, *syn.*, *men.* Bohn became possessed of it, whether from Meerman or not is not known, and sold it to the Rev. Theodore Williams, Vicar of Hendon, for £120. The Rev. Joseph Mendham bought it of Payne for £70 in 1827. It was given by Mr. Mendham's widow to Dean Burgon for his life, afterwards to go to the Bodleian Library, where the Rev. W. F. Rose brought it upon the Dean's death. It is dated on the last leaf by a later hand, A. D. 1322. It is evenly written in pale brown ink with a reed-pen. The last twenty leaves contain the Gospels for Maundy Thursday, for Good Friday, and for St. John's Day. The ornamentation is as fresh and bright as if done yesterday, and its text is of the ordinary type, like lmn^{scr} (Evann. 201, 542, 568). It is a very beautiful MS., and an excellent specimen in all ways. (Greg. 521.)

Mr. James Woodhouse [d. 1866], Treasurer-General of the Ionian Islands, while resident fifty years at Corfu, formed a collection of manuscripts from monasteries in the Levant, which was sold in London in 1869, 1872, 1875. Among them were three copies of the Gospels, two Evangelistaria, one copy of the Acts and St. Paul.

*563. London, Brit. Mus. Egerton 2783 [xiii], $5\frac{3}{8} \times 3\frac{1}{2}$, ff. 337 (22), *Carp.*, *Eus. t.*, *prol.*, *κεφ. t.*, *pict.*, *τίτλ.*, *κεφ.*, *lect.* (*ἀρχαί* and *τέλη*), *subscr.*, *στίχ.*, *vers.*, *syn.*, *men.* It was once fair, but has suffered from damp, and has been sadly cropped by the Western binder. *Mut.* John xx. 17. The headings of the Gospels are in lake. It abounds in curious and unique liturgical notes, whereof Burgon gives specimens, and it has textual corrections by the original scribe. Collated by Rose. Bought by Burgon, then belonged to Rev. W. F. Rose, and bought for the Museum in 1893. (Greg. 714.)

*564. Brit. Mus. Egerton 2785 [xiv], $10\frac{1}{2} \times 8$, ff. 226 (27–29), 2 cols., *syn.*, *men.*, scholium on *τίτλος α'*, *prol.*, *κεφ. t.*, *pict.*, *Am.*, *τίτλ.*, *κεφ.* (*lect.* later), *subscr.*, *ῥήμ.*, *στίχ.* The ornamentation is in lake, and at the end are extracts from Eulogius and Hesychius. Upon collation by Mr. Rose it exhibits here and there suggestive discrepancies from the common text. Evann. 563, 564 were respectively offered for sale in 1871 for £50 and £40. Bought by Burgon, belonged to Rose, and purchased for Museum in 1893. (Greg. 715.)

*565. Brit. Mus. Egerton 2784 [xii, Greg. xiv], $8\frac{3}{8} \times 5\frac{3}{4}$, ff. 213 (22–25), *κεφ. t.*, *τίτλ.*, *κεφ.*, *Am.*, *Eus.*, *lect.*, *ἀναγν.*, *subscr.*, *ῥήμ.*, *στίχ.*, fragment of *syn.* Apparently not from the Woodhouse collection. It is beautifully written and of an uncommon type. Its older binding suggests a Levantine origin. The readings are far more interesting than those of Cod. 564, some of them being quite unique. Belonged to Burgon, then Rose, then to the Museum in 1893. (Greg. 716.)

*566. h^{scr}. Brit. Mus. Arund. 524 [xi], $6\frac{3}{4} \times 5\frac{1}{4}$, ff. 218 (27), *Carp.*, *Eus. t.*, *κεφ. t.*, *κεφ.*, *τίτλ.*, *Am.*, *Eus.*, *lect.*, *syn.*, *men.*, was brought to England (with x^{scr} and many others) by the great Earl of Arundel in 1646. Henry Howard, Evelyn's Duke of Norfolk, presented them to the Royal Society, from whose rooms at Somerset House they were transferred to the Museum in 1831. (Greg. 476.)

567. Brit. Mus. Harl. 5538, described in the Harleian Catalogue as an Evangelistarium, and numbered by Scholz Evst. 149, is a copy of the Gospels [xiv, Greg. xii], $4\frac{3}{4} \times 3\frac{1}{2}$, ff. 226 (23), *orn.*, *lect.*, *Am.* (Greg. 505.)

*568. n^{scr}. (Paul. 259 or j^{scr}.) Brit. Mus., Burney 18 (purchased in 1818, with many other manuscripts, from the heirs of Dr. Charles

Burney), contains the Gospels and two leaves of St. Paul (Hebr. xii. 17—xiii. 25), written by one Joasaph A. D. 1366, 12¾ × 9, ff. 222 (23) + 9 blank, *κεφ. t.*, *κεφ.*, *lect.*, *Am.*, *Eus.*, *ἀναγν.*, *subscr.*, *στίχ.*, very superb in gold letters. Codd. lmn (542, 201, 568) agree pretty closely. (Greg. 480.)

*569. o[scr]. Brit. Mus. Burn. 19 [x], 8½ × 7, ff. 217 (22), *pict.* (Plate iii, No. 8), in the Escurial as late as 1809, is singularly void of the usual apparatus. (Greg. 481.)

*570. p[scr]. Brit. Mus. Burn. 20 [A. D. 1285, Indict. 13, altered into 985, whose indiction is the same], 7½ × 6, ff. 317 (22, 23), written by a monk Theophilus: *pict.*, *Eus. t.*, *κεφ. t.*, *τίτλ.*, *Am.*, *Eus.*, *lect.*, *syn.*, *men.*, the two last in a later hand, which has made many corrections: this copy is quite equal in value to Cod. c[scr] (511), and often agrees closely with w[scr] (507). (Greg. 482.)

*571. r[scr]. Brit. Mus. Burn. 21, by the same scribe as Cod. 543 [A. D. 1292], 13 × 10, ff. 258 (24), on cotton paper in a beautiful but formed hand (*see* Plate vi, No. 15), *syn.*, *κεφ. t.*, *prol.*, *orn.*, *κεφ.*, *τίτλ.*, *Am.*, *lect.*, *subscr.*, *στίχ.*, *men.* A fine copy, much damaged. Codd. 543 and 571 differ only in 183 places. (Greg. 484.)

*572. s[scr]. Brit. Mus. Burn. 23 [xii], 7¾ × 6, ff. 230 (23–25), boldly but carelessly written, ends John viii. 14: *mut.* Luke v. 22—ix. 32; xi. 31—xiii. 25; xvii. 24—xviii. 4. *Syn.*, *Carp.*, *κεφ. t.*, *orn.*, *κεφ.*, *τίτλ.*, *Am.*, *lect.*, *subscr.*, *στίχ.*, with many later changes and weighty readings. (Greg. 485.)

573. Brit. Mus. Add. 5468 [A. D. 1338], 8¼ × 6, ff. 226 (29), *Carp.*, *Eus. t.*, *κεφ. t.*, *τίτλ.*, *κεφ.*, *Am.*, *lect.*, *subscr.*, *στίχ.*, *syn.*, *men.* It was 'John Jackson's book, bought of Conant in Fleet Street, 1777, for five guineas.' *Mut.* Matt. i. 1—vi. 18, and the last leaf of St. Luke (xxiv. 47–53). This copy has the subscriptions at the end of each of the Gospels of SS. Matthew and Mark. There is a probable reference to them at the end of St. John (*ὁμοίως*). It is coarsely written on thick vellum, with much *lect.* in vermilion. The breathings and accents are remarkably incorrect. (Greg. 686.)

574. Brit. Mus. Add. 7141, bought 1825, and once Claudius James Rich's [xiii, Greg. xi], 9¾ × 7½, ff. 192 (27), 2 cols., *Carp.*, *Eus. t.*, *κεφ. t.*, *τίτλ.*, *Am.* (partial), *Eus.*, *lect.* in red, *subscr.* (Greg. 490.)

*575 or k[scr]. Brit. Mus. Add. 11,300, Lebanon [xii], 6¾ × 4½, ff. 268 (26), *Carp.*, *Eus. t.*, *κεφ. t.*, *κεφ.*, *τίτλ.*, *Am.*, *Eus.*, *lect.*, *subscr.*, most elegantly and correctly written, purchased in 1838, and said to come from Caesarea Philippi at the foot of Lebanon. Contains *scholia*: the text is broken up into paragraphs. (Re-examined by Bloomfield.) There is a beautiful facsimile page in the new 'Catalogue of Ancient Manuscripts in the British Museum' (1881), Plate 16. (Greg. 478.)

576. (Act. 226, Paul. 268.) Brit. Mus. Add. 11,836, this and the next two are from Bishop Butler's collection: [xi], 7¼ × 5¼, ff. 305 (34), *Eus. t.* (blank), *pict.*, *κεφ. t.*, *κεφ.*, *τίτλ.*, *Am.*, *subscr.*, *κεφ.* in Epistles, beautifully written in a minute hand and adorned with gold letters, contains Evan.,

Act., Cath., Paul., Psalms, &c. *Mut.* Mark i. 1–28; Acts i. 1–23; vii. 8–39; Ps. i. 1–3. Akin to Cod. 440 in St. Paul (Vansittart). (Greg. 491.)

577. Brit. Mus. Add. 11,838[1] [A. D. 1326, Ind. 9], $9\frac{1}{4} \times 6$, ff. 269 (24), (*syn.*, *men.* later), *κεφ. t.*, *pict.* (*lect.*, some *ἀναγν.* later), *τίτλ.*, from Sinai, most beautifully written by Constantine, a monk. (Greg. 492.)

578. Brit. Mus. Add. 11,839 [xv], $10\frac{1}{2} \times 8$, *chart.*, ff. 157 (27), *lect.* (later, and in latter part), ill-written, with later marginal notes, and no chapter divisions. Matt. iv. 13—xi. 27; Mark i. 1—vi. 1, are later. (Greg. 493.)

579. Brit. Mus. Add. 11,868, from the Butler collection [xi], $9\frac{1}{2} \times 7$, ff. 7 (29), 2 cols. (now bound separately), containing Matt. x. 33—xi. 12; xiii. 44—xiv. 6; xv. 14–18; 20–22; 26–29; 30–32; 34—xvii. 10; 34—xvii. 10; 12–15; 18–20; 22–24; 25 (sic)—xviii. 16, two half-leaves being lost, beautifully written in two columns. Κεφ., *τίτλ.* (*mut.*), *Am.*, *Eus.*, later *lect.* (Greg. 687.)

580. *See* Evan. 272. Instead—
Lord Herries [xiii], $8\frac{1}{2} \times 6\frac{1}{8}$, f. 1 (26), *κεφ.*, *τίτλ.*, *Am.* (*lect.*, *ἀναγν.* later). (*See* Greg. 576.)

581. Brit. Mus. Add. 16,183 (sic) [xii], $6\frac{1}{2} \times 5\frac{3}{4}$, ff. 181 (28, 29), *Carp.* (*mut.* at beg.), space for *Eus. t.*, *κεφ. t.*, *κεφ.*, *τίτλ.*, *lect.*, *Am.*, *Eus.*, *syn.*, *men.*, in a minute hand, bought (as was Cod. 582) of Captain C. K. Macdonald in 1846. The two came probably from Sinai, where he once saw Cod. ℵ. (Greg. 495.)

582. (Act. 227, Paul. 279.) Brit. Mus. Add. 16,184 [xiii or xiv], $7\frac{1}{2} \times 5\frac{1}{2}$, ff. 300 (33, 34), *Carp.*, *prol.*, *κεφ. t.*, *lect.*, *τίτλ.*, *κεφ.*, *Am.*, *Eus.*, *subscr.*, *στίχ.*, *pict.*, *syn.*, *men.*, some later on paper. The whole New Testament, except the Apocalypse, in the usual Greek order. This copy contains many important various readings: e.g. it countenances Codd. ℵBL in Luke xi. 2, 4. (Greg. 496.)

583. Brit. Mus. Add. 16,943 [xi], $6 \times 4\frac{3}{4}$, ff. 184 (22, 23), in a very small hand, *prol.*, *κεφ. t.*, *lect.*, *τίτλ.*, *κεφ.*, *Am.*, *Eus.*, *subscr.*, *στίχ.*, *pict.*, *syn.*, *men.*, from the collection made by the Hon. F. North for the University of Corfu. *See* Evann. 531–2; Act. 198. (Greg. 497.)

584. (Act. 228, Paul. 269, Apoc. 97 or j[scr].) Brit. Mus. Add. 17,469, contains the whole N. T., bought of T. Rodd in 1848 [xiv], $10\frac{1}{4} \times 7$, ff. 187 (35) (very minute writing), with much other matter. *Prol.*, *vers.*, *κεφ. t.*, *κεφ.*, *τίτλ.*, *Am.*, *lect.*, *syn.* *Mut.* Matt. i. 1—ii. 13; Mark v. 2—vi. 11; Acts i. 1—v. 2; James i. 1—v. 4; 3 John; Jude; Rom. i. 1—iv. 9; 2 Thess. ii. 13—1 Tim. i. 13; vi. 19—2 Tim. ii. 19. In Acts *τίτλ.*, *lect.* rubro. *Prol.* to every Epistle. Written by Gerasimus. (Greg. 498.)

585. Brit. Mus. Add. 17,470 [A.D. 1034], 8×6, ff. 287 (20), *syn.*, *men.*, *pict.*, *κεφ. t.* (with *harm.*), *κεφ.*, *τίτλ.* (with *harm.*), *Am.*, *Eus.*, *lect.*, with many marginal corrections of the text. Written by Synesius, a priest, bought of H. Rodd in 1848. 'A singularly genuine specimen.' (Greg. 504.)

[1] For Add. 11,837, which is m[scr], *see* Evan. *201.

586. Brit. Mus. Add. 17,741 [xii], 9¼ × 6¼, ff. 216 (22), begins Matt. xii. 21, ends John xvii. 13: purchased in 1849. *Am.* (not *Eus.*), ἀρχαί and τέλη, *lect.* The genealogy in St. Luke is in three columns. (Greg. 499.)

587. Brit. Mus. Add. 17,982 [xiii], 8 × 6, ff. 244 (23), *Carp.*, space for *Eus. t.*, κεφ. *t.*, κεφ., τίτλ., *Am.*, ἀναγν., *vers.*, *syn.*, *men.*, ending John xix. 39 (eight leaves being lost, also leaf containing xviii. 1–21), and believed to contain important readings. (Greg. 500.)

588. Brit. Mus. Add. 18,211 [xiii], 9½ × 7½, ff. 157 (23), 12 *chart.* [xv] to supply hiatus: κεφ. *t.*, κεφ., *Am.*, some τίτλ., *lect.*, came from Patmos. F. V. J. Arundell, British Chaplain at Smyrna (1834), describes this copy, given him by Mr. Borrell, and a Lectionary sold to him at the same time, in his 'Discoveries in Asia Minor,' vol. ii. p. 268. He there compares it with the beautiful Cod. Ebnerianus (Evan. 105), which it very slightly resembles, being larger and far less elegant. *Mut.* Matt. i. 1–19; Mark i. 1–16; Luke ix. 14—xvii. 4; xxi. 19—John iv. 5. (Greg. 501.)

589. Brit. Mus. Add. 19,387 [xii], 8¼ × 6½, ff. 235 (22), κεφ., τίτλ., *Am.*, *Eus.*, *lect.*, *prol.*, κεφ. *t.*, *subscr.*, *syn.*, *men.*, written by one Leo, and found in a monastery of St. Maximus, begins Matt. viii. 6, and was purchased in 1853 from the well-known Constantine Simonides (Greg. 502) —as was also

590. Brit. Mus. Add. 19,389 [xiii], 4¾ × 3½, ff. 60 (26), κεφ., *Am.*, *lect.*, St. John's Gospel only, elegantly written by Cosmas Vanaretus, a monk. (Greg. 503.)

The foregoing Additional MSS. in the British Museum were examined and collated (apparently only in select passages) by Dr. S. T. Bloomfield for his 'Critical Annotations on the Sacred Text' (1860), designed as a Supplement to the ninth edition of his Greek Testament, and comprising an *opus supremum et ultimum*, the last effort of a long and honourable literary career. He has passed under review no less than seventy manuscripts of the New Testament, twenty-three at Lambeth, the rest in the British Museum. The following have been accumulated since his time.

591. Brit. Mus. Add. 22,506 [A. D. 1305], 9½ × 7, ff. 279 (22), κεφ. *t.*, *pict.*, κεφ., *lect.*, τίτλ., *Am.*, *subscr.*, στίχ., ἀναγν., written by Neophytus a monk of Cyprus, was bought at Milos by H. O. Coxe of a Greek who had it from a relative who had been ἡγούμενος of a Candian monastery. A facsimile is given in the new Museum Catalogue. (Greg. 645.)

592. Brit. Mus. Add. 22,736 [June, A. D. 1179], 9½ × 7½, ff. 226 (24), 2 cols., *syn.*, *prol.*, κεφ. *t.*, *pict.*, κεφ., *lect.*, τίτλ., *Am.*, written by John ἀναγνώστης, with peculiar, almost barbarous, illuminations. (Greg. 688.)

593. Brit. Mus. Add. 22,737 [xii], 8¼ × 6, ff. 313 (20), κεφ. *t.*, κεφ., not τίτλ., *lect.*, *subscr.*, στίχ., *syn.*, *men.*, with decorations in very deep lake. (Greg. 689.)

594. Brit. Mus. Add. 22,738 [xiii], 6¾ × 4⅝, ff. 237 (23, 24), *Carp.*, *Eus. t.*, κεφ. *t.*, κεφ. (τίτλ., *lect.*, *syn.*, *men.*, by another hand), *Am.*, *pict.*, rough and abounding with itacisms. Two rude pictures of Evangelists have been effaced. (Greg. 690.)

595. Brit. Mus. Add. 22,739, has a rather modern look [xiv ?], $7\frac{3}{8} \times 5\frac{3}{8}$, ff. 275 (22), *Carp.*, *Eus. t.*, *κεφ. t.*, *κεφ.*, *pict.*, *τίτλ.*, *Am.*, *lect.*, *στίχ.*, *ἀναγν.*, with rough pictures and illuminations. (Greg. 691.)

596. Brit. Mus. Add. 22,740 [xii], 8 × 6, ff. 237 (23), *prol.*, *κεφ. t.*, *pict.*, *κεφ.*, *τίτλ.*, *Am.*, *Eus.* (in blue), exquisitely written, said to greatly resemble Cod. 71 (g^scr) in text, with illuminated headings to the Gospels. *Mut.* Luke ii. 7–21, and after *τίτλ.* of St. John. This MS. with Evst. 269, 270, 271, 272, and Evann. 592, 597, was bought of Sp. Lampros of Athens in 1859. (Greg. 692.)

597. Brit. Mus. Add. 22,741 [xiv], $10 \times 7\frac{3}{4}$, ff. 208 (22), *Eus. t.*, *Carp.*, *κεφ. t.*, *κεφ.*, *τίτλ.*, *Am.*, *subscr.*, *orn.*, *prol.* (here called *προγράμματα*, a term we have not noticed elsewhere). *Mut.* Mark i. 27–43; ii. 2–16. John vii. 1—xxi. 25. (Greg. 693.)

598. Brit. Mus. Add. 24,112 [xv], $11\frac{1}{2} \times 8\frac{1}{2}$, *chart.*, ff. 211 (33, 34), ($7\frac{1}{4}$ pages Gr. and Lat.), *κεφ. t.*, *κεφ.*, *lect.*, *subscr.*, *στίχ.*, *ἀναγν.*, *syn.*, *men.* Bought at Puttick's, 1861. (Greg. 694.)

599. Brit. Mus. Add. 24,373 [xiii], $9\frac{1}{4} \times 7\frac{1}{2}$, ff. 299 (22), *syn.*, *men.*, *Carp.*, *Eus. t.*, *κεφ. t.*, *prol.*, *pict.*, *orn.*, *κεφ.*, *τίτλ.*, *lect.*, *Am.*, *Eus.*, *subscr.*, very beautiful. *Mut.* Matt. i. 11—xv. 19. Long *lect.*, *ἀρχ.* in marg., *τέλ.* in the text. Bought of H. S. Freeman, Consul at Janina, in 1862. (Greg. 695.)

600. Brit. Mus. Add. 24,376 [xiv], $10\frac{3}{4} \times 8\frac{1}{4}$, ff. 350 (19), 2 cols., *κεφ. t.*, *pict.*, *κεφ.*, *lect.*, *ἀναγν.*, some *Am.*, *subscr.*, *στίχ.*, *syn.*, *men.* Remarkable *pict.* of the Annunciation and of the three later Evangelists, Gospel headings left blank. *See* Evst. 273–7. (Greg. 696.)

601. Brit. Mus. Add. 26,103 [xiv], 8 × 6, ff. 242 (25), *orn.*, *κεφ.*, *τίτλ.*, *Am.* (in gold), *pict.* (John), was found in a village near Corinth, and bought of C. L. Merlin, our Vice-Consul at Athens, in 1865. Beautifully written in very black ink, the first page of each Gospel being in gold. (Greg. 697.)

602. Brit. Mus. Add. 27,861 [xiv], $6\frac{1}{2} \times 5$, ff. 186 (19, 20, &c.), *κεφ. t.*, *κεφ.*, *τίτλ.*, *Am.*, *lect.*, *subscr.*, *syn.*, *men.*, from Sir T. Gage's sale, 1868, rough and dirty, with many marginal notes to supply omissions. St. Matthew's Gospel is wholly lost. No *pict.*, but ornamentation in faded lake. (Greg. 698.)

603. (Act. 231, Paul. 266 and 271.) Brit. Mus. Add. 28,815 [x or xi], $11\frac{1}{2} \times 8\frac{1}{2}$, ff. 302 (30), *κεφ.*, *τίτλ.*, *Am.*, *Eus.*, *lect.*, *pict.*, sumptuously bound with silver-gilt plates. This noble fragment was bought (as were Act. 232, Evst. 279, 280) of Sir Ivor B. Guest in 1871, and contains the Gospels, Acts, Catholic Epistles, Romans, 1, 2 Corinthians, Galatians, the rest of the original volume being evidently torn out of the book when already bound. In the same year 1871 the Baroness Burdett-Coutts also imported from Janina in Epirus sixty-seven leaves containing the rest of St. Paul's Epistles and the Apocalypse (B.-C. II. 4, Paul. 266, Apoc. 89), which fragments were described in the second edition of the present book. Mr. Edward A. Guy, of Miami University, Oxford, Ohio, U.S.A., on examining the Museum fragment in 1875 with my book in his hand, concluded that the two portions originally formed one magnificent copy of the whole New Testament,

and when I brought the two together, I saw that the illuminated heading and initial capital on the first page of B.-C. II. 4 (Eph. i) was worked off through damp on the *verso* of the last leaf (302) of the Museum copy, and the red κεφ. of Gal. vi on the top of B.-C. II. 4, leaf one, *recto.* In the larger fragment we find two *pict.* of St. Luke (one of them before the Acts), one of St. John, with illuminated headings. *Carp.*, *Eus. t.*, &c. must have perished, as the first page opens with Matt. i. 1. It has τίτλ. in gold letters on purple vellum, a Harmony at the foot of fol. 17 b—18 b, and many brief marginal scholia. *See* Paul. 266 (B.-C. II. 4), which is at present five miles off, in the Library of Sir Roger Cholmeley's School, Highgate. (Greg. 699.)

604. Brit. Mus. Egerton 2610 [xii], $5\frac{3}{4} \times 4\frac{1}{4}$, ff. 297 (19), about thirty letters to a line), *Carp.*, *Eus. t.*, *κεφ. t.* (Matt., Mark, Luke), τίτλ., *Am.*, *Eus.*, *pict.* (beautifully executed). First noticed by Dean Burgon, bought for the Museum in 1882, and collated by Mr. H. C. Hoskier, 'Full Account, &c.,' D. Nutt, 1890. According to Mr. Hoskier's analysis it contains no less than 270 quite unique readings, siding at least twenty times alone with D, eleven with B, six with ℵ, six with Evan. 1, twenty-nine with Evan. 473. It has 2724 variations from T. R. There are besides a vast number of almost unique readings, e. g. Luke xi. 2, for which Greg. Nyss. is about the only authority (Hoskier). (Greg. 700.)

605. (Act. 233, Paul. 243, Apoc. 106.) Zittaviensis A. 1 [xv], *chart.*, ff. 775 (30), *prol.*, *κεφ. t.*, *κεφ.*, *τίτλ.*, *subscr.*, *στίχ.*, *vers.*, given to the Senate of Zittau (Lusatian Saxony) in 1620, contains the canonical books of the Old Testament down to Esther, with 1 Esdras, 4 Maccabees, Judith, Tobit, and the whole New Testament. Matthaei collated the Old Testament portion for Dean Holmes's edition of the Septuagint (Cod. 44), and saw its great critical value. It was examined, as so many others have been, by Dr. C. R. Gregory. (Greg. 664.)

The next two were bought for the Bodleian in 1882: they came from Constantinople.

606. Oxf. Bodl. Gr. Misc. 305 [xi], $9\frac{1}{2} \times 7\frac{1}{4}$, ff. 149 (27), *pict.* (Matt., Mark), *κεφ.*, *Am.*, *Eus.*, few *lect.* (later), *subscr.* (Matt.), *orn.* *Mut.* Mark xvi. 19 (*post* καί) 20. The passages Matt. xvi. 2, 3; John v. 4; vii. 53—viii. 11 are obelized in the margin. (Greg. 707.)

607. Oxf. Bodl. Gr. Misc. 306 [xi], $7\frac{1}{4} \times 6$, ff. 200 (32, &c.), *Eus. t.*, *κεφ. t.*, *pict.*, *κεφ.*, *τίτλ.*, *Am.*, *Eus.*, much cropped in binding. *Mut.* (1), fol. 1; (2) tops of pages containing τίτλοι: and (3) Quaternion of 8 ff., Matt. xx. 15—xxiv. 22. (Greg. 708.)

608. Brit. Mus. Add. 11,859–60 (palimpsest) is a Typicum or Rituale [xiv or xv], $10 \times 7\frac{3}{4}$, ff. 39 + 29 (uncertain), from the Butler collection, having written under it an earlier cursive text [xiii] containing, in 11,859, Matt. xii. 33—xiii. 7; xvi. 21—xvii. 15; xx. 1–15; 15—xxi. 5; Mark x. 45—xi. 17: 198 verses; and in 11,860, ~~only~~ twenty-seven verses of the Catholic Epistles, James 1–16; Jude 4–15. This is Act. 234. (Greg. 1274)

609. Camb. Univ. Libr., Hh. 6. 12 [xv], $8 \times 5\frac{3}{4}$, *chart.*, ff. 182 (20, &c.),

κεφ. t., *prol.*, *subscr.* This must be Scholz's 1673 (N. T., vol. i. p. cxix), but it contains the Gospels only, not the Acts, as he supposes. (Greg. 552.)

610. Oxf. Bodl. Barocc. 59 [xi], 8¼ × 5½, ff. 6 (21), 1 *chart.*, κεφ. t. (John), κεφ., τίτλ., *Am.*, *lect.*, containing Luke xxiii. 38–50; xxiv. 46–53; John i. 30—iii. 5 in a book of other matter [xv], *chart.* (Greg. 526.)

611. Rom. Angel. D. 3. 8, olim Cardinalis Passionei [xi], 9⅝ × 6½, ff. 442 (21), *prol.*, κεφ. t. St. Luke with Theophylact's commentary, described with facsimile by Vitali in Bianchini's 'Evan. Quadr.' vol. ii. pt. 1, pp. 506–40, 563, 560. (Greg. 848.)

612. B.-C. I. 11 [xii], 3½ × 2½, ff. 112 (25–28), is a very small and beautiful 'Ωδεῖον, containing the Magnificat and Benedictus, besides the 151 Psalms of the Septuagint version, and the Hymns of Moses (Ex. xv. 1–14; Deut. xxxii. 14–43), of Hannah (1 Sam. ii), of Habakkuk (ch. iii), Isaiah (ch. xxvi), Jonah (ch. ii), with that of the Three Holy Children. Many such books are extant, of which this is inserted in our list as a specimen. *See* 5pe, note.

John Belsheim, editor of the Codex Aureus, found at Upsal in 1875, and described to Burgon in 1882, together with Act. 68, three manuscripts in the University Library there containing the Gospels only.

613. Upsala 4, Sparvenfeldt[1] 45 [xi], 5⅞ × 4½, ff. 208 (25), *Eus. t.*, κεφ. t., *pict.*, last leaf later, bought at Venice in 1678. (Greg. 899.)

614. Upsala 9 [xiii], 9½ × 7⅛, ff. 288 (22), *pict.*, given by a Greek priest in 1784 to A. F. Stiertzenbecker, who bequeathed it to the University Library. (Greg. 900.)

615. Upsala 12, Björnsthal 2 [xii], 6¾ × 4⅞, ff. 328 (31), *syn.*, *men.*, contains the Gospels, Acts, and Epistles, being Act. 237, Paul. 274. (Greg. 901.)

616. Upsala 13, Björnsthal 3 [xii], 6¼ × 4¾, ff. 230 (24), *prol.*, κεφ. t. (Greg. 902.)

These two last and Act. 236 were bequeathed by Professor J. Björnsthal to the University Library.

617. Oxf. Oriel, MS. lxxxiii [xi or xii], 7¾ × 5¾, ff. 236 (22, 23), 2 cols., κεφ. t., *pict.* (cut out), τίτλ., *lect.*, *Am.*, *Eus.*, *syn.*, *men.*, written in gold letters. *Mut.* in many places. Brought in 1878 by Capt. J. Hext from Corfu, and given by him to Mr. Daniel Parsons, who gave it to the College as a 'joint gift.' (Greg. 618.)

618. Camb. Add. 720 [xi], 5½ × 4¼, ff. 278 (19, 20), *Am.*, *Eus.*, κεφ., τίτλ. (fragments of κεφ. t.), *lect.*, *syn.*, *men.*, *pict.* But *Carp.*, *Eus. t.*, κεφ. t. of Matt., and perhaps *prol.* are apparently lost. *Mut.* Matt. xxviii. 1–20; Mark xv. 29—Luke iii. 33. In a later hand is Luke xxiv. 46–53. (Hort and Bradshaw.) (Greg. 672.)

[1] Belsheim (Cod. Aureus, Proleg. p. xvii and note 3) gives a short life of that noble Swede, John Gabriel Sparvenfeldt [1655–1727], who was sent over Europe by his master, Charles XI, to procure manuscripts for the Royal Library, and bought the Latin Codex Aureus at Madrid in 1690.

619. Camb. Add. 1837 [xii or xiii], $8\frac{1}{8} \times 6\frac{1}{2}$, ff. 164 (19), injured in parts by damp. Κεφ., fragment of *κεφ. t.*, *lect.*, *ἀναγν.*, *subscr.*, *στίχ.* No *Am.*, *Eus.*, *τίτλ.*, *prol.* *Mut.* Matt. i. 1—x. 42; xiii. 3–16; xxvii. 24–37; Mark xiv. 21—Luke iii. 16; iv. 35—v. 23; vii. 4–15. Ends Luke xix. 33. (Hort and Bradshaw.) (Greg. 673.)

620. Camb. Add. 1879. 11 [xii], $9 \times 6\frac{3}{4}$, ff. 4 (26), containing Matt. x. 42—xii. 43. *Am.* (not *Eus.*), *κεφ.*, *τίτλ.* *Lect.* are in a later hand. (Hort and Bradshaw.) (Greg. 674.) From Tischendorf's collection, as is also

621. Camb. Add. 1879. 24 [xiii—xiv], $8\frac{1}{8} \times 5\frac{3}{4}$, ff. 2 (25), containing Matt. xxvi. 20–39 and ὑπόθεσις and verses before St. Mark. Κεφ., *τίτλ.*, *lect.* (Hort and Bradshaw.) (Greg. 675.)

The Rev. H. O. Coxe, late Bodley's Librarian, though quite unable to purchase any of the literary treasures he was commissioned to inspect in 1857, added considerably by his research to our knowledge of manuscripts in the East. A list of them was given in groups by Dr. Scrivener in the third edition of this work: but for various reasons they will be found separately placed amongst the ensuing MSS., to fill up gaps which have been since discovered in the supplementary list of cursive manuscripts that was bound up in the beginning of the last edition.

The Evann. 622–735 were reported to Dean Burgon from several Libraries in reply to his sedulous enquiries. Upon subsequent examination by Dr. C. R. Gregory on the spot, many of them were seen not to be Evangelia, but instead of that commentaries of St. Chrysostom, or other commentaries, or Evangelistaria, or MSS. containing other matter. Thus —including the list of the Abbé Martin, who extended Dean Burgon's numeration up to 776—the following must be excised: 643–665, 667, 673, 677–679, 681, 682, 685, 686, 688, 689, 695, 700–702, 706, 711, 712, 715–722, 724–728 (including 726 which Dr. Scrivener noticed as a duplication of 611), 731, 733, 734, 758, 760, 763, 771, 772, 775, 776. Gregory, Prolegomena, pp. 794, 795. The editor has inserted other MSS. in their places, being especially those found by the late Rev. H. O. Coxe in his travels, and enumerated in his Report to Her Majesty's Government.

622. (Act. 242, Paul. 290, Apoc. 110.) Crypta Ferrata, A. α. 1 [xiv], $11\frac{3}{8} \times 8\frac{1}{4}$, ff. 386 (28), *chart.*, *κεφ. t.* with *harm.*, *Am.*, *Eus.* (rare), *lect.*, *ἀναγν.*, *subscr.*, *στίχ.*, *vers.*, *pict.*, *syn.*, *men.*, a beautiful codex of the entire New Testament. Described by the custodian Rocchi (Codices Cryptenses, &c., 1882, pp. 1, 2). (Greg. 824.)

623. Crypta Ferrata, A. α. 2 [xi, Greg. xiii], $9 \times 6\frac{5}{8}$, ff. 337 (21), *prol.*, *κεφ. t.*, *lect.*, *ἀναγν.*, *subscr.*, *pict.*, *syn.*, *men.*, a beautiful codex brought from Corcyra in 1729. Described by Rocchi, pp. 2–4. (Greg. 825.)

*624. Crypta Ferrata, A. α. 3 [xi, Greg. xii], $8\frac{5}{8} \times 6\frac{3}{4}$, ff. 234 (26), in 2 cols., *κεφ. t.*, *κεφ.*, *τίτλ.*, *Am.*, *Eus.*, *lect.*, *subscr.*, *στίχ.*, *syn.*, *men.* Collated by W. H. Simcox (Greg.), agrees with the Ferrar group. A beautiful codex: written probably at Rhegium. (Greg. 826.)

625. Crypta Ferrata, A. α. 4 [xi, Greg. xiii], $8\frac{1}{4} \times 6\frac{5}{8}$, ff. 225 (24), *κεφ.*, *τίτλ.*, *Am.*, *subscr.*, *vers.*; from St. John xix. 21 in a more recent hand. No *Pericope de adulterâ.* (Greg. 827.)

626. Crypta Ferrata, A. a. 5 [xi, Greg. xii], $10\frac{5}{8} \times 7\frac{7}{8}$, ff. 176 (27), 2 cols., *Eus. t.* (beautiful), κεφ. *t.*, κεφ., τίτλ., *Am.*, *Eus.*, *lect.*, *subscr.*, ῥήμ., στίχ., *pict.*, *syn.*, *men.*; with beautiful Eusebian tables. Described by Rocchi, pp. 5, 6. (Greg. 828.)

627. Crypta Ferrata, A. a. 6 [xi, Greg. xii], $8\frac{5}{8} \times 6\frac{3}{4}$, ff. 209 (26), 2 cols., κεφ. *t.*, κεφ., τίτλ., *Am.*, *Eus.*, *lect.*, στίχ., *syn.*, *men.*, *subscr.* to St. Mark like Λ. Begins at St. Matt. xiii. 28. Described by Rocchi, pp. 6, 7. (Greg. 829.)

628. Crypta Ferrata, A. a. 8 [xiii], $8\frac{5}{8} \times 4\frac{3}{4}$, ff. 118 (26), *prol.*, κεφ. *t.*, κεφ., τίτλ., *Am.*, *Eus.*; St. Luke and St. John *mut.* Described by Rocchi, p. 8. (Greg. 830.)

629. Crypta Ferrata, A. a. 17 [xii, Greg. xi], $5\frac{5}{8} \times 5\frac{1}{8}$, ff. 69 (23), κεφ. *t.*, κεφ., *Am.*, *lect.*, *subscr.* A fragment only, beginning at St. Luke xix. 35. The *pericope de adulterâ* is supplied at the end of the codex—imperfect after verse 6. (Greg. 831.)

630. Messina, University Library 88 (Evst. 361) [xiv], $10\frac{1}{4} \times 8\frac{1}{2}$, ff. 260 (22), *chart.*, *pict.*, *Eus. t.* (exquisite), κεφ., τίτλ., *Am.*, *Eus.*, *syn.*, *men.* All in good preservation. (Greg. 839.)

631. Messina, Univ. Libr. 100 [xiii], $10\frac{1}{2} \times 7\frac{7}{8}$, ff. 125 (24), τίτλ. St. Luke i to xxii with a commentary. (Greg. 840.)

632. Lond. Butler, formerly Hamilton 244 [xii], $9\frac{5}{8} \times 6\frac{7}{8}$, ff. ? (22), *Carp.*, *Eus. t.*, *pict.*, κεφ. *t.*, κεφ., τίτλ., *Am.*, *Eus.* (in the same line); superbly illuminated and adorned with effigies of St. Matthew and of the Virgin and Child, on gold ground. The Eusebian Canons written in gold between human figures standing on columns supporting arched arabesque friezes finely painted in gold and colours. (Greg. 662.)

633. Par. Nat. Suppl. 227 [xvi or xvii], $9\frac{3}{4} \times 7$, ff. 212 (22), κεφ., τίτλ., *Am.*; a Western codex. (Greg. 745.)

634. Par. Nat. Suppl. 911 [A.D. 1043], written by Euphemius ἀναγνώστης, in black, blue, and red ink, $6\frac{7}{8} \times 5\frac{3}{8}$, ff. 315 (18), 2 cols., *Am.* St. Luke, Greek and Arabic. (Greg. 609.)

635. Berlin, Royal Gr. 4to, 39 [xii or xi], $9\frac{3}{4} \times 7\frac{5}{8}$, ff. 313, *Carp.*, *Eus. t.*, *prol.*, κεφ. *t.*, κεφ., τίτλ., *Am.*, *Eus.*, *harm.* at foot, *lect.*, *subscr.*, στίχ., *pict.* Note that the *pericope de adulterâ* is found in this Evan. as well as in Evann. 636, 637, 638, 641, and 642. (Greg. 655.)

636. Berl. R. Gr. 4to, 47 [xiii or xii], $9\frac{1}{4} \times 5\frac{3}{4}$, ff. 220, *Carp.*, *Eus. t.*, κεφ. *t.*, κεφ., τίτλ., *Am.*, *Eus.* in same line, *lect.*, *syn.*, *men.* (Greg. 658.)

637. Berl. R. Gr. 4to, 55 [xii], $8\frac{1}{4} \times 6\frac{1}{8}$, ff. 292, *prol.*, κεφ. *t.*, *Am.*, *Eus.*, *lect.*, *subscr.*, *pict.* (Greg. 659.)

638. Berl. R. Gr. 4to, 66 [xii or xi], $8\frac{7}{8} \times 6\frac{1}{2}$, ff. 139 (21), *Eus. t.*, κεφ. *t.*, κεφ., τίτλ., *Am.*, *Eus.*, *lect.*, *pict.* (Greg. 660.)

639. Berl. R. Gr. 4to, 67 [xi], $9\frac{7}{8} \times 7\frac{3}{4}$, ff. 234 (23), κεφ. *t.*, κεφ., τίτλ., *Am.*, *Eus.*, *pict.* (Greg. 661.)

640. Berl. R. Gr. 8vo, 3 [A.D. 1077], $5\frac{7}{8} \times 4\frac{1}{8}$, ff. 266 (16), κεφ. *t.*, κεφ., τίτλ., *Am.*, *Eus.*, *lect.*, *subscr.*, στίχ. (Greg. 653.)

641. Berl. R. Gr. 8vo, 4 [xi or xii], $4\frac{3}{4} \times 3\frac{3}{4}$, ff. 178 (25), κεφ., τίτλ. *Mut.* in places. Contains from St. Matt. ii. 15 to St. John xix. 32. (Greg. 654.)

642. (Act. 252, Paul 302.) Berl. R. Gr. 8vo, 9 [xi, Greg. xiv], $5\frac{3}{8} \times 4$, ff. 140 (32), very minute writing, κεφ. t., κεφ., τίτλ., *Am.*, *Eus.*, *lect.*, *subscr.*, στίχ.; probably once contained all the New Testament. It begins now with St. Luke xxiv. 53: *mut.* after I Thess. (Greg. 656.)

643. Cairo, Patriarchal Library 2 [xiii], Gospels, 4to. (Greg. 601.)

644. Cairo, Patr. Libr. 15 [xi]. *Mut.* Gosp., 4to. (Greg. 602.)

645. Cairo, Patr. Libr. 16 [xi], Gosp., 4to, *syn.*, *men.*, beautifully written. (Greg. 603.)

646. Cairo, Patr. Libr. 17 [xi], Gosp., 4to. (Greg. 604.)

647. Cairo, Patr. Libr. 68 [x], Gosp., 4to. (Greg. 605.)

648. Cairo, Μετοικία of St. Katherine of Mount Sinai 7 [xvi], Synopsis of Gospels with Psalter, fol., *chart.* (Greg. 606.)

649. Jerusalem, Holy Sepulchre (monastery of) 2 [x], Gosp., 4to, beautifully written. (Greg. 607.)

650. Jerus. Holy Sepul. 5 [x], Gosp., 4to, beautifully written. (Greg. 608.)

651. Jerus. Holy Sepul. 6 (Scholz 450) [A. D. 1043], St. Luke (Gr. and Arab.), 4to, by Euphemius. Beautifully written[1]. (Greg. 450.)

652. Jerus. Holy Sepul. 14 [xii], Gosp. with scholia, large 4to. (Greg. 610.)

653. Jerus. Holy Sepul. 17 [xi], Gosp. with few scholia, 4to. (Greg. 611.)

654. Jerus. Holy Sepul. 31 [xi], Gosp., 4to, very beautiful. (Greg. 612.)

655. Jerus. Holy Sepul. 32 [xi], Gosp., 4to. (Greg. 613.)

656. Jerus. Holy Sepul. 33 [xii], Gosp., 4to. (Greg. 614.)

657. (Act. 325, Paul. 152.) Jerus. Holy Sepul. 40 [xii], N. T., except Apoc., 4to. A fine copy. (Greg. 615.)

658. Jerus. Holy Sepul. 41 [xi], Gosp., 4to, beautiful. (Greg. 616.)

659. Jerus. Holy Sepul. 43 [xi], Gosp., fol., scholia (Matt. unc. in golden letters). (Scholz 456?) (Greg. 617.)

660. Jerus. Holy Sepul. 44 [xiv], Gosp., fol. (Greg. 618.)

661. (Act. 260, Paul. 304.) Jerus. Holy Sepul. 45 [xii], Gosp., Paul., Cath., with λέξεις τῶν Πράξεων, 4to. (Greg. 619.)

662. Jerus. Holy Sepul. 46 [xi], Gosp., small 4to. (Greg. 620.)

663. Jerus. Holy Cross, 3 [xi], Gosp., 4to, *syn.*, *men.*, κεφ. (Greg. 621.)

664. St. Saba 27 [xii], Gosp., fol. (Greg. 622.)

665. (Act. 328, Paul. 230.) St. Saba 52 [xi], Gosp., Paul., Cath., 4to, *syn.*, *men.* (Greg. 623.)

[1] Gregory considers this to be (not a duplicate but) the same as Cod. 634.

666. Rom. Vat. Gr. 641 [A. D. 1287], $10 \times 6\frac{5}{8}$, ff. 467 (28), *chart.* The Gospels, with Theophylact's commentary. (Greg. 854.)

667. (Act. 317, Paul. 316.) St. Saba 53 [xi], Gosp., Paul., Cath., 4to. (Greg. 624.)

668. Rom. Vat. Gr. 643 [xii], $10\frac{1}{4} \times 8\frac{3}{4}$, ff. 584 (36), *pict.* The Gospels, with Theophylact's commentary. (Greg. 855.)

669. Rom. Vat. Gr. 644 [A. D. 1280], $13 \times 9\frac{1}{2}$, ff. 349 (44), 2 cols., *chart.*, *Am.*, written by order of Michael Palaeologus. Same contents as the preceding. (Greg. 856.)

670. Rom. Vat. Gr. 645 [xii], $11\frac{1}{2} \times 9\frac{1}{8}$, ff. 391 (28), *prol.*, *κεφ. t.*, *κεφ.*, *τίτλ.* St. Luke and St. John, with Theophylact's commentary. (Greg. 857.)

671. (Paul. 311.) Rom. Vat. Gr. 647 [xv or xiv], $13\frac{1}{2} \times 9\frac{3}{4}$, ff. 338 (48), *chart.* Gospels and Epistles, with commentary of Theophylact. (Greg. 858.)

672. Rom. Vat. Gr. 759 [xv or xvi], $8\frac{5}{8} \times 5\frac{3}{4}$, ff. 261, *chart.* St. Luke, with a commentary. (Greg. 859.)

673. (Act. 318, Paul. 317.) St. Saba 54 [xii], Gosp., Paul., Cath., 4to. (Greg. 625.) (Vat. Gr. 1068 is Evst. 122.—Greg.)

674. Rom. Vat. Gr. 1090 [xvi], $10\frac{3}{4} \times 8\frac{1}{4}$, ff. 509 (40), *chart.* The Gospels, with commentary of Peter of Laodicea. Part i and ii. (Greg. 861.)

675. Rom. Vat. Gr. 1191 [xii], $9 \times 6\frac{3}{4}$, ff. 402 (?), written by one 'Arsenius.' St. John, with Theophylact's commentary. (Greg. 862.)

676. Rom. Vat. Gr. 1221 [xii or xiii], $15\frac{1}{8} \times 10\frac{5}{8}$, ff. 400 (41), 2 cols., *κεφ. t.*, *κεφ.*, *τίτλ.*, *lect.*, *subscr.* The Gospels, with Theophylact's commentary. (Greg. 863.)

No. 677 is a Catech., 678 is Evst. 551, 679 a commentary. (Greg.)

677. St. Saba 56 [x], Gosp., 4to. (Greg. 626.)

678. St. Saba 57 [x], Gosp., 4to. (Greg. 627.)

679. St. Saba 58 [x], Gosp., 4to. (Greg. 628.)

680. Rom. Vat. Gr. 1895 [xv or xiv], $6\frac{1}{2} \times 4\frac{3}{8}$, ff. 223 (20), *prol.*, *κεφ. t.*, with *harm.*, *κεφ.*, *lect.*, *ἀναγν.*, *subscr.*, *στίχ.*, *vers.* (Greg. 867.)

681. St. Saba 59 [x], Gosp., 4to. (Greg. 629.)

682. St. Saba 60 [x], Gosp., 4to. (Greg. 630.)

683. Rom. Vat. Gr. 1933 [xvii], $15\frac{5}{8} \times 10\frac{3}{8}$, ff. 624 (26), *chart.* St. Luke, with a Catena. (Greg. 868.)

684. Rom. Vat. Gr. 1996 [xi or xii], $10\frac{7}{8} \times 8\frac{5}{8}$, ff. 245 (25), *κεφ.*, *τίτλ.*, with a commentary. (Greg. 869.)

685. St. Saba 61 *a* [xi], Gosp., 4to. (Greg. 631.)

686. St. Saba 61 *b* [xi], Gosp., 4to. (Greg. 632.)

687. Rom. Vat. Gr. 2117 [xi], $5\frac{1}{4} \times 4\frac{3}{8}$, ff. 164 (29), *prol.*, *κεφ. t.*, *κεφ.*, *τίτλ.*, *subscr.* (later); a beautiful Evangelium. (Greg. 871.)

688. St. Saba 61 *c* [xi], Gosp., 4to. (Greg. 633.)

689. Rom. Vat. Gr. 2165 [xi], $13\frac{3}{8} \times 9\frac{7}{8}$, ff. 289 (23), 2 cols., *Carp.*,

Eus. t., κεφ. *t.*, κεφ., τίτλ., *Am.*, *Eus.*, *subscr.*, ῥήμ., στίχ., olim Columnensis 4. This was Evst. 391. (Greg. 873.)

690. Rom. Vat. Gr. 2160 [xi or xii], $8\frac{1}{4} \times 6\frac{1}{4}$, ff. 180 (26), 2 cols., *Carp.*, *prol.*, κεφ. *t.*, κεφ., τίτλ., *Am.*, *Eus.*, *lect.*, *subscr.*, στίχ., *vers.*, *pict.* 'Venit e familia principe Romanâ De Alteriis, cujus stemma argenteum in tegmine habet.' (Greg. 872.)

691. Rom. Vat. Gr. 2187 [xii or xiii], $11\frac{1}{4} \times 7\frac{3}{4}$, ff. 383 (27), olim Columnensis 26. St. John, with Commentary of Theophylact. (Greg. 874.)

692. Rom. Vat. Gr. 2247 [?], $7\frac{7}{8} \times 5\frac{7}{8}$, ff. 228 (23), *Eus. t.*, *prol.* (John), κεφ. *t.*, *pict.*, κεφ., τίτλ., *Am.*, *Eus.*, *lect.*, *syn.*; a fine codex. Column. 86. (Greg. 875.)

693. Rom. Vat. Gr. 2275 [xvi], $13\frac{5}{8} \times 9\frac{1}{4}$, ff. 2 + 17 (40), *chart.*, fragments of SS. Matt. and John with comm. (Greg. 876.)

694. Rom. Vat. Gr. 2290 [A. D. 1197], $10\frac{1}{2} \times 8\frac{1}{4}$, ff. 218 (25), 2 cols., *Carp.*, *Eus. t.*, *prol.*, κεφ. *t.*, κεφ., τίτλ., *Am.*, *Eus.*, *vers.* A splendid codex. It has been numbered 2161. (Greg. 877.)

695. St. Saba 61 *d* [xi], Gosp., 4to. (Greg. 634.)

696. Rom. Vat. Reg. Gr. 3 [xiii, Greg. xi], $13\frac{7}{8} \times 10\frac{1}{2}$, ff. 256 (30). St. Luke and St. John, with commentary of Chrys.; begins Luke iii. 1. (Greg. 884.)

697. Rom. Vat. Reg. Gr. 5 [xv], $11\frac{5}{8} \times 8\frac{3}{4}$, ff. 439 (29), *chart.* St. Matthew, with a commentary. (Greg. 885.)

698. (Act. 268, Paul. 324, Apoc. 117.) Rom. Vat. Reg. Gr. 6 [A. D. 1454], $13\frac{1}{2} \times 9\frac{3}{4}$, ff. 336 (59), *chart.*, κεφ. *t.* The Gospels, with commentary of Nicetas of Naupactus; Acts and St. Paul, with commentary of Theophylact; Apoc., with the commentary of an anonymous writer. (Greg. 886.)

699. Rom. Vat. Reg. Gr. 9 [xi], $11\frac{3}{4} \times 9\frac{7}{8}$, ff. 197 (38). St. John, with a commentary. (Greg. 887.)

700. St. Saba 61 *e* [xi], Gosp., 4to. (Greg. 635.)

701. St. Saba 62 *a* [xii], Gosp., 4to. (Greg. 636.)

702. St. Saba 62 *b* [xii], Gosp., 4to. (Greg. 637.)

703. Rom. Vat. Ottob. 37 [xii], $13\frac{1}{2} \times 18\frac{1}{2}$, ff. 248 (46), *Eus. t.*, κεφ. *t.*, κεφ., τίτλ., *Am.*, *Eus.*, *lect.*, *vers.*, with the commentary of Theophylact. Pars i et ii. Olim Altempsianus. (Greg. 878.)

704. Rom. Vat. Ottob. 100 [xvi], ff. 105, *chart.*, part of St. Luke, with commentary. (Greg. 879.)

705. Rom. Vat. Ottob. 208 [xv], $8\frac{3}{8} \times 5\frac{3}{4}$, ff. 255 (17), *chart.*, *pict.*, κεφ., τίτλ., *Am.* A fine Evangelium, with pictures. (Greg. 880.)

706. St. Saba 62 *c* [xii], Gosp., 4to. (Greg. 638.)

707.–709. Rom. Vat. Ottob. 453, 454, 456 [xiii, Greg. xv], $13\frac{3}{4} \times 9\frac{1}{2}$, ff. 171 + 171 + 181 (31), *chart.* The Gospels, with Theophylact's commentary. Dr. Gregory, having examined these three, pronounces them parts of the same MS. (Greg. 881.)

710. St. Saba 62 *d* [xii], Gosp., 4to. (Greg. 639.) Dr. Gregory identifies 710 with Evan. 146.

711. St. Saba 62 *e* [xii], Gosp., 4to. (Greg. 640.)

712. St. Saba, Tower Library 45 [xi], Gosp., 4to. (Greg. 641.)

713. Rom. Vat. Pal. 32 [xi or x], $14\frac{1}{4} \times 10\frac{1}{2}$, ff. 181, 2 cols. St. John, with commentary of Chrys. (Greg. 882.)

714. Rom. Vat. Pal. 208 [xv], $8\frac{1}{8} \times 5\frac{1}{8}$, ff. 247 (24), *chart.* St. John, with Theophylact's commentary. (Greg. 883.)

715. St. Saba, Tower Library 46 [xii], Gosp., 4to. (Greg. 642.)

716. St. Saba, Tower Library 47 [xi], Gosp., 4to. (Greg. 643.)

717. Patmos, St. John 2 [xii], Gosp., scholia, 4to. (Greg. 467.)

718. Patmos, St. John 6 [x], Gosp., 4to, *syn.*, *men.* (Greg. 468.)

719 [1]. Patmos, St. John 21 [xii], Gosp., fol. (Greg. 469.)

720. Cyprus, Larnaca [xii], Gosp., 4to, *syn.* (Greg. 644.) Five more were noted by Mr. Coxe, but he was unable through illness to see them. They have been examined since then by Dr. Gregory.

721. Constantinople ἁγίου τάφου 436 [xiii], $7\frac{7}{8} \times 5\frac{7}{8}$, ff. ? (22), written by several hands, *Eus. t.*, *κεφ. t.*, *Am.*, *Eus.* (*See* Greg. 646.)

722. Constant. ἁγ. τάφ. 520 [xiii], $10 \times 7\frac{3}{8}$, ff. ? (24), 2 cols., *Carp.*, *Eus. t.*, *prol.*, *κεφ. t.*, *pict.*, *Am.*, *Eus.*, *subscr.*, *vers.*, *syn.*, *men.* (*See* Greg. 647.)

723. Rom. Angelic. B. i. 5 [xii, Greg. xiv], $11\frac{1}{2} \times 8\frac{3}{4}$, ff. ? (33), *κεφ. t.*, *subscr.*, *στίχ.*, *syn.* Formerly belonged to Card. Passionei. Matt. and Mark with catena. (Greg. 847.)

724. Constant. ἁγ. τάφ. 574 [xiv], $9\frac{1}{2} \times 7$, ff. ? (23), *κεφ. t.*, *lect.*, *subscr.* *Mut.* end of Mark, beg. and end of Luke, many places in John. (Greg. 648.)

725. Constant. τοῦ ἑλληνικοῦ φιλολογικοῦ συλλόγου 1 [A. D. 1303 ?], $11\frac{1}{2} \times 8\frac{5}{8}$, ff. 294 (44), *chart.*, 2 cols. Gospels with commentary much in a later hand. Written by a certain George. (*See* Greg. 649.)

726. Constant. τ. ἑλλ. φιλ. συλλόγ. 5 [xiii], $5\frac{1}{4} \times 7$, ff. ? (24), *κεφ. t.*, *Am.*, *lect.*, *subscr.*, *στίχ.*, *vers.*, *syn.*, *men.* *Mut.* (*See* Greg. 650.)

727, 728, 731, 733. Chalké, Trinity Monastery, ten miles from Constantinople, seen by Dr. Millingen, and reported by Coxe, four Evang., with silver clasps, numbered by him 1, 2, 3, 4. These four MSS. (727, 728, 731, and 733) seem to be the same as those which Dr. Gregory has recorded as 'Chalcis monasterii Trinitatis 11 et 12,' and 'Chalcis scholae 8' and 27 (A. D. 1370, fol., *κεφ. t.*, *lect.*, *ἀναγν.*, *syn.*, *men.*), the latter of which with two more (*see* below, 734, 735) he saw. Dr. Millingen mentions eight; but Dr. Gregory records only six, which must be taken to be the number. *See* Prolegomena 1144–49, p. 608.

729. Rom. Barberini iv. 86 (olim 228) [x, Greg. xii], $11\frac{1}{8} \times 8\frac{1}{2}$, ff. 381 (35 ?), 2 cols. St. John, with Cyril's commentary. (Greg. 850.)

[1] For the other Evann. at Patmos, *see* No. 1160, &c.

730. Rom. Barb. iv. 77 (ol. 210) [xvii], $10\frac{3}{4} \times 8$, ff. 152 (21), *chart.* St. John, with Books v and vi of Cyril's commentary. (Greg. 849.)

732. Rom. Borgian. (Propag.) L. vi. 10 [A. D. 1300], $9\frac{1}{8} \times 6\frac{1}{2}$, ff. 165, *κεφ.*, *τίτλ.*, *Am.*, *syn.*, *men.* The Gospels, with Menologium. 'Birchius eo usus est:' but he makes no mention of it. (Greg. 852.)

734. Chalké, 'Chalcis scholae' 95 [xiii], 4to, *pict.*

735. Chalké (Act. 288, Paul. 336), 'Chalcis scholae' 133 [xiii], 4to.

736. Bought of Muller, the London bookseller, ~~and collated~~ by H. B. Swete, D.D., Regius Professor of Divinity, Cambridge [xi or xii, Greg. xiv], $7\frac{1}{2} \times 6$, ff. 254, in modern binding. After signature 28 seven leaves [xiv?] containing John xviii. 39, ὑμῖν ἵνα to the end are supplied. *Syn.*, *men.*, *prol.*, *vers.*, *κεφ. t.*, *κεφ.*, *Am.* (*Eus.* later), *lect.*, *subscr.* like Λ, *στίχ.* In the margin are textual corrections, some *primâ manu.* The readings are sometimes curious. (Greg. 718.)

737. Ox. Bodl. Misc. Gr. 314, found at Rhodes in 1882, and procured through Mr. Edmund Calvert [xi], $7\frac{1}{2} \times 6$, ff. 118 (21), 2 cols., *κεφ. t.*, *κεφ.*, *τίτλ.*, *Am.*, *Eus.*, *lect.*, *subscr.*, *στίχ.*, *ῥήμ.* *Mut.* Matt. v. 40—xxi. 1; Luke xv. 4—xxii. 49; xxiv. 34–52; John iv. 14—ix. 11; xiii. 3—xv. 10; xvi. 21—xxi. 25 (some fresh leaves having been lately purchased). It was apparently written by an Armenian scribe (F. Madan). A later hand [xiii] supplies Luke iii. 25—iv. 11; vi. 25–42 in palimpsest, over writing not much earlier than itself. (Greg. 709.)

The following MSS. (738–774) are from the late Abbé Martin's list of MSS. at Paris (*see* 'Description Technique'), and are numbered by him as they are given here:—

738. (Act. 262, Apoc. 123.) Par. Nat. Suppl. Gr. 159 [xiii, Greg. xiv], $15\frac{3}{4} \times 11\frac{3}{8}$, ff. 406 (36), *κεφ. t.*, *κεφ.*, *τίτλ.*, *lect.* (Greg. 743.)

739. Par. Nat. Suppl. Gr. 919 [xiii, Greg. xv], $5\frac{7}{8} \times 4\frac{7}{8}$, ff. 19 (47), *Eus. t.*, *prol.*, *syn.*, *men.* (remarkable), *κεφ.*, *Am.*, *Eus.*, *lect.* Contains Matt. ii. 13—ix. 17. (Greg. 751.)

740. Par. Nat. Suppl. Gr. 611 [x, Greg. xi], $10\frac{1}{2} \times 7\frac{3}{4}$, ff. 396 (47), *Carp.*, *Eus. t.*, *κεφ. t.*, *κεφ.*, *τίτλ.*, *Am.*, *Eus.*, *prol.* Section of adultery omitted, a leaf probably lost. (Greg. 746.)

741. Par. Nat. Suppl. Gr. 612 [A. D. 1164], $9\frac{3}{8} \times 7\frac{1}{2}$, ff. 376 (53), *Carp.*, *Eus. t.*, *κεφ. t.*, *τίτλ.*, *prol.*, *Am.*, *Eus.*, *lect.*, *pict.* Commentary. (Greg. 747.)

742. Par. Nat. Suppl. Gr. 914 [xi–xii], $11\frac{3}{4} \times 8\frac{3}{4}$, ff. 319 (20), *κεφ.*, *τίτλ.*, *Am.*, *pict.*, *subscr.* (Greg. 750.)

743. Par. Nat. Gr. 97 [xiii], $8\frac{5}{8} \times 6\frac{1}{8}$, ff. 152 (28), *κεφ.*, *τίτλ.*, *Am.*, *lect.*, *Mut.* John xx. 15–end. Has a double termination to St. Mark written by George. (Greg. 579.)

744. Par. Nat. Gr. 119 [xi, Greg. xii or xiii], $6 \times 4\frac{1}{8}$, ff. 382 (25), Greg. 388 (16), *Carp.*, *Eus. t.*, *κεφ. t.*, *κεφ.*, *τίτλ.*, *Am.*, *syn.*, *men.*, *lect.* A beautiful MS. (Greg. 580.)

745. Par. Nat. Gr. 179 [xvi, Greg. xiv], $13\frac{1}{2} \times 9\frac{7}{8}$, ff. 246 (50), 2 cols., *κεφ. t.*, *κεφ.*, *τίτλ.* Beautiful; Gospels with Theoph. (Greg. 727.)

746. Par. Nat. Gr. 181 [xiii, Greg. xiv], $11\frac{5}{8} \times 8\frac{1}{2}$, ff. 230 (68), 2 cols., *syn.*, *pict.*, *prol.*, κεφ. *t.*, κεφ., τίτλ., *Am.*, *lect.* Gospels with Theoph. (Greg. 728.)

747. Par. Nat. Gr. 182 [xiii], $11\frac{5}{8} \times 8\frac{1}{2}$, ff. 341 (47), 2 cols., κεφ. *t.*, τίτλ. Gospels with Theoph. (Greg. 729.)

748. Par. Nat. Gr. 183 [xiv], $9\frac{7}{8} \times 6\frac{1}{2}$, ff. 331 (32), *chart.*, *prol.*, κεφ. *t.*, τίτλ. *Mut.* John xvi. 4-end. Gospels with Theoph. (Greg. 730.)

749. Par. Nat. Gr. 184 [xiv], $9\frac{1}{2} \times 5\frac{3}{4}$, ff. 426 (40), *chart.*, *prol.*, κεφ. *t.*, τίτλ., *Am.*, *pict.* Gospels with Theoph. (Greg. 731.)

750. Par. Nat. Gr. 185 [xiii or xiv], ff. 271 (38), *chart.*, *syn.*, *Eus. t.*, *prol.*, *Am.*, *lect.*, κεφ., τίτλ. Gospels with Theoph. (Greg. 732.)

751. Par. Nat. Gr. 190 [xii], $11\frac{5}{8} \times 8\frac{3}{4}$, ff. 347 (42), *prol.*, κεφ. *t.*, *pict.* (Matt.), κεφ., τίτλ. (Greg. 733.)

752. Par. Nat. Gr. 192 [xiv or xv], $11\frac{3}{4} \times 8\frac{5}{8}$, ff. 297 (39), (269–297 *chart.*). SS. John, Matt., Luke with Theoph. (Greg. 734.)

753. Par. Nat. Gr. 196 (xiii, Greg. xv), $9\frac{1}{4} \times 6\frac{1}{8}$, ff. 164 (50), latter part a palimpsest. SS. Matt. and Luke with Theoph. *Mut.* Matt. i. 1—vii. 16 (xii. 33, and other places, Greg.) (Greg. 735.)

754. Par. Nat. Gr. 198 [xi or xii], $10\frac{7}{8} \times 7\frac{3}{4}$, ff. 235 (34), κεφ. *t.*, κεφ., τίτλ. Gospels with Theoph. (Greg. 736.)

755. Par. Nat. Gr. 204 [xiii], $10\frac{1}{2} \times 8\frac{1}{8}$, ff. 176 (30), Matt. with Theoph. (Greg. 737.)

756. Par. Nat. Gr. 205 [A.D. 1327], $11\frac{1}{2} \times 8\frac{1}{4}$, ff. 80 (38), *chart.*, κεφ. *t.*, κεφ., τίτλ. Matt. with Theoph. (Greg. 738.)

757. Par. Nat. Gr. 207 [xv], $13\frac{1}{2} \times 8\frac{7}{8}$, ff. 48 (39). Luke with Theoph. (Greg. 739.)

758. Par. Nat. Suppl. Gr. 903 [xii], ?, ff. 278, κεφ. *t.*, κεφ., τίτλ., *Am.*, *lect.*, *subscr.* *Mut.* in many places. (*See* Greg. 748, who also notes that Nat. Gr. 214 is only a homily.)

759. Par. Nat. Suppl. Gr. 219 [xii or xiii], $9\frac{1}{4} \times 8\frac{1}{4}$, ff. 367 (27), τίτλ. (Matt.), *pict.* (Luke). Gospels with Theoph. (Greg. 744.)

760. Par. Nat. Suppl. Gr. 1035, frag. [viii ?] ff. 12; [xi or xii], 8 × 6, ff. 182 (35), *membr.* and *chart.* (*Am.*, *lect.* later). Matt. xxiii. 11–21. (*See* Greg. 753.)

761. Par. Nat. Gr. 234 [xii or xiii, Greg. xiv or xv], $9\frac{3}{4} \times 7$, ff. 441 (36), (Greg. 444 (33, &c.)), *chart.*, *syn.*, κεφ., τίτλ., *lect.* Gospels with Theoph. (Greg. 740.)

762. Par. Nat. Gr. 235 [xiv], $9\frac{3}{8} \times 6\frac{1}{2}$, ff. 362 (26–52), *chart.*, τίτλ., *lect.* Gospels with Theoph. (Greg. 741.)

763. Par. Nat. Suppl. Gr. 1076 [xi], small fol., ff. 465, *Carp.* Brought from Janina. (*See* Greg. 754.)

764. Par. Nat. Gr. 1775 [xv–xvi], $8\frac{1}{2} \times 6$, ff. 160, *chart.* St. John with Theoph. (Greg. 742.)

765. Par. Nat. Coislin. Gr. 128 [Mart. xi, xii, Greg. xiii], $12\frac{5}{8} \times 9\frac{5}{8}$, ff. 344 (40), *prol.*, *κεφ. t.*, *τίτλ.* Gospels with Theoph. (Greg. 1261.)

766. Par. Nat. Coisl. Gr. 129 [xiii, xiv], $12\frac{7}{8} \times 9\frac{1}{2}$, ff. 317 (43), 2 cols. Gospels with Theoph. (Greg. 1262.)

767. Par. Nat. Coisl. Gr. 198 [xiii, xiv], $9\frac{3}{4} \times 6\frac{1}{2}$, ff. 434 (26), *chart.*, *κεφ. t.*, *τίτλ.*, *Am.*, *Eus.* Gospels with Theoph. (Greg. 1263.)

768. Par. Nat. Coisl. Gr. 203 [xii, xiii], $9\frac{3}{4} \times 7\frac{3}{4}$, ff. 435 (33), *κεφ. t.*, *pict.*, *τίτλ.* *Mut.* in places. Gospels with commentary. (Greg. 1265.)

769. Par. Nat. Coisl. Gr. 206 [x or xi], $11 \times 8\frac{1}{2}$, ff. 432 (25), *syn.*, *κεφ. t.*, *κεφ.*, *τίτλ.*, *lect.* (2 vols., Greg.). (Greg. 1266.)

770. (Paul. 478.) Par. Nat. Coisl. Gr. 207 [xiv], $10\frac{7}{8} \times 7\frac{7}{8}$, ff. 295 (36), *chart.* St. John and Rom., 2 Cor., Gal. i. 1—ii. 15 with Theoph. (Greg. 1267.)

771. Par. Nat. Suppl. Gr. 1080 [xiv], 4to, *chart.*, ff. 332. Brought from Janina. (*See* Greg. 755.)

772. Par. Nat. Suppl. 1083 [xi], 4to, ff. 179. *Mut.* at end. Written by Michaelis. (*See* Greg. 756.)

773. Par. Nat. Suppl. Gr. 904 [xii or xiii], $13 \times 9\frac{1}{2}$, ff. 199 (40), *prol.*, *κεφ.*, *τίτλ.* Fragment of Gosp. with Theoph. (Greg. 749.)

774. Par. Nat. Suppl. Gr. 927 [xii or xiii], $6\frac{1}{8} \times 4\frac{1}{2}$, ff. 199 (26), (*syn.*, *men.*, *chart.*), *κεφ.*, *τίτλ.*, *Am.*, *pict.*, *lect.* (later). (Greg. 572.)

CHAPTER IX.

CURSIVE MANUSCRIPTS OF THE GOSPELS.

PART III.

WE have now come to Dr. Gregory's list, where Dr. Scrivener's and the Abbé Martin's have ceased, and shall follow it, except in the case of MSS. which have been already recorded, and which therefore must be replaced by other MSS. Whenever no independent information is at hand, the MS. will be simply noted, and the reader is referred to Dr. Gregory's 'Prolegomena' under the same number. Information from other sources than Dr. Gregory's book will in each case, where the Editor has discovered it, be duly given. Whenever no reference is made to Dr. Gregory's list, the numbers in both lists are the same.

The particulars added to MSS. at Athens are taken from the Catalogue by K. Alcibiades I. Sakkelion, obligingly lent me with others by Mr. J. Rendel Harris; but the press-marks of the MSS. have apparently been changed since Dr. Gregory examined them, and I have not succeeded in obtaining information upon this point. I have therefore identified the MSS. as best I could, and have inserted queries when there seemed to be doubt. The number in brackets is the present press-mark. The two measurements often differ; I have followed that of Sakkelion.

775. Athens, Nat. Sakkelion 3 (58) [xiii], $4\frac{3}{4} \times 4$, ff. 223. Belonged to John Cantacuzenus.

776. Ath. Nat. Sakkel. 5 (76) [xii], $8\frac{1}{4} \times 5\frac{5}{8}$, ff. 387, *pict.*, *prol.*

777. Ath. Nat. Sakkel. 6 (93) [xiv], $8\frac{5}{8} \times 5\frac{3}{4}$, ff. 185, *pict.*

778. Ath. Nat. Sakkel. 7 (80) [xiv], $9\frac{1}{2} \times 6\frac{3}{4}$, ff. 195, *pict.*

779. Ath. Nat. 1 (127) [xiv], $7\frac{7}{8} \times 5\frac{7}{8}$, ff. 171, *pict.*

780. Ath. Nat. 5 (121) [xi], $8\frac{1}{4} \times 6\frac{3}{8}$, ff. 241, scholia in red.

781. Ath. Nat. 14 (110 ?) [xv], $8\frac{5}{8} \times 5\frac{7}{8}$, ff. 197.

782. Ath. Nat. 16 (81 ?) [xiv], $9 \times 7\frac{1}{8}$, ff. 277.

783. Ath. Nat. 17 (71 ?) [xiv], $11\frac{3}{8} \times 8\frac{5}{8}$, ff. 211, *pict.*

784. Ath. Nat. 20 (87 ? ?) [xiv], $8\frac{5}{8} \times 5\frac{7}{8}$, ff. 161, *cotton*, *pict.* *Mut.* beg., κεφ.

785. Ath. Nat. 21 (118) [xi], $7\frac{1}{2} \times 5\frac{7}{8}$, ff. 230, *pict.*

786. Ath. Nat. 22 (125 ?) [xv], $7\frac{1}{8} \times 4\frac{3}{4}$, ff. 280.

787. Ath. Nat. 23 (108 ?) [xiv], ff. 305.

788. Ath. Nat. 26 (74 ?) [x], $8\frac{5}{8} \times 6\frac{3}{4}$, ff. 219, *pict.*

789. Ath. Nat. 27 (134 ?) [xii–xiv], $5\frac{4}{8} \times 4$, ff. 250 (1–23 and 245–50, *chart.*).

790. Ath. Nat. 39 (95 ? ?), $11 \times 7\frac{7}{8}$, ff. 163, *mut.* beg. (167 ff.) and end (many). SS. John and Luke, with commentary of Titus of Bostra.

791. Ath. Nat. 60 (77) [xiv], $8\frac{5}{8} \times 5\frac{7}{8}$, ff. 229, *pict.*

792. (Apoc. 111.) Ath. Nat. 67 M (107) [xv], $3\frac{1}{2} \times 2\frac{3}{4}$, ff. 145. Beautifully written in very small letters.

793. Ath. Nat. 71 (75) [xiv], $6\frac{3}{4} \times 5\frac{7}{8}$, ff. 255, *pict.*

794. (Act. 269, Paul. 401.) Ath. Nat. 118 (122), $8\frac{1}{4} \times 5\frac{7}{8}$, ff. 269.

795. Ath. Nat. 150 (109 ? ?) [xv], $5\frac{7}{8} \times 4$, ff. 324. (In Greg. '2' for '?': else how could *syn.*, *men.*, &c., occur in two leaves ?)

796. (Act. 321, Paul. 276.) Ath. Nat. 767 (160) [xi], $6\frac{3}{8} \times 4\frac{3}{8}$, ff. 323, *Eus. t.*, *pict.*

797. Ath. Nat. (111 ?) [xv], $7\frac{1}{2} \times 5\frac{1}{2}$, ff. 223.

798. Ath. Nat. (137 ?) [xiv], $6\frac{3}{4} \times 4\frac{3}{8}$, ff. 113, *mut.* ff. 2 at beg., and from Mark viii. 3 to end of Gospels, *pict.*

799. Ath. Nat. 117 [xi], $7\frac{7}{8} \times 5\frac{1}{2}$, ff. 366.

800. Ath. Nat. 150 (65 ?) [xii], $10\frac{3}{4} \times 7\frac{1}{2}$.

801. (Act. 326, Paul. 313.) Ath. Nat. (130) [xv], $8\frac{1}{4} \times 5\frac{1}{2}$, ff. 324.

802. Ath. Nat. (99) [xiv], $9\frac{7}{8} \times 7\frac{1}{2}$, ff. 24. St. Luke i. 1—vi. 13.

803. Ath. Nat. (88) [xvi], $8\frac{5}{8} \times 5\frac{7}{8}$, ff. 176. Gospels except St. John.

804. Ath. τῆς Βουλῆς.

805. Ath. τῆς Βουλῆς.

806. Ath. τῆς Βουλῆς.

807. Ath. τῆς Βουλῆς.

808. (Act. 265, Paul. 403, Apoc. 150.) Ath. Dom. Mamoukae.

809. Ath. Dom. Mamoukae.

810. Ath. Dom. Οἰκονόμου 6.

811. Ath. Soc. Archaeolog. Christ.

812. Corcyra, Abp. Eustathius.

813. Corcyra, Abp. Eustathius.

814. Corcyra, Abp. Eustathius.

815. Corcyra, Comes de Gonemus.

816. Corcyra.

817. Basle, A. N. iii. 15.

818. Escurial Ψ. iii. 13.

819. Escurial Ψ. iii. 14.

820. Escurial Ω. i. 16.

821. Madrid, Reg. O. 10.

822. Madrid, Reg. O. 62.

823. (Act. 266, Paul. 404.) Berlin Reg. 8vo. 13.

824. Vienna, Imp. Gr. Theol. 19. (Greg. 719.)

825. Vienna, Imp. Gr. Theol. 79, 80. (Greg. 720.)

826. Vienna, Imp. Gr. Theol. 90. (Greg. 721.)

827. Vienna, Imp. Gr. Theol. 95. (Greg. 722.)

828. Vienna, Imp. Gr. Theol. 122. (Greg. 723.)

829. Vienna, Imp. Priv. Bibl. 7972. (Greg. 724.)

830. Milan, Ambr. A. 178 supr. (Greg. 589.)

831. Parma, Reg. 15. (Greg. 590.)

832. (Act. 143.) Florence, Laurentian Libr. vi. 5.

833. Florence, Laurent. vi. 26.

834. Flor. Laur. xi. 6.

835. Flor. Laur. xi. 8.

836. Flor. Laur. xi. 18.

837. Milan, Ambr. E. S. iv. 14. Ff. 34–66.

838. Formerly Milan, 'Hoeplii.'

839. Messina, Univ. 88.

840. Messina, Univ. 100.

841. Modena, iii. F. 13.

842. Modena, G. 9.

843. Naples, Nat. Libr. II. AA. 37.

844. Padua, Univ. 695.

845. Pistoia, Fabron. Libr. 307.

846. Athens, Nat. Theol. (150, 12) [xv], $11\frac{3}{4} \times 8\frac{5}{8}$ (Act. 209, Paul. 399, Apoc. 146), ff. 414, *syn.*, *men.*, *κεφ.*, *prol.*, *pict.* (Greg. 757.)

847. Athens, Nat. Theol. (151, 13) [xiv], $5\frac{1}{2} \times 4$, ff. 301, *κεφ. t.*, *κεφ.*, *τίτλ.*, *pict.*, &c. (Greg. 758.)

848. Ath. Nat. Theol. (152, 14) [xiii], $8\frac{5}{8} \times 5\frac{7}{8}$, ff. 295, *Carp.*, *Eus. t.*, *prol.*, *κεφ. t.*, *prol. Theophyl.*, *pict.*, *κεφ.*, *τίτλ.*, &c., *vers.*, *syn.*, *men.*, *ἀναγν.* (Greg. 759.)

849. Ath. Nat. Theol. (153, 15) [xiv], $8\frac{1}{4} \times 6\frac{3}{8}$, ff. 283, *Eus. t.* (Greg. 760.)

850. Ath. Nat. Theol. (154, 16) [xiv], $8\frac{1}{4} \times 6$, ff. 281, *syn.*, *men.*, *Carp.*, *Eus. t.*, *prol.*, *κεφ. t.*, *κεφ.* (Greg. 761.)

851. Rom. Propag. L. vi. 9.

852. Ath. Nat. Theol. (155, 17) [xiv], $9 \times 6\frac{3}{8}$, ff. 332, *syn.* (Greg. 762.)

853. Rom. Casanatensis G. ii. 9.

854. Ath. Nat. Theol. (156, 18) [xv], $9\frac{1}{2} \times 6\frac{3}{8}$, ff. 324 (4 *chart.*), *pict.* (Greg. 763.)

855. Ath. Nat. Theol. (157, 19) [xii], $11\frac{3}{8} \times 7\frac{1}{2}$, ff. 316, *mut.* at beg. and end. (Greg. 764.)

856. Ath. Nat. Theol. (158, 20) [xiv], $7\frac{1}{2} \times 5\frac{1}{8}$, ff. 229. (Greg. 765.)

857. Ath. Nat. Theol. (159, 21) [xiv], $7\frac{7}{8} \times 4\frac{3}{4}$, ff. 316 (12 *chart.*). (Greg. 766.)

858. (Act. 267, Paul. 400.) Ath. Nat. Theol. (160, 22) [xi], ff. 323, *Eus. t.*, *pict.* (Greg. 767.)

859. Ath. Nat. Theol. (161, 23) [xiv], $7\frac{1}{8} \times 5\frac{1}{2}$, ff. 222 (14 *chart.*). (Greg. 768.)

860. Rom. Vat. Gr. 774.

861. Ath. Nat. Theol. (162, 24) [xv], $9 \times 6\frac{3}{8}$, ff. 253. (Greg. 769.)

862. Ath. Nat. Theol. (203, 66) [xi], $10\frac{5}{8} \times 7\frac{7}{8}$, ff. 270, *mut.* beg. and end. (Greg. 770.)

863. Ath. Nat. Theol. (204, 67) [x], $12\frac{1}{2} \times 9$, ff. 153, *mut.* middle and end, *vers.* (Greg. 771.)

864. Rom. Vat. Gr. 1253. 865. Rom. Vat. Gr. 1472.

866. Rom. Vat. Gr. 1882, ff. 10–16 (Apoc. 115).

867. Ath. Nat. Theol. (489, 216) [xv], $10\frac{1}{4} \times 7\frac{1}{2}$, ff. 387 (21 *chart.*, comm. of Theophylact). (Greg. 772.)

868. Ath. Nat. Sakkelion 1 (56) [x], $13\frac{3}{8} \times 9\frac{7}{8}$, ff. 285, *pict.*, *mut.*, *Carp.*, *Eus. t.* (Greg. 773.)

869. Ath. Nat. Sakkel. 2 (57) [xi–xii], $10\frac{3}{4} \times 7\frac{7}{8}$, ff. (368 − 3 plain =) 365, *pict.*, *Carp.*, *Eus. t.*, *vers.* (Greg. 774.)

870. Rom. Vat. Gr. 2115, ff. 166–170.

871. Montpelier, Schol. Med. H. 446. (Greg. 577.)

872. Arras, 970. (Greg. 578.) 873. Rom. Vat. Gr. 2165.

874. Dessau. (Greg. 651.)

875. Munich, Reg. 594. (Greg. 652.)

876. Berlin, Reg. Gr. 4to, 12. (Greg. 657.)

877. Strasburg, Ed. Reuss. (Greg. 663.)

878. Petersburg, Imp. Muralt. 56 (vii). (Greg. 567.)

879. Petersburg, Imp. Muralt. 67. (Greg. 568.)

880. Petersburg, Imp. Muralt. 105. (Greg. 574.)

881. Brussels, Reg. 11,358. (Greg. 725.)

882. Brussels, Reg. 11,375. (Greg. 726.)

883. Rom. Corsin. 41 G. 16. (Greg. 591.)

884. London, Mr. White 2. (Greg. 702.)

885. Formerly London, Quaritch [1251]. (Greg. 703.)

886. Manchester, Rylands Library, formerly Quaritch [xiii], $4\frac{3}{8} \times 3\frac{1}{4}$, ff. 324 (18), 2 cols., with Latin version to St. Matthew. (Greg. 704.)

887. Hackney, Lord Amherst, formerly Quaritch [xiii], $9\frac{1}{2} \times 6\frac{3}{4}$, ff. 253 (18), *κεφ. t.*, *pict.* (Greg. 705.)

888. Venice, St. Mark 26. 889. Venice, St. Mark 30.

890. Venice, St. Mark 31. 891. Venice, St. Mark 32. (Paul. 325.)

892. Lond. Brit. Mus. Add. 33,277 [x], $6 \times 4\frac{1}{2}$, ff. 353 (20), *chart.* at end and later, *syn.*, *men.*, *κεφ. t.*, *κεφ.*, *lect.*, *Am.*, *Eus.*, *vers.*, *subscr.* Beautifully written in minute characters, but damaged and faded. Bought from H. L. Dupuis in 1887. (Collated by J. R. Harris, Journal of Biblical Literature, ix. 1890.)

893. Venice, St. Mark i. 61. 894. Venice, St. Mark ii. 144.

895. Cheltenham, 6899. (Greg. 665.)

896. Edinburgh, Mackellar.

897. Edinburgh, Univ. David Laing 6.
898. Edinburgh, Univ. Laing, 667.
899. Massachusetts, Harvard. (Greg. 666.)
900. New ~~Caesarea~~ (U.S.A.), Madison, Drew 3. (Greg. 667.)
901. Tennessee (U.S.A.), Sewanee, Benton 2. (Greg. 670.)
902. Tennessee, Sewanee, Benton 3. (Greg. 669.)
903. Cairo, Patriarch. Alex. 421.
904. Cairo, Patriarch. Alex. 952.
905. Athos, St. Andrew A'.
906. Athos, St. Andrew E'.
907. Athos, St. Andrew H'.
908. Athos, St. Andrew Θ'.
909. Athos, Vatopedi 206.
910. Athos, Vatopedi 207.
911. Athos, Vatopedi 211.
912. Athos, Vatopedi 212.
913. Athos, Vatopedi 213.
914. Athos, Vatopedi 214.
915. Athos, Vatopedi 215.
916. Athos, Vatopedi 216.
917. Athos, Vatopedi 217.
918. Athos, Vatopedi 218.
919. Athos, Vatopedi 219 [June, 1112, Greg. 1116], 16mo. Written by one Constantine. (Greg. Constantius.)
920. Athos, Vatopedi 220.
921. Athos, Vatopedi 414.
922. Athos, Gregory 3. (Act. 270, Paul. 407, Apoc. 151.)
923. Athos, Gregory τοῦ ἡγουμένου.
924. Athos, Dionysius 4.
925. Athos, Dionysius 5.
926. Athos, Dionysius 7.
927. Athos, Dionysius 8.
928. Athos, Dionysius 9.
929. Athos, Dionysius 12.
930. Athos, Dionysius 22.
931. Athos, Dionysius 23.
932. Athos, Dionysius 24.
933. Athos, Dionysius 25.
934. Athos, Dionysius 26.
935. Athos, Dionysius 27.
936. Athos, Dionysius 28.
937. Athos, Dionysius 29.
938. Athos, Dionysius 30.
939. Athos, Dionysius 31.
940. Athos, Dionysius 32.
941. Athos, Dionysius 33.
942. Athos, Dionysius 34.
943. Athos, Dionysius 35.
944. Athos, Dionysius 36.
945. Athos, Dionysius 37.
946. Athos, Dionysius 38.
947. Athos, Dionysius 39.
948. Athos, Dionysius 40.
949. Athos, Dionysius 64.
950. Athos, Dionysius 67.
951. Athos, Dionysius 80.
952. Athos, Dionysius 310.
953. Athos, Dionysius 311.
954. Athos, Dionysius 312.
955. Athos, Dionysius 313.
956. Athos, Dionysius 314.
957. Athos, Dionysius 315.
958. Athos, Dionysius 316.
959. Athos, Dionysius 317.
960. Athos, Dionysius 318.
961. Athos, Dionysius 319.
962. Athos, Dionysius 320.
963. Athos, Dionysius 321.
964. Athos, Docheiariou 7.

965. Athos, Docheiariou 21.
966. Athos, Docheiariou 22.
967. Athos, Docheiariou 30.
968. Athos, Docheiariou 35.
969. Athos, Docheiariou 39.
970. Athos, Docheiariou 42.
971. Athos, Docheiariou 46.
972. Athos, Docheiariou 49.
973. Athos, Docheiariou 51.
974. Athos, Docheiariou 52.
975. Athos, Docheiariou 55.
976. Athos, Docheiariou 56.
977. Athos, Docheiariou 59.
978. Athos, Docheiariou 76.
979. Athos, Docheiariou 142.
980. Athos, Esphigmenou 25.
981. Athos, Esphigmenou 26.
982. At' os, Esphigmenou 27.
983. Athos, Esphigmenou 29.
984. Athos, Esphigmenou 30.
985. Athos, Esphigmenou 31.
986. Athos, Esphigmenou 186.

987. Athos, Zographou 4 [xii], 8vo, ff. 176. Repaired with paper leaves at beginning and end.

988. Athos, Zographou 14 [1674], 8vo. Written by one Theocletus.

989. Athos, Iveron 2.
990. Athos, Iveron 5.
991. Athos, Iveron 7.
992. Athos, Iveron 9.
993. Athos, Iveron 18.
994. Athos, Iveron 19.
995. Athos, Iveron 21.
996. Athos, Iveron 28. (Act. 278, Paul. 431.)
997. Athos, Iveron 29. (Act. 279, Paul. 432.)
998. Athos, Iveron 30.
999. Athos, Iveron 31. (Act. 280, Paul. 433.)
1000. Athos, Iveron 32.
1001. Athos, Iveron 33.
1002. Athos, Iveron 51.
1003. Athos, Iveron 52.
1004. Athos, Iveron 53.
1005. Athos, Iveron 55.
1006. Athos, Iveron 56.
1007. Athos, Iveron 59.
1008. Athos, Iveron 61.
1009. Athos, Iveron 63.
1010. Athos, Iveron 66.
1011. Athos, Iveron 67.
1012. Athos, Iveron 68.
1013. Athos, Iveron 69.
1014. Athos, Iveron 72.
1015. Athos, Iveron 75.
1016. Athos, Iveron 371.
1017. Athos, Iveron 548.
1018. Athos, Iveron 549.
1019. Athos, Iveron 550.
1020. Athos, Iveron 562.
1021. Athos, Iveron 599.
1022. Athos, Iveron 607.
1023. Athos, Iveron 608.
1024. Athos, Iveron 610.
1025. Athos, Iveron 636.
1026. Athos, Iveron 641.
1027. Athos, Iveron 647.
1028. Athos, Iveron 665.
1029. Athos, Iveron 671.
1030. Athos, Iveron 809.
1031. Athos, Iveron 871.
1032. Athos, Caracalla 19.
1033. Athos, Caracalla 20.

1034. Athos, Caracalla 31.
1035. Athos, Caracalla 34.
1036. Athos, Caracalla 35.
1037. Athos, Caracalla 36.
1038. Athos, Caracalla 37.
1039. Athos, Caracalla 111.
1040. Athos, Caracalla 121.
1041. Athos, Caracalla 128.
1042. Athos, Caracalla 198.
1043. Athos, Constamonitou 1. Theophylact on SS. Matt. and John?
1044. Athos, Constamonitou 61 [xvi], 8vo, *chart.*, *mut.*
1045. Athos, Constamonitou 106 [xiii], 16mo. Begins with St. Luke.
1046. Athos, Coutloumoussi 67.
1047. Athos, Coutloumoussi 68.
1048. Athos, Coutloumoussi 69.
1049. Athos, Coutloumoussi 70.
1050. Athos, Coutloumoussi 71.
1051. Athos, Coutloumoussi 72.
1052. Athos, Coutloumoussi 73.
1053. Athos, Coutloumoussi 74.
1054. Athos, Coutloumoussi 75.
1055. Athos, Coutloumoussi 76.
1056. Athos, Coutloumoussi 77.
1057. Athos, Coutloumoussi 78.
1058. Athos, Coutloumoussi 90[a]. (Act. 283, Paul. 472.)
1059. Athos, Coutloumoussi 278.
1060. Athos, Coutloumoussi 281.
1061. Athos, Coutloumoussi 283.
1062. Athos, Coutloumoussi 284.
1063. Athos, Coutloumoussi 285.
1064. Athos, Coutloumoussi 286.
1065. Athos, Coutloumoussi 287.
1066. Athos, Coutloumoussi 288.
1067. Athos, Coutloumoussi 289.
1068. Athos, Coutloumoussi 290.
1069. Athos, Coutloumoussi 291.
1070. Athos, Coutloumoussi 293.
1071. Athos, Laura *.
1072. (Act. 284, Paul. 476, Apoc. 160.) Athos, Laura *.
1073. (Act. 285.) Athos, Laura *.
1074. Athos, Laura *.
1075. (Act. 286, Paul. 478, Apoc. 161.) Athos, Laura *.
1076. Athos, Laura *.
1077. Athos, Laura *.
1078. Athos, Laura *.
1079. Athos, Laura *.
1080. Athos, Laura *.

* Dr. Gregory has seen these ten MSS., but gives no press-mark.

1081. Athos, Xeropotamou 103.
1082. Athos, Xeropotamou 105.
1083. Athos, Xeropotamou 107.
1084. Athos, Xeropotamou 108.
1085. Athos, Xeropotamou 115.
1086. Athos, Xeropotamou 123.
1087. Athos, Xeropotamou 200.
1088. Athos, Xeropotamou 205.
1089. Athos, Xeropotamou 221.
1090. Athos, in Ecclesia.
1091. Athos, Panteleemon xxv.
1092. Athos, Panteleemon xxvi.
1093. Athos, Panteleemon xxviii.
1094. (Act. 287, Paul. 480, Apoc. 182.) Athos, Panteleemon xxix.
1095. Athos, Paul 4 [xiv], 8vo, *pict.*, *τίτλ.*, *syn.*, *men.*

1096. Athos, Paul 5 [xiii], 8vo. A leaf, 2 cols., of St. Matt. added at the end.

1097. Athos, Protaton 41 [x], 8vo. With histories of the Evangelists.

1098. Athos, Simopetra 25.

1099. Athos, Simopetra 26.

1100. Athos, Simopetra 29.

1101. Athos, Simopetra (34?).

1102. Athos, Simopetra 38.

1103. Athos, Simopetra 39.

1104. Athos, Simopetra 40.

1105. Athos, Simopetra 41.

1106. Athos, Simopetra 63.

1107. Athos, Simopetra 145.

1108. Athos, Simopetra 146.

1109. Athos, Simopetra 147.

1110. Athos, Stauroniketa 43.

1111. Athos, Stauroniketa 53.

1112. Athos, Stauroniketa 54.

1113. Athos, Stauroniketa 56.

1114. Athos, Stauroniketa 70.

1115. Athos, Stauroniketa 97.

1116. Athos, Stauroniketa 127.

1117. Athos, Philotheou 5.

1118. Athos, Philotheou 21.

1119. Athos, Philotheou 22.

1120. Athos, Philotheou 33.

1121. Athos, Philotheou 39.

1122. Athos, Philotheou 41.

1123. Athos, Philotheou 44.

1124. Athos, Philotheou 45.

1125. Athos, Philotheou 46.

1126. Athos, Philotheou 47.

1127. Athos, Philotheou 48.

1128. Athos, Philotheou 51.

1129. Athos, Philotheou 53.

1130. Athos, Philotheou 68.

1131. Athos, Philotheou 71.

1132. Athos, Philotheou 72.

1133. Athos, Philotheou 74.

1134. Athos, Philotheou 77.

1135. Athos, Philotheou 78.

1136. Athos, Philotheou 80.

1137. Athos, Philotheou 86.

1138. Athos, Chiliandari 5 [xii], 8vo, *orn.*

1139. Athos, Chiliandari 19 [xviii], 8vo, *chart.*

1140. Athos, Chiliandari 105 [xiv], 4to. Golden letters, very handsome, 11 lines, 2 cols.

1141. Berat, Archbp.

1142. Berat, Mangalemine Church.

1143. Berat, Church *τοῦ εὐαγγελισμοῦ.*

1144. New York, Syracuse. (Greg. 668.)

1145. Athens, Nat. Libr. 13 [xv], $5\frac{5}{8} \times 4$, ff. 299.

1146. Ath. Nat. Libr. 139 [xv], $6\frac{3}{8} \times 4\frac{3}{8}$, ff. 444. *Mut.* at beg. and end. With commentary. Two palimpsest leaves [viii].

1147. Ath. Nat. Libr. 347 [ix–x], $7\frac{7}{8} \times 5\frac{1}{8}$, ff. 131. Palimpsest. Other writing. Hymns and Prayers [A. D. 1406].

1148. Jerusalem, Patriarchal Library 25 [xi], $11\frac{3}{8} \times 9\frac{1}{2}$, ff. 273 (17), *syn.*, *κεφ. t.*, *proll.*, *στίχ.*, *scholia.* *Mut.* from fire and damp, Luke i. 1–25; John xxi. 17–end; ff. 127, 128 partially mutilated[1].

[1] For all these MSS. (Evann. 1148, 1149, 1261, 1262, 1263, 1265–1268, 1274–1279), *see* Ἱεροσολυμιτικὴ Βιβλιοθήκη, κ.τ.λ., ὑπὸ Α. Παπαδοπούλου Π. Κεραμέως. Τόμος Πρῶτος. Ἐν Πετρουπόλει, 1891.

1149. (Paul. 53.) Jerus. Patr. Libr. 28 [xi], 11 × 9¼, ff. 212 (21), *κεφ. t.*, *στίχ.*, *scholia*. Brought in 1562 by Peter τοῦ Καραμανίτου.

1150. Constantinople, St. Sepulchre 227.

1151. Constantinople, St. Sepulch. 417.

1152. Constantinople, St. Sepulch. 419.

1153. Constantinople, St. Sepulch. 435.

1154. Constantinople, St. Sepulch. 439.

1155. Constantinople, St. Sepulch. 441.

1156. Lesbos, Mon. τοῦ Λείμωνος 356. Commentary of St. Chrysostom on St. John, and commentary of Theophylact on St. Matt., perhaps with St. Matt. [xiv], 12¾ × 10¼, by the hand of Michael the monk, partly on vellum (ff. 1–4, and 121–125, 2 cols.), chiefly on cotton (ff. 116, 1 col.). (Papadop. Kar. Παράρτημα τοῦ ΙϚ τόμου. Constantinople, 1885.)

1157. Lesb. Mon. τοῦ Λείμων. 67 [xi], 9¼ × 7⅛, ff. 395, *κεφ.*, *subscr.* Latin between the lines of John i. 1–12.

1158. Lesb. Mon. τοῦ Λείμων. 97 *chart.* [xv], 7⅞ × 5¾, with two vellum leaves [xi].

1159. Lesb. Mon. τοῦ Λείμων. 99 [xiv, end], 9½ × 6⅜, *l*, *κεφ. t.*, *pict.*, Luke *mut.*, John wanting.

1160. Patmos 58. 1161. Patmos 59 [x], 4to. Seen by Coxe.

1162. Patmos 60. 1163. Patmos 76. 1164. Patmos 80.

1165. Patmos 81. 1166. Patmos 82. 1167. Patmos 83.

1168. Patmos 84. 1169. Patmos 90. 1170. Patmos 92.

1171. Patmos 94. 1172. Patmos 95. 1173. Patmos 96.

1174. Patmos 97. 1175. Patmos 98. 1176. Patmos 100.

1177. Patmos 117. 1178. Patmos 203. 1179. Patmos 275.

1180. Patmos 333. 1181. Patmos 335.

1182. Thessalonica, ἑλληνικοῦ γυμνασίου 6.

1183. Thess. ἑλλην. γυμνασ. 11.

1184. Thess., at the house of *Ku.* Σπυρίου.

1185. Sinai, Mt. Catherine 148. 1186. Sinai, Mt. Catherine 149.

1187. Sinai, Mt. Cath. 150. 1188. Sinai, Mt. Cath. 151.

1189. Sinai, Mt. Cath. 152. 1190. Sinai, Mt. Cath. 153.

1191. Sinai, Mt. Cath. 154. 1192. Sinai, Mt. Cath. 155.

1193. Sinai, Mt. Cath. 156. 1194. Sinai, Mt. Cath. 157.

1195. Sinai, Mt. Cath. 158. 1196. Sinai, Mt. Cath. 159.

1197. Sinai, Mt. Cath. 160. 1198. Sinai, Mt. Cath. 161.

1199. Sinai, Mt. Cath. 162. 1200. Sinai, Mt. Cath. 163.

1201. Sinai, Mt. Cath. 164.

1202. (Act. 417.) Sinai, Mt. Cath. 165.

1203. Sinai, Mt. Cath. 166. 1204. Sinai, Mt. Cath. 167.

1205. Sinai, Mt. Cath. 168.
1206. Sinai, Mt. Cath. 169.
1207. Sinai, Mt. Cath. 170.
1208. Sinai, Mt. Cath. 171.
1209. Sinai, Mt. Cath. 172.
1210. Sinai, Mt. Cath. 173.
1211. Sinai, Mt. Cath. 174.
1212. Sinai, Mt. Cath. 175.
1213. Sinai, Mt. Cath. 176.
1214. Sinai, Mt. Cath. 177.
1215. Sinai, Mt. Cath. 178.
1216. Sinai, Mt. Cath. 179.
1217. Sinai, Mt. Cath. 180.
1218. Sinai, Mt. Cath. 181.
1219. Sinai, Mt. Cath. 182.
1220. Sinai, Mt. Cath. 183.
1221. Sinai, Mt. Cath. 184.
1222. Sinai, Mt. Cath. 185.
1223. Sinai, Mt. Cath. 186.
1224. Sinai, Mt. Cath. 187.
1225. Sinai, Mt. Cath. 188.
1226. Sinai, Mt. Cath. 189.
1227. Sinai, Mt. Cath. 190.
1228. Sinai, Mt. Cath. 191.
1229. Sinai, Mt. Cath. 192.
1230. Sinai, Mt. Cath. 193.
1231. Sinai, Mt. Cath. 194.
1232. Sinai, Mt. Cath. 195.
1233. Sinai, Mt. Cath. 196.
1234. Sinai, Mt. Cath. 197.
1235. Sinai, Mt. Cath. 198.
1236. Sinai, Mt. Cath. 199.
1237. Sinai, Mt. Cath. 200.
1238. Sinai, Mt. Cath. 201.
1239. Sinai, Mt. Cath. 203.
1240. Sinai, Mt. Cath. 259.
1241. Sinai, Mt. Cath. 260.
1242. Sinai, Mt. Cath. 261.
1243. Sinai, Mt. Cath. 262.
1244. Sinai, Mt. Cath. 263.
1245. Sinai, Mt. Cath. 264.
1246. Sinai, Mt. Cath. 265.
1247. Sinai, Mt. Cath. 266.
1248. Sinai, Mt. Cath. 267.
1249. Sinai, Mt. Cath. 268.
1250. Sinai, Mt. Cath. 269.
1251. Sinai, Mt. Cath. 270.
1252. Sinai, Mt. Cath. 302.
1253. Sinai, Mt. Cath. 303.
1254. Sinai, Mt. Cath. 304.
1255. Sinai, Mt. Cath. 305.
1256. Sinai, Mt. Cath. 306.
1257. Smyrna, Schol. Evan. Γ'. 1.
1258. Smyrn. Schol. Evan. Γ'. 2.
1259. Smyrn. Schol. Evan. Γ'. 5.
1260. Cortona, Bibl. Commun. 201.

1261. Jerusalem, Patriarch. Libr. 31 [xi], $10\frac{1}{2} \times 8$, ff. 295 (20), *Eus. t., prol., pict., κεφ. t.* Brought from Tauronesus to Constantinople before 1683.

1262. (Act. 417, Paul. 57, Apoc. 153.) Jerus. Patr. Libr. 37 [xi], $9\frac{3}{8} \times 7$, ff. 355 (31), *κεφ. t., proll., pict., carp., glossary, κεφ. Mut.* end of 1 Pet., Heb.–end. Has signature of Patriarch Sophronius, A.D. 1604–5. According to another note Thomas and Georgilas and their relatives offered it in 1589.

1263. Jerus. Patr. Libr. 41 [xi], $9\frac{1}{4} \times 6\frac{1}{2}$, ff. 298 (21), of which three are plain, *τίτλ., κεφ., pict.* Fine letters.

1264. Paris, Nat. Coislin. Gr. 201.

1265. Jerus. Patr. Libr. 42 [xi], $9 \times 7\frac{1}{2}$, 248 (19), *τίτλ., κεφ.* (gold). *Mut.* at beginning of each Evangelist, and several leaves cut off at the end.

1266. Jerus. Patr. Libr. 46 [xii], $8\frac{1}{2} \times 6\frac{3}{8}$, ff. 278 (25), one leaf cut out after f. 80, and ff. 15 and 16 palimpsest.

1267. (Act. 329, Paul. 380.) Jerus. Patr. Libr. 47 [xi], $8\frac{5}{8} \times 6\frac{1}{2}$, ff. 216 (40), 130–137 being cotton [xiii], *vers.*, *pict.*, *syn.* Very beautiful. Brought from Cyprus.

1268. Jerus. Patr. Libr. 48 [xi], $8 \times 6\frac{3}{8}$, ff. 258 (7 being plain), *κεφ. t.*, *Carp.*, *Eus. t.*, *orn.*

1269. Rom. Vat. Urb. 4.

1270. Cairo, Patriarch. Alex. 82.

1271. Cairo, Patriarch. Alex. 87.

1272. Athens, Nat. 111.

1273. Auckland (New Zealand), City Library.

1274. Jerus. Patr. Libr. 49 [xi, 1st quarter], $8\frac{1}{4} \times 6\frac{5}{8}$, ff. 306 (18), 8 being blank, *κεφ. t.* (gold), *Carp.*, *Eus. t.*, *pict.*, *syn.*, *men.*

1275. Jerus. Patr. Libr. 56 [xi], $7\frac{1}{4} \times 5\frac{3}{4}$, ff. 218 (23), *Eus. t.* (κανόνιον ?), *κεφ. t.*, *pict.*, *syn.* Came from St. Saba.

1276. Jerus. Patr. Libr. 59 [xi], $5\frac{1}{2} \times 4\frac{1}{4}$, ff. 299 (23), 12 blank, *Carp.*, *κεφ. t.*, *pict.*, *lect.* First page in vermilion, rest in gold. Written in Palestine.

1277. Jerus. Patr. Libr. 60 [xi], $5\frac{1}{2} \times 4\frac{3}{8}$, ff. 299 (23), 12 blank, *κεφ. t.*, *Carp.*, *Eus. t.* (κανόνιον), *pict.* First page in vermilion, rest in gold on purple.

1278. Jerus. Patr. Libr. 62 [May 1, 1721], ?, ff. 385, 2 cols., *chart.* In Greek and Turkish (written in Greek letters). *Prol.*, *pict.*

1279. Jerus. Patr. Libr. 139 [xiv], $11\frac{3}{8} \times 8\frac{1}{4}$, ff. 124 (34), *chart.*

1280. Lesbos, τ. Λείμωνος μονῆς 141 [xv], $8\frac{5}{8} \times 5\frac{7}{8}$, ff. ?, *chart.* *Mut.* beginning and end, and in other places.

1281. Lesbos, τ. Λείμωνος μονῆς 145 [xv], $8\frac{1}{2} \times 5\frac{3}{4}$. *Chart.*

1282. Lesbos, τ. Λείμωνος μονῆς 227 [xii], $6\frac{1}{2} \times 5\frac{1}{8}$, ff. 136. *Mut.* Matt. i. 1—vii. 5; Mark i. 1–15; Luke xix. 32—John xxi. 25.

1283. Lesbos, Μανταμάδου, Ταξίαρχοι ΚΑ [xiii], $8\frac{5}{8} \times 6\frac{1}{2}$, ff. 288. Written by one Macarius.

1284. Mitylene, Libr. of Gymnasion 9 [xii–xiii], $10\frac{1}{4} \times 7\frac{1}{2}$, ff. 292 + 8 *chart.*, 2 cols., *pict.*

1285. Mityl. Libr. Gym. 41 [x], $7\frac{1}{8} \times 5\frac{3}{8}$, ff. 258. *Mut.* at beginning, &c. ff. 3 [xiii].

1286. Andros, Μονὴ ἁγία 1 [1156], size not given, ff. 342 (20), *κεφ. t.*, *pict.*

1287. Andros, Μ. ἁγ. 33 [xii–xiii]. One leaf *mut.*

1288. Andros, Μ. ἁγ. 34 [1523], 6 ff. at end *chart.* Well written.

1289. Andros, Μ. ἁγ. 35. Like the last, several perished folios have been replaced by paper ones.

1290. Andros, Μ. ἁγ. 37 [xii]. Sumptuous binding with precious stones and silver tablets.

1291. Andros, Μ. ἁγ. 38. *Chart.*, *vers.*

1292. Andros, Μ. ἁγ. 48 [1709]. Beautiful and perfect. *Κεφ. t.*, *pict.*

1293. Andros, M. ἀγ. 49 [1234]. Κεφ. and other ornaments cut out. Like 34.

1294. Andros, M. ἀγ. 50 [xii–xiii]. *Mut.* at beginning and end, &c.

1295. Kosinitsa, Mon. Libr. 219 [1285].

1296. Kosinitsa, Mon. Libr. 58 [ix–x], 12 × 8, ff. 288. *Pict.*, κεφ. *t.*, *proll.* (various), *scholia.* Written in early minuscules.

1297. (Act. 416, Paul. 377.) Kosinitsa, Mon. Libr. 216 [?], $7\frac{3}{4} \times 5\frac{3}{4}$, *pict.*

1298. Kosinitsa, Mon. Libr. 217, *Carp.*, *Eus. t.*, *pict.*

1299. Kosinitsa, Mon. Libr. 218, *pict.*

1300. Kosinitsa, Mon. Libr. 219. 1301. Kosinitsa, Mon. Libr. 220.

1302. Kosinitsa, Mon. Libr. 222.

1303. Kosinitsa, Mon. Libr. 223 [1471], ?, ff. 201.

1304. Kosinitsa, Mon. Libr. 198.

1305. Athos, Protaton 15 [xi], 2 cols.

1306. Athos, Prot. 44 [xiv], 2 cols., *chart.*

1307. Athos, Paul. 1 [xiv], 4to, ff. 50. Written by one Matthew. *Mut.*

1308. Athos, Chiliandari 6 [xiii], 8vo. *Mut.* at beginning and elsewhere.

1309. Athos, Constamonitou 99 [xiv]. Palimpsest over Latin Lives and Martyrdom of Saints [xii].

1310. Athos, Xenophon 1 [1181], 4to, 2 cols. Written by John, a reader from Buthrotus.

1311. Athos, Xenophon 3 [xiii], 8vo, 2 cols. *Mut.*

1312. Athos, Xenophon 58 [xvi], 8vo, *chart.*

1313. Athens, Nat. Libr. 72 [A. D. 1181], $10\frac{5}{8} \times 7\frac{7}{8}$, ff. 191.

1314. Ath. Nat. Libr. 92 [xiv], $5\frac{1}{8} \times 4$, ff. 277, *Carp.*, *Eus. t.*, κεφ. *t.*, with a peculiar description of the Eusebian Canons.

1315. Ath. Nat. Libr. 113 [xi], $7\frac{1}{2} \times 5\frac{1}{2}$, ff. 232.

1316. Ath. Nat. Libr. 123 [A. D. 1145], $8\frac{1}{4} \times 5\frac{7}{8}$, ff. 189, *pict.*

1317. Ath. Nat. Libr. 128 [xii], $6\frac{3}{4} \times 5\frac{7}{8}$, ff. 181.

1318. Ath. Nat. Libr. 132 [x], $6\frac{3}{8} \times 4\frac{3}{4}$, ff. 210.

1319. Ath. Nat. Libr. 135 [xv], $9 \times 7\frac{1}{8}$, ff. 150.

1320. Earl of Crawford 1 [xi], $8\frac{1}{8} \times 6\frac{1}{8}$, ff. 239 (25), *Carp.*, *Eus. t.* (*prol.*, κεφ., τίτλ. in blue by another hand), *lect.* with ἀρχ. and τέλ. later), *Am.*, *Eus.*, *subscr.*, κεφ. *t.* Exquisitely written and ornamented. Perfect, except that κεφ. *t.* in Matt. is torn out. Memorandum on last leaf of the birth of Theodora [Oct. 2, 1320].

1321. Earl of Crawford 2 [xi–xii], $5\frac{1}{2} \times 4$, ff. 240 (21, 20), κεφ. *t.*, *pict.*, κεφ., τίτλ., *Am.*, *subscr.*, *vers.* (Luke), *syn.*, *men.* Beautifully written, though not equal to the last. Has suffered from age. Written by Paul a monk. The third leaf in St. Luke lost: otherwise perfect.

CHAPTER X.

CURSIVE MANUSCRIPTS OF THE ACTS AND CATHOLIC EPISTLES.

*1. (Evan. 1.)

2. (Paul. 2.) Basil. Univ. A. N. iv. 4 (formerly B. ix. 38) [xiii or xiv Burgon], $5\frac{7}{8} \times 3\frac{7}{8}$, ff. 216 (27), with short Introductions to the books, once belonged to the Preaching Friars, then to Amerbach, a printer of Basle. Erasmus grounded on this copy, in some passages with some alterations of the MS., the text of his first edition (1516), and he calls it 'exemplar mire castigatum.' His binder cut off a considerable part of the margin (Hoskier). It is Mill's B. 2 (Battier, Wetstein).

3. (Evan. 3.)

4. (Paul. 4.) Basil. A. N. iv. 5 (formerly B. x. 20) [xv], $6\frac{1}{8} \times 4\frac{3}{8}$, ff. 287 (18), Mill's B. 3, badly written by several bands, and full of contractions: the Pauline Epistles preceding the Catholic. Erasmus made some use of this copy and of its marginal readings (e. g. Acts viii. 37; xv. 34; xxiv. 6–8) for forming his text (Battier, Wetstein).

5. (Evan. 5.) 6. (Evan. 6.)

7. (Paul. 9.) Paris, Nat. Gr. 102 [x, Greg. xi, Omont xii], $7\frac{1}{4} \times 5\frac{7}{8}$, ff. 390 (20), *prol.*, *κεφ. t.*, *τίτλ.*, *pict.*, seems to be Stephen's *ι'*, although *ι'* is cited in error Luke v. 19; John ii. 17: it nearly resembles Cod. 5 and the Latin version. In this copy, and in Paul. H, 12, 17, 20, 137, Mr. Vansittart re-collated the beginning of the Epistle to the Hebrews.

8. (Paul. 10.) Stephen's *ια'*, now missing, cited about 400 times by that editor, in 276 of which it supports the Latin versions (Mill, N. T., Proleg. § 1171). Stephen cites *ια'* (apparently in error) four times in the Gospels, once in the Apocalypse (Matt. x. 8; 10; xii. 32; John ii. 17; Apoc. xiii. 4).

9. (Paul. 11.) Cambridge, Univ. Libr. Kk. 6. 4 [xi], $6\frac{3}{4} \times 4\frac{3}{4}$, ff. 247 (22), *lect.* *Mut.* Acts iii. 6–17; 1 Tim. iv. 12—2 Tim. iv. 3; Heb. vii. 20—xi. 10; xi. 23–end. Bp. Marsh has fully proved that this copy, which once belonged to Stephen's friend Vatablus, Professor of Hebrew at Paris, is his *ιγ'*. This copy also is twice quoted by Stephen in the Gospels (Matt. xxvii. 64; John ii. 17), through mere oversight. Dr. Hort states that it is rich in detached readings in Cath. Epp., not in Acts or Paul.

10. (Paul. 12, Apoc. 2.) Par. Nat. Gr. 237, Stephen's *ιε'* [x], $8\frac{1}{8} \times 6\frac{3}{8}$, ff. 246 (28), *prol.*, *κεφ. t.*, *τίτλ.*, *κεφ.*, *subscr.*, *στίχ.*, neatly written, with scholia and other matter. Le Long identified this, and about five other

of Stephen's manuscripts: its value in the Apocalypse is considerable (Wetstein, Scholz).

11. (Paul. 140.) Par. Nat. Gr. 103 [x, Greg. xi], $8\frac{1}{2} \times 6\frac{3}{4}$, ff. 333 (18), *prol.*, with scholia. *Mut.* Acts ii. 20–31.

12. (Paul. 16, Apoc. 4.) Par. Nat. Gr. 219 [xi], $12\frac{3}{8} \times 9\frac{1}{8}$, ff. 313 (40), *prol.*, *κεφ. t.*, *κεφ.*, *τίτλ.*, *syn.*, *men.*, neat, with Arethas' commentary on the Apocalypse, and Œcumenius' on the other books. Like Evann. 16, 19, 317, it once belonged to the Medici: in 1518 it was given by the Greek Janus Lascar to 'Petro Masieli' of Constance, and was used by Donatus of Verona for an edition of Œcumenius (Wetstein, Scholz).

*13. (Evan. 33.) 14. (Evan. 35.)

15. Par. Nat. Coislin. 25 [xi], $12\frac{3}{8} \times 9\frac{1}{4}$, ff. 254 (36), *prol.*, *κεφ. t.*, *κεφ.*, *τίτλ.*, *subscr.*, *στίχ.*, described by Montfaucon (as were also Act. 16–18), compared with Pamphilus' revision, *prol.*, and a commentary digested by Andreas, a priest (Wetstein).

16. (Paul. 19.) Par. Nat. Coisl. 26 [xi, Greg. x], $11\frac{5}{8} \times 9$, ff. 381 (40), *prol.*, with a commentary much like that of Œcumenius, and a catena of various Fathers: also a life of St. Longinus on two leaves [ix]. It once belonged to the monastery of St. Athanasius on Athos, *βιβλίον τῆς τετάρτης θέσεως* (Wetstein).

17. (Paul. 21, Apoc. 19.) Par. Nat. Coisl. 205 [~~written~~ by Anthony, a monk, A.D. 1079, Indict. 2], $9\frac{7}{8} \times 7$, ff. 270 (27), *prol.*, *κεφ. t.*, *κεφ.*, *τίτλ.*, *lect.*, *subscr.*, *στίχ.*, *syn.* *Mut.* 1 Cor. xvi. 17—2 Cor. i. 7; Heb. xiii. 15–25; with Apoc. i. 1—ii. 5 in a recent hand (Wetstein).

18. (Paul. 22, Apoc. 18.) Par. Nat. Coisl. 202, 2, ff. 1–26 [xi] on vellum, the rest [xiii] on cotton paper, $9\frac{5}{8} \times 7\frac{1}{8}$, ff. 302 (22), with scholia to the Acts and Catholic Epistles, Andreas' commentary to the Apocalypse, *prol.* to St. Paul's Epistles (Wetstein).

19. (Evan. 38.)

20. (Paul. 25.) Brit. Mus. Royal MS. I. B. I, once Westminster 935 [xiv], $10 \times 7\frac{3}{4}$, ff. 144 (22), *chart.*, *Euthal.*, *prol.* in Cath. and Paul. *Mut.* and in bad condition, almost illegible in parts (Wetstein). The Pauline Epistles precede the Acts and Catholic Epistles. Casley notices one leaf lost in the Hebrews (after *ὡς υἱοῖς ὑμῖν πρός* ch. xii. 7).

21. (Paul. 26.) Cambridge, Univ. Libr. Dd. xi. 90 [xiii], $6\frac{1}{2} \times 5\frac{1}{4}$, ff. 159 (24), *prol.*, *lect.*, *στίχ.* *Mut.* Acts i—xii. 2; xiv. 22—xv. 10; Rom. xv. 14–16; 24–26; xvi. 4–20; 1 Cor. i. 15—iii. 12; 2 Tim. i. 1—ii. 4; Tit. i. 9—ii. 15; Philem. ii–end of Hebrews. *Prol.* to Pauline Epistles only, copy is Mill's *Lu.*, but he forgot to name it in his Prolegomena. It was re-discovered and collated by Wetstein, and is probably Bentley's Q (Ellis, Bentleii Critica Sacra, p. xxix). John Berriman, in the manuscript notes to his own copy of his 'Critical Dissertation on 1 Tim. iii. 16' (1741), which he presented to the British Museum in 1761, tells us that this codex [then Cant. 495] was identified 'by several collations of many texts by different hands (Professor Francklin and others), and by other circumstances' to have been Professor Luke's (MS. note on p. 104).

22. (Paul. 75 in the same hand.) Brit. Mus. Add. 5115 and 5116, once Dr. Mead's (Berriman), then Askew's [xii], $7\frac{5}{8} \times 5\frac{3}{4}$, ff. 127 + 174 (22), *κεφ. t.*, *κεφ.*, *prol.*, *syn.*, *lect.* (later). *Mut.* Acts i. 1–11: (Acts i—xx collated by Paulus for Griesbach: Bloomfield): Scholz's date [ix] is an error.

23. (Paul. 28, Apoc. 6.) Oxf. Bodl. Barocc. 3 [xi], 5 × 4, ff. 297 (21), *prol.* (Euth.), *κεφ. t.*, a beautiful little book, ~~written at Ephesus,~~ beginning Acts xi. 13, ending Apoc. xx. 1: the opening chapters are supplied in a late hand. Tregelles calls this 'a very obscure manuscript.' With scholia on the Epistles, and a full and unique commentary on the Apocalypse, edited by J. A. Cramer, 1840 (Mill, Caspar Wetstein, Griesbach). This copy is Bentley's χ in Trin. Coll. B. xvii. 5 (*see* Evan. 51). *Mut.* Acts iii. 10—xi. 13; xiv. 6—xvii. 19; xx. 28—xxiv. 12; 1 Pet. ii. 2–16; iii. 7–21; 2 Cor. ix. 15—xi. 9; Gal. i. 1–18; Eph. vi. 1–19; Phil. iv. 18–23; Rev. i. 10–17; ix. 12–18; xvii. 10—xviii. 8, and in other places.

*24. (Paul. 29.) Camb. Christ's Coll. F. 1. 13 [xii], $8\frac{1}{8} \times 6$, ff. 303 (22). *Mut.* Acts i. 1–11; xviii. 20—xx. 14; James v. 14—1 Pet. i. 4, and some leaves of this fine copy are torn or decayed: there are also many changes by a later hand (Mill's Cant. 2, Scrivener's 1): unpublished collations were made by Bentley (Trin. Coll. Camb. B. xvii. 10, 11), and by Jo. Wigley for Jackson (Jesus Coll. Camb. O. Θ. 1).

25. (Paul. 31, Apoc. 7.) Brit. Mus. Harl. 5537 [Pentecost, A. D. 1087, Indict. 10], $4\frac{1}{2} \times 3\frac{1}{2}$, ff. 286 (23), (with a lexicon, *chart.*), *prol.*, *κεφ. t.*, *κεφ.*, some *lect.*, *subscr.*, *στίχ.*, an important copy, from the neighbourhood of the Aegean. *Mut.* 1 John v. 14—2 John 6 (Mill, Griesbach, Bloomfield, Scrivener's 1 in Apoc.)[1].

26. (Paul. 32.) Brit. Mus. Harl. 5557 [xii], 7 × 6, ff. 293 (22), *syn.*, *men.* (*prol.*, *κεφ. t.* Paul.), *lect.*, some *subscr.* and *στίχ.* *Mut.* Acts i. 1–11; 1 Cor. xi. 7—xv. 56. This copy and the next bear Covell's emblem '*Luceo*,' and the date Constantinople, 1675, but he got Act. 27 from Adrianople. (Mill, Paulus in Acts i–iii Bloomfield.)

27. (Paul. 33.) Brit. Mus. Harl. 5620 [xv], $8\frac{1}{4} \times 6$, ff. 134 (22), *chart.*, is of some weight: there are no chapter-divisions *primâ manu*; the writing is small and abbreviated (Mill, Griesbach, Bloomfield).

28. (Paul. 34, Apoc. 8.) Brit. Mus. Harl. 5778, is Covell's 5 or Sinai manuscript[2] [xii], $8\frac{3}{4} \times 6\frac{1}{2}$, ff. 156 (30), *κεφ.*, *τίτλ.*, *lect.*, *subscr.*, *στίχ.*, in wretched condition, and often illegible. *Mut.* Acts i. 1–20; Apoc. vi. 14—viii. 1; xxii. 19–21, perhaps elsewhere (Mill, Bloomfield for Act., Paul., Scrivener's d for Apoc.).

29. (Paul. 35.) Geneva, Libr. 20 [xi or xii], $5\frac{3}{8} \times 4$, ff. 269 (18),

[1] Mr. Ellis (Bentleii Critica Sacra, pp. xxviii, xxix) represents, among facts which I am better able to verify, that Act. and Epp. 25, 26, and Epp. 15, were collated by Wetstein, and his labours preserved at Trin. Coll. Cambridge (B. xvii. 10, 11). The manuscripts he indicates so ambiguously must be Paul. 25, 26, and Act. 15, since Wetstein is not known to have worked at Act. 25, 26, or Paul. 15.

[2] Covell once marked this codex 5, but afterwards gave it the name of the Sinai MS. (little anticipating worthier claimants for that appellation), reserving 5 for Harl. 5777 or Evan. 446.

brought from Greece, beautifully but carelessly written, without subscriptions; in text much like Act. 27 (readings sent to Mill, Scholz).

30. (Paul. 36, Apoc. 9.) Oxf. Bodleian Misc. Gr. 74 [xi], $10\frac{3}{4} \times 7$, ff. 333 (24), *prol.*, κεφ. *t.*, some κεφ., *subscr.*, στίχ., brought from the East by Bp. Huntington, beginning Acts xv. 19, but 3 John, Jude, the Apocalypse, and St. Paul's Epistles (which stand last) are in a somewhat earlier hand than the rest. (Mill's Hunt. 1.)

*31. (Evan. 69.) 32. (Evan. 51.)

33. (Paul. 39.) Oxf. Lincoln Coll. Gr. 15 B. 82 [xii], $7\frac{5}{8} \times 6$, ff. 206 (27), *prol.*, *pict.*, *lect.*, some τίτλ., στίχ., *syn.*, *men.*, presented in 1483 by Robert Flemmyng, Dean of Lincoln, a beautiful and interesting codex, with *pict.*, *prol.*, *lect.*, *syn.*, *men.*, and the numbers of the στίχοι noted in the subscriptions. *Mut.* 2 Pet. i. 1–15; Rom. i. 1–20 (Walton's Polyglott, Mill, Dobbin 'Cod. Montfort.,' who regards it as the manuscript from which this portion of the latter was mainly copied). The Epistle of Jude stands between James and 1 Peter. Vansittart notes its affinity in text with Act. 13.

*34. (Evan. 61.) 35. (Evan. 57.)

36. Oxf. New College, 36 (58) [xii, end], $10 \times 7\frac{3}{4}$, ff. 245 (39), *prol.*, κεφ., τίτλ., valuable text, with a catena of Fathers, enumerated by Mill (N. T., Proleg. § 1390), and edited by Cramer, Oxford, 1838 (Walton's Polyglott, Mill).

37. (Paul. 43.) Oxf. New Coll. 37 (59) [xiii], $9\frac{1}{4} \times 6\frac{5}{8}$, ff. 298 (20), *prol.*, κεφ. *t.*, τίτλ., perhaps a little later than Cod. 36, erroneously described by Walton, and after him by Wetstein, as part of Evan. 58, a much later manuscript. Heb. xiii. 21–25 is supplied in a recent hand. It is a beautiful copy, with marginal glosses (Walton's Polyglott, Mill, Dobbin).

*38. (Paul. 44.) Lugduno-Batav. 77, Voss. Gr. Q. 2 [xiii], $7\frac{1}{4} \times 5\frac{1}{4}$, ff. 215 (22), *prol.*, *lect.*, *ἀναγν.*, *subscr.*, στίχ., *syn.*, *men.*, once belonging to Petavius, a Councillor of Paris, given by Queen Christina to Is. Vossius (Mill, Wetstein, Dermout 1825).

39. (Paul. 45, Apoc. 11.) Petavii 2, age and present locality not stated. *Mut.* Acts i. 1—xviii. 22; James i. 1—v. 17; 3 John 9—Jude 25; 1 Cor. iii. 16—x. 13 (Extracts in Mill; J. Gachon).

40. (Paul. 46, Apoc. 12.) Vat. Reg. Gr. 179 [xi], $9\frac{7}{8} \times 7\frac{1}{2}$, ff. 169 (27), *prol.*, κεφ. *t.*, κεφ., τίτλ., *lect.*, *subscr.*, στίχ., *men.*, with a mixed text and the end of Titus (from ch. iii. 3), Philemon, and the Apocalypse in a later hand. This copy, given by Christina to Alexander VIII (1689–91), is of considerable importance, and, as containing all Euthalius' labours on the Acts and the Epistles, was largely used by Laur. Zacagni for his edition of the Prologues, &c., of Euthalius (Extracts in Mill, Zacagni, Birch; Griesbach adds, 'Gagnaeus eundem sub Dionysiani nomine laudasse creditur').

41. (Evan. 175.)

*42. (Paul. 48, Apoc. 13, Evst. 287, Apost. 56.) Frankfort on the Oder Gymnasium, once Seidel's [xi], $8\frac{1}{8} \times 5\frac{7}{8}$, ff. 302 (23), κεφ. *t.*, κεφ., *lect.*, carelessly written, with some rare readings. *Mut.* Acts ii. 3–34 (xxvii. 19–34 is in a later hand); 2 Pet. i. 1, 2; 1 John v. 11–21; Apoc. xviii. 3–13 (N. Westermann, H. Middeldorpf). One leaf of a Lectionary is added, containing Matt. xvii. 16–23; 1 Cor. ix. 2—12. This copy often agrees closely with the Complutensian text and Laud. 81 (Evan. 51) jointly.

43. (Evan. 76.)

44. (Like Evan. 82, Paul. 51, Apoc. 5) certain manuscripts cited by Laurentius Valla. Dr. Hort's Cod. 44 is B.-C. III. 37, which is our Act. 221, Paul. 265.

45. (Paul. 52, Apoc. 16.) Hamburg, City Library, Cod. Gr. 1252 [xv], 7⅞ × 5⅞, ff. 268 (22), *chart.*, *prol.* With its companion Cod. M of St. Paul's Epistles, it was lent to Wetstein in 1717 and to Bengel, by Z. C. Uffenbach. It once belonged to Jo. Ciampini at Rome, is carelessly written, but from a good text: 'plura genuina omittens, quam aliena admiscens,' Bengel.

46. (Paul. 55.) Monacensis Reg. 375 [xi, Greg. x], 12½ × 9⅜, ff. 381 (40), *στίχ.* (marked peculiarly in archaic fashion—J. R. Harris—e. g. 1 Cor. ℍHHHℍΔΔ), is Bengel's Augustan. 6, with Œcumenius' commentary and some rare readings (Bengel, Matthaei, Scholz). All the Augsburg MSS. of the N. T. (*see* Evann. 83, 426–8, Paul. 54, 125, 126) were removed to Munich in 1806.

47. (Evan. 90.) 48. (Evan. 105.) 49. (Evan. 92.)

50. (Paul. 8.) Stephen's ζʹ is unknown, though it was once in the Royal Library at Paris; that is, if Evan. 8, Reg. 49, is Stephen's ζʹ in the Gospels, which Mr. Vansittart seems to have proved. Stephen seldom cites ζʹ, or (as Mill puts the case) 'textus ipsius ferè universus absorptus est in hac editione' (N. T., Proleg. § 1167). *See* Evan. 8.

51. (Paul. 133, Apoc. 52.) Paris, Nat. Gr. 56, once Mazarin's [xii], 10 × 6⅜, ff. 375 (23), *prol.*, *κεφ.*, *lect.*, *subscr.* *Mut.* Apoc. xxii. 17–21.

52. (Paul. 50.) Cod. Rhodiensis, some of whose readings Stunica, the chief of the Complutensian editors, cites in controversy with Erasmus: it may have been his own property, and cannot now be identified. Whatever Mill states (on 1 John iii. 16), it is not now at Alcalá.

*53. (Paul. 30.) Camb. Emman. Coll. i. 4. 35 [xii], 3¾ × 3, ff. 214 (24), *prol.*, *κεφ. t.*, *τίτλ.*, *κεφ.*, the writing being among the minutest and most elegant extant. It is Mill's Cant. 3, Scrivener's n (a facsimile is given Plate xii. No. 33), and is in bad condition, in parts almost illegible. It begins 2 Pet. ii. 4, and there is a hiatus from 1 John iii. 20 to the middle of Œcumenius' Prologue to the Romans: *mut.* also 1 Cor. xi. 7—xv. 56, and ends Heb. xi. 27. From 1 Tim. vi. 5 another and far less careful hand begins: but the manuscript exhibits throughout many abbreviations. Has some marginal notes *primâ manu.* Given to the College 'in Testimonium grati animi' by Sam. Wright, a member of the College, in 1598.

54. (Evan. 43.) Paris, Arsenal Libr. The second volume of this book

(containing the Acts and all the Epistles on 189 leaves) is judged by the present librarian to be a little more modern than the first volume. They were both 'ex dono R. P. de Berziah' (sic) to the Oratory of San Maglorian.

55. Readings of a *second* copy of St. Jude contained in Cod. 47. Tischendorf, in his eighth edition, cites this copy in Acts xvi. 6, apparently by mistake.

56. (Paul. 227.) Oxf. Bodl. E. D. Clarke 4 [xii], 9 × 6, ff. 220 (27), *prol.* (names and miracles of Apostles, &c.), *κεφ. t.*, *κεφ.*, *lect.*, *subscr.*, *στίχ.*, *syn.* (extracts, &c. by Dean Gaisford).

(This number was assigned by Wetstein and Griesbach to certain readings of four Medicean manuscripts (only one in the Acts), which, like those of No. 102 of the Gospels, were found by Wetstein in the margin of Rapheleng's Plantin Greek Testament (1591). Identical with Act. 84, 87–89.—Birch, Scholz.)

57. (Evan. 234.)

58. (Paul. 224.) Oxf. Bodl. Clarke 9 [xiii], 7 × 5, ff. 181 (26), *lect. Mut.* Heb. xiii. 7–25 (Gaisford). (58 of Wetstein is the same codex as 22; Scholz substitutes the above.)

59. (Paul. 62.) Brit. Mus. Harl. 5588 [xiii], 10 × $6\frac{1}{2}$, 132 (36), cotton paper, *prol.*, full *lect.*, *κεφ.*, *subscr.*, *στίχ.* On the first leaf we read 'liber hospitalis de Cusa trevirencis dioc. R^{mi}. . .' *See* Evan. 87 (Griesbach, Bloomfield).

60. (Paul. 63, Apoc. 29.) Brit. Mus. Harl. 5613 [May, A.D. 1407, Indict. 15], $8\frac{1}{2}$ × $5\frac{3}{4}$, ff. 267 (26), *prol.*, *subscr.*, *στίχ.* *Mut.* Apoc. xxii. 2–18. (Griesbach collated fifty-five chapters of Acts and Epp., Griesbach and Scrivener's e in Apocalypse.)

*61. Brit. Mus. Add. 20,003 [April 20, A.D. 1044, Indict. 12], 7 × $6\frac{1}{2}$, ff. 57 (23), *κεφ. t.* in St. James. This has been called the most important cursive copy of the Acts [but is much overrated—Ed.], was formerly called lo^{ti} (p^{scr}), discovered by Tischendorf in Egypt in 1853, and sold to the Trustees of the British Museum in 1854, was written by one John, a monk, with rubrical marks added in a later hand. *Mut.* ch. iv. 8—vii. 17; xvii. 28—xxiii. 9; 297 verses. Independent collations have been made by Tischendorf (Anecd. sacra et prof., pp. 7, 8, 130–46), by Tregelles, and by Scrivener (Cod. Augiensis, Introd., pp. lxviii–lxx). Its value is shown not so much by the readings in which it stands alone, as *by its agreement with the oldest uncial copies*, where their testimonies coincide. ((Paul. 61) comprised extracts made by Griesbach from the margin of a copy of Mill's N. T. in the Bodleian (*see* Evan. 236), where certain readings are cited under the notation *Hal.* These are now known to be taken from Evan. 440, Act. 111, Paul. 221, or Scrivener's v of the Gospels, o of the Acts and Epistles—Tischendorf, Tregelles.)

62. (Paul. 65.) Par. Nat. Gr. 60, once Colbert's [xiv], 14 × $9\frac{1}{8}$, ff. 135 (35), *chart.*, *prol.*, *κεφ. t.*, *κεφ.*, *τίτλ.*, *lect.*, *subscr.*, *στίχ.*, *syn.*, with scholia (Wetstein, Griesbach, Scholz).

63. (Paul. 68.) Vindobon. Caesar, Nessel. 313 [xiv], $7\frac{3}{8}$ × $5\frac{3}{4}$, ff. 157 (26), *prol.*, *κεφ. t.*, *lect.*, *subscr.*, *στίχ.*, *syn.*, scholia (Treschow, Alter, Birch).

64. (Paul. 69.) Vind. Caes. Ness. 303 [xii], 7⅝ × 5¾, ff. 279 (22), *prol.*, *κεφ. t.*, *lect.*, *subscr.*, *syn.*, *men.*, carefully written by one John, brought by Ogier de Busbeck from Constantinople, like Cod. 67 and many others of this collection (Treschow, Alter, Birch).

*65. (Evan. 218.)

66. (Paul. 67, Apoc. 34.) Vind. Caes. Ness. 302 [xii, Greg. xi], 7¼ × 5½, ff. 368 (22), *prol.*, *κεφ. t.*, *pict.*, *lect.*, *subscr.*, *στίχ.*, *vers.*, *syn.*, *men.*, scholia, and other matter: three several hands have made corrections, which Griesbach regarded as far more valuable than the text (cited by him 66**). *Mut.* Apoc. xv. 6—xvii. 3; xviii. 10—xix. 9; xx. 8—xxii. 21. It once belonged to Arsenius Archbishop of Monembasia (*see* Evan. 333, Evst. 113), then to Sebastian Tengnagel and Jo. Sambuc (A. C. Hwiid 1785 for the Acts, Treschow, Alter, Birch).

67. (Paul. 70.) Vind. Caes. Ness. 221 [written by one Leo at Constantinople, December, 1331, Indict. 14], 8¾ × 7, ff. 174 (31), *prol.*, *κεφ. t.*, *lect.*, *subscr.*, *στίχ.*, *syn.*, *men.*, elegant but inaccurate (Treschow, Alter, Birch).

68. (Paul. 73.) Upsal. Univ. Gr. 1, 9 × 6¾, ff. 220 (38), is in fact two separate manuscripts bound together, both of high value. The first part [xii] contains the Acts (commencing ch. viii. 14), Rom., 1 Cor. to ch. xv. 38: the second [xi] begins 1 Cor. xiii. 6, and extends through the Pauline and Catholic Epistles, which follow them. In the text of St. Paul it much resembles Paul. 17. A catena is annexed, which is an abridgement of Œcumenius, and the portion in duplicate (1 Cor. xiii. 6—xv. 38) has contradictory readings (P. F. Aurivill [Orville?], 1786). It was bought at Venice by Sparvenfeldt in 1678 (Belsheim).

69. (Paul. 74, Apoc. 30.) Guelpherbytanus xvi. 7, August., 8⅞ × 6⅛, ff. 204 (29), *chart.*, also in two hands: the first (Acts and Epistles) [xiii], written by George a monk, the Apocalypse [xiv]. It exhibits a remarkable text, and has many marginal readings and *prol.* (Knittel, Matthaei).

All from 70 to 96 were slightly collated by Birch, and except 81, 93–6 by Scholz also.

70. (Evan. 131.) 71. (Evan. 133.)

72. (Paul. 79, Apoc. 37.) Rom. Vat. Gr. 366 [xiii, Greg. xv], 7¾ × 5⅜, ff. 218 (24), *chart.*, *prol.*

73. (Paul. 80.) Rom. Vat. Gr. 367 [xi], 8⅛ × 6⅝, ff. 165 (30), an excellent manuscript used by Caryophilus (*see* Evan. 112).

74. Rom. Vat. Gr. 760 [xii], 10⅛ × 8¼, ff. 257 (24), contains only the Acts with a catena.

75. (Evan. 141.) 76. (Evan. 142.) 77. (Evan. 149.)

78. (Paul. 89.) Rom. Alexandrino-Vat. Gr. 29 [xii, Greg. x], 10 × 7⅛, ff. 177 (21), a good copy, but *mut.* 2 Cor. xi. 15—xii. 1; Eph. i. 9—Heb. xiii. 25. Traced to Strasburg in the possession of H. Boecler, and identified with 201 (Scr., 3rd ed.) by Dr. Gregory.

79. (Paul. 90.) Rom. Urbino-Vat. Gr. 3 [xi], 7⅜ × 5½, ff. 161 (30).

80. (Paul. 91, Apoc. 42.) Rom. Pio-Vat. Gr. 50 [xii], 6⅝ × 5⅛, ff. 327 (21).

81. Rom. Barberin. Gr. vi. 21 [xi, Greg. xiv], $13\frac{3}{4} \times 10\frac{3}{4}$, with a commentary (Birch). Scholz could not find this copy, which has remarkable readings: it contains but one chapter of the Acts and the Catholic Epistles.

82. (Evan. 180.)

83. (Paul. 93.) Naples, Bibl. Nat. ii. Aa. 7 [x, Greg. xii], $10\frac{3}{8} \times 7\frac{3}{8}$, ff. 123 (37), 2 cols., written by Evagrius and compared with Pamphilus' copy at Caesarea (*see* Act. 15): *στίχοι* sometimes in the margin. *See* below, Act. 173.

84. (Paul. 94.) Florence, Laurent. iv. 1 [x], $12\frac{3}{4} \times 10\frac{1}{8}$, ff. 244 (21), has St. Chrysostom's commentary on the Acts, that of Nicetas of Heraclea on all the Epistles.

85. (Paul. 95.) Flor. Laurent. iv. 1 [xiii], $12\frac{1}{8} \times 10$, ff. 288 (31), *chart.*, contains the Acts and *Pauline* Epistles with Theophylact's commentary.

86. (Paul. 96, Apoc. 75.) Flor. Laurent. iv. 30 [xi, Greg. x], $7\frac{1}{2} \times 5\frac{3}{4}$, ff. 377 (18), with a commentary. Tregelles states that this is the same copy as Cod. 147, the press-mark 20 being put by Birch in error for 30.

87. (Paul. 97.) Flor. Laurent. iv. 29 [x], $10\frac{1}{4} \times 7\frac{3}{4}$, ff. 294 (19), with scholia, *prol.*, and a modern interlinear Latin version in the Epistles, for the use of beginners.

88. (Paul. 98.) Flor. Laurent. iv. 31 [xi], $7 \times 5\frac{1}{2}$, ff. 276 (24), *prol. Mut.* in fine Titi.

89. (Paul. 99, Apoc. 45.) Flor. Laurent. iv. 32, $5 \times 3\frac{1}{2}$, 276 (27), written by John Tzutzuna, priest and monk, December, 1092, Indict. 1, in the reign of Alexius Comnenus, Nicolas being Patriarch of Constantinople. *Prol.*, *syn.*, and a treatise of Dorotheus, Bishop of Tyre in Julian's reign, on the seventy disciples and twelve Apostles, which is found also in Act. 10, 179, Burdett-Coutts II. 4 (Paul. 266), in Erasmus' N. T. (1516), and partly in Stephen's of 1550. *See* Cave's 'Hist. Lit.,' vol. i. pp. 164–172.

90. (Evan. 197.) 91. (Evan. 201.) 92. (Evan. 204.)

*93. (Evan. 205.) *94. (Evan. 206.) *95. (Evan. 209.)

*96. (Paul. 109.) Venet. Marc. 11 [xi, Greg. xiii or xiv], $11\frac{1}{4} \times 9\frac{1}{2}$, ff. 304 (?), 3 cols., an important copy, often resembling Act. 142, from the monastery of St. Michael de Troyna in Sicily. It has both a Latin and an Arabic version. *Mut.* Acts i. 1–12; xxv. 21—xxvi. 18; Philemon. Act. 93–96 and Paul. 106–112 were collated by G. F. Rinck, 'Lucubratio Critica in Act. Apost. Epp. Cath. et Paul.' Basileae, 1830.

97. (Paul. 241.) Guelpherbyt. Biblioth. Gud. gr. 104. 2 [xii], $7\frac{1}{4} \times 5\frac{3}{8}$, ff. 226 (27), once belonging to Langer, librarian at Wolfenbüttel, who sent a collation to Griesbach. *Mut.* Acts xvi. 39—xvii. 18: it has marginal scholia from Chrysostom and Œcumenius, prayers and dialogues subjoined. Deposited by one Theodoret in the Catechumens' library of the Laura (monastery) of St. Athanasius on Athos.

Act. 98–107 were accurately collated by Matthaei for his N. T.

*98. (Paul. 113, Apost. 77.) Dresden, Reg. A. 104 [xi], $11\frac{3}{4}\times 8\frac{5}{8}$, ff. 186 (40), 2 cols., once belonged to Jeremias the patriarch of the monastery of Stauroniketa on Athos. Matthaei professes that he chiefly followed this manuscript, which is divided into three parts: viz. a_1 Church Lessons from the Acts, so arranged that no verse is lost, with various readings and scholia in the margin: a_2 (or simply *a*) the text with marginal various readings and scholia: a_3 Church Lessons from the Acts and Epistles. Identified by Gregory with Act. 107.

*99. (Paul. 114.) Mosq. Synod. 5 (Mt. c) [April, A. D. 1445, Greg. 1345], folio, ff. 464, *chart.*, contains also the Life and Speeches of Gregory Naz. and much other matter, from the Iberian or Iveron monastery on Athos, carelessly written by Theognostus, Metropolitan of Perga and Attalia: *prol.*, *syn.*, *men.*, *Euthal.*, and some Patristic writings.

*100. (Paul. 115.) Mosq. Synod. 334 (Mt. d) [xi], 4to, ff. ?, with a catena and scholia.

*101. (Paul. 116.) Mosq. Synod. 333 (Mt. f) [xiii], 4to, ff. 240, *chart. B.*, *prol.*, *syn.*, carefully written, with scholia to the Acts.

*102. [This is Cod. K of the Catholic and Pauline Epistles, cited according to Matthaei's notation. Hort's 102 is k^{scr}.]

*103. (Paul. 118.) Mosq. Synod. 193 (Mt. h) [xii], folio, ff. 236, from the Iveron monastery on Athos, is a volume of scholia, with the entire text in its margin for Acts i. 1—ix. 12; elsewhere only in fragments after the usual manner of scholia.

*104. (Evan. 241.) *105. (Evan. 242.)

*106. (Paul. 122.) Mosq. Synod. 328 (Mt. m) [xi], 4to, ff. 228, *prol.*, *κεφ. t.*, *lect.*, *syn.*, carefully written, from the Vatopedi monastery on Athos, has *prol.*, *syn.*, and the Psalms annexed.

107[1]. (Paul. 491.) Lond. Brit. Mus. Add. 22,734 [xi–xii], $11\frac{5}{8}\times 9\frac{1}{4}$, ff. 248 (13–25), *prol.*, *κεφ.*, *subscr.*, *στίχ.* With comm. of Œcumenius. *Mut.* Acts iv. 15–22; xxiii. 15–30; Rom. v. 13—vi. 21; vi. 22—end of Phil.; Col. iii. 15—iv. 11; Heb. xiii. 24–25 (pt.). Bears name of Jo. Card. de Salviatis, and arms of Pius VI. Bought of Sp. P. Lampros of Athens in 1853. (Greg. 204.)

108. (Evan. 226.) 109. (Evan. 228.)

Codd. 110–181 were first added to the list by Scholz, who states that he collated entire 115, 133, 160; in the greater part 120–3, 126, 127, 131, 137, 161–3, 174; the rest slightly or not at all.

110. (Evan. 568.) (Greg. 247.) Metz, Publ. Library, 4.

Erase Evan. 441, being a printed edition (see p. 239). Hort's 110 is a^{scr}, which is our 182.

*111. (Evan. 440.) This is Scrivener's o Act. and Paul.

112. Cantabrig. 2068 erase: it is the same as Cod. 9. Hort's 112 is c^{scr}, which is our 184. Instead of it Greg. inserts—

[1] *See* under 98.

(Paul. 179.) Modena, Este ii. G. 3 [ix or x], $13 \times 8\frac{7}{8}$, ff. ? (30), *prol.*, *Euthal.*, being part of uncial H in minuscules (*see* under H of Acts).

*113. (Evan. 18.)

Codd. 113, 114, 117, being 132, 134, 137 of St. Paul respectively, together with Act. 127 and Paul. 139, 140, 153, have been collated by J. G. Reiche, in his 'Codicum aliquot Graecorum N. T. Parisiensium nova descriptio: praemissis quibusdam de neglecti MSS. N. T. studii causâ.' Gott. 1847.

*114. (Paul. 134.) Par. Nat. Gr. 57 [xiii, Greg. xi], $11\frac{5}{8} \times 8\frac{3}{4}$, ff. 231 (24), 2 cols., *κεφ.*, *syn.*, *men.*, &c., a valuable copy, with some portions of the Septuagint version, and prayers for the service of the Greek Church.

115. (Paul. 135.) Par. Nat. Gr. 58, once Colbert's (as were 118, 121, 122, 124, 128, 129) [xiii, Greg. xi], $10\frac{1}{8} \times 7\frac{3}{4}$, ff. 174 (28), *prol.*, *κεφ. t.*, *subscr.*, *στίχ.*, begins Acts xiv. 27, ends 2 Tim.; no liturgical notes.

116. (Paul. 136, Apoc. 53.) Par. Nat. Gr. 59, once Teller's [xvi], 11×8, ff. 331 (21), *chart.*, *prol.*, and scholia to the Catholic Epistles.

*117. (Evan. 263, Paul. 137) of some value.

118. (Paul. 138, Apoc. 55.) Par. Nat. Gr. 101 [xiii], $9\frac{1}{8} \times 6\frac{1}{4}$, ff. 200 (28), *chart.*, *prol.*, *κεφ. t.*, *κεφ.*, *subscr.*, *στίχ.* *Mut.* Acts xix. 18—xxii. 17.

119. (Paul. 139, Apoc. 56.) Par. Nat. Gr. 102 A [x, but Apoc. xiii], $9\frac{1}{4} \times 6\frac{3}{4}$, ff. 229 (26, 25), *prol.*, *lect.*, *subscr.*, *στίχ.*, *ἀναγν.*, *men.* *Mut.* 2 Cor. i. 8—ii. 4. Cath. follow Paul., as in Cod. 120.

120. (Paul. 141.) Par. Nat. Gr. 103 A [xi, Greg. xiii], $9\frac{5}{8} \times 6\frac{5}{8}$, ff. 243 (22), *κεφ. t.*, *lect.*, *ἀναγν.*, *subscr.*, *στίχ.*, *prol.* beginning Acts xxi. 20 (v. 38—vi. 7; vii. 6–16; 32—x. 25 *chart.* [xiii]). *Mut.* Acts xxviii. 23—Rom. ii. 26; Phil. i. 5—1 Thess. iv. 1; v. 26—2 Thess. i. 11; 1 John ii. 11—iii. 3; 24—v. 14; 2 John; ending 3 John 11.

121. (Paul. 142.) Par. Nat. Gr. 104 [xiii], $7\frac{1}{4} \times 5$, ff. 257 (24), *chart.*, *prol.*, *κεφ. t.*, *τίτλ.*, *lect.*, *subscr.*, *στίχ.*, *syn.*, August. de Thou's, then Colbert's.

122. (Paul. 143.) Par. Nat. Gr. 105 [xi or x], $8\frac{1}{8} \times 6\frac{1}{4}$, ff. 248 (17), *prol.*, *κεφ.*, *τίτλ.*, *subscr.*, *στίχ.*, correctly written, but fragments, viz. Acts xiii. 48—xv. 22; 29—xvi. 36; xvii. 4—xviii. 26; xx. 16—xxviii. 17; 1 Pet. ii. 20—iii. 2; 1 John iii. 5; 21—v. 9; 2 John 8—3 John 10; Jude 7—Rom. iv. 16; 24—vii. 9; 18—1 Cor. i. 28; ii. 13—viii. 1; ix. 6—xiv. 2; 10—Gal. i. 10; ii. 4—Eph. i. 18; 1 Tim. i. 14—v. 5.

123. (Paul. 144.) Par. Nat. Gr. 106 A [xiv], $8\frac{5}{8} \times 6\frac{1}{8}$, ff. 276 (29), *prol.*, *κεφ. t.*, *κεφ.*, *τίτλ.*, *lect.*, *subscr.*, *στίχ.* Hymns. *Mut.* 1 Pet. i. 9—ii. 7.

124. (Paul. 149, Apoc. 57.) Par. Nat. Gr. 124 [xvi], 16mo, beautifully written by Angelus Vergecius.

125. (Paul. 150.) Par. Nat. Gr. 125 [xiv], $6\frac{5}{8} \times 7\frac{7}{8}$, ff. 394 (16), *prol.*, *lect.*, *subscr.*, *ἀναγν.*, *στίχ.*, from Constantinople.

126. (Paul. 153.) Par. Nat. Gr. 216, from Medici collection [x], $12\frac{3}{4} \times 9\frac{1}{2}$, ff. 333 (21), 2 cols., *prol.*, *κεφ. t.*, *κεφ.*, *τίτλ.*, *subscr.*, *στίχ.*, probably written at Constantinople, with catena, sometimes in uncial, occasionally, esp. in Heb., as late as [xvi].

*127. (Paul. 154.) Par. Nat. Gr. 217 [xi], $12\frac{5}{8}\times 10\frac{1}{8}$, ff. 373 (28–33), *prol.*, κεφ. *t.*, *subscr.*, στίχ., carelessly written (Vansittart), collated by Reiche. It has a catena. Act., scholia (Cath.), Theodoret's commentary (Paul.).

128. (Paul. 155.) Par. Nat. Gr. 218 [xi], $12\frac{1}{2}\times 10$, ff. 317 (37), with a catena.

129. (Paul. 156.) Par. Nat. Gr. 220 [xiii, Greg. xiv], $11\frac{1}{2}\times 8\frac{1}{2}$, ff. 388 (41), 2 cols., a commentary, the text sometimes suppressed.

130. Par. Nat. Gr. 221 [xii], $11\frac{1}{8}\times 8\frac{1}{2}$, ff. 177 (14), from the East, with a catena. *Mut.* Acts xx. 38—xxii. 3; 2 Pet. i. 14—iii. 18; 1 John iv. 11—Jude 8.

131. (Paul. 158.) Par. Nat. Gr. 223, once Boistaller's, contains Paul. with *prol.* and catena, [A. D. 1045], $11\frac{1}{2}\times 8\frac{1}{2}$, ff. 273 (23), by Theopemptus, a reader, followed by Act. and Cath. [xii].

132. (Evan. 330.)

133. (Paul. 166.) Turin, Univ. C. vi. 19 [xiii, Greg. xii], $8\times 5\frac{3}{4}$, ff. 295 (24), *chart.*, *pict.*, *prol.*, in a clear large hand; Dr. Hort noticed remarkable readings in the Catholic Epistles. The Epistle to the Hebrews precedes 1 Timothy, as Pasinus notes in his Catalogue.

134. (Paul. 167.) Turin, Univ. B. v. 19 [xi, Greg. xii or xiii], $8\frac{1}{4}\times 6$, ff. 370 (19), *prol.*, *mut.* Acts i, ii. Pasinus notes that the Pauline precede the Catholic Epistles.

135. (Evan. 339.)

136. (Paul. 169.) Turin, Univ. C. v. 1 [xii], $9\frac{1}{4}\times 7$, ff. 174 (27), *prol.*, κεφ. *t.*, *lect.*, *syn.*. *Mut.* in Heb.

137. (Paul. 176.) Milan, Ambros. E. 97 sup. [xi, Greg. xiii], $10\frac{1}{8}\times 7\frac{3}{8}$, ff. 276 (23), *prol.*, *lect.*, ἀναγν., *subscr.*, στίχ., bought at Corfu: so like Codd. DEc^{scr} (Act. 184) and the margin of the Harkleian Syriac in the Acts, as to assist us when DE are mutilated, especially in additions: e. g. Acts xxvii. 5; xxviii. 16; 19 (*bis*). *See* Scrivener's 'Cod. Bezae,' Introd., p. lix, note.

138. (Paul. 173.) Milan, Ambros. E. 102 sup. [xiv, Greg. xv], $9\frac{3}{4}\times 6\frac{3}{4}$, ff. 202 (19), *chart.*, once J. V. Pinelli's; it contains the Epistles only.

139. (Paul. 174.) Milan, Ambros. H. 104 sup. [written March 20, 1434, Indict. 12, by one Athanasius], $11\frac{1}{2}\times 8\frac{5}{8}$, ff. 164 (31), 2 cols., *prol.*, *subscr.*, στίχ., *chart.*, bought at Padua, 1603.

140. (Paul. 215, Apoc. 74.) Venice, 546 [partly xi on vellum, partly xiii *chart.*], $11\frac{1}{2}\times 9\frac{5}{8}$, ff. 268 (21), *prol.*, στίχ. The Epistles have a catena, the Apocalypse a commentary.

141. (Evan. 189.)

142. (Paul. 178.) Modena, iii. B. 17 [xii], $7\frac{1}{8}\times 5\frac{3}{8}$, ff. ?, *prol.*, *subscr.*, στίχ., valuable, but with many errors; see however Act. 96.

143. (Evan. 832.) Contains the Catholic Epistles, but not the Acts.

144. (Evan. 363.) 145. (Evan. 365.) 146. (Evan. 367.)

147. Ven. St. Mark ii. 61.

148. (Paul. 184.) Flor. Laurent. Convent. Soppr. 191 [written A. D. 984, Indict. 12, by Theophylact, priest and doctor of law], $13\frac{1}{2} \times 9\frac{1}{2}$, ff. 342, *prol.*, once belonged to the Benedictine Library of St. Mary.

149. (Paul. 349, Apoc. 180.) Flor. Laurent. Conv. Soppr. 150 [xiii, Greg. xii], $8\frac{}{8} \times 5\frac{1}{4}$, ff. 144 (32), 2 cols., *subscr.*, *στίχ.*, contains the Catholic Epistles, with a Latin version.

150. (Evan. 368.) 151. (Evan. 386.)

152. (Evan. 1202.) 153. (Evan. 444.)

154. (Paul. 187.) Rom. Vat. Gr. 1270 [xv, Greg. xiv], $8\frac{3}{4} \times 6\frac{1}{2}$, ff. 164 (36), *prol.*, *κεφ. t.*, *lect.*, contains the Acts, Catholic Epistles, Rom., 1 Cor., with a commentary.

155. (Paul. 188.) Rom. Vat. Gr. 1430 [xii], $14 \times 11\frac{1}{4}$, ff. 270 (20), *prol.*, with a commentary in another hand. It does not contain the Acts, but all the Epistles.

156. (Paul. 190.) Rom. Vat. Gr. 1650 [Jan. 1037], $13\frac{1}{2} \times 10\frac{3}{4}$, ff. 187 (43), 2 cols., *prol.*, *κεφ. t.*, *κεφ.*, *τίτλ.*, *lect.*, *subscr.*, *στίχ.*, *vers.*, *Euthal.*, written for Nicolas Archbishop of Calabria by the cleric Theodore. The Pauline Epistles have a commentary: it begins Acts v. 4.

157. (Paul. 191.) Rom. Vat. Gr. 1714 [xii], $8\frac{1}{2} \times 6\frac{3}{4}$, ff. 46 (25), *prol.*, *κεφ. t.*, *κεφ.*, *τίτλ.*, *lect.*, *ἀναγν.*, *subscr.*, *στίχ.*, is a heap of disarranged fragments, containing Acts xviii. 14—xix. 9; xxiv. 11—xxvi. 23; James iii. 1—v. 20; 3 John with *κεφ.* and *ὑπόθεσις* to Jude; Rom. vi. 22—viii. 32; xi. 31—xv. 23; 1 Cor. i. 1—iii. 12.

158. (Paul. 192.) Rom. Vat. Gr. 1761 [xi], $9\frac{1}{2} \times 7\frac{1}{8}$, ff. 481 (21), *prol.*, *κεφ. t.*, *κεφ.*, *τίτλ.* From this copy Mai supplied the lacunae of Cod. B in the Pauline Epistles.

159. Rom. Vat. Gr. 1968, Basil. 7 [xi, Greg. x], $6\frac{1}{4} \times 4\frac{1}{8}$, ff. 84 (22), *prol.*, *κεφ. t.*, *κεφ.*, *τίτλ.*, *lect.*, *subscr.*, contains the Acts, James, and 1 Peter, with scholia, whose authors' names are given. *Mut.* Acts i. 1—v. 29; vi. 14—vii. 11.

160. (Paul. 193, Apoc. 24.) Rom. Vat. Gr. 2062 [xi, Greg. x], $10\frac{5}{8} \times 8$, ff. 287 (26), *κεφ.*, *τίτλ.*, *subscr.*, *στίχ.*, with copious scholia accompanied by the authors' names: it begins Acts xxviii. 19, ends Heb. ii. 1.

161. (Paul. 198, Apoc. 69.) Rom. Vat. Ottob. Gr. 258 [xiii, Greg. xiv], $9\frac{3}{4} \times 7\frac{3}{8}$, ff. 216 (32), 2 cols., *chart.*, *prol.*, *subscr.*, with a Latin version: it begins Acts ii. 27, and the last chapters of the Apocalypse are lost. The latter part was written later [xiv].

162. (Paul. 200.) Rom. Vat. Ottob. Gr. 298 [xv, Greg. xiv], $6\frac{3}{4} \times 4\frac{3}{4}$, ff. 265 (27), 2 cols., with the Latin Vulgate version (with which Scholz states that the Greek has been in many places made to harmonize) in a parallel column, contains many transpositions of words, and unusual readings introduced by a later hand[1].

[1] Cod. 162 has attracted much attention from the circumstance that it is the only unsuspected witness among the Greek manuscripts for the celebrated text 1 John v. 7, 8, whose authenticity will be discussed in Vol. II. Ch. XII. A facsimile of the passage in question was traced in 1829 by Cardinal Wiseman for Bishop Burgess, and published by Horne in several editions of his 'Introduction,'

163. (Paul. 201.) Rom. Vat. Ottob. Gr. 325 [xiv], 7⅝ × 4⅞, ff. 215 (26) *chart.*, *prol.*, *κεφ. t.* *Mut.* Acts iv. 19—v. 1.

164. (Evan. 390.)

165. Rom. Vat. Ottob. Gr. 417 [xiv, Greg. xvi], 8⅜ × 5¾, ff. 339 (21), *chart.*, contains the Catholic Epistles, with works of St. Ephraem and others.

166. (Paul. 204, Apoc. 22.) Rom. Vallicell. B. 86 [xii–xiv, Greg.], 7 × 4⅞, ff. 258 (26), i. e. ff. 1–103 [xii], by George, son of Elias; 104–191 [xiii], by Joachim, a monk; 192–228 [xii] also by George; 229–254 [xiv]; and four prefatory leaves, *chart.*, were added later [xvi]. *Prol.*, *κεφ.*, *τίτλ.*, *subscr.*, *στίχ.* Described with facsimile in Bianchini, Evan. Quadr., vol. ii. pt. 1, pp. 535–8.

167. (Evan. 393.)

168. (Paul. 205.) Rom. Vallicell. F. 13 [xiv], 9¼ × 6⅜, ff. 204 (40), *chart.*, *prol.*, *ἀναγν.*, *subscr.*, *στίχ.*

169. (Paul. 206.) Rom. Chigian. R. v. 29 [June 12, 1394[1]], 11½ × 8½, ff. 248 (21), *prol.*, *κεφ.*, *lect.*, *ἀναγν.*, *syn.*, *men.*, *subscr.*, *στίχ.*, written by Joasaph at Constantinople in the monastery *τῶν ὁδηγῶν*. *See* Evangelistarium 86.

170. (Evan. 394.)

171, 172 (Paul. 209, 210) are both Collegii Romani [xvi], fol., *chart.* Dr. Gregory could not find them in 1886.

173. (Paul. 211.) Naples, Nat. Libr. ii. Aa. 8 [xi], 8¾ × 6⅝, ff. 245 (22), *prol.*, *κεφ. t.*, *κεφ.*, *τίτλ.*, *lect.*, *ἀναγν.*, *subscr.*, *στίχ.*, and *μαρτυρίαι* cited from Scripture and profane writers. This codex has I John v. 7, 8 in the margin, by a recent hand. (Tregelles suggests that this is probably the same copy as Cod. 83, the readings ascribed to it being extracted from the margin of that manuscript.)

174. (Paul. 212.) Naples, Nat. Libr. ii. Aa. 9 [xv], 8½ × 5⅝, ff. 208 (27), *chart.*, *prol.*, *κεφ. t.*, *lect.*, *subscr.*, *στίχ.*

175. (Paul. 216.) Messina, St. Basil 104 [xii], 11⅝ × 8⅞, ff. 241 (25), 2 cols., *prol.*, *κεφ. t.*, *lect.*, *subscr.*, *στίχ.*, *men.*

176. (Evan. 421.) 177. (Evan. 122.)

178. (Paul. 242, Apoc. 87 or m[scr].) Cheltenham, Phillipps 1461 [xi or xii, Greg. xiv and xv], 9½ × 6½, ff. 229 (27), (Hoskier), bought at Meerman's sale in 1824 by the late Sir T. Phillipps, Bart., of Middle Hill, Worcestershire. The Pauline Epistles are written smaller than the rest, but in the same clear hand. *Lect.*, *κεφ. t.*, *prol.*, *κεφ.* (but not in the Apocalypse), flourished rubric capitals. Scrivener in 1856 fully

as also by Tregelles (Horne, vol. iv. p. 217). If the facsimile is at all faithful, this is as rudely and indistinctly written as any manuscript in existence; but the illegible scrawl between the Latin column in the post of honour on the left, and the Greek column on the right, has been ascertained by Mr. B. H. Alford (who examined the codex at Tregelles' request) to be merely a consequence of the accidental shifting of the tracing paper, too servilely copied by the engraver.

[1] Scholz says 1344, and Tischendorf corrects but few of his gross errors in these Catalogues: but A. M. 6902, which he cites from the manuscript, is A. D. 1394.

collated Apoc. (whose text is valuable), the rest slightly. It is sadly mutilated; it begins Acts iv. 24; *mut.* Acts v. 2-16; vi. 2—vii. 2; 16—viii. 10; 38—ix. 13; 26-39; x. 9-22; 43—xiii. 1; xxiii. 32—xxiv. 24; xxviii. 23—James i. 5; iii. 6—iv. 16; 2 Pet. iii. 10—1 John i. 1; iii. 13—iv. 2; Jude 16-25; Rom. xiv. 23 (xvi. 25-27 was there placed)—xv. 14; 1 Cor. iii. 15—xv. 23; 2 Cor. x. 14—xi. 19; xiii. 5-13; Eph. i. 1—ii. 14; v. 29—vi. 24; Col. i. 24-26; ii. 4-7; 2 Thess. i. 1—iii. 5; Heb. ix. 3—x. 29; Apoc. xiv. 4-14: ending Apoc. xxi. 12. The *ὑποθέσεις* and tables of *κεφ.* before each Epistle have suffered in like manner.

179. (Paul. 128, Apoc. 82.) Munich, Royal Libr. 211 [xi, Delitzsch xiii], 10$\frac{5}{8}$ × 8$\frac{3}{8}$, ff. 227 (25), *lect.*, *prol.*, *ὑπογραφαί*, Dorotheus' treatise (*see* Act. 89), fragments of *Eus. t.*, and (in a later hand) marginal scholia to St. Paul. Belonged to Zomozerab, the Bohemian. The text is very near that commonly received. The portion of this manuscript which contains the Apocalypse is described by Delitzsch, Handschriftliche Funde, Leipzig, 1862, pp. 45-48, with a facsimile of Apoc. viii. 12, 13.

180. (Evan. 431.) ~~Important, but seems to have perished in 1870 at Strasburg.~~

181. (Evan. 400 [1].)

The following codices also are described by Scrivener, Cod. Augiens., Introd. pp. lv-lxiv, and their collations given in the Appendix.

*182. a^scr (Paul. 252). Lond. Lambeth 1182 [xii, Greg. xiii], 10$\frac{1}{2}$ × 6$\frac{7}{8}$, ff. 397 (20), *chart.*, brought (as were also 183-6) by Carlyle from a Greek island. A later hand [xiv] supplied Acts i. 1—xii. 3; xiii. 5-15; 2, 3 John, Jude. In this copy and 183 the Pauline Epistles precede the Catholic). *Lect.*, *pict.*, *κεφ.*, *prol.*, *syn.*, *men.*, *ἀποδημίαι παύλου*, *ἀντίφωνα* for Easter, and other foreign matter. The various readings are interesting, and strongly resemble those of Cod. 69 of the Acts, and Cod. 61 hardly less, especially in Acts xiii-xvii. This is Hort's Cod. 110. (Greg. 214.)

*183. b^scr (Paul. 253). Lond. Lamb. 1183 [A. D. 1358], 10 × 7, ff. 236 (27), *chart.*, *mut.* 1 Cor. xi. 7-27; 1 Tim. iv. 1—v. 8. *Syn.*, *prol.*, *κεφ. t.*, *τίτλ.*, *mut.*, *κεφ.*, *lect.*, in a beautiful hand, with many later corrections. (Greg. 215.)

*184. c^scr (Paul. 254). Lond. Lamb. 1184 [xv], 4to, *chart.*, *mut.* Acts vii. 52—viii. 25. Having been restored in 1817 (Evan. 516), its readings (which, especially in the Acts and Catholic Epistles, are very

[1] Here again we banish to the notes Scholz's list from Cod. 182 to Cod. 189, for the reasons stated after Evan. 449.
182. (Paul. 243.) Library of St. John's monastery at Patmos [xii], 8vo, also another [xiii] 8vo.
183. (Paul. 231.) Library of the Great Greek monastery at Jerusalem 8 [xiv], 8vo. This must be Coxe's No. 7 [x], 4to, beginning Acts xii. 6.
184. (Paul. 232, Apoc. 85.) Jerusalem 9 [xiii], 4to, with a commentary. This is evidently Coxe's No. 15, though he dates it at the end of [x].
185. (Paul. 233.) St. Saba, Greek monastery, 1 [xi], 12mo.
186. (Evan. 457.) 187. (Evan. 462.)
188. (Paul. 236.) St. Saba 15 [xii], 4to. 189. (Evan. 466.)

important) are taken from an excellent collation (Lamb. 1255, 10–14) made for Carlyle about 1804 by the Rev. W. Sanderson of Morpeth. The text much resembles that of Act. 61, and is almost identical with that of B.-C. III. 37 (Act. 221) and of Act. 137. This is Hort's Cod. 112. (Greg. 216.)

*185. d^{scr} (Paul. 255). Lond. Lamb. 1185 [xiv?], $8\frac{3}{4} \times 5\frac{3}{4}$, ff. 209 23–5), *prol.*, *κεφ. t.*, *κεφ.*, *lect.*, *subscr.*, *men.*, *στίχ.*, *chart.*, miserably mutilated and ill-written. It must be regarded as a collection of fragments in at least four different hands, pieced together by the most recent scribe. *Mut.* Acts ii. 36—iii. 8; vii. 3–59; xii. 7–25; xiv. 8–27; xviii. 20—xix. 12; xxii. 7—xxiii. 11; 1 Cor. viii. 12—ix. 18; 2 Cor. i. 1–10; Eph. iii. 2—Phil. i. 24; 2 Tim. iv. 12—Tit. i. 6; Heb. vii. 19—ix. 12. We have 1 Cor. v. 11, 12; 2 Cor. x. 8–15, written by two different persons. (Greg. 217.)

*186. e^{scr} (Paul. 321) seems to have been Lond. Lamb. 1181 [xiv], 4to of the Acts, Catholic and Pauline Epistles (as we learn from the Lambeth Catalogue, but having been returned (*see* Evan. 516), we have access only to a tolerable collation of Acts i. 1—xxvii. 12, made by the Rev. John Fenton for Carlyle (Lamb. 1255, 27–33). In its text it much resembles Cod. E. (Greg. 218.)

*187. f^{scr} (Evan. 543). (Greg. 194.)

*188. g^{scr} (Evan. 542). (Greg. 193.)

189. (Evan. 825.) (Greg. 258.) 190. (Evan. 503.)

191. (Paul. 245.) Oxf. Ch. Ch. Wake 38 [xi], $7 \times 5\frac{1}{2}$, ff. 306 (23), *prol.*, *Euthal.*, *κεφ. t.*, *κεφ.*, *τίτλ.*, *subscr.*, *syn.*, *men.*, in small and neat characters, from St. Saba (brought to England with the other Wake manuscripts in 1731), contains a catena, and at the end the date 1312 (ἐτελειώθη τὸ παρὸν ἐν ἔτει ϛωκ΄) in a later hand. *Mut.* Acts i. 1–11.

192. (Paul. 246.) Oxf. Ch. Ch. Wake 37 [xi], 8×6, ff. 237 (23), *κεφ.*, *vers.* *Mut.* Acts xii. 4—xxiii. 32. The last leaf is a palimpsest, *chart.* at end about 1490 A.D., the vellum being about 1070, *mut.* 6 leaves at beginning and 16–24.

*193. (Evan. 492.) (Greg. 199.) 194. (Evan. 451.) (Greg. 206.)

195. Modena, Este ii. A. 13 [xiii, Greg. xv], $4 \times 3\frac{1}{4}$, ff. ?, *lect.*, *syn.*, *men.* (*See* Greg. 238.)

196. Modena, Este ii. C. 4 [xi or xii], $9\frac{5}{8} \times 8$, ff. ? *Prol.* ἀποδημία and μαρτ. Paul., *κεφ.*, *τίτλ.*, *subscr.*, *στίχ.*, *vers.*, *syn.* (*See* Greg. 239.)

197. (Evan. 461.) (Greg. 207.)

198. (Paul. 280.) Cheltenham, Phillipps 7681 [A.D. 1107], $12\frac{1}{4} \times 8\frac{7}{8}$, ff. 268 (24), 2 cols., is a copy of the Acts and all the Epistles from the Hon. F. North's collection. A grand folio in a very large hand (Hoskier). (Greg. 225.)

199. Cheltenham, Phillipps 7682 (Evan. 531). (Greg. 255.)

200. Cheltenham, Phillipps 1284 (Evan. 527). (Greg. 254.)

201. (Paul. 396, Apoc. 86.) Athens, National Library (490, 217) [xiv, Greg. xv], $10\frac{5}{8} \times 6\frac{3}{4}$, ff. 453 (42), *chart.*, *prol.*, *κεφ. t.*, *κεφ.* *mut.* at

beginning and end, with commentary of Theophylact, and Andreas (alone) on Apocalypse. (Greg. 251. *See* Act. 78.)

Besides Evann. 226 and 228, entered above as Act. 108 and 109, Montana sent to Mr. Kelly a list of eight more in the Escurial (Greg. 230–237, who inserts Σ. i. 5 for 206).

202. Escurial ρ. iii. 4 [xiii]. 203. Escurial τ. iii. 12 [xiii].

204. Escurial χ. iii. 3 [xii]. 205. Escurial χ. iii. 10 [xii].

206. Escurial χ. iv. 2 [xiv]. 207. Escurial ψ. iii. 6 [xi].

208. Escurial ψ. iii. 18 [x]. 209. Escurial ω. iv. 22 [xv].

210. (Paul. 247.) Paris, St. Geneviève, A. O. 35 [xiv, Greg. xv], $7 \times 4\frac{3}{4}$, ff. 182 (24), beautifully written and illuminated, contains the Catholic and Pauline Epistles. Some name like Λασκαρις stands on fol. 1 in silver letters enclosed by a laurel-leaf. Described to Burgon by the librarian, M. Ruelle. (Greg. 415.)

The next three are at Oxford:

211. (Evan. 488.) (Greg. 200.)

212. (Paul. 250.) Oxf. Bodl. Canon. Gr. 110 [x], $7\frac{1}{2} \times 5\frac{1}{4}$, ff. 380 (18), *pict.*, *prol.* (Euthal.), *κεφ. t.*, *κεφ.*, *τίτλ.*, *subscr.*, *στίχ.* (Paul.), a beautiful copy of the Acts and all the Epistles. For its collation, *see* Evan. 105. It also contains one leaf from Cyril's Homilies, and two other later. (Greg. 221.)

213. (Paul. 251.) Oxf. Bodl. Misc. Gr. 118 [xiii], $9 \times 6\frac{1}{2}$, ff. 149 (29), *syn.*, *men.*, *prol. Euthal.* (Paul.), *κεφ. t.*, *τίτλ.*, *lect.*, *subscr.* *Mut.*, also contains the Acts and all the Epistles. (Greg. 222.)

214. (Evan. 846.) (Greg. 258.)

215. Parham 6 (Evan. 534). (Greg. 202.)

216. (Paul. 234.) Parham 79. 14 [1009], $10\frac{1}{4} \times 8$, ff. ?, *subscr.*, *στίχ.*, from St. Saba; a facsimile in Parham Catalogue. This copy and the next two contain the Acts and all the Epistles. (Greg. 226.)

217. (Paul. 235.) Parham 80. 15 [xi, Greg. xii], $10\frac{5}{8} \times 8\frac{1}{2}$, ff. ?, *prol.*, *subscr.*, *στίχ.*, from Caracalla, with a marginal commentary. (Greg. 227.)

218. (Paul. 236.) Parham 81. 16 [xiii], $13\frac{1}{2} \times 8\frac{5}{8}$, ff. ?, *prol.*, *κεφ.*, *τίτλ.*, *subscr.*, *syn.*, *men.*, from Simopetra on Athos. (Greg. 228.)

The Baroness Burdett-Coutts has three copies of the Acts, two of the Catholic Epistles, viz.:

*219. B.-C. II. 7 (Evan. 549). (Greg. 201.)

*220. (Paul. 264.) B.-C. III. 1, Acts and all the Epistles, the Pauline preceding the Catholic [xi or xii], $11\frac{1}{2} \times 8$, ff. 375 (22), on fine vellum, with broad margins. This is one of the most superb copies extant of the latter part of the N.T., on which so much cost was seldom bestowed as on the Gospels. The illuminations before each book, the golden titles, subscriptions, and capitals, are very rich and fresh: the rubrical directions are in bright red at the top and bottom of the pages. The preliminary matter consists of *syn.* of the Apostolos, *ὑπόθεσις* to the

Acts, *Εὐθαλίου διακόνου περὶ τῶν χρόνων τοῦ κηρύγματος τοῦ ἁγίου παύλου, κεφ. τ.* of the Acts, in all twenty pages. There are no other tables of *κεφάλαια*, but their *τίτλοι* and *κεφ.* are given throughout the manuscript. To each Epistle is prefixed the ordinary *ὑπόθεσις* or *prol., vers.*, and to eight of them Theodoret's also. Three leaves at the beginning of Epistles (containing portions of *prol.* and 2 Cor. i. 1–3; Eph. i. 1–4; Heb. i. 1–6) have been shamefully cut out for the sake of the illuminations. A complete menology of eighteen pages closes the volume. At the end of Jude we find in golden letters *κέ ἰῦ χε̄ υἱὲ τοῦ θῦ ἐλέησόν με τὸν πολϊαμάρτητον ἀντώνϊον τάχα καὶ μοναχὸν τὸν μαλεύκην.* (Greg. 223.)

*221. (Paul. 265.) B.-C. III. 37 [xii], 6 × 4, 270 (20) + 6 *membran.* [xiv or later], and *chart.* [xv] (beginning and end), *men., lect., subscr.*, contains the Acts, Catholic and Pauline Epistles complete. This copy is full of instructive variations, being nearest akin to the Harkleian Syriac *cum asterisco* and to c^{scr} (184), then to a^{scr} (182), 137, 100, 66**, 69, d^{scr} (185) next to 27, 29, 57**. (Greg. 224.)

222. (Evan. 560.) (Greg. 257.)

*223. (Paul. 262.) Brit. Mus. Egerton 2787 [xiv], $7\frac{3}{4} \times 5\frac{3}{8}$, ff. 244 (22), *mut.* Jude 20–25, containing the Acts and all the Epistles, neatly written and bound in the original oak boards. After being offered for £60 in London from 1869 to 1875, it was bought by Dean Burgon, and, like Evan. 563, passed to his nephew, the Rev. W. F. Rose, and was obtained for the Museum in 1893. *Prol., κεφ. τ., κεφ., τίτλ., ἀρχ.* and *τέλ., subscr., στίχ., syn., men.*, at the beginning, but it has been ill used, and the text corrected by an unskilful hand. Its faded ornaments were executed in lake. (Greg. 229.)

*224. (Evan. 507) w^{scr}. Hort's Act. 102. (Greg. 195.)

Besides the British Museum copies already described (Act. 22, 25–8, 59, 91) we must add:

*225 or j^{scr}. Lond. Brit. Mus. Burney 48 [xiv], $14\frac{3}{4} \times 10\frac{1}{4}$, end of St. Chrysost. vol. ii, ff. (230–244) 15, *chart., prol., κεφ. τ., κεφ., lect., τίτλ., subscr., στίχ.*, elegantly written, contains the Catholic Epistles (except that of St. Jude), with important variations. (Greg. 219.)

226. (Evan. 576.) (Greg. 196.) 227. (Evan. 582.) (Greg. 197.)

228. (Evan. 584.) (Greg. 198.)

229. (Paul. 270.) Lond. Brit. Mus. Add. 19,388 [xiii or xiv], $7\frac{1}{4} \times 5\frac{3}{4}$, ff. 94 (21), *prol., κεφ., subscr., τίτλ., lect.*, very neat, bought of Simonides in 1853, contains only 2 Cor. xi. 25—1 Pet. iii. 15, for which order *see* Vol. I. p. 73. (Greg. 220.)

Act. 226–229 were also examined by Dr. Bloomfield.

230. Lond. Brit. Mus. Add. 19,392 [xi], ff. $14 \times 10\frac{1}{2}$, ff. $(2 + 1 + 2 =) 5$, (1) two leaves of wonderful beauty, containing James i. 1–23, the heading illuminated, *κεφ.* at the tops of the pages, with a commentary on three sides of the text in a very minute hand; (2) one leaf of an Evst. out of a volume which fell into the hands of General Menon, and was presented by Mr. Harris of Alexandria to the Brit. Mus., con-

taining Matt. vi. 13–18 (*see* Evst. 262); (3) two leaves containing Luke xxiv. 25–35; John i. 35–51. (Greg. 203.)

231. (Evan. 603.) (Greg. 256.)

232. (Paul. 271, Apoc. 107.) Lond. Brit. Mus. Add. 28,816 [A. D. 1111, Indict. 4], 11½ × 8½, ff. 149 (32), *prol.*, κεφ. *t.*, κεφ., *lect.* (no τίτλ.), *subscr.*, μαρτ., στίχ., a splendid copy, bought (*see* Evan. 603) of Sir Ivor Guest in 1871. A facsimile is exhibited in the Palaeographical Society's work, Plate 84. It begins with Euthalii ἔκθεσις of the chapters of the Acts. Euthalius' Prologue also precedes the Pauline Epistles, and that of Arethas (σύνοψις σχολική) the Apocalypse, with a table of his seventy-two κεφάλαια. Throughout the volume the numerals indicating the κεφάλαια of each book stand in the margin in red, and a list of the κεφ. before each. There are many marginal glosses in a very minute hand. *Mut.* 1 Cor. xvi. 15—Prol. to 2 Cor., and one leaf (Eph. v. 3—vi. 16) is supplied [xv] *chart.* There are ten leaves at the end containing foreign matter, by the same hand, and in the colophon, besides the date, we read that the monk Andreas wrote it εἰς τὰ ὅρος τοῦ $\overline{\pi\rho\sigma}$ καὶ αγ μελετίου τῆς μυοπάλεως ἐν τῇ μονῇ τοῦ $\overline{\sigma\rho\sigma}$, adding of himself (as well he might) πολλὰ γὰρ ἐκαπίασα ἐν τρισὶν ἔτεσιν κτίζων αὐτήν. The foreign matter includes an exposition of the errors condemned by the seven general councils (ff. 143–5), resembling that in Evan. 69. (Greg. 205.)

233. (Evan. 605.) (Greg. 253.) 234. (Evan. 608.) (Greg. 417.)

235. (Evan. 472.)

Belsheim enables us to add

236. (Paul. 273, Apoc. 108.) Upsal, Univ. Gr. 11 [xii], 6½ × 4¾, ff. 182 (33), containing the Acts, Epistles, and Apocalypse. (Greg. 335.)

237. (Evan. 616, Paul. 274.) (Greg. 269.)

He also found

238. Linköping, Benzel 35, once belonging to Eric Benzel [1675–1743], Archbishop of Upsal [x], 4to, ff. 244, very beautiful, *lect.* at beginning and end, contains the Acts and all the Epistles (Paul. 272), the Epistle to the Hebrews preceding 1 Tim. *Mut.* 2 Thess. iii. 7—Heb. i. 5. (Greg. 334.)

239. Rom. Vat. Gr. 652 [xiv], 11 × 7½, ff. 105, *chart.*, the Acts only for all that appears, with Theophylact's commentary, as printed in full in vol. iii (pp. 189–317, Praef. p. viii) of the Venice edition of Theophylact, 1758. *Lect.*, κεφ., τίτλοι, ἀρχ. and τέλη (Burgon). (Greg. 325.)

Fourteen copies were seen by Mr. Coxe in the East, which are numbered below. Compare Scholz's list.

240. (Paul. 282, Apoc. 109.) Paris Nat. 'Arménien 9' [xi], 11½ × 9, ff. 323 (36), 2 cols., *prol.*, κεφ. *t.*, *lect.*, *subscr.*, στίχ. Greek and Armenian. (Greg. 301.)

241. (Paul. 283.) Messina, Univ. 40 [xii, Greg. xiii], 13⅜ × 10¼, ff. 224 (28), *chart.*, *prol.*, *mut.* Begins at Acts viii. 2, ends at Hebrews viii. 2. Has a commentary. (Greg. 320.)

242. (Evan. 622, Paul. 290, Apoc. 110.) Crypta Ferrata A'. α'. 1. (Greg. 267.)

243. (Paul. 291.) Crypta Ferrata A. β. 1 [x], 9 × 7⅛, ff. 139 (25), 2 cols., *Euth.*, *prol.*, *κεφ. t.*, *κεφ.*, *τίτλ.*, *lect.*, *subscr.*, *στίχ.* John (1, 2, 3), Jude, Paul. (Heb., Tim.). *Mut.* 2 Tim. iv. 8—end. (Greg. 317.)

244. (Paul. 292.) Crypta Ferrata A. β. 3 [xi or xii], 10¼ × 6¾, ff. 172 (29), 2 cols., *prol.*, *lect.*, *subscr.*, *στίχ.*, *syn.*, *men.* (Greg. 318.)

245. (Paul. 293.) Crypta Ferrata A. β. 6 [xi], 9 × 6¾, ff. 193 (26), *prol.* (Paul.), *lect.*, *subscr.*, *στίχ.*, *men.*, *mut.* at the end. (Greg. 319.)

246. (Paul. 294.) Rom. Vat. Gr. 1208, 11 × 7⅞, ff. 395 (19), *pict.*, *κεφ. t.*, *κεφ.*, *τίτλ.* Abbate Cozza-Luzi confirms Berriman's account (pp. 98, 99) of the splendour of this codex. It is written in gold letters and is said to have belonged to Carlotta, Queen of Jerusalem, Cyprus, and Armenia, who died at Rome, A. D. 1487, and probably gave this book to pope Innocent VIII, whose arms are painted at the beginning. It contains effigies of SS. Luke, James, Peter, John, Jude, Paul. (Greg. 326.)

247. (Paul. 295.) Rom. Pal.-Vat. Gr. 38 [xi], 8¾ × 6⅛, ff. 351 (24), *prol.*, *κεφ. t.*, *κεφ.*, *τίτλ.*, *subscr.*, *στίχ.* (Greg. 330.)

248. (Paul. 298.) Berlin, Königl. (Hamilton) 244 (625) [A. D. 1090 ?], 5⅞ × 4⅜, ff. 330 (22), *prol.*, *κεφ. t.*, *subscr.*, *στίχ.*, *syn.*, *men.* It contains the Acts, Cath. and St. Paul, as Dr. C. de Boor informs us. (*See* Greg. 303.)

249. (Paul. 299.) Berlin, Königl. Gr. 4to, 40 [xiii, Greg. xi], 10¾ × 5¾, ff. 222 (26), 2 cols., *prol.*, *κεφ. t.*, *lect.*, *subscr.*, *στίχ.*, same contents as the preceding. (*See* Greg. 252.)

250. (Paul. 300.) Berlin, Königl. Gr. 4to, 43 [xi, Greg. xiv], 9⅝ × 7, ff. 116 (39), *prol.*, *κεφ.*, *τίτλ.*, *lect.*, *subscr.*, *στίχ.*, *syn.*, *men.*, same contents as the preceding, but commences with the Psalms. (*See* Greg. 302.)

251. (Paul. 301.) Berlin, Königl. Gr. 4to, 57 [xiv, Greg. xiii], 8⅝ × 6, ff. ?, *prol.*, *κεφ. t.*, *chart.*, same contents as Act. 248. (*See* Greg. 248.)

252. (Evan. 642, Paul. 302.) Berlin, Königl. Gr. 8vo, 9. (Greg. 213.)

253, 254, 255, 257, 260 were discovered on the spot by Dr. Gregory not to be Codd. Act.

253. (Paul. 248.) Cairo, Patriarch. Alex. Library 8 [xiv], 4to, *chart.*, Cath. (Greg. 240.)

254. (Paul. 275.) Cair. Patr. Alex. Libr. 59 [xi], 4to, Acts and all Epistles. (Greg. 241.)

255. (Paul. 296.) Cair. Patr. Alex. Libr. 88 [xi], fol, Acts and all Epistles, after Psalms. (Greg. 242.)

256. (Paul. 322.) Rom. Vat. Gr. 2099 [x, Greg. xi], 7¼ × 6, ff. 125 (21), *Euth.*, *κεφ.*, *τίτλ.*, *lect.*, *subscr.* Though numbered from 'Acts,' it contains only the Cath. Epp. (*See* Greg. 329.)

257. (Paul. 303.) Jerusalem, Holy Sepulchre 7 [x], 4to. Act., Cath., Paul., begins at Acts xii. 6. (Greg. 183 ?)

258. (Paul. 306.) Jerus. Holy Sep. 15 [x, end], 4to, with rich scholia. (Greg. 184 ?)

259. (Evan. 657.) (Greg. 208.)

260. (Evan. 661.) (Greg. 209.)

261. (Paul. 336.) Rom. Casanatensis G. ii. 6 [xv or xvi], $12\frac{7}{8} \times 23\frac{1}{8}$, ff. ?, *subscr.*, *vers.*, *στίχ.*, Catholic and Pauline Epistles with a catena. (*See* Greg. 321.)

The next three were added by the Abbé Martin.

262. (Evan. 738.) (Greg. 259.)

263. Par. Nat. Suppl. Gr. 906 [xii–xiii], $8\frac{1}{8} \times 5\frac{3}{4}$, ff. 48 (20). *Mut.* Acts xi. 5–22; xvi. 1–16; xxii. 10—xxviii. 31; James i. 1—ii. 18; iv. 3—v. 20. *Prol.* (Greg. 249.)

264. (Paul. 337.) Paris, Nat. Coislin. 224 [xi], 10×8, ff. 379 (20), *syn.*, *Euth.*, Act., Cath., Paul. (Greg. 250.)

We now follow Dr. Gregory's order as far as is possible, and refer students to his pages where Library Catalogues and other sources of information do not supply particulars.

265. (Evan. 808.)

266. (Evan. 823.)

267. (Evan. 858.) (Greg. 261.)

268. (Evan. 698.)

269. (Evan. 794.) (Greg. 262.)

270. (Evan. 922.)

271. (Evan. 927.)

272. (Evan. 935.)

273. (Evan. 941.)

274. (Evan. 945.)

275. (Evan. 956.)

276. (Evan. 959.)

277. (Evan. 986.)

278. (Evan. 996.)

279. (Evan. 997.)

280. (Evan. 999.)

281. (Evan. 1003.)

282. (Evan. 1040.)

283. (Evan. 1058.)

284. (Evan. 1072.)

285. (Evan. 1073.)

286. (Evan. 1075.)

287. (Evan. 1094.)

288. (Evan. 1149.)

289. (Evan. 1240.)

290. (Evan. 1241.)

291. (Evan. 1242.)

292. (Evan. 1243.)

293. (Evan. 1244.)

294. (Evan. 1245.)

295. (Evan. 1246.)

296. (Evan. 1247.)

297. (Evan. 1248.)

298. (Evan. 1249.)

299. (Evan. 1250.)

300. (Evan. 1251.)

301. (Paul. 334, Apoc. 109.) St. Saba 20 [xi, beginning], 4to, Act., Cath. (Greg. 243.)

302. (Paul. 313.) St. Saba 35 [xi], 4to. (Greg. 244.)

303. (Apoc. 185.) Lesbos, τ. Λείμωνος μονῆς 132 [xv], $8\frac{1}{4} \times 5\frac{1}{4}$, *chart.*, *mut.* at beginning and end.

304. (Paul. 331.) Athens, Nat. Theol. (207, 70) [xiii], $6\frac{3}{8} \times 4\frac{3}{4}$, ff. 321. Very beautiful. Written by Cosmas.

305. (Paul. 332.) Ath. Nat. Theol. (208, 7) [xiv], $7\frac{1}{2} \times 5\frac{1}{8}$, ff. 273, with Œcumenius.

306. (Paul. 333.) Ath. Nat. Theol. (209, 72) [A. D. 1364], $8\frac{1}{4} \times 5\frac{7}{8}$, ff. 250. Written by Constantine Alexopoulos. Restored by Nicolaus in A.D. 1464.

307. (Paul. 469, Apoc. 111.) Ath. Nat. 43 (149 ?) [x], $8\frac{5}{8} \times 6\frac{3}{8}$.

308. (Paul. 420.) Ath. Nat. (45).

309. (Paul. 300, Apoc. 124.) Ath. Nat. 64 (91) [x], $9 \times 7\frac{1}{8}$, ff. 327. Apoc. ends at xviii. 22.

310. Ath. Nat. 66 (105) [x], $9\frac{7}{8} \times 7\frac{1}{2}$, ff. 293. Sixteen homilies of St. Chrysostom on the Acts. Eight leaves at the beginning are of cent. xiv.

311. (Paul. 419.) Ath. Nat. 221 (129 ?) [xiii], $5\frac{7}{8} \times 4\frac{1}{4}$, ff. 224.

312. (Paul. 421.) Ath. Nat. (119) [xii], $9\frac{7}{8} \times 5\frac{1}{2}$, ff. 356, *chart.*

313. (Paul. 422.) Ath. Nat. 89 [xii], $11\frac{3}{8} \times 8\frac{1}{4}$, ff. 220. *Mut.* Acts i. 1—vii. 35.

314. Zante.

315. (Paul. 474.) Petersburg, Imp. Porfirianus.

316. Madrid, Royal O. 78.

317. (Evan. 667.) Coxe, St. Saba 53. (Greg. 211.)

318. (Evan. 673.) Coxe, St. Saba 54. (Greg. 212.)

319. (Paul. 318.) Patmos 27 [xii], fol., Act., Cath., Paul., with marginal gloss. Coxe.

320. (Paul. 320.) Patmos 31 [ix], fol., Act., Cath., Paul. Coxe.

321. (Evan. 796.) (Greg. 263.)

322. Athos, Iveron 639.

323. (Paul. 429.) Lesb. τ. Λείμ. 55.

324. Jerusalem, Holy Cross 1.

325. (Paul. 495, Apoc. 187.) Athens, Nat. Libr. 91 [x], $9 \times 7\frac{1}{8}$, ff. 327, *orn.*, *mus.*, *mut.* Apoc. xviii. 22–end.

326. (Evan. 801.) (Greg. 264.)

327. Rom. Vat. Gr. 1227.

328. (Evan. 665.) (Greg. 210.)

329. (Evan. 1267.)

330. (Paul. 491.) Jerus. Patr. Libr. 462 [xiv] ?, 535 pages *chart.*, ff. 60 (58 first and 2 last [xxi], *κεφ. t.*, *syn.*, *proll.*

331. (Paul. 145.) Contains also James, 1 Pet., 2 Pet. i. 1–3.

332. (Paul. 434.) Ven. Marc. ii. 114.

333. (Paul. 435.) Edinburgh, Mr. Mackellar.

334. (Paul. 319.) Rom. Vat. Gr. 1971 [x], $6\frac{3}{4} \times 5\frac{1}{4}$, ff. 247 (31), 2 cols., *Euth.*, *proll.*, *κεφ. t.*, *lect.*, *ἀναγν.*, *subscr.*, *στίχ.*, *men.* (*See* Greg. 268.)

335. (Paul. 329.) Vindob. Caes. Gr. Theol. 141. (Greg. 245.)

336. Athos, Vatopedi 41.

337. Ath. Vat. 201.

338. Ath. Vat. 203.

339. Ath. Vat. 210.

340. Ath. Vat. 259.

341. Ath. Vat. 328.

342. Ath. Vat. 380.

343. Ath. Vat. 419.

344. Ath. Dionysius 68.

345. Ath. Dion. 75.

346. Ath. Dion. 382.
347. Ath. Docheiariou 38.
348. Ath. Doch. 48.
349. Ath. Doch. 136.
350. Ath. Doch. 139.
351. Ath. Doch. 147.
352. Ath. Esphigmenou 63.
353. Ath. Esphig. 64.
354. Ath. Esphig. 65.
355. Ath. Esphig. 66.
356. Ath. Esphig. 67.
357. Ath. Esphig. 68.
358. Ath. Iveron 24.
359. Ath. Iveron 25.
360. Ath. Iveron 37.
361. Ath. Iveron 57.
362. Ath. Iveron 60.
363. Ath. Iveron 642.
364. Ath. Iveron 643.
365. Ath. Iveron 648.
366. Ath. Constamonitou 108.
367. Ath. Coutloumoussi 16.
368. Ath. Coutloum. 57.
369. Ath. Coutloum. 80.
370. Ath. Coutloum. 81.
371. Ath. Coutloum. 82.
372. Ath. Coutloum. 83.
373. Ath. Coutloum. 275.
374. Ath. Paul 2.
375. Ath. Protaton 32.
376. Ath. Simopetra 42.
377. Ath. Stauroniketa 52.
378. Ath. Philotheou 38.
379. Ath. Philoth. 76.
380. Beratinus Archiepisc.
381. Cairo, Patriarch. Alex. 942.
382. Chalcis, Mon. Trin. 16.
383. Chalcis, Schol. 9.
384. Chalcis, Schol. 26.
385. Chalcis, Schol. 33.
386. Chalcis, Schol. 96.
387. Patmos, St. John 14.
388. Patmos, St. John 15.
389. Patmos, St. John 16.
390. Patmos, St. John 263.
391. Thessalonica, Gr. Gymn. 12.
392. Thessalonica, Gr. Gymn. 15.
393. Thessalonica, Gr. Gymn. 16.
394. Sinaitic 274.
395. Sinaitic 275.
396. Sinaitic 276.
397. Sinaitic 277.
398. Sinaitic 278.
399. Sinaitic 279.
400. Sinaitic 280.
401. Sinaitic 281.
402. Sinaitic 282.
403. Sinaitic 283.
404. Sinaitic 284.
405. Sinaitic 285.
406. Sinaitic 287.
407. Sinaitic 288.
408. Sinaitic 289.
409. Sinaitic 290.
410. Sinaitic 291.
411. Sinaitic 292.
412. Sinaitic 293.
413. Sinaitic 300.
414. Sinaitic 301.
415. (Paul. 329.) Vindob. Caes. Gr. Theol. 150. (Greg. 246.)

From Ἱεροσολυμιτικὴ Βιβλιοθήκη, by Papadopoulos Kerameus.

416. (Paul. 58, Apoc. 181.) Jerusalem, Patriarch. Libr. 38 [xi beg.], $9\frac{3}{8} \times 7\frac{1}{2}$, ff. 280 (i.e. 89+234), (*syn.* for July and August [xiii]), *pict.*,

mut. Acts i. 1–11, Life of St. Paul. Heb. at end of Paul. Written at Constantinople by Theophanes. Belonged to Matthew a monk, and to monastery of St. Saba.

417. (Paul. 64.) Jerus. Patr. Libr. 43 [xii], $8\frac{7}{8} \times 6$, ff. 138 (28). *Prol.*, *mut.* Acts i. 1—xii. 9. Epp. of Paul with Heb. at end follow Acts. Came from St. Saba.

From Ἔκθεσις Παλαιογραφικῶν καὶ Φιλολογικῶν Ἐρευνῶν ἐν Θράκῃ καὶ Μοκεδονίᾳ, by Papadopoulos Kerameus.

418. (Paul. 492.) Cosinitsa, Ἁγία Μονή, Ματθαῖος ἱερεύς 54 [A.D. 1344], Acts, Cath. Epp. Written by the aforenamed.

From Καταλόγος τῶν ἐν ταῖς Βιβλιοθήκαις τοῦ Ἁγίου Ὄρους Ἑλληνικῶν Κωδίκων ὑπὸ Σπυρίδωνος Π. Λαμπρός 1888.

419. (Paul. 493, Apoc. 185.) Athos, Monastery of St. Paul 2 [A.D. 800 ? ?], 4to, said to have been written by the Empress Mary, who had been divorced by Constantine VI, and shut up in a convent in Cilicia. At the end of the Apoc. it has the subscription, σταυρέ, φύλαττε βασίλισσαν Μαρίαν. Some leaves in the beginning and middle *chart.* [xviii].

420. (Paul. 494.) Athens, Nat. Libr. 222 [xvii], $12\frac{1}{8} \times 7\frac{7}{8}$, ff. 246. After the Κατηχήσεις of Theodorus Studita, Act., Cath., Paul.

CHAPTER XI.

CURSIVE MANUSCRIPTS OF ST. PAUL'S EPISTLES.

*1. (Evan. 1.) 2. (Act. 2.) 3. (Evan. 3.)

4. (Act. 4.) 5. (Evan. 5.) 6. (Evan. 6.)

7. Basil. A. N. iii. 11, 11¼ × 8½, ff. 387 (11), *prol.*, with notes and a finely written marginal commentary, ends Heb. xii. 18. But Rom., 1, 2 Cor. are in a different hand. It is plain that Erasmus must have used this copy, cf. Rom. v. 21; vi. 19; viii. 35; xv. 31; xvi. 22; 1 Cor. xi. 15; 2 Cor. v. 4; ix. 8; 12; Gal. i. 6; iii. 27; Phil. iii. 9; Col. i. 6; iii. 17; 1 Thess. i. 7; Tit. iii. 8; Philem. 15; Heb. v. 4; vii. 5, in all which places it countenances peculiar readings of his first edition. It contained τό in Rom. iv. 4, but not καὶ πεισθέντες in Heb. xi. 13 (Wetstein, Hoskier).

8. (Act. 50.) 9. (Act. 7.) 10. (Act. 8.)

11. (Act. 9.) 12. (Act. 10.) *See* Act. 7.

13. Certain readings cited by J. le Fevre d'Etaples, in his commentary on St. Paul's Epistles, Paris, 1512.

14. (Evan. 90.)

15. A manuscript cited by Erasmus, belonging to Amandus of Louvain.

16. (Act. 12.) *17. (Evan. 33.) *See* Act. 7.

18. (Evan. 35.) 19. (Act. 16.)

20. Par. Nat. Coislin. Gr. 27, described (as is Cod. 23) by Montfaucon [x], 13¾ × 10½, ff. 252 (39), in bad condition, with *prol.* and a catena, from Laura at Athos (Wetstein). *See* Act. 7.

21. (Act. 17.) 22. (Act. 18.)

23. Par. Nat. Coisl. Gr. 28 [A. D. 1056], 14¾ × 10½, ff. 272 (47), *prol.*, *κεφ.*, *τίτλ.*, *subscr.*, *στίχ.* (Wetstein, Scholz). From Laura.

24. (Evan. 105.) 25. (Act. 20.) 26. (Act. 21.)

27. Cambr. Univ. Libr. Ff. i. 30 [xii], 11¾ × 8¼, ff. 169 (varies), *prol.*, *κεφ. t.*, *κεφ.*, *lect.*, *subscr.*, *στίχ.*, with Œcumenius' commentary: Rom. and 1, 2 Cor. are wanting (Wetstein, 1716). Bradshaw found that this manuscript, which came to Cambridge in 1574, is only the second part of Paul. 42, the last quire of the latter being numbered κα', while the first in Cod. 27 is κβ'. Hort's Paul. 27 is k^{scr} or Paul. 260.

28. (Act. 23.) *29. (Act. 24.) *30. (Act. 53.)

31. (Act. 25.) 32. (Act. 26.) 33. (Act. 27.)
*34. (Act. 28.) 35. (Act. 29.) 36. (Act. 30.)
*37. (Evan. 69.) 38. (Evan. 51.) 39. (Act. 33.)
*40. (Evan. 61.) 41. (Evan. 57.)

42. Oxf. Magdalen Coll. Gr. 7 [xii], $11\frac{3}{4} \times 8\frac{1}{4}$, ff. 170 (varies), *prol.*, *κεφ.*, *lect.*, contains Rom., 1, 2 Cor. surrounded by Œcumenius' commentary (Walton's Polyglott, Mill). First part of Paul. 27.

43. (Act. 37.) *44. (Act. 38.)
45. (Act. 39.) 46. (Act. 40.)

47. Oxf. Bodl. Roe 16 [xi], $11\frac{3}{8} \times 8\frac{1}{2}$, ff. 255 (15), *prol.*, *subscr.*, *στίχ.*, with a Patristic catena, in a small and beautiful hand, having a text much resembling that of Cod. A, and Cod. B still more often when the two stand alone: its history is the same as that of Evan. 49. The Epistle to the Hebrews precedes 1 Tim. (Mill, Roe 2, Tregelles for his edition of the N. T.: inspected by Vansittart.)

*48. (Act. 42.) 49. (Evan. 76.) 50. (Act. 52.)
51. (Evan. 82, Act. 44, Apoc. 5.) 52. (Act. 45.)

53 of Wetstein is now Paul. Cod. M, the portion containing the Hebrews, or Bengel's Uffenbach 2 or 1. Instead—
(Evan. 1149.) (Greg. 336.)

54. Monacensis Reg. Gr. 412 [xii], $11\frac{7}{8} \times 8\frac{3}{8}$, ff. 358 (24), is Bengel's August. 5 (*see* Act. 46), containing Rom. vii. 7—xvi. 24, with a catena from twenty Greek authors (*see* Paul. 127), stated by Bengel to resemble that in the Bodleian described by Mill (N. T., Proleg. § 1448).

55. (Act. 46.)

56. This is worthless as being a transcript of Erasmus' first edition, then just published. Instead—
(Evan. 1262.)

*57. (Evan. 218.)

58. Rom. Vat. Gr. 1650 [1]=Act. 156, Paul. 190. Instead—
(Act. 416.)

59. Par. Nat. Coisl. Gr. 204 [xi], $11 \times 8\frac{7}{8}$, ff. 312 (32). *Mut.* Rom., 1 Cor., 2 Cor. is in the 3rd of 3 vols. *See* Cramer's Catena. (Greg.) Wetstein and Griesbach comprise readings of two Medicean manuscripts of the Ephes. and Philipp., derived from the same source as Evan. 102, Act. 56, Apoc. 23.

60. Codices cited in the Correctorium Bibliorum Latinorum.

*61. (Act. 61.) 62. (Act. 59.) 63. (Act. 60.)

64 of Griesbach is the portion of Evan. M. Instead—
(Act. 417.)

65. (Act. 62.)

[1] From the monastery of Grotta Ferrata, near Tusculum, 'Ubi degunt ab antiquo tempore monachi, ordinis S. Basilii Magni, ritum Italo-Graecum observantes,' Holmes. Praef. ad Pentateuch. on his Cod. 128, which came to the Vatican from the same place. It is the traditional Villa Luculli.

66. Lond. Brit. Mus. Harl. 5552 [xvi], 6½ × 4¼, ff. 233 (18). This number included readings extracted by Griesbach from the margin of this MS., which itself he considers but a transcript of Erasmus' first edition (Symb. Crit., p. 166).

67. (Act. 66.) 67** resembles Cod. B, yet is independent of it (Eph. iii. 9, iv. 9, &c.). 'These marginal readings must have been derived from a MS. having a text nearly akin to that of the fragmentary MS. called M, though not from M itself' (Hort, Introduction, p. 155).

68. (Act. 63.) 69. (Act. 64.) 70. (Act. 67.)

71. Vindobon. Caesar. Gr. 61 [xii, Greg. x or xi], 9½ × 6¾, ff. 170 (29), 2 cols., *prol.*, *κεφ. t.*, *κεφ.*, *τίτλ.*, *lect.*, *μαρτ.*, *subscr.*, *ἀναγν.*, *στίχ.* *Mut.* Rom. i. 1–4; ii. 3–8, &c. Titus; Philem.; with Hebrews before 1 Tim. It includes a commentary and catechetical lectures of St. Cyril of Jerusalem (Alter, Birch, Greg.).

72. (Evan. 234.) 73. (Act. 68.)

74. (Act. 69.)

75. (Brit. Mus. Add. 5116, *see* Act. 22.)

*76. Leipzig, Univ. Gr. 361 [xiii], 12½ × 9½, ff. out of 327, 85 (35), *prol.*, *κεφ.*, contains Rom., 1 Cor., Gal., and part of Eph., with Theophylact's commentary, and other matter (Matthaei, Gregory).

Codd. 77–112 were cursorily collated by Birch, and nearly all by Scholz.

77. (Evan. 131.) 78. (Evan. 133.)

79. (Act. 72.) 80. (Act. 73[1].)

81. Rom. Vat. Gr. 761 [xii], 13¾ × 10, ff. 266, *Euth.*, *κεφ.*, *τίτλ.*, *subscr.*, *στίχ.*, with Œcumenius' commentary. The Epistle to the Hebrews is wanting.

82. Rom. Vat. Gr. 762 [xii], 12⅛ × 9, ff. 411, *Euth.*, contains Rom., 1, 2 Cor., with a catena.

83. Rom. Vat. Gr. 765 [xi], 14⅛ × 11⅝, ff. 177, *Euth.*, with a commentary.

84. Rom. Vat. Gr. 766 [xii], 14¾ × 11⅜, *prol.*, *κεφ.*, *τίτλ.*, with a commentary.

85. (Apoc. 39.) Rom. Vat. Gr. 1136 [xiii, Greg. xiv], 10 × 6¾, ff. 60 (46), contains *first* the Apocalypse (beginning ch. iii. 8) with a Latin version, then St. Paul's Epistles ending 1 Tim. vi. 5, with many unusual readings.

86. (Evan. 141.) 87. (Evan. 142.)

88. (Evan. 149.) 89. (Act. 78.)

90. (Act. 79.) 91. (Act. 80.)

92. (Evan. 180.) 93. (Act. 83.)

94. (Act. 84.) 95. (Act. 85.)

[1] Birch shows the connexion of Caryophilus with this important copy (which much resembles the Leicester manuscript, Evan. Cod. 69) from James v. 5, and especially from 3 John 5 *μισθόν* for *πιστόν*, a *lectio singularis*. In this codex, as in the others cited, Heb. stands before 1 Tim.

96. (Act. 86.) The same copy as Paul. 183 in the last edition.

97. (Act. 87.) 98. (Act. 88.) 99. (Act. 89.)

100. Flor. Laurent. x. 4 [xii], $12\frac{1}{2} \times 9\frac{1}{2}$, ff. 426 (28), with a commentary and additional scholia [xiv], from the Cistercian monastery of S. Salvator de Septimo, in the diocese of Florence.

101. Flor. Laurent. x. 6 [xi, Greg. x], $13\frac{1}{2} \times 10\frac{1}{4}$, ff. 285, *prol.*, *κεφ. t.*, *κεφ.*, *τίτλ.*, *subscr.*, *στίχ.*, with a catena supplying the authors' names.

102. Flor. Laurent. x. 7 [xi], $13 \times 9\frac{5}{8}$, ff. 270, *prol.*, *κεφ.*, *τίτλ.*, *subscr.*, *στίχ.*, *syn.*, *men.*, a life of St. Paul, and catena with such names attached as Theodoret, Chrysostom, Œcumenius, Severianus, &c.

103. Flor. Laurent. x. 19 [xiii], $9\frac{3}{4} \times 7\frac{3}{8}$, ff. 260, *prol.*, *κεφ. t.*, *κεφ.*, *τίτλ.*, *lect.*, *subscr.*, *στίχ.*, *syn.*, *men.*, with a catena. At the end is a date, 'A.D. 1318, Ind. 1, Timotheus.'

*104. (Evan. 201 or h^scr^.) Examined by Bloomfield.

105. (Evan. 204.) Dean Burgon has received a facsimile of 1 Tim. iii. 16 from the librarian at Bologna.

106. (Evan. 205.) 107. (Evan. 206.)

108. (Evan. 209.) *109. (Act. 96.)

*110. Venet. Marc. 33 [xi], $15\frac{3}{4} \times 12\frac{7}{8}$, ff. 369, *prol.*, with a catena, much being taken from Œcumenius (Rink, as also 111, 112 : *see* Act. 96).

*111. Ven. Marc. 34 [xi], $13\frac{1}{8} \times 10\frac{1}{2}$, ff. 332, *prol.*, *κεφ. t.*, *κεφ.*, *τίτλ.*, *vers.*, with a commentary.

*112. Ven. Marc. 35 [xi], $14\frac{1}{2} \times 11\frac{3}{4}$, ff. 159 (40), with a commentary, a fragment beginning 2 Cor. i. 20, ending Heb. x. 25; *mut.* 1 Thess. iv. 13—2 Thess. ii. 14.

Codd. 113–124 were collated by Matthaei.

*113. (Act. 98.) *114. (Act. 99.)

*115. (Act. 100.) *116. (Act. 101.)

*117. (Act. 102.) *118. (Act. 103.)

*119. Mosc. Synod. 292 [x–xii], 4to, ff. 462, from the monastery of Pantocrator on Athos, contains 1, 2 Corinth., with Theophylact's commentary. (Matthaei.)

*120. (Evan. 241.) *121. (Evan. 242.)

*122. (Act. 106.)

*123. Mosc. Syn. 99 [x or xi], fol., ff. 241, *prol.*, *κεφ. t.*, with scholia, from St. Athanasius' monastery (Laura).

*124. Mosc. Syn. 250 (Mt. q) [xiv], 8vo, ff. 40 (i.e. 117–157), on cotton paper, from the monastery of Vatopedi on Athos, contains Rom. i–xiii, with Theophylact's commentary and other writings.

Codd. 125–230 were first catalogued by Scholz, who professes to have collated entire Paul. 177–179, in the greater part Paul. 157, the rest slightly or not at all.

125. Munich, Reg. Gr. 504 [*dated* Feb. 1, 1387, Indict. 10], $8\frac{5}{8} \times 5\frac{1}{2}$, ff. 381 (33), *prol.*, on cotton paper, with Theophylact's commentary in black

ink, and the text (akin to it) in red. Bought by Nicetas 'primicerius sceuophylactus' for eight golden ducats of Rhodes[1]. *Mut.* Philemon.

126. Munich, Reg. Gr. 455, either a copy of, or derived from Cod. 125. [*dated* Feb. 17, Indict. 12, probably A.D. 1389], $10\frac{1}{2} \times 8\frac{1}{4}$, ff. 439 (32), *chart.*, also *mut.* Philem.; with Theophylact's commentary, and some homilies of Chrysostom. From internal reasons 125 is probably the older of the two (J. Rendel Harris).

127. Munich, Reg. Gr. 110 [xvi], $13\frac{1}{8} \times 8\frac{1}{2}$, ff. 112, *chart.*, once at the Jesuits' College, Munich, contains Rom. vii. 7—ix. 21, with a catena. It was found by Scholz to be, what indeed it professes, a mere copy of part of Cod. 54. (Greg. 54[a].)

128. (Act. 179.)

129. Munich, Reg. Gr. 35 [xvi], $13\frac{5}{8} \times 8\frac{1}{2}$, ff. 488 (30), *chart.*, with catena.

130. (Evan. 43.)

131. (Evan. 330.)

*132. (Evan. 18: *see* Act. 113.)

133. (Act. 51.)

*134. (Act. 114.)

135. (Act. 115.)

136. (Act. 116.)

*137. (Evan. 263.) *See* Act. 7.

138. (Act. 118.)

*139. (Act. 119), Reiche, as also

*140. (Act. 11.)

141. (Act. 120.)

142. (Act. 121.)

143. (Act. 122.)

144. (Act. 123.)

145. Par. Nat. Gr. 108, 109, 110, 111 [xvi, Greg. xv], $7 \times 4\frac{3}{4}$, ff. 308 (14), *prol.*, *κεφ. t.*, *κεφ.* *Mut.* Gal., Eph. (2 Cor. xiii. 1–13 later). Written by George Hermonymus. *See* Act. 331. (Gregory under Act. 331.) Once Colbert's, as were 146, 147, 148.

146, 147, 148—included under 145.

149. (Act. 124.)

150. (Act. 125.)

151. Par. Nat. Gr. 126 [xvi], $4\frac{5}{8} \times 3$, ff. 168 (18), *subscr.*, written (like 149) by Angelus Vergecius.

152. Instead of Par. Nat. Gr. 136[a] (omit Greg.)—
(Evan. 657.) (Greg. 264.)

*153. (Act. 126) Reiche.

154. (Act. 127.)

155. (Act. 128.)

156. (Act. 129.)

157. Par. Nat. Gr. 222 [xi], $12\frac{1}{2} \times 10\frac{1}{8}$, ff. 227, *pict.*, once Colbert's, brought from Constantinople in 1676, with a commentary. *Mut.* Rom. i. 1–11; 21–29; iii. 26—iv. 8; ix. 11–22; 1 Cor. xv. 22–43; Col. i. 1–16.

158. (Act. 131.)

159. (Apoc. 64.) Par. Nat. Gr. 224 [xi], $11\frac{3}{4} \times 8\frac{3}{4}$, ff. 274, *prol.*, *pict.*, *κεφ. t.*, *κεφ.*, *τίτλ.*, *subscr.*, *στίχ.*, very elegant. The Pauline Epistles have a catena, the Apocalypse Arethas' commentary.

1 The gold ducat coined for the Military Order of St. John at Rhodes (*see* Ducange) was worth 9*s.* 6*d.* English money.

160. Par. Nat. Gr. 225 [xvi], 12×8, ff. 401 (29), *chart.*, a fragment of St. Paul, with Theophylact's commentary.

161. Par. Nat. Gr. 226 [xvi], $12\frac{1}{4} \times 8\frac{1}{2}$, ff. 96 (34), *chart.*, contains the Romans, with a commentary.

162. Par. Nat. Gr 227 [xvi], $13\frac{1}{2} \times 9$, ff. 213 (31), *chart.*, once Bigot's, contains a catena on 1 Cor. xvi.

163. Par. Nat. Gr. 238 [xiii], $7\frac{3}{4} \times 5\frac{1}{4}$, ff. 391 (23), from Adrianople, contains Heb. i–viii, with a catena.

164. Par. Nat. Gr. 849 [xvi], $12\frac{7}{8} \times 9\frac{1}{8}$, ff. 261 (30), *chart.*, *prol.*, *subscr.*, once a Medicean manuscript, contains Theodoret's commentary with text.

165. Turin, Univ. C. vi. 29 [xvi], $8\frac{1}{8} \times 5\frac{5}{8}$, ff. 71 (17), *chart.*, contains from 1 Thess. to Hebrews.

166. (Act. 133.)

167. (Act. 134.)

168. Turin, Univ. C. v. 10, $8\frac{5}{8} \times 6\frac{3}{8}$, ff. 239 (29), *prol.*, *κεφ. t.*, *στίχ.*, and a commentary: it begins Rom. iii. 19.

169. (Act. 136.)

170. (Evan. 339.)

171. Milan, Ambros. B. 6 inf. [xiii], $13\frac{5}{8} \times 10\frac{1}{4}$, ff. 241, *prol.*, *κεφ. t.*, *κεφ.*, *τίτλ.*, *subscr.*, *στίχ.*, with a commentary: it ends Heb. iv. 7, and Rom. i. 1—2 Cor. v. 19 are later, on cotton paper.

172. Milan, Ambr. A. 51 sup. [xii], $8\frac{1}{8} \times 6\frac{5}{8}$, ff. 175 (35), *lect.*, *subscr.*, with an abridgement of Chrysostom's commentary: bought at Reggio in Calabria, 1606.

173. (Act. 138.)

174. (Act. 139.)

175. Milan, Ambr. F. 125 sup. [xv], $12\frac{1}{8} \times 7\frac{1}{2}$, ff. 341 (30), *chart.*, with a continuous commentary: it was brought from Thessaly.

176. (Act. 137.)

*177. Modena, Este ii. A. 14 [xv], 16mo. Lost (Greg.).

*178. (Act. 142.)

*179. Modena, Este ii. G. 3,—the minuscule part of Act. H. The Pauline Epistles with a commentary are [xii].

180. (Evan. 363.)

181. (Evan. ~~643~~ 365.)

182. (Evan. 367.)

183. (Act. 254.)

184. (Act. 148.)

185. (Evan. 393.)

186. (Evan. 394.)

187. (Act. 154.)

188. (Act. 155.)

189. Rom. Vat. Gr. 1649 [xiii], $12\frac{7}{8} \times 10$, ff. 137 (48), 2 cols., *prol.*, with Theodoret's commentary: Heb. precedes 1 Tim.

190. (Act. 156.)

191. (Act. 157.)

192. (Act. 158.)

193. (Act. 160.)

194. (Evan. 175.)

195. Rom. Vat. Ottob. 31 [x, Greg. xi], $14\frac{5}{8} \times 10\frac{1}{4}$, ff. 181, *mut.* Rom.

and most of 1 Cor.; with a continuous commentary, and such names as Œcumenius, Theodoret, Methodius, occasionally mentioned.

196. Rom. Vat. Ottob. 61 [xv], $9\frac{3}{4} \times 6\frac{3}{4}$, ff. 198 (48), *chart.*, with a commentary: here, as in Paul. 189, the Epistle to the Hebrews precedes 1 Tim.

197. (Apoc. 78.) Rom. Vat. Ottob. 176 [xv], 8vo, *chart.*

198. (Act. 161.) 199. (Evan. 386.)

200. (Act. 162.) 201. (Act. 163.)

202. Rom. Vat. Ottob. 356 [xv], $9\frac{1}{2} \times 6\frac{5}{8}$, ff. 144 (22), *chart.*, 'olim Aug. ducis ab Altamps,' contains Rom. with a catena.

203. (Evan. 390.) 204. (Act. 166.)

205. (Act. 168.) 206. (Act. 169.)

207. Rom. Ghigian. R. v. 32 [A.D. 1394], $10 \times 6\frac{3}{8}$, ff. 279 (42), *chart.*, with a commentary.

208. Rom. Ghigian. R. viii. 55 [xi], $14\frac{3}{4} \times 10\frac{5}{8}$, ff. 168, *prol.*, *κεφ. t.*, *subscr.*, *στίχ.*, with Theodoret's commentary.

209. (Act. 171.) 210. (Act. 172.)

211. (Act. 173.) 212. (Act. 174.)

213. Rom. Barberin. iv. 85 [A.D. 1338, Greg. 1330?], $10\frac{5}{8} \times 8\frac{1}{8}$, ff. 267, *prol.*, *κεφ.*, *τίτλ.*, *subscr.*, *στίχ.*, scholia. From the reading *τοῦ θεοῦ καὶ πατρὸς τοῦ χριστοῦ* Col. ii. 2 (*see* below, Vol. II. Chap. XII), this must be one of the Barberini manuscripts described under Evan. 112.

214. Vindobon. Caesar. theol. 167 (166?) [xv, Greg. xiv], $9\frac{3}{8} \times 6\frac{1}{4}$, ff. 70 (40), on cotton paper, contains Rom. with a catena, 1 Cor. with Chrysostom's and Theodoret's commentaries, which influence the readings of the text.

215. (Act. 140.) 216. (Act. 175.)

217. Palermo, I. E. 11 [xii, Greg. x], $8\frac{5}{8} \times 6\frac{3}{4}$, ff. 61 (23), *prol.*, *κεφ. t.*, *subscr.*, *στίχ.*, begins 2 Cor. iv. 18; *mut.* 2 Tim. i. 8—ii. 14; ends Heb. ii. 9.

218. (Evan. 421.) 219. (Evan. 122.)

220. (Evan. 400.) *221. (Evan. 440) is o[scr].

222. (Evan. 451.) (Greg. 462.) 223. (Evan. 461.) (Greg. 463.)

224. (Act. 58.)

Substitute for 225 (=Cod. 11)—

225. Milan, N. 272 sup. [xvi], $9\frac{3}{8} \times 6\frac{1}{8}$, *chart.*, 'S. Pauli Epistolae, cum notis marginalibus' (Burgon). (*See* Greg. 478.)

Substitute for 226 (=Cod. 27)—

226. Florence, Libreria Riccardi 85, rather modern, 8vo, 'Marsilii Ficini Florentini.'

227. (Act. 56 of Scholz.) 228. (Evan. 226.)

229. (Evan. 228.)

230. (Instead of Evan. 368) (Evan. 665)[1]. (Greg. 266.)

231. (Evan. 531.) (Greg. 305.)

232. Escurial ψ. iii. 2 [xv], Montana after Haenel, *chart.* (Greg. 472.)

233. Parham 6 (Evan. 534). (Greg. 258.)

234. (Act. 216.) (Greg. 281.) 235. (Act. 217.) (Greg. 282.)

236. (Act. 218.) (Greg. 283.) 237. (Act. 309.) (Greg. 300.)

238. (Evan. 431.) 239. (Evan. 189.)

240. (Evan. 444.) (Greg. 240.) 241. (Act. 97.)

242. (Act. 178.) (Greg. 242.) 243. (Evan. 605.) (Greg. 303.)

244. (Evan. 503.) 245. (Act. 191.)

246. (Act. 192.) 247. (Act. 210.)

248. (Instead of Act. 201=89) (Act. 253). (Greg. 284.)

Next follow three at Oxford:

249. (Evan. 488.) (Greg. 247.) 250. (Act. 212.) (Greg. 276.)

251. (Act. 213.) (Greg. 277.)

The next ten are Scrivener's, collated in the Appendix to Codex Augiensis:

*252. (Act. 182.) (Greg. 270.) *253. (Act. 183.) (Greg. 271.)

*254. (Act. 184.) (Greg. 272.) *255. (Act. 185.) (Greg. 273.)

*256. (Apoc. 93.) Lambeth 1186 or e^{scr} [xi], 4to, of which a facsimile is given in the Catalogue of Manuscripts at Lambeth, 1812. It contains the Pauline Epistles and the Apocalypse only. It begins Rom. xvi. 15 and ends Apoc. xix. 4. *Mut.* 1 Cor. iv. 19—vi. 1; x. 1–21; Heb. iii. 14—ix. 19; Apoc. xiv. 16—xv. 7. *Lect.*, *prol.*, τίτλ., κεφ., to each Epistle, and a few marginal glosses. (Greg. 290.)

*257. (Evan. 543.) (Greg. 251.) *258. (Evan. 542.) (Greg. 249.)

*259. (Evan. 568.) *[h^{scr} : *see* Act. 189.] (Greg. 250.)

*260. (Evan. 507.) This is Hort's Paul. 27. (Greg. 252.)

261. Petersburg, Muralt. 8 (Evan. 476). (Greg. 131.)

262. (Act. 223.) (Greg. 248.)

263. *See* Apoc. 91. Contains Heb. ix. 14—xiii. 25 [xv]. (Greg. 293.)

The Baroness Burdett-Coutts has three copies of the Pauline Epistles:

*264. (Act. 220.) (Greg. 278.) *265. (Act. 221.) (Greg. 279.)

*266. (Evan. 603, Apoc. 89.) Burdett-Coutts (Highgate) II. 4 [x or xi], 11½ × 8½, ff. 67, *orn.*, *proll.*, κεφ. *t.*, τίτλ. (not in Apocalypse). The ten Pauline Epistles from the Ephesians onwards (that to the Hebrews preceding 1 Timothy), and the Apocalypse complete. On three leaves at the end is the (unfinished) ἐπίγραμμα of Dorotheus of Tyre described

[1] Here again we set Scholz's codices in a note, substituting others in their room. Scholz's run, 231. (Act. 183.) 232. (Act. 184.) 233. (Act. 185.) 234. (Evan. 457.) 235. (Evan. 462.) 236. (Act. 188.) 237. (Evan. 466.) 243. (Act. 182), two separate codices.

above, Act. 89. Citations from the Old Testament are specially marked, and the margin contains some scholia and corrections, apparently by the first hand. (Greg. 306.)

267. Brit. Mus. Add. 7142 [xiii], $11\frac{3}{4} \times 9$, ff. 198, *prol.*, Life of St. Paul, *κεφ. t.*, *κεφ.*, *τίτλ.* (*lect.* mostly later), *subscr.*, *στίχ.*, with commentary, partly *mut.* (Greg. 291.)

268. (Evan. 576.) (Greg. 253.) 269. (Evan. 584.) (Greg. 255.)

270. (Act. 229.) (Greg. 275.) 271. (Evan. 603.) (Greg. 306.)

272. (Act. 238.) (Greg. 436.) 273. (Act. 236.) (Greg. 437.)

274. (Act. 237.) (Greg. 319.)

275. Instead of Basil. (only a comm., Greg.)—(Act. 254.) (Greg. 285.)

276. (Act. 321.) (Greg. 312.) 277. (Evan. 492.) (Greg. 256.)

278. (Evan. 560.) (Greg. 307.) 279. (Evan. 582.) (Greg. 254.)

280. (Act. 198.) (Greg. 280.) 281. (Evan. 527.) (Greg. 304.)

282. (Act. 240, Apoc. 109.) (Greg. 259.)

283. (Act. 241.) (Greg. 426.) 284. (Act. 195), Rom. i. 1–5.

285. (Act. 196.) (Greg. 476.)

286. Milan, Ambr. E. 2 infra [xiii], $13\frac{1}{4} \times 10\frac{1}{4}$, ff. 268 (32), *chart.* Four leaves in vellum [xii], 2 cols. The catena of Nicetas 'textus particulatim praemittit commentariis.' (*See* Greg. 393.)

287. Milan, Ambr. A. 241 inf. [xvi], $12\frac{7}{8} \times 8\frac{3}{4}$, ff. 104 (20), copy of the preceding. (*See* Greg. 393a.) 'Est Catena ejusdem auctoris ex initio, sed non complectitur totum opus.'

288. Milan, Ambr. D. 541 inf. [xi], $15 \times 12\frac{1}{4}$, ff. 323, *prol.*, *κεφ.*, *τίτλ.*, *subscr.*, *στίχ.* Text and catena on all St. Paul's Epistles. Came from Thessaly. (*See* Greg. 392.)

289. Milan, Ambr. C. 295 inf. [xi], $14 \times 11\frac{1}{8}$, ff. 190, *proll.*, *κεφ.*, *τίτλ.*, *subscr.*, *στίχ.* With a catena. (*See* Greg. 391.)

290. (Evan. 622, Act. 242, Apoc. 110.) (Greg. 316.)

291. (Act. 243.) (Greg. 423.) 292. (Act. 244.) (Greg. 424.)

293. (Act. 245.) (Greg. 425.) 294. (Act. 246.) (Greg. 430.)

295. (Act. 247.) (Greg. 433.)

296. Already mentioned as 213 (Gregory): instead—
(Act. 255.) (Greg. 286.)

297. Rom. Barberini vi. 13 [xi, Greg. xii], $13\frac{5}{8} \times 10\frac{1}{2}$, ff. 195 (18), with scholia, *subscr.*, *στίχ.*, *mut.* (Cf. Greg. 396.)

298. (Act. 248.) (Greg. 261.) 299. (Act. 249.) (Greg. 302.)

300. (Act. 250.) (Greg. 260.) 301. (Act. 251.) (Greg. 298.)

302. (Evan. 642, Act. 252.) (Greg. 269.)

303. Already mentioned as 225 (Gregory): instead—
(Act. 257.) (Greg. 231.)

304. (Evan. 661.) (Greg. 265.)

305. Rom. Vat. Gr. 549 [xii], $8\frac{1}{4} \times 8\frac{1}{4}$ (?), ff. 380 (29), with Theophylact's commentary. (*See* Greg. 398.)

306. Only a commentary of St. Chrysostom, instead—
(Act. 258.) (Greg. 232.)

307. Rom. Vat. Gr. 551 [x], ff. 283, some of St. Paul's Epistles, with commentary of Chrysostom. (Greg. under 398.)

308. Rom. Vat. Gr. 552 [xi], ff. 155, Hebrews, with commentary of Chrysostom. (Greg. under 398.)

Codd. 309, 316, 318, 320, 321, 329, 331–334 are only commentaries of St. Chrysostom (Gregory). Other MSS. are inserted instead.

309. (Act. 301.) (Greg. 242.)

310. Rom. Vat. Gr. 646 [xiv, Greg. xiii], $10\frac{3}{4} \times 7$, ff. 250 ? (31), *chart.*, with commentary of Euthymius, Pars. i et ii. (Greg. 399.)

311. (Evan. 671.) (Greg. 400.)

312. Rom. Vat. Gr. 648 [A. D. 1232], ff. 338, *chart.*, written at Jerusalem by Simeon 'qui et Saba dicitur.' (Greg. 401.)

313. (Act. 239.) (Greg. denies the 'Paul.')

314. Rom. Vat. Gr. 692 [xii, Greg. xi], $13\frac{7}{8} \times 10$, ff. 93, 2 cols., *mut.* Corinthians, Galatians, Ephesians, with commentary. (Greg. 402.)

315. Rom. Vat. Gr. 1222 [xvi], $12 \times 8\frac{1}{8}$, ff. 437 (28), *prol.*, *κεφ. t.*, *subscr.*, *στίχ.*, Rom., Heb., 1, 2 Cor., 1, 2 Tim., Eph., with Theophylact's commentary. (Greg. 403.)

316. (Evan. 667.) (Greg. 267.)

317. (Evan. 673.) (Greg. 268.)

318. (Act. 319.)

319. (Act. 334.) (Greg. 431.)

320. (Act. 320.)

321. (Act. 186.) (Greg. 274.)

322. (Act. 256.) (Greg. 432.)

323. Rom. Vat. Gr. 2180 [xv], $11\frac{5}{8} \times 8\frac{1}{4}$, ff. 294 (36), *chart.*, *κεφ. t.*, *syn.*, *men.*, with commentary of Theophylact. (*See* Greg. 454.)

324. Rom. Vat. Alex. 4 [x], $12\frac{7}{8} \times 10\frac{3}{8}$, ff. 256 (28), 2 cols., Romans with commentary of Chrysostom. 'Fuit monasterii dicti.' (*See* Greg. 480.)

325. (Evan. 698, Apoc. 117.) (Greg. 317.)

326. Rom. Vat. Ottob. 74 [xv], $12\frac{3}{4} \times 9$, ff. 291 (29) ?, *chart.*, Romans, with Theodoret's commentary. (Greg. 476[d].)

327. Rom. Vat. Pal. Gr. 10 [x], $13\frac{1}{8} \times 9\frac{1}{2}$, ff. 268, *proll.*, *κεφ.*, *τίτλ.*, *subscr.*, *στίχ.*, with a Patristic commentary, 'Felkman adnotat.' (Greg. 406.)

328. Rom. Vat. Pal. Gr. 204 [x], $13\frac{1}{4} \times 9\frac{3}{8}$, ff. 181, with commentary of Œcumenius. (Greg. 407.)

329. (Act. 335.) (Greg. 289.)

330. Rom. Vat. Pal. Gr. 423 [xii], $11\frac{3}{4} \times 9\frac{1}{2}$, ff. 2, Coloss. and Thessalon., with commentary. (*See* Greg. 376[e].)

331. (Act. 304.) (Greg. 292.)

332. (Act. 305.) (Greg. 295.)

333. (Act. 306.) (Greg. 296.)

334. (Act. 301.) (Greg. 287.)

335. A theological treatise (Greg.). Instead—
(Act. 415.) (Greg. 297.)

336. (Act. 261.) (Greg. 427.)

Instead of Cod. 337. (Greg.)

337. (Act. 264.) (Greg. 299.)

The next four MSS. are from the Abbé Martin's list.

338. Par. Nat. Suppl. Gr. 1001 [xiv], $11\frac{3}{8} \times 8\frac{3}{8}$, ff. 12 (31). Fragments of Rom., 2 Tim., Col., Heb. (Greg. 376.)

339. Par. Nat. Coisl. Gr. 95 [xi], $13\frac{7}{8} \times 10$, ff. 348 (28), *prol.*, κεφ. *t.*, κεφ., τίτλ., *subscr.*, στίχ. (Greg. 380.)

340. Par. Nat. Coisl. Gr. 217 [xiii], $11 \times 8\frac{1}{8}$, ff. 227 (52), *proll.*, κεφ. *t.*, κεφ., τίτλ., *subscr.*, *vers.*, στίχ. (Greg. 381.)

341. (Evan. 38.) (Martin.) (Greg. 377.)

We now follow Dr. Gregory's order, only stating the MS. where there is only his authority to rely upon, and referring students to his list for the information which he has diligently gathered, often by personal examination upon the spot.

342. (Evan. 1245.)
343. (Evan. 1246.)
344. (Evan. 1247.)
345. (Evan. 1248.)
346. (Evan. 1249.)
347. (Evan. 1250.)
348. (Evan. 1251.)
349. (Act. 149.)
350. Leyden, Univ. 66.
351. (Act. 307.)
352. (Act. 381.)
353. (Act. 382.)
354. (Act. 383.)
355. (Act. 384.)
356. (Act. 385.)
357. (Act. 386.)
358. (Act. 387.)
359. (Act. 388.)
360. (Act. 389.)
361. (Act. 390.)
362. (Act. 391.)
363. (Act. 392.)
364. (Act. 393.)
365. (Act. 394.)
366. (Act. 395.)
367. (Act. 399.)
368. (Act. 400.)
369. (Act. 403.)
370. (Act. 413.)

371. Madison, New Caesarea, America.

372. Lond. Brit. Mus. Arundel 534 [xiv], $10\frac{3}{4} \times 7$, ff. 418 (31). With Theophylact.

373. Vindobon. Caes. Gr. Theol. 157.

374. Besançon, City Libr. 200.
375. Par. Nat. Gr. 224 A.

376. Par. Nat. Suppl. Gr. 1035.

377. Escurial ψ. ii. 20. (Greg. 376c.)

378. Par. Nat. Coisl. Gr. 29.
379. Par. Nat. Coisl. Gr. 30.

380. (Evan. 1267.)
381. (Act. 330.)

382. Athens, Nat. 69 (100) [x], $10\frac{5}{8} \times 7\frac{1}{8}$, ff. 377. *Mut.* beg. and end, with commentary of Œcumenius and others: ff. 44 at beg. [xv].

383. Ath. Nat. 100 (96) [xiii], $12\frac{1}{8} \times 8\frac{5}{8}$, ff. 319. First leaf perished.
384. Escurial χ. iv. 15.
385. Bologna, Univ. 2378.
386. Florence, Laur. vi. 8.
387. Flor. Laur. x. 9.
388. Flor. Laur. xi. 7.
389. Flor. Laur. Conv. Soppr. 21.
390. Milan, Ambr. A. 62 inf.
391. Milan, Ambr. C. (E ?) 295.
392. Milan, Ambr. D. 541 inf.
393. (Act. 309.) (Greg. 300.)
394. Naples, Nat. II. B. 23.
395. Naples, II. B. 24.
396. (Act. 418.) (Greg. 301.)
397. Rome, Casanatensis G. v. 7.
398. (Evan. 825.) (Greg. 308.)
399. (Evan. 757.) (Greg. 309.)
400. (Evan. 767.) (Greg. 310.)
401. (Evan. 794.) (Greg. 311.)
402. (Evan. 801.) (Greg. 313.)
403. (Evan. 808.) (Greg. 314.)
404. (Evan. 823.) (Greg. 315.)
405. Rom. Vat. Ottob. 17.
406. (Evan. 891.) (Greg. 318.)
407. (Evan. 922.) (Greg. 320.)
408. Venet. Marc. 36.
409. Athos, Coutloumoussi 90b.
410. Ath. Coutloum. 129.
411. Constantinople, Holy Sepulchre 2.
412. Constant. H. Sep. 3.
413. Patmos, St. John 61.
414. Patmos, St. John 62.
415. Patmos, St. John 63.
416. Patmos, St. John 116.
417. St. Saba, Tower 41.
418. Groningen, Univ. A. C. 1.
419. (Act. 311.)
420. (Act. 308.)
421. (Act. 312.)
422. (Act. 313.)
423. (Evan. 927.) (Greg. 321.)
424. (Evan. 935.) (Greg. 322.)
425. (Evan. 941.) (Greg. 323.)
426. (Evan. 945.) (Greg. 324.)
427. (Evan. 959.) (Greg. 325.)
428. (Evan. 1267.)
429. (Act. 323.) (Apoc. 127.)
430. (Evan. 986.) (Greg. 326.)
431. (Evan. 996.) (Greg. 327.)
432. (Evan. 997.) (Greg. 328.)
433. (Evan. 999.) (Greg. 329.)
434. (Act. 332.)
435. (Act. 333.)
436. (Evan. 1003.) (Greg. 330.)
437. (Evan. 1040.) (Greg. 331.)
438. (Act. 344.)
439. (Act. 346.)
440. (Act. 347.)
441. (Act. 348.)
442. (Act. 349.)
443. (Act. 350.)
444. (Act. 351.)
445. (Act. 352.)
446. (Act. 353.)
447. (Act. 354.)
448. (Act. 355.)
449. (Act. 356.)
450. (Act. 357.)
451. (Act. 358.)
452. (Act. 359.)
453. (Act. 360.)
454. (Act. 361.)
455. (Act. 362.)
456. (Act. 366.)
457. (Act. 368.)

458. (Act. 369.)
459. (Act. 370.)
460. (Act. 371.)
461. (Act. 372.)
462. (Act. 373.)
463. (Act. 374.)
464. (Act. 375.)
465. (Act. 376.)
466. (Act. 377.)
467. (Act. 378.)
468. (Act. 379.)
469. (Act. 307.)
470. Escurial τ. iii. 17.
471. Athens, Nat. (259)?
472. (Evan. 1058.) (Greg. 332.)
473. (Act. 205.)
474. (Act. 315.)
475. (Act. 209.)
476. (Evan. 1072.) (Greg. 333.)
477. (Act. 232.)
478. (Evan. 1075.) (Greg. 334.)
479. (Act. 195.)
480. (Evan. 1094.) (Greg. 335.)
481. (Evan. 1240.) (Greg. 337.)
482. (Evan. 1241.) (Greg. 338.)
483. (Evan. 1242.) (Greg. 339.)
484. (Evan. 1243.) (Greg. 340.)
485. (Evan. 1244.) (Greg. 341.)
486. (Act. 303.)
487. (Act. 419.)
488. (Act. 420.)
489. (Act. 325.)

490. Dublin, Trin. Coll. D. i. 28 [xiv], 8½ × 5½, ff. 8, Rom. viii. 23 (ἑαυτούς) . . . xiv. 10 κρι | νεις. Inked over in places by another hand [xvi]. Κεφ. Collated by Dr. T. K. Abbott (*Hermathena*, xviii. 233, 1892).

491. (Act. 107.)

CHAPTER XII.

CURSIVE MANUSCRIPTS OF THE APOCALYPSE.

1. Mayhingen, Oettingen-Wallerstein [xii], $9\frac{1}{8} \times 5\frac{7}{8}$, ff. 90 (15 last *chart.*], the only one used in 1516 by Erasmus (who calls it 'exemplar vetustissimum') and long lost, contains the commentary of Andreas of Caesarea, in which the text is so completely imbedded that great care is needed to separate the one from the other. *Mut.* ch. xxii. 16–21, ending with *τοῦ δᾱδ.* This manuscript was happily re-discovered in 1861 by Professor F. Delitzsch at Mayhingen in Bavaria in the library of the Prince of Oettingen-Wallerstein, and a critical account of it published by him (illustrated by a facsimile) in the first part of his 'Handschriftliche Funde' (1861). Tregelles also, in the second part of the same work, published an independent collation of his own (with valuable 'Notes' prefixed), which he had made at Erlangen in 1862. The identity of Apoc. 1 with the recovered copy is manifest from such *monstra* as *ἐβάπτισας* ch. ii. 3, which is found in both; from the reading *συνάγει* ch. xiii. 10, and from the clauses put wrong by Erasmus, as being lost in the commentary, e.g. ch. ii. 17; iii. 5, 12, 15; vi. 11, 15. Of this copy Dr. Hort says (Introd. p. 263) that 'it is by no means an average cursive of the common sort. On the one hand it has many individualisms and readings with small and evidently unimportant attestation: on the other it has a large and good ancient element, . . . and ought certainly (with the somewhat similar 38) to stand high among secondary documents.'

2. (Act. 10, Stephen's *ιε'*.)

3. Codex Stephani *ις'*, unknown; cited only 77 times throughout the Apocalypse in Stephen's edition of 1550, and that very irregularly; only once (ch. xx. 3) after ch. xvii. 8. It was not one of the copies in the King's Library, and the four citations noticed by Mill (N. T., Prol. § 1176) from Luke xxii. 30; 67; 2 Cor. xii. 11; 1 Tim. iii. 3, are probably mere errors of Stephen's press.

4. (Act. 12.)

5. Codices Laurentii Vallae (*see* Evan. 82); the readings of which Erasmus used.

Codd. 6, 26, 27, 28 were rather loosely collated for Wetstein by his kinsman Caspar Wetstein, chaplain to Frederick, Prince of Wales.

6. (Act. 23.)
*7. (Act. 25, l[scr].)
*8. (Act. 28, d[scr].)
9. (Act. 30.)
10. (Evan. 60.)
11. (Act. 39.)
12. (Act. 40.)
*13. (Act. 42.)
*14. (Evan. 69, f[scr].)[1]

15. Fragments of ch. iii, iv, annexed to Cod. E Evan. in a later hand.

16. (Act. 45.)
17. (Evan. 35.)
18. (Act. 18.)
19. (Act. 17.)

20. (Evan. 175), a few extracts made by Bianchini : so Apoc. 24.

21, 22 of Wetstein were two unknown French codices, cited by Bentley in his specimen of Apoc. xxii, and made Wetstein's 23 (Act. 56). Scholz, discarding these three as doubtful, substitutes—

21. Rom. Vallicell. D. 20 [xiv, Greg. xv], $12\frac{7}{8} \times 8\frac{1}{2}$, ff. 93 (28), *chart.*

22. (Act. 166.)
23. (Evan. 367.)[2]
24. (Act. 160.)
25. (Evan. 149.)
*26. (Evan. 492.)
27. (Evan. 503.)

*28. Oxf. Bodl. Bar. 48 [xv], $8 \times 5\frac{1}{2}$, ff. 24 (22), *chart.*, κεφ., τίτλ., contains mixed matter by several hands, and is n[scr] of the Apocalypse, *mut.* ch. xvii. 5—xxii. 21 (ch. v. 1–5 is repeated in the volume in a different hand). This is an important copy, akin to Apocc. 7 and 96. Bentley also named it κ in his collation extant in the margin of Trin. Coll. B. xvii. 5 (*see* Evan. 51).

*29. (Act. 60, e[scr].)
*30. (Act. 69.)

*31. Lond. Brit. Mus. Harl. 5678 [xv], $11\frac{1}{4} \times 8\frac{1}{2}$, ff. 244 (24), *chart.*, *prol.*, is c[scr], but ch. i–viii had been loosely collated for Griesbach by Paulus. Like Evan. 445 it once belonged to the Jesuits' College at Agen, and is important for its readings. Has much miscellaneous matter.

32. Dresdensis, Reg. A. 124 [xv, Griesb. x], $7\frac{3}{4} \times 4\frac{3}{4}$, ff. 16, belonged to Loescher, then to Brühl, collated by Dassdorf and Matthaei (Mt. t). The close resemblance in the text of Apocc. 29–32 is somewhat overstated by Griesbach.

*33. (Evan. 218.)
34. (Act. 66.)

[1] Mr. B. W. Newton superintended the publication of Tregelles' last part of his Greek New Testament under circumstances which disarm criticism, but Tregelles could hardly have meant that in the Apocalypse 'much of Cod. 14 (Leicestrensis) has been supplied by a later hand from the Codex Montfortianus, Apoc. 92' (Introductory Notice, p. 1). The original hand remains unchanged in the Leicester copy, even on the last torn leaf containing portions of Apoc. xix, but the converse supposition is very maintainable, though not quite certain, that the Apocalypse in Cod. 92 was transcribed from Cod. 14.

[2] Gregory has substituted this for Scholz's 23, which he finds does not contain Apoc. Whatever readings he cites under these three numbers, are simply copied from Wetstein (Kelly's 'Revelation,' Introd. p. xi, note). Dr. Gregory has seen all the four.

35. Vindob. Caes. Gr. Theol. 307 [xiv], $7\frac{1}{8} \times 5\frac{5}{8}$, ff. 32 (20), with Andreas' commentary: brought from Constantinople by de Busbeck (Alter). Described by Delitzsch, Handschriftliche Funde (part ii), p. 41 (1862). In text it closely resembles Cod. 87.

36. Vindob. Caes. Suppl. Gr. 93 [xiv, Greg. xiii], $6\frac{3}{8} \times 4\frac{3}{8}$, ff. 56 (36), *prol.*, κεφ., τίτλ., ends ch. xix. 20, with Andreas' commentary: the text is in στίχοι (Alter), having much in common with Codd. ℵ, 7.

37. (Act. 72.)

*38. Rom. Vat. Gr. 579 [xiii, Greg. xv], $8\frac{3}{8} \times 5\frac{1}{4}$, ff. 24 (30), on cotton paper, in the midst of foreign matter. The text (together with some marginal readings (*primâ manu*) closely resembles that of Codd. AC, and was collated by Birch, inspected by Scholz and Tregelles, and subsequently recollated by B. H. Alford at the request of Tregelles (*see* Evan. T).

39. (Paul. 85.)   40. (Evan. 141.)

41. Rom. Vat. Reg. Gr. 68 [xiv, Greg. xv], $9\frac{1}{8} \times 6$, ff. 70 (14), *chart.*, *proll.*, κεφ. *t.*, with extracts from Œcumenius and Andreas' commentary (Birch, Scholz: so Apoc. 43).

42. (Act. 80.)

43. Rom. Barberini iv. 56 [xiv], $9\frac{3}{4} \times 7$, ff. 5 (58) at end, 2 cols., contains ch. xiv. 17—xviii. 20, with a commentary, together with portions of the Septuagint.

44. (Evan. 180.)   45. (Act. 89.)   46. (Evan. 209.)

*47. (Evan. 241.)   *48. (Evan. 242.)

*49. Moscow, Synod. 67 (Mt. o) [xv], fol., ff. 58, *chart.*, with Andreas' commentary, and Gregory Nazianzen's Homilies.

*50. Mosc. Synod. 206 (Mt. p) [xv], fol. *chart.*, ff. 35, like Evann. 69, 206, 233, is partly of parchment, partly paper, from the Iberian monastery on Athos; it also contains lives of the Saints.

*50[2]. Also from the Iberian monastery [x], is Matthaei's r, Tischendorf's 90.

Apocc. 51–84 were added to the list by Scholz, of which he professes to have collated Cod. 51 entirely, as Reiche has done after him; 68, 69, 82 nearly entire; twenty-one others cursorily, the rest (apparently) not at all. Our 87 is Scrivener's m, collated in the Apocalypse only.

*51. (Evan. 18.)   52. (Act. 51.)   53. (Act. 116.)

54. (Evan. 263.)   55. (Act. 118.)   56. (Act. 119.)

57. (Act. 124.)

58. Par. Nat. Gr. 19, once Colbert's [xvi], $7\frac{7}{8} \times 5\frac{3}{4}$, ff. 36 (22), *chart.*, with 'Hiob et Justini cohort. ad Graec.' Scholz.

59. Par. Nat. Suppl. Gr. 99[a] [xvi], $8\frac{1}{8} \times 5\frac{5}{8}$, ff. 83, *chart.*, with a commentary. Once Giles de Noailles'.

60. Rom. Vat. Gr. 656 [xiii or xiv], $6\frac{3}{4} \times 4\frac{5}{8}$, ff. 207 (17), *chart.*, with Andreas'. (*See* Gregory 79.)

61. Par. Nat. Gr. 491, once Colbert's [xiii], $9\frac{1}{2} \times 6\frac{1}{8}$, ff. 13, on cotton paper, *mut.*, with extracts from Basil, &c.

62. Par. Nat. Gr. 239 [A. D. 1422], $8\frac{5}{8} \times 5\frac{5}{8}$, ff. 119 (26), *chart.*, with Andreas' commentary.

63. Par. Nat. Gr. 241 [xvi], $8\frac{1}{8} \times 5\frac{7}{8}$, ff. 294, *chart.*, with Andreas' commentary. Once de Thou's, then Colbert's.

64. (Paul. 159.)

65. Moscow, Univ. Libr. 25 [xii], 4to, ff. 7 (once Coislin's 229), contains ch. xvi. 20—xxii. 21.

66. (Act. 419.)

67. Rom. Vat. Gr. 1743 [dated December 5, 1302], $8\frac{7}{8} \times 6\frac{1}{2}$, ff. ?, κεφ., τίτλ., with Andreas' commentary.

68. Rom. Vat. Gr. 1904, vol. 2 [xi], $11\frac{1}{4} \times 8\frac{1}{8}$, ff. 19, contains ch. vii, 17—viii. 12; xx. 1—xxii. 21, with Arethas' commentary, and much foreign matter. This fragment (as also Apoc. 72 according to Scholz, who however never cites it) agrees much with Cod. A.

69. (Act. 161.)

70. (Evan. 386.)

71. Athens, Nat. Libr. 142 [xv], $5\frac{7}{8} \times 4\frac{3}{8}$, ff. 233, with other matter.

*72. Rom. Ghigianus R. iv. 8 [xvi], $8\frac{1}{8} \times 5\frac{1}{4}$, ff. ?, *chart.*, with Andreas' commentary. Collated hastily by the late W. H. Simcox.

73. Rom. Corsin. 41. E. 37 [xv or xvi], $7\frac{5}{8} \times 4\frac{7}{8}$, ff. 97 (30), κεφ., τίτλ. (*See* Gregory.)

74. (Act. 140.)

75. (Act. 86.)

76. (Act. 421.)

77. Florence, Laur. vii. 9 [xv, Greg. xvi], $8\frac{5}{8} \times 5\frac{1}{2}$, ff. 363 (25), *chart.*, with Arethas' commentary.

78. (Paul. 197.)

*79. Munich, Reg. Gr. 248 [xvi], $9\frac{1}{8} \times 6\frac{1}{4}$, ff. 84 (28), *chart.*, *prol.*, κεφ., τίτλ.; once Sirlet's, the Apostolic chief notary (*see* Evan. 373 and Evst. 132), with Andreas' commentary, whose text it follows. That excellent and modest scholar Fred. Sylburg collated it for his edition of Andreas, 1596, one of the last labours of his diligent life. An excellent copy.

80. Monac. Reg. Gr. 544 (Bengel's Augustan. 7) [xii Sylburg, xiv Scholz, who adds that it once belonged to the Emperor Manuel Palaeologus, A. D. 1400], $8 \times 5\frac{3}{4}$, ff. 169 (20), *prol.*, κεφ., τίτλ., on cotton paper, with Andreas' commentary.

81. Monac. Reg. Gr. 23 [xvi], $14 \times 9\frac{1}{4}$, ff. 83 (30), *chart.*, κεφ., τίτλ., with works of Gregory Nyssen, and Andreas' commentary, used by Theod. Peltanus for his edition of Andreas, Ingoldstadt, 1547. Peltanus' marginal notes from this copy were seen by Scholz.

82. (Act. 179.)

83. (Evan. 339): much like Apoc. B.

84. (Evan. 368.)[1]

85. Escurial ψ. iji. 17 [xii], 'con commentarios Cl. Pablo' (Haenel and Montana).

86. (Act. 251.) (Greg. 122.)

*87. (Act. 178), m^scr. *See* Apoc. 35.

88. (Evan. 205.)

*89. (Paul. 266.) B.-C. II. 4. (Greg. 108.)

*90. Dresd. Reg. A. 95 [x Griesb., Scholz xv], $12\frac{1}{4} \times 9$, ff. 16 (30), 2 cols. This is 50² Scholz (Mt. r).

*91. (Paul. 263.) Rom. Vat. Gr. 1209 [xv], $10\frac{5}{8} \times 10\frac{5}{8}$, ff. ?. Mico's collation of the modern supplement to the great Cod. B, made for Bentley, and published in Ford's 'Appendix' to the Codex Alexandrinus, 1799. The whole supplement from Heb. ix. 14 *ρεῖ τὴν συνείδησιν* including the Apocalypse (but not the Pastoral Epistles) is printed at full length in Vercellone and Cozza's edition of Cod. Vaticanus (1868).

92. (Evan. 61.) Published by Dr. Barrett, 1801, in his Appendix to Evan. Z, but suspected to be a later addition. See Apoc. 14, note.

Wm. Kelly, 'The Revelation of John edited in Greek with a new English Version,' 1860, thus numbers Scrivener's collations of six copies not included in the foregoing catalogue—

*93. (Paul. 256 or e^scr), a^scr. *94. (Evan. 201), b^scr.

*95. Parham 82. 17, g^scr [xii], $10\frac{1}{4} \times 7\frac{3}{4}$, brought by the late Lord de la Zouche in 1837 from Caracalla on Athos: it contains an epitome of the commentary of Arethas, in a cramped hand much less distinct than the text, which ends at ch. xx. 11. There are no divisions into chapters. This 'special treasure,' as Tregelles calls it, was regarded by him and Alford as one of the best cursive manuscripts of the Apocalypse: Dr. Hort judges it inferior to none. It agrees with Cod. A alone or nearly so in ch. xviii. 8, 10, (19), 23; xix. 14: compare also its readings in ch. xix. 6 (bis), 12.

*96. Parham 67 (?). 2, h^scr [xiv], $11\frac{1}{8} \times 7\frac{5}{8}$, ff. 22 (28), κεφ., on glazed paper, very neat, also from Caracalla, complete and in excellent preservation, with very short scholia here and there. These two manuscripts were collated by Scrivener in 1855, under the hospitable roof of their owner.

*97. (Evan. 584.) Brit. Mus. Add. 17,469, j^scr [xiv], collated only in Apoc.

*98. (Evan. 488.) Oxf. Bodl. Can. 34, k^scr [dated in the Apocalypse July 18, 1516]. The Pauline Epistles [dated Oct. 11, 1515] precede the Acts. Collated only in Apoc.

99. (Act. 83 ?) (*See* Greg.) Cited, like the next, by Tischendorf.

[1] After this again we withdraw Scholz's copies, as virtually included in Coxe's, putting others in their room. They are 85. (Act. 184.) 86. (Evan. 462), thrice cited ineunte libro (Tischendorf). 86² of Scholz, being 89 of Tischendorf (Evan. 466).

100. Naples, Nat. II. Aa. 10 ? [xiv or xv], $10\frac{1}{4} \times 7\frac{3}{8}$. (*See* Greg.)

101. (Evan. 206.)

102. (Evan. 451.) (Greg. 103.)

103. Petersburg, Muralt. 129 [xv], 4to, ff. 25 (35), *chart.*, *prol.*

104. (Evan. 531.) (Greg. 107.)

105. (Act. 301.) (Greg. 104.)

106. (Evan. 605.)

107. (Act. 232.) (Greg. 181.)

108. (Act. 236.)

109[1]. (Act. 240.) (Greg. 102.)

110. (Evan. 622.) (Greg. 113.)

111. (Act. 307.) (Greg. 105.)

112. Dresden, Reg. 187 [xvi], 8 × 6, ff. 21 (26). With Andreas. (*See* Greg. 182.)

113. Messina, Univ. 99 [xiii], $10\frac{5}{8} \times 8\frac{3}{8}$, ff. 138 (24), 2 cols., with commentary. (*See* Greg. 146.)

114. Rom. Vat. Gr. 542 [A. D. 1331], $11 \times 8\frac{1}{4}$, ff. 105 (29). With Andreas and Homm. of Chrysostom. (*See* Greg. 153.)

115. (Evan. 866.) (Greg. 114.)

116. Rom. Vat. Gr. 1976 [xvii, Greg. xvi], $8\frac{3}{8} \times 5\frac{5}{8}$, ff. 114 (20), *chart.*, κεφ., τίτλ., with commentary of Andreas. (*See* Greg. 157.)

117. (Evan. 698, Paul. 324.) (Greg. 115.)

118. Rom. Vat. Ottob. Gr. 283 [A. D. 1574, a Jo. Euripiotϕ], $8\frac{3}{8} \times 5\frac{7}{8}$, ff. 123 (22), *chart.*, κεφ., Andreas. (Greg. 160.)

119. Rom. Vat. Pal. Gr. 346 [xv], $14\frac{3}{8} \times 10$, ff. 86 (30), *prol.*, κεφ. *t.*, κεφ., τίτλ., Andreas. (*See* Greg. 161.)

120. Rom. Angelic. A. 4. 1 [A. D. 1447], $8\frac{1}{2} \times 5\frac{1}{2}$, ff. 86 (29), *chart.*, κεφ., τίτλ., Andreas. (*See* Greg. 149.)

121. Rom. Angelic. B. 5. 15 [xv], $8\frac{1}{8} \times 5\frac{3}{4}$, ff. ?, *chart.*, much liturgical information. (*See* Greg. 150.)

122. Rom. Ghig. R. V. 33 [xiv], $10 \times 7\frac{1}{4}$, ff. 28 (32), much theological writing, collated by W. H. Simcox, ff. 347, *chart.* Andreas and Œcumenius. (*See* Greg. 151.)

123. (Evan. 738.)

124. (Act. 309.)

125. (Act. 207.)

126. (Act. 208.)

127. (Act. 323.)

128. (Act. 332.)

129. (Act. 238.)

130. (Act. 359.)

131. (Act. 362.)

132. (Act. 374.)

133. (Act. 384.)

134. (Act. 386.)

135. (Act. 399.)

136. Vindob. Caes. Gr. Theol. 69.

137. Vind. Caes. Theol. 163.

138. Vind. Caes. Gr. Theol. 220.

139. Par. Nat. Gr. 240.

140. Par. Nat. Coisl. Gr. 256.

141. Athens, bibl. τῆς Βουλῆς.

142. (Paul. 202.)

143. Escurial χ. iii. 6.

144. Madrid. O. 19 (7).

[1] We cannot identify 109, Bentley's R (Regis Galliae, 1872): cf. Ellis, Bentleii Critica Sacra, Intr. p. xxix.

145. Florence, Laur. vii. 29.
146. (Evan. 757.) (Greg. 110.)
147. Modena, Este iii. E. 1.
148. Modena, Este iii. F. 12.
149. (Evan. 792.) (Greg. 111.)
150. (Evan. 808.) (Greg. 112.)
151. (Evan. 922.) (Greg. 116.)
152. Rom. Vat. Gr. 370.
153. (Evan. 1262.)
154. Rom. Vat. Gr. 1190.
155. Rom. Vat. Gr. 1426. (Act. 264.) (Greg. 121.)
156. (Act. 159.)
157. (Evan. 986.) (Greg. 117.)
158. Rom. Vat. Gr. 2129. (Cf. Evst. 389.)
159. Rom. Vat. Ottob. Gr. 154.
160. (Evan. 1072.) (Greg. 118.)
161. (Evan. 1075.) (Greg. 119.)
162. Venice, Mark i. 40.
163. Ven. Mark ii. 54.
164. Athos, Anna 11.
165. Athos, Vatopedi 90.
166. Athos, Vatop. 90 (2).
167. Athos, Dionysius 163. (Cf. Evst. 642.)
168. Athos, Docheiariou 81.
169. Athos, Iveron 34.
170. Athos, Iveron 379.
171. Athos, Iveron 546.
172. Athos, Iveron 594.
173. Athos, Iveron 605.
174. Athos, Iveron 644.
175. Athos, Iveron 661.
176. Athos, Constamonitou 29.
177. Athos, Constam. 107.
178. Patmos, St. John 12.
179. Patmos, St. John 64.
180. (Act. 149.)
181. (Act. 417.) 6
182. (Evan. 1094.) (Greg. 120.)
183. Thessalonica, Ἑλληνικὸν Γυμνάσιον 10. (Cf. Apost. 163.)
184. (Act. 422.)

CHAPTER XIII.

EVANGELISTARIES, OR MANUSCRIPT SERVICE-BOOKS OF TH. GOSPELS.

HOWEVER grievously the great mass of cursive manusci of the New Testament has been neglected by Bib critics, the Lectionaries of the Greek Church, partly for ca previously stated, have received even less attention at t hands. Yet no sound reason can be alleged for regarding testimony of these Service-books as of slighter value than of other witnesses of the same date and character. The ne sary changes interpolated in the text at the commencement sometimes at the end of lessons are so simple and obvious the least experienced student can make allowance for the and if the same passage is often given in a different form w repeated in the same Lectionary, although the fact ought t recorded and borne in mind, this occasional inconsistency n no more militate against the reception of the general evidenc the copy that exhibits it, than it excludes from our roll of cri authorities the works of Origen and other Fathers, in which selfsame variation is even more the rule than the except Dividing, therefore, the Lectionaries that have been hith catalogued (which form indeed but a small portion of tl known to exist in Eastern monasteries and Western libra into Evangelistaria, or Evangeliaria, containing extracts f the Gospels, and Praxapostoli or Apostoli comprising extr from the Acts and Epistles; we purpose to mark with an aste the few that have been really collated, including them in same list with the majority which have been examined su ficially, or not at all. Uncial copies (some as late as the eleve

[1] In the sixth lesson for the Holy Passions the prefatory clause to Mar 16 is founded on an obvious misconception : Τῷ καιρῷ ἐκείνῳ οἱ στρατιῶται ἀπή τὸν ῖν̂ εἰς τὴν αὐλὴν τοῦ καϊάφα, ὅ ἐστι πραιτώριον. We remember no si instance of error.

century) will be distinguished by †. The uncial codices of the Gospels amount to one hundred and six, those of the Acts and Epistles only to seven or eight, but probably to more in either case, since all is not known about some of the Codd. recorded here. Lectionaries are usually (yet see below, Evst. 111, 142, 178, 244, 249, 255, 256, 262, 266, 268, 275, Apost. 52, 69) written with two columns on a page, like the Codex Alexandrinus, FGI (1–6, 7) LMN^bPQRTUX$\Theta^d\Lambda$, 8, 184, 207, 360, 418, 422, 463, 509 of the Gospels, and Cod. M of St. Paul's Epistles.

†1. Par. Nat. Gr. 278 [x ? Omont xiv], $11\frac{7}{8} \times 9\frac{1}{2}$, Unc., ff. 265, 2 cols., *mut.* (Wetstein, Scholz).

†2. Par. Nat. Gr. 280 [ix, Greg. x], $11\frac{1}{4} \times 8\frac{1}{2}$, Unc., ff. 257 (18), 2 cols., *mus.*, *mut.* (Wetstein, Scholz).

†3. Oxf. Lincoln Coll. Gr. ii. 15 [x, Greg. xi], $11\frac{1}{4} \times 9$, Unc., ff. 282 (19), *mus. rubr.*, *men.*, with coloured and gilt illuminations and capitals, and red crosses for stops: three leaves are lost near the end (Mill).

4. Cambr. Univ. Libr. Dd. 8. 49, or Moore 2 [xi], $10\frac{3}{4} \times 8\frac{1}{2}$, ff. 199 (24), 2 cols., *mus. rubr.* (Mill).

†5. Oxf. Bodl. Barocc. 202 [x], 12×9, Unc., ff. 150 (19), 2 cols., *mus. rubr.*, ends at Matt. xxiii. 4, being the middle of the Lesson for Tuesday in Holy Week (Burgon). *Mut.* initio (Mill, Wetstein). This is Bentley's *a* in Trin. Coll. B. xvii. 5 marg. (*see* Evan. 51).

*†6. (Apost. 1.) Leyden, Univ. Scaliger's 243 [xi ?], $7\frac{5}{8} \times 5\frac{1}{4}$, Unc., ff. 278 (18), 2 cols., *chart.*, with an Arabic version, contains the Praxapostolos, Psalms, and but a few Lessons from the Gospels (Wetstein, Dermout).

7. Par. Nat. Gr. 301 [written by George, a priest, A.D. 1205], $12 \times 9\frac{1}{8}$, ff. 316 (23), 2 cols. (Evst. 7–12, 14–17, were slightly collated by Wetstein, Scholz.)

8. Par. Nat. Gr. 312 [xiv], $13\frac{1}{2} \times 11$, ff. 309 (29), 2 cols., written by Cosmas, a monk.

9. Par. Nat. Gr. 307 [xiii], $11\frac{3}{4} \times 9\frac{1}{2}$, ff. 260 (24), 2 cols., *mus.*

10. Par. Nat. Gr. 287 [xi, Greg. xiii], $12\frac{5}{8} \times 9\frac{5}{8}$, ff. 142 (23), 2 cols., *mut.*

11. Par. Nat. Gr. 309 [xiii], $11\frac{3}{4} \times 9$, ff. 142, 2 cols., *mus.*, *mut.*

12. Par. Nat. Gr. 310 [xiii], 12×9, ff. 366 (24), 2 cols., *mus.*, *mut.*

†13. Par. Nat. Coisl. Gr. 31 [x, Greg. xi], $14\frac{1}{2} \times 10\frac{1}{4}$, Unc., ff. 283 (18), 2 cols., *mus. aur.*, *pict.*, most beautifully written, the first seven pages in gold, the next fifteen in vermilion, the rest in black ink, described by Montfaucon (Scholz). Wetstein's 13 (Colbert. 1241 or Reg. 1982) contains no Evangelistarium.

14. Par. Nat. Gr. 315 [xv, Greg. xvi], $10\frac{5}{8} \times 7\frac{1}{2}$, ff. 348 (22), 2 cols., *chart.* Wrongly set down as Evan. 322.

15. Par. Nat. Gr. 302 [xiii], $10 \times 7\frac{1}{2}$, ff. 310 (22), 2 cols., *mut.*

16. Par. Nat. Gr. 297 [xii], $10\frac{5}{8} \times 8\frac{1}{2}$, ff. 199 (19), 2 cols., much *mut.*

†17. Par. Nat. Gr. 279 [xii, Greg. ix], $10\frac{1}{4} \times 7\frac{3}{8}$, Unc., ff. 199 (19), 2 cols., *mut.* (Tischendorf seems to have confounded 13 and 17 in his N. T., Proleg. p. ccxvi, 7th edition.)

18. Oxf. Bodl. Laud. Gr. 32 [xii], $11\frac{1}{2} \times 9\frac{1}{2}$, ff. 276 (22), 2 cols., much *mut.*, beginning John iv. 53. Codd. 18–22 were partially examined by Griesbach after Mill.

19. Oxf. Bodl. Misc. Gr. 10 [xiii], $12\frac{1}{4} \times 8\frac{3}{4}$, ff. 332 (24), 2 cols., *mus. rubr.*, *mut.*, given in 1661 by Parthenius, Patriarch of Constantinople, to Heneage Finch, Earl of Winchelsea, our Ambassador there. This and Cod. 18 are said by Mill to be much like Stephen's ϛ′, Evan. 7.

20. Oxf. Bodl. Laud. Gr. 34 [written by Onesimus, April, 1047, Indiction 15], $11\frac{1}{2} \times 9\frac{1}{2}$, ff. 177 (22), 2 cols., *orn.*, *mus. rubr.*, *mut.*[1]

21. Oxf. Bodl. Seld. B. 56 [xiv], $9\frac{1}{2} \times 7\frac{1}{4}$, ff. 59 (28), 2 cols., a fragment containing Lessons in Lent till Easter, coarsely written.

22. Oxf. Bodl. Seld. B. 54 [xiv], $10\frac{1}{4} \times 8$, ff. 63 (25), 2 cols., *men.*, a fragment, with Patristic homilies [xi].

†23. Unc., Mead's, then Askew's, then D'Eon's, by whom it was sent to France. Wetstein merely saw it. Not now known.

†24. Munich, Reg. Gr. 383 [x], $12\frac{1}{2} \times 9\frac{1}{2}$, ff. 265 (21), 2 cols., Unc., *men.*, the Lessons for Saturdays and Sundays (*σαββατοκυριακαί*: *see* Evst. 110, 157, 186, 221, 227, 283, 289), *mut.* (Bengel, Scholz). Is this Cod. Radzivil, with slightly sloping uncials [viii], of which Silvestre gives a facsimile (Paléogr. Univ., ii. 61)?

25. Lond. Brit. Mus. Harl. 5650 [xii], $9\frac{1}{4} \times 6$, ff. 267 (22), a palimpsest, whose later writing is by Nicephorus the reader. The older writing, now illegible, was partly uncial, *mut.*

25[b] represents a few Lessons in the same codex by a later, yet contemporary hand (Bloomfield).

Evst. 25–30 were very partially collated by Griesbach.

†26. (Apost. 28.) Oxf. Bodl. Seld. supra (1) 2 [xiii], $8 \times 5\frac{3}{4}$, ff. 180, *mut.*, a palimpsest, but the earlier uncial writing is illegible, and the codex in a wretched state, the work of several hands.

†27. Oxf. Bodl. 3391, Seld. supra (2) 3, a palimpsest [ix uncial, xiv later writing], $9 \times 6\frac{3}{4}$, ff. 150 (89–95 cursive), 2 cols., *mut.*, in large ill-formed characters.

Evst. 26, 27 were collated by Mangey, 1749, but his papers appear to be lost.

28. Oxf. Bodl. Misc. Gr. 11 [xiii], $9\frac{3}{4} \times 7\frac{1}{2}$, ff. 203 (21), 2 cols., *orn.*, *mut.* at end and on June 14, in two careless hands.

[1] Laud. Gr. 36, which in the Bodleian Catalogue is described as an Evangelistarium, is a collection of Church Lessons from the Septuagint read in Lent and the Holy Week, such as we described above. It has red musical notes, and seems *once* to have borne the date A. D. 1028. It is Dean Holmes' No. 61 (Praef. ad Pentateuch).

29. Oxf. Bodl. Misc. Gr. 12 [xii or xiii], 10 × 8, ff. 156 (23), 2 cols., *mus.*, *mut.* Elegantly written, but much worn.

30. (Apost. 265.) Oxf. Bodl. Cromw. 11 [the whole written in 1225 by Michael, a χωρικὸς καλλιγράφος], 8 × 6, ff. 208. After Liturgies of Chrys., Basil, Praesanctified, εὐαγγέλια ἀναστάσιμα, Evst. (p. 290) and Apost. (p. 149), i.e. lections from Epistles and Gospels for great feasts.

31. Norimberg. [xii], 4to, ff. 281 (Doederlein). Its readings are stated by Michaelis to resemble those of Codd. D (e.g. Luke xxii. 4), L, 1, 69.

*32. Gotha, Ducal Libr. MS. 78 [xii, Greg. xi], 13½ × 9⅞, ff. 273 (20), 2 cols., carelessly written, but with important readings: *see* Luke xxii. 17, &c., Vol. II. Chap. XII. Edited by Matthaei, 1791.

†33. Card. Alex. Albani [xi], 4to, Unc., a menology edited by Steph. Ant. Morcelli, Rome, 1788.

†34. Munich, Reg. Gr. 329 [x, Greg. ix], 11 × 8, 3 vols., ff. 430 (18), 2 cols., Unc., in massive uncials, from Mannheim, the last three out of four volumes, the menology suiting the custom of a monastery on Athos (Rink, Scholz). Burgon refers to Hardt's Catalogue, iii. 314 seq.

Evst. 35–39 were inspected or collated by Birch, 40–43 by Moldenhawer.

†35. Rom. Vat. Gr. 351 [x], 13¼ × 9⅞, ff. 151 (11), Unc., contains only the Lessons for holidays.

*†36. Rom. Vat. Gr. 1067 [ix], 13⅜ × 10, ff. 368 (21), 2 cols., Unc., a valuable copy, completely collated.

37. (Apost. 7.) Rom. Propaganda, Borgian. L. xvi. 6 [xi, Greg. xii], 10¾ × 8½, ff. 160 (24), 2 cols., contains only thirteen Lessons from the Gospels.

For the next two *see* 117, 118. Hort's 38 = x^{scr}, 39 = y^{scr}. (*See* Hort, pp. 77 note, and 296–7.) Instead—

38. Lond. Brit. Mus. 25,881 [xv, Greg. xiv], ff. 4 at end (24), 2 cols., Matt. xviii. 12–18; iv. 25—v. 30; xviii. 18–20. (Greg. 328^a.)

39. Lond. Brit. Mus. 34,059 [xii], 10 × 8¼, ff. 238 (21), 2 cols., ends with ἀναγνώσματα and τὰ διάφορα. Bought of A. Carlenizza of Pola, in 1891.

†40. Escurial I [x], 4to, Unc., *mus.*, kept with the reliques there as an autograph of St. Chrysostom. It was given by Queen Maria of Hungary (who obtained it from Jo. Diassorin) to Philip II. Moldenhawer collated fifteen Lessons. The text is of the common type, but in the oblong shape of the letters, false breathings and accents, the red musical notes, &c., it resembles Evst. 1, though its date is somewhat lower. Omitted by Montana.

†41. Escurial χ. iii. 12 [x, or xi with Montana], 4to, ff. 204, Unc., *mus.*, very elegant: the menology (as also that of Evst. 43) suited to the use of a Byzantine Church.

†42. Escurial χ. iii. 13 [ix, or xi with Montana], 4to, ff. 227, Unc., *mut.* at the beginning. Two hands appear, the earlier leaning a little to the right.

43. Escurial χ. iii. 16 [xi, or xii with Montana], 4to, *mut.* at the beginning, in large cursive letters; with full *men.*

44. (Apost. 8.) Havniens. Reg. 1324 [xv, Greg. xii], 10½ × 7½, ff. 195, 2 cols., *mut.*, and much in a still later hand. Its history resembles that of Evann. 234–5 (Hensler).

†45. Vindobon. Caesar. Jurid. 5 [x], 11⅝ × 7⅞, Unc., 2 cols., six leaves from the binding of a law-book: the letters resemble the Tübingen fragment, Griesbach's R (*see* p. 139) or Wetstein's 98 (Alter).

†46. Vind. Caesar. Suppl. Gr. 12 [ix], 6½ × 5½, ff. 182 (9), Unc., on purple vellum with gold and silver letters. There is a Latin version (Bianchini, Treschow, Alter). Silvestre has a facsimile, Paléogr. Univ., No. 69.

*†47. Moscow, S. Synod. 43 [viii], fol., ff. 246, 2 cols., 'a barbaro scriptus est, sed ex praestantissimo exemplari,' Matthaei (B), whose codices extend down to 57.

*48. Mosc. Syn. 44 (Mt. c) [by Peter, a monk, A.D. 1056], fol., ff. 250, 2 cols., from the Iberian monastery at Athos. In 1312 it belonged to Nicephorus, Metropolitan of Crete.

*49. Mosc. Typograph. Syn. 11 (Mt. f) [x and xi], fol., ff. 437, 2 cols., *pict.* Superior in text to Cod. 48, but much in a later hand.

*†50. Mosc. Typ. Syn. 12 (Mt. H) [viii ?], fol., ff. 231, Unc. A very valuable copy, whose date Matthaei seems to have placed unreasonably high. [Greg. xiv.]

*51. Mosc. Typ. Syn. 9 (Mt. t) [xvi], 4to, ff. 42, *chart.*

*52. (Apost. 16.) Mosc. Syn. 266 (Mt. ξ) [xiv], 4to, ff. 229, contains a Euchology and ἀποστολοευαγγέλια, as also do 53, 54, 55.

*53. (Apost. 17.) Mosc. Syn. 267 (Mt. χ) [xiv or xv], 4to, ff. 333, *chart.*, from the monastery of Simenus on Athos.

*54. (Apost. 18.) Mosc. Syn. 268 (Mt. ψ) [written A.D. 1470, by Dometius, a monk], 4to, ff. 344, *chart.*, from the Vatopedion monastery on Athos.

*55. (Apost. 19.) Mosc. Typ. Syn. 47 (Mt. ω) [the Apost. copied at Venice, 1602], 4to, ff. 586, *chart.*, wretchedly written.

*56. (Apost. 20.) Mosc. Typ. Syn. 9 (Mt. 16) [xv or xvi], 16mo, ff. 42, *chart.*, fragments of little value.

*57. Dresdensis Reg. A. 151 (Mt. 19) [xv], 8½ × 6⅛, ff. 408 (20), *chart.*, came from Italy, and, like Apoc. 32, once belonged to Loescher, then to the Count de Brühl. It is a Euchology, or Greek Service Book (Suicer, Thesaur. Ecclesiast., i. p. 1287), described in Matthaei, Appendix to St. John's Gospel, p. 378.

Evst. 58–157 were added to the list by Scholz, who professes to have collated entire 60; in the greater part 81, 86.

58. Par. Nat. Suppl. Gr. 50 [xv], 11 × 8¼, ff. 49 (11), *chart.*, brought from some church in Greece.

59. Instead of what was really Evan. 289—

Lond. Egerton 2163 [xii–xiii], $12\frac{1}{8} \times 8$, ff. 207 (26, 25), handsome, titles in gold, initials in gold and colours, *mus. rubr.*, *pict.*, *mut.* (Greg. 339.)

*60. (Apost. 12.) Par. Nat. Gr. 375, once Colbert's, formerly De Thou's [A.D. 1022], $9\frac{1}{4} \times 6\frac{3}{4}$, ff. 195 (28); it contains many valuable readings (akin to those of Codd. ADE), but numerous errors. Written by Helias, a priest and monk, 'in castro de Colonia,' for the use of the French monastery of St. Denys.

†61. (Evan. 747.) Par. Nat. Gr. 182 [x], 4to, a fragment.

62. Instead of what was really Evan. 303—

Lond. Brit. Mus. Add. 29,713 [late xi, Greg. xiv], 13×10, ff. 296 (25), very handsome, illuminated head-pieces and initial letters, some in gold. (Greg. 332.)

†63. Par. Nat. Gr. 277 [ix], $11\frac{1}{4} \times 8\frac{1}{4}$, ff. 158 (22), 2 cols., Unc., *mut.* at the beginning and end.

†64. Par. Nat. Gr. 281 [ix], $10\frac{7}{8} \times 8$, ff. 210 (22), 2 cols., Unc., from Constantinople; many leaves are torn.

†65. Par. Nat. Gr. 282 [ix], $11\frac{3}{4} \times 9\frac{1}{4}$, ff. 213 (20), 2 cols., Unc., a palimpsest, with a Church-service in later writing [xiii].

†66. Par. Nat. Gr. 283 [ix], $11\frac{1}{4} \times 8\frac{1}{4}$, ff. 275 (19), 2 cols., Unc., also a palimpsest, with the older writing of course misplaced; the later (*mut.* in fine) a Church-service [xiii].

†67. Par. Nat. Gr. 284 [xi, Greg. xii], $11\frac{1}{2} \times 9\frac{1}{8}$, ff. 270 (18), 2 cols., Unc., *mus.*, *pict.*, 'optimae notae.'

68. Par. Nat. Gr. 285, once Colbert's [xi, Greg. xii], $12\frac{3}{4} \times 9\frac{3}{8}$, ff. 357 (23), 2 cols., *mut.*, initio et fine.

69. Par. Nat. Gr. 286 [xi, Greg. xii], $12 \times 9\frac{1}{8}$, ff. 257 (25), 2 cols., *mut.*, in fine.

70. Par. Nat. Gr. 288 [xi, Greg. xii], $13\frac{1}{2} \times 10\frac{1}{2}$, ff. 313 (25), 2 cols., brought from the East in 1669. A few leaves at the beginning and end later, *chart.*

71. Par. Nat. Gr. 289, once Colbert's [July, A.D. 1066], $12\frac{3}{8} \times 8\frac{7}{8}$, ff. 159 (26), 2 cols., *mut.* Written by John, a priest, for George, a monk, partly on vellum, partly on cotton paper.

72. Par. Nat. Gr. 290 [A.D. 1257], $9\frac{7}{8} \times 7\frac{5}{8}$, ff. 190, 2 cols. Written by Nicolas. To this codex is appended—

†72b, three uncial leaves [ix], *mus.*, containing John v. 1–11; vi. 61–69; vii. 1–15.

73. Par. Nat. Gr. 291 [xii], $10\frac{3}{4} \times 8\frac{3}{8}$, ff. 34 (25), 2 cols., *mus.*, *mut.*

74. Par. Nat. Gr. 292, once Mazarin's [xii], $9\frac{5}{8} \times 8$, ff. 274 (18), 2 cols.

75. Par. Nat. Gr. 293, from the East [xii], $11 \times 8\frac{7}{8}$, ff. 250 (29), 2 cols.

76. Par. Nat. Gr. 295, once Colbert's [xii], $12\frac{7}{8} \times 9\frac{1}{8}$, ff. 182 (2
2 cols., *mus.*, *mut.*

77. Par. Nat. Gr. 296 [xii], $10\frac{7}{8} \times 8\frac{1}{2}$, ff. 258 (20), 2 cols., fr
Constantinople.

78. Par. Nat. Gr. 298, once Colbert's [xii], $10 \times 7\frac{1}{2}$, ff. 95 (28), 2 co
mus., *mut.* Some hiatus are supplied later on cotton paper.

79. Par. Nat. Gr. 299 [xii, Greg. xiv], $12\frac{1}{2} \times 9\frac{7}{8}$, ff. 120 (26), 2 co
mut. initio et fine.

80. Par. Nat. Gr. 300 [xii], $10\frac{1}{2} \times 8\frac{1}{4}$, ff. 128, 2 cols.

81. Par. Nat. Gr. 305 [xiii, Greg. xiv], $11\frac{5}{8} \times 9\frac{1}{4}$, ff. 197 (22), 2 cc
mut., perhaps written in Egypt. Some passages supplied [xv] on cot
paper.

82. (Apost. 31.) Par. Nat. Gr. 276 [xv, Greg. xiv], $9\frac{3}{4} \times 6\frac{1}{2}$, ff. 1
(27), *mut.*, *chart.*, with Lessons from the Prophets.

83. (Apost. 21.) Par. Nat. Gr. 294 [xi, Greg. xii], $11 \times 8\frac{1}{2}$, ff. :
(26), 2 cols.

84. (Apost. 9.) Par. Nat. Suppl. Gr. 32 a [xii, Greg. xiii], $12\frac{5}{8}$ ×
ff. 212 (66), 2 cols., and

85. (Apost. 10.) Par. Nat. Suppl. Gr. 33 [xii], $11\frac{5}{8} \times 8\frac{7}{8}$, ff. 2
2 cols., have Lessons from the Old and New Testament.

86. Par. Nat. Gr. 311 [July, 1336, Indict. 4], $13\frac{3}{8} \times 10$, ff. 382 (:
2 cols. Written by Charito, given by the monk Ignatius to
monastery τῶν ὁδηγῶν or Θεοτόκου at Constantinople (*see* Act. 16
afterwards it was Boistaller's, and is described by Montfaucon. J.
vii. 53—viii. 11 is at the end, obelized, and not appointed for any d
since the names of Pelagia or Theodora are not in the menology of t
copy.

87. Par. Nat. Gr. 313 [xiv], $10 \times 7\frac{3}{4}$, ff. 121, 2 cols., once Colbe
(as were 88–91; 99–101).

88. Par. Nat. Gr. 314 [xiv], $12\frac{3}{4} \times 7\frac{1}{8}$, ff. 190, 2 cols. Many ve:
are omitted, and the arrangement of the Lessons is a little unusual.

89. Par. Nat. Gr. 316 [xiv], $10\frac{1}{8} \times 6\frac{3}{4}$, ff. 208 (25), on cotton pa;
mut. in fine.

90. Par. Nat. Gr. 317 [A.D. 1533, Indict. 6], $11\frac{3}{8} \times 7\frac{7}{8}$, ff. 223 (:
2 cols., *mus. rubr.*, *chart.* Written by Stephen, a reader.

91. Par. Nat. Gr. 318 [xi, Greg. xiv], $10\frac{1}{2} \times 7\frac{3}{4}$, ff. 322, 2 cols., a s
scription, &c., written in Cyprus by the monk Leontius, 1553 (Montfa
Palaeogr. Graec., p. 89).

92. (Apost. 35.) Par. Nat. Gr. 324 [xiii, Greg. xiv], $8\frac{5}{8} \times 5\frac{3}{4}$, ff.
(21), on cotton paper, with fragments of the Liturgies of SS. B
Chrysostom, and the Praesanctified.

93. (Apost. 36.) Par. Nat. Gr. 326 [xiv, Greg. xvi], $8\frac{1}{8} \times 5\frac{3}{8}$, ff. 1
chart., with the Liturgies of SS. Chrysostom and Basil.

94. (Apost. 29.) Par. Nat. Gr. 330 [xiii, Greg. xii], $7\frac{1}{8} \times 5\frac{3}{8}$, ff. 1

mut., with a Euchology and part of a Church-service in a later hand [xv].

95. Par. Nat. Gr. 374 [xiv], $9\frac{1}{4}\times 7$, ff. 114 (32), 2 cols., from Constantinople.

96. (Apost. 262.) Par. Nat. Suppl. Gr. 115 [xii, Greg. xvi], $8\frac{1}{2}\times 5\frac{3}{4}$, ff. 171 (25), *chart.*, *mut.*, initio et fine.

97. (Evan. 324, Apost. 32.) Par. Nat. Gr. 376, only the εὐαγγέλια τῶν πάθων (*see* Evan. 324).

98. Par. Nat. Gr. 377 [xiii, Greg. xv], $9\times 6\frac{7}{8}$, ff. 196 (21). Once Mazarin's; portions are palimpsest, and the older writing seems to belong to an Evangelistarium.

99. Par. Nat. Gr. 380 [xv, Greg. xvi], $8\frac{1}{4}\times 5\frac{7}{8}$, ff. 243 (22), *chart.* Wrongly set down as Evan. 327.

100. Par. Nat. Gr. 381 [A.D. 1550], $8\frac{1}{4}\times 5\frac{7}{8}$, ff. 306 (20), *chart.* Written at Iconium by Michael ~~Maurice~~. Wrongly set down as Evan. 328.

101. Par. Nat. Gr. 303 [xiii, Greg. xiv], $11\frac{1}{8}\times 7\frac{3}{4}$, ff. 279 (25), 2 cols., grandly written. Wrongly set down as Evan. 321.

102. Milan, Ambros. S. 62 sup. [Sept. A.D. 1370], $11\times 8\frac{1}{2}$, ff. 120 (35), *chart.* Written by Stephen, a priest (but with two leaves of parchment at the beginning, two at the end), bought at Taranto, 1606, with 'commentarii incerti auctoris in omnia Evangelia quae per annum in Ecclesia Graeca leguntur,' according to Burgon.

103. Milan, Ambr. D. 67 sup. [xiii], $11\frac{5}{8}\times 8$, ff. 138 (31), 2 cols., *pict.*; bought 1606, 'Corneliani in Salentinis.' *See* Apost. 46.

104. (Apost. 47.) Milan, Ambr. D. 72 sup. [xii], $11\frac{1}{2}\times 8\frac{3}{4}$, ff. 128 (23), 2 cols., *mut.* initio et fine: brought from Calabria, 1607.

105. Milan, Ambr. M. 81 sup. [xiii], $10\times 7\frac{1}{8}$, ff. 157 (20), 2 cols., carefully written, but the first 19 leaves [xvi] *chart.*

106. Milan, Ambr. C. 91 sup. [xiii], $11\frac{3}{4}\times 9\frac{1}{8}$, ff. 355 (20), 2 cols., *mut.*, splendidly written in a large cursive hand. 'Corcyrae emptus.'

107. Venice, St. Mark 548 [xi, Greg. xii], $12\times 9\frac{1}{8}$, ff. 265 (20), 2 cols., *pict.*

108. Ven. St. Mark 549 [xi], $12\frac{5}{8}\times 9\frac{1}{2}$, ff. 292 (23), 2 cols., *mus. rubr.*, a grand and gorgeous fol., *mut.* in fine.

109. Ven. St. Mark 550 [xi, Greg. xiv], $11\frac{1}{8}\times 8$, ff. 206 (28), 2 cols., *mut.* (Burgon), *pict.*, *chart.*

110. Ven. St. Mark 551 [xi, Greg. xiii], $13\frac{3}{4}\times 10\frac{1}{4}$, ff. 278 (22), 2 cols., *mut.*, a glorious codex, containing only the σαββατοκυριακαί (*see* Evst. 24): the last ~~few~~ leaves are ancient, although supplied on paper.

†111. Modena, Este ii. C. 6 [x], $9\frac{3}{4}\times 6\frac{1}{4}$, ff. ?, Unc., *mus. rubr.*, small thick folio in one column on a page. Montfaucon assigns it to the eighth century, and Burgon admits that he might have done so too, but that it contains in the menology (Dec. 16) the name of Queen Theophano, who died A.D. 892.

112. (Apost. 41.) Flor. Laurent. Conv. Soppr. 24 [xi], $7\frac{3}{8} \times 5\frac{3}{8}$, ff. 145 (22), *mut.* initio.

113. Flor. Laur. vi. 2 [ff. 1–213, xii; the rest written by one George, xiv], $14\frac{1}{2} \times 11\frac{5}{8}$, ff. 341 (19), 2 cols. Prefixed are verses of Arsenius, Archbishop of Monembasia (*see* Evan. 333), addressed to Clement VII (1523–34).

114. Flor. Laur. vi. 7 [xii, Greg. xiv], $13\frac{3}{8} \times 10\frac{1}{4}$, ff. 180 (18), 2 cols., magnificently illuminated.

†115. Flor. Laur. vi. 21 [xi, Greg. x], $9\frac{1}{2} \times 7\frac{3}{4}$, ff. 261 (20), 2 cols., Unc., *mus. rubr.*, elegantly written.

†116. Flor. Laur. vi. 31 [x], 12×9, ff. 226 (20), 2 cols., Unc., *mus. rubr.*, elegant.

117. Flor. Laur. 244 [xii], $13\frac{1}{8} \times 10\frac{3}{4}$, ff. 119 (10), 2 cols., most beautifully written in golden cursive letters, *pict.*, once kept among the choicest *κειμήλια* of the Grand Ducal Palace. *See* above, Evst. 38, 39.

†118. Flor. Laur. 243, kept in a chest for special preservation [xi, Greg. xiv], $15 \times 11\frac{1}{4}$, ff. 368 (20), 2 cols., most elegant. Evst. 113–18 were described by Canon Angelo Bandini, 1787.

119. Rom. Vat. Gr. 1155 [xiii], $13\frac{3}{4} \times 10\frac{5}{8}$, ff. 268 (25), 2 cols.

120. Rom. Vat. Gr. 1256 [xiii], $14 \times 10\frac{3}{4}$, ff. 344 (20), 2 cols.

121. Rom. Vat. Gr. 1156 [xiii, Greg. xi], $14\frac{3}{8} \times 10$, ff. 419 (22), very splendid.

122. Rom. Vat. Gr. 1168 [August, 1175], $10\frac{1}{2} \times 7\frac{3}{8}$, ff. 194 (24), 2 cols., *mus. rubr.*, written by the monk Germanus for the monk Theodoret.

†123. Rom. Vat. Gr. 1522 [x], $11\frac{1}{8} \times 8\frac{3}{4}$, ff. 197 (11), 2 cols., Unc., *vers.*, *pict.*, very correctly written, without points.

124. Rom. Vat. Gr. 1988 [xii], $7\frac{3}{4} \times 5\frac{7}{8}$, ff. 162 (24), 2 cols., *mut.* initio et fine.

125. Rom. Vat. Gr. 2017 [xi or xii], $8\frac{5}{8} \times 6\frac{1}{2}$, ff. 123 (23), 2 cols., *mut.*, with a subscription dated 1346, and a memorandum of the death (Oct. 12, 1345) and burial of one Constantia.

126. Rom. Vat. Gr. 2041 [xii], $12\frac{1}{8} \times 8\frac{7}{8}$, ff. 337 (23), 2 cols., written by one George; *διὰ συνδρομῆς γεωργίου*, whatever *συνδρομή* may mean.

†127. Rom. Vat. Gr. 2063 [ix], $10\frac{5}{8} \times 7\frac{1}{4}$, ff. 178 (20), 2 cols., *mus. rubr.*, Unc., *mut.* initio et fine. The first two leaves of the Festival Lessons [xiv]. Two not contemporaneous hands have been engaged upon this copy.

128. Rom. Vat. Gr. 2133 [xiv], $11\frac{1}{2} \times 8\frac{7}{8}$, ff. 393 (13).

129. Rom. Vat. Regin. Gr. 12 [xiii, Greg. xii], $10\frac{1}{4} \times 8\frac{1}{2}$, ff. 339 (24), 2 cols. Ff. 1–40 appear to have been written in France, and have an unusual text: ff. 41–220 [xiii] are by another hand: the other 71 leaves to the end [xv].

†130. Rom. Vat. Ottob. 2 [ix], $13\frac{1}{8} \times 9\frac{5}{8}$, ff. 343 (20), 2 vols., 2 cols., Unc., very beautiful.

131. Rom. Vat. Ottob. 175 [xiv], $9\frac{1}{2} \times 7\frac{1}{8}$, ff. 70 (12), a fragment.

132. Rom. Vat. Ottob. 326 [xv, Greg. xiv], $6\frac{3}{8} \times 5\frac{1}{4}$, ff. ?, in silver letters. Procured at Rome, Sept. 11, 1590, 'a Francisco et Accida' of Messina, and given to Cardinal Sirlet (*see* Evan. 373, Apoc. 79).

133. (Apost. 39.) Rom. Vat. Ottob. 416 [xiv], $8\frac{1}{2} \times 5\frac{1}{4}$, ff. 296 (29), 1 and 2 cols., *chart.*

134. Rom. Barberin. vi. 4 [xiii], $13\frac{1}{4} \times 11\frac{1}{4}$, ff. 343 (21), 2 cols., the first eight and last three leaves being paper.

†135. Rom. Barb. iv. 54, a palimpsest [vi Scholz, Greg. viii], $9\frac{7}{8} \times 7$, ff. 165 (23), is Tischendorf's barb^{ev}, and by him referred to the middle of the seventh century, which is a somewhat earlier date than has hitherto been assigned to Lectionaries. He has given specimens of its readings in 'Monum. sacr. ined.,' vol. i. pp. 207–210 (Matt. xxiv. 34—xxv. 16; John xix. 11–25).

136. Rom. Barb. iv. 54 [xii], the later writing of the palimpsest Evst. 135.

137. Rom. Vallicell. D. 63, once Peter Polidore's [xii], $9\frac{1}{4} \times 7\frac{1}{4}$, ff. 105 (20), 2 cols., *mut.* initio.

138. Naples, I. B. 14 [xv], $10\frac{1}{2} \times 8\frac{1}{8}$, ff. 255 (22), 2 cols., *chart.*, given by Christopher Palaeologus, May 7, 1584, to the Church of SS. Peter and Paul at Naples.

†139. Venice, St. Mark 12 [x], $12\frac{1}{2} \times 9\frac{1}{2}$, ff. 219 (17), 2 cols., *mut.* initio, with many erasures.

140. Instead of one which has no existence—
(Apost. 242.) Cairo, Patriarch. Alex. 18 [xv], 4to, *chart.*, Συναγωγὴ λέξεων ἐκ παλαιᾶς καὶ νέας (Coxe). (Greg. 759.)

141. Ven. St. Mark i. 9 [xi], $11\frac{3}{4} \times 9\frac{3}{4}$, ff. 268 (15), 2 cols., 'Monasterii Divae Catharinae Sinaitarum quod extat Zacynthi.'

142. Ven. St. Mark i. 23 [xiv], $6\frac{1}{2} \times 4\frac{1}{4}$, ff. 45 (15), *mut.*, only 45 pages, with one column on a page.

143. Instead of Evan. 468—
Jerusalem, Holy Sepulchre 12 [xi end], fol. (Coxe). (Greg. 158.)

†144. Biblio. Malatestianae of Cesena xxvii. 4, now at Rome [xii], fol., *mus. rubr.*, Unc., very splendid.

145. Bibl. Cesen. Malatest. xxix. 2 [xii], fol.

146. Cambr. Univ. Libr. Dd. viii. 23 [xi], $15\frac{1}{2} \times 11\frac{1}{2}$, ff. 212 (29), 2 cols., *syn.*, *men.*, *mut.* at end, neatly written for a church at Constantinople.

Evst. 147, 148 are in *Latin*, and 149 is Evan. 567. Instead—

147. St. Saba 17 [xii], 4to (Coxe). (Greg. 165.)

148. St. Saba 23 [xii], fol. (Coxe). (Greg. 168.)

149. St. Saba 24 [xi], fol. (Coxe). (Greg. 169.)

*†150. Lond. Brit. Mus. Harl. 5598 [May 27, A.D. 995, Indict. 8], $13\frac{1}{4} \times 10\frac{1}{2}$, ff. 374 (21), 2 cols., Unc., *mus. rubr.*, *orn.*, written by

Constantine, a priest, is Scrivener's H (Cod. Augiensis, Introd. pp. xlvii –l), for an alphabet formed from it *see* our Plate iii. No. 7. It was brought from Constantinople by Dr. John Covell, in 1677 (Evan. 65), and by him shown to Mill (N. T., Proleg. § 1426); from Covell it seems to have been purchased (together with his other copies) by Harley, Earl of Oxford. It is a most splendid specimen of the uncial class of Evangelistaria, and its text presents many instructive variations. At the end are several Lessons for special occasions, which are not often met with. Collated also by (Bloomfield), and facsimiles given by the Palaeographical Society, Plates 26, 27.

151. Lond. Brit. Mus. Harl. 5785 [xii], 12½ × 9½, ff. 359 (18), 2 cols., *mus. rubr.*, *orn.*, a splendid copy, in large, bold, cursive letters. At the end is a note, written at Rome in 1699, by L. A. Zacagni, certifying that the volume was then more than 700 years old. The date assigned above is more likely (Bloomfield).

†152. Lond. Brit. Mus. Harl. 5787 [x], 12¼ × 9, ff. 224 (24), 2 cols., Unc., *orn.*, the uncials leaning to the right, a fine copy, with small uncial notes, well meriting collation. Called 'Codex Prusensis' [Prusa, near mount Olympus: Scholz's 171] in a MS. note of H. Wanley. It begins John xx. 20, and is *mut.* in some other parts. For a facsimile page *see* the new 'Catalogue of Ancient MSS. in the British Museum' (1881), Plate 17.

153. Meerman 117 [xi], *see* Evan. 436 ?, bought at Meerman's sale by Payne, the bookseller, for £200. Its present owner is unknown. (Compare Evan. 562.)

154. Munich, Reg. Gr. 326 [xiii], 12⅝ × 9⅞, ff. 49 (21), 2 cols., a fine fol., written very small and neatly, containing the Lessons from the season of Lent to the month of December in the menology, once at Mannheim. It seems adapted to the Constantinopolitan use.

†155. Vindobon. Caes. Gr. Theol. 209 [x], 8½ × 6½, ff. 143 (27), *mus. rubr.*, *pict.*, Unc., a palimpsest, over which is written a commentary on St. Matthew [xiv].

156. Rom. Vallicell. D. 4. 1 [xi], fol., ff. 380, 2 cols., described by Bianchini, Evan. Quadr., vol. ii. pt. i. p. 537; now missing. It must have been a superb specimen of ancient art: about thirty of its pictures are enumerated.

157. Oxf. Bodl., Clarke 8 [A.D. 1253], 8 × 6¾, ff. 198 (23), 2 cols., 2 gatherings destroyed, and one leaf torn out. Written by Demetrius Brizopoulos, *σαββατοκυριακαί* (*see* Evst. 24)[1]. (Greg.)

[1] As with the MSS. of the Gospels, and for the reasons assigned above, we remove to the foot of the page, and do not reckon in our numbering, the twenty-one copies seen by Scholz in Eastern Libraries.

158. Library of the Great Greek Monastery at Jerusalem, No. 10 [xiv], fol.

159. 'Biblioth. monasterii virginum *τῆς μεγάλης παναγίας* a S. Melana erect.' [xiii], fol., very neat ('non sec. viii ut monachi putant,' Scholz).

160. (Apost. 33.) St. Saba 4, written there by one Antony [xiv], 8vo.

161. St. Saba 5 [xv], 8vo, *chart.*

162. St. Saba 6 [xv], 16mo, *chart.*

163. St. Saba 13 [xiii], 4to, *chart.*, adapted (as also those that follow) to the use of Palestine.

164. St. Saba [xiv], 4to.

To Dean Burgon's care and industry we owe Codd. 158–178; 181–187.

158. Par. Suppl. Gr. 27 [xi, Greg. xii], $13 \times 10\frac{7}{8}$, ff. 207 (24), 2 cols., *mus. rubr.*, *pict.*, beautifully illuminated: 'Present de Mr. Desalleurs, ambassadeur pour le roy en 1753, remis par ordre de Mr. le Cte. d'Argenson le 7 Juillet, 1753.' (Greg. 261.)

159. Par. Suppl. Gr. 242 [xv, Greg. xvii], $16\frac{1}{4} \times 10\frac{3}{4}$, ff. 265 (27), 2 cols., *chart.*, peculiarly bound, with oriental pictures. (Greg. 262.)

160. Bologna, Univ. 3638 [xiv], $11\frac{3}{8} \times 9\frac{3}{4}$, ff. 233 (27), 2 cols., written by one Anthimus. This is No. xviii in Talman's and J. S. Assemani's manuscript Catalogue, No. 25 in Mezzofanti's Index. (Greg. 281.)

161. Parma, Reg. 14 [xiv], $11\frac{3}{8} \times 9\frac{3}{4}$, ?, 2 cols., *mus. rubr.*, *mut.* Contains the Gospel for St. Pelagia's day. (Greg. 282.)

162. Siena, Univ. X. iv. 1 [xi or xii], $14\frac{3}{8} \times 11\frac{5}{8}$, ff. 313 (23), 2 cols., *mus. rubr.*, *pict.*, one of the most splendid Service-books in the world, the first five columns in gold, the covers enriched with sumptuous silver enamels and graceful scroll-work. Bought at Venice in 1359 by Andrea di Grazia for the Hospital of S. Maria della Scala, of P. di Giunta Torregiani, a Florentine merchant, who a little before had bought it at Constantinople of the agent of the Emperor John Cantacuzenus [1341–55]. (Greg. 283.)

163. Milan, †Ambr. Q. 79 sup. [x], $11\frac{7}{8} \times 8\frac{1}{4}$, a single uncial page of a Lectionary. (Greg. 284.)

164. Milan, Ambr. E. S. v. 14 [xii], $10\frac{1}{2} \times 8\frac{1}{2}$, ff. 37 (22), 2 cols., two separate fragments, one being fol., in two columns, roughly written. (Greg. 285[a].)

165. Milan, Ambr. ol. E. S. v. 13, now bound up with 164 [xiv], at f. 67, $11\frac{1}{4} \times 8\frac{1}{2}$, f. 1, 2 cols. (*See* Greg. 285.)

166. (Apost. 181.) Milan, Ambr. D. 108 sup. [xiii], $11\frac{3}{8} \times 8\frac{1}{2}$, ff. 204 (29), 2 cols. (*See* Greg. 287.)

167. Milan, Ambr. A. 150 sup. [xiii], $11\frac{7}{8} \times 9\frac{1}{2}$, ff. 124 (24), 2 cols., *mut.* (ff. 1–9, 104–123, *chart.*). (*See* Greg. 288.)

168. Milan, Ambr. C. 160 inf. [xiv], $12\frac{3}{4} \times 10$, ff. 156 (27), 2 cols., *mut.* (*See* Greg. 289.)

169. Milan, Ambr. P. 274 sup. [xiv or xv], $10\frac{3}{8} \times 7\frac{1}{2}$, ff. 198 (23), *mut.*, in disorder. (*See* Greg. 290.)

165. St. Saba 17 [xv], 4to, *chart.* 166. St. Saba 21 [xiii], fol.
167. St. Saba 22 [xiv], fol. 168. St. Saba 23 [xiii], fol.
169. St. Saba 24 [xiii], fol. 170. St. Saba 25 [xiii], fol.
171. (Apost. 52.) St. Saba (unnumbered) [written July, 1059, in the monastery of Θεοτόκος, by Sergius, a monk of Olympus in Bithynia], 8vo.
†172. Library of St. John's monastery at Patmos ['iv' Scholz, obviously a misprint], fol. †173. Patmos [ix], 4to. †174. Patm. [x], 4to.
†175. Patm. [x], 4to. 176. Patm. [xii], 4to. 177. Patm. [xiii], 4to.
178. Patm. [xiv], 4to, in the same Library, but not numbered.
Some of these MSS. have been removed to Europe since Scholz made his reckoning, e. g. Parham No. 20 (Evst. 236).

Besides examining the eight Evangelistaria at St. Mark's, Venice, described in the preceding catalogue (Evst. 107–10; 139–42), Burgon found, exclusive of Evst. 175, eight more: viz.

170. Venice, St. Mark i. 4 [A.D. 1381], $8\frac{1}{2} \times 5\frac{7}{8}$, ff. 209 (22), *chart.*, rather barbarously written by the priest John. (*See* Greg. 264.)

†171. Ven. St. Mark i. 45 [x], $13\frac{3}{8} \times 10\frac{1}{2}$, ff. 78 (20), 2 cols., Unc., *mut.* initio. (Greg. 265.)

172. Ven. St. Mark i. 46 [xii?], $10\frac{1}{4} \times 8$, ff. 50 (22), 2 cols., *mus. rubr.*, *mut.* coarse. (*See* Greg. 266.)

173. Ven. St. Mark. i. 47 [A.D. 1046 [1]], $13\frac{1}{8} \times 10\frac{3}{8}$, ff. 350 (24), 2 cols., a grand cursive folio, sumptuously adorned. (*See* Greg. 267.)

174. Ven. St. Mark i. 48 [xii], $10\frac{3}{8} \times 8\frac{1}{4}$, ff. 281 (20), 2 cols., *mus. rubr.*, with unusual contents. (*See* Greg. 268.)

*†175. ven^{ev}. Ven. St. Mark i. 49 [vii or viii], $9\frac{1}{4} \times 8$, Unc., three nearly illegible palimpsest leaves (edited by Tischendorf in 'Monum. sacr. ined.,' vol. i. pp. 199, &c.), (*see* Evst. 135), containing Matt. viii. 32—ix. 1; 9–13; John ii. 15–22; iii. 22–26; vi. 16–26; or twenty-seven verses.

176. Ven. St. Mark i. 50 [xiv or xv], $11\frac{5}{8} \times 7\frac{7}{8}$, ff. 403 (22), 2 cols., *chart.* (*See* Greg. 270.)

177. Ven. St. Mark i. 51 [xv, Greg. xvii], $8 \times 5\frac{1}{2}$, *chart.*, eleven poor leaves. (Greg. 271.)

178. Ven. St. Mark i. 52 [xvi], $10\frac{1}{4} \times 7\frac{1}{2}$, ff. 276 (26), *mus. rubr.*, *chart.*, from Corfu. (*See* Greg. 272.)

*†179. (Apost. 55.) Trèves, Cath. Libr. 143. F [x or xi], $10\frac{1}{8} \times 7\frac{3}{4}$, ff. 202 (24), Unc., called St. Simeon's, and brought by him from Syria in the eleventh century, consists chiefly of Lessons from the Old Testament. It contains many itacisms and some unusual readings. Edited in 1834 by B. M. Steininger in his 'Codex S. Simeonis exhibens lect. eccl. gr. DCCC ann. vetustate insigne.' (Greg. 179.)

†180. Vindob. Caes. 209 [ix, Greg. x], $8\frac{1}{2} \times 6\frac{1}{2}$, ff. 143 (27), Unc. and Minusc., *mus. rubr.*, *pict.*, a palimpsest, with many itacisms (Scholz, Endlicher). Readings are given by Scholz (N.T., vol. ii. pp. lv–lxiii). (Greg. 155.)

In the Treasury of the Church of St. Mark at Venice Burgon found besides those just named, three others, nearly ruined by the damp of the place where they are kept.

181. Ven. St. Mark, Thesaur. i. 53 [xiii, Greg. xii], $11\frac{3}{4} \times 8\frac{5}{8}$, ff. ? 2 cols., splendidly illuminated and bound in silver and enamel. Substitute this for Wake 12 (= Evan. 492), inserted in error as Evst. 181.

[1] At the end in small gold uncials the following very curious colophon was deciphered by Dean Burgon and the learned sub-librarian Signor Veludo jointly: *Μηνὶ μαΐω 'Ινδ. ΙΔ. ἔτους ϛφνδ'. προσηνέχθη παρὰ βασιλείου μοναχοῦ πρεσβυτέρου καὶ ἡγουμένου τῆς σεβασμίας μονῆς τῆς κοιμήσεως τῆς θκου εἰς τὴν αὐτὴν μονὴν βιβλίο τέσσαρα· τὸ αὐτὸ εὐαγγέλιον, ἀπόστολος, προφητεία, καὶ ἀναγνοστικόν, ὁ βίος τοῦ ἁγίου, καὶ ἐστύχηται δίδωσθαι ὑπὲρ τῆς αὐτῆς προσενέξαιως ἐνὶ ἑκάστω χρόνω ἀπὸ τοῦ δοχείοι τῆς αὐτῆς μονῆς ὑπὲρ μνήμης αὐτ νόμισμα ἓν ἥμισον, μέχ[ρι γὰρ τού]του τὰ τῶν χριστιανῶν [συ]νίσταται· περιφυλάττεται δὲ καὶ ἡ ἁγία μονὴ αὕτη· ἐν γὰρ τῷ τυπικῷ τῆς μονῆς περὶ τοῦ κατίδους (sic) τῶν αὐτῆς βιβλίων, καὶ περὶ τῆς διανομῆς τοῦ ἑνὸς ἡμίσου νομίσματος σαφέστερον διερμηνεύει.*

182. Ven. St. Mark, Thes. i. 54 [xii, Greg. xiii], $10\frac{7}{8} \times 8\frac{3}{8}$, ff. ?, 2 cols., once a fine codex, now tied up in a parcel by itself. (Greg. 276.)

183. Ven. St. Mark, Thes. i. 55 [A.D. 1439], $13 \times 10\frac{1}{8}$, ff. ?, 2 cols., *chart.*, written by Sophronius at Ferrara, poor enough inside, but kept in a glass case for the sake of its gorgeous silver cover, which came from St. Sophia's at Constantinople. (Greg. 277.)

The next three are bound in red velvet, and in excellent preservation.

184. Ven. S. Giorgio di Greco A′ [xiv, Greg. xii], $12\frac{1}{4} \times 10\frac{1}{4}$, ff. 413 (21), 2 cols., is very splendidly illuminated, and was once used for the *Greek* service of this church. (Greg. 279.)

185. Ven. S. Giorgio di Greco Γ′ [xiv], $9\frac{5}{8} \times 7\frac{1}{4}$, ff. 240 (28). Professes to be written by *Νικολαος ὁ Μαλωτρ, πρωτέκδικος τῆς ἁγιωτάτης μητροπόλεως Λακεδαίμονι.* It seems to have been brought hither A.D. 1422. (Greg. 280.)

186. Ven. S. Giorgio di Greco B′ [xiii], $11\frac{1}{2} \times 8\frac{1}{2}$, ff. 223 (21), 2 cols., is the largest, but contains only *σαββατοκυριακαί* (*see* Evst. 24). (Greg. 278.)

187. Flor. Laurent. S. Marci 706 [xi or xii], $9\frac{1}{4} \times 7\frac{7}{8}$, ff. 181 (21), 2 cols., *mus. rubr.*, cursive, much used. (Greg. 291.)

188. Rom. Vat. Pii II. Gr. 33 [x or xi], $8\frac{1}{4} \times 6$, ff. 158 (26), 2 cols., a fine specimen. (Greg. 570.)

†189. carp^ev. Carpentras, Bibl. Urb. 11 [ix, Greg. x], $14 \times 10\frac{5}{8}$, ff. 277 (24), 2 cols., Unc., *mus. rubr.*, examined by Tischendorf in 1843. Extracts are given in his 'Anecd. sacr. et prof.,' pp. 151, &c.

†190. tisch^ev. Leipzig, Univ. Libr. Tisch. V [viii or ix], $10\frac{3}{4} \times 8\frac{1}{2}$, ff. 89 (20), 2 cols., *mus. rubr.*, a palimpsest, described 'Anecd. sacr. et prof.,' pp. 29, &c. (Greg. 293.)

†191. (Apost. 178.) Petrop^ev. Petrop. Caes. Muralt. 44 [ix], 4to, ff. 69, ill written, but with a remarkable text; the date being tolerably fixed by Arabic matter decidedly more modern, written 401 and 425 of the Hegira (i.e. about A.D. 1011 and 1035) respecting the birth and baptism of the two Holy infants. There are but ten Lessons from St. Matthew, and nineteen from other parts of the New Testament, enumerated by Tischendorf in 'Notitia. Cod. Sinaitici,' p. 54. This copy contains the two leaves on cotton paper, with writing by the first hand, mentioned above, p. 23, note 2. (Greg. 249.)

†192. (Apost. 73.) Petrop^ev.2. Petrop. Caes. Muralt. 90 [xii], 8vo., ff. 93 (21), a fragment. Tischendorf, Notitia Cod. Sinaitici, p. 63. (Greg. 256.)

193. Besançon, Bibl. Urb. 44 [?], $11\frac{5}{8} \times 7\frac{5}{8}$, ff. 210 (22), 2 cols., *mus. rubr.* (letter from M. Castan, the Librarian, to Burgon). (Greg. 263.)

†194. 1^pe. Petrop. Caes. Muralt. iv. 13 [ix], fol., ff. 2 (21), 2 cols., Unc. Matt. viii. 10–13; xxvii. 1–9; Mark vi. 14–18; Luke iv. 33–36. (Greg. 246.)

195. 3^pe. Petrop. Caes. Muralt. (56) vii. 179 [x], fol., ff. 251 (26), 2

cols., and (Apost. 54) Praxapostolos (Petrop. viii. 80), 'cum Codice G [Angelico] consentiens exc. Act. xxvii. 29; xxviii. 2.' (Greg. 251.)

196. 6pe. Petrop. Caes. Muralt. (71) x. 180 [*dated* Salernum, 1022], 4to, ff. 170 (20), 2 cols., *mut.* throughout. (Greg. 253.)

197. 9pe. Petrop. Caes. Muralt. xi. 3. 181 [xiii], 4to, ff. 3 (20), 2 cols., fragments: Matt. xxviii. 12–18; Luke iv. 16–22; John x. 9–14; xix. 6, 9–11; 14–19, 20; 25–28: 30–35. (Greg. 258.)

198. 10pe. Panticapaeense [of Kertch?], Palaeologi, collated at Odessa, and the collation sent to Muralt. (Greg. 260.)

199. Fragments of two leaves [ix, Greg. xiii], 11¾ × 7¼, ff. 176 (34), bound up in Evan. 68. (Evan. 68.)

200. The cursive Lessons which overlie the uncial fragment of St. Luke (Ξ). (Greg. 299.)

†201. Oxf. Bodl. Barocc. 197 [x], 11¾ × 7¼, ff. 5 (2), 2 cols., *mus. rubr.*, uncial palimpsest leaves, used for binding. (Greg. 205.)

†202. Oxf. Bodl. Canonici Gr. 85 [ix], 13 × 9¼, ff. 259 (18), 2 cols., *mus. rubr.*, passages and directions in later cursive hand, much *mut.* The uncials lean a little to the left. (Greg. 194.)

†203. Oxf. Bodl. Can. Gr. 92 [x], 15¾ × 12, ff. 483 (14), 2 cols., *mus. rubr.*, large folio, very splendid, with gilt initial letters. (Greg. 195.)

204. Oxf. Bodl. Can. Gr. 119 [xv], 11½ × 7⅝, ff. 155 (26), *chart.*, belonging in 1626 to Nicolas, a priest. (Greg. 196.)

205. Oxf. Bodl. Can. Gr. 126, 9½ × 8, ff. 8 (20), *chart.* (Greg. 197.)

206. Oxf. Bodl. Clarke 45 [xii], 11½ × 9, ff. 276 (24), 2 cols., *mus. rubr.*, *orn.* bound up in disorder (Burgon), splendid but spoiled by damp. (Greg. 198.)

207. Oxf. Bodl. Clarke 46 [xiii], 11 × 9, ff. 252 (21), 2 cols., *mut.* initio et fine. 'A fine ruin, miserably cropped by the modern binder: the writing is very dissimilar in parts' (Burgon). (Greg. 199.)

208. Oxf. Bodl. Clarke 47 [xii], 10½ × 8½, ff. 292 (23), 2 cols., *mus. rubr.*, much like Evst. 206. (Greg. 200.)

209. Oxf. Bodl. Clarke 48 [xiii], 10½ × 7¾, ff. 187 (27), 2 cols., carelessly and ill written: *mut.* initio. (Greg. 201.)

210. Oxf. Bodl. Cromw. 27 [xi], 11½ × 8¾, ff. 315 (22), 2 cols., *men.*, from Athos 1727, once Irene's. (Greg. 202.)

211. Oxf. Bodl. Misc. Gr. 119 [A.D. 1067], 11 × 8, ff. 300 (22), *mus. rubr.*, containing two parts, (1) Evst., (2) *Men.* The first two leaves and the last two were evidently written and inserted later in place of two damaged leaves, and bear the date A.D. 1067, probably copied from the vanished leaf. (MS. note in Bodl. Cat. by Mr. E. B. Nicholson.)

† This Evst. was formerly preceded by one uncial palimpsest leaf, containing parts of Rom. xiv, Heb. i. 1–11, which are now bound up in a separate volume. The whole volume was bought of Payne and Foss, London, in 1820. (Greg. 203.)

212. Oxf. Bodl. Misc. 140 [xi], 9×7, ff. 305 (10), *mus. rubr.*, not in regular order, but in order of holy days, a very beautiful copy, one volume only out of a set of four. (Greg. 204.)

†213. Oxf. Christ Church, Wake 13, 12×9, ff. 261, contains three uncial leaves [ix], Matt. xxv. 31–36; vi. 1–18 (doxy. in Lord's Prayer), the rest cursive [xi], *mus. rubr.*, *orn.*, in a very large, bold, peculiar hand. Two palimpsest leaves at the end cursive in later [xv], John xx. 19—xxi. 25. (Greg. 206.)

214. Ch. Ch. Wake 14 [xii], $11\frac{1}{2} \times 9$, ff. 243 (20), 2 cols., *mus. rubr.*, miniatures on pp. 108, 174, 182, ends at Matt. xxviii. 4. Has one leaf *chart.*, and two leaves at the beginning and end from the Old Testament, I Kings xvii. 12, &c. (Greg. 207.)

215. Ch. Ch. Wake 15 [A.D. 1068], $9\frac{1}{2} \times 7\frac{3}{4}$, ff. 217, 2 cols., *mus. rubr.*, and 2 ff. of Old Testament (first and last) being earlier. Written by Leontius of St. Clement's (Bryennios). (Greg. 208.)

216. Ch. Ch. Wake 16 [xiii], $9\frac{1}{2} \times 7\frac{1}{2}$, ff. 217 (21), 2 cols., *mus. rubr.*, *mut.* initio et fine. (Greg. 209.)

217. Ch. Ch. Wake 17 [xiii or xiv], $9\frac{1}{2} \times 7$, ff. 227 (21), 2 cols., 15 ff. (213–227) by a later hand, *mut.* in fine. (Greg. 210.)

218. Ch. Ch. Wake 18 [palimpsest xiv over xi], $12\frac{1}{4} \times 8\frac{1}{4}$, ff. 218 (29), 2 cols., *orn.*, *men.*, ill written. The first leaf contains the history of St. Varus and six martyrs. (Greg. 211.) This is Walker's E: his H is

219. Ch. Ch. Wake 19 [xi], $11 \times 8\frac{1}{2}$, ff. 248 (20), 2 cols., *orn.*, *mus. rubr.* Of this codex the ninth leaf is wanting. (Greg. 212.)

220. Ch. Ch. Wake 23 [xi], $11\frac{3}{4} \times 9\frac{1}{2}$, ff. 256 (25), 2 cols., *mus. rubr.*, *men.*, an elegant copy. The last page has Mark xvi. 9–20. (Greg. 213.)

*221. Camb. Trin. Coll. O. iv. 22 [xii], $12\frac{1}{3} \times 9$, ff. 249 (18), 2 cols., *mus. rubr.*, *orn.*, once Dean Gale's (*see* Evan. 66), in a bold hand, with illuminations and red musical notes. There are daily Lessons from Easter to Pentecost, but afterwards only σαββατοκυριακαί (*see* Evst. 24), with full Saints' Day Lessons. (*See* Scrivener, Critica Sacra, p. xiv.) (Greg. 186.)

*222 or zscr. Camb. Christ's Coll. F. 1. 8 [xi], $11\frac{3}{4} \times 9$, ff. 436 (30), *orn.*, *syn.*, is much fuller than most Lectionaries, and contains many minute variations[1]: it exhibits a subscription dated 1261, Indict. 4, much later than the codex, and a note stating that Francis Tayler, Preacher at Christ's Church, Canterbury [the Cathedral], gave it to the College in 1654. There are also four Lessons from the prophets, and four from St. Paul (Apost. 53). A facsimile is given, Cod. Augiens. Introd., p. li. This is Hort's 59. (Greg. 185.)

The next four were collated by Dr. Bloomfield for his 'Critical Annotations on the Sacred Text.'

[1] Thus 222, with only two other Evangelistaria (6, 18) and Evan. 59 by the first hand, supports Cod. ℵ and Eusebius in the significant omission of υἱοῦ βαραχίου, Matt. xxiii. 35.

Plate XIII.

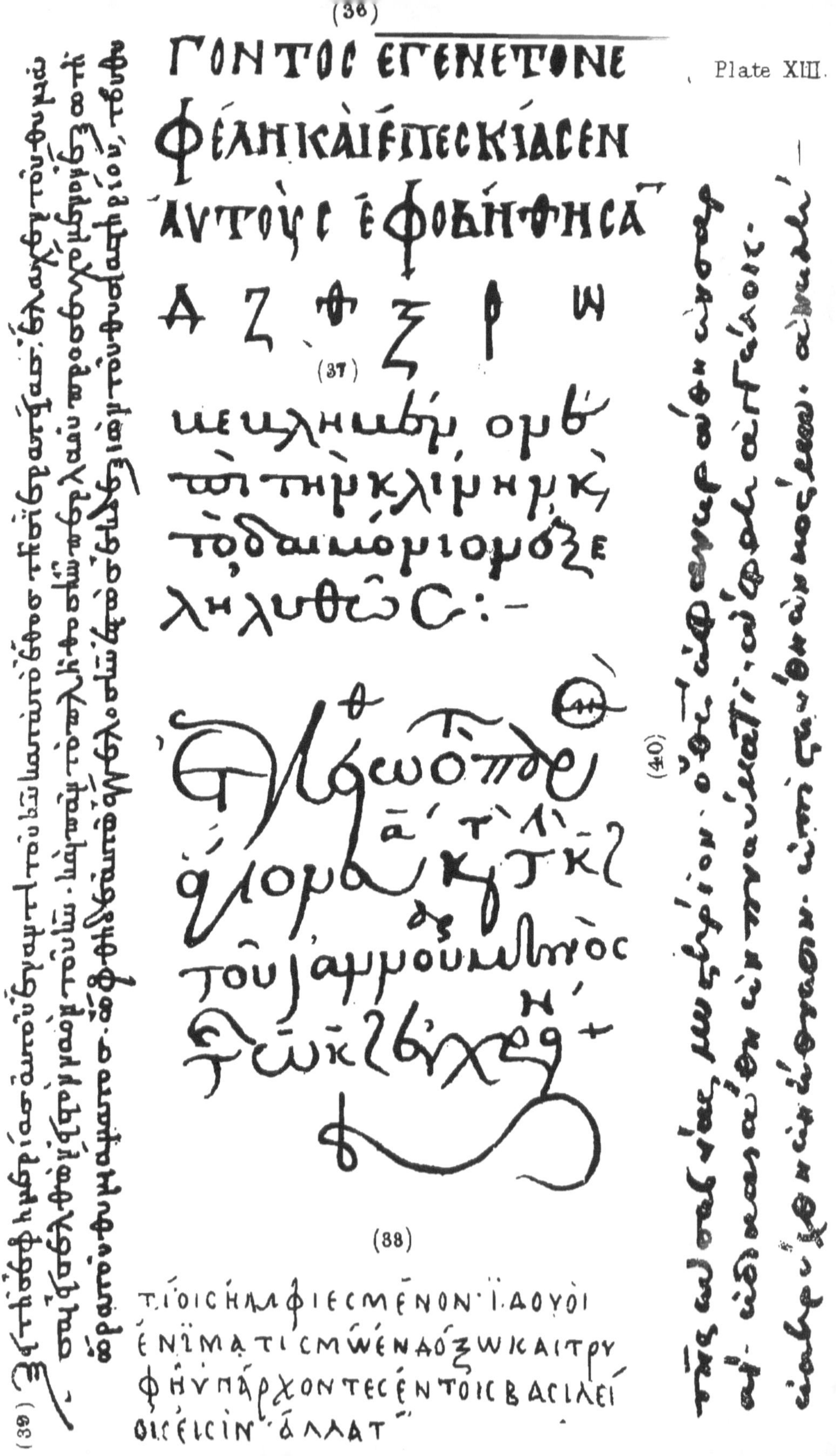

(36)
ΓΟΝΤΟϹ ΕΓΕΝΕΤΟ ΝΕ
ΦΕΛΗ ΚΑΙ ΕΠΕϹΚΙΑϹΕΝ
ΑΥΤΟΥϹ ΕΦΟΒΗΘΗϹΑ
Α Ζ Φ Ξ Ρ Ω
(37)
(38)
ΤΙ ΟΙϹ ΗΜΦΙΕϹΜΕΝΟΝ ΙΔΟΥ ΟΙ
ΕΝ ΙΜΑΤΙϹΜΩ ΕΝΔΟΞΩ ΚΑΙ ΤΡΥ
ΦΗ ΥΠΑΡΧΟΝΤΕϹ ΕΝ ΤΟΙϹ ΒΑϹΙΛΕΙ
ΟΙϹ ΕΙϹΙΝ ΑΛΛΑ Τ
(39)
(40)

223. Lond. Lambeth Archiepiscopal Library 1187 [xiii], $10\frac{1}{4}\times 7\frac{5}{8}$, ff. 177 (26), 2 cols., *mus. rubr.* (Greg. 229.)

224. Lond. Lamb. 1188 [xiii], $11\frac{1}{4}\times 8\frac{1}{2}$, ff. 318 (22–4), 2 cols., *mus. rubr.*, judged by Bloomfield to be the fullest and most accurate here, or at the British Museum. (Greg. 230.)

225. Lond. Lamb. 1189 [xiii], $8\frac{3}{4}\times 7\frac{1}{4}$, ff. 160 (27), 4 cotton (later), *τίτλ.* (Greg. 231.)

226. Lond. Lamb. 1193, $9\frac{1}{4}\times 6\frac{7}{8}$, ff. 153 (26), *mus. rubr.*, *mut.* at the end. Bloomfield assigns this to [ix], but Archdeacon Todd, in his (undated) 'Account of Greek Manuscripts,' &c., at Lambeth, sets it down as [xiii]. (Greg. 232.)

227. Lond. Sion College A. 32. 1, Ev. 1 (2) [xii], $10\frac{1}{2}\times 8\frac{1}{2}$, ff. 246 (19), 2 cols., *mus. rubr.*, *orn.*, 194 leaves of *σαββατοκυριακαί*, a noble copy, one leaf (149) being much mutilated, one leaf in later writing [xvi], and perhaps one leaf lost at the end: otherwise complete, with fair illuminations and red musical notes. (Greg. 234.) For its history *see* Evan. 518, as also that of

228. Lond. Sion Coll. A. 32. 1, Ev. 1 (2) [xiv], $10\frac{1}{4}\times 7\frac{5}{8}$, ff. 142 (23–25), 2 cols., *mus. rubr.*, *mut.* beginning and end. It begins at the Lesson for the third day of the second week (John iii. 19) and ends at Mark vi. 19, in the Lesson for Aug. 29. Two leaves are on paper, not much later than the rest. There is a Lesson for Aug. 1, not very common, *τῶν ἁγίων μακκαβαίων*, Matt. x. 16, &c. (Greg. 235.)

229. Lond. Sion Coll. A. 32. 1, Ev. 1 (4) [xiv, Greg. xiii], $10\times 9\frac{1}{8}$, ff. 217 (19, 20), 2 cols., *mus. rubr.*, *mut.* at end, is complete up to the Lesson for July 20 (Elijah), Luke iv. 22, broken off at *οὐδεὶς αὐτῶν* ver. 27. On the fly-leaf we read Τὰ *παρὸν θύον καὶ ἱερὸν εὐαγγέλιον ὑπάρχι κτῆμα τοῦ θήαυ καὶ ἁγίαυ ναοῦ ταῦ ἁγίαυ ἀπαστώλαυ καὶ εὐαγγελισταῦ μάρκαυ καὶ εἰ τής ἀποξένοι αὐτὰ ἐκ ταῦ ναοῦ ἔχαιτα τῶ ἐπιτίμω*[*-ίω*?] *τῶν ἁγ. πρων*, with the date of *α,χιθ* (1619). (Greg. 236.)

230. Glasgow, Hunterian Museum V. 5. 10 [A.D. 1259], $10\frac{1}{2}\times 7\frac{7}{8}$, ff. 112, 2 cols., *mut.* Belonged to Caesar de Missy. (*See* Greg. 239.)

231. Glasg. Hunt. Mus. V. 3. 3 [xii or xiii], $10\frac{1}{4}\times 8\frac{1}{4}$, ff. 251, 2 cols. From the monastery of *Πρόδρομος*, given by Nicetas. (*See* Greg. 240.)

232. (Apost. 44.) Glasg. Hunt. Mus. V. 4. 3, perhaps [A.D. 1199], $10\frac{3}{4}\times 8\frac{1}{4}$, ff. 176 (26), 2 cols.. Belonged once, like the two last, to De Missy. (*See* Greg. 241.)

The next two were collated by Scrivener—

*†233. P2[scr]. Parham 66. 1 [ix], $10\frac{1}{2}\times 7\frac{5}{8}$, three folio leaves from the monastery of Docheiariou on Athos, containing the thirty-three verses, Matt. i. 1–11; 11–22; vii. 7, 8; Mark ix. 41; xi. 22–26; Luke ix. 1–4. (Greg. 182.)

*†234. P[scr]. (or pa[scr].) Parham 83. 18 [June, A.D. 980], $12\frac{1}{2}\times 8\frac{5}{8}$, ff. 222 (22), 2 cols., belonged to the late Lord de la Zouche, who brought it from Caracalla on Athos in 1837, beautifully written at Ciscissa, in Cappadocia Prima; a note dated 1049 is subjoined by a reviser, who

perhaps made the numerous changes in the text, and added two Lessons in cursive letters. *See* Plate xiii, No. 36. Also 'Cod. Augiens.,' Introd., pp. l–lv. (Greg. 181.)

235. Parham 84. 19 [xi], $14\frac{1}{2} \times 11\frac{1}{2}$, ff. 188 (25), 'the right royal codex,' partly written in gold, perhaps by the Emperor Alexius Comnenus (1081–1118). (Greg. 233.)

236. Parham 85. 20 [xii], $13\frac{3}{8} \times 9\frac{7}{8}$, *mus. rubr.*, brought from St. Saba in 1834, must be on Scholz's list. (Greg. 344.)

237. Ashburnham 205 [xii], $10\frac{3}{8} \times 7\frac{3}{4}$, ff. 127, *mus.*, *mut.*, roughly executed and apparently made up of several copies: seen by Coxe and Burgon. (Greg. 237.) Loose in the book is

†238. Ashburnham 208* [xiii], $10\frac{3}{4} \times 8\frac{1}{2}$, ff. 9, Unc., palimpsest, the fragment of a menology for November and December. These were purchased by the late Earl of Ashburnham at the sale of the library of 'Athenian Aberdeen,' who brought them from Greece. (Greg. 237[a].)

239. Burdett-Coutts I. 2. A fragment of 173 leaves [xiii], $10\frac{3}{4} \times 8\frac{1}{8}$, one being on paper [xv] and 30 leaves palimpsest; having under the Church Lessons, in leaning uncials of two columns [viii or ix], fragments of legends relating to Saints in the menology, including the Apocryphal ἀποδημία of Barnabas. *Pict.*, capitals in red ink. (Greg. 214.)

240. B.-C. I. 8 [xiii], $9\frac{3}{4} \times 7\frac{3}{8}$, is also a palimpsest, with uncial writing in two columns (almost illegible) under the later Church Lessons on the last leaf and the third, fourth, fifth, and seventh leaves from the end: *mut.* at the thirteenth Sunday of St. Matthew, and ends in the tenth εὐαγγέλιον ἀναστάσιμον John xxi. 3 (ἐνέβησαν). (Greg. 215.)

241. B.-C. I. 23 [xiii], $9\frac{1}{4} \times 7\frac{1}{2}$, a poor copy, with illuminations, the last leaf only being lost. (Greg. 217.)

242. B.-C. I. 24 [xiv], $12\frac{1}{2} \times 10\frac{1}{8}$, *chart.*, complete, but the first leaf in a later hand. (Greg. 218.)

243. B.-C. II. 5 [xi or xii], $11 \times 8\frac{3}{8}$, a fine copy, with headings, &c., in gold, and red musical or tone notes. Begins John i. 17, thence complete to the Lesson εἰς ἐπινίκια βασιλέων. At the end are nine later leaves. (Greg. 219.)

244. B.-C. II. 16 [xiii], $8\frac{3}{8} \times 6\frac{1}{2}$, a palimpsest, with only one column on a page. Ends Luke ii. 59. (Greg. 220.)

245. B.-C. II. 30 [xiv], $11\frac{3}{8} \times 7\frac{1}{2}$, on glazed paper, complete. Titles and capitals in red. *Syn.* on a leaf of the binding. (Greg. 221.)

246. B.-C. III. 21 [xiii], *pict.*, *mut.*, with illuminations. Ends in the Lesson for Aug. 29, Mark vi. 22. (Greg. 222.)

247. B.-C. III. 34 [xiii], $10\frac{1}{4} \times 7\frac{3}{4}$, neat and complete. A colophon states the scribe to be Romanus, a priest. (Greg. 224.)

248. B.-C. III. 43 [April 28, 1437, Ind. 15], $11\frac{1}{2} \times 8\frac{3}{8}$, ff. 206, *chart.* (Greg. 225.)

[B.-C. III. 44 is Evst. 289, described below, Apost. 78.]

249. B.-C. III. 46 [xiv], $8\frac{7}{8} \times 7\frac{1}{4}$, ff. 220, *mut.* in the beginning of the Saints' Day Lessons: fifteen leaves are palimpsest, over writing full two centuries earlier, containing in double columns Lessons of the Septuagint from Genesis, Proverbs, and Isaiah. The other 205 leaves have only one column on a page. (Greg. 226.)

250. B.-C. III. 52 [xiii, Greg. xiv], $9\frac{1}{4} \times 7\frac{5}{8}$, *chart.*, is but a fragment. (Greg. 227.)

The following are Euchologies (*see* Evst. 57), and are repeated among the Lectionaries of the Apostolos:

251. (Apost. 64.) B.-C. I. 10 [xii or xiii], $7\frac{3}{8} \times 4\frac{3}{8}$, ff. 60 (17), *orn.*, wherein to the ordinary contents of a Euchology, and the Liturgies of SS. Chrysostom, Basil, and Presanctified, are annexed Church Lessons in a cramped and apparently later hand. (*See* Scrivener, Critica Sacra.) (Greg. 216.)

252. (Apost. 66.) B.-C. III. 29 [xiv or xv], $8\frac{1}{2} \times 6$, ff. 172, *men.* Liturgies as in last, and other matter, on coarse paper, Lessons both from the Gospels and Epistles. (*See* Scrivener, Critica Sacra.) (Greg. 223.)

253. (Apost. 67.) B.-C. III. 42 [xiv], 6 × 4, ff. 310 (22), on stout glazed paper, with the Liturgies as in Evst. 251, and much matter in various hands, has fifteen Lessons from the Gospels, Acts, and Epistles, and three from Isaiah, lxvi–lxviii. (*See* Scrivener, Critica Sacra.) (Greg. 315.)

253^2. (Apost. 68.) B.-C. III. 53 [xv], $8\frac{1}{2} \times 5\frac{3}{4}$, ff. 177 (26), 2 cols., *chart.*, *men.*, *mut.*, rudely written with capitals in red. (Greg. 228.)

254. Coniston, John Ruskin [xiii or xiv, Greg. xi or xii], $12\frac{3}{8} \times 10\frac{1}{4}$, ff. 144 (21), 2 cols., *mus. rubr.*, *mut.*, but well repaired. (Greg. 238.)

255. London, Brit. Mus. Egerton 2786 [xiii], $8\frac{5}{8} \times 6$, ff. 157 (20–27), a palimpsest, *mut.* at the beginning (thirty-two leaves) and end, rather rudely written in single columns, on coarse parchment, with vermilion ornamentation. It abounds in uncouth *itacisms*. After Mr. Woodhouse's death it belonged to Alderman Bragge from 1869 to 1876, then to Dean Burgon, then to Rev. W. F. Rose. Bought in 1893. (Greg. 346.)

256. Lond. Brit. Mus. Arundel 536 [xiii], 9 × 6, ff. 217 (25), besides 3 at beginning, *chart.*, *mus. rubr.*, with Lections from the Epistles. (Greg. 187.)

*†257. Lond. Brit. Mus. Arundel 547, is $\mathrm{x}^{\mathrm{scr}}$ [ix], $11\frac{1}{2} \times 9$, ff. 329 (22), 2 cols., Unc., *mus. rubr.*, *pict.*, *mut.* at the end, but followed by a leaf in a rather later hand, containing John viii. 12–19; 21–23. *See* our facsimile, Plate vi. No. 16. A collation by Bentley is preserved at Trinity College (B. xvii. 8). This is Hort's Cod. 38. (Greg. 183.)

258. (Apost. 53.) Lond. Brit. Mus. Harl. 5561 [xiv], $7\frac{1}{4} \times 5\frac{1}{2}$, ff. 276 (194 vell. + 82 [xv] *chart.*), is a Euchology (*see* Evst. 57), containing many short Lessons from the Gospels, Acts, and Epistles. (Greg. 340.)

259. Lond. Brit. Mus. Burney 22, is $\mathrm{y}^{\mathrm{scr}}$ [A.D. 1319], $11\frac{1}{2} \times 8\frac{1}{2}$, ff. 248 (27), 2 cols. (*see* facsimile, Plate xiii, No. 37), remarkable for its wide departures from the received text, and for that reason often cited by Tischendorf and Alford on the Gospels. See also Westcott, in Smith's

Dictionary of the Bible, 'New Testament.' Part of the first leaf (John i. 11–13) is on paper and later: Evst. 257, 259 are described in Scrivener's 'Collations of the Holy Gospels,' Introd. pp. lix–lxiii. Like Evst. 23 it was once D'Eon's. This is Hort's Cod. 39. (Greg. 184.)

260. Lond. Brit. Mus. Add. 5153 [A.D. 1032], $10\frac{1}{2} \times 7\frac{1}{2}$, 2 vols., ff. 141 and 133 (20), 2 cols., *chart.*, *mus. rubr.*, first five ff. vol. i. *mut.* and damaged. (Greg. 188.)

261. Lond. Brit. Mus. Add. 11,840 [xii], $11 \times 8\frac{1}{2}$, ff. 236 (22), 2 cols., *mus. rubr.*, *mut.*, from Bp. Butler's collection, a very fine specimen. (Greg. 189.)

262. Lond. Brit. Mus. Add. 17,370 [xi], $12\frac{3}{8} \times 9\frac{1}{4}$, three leaves: one in double columns (Matt. vi. 14–21), two in single columns [xiii?] Luke xxiv. 25–35; John i. 35–51. Sir F. Madden's note on the first fragment is 'Presented by Mr. Harris of Alexandria, June 28, 1848. A leaf of a Greek Lectionary taken [*by the Arabs* deleted] out of a volume which afterwards fell into the hands of Gen. Menou.' *See* Act. 230. (Greg. 190.)

263. Lond. Brit. Mus. Add. 18,212 [xii], $11 \times 8\frac{1}{4}$, ff. 297 (21), 2 cols., *mus. rubr.*, much *mut.* at the end, and an older leaf from the Old Testament prefixed (Bloomfield). (Greg. 191.)

264. Lond. Brit. Mus. Add. 19,460 [xiii], $9\frac{1}{4} \times 7\frac{1}{4}$, ff. 104 (31), 2 cols., *mut.* at the beginning and end, in coarse and very unusual black writing (Bloomfield). (Greg. 192.)

265. Lond. Brit. Mus. Add. 19,737 [xiii], $12\frac{3}{4} \times 10$, ff. 279 (23), 2 cols., *mus. rubr.*, bought at Sotheby's, 1854. *Mut.* at the end, with illuminations, and frequent and beautiful gilt letters. (Greg. 318.)

266. Lond. Brit. Mus. Add. 19,993 [A.D. 1335], $9\frac{3}{4} \times 7$, ff. 281 (23), in a bold hand and peculiar style. At the beginning is an Advertisement, signed G. Alefson, which ends literally thus: 'Je l'ai acheté seulement pour le sauver des mains barbares qui allait le destruire intierement au prix de sch. 15 a Chypre, A.D. 1851.' (Bloomfield.) (Greg. 193.)

267. Lond. Brit. Mus. Add. 21,260 [xiii], 12×10, ff. 360 (20), 2 cols., *mus. rubr.*, *orn.*, purchased of Messrs. Boone in 1856. *Mut.* at the end. The first forty leaves of this splendid copy are injured by damp. (Greg. 319.)

268. Lond. Brit. Mus. Add. 21,261 [xiii], $8\frac{1}{2} \times 5\frac{3}{4}$, ff. 196 (19), written by various hands. Purchased of Mr. H. Stevens, 1856. (Greg. 320.)

269. Lond. Brit. Mus. Add. 22,735 [xiii], $12\frac{1}{2} \times 9\frac{1}{2}$, ff. 304 (*sic*), (23), 2 cols., *mus. rubr.*, a fine, complete and interesting codex, bought (like Evann. 596, 597) of Sp. P. Lampros of Athens in 1859: as were also Evst. 270, 271, 272. Seven leaves of Patristic matter are bound up with it at the end. (Greg. 321.)

270. Lond. Brit. Mus. Add. 22,742 [xiii], $11\frac{1}{2} \times 8\frac{3}{4}$, ff. 79 (24), 2 cols., *mus. rubr.* (later), rather old and much mutilated throughout. (Greg. 322.)

271. Lond. Brit. Mus. Add. 22,743 [xii?], 14½ × 9½, ff. 213 (18), 2 cols., *caps.* and *mus. rubr.* in dull brown ink, somewhat roughly executed, apparently written with a reed pen. *Mut.* The last leaf is a fragment of Chrysostom, Hom. xlv, on Genesis. (Greg. 323.)

Evst. 265, 269, 271 sometimes agree with each other in departing from the ordinary week-day Church Lessons, and suggest, as Dean Burgon observes, some local fashion which is well worth investigating for textual purposes. The student will have noticed, in our Table of Lessons appended to Chap. III, how often two other codices, Apost. 64, or B.-C. III. 24 and Evst. 253, or B.-C. III. 42, depart from the common use of Church Lesson books, but only for the middle days of the week: not, it would seem, for Saturdays and Sundays.

272. Lond. Brit. Mus. Add. 22,744 [xiii], 11 × 8¼, ff. 189 (23), 2 cols., a beautiful copy, *mut.* at the beginning (to Sat. of third week), the end, and elsewhere, with red musical notes. *See* Evst. 269. (Greg. 324.)

273. Lond. Brit. Mus. Add. 24,374 [xiii], 11½ × 9, ff. 90 (18), 2 cols., *mus. rubr.*, *mut.* (Greg. 325.)

274. Lond. Brit. Mus. Add. 24,377 [xiv and xii], 12 × 8¾, ff. 350 (21), 2 cols., *mus. rubr.*, the first and some other leaves being lost; fol. 180, which is later, has palimpsest cursive writing under it. (Greg. 326.)

275. Lond. Brit. Mus. Add. 24,378 [xiii], 13 × 8¾, ff. 270, 2 cols., part of a Menaeum, in a small hand, written in a single column: imperfect and damaged in places. (Greg. 927.)

276. Lond. Brit. Mus. Add. 24,379 [xiv], 14¼ × 11, ff. 178 (28), 2 cols., much *mut.* throughout, with liturgical headings and some crosses in red for stops. (Greg. 327.)

277. Lond. Brit. Mus. Add. 24,380 [xiv], 11 × 9, ff. 126, 2 cols., *mus. rubr.*, *mut.* at beginning (to sixth day of seventh week) and end. (Greg. 328.)

Evst. 273–277 were purchased of H. Stanhope Freeman in 1862, as was also Evan. 600.

278. Lond. Brit. Mus. Add. 27,860 [xi or xii], 8 × 5½, ff. 115 (28), 2 cols., belonged to Sir F. Gage. (Greg. 329.)

279. Lond. Brit. Mus. Add. 28,817 [June 9, 1185], 11 × 8¾, ff. 306 (21), 2 cols. *Mut.* throughout, clear, in fine condition and peculiar style. (Greg. 330.) Like Evan. 603, bought in 1871 of Sir Ivor B. Guest, as was

280. Lond. Brit. Mus. Add. 28,818 [July, 1272], 9¾ × 7, ff. 118 (27), 2 cols., *chart.*, begins John xvii. 20. The subscription states that it was written *διὰ χειρὸς ἐμοῦ τοῦ ἁμαρτωλοῦ τολμῶ εἰπεῖν τοῦ ἱερέως τοῦ μεταξάρη.* (Greg. 331.)

*281. Lond. Brit. Mus. Add. 31,208 [xiii], 12½ × 9½, ff. 272 (21), 2 cols., *mus. rubr.*, bought of a dealer at Constantinople, cruelly mutilated (eighty-four leaves being missing), but once very fine. Collated by the Rev. W. F. Rose, who found it much to resemble Evst. 259 (y[scr]).

Burgon gives a French version of an Armenian note, dated 908 of the Armenian era, or A.D. 1460, of no special interest. (Greg. 333.)

282. Lond. Brit. Mus. Add. 31,919 [A.D. 1431], $12\frac{3}{4} \times 10$, ff. 108, formerly Blenheim 3. D. 13, the uncial eighth century palimpsest of the Gospels we have designated as Y, contains Lessons from the Gospels, written by Ignatius, Metropolitan of Selymbria in Thrace, being the February portion of a Menaeum. (Greg. 334.)

283. Lond. Brit. Mus. Add. 31,920 [xi], $9\frac{1}{4} \times 8$, ff. 226 (21), 2 cols., formerly Blenheim 3. C. 14, containing only *σαββατοκυριακαί* (*see* Evst. 24), singularly unadorned, but very interesting and genuine. (Greg. 335.)

284. Lond. Brit. Mus. Add. 31,921 [xiii], 10×8, ff. 178 (24), 2 cols., *mus. rubr.*, *mut.*, formerly Blenheim 3. C. 13, with Church Lessons for every day of the week. Several pages in a recent hand stand at the beginning: the first hand commences Matt. vi. 31. (Greg. 336.)

285. Lond. Brit. Mus. Add. 31,949 [xiii], $11 \times 8\frac{1}{2}$, ff. 103 (27), 2 cols., much dilapidated and *mut.*, was a gift to the Museum. (Greg. 337.)

†286. Sinai, St. Catharine's, Golden Evst. [ix–xi], $11\frac{1}{4} \times 8\frac{1}{2} \times 3\frac{1}{2}$, ff. abt. 200 (16), 2 cols., *pict.*, 'written in large and beautiful golden uncials,' divided into 'verses' like the modern, has breathings and accents. For specimen of writing, &c., *see* Burgon, Aug. 9, 1882. It was seen in 1862 by Burgon, in 1864 by the Rev. E. M. Young, and Mr. Jo. Dury Geden (*Athenaeum*, Nov. 12 and 19, 1864). It is said to be deteriorated by the promiscuous handling of strangers, although E. A. Sophocles tells us that local tradition absurdly assigns it to the Emperor Theodosius [d. 395] as the actual scribe; unless, as Mr. Geden suggests, Theodosius III (A. D. 716) be meant. The volume opens with the Gospels for the first five days of Easter week, which are followed by about sixty-five more from other parts of the yearly services. (Greg. 300.)

*287. (Act. 42, Apost. 56) contains only Matt. xvii. 16–23. (Greg. 923.)

288. Oxf. Bodl. Misc. Gr. 307 [xii], $12 \times 9\frac{1}{2}$, ff. 335 (22), 2 cols., *pict.*, *mus. rubr.*, *men.*, very beautiful. Mr. Madan of the Bodleian transcribed a note on the last leaf, showing that it once belonged to the Palaeologi. (Greg. 341.)

289. Oxf. Bodl. Misc. Gr. 308, from Constantinople [xii or xiii], $11\frac{1}{2} \times 9\frac{1}{4}$, ff. 217 (21), 2 cols., *mus. rubr.*, *men.* Initial letters of Byzantine character, *σαββατοκυριακαί* (*see* Evst. 24), has lost a very few lines at the end. (Greg. 342.)

290. (Apost. 78.) (Greg. 476.)

291. Camb. Univ. Libr. Add. 679. 1 [xii], $10 \times 8\frac{1}{4}$, ff. 170 (18), being a companion book to Apost. 79, containing only the week-day Lessons, except that two sets belong to Saturday and Sunday. Begins Matt. vii. 10, being on the sixth day of the first week of that Evangelist. *Mut.* elsewhere, but the end complete with a colophon, and fragments of two additional leaves. Initial capitals in red. (Greg. 305.)

292. (Apost. 80.) Camb. Univ. Libr. Add. 1836 [xiii], $6\frac{1}{2} \times 5\frac{1}{4}$, ff. (185 − 54 =) 131 (17), *mus. rubr.* Sunday and two Saturday Lessons only for Epistles and Gospels. *Mut.* first fifty and four other leaves. Begins second Sunday in St. Matthew (iv. 23). *Men.* full, followed by two Epistles and Gospels as ἀκολουθία εἰς ὁσίους. Additional Lessons in another hand are inserted about the season of Epiphany. (Greg. 306.)

293. Camb. Univ. Libr. Add. 1839 [xii or xiii], $10 \times 7\frac{1}{2}$, ff. (192 − 88 =) 104 (17), 2 cols.: σαββατοκυριακαί only (*see* Evst. 24). *Mut.* first seventy-seven and ten other leaves. Begins sixth Sunday of St. Luke (viii. 39). *Men.* ending Dec. 26. (Greg. 307.)

294. Camb. Univ. Libr. Add. 1840 [xi or xii], $11\frac{1}{2} \times 8\frac{1}{2}$, ff. 112 (31), 2 cols., *mus. rubr.* From the eleventh Sunday of St. Luke downwards the week-day Lessons are omitted. *Men.* followed by Gospels for several occasions. The arrangement of the week-day Lessons in the Gospels of St. Matthew, St. Mark, and St. Luke differs much from that usually found, though fundamentally akin to it. *Mut.* at the end and many other leaves. (Greg. 308.)

†295. Camb. Univ. Libr. Add. 1879. 2 [x], $11\frac{3}{4} \times 7\frac{7}{8}$, ff. 8 (22), 2 cols., Unc., *orn.*, *mus. rubr.* Σαββατοκυριακαί from eleventh Sunday in St. Luke (xiv. 20) to Sunday of the Publican (xviii. 14). Evst. 295–7 are from Tischendorf's collection. (Greg. 309.)

296. Camb. Univ. Libr. Add. 1879. 12 [xi or xii], $9\frac{1}{2} \times 6\frac{1}{4}$, ff. 4 (25), 2 cols., *mus.*, containing from sixth Saturday in Lent (John xi. 41) to Liturgy for Palm Sunday (John xii. 11), and part of Matins (from Matt. xxi. 36) and Vespers (to Matt. xxiv. 26) for Monday in Holy Week. (Greg. 310.)

297. Camb. Univ. Libr. Add. 1879. 13 [xii], $10 \times 8\frac{1}{2}$, ff. 4, *mut.*, 2 cols., Greek and Arabic, being only the upper part of four leaves of σαββατοκυριακαί in fifth and sixth Sundays of St. Luke (ch. xvi. 24 f.; 28–30; viii. 16–18; 21; 27; 29 f.; 32–34; 38 f.). (Greg. 311.)

298. Oxf. Keble Coll. [xiii], $9\frac{3}{4} \times 6\frac{3}{4}$, ff. 151 (25), 2 cols., some *mus. rubr.*, *syn.*, *men.*, *orn.*, presented in 1882 by Mr. Greville Chester, beginning with the Lesson for the second day of the fifth week after Easter, and ending with the Lesson for St. Helena's day, May 21. (Greg. 343.)

†299. Par. Nat. Gr. 975. B [x], $12\frac{1}{2} \times 9\frac{1}{2}$, ff. 55 (22), 2 cols., *mus. rubr.*, Unc., palimpsest, frag. of St. Luke, *men.* ff. 33, 34, 39, 40 [ix], Chrys. and Zosimus. (*See* Greg. 363.)

300. Messina, Univ. 65 [xii], $13\frac{3}{4} \times 10\frac{1}{2}$, ff. 318 (25), 2 cols., *mus. rubr.* (Greg. 513.)

†301. Mess. Univ. 66 [ix], $13\frac{7}{8} \times 9\frac{5}{8}$, ff. 256 (28), 2 cols., Unc., *mus. rubr.*, *mut.* (Greg. 514.)

302. Mess. Univ. 75 [xiii], $12\frac{1}{4} \times 9\frac{1}{2}$, ff. 136 (22), 2 cols., *mus. rubr.*, *mut.* at beginning and end. (Greg. 516.)

303. Mess. Univ. 96 [xii], $10\frac{1}{2} \times 7\frac{7}{8}$, ff. 298 (24), 2 cols., *mus. rubr.* (Greg. 519.)

304. Mess. Univ. 98 [A.D. 1148], $10\frac{5}{8} \times 8\frac{1}{2}$, ff. 275 (24), 2 cols. (Greg. 520.)

305. Mess. Univ. 73 [xii], $12\frac{7}{8} \times 9\frac{7}{8}$, ff. 223 (28), 2 cols., written at Messina by Nilus the monk in the monastery of St. Salvador: he records (at p. 26^b) the earthquake which happened Sept. 26, 1173, Codex Graeco-Siculus. (Greg. 515.)

306. Mess. Univ. 58 [xiv, Greg. xv or xvi], $11\frac{1}{8} \times 8\frac{1}{8}$, ff. 236 (17), *chart.*, written by three different calligraphers. (Greg. 512.)

307. Mess. Univ. 94 [xii], $10\frac{1}{2} \times 7\frac{3}{4}$, ff. 184 (21), 2 cols., *mus. rubr.*, *mut.* at beginning, breaking off at Sept. 24 in the menology. (Greg. 517.)

308. Mess. Univ. 111 [xii], $9\frac{1}{2} \times 8$, ff. 119 (23), 2 cols., *mut.* at beginning and end. (Greg. 521.)

309. Mess. Univ. 112 [xii], $9\frac{1}{2} \times 7\frac{1}{2}$, ff. 146 (21), 2 cols., *mus. rubr.*, *mut.* at beginning and end. (Greg. 522.)

310. Mess. Univ. 170 [xii], $8\frac{5}{8} \times 6\frac{1}{4}$, ff. 187 (20), 2 cols., *mut.* at beginning and end. (Greg. 524.)

311. Mess. Univ. 95 [xiii], $11\frac{1}{4} \times 8\frac{1}{8}$, ff. 186 (23), 2 cols., *mus. rubr.*, *mut.* from pp. 42–75. (Greg. 518.)

312. (Apost. 112.) Mess. Univ. 150 [xii or xiii], $6\frac{1}{2} \times 5\frac{1}{4}$, ff. 60 (22). A fragment. (*See* Greg. 523.)

313. Crypta Ferrata, A. α. 7 [xii], $9\frac{7}{8} \times 7\frac{7}{8}$, ff. 45 (25), 2 cols., *mus. nigr.*, σαββατοκυριακαί mutilated. (Greg. 463.)

314. Crypt. Ferr. A. α. 9 [xii], $13\frac{3}{8} \times 9\frac{7}{8}$, ff. 292 (25), 2 cols., *mus. rubr.*, *mut.*, a beautiful codex, and very full in its Lections. (Greg. 464.)

315. Crypt. Ferr. A. α. 10 [xi], $12\frac{7}{8} \times 10\frac{1}{4}$, ff. 246 (22), 2 cols., *mus. rubr.*, much foreign matter, a very beautiful codex. (Greg. 465.)

316. Crypt. Ferr. A. α. 11 [xv], $6\frac{1}{4} \times 4\frac{7}{8}$, ff. 181 (14), *mut.* σαββατοκυρ. (Greg. 466.)

317. Crypt. Ferr. A. α. 12 [xiv, Greg. x or xi], $6\frac{3}{8} \times 4\frac{3}{4}$, ff. 97 (22), *mut.* (Greg. 467.)

318. Crypt. Ferr. A. α. 13 [xv], $6\frac{3}{8} \times 4\frac{7}{8}$, ff. 62 (18), partly palimpsest, *mut.* (Greg. 468.)

319. Crypt. Ferr. A. α. 14 [xii], $9\frac{1}{2} \times 6\frac{3}{4}$, ff. 73 (23), 2 cols., *mut.* at beginning and end. (*See* Greg. 469.)

320. Crypt. Ferr. A. α. 15 [xi], $7\frac{1}{8} \times 5\frac{7}{8}$, ff. 69 (23). Closely resembles Evst. 33. (Greg. 470.)

321. Crypt. Ferr. A. α. 16 [xi], $7\frac{7}{8} \times 5\frac{7}{8}$, ff. 55 (26), 2 cols., a fragment from St. John. (Greg. 471.)

322. (Apost. 90.) Crypt. Ferr. A. β. 2 [xi], $5\frac{7}{8} \times 4$, ff. 259 (ff. 159–213), with many excerpts from Fathers. (Greg. 478.)

323. (Apost. 90.) Crypt. Ferr. A. δ. 2 [x], $5\frac{7}{8} \times 4\frac{3}{8}$, ff. 155, much from Old Testament, *mut.* (Greg. 473.)

†324. Par. Nat. Suppl. Gr. 805, ff. 1–7 [ix], $11\frac{1}{8} \times 8\frac{1}{8}$, ff. 7 (19), Unc., palimpsest, *mus. rubr.*, fragm. (*See* Greg. 370.)

325. (Apost. 92.) Crypt. Ferr. A. δ. 4 [xiii], $9\frac{7}{8} \times 7\frac{1}{8}$, ff. 257. Written by 'Johannes Rossanensis.' Contains Lections from Old and New Testaments. (Greg. 475.)

326. St. Saba 25 [xi], fol. Coxe. (Greg. 170.)

327. St. Saba 26 [xi], fol. Coxe.

328. St. Saba 40 [xii], fol. In Greek and Arabic. Coxe.

329. St. Saba 44 [xii], 4to. Coxe.

330. Crypt. Ferr. A. δ. 11 [three fragments] :—

(1) [xi], $9\frac{3}{4} \times 7\frac{1}{2}$, ff. 2 (22), 2 cols.;
(2) [xii], $6\frac{1}{4} \times 4\frac{5}{8}$, ff. 2 (23);
(3) [xiii], $8\frac{5}{8} \times 6\frac{3}{4}$, ff. 4 (22), 2 cols., *mus. rubr.* (*See* Greg. 472.)

331. Crypt. Ferr. A. δ. 16 [x], $9\frac{1}{2} \times 7\frac{1}{8}$, ff. 234 (25), 2 cols., palimpsest. (Greg. 480.)

†332. Crypt. Ferr. A. δ. 17 [x], $7\frac{7}{8} \times 5\frac{7}{8}$, ff. 25 (27), Unc., palimpsest, fragm. (Greg. 481.)

†333. Crypt. Ferr. A. δ. 19 [x], $7\frac{1}{2} \times 5\frac{1}{8}$, ff. 39 (24), 2 cols., Unc., palimpsest, *mut.* (Greg. 482.)

334. (Apost. 95.) Crypt. Ferr. A. δ. 20 [xii, Greg. x or xi], $9 \times 6\frac{3}{4}$, ff. 21 (22), 2 cols., *mut.* (Greg. 483.)

335. Crypt. Ferr. A. δ. 21 [x], 13×9, ff. 97 (31), palimpsest, *mut.* (Greg. 484.)

336. Crypt. Ferr. A. δ. 22 [x or xi], $6\frac{3}{4} \times 5\frac{1}{2}$, ff. 113, 2 cols., palimpsest, *mut.* (Greg. 485.)

†337. (Apost. 96.) Crypt. Ferr. A. δ. 24 [four fragments]:—

(1) Also called Z′. α′. 2 [xiii], $9\frac{3}{4} \times 6\frac{3}{4}$, ff. 2 (28), 2 cols.;
(2) Also B′. α′. 23 [viii or ix], $7\frac{7}{8} \times 5\frac{1}{8}$, palimpsest, Unc., ff. 2 (27), 2 cols.;
(3) Also Z′. α′. 24 (R paul.);
(4) Also Γ. B′. 3 [xi], $7\frac{3}{8} \times 5\frac{1}{2}$. *See* also 340. (Greg. 486^{a-d}.)

338. Crypt. Ferr. Γ. α. 18 [xvii], $10\frac{1}{4} \times 7\frac{7}{8}$, ff. 170, Evangelia ἑωθινά. (Greg. 487.)

339. (Apost. 97.) Crypt. Ferr. Γ. β. 2 [xi], $6\frac{3}{4} \times 5\frac{1}{8}$, ff. 151, a Euchology, contains only a few Lections. (Greg. 488.)

340. (Apost. 98.) Crypt. Ferr. Γ. β. 3 [xiv], $7\frac{3}{8} \times 5\frac{1}{2}$, ff. 201 (19), Euchology. Contains only a few Lessons. (Greg. 486^{d2}.)

341. (Apost. 99.) Crypt. Ferr. Γ. β. 6 [xiii or xiv], $7\frac{1}{8} \times 4\frac{3}{4}$, ff. 101 (21). Contains only a few Lections. (Greg. 489.)

342. Crypt. Ferr. Γ. β. 7 [ix or x], $6\frac{3}{4} \times 5\frac{1}{2}$, ff. 173 (17), Euchology. Contains only a few Lections. (Greg. 490.)

343. Crypt. Ferr. Γ. β. 8 [Greg. xiii], ff. 8 palimpsest at end of ff. 145 [xii]. (*See* Greg. 491.)

344. (Apost. 100.) Crypt. Ferr. Γ. β. 9 [xvi], $4\frac{1}{4} \times 3\frac{1}{8}$, ff. 95, Euchology. Contains only a few Lections. (Greg. 492.)

345. Crypt. Ferr. Γ. β. 11 [xii], $5\frac{1}{2} \times 4\frac{3}{4}$, ff. 20, Euchology. Contains only a few Lections. (Greg. 493.)

346. (Apost. 101.) Crypt. Ferr. Γ. β. 12 [xiv], $5\frac{7}{8} \times 4\frac{3}{4}$, ff. 98, Euchology. Contains only a few Lections. (Greg. 494.)

347. (Apost. 102.) Crypt. Ferr. Γ. β. 13 [xiii], $9 \times 6\frac{1}{4}$, ff. 118 (18), Euchology. Written by 'Johannes Rossanensis.' (Greg. 495.)

348. Crypt. Ferr. Γ. β. 14 [xiii], $7\frac{1}{2} \times 5\frac{1}{2}$, ff. 54 (23). Euchologium with a few Lections. (Greg. 496.)

349. (Apost. 103.) Crypt. Ferr. Γ. β. 15 [xi–xiii], $7\frac{1}{8} \times 5\frac{1}{8}$, ff. 41 (22), Euchology. Contains only a few Lections. (*See* Greg. 497.)

350. (Apost. 104.) Crypt. Ferr. Γ. β. 17 [A.D. 1565], $8\frac{1}{4} \times 5\frac{7}{8}$, ff. 269 (21), *chart.* The Saturday and Sunday Lessons begin at fol. 121. (*See* Greg. 498.)

351. (Apost. 105.) Crypt. Ferr. Γ. β. 18 [xiv], St. Saba 55 [xii], 4to. Coxe. Contains very few Lections.

352. (Apost. 106.) Crypt. Ferr. Γ. β. 19 [xvi], $11\frac{3}{8} \times 8\frac{1}{4}$, ff. 145 (28), *chart.* The Apostolo-Evangeliarium begins at fol. 16. (*See* Greg. 500.)

353. (Apost. 107.) Crypt. Ferr. Γ. β. 23 [A.D. 1641], $12\frac{1}{2} \times 8\frac{5}{8}$, ff. 75. It is a Euchologium with a few Lections. (*See* Greg. 501.)

354. (Apost. 108.) Crypt. Ferr. Γ. β. 24 [xvi], $12\frac{1}{2} \times 9$, ff. 302 (28), *chart.* Liturgical information. (*See* Greg. 502.)

355. Crypt. Ferr. Γ. β. 35 [xiii], $7\frac{1}{8} \times 5\frac{7}{8}$, ff. 83 (21), liturgical. Contains only a few Lections. (*See* Greg. 503.)

356. (Apost. 109.) Crypt. Ferr. Γ. β. 38 [xvii], $11\frac{3}{4} \times 8\frac{5}{8}$, ff. 91. Contains only a few Lections. (*See* Greg. 504.)

357. (Apost. 110.) Crypt. Ferr. Γ. β. 13 [xvi], $10\frac{1}{4} \times 7\frac{1}{2}$, ff. 344, *chart.*, liturgical. (Greg. 505.)

358. (Apost. 111.) Crypt. Ferr. Δ. β. 22 [xviii], $15\frac{5}{8} \times 10\frac{5}{8}$, ff. 77 (27), *chart.* Contains only a few Lections. (Greg. 506.)

359. Crypt. Ferr. Δ. γ. 26 [xiv], $4\frac{1}{4} \times 3\frac{1}{8}$, ff. 115 (19). The Evangelia [ἑωθινά]. (Greg. 507.)

360. Crypt. Ferr. Δ. δ. 6 [xviii], $16 \times 10\frac{5}{8}$, ff. ?, palimpsest. Fragments. (*See* Greg. 508.)

361. St. Saba, Tower Library 12 [xi], 4to. Coxe.

362. Syracuse 'Seminario' 3 [A.D. 1125], $8\frac{3}{8} \times 5\frac{1}{2}$, ff. 255 (25), 2 cols. (Greg. 574.)

363. Lond. Lambeth 1194 [xiii, Greg. xi], $7\frac{1}{2} \times 5\frac{1}{2}$, ff. 218 (17), fifty-one Lessons from Gospels—forty-eight from Acts and Epistles, *mus. rubr.*, *mut.* Menaeum ending in June. (Greg. 477.)

364. St. Saba, Tower 16 [xii], 4to, with Lections from Old Testament. Coxe.

365. St. Saba, Tower 52 [xi], 4to, *mus.* Coxe.

366. Par. Nat. Suppl. Gr. 74 [xiv or xv, Greg. xii], $7\frac{3}{4} \times 5\frac{3}{8}$, ff. 72, 2 cols., *mus. rubr.* Formerly Huet's, who gave it to the Jesuits. Contains the Evangelia *ἑωθινά*. It is rather a Euchologium, and is of little value. (Greg. 366.)

†367. Par. Nat. Suppl. Gr. 567 [xv], 13×10, ff. 173 (14), 2 cols., Unc., apparently modern. Given by the same to the library. Saturday and Sunday Lections. (Greg. 367.)

368. Berlin, Reg. Gr. 'Hamilton 245' [x, Greg. xii], $12\frac{7}{8} \times 9\frac{3}{8}$, ff. 378 (21), 2 cols., *pict.* A magnificent specimen. (Greg. 381.)

369. Berlin, Reg. Gr. 'Hamilton 246' [xiii], $13\frac{1}{3} \times 10\frac{1}{8}$, ff. ?, 2 cols. At the beginning of the volume is a fragment of a more ancient Evangelium, not extending beyond the Eusebian tables of Canons, superbly illuminated. (Greg. 382.)

370. Berlin, Reg. Gr. 51 fol. [xiii, Greg. xii], $12\frac{5}{8} \times 9\frac{1}{2}$, ff. 214 (26), 2 cols. (*See* Greg. 375.)

371. Berlin, Reg. Gr. 52 fol. [xii], $11\frac{5}{8} \times 9$, *mus. rubr.* (Greg. 376.)

372. Berlin, Reg. Gr. 53 fol. [xii, Greg. xi], $11\frac{3}{4} \times 8\frac{3}{4}$, ff. 248 (21), 2 cols., *mus. rubr.* (*See* Greg. 377.)

373. Berlin, Reg. Gr. 4to, 46 [xiii, Greg. xii], $10\frac{3}{4} \times 8$, ff. 46, 2 cols., *mus. rubr.*, ends with the Saturday of Pentecost. (Greg. 378.)

374. Berlin, Reg. Gr. 4to, 61 [xiii], $11\frac{1}{2} \times 8\frac{1}{2}$, *mus. rubr.*, begins with the Saturday after Pentecost, and contains the Menologium. (Greg. 379.)

375. Berlin, Reg. Gr. 4to, 64 [xii, xiii], $10\frac{1}{2} \times 8\frac{1}{8}$, *mut.* at the commencement. (Greg. 380.)

376. Rom. Vat. Gr. 352 [xi, Greg. xiii or xvi], $12\frac{1}{2} \times 9\frac{3}{8}$, ff. 244 (23), 2 cols., with Menology. (Greg. 540.)

†377. Rom. Vat. Gr. 353 [x], $11\frac{5}{8} \times 8\frac{1}{8}$, ff. 237 (20), 2 cols., Unc. Gospel Lections. (Greg. 541.)

†378. Rom. Vat. Gr. 355 [x], $13 \times 10\frac{1}{8}$, ff. 315 (19), 2 cols., Unc. (Greg. 542.)

†379. Rom. Vat. Gr. 357 [x], $15\frac{3}{8} \times 12\frac{3}{4}$, ff. 322 (15), 2 cols., *mus. rubr.* (Greg. 543.)

380. Rom. Vat. Gr. 362 [x, Greg. xi], $7\frac{3}{4} \times 5\frac{7}{8}$, ff. 200 (23). (Greg. 544.)

381. Rom. Vat. Gr. 540 [x], fol., ff. 4 (20), 2 cols., *mus. rubr.*, a fragment prefixed to St. Chrysostom on St. John. (*See* Greg. 545.)

382. Rom. Vat. Gr. 781 [xii, Greg. x or xi], $9\frac{7}{8} \times 7\frac{1}{2}$, ff. 152 (27), 2 cols., 'fuit Blasii praep. Cryptae Ferratae.' (Greg. 546.)

383. Rom. Vat. Gr. 1534 [xiii or xiv], $13\frac{1}{4} \times 10\frac{1}{2}$, ff. 223 (25), 2 cols. (Greg. 549.)

384. Rom. Vat. Gr. 1601 [xiii, Greg. xii], $9\frac{3}{8} \times 7\frac{1}{4}$, ff. 193 (22), 2 cols. (Greg. 550.)

385. Rom. Vat. Gr. 1813 [xiii], $7\frac{1}{8} \times 5\frac{1}{4}$, ff. out of 266 – 3 (19). Evangelia ἑωθινά. (Greg. 552.)

386. Rom. Vat. Gr. 1886 [xiii], $10 \times 7\frac{3}{4}$, ff. 110 (29), 2 cols. (Greg. 553.)

387. (Apost. 118.) Rom. Vat. Gr. 2012 [xv], ff. 211. Contains only a few Gospel Lections. (Greg. 556.)

388. Rom. Vat. Gr. 2100 [xiv], $7 \times 5\frac{1}{4}$, ff. 79 (19), with a commentary. (Greg. 560.)

389. Rom. Vat. Gr. 2129 [xv, Greg. xiv], *chart.*, ff. 5 out of 701. Lections during Lent. (Greg. 561.)

†390. Rom. Vat. Gr. 2144 [viii], $8\frac{1}{4} \times 5\frac{5}{8}$, ff. 193 (22), 2 cols., Unc. Brought from Constantinople. (Greg. 563.)

†391. Patmos 4 [xi], 4to, Unc. Coxe. (Greg. ?)

392. Rom. Vat. Gr. 2167 [xiii], $12\frac{1}{4} \times 9$, ff. 361 (21), 2 cols., *pict.* Olim 'Columnensis.' (Greg. 564.)

†393. Rom. Vat. Gr. 2251 [viii ?], $8\frac{1}{4} \times 5\frac{1}{2}$, ff. 4 (22), 2 cols., Unc. Olim 'Columnensis.' At the beginning and end of a larger MS. (Greg. 565.)

394. Rom. Vat. Alex. Gr. 44 [xvii], $8\frac{1}{4} \times 5\frac{7}{8}$, ff. 355 (20), *chart.*, by different hands, with a commentary. (Greg. 571.)

395. (Apost. 121.) Rom. Vat. Alex. Gr. 59 [xii], $11 \times 7\frac{3}{4}$, ff. 137 (47). Gospels and Epistles for Holy Week. Lections from Old and New Test. (Greg. 573.)

†396. Rom. Vat. Ottob. Gr. 444 A, B [ix], $10 \times 7\frac{3}{8}$, ff. 2 (22), 2 cols., Unc., with fragments of Gospels. (Greg. 566.)

†397. Rom. Vat. Palat. Gr. 1. A [ix or x], $10\frac{1}{4} \times 7\frac{5}{8}$, ff. 2 (23), 2 cols., Unc. A mere fragment. (Greg. 567.)

398. Rom. Vat. Palat. Gr. 221 [xiii, Greg. xv], $9\frac{5}{8} \times 4\frac{1}{8}$ (?), ff. 397 (32), *chart.*, with the commentary of Xiphilinus. (Greg. 568.)

399. Rom. Vat. Palat. Gr. 239 [xv, Greg. xvi], $8\frac{3}{4} \times 5\frac{3}{4}$, ff. 122 (?) (23), *chart.*, with a commentary. (Greg. 569.)

†400. Patmos 10 [xi], 4to, Unc. Coxe. (Greg. ?)

†401. Patmos 22 [xi], fol., Unc. Coxe. (Greg. ?)

†402. Patmos 81 [viii], 4to, Unc. Coxe. (Greg. ?)

403. Rom. Barberini iv. 43 [xii, Greg. xiii or xiv], $9\frac{1}{2} \times 7\frac{1}{4}$, ff. 221 (23), 2 cols., *mus. rubr.*, *pict.*, beautifully illuminated. (Greg. 535.)

404. Rom. Barb. iv. 30 [xii], 9×7, ff. 223 (22), 2 cols. (Greg. 534.)

405. Rom. Barb. iv. 53 [xiii, Greg. xi or xii], $9\frac{3}{4} \times 7\frac{1}{2}$, ff. 161 (22), 2 cols., *mus. rubr.*, *mut.*, *chart.* (Greg. 536.)

406. Rom. Barb. iv. 13 [xii], ff. 143. Contains only a few Lections. (Greg. 531.)

407. Rom. Barb. iv. 25 [xiv, Greg. xi or xii], $9 \times 5\frac{3}{4}$, ff. 159. Contains only certain Lections. (Greg. 532.)

408. (Apost. 218.) Rom. Barb. iv. 1 [xiv–xvi], ff. 323, *chart.* Contains only a few Lections. (Greg. 530.)

409. Rom. Barb. iii. 22 [xv], ff. 254, *chart.* Contains only a few Lections. (Greg. 528.)

410. (Apost. 124.) Rom. Barb. iii. 129 [xiv], ff. 189. (Greg. 529.)

411. Rom. Barb. vi. 18 [xii], $12\frac{3}{8} \times 10\frac{3}{8}$, *mut.*, but beautifully illuminated with Menology. (Greg. 537.)

412. Milos [xii], fol., a fragment. Coxe. (Greg. 804.)

413. Constantinople, Patriarch of Jerusalem 10 [xii], 4to, a palimpsest written over a geometrical treatise [xi]. Coxe.

+414. Rom. Ghig. R. vii. 52 [ix, Greg. x or xi], $11\frac{3}{4} \times 9\frac{3}{8}$, ff. 227 (12), 2 cols., *mus. rubr.*, 'cod. nobilissimus, charact. uncialibus: habet titulum *Hebdomadae magnae Officium Graecorum:* e CP. advectus est ad Conventum Collis Paradisi, et hinc ad Bibliothecam Chisianam.' (Greg. 538.)

415. (Apost. 256.) Par. Nat. 13 [xii–xiii, Greg. xi or xii], $15\frac{5}{8} \times 11\frac{3}{4}$, ff. 478 (68), 2 cols. *See* Martin, p. 165. (Greg. 935.)

416. Par. Nat. Suppl. Gr. 24 [xiii], $13 \times 9\frac{3}{4}$, ff. 339 (22), 2 cols., *mus. rubr.* *See* Martin, p. 165. (Greg. 364.)

417. Par. Nat. Suppl. Gr. 29 [xii], $9\frac{3}{4} \times 7\frac{5}{8}$, ff. 198 (20), 2 cols., *mus. rubr.*, *mut.* *See* Martin, p. 165. (Greg. 365.)

418. Par. Nat. Suppl. Gr. 179, 180 [xiii], $9\frac{1}{4} \times 5\frac{7}{8}$, f. 1 (26). *See* Martin, p. 166. (Greg. 928.)

419. Par. Nat. Suppl. Gr. 1096 [xiii–xiv], $7\frac{1}{4} \times 5\frac{1}{4}$, ff. 33 (26), *men.* (Greg. 374.)

420. Auckland, City Library. (Greg. 474.)

+421. Par. Nat. Suppl. Gr. 686 [xi, Greg. ix], $11\frac{3}{4} \times 9$, ff. 2 (21), 2 cols., *mus. rubr.* Martin, p. 167. (Greg. 368.)

422. Par. Nat. Suppl. Gr. 687 [xii], $13\frac{1}{2} \times 10\frac{1}{8}$, ff. 2 (20), 2 cols., *mus. rubr.* Martin, p. 167. (Greg. 499.)

423. Par. Nat. Suppl. Gr. 758 [xii], $11 \times 8\frac{5}{8}$, ff. 111 (28), 2 cols., *orn.*, *mus. rubr.* Martin, p. 167. (Greg. 369.)

424. Par. Nat. Suppl. Gr. 834 [xiii], $11\frac{5}{8} \times 9$, ff. 90 (27), 2 cols., *mus. rubr.* Martin, p. 168. (Greg. 371.)

425. Par. Nat. Suppl. Gr. 905 [A.D. 1055], $11\frac{7}{8} \times 9\frac{3}{4}$, ff. 254 (20), 2 cols., *pict.*, *men.* Martin, p. 168. (Greg. 372.)

426. Par. Nat. Gr. 235 [xii], $12\frac{3}{8} \times 10$, ff. 235 (24), 2 cols., *mus. rubr.*, *men.*, greatly *mut.* Martin, p. 168. (Greg. 361.)

+427. Par. Nat. Gr. ~~228, Greg.~~ 928 [ix], $11\frac{1}{2} \times 8\frac{1}{2}$, ff. 240 (20), 2 cols., palimpsest with menaeum [xii–xiii] written over, 2 ff. at beginning, and 11 after p. 48, *chart.* and later, *Am.*, Unc. Martin, p. 169. (Greg. 362.)

428. (Apost. 257.) Par. Nat. Gr. 263 [xiii], $15 \times 10\frac{7}{8}$, ff. 200 (62),

2 cols., *mut.* at end. Came from Mon. of Panteleemon at Athos. Martin, p. 170. (Greg. 936.)

For the rest, *see* Gregory, pp. 744, &c. The press-marks in the Athenian MSS. have been changed since Dr. Gregory examined them. I have had great difficulty in identifying them, and am in doubt as to many where a (?) is inserted. The figures in brackets are the present press-marks. Dr. Gregory's are given first.

429. Athens, Nat. Libr. 12 (66 ?) [xi], $11\frac{3}{4} \times 9\frac{1}{2}$, ff. 196.

430. Ath. Nat. 13 (70 ?) [A.D. 1350], $12\frac{1}{2} \times 9$, ff. 199, *pict.*

431. Ath. Nat. 13 (146 ?) [xv], $11 \times 9\frac{1}{2}$, ff. 174, *chart.*

432. Ath. Nat. 15 (64 ?), $13\frac{3}{8} \times 9\frac{1}{2}$, ff. 287, *mut.* at end.

433. Ath. Nat. 17 (82) [xii], $9 \times 7\frac{1}{8}$, ff. 139, *mut.* at end.

434. Ath. Nat. 18 (68 ?) [xii], 11×9, ff. 220, *pict.*, *mut.* at end.

435. Ath. Nat. 19 (79) [xiv], $8\frac{5}{8} \times 7\frac{1}{8}$, ff. 191.

436. Ath. Nat. 19 (73) [A.D. 1545], $12\frac{1}{2} \times 8\frac{1}{4}$, ff. 314 (? 251 + 63 later).

437. Ath. Nat. 24 (67 ?) [x], 11×9, ff. 260, *mus.*

438. Ath. Nat. 25 (112 ?) [xv], $7\frac{1}{2} \times 5\frac{1}{2}$, ff. 119.

439. (Apost. 193.) Ath. Nat. 66 (670 ?) [xii], $8\frac{1}{4} \times 5\frac{7}{8}$, ff. 132, Euchology followed by Apostoloeuaggelia.

440. (Apost. 194.) Ath. Nat. 112 (126) [A.D. 1504], $8\frac{1}{4} \times 5\frac{7}{8}$, ff. 276.

441. Ath. Nat. (69) [xii], $11\frac{3}{8} \times 8\frac{5}{8}$, ff. 200, the last three blank.

442. Ath. Nat. (63 ?) [x end], $11\frac{3}{4} \times 9\frac{1}{2}$, ff. 294.

443. (Apost. 195.) Ath. Nat. 86. I cannot find this, which is a menaeum, or the two next.

†444a. Ath. Nat. ? 444b. Ath. Nat. ?

445. Ath. Nat. (84 ?) [xiv], $11\frac{3}{8} \times 8\frac{5}{8}$, ff. 148.

446. (Apost. 196.) Ath. Nat. (661 ?) [xv], $7\frac{7}{8} \times 6\frac{3}{8}$, ff. 138. Liturgical matter followed by Apostoloeuaggelia.

447. Ath. Nat. (85 ?) [xiv], $11 \times 7\frac{7}{8}$, ff. 102.

448. Ath. Nat. 124 [xii], $10\frac{5}{8} \times 8\frac{5}{8}$, ff. 174, *mus.*

449. Ath. Nat. (62 ?) [xii], $11\frac{3}{4} \times 9$, ff. 329, *mus.*

450. Ath. τῆς Βουλῆς. 451. Ath. M. Bournias.

452a. Ath. M. Bournias. 452b. Ath. M. Bournias.

453. Ath. M. Varouccas.

454. Dublin, Trin. Coll. A. i. 8, fol. 1.

455. Toledo, Conv. Canon. arm. 31, no. 31.

456. Corcyra, Abp. Eustathius. 457. Corcyra, Abp. Eustathius.

458. Corcyra, Abp. Eustathius. 459. Corcyra, M. Eleutherius.

460. Corcyra, M. Eleutherius. 461. Corcyra, M. Eleutherius.

462. Corcyra, M. Arist. St. Varouccas.

463. Andover, Mass. U. S. A., Theol. Seminary 1 [xv or xiv], $8\frac{1}{4} \times 6$, ff. 194 (24), (26 (?) *chart.*), part palimpsest. Hoskier. (Greg. 180.)

464. Athos, Simopetra 148. (Greg. 479.)

†465. Moscow, Syn. 313 (ol. 300). (Greg. 242.)

†466. Petersburg, Caes. Muralt. 21 (69). (Greg. 243.)

†467. Petersburg, Caes. Mur. 35. (Greg. 244.)

†468. Petersburg, Caes. Mur. 36. (Greg. 245a.)

†469. Petersburg, Caes. Mur. 37. (Greg. 245b.)

470. Petersburg, Caes. Mur. 40. (Greg. 247.)

471. Petersburg, Caes. Mur. 43. (Greg. 248.)

472. Petersburg, Caes. Mur. 55. (Greg. 250.)

473. Petersburg, Caes. Mur. 69. (Greg. 252.)

474. Petersburg, Caes. Mur. 80. (Greg. 254.)

475. Petersburg, Caes. Mur. 84. (Greg. 255.)

476. Petersburg, Caes. Mur. 37a. (Greg. 257.)

477. Petersburg, Caes. Mur. 112. (Greg. 259.)

478. Venice, St. Mark ii. 17. (Greg. 273.)

479. Venice, St. Mark ii. 143. (Greg. 274.)

480. Milan, Ambr. E. 101 sup. (Greg. 286.)

481. Tubingen, Univ. 2. (Greg. 294.)

482. Bandur. *ev.* Formerly Montfaucon's. (Greg. 295.)

483. Cambridge, Mass. U.S.A., Harvard Univ. 1h (Dr. 69) [ix], $12\frac{1}{4} \times 8\frac{5}{8}$, ff. 6 (19), 2 cols. *See* Hoskier, MS. 604, App. ii. (Greg. 296.)

484. Camb. Mass. U. S. A., Harv. Univ. 2h [xii], $10\frac{3}{4} \times 8$, ff. 230 (23), 2 cols., *men.* (ff. 171–230), accompanied by an Apost. Hoskier. (Greg. 297.)

485. Camb. Mass. U. S. A., Harv. Univ. 3h (A. R. G. 1. 3) [xiii], $12\frac{1}{2} \times 9\frac{1}{2}$, ff. 202 (25), 2 cols., twelve leaves or parts of leaves later, *mut.*, *mus. rubr.*, *men.* Hoskier. (Greg. 298.)

486. Madison, New ~~Caesarea~~, Theol. Seminary, Drew MS. 2. (Greg. 301.)

487. Sewickley, Pennsylvania, Mr. R. A. Benton. (Greg. 302a.)

488. Cambridge, Clare College [xiv], $8\frac{1}{4} \times 6$, ff. 163 (21), *mut.* at end. Brought from Constantinople, and presented by Mr. J. Rendel Harris, Fellow of the College.

489. Sewickley, Pennsylvania, Mr. R. A. Benton. (Greg. 302b.)

490. Sewanee, Tennessee, Mr. A. A. Benton. (Greg. 302c.)

491. Princetown, New ~~Caesarea~~, Theol. Seminary. (Greg. 303.)

492. Woolwich (?), Mr. Ch. C. G. Bate. (Greg. 304.)

493. Sinaiticus (Λ. 1, *see* under Evan. Λ). (Greg. 312.)

494. Lond. Highgate, Burdett-Coutts II. 5. (Greg. 313.)

495. Lond. Highgate, B.-C. II. 14. (Greg. 314.)

†496. Lond. Brit. Mus. Add. 14,637 [vii], $11\frac{3}{8}\times 7\frac{1}{8}$, ff. 23, 2 cols., Unc., fragments. Palimpsest [x] in Syriac. (Greg. 316.)

†497. Lond. Brit. Mus. Add. 14,638 [viii, Greg. ix], $6\frac{1}{2}\times 4\frac{7}{8}$, ff. (26−8=) 18 (20). Fragments. Palimpsest under Syriac. (Greg. 317.)

498. (Apost. 288.) Jerus. Patr. Libr. 105 [A.D. 1762, May 11]. $12\frac{3}{4}\times 9$, ff. 228, *pict.*, *vers.* Written by Athanasius, ἱερεὺς Σαρασῖτος. (Kerameus.)

†499. London, Brit. Mus. Burney 408 [x], $8\times 6\frac{1}{2}$, ff. 163 (22), 2 cols. Palimpsest, hardly legible, Unc., latter part, as Greg. has discovered, in early minuscules. Bought in 1872. (Greg. 338.)

500. Wisbech, Peckover 70. (Greg. 345.)

501. Vindob. Caes. Gr. Theol. 160. (Greg. 347.)

502. Vindob. Archduke Rainer (1). (Greg. 348.)

503. Vindob. Archd. Rainer (2). (Greg. 349.)

504. Montpelier, School of Medicine H. 405. (Greg. 350.)

505. (Late Henri Bordier.) (Greg. 351.)

506. Paris, late Emman. Miller 4. (Greg. 352.)

†507. Paris, late Emman. Miller 5. (Greg. 353.)

†508. Paris, late Emman. Miller 6. (Greg. 354.)

†509. Paris, late Emman. Miller 7. (Greg. 355.)

510. Florence, Laurent. Gaddianus 124.

511. Flor. Riccardi 69, ff. 111.

†512. Paris, late Emman. Miller 8. (Greg. 356.)

†513. Paris, late Emman. Miller 9. (Greg. 357.)

†514. Paris, late Emman. Miller 10. (Greg. 358.)

†515. Paris, late Emman. Miller 11. (Greg. 359.)

†516. Paris, late Emman. Miller 12. (Greg. 360.)

†517. Par. Nat. Suppl. Gr. 1081. (Greg. 373.)

518. (Apost. 259.) Athens, Nat. Theol. 25 (163) [xii], $12\frac{3}{4}\times 9\frac{7}{8}$, ff. 327, *mut.* at beg. Beautiful and decorated, *mus. rubr.*, *pict.*, *vers.* (Greg. 383.)

519. Ath. Nat. Theol. 26 (164) [xii], $13\frac{3}{4}\times 10\frac{1}{4}$, ff. 291, *mus.* (Greg. 384.)

520. Ath. Nat. Theol. 27 (165) [xiv], $11\frac{3}{4}\times 9$, ff. 162, *mus.* (Greg. 385.)

521. Ath. Nat. Theol. 28 (166) [xiv], $12\frac{7}{8}\times 8\frac{5}{8}$, ff. 236, *mut.* at beg. *mus.* (Greg. 386.)

522. Ath. Nat. Theol. 29 (167) [xiv], $12\frac{1}{8}\times 9$, ff. 243, *mus.* (Greg. 387.)

523. Ath. Nat. Theol. 30 (168) [xv], $12\frac{1}{2}\times 8\frac{1}{4}$, ff. 217, presented to the Church of Christ τοῦ Μαντρί in A.D. 1527. (Greg. 388.)

524. Ath. Nat. Theol. 31 (169) [xiv], $12\frac{1}{2}\times 9$, ff. 212, *mus.* (Greg. 389.)

525. Messina, Univ. 175.

526. Pistoia, Fabronianus.

527. Rom. Angelicus D. ii. 27.

528. Athens, Nat. Theol. 32 (170) [xiv], $12\frac{1}{8} \times 8\frac{5}{8}$, ff. 144. (Greg. 390.)

529. Ath. Nat. Theol. 33 (171) [xvi], $12\frac{1}{2} \times 8\frac{5}{8}$, ff. 355. (Greg. 391.)

530. Ath. Nat. Theol. 34 (172) [xiv], $12\frac{1}{3} \times 9\frac{7}{8}$, ff. 212, *mut.* at beg. and end, *mus.* (Greg. 392.)

531. Ath. Nat. Theol. 35 (173) [xiv], $11\frac{3}{4} \times 9$, ff. 248, *mut.* at beg and end, *vers.*, written by one Michael. (Greg. 393.)

532. Ath. Nat. Theol. 36 (174) [xiv], $11\frac{3}{4} \times 9\frac{1}{2}$, ff. 305, *mut.* at end, *vers.* Very much ornamented; very beautiful and valuable. (Greg. 394.)

533. Rom. Barb. iv. 28.

534. Ath. Nat. Theol. 37 (175) [xiv], $11\frac{3}{4} \times 8\frac{5}{8}$, ff. 180—last 18 *chart.* (Greg. 395.)

535. Ath. Nat. 38 (176) [A. D. 1328], $11\frac{3}{4} \times 8\frac{1}{4}$, ff. 222. Written by Hilarion of Beroea. (Greg. 396.)

536. Ath. Nat. 39 ? (Greg. 397.)

537. Ath. Nat. 40 (177) [xiv], $11 \times 8\frac{1}{4}$, ff. 79, *mut.* at beg. Matt. and Luke. Palimpsest. Under-writing [viii]. Written by Joseph. (Greg. 398[a], [b].)

†538. Ath. Nat. 41 (178) [A. D. 1311], $11 \times 8\frac{1}{4}$, ff. 266. Written by Leon. (Greg. 399[a], [b].)

539. Rom. Vat. Gr. 350.

540. Athos, Dionysius 23. (Greg. 400.)

541. Athens, Nat. Theol. 42 (179) [A. D. 1311], $11 \times 8\frac{1}{4}$, ff. 266, *mus.* Written by Leon. (Greg. 401.)

542. Ath. Nat. Theol. 43 (180) [A. D. 1089], $10\frac{5}{8} \times 8\frac{1}{4}$, ff. 204, *mus.* Written by Andreas. (Greg. 402.)

543. Ath. Nat. Theol. 44 (181) [xiv], $9\frac{7}{8} \times 7\frac{1}{2}$, ff. 257, *mus.* (Greg. 403.)

544. Ath. Nat. Theol. 45 (182) [xii], 11×9, ff. 156, *mut.* at beg. and end, *mus.* (Greg. 404.)

545. Rom. Vallicell. C. 7.

546. Ath. Nat. Theol. 46 (183) [xiv], $10\frac{5}{8} \times 8\frac{5}{8}$, ff. 151. (Greg. 405.)

547. Rom. Vat. Gr. 1217.

548. (Apost. 229.) Rom. Vat. Gr. 1228.

549. Ath. Nat. Theol. 47 (184) [xv], $11\frac{3}{4} \times 8\frac{5}{8}$, ff. 242. (Greg. 406.)

550. Ath. Nat. Theol. 48 (185) [xii], $11 \times 8\frac{1}{4}$, ff. 260, *mus.* (Greg. 407.)

551. Rom. Vat. Gr. 1625.

552. Ath. Nat. Theol. 49 (186) [xii], $11\frac{3}{8} \times 9$, ff. 167, *mus.* (Greg. 408.)

553. Ath. Nat. Theol. 50 (187) [xii], $11\frac{3}{8} \times 8\frac{1}{4}$, ff. 270, *mut.* at beg., *mus.* Written by George. (Greg. 409.)

554. (Apost. 221.) Rom. Vat. Gr. 1973.

555. (Apost. 222.) Rom. Vat. Gr. 1978.

556. Ath. Nat. Theol. 51 (188) [xi], $8\frac{1}{4} \times 5\frac{7}{8}$, ff. 302, *mus.* (Greg. 410.)

557. (Apost. 224.) Rom. Vat. Gr. 2051.

558. (Apost. 225.) Rom. Vat. Gr. 2052.

559. Rom. Vat. Gr. 2061.

560. Ath. Nat. Theol. 52 (189) [xv], $8\frac{1}{4} \times 5\frac{7}{8}$, ff. 156, *mus.* (Greg. 411.)

561. Ath. Nat. Theol. 53 (190) [xii], $9\frac{7}{8} \times 8\frac{1}{4}$, ff. 255, *mus.* (Greg. 412.)

562. Rom. Vat. Gr. 2138.

563. Ath. Nat. Theol. 54 (191) [xii], $11\frac{3}{8} \times 9$, ff. 158, *mut.* at beg. and end, *mus.* (Greg. 413.)

564. Ath. Nat. Theol. 55 (192) [xv], $6\frac{3}{4} \times 5\frac{1}{8}$, ff. 239. Palimpsest, *mut.* at beg. and end. (Greg. 414.)

†565. Ath. Nat. Theol. 56 (193) [xv], $9 \times 6\frac{3}{4}$, ff. 215, much *chart.* The two last leaves are palimpsest [ix], Unc. (Greg. 415.)

566. Ath. Nat. Theol. 57 (194) [xv], $11 \times 8\frac{1}{4}$, ff. 395, *pict.* Note of date, about A. D. 1450, at end. (Greg. 416.)

567. Ath. Nat. Theol. 58 (195) [A. D. 1536], $10\frac{5}{8} \times 8\frac{1}{4}$, ff. 396, *chart.* Beautifully written by John. (Greg. 417.)

568. Ath. Nat. Theol. 59 (196) [xv], $10\frac{1}{4} \times 8\frac{1}{4}$, ff. 206, *chart.*, *mut.* at end. (Greg. 418.)

569. Ath. Nat. Theol. 60 (197) [xv], $7\frac{7}{8} \times 5\frac{7}{8}$, ff. 341, *chart.* (Greg. 419.)

570. Ath. Nat. Theol. 61 (198) [xv], $9 \times 6\frac{3}{4}$, ff. 342, *chart.* (Greg. 420.)

571. (Apost. 188.) Ath. Nat. Theol. 62 (199) [xiv], $9\frac{1}{2} \times 7\frac{1}{8}$, ff. 292, *mus.* (Greg. 421.)

572. (Apost. 189.) Ath. Nat. Theol. 63 (200) [xv], $11 \times 8\frac{1}{4}$, ff. 340, *mut.* at beg. and end, and in other places. Michael of Damascus was the diorthote, or possessor. (Greg. 422.)

573. (Apost. 190.) Ath. Nat. Theol. 64 (201) [A. D. 1732], $8\frac{1}{4} \times 5\frac{7}{8}$, ff. 32. Written by Nicephorus. (Greg. 423.)

574. Ath. Nat. Theol. 65 (202) [xii], $11\frac{3}{8} \times 8\frac{5}{8}$, ff. 68. Separate fragments (four, Greg.), *mus.* (Greg. 424.)

575. (Apost. 113.) Syracuse, Seminary 4.

576. Venice, St. Lazarus 1631.

577. Athos, Dionysius 378.

578. Edinburgh, Univ. Laing 9.

579. Athos, St. Andrew Γ'.

580. Athos, St. Andrew Δ'.

581. Athos, St. Andrew ς'.

582. Athos, St. Andrew Z.

583. Athos, Vatopedi 48.

584. Athos, Vatopedi 192.

585. Athos, Vatopedi 193.

586. Athos, Vatopedi 194.

587. Athos, Vatopedi 195.

588. Athos, Vatopedi 196.

589. Athos, Vatopedi 197.

590. Athos, Vatopedi 198.

591. Athos, Vatopedi 200.

592. Athos, Vatopedi 202.

593. Athos, Vatopedi 204.

594. Athos, Vatopedi 205.

595. Athos, Vatopedi 208.

596. Athos, Vatopedi 209.
597. Athos, Vatopedi 220.
598. Athos, Vatopedi 221.
599. Athos, Vatopedi 223.
600. Athos, Vatopedi 224.
601. Athos, Vatopedi (225).
602. Athos, Vatopedi (226).
603. Athos, Vatopedi (227).
604. Athos, Vatopedi 228.
605. Athos, Vatopedi 229.
606. Athos, Vatopedi 230.
607. Athos, Vatopedi 231.
608. Athos, Vatopedi 232.
609. Athos, Vatopedi 233.
610. Athos, Vatopedi 234.
611. Athos, Vatopedi 235.
612. Athos, Vatopedi 236.
613. Athos, Vatopedi 237.
614. Athos, Vatopedi 238.
615. Athos, Vatopedi 239.
616. Athos, Vatopedi 240.
617. Athos, Vatopedi 241.
618. Athos, Vatopedi 242.
619. Athos, Vatopedi 243.
620. Athos, Vatopedi 253.
621. Athos, Vatopedi 254.
622. Athos, Vatopedi 255.
623. Athos, Vatopedi 256.
624. Athos, Vatopedi 257.
625. Athos, Vatopedi 271.
626. Athos, Vatopedi 291.
627. Athos, Dionysius 1.
628. Athos, Dionysius 2.
629. Athos, Dionysius 3.
630. Athos, Dionysius 6.
631. Athos, Dionysius 11.
632. Athos, Dionysius 13.
633. Athos, Dionysius 14.
634. Athos, Dionysius 15.
635. Athos, Dionysius 16.
636. Athos, Dionysius 17.
637. Athos, Dionysius 18.
638. Athos, Dionysius 19.
639. Athos, Dionysius 20.
640. Athos, Dionysius 21.
641. Athos, Dionysius 85.
642. Athos, Dionysius 163.
643. Athos, Dionysius 302.
644. Athos, Dionysius 303.
645. Athos, Dionysius 304.
646. Athos, Dionysius 305.
647. Athos, Dionysius 306.
648. Athos, Dionysius 307.
649. Athos, Dionysius 308.
650. Athos, Dionysius 309.
651. Athos, Docheiariou 1.
652. Athos, Docheiariou 10.
653. Athos, Docheiariou 13.
654. Athos, Docheiariou 14.
655. Athos, Docheiariou 15.
656. Athos, Docheiariou 19.
657. Athos, Docheiariou 23.
658. Athos, Docheiariou 24.
659. Athos, Docheiariou 36.
660. Athos, Docheiariou 58.
661. Athos, Docheiariou 137.
662. Athos, Esphigmenou 19.
663. Athos, Esphigmenou 20.
664. Athos, Esphigmenou 21.
665. Athos, Esphigmenou 22.
666. Athos, Esphigmenou 23.
667. Athos, Esphigmenou 24.
668. Athos, Esphigmenou 27.
669. Athos, Esphigmenou 28.
670. Athos, Esphigmenou 35.
671. Athos, Esphigmenou 60.
672. Athos, Iveron 1.
673. Athos, Iveron 3.

674. Athos, Iveron 4.
675. Athos, Iveron 6.
676. Athos, Iveron 20.
677. Athos, Iveron 23.
678. Athos, Iveron 35.
679. Athos, Iveron 36.
680. (Apost. 229.) Athos, Iveron 39.
681. Athos, Iveron 635.
682. Athos, Iveron 637.
683. Athos, Iveron 638.
684. Athos, Iveron 639.
685. Athos, Iveron 640.
686. Athos, Iveron 825.
687. Athos, Iveron 826.
688. Athos, Caracalla 3.
689. Athos, Caracalla 11.
690. Athos, Caracalla 15.
691. Athos, Caracalla 16.
692. Athos, Caracalla 17.
693. Athos, Constamonitou 6.
694. Athos, Constamonitou 98.

695. Athos, Constamonitou 100 [xii], 2 cols., *men.* Omitted by Gregory, who has erroneously inserted the Evan. 99 instead (*see* Spyridon P. Lampros).

696. Athos, Coutloumoussi 60.
697. Athos, Coutloumoussi 61.
698. Athos, Coutloumoussi 62.
699. Athos, Coutloumoussi 63.
700. Athos, Coutloumoussi 64.
701. Athos, Coutloumoussi 65.
702. Athos, Coutloumoussi 66.
703. Athos, Coutloumoussi 86.
†704. Athos, Coutloumoussi 90.
705. Athos, Coutloumoussi 279.
706. Athos, Coutloumoussi 280.
707. (Apost. 233.) Athos, Coutloumoussi 282.
708. Athos, Coutloumoussi 292.
709. (Apost. 234.) Athos, Coutloumoussi 356.
710. Athos, Xenophon 1.
711. Athos, Xenophon 58.
712. Athos, Xenophon 59.
713. Athos, Xenophon 68. (Greg. 71.)
714. Athos, Xeropotamou 110.
715. Athos, Xeropotamou 112.
716. Athos, Xeropotamou 118.
717. Athos, Xeropotamou 122.
718. Athos, Xeropotamou 125.
719. Athos, Xeropotamou 126.
720. Athos, Xeropotamou 234.
721. Athos, Xeropotamou 247.
722. Athos, Panteleemon L.
723. Athos, Panteleemon IV. vi. 4.
724. Athos, Panteleemon IX. v. 3.
725. Athos, Panteleemon XXVII. vi. 2.
726. Athos, Panteleemon XXVII. vi. 3.
727. Athos, Panteleemon XXVIII. i. 1.
728. Athos, Paul 1.
729. Athos, Protaton 11.
730. Athos, Protaton 14.
731. Athos, Protaton 15.
732. Athos, Protaton 44.
733. Athos, Protaton 56.
734. Athos, Simopetra 17.
735. Athos, Simopetra 19.

736. Athos, Simopetra 20.
737. Athos, Simopetra 21.
738. Athos, Simopetra 24.
739. Athos, Simopetra 27.
740. Athos, Simopetra 28.
741. (Apost. 237.) Athos, Simopetra 30.
742. Athos, Simopetra 33.
743. (Apost. 238.) Athos, Simopetra 70.
744. Athos, Stauroniketa 1.
745. Athos, Stauroniketa 27.
746. Athos, Stauroniketa 42.
747. Athos, Stauroniketa 102.
748. Athos, Philotheou 1.
749. Athos, Philotheou 2.
750. Athos, Philotheou 3.
751. (Apost. 239.) Athos, Philotheou 6.
752. Athos, Philotheou 18.
753. Athos, Philotheou 25.
754. Athos, Philotheou 61.
755. (Apost. 240.) Athos, Philotheou 213.
756. Athos, Chiliandari 6.
757. Athos, Chiliandari 15.
758. Beratinus, in a Church.
759. Athens, Nat. Sakkelion 4. (Greg. 425.)
760. Cairo, Patr. Alex. 927.
761. Cairo, Patr. Alex. 929.
762. Cairo, Patr. Alex. 943.
763. Cairo, Patr. Alex. 944.
764. Cairo, Patr. Alex. 945.
765. Cairo, Patr. Alex. 946.
766. Cairo, Patr. Alex. 948.
767. Cairo, Patr. Alex. 950.
768. Cairo, Patr. Alex. 951.
769. Cairo, Patr. Alex. 953.
770. Chalcis, Mon. Trinity 1.
771. Chalcis, Mon. Trinity 2.
772. Chalcis, Mon. Trinity 3.
773. Chalcis, Mon. Trinity 4.
774. Chalcis, Mon. Trinity 5.
775. Chalcis, Mon. Trinity 6.
776. Chalcis, Mon. Trinity 7.
777. Chalcis, Mon. Trinity 8.
778. Chalcis, Mon. Trinity 9.
779. Chalcis, Mon. Trinity 10.
780. Chalcis, School 1.
781. Chalcis, School 2.
782. Chalcis, School 3.
783. Chalcis, School 4.
784. Chalcis, School 5.
785. Chalcis, School 6.
786. Chalcis, School 7.
787. Chalcis, School 12.
788. Chalcis, School 74 (75?).
789. Chalcis, School 84.
790. Constantinople, St. George's Church.
791. Constantinople, St. George's.
792. Constantinople, ἁγίου τάφου.
793. Constantinople, ἁγίου τάφου.
794. Constantinople, ἁγίου τάφου 426.
795. Constantinople, ἁγίου τάφου 432.
796. Constantinople, τ. ἑλληνικοῦ φιλολογικοῦ συλλόγου.
797. (Apost. 243.) Jerusalem, Coll. St. Cross 6.

798. Lesbos, *τ. Λείμωνος μονῆς* 1 [ix or x], $11\frac{3}{4} \times 9\frac{1}{2}$, ff. 79 (20), 2 cols., *περικοπαί* from the Evangelists John, Matt., Luke, Mark, *κατὰ παννύχια*, *men.* (Kerameus.)

799. Lesbos, *τ. Λείμωνος μονῆς* 37 [x–xi], $11\frac{3}{4} \times 9\frac{1}{4}$, ff. 288, 2 cols., *mus.* (Kerameus.)

800. Lesbos, *τ. Λείμ. μον.* 38 [xi], $11\frac{3}{4} \times 9\frac{1}{2}$, ff. 208, 2 cols., *mus.* (Kerameus.)

801. Lesbos, *τ. Λείμ. μον.* 40 [xiv], $12\frac{1}{8} \times 8\frac{1}{4}$, *chart.* (Kerameus.)

802. Lesbos, *τ. Λείμ. μον.* 41 [xii–xiii], $12\frac{1}{2} \times 9$, ff. 221, 2 cols., *orn.* (Kerameus.)

803. Lesbos, *τ. Λείμ. μον.* 66 [xii–xiii], $9\frac{5}{8} \times 6\frac{3}{4}$, ff. 428, the last *chart.* written on in A.D. 1558. *Mus.* (Kerameus.)

804. (Apost. 191.) Athens, Nat. 3 (685) [xv], $6\frac{3}{8} \times 4\frac{3}{4}$, ff. 187, *mut.* at beg. Apostoloeuaggelia for the Feasts of the whole year after Liturgical matter. (Greg. 426.)

805. Patmos 68.
806. Patmos 69.
807. Patmos 70.
808. Patmos 71.
809. Patmos 72.
810. Patmos 73.
811. Patmos 74.
812. Patmos 75.
813. Patmos 77.
814. Patmos 78.
815. Patmos 79.
816. Patmos 85.
817. Patmos 86.
818. Patmos 87.
819. Patmos 88.
820. Patmos 89.
821. Patmos 91.
822. Patmos 93.
823. Patmos 99.
824. Patmos 101.
825. Patmos 330.
826. Patmos 331.
827. Patmos 332.

828. (Apost. 192.) Athens, Nat. ϛ? (Greg. 427.)

829. Athens, Nat. 10? (Greg. 428.)

830. Thessalonica, Ἑλλην. γυμνασίου Α΄.

831. Thess. Ἑλλην. γυμνασίου Β΄.
832. Thess. Ἑλλην. γυμνασίου Γ΄.
833. Thess. Ἑλλην. γυμνασίου Δ΄.
834. Thess. Ἑλλην. γυμνασίου Ε΄.
835. Thess. Ἑλλην. γυμνασίου Ζ΄.
836. Thess. Ἑλλην. γυμνασίου Θ΄.
837. Thess. Ἑλλην. γυμνασίου ΙΔ΄.
838. Thess. Μ. Σπύριος.
839. Sinai 205.
840. Sinai 206.
841. Sinai 207.
842. Sinai 208.
843. Sinai 209.
†844. Sinai 210.
†845. Sinai 211.
846. Sinai 212.
†847. Sinai 213.
†848. Sinai 214.
†849. Sinai 215.
850. Sinai 216.

851. Sinai 217.
852. Sinai 218.
853. Sinai 219.
854. Sinai 220.
855. Sinai 221.
856. Sinai 222.
857. Sinai 223.
858. Sinai 224.
859. Sinai 225.
860. Sinai 226.
861. Sinai 227.
862. Sinai 228.
863. Sinai 229.
864. Sinai 230.
865. Sinai 231.
866. Sinai 232.
867. Sinai 233.
868. Sinai 234.
869. Sinai 235.
870. Sinai 236.
871. Sinai 237.
872. Sinai 238.
873. Sinai 239.
874. Sinai 240.
875. Sinai 241.
876. Sinai 242.
877. Sinai 243.
878. Sinai 244.
879. Sinai 245.
880. Sinai 246.
881. Sinai 247.
882. Sinai 248.
883. Sinai 249.
884. Sinai 250.
885. Sinai 251.
886. Sinai 252.
887. Sinai 253.
888. Sinai 254.
889. Sinai 255.
890. Sinai 256.
891. Sinai 257.
892. Sinai 258.
893. Sinai 271.
894. (Apost. 260.) Sinai 272.
895. (Apost. 261.) Sinai 273.
896. Sinai 550.
897. Sinai 659.
898. Sinai 720.
899. Sinai 738.
900. (Apost. 247.) Sinai 748.
901. Sinai 754.
902. Sinai 756.
903. Sinai 775.
904. Sinai 796.
905. Sinai 797.
906. Sinai 800.
907. Sinai 929.
908. (Apost. 248.) Sinai 943.
909. Sinai 957.
910. Sinai 960.
911. (Apost. 249.) Sinai 961.
912. Sinai 962.
913. Sinai 965.
914. Sinai 968.
915. (Apost. 258.) Sinai 972.
916. (Apost. 251.) Sinai 973.
917. (Apost. 252.) Sinai 977.
918. Sinai 981.
919. Sinai 982.
920. Sinai 986.
921. Sinai 1042.
922. Oxf. Bodl. Clarke 9. (*See* Act. 58.)

923. Jerusalem, Patriarchal Library 33 [end of x or beg. of xi], $10\frac{1}{2} \times 8\frac{1}{4}$, ff. 335 (221—252=32) [xiii], *mus. rubr.*, *syn.*, *orn.* (Papadopoulos Kerameus.)

924. (Apost. 253.) Rom. Vat. Reg. 54.

925. Venice, St. Mark 188.

926. Lond. Brit. Mus. Add. 10,068 [?], 9×7, ff. 124, 2 cols., palimpsest, illegible and will not repay investigation.

927. Jerus. Patr. Libr. 161 [xvii], $11\frac{1}{8} \times 8\frac{1}{8}$, *chart.*, collections of bits of Evst. (Kerameus.)

928. Jerus. Patr. Libr. 526 [A. D. 1502], $12\frac{3}{8} \times 8\frac{3}{8}$, ff. 108, 2 cols., *syn.*, with many directions. (Kerameus.)

929. New York, Seminary of Theol. Univ.

930. Lond. Brit. Mus. Add. 19,459 [xii, Greg. xiii], $11\frac{1}{2} \times 9\frac{1}{4}$, ff. 230 (24–8), 2 cols. (ff. 22 inserted later), *mus. rubr.*, *mut.* beg. and end, &c.

931. (Apost. 126.) Venice, St. Mark ii. 130.

932. Jerus. Patr. Libr. 530, *chart.*, Turkish in Greek letters. (Kerameus.)

933. Petersburg, Caes. Muralt. 64 (ix. 1).

934. St. Saba 55 [xii], 4to. Coxe.

935. Quaritch 8 [about A. D. 1200], ff. 346 (26), 2 cols., *mut.*, letters in red, green, blue, yellow, bound in red morocco case. (Catalogue, Dec. 1893.)

936. Lesb. τ. Λείμ. μον. 100. Ἀποστολοευαγγέλια in the midst of the four Liturgies and other matter. (Kerameus.)

937. Lesb. τ. Λείμ. μον. 146 [A. D. 1562–66], $7\frac{7}{8} \times 5\frac{3}{4}$. Begins with St. Matt. (Kerameus.)

938. Lesb. ἐν μονῇ Ἁγίου Ἰωάννου τοῦ Θεολόγου 11 [xii], $9\frac{1}{4} \times 7$, ff. 157 (2, 5, and 6 being chart., one is of the eleventh century). (Kerameus.)

939. Lesb. Ἁγ. Ἰωάνν. 12, $8\frac{7}{8} \times 7\frac{1}{8}$, ff. 110. (Kerameus.)

940. Lesb. Benjamin Library at Potamos ΑΛ [A. D. 1565], $12\frac{1}{8} \times 8\frac{1}{4}$, ff. 378. (Kerameus.)

941. Athos, Constamonitou 98 [xiv], 2 cols., *mus.*, *men.* (Sp. P. Lampros.)

942. Athos, Constam. 100.

†943. Athens, Nat. Libr. 60 [ix], $13\frac{3}{8} \times 5\frac{7}{8}$?, ff. 87, Unc., *mus.*

944. Ath. Nat. Libr. 78 [x], $13\frac{3}{4} \times 10\frac{1}{4}$, ff. 143. Palimpsest under fifteenth century writing. *Mus.*

945. Ath. Nat. Libr. 83 [xv], $11 \times 7\frac{7}{8}$, ff. 324, *chart.*, *mut.* at end.

946. Ath. Nat. Libr. 97 [xii], $12\frac{1}{2} \times 8\frac{5}{8}$, ff. 136, *mut.* at beg. and end, *mus.*

947. (Apost. 227.) Ath. Nat. Libr. 126 [A. D. 1504], $8\frac{1}{4} \times 5\frac{7}{8}$, ff. 276, written by Euthymius.

948. Ath. Nat. Libr. 143 [A. D. 1522], $7\frac{1}{2} \times 5\frac{7}{8}$, ff. 242. A few leaves wanting at beginning.

949. Ath. Nat. Libr. 147 [xii beg.], $9\frac{7}{8} \times 6\frac{3}{4}$, ff. 255—first eight injured. *Mus.*

950. Ath. Nat. Libr. 148 [xv end], $7\frac{1}{2} \times 5\frac{7}{8}$, ff. 104, *mut.* at beg. and end.

The following thirteen MSS. in the National Library at Athens contain portions of Apostoloeuaggelia:—

951. (Apost. 277.) 668, $7\frac{1}{2} \times 5\frac{1}{2}$, ff. 282.

952. (Apost. 278.) 685, $5\frac{7}{8} \times 4\frac{3}{4}$, ff. 187.

953. (Apost. 279.) 700, $5\frac{7}{8} \times 4$, ff. 326.

954. (Apost. 280.) 707, $6\frac{1}{4} \times 4\frac{3}{4}$, ff. 131.

955. (Apost. 281.) 750, $8\frac{5}{8} \times 6\frac{1}{4}$, ff. 117.

956. (Apost. 282.) 757, $8\frac{1}{4} \times 5\frac{1}{2}$, ff. 120.

957. (Apost. 283.) 759, $8\frac{1}{4} \times 6\frac{1}{4}$, ff. 129.

958. (Apost. 284.) 760, $7\frac{7}{8} \times 5\frac{1}{2}$, ff. 262.

959. (Apost. 285.) 766, $8\frac{1}{4} \times 5\frac{7}{8}$, ff. 134.

960. (Apost. 286.) 769, $5\frac{1}{2} \times 4$, ff. 175.

961. (Apost. 287.) 784, $5\frac{7}{8} \times 4\frac{3}{8}$, ff. 36.

962. (Apost. 288.) 786, $5\frac{1}{8} \times 4$, ff. 48.

963. (Apost. 289.) 795, $7\frac{1}{2} \times 5\frac{1}{2}$, ff. 495[1].

[1] †Evan. T^d and T^e and Λ (1) should also properly be classed as Lectionaries. Apost. 15, and perhaps Apost. 24, also contains Lessons from the Gospels. The two copies of the Gospels, Lowes formerly Askew, membr. 4to, mentioned by Scholz (N. T., vol. i. p. cxix), and stated by Marsh on Michaelis, vol. ii. p. 662, to have been bought at Askew's sale by Mr. Lowes, the bookseller, are shown by the sale catalogue to have Evangelistaria. They have not yet been traced. (Ed. 3.)

CHAPTER XIV.

LECTIONARIES CONTAINING THE APOSTOLOS OR PRAXAPOSTOLOS.

*†1. (Evst. 6.)

2. Lond. Brit. Mus. Cotton. Vesp. B. xviii [xi], 11 × 8¼, ff. 230 (16), 2 cols., *mus. rubr.*, *mut.* initio et fine (Casley)[1]. In a fine bold hand. The Museum Catalogue is wrong in stating that it contains Lessons from the Gospels. They exactly correspond with those in our list, five of the Saints' Day Lessons being from the Catholic Epistles.

3. Readings sent to Mill (N. T., Proleg. § 1470) by John Batteley, D.D., as taken from a codex, now missing, in Trinity Hall, Cambridge. The extracts were from 1 Peter and John. Griesbach's Paul. 3 is Bodl. 5 (Evst. 19), cited by Mill only at Hebr. x. 22, 23.

4. (Evst. 112.)

*5. Gottingen, Univ. MS. Theol. 54 [xv], 10¾ × 7⅞, ff. 50 (28), 2 cols., formerly of the monastery Constamonitou on Athos, afterwards De Missy's (Matthaei's v). (Paul. 5 of Griesbach = Evst. 30.)

6. (Evan. 117, ff. 183–202.)

7. (Evst. 37.)

8. (Evst. 44.)

9. (Evst. 84.)

10. (Evst. 85.)

11. Par. Nat. Suppl. Gr. 104 [xii, Greg. xiii], 9¾ × 7½, ff. 139 (24), well written in some monastery of Palestine: with marginal notes in Arabic.

*12. (Evst. 60.)

*13. Moscow, Synod. 4 (Mt. b) [x], fol., ff. 313, 2 cols., important: once belonged to the Iveron monastery; renovated by Joakim, a monk, A. D. 1525. Cited by Tregelles as Frag. Mosq.

*14. Mosc. Synod. 291 (Mt. e) [xii], 4to, ff. 276, well written, from the monastery Esphigmenou on Athos.

*15. Mosc. Typogr. Syn. 31 (Mt. tz) [A. D. 1116], fol., ff. 200, a few Lections from 1 John at the end of Lections from Old Testament.

*16. (Evst. 52.)

*17. (Evst. 53.)

*18. (Evst. 54.)

*19. (Evst. 55.)

*20. (Evst. 56.)

[1] In 1721. *See* Monk's 'Life of Bentley,' vol. ii. p. 149. This is Bentley's O, John Walker's collation of which is preserved at Trin. Coll. (B. xvii. 34). Ellis, Bentleii Critica Sacra, Introd. pp. xxix, xxx.

Apost. 21–48 comprise Scholz's additions to the list, of which he describes none as collated entire or in the greater part. He seems, however, to have collated Cod. 12 entire.

21. (Evst. 83.)

22. Par. Nat. Gr. 304 [xiii, Greg. xiv], $13\frac{5}{8} \times 10\frac{3}{4}$, ff. 302 (22), 2 cols., brought from Constantinople: *mut.* in fine.

23. Par. Nat. Gr. 306 [xii], $13 \times 10\frac{1}{8}$, ff. 187 (28), 2 cols., *mut.* initio et fine.

24. Par. Nat. Gr. 308 [xiii], ff. 201, *mut.*, contains six Lections from 1 John and 1 Pet., more from the Old Testament.

25. Par. Nat. Gr. 319 [xi, Greg. xii], $12\frac{1}{4} \times 8\frac{1}{2}$, ff. 274 (22), ill written, with a Latin version over some portions of the text. Once Colbert's.

26. Par. Nat. Gr. 320 [xii], $9\frac{1}{8} \times 7\frac{3}{4}$, ff. 208 (21), 2 cols., *mus. rubr.*, *mut.*

27. Par. Nat. Gr. 321, once Colbert's [xiii, Greg. xiv], $11\frac{3}{8} \times 8$, ff. 237 (23), *mut.*, and illegible in parts.

28. (Evst. 26.)

29. (Evst. 94.)

30. Par. Nat. Gr. 373 [xiii, Greg. xiv], $8\frac{3}{8} \times 6\frac{3}{4}$, ff. 118 (21), *mut.* initio et fine: with some cotton-paper leaves at the end.

31. (Evst. 82.)

32. (Evan. 324, Evst. 97.)

33. Par. Nat. Gr. 382 [xiii, Greg. x], $9\frac{1}{2} \times 7\frac{1}{8}$, 271 (22), 2 cols., *mus. rubr.* Once Colbert's.

34. Par. Nat. Gr. 383, once Colbert's [xv, Greg. xvi], $8\frac{3}{8} \times 5\frac{1}{4}$, ff. 206 (31), *chart.* In readings it is much with Apost. 12.

35. (Evst. 92.)

36. (Evst. 93.)

37. Ath. Nat. Libr. 103 [xv], $9 \times 6\frac{1}{4}$, ff. 199.

38. Rom. Vat. Gr. 1528 [xv], $8\frac{1}{4} \times 6$, ff. 235 (26), *chart.*, written by the monk Eucholius.

39. (Evst. 133.)

40. Rom. Barberini 18 [x], 4to, a palimpsest (probably uncial, though not so stated by Scholz), correctly written, but mostly become illegible. The later writing [xiv] contains Lessons from the Old Testament, with a few from the Catholic Epistles at the end.

41. Rom. Barb., unnumbered [xi], 4to, *mut.* ff. 1–114.

42. Rom. Vallicell. C. 46 [xvi], $8\frac{1}{2} \times 6\frac{1}{4}$, ff. 115 (24), *chart.*, with other matter.

†43. (Evan. 561.) The palimpsest [viii or ix], written over the Gospels and table of Lessons, and containing Rom. xv. 30–33; 1 Cor. iv. 9–13; xv. 42–5; 2 Cor. ix. 6, 7.

44. (Evst. 232.)

45. Glasgow, Hunt. Mus. V. 3. 4 [A. D. 1199], $11 \times 7\frac{7}{8}$, ff. 239 (22), 2 cols., *mus. rubr.* Written by order of Luke of Antioch. Belonged to Caesar de Missy.

46. Milan, Ambr. C. 63 sup. [xiv], $9\frac{1}{4} \times 5\frac{3}{8}$, ff. 153 (27), *mut.*, bought (like Evst. 103) in 1606, 'Corneliani in Iapygiâ.'

47. (Evst. 104.) 48. (Evst. 222.)[1] (Greg. 59.)

49. Rom. Vat. Gr. 2068 [xi], $9\frac{3}{4} \times 7\frac{1}{2}$, ff. 232 (24), 2 cols., *pict.*, *mut.* at end, formerly Basil 107, described with a facsimile by Bianchini, Evan. Quadr., vol. ii. pt. 1, p. 523 and Plate iv: ἐκλογάδιον τοῦ ἀποστόλου. (Greg. 120.) 505

50. Modena, Este Libr. ii. D. 3 [xv], $11\frac{3}{8} \times 7\frac{7}{8}$, *chart.*, seen by Burgon. (Greg. 89.)

51. Besançon, Public Libr. 41 [xii], $9\frac{1}{8} \times 6\frac{3}{4}$, ff. 141 (21), 2 cols. (M. Castan: *see* Evst. 193). (Greg. 86.)

52. Lond. Brit. Mus. 32,051 [xi, xii, Greg. xiii], $10\frac{1}{2} \times 7\frac{3}{4}$, ff. 192 (29), 2 cols., *mut.* at end, *mus. rubr.*, got from Heraclea by Archd. Payne for the Duke of Marlborough, A. D. 1738. Formerly Blenheim 3. C. 12. (Greg. 65.)

53. (Evst. 258.) (Greg. 186.) 54. (Evst. 195.) (Greg. 73.)

*55. (Evst. 179.) (Greg. 55.)

*56. (Act. 42, Evst. 287) contains only I Cor. ix. 2–12. (Greg. 56.)

57. Lond. Lamb. 1190 [xiii, Greg. xi], 10×7, ff. 130 (25), 2 cols., neatly written, with many letters gilded, *mut.* at the beginning and end, and uninjured. Archdeacon Todd in the Lambeth Catalogue, p. 50, mistakes this for a copy of the Acts and all the Epistles. Bloomfield examined Apost. 57, 59–62. (Greg. 60.)

58. Oxf., Ch. Ch. Wake 33 [A. D. 1172], $11 \times 8\frac{1}{4}$, ff. 266, *mus.*, *men.*, the ink having quite gone in parts. (Greg. 58.)

59. Lambeth 1191 [xiii], $8 \times 6\frac{1}{2}$, ff. 75 (19), much injured, *mut.* at the beginning and end. (Greg. 61.)

60. Lamb. 1194 [xiii], $8\frac{5}{8} \times 7\frac{5}{8}$, ff. 109 (17), *chart.*, *mut.* at the end, the writing very neat, the letters often gilded. (Greg. 62.)

61. Lamb. 1195 [xiii, Greg. xv], $10\frac{3}{8} \times 7\frac{1}{4}$, ff. 75 (17), *chart.*, *mut.* at the beginning. (Greg. 63.)

62. Lamb. 1196 [xiii, Greg. xii], $10\frac{3}{4} \times 8$, ff. 219 (23), 2 cols., *mut.* at the end. (Greg. 64.)

63. Instead of this, which is Act. 315 (Greg.)—

Oxford, Lincoln Coll. 4 [xii], 8×6, ff. 107 (?), *mus. rubr.*, *mut.* beginning and end.

*64. B.-C. I. 10 (Evst. 251). (Greg. 66.)

*65. B.-C. III. 24 [xii or xiii], 4to. (Greg. 68.)

*66. B.-C. III. 29 (Evst. 252). (Greg. 67.)

*67. B.-C. III. 42 (Evst. 253). (Greg. 184.)

[1] As in our preceding lists, we remove to this foot-note Scholz's six copies seen at St. Saba, and occupy their numbers by other manuscripts. They are Apost. 49. St. Saba 16 [xiv], 4to, *chart.* 50. St. Saba 18 [xv], 8vo. 51. St. Saba 26 [xiv], fol. 52. (Evst. 171.) 53. (Evst. 160.) 54. St. Saba (unnumbered) [xiii], 4to.

*68. B.-C. III. 53 (Evst. 253[2]). (Greg. 263.)

69. Brit. Mus. Add. 29,714 [A. D. 1306], 10¾ × 8½, ff. 178 (28), written by one Ignatius; *syn.*, was bought of Nicolas Parassoh in 1874. (Greg. 81.)

70. Bentley's Q=Apost. 52. (*See* Ellis, Bentleii Crit. Sacr. xxx; Berriman, Crit. Dissertation on 1 Tim. iii. 16, p. 105.) Instead—

Cambridge, Mass. U.S.A., Harvard Univ. 2 (A. R. g. 3. 10) [xii], 11½ × 8½, ff. 281 (23), 2 cols., *orn.* (f. 202 *mut.*), *men.*, apparently by the same hand as Evst. 484, but more beautiful. Hoskier, App. H, pp. 3, 4. (Greg. 75.)

*†71. Leipzig, Univ. Libr. Tisch. vi. f. [ix or x], 9¾ × 7, Unc., f. 1 (24), 2 cols., containing Heb. i. 3–12, published in 'Anecd. sacr. et profan.,' p. 73, &c. (Greg. 80.)

*†72. Petrop. Caes. Muralt. 38, 49 [ix], 8vo, one leaf of a double palimpsest, now at St. Petersburg, the oldest writing containing Acts xiii. 10; 2 Cor. xi. 21–23, cited by Tischendorf (N. T., Proleg., p. ccxxvi, 7th edition). (Greg. 70.)

†73. (Evst. 192.) (Greg. 180.)

†74. Oxf. Bodl. Arch. Seld. 9 supr., palimpsest, containing under the Christmas sermons of Proclus, Patriarch of Constantinople, almost illegible Lessons from the Septuagint, with one or two from the Epistles of SS. Peter and John. (Greg. 84.)

75. Lond. Brit. Mus. Add. 11,841 [xii or xiii, Greg. xi], 8 × 5½, ff. 86 (22), 2 cols., *mut.* Amidst Old Test. Lections are (1) ff. 52–54, 1 John iii. 21–24, 26; iv. 9–19; 20–25; v; (2) f. 78 (which should precede f. 74) is a Lesson for June 28 ($\overline{\kappa\eta}$) *τῶν ἁγίων ἀποστόλων πέτρου καὶ παύλου, ἀνάγνωσμα γ*, containing 1 Pet. i. 3–19; ii. 11–24 (*ζήσομεν*). (Greg. 79.)

76. Oxf. Bodl. Misc. Gr. 319 [xiii], 11 × 8, ff. 14 (22), 2 cols., *mus. rubr.*, four leaves being biblical, written by Symeon a reader, *ἁγιοσυμεωνιτης*: the date, if once extant in the red letters of the colophon, being now rubbed away. There are nine *ἀναγνώσματα*. The book is either a Euchology or a Typicum, more probably the former. The first Lesson is 2 Tim. iii. 2–9. The remainder are numbered as Lessons for the *δεκαήμερον*, or Twelve days from Christmas to Epiphany: they run thus, *α´* Rom. v. 18–21: *β´* viii. 3–9: *γ´* ix. 29–33: *δ´* 2 Cor. v. 15–21: *ε´* Gal. iii. 28—iv. 5: *ϛ´* Col. i. 18–22: *ζ´* Phil. iii. 3–9: *η´* Rom. viii. 8–14. Found in a drawer by Mr. E. B. Nicholson, Bodley's Librarian. (Greg. 83.)

77. (Act. 98, portions marked as a_1 and a_3.) (Greg. 82.)

78. (Evst. 290.) Lond. B.-C. III. 44 [xiv], 4to, *chart.*, of 339 surviving leaves, is a *Typicum* in two separate hands, and contains twenty-nine Lessons: viz. eleven from the Old Testament, six from the Apocrypha, two from the Gospels (Matt. xi. 27–30; Mark viii. 34—ix. 1), ten from St. Paul's Epistles. (Greg. 78.)

79. Camb. Univ. Libr. Add. 679. 2 [xii or xiii], 10 × 8¼, ff. 102 (18), being the companion volume to Evst. 291, contains week-day Epistles

from St. Paul. The first quire is in a different hand. *Mut.* six leaves. Ends sixth day of thirty-third week (2 Thess. ii. 1). (Greg. 77.)

80. (Evst. 292.) (Greg. 183.)

81. =Apost. 52. Instead—
Milan, Ambros. C. 16 inf. [xiii], 9 × 7¼, ff. 29 (34), 2 cols. (Greg. 112.)

Scholz says of Evst. 161, and to the same effect Coxe of Evst. Cairo 18, 'continet lect. et pericop.;' which may possibly mean that these copies should be reckoned for the Apostolos also.

82. Messina, Univ. 93 [xii or xiii], 9⅞ × 7¾, ff. 331 (22), 2 cols., perfect. (*See* Greg. 113.)

83. Crypta Ferrata, A. β. 4 [x], 5⅞ × 4¾, ff. 139 (19), *mut.*, Praxapostolos. (*See* Greg. 103.)

84. Crypta Ferrata, A. β. 5 [xi], 7½ × 6¼, ff. 245 (20), 2 cols., *mus. rubr.*, a most beautiful codex. (*See* Greg. 104.)

85. Crypta Ferrata, A. β. 7 [xi], 5⅞ × 4¾, ff. 64 (27), *mut.*, Praxapostolos. (*See* Greg. 105.)

86. Crypta Ferrata, A. β. 8 [xii or xiii, Greg. xiv], 6¼ × 4¾, ff. 27 (16), carelessly written, and injured by damp, fragments, Praxapostolos. (*See* Greg. 106.)

87. Crypta Ferrata, A. β. 9 [xii], 5⅞ × 4¼, ff. 104 (22), Praxapostolos. (*See* Greg. 107.)

88. Crypta Ferrata, A. β. 10 [xiii], 6¼ × 5⅛, ff. 16 (22), *mut.*, fragmentary, with unusual Saints' days. (*See* Greg. 108.)

89. Crypta Ferrata, A. β. 11 [xi], 11⅜ × 8⅝, ff. 191 (25), 2 cols., *mus. rubr.*, *mut.* (*See* Greg. 109.)

90. (Evst. 322.) Crypta Ferrata. (Greg. 102.)

91. (Evst. 323.) Crypta Ferrata. (Greg. 197.)

92. (Evst. 325.) Crypta Ferrata. (Greg. 198.)

93. (Evst. 327.) Crypta Ferrata. (Greg. 172.)

94. (Evst. 328.) Crypta Ferrata. (Greg. 173.)

95. (Evst. 334.) Crypta Ferrata. (Greg. 201.)

96. (Evst. 337.) Crypta Ferrata. (Greg. 200.)

97. (Evst. 339.) Crypta Ferrata. (Greg. 201.)

98. Venice, St. Mark ii. 115 [xi or xii], 12½ × 9¼, ff. 277 (21–23), 2 cols., *mus. rubr.* (*See* Greg. 124.)

99. (Evst. 341.) Crypta Ferrata. (Greg. 202.)

100. (Evst. 344.) Crypta Ferrata. (Greg. 203.)

101. (Evst. 346.) Crypta Ferrata. (Greg. 204.)

102. (Evst. 347.) Crypta Ferrata. (Greg. 205.)

103. (Evst. 349.) Crypta Ferrata. (Greg. 206.)

104. (Evst. 350.) Crypta Ferrata. (Greg. 207.)

105. (Evst. 351.) Crypta Ferrata. (Greg. 169.)

106. (Evst. 352.) Crypta Ferrata. (Greg. 208.)

107. (Evst. 353.) Crypta Ferrata. (Greg. 209.)

108. (Evst. 354.) Crypta Ferrata. (Greg. 210.)

109. (Evst. 356.) Crypta Ferrata. (Greg. 211.)

110. (Evst. 357.) Crypta Ferrata. (Greg. 212.)

111. (Evst. 358.) Crypta Ferrata. (Greg. 213.)

112. (Evst. 312.) Messina, fragm. (Greg. 214.)

113. (Evst. 575.) Syracuse, Seminario 4, *chart.*, ff. 219, *mut.*, given by the Card. Landolina. (Greg. 228.)

114. Venice, St. Mark ii. 128 [xiv], $8\frac{1}{2} \times 6$, ff. 361 (19), *mut.* (*See* Greg. 125.)

115. (Evst. 931.) Ven. St. Mark ii. 130. (Greg. 126.)

116. Rom. Vat. Gr. 368 [xiii], $10 \times 7\frac{3}{4}$, ff. 136 (26), 2 cols., Old Test. Lections at end. (Greg. 118.)

117. (Evst. 381) Vat. (Greg. 264.)

118. (Evst. 387) Vat. (Greg. 223.)

119. Rom. Vat. Gr. 2116 [xiii], $7\frac{1}{2} \times 5\frac{1}{4}$, ff. 111 (21), *mut.* (*See* Greg. 121.)

120. Rom. Vat. Alex. Gr. 11 [xiv, Greg. xii], $11 \times 7\frac{7}{8}$, ff. 169 (24), *mut.* (Greg. 123.)

121. (Evst. 395.) Rom. Vat. Alex. 59. (Greg. 227.)

122. Rom. Vat. Alex. Gr. 70 [A.D. 1544], $7\frac{7}{8} \times 5\frac{1}{4}$, ff. 18, 'in fronte pronunciatio Graeca Latinis literis descripta.' (Greg. 255.)

123. Rom. Vat. Pal. 241 [xv], $8\frac{5}{8} \times 7\frac{3}{4}$, ff. 149 (21), *chart.* (Greg. 122.)

124. (Evst. 410.) Rom. Barb. (Greg. 216.)

125. Rom. Barb. iv. 11 [A.D. 1566], $8\frac{3}{4} \times 6\frac{1}{4}$, ff. 158 (19), *chart.*, *mut.* (Greg. 114.)

126. Rom. Barb. iv. 60 [xi, Greg. xii], $9\frac{7}{8} \times 7\frac{3}{4}$, ff. 322 (22), *mus. rubr.*, a fine codex with *menologium.* (Greg. 115.)

127. Rom. Barb. iv. 84 [xiii, Greg. xii], $11 \times 7\frac{3}{4}$, ff. 189 (24), 2 cols., with *men.*, *mut.* (Greg. 116.)

128. (Evst. 415.) Martin. (Greg. 256.)

129. (Evst. 96.) Martin. (Greg. 262.)

130. Par. Nat Suppl. Gr. 800 [xiv], $8\frac{5}{8} \times 5\frac{7}{8}$, ff. 115 (23), *chart.*, *mut.* at end. Martin, p. 174. (Greg. 88.)

131. Athos, Docheiariou 20.

132. Athos, Docheiariou 27.

133. Athos, Docheiariou 141.

134. Athos, Docheiariou 146.

135. Athos, Iveron 831.

136. Athos, Caracalla 10.

137. Athos, Caracalla 156.

138. Athos, Constamonitou 21 [xvii], 8vo, *chart.*, *mut.*
139. Athos, Constamonitou 22 [xiv], 8vo, cotton.
140. Athos, Constamonitou 23 [xv], 8vo, *chart.* (Σπ. Λαμπρός.)
141. Athos, Coutloumoussi 277. 142. Athos, Coutloumoussi 344.
143. Athos, Coutloumoussi 355. 144. Athos, Protaton 54.
145. Athos, Simopetra 6. 146. Athos, Simopetra 10.
147. (Evst. 479.) Athos, Simopetra 148.
148. Athos, Simopetra 149. 149. Athos, Simopetra 150.
150. Athos, Simopetra 151. 151. Athos, Stauroniketa 129.
152. Athos, Philotheou 17. 153. Beratinus, Abp.
154. Chalcis, Mon. Holy Trinity 13.
155. Chalcis, Mon. Holy Trin. 14.
156. Chalcis, Mon. Holy Trin. 15.
157. Chalcis, School 59. 158. Chalcis, School 74.
159. Chalcis, School 88. 160. Patmos 11.
161. Patmos 12. 162. Thessalonica, Ἑλλην. Γυμν. 8.
163. Thess. Ἑλλην. Γυμν. 10. 164. Thess. Ἑλλην. Γυμν. 13.
165. Sinai 296. 166. Sinai 297.
167. Sinai 298. 168. Sinai 299.
169. Athos, Dionysius 386. (Greg. 127.)
170. (Evst. 642.)
171. Petersburg, Caes. Muralt. 38. (Greg. 70[a].)
172. Petersburg, Caes. Muralt. 49. (Greg. 70[b].)
173. Petersburg, Caes. Muralt. 40[a]. (Greg. 71.)
174. Sinai 294. 175. (Evst. 261.)
176. (Evst. 240.) 177. (Evst. 232.)
178. (Evst. 191.) (Greg. twice, 69 and 178.)
179. (Evst. 472.)
180. Athos, Dionysius 387. (Greg. 128.)
181. (Evst. 166.) 182. (Evst. 169.)
183. Petersburg, Caes. Muralt. 45[a]. (Greg. 72.)
184. Athos, Dionysius 392. (Greg. 129.)
185. (Evst. 275.) 186. Docheiariou 17. (Greg. 130.)
187. (Evst. 420.) 188. (Evst. 571.)
189. (Evst. 572.) 190. (Evst. 573.)
191. (Evst. 804.) 192. (Evst. 828.)
193. (Evst. 439.) 194. (Evst. 440.)
195. (Evst. 443.) 196. (Evst. 446.)
197. Petersburg, Caes. Mur. 110. (Greg. 74.)

198. New York, Astor's Library. (Greg. 76.)
199. (Evst. 290.)
200. Vienna, Caes. Gr. Theol. 308. (Greg. 85.)
201. Par. Nat. Gr. 922, fol. A. (Greg. 87[a].)
202. Par. Nat. Suppl. Gr. 804, ff. 88 and 89. (Greg. 87[b].)
+203. Wisbech, Peckover, Unc., palimpsest. (Greg. 90.)
204. Athens, Nat. 68 (203) [xiii], $10\frac{5}{8} \times 8\frac{5}{8}$, ff. 218, *mus.* (Greg. 91.)
205. Athens, Nat. 69 (206), [xv], $8\frac{5}{8} \times 5\frac{7}{8}$, ff. 347, *mut.* (Greg. 92.)
206. (Evst. 393.) Athens, Nat. (35)? (Greg. 93.)
207. (Evst. 422.) Athens, Nat. (63). (Greg. 94).
208. (Evst. 423.) Athens, Nat. (64) *sic.* (Greg. 95.)
209. Ath. Nat. 95 (115) [A. D. 1576], $8\frac{1}{2} \times 5\frac{7}{8}$, ff. 192, *mut.* at beg. (Greg. 96.)
210. Athens, Nat.? (Greg. 97?)
211. Athens, Nat.? (116?) [xv], $8\frac{5}{8} \times 5\frac{7}{8}$, ff. 141. (Greg. 98.)
212. Athens, Nat.? (114) [xvii], $8\frac{1}{4} \times 6\frac{1}{4}$, ff. 190. (Greg. 99.)
213. Sinai 295. (Greg. 117.)
214. Escurial X. iv. 9. (Greg. 100.)
215. (Evst. 410.)
216. Escurial Ψ. iii. 9. (Greg. 101.)
217. (Evst. 408.)
218. (Evst. 407.)
219. (Evst. 533.)
220. (Evst. 548.)
221. (Evst. 554.)
222. (Evst. 555.)
223. Florence, Laurent. St. Mark 704. (Greg. 111.)
224. (Evst. 557.)
225. (Evst. 558.)
226. (Evst. 572.)
227. Lesbos, τ. Λείμωνος μονῆς 55, Act., Paul., Cath., Apoc., *syn.*, *men.*, *proll.*, *mus. rubr.* (Kerameus.)
228. Lesb. τ. Λείμ. μον. 137 [xv], $8\frac{1}{8} \times 4\frac{7}{8}$, *chart.* (Kerameus.)
229. (Evst. 680.)
230. (Evst. 686.)
231. (Evst. 687.)
232. (Evst. 693.)
233. (Evst. 707.)
234. (Evst. 709.)
235. (Evst. 712.)
236. (Evst. 721.)
237. (Evst. 741.)
238. (Evst. 743.)
239. (Evst. 751.)
240. (Evst. 755.)
241. (Evst. 757.)
242. (Evst. 759.)
243. (Evst. 797.)
244. (Evst. 829.)
245. (Evst. 837.)
246. (Evst. 893.)
247. (Evst. 900.)
248. (Evst. 908.)
249. (Evst. 911.)
250. (Evst. 915.)

251. (Evst. 916.) 252. (Evst. 917.)

253. (Evst. 924.) 254. (Evst. 929.)

255. Andros, Μονὴ 'Αγία 2, ff. 140. Injured, but well written. ('Αντ. Μηλιαράκης.)

256. Andros, Μονὴ 'Αγία 3, *chart.*, moth-eaten. ('Αντώνιος Μηλιαράκης.)

257. (Evst. 428.) 258. (Evst. 272.)

259. (Evst. 518.) 260. (Evst. 894.)

261. (Evst. 895.)

262. Athos, Protaton 32, 4to, amidst other matter, *κεφ. t.*, *syn.*, *men.* (Σπ. Λαμπρός.)

263. Crypta Ferrata, Α'. δ'. 24. (Greg. 110.)

264. (Evst. 952.) 265. (Evst. 30.)

266. Athos, Gregory 60 [xvi], 16mo, *chart.*, *mut.*

267. Kosinitsa, 'Αγία Μονή, 'Ιωάννης ὁ Περευτέσης (?) 198 [A. D. 1503], written by the aforenamed.

268. Kos. 'Αγ. Μον., Νίκολλος 55 [xi], written by the aforenamed.

269. Kos. 'Αγ. Μον., Συμέων Λουτζέρες 195 [A. D. 1505], written by the aforenamed.

270. Ath. Nat. Libr. 101 [xiv], $9 \times 7\frac{1}{8}$, ff. 169, *mut.* at beginning and end.

271. Ath. Nat. Libr. 102 [xvii], $8\frac{5}{8} \times 6\frac{1}{4}$, ff. 229.

272. Ath. Nat. Libr. 106 [xiv–xv], $9\frac{1}{2} \times 7\frac{1}{8}$, ff. 243, *mut.* at beginning and end.

273. Ath. Nat. Libr. 133 [xiv], $8\frac{5}{8} \times 5\frac{1}{2}$, ff. 348, *pict.*

274. Ath. Nat. Libr. 144 [xv], $8\frac{1}{4} \times 5\frac{7}{8}$, ff. 76, *mut.* at beginning and end.

275. (Evst. 956.) 276. (Evst. 957.)

277. (Evst. 958.) 278. (Evst. 959.)

279. (Evst. 960.) 280. (Evst. 961.)

281. (Evst. 962.) 282. (Evst. 963.)

283. (Evst. 964.) 284. (Evst. 965.)

285. (Evst. 966.) 286. (Evst. 967.)

287. (Evst. 968.) 288. (Evst. 498.)

ADDITIONAL UNCIALS.

ג. At Kosinitsa, 'Αγία Μονή 124 [x], $10\frac{7}{8} \times 7$, ff. 339, Evan., Act., Cath., Apoc., Paul. (*sic*). Written by Sabbas, a monk, in tenth century, with marginal writing [xiii].

ד. At Kosinitsa, 'Αγ. Μον. 375 [ix–x], $7\frac{1}{8} \times 13$, ff. 301 (16, 19, or 21). The two first gatherings are mice-eaten. Τίτλοι in vermilion, *ἀναγνώσματα*, *κεφ. t.*, *subscr.*, Evan. *Mut.* Matt. i. 1—ix. 1.

ה. *a.* Athos, Protaton 13 [vi], 4to, ff. 2, appended to Homilies of Chrysostom, and containing fragments of the Evangelists.

b. Athos, Protaton 14 [vi], ff. 3, with fragments of St. John appended at beginning and end to Lives of Saints.

c. Athos, Protaton 20 [vi], 2 cols.

d. Athos, Protaton 56 [vi], ff. 10, 2 cols., at beginning and end of a hortatory discourse [xiv], containing fragments of the Evangelists.

TOTAL NUMBER OF GREEK MANUSCRIPTS AS RECKONED IN THE SIX CLASSES

Uncials :—		
Evangelia	71	
Acts and Catholic Epistles	19	
St. Paul's Epistles . .	27	
Apocalypse	7	
Total . .	——	124
Cursives :—		
Evangelia	1321	
Acts and Catholic Epistles	420	
St. Paul's Epistles . .	491	
Apocalypse	184	
Evangelistaria	963	
Apostolos	288	
Total . .	——	3667
Grand Total		3791

APPENDIX A.

CHIEF AUTHORITIES.

The chief authorities used in corrections and additions in this Edition have been as follows:—

1. MS. Notes and other remains of Dr. Scrivener, such as 'Adversaria Critica Sacra,' just being published.

2. My own examination of the MSS. in London, Oxford, and Cambridge, with obliging help as to those in the British Museum from Mr. G. F. Warner, of the MSS. Department.

3. Burgon's Letters to the *Guardian*, 1873–74, 1882, and 1884.

4. As to Parisian MSS., the Abbé Martin's 'Description technique des MSS. Grecs relatifs au N. Test., conservés dans les Bibliothèques de Paris,' Paris, 1884. And Omont's 'Facsimilés des MSS. Grecs datés de la Bibliothèque Nationale du ix et du xiv.'

5. Κατάλογος τῶν Χειρογράφων τῆς 'Εθνικῆς Βιβλιοθήκης τῆς "Ελλαδος ὑπὸ 'Ιωάννου Σακκελίωνος καὶ 'Αλκιβιάδου 'Ι. Σακκελίωνος. 'Εν 'Αθήναις, 1892.

6. 'Ιεροσολυμιτικὴ Βιβλιοθήκη, ἤτοι Κατάλογος τῶν ἐν ταῖς Βιβλιοθήκαις τοῦ ἁγιωτάτου ἀποστολικοῦ τε καὶ καθολικοῦ ὀρθοδόξου πατριαρχικοῦ θρόνου τῶν 'Ιεροσολύμων κοὶ πάσης Παλαιστίνης ἀποκειμένων 'Ελληνίκων Κωδίκων, κ.τ.λ.: ὑπὸ Παπαδοπούλου Κεραμέως, κ.τ.λ. 'Εν Πετροπόλει, 1891.

7. 'Εν Κωνσταντινουπόλει 'Ελληνικὸς Φιλολογικὸς Σύλλογος. Μαυρογορδάτειος Βιβλιοθήκη. Παραρτήματα τοῦ ΙΕ Τόμου (1884), τοῦ Ιϛ Τόμου (1885), τοῦ ΙΖ Τόμου (1886), τοῦ ΙΗ Τόμου (1888). 'Εν Κωνσταντινουπόλει.

8. 'Υπομνήματα Περιγραφικὰ τὸν Κυκλάδων Νήσων κατὰ μέρος ὑπὸ 'Αντωνίου Μηλιαράκη. "Ανδρος, Κέως, ὑπὸ 'Α. Παπαδυπούλου τοῦ Κεραμέως. 'Εν 'Αθήναις, 1880.

9. "Εκθεσις Παλαιογραφικῶν καὶ Φιλολογικῶν 'Ερεύνων ἐν Θράκῃ καὶ Μακεδονίᾳ: ὑπὸ Α. Παπαδοπούλου Κερυμέως. 'Εν Κωνσταντινουπόλει, 1886.

10. Κατάλογος τῶν ἐν ταῖς Βιβλιοθήκαις τοῦ 'Αγίου "Ορους 'Ελληνικῶν Κωδίκων: ὑπὸ Σπυρίδωνος Π. Λάμπρου.

11. Catalogus Codicum Bibliotheca Imperialis Publicae Gr. et Lat. Edvardus de Muralto. Petropoli, 1840.

12. And especially the learned Prolegomena to Tischendorf, 8th edition, drawn up and issued by Dr. C. R. Gregory, who has with the greatest diligence examined a vast number of MSS. on the spot. I have had a difficult task in steering between my duty to the learned public *in*

the short time allowed me for the preparation of this edition, and the desire of Dr. Gregory that I should not take more of the information supplied in his work than I could help. What I have chiefly done has been to insert his measurements, where I could obtain no others, translating them into inches, and some other particulars upon such MSS. as had been already described in the third edition. In the case of the newly-discovered MSS., which have been first recorded by Dr. Gregory, I have only mentioned them, with a general reference to Dr. Gregory's book, except where information from other sources has come to hand. I have the pleasure of paying a tribute in the case of MSS. which I have examined upon his track to the great skill and accuracy of his examinations.

APPENDIX B.

ON FACSIMILES.

SINCE the application of photography in its more perfect forms to manuscripts for the purpose of representing their character accurately to scholars who have no opportunity of examining the manuscripts for themselves, the older facsimiles have in greater measure lost their value. It seems, therefore, hardly worth while to refer to the collections of facsimiles made by Montfaucon, or Bianchini, or Silvestre, or Westwood, other representations when they are to be had being so much more faithful and instructive.

The following are some of the most valuable of recent collections:—

1. Palaeographical Society, Facsimiles of MSS. and Inscriptions, ed. E. A. Bond, E. M. Thompson, and G. F. Warner, first series, 3 vols., London, 1873–1883; second series, 1884, &c., in progress, fol.

This collection contains the following Gr. Test. MSS.:—

SERIES I.

B, Plate 104.	ℵ, Plate 105.
A, Plate 106.	D, 14, 15.
D, Clarom. 63, 64.	E, Laudianus, 80.
Evst., Parham, 83.	Brit. Mus. Harl. 5598, 26, 27.
Brit. Mus. Add. 17,470, 202.	Rom. Vat. Gr. 1208, 131.
Brit. Mus. Add. 28,816, 843.	Brit. Mus. Add. 28,818, 204.
Brit. Mus. Add. 22,506, 205.	Brit. Mus. Add. 19,993, 206.
Camb. Trin. Coll. B. 17. 1, 127.	Δ, Sangallensis, semi-uncial, 179.
Codex Argenteus (Gothic), 118.	

SERIES II.

Oxf. Bodl. Misc. Gr. 313, 7.	Rom. Vat. Gr. 2138, 87.

2. A considerable selection from the large assemblage of MSS. at Paris has been issued in facsimile by M. Omont, in his three volumes, pub-

lished in 1887, 1890, and 1892 respectively, viz. Facsimilés des Manuscrits Grecs des xv et xiv siècles, reproduits en photolithographie d'après les originaux de la Bibliothèque Nationale, Paris, 4to.

Facsimilés des Manuscrits Grecs datés de la Bibliothèque Nationale du ixe au xive siècle, Paris, fol.

Facsimilés des plus anciens Manuscrits Grecs en onciale et en minuscule de la Bibliothèque Nationale du ive au xiie siècle, Paris, fol.

3. For Spain, Martin (A.), Facsimilés des Manuscrits d'Espagne, gravés d'après les photographies de Charles Graux, 2 vols., Paris, 1891, 8vo and atlas.

4. Wattenbach (W.) and Velsen (A. von), Exempla Codicum Graecorum literis minusculis scriptorum, Heidelberg, 1878, fol.

APPENDIX C.

ON DATING BY INDICTION.

Some account of the old way of dating Greek MSS. by indiction has been already given (p. 42, n. 2), but it may be convenient to our readers to have a fuller description to refer to. Such a description may be found in Mr. Maunde Thompson's admirable Manual on Greek and Latin Palaeography, pp. 322–3, which, by the kind permission of the author, is reproduced here.

'Mediaeval Greek MSS. are dated sometimes by the year of the indiction, sometimes by the year of the world according to the era of Constantinople, sometimes by both indiction and year of the world.

The Indiction was a cycle of fifteen years, which are severally styled Indiction 1, Indiction 2, &c., up to Indiction 15, when the series begins afresh. The introduction of this system is attributed to Constantine the Great. From the circumstance of the commencement of the indiction being reckoned variously from different days, four kinds of indictions have been recognized, viz. :—

i. The Indiction of Constantinople, calculated from the 1st of September, A.D. 312.

ii. The Imperial or Caesarian Indiction (commonly used in England and France), beginning on the 24th of September, A.D. 312.

iii. The Roman or Pontifical Indiction (commonly used in dating papal bulls from the ninth to the fourteenth century), beginning on the 1st of January (or the 25th of December, when that day was reckoned as the first day of the year), A.D. 313.

iv. The Indiction used in the register of the parliament of Paris, beginning in October.

The Greeks made use of the Indiction of Constantinople[1].

To find the indiction of a year of the Christian era, add 3 to the year (because A.D. 1 = Indiction 4), and divide the sum by 15: if nothing remains, the indiction will be 15; if there is a remainder, it will be the number of the indiction. But it must not be forgotten that the Indiction of Constantinople begins on the first of September, and consequently that the last four months of a year of the Christian era belong to the next indiction year.

The year of the Creation of the World was calculated, according to the era of Constantinople, to be B.C. 5508. The first day of the year was the 1st of September.

To reduce the Mundane era of Constantinople to the Christian era, deduct 5508 from the former for the months of January to August; and 5509 for September to December.

A chronological table, showing the corresponding years of the Mundane era, the Christian era, and the Indiction, from A.D. 800 to A.D. 1599, will be found in Gardthausen's "Griechische Palaeographie," pp. 450–459.'

Mr. Thompson also refers to an article by Mr. Kenyon in *The Classical Review*, March, 1893, p. 110, where the Egyptian puzzle is noticed, to one by Wilcken in 'Hermes,' xxviii. p. 230, and one by Viereck in 'Philologus,' lii. p. 219, and generally to the interesting and valuable Introduction to the British Museum upon Greek Papyri.

APPENDIX D.

ON THE ῬΗΜΑΤΑ.

THE following ingenious and probably sound explanation of what has been long a *crux* to Textual Critics, comes from a Lecture by Mr. Rendel Harris, 'On the Origin of the Ferrar Group,' delivered at Mansfield College, Oxford, on Nov. 6, 1893, and since published (C. J. Clay and Sons), and courteously sent to the editor by the accomplished author. The explanation is given in Mr. Harris' own words (pp. 7–10): but the whole of his pamphlet should be consulted by those who are interested in this study.

'In Scrivener's Introduction to the New Testament (ed. 3, p. 65) we are told that "besides the division of the text into στίχοι or lines, we find in the Gospels alone another division into ῥήματα or ῥήσεις, 'sentences,' differing but little from the στίχοι in number. Of these last the precise

[1] An independent mode of reckoning the commencement of the indiction was followed in Egypt under the later Roman Empire. The indiction there began normally in the latter half of the month Pauni, which corresponds to about the middle of June; but the actual day of commencement appears to have been variable and to have depended upon the exact period of the rising of the Nile.—'Catalogue of Greek Papyri in the British Museum,' pp. 197, 198.

numbers vary in different copies, though not considerably, &c." And on p. 66 we find the following statistical statement:

Matthew	has	2522	ῥήματα
Mark	„	1675	„
Luke	„	3803	„
John	„	1938	„

These figures are derived from MSS. of the Gospels, in which we frequently find the attestation given both of the ῥήματα and the στίχοι: e.g. Cod. Ev. 173 gives for

Matthew ͵βφκβʹ ῥήματα,
͵βφξʹ στίχοι,

while the corresponding figures for Mark and Luke are

Mark ͵αχοεʹ } and Luke ͵γωγʹ }
͵αχδʹ } ͵βψνʹ }

No explanation, as far as I know, has ever been given of these curiously numbered ῥήματα. The word is, certainly, a peculiar one to use, if short sentences are intended, such as are commonly known by the terms "cola and commata."

It has occurred to me that perhaps the explanation might lie in the fact that ῥῆμα was here a literal translation of the Syriac word ܦܬܓܡܐ. Let us then see whether ܦܬܓܡܐ is the proper word to describe a verse, either a fixed verse, like a hexameter, or a sense-line. A reference to Payne Smith's Lexicon will show that it may be used in either of these senses, for example, we are told that it is not only used generally of the verses of Scripture, but that it may stand for "*comma, membrum versus, sententia brevior quam versus*, στίχος, Schol. ad Hex. Job. ix. 33; ܦܬܓܡܐ ܡ̄ܕ, Tit. ib. Ps. ix; ܦܬܓ̈ܡܐ ܐܠܦܐ ܕ̄, ib. Ex. xxx. 22 marg.: insunt in Geneseos libro ܦ̈ܬܓܡܐ MMMMDIX, coloph. ad Gen., it. C.S.B. 2 et sic ad fin. cuiusque libri; in libris poeticis sententia est hemistichio minor, e.g. in Ps. i. insunt versus sex sed ܦ̄ܬ ܝ; in Ps. ii. versus duodecim, sed ܦ̄ܬ ܟܚ."

It seems, therefore, to be used in Syriac much in the same way as στίχος in Greek.

Now there is in one of the Syriac MSS. on Mount Sinai (Cod. Sin. Syr.) a table of the Canonical books of the Old and New Testaments with their measured verses. We will give some extracts from this table; but first, notice that the Gospels are numbered as follows:

Matthew	has	2522	ܦ̈ܬܓܡܐ
Mark	„	1675	„
Luke	„	3083	„
John	„	1737	„

and the whole of the four Evangelists 9218, which differs slightly from the total formed by addition, which, as the figures stand, is 9017.

On comparing the table with the numbers given by Scrivener from Greek MSS., viz.

Matt. = 2522 ῥήματα
Mark = 1675 „
Luke = 3803 „
John = 1938 „

we see at a glance that we are dealing with the same system; Luke should evidently have 3083, the Greek number being evidently an excessive one; and if we assume that John should be 1938 the total amounts exactly to the 9218 given for the four Gospels.

This is very curious, and since the ῥήματα are now proved to be rightly equated to ܦ̈ܬܓܡܐ, and this latter word is a proper word to describe a verse or στίχος, the ῥήματα appear to be a translation of a Syriac table.

Perhaps we may get some further idea about the character of the verses in question by turning to the Sinai list, which is not confined to the Gospels, but ranges through the whole of the Old and New Testaments.

The Stichometry in question follows the list of the names of the seventy disciples, which list is here assigned to Irenaeus, bishop of Lugdunum. After which we have

ܗܢܘ ܚܘܫܒܐ ܕܡܢܝܢܐ ܕܦ̈ܬܓܡܐ
ܡܪ̈ܢܝܐ: ܕܟܡܐ ܦ̈ܬܓܡܐ ܐܝܬ
ܠܟܠ ܚܕ ܡܢܗܘܢ: ܒܪܫܝܬ
ܦ̈ܬܓܡܐ ܐܪܒܥܐ ܐܠܦܝܢ ܘܚܡܫܡܐܐ
ܘܫܬܬܥܣܪ:

i.e. Genesis has 4516 verses
followed by

Exodus	3378	„
Leviticus	2684	„
Numbers	3481	„
Deuteronomy	2982	„
Total for the Law	17041	„
Joshua	1953	„
Judges	2088	„
&c.		

When we come to the New Testament, it seems at first sight as if the verses which are there reckoned cannot be the Greek equivalent hexameters: for we are told that Philemon contains 53 verses, and the Epistle to Titus 116, numbers which are in excess of the Euthalian reckoning, 38 and 97 verses respectively, and similarly in other cases. The suggestion arises that the lines here reckoned are sense lines, and this is therefore the meaning to be attached to the ῥήματα of the MSS. But upon this point we must not speak too hastily.

The interest of the Sinai stichometry is not limited to this single point: its list of New Testament books is peculiar in order and contents. There seem to be no Catholic Epistles, and amongst the Pauline Epistles, Galatians stands first; note also the curious order Hebrews, Colossians, Ephesians, Philippians.

* I do not think there can be the slightest doubt that our explanation of the origin of the ῥήματα is correct * * * *.'

APPENDIX E.

TABLE OF DIFFERENCES BETWEEN THE FOURTH EDITION OF DR. SCRIVENER'S PLAIN INTRODUCTION AND DR. GREGORY'S PROLEGOMENA.

I. *Evangelia.*

Greg.	Scriv.	Greg.	Scriv.	Greg.	Scriv.	Greg.	Scriv.	Greg.	Scriv.
450	Scholz	490	574	519	505	548	535	577	871
451	481	491	576	520	506	549	536	578	872
——		492	577	521	562	550	537	579	743
452	Scholz	493	578	522	488	551	538	580	744
|		494	325	523	489	552	539	581	450
466		495	581	524	490	553	540	582	451
467	717	496	582	525	491	554	541	583	452
468	718	497	583	526	610	555	609	584	453
469	719	498	584	527	482	556	526	585	454
470	509	499	586	528	483	557	524	586	455
471	510	500	587	529	484	558	525	587	456
472	511	501	588	530	485	559	518	588	457
473	512	502	589	531	327	560	520	589	830
474	513	503	590	532	545	561	521	590	831
475	515	504	585	533	546	562	522	591	883
476	566	505	567	534	547	563	519	592	461
477	508	506	492	535	548	564	478	593	462
478	575	507	493	536	549	565	473	594	470
479	542	508	494	537	550	566	479	595	468
480	568	509	495	538	552	567	878	596	465
481	569	510	496	539	551	568	879	597	464
482	570	511	497	540	553	569	475	598	466
483	543	512	498	541	554	570	479	599	467
484	571	513	499	542	555	571	474	600	463
485	572	514	500	543	556	572	480	601	643
486	517	515	501	544	557	573	328	602	644
487	516	516	502	545	558	574	880	603	645
488	514	517	503	546	559	575	477	604	646
489	507	518	504	547	534	576	580	605	647

Greg.	Scriv.
606	648
607	649
608	650
609	634
610	652
611	653
612	654
613	655
614	656
615	657
616	658
617	659
618	660
619	661
620	662
621	663
622	664
623	665
624	667
625	673
626	674
627	678
628	679
629	681
630	682
631	685
632	686
633	688
634	695
635	700
636	701
637	702
638	706
639	710
640	711
641	712
642	715
643	716
644	720
645	591
646	721
647	722
648	724
649	725
650	726
651	874
652	875
653	640
654	641

Greg.	Scriv.
655	635
656	642
657	876
658	636
659	637
660	638
661	639
662	632
663	877
664	605
665	895
666	899
667	900
668	1144
669	902
670	901
671	544
672	618
673	619
674	620
675	621
676	527
677	528
678	529
679	530
680	531
681	532
682	533
683	1145
684	1146
685	1147
686	573
687	579
688	592
689	593
690	594
691	595
692	596
693	597
694	598
695	599
696	600
697	601
698	602
699	603
700	604
701	523
702	884
703	885

Greg.	Scriv.
704	886
705	887
706	486
707	606
708	607
709	737
710	81
711	617
712	560
713	561
714	563
715	564
716	565
717	606
718	736
719	824
720	825
721	826
722	827
723	828
724	829
725	881
726	882
727	745
728	746
729	747
730	748
731	749
732	750
733	751
734	752
735	753
736	754
737	755
738	756
739	757
740	761
741	762
742	764
743	738
744	759
745	633
746	740
747	741
748	758
749	773
750	742
751	739
752	774

Greg.	Scriv.
753	760
754	763
755	771
756	772
757	846
758	847
759	848
760	849
761	850
762	851
763	854
764	855
765	856
766	857
767	858
768	859
769	861
770	862
771	863
772	867
773	868
774	869
—	—
824	622
825	623
826	624
827	625
828	626
829	627
830	628
831	629
—	—
839	630
840	631
—	—
847	723
848	611
849	730
850	729
851	
852	732
—	—
854	666
855	668
856	669
857	670
858	671

Greg.	Scriv.
859	672
—	—
861	674
862	675
863	676
—	—
867	680
868	683
869	684
870	
871	687
872	690
873	689
874	691
875	692
876	693
877	694
878	703
879	704
880	705
881	708
882	713
883	714
884	696
885	697
886	698
887	699
—	—
899	613
900	614
901	615
902	616
—	—
1144	727
1145	728
1146	731
1147	733
1148	734
1149	735
—	—
1261	765
1262	766
1263	767
—	—
1265	768
1266	769
1267	770
1268	110

II. *Acts and Catholic Epistles.*

Greg.	Scriv.	Greg.	Scriv.	Greg.	Scriv.	Greg.	Scriv.	Greg.	Scriv.
182	Scholz	204	107	226	216	248	251	301	240
183	257	205	232	227	217	249	263	302	250
184	258	206	194	228	218	250	264	303	248
185		207	197	229	223	251	201	—	
186		208	259	230	202	252	249	317	243
187		209	260	231	203	253	233	318	244
188	Scholz (185–192)	210	328	232	204	254	200	319	245
189		211	317	233	205	255	199	320	241
190		212	318	234	206	256	231	321	261
191		213	252	235	207	257	222	—	
192		214	182	236	208	258	289	325	239
193	188	215	183	237	209	259	260	326	246
194	187	216	184	238	195	260	209	—	
195	224	217	185	239	196	261	267	328	319
196	226	218	186	240	253	262	269	329	256
197	227	219	225	241	254	263	321	330	247
198	228	220	229	242	255	264	326	334	238
199	193	221	212	243	301	—		335	236
200	211	222	213	244	302	267	242	—	
201	219	223	220	245	335	268	334	415	210
202	215	224	221	246	415	269	237	416	147
203	230	225	198	247	110	—		—	

III. *Paul.*

Greg.	Scriv.	Greg.	Scriv.	Greg.	Scriv.	Greg.	Scriv.	Greg.	Scriv.
131	261	248	262	266	230	284	248	302	299
231	303?	249	258	267	316	285	275	303	243
232	306?	250	259	268	317	286	296	304	281
233		251	257	269	302	287	334	305	231
234		252	260	270	252	288	316	306	266
235		253	268	271	253	289	329	307	278
236	Scholz (233–239)	254	279	272	254	290	256	308	398
237		255	269	273	255	291	267	309	399
238		256	277	274	321	292	331	310	400
239		257	249	275	270	293	263	311	401
240	240	258	233	276	250	294	226	312	276
241	Scholz	259	282	277	251	295	332	313	402
242	242	260	300	278	264	296	333	314	403
243	Scholz	261	298	279	265	297	335	315	404
244	244	262	222	280	280	298	301	316	290
245	245	263	223	281	234	299	337	317	325
246	246	264	152	282	235	300	237	318	406
247	247	265	304	283	236	301	396	319	274

Greg.	Scriv.	Greg.	Scriv.	Greg.	Scriv.	Greg.	Scriv.	Greg.	Scriv.
320 ..	407	333 ..	476	376[e] ..	330	401 ..	312	426 ..	283
321 ..	423	334 ..	478	377 ..	341	402 ..	314	427 ..	336
322 ..	424	335 ..	480			403 ..	315	430 ..	294
323 ..	435	336 ..	53	—		404 ..	323	431 ..	319
324 ..	426	337 ..	481	380 ..	339			432 ..	322
325 ..	427	338 ..	482	381 ..	340	—		433 ..	295
326 ..	430	339 ..	487	392 ..	288	406 ..	327	436 ..	272
327 ..	431	340 ..	484	393 ..	286	407 ..	328	437 ..	273
328 ..	432	341 ..	485	393[a] ..	287	—		472 ..	232
329 ..	433			396 ..	297			476 ..	285
330 ..	436	—		398 ..	305	423 ..	291	476[a] ..	326
331 ..	437	376 ..	338	399 ..	310	424 ..	292	478 ..	225
332 ..	472	376[c] ..	377	400 ..	311	425 ..	293	480 ..	324

IV. *Apocalypse.*

Greg.	Scriv.	Greg.	Scriv.	Greg.	Scriv.	Greg.	Scriv.	Greg.	Scriv.
101 ..	103	109 ..	101	117 ..	157	—		158 ..	
102 ..	109	110 ..	146	118 ..	160	149 ..	120	159 ..	
103 ..	102	111 ..	149	119 ..	161	150 ..	121	160 ..	118
104 ..	105	112 ..	150	120 ..	182	151 ..	122	161 ..	119
105 ..	111	113 ..	110	121 ..	153	—		—	
—		114 ..	115	122 ..	86	153 ..	114	181 ..	107
107 ..	104	115 ..	117	—		—		182 ..	112
108 ..	89	116 ..	151	146 ..	113	157 ..	116	—	

V. *Evangelistaries.*

Greg.	Scriv.	Greg.	Scriv.	Greg.	Scriv.	Greg.	Scriv.	Greg.	Scriv.
155 ..	180	174 ..		191 ..	263	208 ..	215	225 ..	248
158 ..		175 ..		192 ..	264	209 ..	216	226 ..	249
159 ..		176 ..		193 ..	266	210 ..	217	227 ..	250
160 ..		177 ..		194 ..	202	211 ..	218	228 ..	253[2]
161 ..		178 ..		195 ..	203	212 ..	219	229 ..	223
162 ..		179 ..	179	196 ..	204	213 ..	220	230 ..	224
163 ..		180 ..	463	197 ..	205	214 ..	239	231 ..	225
164 ..		181 ..	234	198 ..	206	215 ..	240	232 ..	226
165 ..		182 ..	233	199 ..	207	216 ..	251	233 ..	235
166 ..		183 ..	257	200 ..	208	217 ..	241	234 ..	227
167 ..		184 ..	259	201 ..	209	218 ..	242	235 ..	228
168 ..		185 ..	222	202 ..	210	219 ..	243	236 ..	229
169 ..		186 ..	221	203 ..	211	220 ..	244	237 ..	237
170 ..	326	187 ..	256	204 ..	212	221 ..	245	237[a] ..	238
171 ..		188 ..	260	205 ..	201	222 ..	246	238 ..	254
172 ..		189 ..	261	206 ..	213	223 ..	252	239 ..	230
173 ..		190 ..	262	207 ..	214	224 ..	247	240 ..	231

Greg.	Scriv.	Greg.	Scriv.	Greg.	Scriv.	Greg.	Scriv.	Greg.	Scriv.
241	232	289	168	336	284	385	520	467	317
242	465	290	169	337	285	386	521	468	318
243	466	291	187	338	499	387	522	469	319
244	467	292	189	339	59	388	523	470	320
245^{a}	468	293	190	340	258	389	524	471	321
245^{b}	469	294	481	341	288	390	528	472	330
246	194	295	482	342	289	391	529	472^{c}	330
247	470	296	483	343	298	392	530	473	323
248	471	297	484	344	236	393	531	474	420
249	191	298	485	345	500	394	532	475	325
250	472	299	200	346	255	395	534	476	290
251	195	300	286	347	501	396	535	477	363
252	473	301	486	348	502	397	536	478	322
253	196	302^{a}	487	349	503	398^{ab}	537	480	331
254	474	302^{b}	489	350	504	399^{ab}	538	481	332
255	475	303	491	351	505	400	540	482	333
256	192	304	492	352	506	401	541	484	334
257	476	305	291	353	507	402	542	485	336
258	197	306	292	354	508	403	543	486^{a}	337
259	477	307	293	355	509	404	544	486^{d}	340
260	198	308	294	356	512	405	546	487	338
261	158	309	295	357	513	406	549	488	339
262	159	310	296	358	514	407	550	489	341
263	193	311	297	359	515	408	552	490	342
264	170	312	493	360	516	409	553	491	343
265	171	313	494	361	426	410	556	492	344
266	172	314	495	362	427	411	560	493	345
267	173	315	253	363	299	412	561	494	346
268	174	316	496	364	416	413	563	495	347
269	175	317	497	365	417	414	564	496	348
270	176	318	265	366	366	415	565	497	349
271	177	319	267	367	367	416	566	498	350
272	178	320	268	368	421	417	567	499	422
273	478	321	269	369	423	418	568	500	352
274	479	322	270	370	324	419	569	501	353
275	181	323	271	371	424	420	570	502	354
276	182	324	272	372	425	421	571	503	355
277	183	325	273	373	517	422	572	504	356
278	186	326	274	374	419	423	573	505	357
279	184	327	276	375	370	424	574	506	358
280	185	328	277	376	371	425	759	508	359
281	160	328^{a}	38	377	372	426	804	509	360
282	161	329	278	378	373	427	828		
283	162	330	279	379	374	428	829	512	306
284	163	331	280	380	375			513	300
285	164, 5	332	62	381	368	463	313	514	301
286	480	333	281	382	369	464	314	515	305
287	166	334	282	383	518	465	315	516	302
288	167	335	283	384	519	466	316	517	307

Greg.	Scriv.	Greg.	Scriv.	Greg.	Scriv.	Greg.	Scriv.	Greg.	Scriv.
518	311	532	407	545	381	560	388	572	572
519	303	534	404	546	382	561	389	573	395
520	304	535	403	547	547	562	562	574	362
521	308	536	405	548	548	563	390	804	412
522	309	537	411	549	383	564	392	923	288
523	312	538	414	550	384	565	393	—	
524	310	539		551		566	396	927	275
—		540	376	552	385	567	397	928	418
528	409	541	377	553	386	568	398	935	415
529	410	542	378	—		569	399	936	428
530	408	543	379	556	387	570	188		
531	406	544	380	—		571	394		

VI. *Apostolos.*

Greg.	Scriv.	Greg.	Scriv.	Greg.	Scriv.	Greg.	Scriv.	Greg.	Scriv.
49		75	70	100	214	126	115	202	99
50		76	198	101	216	127	169	203	100
51	Scholz	77	79	102	90	128	180	204	101
52		78	78	103	83	129	184	205	102
53		79	75	104	84	130	186	206	103
54		80	71	105	85	—		207	104
55	55	81	69	106	86	169	105	208	106
56	56	82	77	107	87	170	170	209	107
58	58	83	76	108	88	171	70a	210	108
59	48	84	74	109	89	172	93	211	109
60	57	85	200	110	263	173	94	212	110
61	59	86	51	111	223	—		213	111
62	60	87a	201	112	81	180	73	214	112
63	61	87b	202	113	82	—		215	215
64	62	88	130	114	125	183	80	216	124
65	52	89	50	115	126	184	67	—	
66	64	90	203	116	127	185	185	227	121
67	66	91	204	117	213	186	53	228	113
68	65	92	205	118	116	—		—	
69	178	93	206	—		197	91	255	122
70	72	94	207	120	49	198	92	256	128
70b	172	95	208	121	119	199	199	—	
71	173	96	209	122	123	200	96	262	129
72	183	97	210	123	120	201	97	263	68
73	54	98	211	124	98			264	117
74	197	99	212	125	114				

INDEX I.

OF GREEK MANUSCRIPTS.

Index of Greek Manuscripts of the New Testament, arranged according to the countries where they are and the owners to whom they belong.

(N.B.—The Reference is always made to the MSS., which are described in their proper places.)

Add. MSS. (*cont.*)— Total MSS.

14637, 14638 ....Evst. 496–7
14744.....................Evan. 202
15581.....................Evan. 580
16183.....................Evan. 581
16184.....................Evan. 582
16943.....................Evan. 583
17136.....................Evan. N^b
17211.....................Evan. R
17370.....................Evst. 262
17469.....................Evan. 584
17470.....................Evan. 585
17741.....................Evan. 586
17982.....................Evan. 587
18211.....................Evan. 588
18212.....................Evst. 263
19386.....................Evan. 110
19387.....................Evan. 589
19388.....................Act. 229
19389.....................Evan. 590
19392.....................Act. 230
19459.....................Evst. 930
19460.....................Evst. 264
19737.....................Evst. 265
19993.....................Evst. 266
20003.....................Act. 61
21260.....................Evst. 267
21261.....................Evst. 268
22506.....................Evan. 591
22734.....................Act. 107
22735.....................Evst. 269
22736.....................Evan. 592
22737.....................Evan. 593
22738.....................Evan. 594
22739.....................Evan. 595
22740.....................Evan. 596
22741.....................Evan. 597
22742.....................Evst. 270
22743.....................Evst. 271
22744.....................Evst. 272
24112.....................Evan. 598
24373.....................Evan. 599
24374.....................Evst. 273
24376.....................Evan. 600
24377.....................Evst. 274
24378.....................Evst. 275
24379.....................Evst. 276
24380.....................Evst. 277
25881.....................Evst. 38
26103.....................Evan. 601
27860.....................Evst. 278
27861.....................Evan. 602
28815.....................Evan. 603
28816.....................Act. 232
28817.....................Evst. 279
28818.....................Evst. 280
29713.....................Evst. 62
29714.....................Apost. 69
31208.....................Evst. 281
31919.....................Evst. 282
Evan. Υ
31920.....................Evst. 283
31921.....................Evst. 284

Add. MSS. (*cont.*)— Total MSS.

31949.....................Evst. 285
32051.....................Apost. 52
32277.....................Evan. 892
32341.....................Evan. 325
34059.....................Evst. 39
34107.....................Evan. 321
34108.....................Evan. 322

Butler ....Evan. 632 ... 1

Highgate, Burdett-Coutts...... 20

I. 2.....................Evst. 239
I. 3, 4, 7 ....Evann. 545–7
I. 8 ....Evst. 240
I. 9 ....Evan. 548
I. 10 ....Evst. 251
I. 23, 24 ....Evst. 241–2
II. 4 ....Evan. 603
II. 5 ....Evst. 243
II. 5 (?), II. 14 ....Evst. 494–5
II. 7, 13 ....Evann. 549–50
II. 23 ....Evst. 244
II. 26^1, 26^2 ....Evann. 553–4
II. 30 ....Evst. 245
III. 1 ....Act. 220

Sion College 4

A. 32. 1 (1) ....Evst. 227
A. 32. 1 (2) ....Evst. 228
A. 32. 1 (3) ....Evan. 518
A. 32. 1 (4) ....Evst. 229

(Manchester) 1

Rylands Libr. ....Evan. 886

(Oxford)—

BODLEIAN 78

Barocc. 3 ....Act. 23
29 ....Evan. 46
31 ....Evan. 45
48 ....Apoc. 28
59 ....Evan. 610
197 ....Evst. 201
202 ....Evst. 5
Canon. Gr. 33.........Evan. 288
34.........Evan. 488
36.........Evan. 489
85.........Evst. 202
92.........Evst. 203
110.........Act. 212
112.........Evan. 490
119.........Evst. 204
122.........Evan. 491
126.........Evst. 205
E. D. Clarke 4.........Act. 56
5.........Evan. 98
6.........Evan. 107
7.........Evan. 111
8.........Evst. 157
9.........Act. 58
10.........Evan. 112
45.........Evst. 206

Total MSS.

Quaritch i ....Evan. 469 ... 4
ii ....Evan. 471
viii............Evst. 935
Formerly ...Evan. 885

Ruskin, John ....Evst. 254 ... 1

Swete, H. B., Dr........Evan. 736 ... 2
Evan. 737

White, Mr. ....Evan. 523 ... 1

Winchelsea, Earl of Evan. 106 ... 1

(Wisbech)—

PECKOVER 5

1......................Evan. 560
2......................Evan. 561
......................Apost. 43
70 ....Evst. 500
.....................Apost. 203

Woolwich ?, Bate......Evst. 492 ... 1

Wordsworth, Bp. ...Evan. 542 ... 1

IRELAND.

(Dublin)—

TRINITY COLLEGE 3

Evan. Z
D. i. 28 ....Paul. 490
A. i. 2, fol. 1......Evst. 454

SCOTLAND.

Bute ....Evan. 64 ... 1

(Edinburgh) 5

Libr. A. c. 25 ....Evan. 519
Mackellar ....Evan. 896
Act. 333
Univ. D. Laing 6, 667 Evann. 897-8
Univ. Laing ....Evst. 578

(Glasgow)—

HUNTER MUSEUM 7

V. 3. 3..............Evst. 231
V. 3. 4...............Apost. 45
V. 4. 3...............Evst. 232
V. 5. 10 ....Evst. 230
V. 7. 2...............Evan. 520
Q. 7. 10 ....Evan. 521
S. 8. 141...........Evan. 522

Duke of Hamilton's collection.

NEW ZEALAND.

Auckland ....Evan. 1273 2
Evst. 420

Total MSS.

FOREIGN COUNTRIES.

BELGIUM.

Brussels 2

Reg. 11358, 11375 ...Evann. 881-2

DENMARK.

Copenhagen 3

Havniensis 1322 ......Evan. 234
1323 ......Evan. 235
1324 ......Evst. 44

EGYPT.

Cairo 2

Cod. P. Kerameus......Evan. T[g]
Patr. Alex. 2, 15, 16,
17, 68 ....Evann. 643-7
421, 952 ....Evann. 903-4
82, 87 ....Evann. 1270-1
8, 59, 88 ....Act. 253-5
942 ....Act. 381
18 ....Evst. 140
927, 929, 943,
944, 945, 946,
948, 950, 951,
953 ....Evst. 760-9
Μετοικία of St. Cath. 7 Evan. 648

FRANCE.

Arras 970 ....Evan. 872 ... 1

Besançon 41 ....Apost. 51 ... 2
44 ....Evst. 193

Bordier, Henri ......Evst. 505 ... 1

Carpentras 11 ....Evst. 189 ... 1

Dessau.....................Evan. 874... 2
200 ....Paul. 374

Montpelier, Sch. M. 446 Evan. 871... 2
405 Evst. 504

Paris—

NATIONAL LIBRARY 298

Nat. Gr. RI 9 C
13..............Evst. 415
14..............Evan. 33
19..............Apoc. 58
47..............Evan. 18
48..............Evan. M
49..............Evan. 8
50..............Evan. 13
51..............Evan. 260
52..............Evan. 261
53..............Evan. 262
54..............Evan. 16
55..............Evan. 17
56..............Act. 51
57..............Act. 114

Nat. Gr. (*cont.*)—	Total MSS.
227	Paul. 162
228, 263	Evst. 427–8
230	Evan. 12
231	Evan. 319
232	Evan. 320
234	Evan. 761
235	Evan. 762 and Evst. 426
237	Act. 10
238	Paul. 163
239	Apoc. 62
240	Apoc. 139
241	Apoc. 63
276	Evst. 82
277	Evst. 63
278	Evst. 1
279	Evst. 17
280	Evst. 2
281	Evst. 64
282	Evst. 65
283	Evst. 66
284	Evst. 67
285	Evst. 68
286	Evst. 69
287	Evst. 10
288	Evst. 70
289	Evst. 71
290	Evst. 72, 72^{b}
291	Evst. 73
292	Evst. 74
293	Evst. 75
294	Evst. 83
295	Evst. 76
296	Evst. 77
297	Evst. 16
298	Evst. 78
299	Evst. 79
300	Evst. 80
301	Evst. 7
302	Evst. 15
303	Evst. 101
304	Apost. 22
305	Evst. 81
306	Apost. 23
307	Evst. 9
308	Apost. 24
309	Evst. 11
310	Evst. 12
311	Evst. 86
312	Evst. 8
313	Evst. 87
314	Evst. 88 and Evan. W^{a}
315	Evst. 14
316	Evst. 89
317	Evst. 90
318	Evst. 91
319	Apost. 25
320	Apost. 26
321	Apost. 27
324	Evst. 92
326	Evst. 93

Nat. Gr. (*cont.*)—	Total MSS.
330	Evst. 94
373	Apost. 30
374	Evst. 95
375	Evst. 60
376	Evan. 324
377	Evst. 98
378	Evan. 326
379	Evan. 28
380	Evst. 99
381	Evst. 100
382	Apost. 33
383	Apost. 34
491	Apoc. 61
849	Paul. 164
922, fol. A	Apost. 201
975	Evst. 299
1775	Evan. 764
Nat. Suppl. Gr.	
24, 29	Evst. 416–7
27	Evst. 158
32	Evst. 84
33	Evst. 85
50	Evst. 58
74	Evst. 366
75	Evan. 271
79	Evan. 274
99	Apoc. 59
104	Apost. 11
108	Evan. 290
115	Evst. 96
118	Evan. 323
140	Evan. 297
159	Evan. 738
175	Evan. 298
185	Evan. 120
219	Evan. 759
227	Evan. 633
242	Evst. 159
567	Evst. 367
611, 612	Evann. 740–1
686, 687, 758	Evst. 421–3
800	Apost. 130
804	Apost. 202
805	Evst. 324
834	Evst. 424
903	Evan. 758
904	Evan. 773
905	Evst. 425
906	Act. 263
911	Evan. 634
914	Evan. 742
919	Evan. 739
1001	Paul. 338
1035	Evan. 760
1076	Evan. 763
1080	Evan. 771
1081	Evst. 517
1083	Evan. 772
1096	Evst. 419
Nat. Coisl. 1	Evan. F^{a}
19	Evan. 329
20	Evan. 36

Total MSS.

Nüremburg ....Evst. 31 ... 1

Oettingen-Wallerstein, Prince of ....Apoc. 1 ... 1

Pesth.................................... 2

Eubeswald..............Evan. 100
Jancovich ....Evan. 78

Posen.................................... 1

Lycaei Aug. ....Evan. 86

Saxe-Gotha............................ 1

Ducal, MS. 78 ....Evst. 32

[**Strasburg** 3

From Molsheim (destroyed) ....Evan. 431]
Ed. Reuss...............Evan. 877

Trèves 2

Cuzan.....................Evan. 87
Cath. Libr. 143 ....Evst. 179

Tubingen ....Evst. R ... 2

2 ....Evst. 481

Vienna—

IMPERIAL LIBRARY 44

Vind. Caes. Ness.
1 ....Evan. 218
2 ....Evan. N
15 ....Evst. 45
28 ....Evan. 76
29 ....Evan. 77
30 ....Evan. 123
31 ....Evan. 124
32 ....Evan. 219
33 ....Evan. 220
34 ....Act. 66
35 ....Act. 63
36 ....Act. 64
37 ....Act. 67
38 ....Evan. 221
39 ....Evan. 222
40 ....Evan. 223
41 ....Evst. 155
42 ....Evan. 434
46 ....Paul. 214
248 ....Apoc. 35

Vind. Caes. Suppl. Gr.
4 ....Evan. 108
5 ....Evan. 3
6 ....Evan. 125
7 ....Evst. 46
8 ....Evan. 224
9 ....Evan. 225
10 ....Paul. 71
26 ....Apoc. 36

Imp. Priv. Libr. 7972 Evan. 829

Imp. Gr. Theol. 19, 79–80, 90, 95, 122 Evann. 824–8
141 ....Act. 335
150 ....Act. 415
157 ....Paul. 373

Imp. Gr. Theol. (*cont.*)—
69, 163, 210......Apoc. 136–8
Rainer 1, Rainer 2 ....Evst. 502–3
209 ....Evst. 180
308 ....Apost. 200

Wolfenbüttel ....Evan. O[a] ... 6

Carolin. A, B............Evann. P, Q
xvi. 7 ....Act. 69
xvi. 16 ....Evan. 126
Gud. gr. 104. 2 ....Act. 97

Zittau ....Evan. 605 ... 1

GREECE.

Athens 185

Nat. 3 ....Evst. 804
5 ....Evst. 828
10 ?..................Evst. 829

Nat. Sakkel. 58, 76, 93, 80, 127, 121, 110, 81, 71, 87, 118, 125, 108, 74, 134, 95, 77, 107, 75, 122, 109, 160, 111, 137, 117, 65, 130, 99, 88...........Evann. 775–803

150 (12), 151 (13), 152 (14), 153 (15), 154 (16) ....Evann. 846–50

155 (17).............Evan. 852

156 (18), 157 (19), 158 (20), 159 (21), 160 (22), 161 (23)...Evann. 854–9

162 (24), 203 (16)...Evann. 862–3

489 (216), 56, 57 ...Evann. 867–9

13, 139, 347 ....Evann. 1145–7

111 ....Evan. 1272

72, 92, 113, 123, 128, 132, 135..............Evann. 1313–9

207 (70), 208 (71), 209 (72), 43 (149 ?), 45, 64 (91), 66 (105), 221 (129), 119, 89 Act. 304–13

(490, 217) ....Act. 201

69 (100), 100 (96)...Paul. 382–3

259....................Paul. 471

Nat. Libr. 163, 164, 165, 166, 167, 168, 169....................Evst. 518–24

170, 171, 172, 173, 174....................Evst. 528–32

175, 176, ?, 177, 178 Evst. 534–8

179, 180, 181, 182...Evst. 541–4

183 ....Evst. 546

184, 185..............Evst. 549–50

186, 187..............Evst. 552–3

188 ....Evst. 556

189, 190 ....Evst. 560–1

Total MSS.

LIBRERIA RICCARDI 5

5 ....Evan. 370
69 ....Evst. 511
84 ....Evan. 368
85 ....Paul. 226
90 ....Evan. 369

Messina 21

Univ. Libr. 18 ....Evan. 420
40.................Act. 241
88, 100...........Evann. 630–1
93 ....Apost. 82
99.... ....Apoc. 113
65, 66, 75, 96, 98,
73, 58, 94, 111,
112, 170, 95,
150 ....Evst. 300–12
175 ....Evst. 525
St. Basil 104 ....Act. 175

Milan—

AMBROSIAN LIBRARY.............. 46

A. 51 sup. or 15.........Paul. 172
A. 62 inf. ....Paul. 390
A. 152 sup...............Evst. 167
A. 241 inf...............Paul. 287
B. 6 inf. ....Paul. 171
B. 56 ....Evan. 348
B. 62 ....Evan. 350
B. 70 sup. ....Evan. 351
B. 93 ....Evan. 352
C. 16 ....Evst. 81
C. 63 sup. ....Apost. 46
C. 91 sup. ....Evst. 106
C. 160 sup...............Evst. 168
C. 295 inf. ....Paul. 289
D. 67 sup. ....Evst. 103
D. 72 sup. ....Evst. 104
D. 108 sup...............Evst. 166
D. 161 inf. ....Evan. 458
D. 282 inf...............Evan. 459
D. 298 inf...............Evan. 460
D. 541 inf...............Paul. 288
E. 2 inf. ....Paul. 286
E. 63 sup. ....Evan. 457
E. 97 sup. ....Act. 137
E. 101 sup...............Evst. 480
E. 102 sup...............Act. 138
E. 295.....................Paul. 391
F. 61 sup. ....Evan. 349
F. 125 sup...............Paul. 175
G. 16 sup. ....Evan. 344
H. 13 sup. ....Evan. 343
H. 104 sup...............Act. 139
L. 79 sup. ....Evst. 163
M. 48 sup. ....Evan. 456
M. 81 sup. ....Evst. 105
M. 93 ....Evan. 353
N. 272 sup...............Paul. 225
P. 274 sup...............Evst. 169
S. 23 sup. ....Evan. 346
S. 62 sup. ....Evst. 102

Total MSS.

Z. 34 sup. ....Evan. 461
E. S. iii. 13..............Evst. 165
E. S. iv. 14...............Evst. 164, and Evan. 837
17 ....Evan. 345
35 ....Evan. 347
Formerly Hoeplii ......Evan. 838

Modena 16

Este ii. A. 1 ....Evan. 454
ii. A. 5 ....Evan. 455
ii. A. 9 ....Evan. 358
ii. A. 13...........Act. 195
ii. A. 14...........Paul. 177
iii. B. 17...........Act. 142
ii. C. 4 ....Act. 196
ii. C. 6...............Evst. 111
ii. D. 3 ....Apost. 50
ii. G. 3 ....Act. H
Also Act. 112
iii. B. 16 ....Evan. 359
iii. B. 17 ....Act. 142
iii. F. 13 ....Evan. 839
G. 9 ....Evan. 842
iii. E. 1 ....Apoc. 147
iii. F. 12 ....Apoc. 148

Naples 12

I. B. 14 ....Evst. 138
II. AA. 3..............Evan. 401
4..............Evan. 403
5..............Evan. 402
7..............Act. 83
8..............Act. 173
9..............Act. 174
37..............Evan. 843
II. B. 23, 24 ....Paul. 394–5
II. C. 15 ....Evan. R or W[b]
Scotti ....Evan. 404

Padua, Univ. 695 ......Evan. 844... 1

Palermo, I. E. 11 ......Paul. 217... 1

Parma 6

Reg. 5 ....Evan. 452
14 ....Evst. 161
15 ....Evan. 831
95 ....Evan. 453
1821 ....Evan. 361
2319 ....Evan. 360

Pistoia, Fabr. Libr. 307 Evan. 845... 2
Evst. 526

Rome—

VATICAN 213

Vat. Gr. 54 ....Evst. 924
163 ....Evan. 177
165 ....Paul. 58
349 ....Evan. 127
350 ....Evst. 539
351 ....Evst. 35
352, 353......Evst. 376·7
354 ....Evan. S

[1] So Scholz's index, and we may suppose correctly, but in his Catalogue of Evangelistaria he numbers it 1256.

Vat. Gr. (*cont.*)— Total MSS.

2139 ....Evan. 380
2144 ....Evst. 390
2160 ....Evan. 690
2165 ....Evan. 689
2167 ....Evst. 392
2180 ....Paul. 323
2187 ....Evan. 691
2247 ....Evan. 692
2251 ....Evst. 393
2275 ....Evan. 693
2290 ....Evan. 694
3785 ....Evan. N

Vat. Alex. Gr.

3 ....Evan. 696
4 ....Paul. 324
5 ....Evan. 697
9 ....Evan. 699
11 ....Apost. 120
12 ....Evst. 129
28 ....Evan. 154
29 ....Act. 78
33 ....Evst. 188
44, 59 ....Evst. 394-5
68 ....Apoc. 41
70 ....Apost. 122
79 ....Evan. 155
179 ....Act. 40
189 ....Evan. 156

Vat. Ottob. Gr.

2 ....Evst. 130
17 ....Paul. 405
31 ....Paul. 195
37 ....Evan. 703
61 ....Paul. 196
66 ....Evan. 386
74 ....Paul. 326
100 ....Evan. 704
154 ....Apoc. 159
175 ....Evst. 131
176 ....Paul. 197
204 ....Evan. 387
208 ....Evan. 705
212 ....Evan. 388
258 ....Act. 161
283 ....Apoc. 118
297 ....Evan. 389
298 ....Act. 162
325 ....Act. 163
326 ....Evst. 132
356 ....Paul. 202
381 ....Evan. 390
416 ....Evst. 133
417 ....Act. 165
432 ....Evan. 391
444 ....Evst. 396
453, 454, 456......Evann. 707-9

Vat. Palat. Gr.

5 ....Evan. 146
10 ....Paul. 327
20 ....Evan. 381
32 ....Evan. 713
38 ....Act. 247

Vat. Palat. Gr. (*cont.*)— Total MSS.

89 ....Evan. 147
136 ....Evan. 148
171 ....Evan. 149
189 ....Evan. 150
204 ....Paul. 328
208 ....Evan. 714
220 ....Evan. 151
227 ....Evan. 152
229 ....Evan. 153
1. A, 221, 239......Evst. 397-9
241 ....Apost. 123
346 ....Apoc. 119
423 ....Paul. 330

Pio-Vat. Gr. 50 ....Act. 80
55 ....Evan. 158

Vat. Urb. 2 ....Evan. 157
3 ....Act. 79
4 ....Evan. 1269

Rom. Angelica...................... 8

A. 1. 5 ....Evan. 178
A. 2. 15 ....Act. L
A. 4. 1 ....Apoc. 120
A. 4. 11 ....Evan. 179
B. 1. 5 ....Evan. 723
B. 5. 15 ....Apoc. 121
D. ii. 27 ....Evst. 527
D. 3. 8 ....Evan. 611

Rom. Barberini 34

iii. 6 ....Evan. 167
iii. 17 ....Evan. 161
iii. 38 ....Evan. 164
iii. 45 ....Apost. 40
iii. 131 ....Evan. 166
iv. 11, iv. 60, iv. 84 ...Apost. 125-7
iv. 27 ....Evan. 160
iv. 28 ....Evst. 533
iv. 31 ....Evan. 162
iv. 43, iv. 30, iv. 53, iv. 13, iv. 25, iv. 1, iii. 22, iii. 129, vi. 18 ....Evst. 403-11
iv. 54 ....Evst. 135-6
iv. 56 ....Apoc. 43
iv. 64 ....Evan. 159
iv. 85 ....Paul. 213
iv. 86, 77 ....Evann. 729-30
v. 16 ....Evan. 163
v. 17 ....Evann. Y & 392
v. 37 ....Evan. 165
vi. 4 ....Evst. 134
vi. 9 ....Evan. 168
vi. 13 ....Paul. 297
vi. 21 ....Act. 81
No mark..................Apost. 41

Rom. Propaganda 6

? ....Evann. T & T[d]
L. vi. 6 ....Evst. 37
9 ....Evan. 851
10 ....Evan. 732
19 ....Evan. 180

S. Marc. (*cont.*)— Total MSS.
11 .... Act. 96
12 .... Evst. 139
26 .... Evan. 888
27 .... Evan. 210
28 .... Evan. 357
29 .... Evan. 354
30, 31, 32 ...... Evann. 889–91
33 .... Paul. 110
34 .... Paul. 111
35 .... Paul. 112
36 .... Paul. 408
61, 144 .... Evann. 893–4
494 .... Evan. 466
495 .... Evan. 467
539 .... Evan. 211
540 .... Evan. 212
541 .... Evan. 355
542 .... Evan. 213
543 .... Evan. 214
544 .... Evan. 215
545 .... Evan. 356
546 .... Act. 140
548 .... Evst. 107
549 .... Evst. 108
550 .... Evst. 109
551 .... Evst. 110
Nanian. 1. 8 .... Evan. U
1. 9 .... Evst. 141
1. 10 .... Evan. 405
1. 11 .... Evan. 406
1. 12 .... Evan. 407
1. 14 .... Evan. 408
1. 15 .... Evan. 409
1. 17 .... Evan. 410
1. 18 .... Evan. 411
1. 19 .... Evan. 412
1. 20 .... Evan. 413
1. 21 .... Evan. 414
1. 22 .... Evan. 415
1. 23 .... Evst. 142
1. 24 .... Evan. 416
1. 25 .... Evan. 417
1. 28 .... Evan. 418
1. 34 .... Evan. 463
1. 45 .... Evst. 171
1. 46 .... Evst. 172
1. 47 .... Evst. 173
1. 48 .... Evst. 174
1. 49 .... Evst. 175
1. 50 .... Evst. 176
1. 51 .... Evst. 177
1. 52 .... Evst. 178
Ven. Mark Gr.
1. 3 .... Evan. 217
1. 4 .... Evst. 170
1. 56 .... Evan. 468
1. 57 .... Evan. 465
1. 58 .... Evan. 462
1. 59 .... Evan. 464
1. 60 .... Evan. 419

Total MSS.

TREASURY OF ST. MARK'S CHURCH.

Ven. Thesaur. 1. 53 ... Evst. 181
1. 54 ... Evst. 182
1. 55 ... Evst. 183

CHURCH OF S. GIORGIO DI GRECO.

A′ .... Evst. 184
Γ′ .... Evst. 185
B′ .... Evst. 186

Verona 1

Psalter .... Evan. O[c]

PALESTINE.

Jerusalem 42

Holy Cross 1 .... Act. 324
6 .... Evst. 797
46 .... Evan. 663
Holy Sepulc. 2, 5, 6, 14, 17, 31, 32, 33, 40, 41, 43, 44, 45, 46 .... Evann. 649–62
7, 15 .... Act. 257–8
12 .... Evst. 143
Patr. Libr. 28 .... Evan. 1149
31, 37, 41 .... Evann. 1261–3
42, 46, 47, 48 .... Evann. 1265–8
38, 43 .... Act. 416–7
49, 56, 59, 60, 62, 139 Evann. 1274–9
33 .... Evst. 923
105 .... Evst. 925
161, 526 .... Evst. 927–8
462 .... Act. 330
530 .... Evst. 932

St. Saba 27, 52 .... Evann. 664–5 ... 34
54 .... Evan. 673
56, 57, 58 ... Evann. 677–9
59, 60 .... Evann. 681–2
61 *a* and *b* ... Evann. 685–6
61 *c* .... Evan. 688
61 *d* .... Evan. 695
61 *e*, 62 *a*, 62 *b* Evann. 700–2
62 *c* .... Evan. 706
62 *d*, 62 *e* ... Evann. 710–1
Tower Libr. 12 .... Evst. 361
16, 52 .... Evst. 364–5
17, 23, 24 ... Evst. 147–9
20, 35 .... Act. 301–2
25, 26, 40, 44 Evst. 326–9
41 .... Paul. 417
45 .... Evan. 712
46, 47 .... Evann. 715–6

Porphyry, Bp. (*cont.*)— Total MSS.
St. Paul (Q) papyrus
St. Paul (palimpsest)
Olim Coislin. ....Evan. 437
Petropol. (Kiow) ......Evan. 481
98 ....Evan. 474
iv. 13 ....Evst. 194
vi. 470 ......Evan. 473
vii. 179 ......Evst. 195
viii. 80 ......Apost. 54
ix. 3. 471 ...Evan. 475
x. 180.........Evst. 196
xi. 3. 181 ...Evst. 197
Muralt. 10pe ....Evst. 198
38...............Apost. 72
38, 49, 40a ...Apost. 171–3
44...............Evst. 191
45a ....Apost. 183
56, 67, 105 ...Evann. 878–80
64...............Evst. 933
90...............Evst. 192
97...............Evan. 479
99...............Evan. 480
105 ....Evan. 476
110 ....Apost. 197
118 ....Evan. 477
129 ....Apoc. 103

SPAIN.

Escurial i. ....Evst. 40 ... 29
P. iii. 4 ......Act. 202
T. iii. 12......Act. 203
T. iii. 17......Paul. 470
Υ. ii. 8 ......Evan. 233
Φ. iii. 5 ......Evan. 230
Φ. iii. 6 ......Evan. 231
Φ. iii. 7 ......Evan. 232
X. iii. 3 ......Act. 204
X. iii. 6 ......Apoc. 143
X. iii. 10......Act. 205
X. iii. 12......Evst. 41
X. iii. 13......Evst. 42
X. iii. 15......Evan. 227
X. iii. 16......Evst. 43
X. iv. 2 ......Act. 206
X. iv. 9 ......Apost. 214
X. iv. 12......Evan. 228
X. iv. 15......Paul. 384
X. iv. 17......Evan. 226
X. iv. 21......Evan. 229
Ψ. iii. 2 ......Paul. 232
Ψ. iii. 6 ......Act. 207
Ψ. iii. 13, 14 Evann. 818–9
Ψ. iii. 17......Apoc. 85
Ψ. iii. 18......Act. 208
Ω. i. 16.........Evan. 820
Ω. iv. 22......Act. 209

Madrid, Reg. O. 10, 62 Evann. 821–2 4
O. 78 ....Act. 316
O. 19 (7).........Apoc. 144

Toledo ....Evst. 455... 1

Total MSS.

SWEDEN.

Linköping 1
Benzel 35 ....Act. 238

Upsal 6
Univ. Gr. 1 ....Act. 68
4 ....Evan. 613
9 ....Evan. 614
11 ....Act. 236
12 ....Evan. 616
13 ....Evan. 615

SWITZERLAND.

Basle, A. N. iii. 11 ......Paul. 7 ... 9
A. N. iii. 12 ......Evan. E and Apoc. 15
A. N. iii. 15 ......Evan. 817
A. N. iv. 1 ....Evan. 2
A. N. iv. 2 ....Evan. 1
A. N. iv. 4 ....Act. 2
A. N. iv. 5 ....Act. 4
O. ii. 23 ....Evan. 94
O. ii. 27 ....Evan. 92

Geneva 19.................Evan. 75... 2
20.................Act. 29

St. Gall ....Evan. Δ ... 3
17....................Evan. Oe
Evan. Wc

Zurich ....Evan. Od... 1

TURKEY.

Oriental Monasteries.

Albania 7
Beratinus.................Evan. Φ
Berat, Abp...............Evann. 1141
Act. 380
Apost. 153
In churches..............Evann. 1142–43
Evst. 758

Andros 1, 33, 34, 35, 37, ... 11
38, 48, 49, 50 ....Evann. 1286–94
2, 3 ....Apost. 255–6

Chalcis 37
Mon. Trin. 1, 2, 3, 4 ...Evann. 727, –28, –31, –32
Schol. 95, 133...........Evann. 734–5
Trin. 16; Schol. 9, 26, 33, 96 .... Act. 382-6
Trin. 1, 2, 3, 4, 5, 6, 7, 8, 9, 10; Schol. 1, 2, 3, 4, 5, 6, 7, 12, 74, 84........................Evst. 770–89
Trin. 13, 14, 15; School 59, 74, 88..............Apost. 154–9

Dionysius (*cont.*)— Total MSS.
378 ....Evst. 577
386 ....Apost. 169
387 ....Apost. 180
392 ....Apost. 184
Docheiariou 7, 21, 22, 30, 35, 39, 42, 46, 49, 51, 52, 55, 56, 59, 76, 142 ....Evann. 964–79
38, 48, 136, 139, 147 Act. 347–51
81 ....Apoc. 168
1, 10, 13, 14, 15, 19, 23, 24, 36, 58, 137...Evst. 651–61
20, 27, 141, 146 ......Apost. 131–4
Esphigmenou 25, 26, 27, 29, 30, 31, 186......Evann. 980–6
63, 64, 65, 66, 67, 68 Act. 352–7
19, 20, 21, 22, 23, 24, 27, 28, 35, 60 ......Evst. 662–71
Gregory 3, and τ. ἡγουμένου ....Evann. 922–3
In Ecclesia.........Evan. 1090
Iveron 2, 5, 7, 9, 18, 19, 21, 28, 29, 30, 31, 32, 33, 51, 52, 53, 55, 56, 59, 61, 63, 66, 67, 68, 69, 72, 75, 371, 548, 549, 550, 562, 599, 607, 608, 610, 636, 641, 647, 665, 671, 809, 871 ....Evann. 989–1031
639 ....Act. 322
24, 25, 37, 57, 60, 642, 643, 648 ....Act. 358–65
34, 379, 546, 594, 605, 644, 661 ....Apoc. 169–75
1, 3, 4, 6, 20, 23, 35, 36, 39, 635, 637, 638, 639, 640, 825, 826 ....Evst. 672–87
831 ....Apost. 135
Laura ....Evan. Ψ
Evann. 1071–80
Act. S
Paul. S
Panteleemon 25, 26, 28, 29 ....Evann. 1091–4
L, IV. vi. 4, IX. v. 3, XXVII. vi. 2, XXVII. vi. 3, XXVIII. i. 1 ......Evst. 722–7
Paul 4, 5....................Evann. 1095–6
1 ....Evan. 1307
2 ....Act. 374
1 ....Evst. 728
Philotheou 5, 21, 22, 33, 39, 41, 44, 45, 46, 47, 48, 51, 53, 68, 71, 72, 74, 77, 78, 80, 86, Evann. 1117–37

Philotheou (*cont.*)— Total MSS.
38, 76 ....Act. 378–9
1, 2, 3, 6, 18, 25, 61, 213 ....Evst. 748–55
17 ....Apost. 152
Protaton 41..............Evan. 1097
15, 44 ....Evann. 1305–6
32 ....Act. 375
11, 14, 15, 44, 56 ...Evst. 729–33
54 ....Apost. 144
32 ....Apost. 262
Simopetra 25, 26, 29, 34, 38, 39, 40, 41, 63, 145, 146, 147...Evann. 1098–1109
42 ....Act. 376
148 ....Evst. 464
17, 19, 20, 21, 24, 27, 28, 30, 33, 70 ......Evst. 734–43
6, 10, 148, 149, 150, 151 ....Apost. 145–50
St. Andrew...............Evan. ב
Α′, Ε′, Η′, Θ′ ....Evann. 905–8
Γ′, Δ′, ς, Ζ ....Evst. 579–82
Stauroniketa 43, 53, 54, 56, 70, 97, 127......Evann. 1110–6
52 ....Act. 377
1, 27, 42, 102 ....Evst. 744–7
129 ....Apost. 151
Vatopedi 206, 207, 211, 212, 213, 214, 215, 216, 217, 218, 219, 220, 414 ....Evann. 909–21
41, 201, 203, 210, 259, 328, 380, 419 ......Act. 336–43
90, 90 (2)..............Apoc. 165–6
48, 192, 193, 194, 195, 196, 197, 198, 200, 202, 204, 205, 208, 209, 220, 221, 223, 224, 225, 226, 227, 228, 229, 230, 231, 232, 233, 234, 235, 236, 237, 238, 239, 240, 241, 242, 243, 253, 254, 255, 256, 257, 271, 291 ....Evst. 583–626
Xenophon 1, 3, 58......Evann. 1310–2
1, 58, 59, 68 ....Evst. 710–13
Xeropotamou 103, 105, 107, 108, 115, 123, 200, 205, 221 ......Evann. 1081–89
110, 112, 118, 122, 125, 126, 234, 247 Evst. 714–21
Zographou 4, 14.........Evann. 987–8

TOTAL NUMBER OF GREEK MSS., ARRANGED ACCORDING TO COUNTRIES.

British Empire	438
Belgium (2), Denmark (3), Holland (7), Sweden (7)	19
Egypt	26
France	324
Germany	140
Greece	197
Italy	644
Carried forward	1788
Brought forward	1788
Palestine	260
Russia	104
Spain	34
Switzerland	15
Turkey (Oriental Monasteries)	724
United States	17
Places unknown	30
Total	2972

INDEX II.

OF WRITERS, PAST OWNERS, AND COLLATORS OF MSS.

E (Evan.), A (Acts and Cath. Epp.), P (Paul), Apoc. (Apocalypse), Evst. (Evangelistarium), Apost. (Apostolos).

END OF VOL. I.

A

PLAIN INTRODUCTION

TO THE

CRITICISM OF THE NEW TESTAMENT

FOR THE USE OF BIBLICAL STUDENTS

VOLUME II

FREDERICK HENRY AMBROSE
SCRIVENER

CONTENTS.

CHAPTER VII (*continued*).

CHAPTER VIII.

CHAPTER IX.

CHAPTER X.

CHAPTER XI.

CHAPTER XII.

ADDENDA ET CORRIGENDA.

Page 167, l. 16. I am convinced that it is only just measure to a book, which from a strong prejudice is not known nearly as much amongst Textualists as its great merit deserves, to draw more attention to 'The Revision Revised' by the late Dean Burgon. Those who have really studied it, to whichever school they belong, know how it teems with suggestion all through its striking pages. The present book owes a vast debt to him.

P. 248, ll. 8, 9 from bottom, *for* Sir Edmund Beckett *read* Lord Grimthorpe.

Some remains upon sacred Greek MSS. by Dr. Scrivener have been just published under the name of 'Adversaria Critica Sacra,' Cambridge: University Press. Reference has been made in this edition to some of the proof-sheets which were sent to the Editor. Vol. I. Appendix A.

INTRODUCTION

TO

THE CRITICISM OF THE TEXT OF THE NEW TESTAMENT.

CHAPTER I.

ANCIENT VERSIONS.

1. THE facts stated in the preceding volume have led us to believe that no extant manuscript of the Greek Testament yet discovered is older than the fourth century, and that those written as early as the sixth century are both few in number, and (with one notable exception) contain but incomplete portions, for the most part very small portions, of the sacred volume. When to these considerations we add the well-known circumstance that the most ancient codices vary widely and perpetually from the commonly received text and from each other, it becomes desirable for us to obtain, if possible, some evidence as to the character of those copies of the New Testament which were used by the primitive Christians in times anterior to the date of the most venerable now preserved.

Such sources of information, though of a more indirect and precarious kind than manuscripts of the original can supply, are open to us in the Versions of Holy Scripture, made at the remotest period in the history of the Church, for the use of believers whose native tongue was not Greek. After the composition of the writings of the New Testament, it is evident that the Church was in possession of Sacred Books which were of the utmost value, both to those who were already members, and in the conversion of such as had not yet come to the real knowledge of the Faith. The nearness of Syria to Judea, and the growth of the Church at Antioch and Damascus in the earliest days, must have produced a demand for a rendering into the Syriac languages; and the bilingual condition of most of the Roman Empire must have entailed a constant desire amongst vast multitudes to read in their own tongue a verification of the truths taught them. Accordingly translations, certainly of the New and probably also of the Old Testament, were executed not later than the second century in the Syriac and Latin languages, and, so far as their present state enables us to judge of the documents from which they were rendered, they represent to us a modification of the inspired text which existed within a century of the death of the Apostles. Later on, the influence of Alexandria opened the districts to the south and gave birth to the Coptic versions. And about the time of the acceptance of the Christian Religion by the Empire a further impetus was given, and the Vulgate and the Gothic and Ethiopic versions were soon made, followed by others according as the demand arose.

Indeed, the fact that versions as a class go much further back than MSS., constitutes one of the chiefest points of their importance in Textual Criticism; since the range of the ancient versions may be roughly estimated as reaching from the second to the tenth century, whereas the period of extant MSS. did not commence till the fourth century was well advanced, and were continued into the sixteenth. Their respective ages, too, are actually known, and do not rest upon probabilities, as in the first kind of evidence. They are also generally authorized translations, made either by a body of men, or by one eminent authority whose work was adopted amongst the people for whose use the Holy Scriptures had been translated. And they probably represented, either many MSS., or a small body of accepted MSS.

On the other hand, versions as evidence are not without their special drawbacks. It may be found as difficult to arrive at the primitive text of a version, as of the Greek original itself;

whether from variations in the different copies, or from suspicions of subsequent correction. Besides this, some are secondary versions, being derived not from the Greek, but from some version of the Greek. Again, some are 'sense-translations [1],' rather than word-renderings, and it is in many cases difficult to infer their real verdict. Of course, none but an expert, such as Dr. S. C. Malan, or the several revisers of the succeeding chapters of this edition, can pronounce upon the character of the verdict of a version in question.

It will be seen then that versions by themselves cannot be taken to establish any reading, because manuscripts are necessarily first authorities, and there is no lack of abundance in such testimony. Yet they confirm, or help to decide, the conclusions or the leanings of manuscriptal evidence: and taken in connexion with other witnesses, they have much independent force, varying of course according to the character of the version or versions, and the nature and extent of their agreement. In this respect they possess great importance.

The experience of recent years has shown that it is misleading to construct classes of versions in regard to their relative importance. Fuller knowledge casts aside, and often with contumely, such adventitious helps. Readers are therefore referred for information upon each version to the chapter or section which is devoted to it, and are recommended to gather their apprehensions of the several values of those versions from the facts recorded therein, and from use of them in the various passages of Holy Scripture where they are cited. But the following is a list of the chief versions of the New Testament which were made before the introduction of printing, and a few handposts are inserted here and there for elementary guidance in the study of them :—

I. Peshitto Syriac (cent. ii), called 'the Queen of Versions' (Hort, cent. iii).

II. Latin version or versions [2] (ii, or ii–iv). Remarkable for age.

[1] *See* Studia Biblica et Ecclesiastica, ii. 'Evidence of Early Versions and Patristic Quotations, &c.,' by the Rev. Ll. J. M. Bebb, M.A., p. 211. In this chapter, which from press reasons has been curtailed, I am glad to refer to Mr. Bebb's careful and thoughtful essay.

[2] I cannot help expressing my strong opinion that there were a great many

III. Bohairic (or Memphitic) (iii? Stern, iv or v), best of the Egyptian versions.

IV. Sahidic (or Thebaic) (iii?), second Egyptian version.

V. Middle-Egyptian (iii?).

VI. Fayoumic (ii or iii?).

VII. Curetonian (iv), corrupt,—(Hort, ii).

VIII. Vulgate (iv), made by Jerome from the various Latin texts in vogue at the time.

IX. Gothic (iv).

X. Armenian (iv).

XI. Jerusalem (v?).

XII. Ethiopic (v–vi). A large number of MSS. exist.

XIII. Georgian (v, vi?).

XIV. Philoxenian (A.D. 508), corrected by Thomas of Harkel, Harkleian (A.D. 616); very literal.

XV. Arabic versions (ix–xvii), made from Greek, Syriac, Egyptian, &c.

XVI. Anglo-Saxon (x) of the Gospels, made from the Vulgate.

XVII. Frankish (ix).

XVIII. Two Persic, from the Peshitto (xiii), and from the Greek (xiv).

The last four, being secondary, are worth but little as critical helps.

distinct Latin versions, and that they had a great many sources of origin:—briefly speaking,

(*a*) Because of the testimony of Augustine and Jerome;

(*b*) Because Latin translations from the first *must* have been wanted everywhere, and must have been constantly supplied. On the one hand the bilingualism prevalent in the Roman Empire would ensure a large number of translators: and on the other the want of accurate Greek scholarship would account for the numerous errors found in and propagated by the old Latin manuscripts. Copies of one translation could not in those days have been supplied in every place adequately to the want;

(*c*) Because of the multitude of synonyms to be found in Old Latin MSS.;

(*d*) Because on almost all disputed passages Old Latin evidence can be quoted on both sides;

(*e*) Because the various MSS. differ so thoroughly that each MS. is quoted as resting upon its own authority, and no one standard has been reached or is in view, the utmost that has been done in this respect being to group them.

But see next chapter: this is an undecided question.—Ed.

It may be added, that from the literary activity of the last ten years in the closer examination of ancient records, and through discoveries in Egypt and elsewhere, a great deal has been added to the knowledge previously existing upon this part of the subject of this book. Therefore in the succeeding chapters much alteration has been found necessary both in the way of correction, because some theories have been exploded under the increased light of wider information, and by the insertion of additions from the results of investigation and of study. The editor has been readily and generously assisted by several accomplished scholars who are experts in their respective departments; and the names of the various writers who have contributed to the four succeeding chapters will form a sufficient guarantee for the soundness and completeness of the information therein supplied.

CHAPTER II.

SYRIAC VERSIONS.

IN the following account of the earlier Syriac versions, the Editor has received the most valuable help from the Rev. G. H. Gwilliam, B.D., Fellow of Hertford College, who is editing the Peshitto Gospels for the University of Oxford. And upon the Harkleian version, he is indebted for important assistance to the Rev. H. Deane, late Fellow of St. John's College, whose labours have been unfortunately stopped by failure in eyesight.

1. *The Peshitto.*

The Aramaean or Syriac (preserved to this day as their sacred tongue by several Eastern Churches) is an important branch of the great Semitic family of languages, and as early as Jacob's age existed distinct from the Hebrew (Gen. xxxi. 47). As we now find it in books, it was spoken in the north of Syria and in Upper Mesopotamia about Edessa, and survives to this day in the vernacular of the plateau to the north of Mardin and Nisibis [1]. It is a more copious, flexible, and elegant language than the old Hebrew (which ceased to be vernacular at the Babylonish captivity) had ever the means of becoming, and is so intimately akin to the Chaldee as spoken at Babylon, and throughout Syria, that the latter was popularly known by its name (2 Kings xviii. 26; Isa. xxxvi. 11; Dan. ii. 4) [2]. As the Gospel took firm root at Antioch within a few years after the Lord's Ascension (Acts xi. 19–27; xiii. 1, &c.), we might deem it probable that its tidings soon spread from the Greek capital into the native interior, even though we utterly rejected the vener-

[1] Duval, Grammaire Syriaque, p. xi.

[2] Dr. Neubauer in Studia Biblica, vol. i. (Clarendon Press), 'The Dialects of Palestine in the time of Christ,' distinguishes between (1) Babylonian Aramaic, (2) Galilaean Aramaic, (3) the purer Aramaic spoken at Jerusalem, and (4) modernized Hebrew also used at Jerusalem.

able tradition of Thaddaeus' mission to Abgarus, toparch of Edessa, as well as the fable of that monarch's intercourse with Christ while yet on earth (Eusebius, Eccl. Hist., i. 13; ii. 1). At all events we are sure that Christianity flourished in these regions at a very early period; it is even possible that the Syriac Scriptures were seen by Hegesippus in the second century (Euseb., Eccl. Hist., iv. 22); they were familiarly used and claimed as his national version by the eminent Ephraem of Edessa in the fourth. Thus the universal belief of later ages, and the very nature of the case, seem to render it unquestionable that the Syrian Church was possessed of a translation, both of the Old and New Testament, which it used habitually, and for public worship exclusively, from the second century of our era downwards: as early as A.D. 170 ὁ Σύρος is cited by Melito on Gen. xxii. 13 (Mill, Proleg. § 1239)[1]. And the sad history of that distracted Church can leave no room to doubt what that version was. In the middle of the fifth century, the third and fourth general Councils at Ephesus and Chalcedon proved the immediate occasions of dividing the Syrian Christians into three, and eventually into yet more, hostile communions. These grievous divisions have now subsisted for fourteen hundred years, and though the bitterness of controversy has abated, the estrangement of the rival Churches is as complete and hopeless as ever[2]. Yet the same translation of Holy Scripture is read alike in the public assemblies of the Nestorians among the fastnesses of Koordistan, of the Monophysites who are scattered over the plains of Syria, of the Christians of St. Thomas along the coast of Malabar, and of the

[1] I cannot agree with Dr. Field (Origenis Hexaplorum quae supersunt, Proleg. lxxvii, 1874) that the Peshitto is not the Syriac version here quoted by Melito; but, while he admits a frequent resemblance between it and the renderings imputed to 'the Syrian,' he certainly produces not a few instances of diversity between the two. Besides Theodoret, who often opposes ὁ Σύρος to ὁ Ἑβραῖος (Thren. 1. 15 and passim), Field notes the following writers as citing the former,—Didymus, Diodorus, Eusebius of Emesa, Polychronius, Apollinarius, Chrysostom, Procopius (ibid. p. lxvii).

[2] All modern accounts of the unorthodox sects of the East confirm Walton's gracious language two hundred years ago: 'Etsi verò, olim in haereses miserè prolapsi, se a reliquis Ecclesiae Catholicae membris separarint, unde justo Dei judicio sub Infidelium jugo oppressi serviunt, qui ipsis dominantur, ex continuis tamen calamitatibus edocti et sapientiores redditi (est enim Schola Crucis Schola Lucis) tandem eorum misertus Misericordiarum Pater eos ad rectam sanamque mentem, rejectis antiquis erroribus, reduxit (Walton, Prolegomena, Wrangham, Tom. ii. p. 500).

Maronites on the mountain-terraces of Lebanon. Even though these last acknowledged the supremacy of Rome in the twelfth century, and certain Nestorians of Chaldaea in the eighteenth, both societies claimed at the time, and enjoy to this day, the free use of their Syriac translation of Holy Scripture. Manuscripts too, obtained from each of these rival communions, have flowed from time to time into the libraries of the West, yet they all exhibit a text in every important respect the same; all are without the Apocalypse and four of the Catholic Epistles, which latter we know to have been wanting in the Syriac in the sixth century (Cosmas Indicopleustes apud Montfaucon, 'Collectio Nova Patrum et Script. Graec.,' Tom. ii. p. 292), a defect, we may observe in passing, which alone is no slight proof of the high antiquity of the version that omits them; all correspond with whatever we know from other sources of that translation which, in contrast with one more recent, was termed 'old' (ܩܕܝܡܐ) by Thomas of Harkel A.D. 616, and 'Peshitto' (ܦܫܝܛܬܐ) the 'Simple,' by the great Monophysite doctor, Gregory Bar-Hebraeus [1226–86]. Literary history can hardly afford a more powerful case than has been established for the identity of the version of the Syriac now called the *Peshitto* with that used by the Eastern Church, long before the great schism had its beginning in the native land of the blessed Gospel.

The first printed edition of this most venerable monument of the Christian faith was published in quarto at Vienna in the year 1555 (some copies are re-dated 1562), at the expense of the Emperor Ferdinand I, on the recommendation and with the active aid of his Chancellor, Albert Widmanstadt, an accomplished person, whose travelling name in Italy was John Lucretius. It was undertaken at the instance of Moses of Mardin, legate from the Monophysite Patriarch Ignatius to Pope Julius III (1550–55), who seems to have brought with him a manuscript, the text whereof was of the Jacobite family, although written at Mosul, for publication in the West. Widmanstadt contributed a second manuscript of his own, though it does not appear whether either or both contained the whole New Testament. This beautiful book, the different portions of which have separate dedications, was edited by Widmanstadt, by Moses, and by W. Postell jointly, in an elegant type of the modern Syriac character, the vowel and diacritic points, especially the *linea occultans*, being frequently dropped, with subscriptions and titles indicating the Jacobite Church Lessons in the older, or Estrangelo, letter. It omits, as was natural and right, those books which the Peshitto does not contain: viz. the second Epistle of Peter, the second and third of John, that of Jude and the Apocalypse, together with the disputed passage John vii. 53—viii. 11, and the doubtful, or more than doubtful, clauses in Matt. xxvii. 35; Acts viii. 37; xv. 34; xxviii. 29; I John v. 7, 8. It omits Luke xxii. 17, 18, *see* Chap. XII on the passage. This *editio princeps* of the Peshitto New Testament, though now become very scarce (one half of its thousand copies having been sent into Syria), is held in high and deserved repute, as its text is apparently based on manuscript authority alone.

Immanuel Tremellius [1510–80], a converted Jew (the proselyte, first of Cardinal Pole, then of Peter Martyr), and Professor of Divinity at Heidelberg, published the second edition in folio in 1569, containing the New Testament in Hebrew type, with a literal Latin version, accompanied by the Greek text and Beza's translation of it, having a Chaldee and Syriac grammar annexed. Tremellius used several manuscripts, especially one at Heidelberg, and made from them and his own conjecture many changes, that were not always improvements, in the text; besides admitting some grammatical forms which are Chaldee rather than Syriac. His Latin version has been used as their basis by later editors, down to the time of Schaaf. Tremellius' and Beza's Latin versions were reprinted together in London, without their respective originals, in 1592. Subsequent editions of the Peshitto New Testament were those of the folio Antwerp or Royal Spanish Polyglott of Plantin (1571–73), in Hebrew and Syriac type, revised from a copy written about A.D. 1200, which Postell had brought from the East: two other editions of Plantin in Hebrew type without points (1574, 8vo; 1575, 18mo), the second containing various readings extracted by Francis Rapheleng from a Cologne manuscript for his own reprints of 1575 and subsequently of 1583: the smaller Paris edition, also in unpointed Hebrew letters, 1584, 4to, by Guy Le Fevre de la Boderie, who prepared the Syriac portion of the Antwerp Polyglott in 1571: that of Elias Hutter, in two folio volumes (Nuremberg, 1599–1600), in Hebrew characters; this editor venturing to supply in Syriac of his own making the single passages wanting in the *editio princeps* of Widmanstadt, and the spurious Epistle to the Laodiceans. Martin Trost's edition (Anhalt-Cöthen, 1621, 4to), in Syriac characters, with vowel-points, a list of various readings, and a Latin translation, is superior to Hutter's.

The magnificent Paris Polyglott (fol. 1645) is the first which gives us the Old Testament portion of the Peshitto, though in an incomplete state. The Maronite Gabriel Sionita, who superintended this part of the Polyglott, made several changes in the system of vowel punctuation, possibly from analogy rather than from manuscript authority, but certainly for the better. He inserted as integral portions of the Peshitto the version of the four missing Catholic Epistles, which had been published in 1630 by our illustrious oriental scholar, Edward Pococke, from a manuscript in the Bodleian (Orient. 119)[1]: and another of the Apocalypse, edited at Leyden in 1627 by Louis De Dieu, from a manuscript, since examined by Tregelles, in the University Library there (Scaliger MS. 18), and from one sent him by Archbishop Ussher, which is now in the Library of Trinity College, Dublin (B. 5. 16). Of the two, the version of the Catholic Epistles seems decidedly the older, and both bear much resemblance to the later Syriac or Harkleian translation, but neither have claim to be regarded as portions of the original Peshitto, to which, however, they have been appended ever since.

Bp. Walton's, or the London Polyglott (fol. 1654–7), affords us little more than a reprint of Sionita's Syriac text, with Trost's various readings appended, but interpolates the text yet further by inserting John vii. 53—viii. 11. This passage, which is the 'Pericope de adultera,' is found in Archbishop Ussher's copy, dated A.D. 1627, and made from a Maronite MS. of much esteem at Kenobin under Mt. Lebanon; also in Brit. Mus. 14,470, in Cod. Barsalibaei at New College, Oxford, and in the Paris Nat. Library xxii, of which the two last copies are Harkleian, and the one in the British Museum is Peshitto[2]. We are left to conjecture as to the real date and origin of these translations, except that as far

[1] Dean Payne Smith's Catalogue, pp. 109-112. In the great Cambridge manuscript (Oo. I. 1, 2) the Epistles of 2 Peter, 2 and 3 John, and Jude follow 1 John, and are continued on the same quire, as Mr. Bradshaw reports.

[2] See an admirable paper by Dr. Gwynn in 'Transactions of the Royal Irish Academy,' xxvii. 8, 'On a Syriac MS. belonging to Archbishop Ussher.' This MS. was procured for Ussher in 1626 by T. Davies, lent to De Dieu, who used it in 1631, and is now in Trinity College Library, Dublin.

as the Harkleian is concerned, Dr. Gwynn has shown that according to the Paris and Brit. Mus. MSS. they are claimed for Paul, a contemporary of Thomas of Harkel.

Giles Gutbier published at Hamburg (8vo, 1664) an edition containing all the interpolated matter, and 1 John v. 7, 8 in addition, from Tremellius' own version, which he inserted in *his* margin. Gutbier used two manuscripts, by one of which, belonging to Constantine L'Empereur, he corrected Sionita's system of punctuation. A glossary, notes, and various readings are annexed. The Sulzbach edition 12mo, 1684, seems a mere reprint of Plantin's; nor does that published in Rome in 1713 for the use of the Maronites, though grounded upon manuscript authority, appear to have much critical value.

A collation of the various readings in all the preceding editions, excepting those of 1684 and 1713, is affixed to the Syriac N. T. of J. Leusden and Ch. Schaaf (4to, Leyden, 1708–9: with a new title-page 1717). It extends over one hundred pages, and, though most of the changes noted are very insignificant, is tolerably accurate and of considerable value. This edition contains the Latin version of Tremellius not too thoroughly revised, and is usually accompanied with an admirable 'Lexicon Syriacum Concordantiale' of the Peshitto New Testament. Its worth, however, is considerably lessened by a fancy of Leusden for pointing the vowels according to the rules of Chaldee rather than of Syriac grammar: after his death, indeed, and from Luke xviii. 27 onwards, this grave mistake was corrected by Schaaf[1]. Of modern editions the most convenient, or certainly the most accessible to English students, are the N. T. which Professor Lee prepared in 1816 for the British and Foreign Bible Society with the Eastern Church Lessons noted in Syriac, and that of Wm. Greenfield [d. 1831], both in Bagster's Polyglott of 1828, and in a small and separate form; the latter editor aims at representing Widmanstadt's text distinct from the subsequent additions derived from other sources. Lee's edition was grounded on a collation of three fresh manuscripts, besides the application of other matter previously available for the

[1] Yet, besides his error of judgement in bringing into the Peshitto text such passages as we have just enumerated, Schaaf follows the Paris and London Polyglotts when interpolating *τῶν σωζομένων* Apoc. xxi. 24, although the words had been omitted by De Dieu (1627) and Gutbier (1664).

revision of the text; but the materials on which he founded his conclusions have never been printed, although their learned collector once intended to do so, and many years afterwards consented to lend them to Scrivener for that purpose; a promise which his death in 1848 ultimately hindered him from redeeming. An edition of the Gospels printed in 1829 by the British and Foreign Bible Society for the Nestorian Christians was based on a single manuscript brought from Mosul by Dr. Wolff. Besides these, two editions have been published by the American Bible Society, at Oroomia, Persia, in 1846, and at New York (a reprint of the former) in 1878 [1].

From the foregoing statement it will plainly appear that no edition of the Peshitto Syriac has yet been published with that critical care on the part of editors which its antiquity and importance so urgently demand. It is therefore a matter of deep satisfaction that the work commenced by the late Philip Pusey has been brought near conclusion by the Rev. G. H. Gwilliam, for the University of Oxford. Mr. Gwilliam has informed the editor that the Peshitto 'Tetraevangelium' will be the first part published, and will exhibit in its *apparatus criticus* readings taken from forty manuscripts, some of which have been collated throughout, others in parts. From the account given in the third volume of 'Studia Biblica et Ecclesiastica,' we learn that the authorities on which he bases his text in this elaborate edition are as follows:—

1. Brit. Mus. Add. 14,479 [A. D. 534], the fourteen Epistles of St. Paul, Hebrews being always included by the Syrians.
2. Brit. Mus. Add. 14,459 [A. D. 530, last letter illegible], SS. Luke and John. Possibly older than the last.
3. Rome, Vatican [A. D. 548]. A Tetraevangelium, written at Edessa.
4. Florence, Laurentian Library [A. D. 586].
5. Brit. Mus. 14,460 [A. D. 600]. A Nestorian Estrangelo, written in the district of Naarda, near Bagdad.
6. Brit. Mus. 14,471 [A. D. 615]. Another Nestorian MS. of the Gospels, written at Nisibis.
7. Cod. Guelpherbytanus [A. D. 634]. Written in the convent of Beth Chela, near Damascus.
8. Brit. Mus. Add. 14,448 [A. D. 699–700]. A Nestorian MS. Whole of New Testament as received in the Syrian Church.
9. Brit. Mus. Add. 7157 [A. D. 768]. Written at Beth Kuka.

[1] Compare the Printed Editions of the Syriac New Testament, *Church Quarterly Review*, vol. xxvi, no. lii, 1888, and a Bibliographical Appendix by Prof. Isaac H. Hall to Dr. Murdock's Translation of the Peshitto.

10. Brit. Mus. Add. 14,459 [about A. D. 450], SS. Matthew and Mark.
11. Brit. Mus. Add. 17,117 [about A. D. 450].
12. Brit. Mus. Add. 14,470 [v–vi]. Whole of Peshitto New Testament. The Pericope de Adultera has been added as stated above, p. 10.
13. Brit. Mus. Add. 14,453 [v–vi]. A Tetraevangelium.
14. Brit. Mus. Add. 14,476 [v–vi]. Paul.
15. Brit. Mus. Add. 14,480 [v-vi]. Paul.
16. Cod. Crawfordianus I [vi]. A very handsome Tetraevangelium, and in excellent preservation.
17. Codd. Dawkinsiani III, XXVII, in the Bodleian Library.
18. Partial collations of many other MSS. in the British Museum.
19. The editions published by the American Bible Society, which were, at least to some extent, revised on the authority of ancient Nestorian copies.
20. The evidence of the Syriac Massorah of both the Nestorian and the Jacobite (Karkaphensian) recensions.

It is necessary to mention briefly this remarkable wealth of evidence, probably to be largely increased by future investigations, in which the Peshitto presents no inconsiderable parallel to the vast amount of authorities on which the Greek Text of the New Testament depends, because people are apt to underrate the grand position of the Peshitto version, when comparing it with the Curetonian Syriac, of which the sole evidence consists only of two codices, if the newly-discovered one turns out to be what was anticipated.

It is not easy to determine why the name of *Peshitto*, 'Simple,' 'Common,' should have been given to the oldest Syriac version of Scripture, to distinguish it from others that were subsequently made[1]. In comparison with the Harkleian it is the very reverse of a close rendering of the original. Perhaps the title refers to its common and popular use[2]. We shall presently submit to the reader a few extracts from it, contrasted with the same passages in other Syriac versions; for the present we can but assent to the ripe judgement of Michaelis, who, after thirty

[1] Tregelles in 'Smith's Dictionary of the Bible' thinks that the term was originally applied to the Syriac version of the Hebrew Old Testament, in order to discriminate between it and the Greek Hexapla, or the Syro-hexaplar translation derived from it, with their apparatus of obeli and asterisks. To this view Dr. Field adds his weighty authority (Origenis Hexapla, Proleg. p. ix, note 1), adding that for this reason the pure Septuagint version also is called *ἁπλοῦν* (1 Kings vii. 18; xii. 22), to distinguish its rendering from what is given *ἐν τῷ ἑξαπλῷ*. The epithet which was proper to the Old Testament in course of time attached itself to the New.

[2] ܡܦܩܬܐ ܦܫܝܛܬܐ, versio vulgata, popularis, Thes. Syr. 3319.

years' study of its contents, declared that he could consult no translation with so much confidence in cases of difficulty and doubt [1].

2. *The Curetonian Syriac.*

The volume which contained the greater part of the Curetonian portions of the Gospels was brought by Archdeacon Tattam in 1842 from the Monastery of St. Mary Deipara in the Nitrian Desert (p. 140). Eighty leaves and a half were picked out by Dr. Cureton, then one of the officers in the Manuscript department of the British Museum, from a mass of other matter which had been bound up with them by unlearned possessors, and comprise the Additional MS. 14,451* of the Library they adorn, and two more reached England in 1847. They are in quarto, with two columns on a page, in a bold hand and the Estrangelo or old Syriac character, on vellum originally very white, the single points for stops, some titles, &c. being in red ink; there are no marks of Church Lessons by the first hand, which Cureton (a most competent judge) assigned to the middle of the fifth century. The fragments contain Matt. i. 1—viii. 22; x. 32—xxiii. 25; Mark xvi. 17–20; John i. 1–42; iii. 5—vii. 37; (but many words in iii. 6—iv. 6 are illegible); xiv. 10–12; 15–19; 21–23; 26–29; Luke ii. 48—iii. 16; vii. 33—xv. 21; xvii. 23—xxiv. 44, or 1786 verses, so arranged that St. Mark's Gospel is here immediately followed by St. John's. Three more leaves of this version (part, perhaps, of the same MS.) were found among the Syriac MSS. procured by Dr. Sachau, and now at Berlin (Royal Libr. Orient. quart. 528). They contain Luke xv. 22—xvi. 12; xvii. 1–23; John vii. 37–52; viii. 12–19. They were published by Roediger (Monatsbericht, Berlin Royal Academy of Sciences, July, 1872), and were privately printed by the late Professor Wright to range with Cureton's volume. Within the last year the discovery has been announced of another Curetonian MS., which was found in the Library of the Convent on Mount Sinai by Mrs. Lewis. An edition of it is now in progress, but will not be published soon enough for notice in this work. The Syriac text of the London MS. was printed in fine Estrangelo type in 1848, and freely imparted to such scholars

[1] A full list of editions of all the Syriac versions is given in the Syriac Grammar of Nestle (tr. Kennedy), Litteratura, pp. 17–30.

as might need its help; but it was not till 1858 that the work was published[1], with a very literal translation into rather bald English, a beautiful and exact facsimile (Luke xv. 11–13; 16–19) by Mrs. Cureton, and a Preface (pp. xcv), full of interesting and indeed startling matter. Dr. Cureton went so far as to persuade himself that he had discovered in these Syriac fragments a text of St. Matthew's Gospel that 'to a great extent, has retained the identical terms and expressions which the Apostle himself employed; and that we have here, in our Lord's discourses, to a great extent the very same words as the Divine Author of our holy religion Himself uttered in proclaiming the glad tidings of salvation in the Hebrew dialect...' (p. xciii): that here in fact we have *to a great extent* the original of that Hebrew Gospel of St. Matthew of which the canonical Greek Gospel is but a translation. It is beside our present purpose to examine in detail the arguments of Dr. Cureton on this head[2], and it would be the less necessary in any case, since they seem to have convinced no one save himself: but the place his version occupies with reference to the Peshitto is a question upon which there has been and still prevails a controversy which largely concerns the issue between contending schools of textual critics[3].

[1] 'Remains of a very ancient recension of the four Gospels in Syriac, hitherto unknown in Europe, discovered, edited, and translated by William Cureton, D.D. . . . Canon of Westminster,' 4to, London, 1858. *See* also Wright's description of the MSS. in Catalogue of Syriac MSS. in the British Museum, vol. i. pp. 73–5.

[2] Less able writers than Dr. Cureton have made out a strong, though not a convincing case, for the Hebrew origin of St. Matthew's Gospel, and thus far his argument is plausible enough. To demonstrate that the version he has discovered is based upon that Hebrew original, at least so far as to be a modification of it and not a translation from the Greek, he has but a single plea that will bear examination, viz. that out of the many readings of the Hebrew or Nazarene Gospel with which we are acquainted, his manuscript agrees with it in the one particular of inserting the *three kings*, ch. i. 8, though even here the number of *fourteen* generations retained in ver. 17 shows them to be an interpolation. Such cases as *Juda*, ch. ii. 1; *Ramtha*, ver. 18; ܕ for ὅτι or the relative, ch. xiii. 16, can prove nothing, as they are common to the Curetonian with the Peshitto, from which version they may very well have been derived.

[3] The title to St. Matthew is remarkable; for while (in the subscription) we read, 'Gospel of Markos,' and 'Gospel of Juchanan' occurs, as in other Syriac MSS., to St. Matthew is prefixed the title 'Evangeliom dampharsa Mattai.' The meaning of the second word is doubtful in this application. The root means *divide, distinguish, separate*—cf. Daniel v. 28. Cureton (Pref. vi) says (1) that the great authority Bernstein suggested 'Evangelium per anni circulum dispositum.' This is inapplicable, because the copy is not set out in Church Lessons, although

Any one who shall compare the verses we have cited from them in parallel columns (pp. 38–40) will readily admit that the translations have a common origin, whatever that may be; many other passages, though not perhaps of equal length, might be named where the resemblance is closer still; where for twenty words together the Peshitto and the Curetonian shall be positively identical, although the Syriac idiom would admit other words and another order just as naturally as that actually employed. Nor will this conclusion be shaken by the not less manifest fact that throughout many passages the diversity is so great that no one, with those places alone before him, would be led to suspect any connexion between the two versions; for resemblances in such a case furnish a positive proof, not to be weakened by the mere negative presumption supplied by divergencies. Add to this the consideration that the Greek manuscripts from which either version was made or corrected (as the case may prove) were materially different in their character; the Peshitto for the most part favouring Cod. A[1], the Curetonian taking part with Cod. D, or with the Old Latin, or often standing quite alone, unsupported by any critical authority whatever; and the reader is then in possession of the whole case, from whose perplexities we have to unravel our decision, which of these two recensions

some are noted by a much later hand in the margins. (2) Cureton himself, noticing a defect in the vellum before ܡܬܝ, would read ܕܡܬܝ, and render 'The distinct Gospel of Matthew.' This he understood to indicate that the translation of Matthew had a different origin from the other books, and was 'built upon the original Aramaic text, which was the work of the Apostle himself.' But there is nothing to justify the insertion of a ܕ, which is required to connect the title with the following name. The title belongs to the whole work, 'Evangeliom dampharsa—Mattai' [Catalogue Brit. Mus. l.c.]; the other names being preceded by 'Evangeliom' only. (3) 'Dampharsa' has been rendered 'explained' [*see* the review in 'Journal of Sacred Literature,' 1858], viz. from the text of the Peshitto; and this, as we shall see presently, agrees with the character of the Curetonian, for it abounds in deliberate alterations. But (4) from the quotations and references in the 'Thesaurus Syriacus' (R. Payne Smith), col. 3304, it seems almost certain that the epithet means 'separated,' as opposed to 'united in a Harmony.' Such, of course, the Codex Curetonianus is, but further evidence is required to justify the inference that the Curetonian was the offspring of Tatian's Harmony, and became the parent of the Peshitto, an opinion in large measure contradicted by the character of the translation.

[1] 'Si nous devons en croire Scrivener, la version syriaque dite *Peshitto* s'accorde bien plus avec lui [Cod. A] qu'avec (B).' (Les Livres Saints, &c., Pau et Vevey, 1872, Préface, p. iii.) The fact is notoriously true, and of course rests not on Scrivener's evidence, but on universal consent.

best exhibits the text of the Holy Gospels as received from the second century downwards by the Syrian Church.

We must not dissemble the fact that Cureton's view of the superior antiquity of the Curetonian to the Peshitto has been adopted by many eminent scholars. So for example Dr. Hort, who was obliged to account for the relation of the two by a baseless supposition of an imaginary recension at Edessa or Nisibis when the Peshitto was drawn up as a Syrian 'Vulgate' (The New Testament in Greek, pp. 135–7). So with more strength of argument Dr. Nestle in 'Real-Encyclopædie für protestanche Theologie en Kirche[1].'

1. Now it is obvious to remark, in the first place, that the Peshitto has the advantage of *possession*, and that too of fourteen centuries standing. The mere fact that the Syriac manuscripts of the rival sects, whether modern or as old as the seventh century, agree with each other in the most important points, and at least to a large extent with the citations from Ephraem and Aphraates, as will be shown, seems to bring the Peshitto text, substantially in the same state as we have it at present, up to the fourth century of our era. Of this version, again, there are many codices, of different ages and widely diffused; of the Curetonian there is indeed one, of the fifth century, so far as the verdict of a most accomplished judge can determine so delicate a question: yet surely this is not to be much preferred, in respect to antiquity, to those ancient copies of the Peshitto which we have enumerated on pp. 10, 11, and which include a MS. of the fifth century, several others nearly as ancient, and two which are dated in the sixth century, the Florentine of A. D. 586, and the Vatican of A. D. 548. Another 'Curetonian' MS., lately discovered, is still under examination, and we have, as yet, no adequate account of it. From the Peshitto, as the authorized version of the Oriental Church, there are many quotations in Syriac books from the fourth century downwards; Dr. Cureton, perhaps the profoundest Syriac scholar of his day in England, failed to allege any *second* citation from the Gospels by a native writer which

[1] The student may also consult:—Evangelienfragmente, F. Baethgen, 1885. Disputatio de cod. Evangg. Syr. Curetoniano, Hermansen, 1859. Lehir's Etude, Paris, 1859. Dr. Harman in Journal of the Society of Biblical Literature, Boston, 1885. Zeitschrift des Morgenländische Gesellschaft, 1859, p. 472. Dr. Wildeboer in De Waarde der Syrische Evangeliën (Leiden, 1880) gives three pages of the literature of the question.

might serve to keep in countenance the statement of Dionysius Barsalibi, late in the twelfth century, that 'there is found occasionally a Syriac copy made out of the Hebrew, which inserts the three kings in the genealogy' (Matt. i. 8)[1]. With every wish to give to this respectable old writer, and to others who bear testimony to the same reading, the consideration that is fairly their due, we can hardly fail to see that the weight of evidence enormously preponderates in the opposite scale.

2. It will probably be admitted that in external proof Cureton's theory is not strong, while yet the internal character of the version may be deemed by many powerfully to favour his view. Negligent or licentious renderings (and the Curetonian Syriac is pretty full of them) cannot but lessen a version's usefulness as an instrument of criticism, by increasing our difficulty of reproducing the precise words of the original which the translator had before him; but in another point of view these very faults may still form the main strength of Dr. Cureton's case. It is, no doubt, a grave suggestion, that the more polished, accurate, faithful, and grammatical of the two versions—and the Peshitto richly deserves all this praise—is more likely to have been produced by a careful and gradual revision of one much its inferior in these respects, than the worse to have originated in the mere corruption of the better (Cureton, Pref. p. lxxxi). *A priori*, we readily confess that probability inclines this way; but it is a probability which needs the confirmation of facts, and by adverse facts may be utterly set aside. Cureton's remark that 'upon the comparison of several of the oldest copies now in the British Museum of that very text of the Gospels which has been generally received as the Peshitto, the more ancient the manuscripts be, the more nearly do they correspond with the text of these Syriac fragments (Pref. p. lxxiii), is confirmed by other, and subsequent, labourers in the same field. The received text of the Peshitto was printed from MSS. of a late type. It was the opinion of P. E. Pusey (whose name has already been mentioned in these pages) that a revision of the Peshitto text was made in the eighth century. The oldest Syriac Massoretic MS. which we possess is dated A. GR. 1210=A. D. 899[2], but a copy of the Gospels (Add. 14,448), the date of which appears to

[1] Cureton, Preface, pp. xi, xciii.

[2] Brit. Mus. Add. 12,138—*see* p. 36.

be A. H. 80 = A. D. 699–700, contains a text which approximates to the type of the printed Peshitto, but exhibits marginal notes in a later hand, referring, however, chiefly to pronunciation and accentuation. There is no evidence that any formal revision took place; but it would appear certain that as questions of orthography, of grammar, and of pronunciation were fixed by the decisions of the Massoretes and grammarians, the faults (as they were deemed) of the older readings were emended by scribes. Hence it is, that if we open a codex of the Peshitto Gospels of about the date of the Codex Curetonianus, we find many resemblances of the kind indicated by Cureton, between the fifth century Peshitto text and the Curetonian text, because both belong to an early, and perhaps less accurate era of transcription [1]. But the resemblances only extend to matters of grammar and spelling. In more important readings, the fifth century form of the Peshitto does not approximate to the Curetonian text. This was clearly seen by Pusey, as a result of the collation of a large number of Peshitto MSS. He found that the text of the oldest of them was substantially the same as that which is printed in the Polyglotts. The grammar may have been improved, but the translation was not revised. This argument has been elaborated in two volumes of the Oxford 'Studia Biblica,' in part by the use of Philip Pusey's materials, in part by independent researches. In vol. i, paper viii, 'A Syriac Biblical MS. of the fifth century,' the readings which appear to be peculiar to that MS. (about seventy in number, for it only contains SS. Matthew and Mark) are set out [2]. Of these twenty-two can be compared with the Curetonian; and it is found that only *three* approximate more nearly than the printed Peshitto to the text which, it is contended, is older than the Peshitto. Further on [3] a stronger argument is adduced; for it is shown that in eleven passages, where the fifth century codex has a different reading from the printed Peshitto, the Curetonian, instead of agreeing with the ancient text (as *ex hypothesi* it ought) approximates to the printed Peshitto, and sometimes agrees with it. In vol. ii, paper iii, 'The materials for the criticism of the Peshitto New Testament,' other evidence is adduced in support of the same conclusions. St. Matt. v. 31–48

[1] So Roediger in Z. M. D. G., b. 16, p. 550, instances [illegible]; but it proves nothing, for the form occurs also in old Peshitto MSS.

[2] Pages 164–5.

[3] Pages 171–2.

is given, with *varr. lectt.* derived from twenty distinct authorities, so as to place before the reader the Peshitto in its best and most ancient form. The same passage is set out in the Curetonian form. The various readings in the Peshitto in the eighteen verses amount to at least thirty-one; but the majority are the merest minutiae of spelling and pronunciation. Only one deserves serious attention; and even that, more for accuracy than in relation to the sense of the context; so little has the Syriac New Testament been altered, or corrupted, in the course of ages of transcription. Again, when comparison is made with the Curetonian, while twenty-eight variations from the best form of the Peshitto occur in the above passage, only four find any support in an old Peshitto MS., and but one of the four is of any interest. In addition to these there is one place where the Curetonian agrees with the oldest Peshitto MSS., against the printed Peshitto text. It is plain then that, as far as the enquiry has yet been pursued, the peculiar readings of the Curetonian cannot be traced backwards through the form of text in the oldest Peshitto MSS. If such a revision of the Peshitto, as Dr. Hort's theory postulates, ever took place, it must have been made at a very remote period in the history of Syriac Christian literature; and the new text must have been substituted for the old by measures so drastic that the old (as far as we know) survives only in one Nitrian and (as we are told) in one Sinaitic MS. But this is not only improbable in itself, but is contrary to the analogy supplied by the Latin versions.

Those who contend for the superior antiquity of the Curetonian rely in great part on the character of the quotations in the two great Syriac writers, Aphraates and Mar-Ephraem, who flourished in the century preceding the era in which our oldest Peshitto MSS. were transcribed[1]. Both writers abound in quotations from the New Testament, but many of them are very free, or mere adaptations. A large number in St. Ephraem are certainly from the Peshitto. Wright, in his edition of Aphraates, was inclined to attribute that writer's quotations to the same source. This has been traversed by others, who contend that the quotations in Aphraates more nearly resemble the Curetonian, or the text of Tatian's Diatessaron, as far as we know it.

[1] Some of the Homilies of Aphraates were composed between 337 and 345. Ephraem died A.D. 373. Bickell, Conspectus, p. 18.

The question of the source of St. Ephraem's quotations has been fully discussed in 'Studia Biblica,' iii, paper iv, by Rev. F. H. Woods, who has also taken some notice of those in Aphraates. Mr. Woods holds, as do others (though, as we think, on insufficient evidence) that the text of the Peshitto was not fully settled in the days of Aphraates and Ephraem. His conclusion is that it is quite clear that Ephraem, in the main, used the Peshitto text (op. cit., p. 107), but as regards Aphraates, he holds that the quotations approximate more closely to the Curetonian. Yet Dr. Zahn, and many others, think that Aphraates used the Diatessaron. The statement of these differences of opinion is enough in itself to show that the source of quotations in these ancient Syriac books is not always easy to determine. Hence it follows that arguments based on the writings of Aphraates and Ephraem are precarious. Moreover, a variation from the Peshitto does not necessarily indicate the employment of another version. The variation might be derived from a Greek text; for there was constant intercourse between Greek and Syrian Christians, and many of the latter were well acquainted with Greek.

While we seek in vain amongst the readings of MSS., and the writings of Syriac authors, for any satisfactory explanation of the origin of the Curetonian, the work itself may perhaps reveal something of its nature, if not of its history. We have already seen [1] that in the opinion of certain textual critics the history of the Latin Vulgate must have its counterpart in the history of the Bible of Edessa. The origin of Jerome's translation is well known. It is supposed that the Peshitto grew in like manner out of an earlier translation. It is contended that the *Ur-Peshitto* is represented to us by the text of the Curetonian; and the two texts have been compared in order to establish this relation. In so doing, no sufficient account has been taken of the phenomena presented by the differences between the Peshitto and the Curetonian. When it is argued that in some of those differences the Peshitto text bears marks of emendation, of the improving touch of a later hand, we answer [2], that in others there are as evident marks in the Curetonian of alteration and

[1] Page 14.

[2] In the following paragraphs we quote from a MS. exhibiting the results of investigations made by the Rev. Dr. Waller, Principal of St. John's Hall, Highbury, who has most generously permitted us to make use of his labours.

corruption. Indeed, to so large an extent do these prevail, that there are good grounds for the suspicion which has been entertained that the Curetonian (at least as exhibited by the editor from his MS.) is itself the later version. In order to give effect to this argument, it would be necessary to show the entire extant Curetonian text, side by side with the corresponding portions of the Peshitto; otherwise it is scarcely possible to realize (i) how manifestly the Curetonian is an attempt to improve upon the Peshitto text; and (ii) how frequently (as a later composition) it demands an acquaintance with the Gospels on the part of the reader; and (iii) how it is pervaded by views of Gospel history, which belong to the Church rather than to the sacred text. But even the short passages, which we have printed as specimens, afford illustrations of the argument.

1. In St. Matthew xii. 1–4, where the Peshitto exhibits the Textus Receptus, saying that the disciples were hungry, and began to pluck ears of corn and to eat, the Curetonian improves upon the Peshitto thus:—'and the disciples were hungry and began to pluck ears of corn, *and break them in their hands*, and eat'—introducing words borrowed from St. Luke[1].

2. (*a*) But in the next verse of the passage, where the words 'on the sabbath' are absolutely required in order to make the Pharisees' question intelligible to the first readers of St. Matthew, the Curetonian must needs draw on the common knowledge of educated readers by exhibiting the question thus:—'Why are thy disciples doing what is not lawful to do?' Of course the Peshitto is here an 'improvement' on the Curetonian, in reading the words 'on the Sabbath'; but that does not affect our argument. Would a primitive version, intended for first converts, have left the reader ignorant what the action objected to might be? whether to pluck ears in another man's field, or to rub out grain on the Sabbath? But a later editor, who revised the text for some purpose (it matters not, at present, for what purpose), might consider the explanatory words superfluous.

(*β*) In like manner in ver. 4, 'the bread of the table of the Lord,' a simple phrase, which every one could understand, has become in the Curetonian 'face-bread,' an expression which

[1] For other like cases see Mat. iv. 11, 21; v. 12, 47, in the Curetonian.

demands knowledge of the earlier Scriptures on the part of the reader, and displays the erudition of the editor, as do his emendations in the list of names in the first chapter of St. Matthew[1].

3. The other passage which we print (St. Mark xvi. 17–29) will illustrate our third criticism. The Curetonian is, 'Our Lord Jesus then, after He had *commanded* His disciples, *was exalted* to heaven, and sat on the right hand of God.' The simpler Peshitto phrase runs thus, 'Jesus our Lord then, after He had *spoken with them*, *ascended* to heaven, and sat on the right hand of God.' The two slight touches of improvement in the Curetonian are evident, and belong to that aspect of the record which finds expression in the Creeds, and in the obedience of the Church. A similar touch appears in the Curetonian addition to ver. 17—them that believe *on me*.

Again in Matt. v. 32 we read (with all authorities), 'Whosoever shall put away his wife, except for the cause of fornication,' &c.; so the Peshitto; but the Curetonian substitutes *adultery*, and thereby sanctions, not the precept delivered by our Lord, but the interpretation almost universally placed upon it. Now either the Curetonian has alone preserved the true text, or the Curetonian is an emended version. The first supposition is unreasonable; the latter is alone suitable to this and to many other passages.

Not less curious is the addition in ver. 41, 'Whosoever shall compel thee to go a mile, go with him *two others*.' The Curetonian (with D and some Latin copies) make our Lord say, 'Go *three* miles.' If we cannot admit that this is the true text, then it is an emendation; for it is no accidental change.

But there is a distinct group of emendations which vividly illustrates our contention, that the Curetonian form of Syriac text is pervaded by views of Gospel history which belong rather to the Church than to the sacred records. While fully accepting the Catholic dogma of the perpetual virginity of the Blessed Virgin, we must grant that it is in the nature of a pious opinion, which Christian sentiment recognized as true, but which is not explicitly stated in the New Testament. Hence we view with grave suspicion a class of emendations which are obviously

[1] The forms in which O. T. quotations appear in the Curetonian demand attention, as they seem to suggest similar inferences.

framed to confute the heresy of the Helvidians. Such a class is found in St. Matt. i. In ver. 16, Pesh., 'Joseph *the husband of Mary*;' Cur., 'Joseph *to whom was espoused Mary the Virgin*.' Ver. 19, Pesh., 'Joseph *her husband*, being a just man;' Cur., 'Joseph, because he was a righteous man.' Ver. 20, Pesh., 'Fear not to take unto thee Mary *thy wife*;' Cur., 'Mary *thy espoused*.' Ver. 24, Pesh., 'Joseph . . . . took unto him *his wife*;' Cur., 'took *Mary*.' The Curetonian translator, for dogmatic purposes, makes four distinct and separate omissions, in three of which he stands unsupported—of the word *husband* in two places, of the word *wife* in two others. These are emendations of a deliberate and peculiar kind. We cannot account for all these vagaries by remarking that the Curetonian has often the support of the so-called *Western* family of text [1]. We must face the question whether the MS. of an ancient version, which exhibits such singular phenomena on its first page, is worthy to be set above that version, which is the common heritage of the whole Syriac Church, and which appears to be the basis of the Curetonian itself. To determine the place of a document in our Apparatus Criticus, we must know something of its history. Of the history of the Curetonian version we know nothing. Its internal character inspires grave doubts of its trustworthiness. We note its peculiarities with interest; but we do not yet see our way to yield much deference to its authority. The Peshitto bears witness to that form of text, which was received in very ancient times in the Syriac Church. The Curetonian, like the Palestinian, is interesting as showing what readings were accepted locally, or by individual editors [2].

[1] E.g. in the transposition of the Beatitudes in St. Matt. v. 4, 5.

[2] Since the discovery of the Curetonian version in Syriac by Archdeacon Tattam in 1842 and Canon Cureton, some Textualists have maintained that it was older than the Peshitto on these main grounds:—

1. Internal evidence proves that the Peshitto cannot have been the original text.
2. The Curetonian is just such a text as may have been so, and would have demanded revision.
3. The parallels of the Latin texts which were revised in the Vulgate suggests an authoritative revision between A.D. 250 and 350.

These arguments depend upon a supposed historical parallel, and internal evidence.

The parallel upon examination turns out to be illusory:—

1. There was a definite recorded revision of the Latin Texts, but none of the Syrian. If there had been, it must have left a trace in history.

3. *The Harkleian or Philoxenian Syriac.*

Of the history of the Harkleian Syriac version, which embraces the whole New Testament except the Apocalypse, we possess more exact information, though some points of difficulty may still remain unsolved. Moses of Aghel in Mesopotamia, who translated into Syriac certain works of the Alexandrian Cyril about A.D. 550, describes a version of the 'New Testament and Psalter made in Syriac by Polycarp, Rural-Bishop[1] (rest his soul!), for Xenaias of Mabug,' &c. This Xenaias or Philoxenus, from whom the original translation takes its name, was Monophysite Bishop of Mabug (Hierapolis) in Eastern Syria (488–518), and doubtless wished to provide for his countrymen a more literal translation from the Greek than the Peshitto aims at being. His scheme may perhaps have been injudicious, but it is a poor token of the presence of that quality which 'thinketh no evil,' to assert, without the slightest grounds for the suspicion, 'More probable it is that his object was of a less commendable character; and that he meant the version in some way to subserve the advancement of his party[2].' Dr. Davidson will have learnt by this time, that one may lie under the imputation of heresy, without being of necessity a bigot or a dunce.

2. There was an 'infinita varietas' (August. De Doctr. Christ., ii. 11) of discordant Latin texts, but only one Syriac, so far as is known.

3. Badness in Latin texts is just what we should expect amongst people who were poor Greek scholars, and lived at a distance. The Syrians on the contrary were close to Judea, and Greek had been known among them for centuries. It was not likely that within reach of the Apostles and almost within their lifetime a version should be made so bad as to require to be thrown off afterwards.

As to internal evidence, the opinion of some experts is balanced by the opinion of other experts (see Abbé Martin, Des Versions Syriennes, Fasc. 4). The position of the Peshitto as universally received by Syrian Christians, and believed to date back to the earliest times, is not to be moved by mere conjecture, and a single copy of another version [or indeed by two copies]. Textual Guide, Miller, 1885, p. 74, note 1.

[1] On the order, functions, and decay of the Χωρεπίσκοποι, see Bingham's 'Antiquities,' book ii, chap. xiv.

[2] Davidson, Bibl. Crit., vol. ii. p. 186, first edition. The Abbé Martin (see p. 323 note), after stating that this version was never used by any Syrian sect save the Monophysites or Jacobites, goes on to ask 'Est-ce à dire que cette version soit entachée de monophysisme? Nous ne le pensons pas; pour l'affirmer, il faudra l'examiner très minutieusement; car l'hérésie monophysite est, à quelques points de vue, une des plus subtiles qui aient jamais paru' (Des Versions Syriennes, p. 162).

Our next account of the work is even more definite. At the end of the manuscripts of the Gospels from which the printed text is derived, we read a subscription by the first hand, importing that 'this book of the four holy Gospels was translated out of the Greek into Syriac with great diligence and labour ... first in the city of Mabug, in the year of Alexander of Macedon 819 (A.D. 508), in the days of the pious Mar Philoxenus, confessor, Bishop of that city. Afterwards it was collated with much diligence by me, the poor Thomas, by the help of two [*or* three] approved and accurate Greek Manuscripts in Antonia, of the great city of Alexandria, in the holy monastery of the Antonians. It was again written out and collated in the aforesaid place in the year of the same Alexander 927 (A.D. 616), Indiction IV. How much toil I spent upon it and its companions the Lord alone knoweth ... &c.' It is plain that by 'its companions' the other parts of the N. T. are meant, for a similar subscription (specifying but one manuscript) is annexed to the Catholic Epistles.

That the labour of Thomas (surnamed from Harkel, his native place, and like Philoxenus, subsequently Monophysite Bishop of Mabug) was confined to the collation of the manuscripts he names, and whose various readings, usually in Greek characters, with occasional exegetical notes, stand in the margin of all copies but one at Florence, is not a probable opinion. It is likely that he added the asterisks and obeli which abound in the version[1], and G. H. Bernstein (De Charklensi N. T. transl. Syriac. Commentatio, Breslau, 1837) believes that he so modified the text itself, that it remains in the state in which Polycarp left it only in one codex now at Rome, which he collated for a few chapters of St. John.

We have been reminded by Tregelles, who was always ready to give every one his due, that our own Pococke in 1630, in the Preface to his edition of the Catholic Epistles not included in the Peshitto, both quotes an extract from Dionysius Barsalibi, Bishop of Amida (Diarbekr), who flourished in the twelfth

[1] The asterisks (※ ⁜) and obeli (∋ ÷) of this version will be observed in our specimens given below. Like the similar marks in Origen's Hexapla (from which they were doubtless borrowed), they have been miserably displaced by copyists; so that their real purpose is a little uncertain. Wetstein, and after him even Storr and Adler, refer them to changes made in the Harkleian from the Peshitto: White more plausibly considers the asterisk to intimate an addition to the text, the obelus to recommend a removal from it.

century, which mentions this version, and even shows some acquaintance with its peculiar character. Although again brought to notice in the comprehensive 'Bibliotheca Orientalis' (1719–28) of the elder J. S. Assemani [1687–1768], the Harkleian attracted no attention until 1730, in which year Samuel Palmer sent from Diarbekr to Dr. Gloucester Ridley four Syriac manuscripts, two of which proved to belong to this translation, both containing the Gospels, one of them being the only extant copy of the Acts and all the Epistles. Fortunately Ridley [1702–1774] was a man of some learning and acuteness, or these precious codices might have lain disregarded as other copies of the same version had long done in Italy; so that though he did not choose to incur the risk of publishing them in full, he communicated his discovery to Wetstein, who came to England once more, in 1746, for the purpose of collating them for his edition of the N. T., then soon to appear: he could spare, however, but fourteen days for the task, which was far too short a time, the rather as the Estrangelo character, in which the manuscripts were written, was new to him. In 1761 Ridley produced his very careful and valuable tract, De Syriacarum N. F. Versionum Indole atque Usu Dissertatio, and on his death his manuscripts went to New College, of which society he had been a Fellow. The care of publishing them was then undertaken by the Delegates of the Oxford Press, who selected for their editor Joseph White [1746–1814], then Fellow of Wadham College and Professor of Arabic, afterwards Canon of Christ Church; who, though now, I fear, chiefly remembered for the most foolish action of his life, was an industrious, able, and genuine scholar. Under his care the Gospels appeared in two vols. 4to, 1778 [1], with

[1] 'Sacrorum Evangeliorum Versio Syriaca Philoxeniana, ex Codd. MSS. Ridleianis in Bibliotheca Novi Collegii Oxon. repositis; nunc primum edita, cum Interpretatione Latinâ et Annotationibus Josephi White. Oxonii e Typographeo Clarendoniano,' 1778, 2 tom. 4to. And so for the two later volumes. Ridley named that one of his manuscripts which contains only the Gospels Codex Barsalibaei, as notes of revision by that writer are found in it (e. g. John vii. 53—viii. 11). G. H. Bernstein has also published St. John's Gospel (Leipzig, 1853) from manuscripts in the Vatican. In or about 1877 Professor Isaac H. Hall, an American missionary, discovered at Beerût a manuscript in the Estrangelo character, much mutilated (of which he kindly sent me a photographed page containing the end of St. Luke and the beginning of St. John), which in the Gospels follows the Harkleian version, although the text differs much from White's, but the rest of the N. T. is from the Peshitto. Dr. Hall has drawn up a list of over 300 readings differing from White's.

a Latin version and satisfactory Prolegomena; the Acts and Catholic Epp. in 1799, the Pauline in 1803. Meanwhile Storr (Observat. super N. T. vers. Syr., 1772) and Adler (N. T. Version. Syr., 1789) had examined and described seven or eight continental codices of the Gospels in this version, some of which are thought superior to White's[1].

The characteristic feature of the Harkleian is its excessive closeness to the original: it is probably the most servile version of Scripture ever made. Specimens of it will appear on pp. 38–40, by the side of those from other translations, which will abundantly justify this statement. The Peshitto is beyond doubt taken as its basis, and is violently changed in order to force it into rigorous conformity with the very letter of the Greek. In the twenty verses of Matt. xxviii we note seventy-six such alterations: three of them seem to concern various readings (vers. 2–18; and 5 *marg.*); six are inversions in the order; about five are substitutions of words for others that may have grown obsolete: the rest are of the most frivolous description, the definite state of nouns being placed for the absolute, or vice versa; the Greek article represented by the Syriac pronoun; the inseparable pronominal affixes (that delicate peculiarity of the Aramaean dialects) retrenched or discarded; the most unmeaning changes made in the tenses of verbs, and the lesser particles. Its very defects, however, as being servilely accurate, give it weight as a textual authority: there can be no hesitation about the readings of the copies from which such a book was made. While those employed for the version itself in the sixth century resembled more nearly our modern printed editions, the three or more codices used by Thomas at Alexandria must have been nearly akin to Cod. D (especially in the Acts), and, next to D, support BL, 1, 33, 69. 'Taken altogether,' is Dr. Hort's comment, 'this is one of the most confused texts preserved: but it may be rendered more intelligible by fresh collations and better editing, even if they should fail to distinguish the work of Thomas of Harkel from that of his predecessor Polycarpus' (Introd., p. 156).

The number of MSS. of this Harkleian version is far greater

[1] Martin names as useful for the study of a version as yet too little known, the Lectionaries Bodleian 43; Brit. Mus. Addit. 7170, 7171, 7172, 14,490, 14,689, 18,714; Paris 51 and 52; Rome, Vatic. 36 and Barberini vi. 32.

than it was supposed to have been. The important discovery of the Mohl MS., now in the possession of the Cambridge University Library, brings down the Epistle to the Hebrews to the conclusion, so that we now possess the Pauline Epistles complete in this revision.

The following account of the MSS. of the Harkleian, consists in his own words of what Mr. Deane has seen himself, many of which he has collated. The letters are those by which he intended to have designated these MSS. had his sight enabled him to complete his revision.

A. Cod. Mus. Brit. Add. 14,469. Saec. x (Wright's Catalogue cxx). Very important.

B. Cod. Mus. Brit. Rich 7163. Saec. ix. x (Forshall's Catalogue xix). Very important.

C. Cod. Bibl. Bodl. Oxon. 'Cod. Or. 130.' Saec. xii.

D. Cod. Bibl. Coll. Nov. Oxon. 333. Perhaps not so important as R.

F. Cod. Bibl. Bodl. Oxon. Dawk. 50.

G. Cod. Mus. Brit. Rich 7164. Saec. xii (Forshall's Catalogue xx).

H. Cod. Mus. Brit. Rich 7165. Saec. xiii (Forshall's Catalogue xxi). In this MS. the two first lines of each page are for the most part obliterated by damp.

K. Cod. Mus. Brit. Rich 7166. Saec. xv. xvi (Forshall's Catalogue xxii).

L. Cod. Mus. Brit. Rich 7167. Saec. xv. xvi.

Q. Cod. Mus. Brit. Add. 17,124. Saec. xiii (No. 65 Wright's Catalogue).

R. Cod. Bibl. Coll. Nov. Oxon. 334.

S. Cod. Bibl. Bodl. Oxon. Orient. 361. Saec. xiv.

T. Cod. Bibl. Bodl. Oxon. Poc. 316.

U. Cod. Mus. Brit. Rich 7167. Saec. xv. xvi. Fragments on St. Matthew only.

V. Cod. Mohl. Cambridge University Library. Saec. xii.

The last of these would probably be the text from which any new edition would be printed. It is a most remarkable MS., executed with great care, and by a good Syrian scholar. Students should observe especially the curious diacritic point by which he designates the Nom. pendens. 'I have not seen,' Mr. Deane adds, 'that elsewhere, though doubtless it exists[1].'

[1] *See* also Syriac Manuscript Gospels of a Pre-Harklensian version, Acts and Epp. of the Peshitto version . . . by the Monk John. Presented to the Syrian Protestant College, &c., described with phototyped fascimiles by Prof. Isaac H. Hall [viii-ix], ff. 219 + a fragment at end. *Mut.* at beg. and end, &c. Written in old Jacobite characters. Sent courteously to the Editor.

4. *The Palestinian or Jerusalem Syriac.*

There are extant several scattered fragments of the Old and New Testaments, in a form of Syriac entirely distinct from the versions already described. These fragments are all in one dialect, and are apparently parts of a single version. The most considerable portion is an Evangelistarium which was discovered virtually by Adler, who collated, described, and copied a portion of it (Matt. xxvii. 3–32) for that great work in a small compass, his 'N. T. Versiones Syriacae' (1789): S. E. Assemani the nephew had merely inserted it in his Vatican Catalogue (1756). It is a partial Lectionary of the Gospels in the Vatican (MS. Syr. 19), on 196 quarto thick vellum leaves, written in two columns in a rude hand, the rubric notes of Church Lessons in *Carshunic*, i.e. Arabic in Syriac letters, with many mistakes. From a subscription, we learn that the scribe was Elias, a presbyter of Abydos, who wrote it in the Monastery of the Abbat Moses at Antioch, in the year of Alexander 1341, or A.D. 1030. Adler gives a poor facsimile (Matt. xxvii. 12–22): the character is peculiar, and all diacritic points (even that distinguishing *dolath* from *rish*), as well as many other changes, are thought to be by a later hand. Tregelles confirms Assemani's statement, which Adler had disputed, that the first six leaves, showing traces of Greek writing buried beneath the Syriac, proceeded from another scribe. The remarkable point, however, about this version (which seems to be made from the Greek, and is quite independent of the Peshitto) is the peculiar dialect its exhibits, ~~and~~ which has suggested its name. Its grammatical forms are far less Syriac than Chaldee, which latter it resembles even in that characteristic particular, the prefixing of *yud*, not *nun*, to the third person masculine of the future of verbs[1]; and many of the words it employs can be illustrated only from the Chaldee portions of the Old Testament, or from the Jerusalem, or Palestinian, Targum and Talmud[2]. Adler's

[1] Thus also the termination of the definite state plural of nouns is made in ܝܐ for ܐ: the third person affix to plural nouns in ܘܢ for ܘܗܘܢ. In the compass of the six verses we have cited (*below*, p. 39) occur not only the Greek words ܩܐܪܘܣܐ (καιρός), v. 3, and ܢܘܣܐ (ναός), v. 5, which are common enough in all Syriac books, but such Palestinian words and forms as ܕܢ for ܕܝܢ, δέ (vv. 4, 6, 7); ܟܡܢ, v. 3, 'when;' ܬܗܐ, v. 3, 'repented;' ܐܕܡܐ for ܕܡܐ (vv. 4, 6, 8), 'blood;' ܠܢ, v. 4, 'to us;' ܓܪܡܗ, v. 5, 'himself; ܕܡܝܢ, v. 6, 'price' (Pesh. has ܛܝܡܐ, Hark. ܛܝ̈ܡܐ (pl.), τιμή); ܒܟܡܢ, v. 8, 'therefore;' ܗܐܘ, v. 8, 'this.'

[2] Hence the name by which this version is distinguished. For the recensions of Targum and Talmud, *see* Etheridge's 'Hebrew Literature,' pp. 145–6, 195–7.

account of the translation and its copyist is not very flattering, 'satis constat dialectum esse incultam et inconcinnam . . . orthographiam autem vagam, inconstantem, arbitrariam, et ab imperito librario rescribendo et corrigendo denuo impeditam' (Vers. Syr., p. 149). As it is mentioned by no Syriac writer, it was probably used but in a few remote churches of Lebanon or Galilee: but though (to employ the words of Porter) 'in elegance far surpassed by the Peshitto; in closeness of adherence to the original by the Philoxenian' (Principles of Textual Criticism, Belfast, 1848, p. 356); it has its value, and that not inconsiderable, as a witness to the state of the text at the time it was turned into Syriac; whether, with Adler, we regard it as derived from a complete version of the Gospels made not later than the sixth century, or with Tischendorf refer it to the fifth[1]. Tregelles (who examined the codex at Rome) wrongly judged it a mere translation of some Greek Evangelistarium of a more recent date. Of all the Syriac books, this copy and Barsalibi's recension of the Harkleian alone contain John vii. 53—viii. 11; the Lectionary giving it as the Proper Lesson for Oct. 8, St. Pelagia's day. In general its readings much resemble those of Codd. BD, siding with B eighty-five times, with D seventy-nine, in the portions published by Adler; but with D *alone* eleven times, with B alone but three.

The information afforded by Adler respecting this remarkable document gave rise to a natural wish that the whole manuscript should be carefully edited by some respectable scholar. This has now been done by Count Francis Miniscalchi Erizzo, who in 1861–4 published at Verona in two quarto volumes 'Evangeliarium Hierosolymitanum ex Codice Vaticano Palaestino deprompsit, edidit, Latinè vertit, Prolegomenis ac Glossario adornavit Comes F. M. E.' This elaborate work, for such it is, although its execution fails on the whole to satisfy critics of the calibre of Land and the Abbé Martin, ends with a list of those chapters and verses of the Gospels (according to the notation of the Latin Vulgate), which the manuscript contains

[1] Dr. Hort's not very explicit judgement should now be added: 'The Jerusalem Syriac Lectionary has an entirely different text [from the Harkleian], probably not altogether unaffected by the Syriac Vulgate [meaning thereby the Peshitto], but more closely related to the Old Syriac [meaning the Curetonian]. Mixture with one or more Greek texts containing elements of every great type, but especially the more ancient, has however given the whole a strikingly composite character' (Introd., p. 157).

in full. Tischendorf, in the eighth edition of his Greek Testament, enriched his notes with the various readings these Church Lessons exhibit; their critical character being much the same as Adler's slight specimen had given us reason to expect[1]. The Lectionary closely resembles that of the Greek Church, the slight differences in the beginnings and endings of the Lessons scarcely exceeding those subsisting between different Greek copies, as noticed in our Synaxarion. It contains the Sunday and week-day Gospels for the first eight weeks beginning at Easter (with a few verses lost in two places of Week VIII); the Saturday and Sunday Gospels only for the rest of the year; the Lessons for the Holy Week, complete as detailed in Vol. I. 85, with two or three slight exceptions; and the eleven Gospels of the Resurrection. In the Menology or Calendar of Immoveable Feasts, there is a greater amount of variation in regard to the Saints' Days kept, as indeed we might have looked for beforehand. We subjoin a list of those whose Gospels are given at length in the manuscript, together with the portions of Scripture appointed for each day, in order that this curious Syriac service-book may be compared with that of the Greeks.

September 1. Simaan Alepinus Stylites. 3. Commemoratio patris nostri Anthioma, John x. 7–16. 4. Babul et pnerorum et sanctorum qui cum eo, Luke x. 1–12. 5. Zacharias, father of the Baptist, Matt. xxiii. 29–39. 6. Eudoxio, Mark xii. 28–37. 8. Birthday of the Virgin, *Matins*, Luke i. 39–56. *Ad Missam*, as p. 87. Sunday before Elevation of the Cross, as p. 87. 14. Elevation of the Cross, John xi. 53; xix. 6–35. 15. Nikita, Matt. x. 16–22. 16. Eufemia, p. 87, note 2. 20. Eustathios et sociorum ejus, Luke xxi. 12–19. 21. Jonah the Prophet, Luke xi. 29–33. 30. Gregory the Armenian[2], Matt. xxiv. 42–51.

October 3. Dionosios the Bishop, Matt. xiii. 45–54. Blagia (p. 87, note 3), John viii. 1–11. 18. Luke, as p. 87. 21. Patris nostri Ilarion, Luke vi. 17–23. 25. SS. Scriptorum Marciano et Martorio, Luke xii. 2–12. 26. Demetrius et commemoratio terrae motus, Matt. viii. 23–27.

November 1. SS. T[h]aumaturgorum Kezma et Damian, Matt. x. 1–8.

December 4. Barbara, Mark v. 24–34. 20. Ignathios, as p. 88. 22. Anastasia, Mark xii. 28–44. 'Dominica ante Nativitatem, et patrum (compare p. 88). In nocte Nativitatis, as p. 88. 25. Christmas Day, sanctorum,' Matt. i. 1–17. 24. Ad mat. Nativitatis, Matt. i. 18–25

[1] On these readings, and those of the MSS. mentioned below (p. 34), *see* 'The New Syriac Fragments' (F. H. Woods), in the *Expository Times*, Nov., 1893.

[2] *See* the 'Life and Times of Gregory the Illuminator, the Founder and Patron Saint of the Armenian Church,' translated by the Rev. S. C. Malan, London, 1868.

as p. 88. 26. Commemoratio dominae Mart. Mariam, as p. 88. 28. Jacob, frater Domini[1], Mark vi. 1–5 (p. 88).

January 1. Circumcision, as p. 88. 3. Matt. iii. 1, 5–11. Saturday and Sunday 'ante missam aquae,' as p. 88. 5. Nocte missae aquae, p. 88. 6. Missa aquae (both Lessons), as p. 88. 7. Commemoration of John the Baptist, as p. 88. Saturday and Sunday post missam aquae, as p. 88. 8. Luke iii. 19–22. 10. John x. 39–42. 11. Luke xx. 1–8. Theodosis, Luke vi. 17–23. 15. Juhanna Tentorii, Matt. iv. 25; v. 1–12. 28. Patris nostri Efrem, Matt. v. 14–19.

February 2. Ingressus Domini Jesu Christi in templum, as p. 88. 24. Finding of the Head of John the Baptist, *ad Mat.* as p. 88: *ad Missam*, Matt. xi. 2–15.

March 9. Martyrii xl martyrum Sebastis, Matt. xx. 1–16. 25. Annuntiationis Deiparae, *ad Missam*, as p. 88.

April 1. Mariam Aegyptiacae, Luke vii. 36–50 (compare p. 88, note 2).

May 8. Evan. Juhanna fil. Zebdiai[2], as p. 88.

June 14. Proph. Elisha, Luke iv. 22–30[3]. 24. Birth of John the Baptist, as p. 88. 29. Peter, as p. 88. 30. The Twelve Apostles, Matt. ix. 36—x. 8.

July 22. Mariam Magdalanis, Luke viii. 1–3.

August 1. Amkabian Ascemonith, et filiorum suorum, Matt. x. 16–22. 6. Apparitio Domini nostri Jesu Christi in Monte Thabur, Luke ix. 28–36; Matt. xvii. 1–9; 10–22. 29. Beheading of John the Baptist, as p. 88.

Appendix. Sanctae Christianae, Matt. xxv. 1–13 (*see* Sept. 24, p. 88). Justorum, Matt. xi. 27–30. Dominica xi, Matt. xv. 21–28.

This last (*of the Canaanites*, p. 88) had been omitted in its usual place, and two lessons inserted about the same place, which are not in the Greek, viz. 'Jejunio sancto Banscira fer. 4, vesp. Mark xi. 22–25,' and 'fer. 6, vesp. John xv. 1–12.'

A new edition of Adler's Evangelistarium was projected by the late Dr. P. A. de Lagarde, who made a fresh collation of the MS. shortly before his death. The results have been published in a posthumous work entitled 'Bibliothecae Syriacae a Paulo de Lagarde collectae,' 1892. The latter part contains the Evangelistarium, with the text set out in the order of the Gospels, instead of that of the Church Lessons, and notes are added on the readings of the MS. and its correctors, and on the edition of Miniscalchi Erizzo.

Another edition has been announced by Mrs. Lewis[4], the text to be taken from two Lectionaries, which she has recently discovered in the Library of the Convent on Mount Sinai, with a collation of the readings of the Vatican MS.

Some fragments of other MSS. of the same Evangelistarium are preserved in the British Museum (Add. 14,450, fol. 14, and 14,664, foll. 17,

[1] Kept by the Greeks Oct. 23. Gale O. 4. 22 and other Greek Evangelistaria commemorate this holiday.

[2] Dec. 27 in the Western Calendar.

[3] So Gale O. 4. 22, with the same Lesson.

[4] See *Athenaeum*, Oct. 28, 1893.

20, 21), and in the Imperial Library, St. Petersburg. They have been pnblished by Professor Land in 'Anecdota Syriaca,' tom. iv, 1875, with a fragment of Acts (xiv. 6–13), in the St. Petersburg Library.

Mr. J. Rendel Harris has published in 'Biblical Fragments from Mount Sinai' a leaf containing Gal. ii. 3–5, 12–14; iii. 17, 18, 24–28.

The same library is said to contain other remains of Palestiuian literature, patristic translations as well as biblical fragments.

In the Bodleian Library are four fragments, Col. iv. 12–18; 1 Thess. i. 1–3; iv. 3–15; 2 Tim. i. 10—ii. 7; Titus i. 11—ii. 5, an edition of which has been accomplished by the Rev. G. H. Gwilliam[1].

5. '*The Karkaphensian*' or *Syriac Massorah*.

Assemani (Biblioth. Orient., tom. ii. p. 283), on the authority of Gregory Bar-Hebraeus, mentions what has been supposed to have been a Syriac 'version' of the N. T., other than the Peshitto and Harkleian, which was named 'Karkaphensian' (ܩܪܩܦܝܐ), whether, as he thought, because it was used by Syrians of the *mountains*, or from *Carcuf*, a city of Mesopotamia. Adler (Vers. Syr., p. 33) was inclined to believe that Bar-Hebraeus meant rather a revised manuscript than a separate translation. Cardinal Wiseman, in the course of those youthful studies which gave such seemly, precocious, deceitful promise (Horae Syriacae, Rom. 1828), discovered in the Vatican (MS. Syr. 152) a Syriac manuscript of readings from both Testaments, with the several portions of the New standing in the following order; Acts, James, 1 Peter, 1 John, the fourteen Epistles of St. Paul, and then the Gospels, these being the only books contained in the true Peshitto. In the margin also are placed by the first hand many readings indicated by the abbreviation ܛܘ, the title of some scribe or teacher[2]. The codex is on thick yellow vellum, in large folio, with the two columns so usual in Syriac writing; the ink, especially the points in vermilion, has often grown pale, and it has been carefully retouched by a later hand; the original document being all the work of one scribe: some of the marginal notes refer to various readings. There arc several long and tedious subscriptions in

[1] Anecdota Oxoniensia, 'The Palestinian Version of the Holy Scripture;' edited by G. H. Gwilliam, B.D.: Oxford, Clarendon Press, 1893.

[2] The full form (ܛܘܒܢܐ *blessed*) occurs in the scholion to Rom. viii. 15; Wiseman thought it meant the Peshitto; but see 'Studia Biblica,' iii. 60 and note.

the volume, whereof one states that the copy was written 'in the year of the Greeks 1291 (A.D. 980) in the [Monophysite] monastery of Aaron on [mount] Sigara, in the jurisdiction of Calisura, in the days of the Patriarchs John and Menna, by David a deacon of Urin in the jurisdiction of Gera' [Γέρρα, near Beroea or Aleppo]. It may be remarked that Assemani has inserted a letter in the 'Bibliotheca Orientalis' from John the Monophysite Patriarch [of Antioch] to his brother Patriarch, Menna of Alexandria. This manuscript, of which Wiseman gives a rather rude facsimile, is deemed by him of great importance in tracing the history of the Syriac vowel-points. Other Karkaphensian manuscripts have been examined since Wiseman's time; and all, whether containing more, or less, of the actual text, agree in the parts which are common, with, however, some independent readings. We subjoin Matt. i. 19 in four texts, wherein the close connexion of the Karkaphensian and the Nestorian recension with the Peshitto is very manifest.

CURETONIAN.

ܝܘܣܦ ܕܝܢ ܡܟܝܠ ܓܒܪܗ̇ ܗܘܐ
ܟܐܢܐ ܠܐ ܨܒܐ ܗܘܐ ܕܢܦܪܣܝܗ̇ ܠܡܪܝܡ
ܘܐܬܪܥܝ ܗܘܐ ܕܒܫܠܝܐ ܢܫܒܩܝܗ̇ ܀

HARKLEIAN—from *White*.

ܝܘܣܦ ܕܝܢ ܗܘ ܓܒܪܐ ܕܝܠܗ̇ ܟܐܢܐ
ܐܝܬܘܗܝ ܗܘܐ: ܘܠܐ ܨܒܐ ܗܘܐ ܕܢܦܪܣܝܗ̇*:
ܐܬܪܥܝ ܕܒܛܘܫܝܐ ܢܫܪܝܗ̇ ܀

* Marg. παραδειγματίσαι.

NESTORIAN MASSORAH.
Cod. Add. Brit. Mus. 12,138.

ܝܘܣܦ ܕܝܢ ܒܥܠܗ̇ ܟܐܢܐ ܗܘܐ.
ܘܠܐ ܨܒܐ ܕܢܦܪܣܝܗ̇. ܘܐܬܪܥܝ (sic)
ܗܘܐ ܕܒܛܠܝܘܬܐ ܢܫܪܝܗ̇ ܀

JACOBITE MASSORAH ('KARKAPHENSIAN').
Cod. Add. Brit. Mus. 12,178.

ܝܘܣܦ ܕܝܢ ܒܥܠܗ̇ ܟܐܢܐ ܗܘܐ.
ܘܠܐ ܨܒܐ ܕܢܦܪܣܝܗ̇. ܘܐܬܪܥܝ ܗܘܐ
ܕܒܛܠܝܘܬܐ ܢܫܪܝܗ̇ ܀

PESHITTO TEXT—from the MSS.

ܝܘܣܦ ܕܝܢ ܒܥܠܗ̇ ܟܐܢܐ ܗܘܐ. ܘܠܐ ܨܒܐ ܕܢܦܪܣܝܗ̇. ܘܐܬܪܥܝ ܗܘܐ ܕܒܛܠܝܘܬܐ
ܢܫܪܝܗ̇ ܀

The reader must not be misled by this specimen to infer that the Karkaphensian always coincides with the Peshitto. It is not a continuous text, but only those verses or passages are quoted where some word or words occur concerning which some annotation is required in reference to orthography or pronunciation. Whole verses or parts of verses are often omitted[1].

Very recently, since the last illness of Dr. Scrivener had com-

[1] Our specimens show the use in MSS. of *rucaca* and *kushaia*, here printed with fine points. The dots and dashes of the Nestorian Massorah are also shown.

menced, the results of a wider examination of Syriac MSS. in different Libraries have been made more generally known by Mr. Gwilliam's Essay in the third volume of 'Studia Biblica[1].' According to the investigations of the leading Syriac scholars, it appears that the Karkaphensian is not a distinct version, but a kind of Massorah—the attempt to preserve the best traditions of the orthography and pronunciation of the more important or difficult words of the Syriac Vernacular Bible. This Massoretic teaching differs from the Hebrew Massorah, in that whilst the latter supplies us with all that we know of the form of the Jewish Scriptures[2], the Syriac Massorah is younger than our oldest copies of the Syriac Bible. The following are Syriac Massoretic MSS.:—

1. Cod. Add. B. M. 12,138, a Nestorian work, written A. D. 899 at Harran.
2. Cod. Vaticanus 152, A. D. 980 (Wiseman, as above).
3. Cod. Add. B. M. 12,178, a Jacobite work of the ninth or tenth century.
4. Cod. Barberinus, described by Bianchini in 'Evangeliarium Quadruplex,' 1748, and afterwards by Wiseman, A. D. 1089 or 1093.
5. Cod. Add. B. M. 7183, also a Jacobite Massoretic work of the early part of the twelfth century.
6. In the Bibliothèque Nationale of Paris, a Massoretic MS.
7. M. l'Abbé Martin mentions another, A. D. 1015, in the Cathedral of Mosul.

Thus the Massorah is extant in two forms, corresponding to the two branches of the Syrian Church. But only one MS. is Nestorian (Cod. Add. 12,138), whilst all except that one are Jacobite.

The name Karkaphensian is connected with the Jacobite Massorah, and signifies the kind of text which was favoured in the Scriptorium of the Skull Convent[3]. Allusions to the Skull Convent are found; the adjective itself occurs in St. Matt. xxvii. 33, and the parallel passages, as a translation of *κρανίου*. It is known that grammatical and philological studies were pursued by Jacob of Edessa (d. A. D. 710), probably by Joseph Huzita, rector of the school at Nisibis (vi); and a tract attached to Add. 12,178 suggests a connexion between these criticisms and the labours of one 'Thomas the Deacon[4].'

[1] Studia Biblica et Ecclesiastica, iii. 56.

[2] The Codex Babylonicus, A. D. 916, is the oldest Old Testament MS. known at present. Dr. Neubauer, Stud. Bibl. et Eccl., iii. 27.

[3] Karkaphta = skull. See also 'Thes. Syr.,' col. 3762.

[4] Mr. Gwilliam suggests that this may have been the well-known Thomas

We have now traced the history of the several Syriac versions, so far at least as to afford the reader some general idea of their relative importance as materials for the correction of the sacred text. We will next give parallel renderings of Matt. xii. 1–4; Mark xvi. 17–20 from the Peshitto, the Curetonian, and the Harkleian, the only versions known in full; for Matt. xxvii. 3–8, in the room of the Curetonian, which is here lost, we have substituted the Jerusalem Syriac, and have retained throughout Thomas' marginal notes to the Harkleian, its asterisks and obeli. We have been compelled to employ the common Syriac type, though every manuscript of respectable antiquity is written in the Estrangelo character. Even from these slight specimens the servile strictness of the Harkleian, and some leading characteristics of the other versions, will readily be apprehended by an attentive student (e.g. of the Curetonian in Matt. xii. 1; 4; Mark xvi. 18; 20).

We hoped to include in this account some description of the MS. lately discovered by Mrs. Lewis in the Monastery of St. Catherine, at Mount Sinai, and brought in copy last spring to Cambridge. It is now undergoing the careful and skilful examination which the character of the accomplished assistants of Mrs. Lewis ensures, and it is impossible at present to anticipate the verdict upon it which those scholars may recommend, and which may be finally adopted by the learned world at large. The photographic illustration of a page, which has been made public[1], does not suggest that the MS. possesses any very remarkable antiquity. But it is due to our argument upon the mutual relations of the Peshitto and the Curetonian to remark, that the Curetonian will even then rest upon only two MSS., one of them being a palimpsest, in face of the numerous supports of the Peshitto, and that even if the Curetonian be proved, as seems improbable, to date from somewhat further back than we have supposed, the claim of the Peshitto to production in the early part of the second century, and to a superior antiquity, will not thereby be removed.

Heracleensis. M. l'Abbé Martin (Tradition Karkaphienne, ou la Massore chez les Syriens), who carefully studied the subject twenty years ago, suggests Thomas of Edessa, teacher of Mar Abbas. *See* Mr. Gwilliam's Essay in 'Stud. Bibl. et Eccl.,' iii. pp. 56–65.

[1] 'How the Codex was found' (Lewis and Gibson), 1893.

MATTHEW XII. 1–4.

PESHITTO.

(1) ܒܗܘ ܙܒܢܐ: ܡܗܠܟ ܗܘܐ ܝܫܘܥ
ܒܫܒܬܐ ܒܝܬ ܙܪܥܐ. ܘܬܠܡܝܕܘܗܝ
ܟܦܢܘ: ܘܫܪܝܘ ܡܦܪܟܝܢ ܫܒܠܐ ܘܐܟܠܝܢ
(2) ܦܪܝܫܐ ܕܝܢ ܟܕ ܚܙܐܘ ܐܡܪܝܢ
ܠܗ. ܗܐ ܬܠܡܝܕܝܟ ܥܒܕܝܢ ܡܕܡ
ܕܠܐ ܫܠܝܛ ܠܡܥܒܕ ܒܫܒܬܐ. (3) ܗܘ
ܕܝܢ ܐܡܪ ܠܗܘܢ. ܠܐ ܩܪܝܬܘܢ ܡܢܐ
ܥܒܕ ܕܘܝܕ ܟܕ ܟܦܢ ܘܐܝܠܝܢ ܕܥܡܗ:
(4) ܐܝܟܢܐ ܥܠ ܠܒܝܬܗ ܕܐܠܗܐ:
ܘܠܚܡܐ ܕܦܐܬܘܗܝ ܕܡܪܝܐ ܐܟܠ:
ܗܘ ܕܠܐ ܫܠܝܛ ܗܘܐ ܠܗ ܠܡܐܟܠܗ.
ܘܠܐ ܠܐܝܠܝܢ ܕܥܡܗ. ܐܠܐ ܐܢ ܠܟܗܢܐ
ܒܠܚܘܕܝܗܘܢ܀

CURETONIAN.

(1) ܒܗܘ ܙܒܢܐ ܡܗܠܟ ܗܘܐ ܝܫܘܥ
ܒܫܒܬܐ ܒܝܬ ܙܪܥܐ. ܘܬܠܡܝܕܘܗܝ
ܟܦܢܘ. ܘܫܪܝܘ ܡܠܩܛܝܢ ܫܒܠܐ ܘܦܪܟܝܢ
ܒܐܝܕܝܗܘܢ ܘܐܟܠܝܢ. (2) ܟܕ ܚܙܘ
ܐܢܘܢ ܦܪܝܫܐ ܐܡܪܝܢ ܠܗ. ܚܙܝ
ܬܠܡܝܕܝܟ ܥܒܕܝܢ ܡܕܡ ܕܠܐ ܫܠܝܛ
ܠܡܥܒܕ. (3) ܐܡܪ ܠܗܘܢ ܠܐ
ܩܪܝܬܘܢ ܡܢܐ ܥܒܕ ܕܘܝܕ ܟܕ ܟܦܢ
ܘܐܝܠܝܢ ܕܥܡܗ. (4) ܐܝܟܢܐ ܥܠ
ܠܒܝܬܗ ܕܐܠܗܐ. ܘܐܟܠ ܡܢ ܠܚܡ
ܐܦܐ. ܕܠܐ ܠܗ ܫܠܝܛ ܗܘܐ ܠܡܐܟܠܗ
ܐܦܠܐ ܠܐܝܠܝܢ ܕܥܡܗ. ܐܠܐ ܐܢ ܠܟܗܢܐ
ܒܠܚܘܕܝܗܘܢ܀

HARKLEIAN.

(1) ܒܗܘ ܙܒܢܐ: ܡܗܠܟ ܗܘܐ
ܝܫܘܥ ܒܫܒܬܐ ܒܝܬ ܙܪܥܐ.
ܬܠܡܝܕܘܗܝ ܕܝܢ ܟܦܢܘ: ܘܫܪܝܘ
ܡܠܩܛܝܢ ܫܒܠܐ ܘܐܟܠܝܢ. (2) ܦܪܝܫܐ
ܕܝܢ ܟܕ ܚܙܘ ܐܡܪܘ ܠܗ. ܗܐ
ܬܠܡܝܕܝܟ ܥܒܕܝܢ ܗܘ ܡܐ ܕܠܐ ܫܠܝܛ
ܠܡܥܒܕ ܒܫܒܬܐ. (3) ܗܘ ܕܝܢ ܐܡܪ
ܠܗܘܢ. ܠܐ ܩܪܝܬܘܢ ܡܢܐ ܥܒܕ ܕܘܝܕ.
ܟܕ [1]ܟܦܢ ܗܘ ܘܐܝܠܝܢ ܕܥܡܗ: (4) ܐܝܟܢܐ
ܥܠ ܠܒܝܬܗ ܕܐܠܗܐ: ܘܠܚܡܐ
[2]ܕܣܝܡܐ ܩܕܡ ܐܠܗܐ: ܐܟܠ ܘܠܐ
ܫܠܝܛ ܗܘܐ ܠܗ ܠܡܐܟܠܗ ܘܠܐ
ܠܗܢܘܢ ܕܥܡܗ: ܐܠܐ ܐܢ ܠܟܗܢܐ
ܒܠܚܘܕܝܗܘܢ܀

[1] Margo, ܗܘ

[2] Marg. προθησεως ܗܢܘ ܕܝܢ ܕܣܝܡܝܢ ܗܘܘ ܩܕܡ ܐܠܗܐ.

PESHITTO.	JERUSALEM SYRIAC.	HARKLEIAN.
(3) ܗܝܕܝܢ ܝܗܘܕܐ ܡܫܠܡܢܐ܆ ܟܕ ܚܙܐ ܕܐܬܚܝܒ ܝܫܘܥ. ܐܙܠ ܬܘܐ ܘܐܗܦܟ ܗܠܝܢ ܬܠܬܝܢ ܕܟܣܦܐ ܠܪܒܝ ܟܗܢܐ ܘܠܩܫܝܫܐ. (4) ܘܐܡܪ. ܣܟܠܬ ܕܐܫܠܡܬ ܕܡܐ ܙܟܝܐ. ܗܢܘܢ ܕܝܢ ܐܡܪܘ ܠܗ. ܠܢ ܡܐ ܠܢ. ܐܢܬ ܝܕܥ ܐܢܬ. (5) ܘܫܕܐ ܟܣܦܐ ܒܗܝܟܠܐ ܘܫܢܝ. ܘܐܙܠ ܚܢܩ ܢܦܫܗ. (6) ܪܒܝ ܟܗܢܐ ܕܝܢ ܫܩܠܘܗܝ ܠܟܣܦܐ ܘܐܡܪܘ. ܠܐ ܫܠܝܛ ܕܢܪܡܝܘܗܝ ܒܝܬ ܩܘܪܒܢܐ. ܡܛܠ ܕܛܝܡܐ ܕܕܡܐ ܗܘ. (7) ܘܡܠܟܐ ܢܣܒܘ ܘܙܒܢܘ ܒܗ ܐܓܘܪܣܐ ܕܩܘܩܝܐ ܠܒܝܬ ܩܒܘܪܐ ܕܐܟܣܢܝܐ. (8) ܡܛܠ ܗܢܐ ܐܬܩܪܝ ܐܓܘܪܣܐ ܗܘ ܩܪܝܬܐ ܕܕܡܐ ܥܕܡܐ ܠܝܘܡܢܐ܀	(3) ܘܟܕ ܚܡܐ ܝܗܘܕܐ ܡܫܠܡܢܗ ܕܐܬܚܝܒ ܝܫܘܥ ܐܬܬܘܝ ܘܐܗܦܟ ܬܠܬܝܢ ܕܟܣܦܐ ܠܪܒܝ ܟܗܢܝܐ (s. m. ܘܠܣܒܝܐ) (4) ܘܐܡܪ. ܚܛܝܬ ܕܐܫܠܡܬ ܕܡ ܙܟܝ܀ (s. m. ܙܟܝ) ܗܢܘܢ ܕܝܢ ܐܡܪܘ ܡܐ ܠܢ ܘܠܟ ܐܬ ܚܡܝ܀ (5) ܘܪܡܐ ܟܣܦܐ ܒܗܝܟܠܐ ܘܐܙܠ ܚܢܩ ܢܦܫܗ܀ (6) ܘܪܒܝ ܟܗܢܝܐ ܢܣܒܘ ܟܣܦܐ ܘܐܡܪܘ ܠܐ ܫܠܝܛ ܠܢ ܕܢܪܡܝ ܝܬܗ ܒܩܘܪܒܢܐ܀ ܡܛܠ ܕܛܝܡܝ ܕܕܡ ܗܘ܀ (7) ܢܣܒܘ (s. m. *sic* ܡܠܟܐ) ܘܙܒܢܘ ܒܗ ܐܓܘܪܐ ܕܩܘܩܝ ܠܩܒܘܪܬܐ ܠܐܟܣܢܝܐ܀ (8) ܡܛܠ ܗܢܐ ܐܬܩܪܝ ܐܓܘܪܐ ܗܘ ܚܩܠ ܕܕܡ ܥܕ ܝܘܡܐ ܕܝܘܡܢ܀ Ed. Lagarde, p. 314, Cod. fol. 130[3].	(3) ܗܝܕܝܢ ܟܕ ܚܙܐ ܝܗܘܕܐ ܗܘ ܕܐܫܠܡܗ ܕܐܬܚܝܒ܆ ܬܘܐ ܠܗ. ܘܐܗܦܟ ܗܠܝܢ ܬܠܬܝܢ ܕܣܐܡܐ ܠܪܒܝ ܟܗܢܐ ܘܠܩܫܝܫܐ (4) ܟܕ ܐܡܪ. ܚܛܝܬ ܕܐܫܠܡܬ ܕܡܐ ܙܟܝܐ[1]. ܗܢܘܢ ܕܝܢ ܐܡܪܘ. ܡܢܐ ܠܢ. ܐܢܬ ܬܚܙܐ[2]. (5) ܘܟܕ ܫܕܐ ܠܗܝܢ ܠܟܣܦܐ ܒܗܝܟܠܐ܆ ܫܢܝ ܘܐܙܠ ܚܢܩ[3] ܢܦܫܗ. (6) ܪܒܝ ܟܗܢܐ ܕܝܢ ܟܕ ܫܩܠܘ ܐܢܘܢ ܠܟܣܦܐ ܐܡܪܘ. ܠܐ ܫܠܝܛ ܠܡܪܡܝܘ ܐܢܘܢ ܒܩܘܪܒܢܐ[4]. ܡܛܠ ܕܛܝܡܐ ܕܕܡܐ ܐܝܬܝܗܘܢ. (7) ܟܕ ܕܝܢ ܡܠܟܐ ܢܣܒܘ. ܙܒܢܘ ܡܢܗܘܢ ܐܓܘܪܣܐ ܕܩܘܩܝܐ[5] ܠܩܒܘܪܬܐ ܕܐܟܣܢܝܐ. (8) ܡܛܠ ܗܢܐ ܐܬܩܪܝ ܐܓܘܪܣܐ ܗܘ ܚܩܠܐ ܕܕܡܐ ܥܕܡܐ ܠܝܘܡܢܐ܀ Marg. [1] αθωον. [2] οψη. [3] απηγξατο. [4] κορβαναν. [5] κεραμεως.

MARK XVI. 17–20.

PESHITTO.

(17) ܐܬܘܬܐ ܕܝܢ ܠܐܝܠܝܢ ܕܡܗܝܡܢܝܢ
ܗܠܝܢ ܢܩܦܢ. ܒܫܡܝ ܫܐܕܐ
ܢܦܩܘܢ. ܘܒܠܫܢܐ ܚܕܬܐ ܢܡܠܠܘܢ.
(18) ܘܚܘܘܬܐ ܢܫܩܠܘܢ. ܘܐܢ ܣܡܐ
ܕܡܘܬܐ ܢܫܬܘܢ ܠܐ ܢܗܪܐ ܠܗܘܢ. ܘܐܝܕܝܗܘܢ
ܢܣܝܡܘܢ ܥܠ ܟܪܝܗܐ ܘܢܬܚܠܡܘܢ.
(19) ܝܫܘܥ ܕܝܢ ܡܪܢ: ܡܢ ܒܬܪ
ܕܡܠܠ ܥܡܗܘܢ ܠܫܡܝܐ ܣܠܩ.
ܘܝܬܒ ܡܢ ܝܡܝܢܐ ܕܐܠܗܐ. (20) ܗܢܘܢ
ܕܝܢ ܢܦܩܘ ܘܐܟܪܙܘ ܒܟܠ ܕܘܟ. ܘܡܪܢ
ܡܥܕܪ ܗܘܐ ܠܗܘܢ: ܘܡܫܪܪ ܡܠܝܗܘܢ
ܒܐܬܘܬܐ ܕܥܒܕܝܢ ܗܘܘ ܀

CURETONIAN.

(17) . . . ܘܕܡܗܝܡܢܝܢ ܒܝ. ܗܠܝܢ
ܒܫܡܝ ܫܐܕܐ ܢܦܩܘܢ. ܒܠܫܢܐ ܚܕܬܐ
ܢܡܠܠܘܢ. (18) ܚܘܘܬܐ ܢܫܩܠܘܢ
ܒܐܝܕܝܗܘܢ ܘܐܢ ܣܡܐ ܕܡܘܬܐ
ܢܫܬܘܢ ܠܐ ܢܗܪ ܐܢܘܢ. ܥܠ ܟܪܝܗܐ
ܢܣܝܡܘܢ ܐܝܕܝܗܘܢ ܘܢܬܐܣܘܢ ܀
(19) ܡܪܢ ܕܝܢ ܡܢ ܒܬܪ ܕܦܩܕ
ܠܬܠܡܝܕܘܗܝ ܐܣܬܠܩ ܠܫܡܝܐ.
ܘܝܬܒ ܡܢ ܝܡܝܢܐ ܕܐܠܗܐ. (20) ܘܗܢܘܢ
ܕܝܢ ܢܦܩܘ ܘܐܟܪܙܘ ܒܟܠ ܕܘܟ. ܟܕ
ܡܪܢ ܡܥܕܪ ܠܗܘܢ ܒܟܠ. ܘܡܠܬܗܘܢ
ܡܫܪܪ ܗܘܐ ܒܐܬܘܬܐ ܕܥܒܕܝܢ ܗܘܘ ܀

HARKLEIAN.

(17) ܐܬܘܬܐ ܕܝܢ ܠܗܠܝܢ ܕܡܗܝܡܢܝܢ
ܗܠܝܢ ܢܩܦܢ. ܒܫܡܝ ܕܝܠܝ ܫܐܕܐ
ܢܦܩܘܢ. ܒܠܫܢܐ ܚܕܬܐ ܢܡܠܠܘܢ.
(18) ⁜ ܘܒܐܝܕܝܐ ܗ݂ ܚܘܘܬܐ ܢܫܩܠܘܢ.
ܘܐܢ ÷ ܣܡܐ ܗ݂ ܡܡܝܬܢܐ ܡܕܡ ܢܫܬܘܢ
ܠܐ ܢܗܪ ܐܢܘܢ. ܥܠ ܟܪܝܗܐ ܐܝܕܝܐ
ܢܣܝܡܘܢ: ܘܫܦܝܪ ܢܗܘܘܢ ܀ (19) ܗܘ
ܡܢ ܗܟܝܠ ܡܪܢ ܝܫܘܥ: ܒܬܪ
ܕܡܠܠ ܥܡܗܘܢ ܐܣܬܠܩ ܠܫܡܝܐ ܘܝܬܒ
ܡܢ ܝܡܝܢܐ ܕܐܠܗܐ ܀ (20) ܗܢܘܢ
ܕܝܢ ܟܕ ܢܦܩܘ ܐܟܪܙܘ ܒܟܠ ܕܘܟܐ:
ܟܕ ܡܪܢ ܡܥܕܪ ܗܘܐ ܘܡܠܬܐ ܡܫܪܪ
ܗܘܐ: ܒܝܕ ܐܬܘܬܐ ܕܢܩܦܢ ܗܘܝ ܀

CHAPTER III.

THE LATIN VERSIONS.

SINCE the publication of the third edition of this book, exhaustive work on the Old Latin Versions and the Vulgate, commenced before for the University of Oxford, as is well known amongst biblical scholars, by the Right Rev. John Wordsworth, D.D., Bishop of Salisbury, with the assistance of the Rev. H. J. White, has been prosecuted further, resulting in the publication of three volumes of Old Latin Biblical Texts, and of the edition of the Vulgate New Testament as far as the end of St. Luke's Gospel. It was therefore with the liveliest gratitude that the Editor received from the Bishop, in reply to consultation upon a special point, an offer to superintend the entire revision of this chapter, if Mr. White would give him his important help, notwithstanding other laborious occupations. Mr. White has carried out the work under the Bishop's direction, rewriting most of the chapter entirely, but incorporating, where possible, Dr. Scrivener's language.

(1) *The Old Latin, previous to Jerome's Revision.*

There are passages in the works of the two great Western Fathers of the fourth century, Jerome [345 ?–420] and Augustine [354–430], whose obvious and literal meaning might lead us to conclude that there existed in their time *many* Latin translations, quite independent in their origin, and used almost indifferently by the faithful. When Jerome, in that Preface to the Gospels which he addressed to Pope Damasus (in 384), anticipates but too surely the unpopularity of his revision of them among the people of his own generation, he consoles himself by the reflection that the variations of previous versions prove the unfaithfulness of them all: 'verum non esse quod variat etiam maledicorum testimonio comprobatur.' Then follows his celebrated assertion: 'Si enim Latinis exemplaribus fides est adhibenda, respondeant quibus: tot enim sunt exemplaria pene quot codices[1].' The testimony of Augustine seems even more explicit, and at first sight conclusive. In his treatise, De Doctrina Christiana (lib. ii. cc. 11–15), when speaking of 'Latinorum interpretum infinita varietas,' and 'interpretum numerositas,' as not without their benefit to an attentive reader, he uses these strong expressions: 'Qui enim Scripturas ex hebraea lingua in Graecam verterunt, numerari possunt, Latini autem interpretes nullo modo. Ut enim cuique primis fidei temporibus in manus venit codex Graecus, et aliquantulum facultatis sibi utriusque linguae habere videbatur, ausus est interpretari' (c. 11); and he soon after specifies a particular version as preferable to the rest: 'In ipsis autem interpretationibus Itala[2] ceteris praeferatur. Nam est verborum tenacior cum perspicuitate sententiae' (cc. 14–15).

When, however, the surviving codices of the version or versions previous to Jerome's revision came to be studied and published by Sabatier[3] and Bianchini[4], it was obvious that though there were many points of difference, there were still traces of a source common to many, if not to all of them; and on a question of this kind, occasional divergency, however extensive, cannot weaken the impression produced by resemblance, if it be too close and constant to be attributable to chance, as we have just seen. The result of a careful and thorough examination and comparison of the existing Old Latin texts, is a conviction that they are all but off-shoots from one, or at most two, parent stocks. Now when, this fact fairly established, we look back at the language employed by Jerome and Augustine, we can easily see

[1] Of no passage is this judgement more true than of this actual sentence itself, which is hardly quoted in the same way in any three MSS.; see Wordsworth's Vulgate, Fasc. 1, p. 2.

[2] For *Itala* Bentley conjectured *et illa*, changing the following *nam* into *quae*; and he wrote to Sabatier almost ridiculing the idea of a 'Versio Italica;' *see* Correspondence, ed. Wordsworth, 1842, p. 569; and 'Versio Latina Italica, somnium merum,' in Ellis, Bentleii Critica Sacra, pp. 157–159; Kaulen, Gesch. d. Vulgata, Mainz, 1868, p. 116 f.; Abp. Potter conjectured *usitata* for *Itala*; *see* Field, Otium Norvicense, pars tertia, p. 57.

[3] Bibliorum Sacr. Latinae Versiones Ant. seu Vetus Italica etc. opera et studio D. Petri Sabatier, 3 vols., Rheims, 1743–1749; a revised edition of this great work, for the Old Test., is in course of preparation under the auspices of the Munich Academy, and the able superintendence of Professor E. Wölfflin.

[4] Evangeliarium Quadruplex Latinae Versionis Antiquae, seu Veteris Italicae, editum ex codicibus manuscriptis . . . a Josepho Blanchino, 2 vols., Rome, 1749; reprinted by Migne, Patr. Lat. xii, with the works of Eusebius Vercellensis.

that, with some allowance for his habit of rhetorical exaggeration, the former may mean no more by the term 'exemplaria' than that the scattered copies of the Latin translation in his own day varied widely from each other; and though the assertions of Augustine are too positive to be thus disposed of, yet he is here speaking, not from his own personal knowledge so much as from vague conjecture; and of what had been done, not in his own time, but 'in the first ages of the faith.'

On one point, however, Augustine must be received as a competent and most sufficient witness. We cannot hesitate to believe that one of the several recensions current towards the end of the fourth century was distinguished from the rest by the name of *Itala*[1], and in his judgement deserved praise for its clearness and fidelity. It was long regarded as certain that here we should find the Old Latin version in its purest form, and that in Italy it had been thus used from the very beginning of the Church, 'cum Ecclesia Latina sine versione Latina esse non potuerit' (Walton, Proleg. x. 1). Mill indeed reminds us that the early Church at Rome was composed to so great an extent of Jewish and other foreigners, whose vernacular tongue was Greek, that the need of a Latin translation of Scripture would not at first be felt; yet even he would not place its date later than Pius I (142–157), the first Bishop of Rome after Clement who bears a Latin name (Mill, Proleg. § 377). It was not until attention had been specially drawn to the style of the Old Latin version, that scholars began to suggest AFRICA as the place, and the second half of the second century as the time, of its origin. This opinion, which had obtained favour with Eichhorn and some others before him, may be considered as demonstrated by Cardinal Wiseman, in his 'Two letters on some parts of the controversy concerning 1 John v. 7[2].' So far as his argument rests on the Greek character of the *Roman* Church, it may not bring conviction to the reflecting reader. Even though the early Bishops of Rome were of foreign origin, though Clement towards the end of the first, Gaius the presbyter late in the second century, who are proved by their names to be Latins, yet chose to write in Greek;

[1] That is, by scholars who did not live in Italy; Italian Christians would use other names, *vetus, antiqua, usitata, communis, vulgata*; Kaulen, p. 118, Berger, p. 6.

[2] Published in the *Catholic Magazine* for 1832–3; since reprinted in his 'Essays on various subjects,' 1853, vol. i.

it does not follow that the Church would not contain many humbler members, both Romans and Italians, ignorant of any language except Latin, and for whose instruction a Latin version would be required. On the ground of *internal* evidence, however, Wiseman made out a case which all who have followed him, Lachmann, Tischendorf, Davidson, Tregelles, accept as irresistible; indeed it is not easy to draw any other conclusion from his elaborate comparison of the words, the phrases, and grammatical constructions of the Latin version of Holy Scripture, with the parallel instances by which they can be illustrated from African writers, and from them only (Essays, vol. i. pp. 46–66)[1]. It is impossible to exhibit any adequate abridgement of an investigation which owes all its cogency to the number and variety of minute particulars, each one weak enough by itself, the whole comprising a mass of evidence which cannot be gainsaid. In the works of Apuleius and of the African Fathers, Tertullian [150 ?–220 ?], Cyprian [† 258], and in the following century, Arnobius, Lactantius, Augustine, we obtain a glimpse into the genius and character of the dialect in which the earliest form of the Old Latin version is composed. We see a multitude of words which occur in no Italian author so late as Cicero; constructions (e. g. *dominantur eorum*, Luke xxii. 25; *faciam vos fieri*, Matt. iv. 19) or forms of verbs (*sive consolamur . . . sive exhortamur*, 2 Cor. i. 6) abound[2], which at Rome had long been obsolete; while the lack of classic polish is not ill-atoned for by a certain vigour which characterizes this whole class of writers, but never degenerates into barbarism.

The *European* and *Italian* forms of the Old Latin version will be discussed afterwards.

The following manuscripts of the version are extant. They

[1] We have let these sentences stand as Dr. Scrivener penned them in 1883; since that time the opinion of scholars has become less positive as to the African origin of the Latin version. It is true that the words, phrases, &c., of that version in its earlier forms can be illustrated from contemporary African writers, and from them only; but that is because during this period we are dependent almost exclusively on Africa for our Latin literature; and consequently are able to use only the method of *agreement* and not the method of *difference* in testing the origin and characteristics of the Latin New Testament. These characteristics may be the result only of the time and not of the supposed place of writing. Nor can more stress be laid on the use of Greek names in the West than on the use of Latin names (plenty of which could be cited) in the East.

[2] *See* Kaulen, p. 130 f., and also his Handb. d. Vulg., Mainz, 1870.

are usually cited by the small italic letters of the alphabet, according to the custom set by Lachmann (1842–1850), which has been considerably extended, and partially altered, since his time. His *a b c d* of the Gospels, *d e* of the Acts, and *g* of St. Paul, remain the same, but his *f* and *ff* of St. Paul = our *d* and *e*, and his *h* = Primasius.

Old Latin Manuscripts of the Gospels.

a. Codex Vercellensis [iv?], at Vercelli; according to a tradition found in a document of the eighth century, this MS. was written by Eusebius, Bishop of Vercellae († 370); M. Samuel Berger, however, and other scholars would place it later. It is written in silver on purple vellum. Bianchini, when Canon of Verona, collated this treasure in 1727; see E. Mangenot, Joseph Bianchini et les anciennes versions latines (Amiens, 1892), who gives an interesting and sympathetic account of his work. *Mut.* in many letters and words throughout, and entirely wanting in Matt. xxiv. 49—xxv. 16; Mark i. 22–34; iv. 17–25; xv. 15—xvi. 7 (xvi. 7–20 is in a later hand, taken from Jerome's Vulgate); Luke i. 1–12; xi. 12–26; xii. 38–59. Published by J. A. Irici (Sacrosanctus Evangeliorum Codex S. Eusebii Magni), Milan, 1748, and by Bianchini on the left-hand page of his great 'Evangeliarium Quadruplex,' Rome, 1749; the latter edition has been reprinted in Migne, Patr. Lat. tom. xii. Facsimile given in Zangemeister and Wattenbach, Exempla codicum Latinorum, pl. 20 (Heidelberg, 1876); compare Bethmann in Pertz, Archiv, xii. p. 606, and E. Ranke, Fragmenta Curiensia, p. 8. Bianchini's work seems to have been extremely accurate, though he does not keep to the actual division of the lines in the original manuscripts either here or in his edition of *b*. The Gospels are in the usual Western order, Matthew, John, Luke, Mark; so also a_2 *b d e f* ff_2 *i n q r*.

b. Cod. Veronensis [iv or v], also in Bianchini's 'Evangeliarum Quadruplex' on the right-hand page. *Mut.* Matt. i. 1–11, xv. 12–23, xxiii. 18–27; Mark xiii. ~~8–10~~; 24—xvi. 20; Luke xix. 26—xxi. 29; also John vii. 44—viii. 12 is *erased*.

c. Cod. Colbertinus [~~xii~~], at Paris (Lat. 254); New Testament, very important, though so late; edited in full by Sabatier (*see* p. 42, n. 3), and in a smaller and cheaper form by J. Belsheim, Christiania, 1888; Belsheim's work however is, as usual, inaccurate. For the date of the MS. *see* E. Ranke, Fragmenta Curiensia, p. 9. Beyond the Gospels, the version is Jerome's, and in a later hand. *See* below under Vulgate MSS., no. 53.

d. Cod. Bezae [vi], its Latin version; *see* Vol. I. pp. 124–130, and for its defects p. 124, n. 2; also Prof. J. Rendel Harris, A Study of Codex Bezae, Cambridge, 1891; and F. H. Chase, The Syriac element in Codex Bezae, London, 1893.

e. Cod. Palatinus [iv or v], now at Vienna (Pal. 1185), where it was acquired from Trent between 1800 and 1829; on purple vellum,

$14 \times 9\frac{3}{4}$, written with gold and silver letters, as are Codd. *a b f i j*, edited by Tischendorf, Leipzig, 1847. Only the following portions are extant: Matt. xii. 49—xiii. 13; 24—xiv. 11 (*with breaks, twelve lines being lost*); 22—xxiv. 49; xxviii. 2—John xviii. 12; 25—Luke viii. 30; 48—xi. 4; 24—xxiv. 53; Mark i. 20—iv. 8; 19—vi. 9; xii. 37-40; xiii. 2, 3; 24-27; 33-36; i. e. 2627 verses, including all St. John but 13 verses, all St. Luke but 38. Another leaf, bought for Trinity College, Dublin, by Dr. Todd before 1847, containing Matt. xiii. 13-23, was published by Dr. T. K. Abbott in his edition of Cod. Z. It was recognized in 1880 to be a fragment of *e* by Mr. French, the sub-librarian; *see* also H. Linke, Neue Bruchst. des Evang. Pal. (S. B. of the Munich Acad. 1893, Heft ii).

f. Cod. Brixianus [vi], at Brescia, edited by Bianchini beneath Cod. *b*. *Mut.* Matt. viii. 16-26; Mark xii. 5—xiii. 32; xiv. 53-62; 70—xvi. 20. There are some bad slips in Migne's reprint of this MS.

ff_1. Cod. Corbeiensis i [viii or ix], containing the Gospel of St. Matthew, now at St. Petersburg (Ov. 3, D. 326). It formerly belonged to the great monastic Library of Corbey, or Corbie, on the Somme, near Amiens; and with the most important part of that Library was transferred to St. Germain des Prés at Paris, in or about the year 1638, and was there numbered 21. The St. Germain Library, however, suffered severely from theft and pillage during the French Revolution, and Peter Dubrowsky, Secretary to the Russian Embassy at Paris, seems to have used his opportunities during that troublous time to acquire MSS. stolen from public libraries; ff_1 with other MSS. fell into his hands and was transferred to the Imperial Library at St. Petersburg about 1800-1805. In 1695 Dom Jean Martianay, well known as the principal editor of the Benedictine St. Jerome, published ff_1 with a marginal collation of the St. Germain Bible (g_1), and the Corbey St. James (*see* p. 52) in a small volume entitled 'Vulgata antiqua Latina et Itala versio secundum Matthaeum e vetustissimis eruta monumentis illustrata Prolegomenis ac notis nuncque primum edita studio et labore D. J. M. etc. Parisiis, apud Antonium Lambin.' Bianchini reprinted it underneath Cod. *a*, giving in its place a collation of ff_2 in SS. Mark, Luke, and John; Sabatier, however, cites ff_1 in Mark i. 1—v. 11, but it is difficult to know to what MS. he refers. Finally it has been re-edited by Belsheim (Christiania, 1882). For the history of this MS., *see* Wordsworth, Old Lat. Bibl. Texts, i. p. xxii, and Studia Biblica, i. p. 124; and for the history of the Library at Corbey, Delisle, Bibliothèque de l'Ecole des Chartes, 1860, p. 438; R. S. Bensly, The missing fragment of the Latin Translation of the Fourth Book of Ezra, p. 7 (Cambridge, 1875).

ff_2. Cod. Corbeiensis ii [vi], now at Paris (Lat. 17,225), formerly at Corbey, where it was numbered 195; it contains 190 leaves and is written in a beautiful round uncial hand. Quoted by Sabatier, and a collation given by Bianchini in Mark, Luke, and John; published in full by Belsheim (Christiania, 1887). Belsheim's work, however, has been since revised by M. Berger and his revision communicated to the present writer (H. J. White). *Mut.* Matt. i. 1—xi. 6; John xvii. 15—xviii. 9; xx. 22—xxi. 8; Luke ix. 48—x. 21; xi. 45—xii. 6; and a few verses missing in Matt. xi, Mark ix and xvi; Facsimile in Palaeogr. Soc. i. pl. 87.

g_1. COD. SANGERMANENSIS I [ix], now at Paris (Lat. 11,553); formerly in the Library of St. Germain des Prés, where it was first numbered 15 and afterwards 86; it is the second volume of a complete Bible, the first volume of which has been lost. This MS. was known to R. Stephens, who in his Latin Bible, published 1538–40 and again 1546, quotes it as *Germ. Lat.*, in consequence of its breadth; it was also examined by R. Simon, who, writing in 1680, speaks of it at some length; Martianay published a collation of its readings in his edition of the Corbey St. Matthew (*see* under ff_1); and Martianay's collation, which indeed was faulty enough, was reprinted by Bianchini. John Walker, Bentley's coadjutor in his great but unfinished work for the New Testament, collated it carefully in 1720; and finally Bp. Wordsworth published St. Matthew's Gospel with full Introductions in 1883 (Old Latin Biblical Texts, No. 1, Oxford), and has collated the other Gospels for his edition of the Vulgate. J. Walker cited the MS. as μ; Bp. Wordsworth cites it as g_1 in St. Matthew, G in the other books of the New Testament. The text can only be called strictly *Old Latin* in St. Matthew, where it seems to be partly of the European, partly of the Italian type; in the other Gospels it is Vulgate, though largely mixed with Old Latin readings. *See* below under Vulgate, MSS., no. 21.

g_2. COD. SANGERMANENSIS II [x], 116 leaves, Irish hand, with a mixed Old Latin and Vulgate text. Now at Paris (Lat. 13,169), but was originally at Angers, and then apparently at Mans in the province of Tours; possibly brought there by Ulgrinus, Bishop of Mans 1057–65. *See* Berger, Histoire de la Vulgate pendant les premiers Siècles du M.A., p. 48.

h. COD. CLAROMONTANUS [iv or v], now in the Vatican Library (Lat. 7223), for which it was bought by Pius VI (1775–99), contains, like g_1, St. Matthew only in the Old Latin, the other Gospels being Vulgate. *Mut.* Matt. i. 1—iii. 15; xiv. 33—xviii. 12. Sabatier gave extracts, and Mai published St. Matthew in full in his 'Script. Vet. nova collectio Vaticana,' iii. p. 257 (Rom. 1828); it has been republished by Belsheim (Evangelium secundum Matthaeum . . . e codice olim Claromontano nunc Vaticano), Christiania, 1892.

i. COD. VINDOBONENSIS [vii], at Vienna (Lat. 1235), formerly belonging to an Augustinian Monastery at Naples, whence it was brought with ninety-four other MSS. to Vienna in 1717; consists of 142 leaves, and contains Luke x. 6—xxiii. 10; Mark ii. 17—iii. 29; iv. 4—x. 1; 33—xiv. 36; xv. 33–40. The MS. was described and edited by F. C. Alter, the Mark fragments in G. E. H. Paulus' 'N. Repert. d. bibl. u. morgenl. Literatur,' iii. pp. 115–170 (1791), the Luke fragments in Paulus, Memorabilia, vii. pp. 58–95 (1795). Bianchini had, however, previously obtained a collation for his 'Evangeliarium Quadruplex' from the Count of Thun and Hohenstein (afterwards Bishop of Gurk in Carinthia), who had spent some time at the Court of Vienna; and N. Forlosia, the principal Librarian at Vienna, had given him a careful description of the MS.; *see* 'Epistola Blanchinii ad Episcopum Gurcensem' in Bianchini's prolegomena. Finally Belsheim edited the MS. completely in 1885 (Leipzig, Weigel), and Dr. Rudolf Beer revised his edition for Bishop Wordsworth's edition of the Vulgate in 1888.

j. Cod. Sarzannensis or Saretianus [v] was discovered in 1872 in the Church of Sarezzano near Tortona. It consists of eight quires written on purple vellum in silver letters, and contains (much mutilated) 292 verses of St. John, viz. i. 38—iii. 23; iii. 33—v. 20; vi. 29–49; 49–67; 68—vii. 32; viii. 6—ix. 21, written two columns on a page. The text is peculiar, and much with *a b d e*. Guerrino Amelli, sub-librarian of the Ambrosian Library (and now at the Benedictine Monastery of Monte Cassino), published at Milan the same year a 'Dissertazione critico-storica,' 18 pp. (2nd edition, 1885), with a lithographed facsimile, whose characters much resemble the round and flowing shape of those in *a b f*. The MS. is now at Rome undergoing careful restoration, but no part of it has yet been published.

k. Cod. Bobiensis [v or vi], now in the National Library at Turin (G. vii. 15), whither it was brought with a vast number of other books from Bobbio; traditionally asserted to have belonged to St. Columban, who died in the monastery he had founded there, in 615. This MS. is perhaps the most important, in regard to text, of all the Old Latin copies, being undoubtedly the oldest existing representative of the African type. It contains Mark viii. 8–11; 14–16; 19—xvi. 9; Matthew i. 1—iii. 10; iv. 2—xiv. 17; xv. 20–36; the order then was probably John, Luke, Mark, Matthew. It was edited by F. F. Fleck in 1837, and by Tischendorf in 1847–49; but so inaccurately by the former and so inconveniently by the latter as to be little known and used by students. It was finally edited by Bishop Wordsworth (1886) as No. 2 of the 'Old-Latin Bible Texts,' with full introduction, and with a dissertation on the text by Professor Sanday.

l. Cod. Rhedigeranus [vii], in the Rhedigeran Library at Breslau; from a note at the end of St. Luke's Gospel, it appears to have been bought by Thomas von Rhediger at Verona in the year 1569. J. E. Scheibel in 1763 published SS. Matthew and Mark, far from correctly. D. Schulz wrote a dissertation on it in 1814, and inserted his collation of it in his edition of Griesbach's N. T., vol. i. 1827. It was edited in full by H. F. Haase, Breslau (in the 'Index. lect. univ. Vratisl.'), 1865–66. *Mut.* Matt. i. 1—ii. 15; John i. 1–16; vi. 32–61; xi. 56—xii. 10; xiii. 34—xiv. 23; xv. 3–15; xvi. 13 *ad fin.*

m. This letter indicates the readings extracted by Mai from the 'Liber de divinis scripturis sive speculum,' ascribed to St. Augustine, and containing extracts from the whole N. T. except Philemon, Hebrews, and 3 John; it also has a citation from the Epistle to the Laodiceans. It resembles the 'Testimonia' of Cyprian (and indeed one MS. has the subscription *explicit testimoniorum*) in that it consists of extracts from both Testaments, arranged in chapters under various heads. This treatise was published by Mai, first in the 'Spicilegium Romanum,' 1843, vol. ix. part ii. 1–88, and again in the 'Nova Patrum Bibliotheca,'

Rome, 1852, vol. i. part ii. 1–117; and Wiseman had drawn attention to it in his celebrated 'Two Letters' (*see* p. 43), because it contains I John v. 7 in two different places. Mai had published it from the Sessorian MS. (no. 58) of the eighth or ninth century, so called from the library of Sta. Croce in Gerusalemme (Bibliotheca Sessoriana) at Rome, in which it is preserved (see Reifferscheid, Bibl. Patr. Italica, ii. p. 129); he furnished a facsimile. Recently the treatise has been excellently edited by Dr. F. Weihrich in the Vienna 'Corpus script. eccl. lat.,' vol. xii (Vienna, 1887), from six MSS.; one of these is the Codex Floriacensis (Libri MS. 16, now in the Bibl. Nat. at Paris, Nouv. acq. lat. 1596), the readings of which are occasionally cited by Sabatier under the name of *floriac.* (*see* Weihrich, p. xl, and L. Delisle, Cat. des MSS. des fonds Libri et Barrois, 1888, p. 25 and pl. iv. 1; also Palaeographical Soc., series ii. pl. 34).

n. Fragmenta Sangallensia [v or vi], in the Stiftsbibliothek at St. Gall, to which Library they have probably belonged from its foundation. The fragments are bound up in a large book numbered 1394, and entitled 'Veterum fragmentorum manuscriptis codicibus detractorum Collectio;' they contain Matt. xvii. 1—xviii. 20; xix. 20—xxi. 3; xxvi. 56–60; 69–74; xxvii. 62—xxviii. 3; 8–20; Mark vii. 13–31; viii. 32—ix. 10; xiii. 2–20; xv. 22—xvi. 13; to this must be added a whole leaf containing John xix. 28–42, and a slip containing portions of John xix. 13–27, which are in the Stadtbibliothek of the same city, bound up in a MS. numbered 70 and entitled 'Casus monasterii Sancti Galli;' and the conjecture of the Abbé Batiffol and Dr. P. Corssen is undoubtedly right that the fragment from St. Luke known as a_2 (see below) is also a part of this MS.

Tischendorf transcribed these fragments, intending to edit them himself, but died before he had done so; the transcripts were purchased from his widow by the Clarendon Press in 1883, and published in the second volume of 'Old Lat. Bibl. Texts' (Oxford, 1886) by the Rev. H. J. White, who revised them on the spot from the originals; meanwhile they had been published in France by the Abbé Batiffol (Note sur un Evangéliare de Saint-Gall, Paris, Champion, 1884, and 'Fragmenta Sangallensia' in the *Revue archéologique*, pp. 305–321, for 1885). A facsimile was appended to the Oxford edition, and is also given by the Palaeographical Soc., series ii. plate 50.

o [vii], another fragment at St. Gall, bound up in the same volume with *n*, contains Mark xvi. 14–20; it may very possibly have been written to complete the above-named MS. when it had lost its last leaf, as it has the same number of lines to a page and begins exactly at the point where *n* leaves off. Edited by Batiffol with *n*, and also in Old Lat. Bibl. Texts, vol. ii.

p [vii or viii], also at St. Gall, bound up in the second volume of the 'Veterum fragmentorum Collectio' (pp. 430–433). This fragment consists of two leaves written in an Irish hand, and apparently belonging to a 'Missa pro defunctis,' of which it was the Gospel; it contains John xi. 16–44, introduced with the lines from Ps. lxv, 'te decet dñe,' &c. The opening verses of the Gospel are adapted as an introduction of the lection; the rest of the text is of the European type, but (with *r*) contains many peculiar Irish characteristics. *p* has been published three times: by Forbes, in the 'Preface to the Arbuthnott Missal,' p. xlviii (Burntisland, 1864); by Haddan and Stubbs, Councils, vol. i. Appendix G, p. 197 (Oxford, 1869); and in Old Lat. Bibl. Texts, vol. ii.

q. COD. MONACENSIS [vii], now in the Royal Library at Munich (Lat. 6224); it was transferred hither in 1802 with other MSS. from the Chapter Library of Freising, in which it was numbered 24; written by a scribe named Valerianus. Contains the four Gospels, but *mut.* Matt. iii. 15—iv. 23; v. 25—vi. 4; 28—vii. 8; John x. 11—xii. 38; xxi. 8–20; Luke xxiii. 23–35; xxiv. 11–39; Mark i. 7–21; xv. 5–36. Published in full by the Rev. H. J. White in Old Lat. Bibl. Texts, vol. iii (Oxford, 1888); facsimiles given in the Oxford edition and also by Silvestre (Paléog. univ.; quatrième partie, no. 158).

r or r_1. CODEX USSERIANUS I [vii], in the Library of Trinity College, Dublin (A. iv. 15); it is kept among the books which once belonged to Archbishop Ussher, but nothing is known of its early history. The MS. consists of 180 leaves or fragments, written in an Irish hand, but much injured by damp; it contains the four Gospels in the usual Old Latin order, but *mut.* Matt. i. 1—xv. 16; 31—xvi. 13; xxi. 4–21; xxviii. 16–20; John i. 1–15; Mark xiv. 58—xv. 8; 29—xvi. 20. Published in full by Professor T. K. Abbott, Evangeliorum versio antehieronymiana (Dublin, 1884); facsimiles are given in his edition, in the Palaeographical Society, series ii. plate 33, and in the 'Facsimiles of National MSS. of Ireland,' part i (1874), pl. ii. It contains the *pericope de adultera* in St. John, but in the Vulgate, not the Old Latin, text.

r_2. CODEX USSERIANUS II [ix or x], also in the Library of Trinity College, Dublin (A. iv. 6). Contains the four Gospels, St. Matt. in the Old Latin and in a text allied to r_1; St. Mark, the early part of St. Luke, and the small portion (only five leaves) extant of St. John, present a text very near the Vulgate. Dr. Abbott inserted a collation of this MS. in the second volume of his book, and also a facsimile. *Mut.* Matt. i. 1–18; ii. 6—iv. 24; v. 29—xiii. 7; xiv. 1—xvi. 13; xviii. 31—xix. 26; xxvii. 58—xxviii. 20; Mark iii. 23—iv. 19; v. 31—vi. 13; Luke i. 1–13; ii. 15—iii. 8; vi. 39—vii. 11; xi. 53—xii. 45; xiv. 18—xv. 25; xvi. 15—xvii. 7; xxii. 35–59; xxiii. 14—xxiv. 53; John i. 1—v. 12; vi. 24—viii. 7; x. 3—xxi. 25.

s. FRAGMENTA AMBROSIANA [vi], now in the Ambrosian Library at Milan, where they are bound up in a volume (C. 73 inf.) containing various treatises; they belonged originally to the Monastery of St. Columban at Bobbio. Four leaves only remain, containing Luke xvii. 3–29; xviii. 39—xix. 47; xx. 46—xxi. 22. They have been edited by Ceriani, Monumenta sacra et profana, tom. i. fasc. i (Milan, 1861), and again in Old Lat. Bibl. Texts, vol. ii; a facsimile is given by the Palaeographical Society, series i. plate 54.

t. FRAGMENTA BERNENSIA [v], palimpsest fragments, now at Berne, where they are bound up in a volume numbered 611; exceedingly difficult to decipher, as the later writing is parallel to the original text. Contain Mark i. 2–23; ii. 22–27; iii. 11–18. They were first published by Professor H. Hagen under the title 'Ein Italafragment aus einem Berner Palimpsest des VI. Jahrhunderts' in Hilgenfeld's 'Zeitschrift für wissenschaftliche Theologie,' vol. xxvii. p. 470 ff. (Leipzig, 1884); reprinted in Old Latin Bibl. Texts, vol. ii, with rather important alterations in the conjectural restitution of the missing half-columns.

v. Fragmentum Vindobonense [vii], at Vienna, where it is bound up at the beginning of a volume numbered Lat. 502 and entitled 'Pactus legis Ripuariae;' it contains John xix. 27—xx. 11, but the writing is much faded. Transcribed by the Bishop of Salisbury and the Rev. H. J. White in 1887, and published in Old Latin Bibl. Texts, vol. iii.

aur. Codex Aureus or Holmiensis, in the Royal Library at Stockholm; Gospels [vii or viii], 195 leaves, complete with the exception of one leaf, which contained Luke xxi. 8–30. According to an inscription in Old English on the title-page, the book was purchased by Alfred the Alderman from the pagans [Danes?] when Alfred was king and Ethelred archbishop (A.D. 871–89), for the use of Christ Church, Canterbury. It afterwards found its way to Madrid, where Sparvenfeldt bought it in 1690 from the Library of the Marquis de Liche. Edited, with facsimiles, by Belsheim (Christiania, 1878), who classes it as Old Latin; but it is really a Vulgate text, though with a certain admixture of Old Latin readings. Hort's *holm*. (Introd., Notes, p. 5).

a_2. Fragmenta Curiensia [v or vi], formerly preserved amongst the Episcopal archives at Chur or Coire, now placed in the Rhätisches Museum of the same city. M. Batiffol was the first to suggest that these fragments belonged to the same MS. as *n*; and though this view was combated at first by Mr. White, it was reasserted strongly by Dr. Corssen (Göttingsche gel. Anzeigen, 1889, p. 316), and further examination has shown that it is correct. The fragments contain Luke xi. 11–29; xiii. 16–34; they were first discovered by Professor Hidber, of Berne, then described by Professor E. Ranke in the 'Theol. Studien u. Kritiken,' 1872, pp. 505–520, and afterwards edited by him in full, Curiensia Ev. Lucani Fragmenta Latina (Vienna, 1874).

δ. Codex Sangallensis, the interlinear Latin of Cod. Δ, stands remarkable especially for its alternative renderings of the Greek, such as 'uxorem uel coniugem' for τὴν γυναῖκα Matt. i. 20, and in almost every verse. How far the Latin text of these MSS. is independent, and how far it is a mere reproduction of the Greek, or whether the Greek has in turn been influenced by the Latin, is one of those elaborate and obscure problems which are still very far from solution. The reader is referred to Prof. J. Rendel Harris' work, The Codex Sangallensis (Cambridge, 1891), for an interesting discussion of these alternative readings.

In the Acts we have Codd. *d m* as in the Gospels; *e* the Latin version of Cod. E (Laudianus) of the Acts, and also

g. Cod. Gigas Holmiensis [xiii], a Bohemian MS. of the whole N. T., now at Stockholm, so called from its great size. Contains the Acts and

Apocalypse in the Old Latin version, the rest of the N. T. in the Vulgate. Mr. Belsheim published the Acts and Apocalypse in full and a collation of the other books (Christiania, 1878). His edition was carefully revised for the Bishop of Salisbury by Dr. H. Karlsson in 1891.

g_2. FRAGMENTUM MEDIOLANENSE [x or xi], from a lectionary; discovered by Ceriani in the Ambrosian Library at Milan and published by him in 'Monumenta Sacra et Profana,' tom. i. fasc. ii. p. 127 (*see* also preface, pp. vi and vii). Contains Acts vi. 8—vii. 2; 51—viii. 4; i. e. lection for St. Stephen's day.

h. PALIMPSESTUS FLORIACENSIS [vi or vii], now in the Bibl. Nat. at Paris, where it forms foll. 113 to 130 of a volume containing various treatises and numbered Lat. 6400 G; it was formerly numbered 5367, and was as such quoted by Sabatier, tom. iii. p. 507 ff., who had collated the first three pages. An inscription on fol. 130 shows it to have belonged in the eleventh century to the famous Benedictine Abbey of Fleury on the Loire. Mr. A. Vansittart deciphered and published some more in the 'Journal of Philology' (vol. ii, 1869, p. 240, and vol. iv, 1872, p. 219), and M. H. Omont published four pages of the Apocalypse in the 'Bibl. de l'École des chartes' (vol. xliv. 1883, p. 445). Belsheim published an edition of the fragments in 1887 ('Appendix Epist. Paulin. ex cod. Sangerm.,' Christiania); and finally M. Berger published a most careful and complete edition in 1889 (Le Palimpseste de Fleury, Paris, Fischbacher). The MS. contains fragments of the Apocalypse, the Acts, 1 and 2 Peter, and 1 John; in the order above mentioned. Of the Acts in M. Berger's edition we obtain the following:—iii. 2—iv. 18; v. 23—vii. 2; 42—viii. 2; ix. 4–23; xiv. 5–23; xvii. 34—xviii. 19; xxiii. 8–24; xxvi. 20—xxvii. 13. Facsimile given by Berger.

s. COD. BOBIENSIS [v or vi], at Vienna, consisting of a number of palimpsest leaves preserved loose and numbered Lat. 16 (*see* 'Tabulae Codd. MSS. praeter graecos et orientales in bibl. Palatina Vindob. asservatorum,' 1863–1875). They were brought with other MSS. to Vienna from Naples in 1717, and formerly belonged to the famous Monastery at Bobbio. Described by Denis (Codd. MSS. theolog. bibl. Palat. Vindob., tom. ii. p. 1, col. 628) and later by von Eichenfeld (Wiener Jahrb. der Literatur, 1824, Bd. xxvi. p. 20); then by Tischendorf in the same periodical (1847, Bd. cxx. p. 36). Finally published in full by Belsheim (Fragmenta Vindobonensia, Christiania, 1886), who printed all the fragments of this very hard palimpsest which Tischendorf had been able to decipher, and the leaves which he himself had been able to make out in addition. We thus obtain Acts xxiii. 18–23; xxv. 23–27; xxvi. 22—xxvii. 7; 10–24; 28–31; xxviii. 16–28. The same MS. also contains fragments of St. James and 1 Peter; *see* below.

In the Catholic Epistles we have

ff. CODEX CORBEIENSIS [x], of the Epistle of St. James, now in the Imperial Library at St. Petersburg, where it was numbered Qv. i. 39. Formerly belonging to the Corbey Library, where it was numbered 635, it was about 1638 transferred to St. Germain des Prés and was numbered 717 in Dom Poirier's catalogue (made about 1791); and finally was taken to St. Petersburg by Peter Dubrowsky about 1805 (see above on ff_1, p. 46). The Epistle was published in 1695 by Martianay in the same volume which included ff_1; later by Mr. Belsheim (Der Brief des Jacobus, Christiania, 1883); and again, after revision by Professor V. Jernstedt, by Bishop Wordsworth in 'Studia Biblica,' vol. i.

There are also *h*, containing 1 Pet. iv. 17—2 Pet. ii. 6; 1 John i. 8—iii. 20; *m* as in Gospels; *s* as in Acts, containing James i. 1–25; ii. 14—iii. 5; 13—iv. 2; v. 19, 20; 1 Pet. i. 1–12; ii. 4–10.

q. One of the sets of fragments at Munich [vii], published by Ziegler (*see* below): they consist of two leaves, giving us 1 John iii. 8—v. 21, and containing the three Heavenly Witnesses (1 John v. 7), placed, however, *after* v. 8, as in the Vulgate *Codex Cavensis* (*see* Ziegler, p. 5 f.); these leaves are in the collection of fragments marked Clm. 6436 (Fris. 236). Later in the same year Ziegler published more fragments from the same MS., which had been used in covering some other books; these give us 1 Pet. i. 8–19; ii. 20—iii. 7; iv. 10—v. 14; 2 Pet. i. 1–4. *See* Sitzungsberichte der k. b. Akademie der Wissenschaften zu München, 1876, Heft v. pp. 607–660.

In the Pauline Epistles we have *m* as in the Gospels. Codd. *d e f g* are the Latin versions of Codd. DEFG of St. Paul, described above, Cod. D (Clarom.); Cod. E (Sangerm.); Cod. F (Aug.); Cod. G (Boern.). To these must be added

gue. Cod. Guelferbytanus [vi], fragments of Rom. xi. 33—xii. 5; 17—xiii. 5; xiv. 9–20; xv. 3–13, found in the great Gothic palimpsest at Wolfenbüttel (Evann. PQ), published with the other matter by Knittel in 1762, and more fully by Tischendorf, Anecdota sacra et profana, pp. 155–158. In the eighth edition of his N. T. he adds readings from Rom. xiii. 3, 4, 6; 1 Tim. iv. 15.

r. Cod. Frisingensis [v or vi], consisting of twenty-one leaves at Munich, numbered Clm. 6436 (Fris. 236), and containing Rom. xiv. 10—xv. 13; 1 Cor. i. 1—iii. 5; vi. 1—vii. 7; xv. 14–43; xvi. 12—2 Cor. ii. 10; iii. 17—v. 1; vii. 10—viii. 12; ix. 10—xi. 21; xii. 14—xiii. 10; Gal. ii. 5—iii. 5; Eph. i. 16—ii. 16; Phil. i. 1–20; 1 Tim. i. 12—ii. 15; v. 18—vi. 13; Hebr. vi. 6—vii. 5; 8—viii. 1; ix. 27—xi. 7. Eight of these leaves were examined by Tischendorf in 1856, who drew attention to their importance in the 'Deutsche Zeitschr. f. christliche Wissenschaft u. chr. Leben,' 1856, n. 8; he incorporated many of their variant readings into his N. T., and intended to publish the fragments. They were published by L. Ziegler with *q* and r_2 (Italafragm. d. paulinischen Briefe, Marburg, 1876); *see* E. Wölfflin, Freisinger Itala (S. B. of Munich Acad. 1893, Heft ii).

r_2. A single leaf from Munich [vii], containing Phil. iv. 11–23; 1 Thess. i. 1–10; published by Ziegler, *see* above; also numbered Clm. 6436 (Fris. 236).

r_3. Cod. Gottvicensis [vi or vii], fragments of Romans and Galatians, from the Benedictine Abbey of Göttweig on the Danube, and consisting of two leaves taken from the cover of another book. They are numbered 1. (9) foll. 23, 24 in the Library Catalogue, and contain Rom. v. 16—

vi. 4; 6–19; Gal. iv. 6–19; 22—v. 2. Published by H. Roensch in Hilgenfeld's Zeitschrift, vol. xxii (1879), pp. 224–238.

In the Apocalypse we have *m* of the Gospels and *g* of the Acts; also *h* of the Acts (*see* above), containing i. 1—ii. 1; viii. 7—ix. 11; xi. 16—xii. 14; xiv. 15—xvi. 5 (Lachmann cites Primasius' version as *h*).

To these thirty-eight codices must be added extracts from the Latin Fathers, of which the Latin interpreter of Irenaeus, Tertullian, Cyprian, Augustine, Priscillian, and Primasius are the most important for the history of the version. For Tertullian, considerable labour will be saved to the student by the work of H. Roensch (Das neue Testament Tertullians, Leipzig, 1871), who has arranged in order his quotations, direct and indirect; for Cyprian, Hartel's excellent edition (vol. iii in the Vienna Corpus) is marred by his having edited the Testimonia, which consist of direct quotations from the Bible, arranged under various heads, from a late and inferior MS. (*see* O. L. Bibl. Texts, ii. p. xliii). The works of Priscillian, who suffered death as a heretic in 385, have been quite lately discovered and edited by Dr. G. Schepss (vol. xviii in the Vienna Corpus); the quotations in them bear a strong resemblance to those of the so-called 'Speculum' of St. Augustine (*m*), and are mainly from the Epistles. Primasius, bishop of Hadrumetum (d. 558?), was the author *inter alia* of a commentary on the Apocalypse; in this he incorporated nearly the entire text of that book, and as this text agrees almost word for word with the citations found in Cyprian's Testimonia, we thus obtain a complete African text of a book in which so many MSS. are defective. In addition to this he quoted largely from another Latin translation of the Apocalypse—that of the Donatist Ticonius—whose version seems to be a good specimen of a later text approximating more closely to the Vulgate; these have also been published quite recently by Professor Haussleiter (Zahn's Forschungen, iv. Teil, Leipzig, 1891).

When we come to arrange these authorities for the Latin version before Jerome, we find a complicated and difficult task before us; for few of our MSS. present a consistent type of text. We will confine ourselves therefore to grouping them in the three great families described by Dr. Hort (Introd. p. 78), whose division has been accepted by most textual critics, and to pointing out how here and there even that division must be accepted with some modification.

The *African* family is comparatively easy to fix, from the rich store of biblical quotations found in the African Fathers. Tertullian indeed does not give us so much help as we should have expected, as he seems to have largely used a Greek Bible and translated it into Latin himself. Cyprian's quotations, however, are valuable, as he apparently confined himself strictly to the Latin Bible current in his time; he may be taken as the standard of the early African version; to him we must add, for the Gospels, the Bobbio MS. (*k*) and the Codex Palatinus (*e*), which, however, represents a stage somewhat later than *k*; for the Acts, the Fleury palimpsest (*h*); for the Apocalypse, Primasius and *h*; and a later and revised stage in the so-called 'Speculum' (*m*), and in the quotations from Ticonius preserved in Primasius.

Existing simultaneously with the African family we find another type of text current in Western Europe, though whether it is a revision of the African text or is of independent origin, it is hard to say. This type Dr. Hort calls the *European*. It is represented in the Gospels by *b*, which may be taken as the typical European MS.; by *a* in St. Matthew, *i* (Luke and Mark), *n* and a_2 (giving us fragments of all the Gospels from the same MS.); *t* in St. Mark; in a slightly revised form by *h* of St. Matthew; in a form marked by special local characteristics, in the Irish MSS. r_1 and *p* (St. John); to a certain extent also by *q* (i.e. in its renderings, and turns of expression, as distinct from the type of Greek text underlying it); of the early Fathers, the Latin version of Irenaeus may probably be referred to this family.

For the European text in the Acts, Dr. Hort cites the Gigas Holmiensis (*g*), and the Milan Lectionary g_2, and the Bobbio fragments at Vienna (*s*); for the Epistles, the Corbey MS. of St. James (*ff*), though this has possibly a tinge of Africanism in it (*see* Bp. Wordsworth and Dr. Sanday in 'Studia Biblica,' i. pp. 113, 233); and *g* again for the Apocalypse.

The *Italian* family presents us with a type of text mainly European, but doubly revised; first in its renderings, 'to give the Latinity a smoother and more customary aspect,' and secondly in its underlying text, which has been largely corrected from the Greek; in both these points the Italian MSS. are a sort of stepping-stone between the European MSS. and Jerome's Vulgate; and as many of the Biblical quotations in Augustine's works agree closely with them, it is distinctly probable that it was this revision which he praised as the Itala. To this group we would assign *f* in the Gospels, and less notably *g*; in the Epistles the Freisingen fragments *q* of St. John and St. Peter, and *r* r_2 of St. Paul's Epistles, and the Göttweig fragments r_3 of Romans and Galatians.

But it will be seen that this arrangement leaves a large number of MSS. unaccounted for; many of the Old Latin MSS. present texts which it is impossible to class either as African, European, or Italian. Some of them possess all three characteristics; some have been half corrected from the Vulgate; and local variation, independent translation from the Greek, and in the case of the Graeco-Latin MSS., assimilation *to* the Greek, have still further complicated matters. Among these mixed texts must be placed *a* in SS. Mark, Luke, and John (with occasional Africanisms, and a large element quite peculiar to itself); *c*, which gives us a text very near the Vulgate in St. John; *d*, that apparently insoluble problem; ff_1 and ff_2 g_1 *s* δ; *l*, a text which to a large extent is almost pure Vulgate, but which at the same time preserves a number of readings, mostly interpolations, that are quite peculiar.

We must bear in mind too that even the MSS. which seem to represent most consistently one type of text, show here and there strange vacillations; *e*, African throughout as it seems at first sight, must have been copied from an ordinary European MS. in the last few chapters of St. Luke; the parent MS. of *r* obviously did not contain the *pericope de adultera*, for that passage has been supplied in a Vulgate text; and other instances might be added.

(2) *Jerome's revised Latin Version, commonly called the Vulgate.*

The extensive variations then existing between different copies of the Old Latin version, and the obvious corruptions which had crept into some of them, prompted Damasus, Bishop of Rome, in A.D. 382, to commit the important task of a formal revision of the New, and probably of the Old Testament, to Jerome, a presbyter born at Stridon on the confines of Dalmatia and Pannonia, probably a little earlier than A.D. 345. He had just returned to Rome, where he had been educated, from his hermitage in Bethlehem, and in the early ripeness of his scholarship undertook a work for which he was specially qualified, and whose delicate nature he well understood[1]. Whatever prudence and moderation could do in this case to remove objections or relieve the scruples of the simple, were not neglected by Jerome, who not only made as few changes as possible in the Old Latin when correcting its text by the help of 'ancient' Greek manuscripts[2], but left untouched many words and forms of expression, and not a few grammatical irregularities, which in a new translation (as his own subsequent version of the Hebrew Scriptures makes clear) he would most certainly have avoided. The four Gospels, as they stand in the traditional Greek order without Western variation, revised but not re-translated on this wise principle, appeared in A. D. 384, accompanied with his celebrated Preface to Damasus ('summus sacerdos'), who died that same year. Notwithstanding his other literary engagements, it is probable enough that his recension of the whole New Testament for public use was completed A. D. 385, though the proof alleged by Mill (N. T., Proleg., § 862), and by others after his example, hardly meets the case. In the next year (A. D. 386), in his Commentary on Galat., Ephes., Titus, and Philem., he indulges in more freedom of alteration as a translator than he had previously deemed advisable; while his new version of the Old Testament from the Hebrew (completed about A. D. 405) is not founded at all on the Old Latin, which was made from the Greek Septuagint; the Psalter excepted, which he executed at Rome at the same date, and in the same spirit, as the Gospels. The boldness of his attempt in regard to the Old Testament is that portion of his labours which *alone* Augustine disapproved[3] (August. ad

[1] 'Novum opus me facere cogis ex veteri: ut post exemplaria Scripturarum toto orbe dispersa, quasi quidam arbiter sedeam: et quia inter se variant, quae sint illa quae cum Graeca consentiant veritate, decernam. Pius labor, sed periculosa praesumptio, judicare de ceteris, ipsum ab omnibus judicandum: senis mutare linguam, et canescentem jam mundum ad initia retrahere parvulorum.' Praef. ad Damasum.

[2] '[Evangelia] Codicum Graecorum emendata collatione, sed veterum, quae ne multum a lectionis Latinae consuetudine discreparent, ita calamo temperavimus, ut his tantum quae sensum videbantur mutare correctis, reliqua manere pateremur ut fuerant.' *Ibid.* For a signal instance, see below, ch. ix, note on Matt. xxi. 31.

[3] To his well-known censure of Jerome's rendering of the Old Testament from the Hebrew, Augustine adds, 'Proinde non parvas Deo gratias agimus de opere tuo, quod Evangelium ex Graeco interpretatus es: quia pene in omnibus nulla offensio est, cum Scripturam Graecam contulerimus.'

Hieron. Ep. x. tom. ii. p. 18, Lugd. 1586, A.D. 403), and indeed it was never received entire by the Western Church, which long preferred his slight revision of the Old Latin, made at some earlier period of his life. Gradually, however, Jerome's recension of the whole Bible gained ground, as well through the growing influence of the Church of Rome as from its own intrinsic merits: so that when in course of time it came to take the place of the older version, it also took its name of the *Vulgate*, or common translation[1]. Cassiodorus indeed, in the middle of the sixth century, is said to have compared the new and old Latin (of the New, perhaps of both Testaments) in parallel columns, which thus became partially mixed in not a few codices: but Gregory the Great (590–604), while confessing that his Church used both ('quia sedes Apostolica, cui auctore Deo praesideo, utrâque utitur,' Epist. Dedic. ad Leandrum, c. 5), awarded so decided a preference to Jerome's translation from the Hebrew, that this form of his Old Testament version, not without some mixture with his translation from the Septuagint (Walton, Polyglott, Prol. x. pp. 242–244, Wrangham), and his Psalter and New Testament as revised from the Old Latin, came at length to comprise the Vulgate Bible, the only shape in which Holy Scripture was accessible in Western Europe (except to a few scattered scholars) during the long night of the Middle Ages.

But it was not a pure Vulgate text that was thus used; the old versions went on side by side with it for centuries, and even when they were thus nominally superseded, fragments of them found their way into probably all existing MSS. We have already remarked (in *c g* &c.) how the same MS. will present us with an Old Latin text in some books of the New Testament, and with a Vulgate text in others; we shall note the same phenomenon in other MSS., especially the British and Irish (see the MSS. numbered 51, 67, 78, 85, 87 below), which preserve on the whole a pure Hieronymian text, but are coloured here and there from the earlier versions. Variation was still further increased by the apparently numerous local or provincial recensions which were made, sometimes anonymously, some-

[1] Roger Bacon's writings, however, in the thirteenth century, are the first in which Jerome's translation is cited as the 'Vulgate' in the modern sense of the term. *See* Denifle, Die Handschriften der Bibel-correctorien des 13. Jahrhunderts, 1883, p. 278.

times under the editorship of famous men. Many of the Irish MSS., for instance, seem to have been corrected immediately from the Greek; but the two most notable recensions of the text came, not, as we might have expected, directly from Rome, but from Gaul; they are those of Alcuin and Theodulf in the ninth century. That of Alcuin was undertaken at the desire of Charles the Great[1], who bade him (A.D. 797) review and correct certain copies by the best Latin MSS. without reference to the original Greek. Charles' motive was not so much critical as a wish to obtain a standard Bible for church use, and consequently of simple and intelligible Latin. Alcuin obtained bibles for this purpose from his native Northumbria, the scene at the beginning of the eighth century of an earlier recension of the text; for it was to their monasteries at Wearmouth and Jarrow (*see* below, p. 71) that Benedict Biscop and Ceolfrid had brought the bibles and other books collected in Rome and elsewhere during their journeys; and it was in Northumbria that the magnificent Anglian texts (such as those numbered 29, 64, 82, 91, &c.) were written, perpetuating the pure Vulgate text contained at that time in the Roman MSS.[2]

At Christmas in 801, Alcuin presented Charles with a copy of the revised Bible[3]; specimens of this revision are to be found in the MSS. numbered below, 5, 9, 25, 37, 117, and others.

About the same time, Theodulf, Bishop of Orleans (787–821), undertook a similar revision, and not of a less scientific character, but followed a different method. Theodulf, himself a Visigoth and born near Narbonne, seems to have done little more than introduce into France the Spanish type of MSS., which was mixed, confused, full of interpolations, and of very slight critical value[4]; this however he corrected carefully and enriched with a large number of marginal readings. This revision is preserved for us in the Theodulfian Bible at Paris (no. 18 below),

[1] *See* Jaffé, Monumenta Carolina, p. 373, 'Jam pridem universos Veteris ac Novi instrumenti libros . . . examussim correximus;' S. Berger's essay (to be distinguished from his larger work), De l'histoire de la Vulgate en France (1887), p. 3 f.

[2] *See* the Oxford 'Studia Biblica et Ecclesiastica,' ii (1890), p. 278 f.

[3] Fritzsche, 'Latein. Bibelübersetzungen' in Herzog, R. E.[2] viii. p. 449; Westcott, 'Vulgate,' in Smith's Bibl. Dict. iii. p. 1703; Kaulen, Gesch. d. Vulg., p. 229 f.; P. Corssen, in 'Die Trierer Adahandschr.' (Leipzig, 1889), p. 31.

[4] Berger, as above, p. 7.

less correctly in its sister volume at Puy (no. 24), the Paris MS. (no. 22 below), and partly also in the correction of the Bible of St. Hubert (no. 6).

Two centuries later the text had again degenerated, and our Primate Lanfranc (1069–89) attempted a similar task, perhaps rather with a view to theology than textual criticism ('secundum orthodoxam fidem studuit corrigere')[1]. In 1109 Stephen Harding, third abbot of Citeaux, made a further revision, partly from good Latin MSS., partly from the Greek, partly, in the Old Testament, from the Hebrew, as he obtained help from some learned Jewish scholars[2]. In 1150 his example was followed by Cardinal Nicolaus Maniacoria[3]. As these individual efforts seemed to have but slight success, the task was taken up in the thirteenth century more fully and systematically by bodies of scholars, in the so-called 'Correctoria Bibliorum;' here the variant readings with their authorities, Greek, Latin, ancient, modern, and citations from the Fathers, were carefully registered. The most noticeable examples of these correctoria are (1) the 'Correctorium Parisiense' prepared by the Paris theologians. Roger Bacon had a poor opinion of the work done by these students; for some time the MSS. of the Bible that were copied and bought and sold in Paris, he says, were corrupt; they were bad to begin with, and copied carelessly by the booksellers and their scribes, while the theologians were not learned enough to discover and amend the mistakes[4]. This correctorium is also frequently, but according to Denifle (p. 284) wrongly, called *Senonense*, as if it was undertaken at the instance of the Bishop of Sens; there is, however, no *correctorium Senonense*, only the *correctiones Senonenses*, i.e. corrections made in the Paris Correctorium by the Dominicans residing at Sens; (2) the 'Correctorium' of the Dominicans, prepared under the auspices of Hugo de S. Caro, about 1240, the final corrected

[1] *See* the Life of Lanfranc, by Milo Crispinus, a monk of Bec, ch. xv, in Migne, Patr. Lat. 150, col. 55, and his Commentary, *ibid.*, col. 101 f.; Mill, Proleg., § 1058; Cave's remark (Hist. Lit. 1743, vol. ii. p. 148), 'Lanfrancus textum continuo emendat,' seems hardly borne out by the facts.

[2] His corrected Bible in four vols. is now preserved at Dijon, public library, 9 bis, *see* below, p. 68, no. 8; also Denifle, Die Hdss. d. Bibel-correctorien des 13. Jahrh. 1883, p. 267; Kaulen, p. 245.

[3] His criticisms are preserved in a MS. at Venice (Marciana Lat. class. x. cod. 178, fol. 141); *see* Denifle, p. 270, who prints them.

[4] *See* the quotations in Denifle, p. 277 f., and Hody, p. 419 f.

form of which is now preserved at Paris, B. N. Lat. 16719–16722 (*see* below, p. 70, no. 23)[1]; this, however, was again an attempt, not so much to get at Jerome's actual text as, to bring the Latin text into accordance with the Greek or Hebrew[2]; (3) a better and more critical revision, the 'Correctorium Vaticanum,' a good MS. of which is in the Vatican Library (Lat. 3466); the author of this has done his best to restore Jerome's reading throughout, although well learned in Greek and Hebrew; and he has with some probability been identified by Vercellone with a scholar much praised by Roger Bacon as a 'sapientissimus homo,' who had spent nearly forty years in the correction of the text[3] (Denifle suggests Wilh. de Mara).

These remedies, partial and temporary as they were, seemed all that was possible before the invention of printing; and, indeed, by an unfortunate chance, the worst of the three correctoria, the 'Parisiense,' was made use of by Robert Stephen.

Among the earliest productions of the press, Latin Bibles took a prominent position; and during the first half-century of printing at least 124 editions were published[4]. Of these perhaps the finest is the earliest, the famous 'forty-two line' Bible, issued at Mentz between 1452 and 1456, in two volumes, and usually ascribed to Gutenberg[5]. This is usually called the 'Mazarin Bible,' from the copy which first attracted the notice of bibliographers having been discovered in the Library of Cardinal Mazarin; in the New Testament, the order of books is Evv., Paul., Act., Cath., Apoc. Mr. Copinger enumerates twenty-five copies on vellum and paper as still known to exist; there are two in the British Museum. The first Bible published at Rome is dated 1471, and was printed by Conrad Sweynheym and Arnold Pannartz, two vols., folio; the first octavo edition, or 'poor man's

[1] *See* S. Berger, De l'histoire de la Vulgate en France, p. 9 f., 1887, and Revue de Théol. et de Philos. de Lausanne, t. xvi. p. 41, 1883.

[2] *See* Hugo's remark (Denifle, p. 295), 'In multis libris maxime historialibus, non utimur translatione Hieronymi.'

[3] *See* Vercellone, Diss. Acad., Rome, 1864, pp. 44–51; Hody, pp. 426–430; and Denifle, pp. 295–298. This correctorium is cited in Wordsworth's Vulgate as *cor. vat.*; *see* Berger, Notitia Linguae Hebraicae etc., p. 32 (1893).

[4] *See* W. A. Copinger, Incunabula Biblica, or the first half-century of the Latin Bible, p. 3, London, 1892; and L. Delisle, Journ. des Savants, Apr. 1893.

[5] Or to Peter Schoeffer, *see* J. H. Hessels, in the *Academy*, June, 1887, p. 396; August, p. 104; or to Johann Fust. *See* the British Museum 'Catalogue of Printed Books,' Bible, part i. col. 16.

Bible,' was printed at Basle in 1491 by Froben. The early editions, however, reproduced the current mediaeval type of text, or copied from each other, the only exceptions being those printed by Froben, whose copies, says Mr. Copinger, were sought after, for their accuracy, by the best scholars in Europe, and whose edition of 1502 with the 'glossa ordinaria' sometimes stands quite alone in possessing the true reading. The first edition with a collection of various readings appears to be one published at Paris in 1504[1], followed by others at Venice and Lyons in 1511, 1513; and a definite revision of the text was attempted by Cardinal Ximenes, in the famous Complutensian Polyglott (1514, &c.; see Chap. V)[2], in which he made use of the Bible of Alcalá (*see* below, no. 42); but though an advance was made on previous editions, the text was still far from pure. Erasmus, in his famous edition of the Greek Testament, appended a Latin translation; this he made himself directly from the Greek, but in his notes he discusses the current Vulgate text and gives readings from MSS. which he had examined; of these he mentions those at the Royal Library at Mechlin, St. Paul's Cathedral, London, Corsendonk Austin Priory, Constance Cathedral, St. Donatian (Abbaye des Dunes) of Bruges; of these the first and third only can be now identified, *see* below, pp. 84, 81, nos.[3] 134, 109. The first edition of a really critical nature was that of Robert Stephen, in 1528; for this he used three good MSS., the *Exemplar S. Germani parvum* (Par. lat. 11937), the Corbey Bible (Par. lat. 11532–3), and the Bible of St. Denis (Par. lat. 2); *see* below, nos. 22, 20, 10; and he published a more important edition in 1538–40 (reprinted 1546), in which he made use of seventeen MSS., of which the following[4], numbered 19, 21, 22, 100 below, have been identified. *This edition is practically the foundation of the Modern Vulgate*, and is cited by Wordsworth as ς. Later, John Hentenius, in his folio edition of the Bible, (Louvain, 1547, and often reprinted; cited by Wordsworth as 𝔥) seems to have used about thirty-one MSS. and two printed copies; but as no various readings are cited from individual

[1] Westcott, Vulgate, p. 1704. This seems to be that of 'Thielman Kerver, impensis J. Parvi,' with emendations of A. Castellani.

[2] The British Museum possesses a copy (840. d. 1); *see* the 'Catalogue,' part i. col. 1.

[3] For details *see* 'Old Lat. Bibl. Texts,' i. p. 51 f.

[4] *Ibid.*, p. 48 f.

MSS., they cannot well be identified; *see* his preface. Lucas Brugensis (*see* his catalogue at the end of the Hentenian Bible of 1583, p. 6) also gives a long list of MSS., which seem impossible to be identified [1], and we must also bear in mind the corrected editions published by Th. Vivian (Paris), and Junta (Venice), 1534 (both are small copies of the New Testament, corrected occasionally from the Greck), Isidore Clarius (Venice, 1542), J. Benedictus (Paris, 1558), Paul Eber (1565), and Luke Osiander (1578).

When the Council of Trent met, the duty of providing for the members of the Church of Rome the most correct recension of the Latin Bible that skill and diligence could produce was obviously incumbent on it; and in one of its earliest sittings (April 8, 1546) the famous decree was passed, ordaining that of the many published editions of the Holy Scripture 'haec ipsa vetus et vulgata editio, quae longo tot saeculorum usu in ipsa ecclesia probata est' should be chosen, and 'in publicis lectionibus, disputationibus, praedicationibus, et expositionibus pro *authentica* habeatur' (Sess. iv. Decr. 2); and directing that 'posthac sacra Scriptura, potissimum vero haec ipsa vetus et vulgata editio quam emendatissime imprimatur.' No immediate action, however, was taken in the matter, and for forty years the editions were still printed and published by private scholars; the Hentenian, for the time being, becoming almost the standard text of the Roman Catholic Church.

Pope Pius IV had indeed begun the task of correcting the Vulgate Bible, but without immediate result, and under his successors the matter still rested, till the accession of Sixtus V (1585–90) [2], a Pope as energetic in his labours on the Holy

[1] The critical notes of Lucas Brugensis himself appear to be found in three forms:—

(1) The 'Notationes,' published in 1580, and incorporated in the Hentenian Bible of 1583.

(2) The 'Variae Lectiones,' printed in Walton's Polyglott, and taken from the Louvain Bible of 1584. These are simply a list of various readings to the Vulgate, with MS. authorities; he frequently adds the letters Q. N., i. e. 'quaere notationes,' where he has treated the subject more fully in (1).

(3) The 'Notae ad Varias Lectiones,' also printed (for the Gospels) in Walton's Polyglott; a *delectus* of them is given in Sabatier at the end of each book of the New Testament, under the title 'Roman. Correctionum auctore Fr. L. Br. delectus.'

[2] *See* E. Nestle, Ein Jubiläum der lateinischen Bibel, Tübingen, p. 13 f., 1892.

Scripture as in other spheres of activity. He appointed a commission on the subject, under the presidency of Cardinal Carafa; and after they had presented the Pope with the result of their work, in the beginning of 1589, he devoted himself personally to the study, reading through the whole Bible more than once, and using his best endeavours to bring it to the highest pitch of accuracy. The result of this appeared in a folio edition of the Bible in three volumes, in 1590 [1], accompanied by a Bull, in which, after relating the extreme care that had been taken in preparing the volume, Sixtus V declared that it was to be considered as the *authentic* edition recommended by the Council of Trent, that it should be taken as the standard of all future reprints, and that all copies should be corrected by it. The edition itself (cited by Wordsworth as 𝔖) was not without faults, and indeed received a good number of corrections by hand after the proofs were printed off; it presents a text more nearly resembling that of Robt. Stephen than that of John Hentenius. In a few months, however, Sixtus was dead; a number of short-lived Popes succeeded him, and in Jan. 1592, Clement VIII ascended the throne. Almost immediately he gave orders for the copies of the Sixtine Vulgate to be called in; it has been hitherto supposed *simply* on account of its inaccuracy, but Professor Nestle (pp. 17 ff.) argues reasonably enough that this ground is insufficient, and suggests that the revocation was really due to the influence of the Jesuits, whom Sixtus had offended by placing one of Bellarmine's books on the *Index Librorum prohibitorum*. Be that as it may, in the same year the Clementine edition of the Vulgate (Wordsworth's ℭ) was published, differing from the Sixtine in many places, and presenting a type of text more nearly allied to Hentenius' Bible. To avoid the appearance of a conflict between the two Popes, the Clementine Bible was boldly published under the name of Sixtus, with a preface by Bellarmine asserting that Sixtus had intended to bring out a new edition in consequence of errors that had occurred in the printing of the first, but had been prevented by death; now, in accordance with his desire, the work was completed by his successor. The opportunity, however, was too good a one for Protestants to miss, and Thomas James in his 'Bellum Papale sive Concordia discors'

[1] There is a copy in the British Museum, Q. e. 5. It is practically in one volume, as the paging is continuous throughout.

(London, 1600), upbraids the two Popes on their high pretensions and the palpable failure of at least one, possibly both of them [1].

From this time forward the Clementine Vulgate (sometimes under the name of Clement, sometimes under that of Sixtus, sometimes under both names) [2] has been the standard edition for the Roman Church; by the Bull of 1592, every edition must be assimilated to this one, no word of the text may be altered, nor even variant readings printed in the margin [3].

Thus the modern attempts at a scientific and critical revision of this version have come from students mainly outside the communion of the Roman Church.

The design of Bentley for a critical Greek Testament is described below (Chap. V); it was obvious that for its prosecution the MSS. of the Vulgate would have to be collated as carefully as those of the Greek text itself; and accordingly the variant readings of a good number were collected by Bentley himself, nos. 3, 59, 60, 61, 62, 63, 64, 65, 66, 68, 69, 70, 71, 72, 74, 75, 76, 77, 82, 83, 85, 155, 160; other MSS. were collated by his friend and colleague John Walker, who worked much at Paris in 1719 and the following years; to him we owe collations of nos. 10, 11, 15, 16, 19, 20, 21, 52, 96, 97, 102, 151, 164, while he obtained collations of the Tours MSS. (nos. 106, 107, 108, 166) from L. Chevalier, through their common friend Sabatier; and of the Oxford MSS. (nos. 86, 87, 89, 90, 148, 161), from David Casley. Walker died, however, in November, 1741, six months before the great Bentley, and the projected edition came to naught [4]. Their collations have not been published, but are contained in the following volumes, in the Library of Trinity College, Cambridge: B. 17. 5 containing collations by Walker, Chevalier, Casley, and Bentley; and B. 17. 15 containing colla-

[1] He gives a long list of the variations between the Sixtine and Clementine Bibles; Vercellone estimated their number at 3,000. It is to be noticed that the *versing* of the Sixtine ed. differs considerably from the Clementine as well as from Stephen.

[2] The regular form of title, 'Biblia Sacra Vulgatae Editionis Sixti V Pont. Max. jussu recognita et Clementis VIII auctoritate edita,' does not appear in any edition known to the writer before that of Rouille, Lyons, 1604. *See* Brit. Mus. Catalogue, col. 50. The earliest edition with this title known to Masch (Le Long, Bibl. Sacra, 1783, ii. p. 251) is dated 1609; and Vercellone (Variae Lect. i. p. lxxii) names others considerably later as the earliest.

[3] *See* Old Lat. Bibl. Texts, i. p. xvi.

[4] *Ibid.*, p. xxv.

tions by Bentley; and they have been made use of by Bishop Wordsworth in his edition of the Vulgate[1].

Two attempts are being made now to restore the text of St. Jerome: that of Dr. Peter Corssen, of Berlin, and the Oxford edition under the hands of the Bishop of Salisbury. Dr. Corssen's published results at present consist only of the Epistle to the Galatians ('Epistula ad Galatas,' Berlin, Weidmann, 1885), but he has been spending several years in the accumulation of material, and other books of the New Testament will probably be published before very long. The Bishop of Salisbury after nearly eleven years' preparation, in conjunction with the Rev. H. J. White and other friends, published the first volume of his edition, containing St. Matthew's Gospel, in 1889; St. Mark following in 1891, and St. Luke in 1892; and it is hoped that the rest of the New Testament may be published in due course. More than thirty MSS., those numbered 5, 6, 18, 21, 28, 29, 37, 41, 51, 56, 64, 67, 68, 72, 77, 78, 82, 85, 86, 87, 91, 97, 98, 106, 115, 128, 129, 130, 132, 147, 148, 153, 154, 159, 175 below, have been carefully collated throughout for this edition, and a large number of others are cited in all the important passages, besides *correctoria*, and the more noticeable of the earlier printed Bibles.

To enumerate all the known MSS. of the Old Latin version was an easy task; to enumerate those of the Vulgate is almost impossible. It is computed that there are at least 8,000 scattered throughout the various Libraries of Europe, and M. Samuel Berger, the greatest living authority on the subject, has examined more than 800 in Paris alone. Nor would an exhaustive enumeration be of much critical value, as a large number of comparatively late MSS. probably contain the same corrupt type of text.

In the following list it is hoped that most of the really important MSS. are included; the writer has had the unwearied and invaluable aid of M. Samuel Berger[2], besides that of many other kind friends, in its compilation. It has been thought best to arrange the MSS. on a double system; *first* according to their contents:—A. Bibles, whole or incomplete; B. New Testament;

[1] *See* Fasc. i. p. xv, and Ellis, Bentleii Critica Sacra, Cambridge, 1862.

[2] M. Berger, with exceptional kindness, allowed me to see the proof-sheets of his 'History of the Vulgate' as they were printed, and to add a large number of MSS. to this list from that source.

C. Gospels; D. Acts and onwards; E. Epistles and Apocalypse; and *secondly* under each of these heads, A–E, according to countries (alphabetically):—Austria, British Isles, France, Germany, Holland, Italy, Spain, Sweden, Switzerland, United States.

For other lists the student is referred to Le Long, Bibliotheca Sacra, ed. 1723, vol. i. p. 235; Vercellone, Variae Lectiones, Romae, 1860, vol. i. p. lxxxiii f., ii. p. xvii f.; Berger, p. 374 f.; and for a fuller treatment of the history and text of the Vulgate, to Bishop Westcott's article 'Vulgate' in Smith's Bible Dictionary; Kaulen, Geschichte d. Vulgata, Mainz, 1865; Fritzsche, 'Lateinische Bibelübersetzungen' in Herzog, Realencyclopädie, second ed., vol. viii; P. Corssen in Die Trierer Adahandschr., Leipzig, 1889; and the important work of S. Berger, Histoire de la Vulgate pendant les premiers siècles du moyen âge, Paris, 1893; to economize space, this will be quoted below simply as 'Berger.'

After the list of MSS. are added indices of the various notations by which respectively Bentley, Tischendorf, Wordsworth, &c., have cited them.

A. Bibles.

a. *Austria: Vienna.*

1. Imperial Library, Lat. 1190. Bible [early ix], probably copied in the Abbey of St. Vedast at Arras, during the time of the Abbot Rado (795–815); Alcuinian poems. *See* M. Denis' Catalogue, i. p. 167, and Berger, p. 108 f.

b. *British Isles: British Museum.*

2. Reg. I. B. xii. Bible [xiii], written in 1254 by William of Hales for Thomas de la Wile, 'Magister Scolarum Sarum.' Cited by Bishop Wordsworth as W, and incorporated by him into his *apparatus criticus* as furnishing a fair specimen of the current mediaeval text.

3. Reg. I. E. vii, viii. Bible [x], in two large folio volumes, the first few pages of each volume, and the last pages of the second, being supplied in a twelfth-century hand; contains stichometry to several of the books, both in the Old and in the New Testaments; order of New Test., Ev., Act., Cath., Paul. (Laod. after Hebr.), Apoc.; Bentley's R.

4. Harl. 4772, 4773. Bible [xiii], in 2 vols., formerly belonging to the Capucin Monastery of Montpellier; the second volume appears to be somewhat later than the first. The MS. both in handwriting and text seems to come from the south of France. *See* Berger, p. 76.

5. Addit. 10,546. The noble Alcuinian Bible [ix], known usually as 'Charlemagne's' Bible, or the Bible of Grandval (near Basle); became the property of the British Museum in 1836. Probably written about the time of Charles the Bald; a good specimen of the Alcuinian revision; *see*

the Museum Catalogue, i pl. 42, 43, and Westwood, Pal. Sacra Pict., p. 25. Wordsworth's K; collated by the Revs. G. M. Youngman and H. J. White.

6. Addit. 24,142. Bible [ix], formerly belonging to the Monastery of St. Hubert in the Ardennes; written in small minuscule hand, strongly resembling that of the Theodulfian Bible (*see* below, no. 18), three columns to a page; contains Old Test., and in New Test. Ev., Paul., Cath., as far as 1 Pet. iv. 3. Facsimile in 'Catalogue of Anc. MSS. in the B. M.' p. 5, pl. 45. Wordsworth's H.

7. Addit. 28,107. The second volume of a Bible in large folio [dated 1097], 240 leaves, from St. Remacle's at Stavelot, near Liège; with peculiar capitula, and a stichometry. *See* Lightfoot, Journal of Philology, vol. iii. no. 6, p. 197 f.; Facsimile in Palaeogr. Soc. ii. pl. 92, 93.

c. *France: Dijon.*

8. Public Library, 9 bis. Bible, 4 vols. [xii], corrected throughout by Stephen Harding, third abbot of Citeaux; *see* above, p. 60.

Paris.

9. B. N. Lat. 1, formerly 35,612. Bible [middle ix], 423 leaves, fol., 50 × 38 cent., minuscule. This splendid MS., with pictures and initials, was presented to Charles the Bald by Vivian, abbot of St. Martin of Tours, and was for a long time in the Cathedral treasury at Metz; it was given by the Chapter of Metz to Colbert in 1675. *See* Delisle, Cab. des MSS., iii. p. 234 ff.; Berger, p. 215 f.; Le Long, i. p. 237. Alcuinian text.

10. B. N. Lat. 2, formerly 3561 (not, as Le Long and Walker say, 3562). The Bible of St. Denis or of Charles the Bald [ix], 444 leaves, fol., minuscule, with fine initial letters, contains verses in praise of Charles the Bald; in the N. T. the Apoc. is wanting. *See* O. L. Bibl. T., i. p. 55; Delisle, Cab. des MSS., i. p. 200, and pl. xxviii. 1, 4, 5; Les Bibles de Théodulfe, p. 7; De Bastard, c–civ; Jorand, Grammatogr. du ixe siècle, Paris, 1837; Silvestre, Pal. Univ., clxxi; Berger, p. 287 f. Walker's ε; used previously by R. Stephen in his Bible of 1528.

11. Lat. 3, formerly Reg. 3562. Bible [middle ix], fol., thick minuscule; parts of the Apoc. have been supplied by a later hand. Belonged first to the Monastery of Glanfeuil, then to the Abbey of St. Maur des Fossés near Charenton, the library of which was acquired by the St. Germain Abbey in 1716; a good specimen of the Alcuinian revision. *See* Delisle, Cab. des MSS., pl. xxv. 1, 2, xxix. 4; Berger, p. 213 f. Walker's η.

12. Lat. 4, formerly Colbert 157, 158, then Reg. $3571^{12,13}$; 2 vols., fol., 53·5 × 33 cent. [ix or x]; 4^2 contains 193 leaves, with Psalms, Ev., Act., Cath., Apoc., Paul. This MS. was given to Colbert by the Canons of Puy, and called 'Codex Aniciensis.' The first hand presents an Alcuinian text, but a second hand has added a large number of remarkable variant readings, especially in the Acts and Cath. Epp. It appears to belong to Languedoc. *See* Berger, p. 73.

13. Lat. 6. Bible in 4 vols. [x], fol., 48 × 33·5 cent., from the Abbey of Rosas in Catalonia. The fourth volume (6^4) contains the New Test.,

(113 f.) in following order, Ev., Act., Cath., Paul. (Laod. between Col. and Thess.), Apoc. Valuable text, the first hand contains a large number of interesting and Old Latin readings; and in the Acts, the second hand has added a number of Old Latin variants in the margin. From the Noailles Library; *see* Berger, p. 24.

14. Lat. 7, formerly Reg. 3567, one of Card. Mazarin's MSS. Bible, fol., 51 × 34·5 cent. [xi probably], with fine illuminations; order of books in New Test., Ev., Act., Cath., Paul., Apoc. Interesting text in the Acts, and strongly resembling the second hand of Lat. 4^2, this MS. was also probably written in Languedoc. Facsimile in De Bastard. *See* Berger, p. 73.

15. Lat. 45 and 93, formerly Reg. 3563–4. Bible [late ix], fol., thick minuscule; no. 93 has 261 leaves, the New Test. (Ev., Act., Cath., Paul., Apoc.), commencing on fol. 156. This MS. belonged originally to the Monastery of St. Riquier on the Somme; interesting text, especially in the Acts and Cath. Epp. Walker's θ. Berger, p. 96 f.

16. Lat. 47, formerly Reg. 3564^a (Faurianus 32, i. e. in the library of Antoine Faure). Part of a Bible [xi], fol., 176 leaves minuscule; closely resembling no. 11 (Lat. 3) in text and perhaps even more valuable; much *mut.* in N. T. Walker's κ.

17. Lat. 140. Bible [xv], written in Germany, and bearing the name and arms of a Tyrolese, Joachim Schiller ab Herdern. Order of books in the New Test., Ev., Paul., Apoc., Cath., Act. Interesting text, especially in the Acts, where it is more or less mixed; examined by S. Berger.

18. Lat. 9380. Bible [ix], in beautiful and minute minuscule. The famous Theodulfian Bible, formerly belonging to the Cathedral of Orleans, and bearing such a strong resemblance to the other Theodulfian Codex at Puy (*see* below, no. 24), that M. Delisle declares many pages look almost like proofs struck from the same type. It bears a strong resemblance also to the St. Hubert Bible (Brit. Mus. Add. 24,142, *see* no. 6), though it is written in a smaller hand; the Hubert text has been throughout assimilated to this. *See* Berger, p. 149 f.; Delisle, Cab. des MSS., pl. xxi. 3, and Les Bibles de Théodulfe, Paris, 1879. Wordsworth's Θ; collated by Revs. C. Wordsworth and H. J. White.

19. Lat. 11,504–5, formerly St. Germain 3, 4, afterwards 16, 17. Bible [ix], fol., 199 and 215 leaves, minuscule; dated 822. New Test. contains Ev., Act., Rom., 1 and 2 Cor., Gal., Eph., Phil., Col., 1 and 2 Thess., 1 Tim.; then a lacuna; Apoc., Cath. *See* O. L. B. T., i. p. 57; Del., Cab. des MSS., pl. xxiv; Berger, p. 93. Walker's o_2; he collated Act., Cath., Paul., Apoc.

20. Lat. 11,532, 11,533, formerly at Corbey, afterwards St. Germain 1, 2, then 14, 15; 2 vols. Bible [ix], fol., minuscules; probably written after 855 A. D., the year of the accession of Lothair II, who is mentioned in an inscription at the end of the book. Order of books in the New Test., Ev., Act., Cath., Paul., Apoc. Walker's ν; he collated Act., Cath., Paul., Apoc., not Ev.; *see* Wordsworth, O. L. B. T., i. p. 57; Berger, p. 104 f.

21. Lat. 11,553, described above (p. 47) as g_1. Old Latin text in

St. Matthew; in the rest of the New Test. a Vulgate text, but with strong admixture of Old Latin elements. Order of books in New Test., Ev., Act., Cath., Apoc., Paul. Wordsworth's G, Walker's μ; *see* also Berger, p. 65 ff.

22. Lat. 11,937, formerly St. Germain 9, then 645. First volume of Bible [ix], 4to, 179 leaves, containing the Old Test., but incomplete. This MS. was the 'Germ. parv.' of R. Stephen, who cites it also in Matt. v–viii; the volume, however, containing the New Testament has since disappeared. *See* Delisle, Les Bibles de Théodulfe, p. 28.

23. Lat. 16,719–16,722. Bible [xiii], in 4 vols., corrected throughout by the Dominicans under the auspices of Hugo de St. Caro, *see* above, p. 60, often called the Bible of St. Hugo de St. Caro.

Puy.

24. Cathedral Library. The famous Bible [viii or ix], written under the direction of Theodulf, Bishop of Orleans, and closely resembling the Paris Codex B. N. Lat. 9380, though not of equal critical value (*see* above, p. 69, no. 18). Described by Delisle, Les Bibles de Théodulfe; *see* also Le Long, i. p. 235; Berger, p. 171 f.

d. *Germany: Bamberg.*

25. Royal Library, A. I. 5. Bible [ix], large folio, 423 leaves. One of the finest examples of the Alcuinian recension, and a typical specimen of the second period of Caroline writing and ornamentation. Written in the monastery of St. Martin at Tours. Apocalypse wanting. *See* Leitschuh, Führer durch d. kgl. Bibl. zu Bamberg, 1889, p. 82. Wordsworth's B_2 in Acts &c.; collated by the Rev. H. J. White.

Metz.

26. Public Library, no. 7. Second half of Bible [early ix], minuscule. Mixed text, with Languedocian and Irish characteristics. *See* Berger, p. 100.

Würzburg[1].

27. Mp. th. fol. max. 1. Bible [xi], 403 leaves, large folio, formerly belonging to the Cathedral Library. Contains the whole Bible except Pauline Epp. and Book of Baruch, which, together with the Epistle to the Laodiceans, have been abstracted.

e. *Italy: La Cava.*

28. Corpo di Cava (near Salerno); Benedictine Abbey. The well-known 'Codex Cavensis' of the whole Bible [prob. ix], written in Spain, probably in Castile or Leon, in small, round Visigothic minuscules, by a scribe Danila; a copy was made by the Abbate de Rossi early in this century, and is now in the Vatican (Lat. 8484). A good representative of the Spanish type of text, and closely resembling the Codex Toletanus (no. 41). *See* Dom Bernardo Gaetani de Aragona, Cod. diplomat.

[1] For the Würzburg MSS., *see* G. Schepps, Die ältesten Evangelienhandschriften der Universitätsbibliothek, Würzburg, 1887, from which these descriptions are mainly taken.

Cavensis, vol. i, Naples, 1873; Silvestre, Pal. univ., iii; L. Ziegler, Sitzungsber. der k. bayr. Akad. der Wissenschaften phil. phil. Klasse, Munich, 1876, p. 655 f.; Pertz, Archiv, v. p. 542. Collated by Bishop Wordsworth. Tischendorf's *cav.*, Wordsworth's C.

Florence.

29. Laurentian Library. The far-famed Codex Amiatinus of the whole Bible [end of vii or beginning of viii], 1029 leaves, large folio. Till lately it was supposed to have been written by a sixth century scribe in Italy; but now, principally through the acuteness of G. B. de Rossi and the late Professor Hort, it has been proved that it was written by the order of the abbot Ceolfrid either at Wearmouth or Jarrow, and sent by him as a present to the Pope at Rome in 715 A.D. Afterwards placed in the Monastic Library at Monte Amiata, whence it was again sent to Rome for collation at the time of the Sixtine revision (*see* p. 64). The New Testament was badly edited by F. F. Fleck, 1840; carefully, though not without a few slips, by Tischendorf in 1850 (second ed. with some emendations 1854); and by Tregelles in his Greek New Test. 1857. Facsimiles in Zangemeister and Wattenb., Exempla codd. lat., pl. 35, and Palaeogr. Soc. ii. pl. 65, 66. Of the recent literature on this MS., and especially on the first quaternion, with its lists of the books of the Bible closely resembling those of Cassiodorus, *see* G. B. de Rossi, La Biblia offerta da Ceolfr. Abb. al Sepolcro di S. Pietro, Rome, 1887; H. J. White, The Codex Amiatinus and its Birthplace, in 'Studia Biblica,' ii. p. 273 (Oxford, 1890); P. Corssen, Die Bibeln des Cassiodorus und der Cod. Amiatinus, in the 'Jahrb. f. prot. Theologie,' 1883 and 1891; Th. Zahn, Gesch. d. ntl. Kanons, ii. p. 267 f. Tischendorf's *am.*, Wordsworth's A.

Milan.

30. Ambrosian Library, E. 26 *inf.* Part of a Bible [ix or x], commencing with Chron. and finishing with Pauline Epp. Probably written at Bobbio. Mixed text, especially interesting in St. Paul's Epp.; does not contain the last three verses of Romans; *see* Berger, p. 138.

31. E. 53 *inf.* Bible [ix or x], much mutilated; 169 leaves, containing the sacred books in the following order: Octateuch, Jerem., Acts, Cath., Apoc., Kings, Solomon, Job, Tobit, Judith, Esther, Esdras, Maccabees, Ezek., Dan., minor prophets, Isa., Pauline Epp.; i. e. the order in which they are read in ecclesiastical lessons during the year. Formerly at Biasca, a village in the valley of Tessin on the St. Gothard. Vulgate text, but mixed with Old Latin elements; interesting as containing not only the Ep. to the Laodiceans but also the apocryphal correspondence between St. Paul and the Corinthians (cp. the Laon MS., no. 161). *See* Carrière and Berger, La correspondance apocr. de St. Paul et des Corinthiens, Paris, 1891.

Monte Cassino.

32. Monastery of Monte Cassino: codd. 552 and 557 are mentioned by Corssen (Ep. ad Galatas, Berlin, 1885, p. 15) as worthy of note: 552 Bible [xi], 557 Bible [xii–xiii], but both containing an ancient

text. Order of books in both is Ev., Act., Cath., Apoc., Paul. (Ev. lacking in 552). *See* also 'Bibliotheca Casinensis,' ii. pp. 313–352.

Monza.

33. Collegiate Archives, G. 1. Bible [ix], written at Tours by the scribe Amalricus, who was Archbishop of Tours: specimen of the Alcuinian recension and resembling in text and in outward appearance and writing the Parisian Bible, B. N. Lat. 3 (no. 11 above). *See* Corssen, Epist. ad Galatas, p. 10; Berger, p. 221.

Rome.

34. Vat. Lat. 5729, Codex Farfensis. Bible [xi], in one enormous volume; in good preservation, written in three columns. *See* Vercellone, Var. Lect., ii. p. xvii, and Le Long, i. p. 235; the latter wrongly cites it as 6729.

35. Bible of S. Maria ad Martyres (La Rotonda, Pantheon). Bible [x], large folio. The books in the New Test. are in the following order: Ev., Act., Cath., Apoc., Paul.; used by Vercellone.

36. The splendid Bible [ix] preserved in the Library of 'S. Paul without the walls;' belonged to Charles the Bald, and preserves an Alcuinian text, strongly resembling V. *See* Vercellone, Var. Lect., i. p. lxxxv; Le Long, i. p. 237; Berger, p. 292.

37. Vallicellian Library, B. vi. Bible [ix], 347 leaves, large 4to, Caroline minuscules. The Church of Sta. Maria in Vallicella belongs to the Oratorian Fathers, and Bianchini himself was an Oratorian; he refers to this MS. in the 'Evang. Quadr.,' ii. pl. viii. p. 600, and it is probably the best extant specimen of the Alcuinian revision. Bp. Wordsworth collated it, and cites it as V; *see* also Berger, p. 197.

f. *Spain: Leon.*

38. Cathedral Library, 15. Fragments of Bible [vii], palimpsest; 40 leaves, semi-uncial, under some writing in a Visigothic hand of the tenth century. Contains in New Test. portions of Acts, 2 Cor., Col., and 1 John. Vulgate base but with Old Latin elements, especially in 1 John. Discovered by Dr. Rudolf Beer, who is proposing to publish the fragments. *See* Berger, p. 8.

39. Cathedral Library, 6. Second volume of a Bible [x], formerly belonging to the Convent of SS. Cosmas and Damian in the Valle de Torio, and thought to date from the time of Ordogno II (913–923); written by two scribes, Vimara, a presbyter, and John, a deacon; minuscule, like Cavensis, only larger. Order of books in the New Test. is Ev. (followed by a commentary), Act., Paul. (including Laod.), Cath., Apoc.; examined by Bp. Wordsworth in 1882. *See* Berger, p. 17.

40. Church of San Isidro; Codex Gothicus Legionensis. Bible [x], folio, dated 998 of the Spanish era, i.e. 960 A.D.; minuscule of the same type as Cavensis, only larger. Order of books in the New Test.: Ev., Paul., Cath., Act., Apoc. Written 'a notario Sanctioni presbitero,' and was collated on behalf of the Sixtine revision of the Vulgate for Card.

Carafa, and by him called the Codex Gothicus; this collation is preserved in the Vatican, Lat. 4859. Examined by Bp. Wordsworth in 1882. *See* Berger, p. 18.

Madrid.

41. National Library. Bible [x? Berger would date it viii], in three columns, the famous 'Codex Toletanus.' According to a notice in the MS. itself, its 'auctor possessorque' (auctor = legal owner?), Servandus of Seville, gave it to his friend John, Bishop of Cordova, who in turn offered it in the year 988 to the see of Seville; thence it passed in time to Tolédo and ultimately to Madrid. It is written in Visigothic characters, and presents the Spanish type of text, strongly resembling the Cod. Cavensis (no. 28). Collated for the Sixtine revision by Chr. Palomares, whose work, written in a Hentenian Bible of 1569, is now preserved in the Vatican (Lat. 9508); it was not, however, used in that revision, as it reached Cardinal Carafa too late. Bianchini published the collation in his 'Vindiciae Can. Script.,' Rome, 1740, pp. xlvii–ccxvi (=Migne, Patr. Lat., tom. xxix). Bp. Wordsworth collated the New Testament in 1882. *See* Berger, p. 12; Merino, Escuela Paleogr., pl. v. pp. 53–9, Madrid, 1780; Muñoz y Rivero, Paleografia Visigoda, pl. viii, ix, Madrid, 1881; Ewald and Loewe, Exempla Scr. Visig., pp. 7, 8, pl. ix. Tischendorf's *tol.*; Wordsworth's T.

42. University Library, no. 31: Codex Complutensis, i.e. of Alcalá (= Complutum). Bible [ix or x]; in the New Test. Laod. follow Hebrews. Plainly a Spanish text, but with peculiar readings in the Epistles, and especially in the Acts. Purchased at Toledo by Cardinal Ximenes; described by Berger, p. 22, and Westcott, Vulgate, p. 1705.

43. University Library, no. 32. Second volume of a Bible [ix–x], folio, containing from the Proverbs to the Apocalypse, in a Visigothic hand; the ornaments somewhat resembling those of the Codex Cavensis. It formerly belonged to Cardinal Ximenes: *see* Berger, p. 15.

44. Royal Academy of History (Calle del Leon 21), No. F. 186. The second volume of a Bible [x], small folio, written by the monk Quisius. It formerly belonged to the Abbey of St. Emilianus (S. Millan de la Cogolla), between Burgos and Logroño. Order of books in New Test.: Ev., Act., Paul., Cath., Apoc. (fragmentary). The handwriting resembles Cavensis, though it is slightly larger, and the text also belongs to the Spanish group. Examined by Bp. Wordsworth in 1882; *see* Berger, p. 16.

g. Switzerland: Berne.

45. University Library, A. 9. Bible [xi], originally belonging to Vienne in Dauphiné. Contains an interesting text in Cath. Epp. and Acts, where it seems to be much under Theodulfian influence or that of the texts belonging to the South of France; the corrections too are interesting. *See* Berger, p. 62 f.

Einsiedeln.

46. Einsiedeln Library, no. 1. Bible [early x], possibly copied at

Einsiedeln; corrected in accordance with a text like that of St. Gall 75. *See* Berger, p. 132.

47. Einsiedeln Library, nos. 5–7. Bible [x], also corrected and bearing strong resemblance to the one above; same order of books as in 31.

St. Gall.

48. Stiftsbibliothek, no. 11 [viii]. A collection of extracts composed for the use of the monks; written by the monk Winithar. Vulgate text but with a mixture of Old Latin readings. *See* Berger, p. 121 f.

49. Stiftsbibliothek, no. 75. [ix], large folio; contains complete Bible; corrected by the abbot Hartmotus. *See* Berger, p. 129.

Present position unknown.

50. Bible [xiii, but copied from an early exemplar], edited by Matthaei (N. T.) in the Act., Epp., Apoc.; *see* his preface to Cath. Epp., p. xxx f.; belonged to Paul Demidov. Formerly at Lyons; Tischendorf's *demid.*

B. New Testaments.

a. *British Isles: Dublin.*

51. Trin. Coll. The Book of Armagh. New Test. [ix], written by Ferdomnach in a beautiful and small Irish hand. Order of books: Evv., Paul. (Laod. after Col.), Cath., Apoc., Acts. The New Test. was transcribed for Bp. Wordsworth by the Rev. G. M. Youngman; the late Dr. Reeves, Bp. of Down, intended to edit it, and his work is now (1893) being prepared for the press by Professors Gwynn and Bernard, of Dublin. *See* also 'National MSS. of Ireland,' i. pp. xiv–xvii, plates xxv–xxix; Berger, p. 31 f. Wordsworth's D.

b. *France: Paris.*

52. B. N. Lat. 250, formerly Reg. 3572; from Saint-Denis. New Test. [ix], folio, minuscule: Evv., Act., Cath., Paul. (Laod. after Col., which in turn is after Thess.), Apoc. Walker's λ; he collated Cath. and Apoc. Alcuinian text, *see* Berger, p. 243.

53. Lat. 254. New Test. [xii]; has been described above as *c* (p. 45). Text is Old Latin in the Gospels, Vulgate in the rest of the New Test. *See* Berger, p. 74.

54. Lat. 321, formerly belonging to Baluze. New Testament [early xiii], written in the South of France, probably between Carcassonne and Narbonne. Very interesting text; in the Epistles and Acts there are a large number of Old Latin readings; the text of the Acts is especially mixed; orthography incorrect. Berger, p. 77.

55. Lat. 342, formerly Colbert 6155. New Testament [early xiii], written in the South of France; contains large mixture of Old Latin readings throughout; examined by Berger.

c. *Germany: Fulda.*

56. Abbey of Fulda in Prussia. The well-known Codex Fuldensis [vi] of the New Testament, written for Bishop Victor of Capua, and corrected by him A.D. 541–546. The Gospels are arranged in one narrative, based on the order of Tatian's Diatessaron, but with a Vulgate text; the Ep. to the Laodiceans follows that to the Colossians. Described by Schannat in 1723 (Vindemiae Literariae Collectio, pp. 218–21), collated by Lachmann and Ph. Buttmann in 1839, and edited in full by E. Ranke (Marburg, 1868); *see* also Th. Zahn, Tatian's Diatessaron, Erlangen, 1881, pp. 298–313; S. Hemphill, The Diatessaron of Tatian, Dublin, 1888, pp. x, xi, xxiv–v. Facsimiles in Ranke, and Zangem. and Wattenb., Exempla, p. 34. Tischendorf's *fuld.*; Wordsworth's F.

d. *Sweden: Stockholm.*

57. Royal Library: Codex Gigas Holmiensis [xiii]; Old Latin text in Acts and Apoc., Vulgate in the New Testament; described above, p. 51.
This is a Bible, not N.T.

C. GOSPELS.

a. *Austria: Vienna.*

58. *theo* or *theotisc* refers to the Latin version of the 'Fragmenta Theotisca versionis ant. Evang. S. Matthaei . . . ediderunt Steph. Endlicher et Hoffmann Fallerslebensis; Vindobonae, 1834' (2nd edit. cura T. F. Massmann; Viennae, 1841); 15 leaves [viii], containing St. Matt. viii. 33 to the end of the Gospel, but much mutilated; the *recto* side of each leaf contains the Theotisc or Old German version, mixed with Gothic, the *verso* contains the Latin; quoted by Tischendorf in Matt. xx. 28, where it has the common Latin addition. *See* also J. A. Schmeller, Ammonii Alexandrini Harmonia Evangeliorum, Vienna, 1841.

b. *British Isles: British Museum.*

59. Reg. I. A. xviii. Gospels [x], 199 leaves, written in Caroline minuscules, originally belonging to King Athelstan, who gave it to St. Augustine's monastery at Canterbury; *mut.* after John xviii. 21; *see* British Museum Catalogue, p. 37. Bentley's O.

60. Reg. I. B. vii. Gospels [viii], 155 leaves, written in England. The Rev. G. M. Youngman, who has examined this MS. carefully, says the text is very interesting, though rather mixed; has been corrected throughout. Bentley's H in Trin. Coll. Cam. B. 17. 14. *See* Brit. Mus. Catalogue, p. 19, pl. 16, and Morin, Liber Comicus, p. 426, 1893.

61. Reg. I. D. ix. Gospels [x], a handsome 4to volume of 150 leaves, the capitals throughout written in gold, and the initial page to each Gospel finely illuminated; contains prefatory matter and Capitulare, but is *mut.* after John xxi. 18. Formerly belonged to King Canute, as an Anglo-Saxon inscription on fol. 43 *b* testifies. *See* Westwood, A.-S. and Ir. MSS., p. 141; Pal. Sacra Pict., pl. 23. Bentley's A.

62. Reg. I. E. vi. Gospels [end of viii], imperfect; 77 leaves, half uncial

characters, written in England; formerly belonging to St. Augustine's, Canterbury, and in all probability the second volume of the famous 'Biblia Gregoriana' mentioned by Elmham. *See* Westwood, A.-S. and Ir. MSS., pl. 14, 15; British Museum Catalogue, p. 20, pl. 17, 18; Palaeogr. Soc., i. pl. 7; Berger, p. 35. Bentley's P.

63. Cotton Tib. A. ii [early x], written in Germany; Gospels, 216 leaves, written in Caroline minuscules, once the property of King Athelstan; *see* British Museum Catalogue, p. 35. Bentley's E.

64. Cotton Nero D. iv. The magnificent Lindisfarne Gospels [vii or viii], rivalling even the Book of Kells (no. 78) in the beauty of their writing and the richness of their ornamentation. Written by Eadfrith, Bishop of Lindisfarne, 698–721 A.D., and other scribes; preserve a very pure text, agreeing closely with the Codex Amiatinus (no. 29), sometimes against all other known Vulgate MSS. The Latin is accompanied by an interlinear version in the Northumbrian dialect. Edited, rather carelessly, for the Surtees Soc., by Stevenson and Waring, 1854–65; and W. W. Skeat, The Gospel of St. Matthew; Anglo-Saxon and Northumbrian Versions, Cambr., 1887; *see* also Westwood, Anglo-Saxon and Ir. MSS., pp. 33–9, pl. 12, 13; Palaeogr. Sacra Pict., p. 45; Palaeogr. Soc., i. pl. 3–6, 22; Brit. Mus. Catalogue, p. 15, pl. 8–11; Berger, p. 39; Morin, Liber Comicus, p. 426. The Surtees text revised by the Rev. G. M. Youngman. Wordsworth's and Bentley's Y.

65. Cotton Otho B. ix. Gospels [x?], nearly destroyed by fire; there are twelve small fragments containing portions of prefatory matter, and of SS. Matt., Mark, and John, in small Caroline minuscules, but with a large capital at the beginning of St. Mark and interlaced ornamentation. Bentley's D.

66. Cotton Otho C. v. St. Matt. and St. Mark [probably viii], written in Saxon hand, (and *possibly* part of the same MS. as Bentley's C (*see* no. 76).) This Manuscript is now simply a collection of the shrivelled fragments of sixty-four leaves which survived the fire of 1731; the last leaf contains Mark xvi. 6–20. *See* Brit. Mus. Catalogue, p. 20; the editors, however, doubt whether it is part of the same MS. as no. 76. Bentley cites these fragments as ϕ.

67. Egerton 609. Gospels [viii or ix], formerly belonging to the Monastery of Marmoutier (Majus Monasterium) near Tours, where it was numbered 102. It is written, however, in an Irish hand and presents an Irish type of text; it is much *mut.*, especially in St. Mark. *See* Brit. Mus. Catalogue, p. 30. Cited by Calmet, Tischendorf, &c., as *mm*; collated again by the Rev. G. M. Youngman, and cited by Wordsworth as E.

68. Harl. 1775. Gospels [vi or vii], in small but very beautiful uncial hand, and with an extremely valuable text. Formerly numbered 4582 in the Bibliothèque Royale at Paris; stolen from thence by Jean Aymon, it passed into the possession of Harley, Earl of Oxford, and then to the British Museum. Collated in part by Griesbach, Symbolae Criticae, i. pp. 305–26, Halae, 1785; by Bentley or Walker; later by the Rev. G. Williams; and for Bp. Wordsworth's Vulgate by the

Rev. H. J. White; for facsimiles *see* Brit. Mus. Catalogue, p. 14, pl. 3; Palaeogr. Soc., i. p. 16. Wordsworth's and Bentley's Z; Tischendorf's *harl.*

69. Harl. 1802. Gospels [xii], 156 leaves, a small Irish MS., with copious marginal notes, written by the scribe Maelbrigte; stolen from Paris by Jean Aymon. Bentley's W.

70. Harl. 2788. Gospels [end of viii or beginning of ix], 208 leaves folio, an extremely fine MS., written throughout in golden uncials, except the prefatory matter, which is in minuscules; the vellum and also the colours used in the illumination are all wonderfully bright and fresh. *See* Brit. Mus. Catalogue, p. 22, pl. 39–41; Corssen, Ada-H. S. p. 86; Bentley's M in Trin. Coll. Cam. B. 17. 5.

71. Harl. 2826. Gospels [ix or x], 150 leaves, Caroline minuscules; formerly belonging to the monastery of Eller, near Cochem, on the Mosel; *see* Brit. Mus. Catalogue, p. 32. Bentley's H in Trin. Coll. Cam. B. 17. 5.

72. Addit. 5463. Gospels [viii or ix], from the nunnery of St. Peter at Beneventum, formerly belonging to Dr. Richard Mead; written in a fine revived uncial hand. The MS. has usually been supposed to have been written at Beneventum, but Berger doubts this (p. 92). Cited by Bentley as F, by Wordsworth as 𝔉. Facsimiles in Brit. Mus. Catalogue, p. 18, pl. 7, and Palaeogr. Soc., i. p. 236.

Cambridge.

73. University Library, I. i. 6. 32. The Book of Deer; Gospels [viii or ix], small but rather wide 8vo, 86 leaves, but *mut.*; contains Matt. i. 1—vii. 23; Mark i. 1—v. 36; Luke i. 1—iv. 12; John, complete. Belonged originally to the Columbian monastery of Deer in Aberdeenshire: in 1697 belonged to Bp. J. Moore (of Norwich and Ely), and with the rest of his library was bought for the University of Cambridge in 1715. Contains many old and peculiar readings (Westcott, p. 1694). Described by Westwood, A.-S. and Ir. MSS., pp. 89–90; edited in full with facsimiles by J. Stuart (for the Spalding Club), Edinburgh, 1869.

74. Univ. Libr. Kk. 1. 24. St. Luke and St. John [prob. viii], written in Irish hand; collated by Bentley, who cites it as X, and noticed by Westcott, Vulgate, pp. 1695 and 1712; it contains a valuable text.

75. Trin. Coll. B. 10. 4. Gospels [ix], large 4to, written apparently by the same scribe as Brit. Mus. Reg. I. D. ix (no. 61). This is Bentley's T; according to Westcott (p. 1713) it is good Vulgate, with some old readings.

76. Corpus Chr. Coll. CXCVII. Fragments of St. Luke [viii], possibly from the same MS. as Bentley's ϕ; *see* above, no. 66, and also Westwood, A.-S. and Ir. MSS., p. 49; this MS. has been described, and the fragments of St. John published, by J. Goodwin, Publications of the Cambr. Antiq. Soc., no. xiii, 1847. (Bentley's C.)

77. Corpus Chr. Coll. CCLXXXVI Evan. Gospels [vii], formerly belong-

ing to the monastery of St. Augustine at Canterbury, and alleged to have been sent by Pope Gregory to Augustine. They contain an interesting text, the first hand being corrected throughout in accordance with a MS. of the type of the Codex Amiatinus. *See* Westwood, Anglo-Sax. and Ir. MSS., pp. 49, 50; Pal. Sacra Pict., pl. 11. 1–4; Palaeogr. Soc., i. pl. 33, 34, 44. Collated by the Rev. A. W. Streane. Bentley's B; Wordsworth's X.

Dublin.

78. Trinity College A. 1. 6. Gospels [vii or viii], commonly known as the Book of Kells; given to Trinity College, Dublin, by Archbishop Ussher. This MS. is principally known as being perhaps the most perfect specimen of Irish writing and illumination in existence, but it also contains a valuable text, though marked with the characteristics of the Irish family. A collation is given by Dr. Abbott in his edition of the Codex Usserianus, or r_1 (*see* p. 50). Facsimiles in Palaeogr. Soc., i. pl. 55–8, 88, 89; Westwood, A.-S. and Ir. MSS. pp. 25–33, pl. 8–11, and Pal. Sacra Pict., pl. 16, 17; also National MSS. of Ireland, i. pp. x–xii, pl. vii–xvii. Wordsworth's Q.

79. Trinity Coll. A. 4. 5. The Book of Durrow. Gospels [end of vi], 8vo, semi-uncial, the text is allied to Amiatinus; cited by Bp. Wordsworth as *durmach.* According to an inscription on what was the last page, the MS. was written by St. Columba himself in the space of twelve days; the inscription however, like the rest of the book, is probably copied from an earlier exemplar. A collation of this MS. is given by Professor Abbott in his edition of r_1 (*see* p. 50); *see* also his article 'On the colophon of the Book of Durrow' (Dublin Hermathena, 1891, p. 199).

80. Trin. Coll. The Book of Moling. Gospels [viii or ix], small 4to, much the same size, writing, and ornamentation as the Gospels of Macdurnan (*see* 84); but so defaced by damp as to be quite illegible in parts.

81. Royal Irish Academy. The Stowe St. John, formerly in the Ashburnham Library; originally belonging to a Church in Munster. Irish handwriting and text. *See* Berger, p. 42.

Durham.

82. Cathedral Library, A. ii. 16. Gospels [vii or viii], 134 leaves; said to have been written by Bede, and may very possibly have come from the monastery at Jarrow; *mut.* in parts; text allied to the Cod. Amiatinus. Cited by Bentley as K, by Wordsworth (who makes use of it only in St. John) as Δ.

83. Cathedral Library, A. ii. 17. St. John, St. Mark, and St. Luke [prob. viii], with another fragment of St. Luke xxi. 33—xxiii. 34. *See* Westwood, A.-S. and Ir. MSS., p. 47; Bentley's ξ, but to be distinguished from his ξ in Trin. Coll. Camb. B. 17. 5, which is St. Chad's book at Lichfield (*see* no. 85).

Lambeth.

84. Lambeth Palace Library. The Gospels of Macdurnan [x], 216 leaves, Irish writing and ornamentation; an inscription (fol. 3 *b*), in square Saxon capitals, states that it was written by a scribe named Maeielbrith Mac-Durnain. *See* Westwood, Pal. Sacra Pict., pl. 13, 14, 15.

Lichfield.

85. Chapter Library. Gospels [vii or viii], traditionally ascribed to St. Chad, who was Bishop of Lichfield; formerly the MS. was at Llandaff on the altar of St. Telian; 110 leaves, Irish, half-uncial; the writing and ornamentation are very beautiful and resemble the Books of Kells, Lindisfarne, &c.; the text belongs to the Irish group of MSS. Contains Matt., Mark, and Luke i. 1—iii. 9. A careful collation, with full introduction, and three facsimiles, was published by Dr. Scrivener (Cambridge, 1887); *see* also Palaeogr. Soc., i. pl. 20, 21, 35; Westwood, Anglo-Sax. and Ir. MSS., pp. 56–58, pl. 23, and Pal. Sacra Pict., pl. 12. Bentley's ξ in Trin. Coll. B. 17. 5; Wordsworth's L.

Oxford.

86. Bodl. 857, and Auct. D. 2. 14. Gospels [vii], formerly belonging to St. Augustine's Library at Canterbury, and generally known as 'St. Augustine's Gospels;' British text. *See* Westwood, Palaeogr. Sacra Pict., pl. 11, no. 5. Casley's ψ; Tischendorf's *bodl.*; Wordsworth's O, collated for him by F. Madan and Rev. G. M. Youngman.

87. Bodl. Auct. D. 2. 19. Gospels [ix], commonly called the 'Rushworth Gospels' or 'Gospels of Mac Regol,' written by an Irish scribe, who died A.D. 820; has an interlinear Anglo-Saxon version; the Latin text belongs to the Irish type. *Mut.* Luke iv. 29—viii. 38; x. 19–39; xv. 16—xvi. 26. Collation given in the edition of the Surtees Soc., The Lindisfarne and Rushworth Gospels, by Stevenson and Waring, 1854–65; and by W. W. Skeat, The Gospel of St. Matthew; Anglo-Saxon and Northumbrian Versions, Cambridge, 1887. Casley's χ; Wordsworth's R.

88. Bodl. Laud. Lat. 102. Gospels [x], 210 leaves, fol., Saxon minuscule; formerly at Würzburg, where it was bought at the instance of Archbishop Laud. Mixed text, but with traces of Irish influence. *See* Berger, p. 54.

89. Corp. Christi Coll. 122. Gospels [prob. xi], an Irish MS.; *mut.* John i. 1–33; vii. 33—xviii. 20. Bentley's C in Trin. Coll. Cam. B. 17. 5; collated for him by Casley; British type of text.

90. St. John's Coll. 194. Gospels [xi], in very small hand: collated by Casley and cited by Bentley as γ.

Stonyhurst.

91. Stonyhurst, Jesuit College. The Gospel of St. John [~~vii~~]; originally the property, according to a legend which goes back to the thirteenth century, of St. Cuthbert, in whose coffin it was found; it was preserved in Durham Cathedral till the time of Henry VIII. A minute but exquisitely written uncial MS., with a text closely resembling A; facsimiles in Palaeogr. Soc., i. pl. 17; Westwood, Palaeogr. Sacra Pict., pl. 11, no. 6. Wordsworth's S.

c. *France: Angers.*

92. Angers Public Library, no. 20. Gospels [ix–x], written in a French hand, but showing signs of Irish influence both in its ornamentation and text. *See* Berger, p. 48.

Autun.

93. Autun, Grand Séminaire, no. 3. Gospels [dated 755], written for Vosavius by Gundohinus; uncial hand. Vulgate text but with a good many variations. *See* Berger, p. 90.

Avignon.

94. Gospels in the monastery of St. Andrew near Avignon: extracts in Martianay (Vulgata ant. Latina), 1695, and Calmet (Commentaire litt., vii), 1726: cited by Tischendorf as *and.* The MS. has disappeared. *See* Berger, p. 80.

Paris.

95. B. N. Lat. 256. Gospels [vii], in uncial hand; Vulgate text but with a good many Old Latin readings. *See* Berger, p. 91.

96. Lat. 262, formerly Reg. 3706, from Puy. Gospels [ix], with prefatory matter, fol., 247 leaves, thick minuscule; *mut.* in parts. Walker's o_1.

97. Lat. 281 and 298. Gospels [viii], known as 'Codex Bigotianus,' in fine uncial hand, formerly at Fécamp; probably written in France, but both the text and the calligraphy show traces of Irish influence. It is *mut.* in parts; collated by Walker, who cites it as π, and again by Wordsworth, who cites it as B. *See* Delisle, Cab. des MSS., atlas, pl. x. 1, 2; Berger, p. 50.

98. Lat. 9389. Gospels [viii ?], 223 leaves, 4to, formerly belonging to the Benedictine Abbey of St. Willibrord at Echternach; written in an Irish hand, with the interesting subscription on the last page, 'Proemendaui ut potui secundum codicem de bibliotheca eugipi praespiteri quem ferunt fuisse sci hieronimi indictione vi p(ost) con(sulatum) bassilii ū c. anno septimo deximo = A.D. 558.' This, however, must have been in the exemplar from which it was copied, as the MS. itself is at least two centuries later. It presents the Irish type of text, but has been carefully corrected throughout, and the marginal readings represent another type. *See* Delisle, Cab. des MSS., pl. xix. 8; Pal. universelle, pl. ccxxvi; Westwood, Anglo-Sax. and Ir. MSS., p. 58, pl. xxi; Berger, p. 52 f. Cited by Wordsworth as 𝔈𝔓; collated by the Rev. H. J. White.

99. Lat. 10,439. St. John's Gospel [viii], formerly belonging to the Cathedral of Chartres, where it was found in the reliquary containing the sacred vest. A small manuscript, in uncial writing; mixed text, the earlier chapters Old Latin, the rest Vulgate. *See* Berger, p. 89.

100. Lat. 11,955, formerly St. Germain 777, then 663 or 664. 2. St. Matt. and St. Mark [viii ?], 54 leaves, 4to, golden uncials on purple vellum; *mut.* Matt. i. 1—vi. 2; xxvi. 42—xxvii. 49; Mark i. 1—ix. 47; xi. 13—xii. 23. Walker's *a*; Tischendorf's *reg.*; *see* O. L. Bibl. Texts, i. p. 55; Delisle, Cab. des MSS., atlas, pl. i. 2.

101. Lat. 11,959. Gospels [ix], from St. Maur des Fossés. Found by Sabatier in the St. Germain Library and collated by him; cited by Tischendorf as *foss.*

102. Lat. 13,171, formerly St. Germain numbered successively 18, 666, and 223. Gospels [ix], 4to, 223 leaves, small round minuscule. Walker's ϕ.

103. Lat. 17,226. Gospels [vii], in uncials. Vulgate text, but with a certain number of old readings in it. *See* Berger, p. 90.

104. Nouvelles acquisitions lat. 1587 (Libri 14). Gospels [vii–ix], from St. Gatien's, Tours, then in the Ashburnham Library, now at Paris. Quoted by Calmet (Nouv. Dissertations, pp. 448–488), 1720, and by Bianchini, Ev. Quadr.; contains a number of Old Latin readings, and on the whole rather resembles Br. Mus. Egerton 609 (no. 67) in text. Usually cited as *gat.* *See* Berger, p. 46.

105. Nouv. acq. lat. 2196. Evangeliarium [xi], from Luxeuil, written about 105 A.D. by Gerard, abbot of the Benedictine monastery there: sold at Didot's sale in 1879 to the National Library at Paris; cited by Mabillon, Sabatier, and Tischendorf as *lux.* *See* Delisle, Mélanges de Paléographie, p. 154 (1880).

Tours.

106. Public Library 22; formerly at Saint Martin. Gospels [viii or ix], in gold letters, interesting text. Quoted by Sabatier in Mark, Luke, and John. Walker's ρ, Tischendorf's *mt.*, Wordsworth's M; collated for his edition of the Vulgate by the Rev. G. M. Youngman. *See* also Berger, p. 47.

107. Public Libr. 23, formerly St. Martin 174. Gospels [ix], 192 leaves, minuscule. Collated by L. Chevalier, and cited by Walker as σ. *See* Dorange, Cat. des MSS. de Tours, 1875, p. 9.

108. Public Libr. 25, formerly Marmoutier 231 according to Delisle. Gospels [xii], but *mut.* in many parts and wanting after John vii. 5. Collated by Chevalier. Walker's τ.

d. *Germany: Berlin.*

109. Royal Library, MS. Theol. lat. 4to, no. 4. Gospels [ix or x], with prefatory matter; 164 leaves, 25 × 20 cent., minuscule. This MS. formerly belonged to the Augustinian College of Corsendonk near Turnhout in Brabant, and is the 'Corsendonkense Exemplar' of Erasmus, used by him in his second edition, with notes in his own hand. *See* O. L. Bibl. Texts, i. p. 53.

Erlangen.

110. Gospels at Erlangen, used by Sanftl, Dissertatio etc., Ratisbon, 1789, p. 76, and cited by Tischendorf as *erl.*

Karlsruhe.

111. Grand Ducal Library, Cod. Augiensis 211. Gospels [ix], formerly at Reichenau; text strongly marked by Irish readings. *See* Berger, p. 56.

Mayhingen.

112. Library of Prince Œttingen-Wallerstein. Gospels [viii], from

the Abbey of St. Arnoul at Metz; has a note at the end 'Laurentius vivat senio'; the Laurentius referred to being probably the scribe of the celebrated Echternach martyrology. *See* Berger, p. 52.

Munich.

113. Royal Libr. Lat. 13,601 = Cim. 54. Gospels [xi], 119 leaves, folio, from Niedermünster; magnificent pictures and illuminations; *see* Kugler, Museum, 1834, p. 164; Woltmann, Gesch. d. Malerei, i. 258; Berth. Riehl, Zur Bayr. Kunstgesch., i. 16.

114. Lat. 14,000, Cim. 55. Gospels [ix, dated 870], folio, from St. Emmeram's, Ratisbon. This magnificent book is written in golden uncials on fine white vellum, a good deal of purple being employed in the earlier pages; there are splendid illuminations before each Gospel. Collated by C. Sanftl, Dissertatio etc., Ratisbon, 1789. Tischendorf's *em.*

115. ~~Royal Library~~, Gospels [vii], from Ingolstadt; *mut.* in many places, especially in St. Matthew, where it only preserves xxii. 39—xxiv. 19; xxv. 14 *ad fin.* Collated by Tischendorf, who cited it as *ing.* His collation is in the possession of Bp. Wordsworth, who cites the MS. as I.

Nuremberg.

116. Dr. Dombart in Hilgenfeld's Zeitschr., 1881, p. 455 f., has drawn attention to some fragments [probably vi cent.] of St. Luke and St. John now in the Germanisches Museum at Nuremberg; they consist of twenty-eight leaves detached from the covers of books and contain, though *mut.*, Luke v. 19—xxiv. 31, John i. 19–33, written in a most beautiful uncial hand, perhaps not surpassed by any other MS. The text seems to be allied to Amiatinus, but with a considerable mixture of Old Latin readings. More fragments from the same MS. are to be found in the Libri collection; *see* 'Catalogue de la partie réservée de la collection Libri' (1862), p. 45, no. 226, pl. lviii.

Trier.

117. Stadtbibliothek, no. xxii. Gospels [end of viii], 172 leaves, folio, written partly in uncials but mostly in Caroline minuscules; this is the famous 'Codex Aureus,' or 'Adahandschrift,' and is a truly magnificent copy. A full description, both of the palaeography and of the critical value of the text, is given in the fine monograph published at Leipzig in 1889, and entitled 'Die Trierer Adahandschrift;' by several authors. The dissertation on the text is by Dr. P. Corssen.

Wolfenbüttel.

118. A Wolfenbüttel palimpsest [v], quoted occasionally in the Gospels by Tischendorf as *gue. lect.* *See* 'Anecdota sacra et profana,' p. 164 f.

Würzburg.

119. University Library, Mp. Th. q. 1 *a.* Gospels [early vii], 152 leaves, 4to, formerly belonging to the Cathedral Treasury; fine uncial writing, and

beautiful ivory carving on the covers. According to tradition this MS. belonged to St. Kilian and was found in his tomb; *see* however Berger, p. 54. *Mut.* Matt. i. 1—vi. 8; John xx. 23—xxi. 25. Facsimile in Zangemeister and Wattenb., Supplem. ad Exempla codd. lat., pl. lviii—lviii *a*.[1]

120. Mp. th. q. 1. Gospels [x], 194 leaves, 4to, formerly belonging to the Benedictine monastery of St. Stephen. A splendid MS.

121. Mp. th. q. 4. Gospels [xi], 168 leaves, 4to, probably once the property of the monastery at Neumünster. A fine MS. and strongly resembling Mp. th. f. 66 (no. 124).

122. Mp. th. f. 61. St. Matthew [viii], 34 leaves, folio, Anglo-Saxon writing with interlinear glosses; the text is largely intermixed with Old Latin readings. *See* the monograph of K. Köberlin, Eine Würzb. Evang. Hdschr.; Progr. d. Studienanstalt bei S. Anna in Augsburg, 1891.

123. Mp. th. f. 65. Gospels [viii or ix], 182 leaves, folio, formerly belonging to the Cathedral Treasury. Fine minuscule.

124. Mp. th. f. 66. Gospels [viii or ix], 207 leaves, folio, formerly belonging to the Cathedral Treasury. Fine minuscule; was a special treasure of Bishop Heinrich.

125. Mp. th. f. 67. Gospels [vii or viii], 192 leaves, folio, probably from the Cathedral Treasury; semi-uncial, and ivory carving on the cover; there are occasional corrections in an early hand, and the first hand has a large intermixture of Old Latin readings; *mut.* after John xviii. 35, and does not contain John v. 4.

126. Mp. th. f. 68. Gospels [vi or vii], 170 leaves, folio, formerly belonging to the Cathedral Treasury; fine and large uncial, and ivory carving on the cover; corrected frequently in a later minuscule hand, but the reading of the first hand is always visible, and agrees largely with Amiatinus, though in St. John's Gospel there is a good proportion of Old Latin readings.

127. Mp. th. f. 88. Gospels [xii or xiii], 194 leaves, folio; according to an inscription on fol. 194 the MS. was brought from Rome by a Cardinal to the Council of Basle, and used by him there; and then was bought for the Cathedral at Würzburg and handsomely bound.

e. *Holland: Utrecht.*

128. Utrecht. At the end of the famous 'Utrecht Psalter' are bound up some fragments [vii or viii] of St. Matthew (i. 1—iii. 4) and St. John (i. 1-21), written in an Anglian hand, strongly resembling that of the Codex Amiatinus. Facsimiles are given in the well-known edition of the Psalter, which was photographed by the autotype process and published in London in 1873. Wordsworth's U.

[1] For these MSS., *see* as before, G. Schepss, Die ältesten Evangelienhandschriften d. Würzb. Univ. B., 1887.

f. *Italy: Cividale.*

129. Cividale, Friuli. Gospels [vi or vii]. St. Matthew, St. Luke, and St. John are at Cividale in Friuli, from which the MS. is named 'Codex Forojuliensis'; St. Mark partly at Venice in a wretched and illegible plight, partly at Prague. This last portion (xii. 21—xvi. 20) was edited by J. Dobrowsky (Prague, 1778), and is cited by Tischendorf as *prag.*; the other Gospels are edited by Bianchini in the 'Evang. Quadruplex,' ii. app., p. 473 f., and are cited by Tischendorf as *for.*; the MS. is cited throughout by Wordsworth as J. St. John is *mut.* xix. 29–40; xx. 19—xxi. 25. Facsimile in Zangem. and Wattenb., pl. 36.

Milan.

130. Ambrosian Library, C. 39 inf. Gospels [vi], 288 leaves, uncial; with the numbers of the Sections and Canons in small Greek uncials, and some early and interesting lectionary notes in the margins; the text is also very interesting and valuable. *Mut.* Matt. i. 1–6; 25—iii. 12; xxiii. 25—xxv. 41; Mark vi. 10—viii. 12. In a later hand [ix] are Mark xiv. 35–48; John xix. 12–23; also a repeated Passion lesson, John xiii—xviii. Wordsworth's M; transcribed for his edition of the Vulgate by Padre Fortunato Villa, one of the 'Scrittori' of the Library.

131. Ambrosian Library, I. 61 sup. Gospels [viii], Irish hand; interesting text; it has been corrected throughout, and the corrections are as interesting as the original text, giving us good specimens of 'Western' readings; *see* Berger, p. 58.

Perugia.

132. Chapter Library; part of St. Luke's Gospel [vi], in a purple MS.; contains Luke i. 1—xii. 7, but much *mut.* Edited by Bianchini, Evang. Quadr., ii. app., p. 562; Tischendorf's *pe.*; Wordsworth's P.

Turin.

133. Gospels [vii ?], at Turin, used by Tischendorf and cited by him as *taur.*; *see* 'Anecdota Sacra et Profana,' p. 160.

g. *Spain: Escurial.*

134. Gospels [xi], 170 leaves, double columns, written apparently at Spires on the Rhine, in gold letters; now in the Escurial, not numbered, but exhibited under glass; the 'Aureum exemplar' of Erasmus; *see* Old Lat. Bibl. Texts, i. p. 51.

h. *Switzerland: Berne.*

135. University Library, no. 671. Gospels [ix or x], written in a small and graceful Irish hand; mixed text. *See* Berger, p. 56.

Geneva.

136. No. 6. Gospels [viii or ix], Anglo-Saxon text. Berger, p. 57.

St. Gall.

137. Stiftsbibliothek. No. 17 [ix—x], part of a 4to volume of 342

pages, two MSS. bound up together; pp. 3–117 contain the Gospel of St. Matthew; pp. 118–132, St. Mark i. 1—iii. 27 with preface.

138. No. 49 [ix], 4to, 314 pages. Gospels, with prefatory matter.

139. No. 50 [ix–x], 4to, 534 pages. Gospels, with prefatory matter and capitulare.

140. No. 51 [viii], folio, 268 pages, Irish semi-uncial. Gospels; illuminated title-pages and initials, strongly resembling the style of the Books of Kells and Lindisfarne (nos. 78, 64). Vulgate text, but with Old Latin readings, especially in the earlier chapters of St. Matthew. *See* Berger, p. 56.

141. No. 52 [ix], folio, 286 pages. Gospels, with prefatory matter.

142. No. 53 [ix–x], folio, 305 pages. Gospels, with title-pages and initials finely illuminated; written by Sintram, a Deacon at St. Gall, and known as the 'Evangelium longum'; remarkable also for its handsome binding with ivory carvings.

143. No. 60 [viii], folio, 70 pages, Irish writing. St. John's Gospel, with illuminated title-page and picture of St. John; this is one of the thirty 'libri scottice scripti,' mentioned in the ninth century catalogue of the Library; Tischendorf transcribed part of this MS.

144. No. 1394; the book of fragments that contains the Old Latin fragments, *n o p* (*see* p. 49). Pages 101–104 are two leaves small folio [ix] in Irish minuscules, and contain St. Luke i–iii; transcribed by Tischendorf.

145. No. 1395 [vi], being pp. 7–327 of a 4to MS., containing 90 leaves and a number of fragments of a MS. of the Gospels in Roman minuscules; only Matt. vi. 21—John xvii. 18 remain. The scribe says that he had two Latin MSS. before him, and a Greek MS. to which he occasionally referred. *See* below, no. 180. Tischendorf's *san*.

i. *United States: Oswego N. Y.*

146. Library of Th. Irwin, Esq. Gospels [viii], gold letters on purple vellum, formerly in the Hamilton Collection (No. 151); falsely ascribed to Abp. Wilfrid of York (†709); *see* Berger, p. 259.

D. Acts, Epistles, Apocalypse.

a. *British Isles: British Museum.*

147. Add. 11,852. Pauline Epp. (including Laod.), Act., Cath., Apoc. [ix], 215 leaves, small 4to, Caroline minuscule. Written for Hartmotus, Abbot of St. Gall (872–884): it afterwards belonged to the Library of Raymund Kraft at Ulm, and was described by J. G. Schelhorn in 1725 and Häberlin in 1739; bought at Frankfort by Bp. Butler: *see* Dobbin, Cod. Montfort., Introd., p. 44; and the careful examination by E. Nestle, Bengel als Gelehrter, pp. 58–60, Tübingen, 1892. Wordsworth's U_2; collated by the Rev. H. J. White.

Oxford.

148. Bodl. 3418. The Selden Acts, Seld. 30 [vii or viii], *mut.* xiv. 26—xv. 32. A most valuable uncial MS., collated by Casley, who cited it as χ, and by Bp. Wordsworth, who cites it as O_2. *See* Westcott, Vulgate, p. 1696.

b. *France: Paris.*

149. B. N. Lat. 305; Acts, Cath., Paul. (Laod. between Col. and Thess.), Apoc. [xi], texts resembling B. N. 93 (*see* above, no. 15); probably written at Saint Denis. Berger, p. 100.

150. Lat. 309; Acts, Epp., Apoc. [xi], in following order: Pauline Epp. (with Laod. *after* Thess.), Acts, Cath., Apoc. The text, especially in the Acts, resembles that of B. N. 93 (*see* above, no. 15). Berger, p. 99.

151. Lat. 13,174. Formerly St. Germain 23, then 669; Acts, Cath., Apoc. [ix], 139 leaves, 4to, thick minuscule. Valuable text, and contains an interesting note ~~on the~~ passage 1 John v. 7; Berger, p. 103. Walker's γ.

152. Lat. 17,250. Acts and Apocalypse [early xii]; 126 leaves, 32 × 23 cent.; a corrector, apparently of the thirteenth century, has added in the Acts a number of interesting additions from an extremely old version. Formerly at Navarre, and bought in 1445 by Nic. de la Mare from Jean de Mouson. Examined by S. Berger.

c. *Germany: Munich.*

153. Royal Lib. Lat. 6230. Formerly Freisingen 30. Acts, Cath., and Apoc. [early ix?], 126 leaves, large rough Caroline minuscules, Described in the Munich Catalogue as tenth century, but it seems nearer the beginning of the ninth; has a good text, but rather mixed, especially in the Acts, where there are strange conjunctions of good and bad readings. Wordsworth's M_2. Collated by the Rev. H. J. White.

d. *Switzerland: St. Gall.*

154. Stiftsbibliothek. No. 2 [viii], part of a thick 4to volume of 586 pages (not leaves), containing various matter; pp. 301–489 contain Acts and Apoc. in a large minuscule hand, written by the monk and priest Winithar; text interesting, but mixed. Wordsworth's S_2 in Acts and Apoc. Collated by the Rev. H. J. White.

155. No. 63 [ix], 4to, 320 pages. Acts, Epistles, and Apoc. divided as follows: foll. 2–163 Pauline Epp.; 163–244 Acts; 245–283 Catholic Epp. (but not 2 and 3 John), the 'three heavenly witnesses' in 1 John v. 7 being added by a contemporary corrector; 283–320 Apocalypse.

156. No. 72 [ix], folio, 336 pages, containing St. Paul's Epp., Acts, Cath. Epp., and Apoc.

157. No. 83 [ix], large folio, 418 pages; a fine MS., written by the order of Grimaldus and presented by him to the Library. Contains St. Paul's Epp., Acts, Cath. Epp., and Apoc., with prefatory matter.

158–. No. 1398ᵃ [xi], folio. A collection of fragments, of which ff. 230–255 contain fragments of Acts i. 1—v. 36.

E. Epistles (Cath., Paul.) and Apoc.

a. *British Isles: British Museum.*

159. Harl. 1772. Epistles and Apoc. [viii], Col. *after* Thess., and lacking Jude and Laod.; the Apoc. is *mut.* xiv. 16–fin. Formerly at Paris, from whence it was stolen by Jean Aymon. Written in a French hand, but showing traces of Irish influence in its initials and ornamentation; the text is much mixed with Old Latin readings; it has been corrected throughout, and the first hand so carefully erased in places as to be quite illegible. Collated in part by Griesbach, Symb. Crit., i. pp. 326–82, and by the Rev. H. J. White; *see* also Berger, p. 50. Bentley's M in Trin. Coll. Cam. B. 17. 14; Wordsworth's Z_2.

Cambridge.

160. Trin. Coll. B. x. 5 [ix], the Neville MS., 4to, Saxon hand: St. Paul's Epp., beginning 1 Cor. vii. 32. Bentley's S.

Oxford.

161. Bodl. Laud. Lat. 108 [ix], 4to, 117 leaves, Irish hand. Contains St. Paul's Epp. with prefatory matter (ending at Heb. xi. 34), in following order: Rom., 1, 2 Cor., Gal., Eph., Phil., 1, 2 Thess., Col., 1, 2 Tim., Tit., Philem., Heb. A valuable text, corrected apparently by three hands; the original text Old Latin, but has been much erased; in many cases agrees with *d* (Claromontanus) against most, or all, other MSS. *See* Westcott, Vulgate, p. 1696. Casley's χ; Wordsworth's O_3.

b. *France: Laon*

162. Public Library, no. 45. Epistles and Apoc. [xiii], from the monastery of St. Vincent near Laon. 141 leaves, 4to, containing latter part of the Old Testament, and the Epp. Apoc. in following order: Rom., 1, 2 Cor., Gal., Eph., Phil., Col., 1, 2 Thess., 1, 2 Tim., Tit., Philem., Heb., Apoc., James, 1, 2 Pet., 1, 2, 3 John, Jude; and then the apocryphal Petitio Corinthiorum a Paulo apostolo, and 3rd Ep. to the Corinthians. *See* Bratke in Theol. Lt.zeitung, 1892, p. 585 ff.

Orleans.

163. Public Library, no. 16. Consists of a number of fragments of five Biblical MSS.; the two last contain portions of 1 Cor., 1 Thess., Eph., and Phil. [viii?]. Berger, p. 84.

Paris.

164. B. N. 107. The Latin version of Cod. Claromontanus. Walker collated Rom. and 1 Cor. as far as x. 4; he cites it as δ.

165. Lat. 335. Pauline Epp. [viii], in Lombard characters. A valuable MS. Wordsworth's L_2.

166. Lat. 2328. Codex Lemovicensis. Catholic Epp. [ix], mixed text; contains 1 John v. 7, with the 'Three Heavenly Witnesses,' but in a mutilated form. Wordsworth's L_3.

167. Lat. 9553. Formerly Tours 116. St. Paul's Epp., with other matter [xi], 114 leaves, long minuscule; *see* Delisle, Notice sur les MSS. disparus

de la Bibl. de Tours, no. iv. p. 17 (1883). Collated by Chevalier; Walker's *v*.

c. *Germany: Bamberg.*

168. Royal Library, A. ii. 42. Apocalypse and Evangelistarium [x], written in the monastery of Reichenau; a gift from the Empress Kunigunde to the Collegiate foundation of St. Stephan. Noticeable especially for the large number of pictures (fifty-seven) with which the MS. is ornamented; it is perhaps one of the most interesting specimens we have of the pictorial art of this period. *See* Leitschuh, Führer durch d. kgl. Bibl. zu Bamberg, 1889, p. 89 ff.

Munich.

169. Royal Library, Lat. 4577. St. Paul's Epp. [viii ?], with prefatory matter; Col. after Thess., and followed by Laod.; Heb. at end.

170. Lat. 6229, formerly Freisingen 29. St. Paul's Epp. [viii or ix], with prefatory matter. Order as above. The text of this MS. appears to be like 169, and is excellent in the Romans, mixed in the other Epp.; there is an interesting stichometry; examined by Berger.

171. Lat. 14179. St. Paul's Epp. [ix or x]; interesting text.

Würzburg.

172. University Library, Mp. Th. f. 12. Epistles of St. Paul [ix], with Irish glosses. A well-known MS. The glosses have been published by Professor Zimmer (Glossae Hibernicae, Berlin, 1881), and by Mr. Whitley Stokes, with a translation (The Old Irish Glosses of Würzburg and Carlsruhe, Austin, Hertford, 1887); selections published and translated by the Rev. T. Olden (The Holy Scriptures in Ireland a thousand years ago, Dublin, 1888).

173. Mp. Th. f. 69. Pauline Epp. [viii], with Irish initials; Col. after Thess.

d. *Italy: Monza.*

174. Collegiate Archives, no. $1\frac{2}{9}$. Fragments of a Bible [x], Lombard writing; all that is left in the New Test. is part of the Epistles of St. Paul. Probably copied from an ancient MS.; Col. follows Eph.; text strongly resembles that of Milan E. 26 inf. (no. 30 above). Berger, p. 139.

Rome.

175. Vat. Reg. Lat. 9. Pauline Epp. [vii], 114 leaves, 30·3 × 20·3 cent., uncial. Collated for Bp. Wordsworth's Vulgate by Dr. Meyncke, and cited as R_2; *see* also Bianchini, Vindiciae, p. cclxxxiii. Colossians are placed after Thessalonians; *see* Berger, p. 85.

Verona.

176. Chapter Library, no. 74. St. Paul's Epistles [x], a text strongly agreeing with the first corrector of Cod. Fuldensis (*see* above, p. 75, no. 56); Corssen, Ep. ad Galatas, Berlin, 1885, p. 19.

e. *Switzerland : St. Gall.*

177. Stiftsbibliothek, no. 64. [ix], a 4to MS. of 414 pages, of which ff. 1–267 contain St. Paul's Epp.

178. No. 70. [viii], folio, 258 pages, written by the monk Winithar, of which ff. 1–250 contain St. Paul's Epp. (Hebrews being placed after 2 Timothy). *See* Berger, p. 117.

179. No. 907. [viii], 4to, 320 pages, large hand, written by the monk Winithar; pp. 237–297 and 303–318 contain the Epistles of James, Peter, and John, and Apoc. i. 1—vii. 2.

180. No. 908. 219 pages 4to [vi], of which pp. 77–219 form a very valuable palimpsest MS.; the original writing, a Martyrology in Roman semi-uncial hand; over this, St. Paul's Epp. in uncials, beginning Eph. vi. 2 and finishing 1 Tim. ii. 5. Transcribed by Tischendorf and quoted by him as *san.*

181. No. 1395 *See* above, no. 145. Pages 440–441 in the same collection contain fragments of Col. iii. 5–24 in a large Irish hand.

We now subjoin the various notations of these MSS., Bentley's, Walker's, Casley's, Tischendorf's, Wordsworth's:—

Bentley's notation.

A = 61.
B = 77.
C = 76.
C in Trin. Coll. Camb. B. 17. 5 = 89.
D = 65.
E = 63.
F = 72.
H = 60.
H in Trin. Coll. Camb. B. 17. 5 = 71.
K = 82.
M = 159.
M in Trin. Coll. Camb. B. 17. 5 = 70.
O = 59.
P = 62.
R = 3.
S = 160.
T = 75.
W = 69.
X = 74.
Y = 64.
Z = 68.
φ = 66.
ξ = 83.
ξ in Trin. Coll. Camb. B. 17. 5 = 85.

Walker's and Casley's notation.

α = 100.
γ (Walker) = 151.
γ (Casley) = 90.
δ = 164.
ε = 10.
η = 11.
θ = 15.
κ = 16.
λ = 52.
μ = 21.
ν = 20.
o_1 = 96.
o_2 = 19.
π = 97.
ρ = 106.
σ = 107.
τ = 108.
υ = 167.
φ = 102.
χ (Evv.) = 87.
χ (Act.) = 148.
χ (Epp.) = 161.
ψ = 86.

Tischendorf's notation.

am. = 29.
and. = 94.

bodl. = 86.
cav. = 28.
demid. = 50.
em. = 114.
erl. = 110.
for. = 129.
foss. = 101.
fuld. = 56.
gat. = 104.
gue. lect. = 118.
harl. = 68.
ing. = 115.
lux. = 105.
mm. = 67.
mt. = 106.
pe. = 132.
prag. (= *for.*) = 129.
reg. = 100.
san. (*Ev.*) = 145.
san. (*Ep.*) = 180.
taur. = 133.
theotisc. = 58.
tol. = 41.

Wordsworth's notation.

A = 29.
B = 97.
B_2 = 25.
BF = 72.
C = 28.
D = 51.
Δ = 82.
E = 67.
EP = 98.
F = 56.
G = 21.
H = 6.
Θ = 18.
I = 115.
J = 129.
K = 5.
L = 85.
L_2 = 165.
L_3 = 166.
M = 130.
M_2 = 153.
M' = 106.
O = 86.
O_2 = 148.
O_3 = 161.
P = 132.
Q = 78.
R = 87.
R_2 = 175.
S = 91.
S_2 = 154.
T = 41.
U = 128.
U_2 = 147.
V = 37.
W = 2.
X = 77.
Y = 64.
Z = 68.
Z_2 = 159.

CHAPTER IV.

EGYPTIAN OR COPTIC VERSIONS.

THE critical worth of the Egyptian versions has only recently been appreciated as it deserves, and the reader is indebted for the following account of them to the liberal kindness of one of the few English scholars acquainted with the languages in which they are written, the Rev. J. B. Lightfoot, D.D., then Canon of St. Paul's, and Hulsean Professor of Divinity at Cambridge; who, in the midst of varied and pressing occupations, found time to comply with my urgent, though somewhat unreasonable, request for his invaluable aid in this particular for the benefit of the second edition of the present work. His yet more arduous labours, as Bishop of Durham (*cui quando ullum inveniemus parem?*) did not hinder him from revising his contribution for the enriching of the third edition of this work. In this, the fourth edition, the Editor has the pleasure of acknowledging the most valuable help of the Rev. G. Horner, who has in particular revised the description of the MSS. of the Bohairic version, and of the Rev. A. C. Headlam, Fellow of All Souls College, Oxford, who has added the result of more recent research. Mr. Headlam's additions, are, wherever it is possible, distinguished by being enclosed in square brackets.

(1) *The Egyptian or Coptic Versions.*

Most ancient authors, from Herodotus downwards, referring to the heathen period of Egyptian history, mention two distinct modes of writing, the sacred and the common. In place of the former, however, Clement of Alexandria (Strom. v. 4, p. 657), who has left the most precise account of Egyptian writing, substitutes two modes, which he designates *hieroglyphic* and *hieratic* (or priestly) respectively; but since the hieratic is only a cursive adaptation of the hieroglyphic, the two are treated as one by other writers under the common designation of 'sacred' (*ἱερά*). Both these forms of the sacred writing are abundantly represented in extant monuments, the one chiefly in sculptured stone, the other on papyrus rolls, as we might have anticipated.

The common writing is designated by various names. It is sometimes the 'demotic' or 'vulgar' (*δημοτικά* Herod. ii. 36, *δημώδη* Diod. iii. 3); sometimes the 'native' or 'enchorial' (*ἐγχωρία* in the trilingual inscriptions of Rosetta and Philae); sometimes 'epistolographic' or letter-writer's character (Clem. Alex. *l. c.*); and in a bilingual inscription recently (1866) discovered at Tanis (Reinisch u. Roesler, Die zweisprachige Inschrift von Tanis, Wien, 1866, p. 55), it is called 'Egyptian' simply (*ἱεροῖς γράμμασιν καὶ Αἰγυπτίοις καὶ Ἑλληνικοῖς*). This last designation, as Lepsius remarks (Zeitschr. f. Aegyptische Sprache, iv. p. 30, 1866), shows how completely the common writing had outstripped the two forms of sacred character at the time of this inscription, the ninth year of Ptolemy Euergetes I. This demotic character also is represented in a large number of extant papyri of various ages.

These two modes of writing, however—the sacred and the vulgar—besides the difference in external character exhibit also two different languages, or rather (to speak more correctly) two different forms of the same language. Of ancient writers indeed the Egyptian Manetho alone mentions the existence of two such forms (Joseph. c. Ap. i. 14), saying that in the word *Hyksos* the first syllable is taken from 'the sacred tongue' (*τὴν ἱερὰν γλῶσσαν*), the second from the 'common dialect' (*τὴν κοινὴν διάλεκτον*): but this solitary and incidental notice is fully borne out by the extant monuments. The sacred character, whether hieroglyphic or hieratic, presents a much more archaic type of the Egyptian language than the demotic, differing from it very considerably, though the two are used concurrently. The connexion of the two may be illustrated by the relation of the Latin and the Italian, as the ecclesiastical and vulgar tongues respectively of mediaeval Italy. The sacred language had originally been the ordinary speech of Egypt; but having become antiquated in common conversation it survived for sacred uses alone. Unlike the Latin however, it retained its archaic written character along with its archaic grammatical forms. (*See* Brugsch, De Natura et Indole Linguae Popularis Aegyptiorum, Berlin, 1850, p. 1 sq.)

The earliest example of this demotic or enchorial or vulgar writing belongs to the age of Psammetichus (the latter part of the seventh century B.C.); while the latest example of which I have found a notice must be referred to some time between the years A.D. 165–169, as the titles (Armeniacus, Parthicus, &c.) given to the joint sovereigns M. Aurelius and L. Verus show[1]. During the whole of this period, comprising more than eight centuries, the sacred dialect and character are used concurrently with the demotic.

The term *Coptic* is applied to the Egyptian language as spoken and written by Christian people and in Christian times. It is derived from the earliest Arabic conquerors of Egypt, who speak of their native Christian subjects as Copts. No instance of this appellation is found in native Coptic writers, with one very late and doubtful exception (Zoega, Catal., p. 648). Whence they obtained this designation, has been a subject of much discussion. Several theories which have been broached to explain the word will be found in J. S. Assemani, Della Nazione dei Copti, &c., p. 172 (printed in Mai, Script. Vet. Coll., V. P. 2), and in Quatremère, Recherches Critiques et Historiques sur la Langue et la Littérature de l'Égypte, Paris, 1808, p. 30 sq. A very obvious and commonly adopted derivation is that which connects it with the town Coptos in Upper Egypt; but as this place was not at that time prominent or representative, and did not lie directly across the path of the Arab invaders, no sufficient reason appears why it should have been singled out as a designation of the whole country. In earlier ages, however, it seems

[1] My authority for these facts is Brugsch, Grammaire Démotique, p. 4, but what does he mean by the words which I have italicised? 'Au nombre des auteurs les plus récents qui nous aient donné des témoignages sur l'existence du démotique il faut citer St. Clément, prêtre de l'église chrétienne à Alexandrie, et qui vivait vers l'an 190 de notre ère, ou environ le temps où régnait l'empereur Sévère. Mais les monuments nous prouvent que *cette date n'est pas la dernière*; il se trouve encore des inscriptions d'une époque plus rapprochée; telle est par exemple une inscription démotique que M. de Saulcy avait copiée en Égypte et qu'il eut la complaisance de me communiquer pendant mon séjour à Paris; elle date du règne en commun d'Aurélius et de Vérus, ce qui prouve que *dans la première moitié du troisième siècle* le démotique était encore connu et en usage.' L. Verus died A.D. 169.

to have been a much more important place, both strategically and commercially (*see* Brugsch, Die Geographie des alten Ägyptens, i. p. 200; Egypt under the Pharaohs, i. p. 212 sq., Eng. trans.). Even as late as the Roman epoch Strabo (xvii. p. 815) describes it as 'a city with a mixed population of Egyptians and Arabians' (πόλιν κοινὴν Αἰγυπτίων τε καὶ Ἀράβων), and elsewhere (xvi. p. 781) he mentions it as a station of Egyptian traffic with Arabia and India. Possibly therefore this Arabic name for the Egyptians is a survival of those early times. On the whole, however, it seems more probable that the Arabic word is a modification of the Greek Αἰγύπτιος (Schwartze, Das alte Aegypten, i. p. 956). [And this derivation seems now to be generally accepted, the Greek word αἰγύπτιος being represented in Coptic by ⲅⲩⲡⲧⲓⲟⲥ, or ⲕⲩⲡⲧⲁⲓⲟⲥ, whence came *Qibt* (the common form) and our *Coptic*. (Stern, Koptische Grammatik, p. 1.)]

From this account it will appear that the Coptic, as a language, cannot differ materially from the demotic. As a matter of fact the two are found on examination to represent two successive stages of the same language—a result which history would lead us to anticipate. But while the language is essentially the same, the character of the writing is wholly different. The demotic character was derived ultimately from the hieroglyphic. Hence it represents the same medley of signs. Only a small number are truly alphabetic, i. e. denote each a single sound. Others represent syllables. Others again, and these a very large number, are not phonetic at all, but pictorial. Of these pictorial or ideographic signs again there are several kinds; some represent the thing itself directly; others recal it by a symbol; others again are determinative, i. e. exhibit the class or type, to which the object or action belongs. It is strange that this very confused, cumbrous, and uncertain mode of writing should have held its ground for so many centuries, while all the nations around employed strictly phonetic alphabets; but Egypt was proverbially a land of the past, and some sudden shock was necessary to break up a time-honoured usage like this and to effect a literary revolution. This moral earthquake came at length in Christianity. Coincidently with the evangelization of Egypt and the introduction of a Christian literature, we meet with a new and strictly phonetic alphabet. This new Egyptian or Coptic alphabet comprises thirty letters, of which twenty-four are adopted from the Greek alphabet, while the remaining six, of which five represent sounds peculiar to the Egyptian language and the sixth is an aspirate, are signs borrowed from the existing Egyptian writing. If there is no direct historical evidence that this alphabet was directly due to Christianity, yet the coincidence of time and historic probability generally point to this. The Christians indeed had a very powerful reason for changing the character, besides literary convenience. The demotic writing was interspersed with figures of the Egyptian deities, used as symbolic or alphabetical signs. It must have been a suggestion of propriety, if not a dictate of conscience, in translating and transcribing the Scriptures to exclude these profane and incongruous elements from the sacred text.

The date at which this important change was introduced into Egyptian writing has been a matter of much dispute. If it is correctly attributed to Christian influences, the new alphabet must have been coeval with the birth of a native Christian literature in Egypt. The earliest extant remains of such a literature, to which we can fix a date with any certainty, are the Epistles of St. Antony (who was born about the middle of the third century) to Athanasius and Theodore; but, as we shall see presently, one or both of the two principal Egyptian versions must have been already in common use at this time. Indeed, if the date assigned to a recently discovered writing be correct, the introduction of the new character was much earlier than this. On the back of a papyrus in the British Museum, containing the Funeral Oration of Hyperides, is a horoscope in Greek and Egyptian, the latter written in Greek characters, with the additional six letters almost, though not quite, identical with the forms in the ordinary Coptic alphabet. Mr. C. W. Goodwin, who describes this important document in Chabas, 'Mélanges Égyptologiques,' 2me série, p. 294 sq., and in the 'Zeitschrift für Aegyptische Sprache,' vi. p. 18 sq., February, 1868, calculates (though he does not speak confidently) that it is the horoscope of a person born A.D. 154[1].

[1] The date, however, is placed very much earlier by Revillout (Mélanges d'Archéologie Égyptienne et Assyrienne, p. 40), who supposes the Coptic alphabet to have been a work commenced by pagan Gnostics, completed by Christian Gnostics, and adopted when complete by their orthodox successors.

Any account of the Coptic dialects must start from the well-known passage in the Copto-Arabic grammar of Athanasius, bishop of Kos in the Thebaid, who flourished in the eleventh century. 'The Coptic language,' he writes, 'is divided into three dialects; that is to say, the Coptic dialect of Misr, which is the same as the *Sahidic*; the *Bohairic*[1], which gets its name from the province of Bohairah; and the *Bashmuric* in use in the region of Bashmur. At the present time only the Bohairic and Sahidic continue to be used. These different dialects are derived from one and the same language' (quoted in Quatremère, Sur la Langue &c., p. 20 sq.). For the present I will dismiss the Bashmuric, as it will require further investigation hereafter. The remaining two, the Bohairic and Sahidic, were the principal dialects of the language, being spoken in Lower and Upper Egypt respectively; and are largely represented in extant remains of biblical and ecclesiastical literature[2].

The Sahidic and Bohairic dialects are well defined and separate from each other. Among other distinctive features the Sahidic delights in the multiplication of vowels as compared with the Bohairic; thus it has ⲉⲗⲉⲟⲟⲗⲉ for ⲁⲗⲟⲗⲓ, ⲙⲏⲏϣⲉ for ⲙⲏϣ, ϩⲁⲗⲁⲁⲧⲉ for ϩⲁⲗⲁⲧⲓ, ϣⲉⲗⲉⲉⲧ for ϣⲉⲗⲉⲧ, &c. Again the Sahidic has smooth-breathings where the Bohairic has aspirates, e.g. ⲡⲏⲩⲉ for ⲫⲏⲟⲩⲓ 'heavens,' ⲧⲏⲩ for ⲑⲏⲟⲩ 'wind'; and it substitutes the simple aspirate for the stronger guttural, e.g. ⲱⲛϩ for ⲱⲛϧ 'life,' ⲡⲁϩ for ⲫⲁϧ 'rend.' Besides these more general distinctions, the two dialects have special peculiarities, not only in their grammatical forms, but even in their ordinary vocabulary; thus Sah. ⲃⲱⲕ for Boh. ⲓ 'to go,' Sah. ϩⲉ for Boh. ⲣⲏϯ

[1] [That *Bahiric* is a wrong transliteration is shown by Stern, Zeitschr. für Aeg. Sprache, 16 (1878), p. 23.]

[2] [There has been considerable variation in the names given to the different dialects. The terms Thebaic and Memphitic have been commonly adopted as a more convenient nomenclature, but, as will be shown below, the latter name at any rate is incorrect and misleading. Owing to the accident that the Memphitic dialect was the form of Coptic best known and earliest studied in Western Europe, the term Coptic has been sometimes confined to the Bohairic or Memphitic, as distinguished from the Sahidic or Thebaic, and was so used by Tischendorf; this usage also is erroneous and misleading; and the names Bohairic and Sahidic are almost universally employed by scholars at the present day.]

'manner,' Sah. ϩⲁϩ for Boh. ⲙⲏϣ 'a multitude,' 'many,' and so forth. Indeed the relations of the Sahidic and Bohairic dialects to each other may be fairly illustrated, as will have appeared from these facts, by the relation of the Ionic and Attic, though the differences in the Egyptian dialects are greater than in the Greek. Like the Attic, the Bohairic is the more literary and cultivated dialect of the two.

The demotic writing does not give the slightest indication that there were different dialects of the spoken language (*see* Brugsch, Grammaire Démotique, p. 10). In the Coptic, i.e. Christian, literature we learn this fact for the first time; and yet in the earliest age of this literature the dialects are found to be fully developed. Brugsch, however, has shown (De Natura &c., p. 10) that transcriptions of several Egyptian words into Greek in the age of the Ptolemies occur in two different forms, which correspond fairly to the two dialects; and indeed it would seem probable that the separation of the Bohairic and Sahidic should be ascribed to the more remote time, when these regions formed separate kingdoms. The older Egyptian writing, whether sacred or demotic, would obscure the distinction of dialects, partly from a conservative fondness for time-honoured modes of representation, but chiefly owing to the nature of the character itself. Thus this character makes no provision for the nicer distinction of the vowel-sounds, while the dialectic differences depend very largely on the divergent vocalization. Thus again it sometimes represents allied consonants, such as *l* and *r*, by the same sign; while one of the most striking peculiarities of dialect is the common substitution of *l* in the dialect of the Fayoum for *r* in the Sahidic and Bohairic, as e.g. ⲏⲗⲡ for ⲏⲣⲡ 'wine,' ⲗⲁⲙⲡⲓ for ⲣⲟⲙⲡⲓ 'year,' ⲗⲓⲙⲓ for ⲣⲓⲙⲓ 'weeping,' and the like.

Of the time when the Scriptures were translated into the two principal dialects of Egypt no direct record is preserved. Judging, however, from the analogy of the Latin and Syriac and other early versions, and indeed from the exigencies of the case, we may safely infer that as soon as the Gospel began to spread among the native Egyptians who were unacquainted with Greek, the New Testament, or at all events some parts of it, would be translated without delay. Thus we should probably not be exaggerating, if we placed one or both of the principal

Egyptian versions, the Bohairic and the Sahidic, or at least parts of them, before the close of the second century[1]. There are, so far as I am aware, no phenomena whether of text or of interpretation in either, which are inconsistent with this early date. Somewhat later than this we meet with notices which certainly presuppose the common use of a native version or versions of the Scriptures. Quatremère (Sur la Langue &c., p. 9 sq.) and Schwartze (Das alte Aegypten, p. 956 sq.) have collected a number of such notices, from which we may gather that it was the exception and not the rule, when a native Egyptian bishop or monk in the early centuries could speak the Greek language besides his own. Thus for instance St. Antony, who was born about the year 250, could only speak his native tongue, and in conversing with Greeks was obliged to use an interpreter (Athan., Vit. Ant. 74; Hieron., Vit. Hilar. 30; Pallad., Hist. Laus. 26). His own letters, of which fragments are extant, were written in Egyptian. Yet he was a son of Christian parents, and as a boy listened constantly to the reading of the Scriptures (Athan., *l. c.*, § 1). When only eighteen or twenty years old, we are told, he was powerfully influenced by hearing the Gospel read in church (§§ 2, 3); and throughout his life he was a diligent reader and expositor of the Scriptures. Indeed it is quite plain from repeated notices, that the Scriptures in the Egyptian tongue were widely circulated and easily accessible at this time (*see* esp. § 16 ἔλεγεν αὐτοῖς [i.e. τοῖς μοναχοῖς] τῇ Αἰγυπτιακῇ φωνῇ ταῦτα· τὰς μὲν γραφὰς ἱκανὰς εἶναι πρὸς διδασκαλίαν κ. τ. λ.). Again his contemporary Theodore, a famous abbot to whom one of his letters is addressed, was equally ignorant of any language but his own, and had to use an interpreter in speaking with strangers and Alexandrians (Sahid. MS. clxxvii in Zoega, Catal., p. 371). The notices of Theodore's master Pachomius, the founder of Egyptian monasteries, point in the same direction. This famous person, who was converted as a young man in the early years of the fourth century, was till late in life unacquainted with any language but his own. Receiving a visit from an

[1] Schwartze, whose opinion will not be suspected of any theological bias, infers from the historical notices that 'the greatest part of the New Testament writings, if not all, and a part of the Old Testament, especially the Psalms, had been already translated, in the second century, into the Egyptian language, and indeed into that of Lower as well as into that of Upper Egypt' (p. 963).

Alexandrian, another Theodore, be assigned to him as his companion and interpreter a monk who could speak Greek. After some time he himself applied himself to the study of this language that he might be able to converse with his new friend (Zoega, p. 77 sq., and references in Quatremère, Sur la Langue &c., p. 12). Pachomius drew up rules for the guidance of his monastery in the Egyptian language. These rules, which are extant in Greek and Latin translations (Migne, Patrol. Graec., xl. p. 947; Hieron., Op., ii. p. 53 sq.), demand a very diligent study of the Scriptures from the brethren, even from novices before admission into the order. Again and again directions are given relating to the use of manuscripts. These notices indeed refer chiefly to the Thebaid, which was the great seat of the Egyptian monasteries; but the first part of St. Antony's life was spent in the monasteries of Alexandria, and it was only later that he retired to the Thebaid (Athan., Vit. Ant. 49). Though probably more common in Lower than in Upper Egypt, the knowledge of Greek was even there an accomplishment denied to a large number of native Christians. Thus for instance, when Palladius visited John of Lycopolis, an abbot of the Nitrian desert, he found his knowledge of Greek so slight that he could only converse through an interpreter (Hist. Laus. 43). These, it will be remembered, are the most prominent names among the Egyptian Christians; and from such examples it must be plain that the ordinary monk would be wholly dependent on a native version for his knowledge of the Scriptures. Yet the monks swarmed both in Upper and Lower Egypt at this time. Palladius reckons as many as 7,000 brethren under Pachomius in the Tabennitic monastery (Hist. Laus. 38; comp. Hieron., Praef. in Reg. Pach. 2, ii. p. 54), while Jerome states that close upon 50,000 would assemble together at the chief monastery of the order to celebrate the anniversary of the Lord's Passion (ib. § 7). After all allowance made for exaggeration, the numbers must have been very great. Even at a much later date the heads of the Egyptian Church were often wholly dependent on their native tongue. At the Robber Synod of Ephesus (A.D. 449) Calosirius, bishop of Arsinoe, spoke and signed through his deacon, who acted as interpreter (Labb., Conc. iv. p. 1119, 1179, 1188, ed. Colet.). And again two years later, when Dioscorus of Alexandria started for the Council of Chalcedon, he was accompanied by one Macarius, bishop of Tkou, a man of some note in his day, who could not be made to understand a word of Greek (Memph. MS. liv, in Zoega, Catal., p. 99).

[The above was the most complete account of the dialects of the Coptic language and of the early history of the Coptic versions at the time when it was written; but in the last ten years immense additions have been made to our knowledge—additions which have rather complicated than solved the problem. These have been mainly due to the process of new discovery and to the labour of many scholars. A large number of previously unedited Coptic MSS. have been published; many new MSS. have been discovered, and the grammar of the language has been studied with great minuteness. The credit of the discovery and editing of new MSS. must be largely given to the energy and industry of the French school at Cairo, and especially to a former member of it, M. Amélineau, who has published a very large number of texts; the advances in our knowledge of the grammar are due to the labours of the German school of Egyptologists, notably Stern, Erman, and Steindorff. More important in some ways has been the discovery of an immense number of documents of a completely new class, written on papyrus, partly in and near the Fayoum, but also throughout the whole of Upper Egypt. These documents present us with the language in an earlier stage than we had previously known, and in a class of writings such as letters, contracts, and other legal documents, which conform to the spoken language of different parts of Egypt[1].

It is on the subject of the Egyptian dialects that our views have been most modified. We have seen that three dialects in all are mentioned by Athanasius of Cos: the Bohairic, the Sahidic, and a third, the Bashmuric. When therefore fragments of a third version of the Scriptures were discovered, the name Bashmuric was at once assigned to them. The early history of the discussions on this dialect were admirably summed up by Bishop Lightfoot. (3rd edition, pp. 401-403.)]

[1] For convenience the following abbreviations will be used: 'Z. A. S.' for *Zeitschrift für Aegyptische Sprache*; 'Recueil' for the *Recueil de travaux relatifs à la philologie et à l'archéologie égyptiennes et assyriennes*; 'Mémoires' for the *Mémoires de la Mission Archéologique Française au Caire*; and 'Mitt.' for the *Mittheilungen aus der Sammlung der Papyrus Erzherzog Rainer.*

The first fragment, 1 Cor. ix. 9–16, was published at Rome in 1789 by Giorgi, from a MS. in the Borgian Museum, in the work which has been already mentioned. He designated it Bashmuric, and, as the dialect presents affinities to both the Bohairic and Sahidic, he assigned to it a corresponding locality. Herodotus (ii. 42) mentions the inhabitants of the Ammonian Oasis as speaking a language intermediate between the Egyptian and Ethiopian; and on the strength of this passage, combined with the phenomena just mentioned, Giorgi placed Bashmur in this region, deriving the word from the Coptic ⲥⲡⲁⲙⲙⲏⲣ 'the region beyond,' i.e. west of the Nile, and gave the dialect a second name *Ammonian* (p. lxviii sq.). In the same year Münter in his work on the Sahidic dialect (*see* above, p. 393), published this same fragment independently at Copenhagen. He had not seen Giorgi's work, but adopted provisionally his name Ammonian, of which he had heard, while at the same time he stated his own opinion that the variations of form are too slight to constitute a separate dialect (p. 76). In 1808 appeared Quatremère's work, to which I have more than once alluded. In it he included another fragment of this dialect (Baruch iv. 22—v. 22, and Epist. Jerem.), from a MS. in the Imperial Library of Paris. At the same time he pointed out that the passage in Herodotus will not bear the interpretation put upon it by Giorgi, and that, as a matter of fact, the Ammonians speak not a Coptic, but a Berber dialect. He also refuted Giorgi's opinion about the position of Bashmur, and showed conclusively (p. 147 sq.) from several notices in Arabic writers that this region must be placed in the Delta. In a later work (Mémoires Géographiques et Historiques sur l'Égypte, i. p. 233, 1811) he identified it more definitely with Elearchia, the country of the Bucoli, that fierce and turbulent race of herdsmen, who, living in the marshy pasture land and protected by the branches of the Nile, gave so much trouble to their Persian, Greek, and Roman rulers successively (*see* Engelbreth, p. x). The defiant attitude, which in earlier times these Bucoli assumed towards their successive masters, was maintained to the end by the Bashmurites towards their Arab conquerors. While the other Copts succumbed and made terms, they alone stubbornly resisted. At length the Arab invaders were victorious, and the Bashmuric race was extirpated. It would seem, therefore, that Bashmur is the Arabic modification of the Coptic ⲡⲥⲁⲙⲟⲩⲣ, 'regio cincta,' the country girdled by the Nile.

But this being so, Quatremère, looking at the linguistic character of these fragments, denies that they belong to the Bashmuric dialect at all; and suggests for them a locality which will explain their affinities to both the Bohairic and Sahidic, assigning them to the Great and Little Oasis, and accordingly designating them *Oasitic*. In 1810 Zoega's 'Catalogus,' a posthumous work, appeared, in which he published all the fragments of this third Egyptian dialect found in the Borgian collection, comprising (besides a portion of Isaiah) John iv. 28–53; 1 Cor. vi. 19—ix. 16; xiv. 33—xv. 35; Eph. vi. 18–24; Phil. i. 1—ii. 2; 1 Thess. i. 1—iii. 6; Heb. v. 5–9; v. 13—vi. 8–11; 15—vii. 5, 8–13; 16—x. 22, nearly all of these passages being more or less mutilated. And in the following years these same passages were edited by Engelbreth (Fragmenta Basmurico-Coptica Veteris et Novi Testamenti, Havniae, 1811), who had not seen Zoega's edition. Both Zoega and Engelbreth, though agreeing with Quatremère in the position of Bashmur (the former without having seen Quatremère's book), yet claimed these fragments as Bashmuric.

In this opinion there is good reason for acquiescing. It seems highly improbable that Athanasius of Kos, a Christian bishop, can have been ignorant of a dialect so important that the Christian Scriptures were translated into it (for the various fragments oblige us to suppose a complete version of the Old and New Testaments), a dialect moreover which, on Quatremère's hypothesis, was spoken not so very far from his own neighbourhood. And on the other hand it is not very probable that all traces of a dialect which was known to him should have perished, as would be the case if these fragments are not Bashmuric[1]. To counterbalance this twofold difficulty involved in Quatremère's hypothesis, the linguistic objections ought to be serious indeed. But until we are better acquainted with the early history of Egypt than we are ever likely to be, it will be impossible to say why the Bashmuric dialect should not be separated geographically from the Sahidic by a dialect like the Bohairic

[1] Quatremère can only point to a single word accidentally preserved, which according to his hypothesis belongs to the real Bashmuric (Sur la Langue &c., p. 213 sq.).

with which it has fewer, though still some special affinities. The interposition of an Ionic between two Dorian races in Greece will show the insecurity of this mode of argument.

[We must now continue the history. Although Bishop Lightfoot summed up in favour of the theory which would assign these fragments to the Bashmuric, his acuteness had noticed the difficulties which would be involved in the separation of that dialect from the Sahidic, with which it had close affinities by what was then called the Memphitic. The greater knowledge of Egyptian history, which he desired but did not hope for, has become possible. And the objection is supported.

In 1878 Stern examined the history and character of the third Egyptian dialect (Z. A. S. 16, 1878, p. 23), and showed that it was almost impossible on either linguistic or historical grounds to assign it to the district of Bashmur. He pointed out that all the fragments we possessed of it had come from Upper Egypt, that we had positive evidence that there was no version of the Scriptures in the Bashmuric dialect, and that in dialectic affinities it was clearly akin to Sahidic. He also found evidence in Tuki of the existence of another dialect there called Memphiticus Alter, and that this was supported by papyrus documents which came from the site of Memphis (*see* below), which have some, although not a complete, resemblance to the Bashmuric fragments. Hence he concluded that the third dialect was Middle Egyptian, and, guided by two or three words on a fragment of papyrus brought from the Fayoum, he decided that that district must have presented the characters of isolation and independence, which would make the development of a third dialect possible. The proof of his theory was not long to seek. Already in the year 1877 attention had been called to the fragments now known as the Fayoum papyri, and very soon they began to appear in European libraries; it was not long before Berlin and Vienna acquired very large collections. An examination of the Coptic papyri in these collections has proved conclusively the truth of Stern's conclusions. The vast majority of these present the same dialectic affinities as the third Bible translation, and show also (as these had hinted) that the orthography of the dialect was not fixed, in fact that hardly two documents present exactly the same linguistic character, although all are definitely distinguished from the other two dialects.

It may therefore be confidently asserted that all the literature hitherto published as Bashmuric is in the dialect of the Fayoum.

But the discoveries do not stop here. As early as 1876 M. E. Revillont had published (Papyrus Coptes, 1876, p. 103) a collection of documents in the Louvre which came from the Monastery of Abba Jeremias, close to the Serapeum, near the site of the ancient Memphis. These were examined by Stern (Z. A. S. 23, 1885, p. 145 sq.), who shows that here we have again a different dialectic form. It has affinities to the Sahidic, affinities to the Bohairic, and affinities to the Fayoum dialect. It represents in fact the language of ancient Memphis, and an attempt has been made to call it Memphitic, but this would create endless confusion. Stern suggests Lower Sahidic (Unter Sahidisch), but the name Middle Egyptian is the one which has been generally adopted. It is this discovery that shows the necessity of avoiding the term Memphitic for the principal Egyptian version, and substituting the Arabic name 'Bohairic.' That was the language of the province on the sea-coast in the neighbourhood of Alexandria. And it was not until the eleventh century, and the removal of the Patriarchate to Cairo, that it became the language of the district of Memphis, that is, long after the decline of Memphis had begun.

But our knowledge of the dialects of Egypt was still further to be extended. About ten years ago excavations were undertaken by the Egyptian Department of Antiquities in the Coptic Cemetery of Akhmîm, the ancient Chemnis or Panopolis in Upper Egypt. Amongst the results of this discovery were the Apocryphal fragments, which have created a considerable sensation lately. These seem to have been considered by their discoverers to possess so little interest, that they were only accidentally given to the world seven years afterwards. The Coptic fragments were more fortunate, and in 1884 M. Bouriant, head of the French School at Cairo, published considerable fragments of the Old Testament, including a hitherto unknown Apocryphal work, the Testament of Sophonias (Zephaniah), in a fifth dialect, to which, for some reason, he at the time gave the name of Bashmuric (Mémoires, i. 1884, p. 243). This dialect was examined by Stern (Z. A. S. 24, 1886, p. 129), who showed that, while its affinities were with the Middle Egyptian or Lower Sahidic, it represented a more primitive stage in the language, and that these documents are our oldest literary remains of the Coptic language.

In the place then of the two or three dialects known until recent years, we have now at least five: the Bohairic, Sahidic, Fayoumic, Middle Egyptian, and Akhmimic, not to speak of the Bashmuric, in which no literary remains exist. The exact relations of these dialects to one another have not yet been satisfactorily worked out, and the problem is complicated by the fact that most of them had no fixed or standard form, and that papyri (especially those containing documents in the popular speech) vary in every locality and every age. To write the history then of these dialects and of the New Testament in them is not at present possible; but the following may suggest some more or less tentative conclusions.

In the earlier stages of the Egyptian language as we have it now in a written form, there are apparently no certain signs of dialectic variations, although there is certainly evidence that such did exist in the spoken language; and the changes introduced by Christianity are of great interest. The old language was fixed and definite in its orthography, and it represented the traditions of a caste of scribes, and not of the popular speech. Christianity on the other hand was in Egypt a great popular movement; a new and simple alphabet became necessary; the Scriptures were translated, not into the literary language, but into that of the people; and the copies of these translations in each locality reflected the local peculiarities of speech which had existed for centuries, but which up to that time had left behind no literary memorial. Gradually, however, the Christian Church created for itself literary traditions, and a tendency towards unification set in round three centres, the monasteries of the Natron Lakes, the great home of monastic life in Lower Egypt, the monasteries of the Fayoum, and the great White Monastery Deir Amba Shenoudah near Sohag in Upper Egypt. Hence came the three dialects which have a more or less literary character. Then began the decay of the Coptic language. First the dialect of the Fayoum died out, then the Sahidic, until finally Bohairic became, as it is now, the church language of the whole country.

The relation of these changes to the history of the versions has not yet been satisfactorily worked out. It has been sufficiently proved that translations into Coptic existed in the third century, very probably in the second; but in what dialect they were made, and what relation they bore to the existing translations, has not yet been discovered, and the problem remains unsolved.]

(2) *The Bohairic Version*[1].

The Bohairic version was not included in the Polyglotts, though others much later in date and inferior in quality found a place there. The first use of it is found in Bp. Fell's Oxford N. T. (1675), to which many readings were contributed by the Oxford Oriental scholar, T. Marshall, Rector of Lincoln College, who died in 1675, before the Coptic New Testament was published. It was afterwards employed by Mill, who recognized its importance, and gave various readings from it in the notes and appendix to his edition of the Greek Testament (1707). These readings he obtained partly from the papers of Marshall, who had contemplated an edition of the Coptic Gospels, but was prevented by death from accomplishing his design, and partly from the communications of a foreign scholar, Lud. Piques. The MSS. which supplied the former belonged at one time to Marshall himself, and are now in the Bodleian; the latter were taken from MSS. in the Royal Library at Paris (see Mill's 'Prol.,' pp. clii, clx, clxvii).

The *editio princeps* of the Bohairic version appeared a few years later with the title 'Novum Testamentum Aegyptium vulgo Copticum ex MSS. Bodleianis descripsit, cum Vaticanis et Parisiensibus contulit, et in Latinum sermonem convertit David Wilkins Ecclesiae Anglicanae Presbyter, Oxon. 1716.' The editor Wilkins was a Prussian by birth, but an Oxonian by adoption. In his preface he gives an account of the MSS. which he used, and which will be described below. The materials at his disposal were ample, if he had only known how to use them; but unfortunately his knowledge of the language was not thoroughly accurate, nor had he the critical capacity required for such a task. His work was very severely criticized at the time by two eminent Egyptian scholars, Jablonsky and La Croze, whose verdict has been echoed by most subsequent writers; and

[1] Memphitic (Lightfoot), Coptic (Tischendorf and others).

no doubt it is disfigured by many inaccuracies. But he may fairly claim the indulgence granted to pioneers in untrodden fields of learning, and he has laid Biblical scholars under a debt of gratitude which even greater errors of detail could not efface. With some meagre exceptions this was the first work which had appeared in the Egyptian tongue; and under these circumstances much may be forgiven in an editor. The defects which render caution necessary in using it for critical purposes are twofold. *First.* The text itself is not constructed on any consistent or trustworthy principles. It is taken capriciously from one or other of the sources at his disposal; no information is given respecting the authority for the printed text in any particular passage; and, as a rule, no various readings are added. In the prolegomena indeed (p. xi sq.) notices of two or three variations are given, but even here we have no specification of the MSS. from which they are taken. *Secondly.* The translation cannot be trusted. The extent of this inaccuracy may be seen from the examples in Woide, Append. Cod. Alex., p. 16 sq., and Schwartze, Evang. Memph. Praef., p. xxii. One instance will suffice. In 1 Cor. xiii. 3 Wilkins gives the rendering 'ut comburar,' corresponding to the common reading *ἵνα καυθήσωμαι*; though the Memphitic has ⲛ̀ⲧⲁ ϣⲟⲩϣⲟⲩ ⲙ̀ⲙⲟⲓ = *ἵνα καυχήσωμαι*. Yet Wilkins' error has been so contagious that Tattam in his Lexicon gives *καίειν* 'incendere' as a sense of ϣⲟⲩϣⲟⲩ, referring to this passage as an example, though its universal meaning is 'to praise,' 'to glorify.'

In 1829 the British and Foreign Bible Society published an edition of the Four Gospels in Coptic (Bohairic) and Arabic. It is a handsomely printed 4to, intended for the use of the native Christians of Egypt. In the Coptic portion, which was edited by Tattam, the text of Wilkins was followed for the most part, but it was corrected here and there from a recent MS. which will be described below, Evang. 14. This edition has no critical value.

Between the edition of Wilkins and those of Schwartze and Boetticher more than a century and a quarter elapsed; but no important step was taken during this period towards a more critical use of the Bohairic version. Wetstein appears to have been satisfied with the information obtainable from Mill and Wilkins. Bengel was furnished with a few various readings from the Berlin MSS. by La Croze; and Woide again in his preface, p. [13], gave a collation of Mark i. from the Berlin MS. of this Gospel. Griesbach seems not to have gone beyond published sources of information; and this has been the case with later editors of the Greek Testament.

The title of Schwartze's edition is 'Quatuor Evangelia in dialecto linguae Copticae Memphitica perscripta ad Codd. MS. Copticorum in Regia Bibliotheca Berolinensi adservatorum nec non libri a Wilkinsio emissi fidem edidit, emendavit, adnotationibus criticis et grammaticis, variantibus lectionibus expositis atque textu Coptico cum Graeco comparato instruxit M. G. Schwartze.' St. Matthew and St. Mark appeared in 1846, St. Luke and St. John in the following year. The title of the work fully explains its aim. The editor was an exact Egyptian scholar, and so far it is thoroughly trustworthy. The defects of this edition, however, for purposes of textual criticism are not inconsiderable. (1) Schwartze's materials were wholly inadequate. Though the libraries of England, Paris, and Rome contain a large number of MSS. of different ages and qualities, not one of these was consulted; but the editor confined himself to one good MS. and one indifferent transcript, both in the Berlin library. These will be described below. The text of the Bohairic Gospels therefore still remains in a very unsatisfactory state. (2) His collation with the Greek text is at once superfluous and defective. This arises from his capricious choice of standards of comparison, the Codex Ephraem and the printed texts of Lachmann and Tischendorf (1843). If he had given an accurate Latin translation of the whole, and had supplemented this with a distinct statement of the reading of the Bohairic version, where variations are known to exist in other authorities, and where at the same time a Latin version could not be made sufficiently explicit, the result would have been at once more simple, more complete, and more available. As it is, he has contented himself with translating particular sentences (more especially those which are mistranslated in Wilkins), while his method of comparison necessarily overlooks many variations. With all its defects, however, this edition has a far higher value than its predecessor for critical purposes. Not the least useful part of Schwartze's notes is the collation of the published portions of the Sahidic Version, where also he has corrected errors in the edition of Woide and Ford (*see* below, p. 129 sq.).

Schwartze only lived to complete the four Gospels. He had, however, made some collations for the Acts and Epistles during his last visit to England; and after his death they were placed in the hands of P. Boetticher, who continued the work. The titles of Boetticher's editions are 'Acta Apostolorum Coptice,' and 'Epistulae Novi Testamenti Coptice,' both dated Halae, 1852. His plan, however, differs wholly from Schwartze's. He substitutes an 8vo size for the 4to of his predecessor; and he gives no translation or collation with the Greek, but contents himself with noting the variations of his MSS. in Coptic at the foot of the page. Thus his book is absolutely useless to any one who is unacquainted with the language. Moreover his materials, though less scanty than Schwartze's, are far from adequate. For the Acts and for the Catholic Epistles he employed Schwartze's collations of two English MSS., which he calls *tattamianus* and *curetonianus*, and himself collated or obtained collations of two others in the Paris Library (*p*), (*m*); while for the Pauline Epistles he again used Schwartze's collations of the same two English MSS., together with *another* Paris MS. (*p*), and the Berlin MSS., which will be described below. The account, which he gives in his preface, of the MSS. employed by him is so meagre, that in some cases they are with difficulty identified. Nor again are the collations used for this edition nearly complete. I have pointed out below the defects in Schwartze's collation of one of the English MSS., which I have partially examined; and Brugsch in an article in the 'Zeitschr. der Deutschen Morgenl. Gesellsch.,' vii. p. 115 sq. (1853), has given a full collation of the Berlin MS. of the Epistle to the Romans, showing how many variations in this MS. are not recorded in Boetticher's edition. The Apocalypse has never appeared.

About the same time a magnificent edition of the whole of the New Testament in Coptic (Bohairic) and Arabic was published under the auspices of the Society for Promoting Christian Knowledge. The first part, which is entitled ⲡⲓ ϫⲱⲙ ⲛ̀ⲛⲓ ⲇ̅ ⲛ̀ⲛⲓⲉⲩⲁⲅⲅⲉⲗⲓⲟⲛ ⲉⲑⲟⲩⲁⲃ, 'The Book of the Four Holy Gospels,' bears the date 1847, Tattam's Coptic Lexicon having appeared in 1836[1]; the second, comprising the remaining books,

[1] *See* also A. J. Butler's 'Coptic Churches,' vol. ii, Oxford.

including the Apocalypse, is called ⲡⲓ ϫⲱⲙ ⲙⲁϩⲃ ⲛ̀ⲧⲉ ϯⲇⲓⲁⲑⲏⲕⲏ ⲙ̀ⲃⲉⲣⲓ, 'The Second Book of the New Testament,' and appeared in 1852. We are informed in a Coptic colophon at the end, that the Book was edited by 'Henry Tattam the presbyter of the Anglican Church for the Holy Patriarch and the Church of Christ in Egypt.' The type is large and bold, and the volumes are very handsome in all respects, being designed especially for Church use. The editor's eminent services to Coptic literature are well known, but the titles and colophon do not suggest any high expectations of the value of this edition to the scholar. The basis of the text in this edition was a copy belonging to the Coptic Patriarch; but the editor collated it with MSS. in his own possession and with others belonging to the Hon. R. Curzon, adopting from these such variations as seemed to him to agree with the best readings of the Greek MSS. As no various readings are recorded, this edition is quite useless for critical purposes: nor indeed was the aim which the editor set before him consistent with the reproduction of the Bohairic New Testament in its authentic form. The interpolated passages for instance are printed without any indication that their authority is at all doubtful.

The following account of the Bohairic MSS. existing in European libraries, though probably very imperfect, will yet be found much fuller than any which has hitherto been given. Indeed the list in Le Long (Bibl. Sacr., i. p. 140 sq.) is the only one which aims at completeness; and the date of this work (1723) would alone disqualify it, as a guide on such a subject at the present time. Those manuscripts which I describe from personal inspection are marked with an asterisk. In other cases my authorities are given.

A. *The Gospels.*

In the Bodleian Library at Oxford are:

*1. Hunt. 17, fol., paper, Copt. Arab., a very fine and highly important MS. Among other illuminations are seated figures of the four Evangelists prefixed to the several Gospels. The date is given at the close of St. John as the year 890 (of the martyrs), i.e. A.D. 1174[1]. Wilkins

[1] I have always added 284 to the year of the Martyrs for the year A.D.; but this will not give the date accurately in every case, as the Diocletian year began in August or September; *see* Clinton, Fast. Rom., ii. p. 210.

(p. vi), though giving the Coptic numerals correctly ⲱ̅ϥ̅, interprets them 790, i. e. A.D. 1074. This will serve as an example of his inaccuracy; and in future I shall not consider it necessary to point out his errors, which are very numerous, unless there is some special reason for doing so. The scribe's name, John a monk, appears in a colophon at the end of St. Mark.

The importance of this MS. consists in a great measure in its marginal additions, which are very frequent. The text seems to give the original Bohairic version in a very pure form; while the margin supplies all or nearly all the passages which in fewer or greater numbers have crept into the text of other Bohairic MSS., and which (so far as regards the Bohairic version itself) must be regarded as interpolations [1], whatever sanction they may have in Greek MSS. or other ancient authorities. Among these marginal additions I have noted Matt. vi. 13 (the doxology); Mark vi. 11 ἀμὴν λέγω κ.τ.λ., vii. 16 εἴ τις ἔχει ὦτα κ.τ.λ., xiii. 14 τὸ ῥηθὲν ὑπὸ Δανιὴλ τοῦ προφήτου, xv. 28 καὶ ἐπληρώθη κ.τ.λ.; Luke i. 28 εὐλογημένη σὺ ἐν γυναιξίν (in this case, however, not in the margin, but in the text in a smaller hand); xxii. 43, 44 (the agony); xxiii. 17 ἀνάγκην δὲ εἶχεν κ.τ.λ.; xxiii. 34; John vii. 53—viii. 11. On the other hand the descent of the angel, John v. 3, 4, which is wanting in many Bohairic MSS. and can hardly have been part of the original Bohairic version, stands in the text here. At the end of St. Mark the margin gives in an ancient hand (whether coeval with the MS. or not, I am unable to say) the alternative ending of this Gospel substantially as it is found in L and other authorities. This marginal note runs as follows: ⲟⲩⲟϩ ⲛⲏ ⲧⲏⲣⲟⲩ ⲉ̀ⲧⲁϥϩⲟⲛϩⲉⲛ ⲙ̀ⲙⲟϥ [ⲙ̀ⲙⲱⲟⲩ?] ⲛ̀ⲛⲏⲉⲧ ⲁⲩⲓ̀ ⲙⲉⲛⲉⲛⲥⲁ ⲡⲉⲧⲣⲟⲥ ⲟⲩⲟϩ ϧⲉⲛ ⲟⲩⲱⲛϩ ⲉ̀ⲃⲟⲗ ⲁⲩⲥⲁϫⲓ ⲙⲙⲱⲟⲩ ⲟⲩⲟϩ ⲙⲉⲛⲉⲛⲥⲁ ⲛⲁⲓ ⲇⲉ ⲟⲛ ⲁϥⲟⲩⲱⲛϩ ⲉ̀ⲣⲱⲟⲩ ⲛ̀ϫⲉ ⲓ̅ⲏ̅ⲥ̅ ⲓⲥϫⲉⲛ ⲛⲓⲙⲁⲛϣⲁⲓ ⲛ̀ⲧⲉ ⲫⲣⲏ ϣⲁ ⲡⲉϥⲙⲁⲛϩⲱⲧⲡ ⲟⲩⲟϩ ⲁϥⲟⲩⲱⲣⲡⲟⲩ ⲉ ϩⲓ ϣⲉⲛⲛⲟⲩϥⲓ ⲉ̀ⲑⲟⲩⲁⲃ ⲛ̀ⲁⲧⲙⲟⲩⲛⲕ ⲛ̀ⲧⲉ ⲡⲓⲱⲛϧ ⲛ̀ⲉⲛⲉϩ ⲁⲙⲏⲛ ⲛⲁⲓ ⲟⲛ ⲛ̀ⲑⲱⲟⲩ ⲉⲩⲏⲡⲓ ⲛ̀ⲧⲟⲧⲟⲩ ⲟⲩⲟϩ ⲙⲉⲛⲉⲛⲥⲁ ⲛⲁⲓ ⲉ̀ϥⲉⲧⲁϩⲱⲟⲩ [ⲉⲩⲧⲁϩⲱⲟⲩ?] ⲛ̀[ⲛ̀ϫⲉ?] ϩⲁⲛϣⲑⲟⲣⲧⲉⲣ ⲛⲉⲙ ϩⲁⲛϩⲟϫϩⲉϫ ⲟⲩⲟϩ ⲙ̀ⲡⲟⲩϫⲉ ϩⲗⲓ ⲛ̀ϩⲗⲓ ⲛ̀ⲥⲁϫⲓ ⲛⲁⲩⲉⲣⲟϯ ⲅⲁⲣ ⲡⲉ. 'And all those things he commanded to those that went after Peter, and they told them openly, and after these things again also (δέ) Jesus appeared to them from the rising of the sun unto the setting thereof, and sent them to preach the holy and imperishable gospel of eternal life. Amen. These again are reckoned (added) to them; And after these things troubles and afflictions possess them, and they said not a word to any man, for they were afraid.' I have translated the emendations suggested in brackets, for without them it is hardly possible to make sense. But, even when thus corrected, the passage

[1] I have observed Luke xxiii. 17 in at least three wholly distinct forms in different Bohairic MSS.

is not free from confusion. The alternative ending, as here given, most closely resembles the form in the Aethiopic MSS.

*2. Hunt. 20, fol., paper. The titles, initials, &c., are illuminated. The Ammonian Sections and Eusebian Canons are marked, besides Greek and Coptic chapters. This MS. omits the additions in Matt. xviii. 11, Luke xxii. 43, 44; John v. 3, 4; vii. 53—viii. 11, but contains those of Matt. xxiii. 13 (after ver. 14); Luke xxiii. 17, 34. The catalogue ascribes this MS., which is undated, to the thirteenth century; but this is probably too early.

*3. Marshall 5, fol., paper. The titles, initials, &c., illuminated. The Ammonian Sections and Eusebian Canons are marked. This MS. is very like the last in general appearance. In the catalogue the date of a donation is given as A. Mart. 1214 = 1498 A.D. It contains the additions Luke xxii. 43, 44; xxiii. 17, 34; John v. 3, 4; vii. 53—viii. 11; but omits Matt. xviii. 11. Petraeus, who transcribed this MS. in the seventeenth century, calls it very ancient and in ruinous condition.

*4. Marshall 6, fol., paper. The last few pages are supplied by a later hand. A colophon gives the year of the original MS. as A. Mart. 1036 = A.D. 1320, and that of the restoration = 1641 A.D., as A. Mart. 1357. This MS. omits the additions of Luke xxii. 43, 44; xxiii. 17; John v. 3, 4; vii. 53—viii. 11.

*5. Marshall 99, small 8vo, paper, containing the Gospel of St. John only. A comparatively recent but interesting MS. It has no date recorded. It omits John v. 3, 4; vii. 53—viii. 11.

In the British Museum:

*6. Oriental 425, 4to, paper, Copt. Arab. Ff. 2a—6b contain the Eusebian tables, after which originally followed the four Gospels in the common order, ending fol. 116b. The whole of St. Luke however, and the whole of St. John except xix. 6—xx. 13 and xxi. 13–25, are wanting, owing to the mutilation of the MS. The original paging shows that they once formed part of the volume. The subsequent matter is not Biblical. The Ammonian Sections and Eusebian Canons are given throughout. A colophon at the end of St. John gives the name of the scribe John, who must have copied it from the codex in the possession of the Catholic Institute of Paris in the year 1024 of the Martyrs, i.e. A.D. 1308. This MS. was purchased at Archdeacon Tattam's sale. The addition in Matt. xviii. 11 is wanting.

*7. Oriental 426, 4to, paper, Copt. Arab. The Gospel of St. John, of which the beginning as far as i. 13 is wanting. After this Gospel follow some extracts from the New Testament, Eph. iv. 1–13; Matt. xvi. 13–19; Luke xix. 1–10, with other matter. Like the last MS., this was bought at Tattam's sale. It has not the additions John v. 3, 4; vii. 53—viii. 11.

*8. Oriental 1001, large 8vo, paper, with illuminations, Copt. Arab., 'bought of N. Nassif, 21 May, 1869.' The four Gospels complete. Each

Gospel is preceded by introductory matter, table of contents, &c. The first few leaves of the book are supplied by a later hand. A note (fol. 77 b), written by Athanasius, Bishop of Apotheke or Abutij, A.M. 1508 = 1792 A.D., states that the original date of the MS. was A. Mart. 908 (=A.D. 1192). This date is also repeated fol. 264 b. It may possibly be correct, though the MS. does not appear so old. On fol. 125 b this same Athanasius records that he presented the book to the convent of St. Antony, A. Mart. 1508 (= A.D. 1792). It contains Luke xxiii. 34, and the pericope John vii. 53—viii. 11; but omits the additions Luke xxii. 43, 44; John v. 3, 4.

*9. Additional 5995, fol., paper, Copt. Arab. 'brought from Egypt by Major-General Turner, August, 1801.' The four Gospels complete. The few first leaves of St. Matthew and the last leaf of St. John, besides some others in the middle of the volume, are added in a later hand. In an Arabic colophon (fol. 233 b) it is stated that the book was repaired A. Mart. 1492 (i.e. A.D. 1776) by one Ibrahim, son of Simeon, but that its original date was more than four hundred years earlier. This is perhaps an exaggeration. The same colophon says that it was written for the convent of Baramus in the desert of Scete. Coptic chapters are written in uncials while the Ammonian Sections and Eusebian Canons are in cursive letters. It has not Luke xxii. 43, 44; xxiii. 17; nor the pericope John vii. 53—viii. 11; but contains Luke xxiii. 34, and the interpolation in John v. 3, 4.

*10. Additional 14,740 A. A folio volume in which various Bohairic and a few Armenian fragments are bound up together, of various sizes and ages, some on vellum, some on paper. The following fragments of the Bohairic New Testament on vellum are important on account of their antiquity.

(i) Luke viii. 2–7, 8–10, 13–18.
(ii) 2 Cor. iv. 2—v. 4.
(iii) Eph. ii. 10–19; ii. 21—iii. 11.
(iv) 1 Thess. iii. 3–6; iii. 11—iv. 1.

The fragment from the Ephesians, the most ancient of them all, appears from the handwriting to rival in antiquity the oldest Sahidic fragments. They are all more or less mutilated. This volume also contains several paper fragments of the Bohairic New Testament, belonging chiefly (it would appear) to lectionaries, but these are not worth enumerating.

*11. Oriental 1315. The four Gospels, fol., paper, Copt. Arab. The letter to Carpianus, Eusebian tables, &c., are prefixed. This MS., dated A.M. 924=1208 A.D., and bearing a statement of donations in A.M. 973 =1257 A.D., is very similar in writing to Cod. Vat. ix, and the name of the scribe George occurs in both, but the readings do not agree. This and the two following MSS. are from Sir C. A. Murray's collection.

*12. Oriental 1316. The four Gospels, 8vo, paper, Copt. Arab., illuminated, and dated A.D. 1663.

*13. Oriental 1317. The four Gospels, 8vo, paper, Copt. Arab., elaborately illuminated, and dated 1814.

In the British and Foreign Bible Society's Library:

*14. The four Gospels, sm. 8vo size (five leaves in a quire), paper, Copt. Arab. The volume begins with the letter to Carpianus and the tables. Introductions are prefixed to the Gospels. The Ammonian Sections and Eusebian Canons are marked. This volume is a copy made from one in the possession of the Patriarch of Cairo for the Bible Society, and bears the date A.D. 1817 (in a colophon at the end of St. Luke). It was partially used for the Society's edition of the Coptic Gospels (*see* above, p. 107). It contains Luke xxii. 43, 44; xxiii. 17, 34; John v. 3, 4; vii. 53—viii. 11, and seems to represent the common Coptic text of the present day.

In private Libraries in England[1]:

15. The Library of the Earl of Crawford and Balcarres. Fol., paper. The four Gospels. It was written (see colophon at the end of St. Luke) by a scribe, Simon of Tampet, but the date A.M. 1230 = A.D. 1508 is of the donation to a monastery. Several leaves in different parts of the volume were added much later, A. Mart. 1540 (i.e. A.D. 1824), by one George, a monk. It has a rough picture and the Ammonian Sections and Canons throughout. There is a tendency to Sahidic forms. For these particulars my thanks are due to Mr. Rodwell who kindly allowed me to see his catalogue of Lord Crawford's collection. Through inadvertence I omitted to inspect the MS. itself.

*16. Parham 121, 122, 123 (nos. 9, 10, 11 in the printed Catalogue, p. 29), in Lord Zouche's Library at Parham in Sussex. Fol., paper, Copt. Arab. There is a date of donation A.M. 1211 = 1495 A.D. in 123. These three MSS., which contain respectively the Gospels of St. Matthew, St. Luke, and St. John, must originally have formed part of the same volume, which St. Mark is wanted to complete. The last leaf of St. Luke is numbered ⲦⲔ, the first of St. John ⲦⲔⲂ. Several pages at the beginning and end of St. Matthew are supplied by a later hand. The Ammonian Sections and Eusebian Canons are marked. These volumes are written in a large hand, and have illuminations. They contain the additions Luke xxiii. 34; John vii. 53—viii. 11; but not Luke xxii. 43, 44; xxiii. 17; nor John v. 3, 4.

*17. Parham 126 (no. 14, p. 29, in the printed Catalogue), 12mo, paper, Copt. Arab. The four Gospels in a small neat hand, smaller than I remember to have seen in any Coptic MS. There are two dates, A.M. 1392=A.D. 1676, and A.M. 1446=1730 A.D., and it is probable that the book was nearly finished at the earlier time. Introductions and tables

[1] My sincere thanks are due to the late Earl of Crawford and Balcarres, and to Lord Zouche, for their kindness in allowing me free access to their valuable collections of Coptic MSS., and in facilitating my investigations in many ways.

of contents are prefixed to each Gospel. This MS. has the additions Luke xxiii. 34; John vii. 53—viii. 11; but not Luke xxii. 43, 44; xxiii. 17; nor John v. 3, 4; just as was the case with the MS. last described, no. 16[1].

[1] The volume, *Parham 102, described in the printed Catalogue (no. 1, vellum, p. 27) as a MS. of the Gospels of St. Matthew and St. Mark, is really a selection of passages taken in order from the four Gospels, with a patristic catena attached to each. The leaves, however, are much displaced in the binding, and many are wanting. The title to the first Gospel is † ⲉⲣⲙⲏⲛⲓⲁ ⲛ̀ⲧⲉ ⲡⲓⲉⲩⲁⲅⲅⲉⲗⲓⲟⲛ ⲉⲑⲟⲩⲁⲃ ⲕⲁⲧⲁ ⲙⲁⲑⲉⲟⲛ ⲉⲃⲟⲗϩⲓⲧⲉⲛ ϩⲁⲛⲙⲏϣ ⲛ̀ⲥⲁϧ ⲟⲩⲟϩ ⲛ̀ⲫⲱⲥⲧⲏⲣ ⲛ̀ⲧⲉ † ⲉⲕⲕⲗⲏⲥⲓⲁ, &c. 'The interpretation of the Holy Gospel according to Matthew from numerous doctors and luminaries of the Church.' Among the Fathers quoted I observed Athanasius, Basil, Chrysostom, Clement, the two Cyrils (of Jerusalem and of Alexandria), Didymus, Epiphanius, Eusebius, Evagrius, the three Gregories (Thaumaturgus, Nazianzen, and Nyssen), Hippolytus, Irenaeus, Severianus of Gabala, Severus of Antioch (often styled simply the Patriarch), Symeon Stylites, Timotheus, and Titus.

In the account of this MS. in the Catalogue it is stated that 'the name of the scribe who wrote it is Sapita Leporos, a monk of the monastery, or monastic rule, of Laura under the sway of the great abbot Macarius,' and the inference is thence drawn that it must have been written before 395, when Macarius died. This early date, however, is at once set aside by the fact that writers who lived in the sixth century are quoted. Professor Wright (Journal of Sacred Literature, vii. p. 218), observing the name of Severus in the facsimile, points out the error of date, and suggests as an explanation that the colophon (which he had not seen) does not speak of the great Macarius, but of '*an abbot* Macarius.' The fact is, that though the great Macarius is certainly meant, there is nothing which implies that he was then living. The scribe describes himself as ⲁⲛⲟⲕ ϧⲁ ⲡⲓ ⲧⲁⲗⲉⲡⲱⲣⲟⲥ ⲉⲧⲁϥⲥϧⲁⲓ, 'I the unhappy one (*ταλαιπωρος*) who wrote it' (which has been wrongly read and interpreted as a proper name Sapita Leporos). He then gives his name ⲑⲉⲟⲇ ⲡⲟⲩⲥⲓⲣⲓ (Theodorus of Busiris?) and adds, ⲡⲓⲁⲧⲙ̀ⲡϣⲁ ⲙ̀ⲙⲟⲛⲁⲭⲟⲥ ⲛ̀ⲧⲉ †ⲗⲁⲩⲣⲁ ⲉⲑⲟⲩⲁⲃ ⲛ̀ⲧⲉ ⲡⲓⲛⲓϣ† ⲁⲃⲃⲁ ⲙⲁⲕⲁⲣⲓ, 'the unworthy monk of the holy laura of the great abbot Macarius.' He was merely an inmate of the monastery of St. Macarius; see the expression quoted from the Vat. MS. lxi in Tattam's Lexicon, p. 842. This magnificent MS. is dated A.M. 604 = A.D. 888 and has been published by Professor De Lagarde; but its value may not be very great for the Bohairic Version, as it is perhaps translated from the Greek.

The *Parham MS. 106 (no. 5, p. 28) is wrongly described as containing the Gospel of St. John. The error is doubtless to be explained by the fact that the name ⲒⲰⲀⲚⲚⲞⲨ occurs at the bottom of one of the pages; but the manuscript is not Biblical. Another MS. (no. 13, p. 29) is described as 'St. Matthew with an Arabic translation, very large folio: a modern MS. copied at Cairo from an antient one in the library of the Coptic Patriarch.' I was not able to find this, when through the courtesy of Lord Zouche I had access to the Parham collection.

In the Paris National Library :

*18. Cod. Copt. 13, fol., vellum. The four Gospels. A very fine manuscript, elaborately illuminated, with pictures of the principal scenes in the Gospel history. It has the Ammonian Sections and Eusebian Canons in the margin, with the tables at the end of the Gospels. The writer, Michael, bishop of Damietta, gives his name in a colophon at the end of St. Mark. The date at the end of St. Matthew is 894 (or A.D. 1178); of the other Gospels 896 (or A.D. 1180). This MS. is erroneously dated 1173 in the Catalogue, and 1164 in Le Long. The additions Luke xxiii. 17, 34; and John vii. 53—viii. 11, are part of the original text. Also Luke xxii. 43, 44, is written *prima manu* and in the text, but in smaller characters so as to make a distinction. On the other hand the interpolation John v. 3, 4, is wanting.

*19. Cod. Copt. 14, fol., paper, Copt. Arab. The four Gospels. It has the Ammonian Sections and Eusebian Canons, and two other capitulations besides. It contains Luke xxiii. 34, but has not the additions Luke xxii. 43, 44; xxiii. 17; John v. 3, 4; vii. 53—viii. 11. It is referred in the Catalogue to the thirteenth century, which is probably about its date.

*20. Cod. Copt. 15 (Colbert 2913, Reg. 330. 3), 4to. The scribe Victor gives his name in a colophon at the end. It belongs to the more ancient Coptic MSS., though no date is given. The Ammonian Sections and Eusebian Canons are given. The passages Luke xxii. 43, 44; xxiii. 17, 34; Joh. v. 3, 4, are added in the margin, but form no part of the original text. On the other hand John vii. 53—viii. 11 now forms part of the text, but the leaf containing it and several which follow have been supplied by a much later hand. This is the case also with the beginning of St. Matthew and the end of St. John.

*21. Cod. Copt. 16 (De La Mare 579, Reg. 330. 2), 4to, Copt. Arab., paper. Owing to the Calendar at the end beginning 1204 A.D.=A.M. 920, it is assigned to the thirteenth century. It has the Ammonian Sections and Eusebian Canons and (like Cod. Copt. 14) the Greek and Coptic chapters. It contains Luke xxii. 43, 44; xxiii. 17, 34; but not John v. 3, 4; nor John vii. 53—viii. 11.

*22. Cod. Copt. 59 (St. German. 25), 'Ex Bibl. Coisl. olim Seguer.' Fol., paper. The four Gospels. It has the Ammonian Sections and Eusebian Canons, and two other capitulations besides. The date at the end is given as 946 A.M. i. e. 1230 A.D. It does not contain the additions, Luke xxii. 43, 44; xxiii. 17, 34. The earlier part of St. John containing the test passages is wanting.

*23. Cod. Copt. 60, fol., paper, a late MS. The four Gospels. On a fly-leaf is written, 'Quatuor evangelia Coptice Venetiis emta per me Fr. Bernardum de Montfaucon anno 1698, die 11 Augusti.' It has the Ammonian Sections and Canons. The additions, Luke xxii. 43, 44; xxiii. 17; John v. 3, 4, are wanting; but Luke xxiii. 34; John vii. 53—viii. 11 stand as part of the text.

*24. Cod. Copt. 61, 8vo, paper. St. John's Gospel. A late MS.

The leaves are bound up in the wrong order, and some are wanting. It contains John vii. 53—viii. 11.

*25. Cod. Copt. 62, 4to, paper. St. John's Gospel. Arabic words are written interlinearly in the earlier part, but not throughout. It has not v. 3, 4 nor vii. 53—viii. 11. It appears to be of fair antiquity.

In the Berlin Royal Library:

26. MS. Orient. Diez. A. Fol. 40, described by Schwartze (Praef. p. xiii sq.), who collated it for his edition. He says (p. xx), 'decimum saeculum non superat, dummodo aequet.' The great body of this MS. is written by two different scribes, both of whom perhaps wrote in the thirteenth century; the two first and two last leaves are supplied by a third and more recent hand. Of the two earlier scribes the second was not contemporary with the first, as the similarity of the paper and ink might suggest, but the MS. was already mutilated when it came into his hands, and he supplied the missing leaves. The date of A.M. 1125= 1409 A.D. occurs in an Arabic statement but with no mention of writing. There is a tendency to Sahidic forms, more especially in the parts supplied by the second scribe. This MS. is generally free from the interpolated additions, e.g. Luke xxii. 43, 44; xxiii. 17, 34; John v. 3, 4; vii. 53—viii. 11; and seems to be of high value.

27. MS. Orient. Quart. 165, 166, 167, 168, four transcripts by Petraeus, also collated by Schwartze (*see* Praef., p. ix). The first (165) has the lessons for Sundays and Festivals from the four Gospels; the other three (166, 167, 168) contain the Gospels of St. Matthew, St. Mark, and St. Luke respectively, with the exception of the parts included in the ecclesiastical lessons. These transcripts were made in the year 1662, from a MS. which Petraeus describes as 'vetustum' and 'vetustissimum,' and which is now in the Bodleian Library (Maresc. 5).

In the Göttingen University Library:

28. Orientalis 125, described incorrectly by Lagarde, Orientalia, Heft i. p. 4. The four Gospels, written A. Mart. 1073 (A.D. 1357). Some portions are written in another hand and on different paper from the rest when the book was restored in A.D. 1774, but the greater part is of 1357.

In the Vatican Library at Rome:

29. Copt. 8, fol., paper, Copt. Arab. The four Gospels. Some leaves at the beginning, in the middle, and at the end have been supplied more recently. The scribe of these later leaves was one Arcadius, son of John, who gives the date 1303 (i.e. A.D. 1587). The body of the MS. is ascribed by Assemani to the fourteenth century. For further particulars see Mai, Coll. Vet. Script., v. 2, p. 120 sq. From the collection of I. B. Raymund (no. i), left by will to the Vatican Library.

30. Copt. 9 (Raymund iv), fol., paper, Copt. Arab., with fine illuminations. The four Gospels, preceded by the letter of Eusebius to Carpianus and the Eusebian tables. It was given to the Monastery of St. Antony

in the Arabian desert, A. Mart. 986 (=A.D. 1270), by one Michael Abu-Khalîkah, as recorded in a colophon written by Gabriel, who was patriarch of Alexandria at the time. Assemani states that this Michael was also the writer of the MS., but more probably the writer was named George and wrote the book in A. D. 1205=A. M. 921. After the plunder of the monastery by the Arabs, the MS. came into the possession of two other patriarchs of the Copts, John (A. D. 1506) and Gabriel (A. D. 1526), and was afterwards placed (A. D. 1537) in the Church of SS. Sergius and Bacchus at Alexandria. These facts are stated in other colophons. *See* Mai, *l.* c., p. 122 sq.

31. Copt. 10 (Raymund vi), 4to, paper, Copt. Arab. The four Gospels; ascribed to the fourteenth century by Assemani. *See* Mai, *l. c.*, p. 125. There are dates of births and marriages, the earliest being A. D. 1488 = A. M. 1204.

32. Copt. 11 (Pètri de Valle vi), fol., paper, Copt. Arab. The Gospel of St. John. It bears the date 1062 (i. e. A. D. 1346). *See* Mai, *l.* c., p. 125.

33. British Museum; Orient. 3381, fol., paper. The four Gospels. Is not dated, though the writer gives his name as Victor. It is probably of the thirteenth century, and somewhat resembles the writing of Paris 59. The book was restored in A. D. 1793 under the patronage of Athanasius, Bishop of Abu Tij. There is also record of a collation by a priest in A. D. 1801, while a note in English says that the MS. came from Esneh and was bought of the Bishop of Luxor by Mr. Lieder, who sold it in 1864 to Mr. Geden, from whom it passed to the Museum.

34. Paris; Copt. 14 A, Copt. Arab., fol., paper. The four Gospels. Is dated A.M. 1309=A. D. 1593. This date is mentioned in Paris 14 as being the time of a work which was performed on that book, and there can be little doubt that this work was the copying of 14 A from 14.

35. Paris; Copt. 60, fol., paper. The four Gospels. This MS. is not dated, but is not ancient, and appears to be a copy of MS. Diez in its present double form as far as the end of St. Luke. St. John is by another hand, and may be of earlier date. The former copier was a deacon, Abu al Monnâ.

36. Paris, L'Institut Catholique de, Copt. Arab., 4to, paper. The four Gospels. It is dated A. M. 966 = A. D. 1250. The writer Gabriel calls himself monk and priest, and afterwards became Patriarch. A donation of the book to Church of St. Mercurius is recorded in 1750 A. D. The book was brought from Egypt by M. Amélineau and sold to the Institute a few years ago. There are very interesting miniatures, which have been partly published in the Album of M. l'Abbé Hyvernat.

B. *The Pauline Epistles, Catholic Epistles, and Acts.*

In the Bodleian Library at Oxford are:

1. Hunt. 43, fol., paper, Copt. Arab., containing Paul. Ep., Cath. Ep., Acts, and Apocalypse. The paging ceases at the end of the Acts, and

between the Acts and Apocalypse are some blank pages. I did not, however, notice any difference in the handwriting of the two parts. The date given at the end of the Acts is 1398 (i. e. A. D. 1682).

*2. Hunt. 203, 4to, paper. The Pauline Epistles. The beginning, Rom. i. 1—ii. 26, and the end, 2 Tim. iv. 4—Tit. ii. 6, are in a later hand. This later transcriber ends abruptly in the middle of a page with ⲉⲑⲣⲟⲩ, Tit. ii. 6. Thus the end of Titus and the whole of Philemon are wanting. There are several lacunae in the body of the work owing to lost leaves. The description in Wilkins is most inaccurate.

*3. Hunt. 122, 4to, paper, illuminated. The Pauline Epistles. The beginning and end are wanting. The MS. begins with Rom. viii. 29, and ends with 2 Tim. i. 2. The date is given at the end of 2 Corinthians as 1002 of the Diocletian era, i. e. A. D. 1286. The scribe gives his name as 'ⲡⲟⲗϥⲁϫ the son of the bishop.'

In the British Museum:

4. Orient. 424, 4to, paper, Copt. Arab., containing Paul. Ep., Cath. Ep., Acts. At the end of the Pauline Epistles, and at the end of the Acts, are two important Arabic colophons, in which the pedigree of the MS. is given. From these we learn that both portions of this MS. were written A. Mart. 1024 (=A. D. 1308) by one Abu Said. They were copied, however, from a previous MS. in the handwriting of the patriarch Abba Gabriel and bearing the date A. Mart. 966 (=A. D. 1250). This Abba Gabriel stated that 'he took great pains to copy it accurately and correct it, both as to the Coptic and Arabic texts, to the best of human ability.' This MS. of Abba Gabriel again was copied from two earlier MSS., that of the Pauline Epistles in the handwriting of Abba Yuhanna, bishop of Sammanud, that of the Catholic Epistles and Acts in the handwriting of 'Jurja ibn Saksik (?) the famous scribe.' This MS. belonged to Archdeacon Tattam, and was purchased for the British Museum at the sale of his books. It is the MS. designated 'tattamianus' in the edition of Boetticher, who made use of a collation obtained by Schwartze. The corrections in this MS. (designated t in Boetticher) are written in red ink.

5. Oriental 1318, ff. 294, fol., 4to, Copt. Arab., dated A. Mart. 1132 = A. D. 1416.

In private collections in England:

*6. Parham 124 (no. 12, p. 29, in the printed Catalogue), fol., paper, Copt. Arab. Paul. Ep., Cath. Ep., Acts. There are several blank leaves at the end of the Pauline Epistles, and the numbering of the leaves begins afresh with the Catholic Epistles, so that this MS. is two volumes bound together. They are, however, companion volumes and in the same handwriting. This is doubtless the MS. of which Schwartze's collation was used by Boetticher (*see* above, p. 109), and which he calls 'curetonianus.' I am informed that it is designated simply *cur.* by Schwartze himself. It certainly never belonged to Cureton, but was brought with the other Parham MSS. by the Hon.

R. Curzon (afterwards Lord Zouche) from the East, and ever afterwards belonged to his library. Boetticher's designation therefore is probably to be explained by a confusion of names. I gather moreover from private correspondence which I have seen, that some of Mr. Curzon's Coptic MSS. were in the keeping of Cureton at the British Museum about the time when Schwartze's collation was made, and this may have been one. If so, the mistake is doubly explained. I infer the identity of this MS. with the *curetonianus* of Boetticher for the following reasons: (1) Having made all enquiries, I cannot find that Dr. Cureton ever possessed a Coptic MS. of the whole or part of the New Testament; (2) The MS. in question must have been in England, and no other English MS. satisfies the conditions. My first impression was that the MS. next described, Parham 121, would prove to be the *curetonianus*, for I found between the leaves an envelope addressed to Mr. Cureton at the British Museum, and bearing the post mark, January, 1849; this fact indicating that it had been in Mr. Cureton's hands about the time when Schwartze's collation was made. But a comparison of the readings soon showed that this identification must be abandoned. (3) The cipher which Boetticher gives for the date is also found in this MS. in two places, after the Pauline Epistles and again after the Acts. This coincidence is the more remarkable as the cipher is not very intelligible. (4) The readings of our MS., Parham 124, where I compared them, agree with those of Boetticher's *curetonianus*, with an occasional exception which may be accounted for by the inaccuracy of the collation. This is the case with crucial readings, as for instance the marginal alternative in Acts vii. 39. At the same time Schwartze's collation, if Boetticher has given its readings fully, must have been very imperfect. In a short passage which I collated I found more variations omitted than there were verses.

*7. Parham 125 (no. 13, p. 29, printed Catalogue), small 4to, paper, in a very neat hand, with illuminations, Copt. Arab. It contains the Pauline Epistles, Catholic Epistles, and Acts.

In the National Library at Paris:

*8. Copt. 17, fol., paper, Copt. Arab., described in the Catalogue as 'antiquus et elegantissime scriptus.' It contains the fourteen Pauline Epistles. Is this the MS. collated by Boetticher for these Epistles and designated *p* by him?

*9. Copt. 63, small fol., paper. 'Emta per me Bernardum de Montfaucon Venetiis anno 1698, 11 Augusti.' It contains the fourteen Pauline Epistles, and is dated at the end ⲁⲧⲟⲋ, i.e. 1376 = A.D. 1660.

*10. Copt. 64, fol., paper, Copt. Arab. 'Manuscrit de la Bibliothèque de Saumaise acquis par l'abbé Sallier pour le B. R. en 1752.' It contains the fourteen Pauline Epistles.

*11. Copt. 66, 4to, paper, with occasional Arabic notes in the margin. It belonged to the Coislin library, and previously to the Seguerian. It contains the Catholic Epistles and Acts. The date of its completion is given at the end as 1325, i. e. A. D. 1609. A collation of this MS. was used by Boetticher for his edition, and is designated *p* by him.

*12. Copt. 65, fol., paper. 'Emta Venetiis per me Fr. I. Bernardum de Montfaucon anno 1698, 2 Augusti.' This volume contains the Apocalypse, Catholic Epistles, and Acts. It consists of two parts, ff. 1–32 containing the Apocalypse, and ff. 33–102 containing the Catholic Epistles and Acts. The two parts are written on different paper, and apparently in different hands. At the end of the Apocalypse the date is given 1376 = A. D. 1660. At the end of the Acts also the same date 1376 is given, and the scribe there mentions his name ⲓⲱⲁⲛⲛⲓⲡⲣⲉⲥⲃⲩⲧⲉⲣⲟⲥ. Boetticher collated this MS. for his edition and designates it *m*.

In the Royal Library at Berlin:

13. Orient. 615, fol., Copt. Arab., containing the Epistles to the Colossians, Thessalonians, Philemon, Hebrews, Timothy, Titus.

14. Orient. 116, fol., Copt. Arab., containing the Epistles to the Romans and Corinthians.

15. Orient. 169, 4to. A transcript of the Epistles to the Ephesians and Philippians in Coptic, made by Petraeus at Leyden in 1660.

These three were collated by Boetticher, from whom I have extracted this meagre account, which is all that he gives. He designates them *b*.

In the Vatican:

16. Copt. 12 (I. B. Raymund ii), fol., paper, Copt. Arab. The Pauline Epistles, Catholic Epistles, and Acts; ascribed by Assemani to the fourteenth century. In this MS. the Epistle to the Hebrews stands after the Epistle to Philemon, thus departing from the usual Bohairic order, as above, no. 6. *See* Mai, Coll. Vet. Script., v. 2, p. 125 sq.

17. Copt. 13 (I. B. Raymund iii), fol., paper, Copt. Arab., ascribed by Assemani to the thirteenth century. The fourteen Pauline Epistles. *See* Mai, *l. c.*, p. 127 sq.

18. Copt. 14 (I. B. Raymund v), 4to, paper, Copt. Arab., containing the Pauline Epistles, Catholic Epistles, and Acts. It was written by Michael the monk of the city of Bembge in the year 1074 (i.e. A.D. 1358), except the last leaf, which was supplied in 1220 (i. e. A.D. 1504). *See* Mai, *l. c.*, p. 128 sq.

C. *The Apocalypse.*

In England:

*1. Bodleian, Hunt. 43, already described under Epistles 1.

*2. Library of Lord Crawford and Balcarres. A very small folio, paper, with illuminations, Copt. Arab. ϯⲁⲡⲟⲕⲁⲗⲩⲙⲯⲓⲥ ⲛ̀ⲧⲉ ⲓⲱⲁⲛⲛⲏⲥ. The Apocalypse itself is followed by 'The Benediction which is read before the Holy Apocalypse.' The date 1091 (i. e. A. D. 1375) is given at the end of the Apocalypse, where also the scribe mentions his name Peter. On a later page he describes himself as a monk and presbyter. There are corrections in the margin of the Apocalypse, some in red, others in black ink. Some of these contain various readings, e. g. x. 11 ⲡⲉϫⲱⲟⲩ λέγουσι for ⲡⲉϫⲁϥ λέγει. This MS. once belonged to Tattam.

*3. Parham 123 (no. 15, p. 29 in the printed Catalogue). Small fol., paper, rudely written in a recent hand. Copt. Arab. It contains the Apocalypse, followed by the 'Book of the Holy Benediction, &c.' The scribe, who has evidently a very indifferent knowlege of Coptic, gives his name as Matthew the son of Abraham, and states that the work was finished ϧⲉⲛϯⲣⲟⲙⲡⲓⲛ̀ϣⲟⲣ̅ⲉ̅ⲛ̅ⲛ̅ⲓⲙⲁⲣⲧⲩⲣⲟⲥⲉ̅ⲑ̅ⲩ̅. This ought to be the year 1105 of the Martyrs (=A. D. 1389); but the MS. must be later than this date. The colophon itself is perhaps copied from an earlier MS.

*4. Parham 124 (no. 16, p. 29 in the printed Catalogue). A large 12mo, paper, Copt. Arab. It contains about fifteen lines in a page, and about eleven letters in a line. Two or three pages towards the beginning are in a later hand. The date is given at the end, A. Mart. 1037 = A. D. 1321. This Apocalypse is not Sahidic, as described in the printed Catalogue, but Bohairic.

At Paris:

*5. Copt. 65, already described under Epistles 11.

*6. Copt. 91, 8vo, paper, Copt. Arab., containing the Apocalypse alone, ϯⲁⲡⲟⲕⲁⲗⲩⲙⲯⲓⲥ ⲛ̀ⲧⲉ ⲓⲱⲁⲛⲛⲏⲥ ⲡⲓⲉⲩⲁⲅⲅⲉⲗⲓⲥⲧⲏⲥ. It is dated at the end 1117 (?=A. D. 1401).

In the printed Catalogue *Copt. 34 (Delamare 581, Reg. 342. 3) is also stated to contain 'Apocalypsis e Graeca lingua in Copticam conversa,' but there seems to be some mistake about this.

At Rome:

*7. Anglican Library, C. i. 9. The Apocalypse in Copt. Arab. ϯⲁⲡⲟⲕⲁ̀ⲗⲩⲯⲓⲥ ⲛ̀ⲧⲉ ⲓ̅ⲱ̅ⲁ̅ ⲡⲓⲉⲩⲁⲅⲅⲉⲗⲓⲥⲧⲏⲥ ⲟⲩⲟϩ ⲁⲡⲟⲥⲧⲟⲗⲟⲥ, &c., said to belong to the fifteenth century.

8. Library of the Propaganda, large 8vo, paper, in a modern hand. Copt. Arab. The Apocalypse somewhat mutilated. It contains i. 12—ii. 26, and iii. 9—xxii. 12. It is briefly described among the Borgian MSS. by Zoega, p. 3.

9. Vatican, Copt. 15, fol., paper, Copt. Arab. The Apocalypse followed by 'Ordo dominicae palmarum' (fol. 59). Referred by Assemani to the fourteenth century. *See* Mai, Coll. Vet. Script., v. 2, p. 130.

10. Vatican, Copt. 16 (I. B. Raymund, no. xi), 4to, paper, Copt.

Arab. The Apocalypse, followed by a Benedictio. It was written by one John son of Abul-Menna in 1061 (i.e. A.D. 1345). The scribe prays 'omnes amicos suos sinceros ... ut castigent atque corrigant errata illius pro sua prudentia, quoniam ausus sum fungi munere mihi ignoto.' *See* Mai, *l.c.*, p. 130 sq.[1]

Besides these MSS. of different parts of the New Testament there is also a considerable number of Bohairic Lectionaries in the different libraries of Europe.

From this account of the MSS. it appears that, with the single exception of the Apocalypse, the Bohairic New Testament, as far back as we can trace its history, contained all the books of our present Canon. Nor have I noticed any phenomena in the language of the several books, which point to any want of uniformity or separation of date; though it is possible that a more thorough investigation and a more complete mastery of the language might reveal such. It seems clear, however, that the Apocalypse had not a place among the Canonical books. In the majority of cases it is contained in a separate MS. In the exceptions which I have investigated, where it is bound up with other books (the MSS. numbered 1, 12, of the Epistles and Acts), it is distinguished from them in some marked way; and probably this will be found to be the case with any which have not yet been examined. In short, there is not a single authenticated case of a MS. in which it is treated as of equal authority with the other Canonical books. Moreover in Copto-Arabic vocabularies it is omitted from its proper place at the end of the New Testament, all the other books being taken in order. This depreciation of the Apocalypse may perhaps be taken as indicating the date of the completion or codification of the Bohairic version. The earlier Alexandrian writers, Clement and Origen, in the first decades of the third century, quote the Apocalypse without hesitation as the work of St. John. The later Alexandrian Church also from the close of the third century onward seems to have had no doubt about its Apostolic authority (*see* Westcott, Canon, p. 321). But about the middle of the third century doubts were entertained respecting its authorship, to which expression was given by Dionysius of Alexandria (flor. A.D. 233–265), though even

[1] The above account has been throughout revised by the Rev. G. Horner, who has collated or examined all MSS. of the Bohairic versions in European libraries.

Dionysius did not deny its canonicity. The difficulty, however, may have been powerful enough to cause its exclusion from the Egyptian Canon.

The order of the several parts of the New Testament in the MSS. is (1) Gospels, (2) Pauline Epistles, (3) Catholic Epistles, (4) Acts. The Gospels occur in their common order. It is remarkable, however, that in the vocabularies St. John frequently stands first, so that we get the order, John, Matthew, Mark, Luke, which (with the doubtful exception of the Sahidic) is unique. Of this, however, there is no trace in the MSS.; and, as some of these must carry the tradition further back than the vocabularies, the arrangement is perhaps to be explained in some other way. The Pauline Epistles include the Hebrews, which is placed after 1, 2 Thessalonians and before 1, 2 Timothy[1], as in the Greek MSS. ℵABC, &c. (see p. 71). This accords with the general opinion of the Alexandrian school, which regarded this Epistle as the work of St. Paul (*see* Westcott, Canon, p. 323 sq.). In other respects the familiar order is observed in the Pauline Epistles, as is also the case with the Catholic Epistles[2].

The Bohairic version is for the most part a faithful rendering of the original, and the Egyptian language which by this time had borrowed largely from the Greek vocabulary is fairly adequate for the purpose. This version therefore may generally be consulted even for minute variations in the text. The connecting particles are commonly observed; and as the language has both definite and indefinite articles, it may be employed, though with some caution, by the textual critic where other versions fail him. In one point, however, it is quite useless. When the question lies between a participle and a finite verb in the construction of a sentence, the looseness of the Egyptian syntax will seldom afford any clue to the reading which the translator had before him. Perhaps the weakest point in the language is the absence of a passive voice, for which the third person plural active, used impersonally, acts as a substitute. This produces strange awkwardnesses of expression. Thus John i. 6 *ἀπεσταλμένος παρὰ Θεοῦ* is rendered 'whom they sent from God,' ⲉ̀ ⲁⲩⲟⲩⲟⲣⲡϥ ⲉⲃⲟⲗϩⲓⲧⲉⲛ ⲫϯ, and i. 17

[1] The MSS. 7 and 16 are exceptions.

[2] No weight can be given to the abnormal order in no. 12, until we know something more of this MS., which is perhaps a late transcript.

ὁ νόμος διὰ Μωυσέως ἐδόθη 'The law they gave it by Moses,' ⲡⲓ ⲛⲟⲙⲟⲥ ⲁⲩⲧⲏⲓϥ ⲉⲃⲟⲗϩⲓⲧⲉⲛ ⲙⲱⲩⲥⲏⲥ. Another grave defect is the want of a word corresponding to the simple meaning of *ἔχειν*, which has to be rendered by various expedients according to the context.

To the adoption of Greek words there seems to be hardly any limit but the caprice of the translator. Already in the demotic writing we find a few of these foreign intruders naturalized; but in the Coptic, as used for ecclesiastical purposes, they occur in the greatest profusion. Very frequently their adoption cannot be explained by any exigencies of translation. Thus for instance the translator will sometimes render one Greek word by another, e.g. John xiii. 5, *νιπτήρ* by *λακάνη* or *λεκάνη*; Acts xix. 40, *ἐγκαλεῖν* by *κατηγορεῖν*; xxviii. 17, *ἔθος* by *συνήθεια.* Thus again he will diversify the rendering in the same passage, using indifferently the Greek and the Egyptian word for the same original, e.g. ϭⲱⲛⲧ and ⲡⲓⲣⲁⲍⲓⲛ (*πειράζειν*), Matt. iv. 1, 3; ϫⲣⲟϫ and ⲥⲡⲉⲣⲙⲁ, John viii. 33, 37; ⲡⲟⲩⲣⲟ and ⲕⲉⲥⲁⲣ (*Καῖσαρ*), John xix. 12, 15; ⲓϧ and ⲇⲉⲙⲱⲛ (*δαιμόνιον*), Matt. viii. 16, 28, 33. And again and again Greek words are used, where common Egyptian equivalents were ready to hand. The conjunctions *ἀλλά, δέ, γάρ, οὖν*, were doubtless needed to supply a want in the Egyptian language, which, like the Hebrew and Aramaic, was singularly deficient in connecting-particles; but we should hardly have looked for such combinations as *ὅμως μέντοι, πόσῳ μᾶλλον, μήτι, οὐ γάρ, οὐχ ὅτι, ὅτι μὲν γάρ, καί γε, καίτοι, οὐ μόνον δέ, ἐφ' ὅσον, πῶς οὖν, ἵνα κἄν, ἵνα μήπως, μενοῦνγε*, and the like. Nor should we expect to find Greek terms introduced with such reckless prodigality as in the following sentences: John xviii. 3, ⲛⲉⲙ ϩⲁⲛⲫⲁⲛⲟⲥ ⲛⲉⲙ ϩⲁⲛ ⲗⲁⲙⲡⲁⲥ ⲛⲉⲙ ϩⲁⲛ ϩⲟⲡⲗⲟⲛ; Acts xxiii. 8, ⲙ̀ⲙⲟⲛ ⲁⲛⲁⲥⲧⲁⲥⲓⲥ ⲟⲩⲇⲉ ⲁⲅⲅⲉⲗⲟⲥ ⲟⲩⲇⲉ ⲡⲛⲉⲩⲙⲁ; Acts xxvii. 12, ⲕⲁⲧⲁⲛⲧⲁⲛ ⲉ̀ ⲫⲟⲓⲛⲓⲝ ⲉ̀ ⲉⲣ ⲡⲁⲣⲁⲭⲓⲙⲁⲍⲓⲛ ϧⲉⲛ ⲟⲩ ⲗⲩⲙⲏⲛ; Rom. vi. 13, ⲛⲉⲧⲉⲛ ⲙⲉⲗⲟⲥ ⲛ̀ ϩⲟⲗⲡⲟⲛ ⲛ̀ⲧⲉ ϯ ⲁⲇⲓⲕⲓⲁ.

[No definite discussion on the history or critical value of the Bohairic version is possible until the edition which is being prepared by the Rev. G. Horner is published; based as it is on a collation of all known MSS.

An opinion which at present seems to prevail largely among

scholars is that of Stern (Z. A. S. 20, 1882, p. 202), who dates it to the fourth or fifth century, and ascribes it to the literary activity of the monks of the Natron Lakes. He has further suggested that it and the Sahidic may both be derived from, or at any rate connected with, the Akhmîm version (Z. A. S. 24, 1886, p. 134).

The last statement may be definitely dismissed; it is based upon a single sentence quoted from an apocryphal book of the Old Testament, and is definitely disproved in the case of the New Testament by a comparison of the two versions. They are not only different translations, but are based on a different Greek text. The first statement is apparently based upon language, and has undoubtedly an element of truth in it. The language of the version as we have it was probably revised and corrected, and reduced to a fixed orthography and a more definite form, but even here it is not possible to speak quite positively, and we know that there are considerable variations in orthography preserved in some of the MSS. which may represent the tradition of different monasteries. But, granting this, it does not by any means follow that there was not a Bohairic dialect and a Bohairic version at an earlier date, which is closely represented by this, as the Akhmim version was represented by the Sahidic, as regards the Greek text implied. In favour of an early version in the dialect of Lower Egypt is first the *a priori* argument of the probability of Christianity spreading earliest in the Delta. We know that by the middle of the third century it had spread among the native population of Alexandria (Dion. Al. ap. Eus. 'H. E.' vi. 41), and probably had done so in the second century. If Greek had spread so little in the Delta in the fourth or fifth century as to make a Bohairic version necessary, it is not likely to have been more widely prevalent in the third. On these grounds then we should naturally expect Christianity to spread earliest among the native populations of the districts round Alexandria, and also that the New Testament or a portion of it would be translated very early into their language. Nor again does there seem any evidence for deriving the Bohairic dialect from the Akhmimish. It is true that the latter represents the language of Egypt in an earlier form, but it is not an earlier form of Bohairic.

To these *a priori* and negative considerations must be added the positive argument of Krall (Mitt. i. p. 111). He appears to have discovered earlier forms of the Bohairic dialect, and in addition points out that some of the commonest abbreviations in Coptic MSS. could only have been derived from the Bohairic, which seems to show that it was for Bohairic that the alphabet was first used. And this in the New Testament at any rate is supported by the text of the version. A study of this has shown that in the form in which we possess it in most printed editions and late MSS., although as a whole its agreement with the oldest Greek MSS. is undoubted, it contains a considerable number of later additions which agree with the traditional text. But, as Bishop Lightfoot showed, these clearly formed no part of the original Bohairic version, and subsequent investigation has made it clear that the evidence in favour of this statement is even stronger than he represented it (*see* Sanday, Appendices ad Novum Testamentum, App. III. p. 182 sq.). The original Bohairic text then represents a very pure tradition, untouched by the so-called Western additions which are found in the Sahidic version, and it is difficult to believe that a version so singularly free from these should be later than the Sahidic. Christianity spread in the Thebaid certainly as early as the beginning of the third century (Eus. 'H. E.' vi. 1), and that century is the period to which internal evidence would assign the origin of the Sahidic version. An even earlier date is probably demanded both for the extension of Christianity in the Delta and for the text of the Bohairic version.]

(3) *The Sahidic (or Thebaic) Version.*

The Sahidic version did not attract attention till a comparatively late date. When Wilkins published what was then called the Coptic New Testament, he mentioned having found among the Oxford MSS. two which he described as 'lingua plane a reliquis MSS. Copticis, quae unquam vidi, diversa' (Praef. p. vii). These are written in the Thebaic or Sahidic dialect, of which as we may infer from his language, he did not even know the existence. After no long time, however, we find La Croze and Jablonski, with other Egyptian scholars, turning their attention to the dialect of Upper Egypt: and at length in 1778, C. G. Woide issued a prospectus in which he announced his intention of publishing from Oxford MSS. the fragments of the New Testament 'juxta interpretationem dialecti Superioris Aegypti, quae Thebaidica seu Sahidica appellatur.' In the same year he gave to the world some various readings of this version in J. A. Cramer's 'Beyträge zur Beförderung theologischer und andrer wichtigen Kenntnisse,' Pt. iii, Kiel u. Hamburg, 1778. But before Woide's work appeared he was partially anticipated by other labourers in the same field.

In the same year 1778 appeared a grammar of the two Egyptian dialects by Raphael Tuki, Roman Bishop of Arsinoe, with the title 'Rudimenta Linguae Coptae sive Aegyptiacae ad usum Collegii Urbani de Propaganda Fide, Romae.' It contains profuse quotations from the Sahidic version of the Old and New Testaments. This work, which preserves a large number of passages not to be found elsewhere, has been strangely neglected by textual critics[1]. Caution, however, must be observed in the use of it, as the passages are apparently obtained, at least in many instances, not directly from MSS. of the version itself, but through the medium of Arabo-Egyptian grammars and vocabularies; nor is Tuki's work generally at all accurate or critical[2].

In 1785, J. A. Mingarelli published two fasciculi of an account of the Egyptian MSS. in the Nanian Library under the title 'Aegyptiorum codicum reliquiae Venetiis in Bibliotheca Naniana asservatae, Bononiae.' In these he printed at length two portions of the Sahidic New Testament, Matt. xviii. 27—xxi. 15, and John ix. 17—xiii. 1.

In 1789, A. A. Giorgi (Georgius), an Augustinian eremite, brought out a work entitled 'Fragmentum Evangelii S. Joannis Graeco-Copto-Thebaicum Saeculi iv. &c., Romae.' This volume contains John vi. 21–58, and vi. 68—viii. 23, introduced by an elaborate preface and followed by other matter. The MS. from which they are taken belonged to the Borgian collection at Velletri, and has been described already among the Greek MSS., p. 141 sq. It is ascribed to the fourth or fifth century.

[1] It is used in the Apocalypse by Tregelles, and apparently also by Tischendorf in his eighth edition; and in the Rev. S. C. Malan's 'Gospel according to St. John, translated from the Eleven Oldest Versions except the Latin,' London, 1862, all Tuki's Sahidic fragments of this Evangelist are included.

[2] *See* Münter, De Indole, &c., Praef., p. iv. Schwartze (Quat. Evang. p. xx) says, 'Praeterquam quod sicut omnes Tukii libri scatent vitiis, etiam angustioris sunt fidei *Rudimenta*, Sahidicis locis partim e versione Arabica a Tukio concinnatis.' I do not know on what grounds Schwartze makes this last statement.

In the same year, 1789, additional fragments of this version from other Borgian MSS. were published by F. C. C. H. Münter in a volume bearing the title, 'Commentatio de Indole Versionis Novi Testamenti Sahidicae. Accedunt Fragmenta Epistolarum Pauli ad Timotheum ex membranis Sahidicis Musei Borgiani Velitris. Hafniae.' The fragments referred to are 1 Tim. i. 14—iii. 16; vi. 4–21; 2 Tim. i. 1–16. Münter gives also some various readings of this version in different parts of the four Gospels, taken likewise from the Borgian MSS.

Lastly; in 1790 Mingarelli published a third fasciculus of his work on the Egyptian MSS. in the Nanian Library, and in it he printed another important fragment of this version, Mark xi. 29—xv. 32. This third part is very rarely met with, and I have not seen a copy.

Meanwhile Woide was busily engaged on his edition, and had already advanced far when his labours were interrupted by death in May, 1790. His papers were placed in the hands of H. Ford, Professor of Arabic at Oxford, who after several years completed the work. It was published with the title, 'Appendix ad Editionem Novi Testamenti Graeci e Codice MS. Alexandrino a C. G. Woide descripti, in qua continentur Fragmenta Novi Testamenti juxta interpretationem Dialecti Superioris Aegypti quae Thebaidica vel Sahidica appellatur, &c. Oxoniae, 1799.' Woide's materials were:

1. Several MSS. of the Huntington collection in the Bodleian. These consist of (*a*) Two folio lectionaries on paper (Hunt. 3, Hunt. 5); (*b*) A folio likewise on paper, containing fragments of St. John's Gospel (Hunt. 4); (*c*) An 8vo, containing fragments of the Acts and Catholic Epistles (Hunt. 394). Woide gives as the date A. Mart. 1041, and A.D. 1315, 'si recte conjicio,' but the two are not reconcileable; (*d*) A 4to on paper (Hunt. 393), written A. Mart. 1109 (i.e. A.D. 1393) and containing 'De Mysterio literarum Graecarum Discursus Gnostici,' the work of one Seba an anchorite (*see* Ford's 'Praef.,' p. vi. sq., and p. [21], note *a*).

2. A very ancient papyrus belonging to the famous traveller Bruce, who had brought it from Upper Egypt. It contains two Gnostic works, in which are quoted passages from the Old and New Testaments. It is now in the Bodleian [1].

[1] This has now been published. By Amélineau, Notice sur le Papyrus Gnostique Bruce. Texte et Traduction, Notices et Extraits de la Bibliothèque

3. An ancient vellum MS. containing the Gnostic treatise 'Pistis Sophia,' then belonging to Askew and now in the British Museum. It quotes some passages of the Old and New Testaments. The 'Pistis Sophia' has been since transcribed by Schwartze, and published from his papers by Petermann after his death (1853).

4. Several fragments belonging to Woide himself, having been transmitted to him from Upper Egypt while he was employed on the work. Some are Sahidic; others Graeco-Sahidic. These formed a highly important accession to his materials. They now belong to the Clarendon Press at Oxford, and are deposited in the Bodleian.

One of these, a Graeco-Sahidic MS., said to belong to the fourth or fifth century, has been already described (Evan. T). But I am unable to assent to the opinion which is maintained by Tregelles and Tischendorf, and in which Dr. Scrivener there acquiesces, that these Woidian fragments (T^{s} or T^{woi}) were originally part of the same MS. with the Borgian Graeco-Sahidic fragments (T) published by Giorgi. And this for two reasons. (1) The paging of the two sets of fragments is quite inconsistent. The Woidian fragments, Luke xii. 5 (Sahid. Gr. 15)—xiii. 23 (Sahid. Gr. 32) and John viii. 22–32, are paged ⲩⲛⲑ—ⲩⲡⲇ (459–484) and ⲭⲛⲍ, ⲭⲛⲏ (657, 658) respectively (*see* Ford's 'Praef.,' p. [24]). On the other hand the pages of the Borgian fragments, Luke xxii. 12—xxiii. 11; John vi. 21–58; vi. 68—viii. 23, are numbered ⲥⲗⲑ—ⲥⲛⲇ (239–254), ⲧⲗⲇ—ⲧⲙⲅ, ⲧⲙⲋ—ⲧⲝⲁ (334–343, 346–361) respectively (*see* Zoega, p. 184; Georgius, p. 11 sq.). (2) Though the last Woidian fragment begins *somewhere about* where the last Borgian fragment ends, it does not begin at exactly the same place. The Borgian fragment ends ⲁⲛⲅ̄ ⲁⲛⲟⲕ ⲟⲩ ⲉⲃⲟⲗϩⲛ̄ ⲧⲡⲉ ⲛ̄ⲧⲱⲧⲛ̄ ⲛ̄ⲧⲉ (ἐγὼ ἐκ τῶν ἄνω εἰμί· ὑμεῖς), viii. 23; the Woidian fragment begins ⲉ ϯⲛⲁⲃⲱⲕ ⲉⲣⲟϥ (ὅπου ἐγὼ ὑπάγω), viii. 22. Thus the two have several lines in common. For these reasons the later judgement of Tregelles, who pronounces them to be 'certainly parts of the *same* MS.' (Introductory notice to his G. T.), must be abandoned; and we must revert to his earlier and more cautious opinion in which he describes the Woidian fragment as 'a portion of a MS. almost a counterpart of T' (Horne's 'Introduction,' p. 180).

Nationale et autres Bibliothèques. Tome xxix. 1re Partie. Paris, 1891; and Gnostische Schriften in Koptischer Sprache aus dem Codex Brucianus, von Carl Schmidt, Leipzig, 1892.

5. A Sahidic vocabulary in the Royal Library at Paris (Copt. 44), containing several passages from the Sahidic Bible.

6. A few fragments communicated by Adler from the collection of Card. Borgia at Velletri. Besides these Woide incorporated the fragments published by Mingarelli in his first two fasciculi. The works of Giorgi and Münter, however, and the third fasciculus of Mingarelli, were overlooked by him or by his successor Ford.

Besides elaborate prefaces by Ford and Woide this work gives a Latin translation in parallel columns with the Sahidic. It would not be difficult to point out numerous errors in the execution of this volume; but all allowance must be made for a posthumous work completed by a second editor who had to educate himself for the task, and the heavy obligation under which Woide and Ford have laid Biblical scholars may well silence ill-natured criticism[1].

Some years later appeared a highly important contribution to Sahidic literature in G. Zoega's 'Catalogus Codicum Copticorum manuscriptorum qui in Museo Borgiano Velitris adservantur, Romae, 1810,' a posthumous work. The compiler of this catalogue prints at length Eph. v. 21–33; Apoc. xix. 7–18; xx. 7—xxi. 3, and gives besides (p. 200) a full list of the fragments of the Sahidic version, which are found in this rich collection of Egyptian MSS. These would go far towards filling up the gaps in Woide's edition. Thus, for instance, they contain about three-quarters of St. Mark's Gospel, the whole of the Epistle to the Ephesians, and the whole of the Epistle to the Philippians with the exception of five or six verses at the beginning.

In the following year (1811) appeared Engelbreth's work on the Bashmuric version, which has been mentioned above (p. 102). In it he printed, for the sake of comparison with the Bashmuric, the following passages of the Sahidic version: 1 Cor. i. 1–16; xv. 5–33; Phil. i. 7–23; 1 Thess. i. 4—iii. 5; Heb. vii. 11–13; 16–21; ix. 2–10; 24–28; x. 5–10. These were derived wholly

[1] In the interval between Woide and Zoega, Griesbach (1806) appears to have obtained a few readings of this version from the Borgian MSS., e.g. Acts xxiv. 22, 23; xxv. 6; xxvii. 14; Col. ii. 2. At least I have not succeeded in tracing them to any printed source of information.

Of the use which Schwartze has made of the published portions of the Sahidic text in his edition of the Bohairic Gospels, I have already spoken (p. 108). He has added no unpublished materials.

from the Borgian MSS., with the exception of a few verses taken from Woide's book. Beyond this meagre contribution of Engelbreth's, nothing has been done during more than sixty years which have elapsed since the appearance of Zoega's work towards the publication of these valuable remains, important alike for the knowledge of the Egyptian language and for purposes of Biblical criticism. A complete collection of all the fragments of the Sahidic New Testament is now the most pressing want in the province of textual criticism.

The materials for such an edition are the following:

1. The MSS. used by Woide and Ford, which however will require collating afresh.

2. The Nanian fragments published by Mingarelli. The MSS. which he used are said to have disappeared.

3. The MSS. of the Borgian collection, as indicated in the catalogue of Zoega. After the dispersion of the museum at Velletri the Biblical MSS. found their way to the Library of the Propaganda at Rome, where they now are.

4. The quotations in Tuki, though for reasons already stated these must be used with caution. They should be traced, if possible, to their sources.

To these known materials the following, which (so far as I am aware), have never been publicly noticed, must be added:

1. *British Museum, Papyrus xiii, four leaves or eight pages numbered ϭⲙⲁ–ϭⲙⲏ, containing John xx. 1–29 mutilated. It does not differ in any important respects from the text printed by Woide, but I noticed the following variations: ver. 3, *Σίμων Πέτρος*; ver. 8, add *οὖν* after *τότε*; ver. 10, om. *οἱ μαθηταί*; ver. 12, ins. *καὶ* before *θεωρεῖ*; ver. 17, om. *δὲ* after *πορεύου*; ver. 18, om. *δέ* after *ἔρχεται*; ver. 21, *εἶπεν οὖν* for *εἶπεν δέ*; ib. add [*ὁ*] *Ἰησοῦς* after *αὐτοῖς*; ver. 28, add *αὐτῷ* after *ἀπεκρίθη*.

2. *Paris, Copt. 102. Thebaic fragments of various ages, some very old. Those from the New Testament are (*a*) Luke iii. 21—iv. 9; (*b*) John xvii. 17–26, Theb. Arab., paper; (*c*) Acts vii. 51—viii. 3, vellum; (*d*) Apoc. i. 13—ii. 2, vellum. The pages of this last fragment are marked ⲉ–ⲏ.

3. Crawford and Balcarres collection. Several very important Sahidic fragments which formerly belonged to Archdeacon Tattam. These are:

*i. Mark ix. 18—xiv. 26, vellum, six leaves, the pages numbered ⲓⲑ–ⲗ, two columns in a page, and thirty-nine or forty lines in a column. I observed the following readings: ix. 24, om. *μετὰ δακρύων*; 44, 46, om. *ὅπου ὁ σκώληξ κ.τ.λ.*; 50, om. *καὶ πᾶσα θυσία ἁλὶ ἁλισθήσεται*; xi. 26, omitted; xiii. 14, om. *τὸ ῥηθὲν ὑπὸ Δανιὴλ τοῦ προφήτου*; xiv. 22, om. *φάγετε*; 24 has *καινῆς*.

*ii. Luke iii. 8—vi. 37, vellum, two columns in a page, thirty-five lines in a column. A very beautiful MS. The Ammonian Sections and Eusebian Canons are given, and also the *τίτλοι*. There is occasionally a rough concordance in the margin; e.g. on Luke v. 18, ⲓ̅ⲅ̅ ⲉⲧⲃⲉⲡⲉⲧⲥⲏϭ. ⲓⲱ ⲍ̅. ⲙⲑ ⲓ̅ⲅ̅. ⲙⲣ. ⲉ̅, where St. John stands first. I noted down the following readings: iii. 19, om. *Φιλίππου*; 27, *Ἰωανάν*; 30, *Ἰωανάμ*; 32, *Ἰωβήδ*; 32, ⲥⲁⲗⲁ for *Σαλμών*, just as in ver. 35; iv. 26, *Σιδωνίας*; 41, om. *ὁ Χριστός*; ver. 38, om. *καὶ ἀμφότεροι συντηροῦνται*. In vi. 16 *Ἰούδαν Ἰακώβου* is translated 'Judas the son of James.'

*iii. Luke xvii. 18—xix. 30, vellum, two columns in a page, twenty-seven lines in a column, five leaves, paged ⲣⲁ to ⲣⲓ (sic). No sections are marked. It has these readings: xvii. 24, om. *ἐν τῇ ἡμέρᾳ αὐτοῦ*; xviii. 28, *τὰ ἴδια*; xix. 5, om. *εἶδεν αὐτὸν καί*.

*iv. Gal. i. 14—vi. 16, fol., vellum, eight leaves, two columns in a page, twenty-nine lines in a column, the pages marked *ρπθ* onward. It has these readings: i. 15, *ὁ θεός*; ii. 5, *οἷς οὐδέ*; ii. 20, *τοῦ υἱοῦ τοῦ θεοῦ*; iii. 1, om. *τῇ ἀληθείᾳ μὴ πείθεσθαι*; iii. 17, om. *εἰς χριστόν*; iv. 7, *κληρονόμος διὰ* [*τοῦ*] *χριστοῦ*; iv. 14, *τὸν πειρασμόν μου τὸν ἐν κ.τ.λ.*; 15, *ποῦ*; v. 1, *στήκετε οὖν*.

Of these four fragments ii and iv are the most ancient; while i and iii are much later, but still old. Beyond this I do not venture to hazard an opinion as to their date, remembering that Zoega with all his knowledge and experience declines to pronounce on the age of undated Egyptian MSS.[1]

4*. A fragment (a single leaf) of a Graeco-Sahidic lectionary in double columns, belonging to the Rev. G. Horner, who brought it from Upper Egypt in 1873 [ix], $12\frac{1}{4} \times 11$. The Greek and Sahidic are not in opposite columns, but the Greek is followed by the Sahidic. The Greek is Matt. iv. 2–11 *τεσσεράκοντα καὶ τεσσεράκοντα νύκτας . . . διηκόνουν αὐτῷ*; the Sahidic is iv. 1–6 *Τότε . . . ἐπὶ χειρῶν ἀροῦσί σε*. The Coptic character resembles classes v and vi in Zoega. The Greek text has been already numbered as Evst. 299. This has now been presented to the Bodleian by Mr. Horner, MS. Gr. Lit. c. 1.

[Since the above was written, very considerable additions have been made to our knowledge of the Sahidic version.

1. The Biblical MSS. of the Borgian collection preserved in the Library of the Propaganda have been published by M. Amélineau. The Old Testament in the Recueil des Travaux, the New Testament in the 'Zeitschrift für Aegyptische Sprache,' 24 (1886), pp. 41, 103; 25 (1887), pp. 47, 100, 125; 26 (1888), p. 96. This publication was made under

[1] Catal., p. 169: Si de aetate codicum quaeris, scio equidem non defuisse qui singulos ad saecula sua referre satagerent, qui si aliquid profecerunt, ego sane non obstrepo. Sed quoniam meum sit quacumque in re ignorantiam fateri potius quam quae mihi non satisfaciunt, aliis velut explorata offerre, &c.' But since this was written the publication of Hyvernat's 'Album de Paléographie Copte' has given much assistance; and more may be looked for from the publication of the Paris fragments.

considerable disadvantages. M. Amélineau had not the opportunity of seeing the MSS. himself, and merely published a transcript supplied him by the Coptic Archbishop Bschai, then resident in Rome. Moreover he gives no critical notes on various readings in cases where there is more than one copy extant of any passage. Nor again does he edit the fragments completely, but only such portions of the New Testament as were not previously known. His edition therefore is not without inaccuracies, which have been noticed by Ciasca, vol. ii. pp. lix–lxxvii. These defects are, however, being remedied by an edition of all these fragments by Father Ciasca (known as the editor of the Arabic Diatessaron), which is very complete. The first two volumes, containing the Old Testament with many facsimiles, have appeared: the New Testament portion is to follow. (Sacrorum Bibliorum Fragmenta Copto-Sahidica Musei Borgiani iussu et sumptibus S. Congregationis de Propaganda Fide Studio P. Augustini Ciasca. Romae. Typis eiusdem S. Congregationis. Vol. i. 1885; Vol. ii. 1889.)

2. The Crawford and Balcarres fragments mentioned above have also been edited by M. Amélineau in the Recueil des Travaux, v. (1883), p. 105.

3. To O. von Lemm we owe a considerable number of fragments. Bruchstücke der Sahidischen Bibelübersetzung nach Handschriften der kaiserlichen öffentlichen Bibliothek zu St. Petersburg. Leipzig, 1885. And Sieben Sahidische Bibel-Fragmente. Z. A. S. 23 (1885), p. 19.

4. Fragments, mostly smaller in extent, have been edited by the following:

Bouriant	Mémoires, i. 259.
„	Recueil, iv. 1.
Maspero	Recueil, vi. 35; vii. 47.
„	Études Égyptologiques, i. 3. Paris, 1883.
Ceugney	Recueil, ii. 94.
Krall	Mittheilungen, ii. 68.

5. But most important of all are the newly acquired fragments of the Bibliothèque Nationale at Paris. In 1883 that Library had the good fortune to obtain (largely through the influence of M. Amélineau) from the famous White Monastery or Deir Amba Shenoudah of Upper Egypt a large collection of Sahidic fragments. The publication of these has been begun. Considerable sections of the Old Testament have been published by Maspero (Mémoires, vol. vi), and of documents relating to Early Church History by Bouriant (ib. vol. viii). The New Testament fragments have not yet been published, but M. Amélineau, who is entrusted with them, has kindly put at my disposal the following list of contents. I have omitted smaller Fragments:

Matthew (167 leaves): i. 1–20; i. 17—ii. 4; i. 1–22; ii. 4, 5, 8, 11, 14, 15; iii. 1–11; 1–15; iii. 10—iv. 13; iii. 22—iv. 11; iv. 3–19; 21—v. 15; iv. 15—v. 17; v. 17–32; 9–28; v. 25–vi. 3; vii. 6—viii. 4; vii. 8–27; x. 9–28; viii. 1–17; 2–20; ix. 13–33; ix. 25—x. 15;

ix. 33—x. 15; ix. 33—x. 19; ix. 26—x. 19; x. 39—xxviii. 54 (36 leaves); x. 20—xii. 3; xi. 3-10; xi. 15—xii. 16; xi. 16—xii. 4; xii. 6—xiv. 31; xii. 19-40; xiii. 19—xiv. 6; xiii. 22-25; xiii. 35-50; xiii. 41—xiv. 2; xiv. 8—xv. 4; xiv. 8—xv. 4; xiv. 17-35; xiv. 18—xv. 19; xiv. 20-35; xiv. 21—xv. 19; xiv. 24—xv. 11; xiv. 27—xv. 1; xiv. 31-54; xiv. 31—xv. 20; xv. 17—xvi. 19; xviii. 11-35; 15-21; xviii. 26—xix. 1; xix. 7-22; xix. 13—xx. 16; xix. 24—xx. 16; xx. 9-32; xxi. 8-12; 19-21; 12-37; 9-25; 22-33; xxi. 31—xxii. 5; xxi. 32-41; xxi. 38—xxii. 12; xxii. 22—xxiii. 12; xxiv. 7—xxvi. 64; xxiv. 2-42; xxiv. 35—xxv. 36; xxiv. 47—xxvi. 47; xxvi. 41-60; xxvi. 69—xxvii. 5; xxvi. 75—xxviii. 23; xxvii. 26-56; xxvii. 49—xxviii. 4; xxvii. 54—xxviii. 8. Also a fragment containing the last few verses and the beginning of St. Mark.

Mark (43 leaves): i. 1-17; 4-5; i. 30—ii. 1; iv. 1-8; iv. 32—v. 11; v. 30—vii. 36; v. 13-38; vi. 4—viii. 12; vii. 36—viii. 1; viii. 12-31; 23-38; x. 42—xi. 15; xi. 3-27; xi. 11—xiii. 14; xii. 12-35; xii. 31—xiii. 19; xiv. 6—xv. 2; xiv. 12—xv. 21; xiv. 20-40.

Luke (163 leaves): i. 1-26; 1-5; 26-61; 19-35; ii. 10-33; iii. 4—v. 8; iii. 29—iv. 20; iii. 36—iv. 47; iv. 22—viii. 14; iv. 43—v. 29; v. 10—viii. 7; vi. 35—ix. 16; vii. 1—ix. 5; vii. 7-15; vii. 37, 38; 41-45; viii. 2-12; 6-15; 4-37; 7-26; viii. 14—ix. 8; viii. 32-44; ix. 3-22; 9-21; ix. 51—x. 18; x. 39—xii. 37; xi. 23-34; 24-56, xii. 1-8, 36-48; xi. 28-44; xii. 3-12; 37-51; xii. 48—xiii. 10; xii. 53—xiii. 9; xiii. 1-16; xiii. 11-31; xiii. 15—xiv. 15; xiv. 2-20; xiv. 3—xv. 2; xiv. 21-32; xv. 17—xvii. 19; xvi. 18—xvii. 16; xvii. 10-24; xviii. 4—xix. 42; xviii. 21—xix. 22; xix. 3-28; xix. 28—xxi. 22; xix. 49—xx. 6; xxi. 22—xxii. 1; xxii. 11-27; xxii. 8—xxiv. 10; xxiii. 1-39; xxiv. 27-53.

Also the following bilingual (Greek and Sahidic) texts:

iii. 15, 16; x. 11-21; xi. 16-32; xvii. 29—xviii. 1; xviii. 32-42; xxi. 25-31; xxii. 66-xxiii. 17; and two leaves in Greek.

John (207 leaves). One MS. of 48 leaves, Luke iv. 38—v. 1; viii. 10-29; ix. 9-62; John i. 23—vii. 40; ix. 6-27; xix. 13-33; xx. 31—xxi. 17. i. 25-45; 25-36, ii. 7-18; i. 42—iii. 4; i. 43—ii. 11; i. 45—iv. 19; i. 67—ii. 24; ii. 11—iii. 25; ii. 24—iv. 22; iii. 4-10; 13-16; iii. 24—iv. 8; iv. 27-51; iv. 50—vii. 20; v. 24—vi. 5; vi. 12-35; 26-45; 30-41; vi. 62—vii. 17; vi. 65—vii. 10; vii. 20-39; vii. 31—x. 12; vii. 41—viii. 23; vii. 44—viii. 20; viii. 25-44; viii. 22—ix. 28; viii. 36-49; ix. 7—xi. 22; ix. 20-40; 27-39; xii. 4-18; x. 13-19; xi. 27-47; 34-48; 34-45; xi. 44—xii. 2; xii. 25-34; xiii. 7-27; 18-31; xiii. 19—xiv. 1; xiv. 21—xviii. 15; xv. 3—xvi. 15; xv. 6-26; xv. 22—xvi. 16; xvi. 1-23; xvi. 6-26; xvi. 22—xxii. 8; xvii. 14-23; xviii. 3-26; xviii. 5—xix. 40; xviii. 23—xix. 2; xviii. 33—xix. 19; xix. 18-26; xx. 8-18; 19-27; xxi. 2-14.

Also the following bilingual:

i. 19-23; ii. 2-9; iv. 5-13; 15-52; v. 12-21; xii. 36-46.

Acts: ii. 2-17; 18-40; ii. 34—iv. 6; viii. 32—ix. 15; viii. 35—ix. 22; ix. 27-40; x. 3-4; xii. 7—xiii. 5; xii. 23—xiii. 8; xiii.

10—xvi. 4; xiv. 4–22; xviii. 21—xix. 6; xxvii. 38—xxviii. 4; xxviii. 9–23.

ROMANS: i. 26—ii. 25; ii. 28—iii. 13; iii. 20—iv. 4; viii. 35—ix. 22; ix. 12—xi. 11; ix. 15—x. 1; ix. 24—xi. 30; xi. 30—xii. 15; xiv. 4–21; xv. 10–30.

1 COR.: i. 19—ii. 10; ii. 9—iv. 1; ii. 21—vi. 4; vii. 36—ix. 5; ix. 2—x. 7; ix. 12–25; x. 13—xi. 15; xvii. 41–45; xvii. 16–21.

2 COR.: xi. 1–20; xii. 21—xiii. 13 (with Heb. i. 14); xi. 33—xii. 14.

HEB.: ii. 14–20; iv. 7–14; v. 12—vi. 10; ix. 2–14; 20–23; x. 9–10; xii. 16—xiii. 9; xiii. 7–21; xiii. 10–25.

GAL.: i. 1—vi. 18 (with Eph. i. 1–10; vi. 12–24; and Phil. i. 1–7); i. 10–24; iii. 2–16; ii. 9—iii. 10.

EPH.: iv. 17—v. 13 (with Phil. iii. 1—iv. 6).

PHIL.: i. 23—ii. 6; i. 28—ii. 20.

COL.: i. 1–29; 9–11, 15 (with 1 Thess. ii. 15—iv. 4); i. 29—iii. 1.

1 TIM.: iii. 2—v. 2.

1 PET.: i. 18—vi. 14 (with 2 Pet. i. 1—iii. 1); ii. 23—iii. 13; iii. 12—iv. 9; iii. 15—iv. 10.

6. The British Museum has recently acquired a considerable number of fragments on vellum, containing—

MATT.: xv. 11—xvi. 12; xxi. 6–22.

JOHN: ix. 7–26; x. 30–42; xi. 1–10; 37–57.

ACTS: xxii. 12–30; xxiii. 1–15.

And also a large number of papyrus fragments in the Graf collection.

7. Mr. Petrie also has in his possession a valuable papyrus MS. containing considerable portions of St. John. This will probably shortly be published by Mr. Crum.

From the above account it becomes clear that we have now already published, or preserved in European libraries, enough material to produce a complete or almost a complete edition of the Sahidic New Testament. But not only this. We have also a considerable number of fragments written on papyrus, which are much older than any of the MSS. previously known, and will enable us to write a history of the version from an early date. May we express a hope that M. Amélineau, who has made large collections for the purpose, would first of all give us an edition of the Paris fragments as accurate as that of Ciasca, and then of the Sahidic New Testament as a whole? Much more than when Bishop Lightfoot wrote is the publication of it the pressing need of Biblical criticism.]

The order of the books in the Sahidic New Testament, so far as regards the great groups, appears to have been the same as in the Bohairic, i. e. (1) The Four Gospels, (2) The Pauline Epistles, (3) The Catholic Epistles and Acts (*see* above, p. 124). This may be inferred from the order of quotations in the Sahidic vocabulary described by Woide, Praef., p. 18; for the Sahidic MSS. are so fragmentary that no inference on this point can be drawn from them. Like the Bohairic, the original Sahidic Canon seems to have excluded the Apocalypse. In the vocabulary just mentioned it does not appear as part of the New Testament, but liturgical and other matter interposes before it is taken. Moreover in most cases it is evident from the paging of the fragments which remain that the MSS. containing this book formed separate volumes. In the Paris fragment described above this is plainly the case, and it is equally obvious in the Borgian MSS. lxxxviii, lxxxix (Zoega, p. 187). Thus in lxxxviii, pp. 39–44 contain Apoc. xii. 14—xiv. 13; and in lxxxix. pp. 59, 60, 63, 64 contain Apoc. xix. 7–18, xx. 7—xxi. 3. On the other hand in lxxxvii. where Apoc. iii. 20 begins on p. 279, this fragment must have formed part of a much larger volume, which contained (as we may suppose) a considerable portion of the New Testament.

The order of the four Gospels presents a difficulty. In the Sahidic vocabulary already referred to, the sequence is John, Matthew, Mark, Luke; and this order is also observed in the marginal concordance to the Crawford and Balcarres MS. described above. Thus there is reason for supposing that at one time St. John stood first. But the paging of the oldest MSS. does not favour this conclusion. In the Woidian and Borgian fragments of the Graeco-Sahidic Gospels, which belong to the fourth or fifth century, the numbering of the pages (see p. 130) shows that St. Luke stood before St. John. It is possible indeed that in the MSS. the transcriber was guided by the usual Greek arrangement. But in other MSS. also the synoptic evangelists precede St. John, e. g. Borg. xlvi, l, lxiv; while in other fragments again (Borg. lxx, lxxiv) the high numbers of the pages of St. John show that the Evangelist cannot have stood first in the volume, and this seems further supported by the Paris fragments, in which we find St. John following St. Luke in the same MS.

In this version, as in the Bohairic, the Epistle to the

Hebrews was treated as the work of St. Paul; but instead of being placed, as there, after 2 Thessalonians and before 1 Timothy, it stood between 2 Corinthians and Galatians[1]. It clearly occupies this position in the Borgian MS. lxxx (Zoega, p. 186): and by calculating the pages I have ascertained that this must also have been its place in all the other MSS. of the Pauline Epistles of which fragments after 2 Corinthians are preserved. These are the Borgian fragments lxxxii, lxxxv, lxxxvi, (Zoega, p. 186 sq.), and the Crawford and Balcarres fragment (iv) described above (p. 132); all of which happily are paged.

The Oxford MS. Hunt. 394 is a proof that the Acts followed the Catholic Epistles in the Sahidic New Testament, as is the case also in the Memphitic. Woide indeed (Praef., p. [22]), when describing this MS., says, '*exorditur* ab Actis Apostolicis'; but, even if this be so, his own account of the paging shows that the leaves have been displaced in binding, and that the Catholic Epistles originally stood first. The vocabulary also places them before the Acts.

The Sahidic version appears to be in one respect less faithful to the original than the Bohairic. So far as I am able to judge, it pays more respect to the Egyptian idiom, frequently omitting the conjunction and leaving the sentences disconnected. As regards the vocabulary, it adopts Greek words with as great facility as the Bohairic, or even greater. This we should hardly anticipate in Upper Egypt, which must have been comparatively free from Greek influence. Altogether it is a rougher and less polished version than the Bohairic.

The real textual value of the Sahidic cannot under present circumstances be assigned with any certainty. What would be received by one school of critics would not be admitted by another. But the Editor readily records the verdict of Bishop Lightfoot that the text of it, though very ancient, is inferior to the Bohairic, and less pure; that it exhibits a certain infusion of readings which were widely spread in the second century, and may very probably have had, to a considerable extent, a Western origin; that it differs very largely from the Traditional text; and that both in text and in interpretation it is entirely independent of the Bohairic. The coincidences are not greater than must have been exhibited by two separate translations in allied dialects from independent

[1] Its position was before Galatians, and not, as in the archetype of the Codex Vaticanus, after it.

texts of the same original. Of any mutual influence of the versions of Upper and Lower Egypt on each other no traces are discernible.

The following passage from Acts xvii. 12–16 will serve to illustrate the independence of these two versions.

Bohairic.

12 ⲟⲩⲙⲏϣ ⲙⲉⲛ ⲟⲩⲛ ⲉ̀ⲃⲟⲗ
ⲛ̀ϧⲏⲧⲟⲩ ⲁⲩⲛⲁϩϯ ⲛⲉⲙ
ϩⲁⲛⲕⲉⲟⲩⲉⲓⲛⲓⲛ ⲛ̀ϩⲓⲟⲙⲓ
ⲛⲉⲩⲥⲭⲏⲙⲱⲛ ⲛⲉⲙ ϩⲁⲛ-
ⲕⲉⲣⲱⲙⲓ ⲛ̀ ϩⲁⲛⲕⲟⲩϫⲓ ⲁⲛ⳾
13 ⲉⲧⲁⲩⲉ̀ⲙⲓ ⲇⲉ ⲛ̀ϫⲉ ⲛⲓⲓⲟⲩ-
ⲇⲁⲓ ⲛ̀ⲧⲉ ⲑⲉⲥⲥⲁⲗⲟⲛⲓⲕⲏ ϫⲉ
ⲁ̀ ⲡⲁⲩⲗⲟⲥ ϩⲓⲱⲓϣ ϧⲉⲛ
ⲧⲕⲉⲃⲉⲣⲟⲓⲁ ⲙ̀ⲡⲓⲥⲁϫⲓ ⲛ̀ⲧⲉ
ⲫⲛⲟⲩϯ ⲁⲩⲓ ⲉ̀ ⲡⲓⲕⲉⲙⲁ
ⲉ̀ⲧⲉⲙ̀ⲙⲁⲩ ⲉⲩⲕⲓⲙ ⲉ̀
ⲡⲓⲙⲏϣ ⲉⲩϣⲑⲟⲣⲧⲉⲣ ⲙ̀ⲙⲟ-
ⲱⲟⲩ⳾ 14 ⲧⲟⲧⲉ ⲥⲁⲧⲟⲧⲟⲩ
ⲁⲩⲧⲫⲉ ⲡⲁⲩⲗⲟⲥ ⲉ̀ⲃⲟⲗ ⲛ̀ϫⲉ
ⲛⲓⲥⲛⲏⲟⲩ ⲉ̀ ⲑⲣⲉϥϣⲉ ⲉ̀ϫⲉⲛ
ⲫⲓⲟⲙ ⲁⲩⲥⲱϫⲡ ⲇⲉ ⲙ̀ⲙⲁⲩ
ⲛ̀ϫⲉ ⲥⲓⲗⲁⲥ ⲛⲉⲙ ⲧⲓⲙⲟ-
ⲑⲉⲟⲥ⳾ 15 ⲛⲏ ⲇⲉ ⲉⲧⲁⲩⲧⲫⲉ
ⲡⲁⲩⲗⲟⲥ ⲁⲩⲉⲛϥ ⲉ̀ϩⲣⲏⲓ ⲉ̀
ⲁ̀ⲑⲏⲛⲁⲥ ⲟⲩⲟϩ ⲉⲧⲁⲩϭⲓ
ⲉⲛⲧⲟⲗⲏ ⲉ̀ ϭⲓ ⲡϣⲓⲛⲓ ⲛ̀ⲥⲓ-
ⲗⲁⲥ ⲛⲉⲙ ⲧⲓⲙⲟⲑⲉⲟⲥ
ϩⲓⲛⲁ ⲛ̀ⲥⲉⲓ̀ ϩⲁⲣⲟϥ ⲛ̀ϫⲱ-
ⲗⲉⲙ ⲁⲩⲓ ⲉ̀ⲃⲟⲗ ⲁⲩϣⲉ-
ⲛⲱⲟⲩ⳾ 16 ⲡⲁⲩⲗⲟⲥ ⲇⲉ ⲛⲁϥ
ϧⲉⲛ ⲁ̀ⲑⲏⲛⲁⲥ ⲉϥⲥⲟⲙⲥ
ⲉ̀ⲃⲟⲗ ϧⲁϫⲱⲟⲩ ⲁϥϫⲱⲛⲧ
ⲇⲉ ⲛ̀ϫⲉ ⲡⲉϥⲡⲛⲉⲩⲙⲁ
ⲛ̀ϧⲣⲏⲓ ⲛ̀ϧⲏⲧϥ ⲉϥⲛⲁⲩ ⲉ̀
ϯⲡⲟⲗⲓⲥ ⲉⲥⲟϣ ⲙ̀ⲙⲉⲧ-
ϣⲁⲙϣⲉ ⲓ̀ⲇⲱⲗⲟⲛ⳾

Sahidic.

12 ϩⲁϩ ϭⲉ ⲉⲃⲟⲗ ⲉⲛϩⲏⲧⲟⲩ
ⲁⲩⲡⲓⲥⲧⲉⲩⲉ ⲁⲩⲱ ϩⲉⲛ-
ⲥϩⲓⲙⲉ ⲛ̄ϩⲉⲗⲗⲏⲛ ⲛ̄ⲣⲙ̄-
ⲙⲁⲟ ⲙⲛ̄ ϩⲉⲛⲣⲱⲙⲉ ⲉ-
ⲛⲁϣⲱⲟⲩ⳾ 13 ⲛ̄ⲧⲉⲣⲟⲩⲉⲓⲙⲉ
ϭⲉ ⲛ̄ϭⲓ ⲛ̄ⲓⲟⲩⲇⲁⲓ ⲛⲏ ⲉⲃⲟ-
ⲗϩⲛ̄ ⲑⲉⲥⲁⲗⲗⲟⲛⲓⲕⲏ ϫⲉ
ⲁⲩⲧⲁϣⲉⲟⲉⲓϣ ϩⲛ̄ ⲃⲉⲣⲟⲓⲁ
ⲙ̄ⲡϣⲁϫⲉ ⲙ̄ⲡⲛⲟⲩⲧⲉ ⲉ-
ⲃⲟⲗϩⲓⲧⲙ̄ ⲡⲁⲩⲗⲟⲥ ⲁⲩⲉⲓ
ⲟⲛ ⲉⲙⲁⲩ ⲉⲩϣⲧⲟⲣⲧⲣ̄
ⲁⲩⲱ ⲉⲩⲕⲓⲙ ⲉ ⲡⲙⲏⲏϣⲉ⳾
14 ⲛ̄ⲧⲉⲩⲛⲟⲩ ⲇⲉ ⲁ ⲛⲉⲥⲛⲏⲩ
ϫⲟⲟⲩ ⲙ̄ⲡⲁⲩⲗⲟⲥ ⲉ ⲧⲣⲉϥ-
ⲃⲱⲕ ϩⲣⲁⲓ ⲉϫⲛ̄ ⲑⲁⲗⲁⲥⲥⲁ
ⲁ ⲥⲓⲗⲁⲥ ⲇⲉ ϭⲱ ⲙ̄ⲙⲟⲟⲩ
ⲙⲛ̄ ⲧⲓⲙⲟⲑⲉⲟⲥ⳾ 15 ⲛⲉⲧ-
ⲕⲁⲑⲓⲥⲧⲁ ⲇⲉ ⲙ̄ⲡⲁⲩⲗⲟⲥ
ⲁⲩⲛ̄ⲧϥ̄ ϣⲁ ⲁⲑⲉⲛⲛⲁⲓⲁⲥ
ⲁⲩⲱ ⲛ̄ⲧⲉⲣⲟⲩϫⲓ ⲛ̄ⲟⲩⲉⲛ-
ⲧⲟⲗⲏ ⲛ̄ⲧⲟⲟⲧϥ̄ ϣⲁ ⲥⲓⲗⲁⲥ
ⲙⲛ̄ ⲧⲓⲙⲟⲑⲉⲟⲥ ϫⲉ ⲉⲩⲉⲉⲓ
ϣⲁⲣⲟϥ ϩⲛ̄ ⲟⲩϭⲉⲡⲏ ⲁⲩⲉⲓ
ⲉⲃⲟⲗ⳾ 16 ⲉⲣⲉ ⲡⲁⲩⲗⲟⲥ ⲇⲉ
ϭⲱϣⲧ ϩⲏⲧⲟⲩ ϩⲛ̄ ⲁⲑⲏⲛ-
ⲛⲁⲓⲁⲥ ⲁ ⲡⲉϥⲡⲛⲉⲩⲙⲁ
ϩⲟϫϩⲉϫ ⲛ̄ϩⲏⲧϥ̄ ⲉϥⲛⲁⲩ
ⲉⲧⲡⲟⲗⲓⲥ ⲉⲙⲙⲉϩ ⲙ̄ⲙⲁ-
ⲛ̄ⲉⲓⲇⲱⲗⲟⲛ⳾

[(4) *The Fayoum Version.*

The history of the discovery of the third Egyptian version, and the reasons that have caused it to be assigned to the district of the Fayoum, have been given above.

The Fayoum (ⲫⲓⲟⲙ: ⲡⲓⲟⲙ: ⲡⲓⲁⲙ) is a district of Egypt situated to the west of the Nile valley, from which it is separated by a narrow strip of desert, and lying about eighty miles to the south of the apex of the Delta. It is a large depression in the desert, which has been reclaimed and fertilized by an offshoot of the Nile, now called the Bahr-il-Yousouf, and is distinguished at the present day for its extreme fertility. It appears to have been particularly prosperous and thickly populated in Ptolemaic and Roman times; and in the desert surrounding the cultivated land are the remains of several Greek cities, and of large Coptic monasteries; and it is from here that the chief part of the collection of papyrus fragments now in Berlin and Vienna have been obtained.

The dialect of this district, both in the fragments of the Scriptures preserved in it, and in the other documents more recently discovered (Z. A. S. 23, 1885, p. 26), presents very marked peculiarities. As regards vowels it shows the following amongst other variations as compared with Sahidic. It substitutes ⲁ for ⲉ: ⲛⲉⲕ for ⲛⲁⲕ; ⲗⲉⲛ for ⲣⲁⲛ; ⲕⲉⲉⲃ for ϫⲁϥ : ⲕⲁⲁϥ; ⲏ for ⲉ: ⲥⲏⲛⲧⲓ for ⲥⲉⲛϯ : ⲥⲛⲧⲉ; ⲏⲙⲓ for ⲉⲙⲓ : ⲉⲓⲙⲉ; ⲁ for ⲟ: ⲃⲁⲗ for ⲉⲃⲟⲗ; ⲗⲁⲃ for ⲉⲣⲟϥ; ⲟ for ⲱ: ϩⲟⲃ for ϩⲱⲃ; ⲗⲟⲙⲓ for ⲗⲱⲙⲓ (=ⲣⲱⲙⲓ: ⲣⲱⲙⲉ). In consonants it has two very marked features, the substitution of ⲗ for ⲣ, as ⲉⲗ, ⲉⲗⲉ, ⲗⲉⲡ; ϣⲏⲗⲓ for ⲉⲣ, ⲉⲣⲉ, &c., and of ⲃ for final ϥ, as ⲛⲧⲁⲃ for ⲛⲧⲟϥ.

A considerable amount of this version still probably remains unpublished, but specimens may be discovered in the following:

1. Giorgi. Fragmentum Evangelii S. Joannis &c. (*see* p. 128) contains 1 Cor. ix. 9–16.

2. Zoega. Catalogus &c. (*See* p. 102.)

3. Engelbreth. Fragmenta Basmurico-Coptica Veteris et Novi Testamenti. Havniae, 1811.

4. Maspero. Recueil, 11 (1889), p. 116.

5. Mittheilungen, i. p. 69. Matt. xi. 27.

6. Mittelaegyptische Bibelfragmente, in Études Archéologiques Linguistiques et Historiques dédiées à M. le Dr. C. Leemans. Leide, 1885. (But perhaps this and 4 may be more correctly classed as Middle Egyptian or Lower Sahidic.)

On this version Bishop Lightfoot wrote: 'As the Bashmuric is a secondary version, it has no independent value, and is only useful in passages where the Sahidic is wanting.' This opinion would hardly represent the present position. That the Sahidic and Fayoum versions are not independent is quite true, but the relation of them to one another is much more that they are different forms of the same version, of which on the whole perhaps the Fayoum represents the older and more primitive text.

(5) *The Middle Egyptian*[1] *or Lower Sahidic Version.*

It has already been explained that documents found on the site of Memphis exhibit a dialect different in some respects from any of those that we have yet considered. In this also fragments have been found of a translation of the New Testament.

The dialect shows a combination of Sahidic and Bohairic forms. It has ⲓⲱⲧ for Sah. ⲉⲓⲱⲧ; ⲙⲉⲧⲓⲱⲧ for ⲙⲛⲧⲉⲓⲱⲧ; ⲓⲱⲁⲛⲏⲥ for ⲓⲱϩⲁⲛⲛⲏⲥ; ⲛⲧⲟⲧⲕ for ⲛⲧⲟⲟⲧⲕ; ϣⲧⲱⲣⲓ for ϣⲧⲱⲣⲉ. It agrees again with the Fayoum dialect (which is generally considered a variety of it) in its affection for ⲁ, as ⲛⲧⲁⲕ for ⲛⲧⲟⲕ, and apparently in using ⲗ for ⲣ, but only occasionally.

The following specimen from Rom. xi. 31–36 will exhibit the character of the dialect and the version: the Sahidic is taken from the Borgian fragment published by Amélineau, Z. A. S. 25, 1887, p. 49; the Middle Egyptian from 'Mittheilungen,' ii. p. 69.

[1] The term 'Middle Egyptian' is often used as a general term to include the three varieties of Fayoumic, Lower Sahidic or what is properly Memphitic, and Akhmimic.

MIDDLE EGYPTIAN.	SAHIDIC.
xi. 31 ⲧⲉⲓ ⲧⲉ	ⲧⲁⲓ ⲧⲉ
ⲑⲏ ⲛⲛⲉⲓ ϩⲱⲟⲩ ⲧⲉⲛⲟⲩ · ⲉⲁⲩ	ⲑⲏ ⲛⲛⲁⲓ ϩⲱⲟⲩ ⲧⲉⲛⲟⲩ · ⲉⲁⲩ
ⲉⲗⲁⲧⲛⲉϩϯ ⲉⲡⲉⲧⲛ̄ⲛⲁ ·	ⲣ ⲁⲧ ⲛⲁϩ ⲧⲉ ⲉⲡⲉⲧⲛⲛⲁ ·
ϫⲉⲕⲁⲥ ϩⲱⲟⲩ ⲉⲩⲉⲛⲉⲉ̈ ⲛⲏⲩ	ϫⲉⲕⲁⲥ ϩⲱⲟⲩ ⲉⲩⲉⲛⲁ ⲛⲁⲩ
32 ⲙ̄ⲙ̄ⲛ̄ⲛⲥⲟⲥ · ⲁ ⲡⲛⲟⲩϯ ⲅⲁⲣ	ⲙⲛⲛⲥⲱⲥ ⲁ ⲡⲛⲟⲩⲧⲉ
ⲁⲡⲧ ⲟⲩⲁⲛ ⲛⲓⲙ ⲉϩⲟⲩⲛ ⲉⲩ	ⲉⲧⲡ ⲟⲩⲟⲛ ⲛⲓⲙ ⲉϩⲟⲩⲛ ⲉⲟⲩ
ⲙⲉⲧⲁⲧⲛⲉϩϯ · ϫⲉⲕⲁⲁⲥ	ⲙⲛⲧⲁⲧⲛⲁϩⲧⲉ · ϫⲉⲕⲁⲥ
ⲉϥⲉⲛⲁ ⲛⲁⲩ ⲧⲏⲣⲟⲩ :	ⲉϥⲉⲛⲁ ⲛⲁⲩ ⲧⲏⲣⲟⲩ
33 ⲱ ⲡϣⲱⲕ ⲛⲧⲙⲉⲧⲣⲉⲙ	ⲱ ⲡϣⲓⲕⲉ ⲛⲧⲙⲛⲧⲣⲙ
ⲙⲁⲟ · ⲙ̄ⲛ̄ ⲧⲥⲟⲫⲓⲁ · ⲙ̄ⲛ̄	ⲙⲁⲟ ⲙⲛ ⲧⲥⲟⲫⲓⲁ ⲁⲩⲱ
ⲡⲥⲟⲟⲩⲛ ⲙⲡⲫ̄ϯ̄ · ⲛⲑⲏ	ⲡⲥⲟⲟⲩⲛ ⲙⲡⲛⲟⲩⲧⲉ ⲛⲑⲉ
ⲉⲧⲉⲙⲉⲩϣⲙⲁϣⲧ ⲛⲉϩⲉⲛ	ⲉⲧⲉ ⲛⲛⲉⲩⲉϣⲙⲉϣⲧ ⲛⲉϥϩⲁⲡ
ⲙⲡⲛⲟⲩϯ · ⲁⲩⲱ ϩⲉⲛ	ⲁⲩⲱ ⲉⲧⲉ ⲛⲛⲉⲩⲉϣⲉⲛ
ⲁⲧϭⲉⲛⲗⲉⲧⲟⲩ ⲛⲉ ⲛⲉϥϩⲓⲁⲩⲓ ·	ⲣⲁⲧⲟⲩ ⲛⲛⲉϥϩⲓⲟⲟⲩⲉ
34 ⲛⲓⲙ ⲅⲁⲣ ⲡⲉⲧⲉ ⲁϥⲓⲙⲓ ⲉⲛ	ⲛⲓⲙ ⲅⲁⲣ ⲡⲉⲛⲧⲁϥⲉⲓⲙⲉ ⲉⲡ
ϩⲏⲧ ⲙⲡⲟ̄ⲥ̄ · ⲡⲉⲓ ⲉⲧⲛⲁ	ϩⲏⲧ ⲙⲡϫⲟⲉⲓⲥ · ⲡⲁⲓ ⲉⲧⲛⲁ
35 ⲥⲉ ⲃⲓⲛⲧ̄ϥ̄ ⲉⲃⲟⲗ · ⲓ̈ⲉ ⲛⲓⲙ ⲡⲉ	ⲥⲁⲃⲉ ⲉⲓⲁⲧϥ ⲉⲃⲟⲗ ⲏ ⲛⲓⲙ ⲡⲉ
ⲧⲉ ⲁϥϣⲱⲡⲓ ⲛⲏϥ ⲛⲗⲉϥ	ⲛⲧⲁϥϣⲱⲡⲉ ⲛⲁϥ ⲛⲣⲉϥ
ϫⲓϣⲁϫⲛⲓ · ⲓ̈ⲉ ⲛⲓⲙ ⲡⲉ	ϫⲓ ϣⲟϫⲛⲉ · ⲏ ⲛⲓⲙ ⲡⲉ
ⲧⲉ ⲁϥⲓⲗⲓ ⲛⲏϥ ⲛϣⲁⲣⲉⲛ ·	ⲛⲧⲁϥⲉⲓⲣⲉ ⲛⲁϥ ⲛϣⲟⲣⲡ
36 ⲛⲧⲁⲗⲉϥⲧⲟⲩⲓⲁ ⲛⲏϥ · ϫⲉ	ⲧⲁⲣⲉϥ ⲧⲟⲩⲉⲓⲟ ⲛⲁϥ · ϫⲉ
ⲡⲧⲏⲣϥ̄ ϩ̄ⲛ̄ ⲉⲃⲟⲗ ⲙⲙⲁϥ	ⲡⲧⲏⲣϥ ϩⲉⲛ ⲉⲃⲟⲗ ⲙⲙⲟϥ
ⲡⲉ · ⲁⲩⲱ ⲉⲃⲟⲗϩⲓⲧⲁ	ⲡⲉ · ⲁⲩⲱ ⲉⲃⲟⲗϩⲓⲧⲟ
ⲁⲧ̄ϥ̄ · ⲁⲩⲱ ⲉⲩⲛⲁⲕⲁⲧⲟⲩ	ⲟⲧϥ ⲁⲩⲱ ⲉⲩⲛⲁⲕⲟⲧⲟⲩ
ⲉⲗⲁϥ · ⲡⲱϥ ⲡⲉ ⲡⲉⲟⲟⲩ	ⲉⲣⲟϥ · ⲡⲱϥ ⲡⲉ ⲡⲉⲟⲟⲩ
ⲛϣⲁ ⲛⲓⲉⲛϩ̄ ϩⲁⲙⲏⲛ.	ϣⲁ ⲛⲓⲉⲛⲉϩ ϩⲁⲙⲏⲛ.

Specimens of this version may be found in—

1. Mémoires de l'Institut égyptien, II. ii, edited by Bouriant.
2. Mittheilungen, ii. p. 69.
3. Coptic MSS. brought from the Fayoum by W. M. Flinders Petrie, Esq., D.C.L., edited by W. E. Crum, p. 1.
4. It is also said to be contained in some Graeco-Coptic fragments recently acquired by the British Museum.

The lines between this dialect and version and that of the

Fayoum are not, however, clearly defined, and further research may make it necessary to rearrange the different specimens mentioned in this and the preceding sections.

Textually the version is of equal value with that of the Fayoum, that is, it represents another tradition of the version of Upper Egypt, of which Sahidic was the most important representative.

(6) *The Akhmîm Dialect.*

It would have probably been more scientific to have begun our discussion of the versions of Upper Egypt with a description of the Akhmîm dialect. It certainly represents the language in an older form than any other dialect we have examined; unfortunately such a very small fragment of the New Testament version exists that its importance at present can hardly be estimated.

The Akhmîm dialect is known to us by a series of Apocryphal and Biblical fragments published by M. Bouriant (Mémoires, i. p. 243), and has the following characteristics. In its vowels its affinities are nearest to the Middle Egyptian; it has ⲁ for ⲟ, ⲁⲩ for ⲟⲩ, and ⲉ for ⲁ. It does not use ⲗ for ⲣ. Like the Sahidic it has double vowel-endings, and the weak final ⲉ, but not ⲫ, ⲑ, ⲭ for ⲡϩ, ⲧϩ, ⲕϩ. It also has some Bohairic forms, such as ⲛⲟⲩ, ⲁⲣⲉ, ⲁϥ. In the vowels it has the following peculiarities: ⲁ for ⲉ (Sah.), ⲁϩⲟⲩⲛ, ⲁϩⲣⲏⲓ, ⲁⲣⲁⲕ, ⲁⲃⲁⲗ; ⲓ or ⲉⲓ for ⲏ, ⲣⲓ (sun), ⲥⲙⲉⲓ, ⲧϩⲉⲓ; ⲟⲩ for ⲱ, ⲕⲟⲩ, ϫⲟⲩ, ⲥⲃⲟⲩ; ⲟ for ⲁⲩ, ⲛⲟ, ⲥⲛⲟ.

But its most distinguishing feature is an entirely new letter, ϩ: this may represent ϣ of other dialects; ϩ for ⲉϣ (to know), ⲉϩ for ⲁϣ; or ϫ as ⲧϩⲛⲟ for ϫⲛⲟ; or ϧ: ϩ, as ⲱⲛϩ for ⲱⲛϧ; ⲥϩⲉⲓ for ⲥϧⲁⲓ.

The textual affinities can hardly be worked out with the small amount of material we possess, but there seems to be little doubt that it represents in a very early form the same version that we are acquainted with in Sahidic. Further discoveries in this dialect may do much to make us acquainted with the early history of the version of Upper Egypt.

Only two short fragments of this version are known, which have been edited by Mr. W. E. Crum in his edition of the Coptic

MSS. brought from the Fayoum by W. M. Flinders Petrie (p. 2). They are contained in a parchment MS. of very great antiquity (Mr. Crum suggests the fourth century, but this is certainly too early), and contain St. James iv. 12–13, St. Jude 17–20. The following comparison of it with the Sahidic will show both the similarity of the versions and the differences of the dialect.

AKHMIMIC.

Jude [17] ⲛⲛϣⲉϫⲉ ⲙⲡⲛϫⲁⲉⲓⲥ ⲓⲥ
ⲡⲭⲥ ⲛⲉï ⲉⲧⲁ ⲛⲉϥⲁⲡⲟⲥⲧⲟⲗⲟⲥ
ϫⲟⲟⲩ ⲉϫⲛ ⲛϩⲁⲣⲡ’ ⲁⲃⲁⲗ·
[18] ϫⲉ ⲁⲩⲇⲟⲟⲥ ϫⲉ ϩⲛ ⲧϩⲁⲉⲓ
ⲛⲛⲟⲩⲁⲉⲓϣ ⲟⲩⲛ ϩⲉⲛⲣⲉϥϫⲣϫⲣⲉ
ⲛⲏⲩ ⲉⲩⲙⲁⲁϩⲉ ⲕⲁⲧⲁ ⲛⲉⲡⲓ
ⲑⲩⲙⲓⲁ ⲛⲛⲟⲩⲙⲛⲧ’ ϩⲉϥⲧ·
[19] ⲛⲉï ⲛⲉⲧⲡⲱⲣϫ ⲁⲃⲁⲗ ⲉϩⲉⲛ
ⲯⲩⲭⲓⲕⲟⲥ ⲛⲉ ⲉⲙⲛⲧⲉⲩ ⲡⲡⲛⲁ
ⲙⲙⲟ· [20] ⲛⲧⲱⲧⲛⲉⲇⲉ ⲛⲁⲙⲣⲣⲉ-
ⲧⲉ ϩⲱⲡⲉ ⲉⲧⲉⲧⲛ ⲕⲱⲧ ⲙⲙⲱⲧ-
ⲛⲉ ϩⲛ ⲧⲉⲧⲛⲡⲓⲥⲧⲓⲥ ⲉⲧⲟⲩⲁⲁⲃⲉ
ⲙⲡϣⲁ ⲉⲧⲉⲧⲛϣⲗⲏⲗ ϩⲙ
ⲡⲡⲛⲁ ⲉⲧⲟⲩⲁⲁⲃⲉ

SAHIDIC.

[17] ⲛⲛϣⲁϫⲉ ⲙⲡⲉⲛϫⲟⲉⲓⲥ ⲓⲥ
ⲡⲉⲭⲥ· ⲛⲁⲓ ⲛⲧⲁ ⲛⲉϥⲁⲡⲟⲥⲧⲟⲗⲟⲥ
ϫⲟⲟⲩ ϫⲓⲛ ⲛϣⲟⲣⲡ · ⲉⲃⲟⲗ
[18] ϫⲉ ⲁⲩϫⲟⲟⲥ ϫⲉ ϩⲛ ⲑⲁⲏ
ⲛⲛⲉⲟⲩⲟⲉⲓϣ ⲟⲩⲛ ϩⲉⲛⲣⲉϥϫⲏⲣ
ⲛⲏⲩ ⲉⲩⲙⲟⲟϣⲉ ⲕⲁⲧⲁ ⲛⲉⲡⲓ
ⲑⲩⲙⲓⲁ ⲛⲛⲉⲩⲙⲛⲧϣⲁϥⲧⲉ·
[19] ⲛⲁⲓ ⲛⲉⲧⲡⲱⲣϫ ⲉⲃⲟⲗ ⲉϩⲉⲛ
ⲯⲩⲭⲓⲕⲟⲛ ⲛⲉ ⲉⲙⲛⲧⲟⲩ ⲡⲛⲁ
ⲙⲙⲁⲩ· [20] ⲛⲧⲱⲧⲛ ⲇⲉ ⲛⲁⲙⲉⲣⲁ·
ⲧⲉ ⲉⲧⲉⲧⲛ ⲕⲱⲧ ⲙⲡⲱⲧⲉⲛ....

It has only been possible in the above account to give a rough outline of more recent discovery. Further investigation is necessary, and the lines which divide the different dialects, especially those between Fayoumic and Middle Egyptian, require to be more accurately defined. Much may be hoped also from the results of future discovery. The rubbish heaps of the monasteries, the concealed libraries, the graves, have yielded up some of their treasures, but all has not yet been brought to light. Enough has been written to suggest that discoveries of great interest for the life and character of early Egyptian Christianity have been made, and that much still remains to be found, which may indirectly throw a flood of light on the early history of Christianity as a whole[1].]

[1] The writer must express his regret that, owing to the haste with which the additions to this article had to be written, much must have been passed over.

CHAPTER V.

THE OTHER VERSIONS OF THE NEW TESTAMENT.

THE remaining Versions are of less importance in the ascertainment of the sacred text. But some of them have recently received more attention in the general widening of research, and in becoming better known have strengthened their claims to recognition and value. Three of them, at all events, date from the period of the oldest manuscripts of the New Testament now known to be in existence. And the presence amongst us of eminent scholars acquainted with them renders reference to them more easy than it was a few years ago.

Nevertheless, some are of slight service to the critic, being secondary versions, and as such becoming handmaids, not of the Greek, but of some other version translated from the Greek.

In the account of these versions, the Editor of this edition is indebted for most valuable assistance to Mr. F. C. Conybeare, late Fellow of University College, Oxford, who has re-written the sections on the Armenian and Georgian versions; to Professor Margoliouth, who has also re-written those on the Ethiopic and Arabic; to the Rev. Llewellyn J. M. Bebb, Fellow of Brasenose College, who has re-written the account of the Slavonic; and to Dr. James W. Bright, Assistant-Professor of English Philology in the John Hopkins University, who has contributed what is known on the Anglo-Saxon Version.

(1) The Gothic Version (Goth.).

The history of the Goths, who from the wilds of Scandinavia overran the fairest regions of Europe, has been traced by the master-hand of Gibbon (Decline and Fall, Chapters x, xxvi, xxxi, &c.), and needs not here be repeated. While the nation was yet seated in Moesia, Ulphilas or Wulfilas [318–388], a Cappadocian, who succeeded their first Bishop Theophilus in A. D. 348, though himself an Arian and a teacher of that subtil heresy to his adopted countrymen, became their benefactor, by translating both the Old[1] and New Testament into the Gothic, a dialect of the great Teutonic stock of languages, having previously invented or adapted an alphabet expressly for their use. There can be no question, from internal evidence, that the Old Testament was rendered from the Septuagint, the New from the Greek original[2]: but the existing manuscripts testify to some corruption from Latin sources, very naturally arising during the occupation of Italy by the Goths in the fifth century. These venerable documents are principally three, or rather may be treated under two MSS. and one group.

1. Codex Argenteus, the most precious treasure of the University of Upsal, in the mother-country of the Gothic tribes. It appears to be the same copy as Ant. Morillon saw at Werden in Westphalia towards the end of the sixteenth century, and was taken by the Swedes at the siege of Prague in 1648. Queen Christina gave it to her librarian, Isaac Vossius, and from him it was very rightly purchased about 1662 by the Swedish nation and deposited at Upsal. This superb codex contains fragments of the Gospels (in the Western order, Matthew, John, Luke, Mark) on 187 leaves, 4to (out of 330), of purple vellum; the bold, uncial, Gothic letters being in silver, sometimes in gold, of course much faded, and so regular that some have imagined, though erroneously, that they were impressed with a stamp. The date assigned to it is the fifth or early in the sixth century, although the several words are divided, and some various readings stand in the margin *primâ manu*.

2. Codex Carolinus, described above for Codd. PQ, and for the Old Latin *gue*, contains in Gothic about forty verses of the Epistle to the Romans, first published by Knittel, 1762.

3. Codices Ambrosiani, or palimpsest fragments of five manuscripts, apparently like Cod. Carolinus, from Bobbio, and of about the same date, discovered by Mai in 1817 in the Ambrosian Library at Milan, and published by him and Count C. O. Castiglione (Ulphilæ Partium Ineditarum . . . Specimen, in five parts, Milan, 1819, 1820, 1834, 1835, 1839). The last-named manuscripts are minutely described and illustrated by a rude facsimile in Horne's 'Introduction,' and after him in Tregelles' 'Horne,' vol. iv.

[1] 'But he prudently suppressed the four books of Kings, as they might tend to irritate the fierce and sanguinary spirit of the barbarians;' Gibbon, ch. xxxvii.

[2] 'A faithful, a stern and noble Teutonic rendering of the Greek,' is the verdict of Prebendary S. C. Malan (St. John's Gospel, translated from the Eleven Oldest Versions except the Latin, &c., 4to, 1872, Preface, p. viii). Bishop Ellicott also praises this version as usually faithful and accurate, yet marks an Arian tinge in the rendering of Phil. ii. 6–8.

pp. 304–7. They consist of (1) a portion of St. Paul's Epistles, under Homilies of Gregory the Great (viii); (2) portions of St. Paul, under Jerome on Isaiah (viii or ix); (3) parts of the Old Testament, under Plautus and part of Seneca; (4) under four pages of St. John in Latin part of St. Matt. xxvi, xxvii. The fifth fragment consists of Acts of the Council of Chalcedon with no extracts from the Bible. Mai refers some of the Gothic writing to the sixth century and some as far back as the fourth or beginning of the fifth. Unlike the Codex Argenteus (at least if we trust Dr. E. D. Clarke's facsimile of the latter), the words in Mai's palimpsests are continuous: they contain parts of Esther, Nehemiah (apparently no portion of the books of Kings), a few passages of the Gospels, and much of St. Paul [1]. H. F. Massmann (Ulfilas, Stuttgart, 1855–57) also added from an exposition a few verses of St. John, and there are fragments at Vienna and Rome [2]. and Turin

These fragments (for such they still must be called) [3], in spite of the influence of the Latin, approach nearer to the received text, in respect of their readings, than the Egyptian or one or two other versions of about the same age; and from their similarity in language to the Teutonic have been much studied in Germany. The fullest and best edition of the whole collected, with a grammar and lexicon, is by H. C. von der Gabelentz and J. Loebe (Ulfilas Vet. et N. Testamenti versionis Gothicae fragmenta quae supersunt, Leipsic, 1836–46, viz. vol. i. Text, 1836; Pars ii. Glossarium, 1843; Pars ii. Grammatik, 1846), and of the Codex Argenteus singly that of And. Uppstrom (with a good facsimile), Upsal, 1854. This scholar published separately in 1857 ten leaves of the manuscript which had been stolen between 1821 and 1834, and were restored through him by the penitent thief on his death-bed. The Gothic Gospels, however, had been cited as early as 1675 in Fell's N. T., and more fully in Mill's, through Francis Junius' edition (with Marshall's critical notes), which was printed at Dort in 1665, from Derrer's accurate

[1] Goth. Version. Paul. Epist. quae supersunt, C. O. Castiglione, Milan, 1834.

[2] Skeat, St. Mark, 1882.

[3] Matt. iii. 11; v. 8; 15—vi. 32; vii. 12—x. 1; 23—xi. 25; xxv. 38—xxvi. 3; 65—xxvii. 19; 42–66; Mark i. 1; vi. 30; 58—xii. 38; xiii. 16–29; xiv. 4–16; 41—xvi. 12; Luke i. 1—x. 30; xiv. 9—xvi. 24; xvii. 3—xx. 46; John i. 29; iii. 3–5; 23–26; 29–32; v. 21–23; 35–38; 45—xi. 47; xii. 1–49; xiii. 11—xix. 13; Rom. vi. 23; vii. 1—viii. 10; 34—xi. 1; 11—xii. 5; 8—xiv. 5; 9–20; xv. 3–13; xvi. 21–24; 1 Cor. i. 12–25; iv. 2–12; v. 3—vi. 1; vii. 5–28; viii. 9—ix. 9; 19—x. 4; 15—xi. 6; 21–31; xii. 10–22; xiii. 1–12; xiv. 20–27; xv. 1–35; 46—Gal. i. 7; 20—iii. 6; 27—Eph. v. 11; 17–29; vi. 8–24; Phil. i. 14—ii. 8; 22—iv. 17; Col. i. 6–29; ii. 11—iv. 19; 1 Thess. ii. 10—2 Thess. ii. 4; 15—1 Tim. v. 14; 16—2 Tim. iv. 16; Tit. i. 1—ii. 1; Philem. 1–23; but no portion of the Acts, Hebrews, Catholic Epistles, or Apocalypse.

transcript of the Upsal manuscript, made in or about 1655, when it was in Isaac Vossius' possession. Other editions of the Codex Argenteus were published by G. Stiernhielm in 1671 for the College of Antiquaries at Stockholm; by E. Lye at the Clarendon Press in 1750 from the revision of Eric Benzel, Archbishop of Upsal; and (with the addition of the fragments in the Codex Carolinus) by Jo. Ihre in 1763, and by J. C. Zahn in 1805. And also the Gothic and Anglo-Saxon Gospels in parallel columns with the Versions of Wycliffe and Tyndale, London, 1865, and Ulfila, oder die Gotische Bibel (N. T.), E. Bernhardt, Halle, 1875, and St. Mark with a grammatical commentary, R. Müller and H. Hoeppe, 1881, and Skeat, Gospel of St. Mark in Gothic, Clarendon Press, 1882.

(2) The Armenian Version.

The existing Armenian version is a recension made shortly after the Council of Ephesus of a still earlier version, which was based in part upon a Syriac, in part upon a Greek original. This latest recension was made according to 'accurate and reliable copies' of the Greek Bible, which, along with the Canons of the Council of Ephesus, were brought from Constantinople about the year 433. One would naturally wish for more details than the above brief statement contains; yet it is all that one can definitely infer from the history of the version as related by three nearly contemporary writers, whose accounts we now subjoin, namely, Koriun, Lazar of Pharpi, and Moses Khorenatzi.

Koriun[1] in his life of St. Mesrop (written between 441 and 452 A.D.) relates as follows:—

In the fifth year of the reign of Vramshapho [i.e. about 397 A.D.], St. Mesrop was first in Edessa, then in Amid, lastly in Samosata, busy all the time about his discovery of the Armenian characters[2]. In Samosata, where he was received with great respect by the clergy and bishop, Mesrop met with a Greek scribe, Hrofanos (? Rufinus), in conjunction with whom, and

[1] *See* p. 10 of the Armenian edition; Venice, 1833. The French translation of this in the 'Collection des Historiens de l'Arménie,' Paris, 1869, is untrustworthy in all ways, and especially because the translator both adds to and omits from the Armenian text at random.

[2] The true history of which we cannot now make out, for, as given by his contemporaries, it is already obscured by legend and miracle.

with the help of two pupils named John and Joseph, he undertook a translation of the Bible. They began—and this is noteworthy—with the book of the Proverbs of Solomon; Hrofanos or Rufinus writing down the translation with his own hand. Mesrop next visited the Bishop of the Syrians, who congratulated him on his work. He then returned to Nor Chalach, or new city, as Valarshapat was called by the Romans, in the sixth year of Vramshapho's reign, A.D. 398. At a later time, Koriun, the writer, was himself sent with Eznik to Constantinople, apparently in quest of books to translate; for they returned with a *sure* copy of the Scriptures, with works of the Fathers, and with the canons of the Councils of Nice and Ephesus. 'Now St. Sahak had long before translated the collection of Church books from Greek into Armenian, as well as much true wisdom of the holy Patriarchs. But he now resumed, and taking with the help of Eznik the former translations made hurriedly and offhand, he confirmed them by the help of the true copies now brought, and they translated much commentary on the books.' The above is the gist of what Koriun has to tell us, though he mentions that scholars were sent to Edessa to translate and bring back the works of the Fathers. Why Mesrop began with the Book of Proverbs, whether he translated more than that, and from which language, we do not learn from Koriun. Lazar of Pharpi [1], who wrote in the last half of the sixth century, is our next authority. He states that up to the last decade of the fourth century, the offices of religion were still read in Greater Armenia in Syriac, a language which the people did not understand. The edicts of the kings of Armenia were also written out in Syriac or Greek characters. But as soon as the Armenian alphabet was discovered, St. Sahak—who was patriarch 390–428 A.D. and an expert in Greek—set himself, in response to the patriotic exhortations of St. Mesrop, of Vramshapho the king, and of the clergy and nobles, to translate the Holy Scriptures. He states that St. Sahak's version comprised the whole of the Old and New Testaments, and was made from Greek.

Moses of Chorene, bk. iii. ch. 36 ff., copies, confuses, and adds to Koriun's account. A little before 370 A.D. the Persians

[1] The translation of this writer in Langlois' second volume is reliable.

overran Armenia, and Meroujah, their leader, burned all the books he could find in the country, proscribed the study of the Greek language, and enacted penalties against any who should speak it or translate from it. At that time, adds Moses, the offices of the church were performed in Greek, because the Armenian alphabet did not yet exist. On the death of Theodosius (Jan. 395 A.D.) there was a partition of Armenia between his successor Arcadius and the king of Persia, by which the latter took undisputed possession of the eastern provinces, including the basin of Ararat, in which lay the new religious centre Valarshapat or Edschmiadzin, the νέα πόλις of the Romans. The new Mesropic alphabet was at first used only in Persian Armenia; for, says Moses, in the parts dependent on the Greeks, all writing had to be in Greek characters, Syriac being forbidden. As soon as Mesrop had elaborated his alphabet with the aid of Hrophanos, he betook himself to the work of translation; and with the aid of his pupils John and Joseph, translated the entire twenty-two authentic books along with the New Testament, taking care to begin with the Book of Proverbs. About the year 406 he returned to Armenia, and found St. Sahak engaged in translating the Syriac Bible. He hints that Sahak would have preferred a Greek original, if Meroujah had not burned all the Greek books nearly thirty years before. This perhaps implies that the version, on which Mesrop had been engaged in Samosata, was made from Greek. Nor is that unlikely; for Rufinus, who helped him, was a Greek, and we learn from Koriun that there were Armenians in Edessa studying both Greek and Syriac. We read in bk. iii. ch. 60 of the History of Moses, about missions sent to Edessa and Byzantium in order to the translation of the works of the Fathers, but we hear nothing more expressly touching the Version of the Bible, save this, that after the Council of Ephesus, Sahak and Mesrop, then in Ashtishat in Taron, received from Byzantium, as aforesaid, the canons of the council recently held, along with accurate copies of the Greek Bible. On receipt of these, Sahak and Mesrop translated afresh what had already been translated, and were zealous in recasting the text. But they were not, it seems, after all, satisfied with their work, and sent Moses to Alexandria to learn the 'beautiful tongue' (i. e. Greek), with a view to a more accurate articulation and division (of the Armenian scriptures).

The above summary exhausts the evidence of Moses of Khorene[1]. It would appear therefrom that the Bible was translated twice into Armenian before the end of the fourth century; by Mesrop from Greek, and by Sahak from Syriac. The circumstance that Mesrop in Samosata began with the Proverbs of Solomon raises a suspicion that the earlier books had already been rendered, when and by whom is unknown. Certainly the reasons given by Koriun and by Moses for Mesrop beginning with Proverbs are insufficient. Moses again in stating that Sahak rendered the entire Bible from Syriac contradicts both Koriun and Lazar. Are we to infer that Sahak and Mesrop after 430 A.D. retranslated according to the Constantinople Bibles what they had already translated from Syriac, and also it would seem from a presumably less perfect Greek text? Anyhow it is unlikely that they would wholly sacrifice their own work, and we should therefore expect to find in the Armenian version a mixture of texts, namely of some old Syriac text, which must have been in vogue as late as 380, of some older Greek text supplied in Edessa or Samosata, and of the Constantinopolitan texts; which last may well have been among the fifty splendid copies which had been prepared under the order of Constantine by Eusebius a century before. If, and how far, these different elements enter into the Version can only be determined by a careful analysis of its readings. It may be that in some MSS. there lurks more of the unrevised text than in others[2]. The entire history is an apt illustration of that political see-saw between the Roman and the Persian powers which went on in Armenia during the fourth and fifth centuries, and out of which the patriotic vigour and devotion of St. Mesrop and St. Sahak carved at last a truly national Armenian Church, with an independent life and literature of its own.

The Armenian Version was collated for Robert Holmes' edition of the Septuagint, though not with desirable accuracy nor from the oldest MSS. For example, the Codex Arm. 3 of the Pentateuch, which Holmes declares, *teste Adlero*, to be of the year 1063,

[1] Some critics bring down the date of Moses as late as the seventh or eighth century.

[2] Dr. Baronean thinks that the varieties of readings in the oldest Armenian MSS. is due to the fact that more than one *sure* copy was brought from Constantinople on which to base the final revision.

is but an eighteenth century codex. The collation of the New Testament in the eighth edition of Tischendorf's N. T. is accurate so far as it goes, but is far from being exhaustive or based on a consensus of the oldest MSS. Old codices of the Armenian Gospels are very common, and the present writer knows of as many as eight, none of them later than the year A.D. 1000; of four of these he has complete collations. The rest of the N. T. is only found in codices of the whole Bible, which are rare and always written in minuscules, never in uncials as are the Gospels. He knows of no copies of the whole Bible older than the twelfth century.

Two further questions call for brief answer:—1. Have we the Armenian version as it left the hands of the fifth century translators? 2. Did the fifth century version comprise the whole of the Old and New Testament?

In regard to the first question, it must be admitted as probable that changes were subsequently made, at least in the New Testament, in the way both of omission and addition; e.g. in St. Luke xxii. 44, out of four very early uncial codices collated by the writer, the words: *ἐγένετο δὲ ὁ ἱδρῶς αὐτοῦ ὡσεὶ θρόμβοι αἵματος καταβαίνοντες ἐπὶ τὴν γῆν*, are found only in one, and that one the earliest, being dated 902 A.D. The words which precede *ὤφθη δ'—ἐπροσηύχετο* are omitted in all four of them. We may infer that ver. 44 was in the original version, and was omitted from the three codices for doctrinal reasons. The additions made to the text after the fifth century are easier to detect; because they only come in some MSS. and not in others, and also because there is so much discrepancy of readings between those codices which add them, that they are at once seen to be lacunas supplied by different hands. This is the case, for example, with the end of St. Mark's Gospel, which only comes in one of the four codices mentioned, namely in the oldest Edschmiadzin Codex, under the heading 'of the Elder Ariston,' which may refer to Aristion, teacher of Papias, or to Ariston of Pella. The case is the same with the episode of the woman taken in adultery. For the settlement of such points there is wanted a careful collation of the oldest codices.

In answer to the other question we may state, without entering into the proof of it, that the fifth century version included all the books of the Old and New Testament save the third book of Ezra, Esther, Tobit, Judith, Wisdom of Solomon, and perhaps the Maccabees. For as we read in Elisaeus that Vartan Mamikonean in the middle of the fifth century inspired his troops to deeds of valour against the Persians by reading to them the Book of Maccabees, we may fairly infer that that also was already then rendered. It may be added that the Psalms were rendered for church use prior to the rest of the Bible, and were translated afresh by Mesrop and his disciples; also that the Book of Revelations was translated twice. The double translation of both these books is a fact which can be traced in various MSS.

One other point must be noticed. From the history of Moses of Chorene, it is not clear what were the imperfections of the Armenian version, to remedy which Moses was sent to Alexandria. We cannot suppose that Mesrop and Sahak and Eznik, and the other doctors who had already translated the Greek codices brought from Byzantium, were incompetent Greek scholars. The object therefore of Moses' voyage to Alexandria was probably that he might add to the Armenian text the Sections of Ammonius, and also the asterisks and obeli of Origen's Hexaplaric copy[1]. The Ammonian Sections are found in all Armenian New Testaments, and in some copies of the Bible the Origenian marks as well; for instance, in Codex 3270 of the Bibliotheca Vindobonensis. There is no evidence that the Armenians ever used a version of Tatian's Diatessaron.

The following is a list—not exhaustive—of the oldest known codices of the Armenian Gospels, or 'Avetaran':—

1. In the Library of the Lazareffski Institute in Moscow, written in large uncials on parchment, dated in the year 336 of the Armenian era = A.D. 887. Size, 37·75 × 28 cent.; 229 folios.

2. In the Library of the Mechitarists in the island of San Lazaro, in Venice, an uncial codex, on parchment, written in the year 351 of the Armenian era = A. D. 902.

3. In the same Library, on parchment, in large uncials, dated 1006.

4. In the same Library, in large uncials, on parchment, undated, but evidently older than No. 2.

5. In the Patriarchal Library of Edschmiadzin in Russian Armenia, No. 222 of the printed catalogue of Jacob Kareneantz (Tiflis, 1863).

[1] This is the conclusion at which P. P. Carékin arrives. See his 'Catalogue of Ancient Armenian Translations,' Venice, 1889, p. 228.

This book is bound in ivory covers, carved, as it would seem, in the Ravennese style in the fifth or sixth century. In large uncials, on parchment, written A.D. 989.

6. In the same Library is No. 223, an uncially written parchment codex. The earliest of the colophons dates from A.D. 1260 and is in majuscule, but the codex itself seems to be at least two centuries and a half earlier.

7. In the same Library, No. 229, written in minuscule, on parchment, A.D. 1035.

8, 9. In the same Library, Nos. 224, 225, in large uncials, on parchment, presumably as old as the eleventh century, but undated.

10. In Tiflis, in an Armenian church. In large uncials, on parchment. Undated, but certainly prior to A.D. 1000.

11. In the Library of the British Museum, in large uncials, on parchment, undated. Probably of the ninth century, but not after the tenth, according to Dr. Baronean, author of the British Museum Catalogue.

12. In Karin or Erzeroum, in large uncials, on parchment. Dated A.D. 986.

13. In the Library of the Fathers of St. Anthony, in Constantinople. Dated A.D. 960.

14. In the island monastery of Sevan, on the lake of that name in Russian Armenia. In large uncials, on parchment. Written during primacy of Vahan, *circa* A.D. 966.

15. In uncials, on parchment; written in Macedonia, under the Emperor Basil, A.D. 1011. (Carékin, Catalogue des Traductions, omits to specify in what library.)

16. Bibliothèque Nationale in Paris. Codex Armenus VII contains the Four Gospels. Codex Bombyc, litteris uncialibus scriptus.

17. In the same Library, Cod. Arm. VIII. Membranaceus, litteris uncialibus scriptus.

(3) The Ethiopic Version (Eth.).

The Ethiopic translation of the Bible is assigned by Guidi to the end of the fifth, or beginning of the sixth century, the time at which Christianity became the dominant religion in Abyssinia. That religion after a period of decadence began to flourish again in the twelfth century, but in dependence on the Patriarchate of Alexandria. The two principal classes of Ethiopic Biblical MSS. are connected with these periods respectively; the first class being derived from the Greek text before, and the latter after the Alexandrian recension. The corrections, however, vary in different copies, and appear to be the result of desultory rather than of systematic alteration. The MSS. of the Ethiopic N. T. are rarely complete; ordinarily the Gospels, the Epistles of St. Paul, and the Catholic Epistles with the Acts and the Apocalypse constitute separate volumes. The oldest copy of the Gospels would seem to be no. 32 of the Bibliothèque Nationale in Paris, written in the reign of Yekūnō Amlāk; whereas MS. 33 of the same collection represents the later text. Examples of the different recensions are given by Guidi, Atti della R. Academia dei Lincei: Classe di scienze morali &c., iv. 1888, from whom most of the above statements are taken.

Copies of the N. T., especially of the Gospels, are to be found in most collections of Ethiopic MSS.; *see* especially Wright, Ethiopic MSS. of the British Museum, pp. 23–39, and Zotenberg, Catalogue des MSS. Éthiopiens de la Bibliothèque Nationale (nos. 32–48; in the preface to this latter work a list of other collections are given); also Dillmann, Abessinische Handschriften der Königlichen Bibliothek zu Berlin (no. 20, the four Gospels; 21, the Gospel of St. John); D'Abbadie, Catalogue Raisonné de MSS. Éthiopiens (Paris, 1859; nos. 2, 47, 82, 95, 112, 173, the four Gospels; no. 119, St. Paul's Epistles; no. 164, Catholic Epp., Apoc., and Acts); Dillmann, Catalogus MSS. Aethiop. in Bibliotheca Bodleiana, nos. 10–15; Fr. Müller, Aethiop. Handschriften der K. K. Hofbibliothek in Wien (Z. D. M. G., xvi. p. 554, no. v, the Gospels; no. vi, St. John's Gospel); 'Bulletin Scientifique de S. Pétersbourg,' ii. 302 (account of a MS. of the Gospels in the Asiatic Institute at St. Petersburg), iii. 148 (account of a MS. of the four Gospels, bearing the date 78=1426 A.D., in the Public Library at St. Petersburg, and another of St. John's Gospel).

The Ethiopic N. T. was first printed in Rome, 1548, cum epistola Pauli ad Hebraeos tantum, cum concordantiis Evangelistarum Eusebii et numeratione omnium verborum eorundem. Quae omnia curavit Fr. Petrus Ethyops auxilio priorum sedente Paulo iii. Pont. Max. et Claudio illius regni imperatore (edition of Tasfā Sion). The remaining thirteen Epistles of St. Paul were printed in 1549. This edition was reproduced in the London Polyglott. Another was issued by T. P. Platt (for the Bible Society) in 1830, reprinted 1844 and 1874. These editions are based on MSS. containing mixed recensions, and are therefore of no critical value.

(4) The Georgian Version (Georg.).

The Church of the Iberians was founded during the reign of Constantine according to tradition; though, if we consider how intimate and frequent had been from a much earlier period their intercourse with the Greeks, we may safely infer that the seeds of Christianity had been long before sown among them. There is no certain evidence of the date at which they translated the Scriptures; but it is probable that their version of the New Testament was made in the fifth and sixth centuries; and that it was made from a Greek text the most perfunctory examination suffices to prove. According to Armenian historians of the fifth century, St. Mesrop, at the same time that he invented the Armenian characters and made the Armenian version for his own countrymen, fulfilled the same service for the Georgians also. In this tradition, however, the Georgians do not concur; and, no doubt, rightly, seeing that their ancient alphabet and their version are alike independent of the Armenian. It is said by some native Georgian scholars that before the tenth century a revision was made of their version, in order to make it more complete.

The present writer knows of no manuscript of the entire Bible in Europe except at Mount Athos, where there is one reputed to be of the tenth century. Others are preserved in the Convents of the Holy Cross at Jerusalem, and of Mount Sinai. In the Vatican Library there is a codex of the New Testament, neatly written on parchment in majuscule, parts of which the present writer has collated with the printed text. This codex is at least as old as the thirteenth century, and in the collations ~~below~~ is referred to as *a*. Beside this codex the writer has examined in the Georgian Library at Tiflis three very ancient codices of the Gospels, written in uncials on parchment. These books were smaller in size than are, as a rule, the copies of the Gospels used in Eastern Churches.

Of the accompanying collations, nos. i–iv are made from them, and the passages collated were photographed by the present writer. These photographs, which represent the originals on a reduced scale, have been deposited by him in the Bodleian Library for the inspection of the curious. The text referred to as *b* is probably of the tenth century or earlier; the one referred to as *c* cannot be much later than the eleventh, while that indicated by *d* must belong to the twelfth, and is the most beautifully written of them.

The Bible was not printed in Georgian until the year 1743 at Moscow in large folio. It is a rare volume, and has never been reprinted. The character is that called ecclesiastical or priestly majuscule, which differs wholly from the civil characters and can, as a rule, be read by the priests only. The New Testament and Psalms have been reprinted at various times from this original edition, both in priestly and civil characters, and of the latter kind very good and cheap copies can be obtained at the British and Foreign Bible Society, printed, however, at Tiflis. It is said that the edition of 1743 was conformed to the Slavonic version of the Bible; and if this were true, it would, of course, impair its value for critical purposes. Of this statement, however, the writer's collations, so far as they go, afford no proof. Such variations as there are between the printed edition and the manuscript texts are notified in these collations. The point, however, could easily be settled by a thorough comparison of the printed text with the Slavonic.

The MSS. of Tiflis include the last verses of Mark, and the Vatican MS. contains the narrative of the woman taken in adultery, but places it after ver. 44, instead of after ver. 52 of the seventh chapter of John. The printed edition places it after ver. 52, and this uncertainty as to where to insert the narrative, in itself indicates that it is a later interpolation. The printed text also contains the text about the three witnesses; but it is pieced into the context in an awkward and ungrammatical way; and whether it is in any MS. the writer cannot say. The following all too brief collations prove that the printed text fairly represents the MSS.; from which, indeed, it differs very little except in its more modern orthography. It is certain, however, that the most ancient MSS. of this version must be collated and a critical text of it prepared, before it can be quite reliably used as an early witness to the Greek text in regard to any particular points. Where the earliest Greek authorities waver as to the particles by which the parts of the narrative shall be connected —some, e.g. giving καί, others δέ, others οὖν—the Georgian constantly passes abruptly to the new matter without any connecting particle at all—and this, although as a language

Georgian is richer in such connecting particles than is Greek. This peculiarity of the version, which is also shared by the old Armenian version, seems to prove that it was made from a primitive text, in which editors had not yet begun to smooth away the sudden transitions.

(5) The Slavonic Version (Slav.[1]).

This version of the Bible is ascribed to Cyril and Methodius, who lived at the end of the ninth century. It is uncertain, however, how much of the New Testament was translated at that date, and how much was the work of a later time. The manuscripts of the version exist in two characters called Glagolitic and Cyrillic: of these it is now generally agreed that the former is the earlier. In considering the version from the point of view of the textual criticism of the New Testament, we need not deal with its later history except in so far as that throws light on its original form. The chief points to which reference will be made will be (i) the different Manuscripts in which the version exists, with their distinctive characteristics, and the evidence they afford as to the earliest form—the *Urtext*—of the version, and (ii) the Greek text presupposed by the version in the form in which we have it.

It will be convenient to divide the New Testament into three component parts, (i) the Gospels, (ii) the Acts and Epistles, or the *Apostol* as it is called in Slavonic, (iii) the Apocalypse. There can be little doubt that the Gospels were the earliest part to be translated or that this translation was made for liturgical purposes. This last point explains the great preponderance of

[1] Among the chief authorities on the Slavonic version are the following:—

(i) Горскій и Невоструевъ, описаніе славянскихъ рукописей Московской Синодальной Библіотеки. Москва, 1855.

(ii) Астафьевъ, Опытъ исторіи библии въ Россіи въ связи съ просвѣщеніемъ и нравами. С. Петербургъ, 1892.

(iii) Voskresenski, Характеристическія черты главныхъ редакцій славянскаго перевода Евангелія.

(iv) Voskresenski, Древній славянскій переводъ Апостола и его судьбы до xv вѣка.

(v) Oblak, Die Kirchenslavische Uebersetzung der Apocalypse [in the 'Archiv für Slavische Philologie,' xiii. pp. 321–361].

(vi) Prolegomena to the editions of the Codex Marianus and the Codex Zographensis, &c., by Jagić.

(vii) Kaluzniacki, Monumenta Linguae Palaeoslavonicae, vol. i.

MSS. of the version in which the Gospels are arranged in the form of a lectionary [1].

Amongst the earliest manuscripts of the Gospels are the Codex Zographensis, Codex Marianus, and the Codex Assemanicus. The two first Jagić ascribes to the tenth or eleventh century. All these are written for the most part in the Glagolitic character. Besides these, mention must be made of the Ostromir Codex, written in Cyrillic characters, by Gregory, a deacon at Novgorod, and dating from the year 1056–7. In considering the distinctive characteristics of these manuscripts of the version, the first point to notice is that they each preserve certain dialectical forms and expressions by which their place of origin and to some extent their date can be determined. Thus Miklosich regards the Codex Zographensis and Codex Assemanicus as preserving Bulgarico-Slovenish forms, the Ostromir Codex as representative of Russo-Slovenish, and so on. It is mainly in these particulars that the manuscripts differ, though there are also other differences by means of which it has been determined that some Codices, especially those in the Glagolitic character, preserve the version in a more original form than others, as for example the Ostromir Codex. These differences consist [2], (i) in orthography, (ii) in the fact that the later forms of the version translate Greek words left untranslated in the older forms, (iii) in the substitution of later and easier words for archaisms. It may also be noted that alterations are more numerous, as might be expected, in copies of the Gospels made for liturgical purposes than in other copies.

The same remarks would be true of the second part of the Bible, the *Apostol*. This is pointed out by Voskresenski in the book to which reference has been made, but which is known to the writer of these lines only from a review. A very careful examination of the text of the 'Apostol,' based on the manuscripts of the Synodal Library, is made by Gorski and Nevostruiev in the work referred to above, pp. 292 ff.

Oblak has examined the Slavonic version of the Apocalypse, of which the manuscripts are fewer and later. The earliest

[1] In the Synodal Library at Moscow this proportion is as nine to two, and in another library as twelve to one. *See* Описаніе славянскихъ рукописей и т. д. (as above), p. 299.

[2] Kaluzniacki, *l. c.*, p. xlv, gives instances.

manuscript is ascribed to the thirteenth century, but the textual corruption which it exhibits in comparison with other manuscripts requires that the version which it embodies should be referred at least to the twelfth century. We do indeed find a quotation of the Apocalypse (ix. 14) as early as the Isbornik of Sviatoslav of the year 1073, but in a form so different from the MSS. of the version now extant, that we must regard it as a quotation from memory. The MSS. have many small variations, sometimes merely dialectical, sometimes based on a different Greek text. They also show marks in places of having been corrected with the help of the Latin. But in spite of all their variations Oblak believes that all the manuscripts are to be referred to one common translation made from a Greek text of the Constantinopolitan type, which has been here and there corrupted by Western influence.

It may be noted in conclusion that the earliest dated complete manuscript of the Gospels is dated 1144, the earliest manuscript of the whole Bible, A.D. 1499, and that the earliest printed edition is the famous Ostrog Bible of 1581.

It remains to say something of the Greek text underlying the Slavonic version, for this is the special point of view from which the versions are being here considered. The instances will all be taken from the Gospels, though others might have been added from those collected by Gorski. In the first place it is necessary to draw attention to the fact that for critical purposes a modern edition of the version will be found insufficient. The following are cases[1] where the edition published by the British and Foreign Bible Society, probably based on the Textus Receptus, is misleading as to the real original reading of the version. In St. Matt. xi. 2 Codd. Assem., Zograph., Ostrom., all imply the reading *διά*, the modern edition *δύο*: in St. John i. 28 the MSS. have Bethany, the edition Bethabara; in St. John vii. 39 the MSS. insert, the edition omits, *δεδομένον*; in St. Matt. xxv. 2 the MSS. put *μωραί* before *φρόνιμοι*, the edition inverts the order. The Ostromir Codex presents a later form of the version, and so we find instances where the other two MSS., just referred to, preserve what is probably a better reading. Thus in St. Luke ii. 3 they have *οἱ γονεῖς αὐτοῦ*, the Ostromir *Ἰωσὴφ καὶ ἡ μήτηρ αὐτοῦ*; in

[1] *See* Jagić, Codex Zographensis, pp. xxvii ff.

St. John ix. 8 they have προσαίτης, it has τυφλός; in St. John xix. 14 they have τρίτη, it reads ἕκτη; in St. John xxi. 15 they have ἀρνία, it has πρόβατα. Again there are cases where one MS. of the version stands alone. Thus Codex Zogr. stands alone, as against Assem. and Ostrom., in omitting St. Luke xiv. 24, and inserting δευτεροπρώτῳ in St. Luke vi. 1. Again in the choice of Slavonic words for the same Greek original, Cod. Zogr. will agree with Codex Assem. against Codex Ostrom., though where the Codex Assemanicus is freer in its rendering, the Ostromir Codex and Codex Zographensis agree. Sometimes again the Codex Zographensis is alone in curious readings which seem to be conflations of the texts found in the other two manuscripts, or based on a conflate Greek text.

This version and the various manuscripts which contain it have received most attention from Slavonic philologists engaged in examining the earliest monuments of their language; but the readings which have been given will be enough to show that it does not deserve to be dismissed, as summarily as has been sometimes the case, from the number of those versions which have a value for purposes of the Textual Criticism of the New Testament.

(6) The Arabic Version (Arab.).

Arabic versions (Arab.) are many, though of the slightest possible critical importance; their literary history, therefore, need not be traced with much minuteness. A notice is quoted from Bar-hebraeus (Assemani, Bibl. Or., ii. 335) to the effect that John, Patriarch of the Monophysites from 631–640, translated the 'Gospel' from Syriac into Arabic; and some scholars have believed in the existence of a pre-Mohammedan version of parts at least of the New Testament on other grounds; from such a version (written in the 'Hebrew' character) in the opinion of Sprenger (Das Leben und die Lehre Muhammads, i. 131) come the verses of St. John's Gospel (xv. 23–27, xvi. 1), cited by Ibn Ishaq (ob. 768) in his 'Life of Mohammed' (ed. Wüstenfeld, i. 150)[1]. These verses are evidently translated from the (Jerusalem ?) Syriac; but the translation of the Gospel, from the Syriac

[1] The statement that John Bishop of Seville translated the Bible into Arabic in A.D. 719 is disproved by Lagarde (Die vier Evangelien Arabisch, p. xv).

into Arabic, existing in a Leipzig MS. brought by Tischendorf from the East and described at length by Gildemeister (De evangeliis in Arabicum e simplici Syriaco translatis, Bonn, 1865) is shown by internal evidence to be posterior to Islam (pp. 30 sq.). The Arabic versions of the Gospel existing in MS. are divided by Guidi (Atti della R. Academia dei Lincei, classe di scienze morali &c., 1888, 1–30) into five sorts: (1) those made directly from the Greek; (2) made directly or corrected from the Peshitto; (3) made directly or corrected from the Coptic; (4) MSS. of two distinct eclectic recensions made in the Alexandrian Patriarchate in the thirteenth century; (5) MSS. (chiefly derived from the Syriac) which are distinguished by their style; being in rhymed prose or elegant Arabic. MSS. of the first sort can all, he says, be traced to the convent of St. Saba near Jerusalem, and are preceded by the lives of its founders, St. Eutimius and St. Saba; the version they contain is to be ascribed to the time of the Caliph Mamun (ninth century). Of the MSS. of class 4, one set represents a recension made by Ibn El-Assāl, circ. 1250; while another represents a less elaborate recension made shortly afterwards, in which the passages omitted in the other were restored, while marginal notes recorded their omission in other versions. Versions of the fifth class were made in the tenth, fourteenth, and seventeenth centuries. A list of MSS. containing the different recensions of all these classes is given by Guidi, *l. c.*, pp. 30–33.

The printed texts all represent varieties of the second eclectic recension of class 4, of which five editions are enumerated by Gildemeister (*l.c.*, pp. 42, 3, and iv). 1. Roman edition of the Gospels from the Medicean Press, 1591 (ar.^{r}), edited by J. Baptista Raymundi, some copies having a Latin translation by Antonius Sionita. The MS. on which this edition was based is unknown. 2. Edition of Thomas Erpenius (1584–1624, Leyden, 1616, containing the whole New Testament (ar.^{e}). This edition was based on the Leyden MS., Scaliger 217, written in Egypt in the year of the Martyrs 1059 (A.D. 1342–3); two other manuscripts also employed by Erpenius for the Gospels are now in the Cambridge University Library (G. 5. 33, and G. 5. 27, written A.D. 1285). A third MS. employed for this edition was in the Carshunic character. The Acts and Pauline Epistles, the Epistles of St. James, St. Peter I and St. John I in this edition are translated from the Peshitto; the remaining Catholic Epistles and the Apocalypse are from some other source; the latter shows some remarkable agreement with the Memphitic (Hug, Einleitung in das N.T., pp. 433–5). 3. Edition of the whole N.T. in the Paris Polyglott (ar.[p]), 1645, reprinted with little alteration in the London Polyglott (1657). Gildemeister, *l. c.*, proves against Lagarde (*l. c.*, xi) that this recension in the Gospels is not an interpolated reprint of the Roman edition, but is based on a MS. similar to Paris Anc. f. 27 (of A.D. 1619) and Coisl. 239 (new Suppl. Ar. 27) described by Scholz, 'Bibl. Krit. Reise,' pp. 56, 58. The Acts, Epistles, and Apocalypse follow the Greek, but are by another translator. 4. Edition of the whole N. T. in the Carshunic character (Rome, 1703), edited by Faustus Naironus, for the use of the Maronites, from a MS. brought from Cyprus, reprinted Paris, 1827; the Acts, Epistles, and Apocalypse represent the same version as that of Erpenius, but in a different recension. 5. Edition of the four Gospels from a Vienna MS. (previously described by S. C. Storr, Dissertatio inauguralis critica de evangeliis Arabicis, Tübingen, 1875, p. 17 sq.), by P. de Lagarde (Die vier Evangelien Arabisch, Leipzig, 1864). The MS. contains various readings from the Coptic, Syriac, and Latin (according to Lagarde, Gildemeister more naturally renders *rūmī* by Greek). The editor has prefixed a table of variants between his text and that of Erpenius, but regards the relation of the former to the original as involving questions too complicated for immediate discussion (p. xxxi).

Extracts from MSS. of Arabic versions in French and Italian libraries are given by J. M. A. Scholz, Biblisch-Kritische Reise, Leipzig and Sorau, 1823; a description of several others, some of great antiquity, is to be found in Tischendorf's 'Anecdota Sacra et Profana,' pp. 70–73 (2nd ed.); and Professor Rendel Harris, in 'Biblical Fragments from Sinai' (Cambridge, 1890) has published a facsimile of a fragment of an Arabic version from a bilingual MS. of the ninth century; the version whence it is derived agrees with none of those that have been published, and was probably older than any of them.

The repeated revision and correction which these translations have undergone (Gildemeister, *l. c.*, 1–3), while they give evidence of the industry and zeal of the Arabic-speaking Christians, have made scholars despair of employing them for critical purposes;

'they rather serve,' says Gildemeister, 'to illustrate the history of biblical and Christian studies.'

(7) The Anglo-Saxon Version (Sax.).

There is but one known version of the four Gospels (the only portion of the N. T. that was translated into A.-S.); this version was made, probably in the South-West of England at or near Bath, in the last quarter of the tenth century. It is preserved in four MSS.: (Corp.) Corpus Christi Coll. Camb. MS. 140; (B) Bodleian Lib. MS. 441; (C) Cotton MS. Otho C. I (seriously injured by fire), and (A) Camb. Univ. Lib. MS. Ii. 2. 11. Of these the first three may be dated, in round number, about the year 1000; the fourth (A) belongs to the following half-century. The Bodl. Lib. has also recently acquired a fragment of four leaves of St. John's Gospel, which agrees closely with A. [Published by Napier in 'Archiv f. n. Sprachen,' vol. lxxxvii. p. 255 f.]

It may also be mentioned that there are in the Brit. Mus. two additional copies of this version (Bibl. Reg. MS. I. A. xiv, and Hatton MS. 38). These belong to a period after the Conquest and have no critical value, for the first is copied from B, and the second is copied from the first.

This version is based upon a type of the Vulgate MSS. that has not yet been definitely determined. Old Latin readings make it certain that the original MS. was of the mixed type.

Next in importance to this version are the two following Latin MSS. of the four Gospels, with an interlinear Anglo-Saxon gloss. (1) MS. Nero D. 4 (the Lindisfarne MS., also known as the Durham Book). The Latin was written by Eadfrith, bishop of Lindisfarne 698–721; the interlinear gloss being about two and a half centuries later, made near Durham about the year 950. (2) The Rushworth MS. (Bodl. Lib. Auct. D. ii. 19). The Latin was written by the scribe Macregol, probably in the eighth century. The gloss, by the scribes Farman and Owun, is referred to the latter half of the tenth century. These two Latin texts differ but slightly; they are also of the Vulgate types.

All the MSS. that have now been mentioned are published in one volume (of four parts) by Professor W. W. Skeat: 'The Holy Gospels in Anglo-Saxon, Northumbrian, and Old Mercian

Versions, synoptically arranged, with collations exhibiting all the readings of all the MSS.; together with the Early Latin Version as contained in the Lindisfarne MS.; collated with the Latin Version in the Rushworth MS. Cambridge: University Press, 1871–1887.' Dr. James W. Bright has published an edition of St. Luke's Gospel of the A.-S. Version, Oxford, 1892, and has in preparation a critical edition of the entire Version [which has been published recently]. The earlier editions of the Anglo-Saxon Gospels are by Archbishop Parker, 1571; Dr. Marshall (rector of Lincoln College), 1665; Benjamin Thorpe, 1842; Dr. Joseph Bosworth, 1865.

(8) The Frankish Version (Fr.).

A Frankish version of St. Matthew, from a manuscript of the ninth century at St. Gall, in the Frankish dialect of the Teutonic, was published by J. A. Schmeller in 1827. Tischendorf (N. T., Proleg., p. 225) thinks it worthy of examination, but does not state whether it was translated from the Greek or Latin: the latter supposition is the more probable.

(9) Persic Versions (Pers.).

Persic versions of the Gospels only, in print, are two: (1) one in Walton's Polyglott ($pers.^p$) with a Latin version by Samuel Clarke (which C. A. Bode thought it worth his while to reconstruct, Helmstedt, 1750-51, with a learned Preface), obviously made from the Peshitto Syriac, which the Persians had long used ('yet often so paraphrastic as to claim a character of its own,' Malan, *ubi supra*, p. xi), 'interprete Symone F. Joseph Taurinensi,' and taken from a single manuscript belonging to E. Pocock[1], *probably* dated A. D. 1341. This version may prove of some use in restoring the text of the Peshitto. (2) The second, though apparently modern [xiv?] was made from the Greek ($pers.^w$). Its publication was commenced in 1652 by Abraham Wheelocke, Professor of Arabic and Anglo-Saxon and University Librarian at Cambridge, at the expense of Sir Th. Adams, the generous and loyal alderman

[1] Edward Pocock, Professor of Hebrew at Oxford (1648–91) and a great Oriental scholar, should be distinguished from Richard Pococke, an Eastern traveller and Bishop of Meath, who died in 1765.

of London. The basis (as appears from the volume itself) was an Oxford codex (probably Laud. A. 96 of the old notation), which Wheelocke, in his elaborate notes at the end of each chapter, compared with Pocock's and with a third manuscript at Cambridge (Gg. v. 26), dated 1014 of the Hegira (A. D. 1607). On Wheelocke's death in 1653 only 108 pages (to Matt. xviii. 6) were printed, but his whole text and Latin version being found ready for the press, the book was published with a second title-page, dated London, 1657, and a short Preface by an anonymous editor (said to be one Pierson), who in lieu of Wheelocke's notes, which break off after Matt. xvii., appended a simple collation of the Pocock manuscript from that place. The Persians have older versions, parts of both Testaments, still unpublished. There is another copy of the Persian Gospels at Cambridge, which once belonged to Archbishop Bancroft, and was brought from Lambeth in 1646, but was not restored in 1662 with the other books belonging to the Lambeth Library.

CHAPTER VI.

ON THE CITATIONS FROM THE GREEK NEW TESTAMENT OR ITS VERSIONS MADE BY EARLY ECCLESIASTICAL WRITERS, ESPECIALLY BY THE CHRISTIAN FATHERS.

1. WE might at first sight be inclined to suppose that the numerous quotations from the New Testament contained in the remains of the Fathers of the Church and other Christian writers from the first century of our era downwards, would be more useful even than the early versions, for enabling us to determine the character of the text of Scripture current in those primitive times, from which no manuscripts of the original have come down to us [1]. Unquestionably the testimony afforded by these venerable writings will be free from some of the objections that so much diminish the value of translations for critical purposes which have been stated at the commencement of this volume: and the use made of it by Dean Burgon in his remarkable volume entitled the 'Revision Revised [2],' has shown scholars how vast a body of valuable illustrations has received inadequate attention. But not to insist on the fact that many important passages of the New Testament have not been cited at all in any very ancient work now extant, this species of evidence labours under difficulties peculiarly its own. Not only is this kind of testimony fragmentary and not (like that of versions) continuous, so that it often fails us where we should most wish for information: but the Fathers were better theologians than critics; they

[1] I have been obliged to alter the first paragraph in this chapter because of Dr. Scrivener's private confession to myself of the great value of Dean Burgon's services in this province of Sacred Textual Criticism. I am convinced that he could not have continued to maintain an opinion so adverse to the value of early citations as that which he formed when people were not sufficiently aware of the wealth of illustrative evidence that lay ready to their hands. As Editor I owe very much in this chapter, both to the express teaching in Dean Burgon's great book, and to his method of argument in respect to patristic citations. The Dean did not leave this province at all as he found it.

[2] The Revision Revised, by John William Burgon, B.D., Dean of Chichester. John Murray, 1883.

sometimes quoted loosely, or from memory, often no more of a passage than their immediate purpose required; and what they actually wrote has been found liable to change on the part of copyists and unskilful editors. But when all is considered, the Fathers must be at least held under due limitations to be witnesses to the readings found in the codices which they used. If theirs is secondary evidence, it is nevertheless in many cases virtually older than any that can be had from MSS. of the entire text. The fewness of early MSS. adds importance to other early testimony. And the strength of this kind of evidence is found at the highest, when the issue is of a somewhat broader character than usual, and when a large number of quotations are found to corroborate testimony from MSS. and the testimony of Versions. In fact the strength of their evidence is to be seen especially in three aspects: First, they supply us with numerous codices, though at second hand, at a very early date; secondly, there is no doubt whatever that the date of the codices used by them is not later than when they wrote, and their own date is usually a matter of no question; and thirdly, they help us to assign the locality to remarkable readings[1]. In other words, the unknown MS. derives life and character from the Father who uses it[2]. On the other hand, the same author perpetually cites the selfsame text under two or more various forms; in the Gospels it is often impossible to determine to which of the three earlier ones reference is made; and, on the whole, where Scriptural quotations from ecclesiastical writers are single and unsupported, they may safely be disregarded altogether. An *express* citation, however, by a really careful Father of the first four or five centuries (as Origen, for example), if supported by manuscript authority, and countenanced by the best versions, claims our respectful attention, and powerfully vindicates the reading which it favours[3]. In fact, like Versions, Patristic citations

[1] *See* some very thoughtful and cautious remarks by the Rev. Ll. J. M. Bebb in the second volume of the Oxford 'Studia Biblica (et Ecclesiastica).' Mr. Bebb's entire Article on 'The Evidence of the Early Versions and Patristic Quotations on the Text of the Books of the New Testament' is well worth careful study.

[2] 'Dated codices, in fact they are, to all intents and purposes.' Burgon, Revision Revised, p. 292. 'Every Father is seen to be a dated witness and an independent authority,' p. 297.

[3] I am glad to be able to coincide thus far with the judgement of Mr. Hammond, who says: 'The value of even the most definite Patristic citation is only corroborative. Standing by itself, any such citation might mean no more

cannot be taken primarily to establish any reading. But they are often invaluable in supplying support to manuscriptal authority, whether by proving a primitive antiquity, or in demonstrating by an overwhelming body of testimony that the passage or reading was accepted in all ages and in many provinces of the earlier church. Frequently also, they are of unquestionable use, when they bear witness in a less striking manner, or in smaller number.

2. The practice of illustrating the various readings of Scripture from the reliques of Christian antiquity is so obvious and reasonable, that all who have written critical annotations on the sacred text have resorted to it, from Erasmus downwards: the Greek or Latin commentators are appealed to in four out of the five marginal notes found in the Complutensian N. T. When Bishop Fell, however, came to prepare the first edition of the Greek Testament attended with any considerable apparatus for improving the text, he expressly rejected 'S. Textus loca ab antiquis Patribus aliter quam pro recepto more laudata,' from which the toil of such a task did not so much deter him, 'quam cogitatio quod minus utile esset futurum iisdem insistere.' (N. T. 1675, Praef.). 'Venerandi enim illi scriptores,' he adds, 'de verborum apicibus non multum soliciti, ex memoriâ quae ad institutum suum factura videbantur passim allegabant; unde factum ut de priscâ lectione ex illorum scriptis nil ferè certi potuerit hauriri.' It is certainly to the credit of Mill's sagacity that he did not follow his patron's example by setting aside Patristic testimony in so curt and compendious a manner[1]. Nevertheless, no one can study Mill's 'Prolegomena' without being conscious of the fact, that the portion of them relating to the history of the text, as gathered from ecclesiastical writers, and the accumulation of that mass of quotations from the Fathers which stands below his Scripture text, must have been, what he asserts, the result of some years' labour (N. T. Proleg. § 1513): yet these

than that the writer found the passage in his own copy, or in those examined by him, in the form in which he quotes it. The moment, however, it is found to be supported by other good evidence, the writer's authority may become of immense importance' (Outlines of Textual Criticism, p. 66, 2nd edition). His illustration is the statement of Irenaeus in Matt. i. 18, which is discussed below, Chap. XI. (Third Edition.)

[1] He speaks (N. T., Proleg., § 1478) of Bp. Fell's 'praepropera opinio;' he merely stated as *universally* true what for the most part certainly is so.

are just the parts of his celebrated work that have given the least satisfaction. The field indeed is too vast to be occupied by one man. A whole library of authors has to be thoroughly searched; each cited passage must be patiently examined; the help of *indices* should be employed critically and warily; the best editions must be used, and even then the text of the very writers is to be corrected, so far as may be, by the collation of other manuscripts [1].

3. To Griesbach must be assigned the merit of being the earliest editor of the Greek Testament who saw, or at least who acted upon the principle, that it is far more profitable as well as more scholarlike to do one thing well, than to attempt more than can be performed completely and with accuracy. He was led by certain textual theories he had adopted, and which we shall best describe hereafter, to a close examination of the works of Origen, the most celebrated Biblical critic of antiquity. The result, published in the second volume of his Symbolae Criticae, is a lasting monument both of his industry and acuteness; and, if not quite faultless in point of correctness, deserves to be taken as a model by his successors. Tregelles, of whose Greek Testament we shall presently speak, has evidently bestowed much pains on his Patristic citations; to Eusebius of Caesarea, especially to those portions of his works which have been recently edited or brought to light, he has paid great attention: but besides many others, Chrysostom has been grievously neglected, although the subjects of a large portion of his writings, the early date of some of his codices [2], the extensive collations of Matthaei, and the excellent modern editions of most of his Homilies, might have sufficed to commend him to our particular regard. The custom, commenced by Lachmann, and adopted by Tregelles (though not uniformly by Tischendorf), of recording the exact edition, volume, and page of the writer

[1] Take the case of Irenaeus, in some respects the most important of them all. The *editio princeps* of Erasmus (1526) was printed from manuscripts now unknown. The three best manuscripts are in Latin only. The oldest of them I saw at Middle-hill, an exquisite specimen of the tenth or eleventh century, *olim* Claromontanus; another, of the twelfth, is in the Arundel collection in the British Museum; the third once belonged to Vossius.

[2] Tischendorf (N. T., Proleg., p. 256, 7th edition) speaks of one Wolfenbüttel manuscript of the sixth century containing the Homilies on St. Matthew, which he designed to publish in his 'Monumenta Sacra Inedita,' vol. vii. He indicates its readings by Chr^{gue}.

quoted, and in important cases of copying his very words, cannot be too much praised: we would suggest, however, the expediency of further indicating, by an asterisk or some such mark, those passages about which there can be no ambiguity as to the reading adopted by the author, in order to distinguish them from others which are of infinitely less weight and importance.

4. But the greatest step of all towards an extended use of Patristic testimony has been taken by Dean Burgon, and since his much lamented death the results of his labours have been made public. In the early stages of his studies in Sacred Textual Criticism, Burgon saw the extreme value—afterwards recognized by Dr. Scrivener—of an exhaustive use of citations from the Fathers and other ecclesiastical authors; and after a conversation with the Earl of Cranbrook, then Mr. Gathorne Hardy, he set himself upon the vast task of collecting indices of New Testament quotations occurring in the books of those writers. 'This involved his looking through all the Greek and Latin folios of the Fathers, and marking the texts in the margin. Then the folios passed into the hands of his assistants, who arranged the references in the order of the Books of the New Testament, and copied them out; so that it might be only the work of a minute to ascertain how Cyril, or Eusebius, or Gregory of Nyssa quoted such a text[1],' and how many times it was quoted by the Father in question. They were revised and enlarged some years after their first collection. The striking use to which Burgon put his own indices has been already noticed. After his death the sixteen stout volumes containing them were acquired by the authorities of the British Museum, where they have been found to be of much use in cataloguing. Steps have been already taken for the publication of the part relating to the Gospels with Dean Burgon's other works on this great subject.

5. It may be convenient to subjoin an alphabetical list of the ecclesiastical writers, both in Greek and Latin and in other languages (with the usual abridgements for their names), which are the most often cited in critical editions of the New Testament. The Latin authors are printed in italics, and unless they happen to appeal unequivocally to the evidence of Greek codices, are available only for the correction of their vernacular transla-

[1] Life of Dean Burgon, by Dean Goulburn, p. 82, note. Murray, 1892.

tion. The dates annexed generally indicate the death of the persons they refer to, except when 'fl.' (=*floruit*) is prefixed.

Alcimus (Avitus), fl. ~~300.~~ 500
Ambrose, Bp. of Milan, A.D. 397 (Ambr.).
Ambrosiaster, the false Ambrose, perhaps *Hilary* the Deacon, of the fourth century (Ambrst.).
Ammonius of Alexandria, circa 438 (Ammon.) *in Catenis.*
Amphilochius, fl. 380.
Anastasius, Abbot, fl. ~~650.~~ 741
Anastasius Sinaita, fl. 570.
Andreas, Bishop of Caesarea, sixth century? (And.)
Andreas of Crete, seventh century.
Antiochus, monk, fl. 614.
Antipater, Bp. of Bostra, fl. 450.
Aphraates, the Syrian, fourth century.
Archelaus and Manes, fl. 278.
Arethas, Bp. of Caesarea Capp., tenth century? (Areth.)
Aristides, fl. 139.
Arius, fl. 325.
Arnobius of Africa, 306 (Arnob.).
Asterius, fourth century.
Athanasius, Bp. of Alexandria, 373 (Ath.).
Athenagoras of Athens, 177 (Athen.).
Augustine, Bp. of Hippo, 430 (Aug.).
Barnabas, first or second century? (Barn.)
Basil, Bp. of Caesarea, 379 (Bas.).
Basil of Cilicia, fl. 497.
Basil of Seleucia, fl. 440 (Bas. Sel.).
Bede, the Venerable, 735 (Bede).
Caesarius of Arles, fl. 520.
Caesarius (Pseudo-) of Constantinople, 340 (Caes.).
Candidus Isaurus, fl. 500.
Capreolus, fl. 430.
Carpathius, John, fl. 490.
Cassianus, fl. 415.
Cassiodorus, 468–560 (?) (Cassiod.)
Chromatius, Bp. of Aquileia, fl. 390 (Chrom.).
Chrysostom, Bp. of Constantinople, 407 (Chrys.).
Chrysostom (Pseudo-), fl. eighth century.
Clement of Alexandria, fl. 194 (Clem.).
Clement, Bp. of Rome, fl. 90 (Clem. Rom.).
Clementines, the, second century.
Corderius,
Cosmas, Bp. of Maiuma, fl. 743.
Cosmas Indicopleustes, 535 (Cosm.).
Cyprian, Bp. of Carthage, 258 (Cypr.).
Cyril, Bp. of Alexandria, 444 (Cyr.).
Cyril, Bp. of Jerusalem, 386 (Cyr. Jer.).
Dalmatius, fl. 450.
Damascenus, John, 730 (Dam.)[1].
Damasus, Pope, fl. 366.
Didache, 80–120.
Didymus of Alexandria, 370 (Did.).
Diodorus of Tarsus, fl. 380.
Dionysius, Bp. of Alexandria, 265 (Dion.).
Dionysius of Alexandria (Pseudo-), third century.
Dionysius (Pseudo-) Areopagita, fifth century (Dion. Areop.).
Dionysius Maximus, fl. 259 (?).
Ephraem the Syrian, 378 (Ephr.).
Ephraem the Syrian (Pseudo-), fourth century.
Ephraim, Bp. of Cherson.
Epiphanius, Bp. of Cyprus, 403 (Epiph.).
Epiphanius, Deacon of Catana, fl. 787.
Erechthius, fl. 440.
Eudocia, wife of Theodosius II, fl. 430.
Eulogius, sixth century.
Eusebius of Alexandria,
Eusebius, Bp. of Caesarea, 340 (Eus.).
Eustathius, Bp. of Antioch, fl. 350.
Eustathius, monk,
Euthalius, Bp. of Sulci, 458 (Euthal.).
Eutherius, fl. 431.
Euthymius Zigabenus, 1116 (Euthym.).

[1] Dam$^{\text{par cod}}$. i. e. 'Joh. Damasceni parallela sacra ex cod. Rupefuc. saeculi ferè 8.' Tischendorf, N. T., Preface to vol. i of the eighth edition, 1869. He promised full information in his 'Prolegomena,' which never appeared. (Here we have a manuscript ascribed to the same century as the Father whose work it contains.) One MS. is at Paris (collated by Mr. Rendel Harris, A.D. 1884); another in Phillipps collection at Cheltenham.

Eutychius, fl. 553.
Evagrius of Pontus, 380 (Evagr.).
Evagrius Scholasticus, the historian, fl. 492.
Facundus, fl. 547.
Faustus, fl. 400.
Ferrandus, fl. 356.
Fulgentius of Ruspe, fl. 508 (Fulg.).
Gaudentius, fl. 405 (Gaud.).
Gelasius of Cyzicus, fl. 476.
Gennadius, fl. 459.
Germanus of Constantinople, fl. 715.
Gregentius, fl. 540.
Gregory of Nazianzus, the Divine, Bp. of Constantinople, 389 (Naz.).
Gregory Naz. (Pseudo-).
Gregory, Bp. of Nyssa, 396 (Nyss.).
Gregory Thaumaturgus, Bp. of Neocaesarea, 243 (Thauma.).
Gregory the Great, Bp. of Rome, 605 (Greg.).
Haymo, Bp. of Halberstadt, ninth century (Haym.).
Hegesippus, fl. 180.
Hermas, second century.
Hieronymus (Jerome), 420 (Hier.) or (Jer.).
Hilary, Bp. of Arles, 429.
Hilary, Bp. of Poictiers, fl. 354 (Hil.).
Hilary, the deacon, fourth century.
Hippolytus, Bp. of Portus (?), fl. 220 (Hip.).
Ignatius, Bp. of Antioch, 107 (Ign.).
Ignatius (Pseudo-), fourth century.
Irenaeus, Bp. of Lyons, fl. 178; chiefly extant in an old Latin version (Iren.).
Isidore of Pelusium, 412 (Isid.).
Jacobus Nisibenus, fl. 335.
Jobius, sixth century.
Julian, heretic, fl. 425.
Julius Africanus, fl. 220.
Justin Martyr, 164 (Just.).
Justin Martyr (Pseudo-), fourth century.
Justinian, Emperor, fl. 527–565.
Juvencus, fl. 320 (Juv.).
Lactantius, 306 (Lact.).
Leo the Great, fl. 440.
Leontius of Byzantium, fl. 348.
Liberatus of Carthage, fl. 533.
Lucifer, Bp. of Cagliari, 367 (Luc.).
Macarius Magnes, third or fourth century.
Macarius Magnus, fourth century.
Manes, fl. 278. *See* Archelaus.
Marcion the heretic, 139 (Mcion.), cited by Epiphanius (Mcion-e) and by *Tertullian* (Mcion-t).
Maxentius, sixth century.
Maximus the Confessor, 662 (Max. Conf.).
Maximus Taurinensis, 466 (Max. Taur.).
Mercator, Marius, fl. 218.
Methodius, 311 (Meth.).
Modestus, patriarch of Jerus. seventh century.
Nestorius of C. P., fifth century.
Nicephorus, fl. 787.
Nicetas of Aquileia, fifth century.
Nicetas of Byzantium, 1120.
Nilus, monk, fl. 430.
Nonnus, fl. 400 (Nonn.).
Novatianus, fl. 251 (Novat.).
Oecumenius, Bp. of Tricca, tenth century ? (Oecu.)
Optatus, fl. 371.
Origen, b. 186, d. 253 (Or.).
Pacianus, Bp. of Barcelona, fl. 370.
Pamphilus the Martyr, 308 (Pamph.).
Papias, fl. 160.
Paschasius, the deacon ?
Paulus, Bp. of Emesa, fl. 431.
Paulus, patriarch of Constantinople, fl. 648.
Peter, Bp. of Alexandria, 311 (Petr.).
Petrus Chrysologus, Archbp. of Ravenna, fl. 440.
Petrus, Deacon, fl. sixth century.
Petrus Siculus, fl. 790.
Philo of Carpasus, fourth century.
Phoebadius, Bp. of Agen, fl. 358.
Photius, Bp. of Constantinople, 891 (Phot.).
Polycarp, Bp. of Smyrna, 166 (Polyc.).
Porphyrius, fl. 290.
Primasius, Bp. of Adrumetum, fl. 550 (Prim.).
Prosper of Aquitania, fl. 431.
Prudentius, 406 (Prud.).
Rufinus of Aquileia, 397 (Ruf.).
Severianus, a Syrian Bp., 409 (Sevrn.).
Severus of Antioch, fl. 510.
Socrates } Church } fl. 440 (Soc.).
Sozomen } Historians } 450 (Soz.).
Suidas the lexicographer, 980 ? (Suid.).

Symeon, fl. 1000.
Symmachus, fourth century.
Tatian of Antioch, 172 (Tat.).
Tatian (Pseudo-), third century.
Tertullian of Africa, fl. 200 (Tert.)[1].
Theodore, Bp. of Mopsuestia, 428 (Thdor. Mops.).
Theodoret, Bp. of Cyrus or of Cyrrhus in Commagene, 458 (Thdrt.).
Theodorus of Heracleia, fl. 336.
Theodorus, Lector, fl. 525.
Theodorus Studita, fl. 794.
Theodotus of Ancyra, fl. 431.
Theophilus of Alexandria, fl. 388.
Theophilus, Bp. of Antioch, 182 (Thph. Ant.).
Theophylact, Archbp. of Bulgaria, fl. 1077 (Theophyl.).
Tichonius the Donatist, fl. 390 (Tich.).
Timotheus of Antioch, fifth century.
Timotheus of Jerusalem, sixth century.
Titus, Bp. of Bostra, fl. 370 (Tit. Bost.).
Victor of Antioch, 430 (Vict. Ant.)[2].
Victor, Bp. of Tunis, 565 (Vict. Tun.).
Victorinus, Bp. of Pettau, 360 (Victorin.).
Victorinus of Rome, fl. 361.
Vigilius of Thapsus, 484 (Vigil.).
Vincentius Lirinensis, fl. 434.
Zacharias, patriarch of Jerusalem, fl. 614.
Zacharias, Scholasticus, fl. 536.
Zeno, Bp. of Verona, fl. 463.

Besides the writers, the following anonymous works contain quotations from the New Testament:—

Auctor libri de xlii. mansionibus (auct. mans.), fourth century.
Auctor libri de Promissionibus dimid. temporis (Prom.), third century.
Auctor libri de Rebaptismate (Rebapt.), fourth century.
Auctor libri de singularitate clericorum (auct. sing. cler.), fourth century.
Auctor libri de Vocatione gentium (Vocat.), fourth century.
Acta Apostolica (Syriac), fourth century.
Acta Philippi, fourth century.
Acta Pilati, third or fourth century.
Anaphora Pilati, fifth century.
Apocalypse of Peter, 170 (?)
Apocryphal Gospels, second century, &c.
Apostolic Canons, third to fifth century.
Apostolic Constitutions, third and fourth centuries.
Chronicon Paschale, 628.
Concilia, Labbè or Mansi.
Cramer's Catena.
Dialogus, fourth or fifth century.
Eastern bishops at Ephesus, 431.
Gospel of Peter, about 165.
Opus Imperfectum, fifth century.
Quaestiones ex utroque Testamento, fourth century[3].

[1] This important witness for the Old Latin version must now be used with H. Roensch's 'Das Neue Testament Tertullian's,' Leipzig, 1871, wherein all his citations from the N. T. are arranged and critically examined.

[2] *See* Dean Burgon's Appendix (D) to his 'Last Twelve Verses of St. Mark,' pp. 269–287, which well deserves the praise accorded to it by a not very friendly critic. The Dean discusses at length the genius and character of Victor of Antioch's Commentary on St. Mark, and enumerates the manuscripts which contain it.

[3] It should be stated that some of the dates in the two tables just given are doubtful, authorities differing.

CHAPTER VII.

EARLY PRINTED EDITIONS.

IT would be quite foreign to our present design, to attempt to notice all the editions of the New Testament in Greek which have appeared in the course of the last three centuries and a half, nor would a large volume suffice for such a labour. We will limit our attention, therefore, to those early editions which have contributed to form our commonly received text, and to such others of more recent date as not only exhibit a revised text, but contain an accession of fresh critical materials for its more complete emendation [1].

Since the Latin or 'Mazarin' Bible, printed between 1452 and 1456, was the first production of the new-born printing-press (*see* above, p. 61), and the Jews had published the Hebrew Bible in 1488, we must impute it to the general ignorance of Greek among divines in Western Europe, that although the two songs, *Magnificat* and *Benedictus* (Luke i), were annexed to a Greek Psalter which appeared first at Milan in 1481, without a printer's

[1] Since the first edition of this book was issued, Ed. Reuss has published 'Bibliotheca Novi Testamenti Graeci, cuius editiones ab initio typographiae ad nostram aetatem impressas quotquot reperiri potuerunt collegit digessit illustravit E. R. Argentoratensis' (Brunsvigae, 1872), to which the reader is referred for editions which our purpose does not lead us to notice. Some of his statements regarding the text of early editions we have repeated in the notes of the present chapter. His enumeration is not grounded on a complete collation of any book, but from the study of a thousand passages (p. 24) selected for his purpose. Hence his numerical results are perpetually less than our own, or even than Mill's. Professor Isaac H. Hall in Schaff's 'Companion to the Greek Testament and the English Version,' D. I. Macmillan, 1883, has improved upon Reuss, and given a list of editions which as to America is, I believe, exhaustive (*see* also his 'American Greek Testaments—a Critical Bibliography of the Greek New Testament as published in America'—Philadelphia, Pickwick and Company, 1883), and is very full as regards English and other editions. I should like to have availed myself of the Professor's kind permission to copy that list, but it would have been going out of the way to do so, since these two chapters are simply upon the *Early* Printed and the *Critical* Editions of the Text.—ED.

name; next at Venice in 1486, being edited by a Greek; again at Venice from the press of Aldus in 1496 or 1497: and although the first six chapters of St. John's Gospel were published at Venice by Aldus Manutius in 1504, and John vi. 1—14 at Tübingen in 1514, yet the first *printed* edition of the whole in N. T. the original is that contained in—

1. The Complutensian Polyglott[1] (6 vols., folio), the munificent design of Francis Ximenes de Cisneros [1437–1517], Cardinal Archbishop of Toledo, and Regent of Castile (1506–1517). This truly eminent person, six years of whose humble youth were spent in a dungeon through the caprice of one of his predecessors in the Primacy of Spain, experienced what we have seen so conspicuously illustrated in other instances, that long imprisonment ripens the intellect which it fails to extinguish. Entering the Franciscan order in 1482, he carried the ascetic habit of his profession to the throne of Toledo and the palace of his sovereign. Becoming in 1492 Confessor to Queen Isabella the Catholic, and Primate three years later, he devoted to pure charity or to public purposes the enormous revenues of his see; founding the University at Alcalá de Henares in New Castile, where he had gone to school, and defraying the cost of an expedition which as Regent he led to Oran against the Moors. In 1502 he conceived the plan of the first Polyglott Bible, to celebrate the birth of him who afterwards became the Emperor Charles V, and gathered in his University of Alcalá (*Complutum*) as many manuscripts as he could procure, with men he deemed equal to the task, of whom James Lopez de Stunica (subsequently known for his controversy with Erasmus) was the principal: others being Æ. Antonio of Lebrixa, Demetrius Ducas of Crete, and Ferdinand of Valladolid (*Pintianus*). The whole outlay of Cardinal Ximenes on the Polyglott is stated to have exceeded 50,000 ducats or about £23,000, a vast sum in those days:—but his yearly income as Primate was four times as great. The first volume printed, Tom. v, contains the New Testament in two parallel columns, Greek and Latin, the latter being that modification of the Vulgate then current: the colophon on the last page of the Apocalypse states

[1] 'Novum Testamentum Grece et Latine in academia complutensi noviter impressum,' Tom. v.

that it was completed January 10, 1514, the printer being Arnald William de Brocario. Tom. vi, comprising a Lexicon, indices, &c., bears date March 17, 1515; Tom. i–iv of the Old Testament and Apocrypha, 1517 (Tom. iv dated July 10), on November 8 of which year the Cardinal died, full of honours and good deeds. This event must have retarded the publication of the whole, since Pope Leo's licence was not granted until March 22, 1520, and Erasmus did not see the book before 1522. As not more than six hundred copies were printed, this Polyglott must from the first have been scarce and dear, and is not always met with in Public Libraries.

The Apocryphal books, like the N. T., are of course given only in two languages; in the Old Testament the Latin Vulgate holds the chief place in the middle, between the Hebrew and the Septuagint Greek[1]. The Greek type in the other volumes is of the common character, with the usual breathings and accents; in the fifth, or New Testament volume, it is quite different, being modelled after the fashion of manuscripts of about the thirteenth century, very bold and elegant (*see* Plate x, No. 26), without breathings, and accentuated according to a system defended and explained in a bilingual preface πρὸς τοὺς ἐντευξομένους, but never heard of before or since: monosyllables have no accent, while in other words the *tone* syllable receives the acute, the grave and circumflex being discarded. The Latin is in a noble church-character, references are made from the one text to the other by means of small letters, and where in either column there is a void space, in consequence of words omitted or otherwise, it is filled up by such curves as are seen in the bottom line of our specimen. The foreign matter in this volume consists of the short Preface in Latin and Greek, Eusebius Carpiano (but without the canons), Jerome's letter to Damasus, with the ordinary Latin Prologues

[1] Quite enough has been made of that piece of grim Spanish humour, 'Mediam autem inter has latinam beati Hieronymi translationem velut inter Synagogam et Orientalem Ecclesiam posuimus: tanquam duos hinc et inde latrones, medium autem Jesum, hoc est Romanam sive latinam Ecclesiam collocantes' (Prol. Tom. i). The editors plainly meant no disparagement to the original Scriptures, *as such;* but they had persuaded themselves that Hebrew codices had been corrupted by the Jew, the Septuagint by the schismatical Greek, and so clung to the Latin as the only form (even before the Council of Trent) in which the Bible was known or studied in Western Europe.

and Arguments before each book. St. Paul's Epistles precede the Acts, as in Codd. ℵ, 61, 69, 90, &c. and before them stand the *ἀποδημία παύλου*, Euthalii *περὶ χρόνων*, the ordinary *ὑποθέσεις* to all the twenty-one Epistles (grouped together), with Theodoret's *prologues* subjoined to thirteen of the *ὑποθέσεις*. By the side of the Latin text are numerous parallel passages, and there are also five marginal notes (on Matt. vi. 13; 1 Cor. xiii. 3; xv. 31; 51; 1 John v. 7, 8). The only divisions are the common Latin chapters, subdivided by the letters A, B, C, D, &c. Copies of laudatory verses[1], an interpretation of Proper Names, and a Greek Lexicon of the N. T., close the volume.

It has long been debated among critics, what manuscripts were used by the Complutensian editors, especially in the N. T. Ximenes is reported to have spent 4,000 ducats in the purchase of such manuscripts; in the Preface to the N. T. we are assured that 'non quevis exemplaria impressioni huic archetypa fuisse: sed antiquissima emendatissimaque: ac tante preterea vetustatis, ut fidem eis abrogare nefas videatur: Que sanctissimus in Christo pater et dominus noster Leo decimus pontifex maximus, huic instituto favere cupiens ex apostolica bibliotheca educta misit. . . .' Yet these last expressions can hardly refer to the N. T., inasmuch as Leo X was not elected Pope till March 11, 1513, and the N. T. was *completed* Jan. 10 of the very next year[2]. Add to this that Vercellone, whose services to sacred literature have been spoken of above, brought to light the fact that only two manuscripts are recorded as having been sent to the Cardinal from the Vatican in the first year of Leo, and neither of them (Vat. 330, 346) contained any part of

[1] Of these, two copies are in Greek, three in Latin Elegiacs. I subjoin those of the native Greek editor, Demetrius Ducas, as a rather favourable specimen of verse composition in that age: the fantastic mode of accentuation described above was clearly not *his* work.

Ειπράξεις ὅσιαι ἀρετῆτε βροτοὺς ἐς ὄλυμπον,
ἐσμακάρων χῶρον καὶ βίον οἶδεν ἄγειν,
ἀρχιερεὺς ξιμένης θεῖος πέλει. ἔργα γὰρ αὐτοῦ
ἥδε βίβλος. θνητοῖς ἄξια δῶρα τάδε.

[2] Tregelles (Account of the Printed Text, p. 7, note) states that he was *elected* Feb. 28, crowned March 11: Sir Harris Nicolas ('Chronology of History,' p. 194) that he was elected March 11, without naming the date of his coronation as usual, but mentioning that 'Leo X, in his letters, dated the commencement of his pontificate before his coronation.'

the N. T.[1] The only one of the Complutensian codices specified by Stunica, the Cod. Rhodiensis (Act. 52), has entirely disappeared, and from a Catalogue of the thirty volumes of Biblical manuscripts once in the library at Alcalà, but now at Madrid, communicated in 1846 by Don José Gutierrez, the Librarian, we find that they consist exclusively of Latin and Hebrew books, with the exception of two which contain portions of the Septuagint in Greek[2]. Thus we seem cut off from all hope of obtaining direct information as to the age, character, and present locality of the materials employed for the Greek text of this edition.

It is obvious, however, that in the course of twelve years (1502–14), Ximenes may have obtained *transcripts* of codices he did not himself possess, and since some of the more remarkable readings of the Complutensian are found in but one or two manuscripts (e. g. Luke i. 64 in Codd. 140, 251; ii. 22 in Cod. 76), such copies should of course be narrowly watched. We have pointed out above the resemblance that Siedel's codex (Act. 42, Paul. 48, Apoc. 13) bears to this edition: so too Cod. 4 of the Gospels. Mill first noticed its affinity to Laud. 2 or Evan. 51, Act. 32, Paul. 38 (Evan. 51), and though this is somewhat remote in the Gospels, throughout the Acts and Epistles it is close and indubitable[3]. We see, therefore,

[1] The following is the document (a curiosity in its way) as cited by Vercellone: 'Anno primo Leonis PP. X. Reverendiss. Dom. Franciscus Card. Toletanus de mandato SS. D. N. Papae habuit ex bibliotheca a Dom. Phaedro Bibliothecario duo volumina graeca: unum in quo continentur libri infrascripti; videlicet Proverbia Salomonis, Ecclesiastes, Cant. Cant., Job, Sapientia, Ecclesiasticus, Esdras, Tobias, Judith [this is Vat. 346, or 248 of Parsons]. Sunt in eo folia quingenta et duodecim ex papyro in nigro.' Fuit extractum ex blancho primo bibliothecae graecae communis. Mandatum Pontificis super concessione dictorum librorum registratum fuit in Camera Apostolica per D. Franciscum De Attavantes Notarium, ubi etiam annotata est obligatio. Promisit restituere intra annum sub poena ducentorum ducatorum.'—'Restituit die 9 Julii, MDXVIII. Ita est. Fr. Zenobius Bibliothecarius.'

[2] The Catalogue is copied at length by Tregelles (Account of the Printed Text, pp. 15–18). It is scarcely worth while to repeat the silly story taken up by Moldenhawer, whose admiration of *las cosas de España* was not extravagantly high, that the Alcalà manuscripts had been sold to make sky-rockets about 1749; to which statement Sir John Bowring pleasantly adds in 1819, 'To celebrate the arrival of some worthless grandee.' Gutierrez's recent list comprehends all the codices named in the University Catalogue made in 1745; and we may hope that even in Spain all grandees are not necessarily worthless.

[3] Thus in St. Mark the Complutensian varies from Laud. 2 in fifty-one places, and nowhere agrees with it except in company with a mass of other copies. In

no cause for believing that either Cod. B, or any manuscript much resembling it in character, or any other document of high antiquity or first-rate importance, was employed by the editors of this Polyglott. The text it exhibits does not widely differ from that of most codices written from the tenth century downwards.

That it was corrupted from the parallel Latin version was contended by Wetstein and others on very insufficient grounds. Even the Latinism βεελζεβούβ Matt. x. 25, seems a mere inadvertence, and is corrected immediately afterwards (xii. 24, 27), as well as in the four other places wherein the word is used. We need not deny that 1 John v. 7, 8 was interpolated, and probably translated from the Vulgate; and a few other cases have a suspicious look (Rom. xvi. 5; 2 Cor. v. 10; vi. 15; and especially Gal. iii. 19); the articles too are employed as if they were unfamiliar to the editor (e. g. Acts xxi. 4; 8): yet we must emphatically deny that on the whole the Latin Vulgate had an appreciable effect upon the Greek. This last point had been demonstrated to the satisfaction of Michaelis and of Marsh by Goeze[1], in whose short tract many readings of Cod. Laud. 2 are also examined. In the more exact collation of the N. T., which we have made with the common text (Elzevir 1624), and which appeared in the first edition of the present work, out of 2,780 places in all, wherein the Complutensian edition differs from that of Elzevir (viz. 1,046 in the Gospels, 578 in the Pauline Epistles, 542 in the Acts and Catholic Epistles, 614 in the Apocalypse), in no less than 849 the Latin is at variance with the Greek; in the majority of the rest the difference cannot be expressed in another language. Since the Complutensian N. T. could only have been published from manuscripts, it deserves more minute examination than it has received from Mill or Wetstein; and it were much to

the Acts on the contrary they agree 139 times, and differ but forty-one, some of their *loci singulares* being quite decisive: e. g. x. 17; 21; xii. 12; xvii. 31; xx. 38; xxiv. 16; 1 Pet. iii. 12; 14; 2 Pet. i. 11. In most of these places Seidel's Codex, in some of them Act. 69, and in nearly all Cod. Havn. 1 (Evan. 234, Act. 57, Paul. 72) are with Laud. 2. On testing this last at the Bodleian in some forty places, I found Mill's representation fairly accurate. As might have been expected, his Oxford manuscripts were collated much the best.

[1] Goeze's 'Defence of the Complutensian Bible,' 1766. He published a 'Continuation' in 1769. *See* also Franc. Delitzsch's 'Studies on the Complutensian Polyglott' (Bagster, 1872), derived from his Academical Exercise as Dean of the Theological Faculty at Leipzig, 1871–2.

be desired that minute collations could be made of several other early editions, especially the whole five of Erasmus.

Since this Polyglott has been said to be very inaccurately printed, it is necessary to state that we have noted just fifty pure errors of the press; in one place, moreover (Heb. vii. 3), part of the ninth Euthalian κεφάλαιαν (εν ω ότι και του αβραάμ πραετιμήθη) has crept into the text. All the usual peculiarities observable in later manuscripts are here, e.g. 224 itacisms (chiefly ω for υ, η for ει, ει for ι, υ for η, οι for ει, and vice versâ); thirty-two instances of ν ἐφελκυστικόν, or the superabundant ν, before a consonant; fifteen cases of the hiatus for the lack of ν before a vowel; ουτως is sometimes found before a consonant, but ουτω sixty-eight times; ουκ and ουχ are interchanged twelve times. The following peculiarities, found in many manuscripts, and here retained, may show that the grammatical forms of the Greek were not yet settled among scholars; παρήγγελεν Mark vi. 8; διάγγελε Luke ix. 60; καταγγέλειν Acts iv. 2; διαγγέλων Acts xxi. 26; καταγγέλων 1 Cor. ii. 1; παραγγέλω 1 Cor. vii. 10; αναγγέλλων 2 Cor. vii. 7; παραγγέλομεν 2 Thess. iii. 4; παράγγελε 1 Tim. iv. 11; v. 7; vi. 17. The augment is omitted nine times (Matt. xi. 17; Acts vii. 42; xxvi. 32; Rom. i. 2; Gal. ii. 13; 1 Tim. vi. 10; 2 Tim. i. 16; Apoc. iv. 8; xii. 17); the reduplication twice (John xi. 52; 1 Cor. xi. 5); μέλλω and μέλει are confounded, Mark iv. 38; Acts xviii. 17; Apoc. iii. 2; xii. 4. Other anomalous forms (some of them would be called Alexandrian) are παμπόλου Mark viii. 1; νηρέαν Rom. xvi. 15; εξαιρείτε 1 Cor. v. 13; αποκτένει 2 Cor. iii. 6, *passim*; στιχαύμεν Gal. v. 25; είπα Heb. iii. 10; ευράμενος *ibid.* ix. 12; απεσχέσθαι 1 Pet. ii. 11; καταλειπόντες 2 Pet. ii. 15; περιβαλλείται Apoc. iii. 5; δειγνύντος *ibid.* xxii. 8. The stops are placed carelessly in the Greek, being (.), (,), rarely (·), never (;). In the Latin the stops are pretty regular, but the abbreviations very numerous, even such purely arbitrary forms as x̄p̄s for *Christus*. In the Greek σ often stands at the end of a word for ς, ϊ and often ϋ or ῡ are set at the beginning of syllables: there are no instances of ι *ascript* or *subscript*, and no capital letters except at the beginning of a chapter, when they are often flourished. The following forms are also derived from the general practice of manuscripts, and occur perpetually: απάρτι, απάρχης, δαν (for δ' ἂν), ειμή, εξαυτής, επιτοαυτό, εφόσον, εωσότου, καίτοιγε, καθημέραν, κατιδίαν, κατόναρ, μεθήμων, μέντοι, ουμή, τουτέστι; and for the most part διαπαντός, διατί, διατούτο, είτις, ουκέτι. Sometimes the preposition and its case make but a single word, as παραφύσιν, and once we find ευποιήσαι, Vulg. *benefacere* (Mark xiv. 7).

The Complutensian text has been followed in the main by only a few later editions, chiefly by Chr. Plantin's Antwerp Polyglott (1569–72)[1].

[1] Reuss says boldly that the Complutensian text 'purus et authenticus a veteribus nunquam repetitus est' (p. 25), and gives a list of forty-four places in which the Complutensian and Plantin editions are at variance (pp. 16, 17). He subjoins a list of 185 cases in which the two are in unison against Erasmus and Stephen jointly (pp. 18–21), so that the influence of the former over the latter cannot be disputed.

2. ERASMUS' NEW TESTAMENT was by six years the earlier published, though it was printed two years later than the Complutensian. Its editor, both in character and fortunes, presents a striking contrast with Ximenes; yet what he lacked of the Castilian's firmness he more than atoned for by his true love of learning, and the cheerfulness of spirit that struggled patiently, if not boldly, with adversity. Desiderius Erasmus (ἐράσμιος, i.e. Gerald) was born at Rotterdam in 1465, or, perhaps, a year or two later, the illegitimate son of reputable and (but for that sin) of virtuous parents. Soon left an orphan, he was forced to take reluctantly the minor orders, and entered the priesthood in 1492. Thenceforward his was the hard life of a solitary and wandering man of letters, earning a precarious subsistence from booksellers or pupils[1], now learning Greek at Oxford (but αὐτοδίδακτος)[2], now teaching it at Cambridge (1510); losing by his reckless wit the friends his vast erudition had won; restless and unfrugal, perhaps, yet always labouring faithfully and with diligence. He was in England when John Froben, a celebrated publisher at Basle, moved by the report of the forthcoming Spanish Bible and eager to forestall it, made application to Erasmus, through a common friend, to undertake immediately an edition of the N. T.: 'se daturum pollicetur, quantum alius quisquam,' is the argument employed. This proposal was sent on April 17, 1515, years before which time Erasmus had prepared numerous annotations to illustrate a revised Latin version he had long projected. On September 11 it was yet unsettled whether this improved version should stand by the Greek in a parallel column (the plan actually adopted), or be printed separately:

[1] At forty he obtained the countenance of that good and bountiful rather than great prelate, William Wareham, Archbishop of Canterbury (1502–32), who, prosperous in life, was so singularly 'felix opportunitate mortis.' It gladdens and makes sad at once an English heart to read what Erasmus writes about him ten years later: 'Cujusmodi Maecenas, si mihi primis illis contigisset annis, fortassis aliquid in bonis literis potuissem. Nunc natus saeculo parum felici, cum passim impunè regnaret barbaries, praesertim apud nostrates, apud quos tum crimen etiam erat quicquam bonarum literarum attigisse, tantum aberat ut honos aleret hominum studia in eâ regione, quae Baccho Cererique dicata sunt verius quam musis' (N. T. 1516, Annot. 1 Thess. ii. p. 554).

[2] Bishop Middleton may have lost sight of this pregnant fact when he wrote of Erasmus, 'an acquaintance with Greek criticism was certainly not among his best acquirements, as his Greek Testament plainly proves: indeed he seems not to have had a very happy talent for languages' (Doctrine of the Greek Article, p. 395, 3rd edition).

yet the colophon at the end of Erasmus' first edition, a large folio of 1,027 pages in all, is dated February, 1516; the end of the Annotations, March 1, 1516; Erasmus' dedication to Leo X, Feb. 1, 1516; and Froben's Preface, full of joyful hope and honest pride in the friendship of the first of living authors, Feb. 24, 1516. Well might Erasmus, who had besides other literary engagements to occupy his time, declare subsequently that the volume 'praecipitatum fuit verius quam editum;' yet both on the title-page, and in his dedication to the Pope, he allows himself to employ widely different language [1]. When we read the assurance he addressed to Leo, 'Novum ut vocant testamentum universum ad Graecae originis fidem recognovimus, idque non temere neque levi opera, sed adhibitis in consilium compluribus utriusque linguae codicibus, nec iis sane quibuslibet, sed vetustissimis simul et emendatissimis,' it is almost painful to be obliged to remember that a portion of ten months at the utmost could have been devoted to his task by Erasmus; while the only manuscripts he can be imagined to have constantly used are Codd. Evan. 2, Act. Paul. 2 and Paul. 7, with occasional reference to Evan. Act. Paul. 1 and Act. Paul. 4 (all still at Basle) for the remainder of the New Testament, to which add Apoc. 1, now happily recovered, alone for the Apocalypse. All these, excepting Evan. Act. Paul. 1, were neither ancient nor particularly valuable, and of Cod. 1 he professed to make but small account [2]. As Apoc. 1 was mutilated in the last six

[1] The title-page is long and rather boastful. 'Novum Instrumentum omne, diligenter ab Erasmo Roterodamo recognitum et emendatum, non solum ad graecam veritatem, verum etiam ad multorum utriusque linguae codicum, eorumque veterum simul et emendatorum fidem, postremo ad probatissimorum autorum citationem, emendationem, et interpretationem, praecipue, Origenis, Chrysostomi, Cyrilli, Vulgarii, Hieronymi, Cypriani, Ambrosii, Hilarii, Augustini, una cum Annotationibus, quae lectorem doceant, quid qua ratione mutatum sit. Quisquis igitur amas veram theologiam, lege, cognosce, ac deinde judica. Neque statim offendero, si quid mutatum offenderis, sed expende, num in molius mutatum sit. Apud inclytam Germaniae Basilaeam.' The Vulgarius of Erasmus' first edition is no less a person than Theophylact, Archbishop of Bulgaria, as appears plainly from his Annotations, p. 319, 'nec in ullis graecorum exemplaribus addita reperi [ἐκ σοῦ, Luke i. 35], ne apud Vulgarium quidem, nec in antiquis codicibus Latinis.' He had found out his portentous blunder by 1528, when, in his 'Responsio ad Object. xvi. Hispanorum,' he gives that commentator his right name.

[2] Yet he could have followed none other than Cod. 1 in Matt. xxii. 28; xxiii. 25; xxvii. 52; xxviii. 3, 4, 19, 20; Mark vii. 18, 19, 26; x. 1; xii. 22; xv. 46; Luke i. 16, 61; ii. 43; ix. 1, 15; xi. 49; John i. 28; x. 8; xiii. 20; in

verses, Erasmus turned these into Greek from the Latin; and some portions of his self-made version, which are found (however some editors may speak vaguely) *in no one known Greek manuscript whatever*, still cleave to our received text[1]. Besides this scanty roll, however, he not rarely refers in his Annotations to other manuscripts he had seen in the course of his travels (e.g. on Heb. i. 3; Apoc. i. 4; viii. 13), yet too indistinctly for his allusions to be of much use to critics. Some such readings, as alleged by him, have not been found elsewhere (e.g. Acts xxiv. 23; Rom. xii. 20), and may have been cited loosely from distant recollection (comp. Col. iii. 3; Heb. iv. 12; 2 Pet. iii. 1; Apoc. ii. 18).

When Ximenes, in the last year of his life, was shown Erasmus' edition which had thus got the start of his own, and his editor, Stunica, sought to depreciate it, the noble old man replied, 'would God that all the Lord's people were prophets! produce better, if thou canst; condemn not the industry of another[2].' His generous confidence in his own work was not misplaced. He had many advantages over the poor scholar and the enterprising printer of Basle, and had not let them pass unimproved. The

all which passages the Latin Vulgate is neutral or hostile. See also Hoskier, Cod. Ev. 604, App. F. p. 4.

[1] Such are *ὀρθρινός*; Apoc. xxii. ver. 16; *ἐλθέ bis, ἐλθέτω, λαμβανέτω τό*, ver. 17; *συμμαρτυροῦμαι γάρ, ἐπιτιθῇ πρὸς ταῦτα,—τῷ (ante βιβλίῳ)* ver. 18; *ἀφαιρῇ, βίβλου, ἀφαιρήσει, βίβλου secund., καί ult.—τῷ (ante βιβλίῳ)* ver. 19; *ἡμῶν, ὑμῶν*, ver. 21. Erasmus in his Annotations fairly confesses what he did: 'quanquam in calce hujus libri, nonnulla verba reperi apud nostros, quae aberant in Graecis exemplaribus, ea tamen ex latinis adjecimus.' But since the text and commentary in Cod. Reuchlini are so mixed up as to be undistinguishable in parts without the aid of a second manuscript (Tregelles' 'Delitzsch's Handschriftliche Funde,' Part ii. pp. 2–7), it is no wonder that in other places Erasmus in his perplexity was sometimes tempted to translate into his own Greek from the Latin Vulgate such words or clauses as he judged to have been wrongly passed over by his sole authority, e. g. ch. ii. 2, 17; iii. 5, 12, 15; vi. 11, 15 (*see* under Apoc. 1); vii. 17; xiii. 4, 5; xiv. 16; xxi. 16; xxii. 11, where the Greek words only of Erasmus are false; while in ch. ii. 3; v. 14 (*bis*); vi. 1, 3, 5, 7; xiii. 10; xiv. 5 (as partly in xxii. 14), he was misled by the recent copies of the Vulgate, whereto alone he had access, to make additions which no Greek manuscript is known to support. Bengel's acuteness had long before suspected that ch. v. 14; xxii. 11, and the form *ἀκαθάρτητος*, ch. xvii. 4 (where Apoc. 1 has *τὰ ἀκάθαρτα*) had their origin in no Greek copy, but in the Vulgate. Nor does Apoc. 1 lend any countenance to ch. xvii. 8, *καίπερ ἔστι*, or to ver. 13, *διαδιδώσουσιν*. For Erasmus' *πληρώσονται* ch. vi. 11, Apoc. 1 has *πληρώσωσιν*, the Latin *impleantur*; for his *σφραγίζωμεν*, ch. vii. 3, we find *σφραγίσωμεν* in Apoc. 1, but the latter omits *τῆς ἀμπέλου*, ch. xiv. 18, and so does Erasmus on its authority.

[2] Tregelles, Account of the Printed Text, p. 19.

typographical errors of the Complutensian Greek have been stated; Erasmus' first edition is in that respect the most faulty book I know. Oecolampadius, or John Hausschein of Basle [1482–1531], afterwards of some note as a disputer with Luther on the Sacramentarian controversy, had undertaken this department for him, and was glad enough to serve under such a chief; but Froben's hot haste gave him little leisure to do his part. No less than 501 *itacisms* are imported from the manuscripts into his printed text, and the ν ἐφελκυστικόν is perpetually used with verbs, before a consonant beginning the next word. We must, however, impute it to design that ι *subscript*, which is elsewhere placed pretty correctly, is here set under η in the plural of the subjunctive mood active, but not in the singular (e.g. James ii. 8 ἐπιβλέψῃτε, εἴπῃτε *bis*, but ver. 2 εἰσέλθη *bis*). With regard to the text, the difference between the two editions is very wide in the Apocalypse, the text of the Complutensian being decidedly preferable; elsewhere they resemble each other more closely, and while we fully admit the error of Stunica and his colleagues in translating from the Latin version into Greek, 1 John v. 7, 8, it would appear that Erasmus has elsewhere acted in the same manner, not merely in cases which for the moment admitted no choice, but in places where no such necessity existed: thus in Acts ix. 5, 6, the words from σκληρόν to πρὸς αὐτόν are interpolated from the Vulgate, partly by the help of Acts xxvi[1].

Erasmus died at Basle in 1536, having lived to publish four editions besides that of 1516. The second has enlarged annotations, and very truly bears on its title the statement, 'multo quam antehac diligentius ab Er. Rot. recognitum;' for a large portion of the misprints, and not a few readings of the first edition, are herein corrected, the latter chiefly on the authority of a fresh codex, Evan. Act. Paul. 3. The colophon to the Apocalypse is dated 1518, Froben's Epistle to the reader, Feb. 5, 1519. In this edition ι *subscript* is for the most part set right; *Carp.*, *Eus. t.*, κεφ. *t.*, τίτλοι, *Am.*, *Eus.* are added

[1] It sometimes happens that a reading cited in the Annotations is at variance with that given in the text; but Erasmus had been engaged in writing the former for about ten years at intervals, and had no leisure to revise them then. Thus John xvii. 2 δώσει (after Cod. 1, but corrected to δώσῃ in the errata); 1 Thess. ii. 8; iii. 1; 1 Tim. v. 21; Apoc. i. 2; ii. 18; xiv. 10, 13; xxi. 6.

in the Gospels; Dorotheus' 'Lives of the Four Evangelists' (*see* Act. 89) stood before St. Matthew in 1516; but now the longer 'Lives' by Sophronius, with Theophylact's 'Prologues,' are set before each Gospel. Κεφάλαια (not the Euthalian) are given in both editions in Rom. 1, 2 Corinth. only, but the Latin chapters are represented in the margin throughout, with the subdivisions A, B, C, D. Of these two editions put together 3,300 copies were printed. The third edition (1522) is chiefly remarkable for its insertion of 1 John v. 7, 8 in the Greek text[1], under the circumstances described above, Vol. I. p. 200, in consequence of Erasmus' controversy with Stunica and H. Standish, Bp. of St. Asaph (d. 1534), and with a much weaker antagonist, Edward Lee, afterwards Archbishop of York, who objected to his omission of a passage which no Greek codex was then known to contain. This edition again was said to be 'tertio jam ac diligentius . . . recognitum,' and contains also 'Capita argumentorum contra morosos quosdam ac indoctos,' which he subsequently found reason to enlarge. The fourth edition (dated March, 1527) contains the text in three parallel colums, the Greek, the Latin Vulgate, and Erasmus' recension of it. He had seen the Complutensian Polyglott in 1522, shortly after the publication of his third edition, and had now the good sense to avail himself of its aid in the improvement of the text, especially in the Apocalypse, wherein he amended from it at least ninety readings. His last edition of 1535 once more discarded the Latin Vulgate, and differs very little from the fourth as regards the text[2].

A minute collation of all Erasmus' editions is a desideratum we may one day come to see supplied. The present writer hopes

[1] The first complete printed English N. T. (Tyndale 1526) followed Erasmus' third edition rather than his second: cf. Rom. viii. 20, 21 as well as 1 John v. 7, 8.

[2] I never saw the Basle manuscripts, and probably Dean Alford had been more fortunate, otherwise I do not think he has evidence for his statement that 'Erasmus tampered with the readings of the very few MSS. which he collated' (N. T., vol. i. Proleg. p. 74, 4th edition). The truth is, that to save time and trouble, he used them as *copy* for the press, as was intimated above, where Burgon's evidence is quite to the point. For this purpose corrections would of course be necessary (those made by Erasmus were all too few), and he might fairly say, in the words cited by Wetstein (N. T., Proleg., p. 127), 'se codices suos praecastigasse. Any wanton 'tampering' with the text I am loth to admit, unless for better reasons than I yet know of.

soon to publish a full comparison of his first and second editions with the Complutensian text[1], as also with that of Stephen 1550, of Beza 1565, and of Elzevir 1624. All who have followed Mill over any portion of the vast field he endeavoured to occupy, will feel certain that his statements respecting their divergences are much below the truth: such as they are, we repeat them for want of more accurate information. He estimates that Erasmus' second edition contains 330 changes from the first for the better, seventy for the worse (N. T., Proleg. § 1134); that the third differs from the second in 118 places (*ibid.* § 1138)[2]; the fourth from the third in 106 or 113 places, ninety being those from the Apocalypse just spoken of (*ibid.* § 1141)[3]. The fifth he alleges to differ from the fourth only four times, so far as he noticed (*ibid.* § 1150): but we meet with as many variations in St. James' Epistle alone[4].

3. In 1518 appeared the Graeca Biblia at Venice, from the celebrated press of Aldus: the work professes to be grounded on a collation of many most ancient copies[5]. However true this must be with regard to the Old Testament, which was now published in Greek for the first time, Aldus follows the first edition of Erasmus so closely in the New as to reproduce his very errors of the press (Mill, N. T., Proleg. § 1122), even those which Oecolampadius had corrected in the list of errata; though Aldus is stated to differ from Erasmus in about 200 places, for the better or worse[6]. If this edition was really

[1] Reuss (p. 24) enumerates 347 passages wherein the first edition of Erasmus differs from the Complutensian, forty-two of which were changed in his second edition. In fifteen places the first edition agrees with the Complutensian against the second (p. 30).

[2] Besides the weighty insertion of 1 John v. 7, 8, Reuss (p. 32) gives us only seven changes in the third edition from the second: Mill's other cases, he says, must be mere trifles.

[3] Here again Reuss declares 'paucissimas novas habet' (p. 36), and names only six.

[4] 'Non deserit quartam nisi duobus in locis: 1 Cor. xii. 2; Acts ix. 28' (Reuss, p. 37). Reuss had evidently not seen the first edition of the present work.

[5] Multis vetustissimis exemplaribus collatis, adhibita etiam quorundam eruditissimorum hominum cura, Biblia (ut vulgo appellant) graece cuncta eleganter descripsi (Andreas Aesulanus Cardinali Aegidio).

[6] This is Mill's calculation, but Wetstein followed him over the ground, adding (especially in the Apocalypse) not a few variations of Aldus which Mill had overlooked, now and then correcting his predecessor's errors (e.g. 2 Cor.

revised by means of manuscripts (Cod. 131) rather than by mere conjecture, we know not what they were, or how far intelligently employed.

Another edition out of the many which now began to swarm, wherein the testimony of manuscripts is believed to have been followed, is that of Simon Colinaeus, Paris, 1534, in which the text is an eclectic mixture of the Complutensian and Erasmian [1]. Mill states (Proleg. § 1144) that in about 150 places Colinaeus deserts them both, and that his variations are usually supported by the evidence of known codices (Evan. 119, 120 at Paris, and Steph. ια′, i. e. Act. 8, Paul. 10, have been suggested), though a few still remain which may perhaps be deemed conjectural. Wetstein (N. T., Proleg. vol. i. p. 142) thinks that for Bogard's Paris edition of 1543 with various readings Evan. 120 or Steph. ιδ′ might have been used, but his own references hardly favour that notion.

4. The editions of Robert Stephen (Estienne), mainly by reason of their exquisite beauty, have exercised a far wider influence than these, and Stephen's third or folio edition of 1550 is by many regarded as the received or standard text. This eminent and resolute man [1503–59], 'whose Biblical work taken altogether had perhaps more influence than that of any other single man in the sixteenth century [2],' early commenced his useful career as a printer at Paris, and, having incurred the enmity of the Doctors of the Sorbonne for his editions of the Latin Vulgate, was yet protected and patronised by Francis I [d. 1547] and his son Henry II. It was from the Royal Press that his three principal editions of the Greek N. T. were issued, the

xi. 1; Col. ii. 23), not without mistakes of his own (e.g. Luke xi. 34; Eph. vi. 22). Since Wetstein's time no one seems to have gone carefully through the Aldine N. T., except Delitzsch in order to illustrate the Codex Reuchlini (1) in the Apocalypse. Reuss (p. 28) notes eleven places in which it agrees with the Complutensian against Erasmus; seven wherein it rejects both books.

[1] The title-page runs *εν λευκετια των παρησιων, παρα σιμωνι τω κολιναιω δεκεμβριου μηνος δευτερα φθινοντος, ετει απο της θεογονιας αφλδ.* This book has no Preface, and the text does not contain 1 John v. 7, 8. It stands alone in reading ἀγγελία, 1 John i. 5. Reuss (p. 46), who praises Colinaeus highly, states that he deserts Erasmus' third edition 113 times out of his own thousand, fifty-three of them to side with the Complutensian, and subjoins a list of fifty-two passages wherein he stands alone among early editors, for most of which he may have had manuscript authority.

[2] Wordsworth, Old Latin Biblical Texts, I. xv.

fourth and last being published in 1551 at Geneva, to which town he finally withdrew the next year, and made public profession of the Protestant opinions which had long been gathering strength in his mind. The editions of 1546, 1549 are small 12mo in size, most elegantly printed with type cast at the expense of Francis: the opening words of the Preface common to both, "*O mirificam* Regis nostri optimi et praestantissimi principis liberalitatem...' have given them the name by which they are known among connoisseurs. Erasmus and his services to sacred learning Stephen does not so much as name, nor indeed did he as yet adopt him for a model: he speaks of "codices ipsa vetustatis specie pene adorandos" which he had met with in the King's Library, by which, he boldly adds, 'ita hunc nostrum recensuimus, ut nullam omnino literam secus esse pateremur quam plures, iique meliores libri, tanquam testes, comprobarent.' The Complutensian, as he admits, assisted him greatly, and he notes its close connexion with the readings of his manuscripts [1]. Mill assures us (Proleg. § 1220) that Stephen's first and second editions differ but in sixty-seven places. My own collation of the two books gives 139 cases of divergence in the text, twenty-eight in punctuation. They differ jointly from the third edition 334 times in the text, twenty-seven in punctuation. In the Apocalypse the first and second editions are close to the text of Erasmus, differing from each other but in eleven places, while the third edition follows the Complutensian or other authorities against the first in sixty-one places. In the folio or third edition of 1550 the various readings of the codices, obscurely referred to in the Preface to that of 1546, are entered in the margin. This fine volume (bearing on its title-page, in honour of Henry II, the inscription Βασιλεῖ τ' ἀγαθῷ, κρατερῷ τ' αἰχμητῇ) derives much importance from its being the earliest ever published with critical apparatus. In the Preface or Epistle to the Reader, written after the example of the Complutensian editors both in Greek and Latin, his authorities are declared to be sixteen; viz. α′, the Spanish Polyglott; β′, which we have already discussed (*above*,

[1] Reuss (pp. 50, 51, 54) mentions only nine places wherein Stephen's first edition does not agree either with the Complutensian or Erasmus; in the second edition four (or rather three) more; in the third nine, including the great erratum, 1 Pet. iii. 11. He further alleges that in the Apocalypse whatever improvements were introduced by Stephen came from the fourth edition of Erasmus, not from the Complutensian.

p. 124, *note* 3), γ′, δ′, ϵ′, ϛ′, ζ′, η′, ι′, ιϵ′ taken from King Henry II's Library; the rest (i. e. θ′, ια′, ιβ′, ιγ′, ιδ′, ιϛ′) are those ἃ αὐτοὶ πανταχόθεν συνηθροίσαμεν, or, as the Latin runs, 'quae undique corrogare licuit:' these, of course, were not necessarily his own, one at least (ιγ′, Act. 9, Paul. 11) we are sure was not. Although Robert Stephen professed to have collated the whole sixteen for his two previous editions, and that too ὡς οἷόν τε ἦν ἐπιμελέστατα, this part of his work is now known to be due to his son Henry [1528–98], who in 1546 was only eighteen years old (Wetstein, N. T., Proleg., vol. i. pp. 143–4). The degree of accuracy attained in this collation may be estimated from the single instance of the Complutensian, a book printed in very clear type, widely circulated, and highly valued by Stephen himself. Deducting mere *errata*, itacisms, and such like, it differs from his third edition in more than 2,300 places, of which (including cases where π. or πάντες stands for *all* his copies) it is cited correctly 554 times (viz. 164 in the Gospels, ninety-four in St. Paul, seventy-six in the Acts and Catholic Epistles, 220 in the Apocalypse), and falsely no less than fifty-six times, again including errors from a too general use of πάντες [1]. I would not say with some that these authorities stand in the margin more for parade than use, yet the text is perpetually at variance with the majority of them, and in 119 places with them all [2]. If we trust ourselves once more to the guidance of Mill (Proleg. § 1228), the folio of 1550 departs from its smaller predecessors of 1546, 1549, in 284 readings [3], chiefly to adopt the text of Erasmus' fifth

[1] Mill states that Stephen's citations of the Complutensian are 598, Marsh 578, of which forty-eight, or one in twelve, are false; but we have tried to be as exact as possible. Certainly some of Stephen's inaccuracies are rather slight, viz. Acts ix. 6; xv. 29; xxv. 5; xxviii. 3; Eph. iv. 32; Col. iii. 20; Apoc. i. 12; ii. 1, 20, 24; iii. 2, 4, 7, 12; iv. 8; xv. 2: β′ seems to be put for α′ Matt. x. 25.

[2] Viz. in the Gospels 81, Paul. 20, Act. Cath. 17, Apoc. 1 (ch. vii. 5): but for the Apocalypse the margin had only three authorities, α′, ιϵ′, ιϛ′ (ιϛ′ ending ch. xvii. 8), whose united readings Stephen rejects no less than fifty-four times. *See*, moreover, above, p. 1 4, note 3.

[3] Here, again, my own collation represents Stephen's first edition as differing from his third in 797 places, of which 372 only are real various readings, the rest relating to accents, or being mere errata. Of these 372 places, the third edition agrees in fifty-six places with π. or πάντες of its own margin, and in fifty five with some of the authorities cited therein. Stephen no doubt knew of manuscript authority for many of his other changes, though some may be mere errata.

edition, though even now the Complutensian is occasionally preferred (e.g. εὐλογήσας Matt. xxvi. 26), most often in the Apocalypse, and that with very good reason. Of his other fifteen authorities, ια′ (=Act. 8) and ιϛ (=Apoc. 3) have never been identified, but were among the six in private hands: β′ certainly is Cod. D or Bezae; the learned have tried, and on the whole successfully, to recognize the remainder, especially those in the Royal (or Imperial, or National) Library at Paris. In that great collection Le Long has satisfied us that γ′ is probably Evan. 4; δ′ is certainly Evan. 5; ϵ′ Evan. 6; ϛ′ Evan. 7; η′ Evan. L; ζ′ he rightly believed to be Evan. 8 (above, p. 191, note); ι′ appears to be Act. 7. Of those in the possession of individuals in Stephen's time, Bp. Marsh (who in his 'Letters to Mr. Archdeacon Travis,' 1795, was led to examine this subject very carefully) has proved that ιγ′ is Act. 9; Wetstein thought θ′ was Evan. 38 (which however see); Scholz seems to approve of Wetstein's conjecture which Griesbach doubted (N.T., Proleg., Sect. I. p. xxxviii), that ιβ′ is Evan. 9: Griesbach rightly considers ιδ′ to be Evan. 120; ιϵ′ was seen by Le Long to be Act. 10: these last four are now in the Royal Library. It has proved the more difficult to settle them, as Robert Stephen did not even print all the materials that Henry had gathered; many of whose various readings were published subsequently by Beza[1] from the collator's own manuscript, which itself must have been very defective. With all its faults, however, the edition of 1550 was a foundation on which others might hereafter build, and was unquestionably of great use in directing the attention of students to the authorities on which alone the true text of Scripture is based. This standard edition contains the following supplementary matter besides the Epistle to the reader: Chrysostom's Hom. I in S. Matthaeum (then first

[1] Wetstein (N. T., Prol., vol. i. p. 36) instances the readings of Cod. D (indicated as 'quidam codex' by Beza in 1565) in Mark ix. 38; x. 50; Luke vii. 35. We may add that Beza in 1565 cites the evidence of one Stephanic manuscript for the omission of ὑμῶν, Matt. xxiii. 9; of two for κατεδίωξεν Mark i. 36; in later editions of two also in Luke xx. 4, and Acts xxii. 25; of three for ἑτέρῳ Matt. xxi. 30, two of which would be Cod. D and Evan. 9 (Steph. ιβ′). In his dedication to Queen Elizabeth in 1565, Beza speaks plainly of an 'exemplar ex Stephani nostri bibliotheca cum viginti quinque plus minus manuscriptis codicibus, et omnibus paenè impressis, ab Henrico Stephano ejus filio, et paternae sedulitatis haerede, quam diligentissimè collatum.'

published): *Carp.*, *Eus. t.*: Πίναξ μαρτυριῶν of O. T. passages cited in the N.T. being (1) literal, (2) virtual: seventy-two Hexameter lines, headed Ερρικος ο Ρωβερτου Στεφανου, φιλοθεω παντι: *prol.* by Theophylact following 'Lives' by Sophronius and Dorotheus of Tyre, with κεφ. *t.* before each Gospel: τίτλ., κεφ., *Am.*, *Eus.* Before the Acts stand 'Αποδημία Παύλου and Euthalius περὶ τῶν χρόνων, κεφ. *t.* Before the Epistles is a new title-page. Chrysostom's *prol.* on the Pauline Epistles begins the new volume. Each separate Epistle has prefixed *prol.* (chiefly by Theodoret) and κεφ. *t.* The Acts and Epistles have κεφ., but the Apocalypse no *prol.* or κεφ., except the ordinary Latin chapters, which are given throughout the N. T., subdivided by letters.

R. Stephen's smaller edition (16mo), published in 1551 at Geneva, though that name is not on the title-page, is said to contain the Greek Text of 1550 almost unchanged [1], set between the Vulgate and Erasmus' Latin versions. In this volume we first find our present division of the N. T. into verses: 'triste lumen,' as Reuss calls it (p. 58), 'nec posthac extinguendum.'

5. Theodore de Bèze [1519–1605], a native of Vezelai in the Nivernois, after a licentious youth, resigned his ecclesiastical preferments at the age of twenty-nine to retire with the wife of his early choice to Geneva, that little city to which the genius of one man has given so prominent a place in the history of the sixteenth century. His noble birth and knowledge of the world, aided by the impression produced at the Conference at Poissy (1561) by his eloquence and learning, easily gained for Beza the chief place among the French Reformed on the death of their teacher Calvin in 1564. Of his services in connexion with the two Codd. D we have already spoken: he himself put forth at intervals, besides his own elegant Latin version published in 1556, ten editions of the N. T. (viz. four in folio in the years 1565, 1582, 1588, 1598, and six in octavo in 1565, 1567, 1580, 1591, 1604, and 1611), the Latin Vulgate, and Annotations [2]. A better

[1] But here again we must qualify previous statements. Reuss (p. 58) cites six instances wherein Stephen's third and fourth editions differ (Matt. xxi. 7; xxiii. 13, 14; xxiv. 15; Luke xvii. 36; Col. i. 20; Apoc. iii. 12): to which list add Mark xiv. 21; xvi. 20; Luke i. 50; viii. 31; xii. 1; Acts xxvii. 13; 2 Cor. x. 6; Heb. vii. 1.

[2] Professor Isaac H. Hall, who has the advantage of Dr. Scrivener in actually

commentator perhaps than a critic, but most conspicuous as the earnest leader of a religious party, Beza neither sought very anxiously after fresh materials for correcting the text, nor made any great use of what were ready at hand, namely, his own two great codices, the papers of Henry Stephen, and Tremellius' Latin version of the Peshitto. All his editions vary somewhat from Stephen and from each other, yet there is no material difference between any of them [1]. He exhibits a tendency, not the less blameworthy because his extreme theological views would tempt him thereto, towards choosing that reading out of several which might best suit his own preconceived opinions. Thus in Luke ii. 22 he adopts (and our Authorized English version condescends to follow his judgement) *τοῦ καθαρισμοῦ αὐτῆς* from the Complutensian, for which he could have known of no manuscript authority whatever: *ejus* of the Vulgate would most naturally be rendered by *αὐτοῦ* (*see* Campbell in loc.). Wetstein calculates that Beza's text differs from Stephen's in some fifty places (an estimate we shall find below the mark), and that either in his translation or his Annotations he departs from Stephen's Greek text in 150 passages (Wetst. N. T., Proleg., Tom. ii. p. 7).

6. The brothers Bonaventure and Abraham Elzevir set up a printing-press at Leyden, which maintained its reputation for

himself possessing all the ten editions of Beza, as he states in MS. in a copy of his 'American Greek Testaments' kindly given to me, says, p. 60, note, that in the edition of 1556 the Greek does not occur, and that Beza's first *Greek* text was published in 1565. Beza must have reckoned his Latin amongst his editions when he spoke of his folio of 1565 as his second edition, and must generally have dated from 1556 as the beginning of his labours. The dates of the ten editions given above are extracted from Professor Hall's list in Schaff's 'Companion to the Bible,' pp. 500–502.

[1] Reuss says fairly enough (p. 85) that Beza was the true author of what is called the received text, from which the Elzevir of 1624 rarely departs. He used as his basis the fourth edition of Stephen, from which he departed in 1565, so far as Reuss has found, only twenty-five times, nine times to side with the Complutensian, four times with Erasmus, thrice with the two united; the other nine readings are new, whereof two (Acts xvii. 25; James v. 12) had been adopted by Colinaeus. The second edition of 1582 withdraws one of the peculiar readings of its predecessor, but adds fourteen more. The third edition (1588), so far as Reuss knows, departs from the second but five times, and the fourth (1598) from the third only twice, Matt. vi. 1 (*δικαιοσύνην*); Heb. x. 17 (add. *τότε εἴρηκε*), neither of which I can verify. These results, on Reuss's system of investigation, can be only approximately true (*see* p. 154, note), and do not include some changes silently introduced into Beza's Latin version, as suggested in his Annotations.

elegance and correctness throughout the greater part of the seventeenth century. One of their minute editions, so much prized by bibliomanists, was a Greek Testament, 24mo, 1624, alleging on the title-page (there is no Preface whatever) to be *ex Regiis aliisque optimis editionibus cum curâ expressum:* by *Regiis,* we presume, Stephen's editions are meant, and especially that of 1550. The supposed accuracy (for which its good name is not quite deserved) and the great neatness of this little book procured for it much popularity. When the edition was exhausted, a second appeared in 1633, having the verses broken up into separate sentences, instead of their numbers being indicated in the margin, as in 1624. In the Preface it seems to allude to Beza's N. T., without directly naming him: 'Ex regiis ac *ceteris editionibus*, quae maxime ac prae ceteris nunc omnibus probantur.' To this edition is prefixed, as in 1624, a table of quotations (*πίναξ μαρτυριῶν*) from the Old Testament, to which are now added tables of the *κεφάλαια* of the Gospels, *ἔκθεσις κεφαλαίων* of the Acts and all the Epistles. Of the person entrusted with its superintendence we know nothing; nearly all his readings are found either in Stephen's or Beza's N. T. (he leans to the latter in preference[1]); but he speaks of the edition of 1624 as that 'omnibus acceptam;' and boldly states, with a confidence which no doubt helped on its own accomplishment, 'textum ergo habes nunc ab omnibus receptum, in quo nihil immutatum aut corruptum damus.' His other profession, that of superior correctness, is also a little premature: 'ut si quae vel minutissimae in nostro, aut in iis, quos secuti sumus libris, superessent mendae, cum judicio ac cura tollerentur.' Although some of the worst misprints of the edition of 1624 are amended in that of 1633 (Matt. vi. 34; Acts xxvii. 13; 1 Cor. x. 10; Col. ii. 13; 1 Thess. ii. 17; Heb. viii. 9; 2 Pet. i. 7), others just as gross are retained (Acts ix. 3; Rom. vii. 2; xiii. 5; 1 Cor. xii. 23; xiii. 3; 2 Cor. iv. 4; v. 19; viii. 8; Heb. xii. 9; Apoc. iii. 12; vii. 7; xviii. 16), to which much be added a few peculiar to itself (e.g. Mark iii. 10; Rom. xv. 3; 1 Cor. ix. 2; 2 Cor. i. 11; vi. 16; Col. i. 7; iv. 7; Apoc. xxii. 3): *ἐθύθη* in 1 Cor. v. 7 should not be reckoned as an

[1] Reuss (p. 109) states that out of his thousand select examples Elzevir 1624 differs from Beza's smaller New Testament of 1565 in only eight readings, all of which may be found in some of Beza's other editions (e.g. the small edition of 1580), except one misprint (Rom. vii. 2).

erratum, since it was adopted designedly by Beza, and after him by both the Elzevir editions. Of real various readings between the two Elzevirs we mark but seven or eight instances (in six of which that of 1633 follows the Complutensian); viz. Mark iv. 18; viii. 24; Luke xi. 33; xii. 20; John iii. 6 *bis*; 2 Tim. i. 12; i~~v. 51~~[1]; Apoc. xvi. 5: and in 2 Pet. i. 1 (as also in ed. 1641) ἡμῶν is omitted after σωτῆρος[2].

Since Stephen's edition of 1550 and that of the Elzevirs have been taken as the standard or *Received* text[3], the former chiefly in England, the latter on the Continent, and inasmuch as nearly all collated manuscripts have been compared with one or the other of these, it becomes absolutely necessary to know the precise points in which they differ from each other, even to the minutest errors of the press. Mill (N. T., Proleg., 1307) observed but twelve such variations; Tischendorf gives a catalogue of 150 (N. T., Proleg., p. lxxxv, seventh edition). For the first edition of the present work a list of 287 was drawn up, which, it is hoped, will soon be reprinted, in a more convenient shape, in a volume now in preparation[4].

[1] Οἱ δοῦλος is disputed by Hoskier (App. C. p. 18, n.), who says that he has seen besides his own copy of 1624 several which read οἱ δοῦλου. He had also inspected mine. 'And although he says it reads δοῦλος, I read easily δοῦλοι. The type is rather faulty, that is all.' The point is not worth disputing.

[2] 'American Additions and Corrections,' p. 50.

[3] Professor Hall states (Schaff's 'Companion,' p. 501) that Beza's editions of 1588 and 1598 were the chief foundations of the Authorized Version of 1611. Archdeacon Palmer (Preface to Greek Testament with Revisers' Readings, p. vii) refers chiefly to Stephen's edition of 1550. Dr. Scrivener (to whom Archdeacon Palmer refers), Cambridge Greek Testament, Praef., p. vi, in taking the Elzevir edition of 1624 as the authority for the 'Textus Receptus,' says that it rests upon Stephen's 1550, and Beza's 1565, 1582, 1589 (=1588), and 1598 (especially the later editions, and particularly 1598, Authorized Edition of the British Bible, p. 60), besides also Erasmus, the Complutensian, and the Vulgate (Authorized Edition, p. 60). Dr. Scrivener adds in the passage just named that out of 252 passages the 'Translators abide with Beza against Stephen in 113, with Stephen against Beza in fifty-nine, with the Complutensian, Erasmus, or the Vulgate against both Stephen and Beza in eighty.'

[4] 'The Authorized Edition of the English Bible (1611), its subsequent Reprints and Modern Representatives.' By F. H. A. Scrivener, M.A., D.C.L., LL.D., &c., Cambridge, University Press, 1884. Appendix E.

CHAPTER VII (*continued*).

CRITICAL EDITIONS.

THE Science of Sacred Textual Criticism was built up in successive Critical Editions of the Greek Testament, and to a brief description of those this chapter will be devoted. It will not include therefore any notice of editions like that of Valpy, or of Bloomfield, or Alford, or Wordsworth, in which the textual treatment did not assume prominence or involve advancement in this province. Still less is there space for such a list of general editions of the New Testament as the very valuable one compiled by Dr. Isaac H. Hall, and found in Schaff's 'Companion to the New Testament,' to which notice has been already directed. The progress of Textual Science has involved two chief stages; the first, in which all evidence was accepted and registered, and the second, when a selection was made and the rest either partially or totally disregarded. Lachmann was the leader in the second stage, of which to some extent Griesbach was the pioneer. It is evident that in the future a return must be made, as has been already advocated by many, to the principles of the first stage[1].

1. R. Stephen was the first to bring together any considerable body of manuscript evidence, however negligently or capriciously he may have applied it to the emendation of the sacred text. A succession of English scholars was now ready to follow him in the same path, the only direct and sure one in criticism; and for about eighty years our countrymen maintained the foremost place in this important branch of Biblical learning. Their van

[1] *See* Miller's 'Textual Guide,' George Bell & Sons, 1885. Also Dr. Scrivener's 'Adversaria et Critica Sacra' (not yet published).—Postscript.

was led by Brian Walton [1600–61], afterwards Bishop of Chester, who published in 1657 the London Polyglott, which he had planned twelve years before, as at once the solace and meet employment of himself and a worthy band of colleagues during that sad season when Christ's Church in England was for a while trodden in the dust, and its ministers languished in silence and deep poverty. The fifth of his huge folios was devoted to the New Testament in six languages, viz. Stephen's Greek text of 1550[1], the Peshitto-Syriac, the Latin Vulgate, the Ethiopic, Arabic, and (in the Gospels only) the Persic. The exclusively critical apparatus, with which alone we are concerned, consists of the readings of Cod. A set at the foot of the Greek text, and, in the sixth or supplementary volume, of Lucas Brugensis' notes on various readings of the Gospels in Greek and Latin; of those given by the Louvain divines in their edition of the Vulgate (Walton, Polygl., Tom. vi. No. xvii); and especially of a collation of sixteen authorities, whereof all but three, viz. Nos. 1, 15, 16[2], had never been used before (Walton, Tom. vi. No. xvi). These various readings had been gathered by the care and diligence of Archbishop Ussher [1580–1656], then living in studious and devout retirement near London[3]. They are as follows:—(1) *Steph.* the sixteen copies extracted from Stephen's margin: (2) *Cant.* or Evan. D: (3) *Clar.* or Paul. D: (4) *Gon.* or Evan. 59: (5) *Em.* or Evan. 64, and also Act. 53: (6) *Goog.* or Evan. 62: (7) *Mont.* or Evan. 61: (8) *Lin.* or Evan. 56, and also Act. 33: (9) *Magd.* 1 or Evan. 57: (10) *Magd.* 2 or Paul. 42: (11) *Nov.* 1 or Evan. 58: (12) *Nov.* 2 or Act. 36: (13) *Bodl.* 1 or Evan. 47: (14) *Trit.* or *Bodl.* 2, Evan. 96: (15) *March. Veles.*, the Velesian readings, described above, Vol. i. p. 209: (16) *Bib. Wech.*, the Wechelian readings, which deserve no more regard than the Velesian. They were derived

[1] Reuss (p. 56) excepts Matt. ix. 17; 2 Tim. iv. 13; Philem. 6, where Walton prefers the Complutensian reading.

[2] Nos. 2 and 3 had been partially used by Beza (American Additions, p. 50).

[3] If Ussher lacked severe accuracy in collating his manuscripts, as well as skill in deciphering them, we have not to look far for the cause. In a Life prefixed to Ussher's 'Body of Divinity,' 1678, p. 11, we are told that 'in the winter evenings he constantly spent two hours in comparing old MSS. of the Bible, Greek and Latin, taking with his own hand the *variae lectiones* of each:' on which statement Dean Burgon (Letter in the *Guardian*, June 28, 1882) makes the pregnant comment, 'Such work carried on at seventy or more by candlelight, is pretty sure to come to grief, especially when done with a heart-ache.'

from the margin of a Bible printed at Frankfort, 1597, by the heirs of And. Wechel. It is indifferent whether they be referred to Francis Junius or F. Sylburg as editors, since all the readings in the New Testament are found in Stephen's margin, or in the early editions.

Walton was thus enabled to publish very extensive additions to the existing stock of materials. That he did not try by their means to form thus early a corrected text, is not at all to be regretted; the time for that attempt was not yet arrived. He cannot, however, be absolved from the charge to which R. Stephen had been before amenable, of suppressing a large portion of the collations which had been sent him. The Rev. C. B. Scott, Head Master of Westminster School, found in the Library of Emmanuel College, Cambridge, the readings of Codd. D. 59, 61, 62, prepared for Walton (Dobbin, Cod. Montfort., Introd. p. 21), which Mill had access to, and in his N. T. made good use of, as well as of Ussher's other papers (Mill, Proleg. § 1505).

2. Steph. Curcellaeus or Courcelles published his N. T. at Amsterdam in 1658, before he had seen Walton's Polyglott. The peculiar merit of his book arises from his marginal collection of parallel texts, which are more copious than those of his predecessors, yet not too many for convenient use: later editors have been thankful to take them as a basis for their own [1]. There are many various readings [2] (some from two or three fresh manuscripts) at the foot of each page, or thrown into an appendix, mingled with certain rash conjectures which betray a Socinian bias: but since the authorities are not cited for each separate reading, these critical labours were as good as wasted [3].

[1] 'Sed, cum aliqui ex editoribus N. T. in analogiis discernendis nimis fortasse curiosi loca Parallela ad infinitum fere numerum auxerint, quorum alia parum definitae similitudinis, alia remotioris sunt argumenti quam quae servatis sanae interpretationis legibus possint adhiberi, satius habuimus Curcellaeum sequi, qui nec parcior est, nec nimis minutus in locis allegandis, nec dissimilia unquam aut prorsus ἀπροσδιόνυσα ad marginem locavit.'—Car. Oxon. (Bishop C. Lloyd) Monitum N. T. Oxonii, 1827.

[2] 1 John v. 7, 8 is included in brackets. Reuss (p. 130) thinks that the text follows Elzevir 1633 everywhere else but in Luke x. 22. Mill (N. T., Proleg. § 1397) says that it was printed 'ad editiones priores Elzevirianas, typis Elzevirianis nitidissimis.'

[3] 'Stephani Curcellaei annotationes variantium lectionum, pro variantibus lectionibus non habendae, quia ille non notat codices, unde eas habeat, an ex

3. A more important step in advance was taken in the Greek Testament in 8vo, issued from the Oxford University Press in 1675. This elegant volume (whose Greek text is mainly that of Elzevir 1633[1]) was superintended by John Fell [1625–86], Dean of Christ Church, soon afterwards Bishop of Oxford, the biographer of saint-like Hammond, himself one of the most learned and munificent, if not quite the most popular Prelate, of that golden age of the English Church, in whose behalf Anthony à Wood designates him 'the most zealous man of his time.' His brief yet interesting Preface not only discusses the causes of various readings[2], and describes the materials used for his edition, but touches on that weak and ignorant prejudice which had been already raised against the collection of such variations in the text of Scripture; and that too sometimes by persons like John Owen[3] the Puritan, intrusive Dean of Christ Church under Cromwell, who, but that we are loth to doubt his integrity, would hardly be deemed a victim of the panic he sought to spread. In reply to all objectors the Bishop pleads the comparative insignificance of the change produced by various readings in the general sense of Holy Writ, and especially urges that God hath dealt so bountifully with His people 'ut necessaria quaeque et ad salutis summam facientia in S. literis saepius repeterentur; ita ut si forte quidpiam minus commode alicubi expressum, id damnum aliunde reparari possit' (Praef. p. 1).

manuscriptis, an vero ex impressis exemplaribus. Possunt etiam pro uno codice haberi.' Canon xiii. pp. 11, 69–70 of the N. T. by G. D. T. M. D. (*see* below, p. 204).

[1] But it goes with Elz. 1624 in Mark iv. 18; 2 Tim. i. 12; Apoc. xvi. 5, and sometimes prefers the readings of Stephen 1550, e. g. Mark i. 21; vi. 29, and notably Luke ii. 22 (*αὐτῶν*); Luke x. 22; Rom. vii. 2; Philem. 7. Peculiarities of this edition are Εἰ δὲ for Εἶτα Heb. xii. 9; *συγκληρονόμοις* 1 Pet. iii. 7. Wetstein's text follows its erratum, Acts xiii. 29 *ἐτέλησαν*. Mill seems to say (N. T., Proleg. § 1409) that Fell's text was taken from that of Curcellaeus.

[2] Fell imputes the origin of various readings to causes generally recognized, adding one which does not seem very probable, that accidental slips once made were retained and propagated through a superstitious feeling of misplaced reverence, citing in illustration Apoc. xxii. 18, 19. He alleges also the well-known subscription of Irenaeus, preserved by Eusebius, which will best be considered hereafter; and remarks, with whatever truth, that contrary to the practice of the Jews and Muhammedans in regard to their sacred books, it was allowed 'e vulgo quibusvis, calamo pariter et manu profanis, sacra ista [N. T.] tractare' (Praef. p. 4).

[3] 'Considerations on the Biblia Polyglotta,' 1659: to which Walton rejoined, sharply enough, in 'The Considerator considered,' also in 1659.

On this assurance we may well rest in peace. This edition is more valuable for the impulse it gave to subsequent investigators than for the richness of its own stores of fresh materials, although it is stated on the title-page to be derived '*ex plus* 100 *MSS. Codicibus*.' Patristic testimony, as we have seen, Bishop Fell rather undervalued: the use of versions he clearly perceived, yet of those at that time available, he only attends to the Gothic and Coptic as revised by Marshall: his list of manuscripts hitherto untouched is very scanty. To those used by Walton we can add only *R*, the Barberini readings, then just published (*see* p. 210); *B*, twelve Bodleian codices 'quorum plerique intacti prius,' in no-wise described, and cited only by the number of them which may countenance each variation; *U*, the two Ussher manuscripts Evan. 63, 64 as collated by H. Dodwell; *P*, three copies from the Library of Petavius (Act. 38, 39, 40); *Ge.*, another from St. Germains (Paul. E): the readings of the last four were furnished by Joh. Gachon. Yet this slight volume (for so we must needs regard it) was the legitimate parent of one of the noblest works in the whole range of Biblical literature, of which we shall speak next.

4. Novum Testamentum Graecum of Dr. John Mill, Oxford, 1707, in folio. This able and laborious critic, born in 1645, quitted his native village in Westmoreland at sixteen for Queen's College, Oxford, of which society he became a Fellow, and was conspicuous there both as a scholar and as a ready extemporary preacher. In 1685 his College appointed him Principal of its affiliated Hall, St. Edmund, so honourably distinguished for the Biblical studies of its members; but Mill had by that time made good progress in his Greek Testament, on which he gladly spent the last thirty years of his life, dying suddenly in 1707, a fortnight after its publication. His attention was first called to the subject by his friend, Dr. Edward Bernard, the Savilian Professor at Oxford, whom he vividly represents as setting before him an outline of the work, and encouraging him to attempt its accomplishment. 'Vides, Amice mi, opus . . . omnium, mihi crede, longè dignissimum, cui in hoc aetatis tuae flore, robur animi tui, vigilias ac studia, liberaliter impendas' (Proleg. § 1417). Ignorant as yet both of the magnitude and difficulty of his task,

Mill boldly undertook it about 1677, and his efforts soon obtained the countenance of Bishop Fell, who promised to defray the expense of printing, and, mindful of the frailty of life, urged him to go to press before his papers were quite ready to meet the public eye. When about twenty-four chapters of St. Matthew had been completed, Bishop Fell died prematurely in 1686, and the book seems to have languished for many following years from lack of means, though the editor was busy all the while in gathering and arranging his materials, especially for the Prolegomena, which well deserve to be called 'marmore perenniora.' As late as 1704 John Sharp [1644–1714], Archbishop of York, whose remonstrances to Queen Anne some years subsequently hindered the ribald wit that wrote 'A Tale of a Tub' from polluting the episcopal throne of an English see, obtained from her for Mill a stall at Canterbury, and the royal command to prosecute his New Testament forthwith. The preferment came just in time. Three years afterwards the volume was given to the Christian world, and its author's course was already finished: his life's work well ended, he had entered upon his rest. He was spared the pain of reading the unfair attack alike on his book and its subject by our eminent Commentator, Daniel Whitby ('Examen Variantium Lectionum,' 1710), and of witnessing the unscrupulous use of Whitby's arguments made by the sceptic Anthony Collins in his 'Discourse of Free Thinking,' 1713.

Dr. Mill's services to Biblical criticism surpass in extent and value those rendered by any other, except perhaps one or two men of our own time. A large proportion of his care and pains, as we have seen already, was bestowed on the Fathers and ancient writers of every description who have used or cited Scripture. The versions are usually considered his weakest point, although he first accorded to the Vulgate and to its prototype the Old Latin the importance they deserve. His knowledge of Syriac was rather slight, and for the other Eastern tongues, if he was not more ignorant than his successors, he had not discovered how little Latin translations of the Ethiopic, &c., can be trusted. As a collator of manuscripts the list subjoined will bear full testimony to his industry: without seeking to repeat details we have entered into before under the Cursive MSS., it is right to state that he either himself re-examined, or otherwise represented more fully and exactly, the codices that had been previously used for the London Polyglott and the Oxford N. T. of 1675. Still it would be wrong to dissemble the fact that Mill's style of collation is not such as the strictness of modern scholarship demands. He seldom notices at all such various readings as arise from the transposition of words, the insertion or omission of the Greek article, from homoeoteleuta, or itacisms, or from manifest errors of the pen; while in respect to general accuracy he is as much inferior to those who have trod in his steps, as he rises above Stephen and Ussher, or the persons employed by Walton and Fell. It has been my fortune to collate not a few manuscripts after this great critic, and I have elsewhere been obliged to notice these plain facts, I would fain trust in no disparaging temper. During the many years that Mill's N. T. has been my daily companion, my reverence for that diligent and earnest man has been constantly growing: the principles of internal evidence which guided his choice between conflicting authorities were simple (as indeed they ought to be), but applied with rare judgement, sagacity, and moderation: his zeal was unflagging, his treatment of his sacred subject deeply reverential. Of the criticism of the New Testament in the hands of Dr. John Mill it may be said, that he found the edifice of wood, and left it marble.

The following Catalogue of the manuscripts known to Mill exhibits the abridged form in which he cites them, together with the more usual notation, whereby they are described in this work, and will tend, it is believed, to facilitate the use of Mill's N. T.

Alex.	Cod. A
Barb.	Evan. 112 (Wetstein)
Baroc.	Act. 23
B. 1	Evan. E
B. 2	Act. 2
B. 3	Act. 4
Bodl. 1	Evan. 45
Bodl. 2	Evan. 46
Bodl. 3	Evst. 5
Bodl. 4	Evst. 18
Bodl. 5	Evst. 19
Bodl. 6	Evan. 47
Bodl. 7	Evan. 48
Bu.	Evan. 70
Cant.	Evan. Act. D
Cant. 2	Act. 24
Cant. 3	Act. 53
Clar.	Paul. D
Colb. 1	Evan. 27
Colb. 2	Evan. 28
Colb. 3	Evan. 29
Colb. 4	Evan. 30, 31
Colb. 5	Evan. 32
Colb. 6	Act. 13
Colb. 7	Paul. 17
Colb. 8	Evan. 33
Colb. 9 = Colb. 1	
Colb. 10 = Colb. 2	
Colb. 11 = Colb. 1	
Cov. 1	Evan. 65
Cov. 2	Act. 25
Cov. 3	Act. 26
Cov. 4	Act. 27
Cov. 5 *Sin.*	Act. 28
Cypr.	Evan. K
Em.	*see* Evan. 64
Eph.	Evan. 71
Gal.	Evan. 66
Ger.	Paul. E
Genev.	Act. 29
Go.	Evan. 62
Gon.	Evan. 59
Hunt. 1	Act. 30
Hunt. 2	Evan. 67
L.	Evan. 69
Laud. 1	Evan. 50
Laud. 2	Evan. 51

Laud. 3 ......Act. E
Laud. 4 ......Evst. 20
Laud. 5 ......Evan. 52
Lin. ....Evan. 56
Lin. 2 ....Act. 33
Lu. ....Act. 21
M. 1............Evan. 60
M. 2............Evst. 4
Magd. 1 ......Evan. 57
Magd. 2 ......Paul. 42
Med.............Evan. 42
Mont. ....Evan. 61
N. 1............Evan. 58
N. 1............Act. 36
N. 2............Act. 37
Per. ....Evan. 91
Pet. 1 ....Act. 38
Pet. 2 ....Act. 39
Pet. 3 ....Act. 40
Roe. 1 ....Evan. 49
Roe. 2 ....Paul. 47
Seld. 1 ....Evan. 53
Seld. 2 ....Evan. 54
Seld. 3 ....Evan. 55
Seld. 4 ....Evst. 21
Seld. 5 ....Evst. 22
Steph. codices XVI. *videas* pp. 190–191
Trin. ....Apost. 3
Trit. ....Evan. 96
Vat. ....Cod. B
Vel. ....Evan. 111 (Wetstein)
Vien. ....Evan. 76
Usser. 1 ......Evan. 63
Usser. 2 ......Evan. 64
Wheel. 1 ......Evan. 68
Wheel. 2 ......Evan. 95
Wheel. 3 ......Evst. 3
Wech. videas p. 191

Mill merely drew from other sources *Barb.*, *Steph.*, *Vel.*, *Wech.*; the copies deposited abroad (*B* 1–3, *Clar.*, *Colb.* 1–11, *Cypr.*, *Genev.*, *Med.*, *Per.*, *Pet.* 1–3, *Vat.*, *Vien.*), and *Trin.* or Apost. 3 he only knew from readings sent to him; all the rest, not being included in Walton's list, and several of them also, he collated for himself.

The Prolegomena of Mill, divided into three parts—(1) on the Canon of the New Testament; (2) on the History of the Text, including the quotations of the Fathers and the early editions; and (3) on the plan and contents of his own work,—though by this time too far behind the present state of knowledge to bear reprinting, comprise a monument of learning such as the world has seldom seen, and contain much information the student will not even now easily find elsewhere. Although Mill perpetually pronounces his judgement on the character of disputed readings [1], especially in his Prolegomena, which were printed long after some portions of the body of the work, yet he only aims at reproducing Stephen's text of 1550, though in a few places he departs from it, whether by accident or design [2].

In 1710 Ludolph Kuster, a Westphalian, republished Mill's

[1] Dr. Hort says that 'his comprehensive examination of individual documents, seldom rising above the wilderness of multitudinous details, [is] yet full of sagacious observations' (Introd. p. 180).

[2] As Mill's text is sometimes reprinted in England as if it were quite identical with that commonly received, it is right to note the following passages wherein it does not coincide with Stephen's of 1550, besides that it corrects his typographical errors: Matt. xx. 15; 22; xxiv. 15; Mark ix. 16; xi. 22; xv. 29; Luke vii. 12 *bis*; x. 6; xvii. 1; John viii. 4; 25; xiii. 30–31; xix. 7; Acts ii. 36; vii. 17; xiv. 8; Rom. xvi. 11; 1 Cor. iii. 15; x. 10; xv. 28; 2 Cor. vi. 16; Eph. iv. 25; Tit. ii. 10; 1 Pet. iii. 11; 21; iv. 8; 2 Pet. ii. 12; Apoc. ii. 5; xx. 4. Reuss (p. 149) tells us that Kuster's edition recalls the Stephanic readings in Matt. xxiv. 15; Apoc. ii. 5.

Greek Testament, in folio, at Amsterdam and Rotterdam (or with a new title page, Leipsic, 1723, Amsterdam, 1746), arranging in its proper place the matter cast by Mill into his Appendix, as having reached him too late to stand in his critical notes, and adding to those notes the readings of twelve fresh manuscripts, one collated by Kuster himself, which he describes in a Preface well worth reading. Nine of these codices collated by, or under, the Abbé de Louvois are in the Royal Library at Paris (viz. *Paris.* 1, which is Evan. 285; *Paris.* 2=Evan. M; *Paris.* 3=Evan. 9; *Paris.* 4=Evan. 11; *Paris.* 5=Evan. 119; *Paris.* 6=Evan. 13; *Paris.* 7=Evan. 14; *Paris.* 8=Evan. 15; *Paris.* 9=the great Cod. C): but *Lips.*=Evan. 78 was collated by Boerner; *Seidel.*=Act. 42 by Westermann; *Boerner.*=Paul. G by Kuster himself. He keeps his own notes separate from Mill's by prefixing and affixing the marks ǂ, ⫰, and his collations both of his own codices and of early editions will be found more complete than his predecessor's.

5. In the next year after Kuster's Mill (1711), appeared at Amsterdam, from the press of the Wetsteins, a small N. T., 8vo, containing all the critical matter of the Oxford edition of 1675, a collation of one Vienna manuscript (*Caes.*=Evan. 76), 43 canons 'secundum quos variantes lectiones N. T. examinandae,' and discussions upon them, with other matter, especially parallel texts, forming a convenient manual, the whole by G. D. T. M. D., which being interpreted means Gerhard de Trajecto Mosae Doctor, this Gerhard von Mästricht being a Syndic of Bremen. The text is Fell's, except in Apoc. iii. 12, where the portentous erratum λαῷ for *ναῷ* of Stephen is corrected. A second and somewhat improved edition was published in 1735, but ere that date the book must have become quite superseded.

6. We have to return to England once more, where the criticism of the New Testament had engrossed the attention of RICHARD BENTLEY [1662—1742], whose elevation to the enviable post of Master of Trinity College, Cambridge, in 1699, was a just recognition of his supremacy in the English world of letters. As early as 1691 he had felt a keen interest in sacred criticism, and in his 'Epistola ad Johannem Millium' had urged that editor, in language fraught with eloquence and native vigour, to

hasten on the work (whose accomplishment was eventually left to others) of publishing side by side on the opened leaf Codd. A, D (*Bezae*), D (*Clarom.*), E (*Laud.*). For many years afterwards Bentley's laurels were won on other fields, and it was not till his friend was dead, and his admirable labours were exposed to the obloquy of opponents (some honest though unwise, others hating Mill because they hated the Scriptures which he sought to illustrate), that our Aristarchus exerted his giant strength to crush the infidel and to put the ignorant to silence. In his 'Remarks upon a late Discourse of Free Thinking in a letter to F[rancis] H[are] D.D. by Phileleutherus Lipsiensis,' 1713, Bentley displayed that intimate familiarity with the whole subject of various readings, their causes, extent, and consequences, which has rendered this occasional treatise more truly valued (as it was far more important) than the world-renowned 'Dissertation upon the Epistles of Phalaris' itself. As his years were now hastening on and the evening of life was beginning to draw nigh, it was seemly that the first scholar of his age should seek for his rare abilities an employment more entirely suited to his sacred office than even the most successful cultivation of classical learning; and so, about this time, he came to project what he henceforth regarded as his greatest effort, an edition of the Greek New Testament. In 1716 we find him in conference with J. J. Wetstein, then very young, and seeking his aid in procuring collations. In the same year he addressed his memorable 'Letter' to Wm. Wake [1657–1737], Archbishop of Canterbury, whose own mind was full of the subject, wherein he explains, with characteristic energy and precision, the principles on which he proposed to execute his great scheme. As these principles must be reviewed afterwards, we will but touch upon them now. His theory was built upon the notion that the oldest manuscripts of the Greek original and of Jerome's Latin version resemble each other so marvellously, even in the very order of the words, that by this agreement he could restore the text as it stood in the fourth century, 'so that there shall not be twenty words, or even particles, difference.' 'By taking two thousand errors out of the Pope's [i.e. the Clementine] Vulgate, and as many out of the Protestant Pope Stephen's [1550], I can set out an edition of each in columns, without using any book under nine hundred years old, that shall so exactly agree word for word, and, what at first amazed me, order for order, that no two tallies, nor two indentures, can agree better[1].' In 1720, some progress having been made in the task of collation, chiefly at Paris, by John Walker, Fellow of Trinity, who was designated by Bentley 'overseer and corrector of the press,' but proved in fact a great deal more; Bentley published his Proposals for Printing[2], a work which 'he consecrates, as a κειμήλιον, a κτῆμα ἐσαεί, a *charter*, a *magna charta*, to the whole Christian Church; to last when all the ancient MSS. here quoted may be lost and extinguished.' Alas for the emptiness of human anticipations! Of this noble design, projected by one of the most diligent, by one of the most highly gifted men our dear mother Cambridge ever nourished, nothing now remains but a few scattered notices in treatises on Textual Criticism, and large undigested stores of various readings and random observations, accumulated in his College Library; papers which no real student ever glanced through, but with a heart saddened—almost sickened—at the sight of so much labour lost[3]. The specimen chapter (Apocalypse xxii) which accompanied his Proposals shows clearly how little had yet been done towards arranging the materials that had been collected; codices are cited there, and in many of his loose notes, not separately and by name, as in Mill's volume, but mostly as 'Anglicus unus, tres codd. veterrimi, Gall. quatuor, Germ. unus,' &c., in the rough fashion of the Oxford N. T. of 1675[4].

[1] Ellis, Bentleii Critica Sacra, Introductory Preface, p. xv.

[2] Ellis, *ubi supra*, pp. xvii–xix. These *Proposals* were also very properly reprinted by Tischendorf (N. T., Proleg. lxxxvii–xcvi, 7th edition), together with the specimen chapter (Apoc. xxii). The full title was to have been: 'Η ΚΑΙΝΗ ΔΙΑΘΗΚΗ Graece. Novum Testamentum Versionis Vulgatae, per s^{tum} Hieryonymum ad vetusta exemplaria Graeca castigatae et exactae. Utrumque ex antiquissimis Codd. MSS., cum Graecis tum Latinis, edidit Richardus Bentleius.'

[3] This is all the more lamentable, inasmuch as Bentley was not accurate enough as a collator to make it unnecessary to follow him over the same ground. Dr. Westcott confirms my own experience in this respect when in a MS. note inserted by him on a blank leaf of Trin. Coll. B. xvii. 14, he states that 'Bentley's testimony, when he quotes a reading, may always be taken as true; but it is not so when he notes no variation in particular. On an average he omits *one-third* of the variations of the MSS., without following, as far as I can discover, any law in the selection of readings.'

[4] Bp. John Wordsworth would vindicate both Bentley and Walker from the suspicion of lightly taking up and lightly dropping so important a task. Walker, whom Bentley, as is said, called 'Clarissimus Walker,' died on Nov. 9,

It has been often alleged that Bentley seems to have worked but little on the Greek Testament after 1729: that his attention was diverted by his editions of Paradise Lost (1732) and of Manilius (1739), by his Homeric studies and College litigation, until he was overtaken by a paralytic stroke in 1739, and died in his eighty-first year in 1742. Walker's collations of cursive manuscripts at Christ Church (Evan. 506), however, obviously made for Bentley's use, bear the date of 1732[1], and a closer examination of his papers, bequeathed in 1786 by his nephew Richard Bentley to Trinity College, shows that much more progress had been made by him than has been usually supposed. Besides full collations of the uncial Codd. AD (Gospels and Acts), of Cod. F (his θ) and G of St. Paul, of Arundel 547 (Evst. 257) executed by Bentley himself, of Codd. B and C by others at his cost, three volumes are found there full of critical materials, which have been described by Mr. Ellis, and digested by Dr. Westcott. One of these (B. xvii. 5) I was allowed by the Master and Seniors to study at leisure at home. It is a folio edition of the N.T., Greek and Latin (Paris. ap. Claud. Sonnium, 1628, the Greek text being that of Elzevir 1624), whose margin and spaces between the lines are filled with various readings in Bentley's hand, but not all of them necessarily the results of his own labour, collected out of ten Greek and thirty Latin manuscripts. The Greek are all cursives save Evst. 5, and his connexion with them has been referred to above under the Cursive MSS. They are

Evan. 51 (γ),	Evan. 507 (τ),
... 54 (κ),	... 508 (δ),
... 60 (ϵ),	Act. 23 (χ),
... 113 (θ ?),	Apoc. 28 (κ),
... 440 (o),	Evst. 5 (a).

The Latin copies, which alone are described by Bentley in the fly-leaves of the volume, may not be as easily identified, but

1741, at the age of forty-eight.—Wordsworth, Old Biblical Texts, I. xxv. p. 65. And for the Latin and Greek Texts collated by him wholly or partially, *see* pp. 55–68.

[1] He continued this work till after 1735. *See* paper found by Dr. Ince at Christ Church, quoted by Bp. J. Wordsworth, Old Latin Biblical Texts, I. xxv. note 2.

some of them are of great value, and are described above in Chap. III. These are

chad. (ξ),	*oxon.* (C),
dunelm. (K),	*oxon.* (Paul. χ),
harl.[3] (M),	*seld.* (Act. χ),
lind. (η),	*vall.*,
mac-regol (χ),	Westcott adds *harl.*[4] (H).

A second mass of materials, all Latin, about twenty in number, and deposited in England, is contained in the first volume of the Benedictine edition of St. Jerome's works (Paris, 1693). In this book (B. xvii. 14) Dr. Westcott has pasted a valuable note, wherein he identifies the manuscripts used by Bentley by the means of his own actual collation. Those described above in Chap. III are the following:

B. M. Harl. 1802 (W),
harl.[2] (M. of Epistles, &c.),
Addit. 5463 (F),
King's Lib. I. A. 18 (O),
I. B. VII. (H),
I. E. VI. (P),
C. C. C. Camb. 286 (B),
Trin. Coll. Camb. B. x. 5 (S),
B. x. 4 (T, *ibid.*),
lind. (Y : as in B. XVII. 5),
Camb. Univ. Lib. Kk. I. 24 (χ).

Westcott further appropriates B. M. Cotton, Otho B. ix, as Bentley's D; Cotton Tib. A. ii ('the Coronation book') as his ϵ; Cotton Otho C. v as his φ; C. C. C. Camb. 197 as his C; King's Library 1 D. ix as his A. His ξ in B. xvii. 14 seems unrecognized.

These, of course, are no more than the rough materials of criticism. Another copy of the N. T. has been carefully and curiously made available for my use by the goodness of my friend Edwin Palmer, D.D., Archdeacon of Oxford. It is numbered B. xvii. 6, and is a duplicate copy (without its title-page) of the same printed book as B. xvii. 5. It is interleaved throughout, and was prepared very early in the course of this undertaking, inasmuch as Bentley describes it in an undated letter to Wetstein, which the latter answered Nov. 3, 1716. In the printed text itself, both Greek and Latin, as they stand in parallel columns, Bentley makes the corrections which he at that period was willing to adopt. There is no critical apparatus to justify his changes in the Latin version, but on the blank leaves of the book he sets down his Greek authorities, always cited by name, as *Alex.*, *Cant.*, *Rom.* (Cod. B.), *Ox.* in the Acts (Cod. E), θ in St. Paul for Cod. Augiensis (F), though this last did not reach him before 1718. Cod. C is sometimes called *Eph.*, sometimes it is mixed up with Wetstein's other copies (1 Wetstein, 2 Wetstein, &c.). This most interesting volume, therefore, contains the first draft of Bentley's great design, and must have been nearly in its present state when the 'Proposals' were published in 1720, since the specimen chapter (Apoc. xxii) which accompanied them is taken *verbatim* from B. xvii. 6, save that authorities are added to vindicate the alterations of the Latin text, which is destitute of them in the printed book. Mr. Ellis too has printed the Epistle to the Galatians from the same source, and this specimen also produces much the same impression of meagreness and imperfection. It was doubtless in some degree to remedy an apparent crudeness that cursive copies were afterwards called in, as in B. xvii. 5 and in Walker's Oxford collections. The fact is that Bentley's main principle, as set forth by him from 1716 to 1720, that of substantial identity between the oldest Greek and Latin copies, is more favoured by Cod. A, which he knew soonest and best, than by any other really ancient documents, least of all by Cod. B, with which he obtained fuller acquaintance in or about 1720. Our Aristarchus then betook himself at intervals to cursive codices in the vain hope of getting aid from them, and so lost his way at last in that wide and pathless wilderness. We cannot but believe that nothing less than the manifest impossibility of maintaining the principles which his 'Letter' of 1716 enunciated, and his 'Proposals' of 1720 scarcely modified, in the face of the evidence which his growing mass of collations bore against them [1], could have had power enough to break off in the midst

[1] Mr. Jebb (Life of Bentley, p. 164) imputes the failure of Bentley's grand scheme partly to the worry of litigation which harassed him from 1729 to 1738; partly to a growing sense of complexity in the problem of the text, especially after he became better acquainted with the Vatican readings, i. e. about 1720 and 1729. Reuss (p. 172) ought never to have conditioned the ultimate success of such a man by the proviso 'si consilio par fuerit perseverantia.'

that labour of love from which he had looked for undying fame [1].

7. The anonymous text and version of William Mace, said to have been a Presbyterian minister ('The New Testament in Greek and English,' 2 vols. 8vo, 1729), are alike unworthy of serious notice, and have long since been forgotten [2]. And now original research in the science of Biblical criticism, so far as the New Testament is concerned, seems to have left the shores of England, to return no more for upwards of a century [3]; and we must look to Germany if we wish to trace the further progress of investigations which our countrymen had so auspiciously begun. The first considerable effort made on the Continent was

8. The New Testament of John Albert Bengel, 4to, Tübingen, 1734 [4]: his 'Prodromus N. T. Gr. rectè cautèque adornandi' had appeared as early as 1725. This devout and truly able man [1687–1752], who held the office (whatever might be its func-

[1] 'This thought has now so engaged me, and in a manner inslaved me, that *vae mihi* unless I do it. Nothing but sickness (by the blessing of God) shall hinder me from prosecuting it to the end' (Bentley to Archbp. Wake, 1716: Ellis, *ubi supra*, p. xvi). A short article in the *Edinburgh Review* for July, 1860, apparently from the pen of Tregelles, draws attention to 'Nicolai Toinardi Harmonia Graeco-Latina,' Paris, 1707, fol. ('liber rarissimus,' Reuss, p. 167), who so far anticipates Bentley's labours, that he forms a new Greek text by the aid of two Roman manuscripts (Cod. B being one of them) and of the Latin version.

[2] Dr. Gregory says that though Mace's edition had no accents or soft breathing, he anticipates most of the changes accepted by some critics of the present day.

[3] I cannot help borrowing the language of Donaldson, used with reference to an entirely different department of study, in the opening of one of his earliest and by far his most enduring work: 'It may be stated as a fact worthy of observation in the literary history of modern Europe, that generally, when one of our countrymen has made the first advance in any branch of knowledge, we have acquiesced in what he has done, and have left the further improvement of the subject to our neighbours on the continent. The man of genius always finds an utterance, for he is urged on by an irresistible impulse—a conviction that it is his duty and vocation to speak: but we too often want those who shall follow in his steps, clear up what he has left obscure, and complete his unfinished labours' (New Cratylus, p. 1). Dr. Gregory quotes against Dr. Scrivener, Mace (1729), Bowyer, a follower of Wetstein (1763), Harwood (1776), besides Whitby, Middleton, and Twells: but Dr. S. looked for greater names, and till Middleton, a more advancing study.

[4] The full title is 'Ἡ καινὴ διαθήκη. Novum Testamentum Graecum ita adornatum ut Textus probatarum editionum medullam, Margo variantium lectionum in suas classes distributarum locorumque parellelorum delectum, Apparatus subjunctus criseos sacrae Millianae praesertim compendium limam supplementum ac fructum exhibeat, inserviente J. A. B.'

tions) of Abbot of Alpirspach in the Lutheran communion of Württemberg, though more generally known as an interpreter of Scripture from his invaluable 'Gnomon Novi Testamenti,' yet left the stamp of his mind deeply imprinted on the criticism of the sacred volume. As a collator his merits were not high; nearly all his sixteen codices have required and obtained fresh examination from those who came after him[1]. His text, which he arranged in convenient paragraphs, as has been said, is the earliest important specimen of intentional departure from the received type; hence he imposes on himself the strange restriction of admitting into it no reading (excepting in the Apocalypse) which had not appeared in one or more of the editions that preceded his own. He pronounces his opinion on other *select* variations by placing them in his lower margin with Greek numerals attached to them, according as he judged them decidedly better (α), or somewhat more likely (β), than those which stand in his text: or equal to them (γ); or a little (δ), or considerably (ε), inferior. This notation has advantages which might well have commended it to the attention of succeeding editors. In his 'Apparatus Criticus' also, at the end of his volume, he set the example, now generally followed, of recording definitely the testimony in favour of a received reading, as well as that against it.

But the peculiar importance of Bengel's N. T. is due to the critical principles developed therein. Not only was his native acuteness of great service to him, when weighing the conflicting probabilities of internal evidence, but in his fertile mind sprang up the germ of that theory of *families* or *recensions*, which was afterwards expanded by J. S. Semler [1725–91], and grew to such formidable dimensions in the skilful hands of Griesbach. An attentive student of the discrepant readings of the N. T., even in the limited extent they had hitherto been collected, could hardly fail to discern that certain manuscripts, versions, and ecclesiastical writers have a manifest

[1] They consist of seven Augsburg codices (*Aug.* 1=Evan. 83; *Aug.* 2=Evan. 84; *Aug.* 3=Evan. 85; *Aug.* 4=Evst. 24; *Aug.* 5=Paul. 54; *Aug.* 6=Act. 46; *Aug.* 7=Apoc. 80); *Poson.*=Evan. 86; extracts sent by Isel from three Basle copies (*Bas.* α=Evan. E; *Bas.* β=Evan. 2; *Bas.* γ=Evan. 1); *Hirsaug.*=Evan. 97; *Mosc.*=Evan. V; extracts sent by F. C. Gross. To these add Uffenbach's three, *Uffen.* 2 or 1=Paul. M; *Uffen.* 1 or 2=Act. 45; *Uffen*, 3=Evan. 101.

affinity with each other; so that one of them shall seldom be cited in support of a variation (not being a manifest and gross error of the copyist), unless accompanied by several of its kindred. The inference is direct and clear, that documents which thus withdraw themselves from the general mass of authorities, must have sprung from some common source, distinct from those which in characteristic readings they but slightly resemble. It occurred, therefore, to Bengel as a hopeful mode of making good progress in the criticism of the N. T., to reduce all extant testimony into 'companies, families, tribes, and nations,' and thus to simplify the process of settling the sacred text by setting class over against class, and trying to estimate the genius of each, and the relative importance they may severally lay claim to. He wished to divide all extant documents into two nations: the *Asiatic*, chiefly written in Constantinople and its neighbourhood, which he was inclined to disparage; and the *African*, comprising the few of a better type ('Apparatus Criticus,' p. 669, 2nd edition, 1763). Various circumstances hindered Bengel from working out his principle, among which he condescends to set his dread of exposing his task to senseless ridicule[1]; yet no one can doubt that it comprehends the elements of what is both reasonable and true; however difficult it has subsequently proved to adjust the details of any consistent scheme. For the rest, Bengel's critical verdicts, always considered in relation to his age and opportunities, deserve strong commendation. He saw the paramount worth of Cod. A, the only great uncial then much known (N. T., Apparat. Crit., pp. 390–401). The high character of the Latin version, and the

[1] It is worth while to quote at length Bengel's terse and vigorous statement of his principle: 'Posset variarum lectionum ortus, per singulos codices, per paria codicum, per syzygias minores majoresque, per familias, tribus, nationesque illorum, investigari et repraesentari; et inde propinquitates discessionesque codicum ad schematismos quosdam reduci, et schematismorum aliquae concordantiae fieri; atque ita res tota per tabulam quandam quasi genealogicam oculis subjici, ad quam tabulam quaelibet varietas insignior cum agmine suorum codicum, ad convincendos etiam tardissimos dubitatores exigeretur. Magnam conjectanea nostra sylvam habent: sed manum de tabulâ, ne risuum periculo exponatur veritas. Bene est, quod praetergredi montem hunc, et planiore via pervenire datur ad codices discriminandos. Datur autem per hanc regulam aequissimam: Quo saepius non modo singuli codices, sed etiam syzygiae minores eorum vel majores, in aberrationes manifestas tendunt; eo levius ferunt testimonium in discrepantiis difficilioribus, eoque magis lectio ab eis deserta, tanquam genuina retineri debet' (N. T., Apparat. Crit., p. 387).

necessity for revising its text by means of manuscripts (*ibid.*, p. 391), he readily conceded, after Bentley's example. His mean estimate of the Greek-Latin codices (Evan. Act. D; Act. E; Paul. DFG) may not find equal favour in the eyes of all his admirers; he pronounces them 're verâ bilingues;' which, for their perpetual and wilful interpolations, 'non pro codicibus sed pro rhapsodiis, haberi debeant' (*ibid.*, p. 386)[1].

9. The next step in advance was made by John James Wetstein [1693–1754], a native of Basle, whose edition of the Greek New Testament ('cum lectionibus variantibus Codicum MSS., Editionum aliarum, Versionum et Patrum, necnon Commentario pleniore ex scriptoribus veteribus, Hebraeis, Graecis, et Latinis, historiam et vim verborum illustrante') appeared in two volumes, folio, Amsterdam, 1751–2. The genius, the character, and (it must in justice be added) the worldly fortunes of Wetstein were widely different from those of the good Abbot of Alpirspach. His taste for Biblical studies showed itself early. When ordained pastor at the age of twenty he delivered a disputation, 'De variis N. T. lectionibus,' and zeal for this fascinating pursuit became at length with him a passion—the master-passion which consoled and dignified a roving, troubled, unprosperous life. In 1714 his eager search for manuscripts led him to Paris, in 1715–16 and again in 1720 he visited England, and was employed by Bentley in collecting materials for his projected edition, but he seems to have imbibed few of that great man's principles: the interval between them, both in age and station, almost forbade much sympathy. On his return home he gradually became suspected of Socinian tendencies, and it must be feared with too much justice; so that in the end he was deposed from the pastorate (1730), driven into exile, and after having been compelled to serve in a position the least favourable to the cultivation of learning, that of a military chaplain, he obtained at length (1733) a Professorship among the Remonstrants at Amsterdam (in succession to the celebrated Leclerc), and there continued till his death in 1754, having made his third visit to England in 1746. His 'Pro-

[1] See a eulogistic yet discriminating discussion upon Bengel in *Bengel als Gelehrter, ein Bild für unsere Tage*, from the eminent pen of Dr. Nestle, which has been courteously sent to the editor through the Rev. H. J. White.

legomena,' first published in 1730, and afterwards, in an altered form, prefixed to his N. T.[1], present a painful image both of the man and of his circumstances. His restless energy, his undaunted industry, his violent temper, his love of paradox, his assertion for himself of perfect freedom of thought, his silly prejudice against Jesuits and bigots, his enmities, his wrongs, his ill-requited labours, at once excite our respect and our pity: while they all help to make his writings a sort of unconscious autobiography, rather interesting than agreeable. *Non sic itur ad astra*, whether morally or intellectually; yet Wetstein's services to sacred literature were of no common order. His philological annotations, wherein the matter and phraseology of the inspired writers are illustrated by copious—too copious—quotations from all kinds of authors, classical, Patristic, and Rabbinical, have proved an inexhaustible storehouse from which later writers have drawn liberally and sometimes without due acknowledgement; but many of the passages are of such a tenor as (to use Tregelles' very gentle language respecting them) 'only to excite surprise at their being found on the same page as the text of the New Testament' (Account of Printed Text, p. 76). The critical portion of his work, however, is far more valuable, and in this department Wetstein must be placed in the very first rank, inferior (if to any) to but one or two of the highest names. He first cited the manuscripts under the notation by which they are commonly known, his list already embracing A–O, 1–112 of the Gospels; A–G, 1–58 of the Acts; A–H, 1–60 of St. Paul; A–C, 1–28 of the Apocalypse; 1–24 Evangelistaria; 1–4 of the Apostolos. Of these Wetstein himself collated about one hundred and two[2]; if not as fully or accurately as is now expected, yet with far greater care than had hitherto been usual: about eleven were examined for him by other hands. On the versions and early editions he has likewise bestowed great pains; and he improved upon quotations from the Fathers. His text is that of Elzevir (1633), not very exactly printed[3], and immediately below it he

[1] The opposition of Frey and his other adversaries delayed that *opus magnum* for twenty years (N. T., Proleg., vol. i. p. 218).

[2] We here reckon separately, as we believe is both usual and convenient, every distinct portion of the N. T. contained in a manuscript. Thus Codd. C and 69 Evan. will each count for four.

[3] Errors of Wetstein's text will be found in John xi. 31; Acts i. 26; xiii. 29

placed such readings of his manuscripts as he judged preferable to those received. The readings thus approved by Wetstein (which do not amount to five hundred, and those chiefly in the Apocalypse) were inserted in the text of a Greek Testament published in London, 1763, 2 vols., by W. Bowyer, the learned printer, with a collection of critical conjectures annexed, which were afterwards published separately.

Wetstein's Prolegomena have also been reproduced by J. S. Semler (Halle, 1764), with good notes and facsimiles of certain manuscripts, and more recently, in a compressed and modernized form, by J. A. Lotze (Rotterdam, 1831), a book which neither for design nor execution can be much praised. The truth is that both the style and the subject-matter of much that Wetstein wrote are things of the past. In his earlier edition of his Prolegomena (1730) he had spoken of the oldest Greek uncial copies as they deserve ; he was even disposed to take Cod. A as the basis of his text. By the time his N. T. was ready, twenty years later, he had come to include it, with all the older codices of the original, under a general charge of being conformed to the Latin version. That such a tendency may be detected in some of the codices accompanied by a Latin translation, is both possible in itself, and not inconsistent with their general spirit ; but he has scattered abroad his imputations capriciously and almost at random, so as greatly to diminish the weight of his own decisions. Cod. A, in particular, has been fully cleared of the charge of Latinizing by Woide, in his excellent Prolegomena (§ 6). His thorough contempt for that critic prevented Wetstein from giving adequate attention to Bengel's theory of

(ἐτέλησαν, from the Oxford N. T. 1675), though Wetstein himself remarks this. He corrects a few obvious misprints of Elzevir 1633, but his note shows that he does not *intend* to read τῷ in Mark vi. 29. The following seem to be deliberate variations from the Elzevir text : Matt. xiii. 15 ; xxi. 41 ; Mark xiv. 54 ; Luke ii. 22 ; xi. 12 ; xiii. 19 ; 1 Cor. i. 29 ; v. 11 ; xii. 28 ; xiv. 15 ; Phil. iii. 5 ; 1 Tim. iii. 2, 11 (yet not Tit. ii. 2) ; Philem. 7 ; 1 Pet. i. 3 ; iii. 7. All these deliberate variations are found in Von Mastricht's edition of 1735, which seems to have been used by Wetstein as the basis of his text ; and in all of them (except Matt. xxi. 41 ; Luke xi. 12, and Phil. iii. 5) Fell's text agrees with Wetstein's. In Matt. xiii. 15 ; Mark xiv. 54 ; 1 Cor. i. 29 ; v. 11 ; xii. 23 ; xiv. 15 ; Phil. iii. 5 ; 1 Pet. iii. 7, the Elzevir editions vary. (American Additions and Corrections, p. 51.) He spells *ναζαρέτ* uniformly, except in John i. 46, 47. Reuss (p. 183) adds nine changes made by Wetstein in the text for critical reasons : Matt. viii. 28 ; Luke xi. 2 ; John vii. 53—viii. 11 ; Acts v. 36 ; xx. 28 ; 1 Tim. iii. 16 (ὃ) ; Apoc. iii. 2 ; x. 4 ; xviii. 17.

families; indeed he can hardly be said to have rejected a scheme which he scorned to investigate with patience. On the other hand no portion of his labours is more valuable than the 'Animadversiones et Cautiones ad examen variarum lectionum N. T. necessariae' (N. T., Tom. ii. pp. 851–74). In this tract his natural good sense and extensive knowledge of authorities of every class have gone far to correct that impetuous temperament which was ever too ready to substitute plausible conjecture in the room of ascertained facts.

During the twenty years immediately ensuing on the publication of Wetstein's volumes, little was attempted in the way of enlarging or improving the domain he had secured for Biblical science. In England the attention of students was directed, and on the whole successfully, to the criticism of the Hebrew Scriptures; in Germany, the younger (J. D.) Michaelis [1717–91] reigned supreme, and he seems to have deemed it the highest effort of scholarship to sit in judgement on the labours of others. In process of time, however, the researches of John James Griesbach [1745–1812], a native of Hesse Darmstadt and a pupil of Semler, and J. A. Ernesti [1707–81] (whose manual, 'Institutio Interpretis N. T.,' 1761, has not long been superseded), began to attract general notice. Like Wetstein, he made a literary tour in England early in life (1769), and with far more profit; returning to Halle as a Professor, he published before he was thirty (1774–5) his first edition of the N. T., which contained the well-defined embryo of his future and more elaborate speculations. It will be convenient to reserve the examination of his views until we have described the investigations of several collators who unknowingly (and in one instance, no doubt unwillingly) were busy in gathering stores which he was to turn to his own use.

10. Christian Frederick Matthaei, a Thuringian [1744–1811], was appointed, on the recommendation of his tutor Ernesti, to the Professorship of Classical Literature at Moscow: so far as philology is concerned, he probably merited Bp. Middleton's praise, as 'the most accurate scholar who ever edited the N. T.' (Doctrine of the Greek Article, p. 244, 3rd edition.) At Moscow he found a large number of Greek manuscripts, both Biblical and Patristic, originally brought from Athos, quite uncollated,

and almost entirely unknown in the west of Europe. With laudable resolution he set himself to examine them, and gradually formed the scheme of publishing an edition of the New Testament by the aid of materials so precious and abundant. All authors that deserve that honourable name may be presumed to learn not a little, even on the subject they know best, while preparing an important work for the public eye; but Matthaei was as yet ignorant of the first principles of the critical art; and beginning thus late, there was much, and that of a very elementary character, which he never understood at all. When he commenced writing he had not seen the volumes of Mill or Wetstein; and to this significant fact we must impute that inability which clave to him to the last, of discriminating the relative age and value of his own or others' codices. The palaeographical portion of the science, indeed, he gradually acquired from the study of his documents, and through the many facsimiles of them he represents in his edition; but what can be thought of his judgement, when he persisted in asserting the intrinsic superiority of Cod. 69 of the Acts to the great uncials AC (N. T., Tom. xii. p. 222)[1]? Hence it results that Matthaei's text, which of course he moulded on his own views, must be held in slight esteem: his services as a collator comprehend his whole claim (and that no trifling one) to our thankful regard. To him solely we are indebted for Evan. V; 237–259; Act. 98–107; Paul. 113–124; Apoc. 47–50[2] (i. e. r); Evst. 47–57; Apost. 13–20; nearly all at Moscow: the whole seventy[2], together

[1] One other specimen of Matthaei's critical skill will suffice: he is speaking of his Cod. H, which is our Evst. 50. 'Hic Codex scriptus est literis quadratis, estque eorum omnium, qui adhuc in Europa innotuerunt et vetustissimus et praestantissimus. Insanus quidem fuerit, qui cum hoc aut Cod. V [p. 144] comparare, aut aequiparare voluerit Codd. Alexandr. Clar. Germ. Boern. Cant. [Evan. AD, Paul. ADEG], qui sine ullo dubio pessimè ex scholiis et Versione Latinâ Vulgatâ interpolati sunt' (N. T., Tom. ix. p. 254).

[2] In using Matthaei's N. T. the following index of manuscripts first collated by him will be found useful: a = Evan. 259, Act. 98 (a 1), Paul. 113 (a or a 2), Apost. 82 (a 3): B = Evst. 47: b = Apost. 18: c = Act. 99, Paul. 114, Evst. 48: d = Evan. 237, Act. 100, Paul. 115: e = Evan. 238, Apost. 14: f = Act. 101, Paul. 116, Evst. 49: g = Evan. 239, Act. 102, Paul. 117: H = Evst. 50: h = Act. 103, Paul. 118: i = Evan. 240, Paul. 119: k = Evan. 241, Act. 104, Paul. 120, Apoc. 47: l = Evan. 242, Act. 105, Paul. 121, Apoc. 48: m = Evan. 243, Act. 106, Paul. 122: n = Evan. 244, Paul. 123: o = Evan. 245, Apoc. 49: p = Evan. 246, Apoc. 50: q = Evan. 247, Paul. 124: r = Evan. 248, also Apoc. 50[2], Apoc. 90: s = Evan. 249, Paul. 76: t = Apoc. 32, Evst. 51: tz = Apost. 15: V = V: v = Evan. 250, Apost. 5: x = Evan. 251, Act. 69, Paul. 74, Apoc. 30 (from Knittel); z = Evan.

with the citations of Scripture in thirty-four manuscripts of Chrysostom[1], being so fully and accurately collated, that the reader need not be at a loss whether any particular copy supports or opposes the reading in the common text. Matthaei's further services in connexion with Cod. G Paul. and a few others (Act. 69, &c.) have been noticed in their proper places. To his Greek text was annexed the Latin Vulgate (the only version, in its present state, he professes to regard, Tom. xi. p. xii) from the Cod. Demidovianus. The first volume of this edition appeared in 1782, after it had been already eight years in preparation: this comprised the Catholic Epistles. The rest of the work was published at intervals during the next six years, in eleven more thin parts 8vo, the whole series being closed by SS. Matthew and Mark in 1788. Each volume has a Preface, much descriptive matter, and facsimiles of manuscripts (twenty-nine in all), the whole being in complete and almost hopeless disorder, and the general title-page absurdly long. Hence his critical principles (if such they may be termed) must be picked up piecemeal; and it is not very pleasant to observe the sort of influence which hostile controversy exercised over his mind and temper. While yet fresh at his task (1782), anticipating the fair fame his most profitable researches had so well earned, Matthaei is frank, calm, and rational: even at a later period J. D. Michaelis is, in his estimation, the keenest of living judges of codices, and he says so the rather 'quod ille vir doctissimus multis modis me, *quâ de causâ ipse ignoro*, partim jocosè, partim seriò, vexavit' (Tom. ii, 1788, p. xxxi). Bengel, whose sentiments were very dissimilar from those of the Moscow Professor, 'pro acumine, diligentiâ et religione suâ,' would have arrived at other conclusions, had his Augsburg codices been better (*ibid.*, p. xxx). But for Griesbach and his recension-theory no terms of insult are strong enough;

252: 10 = Evan. 253: 11 = Evan. 254: 12 = Evan. 255: 14 = Evan. 256: 15 = O, 16 = Evst. 56, Apost. 20: 17 = Evan. 258: 18 = Evan. 99: 19 = Evst. 57: 20 = Evan. 89: ξ = Evst. 52, Apost. 16: χ = Evst. 53, Apost. 17: ψ = Evst. 54, Apost. 18: ω = Evst. 55, Apost. 19: Frag. Vet. = part of H: G^Paul. It should be noted, that in several of these cases different MSS. are included under one letter: e. g. c = Evst. 48 is a different MS. from c = Act. 99.

[1] The copies of Chysostom's homilies on the Gospels freshly collated by this editor are noted 1, 2, 3, 4, 5, 6, 7, 8, 9, 13, α, β, γ, δ, ε, ζ, η, θ, λ, μ, π, ρ, φ: those on St. Paul's Epistles are noted 1, 2, 3, 4, 5, 6, 7, 8, 9, α, β.

'risum vel adeo pueris debet ille Halensis criticus,' who never saw, '*ut credibile est*,' a manuscript even of the tenth century (*ibid.*, p. xxiii), yet presumes to dictate to those who have collated seventy. The unhappy consequence was, that one who had taken up this employment in an earnest and candid spirit, possessed with the simple desire to promote the study of sacred literature, could devise no fitter commencement for his latest Preface than this: 'Laborem igitur molestum invidiosum et infamem, inter convicia ranarum et latratus canum, aut ferreâ patientiâ aut invictâ pertinaciâ his quindecim annis vel sustinui, vel utcunque potui perfeci, vel denique et fastidio et taedio, ut fortasse non nulli opinantur, deposui et abjeci' (Tom. i, Praef. p. 1): he could find no purer cause for thankfulness, than (what we might have imagined but a very slight mercy) that he had never been commended by those 'of whom to be dispraised is no small praise;' or (to use his own more vigorous language) 'quod nemo scurra . . . nemo denique de grege novorum theologorum, hanc qualemcunque operam meam ausus est ore impuro suo, laudeque contumeliosâ comprobare.' Matthaei's second edition in three volumes (destitute of the Latin version and most of the critical notes) bears date 1803–7[1]. For some cause, now not easy to understand, he hardly gave to this second edition the advantages of his studies during the fifteen years which had elapsed since he completed his first. We saw his labours bestowed on the Zittau N. T. in 1801–2 (Evan. 605). On the last leaf of the third volume of his second edition, writing from Moscow in May, 1805, he speaks of a book containing collations of no less than twenty-four manuscripts, partly fresh, partly corrected, which, when he returned into Russia, he delivered to Augustus Schumann, a bookseller at Ronneburg (in Saxe Altenburg), to be published in close connexion with his second edition against the Easter Fair at Leipzig in 1805. Another book contained extracts from St. Chrysostom with a commentary and index, to be published at the same time, and both at Schumann's risk. 'Utrum isti libri jam prodierint necne,' our author adds pathetically, 'nondum factus sum certior. Certe id vehementer opto.' But in 1805 evil times were hastening upon Germany,

[1] Reuss (p. 207) calculates that, besides misprints, Matthaei's second and very inferior edition differs in text from his first in but twenty-four places, none of them being in the Gospels.

and so unfortunately for the poor man and for textual students these collections have disappeared and left no trace behind.

10.[a] The next, and a far less considerable contribution to our knowledge of manuscripts of the N. T., was made by Francis Karl Alter [1749–1804], a Jesuit, born in Silesia, and Professor of Greek at Vienna. His plan was novel, and, to those who are compelled to use his edition (N. T. Graecum, ad Codicem Vindobonensem Graecè expressum, 8vo, Vienna, 2 tom., 1786–7), inconvenient to the last degree. Adopting for his standard a valuable, but not very ancient or remarkable, manuscript in the Imperial Library (Evan. 218, Act. 65, Paul. 57, Apoc. 83), he prints this copy at full length, retaining even the ν ἐφελκυστικόν when it is found in his model, but not (as it would seem) all the itacisms or errors of the scribe, conforming in such cases to Stephen's edition of 1546. With this text he collates in separate Appendices twenty-one other manuscripts of the same great Library, comprising twelve copies of the Gospels (Codd. N, a fragment, 3, 76, 77, 108, 123, 124, 125, 219, 220, 224, 225); six of the Acts, &c. (3, 43, 63, 64, 66, 67); seven of St. Paul (3, 49, 67–71); three of the Apocalypse (34, 35, 36), and two Evangelistaria (45, 46). He also gives readings from Wilkins' Coptic version, four Slavonic codices and one Old Latin (*i*). In employing this ill-digested mass, it is necessary to turn to a different place for every manuscript to be consulted, and Alter's silence in any passages must be understood to indicate resemblance to his standard, Evan. 218, and not to the common text. As this silence is very often clearly due to the collator's mere oversight, Griesbach set the example of citing these manuscripts in such cases within marks of parenthesis: thus '218 (108, 220)' indicates that the reading in question is certainly found in Cod. 218, and (so far as we may infer *ex Alteri silentio*) not improbably in the other two. Most of these Vienna codices were about the same time examined rather slightly by Andrew Birch.

11. This eminent person, who afterwards bore successively the titles of Bishop of Lolland, Falster, and Aarhuus, in the Lutheran communion established in Denmark, was one of a company of learned men sent by the liberal care of Christian VII to examine Biblical manuscripts in various countries. Adler

pursued his Oriental studies at Rome and elsewhere; D. G. Moldenhawer and O. G. Tychsen (the famous Orientalist of Rostock) were sent into Spain in 1783–4; Birch travelled on the same good errand in 1781–3 through Italy and Germany. The combined results of their investigations were arranged and published by Birch, whose folio edition of the Four Gospels (also in 4to) with Stephen's text of 1550[1], and the various readings contributed by himself and his associates, full descriptive Prolegomena and facsimiles of seven manuscripts (Codd. S, 157 Evan.; and five in Syriac), appeared at Copenhagen in 1788. Seven years afterwards (1795) a fire destroyed the Royal Printing-house, the type, paper, and unsold stock of the first volume, the collations of the rest of the N. T. having very nearly shared the same fate. These poor fragments were collected by Birch into two small 8vo volumes, those relating to the Acts and Epistles in 1798, to the Apocalypse (with facsimiles of Codd. 37, 42) in 1800. In 1801 he revised and re-edited the various readings of the Gospels, in a form to correspond with those of the rest of the N. T. Nothing can be better calculated to win respect and confidence than the whole tone of Birch's several Prolegomena: he displays at once a proper sense of the difficulties of his task, and a consciousness that he had done his utmost to conquer them[2]. It is indeed much to be regretted that, for some cause he does not wish to explain, he accomplished but little for Cod. B; many of the manuscripts on his long list were beyond question examined but very superficially; yet he was almost the first to open to us the literary treasures of the Vatican, of Florence, and of Venice. He more or less inspected the uncials Cod. B, Codd. ST of the Gospels, Cod. L of the Acts and Epistles. His catalogue of cursives comprises Codd. 127–225 of the Gospels; Codd. 63–7, 70–96 of the Acts; Codd. 67–71, 77–112 of St. Paul; Codd. 33-4, 37–46

[1] 'Textui ad Millianum expresso' says Reuss (p. 151), which is not quite the same thing: *see* p. 203, note 2.

[2] 'Conscius sum mihi, me omnem et diligentiam et intentionem adhibuisse, ut haec editio quam emendatissima in manus eruditorum perveniret, utque in hoc opere, in quo ingenio non fuit locus, curae testimonium promererem; nulla tamen mihi est fiducia, me omnia, quae exigi possint, peregisse. Vix enim potest esse ulla tam perpetua legentis intentio, quae non obtutu continuo fatigetur, praesertim in tali genere, quod tam multis, saepe parvis, observationibus constat.' (Lecturis Editor, p. v. 1788.) Well could I testify to the truth of these last words!

of the Apocalypse; Evangelistaria 35–39; Apostolos 7, 8: in all 191 copies, a few of which were thoroughly collated (e.g. Evan. S, 127, 131, 157, Evst. 36). Of Adler's labours we have spoken already; they too are incorporated in Birch's work, and prefaced with a short notice (Birch, Proleg. p. lxxxv) by their author, a real and modest scholar. Moldenhawer's portion of the common task was discharged in another spirit. Received at the Escurial with courtesy and good-will, his colleague Tyschen and he spent four whole months in turning over a collection of 760 Greek manuscripts, of which only twenty related to the Greek Testament. They lacked neither leisure, nor opportunity, nor competent knowledge; but they were full of dislike for Spain and its religion, of overweening conceit, and of implicit trust in Griesbach and his recensions. The whole paper contributed by Moldenhawer to Birch's Prolegomena (pp. lxi–lxxxiv) is in substance very disappointing, while its arrogance is almost intolerable. What he effected for other portions of the N. T. I have not been able to trace (226, 228 Evan., which also contain the Acts and Epistles, are but nominally on Scholz's list for those books); the fire at Copenhagen may probably have destroyed his notes. Of the Gospels he collated eight codices (226–233), and four Evangelistaria (40–43), most of them being dismissed, after a cursory review, with some expression of hearty contempt. To Evann. 226, 229, 230 alone was he disposed to pay any attention; of the rest, whether 'he soon restored them to their primitive obscurity' (p. lxxi), or 'bade them sweet and holy rest among the reliques of Saints and Martyrs' (p. lxvii), he may be understood to say, once for all, 'Omnino nemo, qui horum librorum rationem ac indolem . . . perspectam habet, ex iis lectionis varietatem operose eruere aggredietur, nec, si quam inde conquisiverit, operae pretium fecisse a peritis arbitris existimabitur' (p. lxxiv). It was not thus that Matthaei dealt with the manuscripts at Moscow.

12. Such were the materials ready for Griesbach's use when he projected his second and principal edition of the Greek Testament (vol. i. 1796, vol. ii. 1806). Not that he was backward in adding to the store of various readings by means of his own diligence. His 'Symbolae Criticae[1]' (vol. i. 1785, vol. ii. 1793)

[1] 'Symbolae Criticae ad supplendas et corrigendas variarum N. T. lectionum Collectiones. Accedit multorum N. T. Codicum Graecorum descriptio et examen.'

contained, together with the readings extracted from Origen, collations, in whole or part, of many copies of various portions of the N. T., Latin as well as Greek. Besides inspecting Codd. AD (Evann.), and carefully examining Cod. C[1], he consulted no less than twenty-six codices (including GL) of the Gospels, ten (including E) of the Acts, &c., fifteen (including DEH) of St. Paul, one of the Apocalypse (Cod. 29) twelve Lectionaries of the Gospels, and two of the Apostolos, far the greater part of them being deposited in England. It was not, however, his purpose to exhibit in his N. T. (designed, as it was, for general use) all the readings he had himself recorded elsewhere, much less the whole mass accumulated by the pains of Mill or Wetstein, Matthaei or Birch. The distinctive end at which he aims is to form such a selection from the matter their works contain, as to enable the theological student to decide for himself on the genuineness or corruption of any given reading, by the aid of principles which he devotes his best efforts to establish. Between the text (in which departures from the Elzevir edition of 1624 are generally indicated by being printed in smaller type[2]) and the critical notes at the foot of each page, intervenes a narrow space or inner margin, to receive those portions of the common text which Griesbach has rejected, and such variations of his authorities as he judges to be of equal weight with the received readings which he retains, or but little inferior to them. These decisions he intimates by several symbols, not quite so simple as those employed by Bengel, but conceived in a similar spirit; and he has carried his system somewhat further in his small or manual edition, published at Leipzig in 1805, which may be conceived to represent his last thoughts with regard to the recension of the Greek text of the N. T. But though we may trace some slight discrepancies of opinion between his earliest[3] and his latest works[4], as might

[1] Yet Tischendorf (N. T., Proleg., p. xcvii, 7th ed.) states that he only added two readings (Mark vi. 2, 4) to those given by Wetstein for Cod. C. From Cod. D too he seems to have taken only one reading, and that erroneously, επηγειραν, Acts xiv. 2.

[2] In the London edition of 1809 ἄλλοι is printed for the first οὗτοί, Mark iv. 18. Griesbach also omits καί in 2 Pet. i. 15: no manuscript except Cod. 182 (a^{scr}) is known to do so.

[3] 'Dissertatio critica de Codicibus quatuor Evangeliorum Origenianis,' Halae, 1771: 'Curae in historiam textûs Graeci epistolarum Paulinarum,' Jenae, 1777.

[4] 'Commentarius Criticus in textum Gr. N. T.,' Part i. 1798; Part ii. 1811.

well be looked for in a literary career of forty years, yet the theory of his youth was maintained, and defended, and temperately applied by Griesbach even to the last. From Bengel and Semler he had taken up the belief that manuscripts, versions, and ecclesiastical writers divide themselves, with respect to the character of their testimony, into races or families. This principle he strove to reduce to practice by marshalling all his authorities under their respective heads, and then regarding the evidence, not of individuals, but of the classes to which they belong. The advantage of some such arrangement is sufficiently manifest, if only it could be made to rest on grounds in themselves certain, or, at all events, fairly probable. We should then possess some better guide in our choice between conflicting readings, than the very rough and unsatisfactory process of counting the *number* of witnesses produced on either side. It is not that such a mode of conducting critical enquiries would not be very convenient, that Griesbach's theory is universally abandoned by modern scholars, but because there is no valid reason for believing it to be true.

At the onset of his labours, indeed, this acute and candid enquirer was disposed to divide all extant materials into five or six different families; he afterwards limited them to *three*, the Alexandrian, the Western, and the Byzantine recensions. The standard of the Alexandrian text he conceived to be Origen; who, although his works were written in Palestine, was assumed to have brought with him into exile copies of Scripture, similar to those used in his native city. To this family would belong a few manuscripts of the earliest date, and confessedly of the highest character, Codd. ABC, Cod. L of the Gospels, the Egyptian and some lesser versions. The Western recension would survive in Cod. D of the Gospels and Acts, in the other ancient copies which contain a Latin translation, in the Old Latin and Vulgate versions, and in the Latin Fathers. The vast majority of manuscripts (comprising perhaps nineteen-twentieths of the whole), together with the larger proportion of versions and Patristic writings, were grouped into the Byzantine class, as having prevailed generally in the Patriarchate of Constantinople. To this last class Griesbach hardly professed to accord as much weight as to either of the others, nor, if he had done so, would the result have been materially different. The joint testimony of two classes was, *ceteris paribus*, always to prevail; and since the very few documents which comprise the Alexandrian and Western recensions seldom agree with the Byzantine even when at variance with each other, the numerous codices which make up the third family would thus have about as much share in fixing the text of Scripture, as the poor citizens whose host was included in one of Servius Tullius' lower classes possessed towards counterbalancing the votes of the wealthy few that composed his first or second [1].

Inasmuch as the manuscripts on which our received text was based must, beyond question, be referred to his Byzantine family, wide as were the variations of Griesbach's revised text from that of Elzevir [2], had his theory been pushed to its legitimate consequences, the changes it required would have been greater still. The very plan of his work, however, seemed to reserve a slight preference for the received text *as such*, in cases of doubt and difficulty; and this editor, with a calmness and sagacity which may well be called judicial, was usually disposed to relax his stern mechanical law when persuaded by reasons founded on internal probabilities, which (as we cheerfully admit) few men have been found able to estimate with so much patience and discrimination. The plain fact is, that while disciples like Moldenhawer and persons who knew even less than he were regarding Griesbach's system as self-evidently true, their wiser master must have had many a misgiving as to the safety of that imposing structure his rare ingenuity had built upon the sand. The very essence of his theory consisted in there being not two

[1] The following specimen of a reading, *possessing no internal excellence*, preferred or favoured by Griesbach on the slightest evidence, will serve to illustrate the dangerous tendency of his system, had it been consistently acted upon throughout. In Matt. xxvii. 4 for ἀθῷον he indicates the mere gloss δίκαιον as equal or preferable (though in his later manual edition of 1805 he marks it as an inferior reading), on the authority of the *later* margin of Cod. B, of Cod. L, the Sahidic Armenian, and Latin versions and Fathers, and Origen in four places (ἀθῷον once). He adds the Syriac, but this is an error as regards the Peshitto or Harkleian; the Jerusalem may countenance him; though in such a case the testimony of versions is precarious on either side. Here, however, Griesbach defends δίκαιον against all likelihood, because BL and Origen are Alexandrian, the Latin versions Western.

[2] Reuss (p. 198) calculates that in his second edition out of Reuss' thousand chosen passages Griesbach stands with the Elzevir text in 648, sides with other editions in 293, has fifty-nine peculiar to himself. The second differs from the first edition (1774-5) in about fifty places only.

distinct families, but *three*; the majority deciding in all cases of dispute. Yet he hardly attempted, certainly neither he nor any one after him succeeded in the attempt, to separate the Alexandrian from the Western family, without resorting to arguments which would prove that there are as many classes as there are manuscripts of early date. The supposed accordance of the readings of Origen, so elaborately scrutinized for this purpose by Griesbach, with Cod. A, on which our editor lays the greatest stress, has been shown by Archbishop Laurence (Remarks on Griesbach's Systematic Classification, 1814) to be in a high degree imaginary[1]. It must have been in anticipation of some such researches, and in a partial knowledge of their sure results, that Griesbach was driven to that violent and most unlikely hypothesis, that Cod. A follows the Byzantine class of authorities in the Gospels, the Western in the Acts and Catholic Epistles, and the Alexandrian in St. Paul.

It seems needless to dwell longer on speculations which, however attractive and once widely received, will scarcely again find an advocate. Griesbach's text can no longer be regarded as satisfactory, though it is far less objectionable than such a system as his would have made it in rash or unskilful hands. His industry, his moderation, his fairness to opponents, who (like Matthaei) had shown him little forbearance, we may all imitate to our profit. His logical acuteness and keen intellectual perception fall to the lot of few; and though they may have helped to lead him into error, and have even kept him from retracing his steps, yet on the whole they were worthily exercised in the good cause of promoting a knowledge of God's truth, and of keeping alive, in an evil and unbelieving age, an enlightened interest in Holy Scripture, and the studies which it serves to consecrate.

13. Of a widely different order of mind was John Martin Augustine Scholz [d. 1852], Roman Catholic Dean of Theology in the mixed University of Bonn. It would have been well for the progress of sacred learning and for his own reputation had

[1] Laurence, in the Appendix to his 'Remarks,' shows that while Cod. A agrees with Origen against the received text in 154 places, and disagrees with the two united in 140, it sides with the received text against Origen in no less than 444 passages.

the accuracy and ability of this editor borne some proportion to his zeal and obvious anxiety to be useful. His first essay was his 'Curae Criticae in historiam textûs Evangeliorum,' in two dissertations, Heidelberg, 4to, 1820, containing notices of forty-eight Paris manuscripts (nine of them hitherto unknown) of which he had fully collated seventeen: the second Dissertation is devoted to Cod. K of the Gospels. In 1823 appeared his 'Biblisch-Kritische Reise,' Leipsic, 8vo, Biblio-Critical Travels in France, Switzerland, Italy, Palestine and the Archipelago, which Schulz laid under contribution for his improved edition of Griesbach's first volume[1]. Scholz's 'N. T. Graece,' 4to, was published at Leipsic, vol. i, 1830 (Gospels); vol. ii, 1836.

The accession of fresh materials made known in these works is almost marvellous: Scholz was the first to indicate Codd. 260–469 of the Gospels; 110–192 of the Acts, &c.; 125–246 of St. Paul; 51–89 of the Apocalypse; 51–181 Evangelistaria; 21–58 Lectionaries of the Apostolos; in all 616 cursive codices. His additions to the list of the uncials comprise only the three fragments of the Gospels W^a Y and the Vatican leaves of N. Of those examined previously by others he paid most attention to Evan. KX (M also for its synaxaria), and G (now L) Act., Paul.; he moreover inspected slightly eighty-two cursive codices of the Gospels after Wetstein, Birch, and the rest; collated entire five (Codd. 4, 19, 25, 28, 33), and twelve in the greater part, adding much to our knowledge of the important Cod. 22. In the Acts, &c., he inspected twenty-seven of those known before, partially collated two; in St. Paul he collated partially two, slightly twenty-nine; in the Apocalypse sixteen, cursorily enough it would seem (*see* Codd. 21–3): of the Lectionaries he touched more or less thirteen of the Gospels, four of the Apostolos. On turning to the 616 codices Scholz placed on the list for the first time, we find that he collated entire but thirteen (viz. five of the Gospels, three of the Acts, &c., three of St. Paul, one each of the Apocalypse and Evangelistaria): a few of the rest he examined throughout the greater part; many in only a few chapters; while some were set down from printed

[1] David Schulz published at Berlin, 1827, 8vo, a third and much improved edition of his N. T., vol. i (Gospels), containing also collations of certain additional manuscripts, unknown to Griesbach.

Catalogues, whose plenteous errors we have used our best endeavours to correct in the present volume, so far as the means were within our reach.

Yet, after making a large deduction from our first impressions of the *amount* of labour performed by Scholz, enough and more than enough would remain to entitle him to our lasting gratitude, if it were possible to place any tolerable reliance on the correctness of his results. Those who are, however superficially, acquainted with the nature of such pursuits, will readily believe that faultless accuracy in representing myriads of minute details is not to be looked for from the most diligent and careful critic. Oversights will mar the perfection of the most highly finished of human efforts; but if adequate care and pains shall have been bestowed on detecting them, such blemishes as still linger unremoved are no real subject of reproach, and do not greatly lessen the value of the work which contains them. But in the case of Scholz's Greek Testament the fair indulgence we must all hope for is abused beyond the bounds of reason or moderation. The student who has had much experience of his volumes, especially if he has ever compared the collations there given with the original manuscripts, will never dream of resorting to them for information he can expect to gain elsewhere, or rest with confidence on a statement of fact merely because Scholz asserts it. J. Scott Porter (Principles of Textual Criticism, Belfast, 1848, pp. 263–66) and Tischendorf (N. T., Proleg. c–cii, 7th edition) have dwelt upon his strange blunders, his blind inconsistencies, and his habitual practice of copying from his predecessors without investigation and without acknowledgement; so that it is needless for us to repeat or dwell on that ungracious task[1]; but it is our duty to put the student once for

[1] One of Porter's examples is almost amusing. It was Scholz's constant habit to copy Griesbach's lists of critical authorities (errors, misprints, and all) without giving the reader any warning that they were not the fruit of his own labours. The note he borrowed from Griesbach on 1 Tim. iii. 16, contains the words 'uti docuimus in Symbolis Criticis:' this too Scholz appropriates (Tom. ii. p. 334, col. 2) so as to claim the 'Symbolae Criticae' of the Halle Professor as his own! See also p. 217, Evan. 365; p. 253, Act. 86, and Tischendorf's notes on Acts xix. 25; 2 Pet. i. 15 (N. T., eighth edition). His very text must have been set up by Griesbach's. Thus, since the latter, by a mere press error, omitted με in 2 Cor. ii. 13, Scholz not only follows him in the omission, but cites in his note a few cursives in which he had met with με, a word really absent from no known copy. In Heb. ix. 5 again, both editors in error prefix τῆς to δόξης. Scholz's

all on his guard against what could not fail to mislead him, and to express our sorrow that twelve years and more of hard and persevering toil should, through mere heedlessness, have been nearly thrown away.

As was natural in a pupil of J. L. Hug of Freyburg (*see* vol. i. p. 111), who had himself tried to build a theory of recensions on very slender grounds, Dr. Scholz attempted to settle the text of the N. T. upon principles which must be regarded as a modification of those of Griesbach. In his earliest work, like that great critic, he had been disposed to divide all extant authorities into five separate classes; but he soon reduced them to two, the Alexandrian and the Constantinopolitan. In the Alexandrian family he included the whole of Griesbach's Western recension, from which indeed it seems vain to distinguish it by any broad line of demarcation: to the other family he referred the great mass of more recent documents which compose Griesbach's third or Byzantine class; and to this family he was inclined to give the preference over the other, as well from the internal excellency of its readings, as because it represents the uniform text which had become traditional throughout the Greek Church. That such a standard, public, and authorized text existed he seems to have taken for granted without much enquiry. 'Codices qui hoc nomen [Constantinopolitanum] habent,' he writes, 'parum inter se dissentiunt. Conferas, quaeso, longè plerosque quos huic classi adhaerere dixi, atque lectiones diversas viginti trigintave in totidem capitibus vix reperies, unde conjicias eos esse accuratissimè descriptos, eorumque antigrapha parum inter se discrepasse' (N. T., Proleg., vol. i. § 55). It might have occurred to one who had spent so many years in studying Greek manuscripts, that this marvellous concord between the different Byzantine witnesses (which is striking enough, no doubt, as we turn over the pages of his Greek Testament) is after all due to

inaccuracy in the description of manuscripts which he must have had before him when he was writing is most wearisome to those who have had to trace his steps, and to verify, or rather to falsify, his statements. He has half filled our catalogues with duplicates and codices which are not Greek or are not Biblical at all. After correcting not a few of his misrepresentations of books in the libraries at Florence, Burgon breaks out at last: 'What else but calamitous is it to any branch of study that it should have been prosecuted by such an incorrigible blunderer, a man so abominably careless as this?' (*Guardian*, Aug. 27, 1873.)

nothing so much as to the haste and carelessness of collators. The more closely the cursive copies of Scripture are examined, the more does the individual character of each of them become developed. With certain points of general resemblance, whereby they are distinguished from the older documents of the Alexandrian class, they abound with mutual variations so numerous and perpetual as to vouch for the independent origin of nearly all of them, and their exact study has 'swept away at once and for ever' (Tregelles' 'Account of Printed Text,' p. 180) the fancy of a standard Constantinopolitan text, and every inference that had been grounded upon its presumed existence. If (as we firmly believe) the less ancient codices ought to have their proper weight and appreciable influence in fixing the true text of Scripture, our favourable estimate of them must rest on other arguments than Scholz has urged in their behalf.

Since this editor's system of recensions differed thus widely from Griesbach's, in suppressing altogether one of his three classes, and in yielding to the third, which the other slighted, a decided preference over its surviving rival, it might have been imagined that the consequences of such discrepancy in theory would have been strongly marked in their effects on his text. That such is not the case, at least to any considerable extent (especially in his second volume), must be imputed in part to Griesbach's prudent reserve in carrying out his principles to extremity, but yet more to Scholz's vacillation and evident weakness of judgement. In fact, on his last visit to England in 1845, he distributed among Biblical students here a 'Commentatio de virtutibus et vitiis utriusque codicum N. T. familiae,' that he had just delivered on the occasion of some Encaenia at Bonn, in which (after various statements that display either ignorance or inattention respecting the ordinary phenomena of manuscripts which in a veteran collator is really unaccountable[1]) he declares his purpose, chiefly it would seem from considerations of internal evidence, that if ever it should be his lot to prepare another edition of the New Testament, 'se plerasque codicum Alexandrinorum lectiones illas quas in margine interiore textui editionis suae Alexandrinas dixit, in textum recepturum' (p. 14).

[1] Some of these statements are discussed in Scrivener's 'Collation of the Greek Manuscripts of the Holy Gospels,' Introd. pp. lxix–lxxi.

The text which its constructor distrusted, can have but small claim on the faith of others.

14. 'Novum Testamentum Graece et Latine, Carolus Lachmannus recensuit, Philippus Buttmannus Ph. F. Graecae lectionis auctoritates apposuit' is the simple title-page of a work, by one of the most eminent philologists of his time, the first volume of which (containing the Gospels) appeared at Berlin (8vo), 1842, the second and concluding one in 1850, whose boldness and originality have procured it, as well for good as for ill, a prominent place in the history of the sacred text. Lachmann had published as early as 1831 a small edition containing only the text of the New Testament, with a list of the readings wherein he differs from that of Elzevir, preceded by a notice of his plan not exceeding a few lines in length, itself so obscurely worded that even to those who happened to understand his meaning it must have read like a riddle whose solution they had been told beforehand; and referring us for fuller information to what he strangely considered 'a more convenient place,' a German periodical of the preceding year's date[1]. Authors who take so little pains to explain their fundamental principles of criticism, especially if (as in the present case) these are novel and unexpected, can hardly wonder when their drift and purpose are imperfectly apprehended; so that a little volume, which we now learn had cost Lachmann five years of thought and labour, was confounded, even by the learned, with the mass of common,

[1] The following is the *whole* of this notice, which we reprint after Tregelles' example: 'De ratione et consilio hujus editionis loco commodiore expositum est (Theol. Studien und Kritiken, 1830, pp. 817–845). Hic satis erit dixisse, editorem nusquam judicium suum, sed consuetudinem antiquissimarum orientis ecclesiarum secutum esse. Hanc quoties minus constantem fuisse animadvertit, quantum fieri potuit quae Italorum et Afrorum consensu comprobarentur praetulit: ubi pervagatam omnium auctorum discrepantiam deprehendit, partim uncis partim in marginibus indicavit. Quo factum est ut vulgatae et his proximis duobus saeculis *receptae lectionis* ratio haberi non posset. Haec diversitas hic in fine libri adjecta est, quoniam ea res doctis judicibus necessaria esse videbatur.' Here we have one of Lachmann's leading peculiarities—his absolute disregard of the received readings—hinted at in an incidental manner: the influence he was disposed to accord to the Latin versions when his chief authorities were at variance is pretty clearly indicated: but no one would guess that by the 'custom of the oldest Churches of the East' he intends the few very ancient codices comprising Griesbach's Alexandrian class, and not the great mass of authorities, gathered from the Churches of Syria, Asia Minor, and Constantinople, of which that critic's Byzantine family was made up.

hasty, and superficial reprints. Nor was the difficulty much removed on the publication of the first volume of his larger book. It was then seen, indeed, how clean a sweep he had made of the great majority of Greek manuscripts usually cited in critical editions:—in fact he rejects all in a heap excepting Codd. ABC, the fragments PQTZ (and for some purposes D) of the Gospels; DE of the Acts only; DGH of St. Paul. Yet even now he treats the scheme of his work as if it were already familiarly known, and spends his time in discursive controversy with his opponents and reviewers, whom he chastises with a heartiness which in this country we imputed to downright malice, till Tregelles was so good as to instruct us that in Lachmann it was but 'a tone of pleasantry,' the horseplay of coarse German wit (Account of Printed Text, p. 112). The supplementary Prolegomena which preface his second volume of 1850 are certainly more explicit: both from what they teach and from the practical examples they contain, they have probably helped others, as well as myself, in gaining a nearer insight into his whole design.

It seems, then, to have been Lachmann's purpose, discarding the slightest regard for the *textus receptus* as such, to endeavour to bring the sacred text back to the condition in which it existed during the fourth century, and this in the first instance by documentary aid alone, without regarding for the moment whether the sense produced were probable or improbable, good or bad; but looking solely to his authorities, and following them implicitly wheresoever the numerical majority might carry him. For accomplishing this purpose he possessed but one Greek copy written as early as the fourth century, Cod. B; and of that he not only knew less than has since come to light (and even this is not quite sufficient), but he did not avail himself of Bartolocci's papers on Cod. B, to which Scholz had already drawn attention. His other codices were not of the fourth century at all, but varying in date from the fifth (ACT) to the ninth (G); and of these few (of C more especially) his assistant or colleague Buttmann's representation was loose, careless, and unsatisfactory. Of the Greek Fathers, the scanty Greek remains of Irenaeus and the works of Origen are all that are employed; but considerable weight is given to the readings of the Latin version. The Vulgate is printed at length as revised, after a fashion, by Lachmann himself, from the Codices Fuldensis and Amiatinus: the Old Latin manuscripts *abc*, together with the Latin versions accompanying the Greek copies which he receives[1], are treated as primary authorities: of the Western Fathers he quotes Cyprian, Hilary of Poictiers, Lucifer of Cagliari, and in the Apocalypse Primasius also. The Syriac and Egyptian translations he considers himself excused from attending to, by reason of his ignorance of their respective languages.

The consequence of this voluntary poverty where our manuscript treasures are so abundant, of this deliberate rejection of the testimony of many hundreds of documents, of various countries, dates, and characters, may be told in a few words. Lachmann's text seldom rests on more than four Greek codices, very often on three, not unfrequently on two; in Matt. vi. 20—viii. 5, and in 165 out of the 405 verses of the Apocalypse, on but *one*. It would have been a grievous thing indeed if we really had no better means of ascertaining the true readings of the New Testament than are contained in this editor's scanty roll; and he who, for the sake of some private theory, shall presume to shut out from his mind the great mass of information God's Providence has preserved for our use, will hardly be thought to have chosen the most hopeful method for bringing himself or others to the knowledge of the truth.

But supposing, for the sake of argument, that Lachmann had availed himself to the utmost of the materials he has selected, and that they were adequate for the purpose of leading him up to the state of the text as it existed in the fourth century, would he have made any real advance in the criticism of the sacred volume? Is it not quite evident, even from the authorities contained in his notes, that copies in that age varied as widely—nay even more widely—than they did in later times? that the main corruptions and interpolations which perplex the student in Cod. Bezae and its Latin allies, crept in at a period anterior to the age of Constantine? From the Preface to his second volume (1850) it plainly appears (what might, perhaps, have been gathered by an esoteric pupil from the Preface to his first,

[1] These are *d* for Cod. Bezae, *e* for Cod. Laud. 35, *f* being Lachmann's notation for Paul. Cod. D, as *ff* is for Paul. Cod. E (whose Latin translation is cited independently), *g* for Paul. Cod. G.

pp. v, xxxiii), that he regarded this fourth century text, founded as it is on documentary evidence alone, as purely provisional; as mere subject-matter on which individual *conjecture* might advantageously operate (Praef. 1850, p. v). Of the many examples wherewith he illustrates his principle we must be content with producing one, as an ample specimen both of Lachmann's plan and of his judgement in reducing it to practice. In Matt. xxvii. 28 for ἐκδύσαντες, which gives a perfectly good sense, and seems absolutely required by τὰ ἱμάτια αὐτοῦ in ver. 31, *BDabc* read ἐνδύσαντες, a variation either borrowed from Mark xv. 17, or more probably a mere error of the pen. Had the whole range of manuscripts, versions, and Fathers been searched, no other testimony in favour of ἐνδύσαντες could have been found save Cod. 157, *ff*² and *q* of the Old Latin, the Latin version of Origen, and a few codices of Chrysostom [1]. Against these we might set a vast company of witnesses, exceeding those on the opposite side by full a hundred to one; yet because Cod. A and the Latin Vulgate alone are on Lachmann's list, he is compelled by his system to place ἐνδύσαντες in the text as the reading of his authorities, reserving to himself the privilege of removing it on the ground of its palpable impropriety: and all this because he wishes to keep the 'recensio' of the text distinct from the 'emendatio' of the sense (Praef. 1850, p. vi). Surely it were a far more reasonable, as well as a more convenient process, to have reviewed from the first the entire case on both sides, and if the documentary evidence were not unevenly balanced, or internal evidence strongly preponderated in one scale, to place in the text once for all the reading which upon the whole should appear best suited to the passage, and most sufficiently established by authority.

But while we cannot accord to Lachmann the praise of wisdom in his design, or of over-much industry and care in the execution of it (*see* Tischendorf, N. T., Proleg. pp. cvii–cxii), yet we would not dissemble or extenuate the power his edition has exerted over candid and enquiring minds. Earnest, single-

[1] We must now except the seventh century corrector of Cod. א called by Tischendorf C^a, who actually changes the original reading ἐκδ. into ἐνδ., to be himself set right by a later hand C^b. This is one out of many proofs of something more than an accidental connexion between Codd. א and B at a remote period. *See* vol. i. p. 96, and note.

hearted, a true scholar both in spirit and accomplishments, he has had the merit of restoring the Latin versions to their proper rank in the criticism of the New Testament, which since the failure of Bentley's schemes they seem to have partially lost. No one will hereafter claim for the received text any further weight than it is entitled to as the representative of the manuscripts on which it was constructed: and the principle of recurring exclusively to a few ancient documents in preference to the many (so engaging from its very simplicity), which may be said to have virtually originated with him, has not been without influence with some who condemn the most strongly his hasty and one-sided, though consistent, application of it. Lachmann died in 1851.

15. 'Novum Testamentum Graece. Ad antiquos testes denuo recensuit, apparatum criticum omni studio perfectum apposuit, commentationem isagogicam praetexuit Aenoth. Frid. Const. Tischendorf, editio octava:' Lipsiae, 1865–1872. This is beyond question the most full and comprehensive edition of the Greek Testament existing; it contains the results of the latest collations and discoveries, and as copious a body of various readings as is compatible with the design of adapting it for general use: though Tischendorf's notes are not sufficiently minute (as regards the cursive manuscripts) to supersede the need of perpetually consulting the labours of preceding critics. His earliest enterprise [1] in connexion with Biblical studies was a small edition of the New Testament (12mo, 1841), completed at Leipzig in 1840, which, although greatly inferior to his subsequent works, merited the encouragement which it procured for him, and the praises of D. Schulz, which he very gratefully acknowledged. Soon afterwards he set out on his first literary journey: 'quod quidem tam pauper suscepi,' he ingenuously declares, 'ut pro paenula quam portabam solvere non possem;' and, while busily engaged on Cod. C, prepared three other editions of the New Testament, which appeared in 1843 at Paris, all of them being booksellers' speculations on which, perhaps, he set no high value; one inscribed to Guizot, the Protestant statesman, a second (having

[1] In dedicating the third volume of his 'Monumenta sacra inedita' in 1860 to the Theological Faculty at Leyden, Tischendorf states that he took to these studies twenty-three years before, that is, at about twenty-two years of age.

the Greek text placed in a parallel column with the Latin Vulgate, and somewhat altered to suit it) dedicated to Denys Affre, the Archbishop of Paris who fell so nobly at the barricades in June, 1848. His third edition of that year contained the Greek text of the second edition, without the Latin Vulgate. It is needless to enlarge upon the history of his travels, sufficiently described by Tischendorf in the Preface to his seventh edition (1859); it will be enough to state that he was in Italy in 1843 and 1866; four times he visited England (1842, 1849, 1855, 1865); and thrice went into the East, where his chief discovery —that of the Cod. Sinaiticus—was ultimately made. In 1849 came forth his second Leipzig or fifth edition of the New Testament, showing a very considerable advance upon that of 1841, though, in its earlier pages more especially, still very defective, and even as a manual scarce worthy of his rapidly growing fame. The sixth edition was one stereotyped for Tauchnitz in 1850 (he put forth another stereotyped edition in 1862), representing the text of 1849 slightly revised: the seventh, and up to that date by far the most important, was issued in thirteen parts at Leipsic during the four years 1856–9. It is indeed a monument of persevering industry which the world has not often seen surpassed: yet it was soon to be thrown into the shade by his eighth and latest edition, issued in eleven parts, between 1864 and 1872, the text of which is complete, but the Prolegomena, to our great loss, were never written, by reason of his illness and death (Dec. 7, 1874)[1].

Yet it may truly be asserted that the reputation of Tischendorf as a Biblical scholar rests less on his critical editions of the N. T., than on the texts of the chief uncial authorities which in rapid succession he has given to the world. In 1843 was published the New Testament, in 1845 the Old Testament portion of 'Codex Ephraemi Syri rescriptus (Cod. C), 2 vols. 4to, in uncial type, with elaborate Prolegomena, notes, and facsimiles. In 1846 appeared 'Monumenta sacra inedita,' 4to, containing transcripts of Codd. $F^{a}LNW^{a}Y\Theta^{a}$ of the Gospels, and B of the Apocalypse;

[1] Tischendorf left almost no papers behind him. Hence the task of writing Prolegomena to his eighth edition, gallantly undertaken by two American scholars, Dr. Caspar René Gregory of Leipzig, and Dr. Ezra Abbot of Cambridge, U. S., but for their own independent researches, might seem to resemble that of making bricks without straw.

the plan and apparatus of this volume and of nearly all that follow are the same as in the Codex Ephraemi. In 1846 he also published the Codex Friderico-Augustanus in lithographed facsimile throughout, containing the results of his first discovery at Mount Sinai: in 1847 the Evangelium Palatinum ineditum of the Old Latin: in 1850 and again in 1854 less splendid but good and useful editions of the Codex Amiatinus of the Latin Vulgate. His edition of Codex Claromontanus (D of St. Paul), 1852, was of precisely the same nature as his editions of Cod. Ephraemi, &c., but his book entitled 'Anecdota sacra et profana,' 1855 (second and enlarged edition in 1861), exhibits a more miscellaneous character, comprising (together with other matter) transcripts of O^a of the Gospels, M of St. Paul; a collation of Cod. 61 of the Acts *being the only cursive copy he seems to have examined;* notices and facsimiles of Codd. ΙΓΛ tisch.^{1} or Evan. 478 of the Gospels, and of the lectionaries tisch.^{ev} (Evst. 190) and tisch.$^{6.\ f.}$ (Apost. 71). Next was commenced a new series of 'Monumenta sacra inedita' (projected to consist of nine volumes), on the same plan as the book of 1846. Much of this series is devoted to codices of the Septuagint version, to which Tischendorf paid great attention, and whereof he published four editions (the latest in 1869) hardly worthy of him; but vol. i (1855) contains transcripts of Codd. I, ven^{ev}. (Evst. 175); vol. ii (1857) of Codd. $N^bR\Theta^a$; vol. iii (1860) of Codd. QW^c, all of the Gospels; vol. iv (1869) was given up to the Septuagint, as vol. vii would have been to the Wolfenbüttel manuscript of Chrysostom, of the sixth century[1]; but Cod. P of the Acts, Epistles, and Apocalypse comprises a portion of vols. v (1865) and of vi (1869); while vol. viii was to have been devoted to palimpsest fragments of both Testaments, such as we have described amongst the Uncials: the Appendix or vol. ix (1870) contains Cod. E of the Acts, &c. An improved edition of his system of Gospel Harmony (Synopsis Evangelica, 1851) appeared in 1864, with some fresh critical matter, a better one in 1871, and the fifth in 1884. His achievements in regard to Codd. ℵ and B we have spoken of in

[1] Through his haste to publish Cod. E of the Acts, in which design he feared to be forestalled by a certain Englishman, Tischendorf postponed to it vols. vii and viii, which he did not live to resume. Oscar von Gebhardt, now of Berlin, will complete vol. vii; Caspar René Gregory hopes to do what is possible for vol. viii.

their proper places. He published his 'Notitia Cod. Sinaitici' in 1860, his great edition of that manuscript in 1862, with full notes and Prolegomena; smaller editions of the New Testament only in 1863 and 1865; 'an Appendix Codd. celeberrimorum Sinaitici, Vaticani, Alexandrini with facsimiles' in 1867. His marvellous yet unsatisfactory edition of Cod. Vaticanus, prepared under the disadvantages we have described, appeared in 1867; its 'Appendix' (including Cod. B of the Apocalypse) in 1869; his unhappy 'Responsa ad calumnias Romanas' in 1870. To this long and varied catalogue must yet be added exact collations of Codd. EGHKMUX Gospels, EGHL Acts, FHL of St. Paul, and more, all made for his editions of the N. T. A poor issue of the Authorized English Version of the N. T. was put forth in his name in 1869, being the thousandth volume of Tauchnitz's series.

The consideration of the text of Tischendorf's several editions will be touched upon in Chapter X. To the *general* accuracy of his collations every one who has followed him over a portion of his vast field can bear and is bound to bear cheerful testimony. For practical purposes his correctness is quite sufficient, even though one or two who have accomplished very much less may have excelled in this respect some at least of his later works. For the unflinching exertions and persevering toil of full thirty years Tischendorf was called upon in 1873 to pay the natural penalty in a stroke of paralysis, which prostrated his strong frame, and put a sudden end to his most fruitful studies. He was born at Lengenfeld in the kingdom of Saxony in 1815 and died in 1874, having nearly completed his sixtieth year[1].

16. 'The Greek New Testament, edited from ancient authorities; with the various readings of all the ancient MSS., the ancient versions, and other ecclesiastical writers (to Eusebius inclusive); together with the Latin version of Jerome, from the Codex Amiatinus of the sixth century. By Samuel Prideaux Tregelles, LL.D.' 4to, 1857–1872, pp. 1017. [Appendix by Dr. Hort, 1879, pp. i–xxxii; 1018–1069.]

[1] For further information respecting this indefatigable scholar and his labours we may refer to a work published at Leipzig in 1862, 'Constantin Tischendorf in seiner fünfundzwanzigjährigen schriftstellerischen wirksamkeit. Literar-historische skizze von Dr. Joh. Ernst Volbeding.' I have also seen, by Dr. Ezra Abbot's courtesy, his paper in the *Unitarian Review*, March, 1875.

The esteemed editor of the work of which the above is the full title, first became generally known as the author of 'The Book of Revelation in Greek, edited from ancient authorities; with a new English Version,' 1844: and, in spite of some obvious blemishes and defects, his attempt was received in the English Church with the gratitude and respect to which his thorough earnestness and independent views justly entitled him. He had arranged in his own mind as early as 1838 the plan of a Greek Testament, which he announced on the publication of the Apocalypse, and now set himself vigorously to accomplish. His fruitless endeavour to collate Cod. B has already been mentioned, but when he was on the continent in 1845-6, and again in 1849–50, also in 1862, he thoroughly examined all the manuscripts he could meet with, that fell within the compass of his design. In 1854 he published a volume full of valuable information, and intended as a formal exposition of his critical principles, intituled 'An Account of the Printed Text of the Greek New Testament.' In 1856 he re-wrote, rather than re-edited, that portion of the Rev. T. Hartwell Horne's well-known 'Introduction to the Critical Study and Knowledge of the Holy Scriptures' which relates to the New Testament, under the title of 'An Introduction to the Textual Criticism of the New Testament,' &c.[1] In 1857 appeared, for the use of subscribers only, the Gospels of SS. Matthew and Mark, as the first part of his 'Greek New Testament' (pp. 1–216); early in 1861 the second part, containing SS. Luke and John (pp. 217–488), with but a few pages of 'Introductory Notice' in each. In that year, paralysis, *mercurialium pestis virorum*, for a while suspended our editor's too assiduous labours: but he recovered health sufficient to publish the Acts and Catholic Epistles in 1865, the Epistles of St. Paul down to 2 Thess. in 1869. Early in 1870, while in the act of revising the concluding

[1] A pamphlet of thirty-six pages appeared late in 1860, 'Additions to the Fourth Volume of the Introduction to the Holy Scriptures,' &c., by S. P. T. Most of this industrious writer's other publications are not sufficiently connected with the subject of the present volume to be noticed here, but as throwing light upon the literary history of Scripture we may mention his edition of the 'Canon Muratorianus,' liberally printed for him in 1867 by the Delegates of the Oxford University Press. Burgon, however, on comparing Tregelles' book with the document itself at Milan, cannot overmuch laud his minute correctness (*Guardian*, Feb. 5, 1873). Isaac H. Hall made the same comparison at Milan and confirms Burgon's judgement. The custodian of the Ambrosian Library at Milan, the famous Ceriani, had nothing to do with the work or with the lithograph facsimile.

chapters of the Apocalypse, he was visited by a second and very severe stroke of his fell disease. The remaining portion of the Pauline Epistles was sent out in 1870 as he had himself prepared it; the Revelation (alas! without the long-desired Prolegomena) in 1872, as well as the state of Tregelles' papers would enable his friends S. J. B. Bloxsidge and B. W. Newton to perform their office. The revered author could contribute nothing save a message to his subscribers, full of devout thankfulness and calm reliance on the Divine wisdom. The text of the Apocalypse differs from that which he arranged in 1844 in about 229 places.

Except Codd. OΞ, which were published in 1861 (*see* under those MSS.), this critic has not edited in full the text of any document, but his renewed collations of manuscripts are very extensive: viz. Codd. EGHKMN^{b}RUXZΓΛ 1, 33, 69 of the Gospels; HL 13, 31, 61 of the Acts; DFL 1, 17, 37 of St. Paul, 1, 14 of the Apocalypse, *Am.* of the Vulgate. Having followed Tregelles through the whole of Cod. 69 (Act. 31, Paul. 37, Apoc. 14), I am able to speak positively of his scrupulous exactness, and in regard to other manuscripts now in England it will be found that where Tischendorf and Tregelles differ, the latter is seldom in the wrong. To the versions and Fathers (especially to Origen and Eusebius) he has devoted great attention. His volume is a beautiful specimen of typography [1], and its arrangement is very convenient, particularly his happy expedient for showing at every open leaf the precise authorities that are extant at that place.

The peculiarity of Tregelles' system is intimated, rather than stated, in the title-page of his Greek N. T. It consists in resorting to 'ancient authorities' alone in the construction of his revised text, and in refusing not only to the received text, but to the great mass of manuscripts also, all voice in determining the true readings. This scheme, although from the history he gives of his work (An Account of Printed Text, pp. 153, &c.), it was apparently devised independently of Lachmann, is in fact essentially that great scholar's plan, after those parts of it are withdrawn which are manifestly indefen-

[1] As a whole it may be pronounced very accurate as well as beautiful, with the conspicuous drawback that the Greek accents are so ill represented as to show either strange ignorance or utter indifference about them on the part of the person who revised the sheets for the press.

sible. Tregelles' 'ancient authorities' are thus reduced to those manuscripts which, not being Lectionaries, happen to be written in uncial characters, with the remarkable exceptions of Codd. 1, 33, 69 of the Gospels, 61 of the Acts, which he admits because they 'preserve an ancient text.' We shall hereafter enquire (Chap. X) whether the text of the N. T. can safely be grounded on a basis so narrow as that of Tregelles.

This truly eminent person, born at Falmouth of a Quaker family January 30, 1813, received what education he ever got at Falmouth Classical School (of which I was Master twenty years later), from 1825 to 1828. At an early age he left the communion in which he was bred, to join a body called the Plymouth Brethren, among whom he met with much disquietude and some mild persecution: his last years were more happily spent as a humble lay member of the Church of England, a fact he very earnestly begged me to keep in mind[1]. The critical studies he took up as early as 1838, when he was only twenty-five years old, were the main occupation of his life. The inconvenient and costly form in which he published his Greek Testament, brought upon him pecuniary loss, and even trenched upon the moderate fortune of his true and loving wife. After several years of deep retirement he died at Plymouth, April 24, 1875: and whereas his widow, who has since followed him to the other world, was anxious that his great work should be as far as possible completed, Dr. Hort has manifested his veneration for an honoured memory by publishing in 1879 an 'Appendix' to the Greek New Testament, embracing what materials for Prolegomena Tregelles' published writings supplied, and supplementary corrections to every page of the main work, compiled by the Rev. A. W. Streane, Fellow of C. C. C., Cambridge, which comprise a wonderful monument of minute diligence and devotion.

Of Tischendorf and Tregelles, that duumvirate of Biblical critics, I may be allowed to repeat a few words, extracted from the Preface to the Greek Testament of 1876, in the series of 'Cambridge Texts:' 'Eheu quos viros! natu ferè aequales, indole et famâ satis dispares, ambo semper in adversum nitentes, ambo piis laboribus infractos, intra paucos menses mors abripuit immatura.'

[1] He gave the same assurance to A. Earle, D.D., Bishop of Marlborough, assigning as his reason the results of the study of the Greek N. T.

17. 'The New Testament in the original Greek. The text revised by Brooke Foss Westcott, D.D. [Regius Professor of Divinity in the University of Cambridge], and Fenton John Anthony Hort, D.D. [Hulsean Professor of Divinity there]. Vol. I. Cambridge and London, 1881.' 'Introduction and Appendix,' in a separate volume, by Dr. Hort only, 1881. This important and comprehensive work, the joint labour of two of the best scholars of this age, toiling, now separately, now in counsel, for five and twenty years, was published, the text a few days earlier than the Revised English Version (May 17, 1881), the Introduction about four months later. The text, or one almost identical with it, had been submitted to the Revisers of the N. T., and to a few other Biblical students, several years before, so that the general tenor and spirit of our authors' judgement was known to many: the second edition of my present work was enriched by the free permission granted by them to announce their conclusions regarding passages which come up for discussion in Chapter XII, and elsewhere. Drs. Westcott and Hort depart more widely from the *textus receptus* than any previous editor had thought necessary; nor can they be blamed for carrying out their deliberate convictions, if the reasons they allege shall prove sufficient to justify them. Those reasons are given at length by Dr. Hort in his 'Introduction,' a treatise whose merits may be frankly acknowledged by persons the least disposed to accept his arguments: never was a cause, good or bad in itself, set off with higher ability and persuasive power. On the validity of his theory we shall have much to say in Chapters X and XII, to which we here refer once for all. The elegant volume which exhibits the Greek text contains in its margin many alternative readings, chiefly recorded in passages wherein a difference of opinion existed between the two illustrious editors. Words or passages supposed to be of doubtful authority are included in brackets ([]), those judged to be probably or certainly spurious —and their number is ominously large—in double brackets ([[ ]]). Mark xvi. 9–20; John vii. 53—viii. 11 are banished to the end of their respective Gospels, as if they did not belong to them. Finally, quotations from and even slight allusions to the Old Testament, in great but judicious plenty, are printed in a kind of uncial letter, to the great benefit of the student.

This notice cannot be left without an expression of deep

regret upon the loss of Dr. Hort at a comparatively early age. Much as the author of this work and the editor of this edition has differed from the views of that distinguished man, the services which he has rendered in many ways to the cause of sacred textual criticism cannot here be forgotten or unrecognized. His assiduity and thoroughness are a pattern to all who come after him.

18. The text constructed by the English Revisers in preparation for their Revised Translation was published in two forms at Oxford and Cambridge respectively in 1881. The Oxford edition, under the care of Archdeacon Palmer, incorporated in the text the readings adopted by the Revisers with the variations at the foot of the Authorized edition of 1611, of Stephanus' third edition published in 1550, and of the margin of the Revised Version. The Cambridge edition, under the care of Dr. Scrivener, gave the Authorized text with the variations of the Revisers mentioned at the foot. Both editions are admirably edited. The number of variations adopted by the Revisers, which are generally based upon the principles advocated by Westcott and Hort, has been estimated by Dr. Scrivener at 5,337 (Burgon's 'Revision Revised,' p. 405). The titles in full of these two editions are:—

1. The New Testament in the Original Greek, according to the Text followed in the Authorized Version, together with the Variations adopted in the Revised Version. Edited for the Syndics of the Cambridge University Press, by F. H. A. Scrivener, M.A., D.C.L., L.L.D., Prebendary of Exeter and Vicar of Hendon. Cambridge, 1881.

2. 'Η ΚΑΙΝΗ ΔΙΑΘΗΚΗ. The Greek Testament, with the Readings adopted by the Revisers of the Authorized Version. Oxford, at the Clarendon Press, 1881. [Preface by the Editor, Archdeacon Palmer, D.D.]

CHAPTER VIII.

INTERNAL EVIDENCE.

WE have now described, in some detail, the several species of external testimony available for the textual criticism of the New Testament, whether comprising manuscripts of the original Greek, or ancient translations from it, or citations from Scripture made by ecclesiastical writers. We have, moreover, indicated the chief editions wherein all these materials are recorded for our use, and the principles that have guided their several editors in applying them to the revision of the text. One source of information, formerly deemed quite legitimate, has been designedly passed by. It is now agreed among competent judges that *Conjectural Emendation* must never be resorted to, even in passages of acknowledged difficulty[1]; the absence of proof that a reading proposed to be substituted for the common one is actually supported by some trustworthy document being of itself a fatal objection to our receiving it[2]. Those that have

[1] Dr. Hort (Introd. p. 277) hardly goes so far as this: 'Those,' he says, 'who propose remedies which cannot possibly avail are not thereby shown to have been wrong in the supposition that remedies were needed; and a few have been perhaps too quickly forgotten.'

[2] I hope that the change made in the wording of the above sentence from what stood in the first edition will satisfy my learned and acute critic, Mr. Linwood (Remarks on Conjectural Emendations as applied to the New Testament, 1873, p. 9, note); although I fear that the difference between us is in substance as wide as ever. At the same time I would hardly rest the main stress of the argument where Dr. Roberts does when he says that 'conjectural criticism is entirely banished from the field, &c., simply because all sober critics feel that there is no need for it' (Words of the N. T., p. 24). There are texts, no doubt, some of those for example which Dr. Westcott and Dr. Hort have branded with a marginal † in their edition; e. g. Acts vii. 46; xiii. 32; xix. 40; xxvi. 28; Rom. viii. 2; 1 Cor. xii. 2 (where Eph. ii. 11 might suggest ὅτι ποτέ); 1 Tim. vi. 7, and especially in the kindred Epistles, 2 Pet. iii. 10; 12; Jude 5; 22, 23, wherein, whether from internal difficulties or from the actual state of the external

been hazarded aforetime by celebrated scholars, when but few codices were known or actually collated, have seldom, very seldom, been confirmed by subsequent researches: and the time has now fully come when, in the possession of abundant stores of variations collected from memorials of almost every age and country, we are fully authorized in believing that the reading to which no manuscript, or old version, or primitive Father has borne witness, however plausible and (for some purposes) convenient, cannot safely be accepted as genuine or even as probable; even though there may still remain a few passages respecting which we cannot help framing a shrewd suspicion that the original reading differed from any form in which they are now presented to us[1].

In no wise less dangerous than bare conjecture destitute of external evidence, is the device of Lachmann for unsettling by means of emendation (*emendando*), without reference to the balance of conflicting testimony, the very text he had previously fixed by revision (*recensendo*) through the means of critical authorities: in fact the earlier process is but so much trouble misemployed, if its results are liable to be put aside by

evidence, we should be very glad of more light than our existing authorities will lend us. What I most urge is the plain fact, that the conjectures, even of able and accomplished men, have never been such as to approve themselves to any but their authors, much less to commend themselves to the judgement of scholars as intuitively true.

[1] Bentley, the last great critic who paid much regard to conjectural emendations, promised in his Prospectus of 1720 that 'If the author has anything to suggest towards a change of the text, not supported by any copies now extant, he will offer it separate in his Prolegomena.' It is really worth while to turn over Wm. Bowyer's 'Critical Conjectures and Observations on the N. T.,' or the summary of them contained in Knappe's N. T. of 1797, if only to see the utter fruitlessness of the attempt to illustrate Scripture by ingenious exercise of the imagination. The best (*e.g.* συναλιζομένοις Acts i. 4; πορκείας for πορνείας *ibid.* xv. 20, 29), no less than the most tasteless and stupid (*e.g.* νηνεμίαν for νηστείαν Acts xxvii. 9), in the whole collection, are hopelessly condemned by the deep silence of a host of authorities which have since come to light. Nor are Mr. Linwood's additions to the over-copious list likely to fare much better. Who but himself will think πρώτη in Luke ii. 2 corrupted through the intermediate πρώτει from πρώτῳ ἔτει (*ubi supra* p. 5); or that τὰ πολλά in Rom. xv. 22 ought to be ἔτη πολλά (p. 13)? Add to this, that he gives up existing readings much too easily, even where his emendations are more plausible than the foregoing, as when he would adopt ὃς ἄν for ὅταν in John viii. 44 (p. 6); and this is perhaps his best attempt. His worst surely is OC for $\overline{\Theta C}$ (θεός) Rom. ix. 5, which could not be endured unless ἐστιν followed ὅς, as it does in the very passage (Rom. i. 25) which he cites in illustration (p. 13).

abstract judgement or individual prejudices. Not that the most sober and cautious critic would disparage the fair use of internal evidence, or withhold their proper influence from those reasonable considerations which in practice cannot, and in speculation should not, be shut out from every subject on which the mind seeks to form an intelligent opinion. Whether we will or not, we unconsciously and almost instinctively adopt that one of two opposite statements, *in themselves pretty equally attested to*, which we judge the better suited to recognized phenomena, and to the common course of things. I know of no person who has affected to construct a text of the N. T. on diplomatic grounds exclusively, without paying some regard to the character of the sense produced; nor, were the experiment tried, would any one find it easy to dispense with discretion and the dictates of good sense: nature would prove too strong for the dogmas of a wayward theory. 'It is difficult not to indulge in *subjectiveness*, at least in some measure,' writes Dr. Tregelles (Account of Printed Text, p. 109): and, thus qualified, we may add that it is one of those difficulties a sane man would not wish to overcome.

The foregoing remarks may tend to explain the broad distinction between mere conjectural emendation, which must be utterly discarded, and that just use of internal testimony which he is the best critic who most judiciously employs. They so far resemble each other, as they are both products of the reasoning faculty exercising itself on the sacred words of Scripture: they differ in this essential feature, that the one proceeds in ignorance or disregard of evidence from without, while the office of the other has no place unless where external evidence is evenly, or at any rate not very unevenly, balanced. What degree of preponderance in favour of one out of several readings, all of them affording some tolerable sense, shall entitle it to reception as a matter of right; to what extent canons of subjective criticism may be allowed to eke out the scantiness of documentary authority; are points that cannot well be defined with strict accuracy. Men's decisions respecting them will always vary according to their temperament and intellectual habits; the judgement of the same person (the rather if he be by constitution a little unstable) will fluctuate from time to time as to the same evidence brought to bear on the self-same passage. Though the *canons* or rules of internal testimony be themselves grounded either on principles of common sense, or on certain peculiarities which all may mark in the documents from which our direct proofs are derived; yet has it been found by experience (what indeed we might have looked for beforehand), that in spite, perhaps in consequence, of their extreme simplicity, the application of these canons has proved a searching test of the tact, the sagacity, and the judicial acumen of all that handle them. For the other functions of an editor accuracy and learning, diligence and zeal are sufficient: but the delicate adjustment of conflicting probabilities calls for no mean exercise of a critical genius. This innate faculty we lack in Wetstein, and notably in Scholz; it was highly developed in Mill and Bengel, and still more in Griesbach. His well-known power in this respect is the main cause of our deep regret for the failure of Bentley's projected work, with all its faults whether of plan or execution.

Nearly all the following rules of internal evidence, being founded in the nature of things, are alike applicable to all subjects of literary investigation, though their general principles may need some modification in the particular instance of the Greek Testament.

I. Proclivi Scriptioni praestat ardua: the more difficult the reading the more likely it is to be genuine. It would seem more probable that the copyist tried to explain an obscure passage, or to relieve a hard construction, than to make that perplexed which before was easy: thus in John vii. 39, Lachmann's addition of δεδομένον to οὔπω ἦν πνεῦμα ἅγιον is very improbable, though countenanced by Cod. B and (of course) by several of the chief versions. We have here Bengel's prime canon, and although Wetstein questioned it (N. T., vol. i. Proleg. p. 157), he was himself ultimately obliged to lay down something nearly to the same effect[1]. Yet this excellent rule may easily

[1] 'vii. Inter duas variantes lectiones, si quae est εὐφωνότερος aut planior aut Graecantior, alteri non protinus praeferenda est, sed contra saepius. viii. Lectio exhibens locutionem minus usitatam, sed alioqui subjectae materiae convenientem, praeferenda est alteri, quae, cum aeque conveniens sit, tamen phrasim habet minus insolentem, usuque magis tritam.' Wetstein's whole tract, 'Animadversiones et Cautiones ad examen variarum lectionum N. T. necessariae' (N. T.,

be applied on a wrong occasion, and is only true *ceteris paribus*, where manuscripts or versions lend strong support to the harder form. 'To force readings into the text merely because they are difficult, is to adulterate the divine text with human alloy; it is to obtrude upon the reader of Scripture the solecisms of faltering copyists, in the place of the word of God' (Bp. Chr. Wordsworth, N. T., vol. i. Preface, p. xii) [1]. See Chap. XII on Matt. xxi. 28–31. Compare also above, Vol. I. i. § 11.

II. That reading out of several is preferable, from which all the rest may have been derived, although it could not be derived from any of them. Tischendorf (N. T., Proleg. p. xlii. 7th edition) might well say that this would be 'omnium regularum principium,' if its application were less precarious. Of his own two examples the former is too weakly vouched for to be listened to, save by way of illustration. In Matt. xxiv. 38 he [2] and Alford would simply read ἐν ταῖς ἡμέραις τοῦ κατακλυσμοῦ on the very feeble evidence of Cod. L, one uncial Evst. (13), *a e ff*[1], the Sahidic version, and Origen (in two places); because the copyists, knowing that the eating and drinking and marrying took place not in the days of the flood, but before them (καὶ οὐκ ἔγνωσαν ἕως ἦλθεν ὁ κατακλυσμός ver. 39), would strive to evade the difficulty, such as it was, by adopting one of the several forms found in our copies: ἡμέραις πρὸ τοῦ κατακλ.,

vol. ii. pp. 851–874) deserves attentive study. See also the 43 Canones Critici and their Confirmatio in N. T. of G. D. T. M. D.

[1] So even Dr. Roberts, whose sympathies on the whole would not be the same as the Bishop of Lincoln's: 'Of course occasions might occur on which, from carelessness or oversight, a transcriber would render a sentence obscure or ungrammatical which was clear and correct in his exemplar; but it is manifest that, so far as intentional alteration was concerned, the temptation all lay in the opposite direction' ('Words of the New Testament,' p. 7). So again speaks E. G. Punchard on James iii. 3 in Bp. Ellicott's Commentary, 'The supporters of such curious corrections argue that the less likely is the more so; and thus every slip of a copyist, either in grammar or spelling, becomes more sacred in their eyes than is the Received text with believers in verbal inspiration.' Sir Edmund Beckett ('Should the Revised New Testament be Authorised?' 1882) writes in so scornful a spirit as to neutralize the effects on a reader's mind of his native acuteness and common sense, but he deals well with the argument 'that an improbable reading is more likely right, because nobody would have invented it.' 'I suppose,' he rejoins, 'an accidental piece of carelessness can produce an improbable and absurd error in copying as well as a probable one.' (p. 7.)

[2] In his seventh edition, not in his eighth.

or *ἡμέραις ταῖς πρὸ τοῦ κατακλ.*, or *ἡμέραις ἐκείναις πρὸ τοῦ κατακλ.*, or *ἡμέραις ἐκείναις ταῖς πρὸ τοῦ κατακλ.*, or even *ἡμέραις τοῦ νῶε.* In his second example Tischendorf is more fortunate, unless indeed we choose to refer it rather to Bengel's canon. James iii. 12 certainly ought to run *μὴ δύναται, ἀδελφοί μου, συκῆ ἐλαίας ποιῆσαι, ἢ ἄμπελος σῦκα ; οὔτε* (*vel οὐδὲ*) *ἁλυκὸν γλυκὺ ποιῆσαι ὕδωρ*, as in Codd. ℵABC, in not less than six good cursives, the Vulgate and other versions. To soften the ruggedness of this construction, some copies prefixed *οὕτως* to *οὔτε* or *οὐδέ*, while others inserted the whole clause *οὕτως οὐδεμία πηγὴ ἁλυκὸν καί* before *γλυκὺ ποιῆσαι ὕδωρ*. Other fair instances may be seen in Chap. XII, notes on Luke x. 41, 42 ; Col. ii. 2 [1]. In the Septuagint also the reading of ℵ *συνεισελθόντας* 1 Macc. xii. 48 appears to be the origin both of *συνελθόντας* with A, the uncial 23, and four cursives at least, and of *εἰσελθόντας* of the Roman edition and the mass of cursives.

III. 'Brevior lectio, nisi testium vetustorum et gravium auctoritate penitus destituatur, praeferenda est verbosiori. Librarii enim multò proniores ad addendum fuerunt, quam ad omittendum' (Griesbach, N. T., Proleg. p. lxiv. vol. i). This canon bears an influential part in the system of Griesbach and his successors, and by the aid of Cod. B and a few others, has brought great changes into the text as approved by some critics. Dr. Green too (Course of Developed Criticism on Text of N. T.) sometimes carries it to excess in his desire to remove what he considers *accretions*. It is so far true, that scribes were no doubt prone to receive marginal notes into the text which they were originally designed only to explain or enforce (e. g.

[1] One other example to illustrate this rule, so difficult in its practical use, may be added from Alford on Mark ii. 22, where the reading *καὶ ὁ οἶνος ἀπόλλυται καὶ οἱ ἀσκοί* (whether the verse end or not in these words) appears to have been the original form, since 'it fully explains all the others, either as emendations of construction, or corrections from parallel places.' The reader may apply this canon, if he pleases, to Aristotle, Ethic. iv. 9, in selecting between the three different readings *ὀκνηροί* or *νωθροί* or *νοεροί* to close the sentence *οὐ μὴν ἠλίθιοί γε οἱ τοιοῦτοι δοκοῦσιν εἶναι, ἀλλὰ μᾶλλον* . . . having careful reference to the context in which it stands : or to the easier case of *καίτοιγε* and its variations in Acts xvii. 27 : or to Rom. viii. 24, where the first hand of B and the margin of Cod. 47 (very expressly), by omitting *τί καί*, appear to present the original text.

1 John v. 7, 8)[1]; or sought to amplify a brief account from a fuller narrative of the same event found elsewhere, whether in the same book (e.g. Act. ix. 5 compared with ch. xxvi. 14), or in the parallel passage of one of the other synoptical Gospels. In quotations, also, from the Old Testament the shorter form is always the more probably correct (*ibid.*). Circumstances too will be supplied which were deemed essential for the preservation of historical truth (e.g. Act. viii. 37), or names of persons and places may be inserted from the Lectionaries: and to this head we must refer the graver and more deliberate interpolations so frequently met with in Cod. D and a few other documents. Yet it is just as true that words and clauses are sometimes wilfully omitted for the sake of removing apparent difficulties (e.g. *υἱοῦ βαραχίου*, Matt. xxiii. 35 in Cod. ℵ and a few others), and that the negligent loss of whole passages through *ὁμοιοτέλευτον* is common to manuscripts of every age and character. On the whole, therefore, the indiscriminate rejection of portions of the text regarded as supplementary, on the evidence of but a few authorities, must be viewed with considerable distrust and suspicion.

IV. That reading of a passage is preferable which best suits the peculiar style, manner, and habits of thought of an author; it being the tendency of copyists to overlook the idiosyncrasies of the writer. For example, the abrupt energy of St. James' *asyndeta* (e.g. ch. i. 27), of which we have just seen a marked instance, is much concealed by the particles inserted by the common text (e.g. ch. ii. 4, 13; iii. 17; iv. 2; v. 6): St. Luke in the Acts is fond of omitting 'said' or 'saith' after the word indicating the speaker, though they are duly supplied by recent scribes (e.g. ch. ii. 38; ix. 5; xix. 2; xxv. 22; xxv. 28, 29). Thus again, in editing Herodotus, an Ionic form is more eligible than an Attic one equally well attested, while in the Greek Testament an Alexandrian termination should be chosen under similar circumstances. Yet even this canon has a double edge: habit or the love of critical correction will sometimes lead

[1] 'Though the theory of explanatory interpolations of marginal glosses into the text of the N. T. has been sometimes carried too far (e.g. by *Wassenberg* in "Valcken." Schol. in N. T., Tom. i), yet probably this has been the most fertile source of error in some MSS. of the Sacred Volume.' (Bp. Chr. Wordsworth, N. T., on 2 Cor. iii. 3.) Yes, in *some* MSS.

the scribe to change the text to his author's more usual style, as well as to depart from it through inadvertence (*see* Acts iv. 17; 1 Pet. ii. 24): so that we may securely apply the rule only where the external evidence is not unequally balanced.

V. Attention must be paid to the genius and usage of each several authority, in assigning the weight due to it in a particular instance. Thus the testimony of Cod. B is of the less influence in omissions, that of Cod. D (Bezae) in additions, inasmuch as the tendency of the former is to abridge, that of the latter to amplify the sacred text. The value of versions and ecclesiastical writers also much depends on the degree of care and critical skill which they display.

Every one of the foregoing rules might be applied *mutatis mutandis* to the emendation of the text of any author whose works have suffered alteration since they left his hands: the next (so far as it is true) is peculiar to the case of Holy Scripture.

VI. 'Inter plures unius loci lectiones ea pro suspectâ merito habetur, quae orthodoxorum dogmatibus manifestè prae ceteris favet' (Griesbach, N.T., Proleg., p. lxvi. vol. i). I cite this canon from Griesbach for the sake of annexing Archbishop Magee's very pertinent corollary: 'from which, at least, it is reasonable to infer, that whatever readings, in favour of the Orthodox opinion, may have had *his* sanction, have not been preferred by him from any bias in behalf of Orthodoxy' (Discourses on Atonement and Sacrifice, vol. iii. p. 212). Alford says that the rule, 'sound in the main,' does not hold good, when, '*whichever reading is adopted, the orthodox meaning is legitimate*, but *the adoption of the stronger orthodox reading is absolutely incompatible with the heretical meaning*,—then it is probable that *such stronger orthodox reading was the original*' (N.T., Proleg., vol. i. p. 83, note 6, 4th edition): instancing Act. xx. 28, where the weaker reading τὴν ἐκκλησίαν τοῦ κυρίου would quite satisfy the orthodox, while the alternative reading τοῦ θεοῦ 'would have been certain to be altered by the heretics.' But in truth there seems no good ground for believing that the rule is 'sound in the main,' though two or three such instances as

1 Tim. iii. 16[1] and the insertion of *θεόν* in Jude, ver. 4, might seem to countenance it. We dissent altogether from Griesbach's statement, 'Scimus enim, lectiones quascunque, etiam manifestò falsas, dummodo orthodoxorum placitis patrocinarentur, inde a tertii seculi initiis mordicus defensas seduloque propagatas, ceteras autem ejusdem loci lectiones, quae dogmati ecclesiastico nil praesidii afferrent, haereticorum perfidiae attributas temere fuisse' (Griesb. *ubi supra*), if he means that the orthodox forged those great texts, which, *believing them to be authentic*, it was surely innocent and even incumbent on them to employ[2]. The Church of Christ 'inde a tertii seculi initiis' has had her faults, many and grievous, but she never did nor shall fail in her duty as a faithful 'witness and keeper of Holy Writ.' But while vindicating the copyists of Scripture from all wilful tampering with the text, we need not deny that they, like others of their craft, preferred that one out of several extant readings that seemed to give the fullest and most emphatic sense: hence Davidson would fain account for the addition *ἐκ τῆς σαρκὸς αὐτοῦ καὶ ἐκ τῶν ὀστέων αὐτοῦ* (which, however, is not unlikely to be genuine[3]) in Eph. v. 30. Since the mediaeval scribes belonged almost universally to the monastic orders, we will not dispute the truth of Griesbach's rule, 'Lectio prae aliis sensum pietati (praesertim monasticae) alendae aptum fundens, suspecta est,' though its scope is doubtless very limited[4]. Their

[1] On this passage Canon Liddon justly says, 'The question may still perhaps be asked ... whether here, as elsewhere, the presumption that copyists were always anxious to alter the text of the New Testament in theological interests, is not pressed somewhat excessively' (Bampton Lectures, 1866, p. 467, note).

[2] Griesbach's 'etiam manifestò falsas' can allude only to 1 John v. 7, 8; yet it is a strong point against the authenticity of that passage that it is *not* cited by Greek writers, who did not find it in their copies, but only by the Latins who did.

[3] The clause might have been derived from Gen. ii. 23, yet the evidence against it is strong and varied (ℵAB, 17, 67**, Bohair., &c.).

[4] Alford's only *definite* example (and that derived from Wetstein, N. T., vol. ii. p. 11) is found but in a single cursive (4) in Rom. xiv. 17, *οὐ γάρ ἐστιν ἡ βασιλεία τοῦ Θεοῦ βρῶσις καὶ πόσις, ἀλλὰ δικαιοσύνη καὶ ἄσκησις καὶ εἰρήνη.* Tregelles (An Account of Printed Text, p. 222) adds 1 Cor. vii. 5; Act. x. 30; Rom. xii. 13 (!) More to their purpose, perhaps, if we desired to help them on, would be the suspected addition of *καὶ νηστείᾳ* in Mark ix. 29, and of the whole verse in the parallel place Matt. xvii. 21; the former being brought into doubt on the very insufficient authority of Codd. ℵ (by the first hand) B, of the beautiful Latin copy *k* from Bobbio, and by reason of the silence of Clement of Alexandria: the latter on the evidence of the same Greek manuscripts (*k* being

habit of composing and transcribing Homilies has also been supposed to have led them to give a hortatory form to positive commands or dogmatic statements (*see* Vol. I. p. 17), but there is much weight in Wordsworth's remark, that 'such suppositions as these have a tendency to destroy the credit of the ancient MSS.; and if such surmises were true, those MSS. would hardly be worth the pains of collating them' (*note on* 1 Cor. xv. 49).

VII. 'Apparent probabilities of erroneous transcription, permutation of letters, itacism and so forth,' have been designated by Bp. Ellicott '*paradiplomatic* evidence' (Preface to the Galatians, p. xvii, first edition), as distinguished from the '*diplomatic*' testimony of codices, versions, &c. This species of evidence, which can hardly be deemed internal, must have considerable influence in numerous cases, and will be used the most skilfully by such as have considerable practical acquaintance with the rough materials of criticism. We have anticipated what can be laid before inexperienced readers on this topic in the first chapter of our first volume, when discussing the sources of various readings[1]: in fact, so far as canons of internal

defective) with Cod. 33, both (?) Egyptian, the Curetonian and Jerusalem Syriac, the Latin *e ff*[1], some forms of the Ethiopic version, and from the absence of the Eusebian canon, which ought to have referred us to the parallel place in St. Mark, whereas that verse is assigned to the *tenth* canon. In the face of such readings of ℵB it is hard to understand the grounds of Mr. Darby's vague suspicion that they 'bear the marks of having been in ecclesiastical hands.' (N.T., Preface, p. 3.)

[1] See (6), (7), (17), (18). The uncial characters most liable to be confounded by scribes (p. 10) are AΔΛ, ЄC, OΘ, NΠ, and less probably ΓIT. An article in a foreign classical periodical, written by Professor Cobet, the co-editor of the Leyden reprint of the N.T. portion of Cod. B, unless regarded as a mere *jeu d'esprit*, would serve to prove that the race of conjectural emendators is not so completely extinct as (before Mr. Linwood's pamphlet) I had supposed. By a dexterous interchange of letters of nearly the same form (Δ for A, Є for C, I for T, C for Є, K for IC, T for I) this modern Bentley—and he well deserves the name—suggests for ACTЄIOC *τῷ θεῷ* Act. vii. 20 [compare Heb. xi. 23] the common-place ΔЄKTOC *τῷ θεῷ*, from Act. x. 35. Each one of the *six* necessary changes Cobet profusely illustrates by examples, and even the reverse substitution of *δεκτός* for *ἀστεῖος* from Alciphron: but in the absence of all manuscript authority for the very smallest of these several permutations in Act. vii. 20, he excites in us no other feeling than a sort of grudging admiration of his misplaced ingenuity. In the same spirit he suggests HΔЄIONA for ΠΛЄIONA, Heb. xi. 4; while in 1 Cor. ii. 4 for *ἐν πειθοῖς σοφίας λόγοις* he simply reads *ἐν πειθοῖ σοφίας*, the *σ* which begins *σοφίας* having become accidentally doubled and *λόγοις* subsequently added to explain *πειθοῖς*, which he holds to be no Greek word at all: it seems indeed to be met with nowhere else. Dr. Hort's comment on this learned

or of paradiplomatic evidence are at all trustworthy, they instruct us in the reverse process to that aimed at in Vol. I. Chap. I; the latter showing by what means the pure text of the inspired writings was brought into its present state of *partial* corruption, the former promising us some guidance while we seek to retrace its once downward course back to the fountain-head of primeval truth[1]. To what has been previously stated in regard to paradiplomatic testimony it may possibly be worth while to add Griesbach's caution 'lectiones RHYTHMI fallaciâ facillimè explicandae nullius sunt pretii' (N. T., Proleg. p. lxvi), a fact whereof 2 Cor. iii. 3 affords a memorable example. Here what once seemed the wholly unnatural reading ἐν πλαξὶ καρδίαις σαρκίναις, being disparaged by dint of the rhyming termination, is received by Lachmann in the place of καρδίας, on the authority of Codd. AB (*sic*) CDEGLP, perhaps a majority of cursive copies (seven out of Scrivener's twelve, and Wake 12 or Paul. 277); to which add Cod. ℵ unknown to Lachmann, and that abject slave of manuscripts, the Harkleian Syriac. Codd. FK have καρδίας, with all the other versions. If we attempt to interpret καρδίαις, we must either render with Alford, in spite of the order of the Greek, 'on fleshy tables, [your] hearts:' or with the Revisers of 1881 'in tables *that are* hearts of flesh;' yet surely σαρκίναις as well as λιθίναις must agree with πλαξί. Dr. Hort in mere despair would almost reject the second πλαξί (Introd., Notes, p. 119).

It has been said that 'when the cause of a various reading is known, the variation usually disappears[2].' This language may seem extravagant, yet it hardly exaggerates what may be effected by internal evidence, when it is clear, simple, and unambiguous. It is, therefore, much to be lamented that this is seldom the case in practice. Readings that we should uphold in virtue of one canon, are very frequently (perhaps in a majority of really doubtful passages) brought into suspicion by means of

trifling is instructive: 'Though it cannot be said that recent attempts in Holland to revive conjectural criticism for the N. T. have shown much felicity of suggestion, they cannot be justly condemned on the ground of principle' (Introd., p. 277).

[1] Thus Canon I of this chapter includes (12), (19): Canon III includes (2), (3), (4), (8), (9), (10); while (13) comes under Canon IV; (20) under Canon VI.

[2] 'Canon Criticus' xxiv, N. T., by G. D. T. M. D., p. 12, 1735.

another; yet they shall each of them be perfectly sound and reasonable in their proper sphere. An instance in point is Matt. v. 22, where the external evidence is divided. Codd. ℵB (in Δ *secundâ manu*), 48, 198, 583, 587, Origen *twice*, the Ethiopic and Vulgate, omit εἰκῆ after πᾶς ὁ ὀργιζόμενος τῷ ἀδελφῷ αὐτοῦ, Jerome fairly stating that it is 'in quibusdam codicibus,' not 'in veris,' which may be supposed to be Origen's MSS., and therefore removing it from his revised Latin version. It is found, however, in all other extant copies (including ΣDEKLMSUVΔ (*primâ manu*) Π, most cursives, all the Syriac (the Peshitto inserting, not a Syriac equivalent, but the Greek word εἰκῆ) and Old Latin copies, the Bohairic, Armenian, and Gothic versions), in Eusebius, in many Greek Fathers, in the Latin Fathers from Irenaeus downwards [1], and even in the Old Latin Version of Origen himself; the later authorities uniting with Codd. ΣD and their associates against the two oldest manuscripts extant. Under such circumstances the suggestions of internal evidence would be precious indeed, were not that just as equivocal as diplomatic proof. 'Griesbach and Meyer,' says Dean Alford, 'hold it to have been expunged from motives of moral rigorism:—De Wette to have been inserted to soften the apparent rigour of the precept [2].' Our sixth Canon is here opposed to our first [3]. The important yet precarious and strictly auxiliary nature of rules of internal evidence will not now escape the attentive student; he may find them exemplified very slightly and imperfectly in the twelfth Chapter of this volume, but more fully by recent critical editors of the Greek Testament; except perhaps by Tregelles, who usually passes them by in silence, though to

[1] Dean Burgon cites (Revision Revised, pp. 359, 360) 'no less than thirty ancient witnesses.'

[2] 'The precept, if we omit the phrase, is in striking harmony with the at first sight sharp, extreme, almost paradoxical character of various other precepts of the 'Sermon on the Mount.' Milligan, Words of the N. T., p. 111.

[3] Very similar in point of moral feeling is the variation between ὀλιγοπιστίαν, the gentler, intrinsically perhaps the more probable, and ἀπιστίαν, the more emphatic term, in Matt. xvii. 20. Both must have been current in the second century, the former having the support of Codd. ℵB, 13, 22, 33, 124, 346 [*hiat* 69], the Curetonian Syriac (and that too against Cod. D), both Egyptian, the Armenian and Ethiopic versions, Origen, Chrysostom (very expressly, although his manuscripts vary), John Damascene, but of the Latins Hilary alone. All the rest, including Codd. CD, the Peshitto Syriac, and the Latins among first class witnesses, maintain ἀπιστίαν of the common text.

some extent they influence his decisions; by Lachmann, in the formation of whose provisional text they have had no share; and by Dean Burgon, who held that 'we must resolutely maintain, that External Evidence must after all be our best, our only safe guide' (The Revision Revised, p. 19)[1]. We will close this investigation by citing a few of those crisp little periods (conceived in the same spirit as our own remarks) wherewith Davidson is wont to inform and sometimes perhaps to amuse his admirers:

> 'Readings must be judged on internal grounds. One can hardly avoid doing so. It is natural and almost unavoidable. It must be admitted indeed that the choice of readings on internal evidence is liable to abuse. Arbitrary caprice may characterize it. It may degenerate into simple *subjectivity*. But though the temptation to misapply it be great, it must not be laid aside. . . . While allowing superior weight to the external sources of evidence, we feel the pressing necessity of the subjective. Here, as in other instances, the objective and subjective should accompany and modify one another. They cannot be rightly separated.' (Biblical Criticism, vol. ii. p. 374, 1852.)

[1] Perhaps I may refer to my 'Textual Guide,' p. 120. The utmost caution should be employed in the use of this kind of evidence: perhaps nowhere else do authorities differ so much.—Ed.

CHAPTER IX.

HISTORY OF THE TEXT.

AN adequate discussion of the subject of the present chapter would need a treatise by itself, and has been the single theme of several elaborate works. We shall here limit ourselves to the examination of those more prominent topics, a clear understanding of which is essential for the establishment of trustworthy principles in the application of *external* evidence to the correction of the text of the New Testament.

1. It was stated at the commencement of this volume that the autographs of the sacred writers 'perished utterly in the very infancy of Christian history:' nor can any other conclusion be safely drawn from the general silence of the earliest Fathers, and from their constant habit of appealing to 'ancient and approved copies[1],' when a reference to the originals, if extant, would have put an end to all controversy on the subject of various readings. Dismissing one passage in the genuine Epistles of Ignatius (d. 107), which has no real connexion with the matter[2], the only allusion to the autographs of Scripture met with in the primitive ages is the well-known declaration of

[1] E. g. Irenaeus, Contra Haereses, v. 30. 1, for which see below, p. 261: the early date renders this testimony most weighty.

[2] In deference to Lardner and others, who have supposed that Ignatius refers to the sacred autographs, we subjoin the sentence in dispute. *Ἐπεὶ ἤκουσά τινων λεγόντων, ὅτι ἐὰν μὴ ἐν τοῖς ἀρχαίοις εὕρω, ἐν τῷ εὐαγγελίῳ οὐ πιστεύω· καὶ λέγοντός μου αὐτοῖς, ὅτι γέγραπται, ἀπεκρίθησάν μοι, ὅτι πρόκειται. Ἐμοὶ δὲ ἀρχεῖά ἐστιν Ἰησοῦς Χριστός κ. τ. λ.* (Ad Philadelph. c. 8.) On account of *ἀρχεῖα* in the succeeding clause, *ἀρχείοις* has been suggested as a substitute for the manuscript reading *ἀρχαίοις*, and so the interpolators of the genuine Epistle have actually written. But without denying that a play on the words was designed between *ἀρχαίοις* and *ἀρχεῖα*, both copies of the Old Latin version maintain the distinction made in the Medicean Greek ('si non in veteribus invenio' and 'Mihi autem principium est Jesus Christus'), and any difficulty as to the sense lies not in

Tertullian (fl. 200): 'Percurre Ecclesias Apostolicas, apud quas ipsae adhuc Cathedrae Apostolorum suis locis praesident, apud quas ipsae Authenticae Literae eorum recitantur, sonantes vocem, et repraesentantes faciem uniuscujusque. Proximè est tibi Achaia, habes Corinthum. Si non longè es a Macedoniâ, habes Philippos, habes Thessalonicenses. Si potes in Asiam tendere, habes Ephesum. Si autem Italiae adjaces, habes Romam . . .' (De Praescriptione Haereticorum, c. 36.) Attempts have been made, indeed, and that by eminent writers, to reduce the term 'Authenticae Literae' so as to mean nothing more than 'genuine, unadulterated Epistles,' or even the authentic Greek as opposed to the Latin translation [1]. It seems enough to reply with Ernesti, that any such non-natural sense is absolutely excluded by the word 'ipsae,' which would be utterly absurd, if 'genuine' only were intended (Institutes, Pt. iii. Ch. ii. 3) [2]: yet the African Tertullian was too little likely to be well informed on this subject, to entitle his rhetorical statement to any real attention [3]. We need not try to explain away his obvious meaning, but we may fairly demur to the evidence of this honest, but impetuous and wrong-headed man. We have no faith in the continued existence of autographs which are vouched

ἀρχαίοις but in πρόκειται. Chevallier's translation of the passage is perfectly intelligible, 'Because I have heard some say, Unless I find it in the ancient writings, I will not believe in the Gospel. And when I said to them, "It is written [in the Gospel]," they answered me, "It is found written before [in the Law]."' Gainsayers set the first covenant in opposition to the second and better one.

[1] Thus Dr. Westcott understands the term, citing from Tertullian, De Monogamia, xi: 'sciamus planè non sic esse in Graeco authentico.' Dean Burgon refers us to Routh's 'Opuscula,' vol. i. pp. 151 and 206.

[2] Compare too Jerome's expression 'ipsa authentica' (Comment. in Epist. ad Titum), when speaking of the autographs of Origen's Hexapla : below, p. 263.

[3] The view I take is Coleridge's (Table Talk, p. 89, 2nd ed.). 'I beg Tertullian's pardon; but among his many *bravuras*, he says something about St. Paul's autograph. Origen expressly declares the reverse;' referring, I suppose, to the passage cited below, p. 263. Bp. Kaye, the very excellence of whose character almost unfitted him for entering into the spirit of Tertullian, observes: 'Since the whole passage is evidently nothing more than a declamatory mode of stating the weight which he attached to the authority of the Apostolic Churches; to infer from it that the very chairs in which the Apostles sat, or that the very Epistles which they wrote, then actually existed at Corinth, Ephesus, Rome, &c., would be only to betray a total ignorance of Tertullian's style' (Kaye's 'Ecclesiastical History . . . illustrated from the writings of Tertullian,' p. 313, 2nd ed.). Just so: the autographs were no more in those cities than the chairs were: but it suited the purpose of the moment to suppose that they were extant; and, *knowing nothing to the contrary*, he boldly sends the reader in search of them.

for on no better authority than the real or apparent exigency of *his* argument [1].

2. Besides the undesigned and, to a great extent, unavoidable differences subsisting between manuscripts of the New Testament within a century of its being written, the wilful corruptions introduced by heretics soon became a cause of loud complaint in the primitive ages of the Church [2]. Dionysius, Bishop of Corinth, addressing the Church of Rome and Soter its Bishop (A. D. 168–176), complains that even his own letters had been tampered with: *καὶ ταύτας οἱ τοῦ διαβόλου ἀπόστολοι ζιζανίων γεγέμικαν, ἃ μὲν ἐξαιροῦντες, ἃ δὲ προστιθέντες· οἷς τὸ οὐαὶ κεῖται*: adding, however, the far graver offence, *οὐ θαυμαστὸν ἄρα εἰ καὶ τῶν κυριακῶν ῥαδιουργῆσαί τινες ἐπιβέβληνται γραφῶν* (Euseb., Eccl. Hist., iv. 23), where *αἱ κυριακαὶ γραφαί* can be none other than the Holy Scriptures. Nor was the evil new in the age of Dionysius. Not to mention Asclepiades, or Theodotus, or Hermophylus, or Apollonides, who all under the excuse of correcting the sacred text corrupted it [3], or the Gnostics Basilides (A. D. 130?) and Valentinus (A. D. 150?) who published additions to the sacred text which were avowedly of their own composition, Marcion of Pontus, the

[1] I do not observe, as some have thought, that Eusebius (Hist. Eccl. v. 10) intimates that the copy of St. Matthew's Gospel in Hebrew letters, left by St. Bartholomew in India, was the Evangelist's autograph; and the fancy that St. Mark wrote with his own hand the Latin fragments now at Venice (*for.*) is worthy of serious notice. The statement twice made in the 'Chronicon Paschale,' of Alexandria, compiled in the seventh century, *but full of ancient fragments*, that *ὡσεὶ τριτὴ* was the true reading of John xix. 14 '*καθὼς τὰ ἀκριβῆ βιβλία περιέχει, αὐτό τε τὸ ἰδιόχειρον τοῦ εὐαγγελιστοῦ ὅπερ μέχρι τοῦ νῦν πεφύλακται χάριτι Θεοῦ ἐν τῇ ἐφεσίων ἁγιωτάτῃ ἐκκλησίᾳ καὶ ὑπὸ τῶν πιστῶν ἐκεῖσε προσκυνεῖται*' (Dindorf, Chron. Pasch., pp. 11 and 411), is simply incredible. Isaac Casaubon, however, a most unimpeachable witness, says that this passage, and another which he cites, were found by himself in a fine fragment of the Paschal treatise of 'Peter Bp. of Alexandria and martyr' [d. 311], which he got from Andrew Damarius, a Greek merchant or calligrapher (Pattison, Life of Is. Casaubon, p. 38). Casaubon adds to the assertion of Peter 'Hec ille. Ego non ignoro quid adversus hanc sententiam possit disputari: de quo judicium esto eruditorum' (Exercit. in Annal. Eccles. pp. 464, 670, London, 1614).

[2] 'I have no doubt,' says Tischendorf, 'that in the very earliest ages after our Holy Scriptures were written, and before the authority of the Church protected them, wilful alterations, and especially additions, were made in them,' English N. T., 1869, Introd. p. xv.

[3] Caius (175–200) in Routh's 'Reliquiae,' ii. 125, quoted in Burgon's 'Revision Revised,' p. 323.

arch-heretic of that period, coming to Rome on the death of its Bishop Hyginus (A.D. 142)[1], brought with him that mutilated and falsified copy of the New Testament, against which the Fathers of the second century and later exerted all their powers, and whose general contents are known to us chiefly through the writings of Tertullian and subsequently of Epiphanius. It can hardly be said that Marcion deserves very particular mention in relating the history of the sacred text[2]. Some of the variations from the common readings which his opponents detected were doubtless taken from manuscripts in circulation at the time, and, being adopted through no private preferences of his own, are justly available for critical purposes. Thus in 1 Thess. ii. 15, Tertullian, who saw only *τοὺς προφήτας* in his own copies, objects to Marcion's reading *τοὺς ἰδίους προφήτας* ('licet *suos* adjectio sit haeretici'), although *ἰδίους* stands in the received text, in Evann. KL (DE in later hands) and all cursives except eight, in the Gothic and both (?) Syriac versions, in Chrysostom, Theodoret, and John Damascenus. Here the heretic's testimony is useful in showing the high antiquity of *ἰδίους*, even though ℵABDEFGP, eight cursives, Origen thrice, the Vulgate, Armenian, Ethiopic, and all three Egyptian versions, join with Lachmann, Tischendorf, Tregelles, Westcott and Hort in rejecting it, some of them perhaps in compliance with Tertullian's decision. In similar instances the evidence of Marcion, as to matters of fact to which he could attach no kind of importance, is well worth recording[3]: but where on the contrary the dogmas of his own miserable system are touched, or no codices or other witnesses countenance his changes (as is perpetually the case in his edition of St. Luke, the only Gospel—and that maimed or interpolated from the others—he seems to have acknowledged at all), his blasphemous extravagance may very well be forgotten. In such cases he

[1] 'Necdum quoque Marcion Ponticus de Ponto emersisset, cujus magister Cerdon sub Hygino tunc episcopo, qui in Urbe nonus fuit, Romam venit: quem Marcion secutus...' Cyprian., Epist. 74. Cf. Euseb., Eccl. Hist., iv. 10, 11.

[2] Dean Burgon attributes more importance to Marcion's mutilations. *See* e. g. 'The Revision Revised,' pp. 84–35.

[3] In 1 Cor. x. 9 Marcion seems to uphold the true reading against the judgement of Epiphanius: *ὁ δὲ μαρκίων ἀντὶ τοῦ κ̅ν̅ χ̅ν̅ ἐποίησεν.* Consult also Bp. Lightfoot's note (Epistle to the Colossians, p. 336, n. 1) on Heracleon's variation of *πέντε* for *ἕξ* in John ii. 20. 'There is no reason to think,' he says, 'that Heracleon falsified the text here; he appears to have found this various reading already in his copy.'

does not so much as profess to follow anything more respectable than the capricious devices of his misguided fancy.

3. Nothing throws so strong a light on the real state of the text in the latter half of the second century as the single notice of Irenaeus (fl. 178) on Apoc. xiii. 18. This eminent person, the glory of the Western Church in his own age, whose five books against Heresies (though chiefly extant but in a bald old Latin version) are among the most precious reliques of Christian antiquity, had been privileged in his youth to enjoy the friendly intercourse of his master Polycarp, who himself had conversed familiarly with St. John and others that had seen the Lord (Euseb., Eccl. Hist., v. 20). Yet even Irenaeus, though removed but by one stage from the very Apostles, possessed (if we except a bare tradition) no other means of settling discordant readings than are now open to ourselves; namely, to search out the best copies and exercise the judgement on their contents. His *locus classicus* must needs be cited in full, the Latin throughout, the Greek in such portions as survive. The question is whether St. John wrote χξϛ′ (666), or χιϛ′ (616).

'Hic autem sic se habentibus, et in omnibus antiquis et probatissimis et veteribus scripturis numero hoc posito, et testimonium perhibentibus his qui facie ad faciem Johannem viderunt (*τούτων δὲ οὕτως ἐχόντων, καὶ ἐν πᾶσι δὲ τοῖς σπουδαίοις καὶ ἀρχαίοις ἀντιγράφοις τοῦ ἀριθμοῦ τούτου κειμένου, καὶ μαρτυρούντων αὐτῶν ἐκείνων τῶν κατ' ὄψιν τὸν Ἰωάννην ἑωρακότων, καὶ τοῦ λόγου διδάσκοντος ἡμᾶς ὅτι ὁ ἀριθμὸς τοῦ ὀνόματος τοῦ θηρίου κατὰ τὴν τῶν Ἑλλήνων ψῆφον διὰ τῶν ἐν αὐτῷ γραμμάτων* [*ἐμφοίνεται*]), et ratione docente nos quoniam numerus nominis bestiae, secundum Graecorum computationem, per literas quae in eo sunt sexcentos habebit et sexaginta et sex: ignoro quomodo erraverunt quidam sequentes idiotismum et medium frustrantes numerum nominis, quinquaginta numeros deducentes, pro sex decadis unam decadem volentes esse (*αὐκ οἶδα πῶς ἐσφάλησάν τινες ἐπικολουθήσαντες ἰδιωτισμῷ καὶ τὸν μέσον ἠθέτησαν ἀριθμὸν τοῦ ὀνόματος, ν′ ψήφισμα ὑφελόντες καὶ ἀντὶ τῶν ἓξ δεκάδων μίαν δεκάδα βουλόμενοι εἶναι*). Hoc autem arbitror scriptorum peccatum fuisse, ut solet fieri, quoniam et per literas numeri ponuntur, facilè literam Graecam quae sexaginta enuntiat numerum, in iota Graecorum literam expansam. . . . Sed his quidem qui simpliciter et sine malitia hoc fecerunt, arbitramur veniam dari a Deo.' (Contra Haeres. v. 30. 1: Harvey, vol. ii. pp. 406–7.)

Here we obtain at once the authority of Irenaeus for receiving the Apocalypse as the work of St. John; we discern the living interest its contents had for the Christians of the second century, even up to the *traditional* preservation of its minutest readings;

we recognize the fact that numbers were then represented by letters[1]; and the far more important one that the original autograph of the Apocalypse was already so completely lost, that a thought of it never entered the mind of the writer, though the book had not been composed one hundred years, perhaps not more than seventy[2].

4. Clement of Alexandria is the next writer who claims our attention (fl. 194). Though his works abound with citations from Scripture, on the whole not too carefully made ('in adducendis N. T. locis creber est et *castus*,' is rather too high praise, Mill, Proleg. § 627), the most has not yet been made of the information he supplies. He too complains of those who tamper with (or metaphrase) the Gospels for their own sinister ends, and affords us one specimen of their evil diligence[3]. His pupil Origen's [185–253] is the highest name among the critics and expositors of the early Church; he is perpetually engaged in the discussion of various readings of the New Testament, and employs language in describing the then existing state of the text, which would be deemed strong if applied even to its present

[1] *See* Chap. XI on Acts xxvii. 37.

[2] Irenaeus' anxiety that his own works should be kept free from corruption, and the value attached by him to the labours of the corrector, are plainly seen in a remarkable subscription preserved by Eusebius (Eccl. Hist. v. 20), which illustrates what has been said above, *'Ορκίζω σε τὸν μεταγραψόμενον τὸ βίβλιον τοῦτο, κατὰ τοῦ κυρίου ἡμῶν Ιησοῦ χριστοῦ, καὶ κατὰ τῆς ἐνδόξου πορουσίας αὐτοῦ, ἧς ἔρχεται κρῖναι ζῶντας καὶ νεκρούς, ἵνα ἀντιβάλλῃς ὃ μετεγράψω, καὶ κατορθώσῃς αὐτὸ πρὸς τὸ ἀντίγραφον τοῦτο, ὅθεν μετεγράψω ἐπιμελῶς, καὶ τὸν ὅρκον τοῦτον ὁμοίως μεταγράψῃς, καὶ θήσεις ἐν τῷ ἀντιγράφῳ.* Here the copyist (*ὁ μεταγραφόμενος*) is assumed to be the same person as the reviser or corrector. Mr. Linwood also (*ubi supra*, p. 11) illustrates from Martial (Lib. vii. Epigram. x) the reader's natural wish to possess an author's original manuscript rather than a less perfect copy: *Qui vis* archetypas *habere nugas*. A still stronger illustration of the passage in Irenaeus (v. 30) is Linwood's citation of a well-known passage in Aulus Gellius, a contemporary of that Father, wherein he discusses with Higinus the corrupt variation *amaro* for *amaror* in Virgil, Geor. ii. 247 (Noctes Atticae, Lib. i. cap. 21).

[3] *Μακάριοι, φησίν, οἱ δεδιωγμένοι ἕνεκεν δικαιοσύνης, ὅτι αὐτοὶ υἱοὶ Θεοῦ κληθήσονται· ἤ, ὥς τινες τῶν μετατιθέντων τὰ Εὐαγγέλια, Μακάριοι, φησίν, οἱ δεδιωγμένοι ὑπὸ τῆς δικαιοσύνης, ὅτι οὗτοι ἔσονται τέλειοι· καί, μακάριοι οἱ δεδιωγμένοι ἕνεκα ἐμοῦ, ὅτι ἕξουσι τόπον ὅπου οὐ διωχθήσονται* (Stromata, iv. 6). Tregelles (Horne, p. 39, note 2) pertinently remarks that Clement, in the very act of censuring others, subjoins the close of Matt. v. 9 to v. 10, and elsewhere himself ventures on liberties no less extravagant, as when he thus quotes Matt. xix. 24 (or Luke xviii. 25): *πειστέον οὖν πολλῷ μᾶλλον τῇ γραφῇ λεγούσῃ, Θᾶττον κάμηλον διὰ τρυπήματος βελόνης διελεύσεσθαι, ἢ πλούσιον φιλοσοφεῖν* (Stromata, ii. 5).

condition, after the changes which sixteen more centuries must needs have produced. His statements are familiar enough to Biblical enquirers, but, though often repeated, cannot be rightly omitted here. Seldom have such warmth of fancy and so bold a grasp of mind been united with the life-long patient industry which procured for this famous man the honourable appellation of *Adamantius*. Respecting the sacred autographs, their fate or their continued existence, he seems to have had no information, and to have entertained no curiosity: they had simply passed by and were out of reach. Had it not been for the diversities of copies in all the Gospels on other points (he writes)—*καὶ εἰ μὲν μὴ καὶ περὶ ἄλλων πολλῶν διαφωνία ἦν πρὸς ἄλληλα τῶν ἀντιγράφων* —he should not have ventured to object to the authenticity of a certain passage (Matt. xix. 19) on internal grounds: *νυνὶ δὲ δηλονότι πολλὴ γέγονεν ἡ τῶν ἀντιγράφων διαφορά, εἴτε ἀπὸ ῥαθυμίας τινῶν γραφέων, εἴτε ἀπὸ τόλμης τινῶν μοχθηρᾶς τῆς διορθώσεως τῶν γραφομένων, εἴτε καὶ ἀπὸ τῶν τὰ ἑαυτοῖς δοκοῦντα ἐν τῇ διορθώσει προστιθέντων ἢ ἀφαιρούντων* (Comment. on Matt., Tom. iii. p. 671, *De la Rue*). 'But now,' saith he, 'great in truth has become the diversity of copies, be it from the negligence of certain scribes, or from the evil daring of some who correct what is written, or from those who in correcting add or take away what they think fit[1]:' just like Irenaeus had previously described revisers of the text as persons 'qui peritiores apostolis volunt esse' (Contra Haeres. iv. 6. 1).

5. Nor can it easily be denied that the various readings of the New Testament current from the middle of the second to the middle of the third century, were neither fewer nor less considerable than such language would lead us to anticipate. Though no

[1] In this place (contrary to what might have been inferred from the language of Irenaeus, cited above, p. 262, note 2) the copyist (*γραφεύς*) is clearly distinct from the corrector (*διορθωτής*), who either alters the words that stand in the text, or adds to and subtracts from them. In Cobet's masterly Preface to his own and Kuenen's 'N. T. ad fidem Cod. Vaticani,' Leyden, 1860, pp. xxvii-xxxiv, will be found most of the passages we have used that bear on the subject, with the following from classical writers, 'Nota est Strabonis querela xiii. p. 609 de bibliopolis, qui libros edebant γραφεῦσι φαύλοις χρώμενοι, καὶ οὐκ ἀντιβάλλοντες... Sic in Demosthenis Codice Monacensi ad finem Orationis xi annotatum est Διωρθώθη πρὸς δύο 'Αττικιανά, id est, *correctus est* (hic liber) *ex duobus codicibus ab Attico* (nobili calligrapho) *descriptis*.' Just as at the end of each of Terence's plays the manuscripts read 'Calliopius recensui.'

surviving manuscript of the Old Latin version, or versions, dates before the fourth century, and most of them belong to a still later age, yet the general correspondence of their text with that used by the first Latin Fathers is a sufficient voucher for its high antiquity. The connexion subsisting between this Latin version, the Curetonian Syriac, and Codex Bezae, proves that the text of these documents is considerably older than the vellum on which they are written; the Peshitto Syriac also, most probably the very earliest of all translations, though approaching far nearer to the received text than they, sufficiently resembles these authorities in many peculiar readings to exhibit the general tone and character of one class of manuscripts extant in the second century, two hundred years anterior to Codd. ℵB. Now it may be said without extravagance that no set of Scriptural records affords a text less probable in itself or less sustained by any rational principles of external evidence, than that of Cod. D, of the Latin codices, and (so far as it accords with them) of Cureton's Syriac. Interpolations, as insipid in themselves as unsupported by other evidence, abound in them all[1]: additions so little in accordance with the genuine spirit of Holy Writ that some critics (though I, for one, profess no skill in such alchemy) have declared them to be as easily separable from the text which they encumber, as the foot-notes appended to a modern book are from the main body of the work (Tregelles, An Account of the Printed Text, p. 138, note). It is no less true to fact than paradoxical in sound, that the worst corruptions to which the New Testament has ever been subjected, originated within a hundred years after it was composed; that Irenaeus and the African Fathers and the whole Western, with a portion of the Syrian Church, used far inferior manuscripts to those employed by Stunica, or Erasmus, or Stephen thirteen centuries later, when

[1] No doubt certain that are quite or almost peculiar to Cod. D would deserve consideration if they were not destitute of adequate support. Some may be inclined to think the words cited above in vol. I. p. 8 not unworthy of Him to whom they are ascribed. The margin of the Harkleian Syriac alone countenances D in that touching appendage to Acts viii. 24, which every one must wish to be genuine, *ος πολλα κλαιων ου διελυ[ι]μπανεν*. Several minute facts are also inserted by D in the latter part of the same book, which are more likely to rest on traditional knowledge than to be mere exorcises of an idle fancy. Such are *απο ωρας ε̄ εως δεκατης* annexed to the end of Acts xix. 9: *και Μυρα* to Acts xxi. 1; the former of which is also found in Cod. 137 and the Harkleian margin; the lattor in the Sahidic and one or two Latin copies.

moulding the Textus Receptus. What passage in the Holy Gospels would be more jealously guarded than the record of the heavenly voice at the Lord's Baptism? Yet Augustine (De Consensu Evangelist. ii. 14) marked a variation which he thought might be found 'in aliquibus fide dignis exemplaribus,' though not 'in antiquioribus codicibus Graecis,' where, in the place of ἐν σοὶ ηὐδόκησα (Luke iii. 22), the words ἐγὼ σήμερον γεγέννηκά σε are substituted from Psalm ii. 7: so also reads the Manichaean Faustus apud Augustin.; Enchiridion ad Laurentium, c. 49. The only Greek copy which maintains this important reading is D: it is met with moreover in *abc* (in *d* of course), in *ff*[1] *primâ manu*, and in *l*, whose united evidence leaves not a doubt of its existence in the primitive Old Latin; whence it is cited by Hilary three times, by Lactantius and Juvencus, to which list Abbot adds Hilary the deacon (Quaestiones V. et N. T.). Among the Greeks it is known but to Methodius, and to those very early writers, Justin Martyr and Clement of Alexandria, who seem to have derived the corruption (for such it must doubtless be regarded) from the Ebionite Gospel (Epiphan., Haeres., xxi. 13)[1]. So again of a doubtful passage which we shall examine in Chapter XII, Irenaeus cites Acts viii. 37 without the least misgiving, though the spuriousness of the verse can hardly be doubted; and expressly testifies to a reading in Matt. i. 18 which has not till lately found many advocates. It is hard to believe that I John v. 7, 8 was not cited by Cyprian, and even the interpolation in Matt. xx. 28 was widely known and received. Many other examples might be produced from the most venerable Christian writers, in which they countenance variations (and those not arbitrary, but resting on some sort of authority) which no modern critic has ever attempted to vindicate.

6. When we come down to the fourth century, our information grows at once more definite and more trustworthy. Copies of Scripture had been extensively destroyed during the long and terrible period of affliction that preceded the conversion of

[1] Considering that Cod. D and the Latin manuscripts contain the variation in Luke iii. 22, but not in Matt. iii. 17, we ought not to doubt that Justin Martyr (p. 331 B, ed. Paris, 1636) and Clement (p. 113, ed. Potter) refer to the former. Hence Bp. Kaye (Account of the Writings of Clement, p. 410) should not have produced this passage among others to show (what in itself is quite true) that 'Clement frequently quotes from momory.'

Constantine. In the very edict which marked the beginning of Diocletian's persecution, it is ordered that the holy writings should be burnt (τὰς γραφὰς ἀφανεῖς πυρὶ γενέσθαι, Eusebius, Eccl. Hist., viii. 2); and the cruel decree was so rigidly enforced that a special name of reproach (*traditores*), together with the heaviest censures of the Church, was laid upon those Christians who betrayed the sacred trust (Bingham, Antiquities, book xvi. ch. vi. 25). At such a period critical revision or even the ordinary care of devout transcribers must have disappeared before the pressure of the times. Fresh copies of the New Testament would have to be made in haste to supply the room of those seized by the enemies of our Faith; and, when made, they had to circulate by stealth among persons whose lives were in jeopardy every hour. Hence arose the need, when the tempest was overpast, of transcribing many new manuscripts of the Holy Bible, the rather as the Church was now receiving vast accessions of converts within her pale. Eusebius of Caesarea, the ecclesiastical historian, seems to have taken the lead in this happy labour; his extensive learning, which by the aid of certain other less commendable qualities had placed him high in Constantine's favour, rendered it natural that the emperor should employ his services for furnishing with fifty copies of Scripture the churches of his new capital, Constantinople. Eusebius' deep interest in Biblical studies is exhibited in several of his surviving works, as well as in his Canons for harmonizing the Gospels: and he would naturally betake himself for the text of his fifty codices to the Library founded at his Episcopal city of Caesarea by the martyr Pamphilus, the dear friend and teacher from whom he derived his own familiar appellation *Eusebius Pamphili*. Into this Library Pamphilus had gathered manuscripts of Origen as well as of other theologians, and of these Eusebius made an index (τοὺς πίνακας παρεθέμην: Eccles. Hist., vi. 32). From this collection Cod. H of St. Paul and others are stated to have been derived, nay even Cod. ℵ in its Old Testament portion (*see* vol. I. p. 55 and note), which is expressly declared to have been corrected to the Hexapla of Origen. Indeed we know from Jerome (Comment. in Epist. ad Tit.) that the very autograph ('ipsa authentica') of Origen's Hexapla was used by himself at Caesarea, and Montfaucon (Praeliminaria in Hexapl., chap. i. 5) cites from one manuscript the following subscription to Ezekiel, 'Ο Εὐσέβιος ἐγὼ σχόλια παρέθηκα. Πάμφιλος καὶ Εὐσέβιος ἐδιωρθώσαντο.

7. We are thus warranted, as well from direct evidence as from the analogy of the Old Testament, to believe that Eusebius mainly resorted for his Constantinopolitan Church-books to the codices of Pamphilus, which might once have belonged to Origen. What critical corrections (if any) he ventured to make in the text on his own judgement is not so clear. Not that there is the least cause to believe, with Dr. Nolan (Inquiry into the Integrity of the Greek Vulgate, p. 27), that Eusebius had either the power or the will to suppress or tamper with the great doctrinal texts 1 John v. 7, 8; 1 Tim. iii. 16; Acts xx. 28; yet we cannot deny that his prepossessions may have tempted him to arbitrary alterations in other passages, which had no direct bearing on the controversies of his age [1]. Codd. ℵB are quite old enough to have been copied under his inspection [2], and it is certainly very remarkable that these two early manuscripts omit one whole paragraph (Mark xvi. 9-20) with his sanction, if not after his example (*see* below, Chap. XII). Thus also in Matt. xxiii. 35 Cod. ℵ, with the countenance only of Evan. 59, Evst. 6, 13, 222 (*see* under Evst. 222), discards υἱοῦ βαραχίου, for which change Eusebius (*silentio*) is literally the only authority among the Fathers, Irenaeus and even Origen retaining the words, in spite of their obvious difficulty. The relation in which Cod. ℵ stands to the other four chief manuscripts of the Gospels, may be roughly estimated from analyzing the transcript of four pages first published by Tischendorf [3], as well as in any other

[1] This point is exceedingly well stated by Canon Cook (Revised Version of the first three Gospels, p. 176): 'I will not dwell upon indications of Arian tendencies. They are not such as we should be entitled to rely upon..... Eusebius was certainly above the suspicion of consciously introducing false statements or of obliterating true statements. As was the case with many supporters of the high Arian party, which came nearest to the sound orthodox faith, Eusebius was familiar with all scriptural texts which distinctly ascribe to our Lord the divine attributes and the divine name, and was far more likely to adopt an explanation which coincided with his own system, than to incur the risk of exposure and disgrace by obliterating or modifying them in manuscripts which would be always open to public inspection.'

[2] 'This is possible, though there is no proof of it,' is Professor Abbot's comment (*ubi supra*, p. 190, but *see* above, vol. i. p. 118, note 2).

[3] In the 'Notitia Editionis Cod. Sin.,' 1860. They are Matt. xxvii. 64—xxviii. 20; Mark i. 1-35; Luke xxiv. 24-53; John xxi. 1-25. Other like calcula-

way. Of the 312 variations from the common text therein noted, ℵ stands alone in forty-five, in eight agrees with ABCD united (much of C, however, is lost in these passages), with ABC together thirty-one times, with ABD fourteen, with AB thirteen, with D alone ten, with B alone but once (Mark i. 27), with C alone once: with several authorities against AB thirty-nine times, with A against B fifty-two, with B against A ninety-eight. Hence, while the discovery of this precious document has unquestionably done much to uphold Cod. B (which is the more correctly written, and doubtless the more valuable of the two) in many of its more characteristic and singular readings, it has made the mutual divergencies of the very oldest critical authorities more patent and perplexing than ever [1].

8. Codd. ℵB were apparently anterior to the age of Jerome, the latest ecclesiastical writer whose testimony need be dwelt upon, since from his time downwards the stream of extant and direct manuscript evidence, beginning with Codd. AC, flows on without interruption. Jerome's attention was directed to the criticism of the Greek Testament by his early Biblical studies, and the knowledge he thus obtained had full scope for its exercise when he was engaged on revising the Old Latin version. In his so-often cited 'Praefatio ad Damasum,' prefixed to his recension of the Gospels, he complains of certain 'codices, quos a Luciano et Hesychio nuncupatos, paucorum hominum asserit perversa contentio,' and those not of the Old Testament alone, but also of the New. This obscure and passing notice of corrupt and (apparently) interpolated copies has been made the foundation of more than one theory as fanciful as ingenious. Jerome further informs us that he had adopted in his translation the canons which Eusebius 'Alexandrium secutus Ammonium' (*but*

tions, with much the same result, are given in Scrivener's 'Cod. Sin.,' Introd. pp. xlii, xliii.

[1] And that too hardly to the credit of either of them. 'Ought it not,' asks Dean Burgon, 'sensibly to detract from our opinion of the value of their evidence to discover that *it is easier to find two consecutive verses in which the two MSS. differ, the one from the other, than two consecutive verses in which they entirely agree?* . . . On every such occasion only one of them can possibly be speaking the truth. Shall I be thought unreasonable if I confess that these perpetual inconsistencies between Codd. B and ℵ—grave inconsistencies, and occasionally even gross ones—altogether destroy my confidence in either?' (Last Twelve Verses of St. Mark, pp. 77-8.)

see Vol. I. pp. 59, &c.) had invented or first brought into vogue; stating, and, in his usual fashion, somewhat exaggerating[1], an evil these canons helped to remedy, the mixing up of the matter peculiar to one Evangelist with the narrative of another. Hence we might naturally expect that the Greek manuscripts he would view with special favour, were the same as Eusebius had approved before him. In the scattered notices throughout his works, Jerome sometimes speaks but vaguely of 'quaedam exemplaria tam Graeca quam Latina' (Luke xxii. 43–4, almost in the words of Hilary, his senior); or appeals to readings 'in quibusdam exemplaribus et maximè in Graecis codicibus' (Mark xvi. 14). Occasionally we hear of 'multi et Graeci et Latini codices' (John vii. 53), or 'vera exemplaria' (Matt. v. 22; xxi. 31), or 'antiqua exemplaria' (Luke ix. 23), without specifying in which language: Mark xvi. 9–20 'in raris fertur Evangeliis,' since 'omnes Graeciae libri paene' do not contain it[2]. In two places, however, he gives a more definite account of the copies he most regarded. In Galat. iii. 1 τῇ ἀληθείᾳ μὴ πείθεσθαι is omitted by Jerome, because it is not contained 'in exemplaribus Adamantii,' although (as he elsewhere informs us) 'et Graeca exemplaria hoc errore confusa sint.' In the other of the two passages Jerome remarks that in some Latin copies of Matt. xxiv. 36 *neque filius* is added, 'quum in Graecis, et maxime Adamantii et Pierii exemplaribus, hoc non habeatur adscriptum.' Pierius the presbyter of Alexandria, elsewhere called by Jerome 'the younger Origen' (Cat. Scriptt. Eccl., i. p. 128), has been deprived by fortune of the honour due to his merit and learning. A contemporary, perhaps the teacher of Pamphilus (Euseb., Eccl. Hist., vii. 32) at Caesarea, his copies of Scripture would naturally be preserved with those of Origen in the great Library of that city. Here they were doubtless seen by Jerome when, to his deep joy, he found Origen's writings copied in Pamphilus' hand (Cat. Scriptt. Eccl.,

[1] Magnus siquidem hic in nostris codicibus error inolevit, dum quod in eadem re alius Evangelista plus dixit, in alio, quia minus putaverint, addiderunt. Vel dum eundem sensum alius aliter expressit, ille qui unum e quatuor primum legerat, ad ejus exemplum ceteros quoque existimaverit emendandos. *Unde accidit ut apud nos mixta sint omnia* (Praef. ad Damasum).

[2] The precise references may be seen in Tischendorf's, and for the most part more exactly in Tregelles' N. T. That on Matt. xxiv. 36 is Tom. vii. p. 199, or vi. p. 54; on Galat. iii. 1 is Tom. vii. pp. 418, 487.

ubi supra), which volumes Acacius and Euzoius, elder contemporaries of Jerome himself, had taken pious care to repair and renew (*ibid.* i. p. 131; ad Marcell. Ep. cxli). It is not therefore wonderful if, employing as they did and setting a high value on precisely the same manuscripts of the N. T., the readings approved by Origen, Eusebius, and Jerome should closely agree.

9. Epiphanius [d. 403], who wrote at about the same period as Jerome, distinguishes in his note on Luke xix. 41 or xxii. 44 (Tom. ii. p. 36) between the uncorrected copies (*ἀδιορθώτοις*), and those used by the Orthodox [1]. Of the function of the 'corrector' (*διορθωτής*) of an ancient manuscript we have spoken several times before: but a system was devised by Professor J. L. Hug of Freyburg (Einleitung, 1808), and maintained, though with some modifications, by J. G. Eichhorn, which assigned to these occasional, and (as they would seem to be) unsystematic labours of the reviser, a foremost place in the criticism of the N. T. Hug conceived that the process of corruption had been going on so rapidly and uniformly from the Apostolic age downwards, that by the middle of the third century the state of the text in the general mass of codices had degenerated into the form exhibited in Codd. D, 1, 13, 69, 124 of the Gospels, the Old Latin and Sahidic (he would now have added the Curetonian Syriac) versions, and to some extent in the Peshitto and in the citations of Clement of Alexandria and of Origen in his early works. To this uncorrected text he gave the name of *κοινὴ ἔκδοσις*, and that it existed, substantially in the interpolated shape now seen in Cod. D, the Old Latin, and Cureton's Syriac, as early as the second century, need not be doubted. There is some foundation for this position, but it was marred by Hug's lack of sobriety of judgement. What we may fairly dispute is that this text ever

[1] See our note on Luke xxii. 44 below in Chap. XI. This same writer testifies to a practice already partially employed, of using breathings, accents, and stops in copies of Holy Scripture. *Ἐπειδὴ δέ τινες κατὰ προσῳδίαν ἔστιξαν τὰς γραφὰς καὶ περὶ τῶν προσῳδῶν τάδε· ὀξεῖα ´, δασεῖα ῾, βαρεῖα `, ψιλὴ ᾿, περισπωμένη ῀, ἀπόστροφος ᾽, μακρὰ –, ὑφὲν ‿, βραχεῖα ˘, ὑποδιαστολή , . Ὡσαύτως καὶ περὶ τῶν λοιπῶν σημείων κ. τ. λ.* (Epiphan., De Mensur., c. 2, Tom. iii. p. 237 Migne). This passage may tend to confirm the statements made above, Vol. I. pp. 45-8, respecting the presence of such marks in very ancient codices, though on the whole we may not quite vouch for Sir F. Madden's opinion as regards Cod. A.

had extensive circulation or good repute in the Churches whose vernacular language was Greek. This 'common edition' Hug supposes to have received three separate emendations in the middle of the third century; one made by Origen in Palestine, which he thinks Jerome adopted and approved; two others by Hesychius and Lucian (a presbyter of Antioch and Martyr), in Egypt and Syria respectively, both which Jerome condemned, and Pope Gelasius (A.D. 492–6) declared to be apocryphal[1]. To Origen's recension he referred such copies as AKM, 42, 106, 114, 116, 253 of the Gospels, the Harkleian Syriac, the quotations of Chrysostom and Theodoret; to Hesychius the Alexandrian codices BCL; to Lucian the Byzantine documents EFGHSV and the mass of later books. The practical effect of this elaborate theory would be to accord to Cod. A a higher place among our authorities than some recent editors have granted it, even than it quite deserves, yet its correspondence with Origen in many characteristic readings would thus be admitted and accounted for (*but see* p. 226). But in truth Hug's whole scheme is utterly baseless as regards historical fact, and most insufficiently sustained by internal proof. Jerome's slight and solitary mention of the copies of Lucian and Hesychius abundantly evinces their narrow circulation and the low esteem in which they were held; and even Eichhorn perceived that there was no evidence whatever to show that Origen had attempted a formal revision of the text. The passages cited above, both from Eusebius and Jerome —and no others are known to bear on the subject—will carry us no further than this:—that these Fathers had access to codices of the N.T. once possessed by Adamantius, and here and there, perhaps, retouched by his hand. The manuscripts copied by Pamphilus were those of Origen's own works; and while we have full and detailed accounts of what he accomplished for the Greek versions of the Old Testament, no hint has been thrown out by any ancient writer that he carried his pious labour into

[1] 'Evangelia quae falsavit Lucianus, apocrypha.' 'Evangelia quae falsavit Esitius [*alii* Hesychius *vel* Isicius], apocrypha,' occur separately in the course of a long list of spurious books (such as the Gospels of Thaddaeus, Matthias, Peter, James, that 'nomine Thomae quo utuntur Manichaei,' &c.) in Appendix iii to Gelasius' works in Migne's Patrologia, Tom. lix. p. 162 [A. D. 494]. But the authenticity of those decrees is far from certain, and since we hear of these falsified Gospels nowhere else, Gelasius' knowledge of them might have been derived from what he had read in Jerome's 'Praef. ad Damasum.'

the criticism of the New. On the contrary, he seems to disclaim the task in a sentence now extant chiefly in the old Latin version of his works, wherein, to a notice of his attempt to remove diversity of reading from codices of the Septuagint by the help of 'the other editions' (κριτηρίῳ χρησάμενοι ταῖς λοιπαῖς ἐκδόσεσιν, i.e. the versions of Aquila and the rest), he is represented as adding, 'In exemplaribus autem Novi Testamenti, hoc ipsum me posse facere sine periculo non putavi' (Origen, Tom. iii. p. 671).

10. Hug's system of recensions was devised as a corrective to those of Bengel and of Griesbach, which have been adequately discussed in Chapter VII. The veteran Griesbach spent his last effort as a writer in bringing to notice the weak points of Hug's case, and in claiming him, where he rightly could, as a welcome ally[1]. But neither did Hug's scheme, nor that propounded by Scholz some years later, obtain the general credit and acceptance which had once been conceded to Griesbach's. It was by this time plainly seen that not only were such theories unsupported by historical testimony (to which indeed the Professor of Halle had been too wise to lay claim), but that they failed to account for more than a part, and that usually a small part, of the phenomena disclosed by minute study of our critical materials. All that can be inferred from searching into the history of the sacred text amounts to no more than this: that extensive

[1] Griesbach rejoices to have Hug's assent 'in eo, in quo disputationis de veteribus N. T. recensionibus cardo vertitur; nempe extitisse, inde a secundo et tertio saeculo, plures sacri textûs recensiones, quarum una, si Evangelia spectes, supersit in Codice D, altera in Codd. BCL, alia in Codd. EFGHS et quae sunt reliqua' (Meletemata, p. lxviii, prefixed to 'Commentarius Criticus,' Pars ii, 1811). I suppose that Tregelles must have overlooked this decisive passage (probably the last its author wrote for the public eye) when he states that Griesbach now 'virtually gave up his system' as regards the possibility of 'drawing an actual line of distinction between his Alexandrian and Western recensions' (An Account of the Printed Text, p. 91). He certainly showed, throughout his 'Commentarius Criticus,' that Origen does not lend him the support he had once anticipated; but he still held that the theory of a triple recension was the very *hinge* on which the whole question turned, and clung to that theory as tenaciously as ever. THIRD EDITION. Dr. Hort (N. T., Introd. p. 186) has since confirmed our opinion that Griesbach was faithful to the last to the essential characteristics of his theory, adding that 'the Meletemata of 1811 . . . reiterate Griesbach's familiar statements in precise language, while they show a growing perception of mixture which might have led him to further results if he had not died in the following spring.'

variations, arising no doubt from the wide circulation of the New Testament in different regions and among nations of diverse languages, subsisted from the earliest period to which our records extend. Beyond this point our investigations cannot be carried, without indulging in pleasant speculations which may amuse the fancy, but cannot inform the sober judgement. Such is the conclusion to which we are reluctantly brought after examining the principles laid down, as well by the critics we have named above, as by Lachmann, by his disciple Tregelles, and even by the *par nobile* of Cambridge Doctors, Professor Hort and Bishop (formerly, Canon) Westcott, of whose labours we shall speak presently.

CHAPTER X.

RECENT VIEWS OF COMPARATIVE CRITICISM.

YET is it true that we are thus cast upon the wide ocean without a compass or a guide? Can no clue be found that may conduct us through the tangled maze? Is there no other method of settling the text of the New Testament than by collecting and marshalling and scrutinizing the testimony of thousands of separate documents, now agreeing, now at issue with each other :—manuscripts, versions, ecclesiastical writers, whose mutual connexion and interdependence, as far as they exist (and to some extent they do and *must* exist), defy all our skill and industry to detect and estimate aright? This would surely be a discouraging view of critical science as applied to the sacred volume, and it is by no means warranted by proved and admitted facts. Elaborate systems have failed, as might have been looked for from the first. It was premature to frame them in the present stage of things, while the knowledge we possess of the actual contents of our extant authorities is imperfect, vague, and fragmentary; while our conclusions are liable to be disturbed from time to time by the rapid accession of fresh materials, of whose character we are still quite ignorant. But if we be incompetent to devise theories on a grand or imposing scale, a more modest and a safer course is open. Men of the present generation may be disqualified for taking a general survey of the whole domain of this branch of divine learning, who may yet be employed, serviceably and with honour, in cultivating each one for himself some limited and humble field of special research, to which his taste, his abilities, or opportunities have attached him: those persons may usefully improve a farm, who cannot hope to conquer a kingdom. Out of the long array of uncollated manuscripts which swell our catalogues, let the student choose from the mass a few within his reach which he may deem worthy of complete examination; or exhaust the information some ecclesiastical writer of the first six centuries can afford; or contribute what he can to an exact acquaintance with some good ancient version, ascertaining the genius of its language and (where this is attainable) the literary history of its text. If, in the course of such quiet toil, he shall mark (as a patient observer will find cause to mark) resemblances and affinities more than accidental, between documents of widely different ages and countries; he will not only be contributing to the common stock what cannot fail to be available hereafter as raw material, but he will be helping to solve that great problem which has hitherto in part eluded the most earnest inquiries, the investigation of the true laws and principles of COMPARATIVE CRITICISM.

The last-mentioned term has been happily applied by Tregelles to that delicate and important process, whereby we seek to determine the *comparative* value, and trace the mutual relation, of authorities of every kind upon which the original text of the N.T. is based. Thus explained (and in this enlarged sense scholars have willingly accepted it), its researches may be pursued with diligence and interest, without reference to the maintenance or refutation of any particular system or scheme of recensions. The mode of procedure is experimental and tentative, rather than dogmatical; the facts it gradually develops will eventually (as we trust) put us on the right road, although for the present we meet with much that is uncertain, perplexing, ambiguous. It has already enabled critics in some degree to classify the documents with which they have to deal; it may possibly lead them, at some future period, to the establishment of principles more general, and therefore more simple, than we can now conceive likely or even possible to be attained to.

1. In the course of investigations thus difficult and precarious, designed to throw light on a matter of such vast consequence as the genuine condition of the text of Scripture, one thing would appear at first sight almost too clear for argument, too self-evident to be disputed,—that it is both our wisdom and our duty *to weigh the momentous subject at issue in all its parts*, shutting out from the mind no source of information which can reasonably be supposed capable of influencing our decision. Nor can such a course become less right or expedient because it must perforce involve us in laborious, extensive, and prolonged examination of a vast store of varied and voluminous testimony. It is essential

that divines should strive to come to definite conclusions respecting disputed points of sacred criticism; it is not necessary that these conclusions should be drawn within a certain limited period, either this year, or even in the lifetime of our generation. Hence such a plan as that advocated by Lachmann, for abridging the trouble of investigation by the arbitrary rejection of the great mass of existing evidence, must needs be condemned for its rashness by those who think their utmost pains well bestowed in such a cause; nor can we consistently praise the determination of others, who, shunning the more obvious errors into which Lachmann fell, yet follow his example in constructing the text of the N. T. on a foundation somewhat less narrow, but scarcely more firm than his. As the true science of Biblical criticism is in real danger of suffering harm from the efforts of disciples of this school, it cannot be out of place if we examine the pleas which have been urged in vindication of their scheme, and assign (as briefly as we may) our reasons for believing that its apologists are but labouring in vain.

2. *Brevis vita, ars longa.* For this lawful cause, if for no other, the most ardent student of Biblical criticism would fain embrace some such system as is advocated by Lachmann and his followers, if only it could be done in tolerable safety. The process of investigation might thus be diminished twentyfold, and the whole subject brought within a compass not too vast for one man's diligence or the space of an ordinary lifetime. The simplicity and comparative facility of this process of resorting to the few for instruction hitherto supposed to be diffused among the many, has created in its favour a strong and not unnatural prejudice, which has yielded, so far as it has yet yielded at all, to nothing but the stubborn opposition of indisputable facts. It will also readily be admitted, that certain principles, not indeed peculiar to this theory, but brought by it into greater prominence, are themselves most reasonable and true. No one will question, for example, that 'if the reading of the ancient authorities in general is unanimous, there can be but little doubt that it should be followed, whatever may be the later testimonies; for it is most improbable that the independent testimony of early MSS., versions, and Fathers should accord with regard to something entirely groundless' (Tregelles, N. T.,

Introductory Notice, p. 2). No living man, possessed of a tincture of scholarship, would dream of setting up testimony exclusively modern against the unanimous voice of antiquity. The point on which we insist is briefly this:—that the evidence of ancient authorities is anything but unanimous; that they are perpetually at variance with each other, even if we limit the term ancient within the narrowest bounds. Shall it include, among the manuscripts of the Gospels, none but the five oldest copies Codd. ℵABCD[1]? The reader has but to open the first recent critical work he shall meet with, to see them scarcely ever in unison; perpetually divided two against three, or perhaps four against one. All the readings these venerable monuments contain must of course be *ancient*, or they would not be found where they are; but they cannot all be true. So again, if our search be extended to the versions and primitive Fathers, the same phenomenon unfolds itself, to our grievous perplexity and disappointment. How much is contained in Cureton's Syriac and the Old Latin for which no Greek original can now be alleged? Do not the earliest ecclesiastical writers describe readings as existing and current in their copies, of which few traces can be met with at present[2]? If the question be fairly proposed, 'What right have we to set virtually aside the agreement in the main of our oldest uncials, at the distance of one or two centuries—of which, owing probably to the results of persecution, we have no MS. remains—with the citations of the primitive Fathers, and with the earliest versions?': the answer must be rendered, without hesitation, *no right whatever*. Where the oldest of these authorities really agree, we accept their united testimony as practically conclusive. It is not at all our design to seek our readings from the later uncials, supported as they usually are by the mass of cursive manuscripts; but to employ their confessedly secondary evidence in those numberless instances wherein their elder brethren are hopelessly at variance[3]. We do not claim for the recent documents the high consideration and deference fitly

[1] It should be also observed that ΦΣ containing SS. Matthew and Mark are probably older than D.

[2] E. g. Matt. i. 18; Acts viii. 37 for Irenaeus: Acts xiii. 33 for Origen. It is rare indeed that the express testimony of a Father is so fully confirmed by the oldest copies as in John i. 28, where Βηθανίᾳ, said by Origen to be *σχεδὸν ἐν πᾶσι τοῖς ἀντιγράφοις*, actually appears in ℵ*ABC*.

[3] This view is controverted in Burgon's 'Remains.'

reserved for a few of the oldest; just as little do we think it right to pass them by in silence, and allow to them no more weight or importance than if they had never been written. 'There are passages,' to employ the words of a very competent judge, 'where the evidence of the better cursives may be of substantial use in confirming a good reading, or in deciding us between two of nearly equal merit to place one in the text and assign the other to the margin [1].'

3. It may readily be supposed that the very few manuscripts which, being ancient themselves, are regarded by the school of Lachmann as alone preserving an ancient and genuine form, have not been selected as virtually the sole authorities for the settling of the sacred text, except for reasons which those who thus adopt them regard as weighty, and which merit at any rate our best consideration before we put them aside as insufficient. The great uncials, we are told, are treated with so much deference, not only or chiefly because they are old, but because they have been rigorously tested and have proved on trial to deserve the confidence which has been reposed in them. The process of investigation shall now be stated, as fairly and even favourably as possible. It is not worth while, as it certainly is not our desire, to snatch a transient advantage by misrepresenting the views we are controverting. We would rather comprise in our own system all that is sound and exact in them, while we withstand the attempt to carry them beyond the limits which they may legitimately occupy, and refuse to generalize on the strength of facts which are only partially true.

We have already laid down the axiom admitted by all, that manuscripts of the original hold the first rank among our critical materials; versions, and, yet more, the citations of ecclesiastical authors being subordinate to them. Yet whatever other disadvantages the Patristic writings may labour under, we are at

[1] Mr. A. A. Vansittart, Journal of Philology, vol. ii. No. 3, p. 35. I suppose too that Mr. Hammond means much the same thing when he says, 'It seems almost superfluous to affirm that *every element of evidence must be allowed its full weight;* but it is a principle that must not be forgotten.' (Outlines of Textual Criticism, p. 93, 2nd edition.) Truly it is not superfluous to insist on this principle when we so perpetually find the study of the cursive manuscripts disparaged by the use of what we may venture to call the Caliph Omar's argument, that if they agree with the older authorities their evidence is superfluous, if they contradict them, it is necessarily false.

any rate certain respecting the age in which they were composed, the works themselves being assumed to be authentic. If Irenaeus, or Tertullian, or Origen, expressly assure us that particular words which they name were read in their copies of Scripture, we cannot withstand their testimony that such words were really found in manuscripts of the New Testament in the second and third centuries, one or two hundred years before Codd. אB were in existence. If, therefore, we take a various reading of the text for which any one of these venerable men has vouched, and observe that it is supported perhaps by a few manuscripts of various ages, then by a version or two, especially if they be natives of different countries, and flow together into the same stream from sources remote from each other;—the rather too if the reading be plausible and even probable in itself:—and if, after having formed an opinion that on the whole it deserves to be respectfully considered, we then turn to א or B, or to both, and discover the same reading in them also:—not only has the variation itself made out an urgent case for our acceptance, but the character of א and B as faithful witnesses is largely enhanced. It is moreover evident, that if the same method of investigation be pursued many times over with the same, or something approaching to the same success, the value of א and B as truthful codices will be proportionally increased.

A single good example of this process will make it yet more intelligible to the careful student. It shall be one that has been chosen for the purpose by more than one of the advocates of the system we are on the whole opposing. Of the two forms in which the Lord's Prayer is delivered to us, Matt. vi. 13 has the clause *ἀλλὰ ῥῦσαι ἡμᾶς ἀπὸ τοῦ πονηροῦ* in every known authority: in Luke xi. 4 the case is far otherwise. That Tertullian, when citing the words before and after it, should take no notice of it, would of itself prove little. Origen, however, once passes it by in like manner, once more expressly declares that it was not in St. Luke (*παρὰ τῷ Λουκᾷ σεσιώπηται*), a third time explains in his most happy manner why it was omitted by the one Evangelist, inserted by the other. The question thus raised sets us upon the inquiry what other evidence we have for rejecting the clause in St. Luke. It appears to be wanting in several Greek manuscripts, such as L, 1, 22, 57, 130 both Greek and Latin, 131, 226*, 237, 242, 426, 582, 604, and in the catenas annexed to 36,

237, 239, 253, 259, 426; several of these codices (as 57, 226, 242) not being much found in such company. It is absent from the Vulgate version, and apparently from some forms of the Old Latin, the rather as Augustine says that St. Luke gives five petitions in the Lord's Prayer, St. Matthew seven, and attributes the omission of our clause to some such reason as Origen had assigned. It is omitted also in the Armenian version, which, except for the later translation by Sahak from Syriac, might be supposed to differ *toto caelo* from the Latin in country and genius. The list is closed by the younger Cyril, a pure witness from another region, very different lines of evidence thus converging into one. Then comes the probability that if one of the Gospels contained the Lord's Prayer in a shorter form than the other, nothing was so likely as that a scribe in perfect innocence would supply what he considered an undoubted defect, without staying to reflect with Origen and Augustine that the two were delivered on different occasions, to different classes of persons, with different ends in view. Turning therefore now, with a strong case already made out for the omission of the clause, to ℵ and B, which have been hitherto kept out of sight, we find that B has not the disputed words at all, nor had ℵ by the first hand, but in one three centuries later. The clear result, so far as it goes, is at once to vindicate the claim of ℵB to high consideration, and to make out a formidable case against the genuineness of the six words involved. We say advisedly a formidable, not necessarily a fatal case, for the counter evidence is still very strong, and comes as much as that alleged above from different quarters, being also as early as widely diffused. It consists of Codd. ACDEFGHKMR[1] SUVΓΔΛΠ, of

[1] The evidence of Evan. R, which contains only the decisive letters ΝΗΡΟΥ·, is the more valuable, inasmuch as it has been alleged to support the readings of documents of the other class (which no doubt it often does) and thus to afford a confirmation of their authority; it cannot help them much when its vote is against them. On analyzing the 908 readings for which R is cited in Tischendorf's eighth edition, I find that it sides with A, the representative of the one class, 356 times; with its better reputed rival B 157 times, where A and B are at variance. It is with A alone of the great uncials 101 times, with B alone four, with ℵ alone five, with C alone (but C is lost in 473 places out of the 908) six; with D alone twenty-four. Some of its other combinations are instructive. It is with AC forty-two times and with ACL sixteen; with AD fifty-one and with ADL eighteen; with ℵB eleven and with ℵBL twenty-nine; with ℵL nine times; with AL nineteen; with BL fifteen; with CL never;

all cursives not named above, of the Old Latin *b c f ff i l q*, whereof *f* mostly goes with the Vulgate (*hiant a e*), the Bohairic, Peshitto, Curetonian, Harkleian Syriac (the Jerusalem not containing this week-day Lesson), and the Ethiopic versions. So far as this side as stated is weak at all, it lacks Patristic evidence (which cannot now be investigated for our purpose), and the balance of internal evidence is decidedly adverse to it.

4. The student may try the same experiments on two other passages often urged in this debate, Matt. v. 22, for which he will find the materials above, p. 255, and Matt. xix. 17, which will be discussed in Chap. XII. We freely admit that these are but a few out of many cases where the statements of ancient writers about whose date there can be no question are borne out by the readings of the more ancient codices, especially of א or B, or of the two united. Undoubtedly this circumstance lends a weight and authority to these manuscripts, and to the few which side with them, which their mere age would not procure for them: it does not entitle them to be regarded as virtually the only documents worthy of being consulted in the recension of the sacred text; as qualifying to be sole arbiters in critical questions relating to the New Testament, against whose decision there can be no appeal. Yet nothing less than this is claimed in behalf of one or two of them by their devoted admirers. In a court of justice, we are told, when once the evidence of a witness has been thoroughly probed and tested, it is received thenceforth as true, even on those points where it stands alone, and in the face of strong antecedent improbabilities. Now reasoning in metaphor has its advantages, as well for the sake of clearly expressing our meaning, as of making an impression on those we address; but it is attended with this grave inconvenience, that, since the analogy between no two things that can be compared is quite complete, we are sorely tempted to apply to the one of them properties which appertain exclusively to the other. In the present instance, besides the properties wherein documentary can be assimilated to oral testimony, such as

with DL twice. Cod. R stands unsupported by any of the preceding eighty-nine times, seldom without some countenance (but see Luke xi. 24 ἐκ), such as the Memphitic version, or later codices. In the places where its fragments coincide with those of Cod. Ξ (which is much more friendly to B) they agree 127 times, differ 105.

general accuracy and means of information, an important element is present in the latter, to which the former has nothing parallel, namely, moral character, that full persuasion of a witness's good faith and disinterested integrity to which a jury will often surrender, and rightly surrender, all earlier impressions and predilections. Of this we can have nothing in the case of the manuscripts of Scripture which we now possess. In the second century we have seen too many instances of attempts to tamper with the text of Scripture, some merely injudicious, others positively dishonest; but all this was over long before the scribes of the fourth and fifth centuries began their happy task, as simple and honest copyists of the older records placed before them. Let their testimony be received with attention at all times; let it be accepted as conclusive whensoever there are no grave reasons to the contrary, but let not their paramount authority shut out all other considerations, external and internal, which might guide us to the true reading of a passage; nor let us be so illogical as to conclude, because ℵ and B are sometimes right, that therefore they never are in the wrong [1].

The results of this excessive and irrational deference to one of our chief codices, that which he was so fortunate as to bring to the light twenty-five years ago, appears plainly in Tischendorf's eighth edition of the New Testament. That great critic had never been conspicuous for stability of judgement. His third edition was constructed almost without any reference to the cursive manuscripts, which, unless they be, what no one asserts or imagines, merely corrupt copies, or copies of copies, of existing uncials, must needs be the representatives of yet older codices which have long since perished: 'respectable ancestors' (as one has quaintly put the matter) 'who live only in their descendants' (Long, Ciceronis Verrin. Orat., Praef. p. vi) [2]. In Tischendorf's

[1] Dean Burgon avers that he is thoroughly convinced that 'no reading can be of real importance—I mean has a chance of being *true*—which is witnessed to exclusively by a very few copies, whether uncial or cursive. . . Nothing else are such extraordinary readings, *wherever they may happen to be found*, but fragments of primitive error, repudiated by the Church ('a witness and keeper of Holy Writ') in her corporate capacity.' (Letter in the *Guardian*, July 12, 1882.) I cannot go quite so far as this. [Dean Burgon has left his reply.]

[2] Not that we can in any way assent to the notions of Canon T. R. Birks (Essay on the right estimation of manuscript evidence in the text of the N. T., 1878), whose proposition that 'Constant increase of error is no certain and inevitable result of repeated transcription' (p. 33) is true enough in itself,

seventh edition, completed in 1859, that error was rectified, and the sum of textual variations between the third and seventh edition in consequence amounted to 1296, in no less than 595 of which (430 of the remainder being mere matters of spelling) he returned to the readings of the Received text, which he had before deserted, but to which fresh materials and larger experience had brought him back[1]. In the eighth edition another disturbing element is introduced, and that edition differs from his seventh in as many as 3369 places, to the scandal of the science of Comparative Criticism, as well as to his own grave discredit for discernment and consistency. The evidence of Cod. ℵ, supported or even unsupported by one or two authorities of any description, proved with him sufficient to outweigh all other witnesses, whether manuscripts, versions, or ecclesiastical writers.

The foregoing examination will probably have satisfied the student that we have no right to regard Cod. B as a second Infallible Voice proceeding from the Vatican, which, when it has once spoken, must put an end to all strife. Yet nothing less than this is claimed for it by writers, who yet have bestowed

though we cannot follow him when he adds that 'Errors, after they have found entrance, may be removed as well as increased in later copies. A careful scribe may not only make fewer mistakes of his own, but he may correct manifest faults of the manuscript from which he copies, and avail himself of the testimony of others, so as to revise and improve the text of that on which he chiefly relies.' Only such a scribe would no longer be a witness for the state of the text as extant in his generation, but a critical editor, working on principles of his own, whether good or bad alike unknown to us.

[1] Very pertinent to this matter is a striking extract from J. G. Reiche (a critic 'remarkable for extent and accuracy of learning, and for soundness and sobriety of judgement,' as Canon Cook vouches, Revised Version, p. 4), given in Bloomfield's 'Critical Annotations on the Sacred Text,' p. 5, note: 'In multis sanè N. T. locis lectionis variae, iisque gravissimi argumenti, de verâ scripturâ judicium firmum et absolutum, quo acquiescere possis, ferri nequit, nisi omnium subsidiorum nostrorum alicujus auctoritatis suffragia, et interna veri falsique indicia, diligenter explorata, justâ lance expendantur . . . Quod in causâ est, ut re non satis omni ex parte circumspectâ, non solum critici tantopere inter se dissentiant, sed etiam singuli sententiam suam toties retractent atque commutent.' In the same spirit Lagarde, speaking of the more recent manuscripts of the Septuagint, thus protests: 'Certum est eos non a somniis monachorum undecimi vel alius cujusquam saeculi natos, sed ex archetypis uncialibus aut ipsos aut intercedentibus aliis derivatos. Unde elucet criticum acuto judicio et doctrinâ probabili instructum codicibus recentioribus collectis effecturum esse (?) quid in communi plurium aliquorum archetypo scriptum fuerit' (Genesis, p. 19). Compare also Canon Cook, Revised Version of the First Three Gospels, p. 5.

much thought and labour on this controversy. 'Seeing that the Vatican manuscript does not contain one single passage that can be demonstrated to be spurious, or that by the evidence of other manuscripts and of the context, admits of just doubt as to its authenticity, a position that no other manuscript enjoys, man is bound to accept the testimony of that manuscript alone, as his present text of the sacred record, wherever he possesses its teaching[1].' I am not sure whether, if we conceded this writer's premisses, we should be bound to accept his conclusion; but the easiest way of disposing of his argument, as well as of that of persons, who, in heart agreeing with him, would hardly like to enunciate their principle so broadly, is presently to lay before the student a few readings of Cod. B, either standing alone, or supported by ℵ and others, respecting whose authenticity, or rather genuineness, some of us must be forgiven if we cherish considerable doubts. It is right, however, to declare that this discussion is forced upon us through no wish to dissemble the great value of the Codex Vaticanus, which in common with our opponents we regard as the most weighty single authority that we possess, but entirely by way of unavoidable protest against a claim for supremacy set up in its behalf, which can belong of right to no existing document whatsoever.

5. But indeed the theories of preceding critics, as well as the practical application of those theories to the sacred text, have been thrown into the shade by the more recent and elaborate publications of Drs. Hort and Westcott, briefly noticed in a preceding chapter, and claiming in this place our serious attention[2].

[1] 'So extravagant a statement could scarcely be deemed worthy of the elaborate confutation with which Dr. Scrivener has condescended to honour it' (*Saturday Review*, Aug. 20, 1881). Yet this scheme of 'Comparative Criticism made easy' has obtained, for its childlike simplicity, more acceptance than the reviewer could reasonably suppose. Dr. Hort, of course, speaks very differently: 'B must be regarded as having preserved not only a very ancient text, but a very pure line of very ancient text, and that with comparatively small depravation either by scattered ancient corruptions otherwise attested or by individualisms of the scribe himself. On the other hand, to take it as the sole authority except where it contains self-betraying errors, as some have done, is an unwarrantable abandonment of criticism, and in our opinion inevitably leads to erroneous results' (Introd. p. 250).

[2] The textual labours of the Cambridge duumvirate have received all the fuller consideration in the learned world by reason of their authors having been members of the New Testament Revision Company, in whose deliberations they

The system on which their text has been constructed has been vindicated, so far as vindication was possible, in Dr. Hort's 'Introduction,' a very model of earnest reasoning, calling for and richly rewarding the close and repeated study of all who would learn the utmost that can be done for settling the text of the New Testament on dogmatic principles. The germ of this theory can be traced in the speculations of Bentley and Griesbach; its authors would confess themselves on many points disciples of Lachmann, although their process of investigation is far more artificial than his. But there is little hope for the stability of their imposing structure, if its foundations have been laid on the sandy ground of ingenious conjecture: and since barely the smallest vestige of historical evidence has ever been alleged in support of the views of these accomplished editors, their teaching must either be received as intuitively true, or dismissed from our consideration as precarious, and even visionary. This much said by way of preface, we will endeavour to state the principles they advocate, as fairly and concisely as we can.

(*a*) The books of the New Testament, even the Holy Gospels themselves, could not well have been collected into one volume till some time after the death of St. John. During this early period, each portion of the inspired record would be circulated separately, until at length the four Gospels would be brought together in one book or Quaternion, and, since each component member had to receive a distinctive appellation, the simplest and

had a real influence, though, as a comparison of their text with that adopted by the Revisionists might easily have shown, by no means a preponderating one. I have carefully studied the chief criticisms which have been published on the controversy, without materially adding to the acquaintance with the subject which nearly eleven years of familiar conference with my colleagues had necessarily brought to me. The formidable onslaught on Dr. Hort's and Bishop Westcott's principles in three articles in the *Quarterly Review* [afterwards published together with additions in 'The Revision Revised'] especially in the number for April, 1882, and Canon F. C. Cook's 'Revised Version of the First Three Gospels' (1882), must be known to most scholars, and abound with materials from which a final judgement may be formed. 'The Ely Lectures on the Revised Version of the N. T.' (1882), which my friend and benefactor Canon Kennedy was pleased to inscribe to myself, are none the less valuable for their attempt to hold the balance even between opposite views of the questions at issue. The host of pamphlets and articles in periodicals which the occasion has called forth could hardly be enumerated in detail, but some of them have been used with due acknowledgement in Chap. XII.

the earliest headings would ascribe them to their respective authors, κατὰ Ματθαῖον, κατὰ Μάρκον, κ.τ.λ., the general title of the four being Εὐαγγέλιον. 'It is quite uncertain to what extent the whole N. T. was ever included in a single volume in Ante-Nicene times' (Hort, Introduction, pp. 223, 268), only that the Gospels had certainly been collected together when Justin Martyr wrote his first Apology between A. D. 139 and 150, inasmuch as he appeals thrice over to the Memoirs of the Apostles, which he once identifies with the Gospels (οἱ ἀπόστολοι ἐν τοῖς γενομένοις ὑπ' αὐτῶν ἀπομνημονεύμασιν ἃ καλεῖται εὐαγγέλια). Justin's disciple Tatian, again, composed a Harmony of the Four (Διὰ τεσσάρων), respecting the precise nature of which we have recently gained very seasonable information. 'The idea, if not the name, of a collective "Gospel" is implied throughout the well-known passage in the third book of Irenaeus, who doubtless received it from earlier generations' (Hort, p. 321). Hence it is not unreasonable to suspect that our great codices (ℵABC), which originally contained the whole N. T., may have been transcribed in their several parts from copies differing from each other in genius and in date. With such a possibility before us we ought not to be perplexed if the character of the text whether of Cod. A or of Cod. B differs in the Gospels from that which it bears in the Acts and the Epistles; or if Cod. C in the Apocalypse, and Cod. Δ in St. Mark, as has been already explained under those MSS., appear to belong to a family or group apart from that of the rest of their respective codices.

(β) At this remote period, during the first half of the second century, must have originated the wide variations from the prevailing text on the part of our primary authorities, both manuscripts and versions, which survive in Cod. Bezae of the Greek, and in the Old Latin codices or at least in some of them. The text they exhibit is distinguished as Western, and they have been joined by a powerful ally, the Curetonian Syriac. Critics of every school agree in admitting the primitive existence of this Western recension, and in their estimate of its general spirit. 'The earliest readings which can be fixed chronologically belong to it . . . But any prepossessions in its favour that might be created by this imposing early ascendency are for the most part soon dissipated by continuous study of its internal character' (Hort, p. 120). 'The chief and most constant characteristic of the Western readings is a love of paraphrase. Words, clauses, and even whole sentences were changed, omitted, and inserted with astonishing freedom, wherever it seemed that the meaning could be brought out with greater force and definiteness' (*ibid.* p. 122). 'Another equally important characteristic is a disposition to enrich the text at the cost of its purity by alterations or additions taken from traditional and perhaps from apocryphal and other non-biblical sources' (*ibid.* p. 123). Especially may we note among other interpolations the long passage after Matt. xx. 28 which we cited above, Vol. I. p. 8.

(γ) We now come to the feature which distinguishes Dr. Hort's system from any hitherto propounded; by the acceptance or non-acceptance of which his whole edifice must stand or fall. He seems to exaggerate the force of extant evidence when he judges that the corrupt Western 'was the more widely-spread text of Ante-Nicene times' (*ibid.* p. 120); but he tacitly assumes that many codices, versions, and ecclesiastical writers remained free from its malignant influence. The evidence of this latter class was preserved comparatively pure until the middle of the third century, when it was taken in hand, at some time between A. D. 250 and 350, 'at what date it is impossible to say with confidence, and even for conjecture the materials are scanty' (*ibid.* p. 137), by the Syrian bishops and Fathers of the Patriarchate of Antioch, who undertook (1) 'an authoritative revision at Antioch' of the Greek text, which (2) was then taken as a standard for a similar authoritative revision of the Syriac text, and (3) was itself at a later time subjected to a second authoritative revision, carrying out more completely the purposes of the first' (*ibid.* p. 137). Of this twofold authoritative revision of the Greek text, of this formal transmutation of the Curetonian Syriac into the Peshitto (for this is what Dr. Hort means, though his language is a little obscure), although they must have been of necessity public acts of great Churches in ages abounding in Councils General or Provincial, not one trace remains in the history of Christian antiquity; no one writer seems conscious that any modification either of the Greek Scriptures or of the vernacular translation was made in or before his time. It is as if the Bishops' Bible had been thrust out of the English Church service and out of the studies of her divines, and the Bible of 1611 had silently taken its place, no one knew how, or when, or why, or indeed that any change whatever had been made. Yet regarding his speculative conjecture as undubitably true, Dr. Hort proceeds to name the text as it stood before his imaginary era of transfusion a *Pre-Syrian* text, and that into which it was changed, sometimes *Antiochian*, more often *Syrian*[1]; while of the latter recension, though made deliberately, as our author believes, by the authoritative voice of the Eastern Church, he does not shrink from declaring that 'all distinctively Syrian readings must be at once rejected' (*ibid.* p. 119), thus making a clean sweep of all critical materials, Fathers, versions, manuscripts uncial or cursive, comprising about nineteen-twentieths of the whole mass, which do not correspond with his preconceived opinion of what a correct text ought to be (*ibid.* p. 163).

(δ) But one or two steps yet remain in this thorough elimination of useless elements. A few authorities still survive which are honoured as *Pre-Syrian*, and continued unaffected by the phantom revisions, which, for critical purposes, have reduced their colleagues to ignominious silence. Besides the Western, Dr. Hort has in reserve two other groups, the Alexandrian and the Neutral. The former retains a text essentially pure from Syrian (though not from Western) mixture, but its component members are portentously few in number, being tolerably void of corruption as regards the substance, with 'no incorporation of matter extraneous to the canonical text of the Bible, and no habitual or extreme license of paraphrase . . . the changes made having usually more to do with language than with matter, and being marked by an effort after correctness of phrase' (*ibid.* p. 131). There are no unmixed vouchers for this Non-Western, Pre-Syrian, Alexandrian class, though Cyril of Alexandria seems to come the nearest to purity (*ibid.* p. 141),

[1] We are concerned not with names but with things, so that Dr. Hort may give his *ignis fatuus* what appellation he likes, only why he calls it Syrian it is hard to determine. The notices connecting his imaginary revision with Lucian of Antioch which we have given above he feels to be insufficient, for he says no more than that 'the conjecture derives some little support from a passage of Jerome, which is not itself discredited by the precariousness of the modern theories which have been suggested by it' (Hort, p. 138).

then Origen, occasionally other Alexandrian Fathers, also the Sahidic, and especially the Bohairic version (*ibid.* p. 131). No extant MS. has preserved so many Alexandrian readings as Cod. L (*ibid.* p. 153). Cod. C has some, T and Ξ more: in the Gospels they are chiefly marked by the combination ℵCLXZ, 33 (*ibid.* p. 166). In Cod. A, for the Acts and Epistles, the Alexandrian outnumber both the Syrian and Western readings (Hort, p. 152), but they all are mere degenerations so far as they depart from Dr. Hort's standard

(ε) The *Neutral* type of text: so called because it is free from the glaring corruption of the Western, from the smooth assimilations of the Syrian, and from the grammatical purism of the Alexandrian. Only two documents come under this last head, Codd. B and ℵ, and of these two, when they differ, B is preferable to ℵ, which has a not inconsiderable Western element, besides that the scribe's bold and rough manner has rendered 'all the ordinary lapses due to rapid and careless transcription more numerous' than in B (*ibid.* p. 246). Yet, with certain slight exceptions which he carefully specifies, it is our learned author's belief '(1) that the readings of ℵB should be accepted as the true readings until strong internal evidence is found to the contrary, and (2) that no readings of ℵB can safely be rejected absolutely, though it is sometimes right to place them only on an alternative footing, especially where they receive no support from Versions and Fathers' (*ibid.* p. 225): and this their pre-eminence, in our critic's judgement, 'is due to the extreme, and, as it were, primordial antiquity of the common original from which the ancestries of the two MSS. have diverged, the date of which cannot be later than the earlier part of the second century, and may well be yet earlier' (*ibid.* p. 223).

That ℵB should thus lift up their heads against all the world is much, especially having regard to the fact that several versions and not a few Fathers are older than they: for, while we grant that a simple patristic citation, standing by itself, is of little value, yet when the context or current of exposition renders it clear what reading these writers had before them, they must surely for that passage be equivalent as authorities to a manuscript of their own age. Nor will Dr. Hort allow us to make any deduction from the weight of the united testimony of ℵB by reason of the curious fact, demonstrated as well to his satisfaction (Hort, p. 213) as to our own, that the scribe of B was the actual writer of parts of three distinct quires, forming three pairs of conjugate leaves of ℵ (*see* above, p. 96, note 1); but on this head we think he will find few readers to agree with him. His devotion to Cod. B when it stands alone is of necessity far more intelligent than that of the unnamed writer mentioned already, yet we believe that his implied confidence is scarcely the less misplaced. He is very glad when he can to find friends for his favourite, and discusses with great care the several binary combinations, such as BL, BC, BT, BΞ, BD (which last, indeed, is unsafe enough), AB, BZ, B 33 or BΔ (for St. Mark) in the Gospels; AB, BC, &c., in the rest of the N. T. (Hort, p. 227). He does not disparage the *subsingular* readings of B, meaning by this convenient, perhaps novel, term, the agreement of B with 'inferior Greek MSS., Versions, or Fathers, or combinations of documentary evidence of these kinds' (*ibid.* p. 230). But, when the worst comes to the worst, and Cod. B is left absolutely alone, its advocates need not despair, inasmuch as no readings of that manuscript, not involving clerical error (and 'the scribe reached by no means a high standard of accuracy,' *ibid.* p. 233), must be lightly or hastily rejected, so powerfully do they commend themselves on their own merits (*ibid.* p. 238). This transcendent excellency, however, belongs to it chiefly in the Gospels. In the Acts and Catholic Epistles, if the value of A increases as has been said, that of B is somewhat diminished; while in the Pauline Epistles a 'local Western element of B' (Hort, p. 240) brings it into the less reputable company of DFG or even of D alone. Hence in the formation of Westcott and Hort's Pauline text we sometimes meet with what appears the paradoxical result that the evidence of B alone is accepted, while that of B attended by other codices is laid aside as insufficient.

It is very instructive to compare the foregoing sketch of Dr. Hort's system, brief and inadequate, yet not we trust unfair, as it is, with the theory of Griesbach, for whose labours and genius we share much of his successor's veneration. As regards the modification of text called Western their views are nearly identical, only that Griesbach was necessarily ignorant of such important constituents of it as the Curetonian Syriac and the

Old Latin codices which have come to light since his day, and thus was exempted from the temptation to which Dr. Hort has unhappily yielded, of believing that Codd. ℵB, with all their comparative purity, represent a primitive text already corrupted by certain accretions from which the Western copies were free (*see* below, p. 299 and note 1): a violent supposition which seriously impairs the homogeneousness and self-consistency of his whole argument (Hort, pp. 175–6). Griesbach's Alexandrian class includes not only that which Dr. Hort understands by the name, but the later critic's *Neutral* class also, which indeed we fail to distinguish from the other by any marked peculiar characteristics. The more mixed text which Griesbach called Constantinopolitan, and which is represented by Cod. A in the Gospels, in part by Cod. C, the Latin Vulgate, and later authorities, differs from Dr. Hort's Syrian in much more than name. Wider and deeper researches have made it evident that Griesbach's notion of a gradual modernizing of the text used from the fourth century downwards in the Patriarchate of Constantinople, would not adequately account for the phenomena wherewith we have to deal. The general, almost universal, prevalence of such a departure from the readings of ℵB, met with in ecclesiastical writers at least as early in date as the parchment of those manuscripts themselves, can be explained by nothing less than a comprehensive, deliberate, authoritative recension of the sacred books, undertaken by the chief rulers of the Antiochene Church, accepted throughout that great Patriarchate, yet, in spite of all this, never noticed even in the way of passing reference by writers of any description from that period onwards, until its consequences, not its process, became known to eminent critics in the latter half of the nineteenth century. Nothing less than the exigency of his case could have driven our author to encumber himself with a scheme fraught with difficulties too great even for his skill to overcome.

Dr. Hort's system, therefore, is entirely destitute of historical foundation[1]. He does not so much as make a show of pretending to it: but then he would persuade us, as he has persuaded himself, that its substantial truth is proved by results; and for results of themselves to establish so very much, they must needs be unequivocal, and admit of no logical escape from the con-

[1] *See* Burgon's 'The Revision Revised,' pp. 271–288.

clusions they lead up to. But is this really the case? 'Two Members of the New Testament Company' of Revisers, in a temperate and very able pamphlet, have answered in the affirmative, and have assigned, after Dr. Hort, but with greater precision than he, *three* reasons 'for the belief that the Syrian text is posterior in origin to those which he calls Western, Alexandrian, and Neutral' (The Revisers and the Greek text of the N. T., p. 25). Granting for our present purpose the reality of this Syrian text, of whose independent existence we have no direct proof whatever, let us see what the three reasons will amount to.

(*a*) 'The first reason appears to us almost sufficient to settle the question by itself. It is founded on the observation . . . that the Syrian text presents numerous instances of readings which, according to all textual probability, must be considered to be combinations of early readings still extant.' . . . 'The reader will find in Dr. Hort's own pages abundant illustration of the fact in eight examples rigorously analyzed, which seem to supply a proof, as positive as the subject admits, that Syrian readings are posterior both to Western readings, and to other readings which may be properly described as Neutral' (*ibid.* pp. 25–6). But the misfortune is that the subject does not admit of positive proof; that what appears to one scholar 'textual probability,' appears to another a mere begging of the whole question. These eight examples have been re-analyzed by Canon Cook (Revised Version, pp. 205–18), and just before him by the *Quarterly Reviewer* (Revision Revised, pp. 258–65), writers not destitute either of learning or of natural acuteness, who would fain lead us to draw directly opposite inferences from Dr. Hort's. We will take but one specimen, the eighth and last, to make our meaning as clear as possible. 'This simple instance,' says Dr. Hort complacently, 'needs no explanation' (Hort, p. 104).

Luke xxiv. 53. *καὶ ἦσαν διαπαντὸς ἐν τῷ ἱερῷ, αἰνοῦντες καὶ εὐλογοῦντες τὸν Θεόν.* Thus it stands in the Received text with AC**FHKMSUVXΓΔΛΠ, all cursives, even those most esteemed by Westcott and Hort, with *c f g*, the Vulgate, Peshitto and Harkleian Syriac, the Armenian, and Ethiopic virtually (*εὐλογοῦντες καὶ αἰνοῦντες τὸν Θεόν*). This is called the Syrian reading.

The two so-termed Pre-Syrian forms are,

om. *αἰνοῦντες καὶ* ℵBCL*, Bohairic (Hort), Jerusalem Syriac. This is the Neutral and Alexandrian text.

om. *καὶ εὐλογοῦντες* D, *a b e ff l*, *gat. bodl.*, Bohairic (Tischendorf). This is the Western text.

The assumption of course is that the Syrian reading is a *conflation* of those of the other two classes, so forming a full but not overburdened clause. But if this *praejudicium* be met with the plea that D and the Latins perpetually, B and its allies very often, seek to abridge the sacred original, it would be hard to demonstrate that the latter explanation is more improbable than the former. Beyond this point of subjective feeling the matter cannot well be carried, whether on one side or the other.

Dr. Hort's other examples of conflation have the same double edge as Luke xxiv. 53, and there is no doubt that Dr. Sanday is right in asserting that like instances may be found wheresoever they are looked for ; but they prove nothing to any one who has not made up his mind beforehand as to what the reading ought to be. We have already confessed that there is a tendency on the part of copyists to assimilate the narratives of the several Gospels to each other ; and that such Harmonies as that of Tatian would facilitate the process ; that synonymous words are liable to be exchanged and harsh constructions supplied. Part of the value of the older codices arises from their comparative freedom from such corrections: but then this modernizing process is on the part of copyists unsystematic, almost unconscious ; it is wholly different from the deliberate formal emendations implied throughout Dr. Hort's volume.

(β) The second reason adduced by the *Two Revisers* 'is almost equally cogent' in their estimation. It is that while the Ante-Nicene Fathers 'place before us from separate and in some cases widely distant countries examples of Western, Alexandrian, and Neutral readings, it appears to be certain that before the middle of the third century we have no historical traces of readings which can properly be entitled distinctively Syrian' (The Revisers, &c., p. 26). Now the middle of the third century is the earliest period assigned by Dr. Hort for the inception of his phantom scheme of Syrian revision, and we feel sure that the epoch of Patristic evidence was not put thus early, in order to exclude Origen, whose support of his Alexandrian readings Griesbach found so partial and precarious (*see* above, p. 226). In fact Dr. Hort expressly states that 'The only period for which we have anything like a sufficiency of representative knowledge consists roughly of three-quarters of a century from about 175 to 250: but the remains of four eminent Greek Fathers, which range through this period, cast a strong light on textual history backward and forward. They are Irenaeus, of Asia Minor, Rome, and Lyons; his disciple Hippolytus, of Rome; Clement, of Athens and Alexandria; and his disciple, Origen, of Alexandria and Palestine' (Hort, p. 112). Even if the extant writings of these Fathers had been as rigorously examined and as thoroughly known as they certainly are not, 'their scantiness and the comparative vagueness of the textual materials contained in them' (*ibid.*) would hinder our drawing at present any positive conclusions regarding the sacred text as known to them. Even the slender specimens of controverted readings collected in our Chap. XII would suffice to prove that their evidence is by no means exclusively favourable to Dr. Hort's opinions, a fact for which we will allege but one instance out of many, the support given to the Received text by Hippolytus in that grand passage, John iii. 13[1].

There are three considerable works relating to the criticism of the N. T. still open to the enterprise of scholars, and they can hardly be taken up at all except by the fresh hopefulness of scholars yet young. We need a fuller and more comprehensive collation of the cursive manuscripts (Hort, pp. 76–7): 'a complete collection of all the fragments of the Thebaic New Testament is now the most pressing want in the province of textual criticism,' writes Bp. Lightfoot, and he might have added a better edition of the Bohairic also: but for the demands of the present controversy we must set in the first rank the necessity for a complete survey of the Patristic literature of the first five centuries at the least. While we concede to Dr. Hort that as

[1] Other examples may be seen in our notes in Chap. XII on Luke ii. 14 for Methodius; Luke xxii. 43, 44 for Hippolytus again; Luke xxiii. 34 for Irenaeus and Origen. Add Luke x. 1 for Irenaeus (p. 546, note 1); xxiii. 45 (Hippolytus); John xiii. 24 (Clem. Alex.); 2 Cor. xii. 7 (Iren. Orig.); Mark xvi. 17, 18 (Hippol.). *See* also Miller's 'Textual Guide,' pp. 84, 85, where 165 passages on fifteen texts are gathered from writers before St. Chrysostom.

a rule 'negative patristic evidence'—that derived from the mere silence of the writer, 'is of no force at all' (Hort, p. 201), and attach very slight importance to citations which are not express, it is from this source that we must look for any stable decision regarding the comparative purity in reference to the sacred autographs of the several classes of documents which have passed under our review.

(γ) Hence the second reason for supporting the text of Westcott and Hort urged by the *Two Revisers* relates to an investigation of facts hitherto but partially ascertained: the third, like the first, involves only matters of opinion, in which individual judgements and prepossessions bear the chief part. 'Yet a third reason is supplied by Internal Evidence, or, in other words, by considerations...of intrinsic or of Transcriptional Probability' (The Revisers &c., p. 26): and 'here,' they very justly add, "it is obvious that we enter at once into a very delicate and difficult domain of textual criticism, and can only draw our conclusions with the utmost circumspection and reserve' (*ibid.*). On the subject of Internal Evidence enough for our present purpose has been said, and Dr. Hort's Transcriptional head appears to be Bp. Ellicott's *paradiplomatic* under a more convenient name. Our author's discussion of what he calls the 'rudimental criticism' of Internal evidence (Hort, Part ii. pp. 19–72), if necessarily somewhat abstruse, is one of the most elaborate and interesting in his admirable volume. It is sometimes said that all reasoning is analytical, not synthetical; the reducing a foregone conclusion to the first principles on which it rests, rather than the building upon those first principles the materials wherewith to construct the conclusion. Of this portion of Dr. Hort's labours the *dictum* is emphatically true. Cod. B and its characteristic peculiarities are never out of the author's mind, and those lines of thought are closely followed which most readily lead up to the theory of that manuscript's practical impeccability. We allege this statement in no disparaging spirit, and it may be that Dr. Hort will not wholly disagree with us. Not only is he duly sensible of the precariousness of Intrinsic evidence, inasmuch as 'the uncertainty of the decision in ordinary cases is shown by the great diversity of judgement which is actually found to exist' (Hort, p. 21), but he boldly, and no less boldly than truly, intimates that in such cases the ultimate decision must rest with the individual critic: 'in almost all texts variations occur where personal judgement inevitably takes a large part in the final decision... Different minds will be impressed by different parts of the evidence as clearer than the rest, and so virtually ruling the rest: here therefore personal discernment would seem the surest ground for confidence' (*ibid.* p. 65). For the critic's confidence perhaps, not for that of his reader.

The process of grouping authorities, whether by considerations of their geographical distribution or (more uncertainly) according to their genealogy as inferred from internal considerations (*ibid.* pp. 49–65), occupies a large measure of Dr. Hort's attention. The idea has not indeed originated with him, and its occasional value will be frankly acknowledged in the ensuing pages, so that on this head we need not further enlarge. In conclusion we will say, that the more our Cambridge Professor's 'Introduction' is studied the more it grows upon our esteem for fulness of learning, for patience of research, for keenness of intellectual power, and especially for a certain marvellous readiness in accounting after some fashion for every new phenomenon which occurs, however apparently adverse to the acceptance of his own theory. With all our reverence for his genius, and gratitude for much that we have learnt from him in the course of our studies, we are compelled to repeat as emphatically as ever our strong conviction that the hypothesis to whose proof he has devoted so many laborious years, is destitute not only of historical foundation, but of all probability resulting from the internal goodness of the text which its adoption would force upon us [1].

This last assertion we will try to verify by subjoining a select

[1] For reasons which will be readily understood, we have quoted sparingly from the trenchant article in the *Quarterly Review*, April, 1882, but the following summary of the consequences of a too exclusive devotion to Codd. ℵB seems no unfit comment on the facts of the case: 'Thus it would appear that the Truth of Scripture has run a very narrow risk of being lost for ever to mankind. Dr. Hort contends that it more than half lay *perdu* on a forgotten shelf in the Vatican Library;—Dr. Tischendorf that it had found its way into a waste-paper basket in the convent of St. Catherine at the foot of Mount Sinai—from which he rescued it on February 4, 1859:—neither, we venture to think, a very likely supposition. We incline to believe that the Author of Scripture hath not by any means shown Himself so unmindful of the safety of the Deposit, as these learned persons imagine' (p. 365). The Revision Revised, p. 343.

number of those many passages in the N. T. wherein the two great codices ℵ and B, one or both of them, are witnesses for readings, nearly all of which, to the best of our judgement, are corruptions of the sacred originals[1].

6. Those who devote themselves to the criticism of the text of the New Testament have only of late come to understand the full importance of attending closely to the mutual connexion subsisting between their several materials of every description, whether manuscripts, versions, or Fathers. The study of *grouping* has been recently and not untruly said to be the foundation of all enduring criticism[2]. Now that theories about the formal recensions of whole classes of these documents have generally been given up as purely visionary, and the very word *families* has come into disrepute by reason of the exploded fancies it recalls, we can discern not the less clearly that certain groups of them have in common not only a general resemblance in regard to the readings they exhibit, but characteristic peculiarities attaching themselves to each group. Systematic or wilful corruption of the sacred text, at least on a scale worth taking into account, there would seem to have been almost none; yet the tendency to licentious paraphrase and unwarranted additions distinguished one set of our witnesses from the second century downwards; a bias towards grammatical and critical purism and needless omissions appertained to another; while

[1] *See* Appendix of passages at the end of this chapter. Yet while refusing without hesitation the claim of the *monstra* which follow to be regarded as a part of the sacred text, we are by no means insensible to the fact impressed upon us by the Dean of Llandaff, that there are readings which conciliate favour the more we think over them: it being the special privilege of Truth always to grow upon candid minds. We subjoin his persuasive words: 'It is deeply interesting to take note of the process of thought and feeling which attends in one's own mind the presentation of some unfamiliar reading. At first sight the suggestion is repelled as unintelligible, startling, almost shocking. By degrees, light dawns upon it—it finds its plea and its palliation. At last, in many instances, it is accepted as adding force and beauty to the context, and a conviction gradually forms itself that thus and not otherwise was it written.' (Vaughan, Epistle to Romans, Preface to the third edition, p. xxi.)

[2] Thus far we are in agreement with the 'Two Members of the N. T. Company,' however widely we may differ from their general views: 'The great contribution of our own times to a mastery over materials has been the clearer statement of the method of genealogy, and, by means of it, the corrected distribution of the great mass of documentary evidence' (p. 19). Only that arbitrary theories ought to be kept as far as possible out of sight.

a third was only too apt to soften what might seem harsh, to smooth over difficulties, and to bring passages, especially of the Synoptic Gospels, into unnatural harmony with each other. All these changes appear to have been going on without notice during the whole of the third and fourth centuries, and except that the great name of Origen is associated (not always happily) with one class of them, were rather the work of transcribers than of scholars. Eusebius and Jerome, in their judgements about Scripture texts, are more the echoes of Origen than independent investigators.

Now, as a first approximation to the actual state of the case, the several classes of changes which we have enumerated admit of a certain rude geographical distribution, one of them appertaining to Western Christendom and the earliest Fathers of the African and Gallic Churches (including North Italy under the latter appellation); a second to Egypt and its neighbourhood; the third originally to Syria and Christian Antioch, in later times to the Patriarchate of Constantinople. We have here, no doubt, much to remind us of Griesbach and his scheme of triple recensions, but with this broad distinction between his conclusions and those of modern critics, that whereas he regarded the existence of his families as a patent fact, and grounded upon it precise and mechanical rules for the arrangement of the text, we are now content to perceive no more than unconscious tendencies, liable to be modified or diverted by a thousand occult influences, of which in each single case it is impossible to form an estimate beforehand. Even that marked bias in the direction of adding to the record, which is the reproach of Codex Bezae and some of its compeers, and renders the text of the Acts as exhibited by DE, by the cursive 137, and the margin of the Harkleian Syriac, as unlike that commonly read as can well be imagined[1], is mixed up with a proneness to omissions which we should look for rather from another class of documents (e. g. the rejection of *ψευδόμενοι* Matt. v. 11), and which in the latter part of St. Luke's Gospel almost suggests the idea of representing an earlier edition than that now in ordinary use,

[1] So that we may be sure what we should have found in Cod. D, and with high probability in Cod. E, were they not defective, when in Acts xxvii. 5 we observe *δι' ἡμερῶν δεκάπεντε* inserted after *διαπλεύσαντες* in 137, 184, and the Harkleian margin with an asterisk; as also when we note in Acts xxviii. 16 *ἔξω τῆς παρεμβολῆς* before *σύν* in the last two and in *demid.*

yet proceeding from the Evangelist's own hand (*see* p. 18)[1]. Again, the process whereby the rough places are made plain and abrupt constructions rounded, is abundantly exemplified in the readings of the great uncial A, supported as it is by the mass of later manuscripts (e. g. Mark i. 27; Acts xv. 17, 18; xx. 24); yet in innumerable instances (*see* Appendix to this chapter) these self-same codices retain the genuine text of the sacred writers which their more illustrious compeers have lost or impaired.

Hence it follows that in judging of the character of a various reading proposed for our acceptance, we must carefully mark whether it comes to us from many directions or from one. And herein the native country of the several documents, even when we can make sure of it, is only a precarious guide. If the Ethiopic or the Armenian versions have really been corrected by the Latin Vulgate, the geographical remoteness of their origin must go for nothing where they agree with the latter version. The relation in which Cod. L and the Bohairic version stand to Cod. B is too close to allow them their full value as independent witnesses unless when they are at variance with that great uncial, wheresoever it may have been written: the same might be said of the beautiful Latin fragment *k* from Bobbio. To whatever nations they belong, their resemblances are too strong and perpetual not to compel us to withhold from them a part of the consideration their concord would otherwise lay claim to. The same is incontestably the case with the Curetonian and margin of the Harkleian Syriac in connexion with Cod. D. Wide as is the region which separates Syria from Gaul, there

[1] E. g. Luke xxiv. 3 τοῦ κυρίου Ἰησοῦ omitted by D, *a b e ff*[2] *l*; ver. 6 οὐκ ἔστιν ὧδε ἀλλὰ ἠγέρθη (comp. Mark xvi. 6), omitted by the same; ver. 9 ἀπὸ τοῦ μνημείου by the same, by *c* and the Armenian; the whole of ver. 12, by the same (except *ff*[2]) with *fuld.*, but surely not by the Jerusalem Syriac, even according to Tischendorf's showing, or by Eusebius' canon, for he knew the verse well (comp. John xx. 5); ver. 36 καὶ λέγει αὐτοῖς, εἰρήνη ὑμῖν omitted by D, *a b e ff*[2] *l* as before (comp. John xx. 19, 26); the whole of ver. 40, omitted by the same and by Cureton's Syriac (comp. John xx. 20); ver. 51 καὶ ἀνεφέρετο εἰς τὸν οὐρανόν and ver. 52 προσκυνήσαντες αὐτόν omitted by the same and by Augustine, the important clause in ver. 51 by א* also, and consequently by Tischendorf. Yet, as if to show how mixed the evidence is, D deserts *a b ff*[2] *l* when, in company with a host of authorities, both manuscripts and versions (*f q*, Vulgate, Bohairic, Syriac, and others), they annex καὶ ἀπὸ μελισσίου κηρίου to the end of ver. 42. *See* also Luke x. 41, 42; xxii. 19, 20, discussed in Chap. XII.

must have been in very early times some remote communication by which the stream of Eastern testimony or tradition, like another Alpheus, rose up again with fresh strength to irrigate the regions of the distant West. The Peshitto Syriac leans at times in the same direction, although both in nation and character it most assimilates to the same class as Cod. A.

With these, and it may be with some further reservations which experience and study shall hereafter suggest, the principle of grouping must be acknowledged to be a sound one, and those lines of evidence to be least likely to lead us astray which converge from the most varied quarters to the same point. It is strange, but not more strange than needful, that we are compelled in the cause of truth to make one stipulation more: namely, that this rule be henceforth applied impartially in all cases, as well when it will tell in favour of the Received text, as when it shall help to set it aside. To assign a high value to cursive manuscripts of the best description (such as 1, 33, 69, 157, Evst. 259, or 61 of the Acts), and to such uncials as LRΔ, or even as ℵ or C, whensoever they happen to agree with Cod. B, and to treat their refined silver as though it had been suddenly transmuted into dross when they come to contradict it, is a practice too plainly unreasonable to admit of serious defence, and can only lead to results which those who uphold it would be the first to deplore[1].

7. It is hoped that the general issue of the foregoing discussion may now be embodied in these four practical rules[2]:—

(1) That the true readings of the Greek New Testament cannot safely be derived from any one set of authorities, whether manuscripts, versions, or Fathers, but ought to be the result of

[1] So of certain of the chief versions we sometimes hear it said that they are less important in the rest of the N.T. than in the Gospels; which means that in the former they side less with ℵB.

[2] Canon Kennedy, whose 'Ely Lectures' exhibit, to say the least, no prejudice against the principles enunciated in Dr. Hort's Introduction, is good enough to commend the four rules here set forth to the attention of his readers (p. 159, note). The first three were stated in my first edition (1861), the fourth added in the second edition (1874), and, while they will not satisfy the advocates of extreme views on either side, suffice to intimate the terms on which the respective claims of the uncial and cursive manuscripts, of the earlier and the more recent authorities, may, in my deliberate judgement, be equitably adjusted.

a patient comparison and careful estimate of the evidence supplied by them all.

(2) That where there is a real agreement between all documents containing the Gospels up to the sixth century, and in other parts of the New Testament up to the ninth, the testimony of later manuscripts and versions, though not to be rejected unheard, must be regarded with great suspicion, and, UNLESS UPHELD BY STRONG INTERNAL EVIDENCE, can hardly be adopted[1].

(3) That where the more ancient documents are at variance with each other, the later uncial and cursive copies, especially those of approved merit, are of real importance, as being the surviving representatives of other codices, very probably as early, perhaps even earlier, than any now extant[1].

(4) That in weighing conflicting evidence we must assign the highest value not to those readings which are attested by the greatest number of witnesses, but to those which come to us from several remote and independent sources, and which bear the least likeness to each other in respect to genius and general character.

[1] Dean Burgon held that too much deference is here paid to the mere antiquity of those which happen to be the oldest MSS., but are not the oldest authorities. He would therefore enlarge the grounds of judgement.

APPENDIX TO CHAPTER X.

Matt. vi. 8. The transparent gloss ὁ θεός is inserted before ὁ πατὴρ ὑμῶν by Codd. ℵ*B and the Sahidic version[1].

Ver. 22. Ὁ λύχνος τοῦ σώματός ἐστιν ὁ ὀφθαλμός σου B, *a b c ff*[1] *n*[1.2] *h l*, the printed Vulgate, some Latin writers, and the Ethiopic. The addition of σου is more strongly attested in Luke xi. 34 by ℵ*ABCDM, but is intolerable in either place.

Matt. xvi. 21. Ἀπὸ τότε ἤρξατο ἰησοῦς χριστός: so the first hands of ℵ and B, with the Bohairic version only, their very frequent companion.

Matt. xxvii. 28. On the impossible reading of ℵ[c]BD, *a b c ff*[2] *q*, and a few others, enough has been said in Chap. VII. p. 234.

Ver. 49. We are here brought face to face with the gravest interpolation yet laid to the charge of B, whose tendency is usually in the opposite direction. Westcott and Hort alone among the editors feel constrained to insert in the text, though enclosed in their double brackets and regarded as 'most probably an interpolation,' a sentence which neither they nor any other competent scholar can easily believe that the Evangelist ever wrote[2]. After σώσων αὐτόν are set the following words borrowed from John xix. 34, with a slight verbal change, and representing that the Saviour was pierced before his death: ἄλλος δὲ λαβὼν λόγχην ἔνυξεν αὐτοῦ τὴν πλευράν, καὶ ἐξῆλθεν ὕδωρ καὶ αἷμα. Thus we read in ℵBCLU (which has εὐθέως before ἐξῆλθεν αἷμα καὶ ὕδωρ) Γ, 5, 48, 67, 115, 127*, five good manuscripts of the Vulgate, *Kells*, *gat.*, *mm.*, *chad.*, *mac-regol.*, and *Oxon.*, *C. C.* (*not* in *Bodl.*), *Harl.* 1023 and 1802*, and the margin of 1 E. VI, the Jerusalem Syriac once when the Lesson occurs, and the Ethiopic. Chrysostom thus read in his copy, but used the clause with so little reflection that he regarded the Lord as dead already. Severus of Antioch [d. 539], who himself protested against this gross corruption, tells us that Cyril of Alexandria as well as Chrysostom received it. A scholion found in Cod. 72 refers this addition εἰς τὸ καθ' ἱστορίαν εὐαγγέλιον Διοδώρου καὶ Τατιάνου καὶ ἄλλων διαφόρων ἁγίων πατέρων, on the authority of Chrysostom; and from the unintentional blunders of Harmonists like Tatian such an insertion might very well have crept in. The marvel is that it found favour so widely as it did[3].

[1] The harmony subsisting between B and the Sahidic in characteristic readings, for which they stand almost or quite alone, is well worth notice: e. g. Acts xxvii. 37; Rom. xiii. 13; Col. iii. 6; Heb. iii. 2; 1 John ii. 14; 20.

[2] 'The intrinsic evidence seems immoveable against the insertion.' Textual Criticism of the N. T., B. B. Warfield, D.D., p. 135.

[3] Yet in Penn's 'Annotations to the Vatican Manuscripts' (1837) 'The restoration of this verse to its due place' is described as 'the most important

Matt. xxviii. 19. βαπτίσαντες occurs only in BD (whose Latin has *baptizantes*), as though Baptism were to precede instruction in the faith. Tregelles alone dares to place this reading in the text: Westcott and Hort have it in their margin.

Mark iii. 14, 16. After noticing the evidence which supported the corrupt sentence in Matt. xxvii. 49, we are little disposed to accept what is in substance the same for such feeble glosses as are afforded us in these two verses; namely, οὓς καὶ ἀποστόλους ὠνόμασεν after δώδεκα in ver. 14 (derived from Luke vi. 13), and καὶ ἐποίησε τοὺς δώδεκα at the beginning of ver. 16. Westcott and Hort receive both clauses, Tischendorf only the latter, with ℵBC*Δ and an Ethiopic manuscript: yet the former, if less likely to be genuine, is the better supported. It is found in ℵBC*Δ (with some variation), in 13, 28, 69, 124, 238, 346, the Bohairic, the margin of the Harkleian Syriac, the Ethiopic, the Arabic of the Polyglott: a goodly array from divers sources to uphold so bad a reading.

Mark vi. 2. οἱ πολλοί is read by Westcott and Hort (so Tischendorf) instead of πολλοί with BL, 13, 28, 69, 346. Three out of the four cursives belong to Professor Ferrar's group.

Ver. 22. In the room of τῆς θυγατρὸς αὐτῆς τῆς Ἡρωδιάδος a serious variation of ℵBDLΔ, 238, 473, 558 is admitted into the text by Westcott and Hort, τῆς θυγατρὸς αὐτοῦ (+τῆς 238, 558) Ἡρῳδιάδος, thus bringing St. Mark into direct contradiction with Josephus, who expressly states that the wretched girl was named Salome, and was the daughter of Herod Philip by Herodias, who did not leave her husband till after Salome's birth (Josephus, Antiq., lib. xviii. ch. v. § 4). Add to this the extreme improbability that even Herod the Tetrarch should have allowed his own child to degrade herself in such wise as Salome did here, or that she could not have carried her point with her father without resorting to licentious allurements. We must therefore regard αὐτοῦ as certainly false, while αὐτῆς strongly expresses the writer's feeling that even Herodias could stoop so low, and being used emphatically has so much offended a few that they omit it altogether. Such are 1, 118, 209, and some versions (*b c f*, the Bohairic, Armenian, Ethiopic, and Gothic) which did not understand it. Tischendorf was hardly right in adding the Peshitto to the list[1].

Mark ix. 1. ὧδε τῶν for τῶν ὧδε (ἑστηκότων) is the almost impossible reading of BD*, *c k** (*a d q n* are uncertain), adopted the more readily by Tischendorf, Tregelles, Westcott and Hort, because all have the proper order τῶν ὧδε in Matt. xvi. 28.

Mark xiii. 33. Lachmann, Tischendorf, Westcott and Hort reject (Tregelles more fitly sets within brackets) καὶ προσεύχεσθε with BD, 122, and the Latin *a c k* and *tol.** of the Vulgate only. It is in the favour of the two words that they cannot have come from the parallel place in

circumstance of this [sc. his own] revision.' Its omission is imputed to 'the undue influence of a criticism of Origen [ἤδη δὲ αὐτοῦ ἀποθανόντος], whom Jerome followed.'

[1] 'This gross perversion of the truth, alike of Scripture and of history—a reading as preposterous as it is revolting,' is the vigorous protest of Dean Burgon, The Revision Revised, p. 68, note.

St. Matthew (ch. xxiv. 42), nor is the preceding verb the same in ch. xiv. 38. Here even ℵLΔ side against B with AC and all other authorities, including the Egyptian and most Latin, as well as the Syriac versions.

Luke iv. 44. The wonderful variation Ἰουδαίας is brought into the text of Hort and Westcott, the true reading Γαλιλαίας being banished to their margin. Their change is upheld by a strong phalanx indeed: ℵBCLQR, 1, 21, 71, Evst. 222, 259 and some twenty other cursives (Evan. 503 and two Lectionaries read αὐτῶν instead of either), the Bohairic and the text of the Harkleian: authorities enough to prove anything not in itself impossible, as Ἰουδαίας is in this place. Not only is Galilee the scene of the events recorded immediately before and after the present verse, but the passage is manifestly parallel to Mark i. 39. The three Synoptic Gospels are broadly distinguished from that of St. John by their silence respecting the Lord's ministry in Judaea before He went up to the last passover. Yet Alford *in loco*, while admitting that 'our narrative is thus brought into the more startling discrepancy with that of St. Mark, in which unquestionably the same portion of the sacred history is related,' most strangely adds, 'Still these are considerations which must not weigh in the least degree with the critic. It is his province simply to track out what is the sacred text, not what, in his own feeble and partial judgement, *it ought to have been.*'

Luke vi. 48. It is surprising how a gloss so frigid as διὰ τὸ καλῶς οἰκοδομῆσθαι αὐτήν could have been accepted by Tischendorf, Tregelles, Westcott and Hort, in the room of τεθεμελίωτο γὰρ ἐπὶ τὴν πέτραν, chiefly, it may be presumed, because the latter is the expression of St. Matthew (ch. vii. 25). Yet such is the reading of ℵBLΞ, of the two best cursives 33, 157, of the Bohairic (with some variation in its copies), of the margin of the Harkleian, and of Cyril of Alexandria. The Ethiopic preserves both forms. As the present οἰκοδομοῦντι early in the verse involves a plain contradiction when compared with the perfect οἰκοδομῆσθαι at the end, Tregelles changes the latter into οἰκοδομεῖσθαι on the feeble authority of the third hand of B, of 33, and possibly of 157.

Luke viii. 40. For αὐτόν after προσδοκῶντες we find τὸν θεόν in ℵ only. Of course the variation is quite wrong, but it is hard to see the pertinency of Dr. Vance Smith's hint (*Theological Review*, July, 1875) 'that it cannot have got in by accident.'

Luke x. 1. This case is interesting, as being one wherein B (not ℵ) is at variance with the very express evidence of the earliest ecclesiastical writers, while it makes the number of these disciples, not seventy, but seventy-two [1]. With B are DM, also R ('ita enim certè omnino videtur,'

[1] 'Post enim duodecim apostolos septuaginta alios Dominus noster ante se misisse invenitur; septuaginta autem nec octonario numero neque denario' (Irenaeus, p. 146, Massuet). Tertullian, just a little later (re-echoed by the younger Cyril), compares the Apostles with the twelve wells at Elim (Ex. xv. 27), the seventy with the three-score and ten palm-trees there (Adv. Marc. iv. 24). So Eusebius thrice, Basil and Ambrose. On the other hand in the Recognitions of Clement, usually assigned to the second or third century, the number adopted is seventy-two, 'vel hoc modo recognitâ imagine Moysis' and of his

Tisch., Monum. sacra inedita, vol. ii. Proleg. p. xviii), in the prefixed table of τίτλοι (Vol. I. p. 57, *n*), its text being lost, Codd. 1, 42, *a c e g*[1.2] *? l*, the Vulgate, Curetonian Syriac, and Armenian. Lachmann with Westcott and Hort insert δύο, but within brackets, for the evidence against it is overwhelming both in number and in weight: namely, Codd. ℵACEGHKLSUVXΓΔΛΞΠ, all other cursives, *b f g* of the Old Latin, the Bohairic, the three other Syriac, the Gothic, and Ethiopic versions.

Luke xiv. 5. Here again we have a strong conviction that ℵ, though now in the minority, is more correct than B, supported as the latter is by a dense array of witnesses of every age and country. In the clause τίνος ὑμῶν ὄνος ἢ βοῦς of the Received text all the critical editors substitute υἱὸς for ὄνος, which introduces a bathos so tasteless as to be almost ludicrous[1]. Yet υἱὸς is found with or without ὁ before it in AB (*hiant* CF)EGHMSUVΓΔΛ, in no less than 125 cursive copies already cited by name[2] (also υἱὸς ὑμῶν Evst. 259), in *e f g*, the Sahidic, Peshitto and Harkleian[3] Syriac versions: Cod. 508 and the Curetonian combine both forms υἱὸς ἢ βοῦς ἢ ὄνος, and Cod. 215 has υἱὸς ἢ ὄνος without βοῦς. Add to these Cyril of Alexandria (whose words are cited in catenas, as in the scholia to X, 253, 259), Titus of Bostra the commentator, Euthymius, and Theophylact. For ὄνος are ℵKLXΠ, 1, 33, 66 *secundâ manu*, 69 (ὄρος), 71, 207 *sec. man.*, 211, 213, 407, 413, 492, 509, 512, 549, 550, 555, 556, 569, 570, 599, 602, and doubtless others not cited: also the text of X, 253, 259 in spite of the annexed commentary; of the versions *a b c i l* of the Old Latin, the Vulgate, Bohairic, Jerusalem Syriac, Armenian, and Ethiopic (*bos eius aut asinus*), though the Slavonic codices and Persic of the Polyglott make for υἱός. Cod. 52 (*sic*) and the Arabic of the Polyglott omit ὄνος ἤ, while D has πρόβατον (*ovis d*) for ὄνος (comp. Matt. xii. 11), and 557 exhibits βοῦς ἢ ὄνος. YC or OIC mistaken as the contraction for YIOC is a mere guess, and we are safest here in clinging to common sense against a preponderance of outward evidence.

Luke xv. 21. Here by adding from ver. 19 ποίησόν με ὡς ἕνα τῶν μισθίων σου (placed in the text by Westcott and Hort within brackets) the great codices ℵBD, with UX, 33, 512, 543, 558, 571, a catena, and four manuscripts of the Vulgate (*bodl. gat. mm. tol.*), manage to keep out of sight that delicate touch of true nature which Augustine points out, that the son never carried out his purpose of offering himself for a hireling, 'quod post osculum patris generosissime jam dedignatur.'

Luke xvi. 12. It is hard to tell how far thorough scholars and able critics are prepared to push a favourite theory, when Westcott and Hort place τὸ ἡμέτερον τίς δώσει ὑμῖν in the text, reserving ὑμέτερον for the margin. Not to mention that the interchange of η and υ in these pro-

elders, traditionally set down at that number. Compare Num. xi. 16. Epiphanius, Hilary (Scholz), and Augustine are also with Cod. B.

[1] To enable us to translate 'a son, nay even an ox,' would require ἢ καί, which none read The argument, moreover, is one *a minori ad majus*. Compare Ex. xxi. 33 with Ex. xxiii. 4; ch. xiii. 15.

[2] Let me add *ex meo* Codd. 22, 219, 492, 547, 549, 558, 559, 576, 582, 584, 594, 596, 597, 598, 601, being no doubt a large majority of cursives. So Cod. 662, apparently after correction.

[3] But not in the Beirût MS. discovered in 1877 by Dr. Is. H. Hall.

nouns is the most obstinate of all known itacisms, and one to which B is especially prone (e. g. Acts xvii. 28; 1 Pet. ii. 24; 1 John ii. 25; iii. 1, Vol. I. p. 11), ἡμέτερον is found only in BL, Evst. 21, and Origen once: in 157, *e i l*, and in Tertullian twice it is softened down to ἐμόν.

Luke xxi. 24: ἄχρι οὗ πληρωθῶσιν [καὶ ἔσονται] καιροὶ ἐθνῶν. The words within brackets appear thus in Westcott and Hort's text alone; what possible meaning can be assigned to them in the position they there occupy it is hard to see. They are obviously derived by an error of the scribe's eye from καὶ ἔσονται (the reading of ℵBD, &c.) at the beginning of ver. 25. This unintelligible insertion is due to B; but L, the Bohairic, and a codex cited in the Harkleian margin also have it with another καιροί prefixed to καὶ ἔσονται. D runs on thus: ἄχρις οὗ πληρωθῶσιν καὶ ἔσονται σημεῖα (om. καιροὶ ἐθνῶν). Those who discover some recondite beauty in the reading of B compare with this the genuine addition καὶ ἐσμέν after κληθῶμεν in 1 John iii. 1. *Nempè amatorem turpia decipiunt caecum vitia, aut etiam ipsa haec delectant.*

Luke xxiii. 32. For ἕτεροι δύο κακοῦργοι, which is unobjectionable in the Greek, though a little hard in a close English translation, ℵB and the two Egyptian versions, followed by Westcott and Hort, have the wholly impossible ἕτεροι κακοῦργοι δύο.

John ii. 3. The loose paraphrase of Cod. ℵ in place of ὑστερήσαντος οἴνου commends itself to no one but Tischendorf, who in his turn admires the worst deformities of *his* favourite: it runs καὶ οἶνον οὐκ εἶχον ὅτι συνετελέσθη ὁ οἶνος τοῦ γάμου, in which few readers will be able to discern with him the manner and style of St. John. The Old Latin *a b ff*^{2} and Gaudentius [IV]; also *e l*, the Ethiopic, and the margin of the Harkleian in part, exhibit the same vapid circumlocution. Cod. ℵ in this Gospel, and sometimes elsewhere, has a good deal in common with the Western codices and Latin Fathers, and some of its glosses are simply deplorable: e. g. καλοκαγαθίας for κακοπαθείας, James v. 10; συνομιλοῦντες for συνοικοῦντες, 1 Pet. iii. 7; ἀποθανόντος for παθόντος, 1 Pet. iv. 1 after ch. ii. 21, where it does not stand alone, as here. Of a better character is its bold supplement of ἐκκλησία before συνεκλεκτή in 1 Pet. v. 13, apparently borrowed from primitive tradition, and supported by the Peshitto, Vulgate (in its best manuscripts and editions), and Armenian versions.

John iv. 1. After βαπτίζει we find ἤ omitted in AB* (though it is added in what Tischendorf considers an ancient hand, his B^2) GLΓ, 262, Origen and Epiphanius, but appears in ℵCD and all the rest. Tregelles rejects ἤ in his margin, Hort and Westcott put it within brackets. Well may Dr. Hort say (Notes, p. 76), 'It remains no easy matter to explain how the verse as it stands can be reasonably understood without ἤ, or how such a mere slip as the loss of Η after ΕΙ should have so much excellent Greek authority, more especially as the absence of ἤ increases the obvious no less than the real difficulty of the verse.'

John vii. 39. One of the worst faults a manuscript (the same is not true of a version) can have is a habit of supplying, either from the margin or from the scribe's misplaced ingenuity, some word that may clear up a difficulty, or limit the writer's meaning. Certainly this is not a common fault with Cod. B, but we have here a conspicuous example of it. It stands almost alone in receiving δεδαμέναν after πνεῦμα: one cursive (254) has δοθέν, and so read *a b c e ff² g l q*, the Vulgate, the Peshitto, and the Georgian (Malan, St. John), the Jerusalem Syriac, the Polyglott Persic, a catena, Eusebius and Origen in a Latin version: the margin of the Harkleian Syriac makes a yet further addition. The Sahidic, Ethiopic, and Erpenius' Arabic also supply some word. But the versions and commentators, like our own English translations, probably meant no more than a bold exposition. The whole blame of this evident corruption rests with the two manuscripts. No editor follows B here.

John ix. 4. Most readers will think with Dean Burgon that the reading ἡμᾶς δεῖ ἐργάζεσθαι τὰ ἔργα τοῦ πέμψαντος (whether followed by με or ἡμᾶς) 'carries with it its own sufficient condemnation' (Last Twelve Verses, &c., p. 81). The single or double ἡμᾶς, turning the whole clause into a general statement, applicable to every one, is found in ℵ*BDL, the two Egyptian, Jerusalem Syriac, Erpenius' Arabic, and Roman Ethiopic versions, in the younger Cyril and the versifier Nonnus. Origen and Jerome cite the passage as if the reading were ἐργάζεσθε, which, by a familiar *itacism* (*see* p. 11), is the reading of the first hand of B. The first ἡμᾶς is adopted by Tischendorf, Tregelles, Westcott and Hort: the second by Tischendorf alone after ℵ*L, the Bohairic, Roman Ethiopic, Erpenius' Arabic, and Cyril. Certainly με of BD, the Sahidic, and Jerusalem Syriac, is very harsh.

John x. 22. For δέ after ἐγένετο Westcott and Hort read τότε with BL, 33, the Sahidic, Gothic, Slavonic, and Armenian versions. No such use of τότε in this order, and without another particle, will be found in the New Testament, or easily elsewhere. The Bohairic and *gat.* of the Vulgate have δὲ τότε, which is a different thing. Moreover, the sense will not admit so sharp a definition of sameness in time as τότε implies. Three months intervened between the feast of Tabernacles, in and after which all the events named from ch. vii downwards took place, and this winter feast of Dedication.

John xviii. 5. For λέγει αὐτοῖς ὁ Ἰησοῦς ἐγώ εἰμι, B and *a* have the miserable variation λέγει αὐτοῖς ἐγώ εἰμι Ἰησοῦς, which Westcott and Hort advance to a place in their margin. The first IC (omitting ὁ) was absorbed in the last syllable of AYTOIC, the second being a mere repetition of the first syllable of ICTHKEI (*sic* B *primâ manu*). Compare Vol. I. p. 10. With so little care was this capital document written [1].

Acts iv. 25. We have here, upheld by nearly all the authorities to which students usually defer, that which cannot possibly be right, though critical editors, in mere helplessness, feel obliged to put it in their text: ὁ τοῦ πατρὸς ἡμῶν διὰ πνεύματος ἁγίου στόματος δαυεὶδ παιδός σου εἰπών. Thus read ℵABE, 13, 15, 27, 29, 36, 38. Apost. 12, a catena and Athanasius. The Vulgate and Latin Fathers, the Harkleian Syriac and Armenian versions conspire, but with such wide variations as only serve to display their perplexity. We have here two several

[1] A more ludicrous blunder of Cod. B has been pointed out to me in the Old Testament, Ps. xvii. 14 'they have children at their desire': εχορτασθησαν υἱων Cod. A, but εχορτασθησαν ὑειων Cod. B. The London papyrus has υων for υιων.

readings, either of which might be true, combined into one that cannot. We might either adopt with D ὃς διὰ μυό ἁγίου διὰ τοῦ στόματος λαλήσας δαυεὶδ παιδός σου (but *david puero tuo* d), or better with Didymus ὁ διὰ πνεύματος ἁγίου στόματος δὲ δαυεὶδ παιδός σου εἰπών (which will fairly suit the Peshitto and Bohairic); or we might prefer the easier form of the Received text ὁ διὰ στόματος δαβὶδ τοῦ παιδός σου εἰπών, which has no support except from P[1] and the cursives 1, 31, 40, 220, 221, &c. (the valuable copy 224 reads ὁ διὰ τοῦ πατρὸς ἡμῶν ἐν δᾱδ), and from Theophylact, Chrysostom being doubtful. Tischendorf justly pleads for the form he edits that it has second, third, and fourth century authority, adding 'singula verba praeter morem sed non sine caussâ collocata sunt.' *Praeter morem* they certainly are, and *non sine caussâ* too, if this and like examples shall lead us to a higher style of criticism than will be attained by setting up one or more of the oldest copies as objects of unreasonable idolatry.

Acts vii. 46. ᾐτήσατο εὑρεῖν σκήνωμα τῷ θεῷ Ἰακώβ. The portentous variant οἴκῳ for θεῷ is adopted by Lachmann, and by Tischendorf, who observes of it 'minimè sensu caret:' even Tregelles sets it in the margin, but Westcott and Hort simply obelize θεῷ as if they would read τῷ Ἰακώβ (compare Psalm xxiv. 6, cxxxii. 5 with Gen. xlix. 24). Yet οἴκῳ appears in ℵ*BDH against ℵ^cACEP, all cursives (including 13, 31, 61, 220, 221), all versions. Observe also in ch. viii. 5 καισορίας in ℵ* for σαμαρείας on account of ver. 40 and ch. xxi. 8.

Acts x. 19. Ἰδοὺ ἄνδρες δύο is the reading of Westcott and Hort's text ([τρεῖς] margin) after B only, the true number being three (ver. 7): in ch. xi. 11 Epiphanius only has δύο. There might be some grounds for omitting τρεῖς here, as Tischendorf does, and Tregelles more doubtfully in his margin (with DHLP, 24, 31, 111, 182, 183, 184, 185, 188, 189, 220, 221, 224, *m*, the later Syriac, the Apostolical Constitutions, the elder Cyril, Chrysostom and Theophylact, Augustine and Ambrose), no reason surely for representing the Spirit as speaking only of the δύο οἰκέται.

Acts xii. 25. An important passage for our present purpose. That the two Apostles returned from, not to, Jerusalem is too plain for argument (ch. xi. 29, 30), yet εἰς Ἱερουσαλήμ (which in its present order surely cannot be joined with πληρώσαντες) is the reading of Westcott and Hort's text (ἐξ and the fatal obelus † being in their margin) after ℵBHLP, 61, four of Matthaei's copies, Codd. 2, 4, 14, 24, 26, 34, 64, 78, 80, 95, 224, and perhaps twenty other cursives, but besides these only the margin of the Harkleian, the Roman Ethiopic, the Polyglott Arabic, some copies of the Slavonic and of Chrysostom, with Theophylact and Erasmus' first two editions, who says in his notes 'ita legunt Graeci,' i.e. his Codd. 2, 4. A few which substitute 'Antioch' for 'Jerusalem' (28, 38, 66 *marg.*, 67**, 97 *marg.*, Apost. 5) are witnesses for εἰς, but not so those which, reading ἐξ or ἀπό, add with the Complutensian εἰς Ἀντιόχειαν (E, 7, 14**, 27, 29, 32, 42, 57, 69, 98 *marg.*, 100, 105, 106,

[1] Codex P is of far greater value than others of its own date. It is frequently found in the company of B, sometimes alone, sometimes with other chief authorities, especially in the Catholic Epistles, e.g. James iv. 15; v. 4; 14; 2 Pet. i. 17 (partly); ii. 6; 1 John ii. 20.

111, 126**, 182, 183, 186, 220, 221, the Sahidic, Peshitto, and Erpenius' Arabic): Cod. 76 has *εἰς Ἀντιόχειαν ἀπὸ Ἱερουσαλήμ*. C is defective here, and the only three remaining uncials are divided between *ἐξ* (A, 13, 27, 29, 69, 214, Apost. 54, Chrysostom sometimes) and *ἀπό* (DE, 15, 18, 36, 40, 68, 73, 76, 81, 93, 98, 100, 105, 106, 111, 113, 180, 183, 184, a copy of Chrysostom, and the Vulgate *ab*). The two Egyptian, the Peshitto, the Philoxenian text, the Armenian and Pell Platt's Ethiopic have 'from,' the only possible sense, in spite of ℵB. Tischendorf in his N. T. Vaticanum 1867 alleges that in that codex 'litterae *εισ ιερου* primâ ut videtur manu rescriptae. Videtur primum *απο* pro *εισ* scriptum fuisse.' But since he did not repeat the statement three years later in his eighth edition, he may have come to feel doubtful about it. Dr. Hort conjectures that the original order was *τὴν εἰς Ἱερουσαλὴμ πληρώσαντες διακονίαν*.

Acts xvii. 28. Here Westcott and Hort place *ὑμᾶς* in their text, *ἡμᾶς* in the margin. For *ἡμᾶς* we find only B, 33, 68, 95, 96, 105, 137, and rather wonder than otherwise that the itacism is not met with in more cursives than six. The Bohairic has been cited in error on the same side. It needs not a word to explain that the stress of St. Paul's argument rests on *ὑμᾶς*. To the Athenians he quotes not the Hebrew Scriptures, but the poets of whom they were proud. Compare Luke xvi. 12, above.

An itacism not quite so gross in ch. xx. 10 *μὴ θορυβεῖσθαι* (B*, 185, 224*) is likewise honoured with a place in Westcott and Hort's margin. In Matt. xi. 16 they follow Tischendorf and Tregelles in adopting *ἑτέροις* for *ἑταίροις* with BCDZ, and indeed the mass of copies. This last itacism (for it can be nothing better) was admitted so early as to affect many of the chief versions.

Acts xx. 30. Cod. B omits *αὐτῶν* after *ὑμῶν*, where it is much wanted, apparently with no countenance except from Cod. 186, for this is just a point in which versions (the Sahidic and both Ethiopic) can be little trusted. The present is one of the countless examples of Cod. B's inclination to abridge, which in the Old Testament is carried so far as to eject from the text of the Septuagint words that are, and always must have been, in the original Hebrew. Westcott and Hort include *αὐτῶν* within brackets.

Acts xxv. 13. Agrippa and Bernice went to Caesarea to greet the new governor (*ἀσπασόμενοι*), not surely after they had sent their greeting before them (*ἀσπασάμενοι*), which, if it had been a fact, would not have been worth mentioning. Yet, though the reading is so manifestly false, the evidence for the aorist seems overwhelming (ℵABHLP, the Greek of E, 13, 24*, 31, 68, 105, 180, 220, 224*, a few more copies, and the Coptic and Ethiopic versions). The future is found possibly in C, certainly in 61, 221, and the mass of cursives, in *e* and other versions, in Chrysostom, and in one form of Theophylact's commentary. Here again Dr. Hort suspects some kind of prior corruption (Notes, p. 100).

Acts xxviii. 13. For *περιελθόντες* of all other manuscripts and versions ℵ*B have *περιελόντες*, evidently borrowed from ch. xxvii. 40. Even this vile error of transcription is set in Westcott and Hort's text, the alternative not even in their margin. In ver. 15 they once set *οἱ* within brackets[1] on the evidence of B, 96 only. Cod. B is very prone to omit the article, especially, but not exclusively, with proper names.

Rom. vii. 22. The substitution of τοῦ νοός (cf. ver. 23) for τοῦ θεοῦ seems peculiar to Cod. B.

Rom. xv. 31. Lachmann and Tregelles (in his margin only) accept the manifest gloss δωροφορία for διακονία with B (*see* Vol. I. p. 290 for its '*Western* element') D*FG (*d e* have *remuneratio*) and Ambrosiaster (*munerum meorum ministratio*). But διακονία is found in ℵACD² and ³ and consequently in E (*see* Vol. I. p. 176), *f* (*ministratio*), *g* (*administratio*), Vulg. (*obsequii mei oblatio*), so *d****, *fuld.* and Origen in the Latin (*ministerium*), with both Syriac, the Bohairic, Armenian and Ethiopic versions, Chrysostom, Theodoret, and John Damascene.

1 Cor. xiii. 5. Never was a noble speech more cruelly pared down to a trite commonplace than by the reading of B and Clement of Alexandria (very expressly) οὐ ζητεῖ τὰ μὴ ἑαυτῆς, in the place of οὐ ζητεῖ τὰ (or τὸ) ἑαυτῆς of the self-same Clement just as expressly elsewhere (*see* p. 262 and note 3), and of all other authorities of every description. Here Westcott and Hort place τὸ μὴ in their margin.

Col. iv. 15. For αὐτοῦ Lachmann, Tregelles' margin, Hort and Westcott have αὐτῆς from B, 67**, and the text of the later Syriac, thus implying that νύμφα is the Doric feminine form, which is very unlikely.

1 Thess. v. 4. Lachmann with Hort and Westcott (but not their margin) reads κλέπτας for κλέπτης with AB and the Bohairic, but this cannot be right.

Heb. vii. 1. For ὁ συναντήσας Lachmann, Tregelles, Hort and Westcott's text have ὃς συναντήσας with ℵABC**DEK, 17, a broken sentence: but this is too much even for Dr. Hort, who says, in the language habitual to him, that ὁ seems 'a right emendation of the Syrian revisers' (Notes, p. 130).

James i. 17. What can be meant by ἀποσκιάσματος of ℵ*B it is hard to say. The versions are not clear as to the sense, but *ff* alone seems to suggest the genitive (*modicum obumbrationis*). That valuable Cod. 184, now known only by Sanderson's collation at Lambeth (No. 1255, 10–14)[2], is said by him to *add* to the end of the verse οὐδὲ μέχρι ὑπονοίας τινὸς ὑποβολὴ ἀποσκιάσματος, which seems like a scholion on the preceding clause, and is found also in Cod. 221.

Nor will any one praise certain readings of Cod. B in James i. 9; 1 Pet. i. 9; 11; ii. 1; 12; 25; iii. 7; 14; 18 (*om.* τῷ θεῷ); iv. 1; v. 3;

[1] We note many small variations between the text of these critics as communicated to the Revisers some years before, and that finally published in 1881. The latter, of course, we have treated as their standard.

[2] This precious cursive forms one of a small class which in the Catholic Epistles and sometimes in the Acts conspire with the best uncials in upholding readings of the higher type: the other members are 69, 137, 182, to which will sometimes be added the text or margin of the Harkleian Syriac, Codd. 27, 29, the second hands of 57 and 66, 100, 180, 185, and particularly 221, which is of special interest in these Epistles. The following passages, examined by means of Tischendorf's notes, will prove what is here alleged: 1 Pet. iii. 16; 2 Pet. i. 4; 21; ii. 6; 11; 1 John i. 5; 7; 8; ii. 19; iii. 1; 19; 22; iv. 19; v. 5.

2 Pet. i. 17; 1 John i. 2; ii. 14; 20; 25; 27; iii. 15; 3 John 4; 9; Jude 9, which passages the student may work out for himself.

Enough of the weary and ungracious task of finding fault. The foregoing list of errors patent in the most ancient codices might be largely increased: two or three more will occur incidentally in Chapter XII (1 Cor. xiii. 3; Phil. ii. 1; 1 Pet. i. 23; *see* also pp. 254, 319). Even if the reader has not gone with me in every case, more than enough has been alleged to prove to demonstration that the true and pure text of the sacred writers is not to be looked for in ℵ or B, in ℵB, or BD, or BL, or any like combination of a select few authorities, but demands, in every fresh case as it arises, the free and impartial use of every available source of information. Yet after all, Cod. B is a document of such value, that it grows by experience even upon those who may have been a little prejudiced against it by reason of the excessive claims of its too zealous friends [1]. Its best associate, in our judgement, is Cod. C, where the testimony of that precious palimpsest can be had. BC together will often carry us safe through difficulties of the most complicated character, as for instance, through that vexatious passage John xiii. 25, 26. Compare also Acts xxvi. 16. Yet even here it is necessary to commend with reserve: BC stand almost alone in maintaining the ingenious but improbable variation *ἐκσῶσαι* in Acts xxvii. 39 (*see* Chap. XII), and the frigid gloss *κρίνοντι* in 1 Pet. iv. 5: they unite with others in foisting on St. Matthew's text its worst corruption, ch. xxvii. 49. In Gal. iii. 1, C against AB contains the gloss *τῇ ἀληθείᾳ μὴ πείθεσθαι*. Again, since no fact relating to these pursuits is more certain than the absolute independence of the sources from which A and B are derived, it is manifest that their occasional agreement is always of the greatest weight, and is little less than conclusive in those portions of the N. T. where other evidence is slender in amount or consideration, e. g. 1 Pet. i. 21 and v. 10 (with the Vulgate); v. 11: also supported by those admirable cursives 27, 29, in 1 Pet. v. 14; 1 John iv. 3; 19; 2 John 3; 12. See also 1 John v. 18, to be discussed in Chap. XII.

[1] Notice especially those instances in the Catholic Epistles, wherein the primary authorities are comparatively few, in which Cod. B accords with the later copies against Codd. ℵA(C), and is also supported by internal evidence: e.g. 1 Pet. iii. 18; iv. 14; v. 2; 2 Pet. ii. 20; 1 John ii. 10; iii. 23, &c. In 1 John iii. 21, where the first *ἡμῶν* is omitted by A and others, the second by C almost alone, B seems right in rejecting the word in both places. So in other cases internal probabilities occasionally plead strongly in favour of B, when it has little other support: as in Rom. viii. 24, where *τίς ἐλπίζει;* as against *τις, τί καὶ ἐλπίζει;* though B and the margin of Cod. 47 stand alone here, best accounts for the existence of other variations (*see* p. 248). In Eph. v. 22, B alone, with Clement and Jerome, the latter very expressly, omits the verb in a manner which can hardly fail to commend itself as representing the true form of the passage. In Col. iii. 6, B, the Sahidic, the Roman Ethiopic, Clement (twice), Cyprian, Ambrosiaster, and auct. de singl. cler., are alone free from the clause interpolated from Eph. v. 6.

CHAPTER XI.

CONSIDERATIONS DERIVED FROM THE PECULIAR CHARACTER AND GRAMMATICAL FORM OF THE DIALECT OF THE GREEK TESTAMENT.

1. IT will not be expected of us to enter in this place upon the wide subject of the origin, genius, and peculiarities, whether in respect to grammar or orthography, of that dialect of the Greek in which the N. T. was written, except so far as it bears directly upon the criticism of the sacred volume. Questions, however, are perpetually arising, when we come to examine the oldest manuscripts of Scripture, which cannot be resolved unless we bear in mind the leading particulars wherein the diction of the Evangelists and Apostles differs not only from that of pure classical models, but also of their own contemporaries who composed in the Greek language, or used it as their ordinary tongue.

2. The Greek style of the N. T., then, is the result of blending two independent elements, the debased vernacular speech of the age, and that strange modification of the Alexandrian dialect which first appeared in the Septuagint version of the Old Testament, and which, from their habitual use of that version, had become familiar to the Jews in all nations under heaven; and was the more readily adopted by those whose native language was Aramaean, from its profuse employment of Hebrew idioms and forms of expression. It is to this latter, the Greek of the Septuagint, of the Apocalypse, and of the foreign Jews, that the name of *Hellenistic* (Acts vi. 1) strictly applies. St. Paul, who was born in a pure Greek city (Juvenal, iii. 114–118);

perhaps even St. Luke, whose original writings[1] savour strongly of Demosthenes and Polybius, cannot be said to have *affected* the Hellenic, which they must have heard and spoken from their cradles. Without denying that the Septuagint translation and (by reason of their long sojourning in Palestine) even Syriac phraseology would powerfully influence the style of these inspired penmen, it is not chiefly from these sources that their writings must be illustrated, but rather from the kind of Greek current during their lifetime in Hellenic cities and colonies.

3. Hence may be seen the exceeding practical difficulty of fixing the orthography, or even the grammatical forms, prevailing in the Greek Testament, a difficulty arising not only from the fluctuation of manuscript authorities, but even more from the varying circumstances of the respective authors. To St. John, for example, Greek must have been an alien tongue; the very construction of his sentences and the subtil current of his thoughts amidst all his simplicity of mere diction, render it evident (even could we forget the style of his Apocalypse) that he *thought* in Aramaean: divergences from the common Greek type might be looked for in him and in those Apostles whose situation resembled his, which it is very unlikely would be adopted by Paul of Tarsus. Bearing these facts always in mind (for the style of the New Testament is too apt to be treated as an uniform whole), we will proceed to discuss briefly, yet as distinctly as may be, a few out of the many perplexities of this description to which the study of the original codices at once introduces us[1].

[1] Viz. Luke i. 1–4, some portion of the Gospel and most of the Acts: excluding such cases as St. Stephen's speech, Acts vii, and the parts of his Gospel which resemble in style, and were derived from the same sources as, those of SS. Matthew and Mark.

[2] Dr. Hort (Introd., Notes, p. 141) confirms the foregoing statements, which we have repeated unchanged from our former editions. 'What spellings are sufficiently probable to deserve inclusion among alternative readings, is often difficult to determine. Although many deviations from classical orthography are amply attested, many others, which appear to be equally genuine, are found in one, two, or three MSS. only, and that often with an irregularity which suggests that all our MSS. have to a greater or less extent suffered from the effacement of unclassical forms of words. It is no less true on the other hand that a tendency in the opposite direction is discernible in Western MSS.: the orthography of common life, which to a certain extent was used

4. One of the most striking of them regards what is called ν ἐφελκυστικόν, the 'ν attached,' which has been held to be an arbitrary and secondary adjunct. This letter, however, which is 'of more frequent occurrence at the end of words, is itself of such a weak and fleeting consistency, that it often becomes inaudible, and is omitted in writing' (Donaldson, Greek Grammar, p. 53, 2nd edit.). Hence, though, through the difficulty of pronunciation, it became usual to neglect it before a consonant, it always comprised *a real portion of the word to which it was annexed*, and the great Attic poets are full of verses which cannot be scanned in its absence[1]: on the other hand, the cases are just as frequent where its insertion before a consonant would be fatal to the metre. In these instances the laws of prosody infallibly point out the true reading, and lead us up to a general rule, that the weak or moveable ν is more often dropped before a consonant than otherwise. This conclusion is confirmed by the evidence of surviving classical manuscripts, although but few of them are older than the tenth century, and would naturally be conformed, in such minute points, to the fashion of that period. Codices of the Greek Testament, and of the Septuagint, however, which date from the fourth century downwards, present to us this remarkable phenomenon, that they exhibit the final ν before a consonant full as often as they reject it, and, speaking generally, the most ancient (e.g. Evan. ℵABCD)[2] are the most constant in retaining it, though it is met with frequently in many cursive copies, and occasionally in almost all[3]. Hence arises a difficulty, on the part of modern editors, in dealing with

by all the writers of the New Testament, though in unequal degrees, would naturally be introduced more freely in texts affected by an instinct of popular adaptation.'

[1] E.g. Aeschylus, Persae, 411: *κόρυμβ', ἐπ' ἄλλην δ' ἄλλος ἴθυνεν δόρυ*, or Sophocles, Antigone, 219: *τὸ μὴ 'πιχωρεῖν τοῖς ἀπιστοῦσῖν τάδε.*

[2] Cod. ℵ, for instance, does not omit it above 208 times throughout the N. T., out of which 134 occur with verbs (three so as to cause a hiatus), 29 with nouns, 45 with adjectives (chiefly *πᾶσι*) or participles (Scrivener, Collation, &c., p. liv). Its absence produces the hiatus in B*C in 1 Pet. ii. 18 (*ἐπιεικέσι*), and not seldom in B, e.g. 1 Pet. iv. 6, where we find *κριθῶσι* and *ζῶσι*, which latter is countenanced by A, and both by ℵL.

[3] Wake 12 (Evan. 492), of the eleventh century, may be taken for a fair representative of its class and date. It retains ν with *εἶπεν* thirty-three times in St. Matthew, thirteen in St. Mark, as often as 130 in St. Luke. With other words it mostly reserves ν to indicate emphasis (e.g. Luke xxii. 14; xxiv. 30), or to stand before a break in the sense.

this troublesome letter. Lachmann professes to follow the balance of evidence (such evidence as he received) in each separate case, and, while he usually inserted, sometimes omitted *nu* where he had no cause for such inconsistency except the purely accidental variation of his manuscripts; Tischendorf admits it almost always (N. T., Proleg. p. liii, 7th edition), Tregelles (I think), as also Westcott and Hort, invariably. Whether it be employed or not, the practice should at any rate be uniform, and it is hard to assign any reason for using it which would not apply to classical writers, whose manuscripts would no doubt contain it as often as those of the N. T., were they as remote in date[1]. The same facts are true, and the same remarks equally apply to the representing or withdrawing of the weak ς in οὕτως before a consonant. Each of the aforenamed editors, however, for the sake of euphony, prefers οὕτω before σ at the beginning of the next word, except that Tregelles ventures on οὕτως σε δεῖ in Acts xxiii. 11. Cod. ℵ has οὕτω about fourteen times in the N. T.

5. In the mode of spelling proper names of places and persons peculiar to Judaea, the general practice of some older codices is to represent harsher forms than those met with in later documents. Thus in Mark i. 21 καφαρναούμ is found in ℵBDΔ, 33, 69, Origen (*twice*), the Latin, Bohairic, and Gothic (*but not the Syriac:* ܟܦܪܢܚܘܡ) versions, and, from the facility of its becoming softened by copyists, this may be preferred to καπερναούμ of AC and the great numerical majority: yet we see LP with C in Matt. iv. 13, where Z sides with BD. In other instances the practice varies, even in the same manuscript, or in different parts of the N. T. Tischendorf, for example, decides that we ought always to read ναζαρέθ in St. Matthew, ναζαρέτ in St. John (N. T., Proleg. p. lv, note): yet the Peshitto in all twelve places that the name occurs, and the Curetonian in the four wherein it is extant (Matt. ii. 23; iv. 13; xxi. 11; Luke ii. 51), have the aspirate (ܢܨܪܬ), and being written in a kindred dialect, claim all the more consideration. Everywhere the manuscripts vary considerably: thus in Mark i. 9 ναζαρέτ is found in ℵBLΓΔ,

[1] The terminations which admit this moveable ν (including -ει of the pluperfect) are enumerated by Donaldson (Gr. Gram. p. 53). Tischendorf, however (N. T., Proleg. p. liv), demurs to εἴκοσιν, even before a vowel.

33, 69, and most cursives (seventeen of Scrivener's), Origen, the Harkleian Syriac and Old Latin *a b f*: Ναζαράτ in AP: but ναζαρέθ in D (not its Latin version, *d*) EFHKMUVΠ, 1, and at least sixteen other cursives (but not Cod. 69 by the first hand, as Tregelles states), the Old Latin *c*, the Vulgate, the Bohairic and Gothic as well as the elder Syriac. In Matt. iv. 13 Cod. B has Ναζαρά by the first hand (but -έτ ch. ii. 23), Cod. ℵ by a later one, with Z, 33 (so Ξ in Luke iv. 16); CPΔ Ναζαράθ, which is found in Δ nine times, in A twice: so that regarding the orthography of this word (which is inconstant also in the Received text), no reasonable certainty is to be attained. For Μαθθαῖος, again (the variation from the common form Ματθαῖος adopted by Lachmann, Tischendorf, Tregelles, Westcott and Hort), the authority is but slender, nor is the internal probability great. Codd. ℵBΔ read Μαθθαῖος in the title and headings to the first Gospel, while, in the five places where it occurs in the text, B (*primâ manu*), the fragment T^{e}, and D have it always, ℵ three times (but μαθθεος Matt. x. 3, ματθαιου Mark iii. 18 with Σ in the subscription to the first Gospel), the Sahidic and Gothic each twice: the Peshitto and title of the Curetonian too (all that is extant) have ܡܬܝ. For Ἰωάνης the proof is yet weaker, for here Cod. B alone, and not quite consistently (e.g. Luke i. 13; 60; 63; Acts iii. 4, &c.), reads Ιωανης, Cod. ℵ Ιωαννης[1], while Cod. D fluctuates between the two. In questions of orthography Westcott and Hort, as also the other editors in some degree, adopt a uniform mode of spelling, without reference to the state of the evidence in each particular case.

6. Far more important than these are such variations in orthography as bear upon the dialect of the N. T. Its affinity to the Septuagint is admitted on all hands, the degree of that affinity must depend on the influence we grant to certain very old manuscripts of the N. T., which abound in Alexandrian forms for the most part absent in the great mass of codices. Such are the verbal terminations -αμεν, -ατε, -αν in the plural of the second aorist indicative, -οσαν for -ον in the plural imperfect

[1] With the remarkable exception of those six leaves of Cod. ℵ which Tischendorf assigns to the scribe who wrote Cod. B. In these leaves of Cod. ℵ Ἰωάνης occurs four times: Matt. xvi. 14; xvii. 1; 13; Luke i. 13, in which last passage, however, B has the double *nu*.

or second aorist, -ουσαν for -ουν, -αν for -ασι of the perfect, -άτω for -έτω, -ατο for -ετο, -άμενος for -όμενος. In nouns the principal changes are -αν for -α in the accusative of the third declension, and (more rarely) the converse α for -αν in the first [1]. We have conceded to these forms the name of Alexandrian, because it is probable that they actually derived their origin from that city [2], whose dialectic peculiarities the Septuagint had propagated among all Jews that spoke Greek; although some of them, if not the greater part, have been clearly traced to other regions; as for example -αν for -ασι to Western Asia Minor also and to Cilicia (Scholz, Commentatio, p. 9, notes w, x), occurring too in the Pseudo-Homeric 'Batrachomyomachia' (ἐπεὶ κακὰ πολλά μ' ἔοργαν, ver. 179). Now when we come to examine our manuscripts closely we find the forms we have enumerated not quite banished from the most recent, but appearing far more frequently in such copies as ℵABC (especially D) LZ than in those of lower date. It has been usual to ascribe such anomalous (or, at all events, unclassical) inflexions to the circumstance that the first-rate codices were written in Egypt; but an assumption which might be plausible in the case of two or three is improbable as regards them all; it will not apply at all to those Greek-Latin manuscripts which must have been made in the West, or to the cursives in which such forms are sparsely met with, but which were certainly not copied from *surviving* uncials [3]. Thus we are led to the conclusion that the older documents retained these irregularities, because they were found in *their* prototypes, the copies first taken from the sacred originals: that some of them were in all likelihood the production of the skilful scribes of Alexandria,

[1] These last might be supposed to have originated from the omission or insertion of the faint line for ν over the preceding letter, which (especially at the end of a line) we stated in Vol. I. p. 50 to be found even in the oldest manuscripts. Sometimes the anomalous form is much supported by junior as well as by ancient codices: e. g. θυγατέραν, Luke xiii. 16 by ΚΧΓ*Λ, 209, also by 69, and ten others of Scrivener's.

[2] Thus Canon Selwyn cites from Lycophron κἀπὸ γῆς ἐσχάζοσαν, and Dr. Moulton (Winer, p. 91, note 5), after Mullach, ἔσχοσαν from Scymnus Chius.

[3] Tregelles presses yet another argument: 'If Alexandrian forms had been introduced into the N. T. by Egyptian copyists, how comes it that the classical MSS. written in that country are free from them?' (An Account of the Printed Text, p. 178). But what classical MSS. does he know of, written while Egypt was yet Greek or Christian, and now extant for our inspection? I can only think of Cureton's Homer and Babington's papyri.

though their exhibiting these forms does not prove the fact, or even render it very probable: and that the sacred penmen, some perhaps more than others, but all to some extent, were influenced by their recollections and habitual use of the Septuagint version. Our practical inference from the whole discussion will be, not that Alexandrian inflexions should be invariably or even usually received into the text, as some recent editors have been inclined to do, but that they should be judged separately in every case on their merits and the support adduced in their behalf; and be held entitled to no other indulgence than that a lower degree of evidence will suffice for them than when the sense is affected, inasmuch as idiosyncrasies in spelling are of all others the most liable to be gradually and progressively modernized even by faithful and painstaking transcribers.

7. The same remarks will obviously apply to those other dialectic forms, which, having been once peculiar to some one race of the great Greek family, had in the Apostles' time spread themselves throughout the Greek colonies of Asia and Africa, and become incorporated into the common speech, if they did not enter into the cultivated literary style, of the whole nation. Such are the reputed Dorisms ὀδυνᾶσαι Luke xvi. 25, καυχᾶσαι Rom. ii. 17, 1 Cor. iv. 7 of the Received text, with no real variation in any known manuscript: all such examples must stand or fall on their own proper grounds of external evidence, the internal, so far as it ought to go, being clearly in their favour. Like to them are the Ionisms μαχαίρης Luke xxi. 24 (B*Δ *only*); Heb. xi. 34 (ℵAD*); 37 (ℵD*): μαχαίρῃ Luke xxii. 49 (ℵB*DLT *only*); Acts xii. 2 (ℵAB*D**, 61): συνειδυίης Acts v. 2 (AB³E *only*, συνιδυης ℵ, συνιδυιης B*): σπείρης Acts xxvii. 1 of the common text, where the only authorities for the more familiar σπείρας seem to be Chrysostom, the cursives 37, 39, 56, 66, 100, 111, 183, 186, 188, 189. To this class belong such changes of conjugation as κατεγέλουν Mark v. 40 in K, 228, 447, 511 or c[scr]; or *vice versâ*, as ἀγανακτῶντες Cod. 69, in Mark xiv. 4. The form ἔστηκεν for ἕστηκεν John viii. 44; Apoc. xii. 4, adopted by Westcott and Hort as the imperfect of στήκω (Mark xi. 25, &c.), does not seem suitable to the context in either place, although οὐκ precedes in the former passage in ℵB*DLXΔΛ*, 1, 69*, 253, 507, 508, Evst. 234.

8. One caution seems called for in this matter, at least if we may judge from the practice of certain critics of high and merited fame. The sacred penmen may have adopted orthographical forms from the dialect of the Septuagint, or from the debased diction of common life, but they did not, and could not, write what was merely inaccurate or barbarous. Hence repudiate, in St. Paul especially, expressions like Tischendorf's ἐφ' ἐλπίδι Rom. viii. 20, as simply incredible on any evidence[1]. He may allege for it Codd. ℵB*D*FG, of which the last three are bilingual codices, the scribes of FG showing marvellous ignorance of Greek[2]. That Codd. ℵB should countenance such a *monstrum* only enables us to accumulate one example the more of the fallibility of the very best documents, and to put in all seriousness the inquiry of Cobet in some like instance: 'Quot annorum Codex te impellet ut hoc credas? . . . ecquis est, cui *fides veterum membranarum* in tali re non admodum ridicula et inepta videatur?' (N. T. Vatic., Praef. p. xx). In the same way we utterly disregard the manuscripts when they confound οὐχ with οὐκ (but *see* p. 318), μέλλει with μέλει, sense with nonsense.

The reader has, we trust, been furnished with the leading principles on which it is conceived that dialectic peculiarities should be treated in revising the text of the N. T. It would have been out of place to have entered into a more detailed account of variations which will readily be met with (and must be carefully studied) in any good Grammar of the Greek New Testament. Dr. Moulton's translation of Winer ought to be in the hands of every student, and leaves nothing to be regretted, except that accurate scholarship and unsparing diligence should

[1] 'It is hard to make St. Paul responsible for vulgarisms or provincialisms, which certainly his pen never wrote, and which there can be no proof that his lips ever uttered' (Epistle to the Romans, Preface to the third edition, p. xxi) is Dean Vaughan's comment on this 'barbarism.' He regards the Apostle's habit of dictating his letters as a 'sufficient reason for broken constructions, for participles without verbs, for suspended nominatives, for sudden digressions, for fresh starts.'

[2] Dr. Hort, however, accepts the form ἐφ' in this place, aspirating ἐλπίδι, and in the same way favours but does not print οὐχ ὀλίγος eight times in the Acts, adding that although ὀλίγος 'has no lost digamma to justify it, like some others, it may nevertheless have been in use in the apostolic age: it occurs in good MSS. of the LXX' (Introd., Notes, p. 148).

have been expended on improving another man's work, by one who is well able to produce a better of his own[1].

[1] 'A Treatise on the Grammar of New Testament Greek regarded as the basis of N. T. Exegesis. By Dr. G. B. Winer. Translated from the German with large additions and full indices by Rev. W. F. Moulton, M.A., D.D.,' third edition revised, 8vo, Edinburgh, 1882. The forthcoming 'Prolegomena' to Tischendorf's N. T. eighth edition (pp. 71–126), to which the kindness of Dr. Caspar René Gregory has given me access, contain a store of fresh materials on this subject; and Dr. Hort's 'Notes on Orthography' (Introd., Notes, pp. 143–173) will afford invaluable aid to the student who is ever so little able to accept some of his conclusions. See also on the more general subject Dr. Neubauer's Article in the first issue of the Oxford 'Studia Biblica' on 'The Dialects of Palestine in the Time of Christ.' He controverts Dr. Roberts' opinion that 'Christ spoke for the most part in Greek, and only now and then in Aramaic.' And he distinguishes between the Babylonian Aramaic, the Galilean Aramaic, and the dialect spoken at Jerusalem, which had more of Hebrew.

CHAPTER XII.

APPLICATION OF THE FOREGOING MATERIALS AND PRINCIPLES TO THE CRITICISM OF SELECT PASSAGES OF THE NEW TESTAMENT.

IN applying to the revision of the sacred text the diplomatic materials and critical principles it has been the purpose of the preceding pages to describe, we have selected the few passages we have room to examine, chiefly in consideration of their actual importance, occasionally also with the design of illustrating by pertinent examples the canons of internal evidence and the laws of Comparative Criticism. It will be convenient to discuss these passages in the order they occupy in the volume of the New Testament: that which stands first affords a conspicuous instance of undue and misplaced *subjectivity.*

First Series. Gospels.

1. MATT. i. 18. Τοῦ δὲ Ἰησοῦ Χριστοῦ . . . is altered by Tregelles into Τοῦ δὲ Χριστοῦ, Ἰησοῦ being omitted: Westcott and Hort place Ἰησοῦ between brackets, and Τοῦ δὲ Χριστοῦ Ἰησοῦ of Cod. B in the margin: Tischendorf, who had rejected Ἰησοῦ in his fifth and seventh editions, restored it in his eighth. Michaelis had objected to the term τὸν Ἰησοῦν Χριστόν, Acts viii. 37 (see that verse, to be examined below), on the ground that 'In the time of the Apostles the word Christ was never used as the Proper Name of a Person, but as an epithet expressive of the ministry of Jesus;' and although Bp. Middleton has abundantly proved his statement incorrect (Doctrine of the Greek Article, note on Mark ix. 41), and Ἰησοῦς Χριστός [1], especially in some one of the oblique cases after prepositions, is very common, yet the

[1] In Acts ix. 34 Ἰησοῦς Χριστός, the article between them being rejected, is read by Lachmann, Tischendorf, Tregelles, Westcott and Hort, on the adequate authority of ℵB*C, 13, 15, 18, 68, 111, 180, and a catena (probably also Cod. 36), with one or two Fathers, although against AEP, 31, 61, &c.

precise form ὁ Ἰησοῦς Χριστός occurs only in these places and in 1 John iv. 3; Apoc. xii. 17, where again the reading is more than doubtful. Hence, apparently, the determination to change the common text in St. Matthew, on evidence however slight. Now Ἰησοῦ is omitted *in no Greek manuscript whatsoever*[1]. The Latin version of Cod. D (*d*) indeed rejects it, the parallel Greek being lost; but since *d* sometimes agrees with other Latin copies against its own Greek, it cannot be deemed quite certain that the Greek rejected it also[2]. Cod. B reads τοῦ δὲ Χριστοῦ Ἰησοῦ, in support of which Lachmann cites Origen, iii. 965 *d* in the Latin, but on very precarious grounds, as Tregelles (An Account of the Printed Text, p. 189, note †) candidly admits. Tischendorf quotes Cod. 74 (after Wetstein), the Persic (of the Polyglott and in manuscript), and Maximus, Dial. de Trinitate, for τοῦ δὲ ἰησοῦ. The real testimony in favour of τοῦ δὲ Χριστοῦ consists of the Old Latin copies *a b c d f ff*[1], the Curetonian Syriac (I know not why Cureton should add 'the Peshitto'), the Latin Vulgate, the Frankish and Anglo-Saxon, Wheelocke's Persic, and Irenaeus in three places, 'who (after having previously cited the words "*Christi autem generatio sic erat*") continues 'Ceterum potuerat dicere Matthaeus, *Jesu vero generatio sic erat*; sed praevidens Spiritus Sanctus depravatores, et praemuniens contra fraudulentiam eorum, per Matthaeum ait: *Christi autem generatio sic erat*' (Contra Haeres., lib. iii. 16. 2). This is given in proof that Jesus and Christ are one and the same Person, and that Jesus cannot be said to be the receptacle that afterwards received Christ; for *the Christ was born*' (An Account of the Printed Text, p. 188). To this most meagre list of authorities Scholz adds, 'Pseudo-Theophil. in Evang.,' manuscripts of Theophylact, Augustine, and one or two of little account: but even in Irenaeus (Harvey, vol. ii. p. 48) τοῦ δὲ $\overline{ιυ}$ $\overline{χυ}$ (*tacitè*), as preserved by Germanus, Patriarch of Constantinople [viii], stands over against the Latin 'Christi.'

We do not deny the importance of Irenaeus' express testimony[3] (a little impaired though it be by the fanciful distinction

[1] I know not why Tischendorf cites Cod. 71 (g^{scr}) for the omission of Ἰησοῦ. I have again consulted the MS. at Lambeth, and find $\overline{ιυ}$ in this place.

[2] *See* above, I. 130. The precise relation of the Latin Version of Cod. D to the parallel Greek text is fully examined in Scrivener's 'Codex Bezae,' Introduction, chap. iii.

[3] Mr. E. B. Nicholson, Bodley's Librarian, doubts the conclusiveness of Ire-

which he had taken up with), had it been supported by something more trustworthy than the Old Latin versions and their constant associate, the Curetonian Syriac. On the other hand, all uncial and cursive codices (ℵCΣEKLMPSUVZΓΔΠ: ADFGΦ &c. being defective here), the Syriac of the Peshitto, Harkleian, and Jerusalem (δέ only being omitted, since the Church Lesson begins here), the Sahidic, Bohairic, Armenian, and Ethiopic versions, Tatian, Irenaeus, Origen (in the Greek), Eusebius, Didymus, Epiphanius, Chrysostom, and the younger Cyril, comprise a body of proof, not to be shaken by subjective notions, or even by Western evidence from the second century downwards[1].

2. Matt. vi. 13. *ὅτι σοῦ ἐστιν ἡ βασιλεία καὶ ἡ δύναμις καὶ ἡ δόξα εἰς τοὺς αἰῶνας. ἀμήν.* It is right to say that I can no longer regard this doxology as *certainly* an integral part of St. Matthew's Gospel: but (notwithstanding its rejection by Lachmann, Tischendorf, Tregelles, Westcott and Hort) I am not yet absolutely convinced of its spuriousness [i.e. upon much less evidence than is now adduced]. It is wanting in the oldest uncials extant, ℵBDZ, and since ACP (whose general character would lead us to look for support to the Received text in such a case) are unfortunately deficient here, the burden of the defence is thrown on Φ and Σ and the later uncials EGKLMSUVW^{f}ΔΠ (*hiat* Γ), whereof L is conspicuous for usually siding with B. Of the cursives only *five* are known to omit the clause, 1, 17 (*habet ἀμήν*), 118, 130, 209, but 566 or h^{scr} (and as it would seem some others) has it obelized in the margin, while the scholia in certain other copies indicate that it is doubtful: even 33 contains it, 69 being defective, while 157, 225, 418 add to *δόξα, τοῦ πατρὸς καὶ τοῦ υἱοῦ καὶ τοῦ ἁγίου πνεύματος*, but 422 *τοῦ πρσ* only. Versions have much influence on such a question, it is therefore important to notice that it is found in all the four Syriac (Cureton's omitting *καὶ ἡ δύναμις*, and some editions of the Peshitto *ἀμήν*, which

naeus' Latin here 'because his copyist was in the habit of altering him into accordance with the oldest Latin version; and because his argument is just as strong if we read *Jesu Christi autem* as if we read *Christi*. The argument requires *Christi*, but does not in the least require it as against *Jesu Christi*.'

[1] 'The clearly Western Τοῦ δὲ χριστοῦ,' as Dr. Hort admits, 'is intrinsically free from objection, . . . yet it cannot be confidently accepted. The attestation is unsatisfactory, for no other Western omission of a solitary word in the Gospels has any high probability' (N. T., Notes, p. 7). He retains *ψευδόμενοι*, Matt. v. 11.

is in *at least* one manuscript), the Sahidic (omitting καὶ ἡ δόξα), the Ethiopic, Armenian, Gothic, Slavonic, Georgian, Erpenius' Arabic, the Persic of the Polyglott from Pococke's manuscript, the margin of some Bohairic codices, the Old Latin *k* (quoniam est tibi virtus in saecula saeculorum), *f* g^1 (omitting *amen*) *q*. The doxology is not found in most Bohairic (but is in the margin of Hunt. 17 or Bp. Lightfoot's Cod. 1) and Arabic manuscripts or editions, in Wheelocke's Persic, in the Old Latin *a b c* ff^1 g^1 *h l*, in the Vulgate or its satellites the Anglo-Saxon and Frankish (the Clementine Vulg. and Sax. add *amen*). Its absence from the Latin avowedly caused the editors of the Complutensian N. T. to pass it over, though it was found in their Greek copies: the earliest Latin Fathers naturally did not cite what the Latin codices for the most part do not contain. Among the Greeks it is met with in Isidore of Pelusium (412), and in the Pseudo-Apostolic Constitutions, probably of the fourth century: soon afterwards Chrysostom (Hom. in Matt. xix. vol. i. p. 283, Field) comments upon it without showing the least consciousness that its authenticity was disputed. The silence of some writers, viz. Tertullian, Cyprian, Origen, Augustine, Cyril of Jerusalem, and Maximus, especially when expounding the Lord's Prayer, may be partly accounted for by the fact of the existence of the shorter form of the Lord's Prayer as given in St. Luke without the doxology; or upon the supposition that the doxology was regarded not so much a portion of the Prayer itself, as a hymn of praise annexed to it; yet this latter fact would be somewhat unfavourable to its genuineness, and would be fatal unless we knew the precariousness of any argument derived from such silence. The Fathers are constantly overlooking the most obvious citations from Scripture, even where we should expect them most, although, as we learn from other passages in their writings, they were perfectly familiar with them. Internal evidence is not unevenly balanced. It is probable that the doxology was interpolated from the Liturgies, and the variation of reading renders this all the more likely; it is just as probable that it was cast out of St. Matthew's Gospel to bring it into harmony with St. Luke's (xi. 4): I cannot concede to Scholz that it is 'in interruption of the context,' for then the whole of ver. 13 would have to be cancelled (a remedy which no one proposes), and not merely this concluding part of it.

It is vain to dissemble the pressure of the adverse case, though it ought not to be looked upon as conclusive. The Διδαχή (with variation) and the Syriac and Sahidic versions bring up the existence of the doxology to the second century; the Apostolic Constitutions in the third; Ambrose, Caesarius, Chrysostom, the Opus Imperfectum, Isidore, and perhaps others[1], attest for it in the fourth; then come the Latin codices[2] *f* g^1 *k q*, the Gothic, the Armenian, the Ethiopic, and lastly Codd. Φ and Σ of the fifth or sixth century, and the whole flood-tide of Greek manuscripts from the eighth century downwards, including even L, 33, with Theophylact and Euthymius Zigabenus in the eleventh and twelfth. Perhaps it is not very wise '*quaerere quae habere non possumus*,' yet those who are persuaded, from the well-ascertained affinities subsisting between them, that ACP, or at least two out of the three, would have preserved a reading sanctioned by the Peshitto, by Codd. *f k*, by Chrysostom, and by nearly all the later documents, may be excused for regarding the indictment against the last clause of the Lord's Prayer as hitherto *unproven*, in Dr. Scrivener's judgement passed upon much less than the evidence in favour adduced above; and for supposing the genuineness of the clause to be proved when the additional evidence is taken into consideration.

3. Matt. xi. 19. The change of τέκνων of the Received text into ἔργων, as made by Tischendorf, Tregelles (who retains τέκνων in his margin), by Hort and Westcott, is quite destructive to the sense, so far as we can perceive, for Jerome's exposition ('Sapientia quippe non quaerit vocis testimonium, sed operum') could

[1] Why should Gregory Nyssen (371) be classed among the opponents of the clause, whereas Griesbach honestly states, 'suam expositionem his quidem verbis concludit: [ἀπὸ τοῦ πονηροῦ τοῦ ἐν τῷ κόσμῳ τούτῳ τὴν ἰσχὺν κεκτημένου, οὗ ῥυσθείημεν] χάριτι [τοῦ] χριστοῦ, ὅτι αὐτοῦ ἡ δύναμις καὶ ἡ δόξα ἅμα τῷ πατρὶ καὶ τῷ ἁγίῳ πνεύματι, νῦν καὶ ἀεὶ καὶ εἰς τοὺς αἰῶνας τῶν αἰώνων, ἀμήν'? Griesbach adds indeed, 'sed pro parte sacri textûs neutiquam haec habuisse videtur;' and justly: they were rather a *loose paraphrase* of the sentence before him. *See* Textual Guide, Edward Miller, App. V.

[2] Canon Cook (Revised Version, p. 57) alleges as a probable cause of the general omission of the doxology in early Latin Versions and Fathers, that in all the Western liturgies it is separated from the petitions preceding by an intercalated *Embolismus*. More weighty is his observation that all the Greek Fathers, from Chrysostom onwards, who deal with the interpretation of the Lord's Prayer, 'agree with that great expositor in maintaining the important bearings [of the doxology] upon the preceding petitions.'

hardly satisfy any one but himself. The reading ἔργων is supported by ℵB* (with τέκνων in the margin by the hand B², 124, the Peshitto Syriac (apparently; for all the older editions we know punctuate ܥܒ̈ܕܝܗ̇ 'doers,' no ܥܒ̈ܕܝܗ̇ 'works'), the Harkleian text (but not its margin), the Bohairic, some copies known to Jerome, Armenian manuscripts, the Ethiopic (one MS. contains both forms), and (after the Peshitto Syriac) the Persic of the Polyglott and its codices. We can hardly question that the origin of the variation arose from the difficulty on the part of translators and copyists to understand the Hellenistic use of τέκνων in this place, and modern editors have been tempted to accept it from a false suspicion that the present passage has been assimilated to Luke vii. 35, where indeed Cod. ℵ and St. Ambrose have ἀπὸ πάντων τῶν ἔργων αὐτῆς. As we have alleged that Jerome's explanation is unsatisfactory in St. Matthew's Gospel, we subjoin that of Ambrose, which is certainly no less obscure, on the parallel place of St. Luke: 'Bene *ab omnibus* quia circa omnes justitia servatur, ut susceptio fiat fidelium, rejectio perfidorum. Unde plerique Graeci sic habent: *justificata est sapientia ab omnibus operibus suis*, quod opus justitiae sit, circa uniuscujusque meritum servare mensuram.' In the face of the language of these two great Latin Fathers it is remarkable that all other Latin authorities agree with the Curetonian Syriac and the mass of Greek manuscripts in upholding τέκνων, which is undoubtedly the only true reading.

4. MATT. xvi. 2, 3. The whole passage from Ὀψίας ver. 2 to the end of ver. 3 is set within brackets by Tischendorf in his eighth edition, within double brackets by Westcott and Hort, who holds (Notes, p. 13) that 'both documentary evidence and the impossibility of accounting for omission prove these words to be no part of the text of Mt.' Yet it might seem impossible for any one possessed of the slightest tincture of critical instinct to read them thoughtfully without feeling assured that they were actually spoken by the Lord on the occasion related in the Received text, and were omitted by copyists whose climate the natural phenomena described did not very well suit, the rather as they do not occur in the parallel text, ch. xii. 38, 39. Under these circumstances, the internal evidence in favour of the passage being thus clear and irresistible, the witnesses against it are

more likely to damage their own authority than to impair our confidence in its genuineness. These witnesses are ℵBVXΓ, 2, 13, 34, 39, 44, 84, 124 *primâ manu*, 157, 180, 194, 258, 301, 511, 575. Cod. 482 has the words, but only in a later hand at the foot of the page (Nicholson). Of these cursive codices 157 alone is of the first class for importance, and the verses are explained in the scholia of X (for ver. 3) and of 39. E and 606 have them with an asterisk; but they are wanting in the Curetonian Syriac, the Bohairic according to Mill (but not so other Coptic manuscripts and editions), and the Armenian, as unaltered from the Latin. Origen passes them over in his commentary, and Jerome, in his sweeping way, declares 'hoc in plerisque codicibus non habetur.' They are recognized in the Eusebian canons (Tregelles, An Account of the Printed Text, p. 205).

The united testimony of ℵB and the Curetonian version suffices to show that the omission was current as early as the second century, while the accordance of CD, of all the Latins and the Peshitto, with the mass of later codices assures us that the words were extant at the same early date. If any one shall deem this a case best explained by the existence of two separate recensions of the same work, one containing the disputed sentences, the other derived from copies in which they had not yet been inserted, he may find much encouragement for his conjecture by considering certain passages in the latter part of St. Luke's Gospel, where the same sort of omissions, supported by a class of authorities quite different from those we have to deal with here, occur too often to be merely accidental.

5. MATT. xix. 17. For Τί με λέγεις ἀγαθόν; οὐδεὶς ἀγαθός, εἰ μὴ εἷς, ὁ Θεός, Griesbach, Lachmann, Tischendorf, Tregelles, Alford, Westcott and Hort read Τί με ἐρωτᾷς περὶ τοῦ ἀγαθοῦ; εἷς ἐστὶν ὁ ἀγαθός. The self-same words as in the Received text occur in the parallel places Mark x. 18, Luke xviii. 19 with no variation worth speaking of; a fact which (so far as it goes) certainly lends some support to the supposition that St. Matthew's autograph contained the other reading [?]. Add to this that any change made from St. Matthew, *supposing the common reading to be true*, must have been wilfully introduced by one who was offended at the doctrine of the Divine Son's inferiority to the

Father which it seemed to assert or imply. Internal evidence, therefore, would be a little in favour of the alteration approved by Lachmann, Tischendorf, and the rest; and in discussing external authority, their opponents are much hampered by the accident that A is defective in this place, while ℵ has recently been added to the list of its supporters [though more recently Φ and Σ have come into the opposite balance]. Under these circumstances we might have been excused from noticing this passage at all, as we are no longer able to uphold the Received text with the same confidence as before, but that it seemed dishonest to suppress a case on which Tregelles (An Account of the Printed Text, pp. 133–8) has laid great stress, and which, when the drift of the internal evidence is duly allowed for, tells more in his favour than any other he has alleged, or is likely to be met with elsewhere[1].

The alternative reading Τί με ἐρωτᾷς περὶ τοῦ ἀγαθοῦ κ. τ. λ. occurs in ℵBD (omitting τοῦ and ὁ) L, 1 (omitting ὁ), 22, 604. In 251 both readings are given, the Received one first, in ver. 17, the other interpolated after ποίας ver. 18, prefaced by ὁ δὲ ἰησοῦς εἶπεν αὐτῷ. Excepting these seven, all other extant codices reject it, CEFGHKMSUVΓΔ (Γ omits τί με λέγεις ἀγαθόν; Δ omits λέγεις, Π is defective here), even Codd. 33, 69. The versions are more seriously divided. The Peshitto Syriac, the Harkleian text, the Sahidic (Oxford fragments), the Old Latin *f q*, the Arabic, &c., make for the common reading; Cureton's and the Jerusalem Syriac, the Old Latin *a b c e ff*$^{1.2}$ *l*, the Vulgate (the Anglo-Saxon and Frankish, of course), Bohairic and Armenian, for that of Lachmann and his followers. Several present a mixed form: τί με ἐρωτᾷς περὶ τοῦ ἀγαθοῦ; οὐδεὶς ἀγαθὸς εἰ μὴ εἷς: viz. the margin of the Harkleian, the Ethiopic, and *g*^{1} *h m* of the Old Latin. A few (Cureton's Syriac, *b c ff*$^{1.2}$ *g*^{1} *h l m*, Jerome and the Vulgate) add ὁ θεός, as in the common text; but this is unimportant.

Tregelles presses us hard with the testimony of Origen in favour of the reading he adopts: ὁ μὲν οὖν Ματθαῖος, ὡς περὶ ἀγαθοῦ ἔργου ἐρωτηθέντος τοῦ σωτῆρος ἐν τῷ, Τί ἀγαθὸν ποιήσω; ἀνέγραψεν. Ὁ δὲ Μάρκος καὶ Λουκᾶς φασὶ τὸν σωτῆρα εἰρηκέναι, Τί με λέγεις ἀγαθόν; οὐδεὶς ἀγαθός, εἰ μὴ εἷς, ὁ Θεός (Tom. iii. p. 644 *d*). 'The reading which is *opposed* to the common text,' Tregelles

[1] 'Quite a test-passage' Mr. Hammond calls it (Outlines of Text. Crit., p. 76).

writes, 'has the express testimony of Origen in its favour' (p. 134); 'might I not well ask for some *proof* that the other reading existed, in the time of Origen, in copies of St. Matthew's Gospel?' (p. 137). I may say in answer, that the testimony of Origen applies indeed to the former part of the variation which Tregelles maintains (*τί με ἐρωτᾷς περὶ τοῦ ἀγαθοῦ*), but not at all to the latter (*εἷς ἐστιν ὁ ἀγαθός*), and that the Peshitto Syriac version of the second, as also the Sahidic of the third century, uphold the common text, without any variation in the manuscripts of the former, that we know of. Or if he asks for the evidence of Fathers to counterbalance that of a Father, we have Justin Martyr: *προσελθόντος αὐτῷ τινὸς καὶ εἰπόντος* (words which show, as Tischendorf observes, that St. Matthew's is the only Gospel that can be referred to) *Διδάσκαλε ἀγαθέ, ἀπεκρίνατο λέγων, Οὐδεὶς ἀγαθὸς εἰ μὴ μόνος ὁ Θεὸς ὁ ποιήσας τὰ πάντα*, citing loosely, as is usual with him, but not ambiguously. Or if *half* the variation will satisfy, as it was made to do for Origen, Tregelles' own note refers us to Irenaeus 92 for *τί με λέγεις ἀγαθόν; εἷς ἐστὶν ἀγαθός*, and to Eusebius for the other half in the form above quoted from the Ethiopic, &c. Moreover, since he cites the last five words of the subjoined extract *as belonging to St. Matthew*, Tregelles entitles us to employ for our purpose the whole passage, Marcos. apud Iren. 92, which we might not otherwise have ventured to do; *καὶ τῷ εἰπόντι αὐτῷ Διδάσκαλε ἀγαθέ, τὸν ἀληθῶς ἀγαθὸν θεὸν ὡμολογηκέναι, εἰπόντα Τί με λέγεις ἀγαθόν; εἷς ἐστιν ἀγαθός, ὁ πατὴρ ἐν τοῖς οὐρανοῖς.* Jerome and Augustine (for the first clause only, though very expressly: de Consensu Evan. ii. 63) are with the Latin Vulgate, Hilary with the common Greek text, as are also Optatus, Ambrose, Chrysostom, and the main body of later Fathers. Thus the great mass of manuscripts, headed by C [followed by Φ and Σ], is well supported by versions, and even better by ecclesiastical writers; yet, in virtue of the weight of internal evidence [?], we dare not hold out unreservedly against the reading of BDL, &c., now that Cod. ℵ is found to agree with them, even though subsequent investigations have brought to light so close a relation between ℵ and B as to render it impossible, in our opinion, to regard them as independent witnesses [1].

[1] THIRD EDITION. I would fain side in this instance with my revered friend and Revision colleague Dr. David Brown of Aberdeen, and all my prepossessions are strongly in favour of the *textus receptus* here. He is quite right in perceiving

6. MATT. xx. 28. The extensive interpolation which follows this verse in some very ancient documents has been given above (I. 8), in the form represented in the Curetonian Syriac version. It bears the internal marks of evident spuriousness, the first sentence consisting of a rhetorical antithesis as unsuitable as can be imagined to the majestic simplicity of our Lord's usual tone, while the sentiment of the rest is manifestly borrowed from Luke xiv. 8–10, although there is little or no resemblance in the words. The only extant Greek for the passage is in Codd. Φ and D, of which D gives the fullest text, as follows: *υμεις δε ζητειτε · εκ μεικρου αυξησαι και εκ μειζονος ελαττον ειναι Εισερχομενοι δε και πορακληθεντες δειπνησαι · μη ανακλεινεσθαι εις τους εξεχοντας τοπους μη ποτε ενδοξοτερος σου επελθη και προσελθων ο δειπνοκλητωρ ειπη σοι ετι κατω χωρει · και καταισχυνθηση Εαν δε αναπεσης· εις τον ηττονα τοπον και επελθη σου ηττων ερει σοι ο δειπνοκλητωρ· συναγε ετι ανω και εσται σοι τουτο χρησιμον.* The codices of the Old Latin version (*a b c e ff*[1.2] *h n* and *and. em.* of the Vulgate[1]) mostly support the same addition, though with many variations: *d*, as usual, agrees with none; g^2 has not the first clause down to *εἶναι*, while g^1 *m* have nothing else. Besides the Curetonian Syriac, the margin of the Harkleian contains it in a shape much like *d*, noting that the paragraph is 'found in Greek copies in this place, but in ancient copies only in St. Luke, κεφ. 53' [ch. xiv. 8, &c.]: Cureton has also seen it in one manuscript of the Peshitto (Brit. Mus. 14,456), but there too in the margin. Marshall states that it is contained in four codices of the Anglo-Saxon version, which proves its wide reception in the West. Of the Fathers, Hilary recognizes it, as apparently do Juvencus and Pope Leo the Great (A. D. 440–461). It must have been

(Christian Opinion and Revisionist, p. 435) that the key of his position lies in the authenticity of ἀγαθέ ver. 16, which is undoubtedly found in Mark x. 17; Luke xviii. 18. If that word had abided unquestioned here, the form of reply adopted in the other two Gospels would have inevitably followed. As the case stands, there is not considerably less evidence for omitting ἀγαθέ (אBDL, 1, 22, 479, Evst. 5 [*not* 'five Evangelistaria'], *a e ff*[1], Eth., Origen twice, Hilary) than for Τί με ἐρωτᾷς κ.τ.λ., although Cureton's and the Jerusalem Syriac, the Bohairic, and the Vulgate with some other Latin copies, change sides here. It is upon these recreant versions that Dr. Brown must fix the charge of inconsistency. If ἀγαθέ be an interpolation, surely τί ἀγαθὸν ποιήσω is pertinently answered by Τί με ἐρωτᾷς περὶ τοῦ ἀγαθοῦ.

[1] Canon Westcott (Smith's 'Dictionary of the Bible,' Vulgate Version) adds Bodl. 857; Brit. Mus. Reg. I B. vii, and Reg. I. A. xviii in part, also Addit. 24,142 by the second hand. Tischendorf also cites *theotisc.*

rejected by Jerome, being entirely absent from the great mass of Vulgate codices, nor is it in the Old Latin *f l q*. No other Greek codex, or version, or ecclesiastical writer, has any knowledge of the passage: while the whole language of the Greek of Cod. D, especially in such words as δειπνοκλήτωρ, ἐξέχοντας, ἥττων, χρήσιμος, is so foreign to the style of St. Matthew's Gospel, that it seems rather to have been rendered from the Latin [1], although in the midst of so much variation it is hard to say from what copy. Cureton too testifies that the Syriac of the version named from him must have been made quite independently of that in the margins of the Harkleian and Peshitto.

No one has hitherto ventured to regard this paragraph as genuine, however perplexing it may be to decide at what period or even in what language it originated. The wide divergences between the witnesses must always dismiss it from serious consideration. Its chief critical use must be to show that the united testimony of the Old Latin, of the Curetonian Syriac, and of Cod. D, are quite insufficient in themselves to prove any more than that the reading they exhibit is ancient: certainly as ancient as the second century.

7. MATT. xxi. 28–31. This passage, so transparently clear in the common text, stands thus in the edition of Tregelles: (28) Τί δὲ ὑμῖν δοκεῖ; ἄνθρωπος εἶχεν τέκνα δύο, καὶ προσελθὼν τῷ πρώτῳ εἶπεν, Τέκνον, ὕπαγε σήμερον ἐργάζου ἐν τῷ ἀμπελῶνι. (29) ὁ δὲ ἀποκριθεὶς εἶπεν, Οὐ θέλω· ὕστερον δὲ μεταμεληθεὶς ἀπῆλθεν. (30) προσελθὼν δὲ τῷ δευτέρῳ εἶπεν ὡσαύτως. ὁ δὲ ἀποκριθεὶς εἶπεν, Ἐγώ, κύριε· καὶ οὐκ ἀπῆλθεν. (31) τίς ἐκ τῶν δύο ἐποίησεν τὸ θέλημα τοῦ πατρός; λέγουσιν, Ὁ ὕστερος. The above is indeed a brilliant exemplification of Bengel's Canon, 'Proclivi orationi praestat ardua.' Lachmann in 1842 had given the same reading, with a few slight and unimportant exceptions. The question is pro-

[1] No passage more favours Bp. Middleton's deliberate conclusion respecting the history of the Codex Bezae: 'I believe that no fraud was intended: but only that the critical possessor of the basis filled its margin with glosses and readings chiefly from the Latin, being a Christian of the Western Church; and that the whole collection of Latin passages was translated into Greek, and substituted in the text by some one who had a high opinion of their value, and who was, as Wetstein describes him, 'καλλιγραφίας quàm vel Graecae vel Latinae linguae peritior.' (Doctrine of the Greek Article, Appendix I. p. 485, 3rd edition.)

posed which of the two sons did their father's will; the reply is ὁ ὕστερος, the one that promised and then failed! Lachmann in 1850 (N. T., vol. ii. Praef. p. 5) remarks that had he been sure that πρῶτος (ver. 31) was the reading of Cod. C, he should have honoured it, *the only word that makes sense,* with a place in his margin: 'Nihilo minus,' he naïvely adds, 'id quod nunc solum edidi... ὁ ὕστερος veri similius est altero, quod facile aliquis correctori adscribat, illud non item;' and we must fairly confess that no copyist would have sought to introduce a plain absurdity into so beautiful and simple a parable. 'Quid vero,' he goes on to plead, 'si id quod veri similius esse dixi ne intellegi quidem potest?' (a pertinent question certainly) 'CORRIGETUR, SI MODO NECESSE ERIT:' critical conjecture, as usual, is his panacea. Conjecture, however, is justly held inadmissible by Tregelles, whose mode of interpretation is a curiosity in its way. 'I believe,' he says, 'that ὁ ὕστερος refers not to the order in which the two sons have been mentioned, but to the previous expression about the elder son, ὕστερον δὲ μεταμεληθεὶς ἀπῆλθεν, *afterwards* he repented and went.' 'Which of the two did his father's will! ὁ ὕστερος. *He who afterwards* [repented and went]. This answers the charge that the reading of Lachmann is void of sense' (An Account of the Printed Text, p. 107). I entertain sincere veneration for the character and services of Dr. Tregelles, but it is only right to assert at once that what stands in his text is impossible Greek. Even granting that instead of the plain answer 'the first,' our Lord's adversaries resorted to the harsh and equivocal reply 'he who afterwards,' they would not have said ὁ ὕστερος, but ὁ ὕστερον, or (the better to point out their reference to ὕστερον in ver. 29) ὁ τὸ ὕστερον.

Why then prefer nonsense, for the mere purpose of carrying out Bengel's canon to the extremity? The passage, precisely as it stands in Tregelles' N. T., *is sanctioned by no critical authority whatsoever.* Cod. B indeed has ὕστερος (which is here followed by Westcott and Hort), Cod. 4 δεύτερος, Codd. 13, 69, 124, 346 (Abbott's four), and 238, 262, 556, 604, perhaps others, ἔσχατος, one or other of which is in the Jerusalem Syriac and Bohairic, the Ethiopic (two manuscripts), the Armenian and two chief Arabic versions; but all these authorities (with *tol.* of the Vulgate *secundâ manu,* as also Isidore, the Pseudo-Athanasius, and John Damascene), transpose the order of the two sons in vv. 29, 30, so that the result produces just the same sense as in the Received text. The suggestion that the clauses were transferred in order to reconcile ὕστερος or ἔσχατος with the context may be met by the counter-statement that ὕστερος was just as likely to be substituted for πρῶτος to suit the inversion of the clauses. Against such inversion (which we do not pretend to recommend, though Westcott and Hort adopt it) Origen is an early witness, so that Cod. B and its allies are no doubt wrong: yet as that Father does not notice any difficulty in ver. 31, the necessary inference ought to be that he read πρῶτος[1]. Hippolytus testifies to ἔσχατος in ver. 31, but his evidence cannot be used, since he gives no indication in what order he took the clauses in vv. 29, 30. The indefensible part of Tregelles' arrangement is that, allowing the answers of the two sons to stand as in our common Bibles, he receives ὕστερος in the room of πρῶτος on evidence that really tells against him. The only true supporters of his general view are Cod. D αισχατος (i.e. ἔσχατος), the Old Latin copies *a b e ff*^{1,2} *g*^{1} *h l*, the best codices of the Vulgate (*am. fuld. for. san. tol. harl.**), the Anglo-Saxon version, and Augustine, though not the Clementine edition of the Vulgate. Hilary perplexes himself by trying to explain the same reading; and Jerome, although he says 'Sciendum est in veris exemplaribus non haberi *novissimum* sed *primum*,' has an expedient to account for the former word[2], which, however (if *am. fuld.*, &c. may be trusted), he did not venture to reject when revising the Old Latin. On no true principles can Cod. D and its Latin allies

[1] I see no reasonable ground for imagining with Lachmann that Origen who, as he truly observes, 'non solet difficilia praeterire,' did not find in his copy anything between πατρός; and Ἀμήν in ver. 31. On the supposition that he read πρῶτος there was no difficulty to slur over. Moreover, there is not a vestige of evidence for omitting λέγει αὐτοῖς ὁ Ἰησοῦς, the existence of which words Lachmann clearly perceived to be fatal to his ingenious guess, although Dr. Hort will only allow that it 'weakens his suggestion,' adding in his quiet way 'This phrase might easily seem otiose if it followed immediately on words of Christ, and might thus be thought to imply the intervention of words spoken by others' (Notes, p. 17).

[2] Jerome conceives that the Jews 'intellegere quidem veritatem, sed tergiversari, et nolle dicere quod sentiunt;' and so Canon G. F. Goddard, Rector of Southfleet, believed that their wantonly false answer brought on them the Lord's stern rebuke. Hilary's idea is even more far-fetched: viz. that though the second son disobeyed, it was because he *could* not execute the command. 'Non ait noluisse sed non abisse. Res extra culpam infidelitatis est, quia in facti erat difficultate ne fieret.'

avail against such a mass of opposing proof, whereof Codd. ℵCΦΣLX lead the van. Even the Curetonian Syriac, which so often favours Cod. D and the Old Latin, is with the *textus receptus* here.

8. MATT. xxvii. 35. After βάλλοντες κλῆρον the Received text, but not the Complutensian edition, has ἵνα πληρωθῇ τὸ ῥηθὲν ὑπὸ τοῦ προφήτου, Διεμερίσαντο τὰ ἱμάτιά μου ἑαυτοῖς καὶ ἐπὶ τὸν ἱματισμόν μου ἔβαλον κλῆρον. Internal evidence may be about equal for the omission of the clause by homoeoteleuton of κλῆρον, and for its interpolation from John xix. 24, 'with just the phrase τὸ ῥηθὲν ὑπὸ (or ἀπὸ) τοῦ προφήτου assimilated to Matthew's usual form of citation' (Alford, *ad loc.*). External evidence, however, places the spuriousness of the addition beyond doubt. It is first heard of in citations of Eusebius, and is read in the Old Latin codices *a b c* g^2 (not g^1) *h q*, the Clementine (not the Sixtine) Vulgate and even in *am. lux.*, Harl. 2826, *lind.*, in King's Libr. 1. D. ix and the margin of 1. E. vi (but not in *fuld. for. tol.* em. ing. jac. san.* nor in *f* $ff^{1.2}$ g^1 *l*), the Armenian (whose resemblance to the Vulgate is so suspicious), the Frankish and Anglo-Saxon, and as a matter of course in the Roman edition of the Arabic, and in the Persic of the Polyglott. The clause seems to be found in no manuscript of the Peshitto Syriac, and is consequently absent from Widmanstadt's edition and the Antwerp, Paris, and London Polyglotts. Tremellius first turned the Greek words into Syriac and placed them in the margin of his book, whence they were most unwisely admitted into the text of several later editions (but not into Lee's), without the slightest authority. They also appear in the text of the Harkleian, but the marginal note states that 'this passage from the prophet is not in two ['three' Codd. Assemani] Greek copies, nor in the ancient Syriac.' All other versions and Fathers (except Eusebius and the Pseudo-Athanasius), and all Greek manuscripts reject the clause, except Δ, 1, 17, 58 (*marg.*), 69, 118, 124, 262, 300, 503, 550, Evst. 55 : Scholz adds 'aliis multis,' which (judging from my own experience) I must take leave to doubt. Besides other slight changes (αυτοις Δ, κλήρους 69 *secundâ manu*) Codd. Δ, 61, 69, 503 and Eusebius read διά for ὑπό. The present case is one out of many that show an intimate connexion subsisting between Codd. 61 and 69.

9. Mark vi. 20. καὶ ἀκούσας αὐτοῦ πολλὰ ἐποίει, καὶ ἡδέως αὐτοῦ ἤκουε. '"Did many things" Engl. vers. I think it must have occurred to many readers that this is, to say the least, a very singular expression.' So writes Mr. Linwood, very truly, for nothing can well be more tame or unmeaning. His remedy we can say little for. 'I think that for πολλὰ ἐποίει we should read πολλοῦ ἐποίει, i.e. magni faciebat. It is true that classical usage would require the middle voice, sc. πολλοῦ ἐποιεῖτο. But this rule is not always observed by the N. T. writers[1]' (Linwood, p. 11). If, instead of resorting to conjecture, he had opened Tischendorf's eighth edition, he would have found there a reading, adopted as well by that editor as by Westcott and Hort, whose felicity, had it been nothing more than a happy conjecture, he might well have admired. Codd. ℵBL for πολλὰ ἐποίει[2] have πολλὰ ἠπόρει 'was much perplexed,' which the Bohairic confirms, only that, in translating, it joins πολλά with ἀκούσας. This close resemblance between the Bohairic version and Codd. ℵB (especially Cod. B) is very apparent throughout the N. T.; a single example being their united omission of ἰσχυρόν in Matt. xiv. 30 in company with but one other authority, the great cursive Cod. 33. Hence we do not hesitate to receive a variation supported by only a few first-rate authorities, where internal evidence (Canon II, p. 248) pleads so powerfully in its favour. Although the middle voice is found elsewhere in the N. T., yet the active in this precise sense may be supported by good examples, even when used absolutely, as here: e.g. ἄλλος οἱ ἀπορέοντι ὑπεθήκατο Herod. i. 191: ὁ δ' ἀπορῶν, ὥς φασι, μόλις κατενόησε τὴν πρόσχωσιν ταύτην τοῦ 'Αχελῴου Thuc. ii. 102.

Another less considerable but interesting variation, occurring just before, in chap. v. 36, παρακούσας 'overhearing' instead of ἀκούσας, may be deemed probable on the evidence of ℵ*BLΔ and the Latin *e*, which must have had the reading, though it is mistranslated *neglexit*[3]. We gladly credit the same group (ℵBCLΔ, 473, Evst. 150, 259) with another rare compound, κατευλόγει in ch. x. 16, whose intensive force is very excellent.

[1] His sole example is ὁδὸν ποιεῖν Mark ii. 23, which seems not at all parallel. The phrase may as well signify to 'clear away' as 'make their way.'

[2] πολλὰ ἃ ἐποίει is the reading of Abbott's four and of Codd. 28, 122, 541, 561, 572, Evst. 196.

[3] Which is certainly its meaning in Lucian, Tom. ii. p. 705 (Salmur. 1619); I know no example like that in St. Mark.

In ch. xii. 17 a similar compound ἐξεθαύμαζον is too feebly vouched for by ℵB alone.

[THIRD EDITION. It is only fair to retain unchanged the note on Mark vi. 20, inasmuch as the 'Two Members of the N. T. Company' have exercised their right of claiming my assent to the change of ἐποίει into ἠπόρει. I must, however, retract that opinion, for the former reading now appears to me to afford an excellent sense. Herod gladly heard the Baptist, and *did many things* at his exhortation; every thing in fact save the one great sacrifice which he could not persuade himself to make.]

10. MARK vii. 19. The substitution of καθαρίζων for καθαρίζον, so far from being the unmeaning itacism it might seem at first sight, is a happy restoration of the true sense of a passage long obscured by the false reading. For the long vowel there is the overwhelming evidence of ℵAB (*hiat* C) EFGH LSXΔ, 1, 13, 28, 48, 50, 53, 58, 59 (*me teste*), 61**, 64, 65, 69, 122*, 124, 229, 235, 244, 251, 282, 346, 435, 473, 492, 508, 515, 570, 622, Evst. 49, 259, and Erasmus' first edition: his second reads ἐκκαθαρίζων, his third καθαρίζον of ΦΣΚΜUVΓΠ, 547, 558, and perhaps a majority of the cursives. The reading of D καθαρίζει (καθαρίζειν 61 *primâ manu*), as also καὶ καθαρίζει of Evst. 222 and the Latin *i*, seem to favour the termination -ον: *purgans* of *a b c* (enen *d*) *ff*^{2} *g*$^{1.2}$ *l* ? *n q* and the Vulgate, is of course neutral. The Peshitto ܕܡܕܟܐ (qui purgat) refers in gender to the noun immediately preceding, and would require καθαρίζοντα. Will any one undertake to say what is meant by the last clause of the verse as it stands in the Authorized English version, and as it must stand, so long as καθαρίζον is read? If, on the other hand, we follow Lachmann, Tregelles, Tischendorf, Westcott and Hort, we must take the Lord's words to end with ἐκπορεύεται, and regard καθαρίζων πάντα τὰ βρώματα as the Evangelist's comment upon them: '*This he said*, to make all things clean.' Compare Acts x. 15. This, and none other, seems to have been the meaning assigned to the passage by the Greek Fathers. It is indeed most simply expressed by Chrysostom (Hom. II. in Matt. p. 526 A): Ὁ δὲ Μάρκος φησίν, ὅτι καθαρίζων τὰ βρώματα, ταῦτα ἔλεγεν, where Dr. Field's elaborate note should be con-

sulted. He rightly judges that Chrysostom was treading in the steps of Origen: καὶ μάλιστα ἐπεὶ κατὰ τὸν Μάρκον ἔλεγε ταῦτα ὁ Σωτήρ, καθαρίζων πάντα τὰ βρώματα. Hence Gregory Thaumaturgus designates the Lord as ὁ σωτὴρ ὁ πάντα καθαρίζων τὰ βρώματα. I know not how Tischendorf came to overlook the passage from Chrysostom: Tregelles very seldom uses him. It is obvious how well the elliptical form of the expression suits this Evangelist's style, which is often singularly concise and abrupt, yet never obscure.

11. MARK xvi. 9–20. In Vol. I. Chap. I, we engaged to defend the authenticity of this long and important passage, and that without the slightest misgiving (p. 7). Dean Burgon's brilliant monograph, 'The Last Twelve Verses of the Gospel according to St. Mark vindicated against recent objectors and established' (Oxford and London, 1871), has thrown a stream of light upon the controversy, nor does the joyous tone of his book misbecome one who is conscious of having triumphantly maintained a cause which is very precious to him. We may fairly say that his conclusions have in no essential point been shaken by the elaborate and very able counter-plea of Dr. Hort (Notes, pp. 28–51). This whole paragraph is set apart by itself in the critical editions of Tischendorf and Tregelles. Besides this, it is placed within double brackets by Westcott and Hort, and followed by the wretched supplement derived from Cod. L (*vide infra*), annexed as an alternative reading (ⲁⲗⲗⲱⲥ). Out of all the great manuscripts, the two oldest (ℵB) stand alone in omitting vers. 9–20 altogether[1]. Cod. B, however, betrays consciousness on the scribe's part that something is left out, inasmuch as after ἐφοβοῦντο γάρ ver. 8, a whole column is left perfectly blank (*the only blank one in the whole volume*[2]), as well as the rest of the column containing ver. 8, which is usual

[1] I have ventured but slowly to vouch for Tischendorf's notion, that six leaves of Cod. ℵ, *that containing* Mark xvi. 2—Luke i. 56 *being one of them*, were written by the scribe of Cod. B. On mere identity of handwriting and the peculiar shape of certain letters who shall insist? Yet there are parts of the case which I know not how to answer, and which have persuaded even Dr. Hort. Having now arrived at this conclusion our inference is simple and direct, that at least in these leaves, Codd. ℵB make but one witness, not two.

[2] The cases of Nehemiah, Tobit, and Daniel, in the Old Testament portion of Cod. B, are obviously in no wise parallel in regard to their blank columns.

in Cod. B at the end of every other book of Scripture. (No such peculiarity attaches to Cod. ℵ.) The testimony of L, that close companion of B, is very suggestive. Immediately after ver. 8 the copyist breaks off; then in the same hand (for all corrections in this manuscript seem *primâ manu* : *see* p. 138), at the top of the next column we read... *φερετε που και ταυτα*+... *πάντα δὲ τα παρηγγελμενα τοῖς περι τον πετρον συντομωσ ἐξηγγιλαν*+ *μετα δὲ ταῦτα καὶ αὐτος ὁ ισ̅, ἀπο ἀνατολησ καὶ ἄχρι δυσεωσ ἐξαπεστιλεν δι ἀυτων το ϊἐρον καὶ ἀφθαρτον κηρυγμα*+*τησ αἰῶνιου σωτηριασ*+ ... *εστην δε και ταῦτα φερομενα μετα το ἐφοβουντο γαρ*+... *Αναστὰσ δὲ πρωϊ πρωτη σαββατȣ*+*κ.τ.λ.*, ver. 9, *ad fin. capit.* (Burgon's *facsimile*, facing his p. 113: our *facsimile* No. 21): as if vv. 9–20 were just as little to be regarded as the trifling apocryphal supplement[1] which precedes them. Besides these, the twelve verses are omitted in none but some old Armenian codices[2] and two of the Ethiopic, *k* of the Old Latin, and an Arabic Lectionary [ix] No. 13, examined by Scholz in the Vatican. The Old Latin Codex *k* puts in their room a corrupt and careless version of the subscription in L ending with *σωτηρίας* (*k* adding *amen*): the same subscription being appended to the end of the Gospel in the two Ethiopic manuscripts, and (with *ἀμήν*) in the margin of 274 and the Harkleian. Not unlike is the marginal note in Hunt. 17 or Cod. 1 of the Bohairic, translated by Bp. Lightfoot above. Of cursive Greek manuscripts 137, 138, which Birch had hastily reported as marking the passage with an asterisk, each contains the marginal annotation given below, which claims the passage as genuine, 138 with no asterisk at all, 137 (like 36 and others) with an ordinary mark of reference from the text to the note, where (of course) it is repeated[3]. Other manuscripts contain marginal scholia respecting it, of which the following is

[1] Of which supplement Dr. Hort says unexpectedly enough, 'In style it is unlike the ordinary narratives of the Evangelists, but comparable to the four introductory verses of St. Luke's Gospel' (Introduction, p. 298).

[2] We ought to add that some Armenian codices which contain the paragraph have the subscription 'Gospel after Mark' at the end of ver. 8 as well as of ver. 20, as though their scribes, like Cod. L's, knew of a double ending to the Gospel.

[3] Burgon (*Guardian*, July 12, 1882) speaks of seven manuscripts (Codd. 538, 539 being among them) wherein these last twelve verses begin on the right hand of the page. This would be more significant if a space were left, as is not stated, at the foot of the preceding page. In Cod. 550 the first letter *α* is small, but covers an abnormally large space

the substance. Cod. 199 has τέλος[1] after ἐφοβοῦντο γάρ and before Ἀναστὰς δέ, and in the same hand as τέλος we read, ἔν τισι τῶν ἀντιγράφων οὐ κεῖται ταῦτα, ἀλλ' ἐνταῦθα καταπαύει. The kindred Codd. 20, 215, 300 (but after ver. 15, not ver. 8) mark the omission in some (τισί) copies, adding ἐν δὲ τοῖς ἀρχαίοις πάντα ἀπαράλειπτα κεῖται, and these had been corrected from Jerusalem copies (*see* pp. 161 and note, 193). Cod. 573 has for a subscription ἐγράφη καὶ ἀντεβλήθη ὁμοίως ἐκ τῶν ἐσπουδασμένων κεφαλαίοις σλζ: where Burgon, going back to St. Matthew's Gospel (*see* p. 161, note) infers that the old Jerusalem copies must have contained our twelve verses. Codd. 15, 22 conclude at ἐφοβοῦντο γάρ, then add in red ink that in some copies the Evangelist ends here, ἐν πολλοῖς δὲ καὶ ταῦτα φέρεται, affixing vers. 9–20. In Codd. 1, 205 (in its duplicate 206 also), 209 is the same notice, ἄλλοις standing for πολλοῖς in 206, with the additional assertion that Eusebius 'canonized' no further than ver. 8, a statement which is confirmed by the absence of the Ammonian and Eusebian numerals beyond that verse in ℵALSU and at least eleven cursives, with *am. fuld. ing.* of the Vulgate. It would be no marvel if Eusebius, the author of this harmonizing system, had consistently acted upon his own rash opinion respecting the paragraph, an opinion which we shall have to notice presently, and such action on his part would have added nothing to the strength of the adverse case. But it does not seem that he really did so. These numerals appear in most manuscripts, and in all parts of them, with a good deal of variation which we can easily account for. In the present instance they are annexed to ver. 9 and the rest of the passage in Codd. CEKVΠ, and (with some changes) in GHMΓΔΛ and many others: in Cod. 566 the concluding sections are there (σλδ ver. 11, σλε ver. 12, σλς ver. 14) without the canons. In their respective margins the annotated codices 12 (of Scholz), 24, 36, 37, 40, 41, 108, 129, 137, 138, 143, 181, 186, 195, 210, 221, 222, 237, 238, 255, 259, 299, 329, 374 (twenty-four in all), present in substance[2] the same

[1] Of course no notice is to be taken of τέλος after ἐφοβοῦντο γάρ, as the end of the ecclesiastical lesson is all that is intimated. The grievous misstatements of preceding critics from Wetstein and Scholz down to Tischendorf, have been corrected throughout by means of Burgon's laborious researches (Burgon, pp. 114–123).

[2] The minute variations between these several codices are given by Burgon (Appendix E, pp. 288–90). Cod. 255 contains a scholion imputed to Eusebius,

weighty testimony in favour of the passage: παρὰ πλείστοις ἀντιγράφοις οὐ κεῖται (thus far also Cod. 119, adding only ταῦτα, ἀλλ' ἐνταῦθα καταπαύει) ἐν τῷ παρόντι εὐαγγελίῳ, ὡς νόθα νομίσαντες αὐτὰ εἶναι· ἀλλὰ ἡμεῖς ἐξ ἀκριβῶν ἀντιγράφων ἐν πλείστοις εὑρόντες αὐτὰ καὶ κατὰ τὸ Παλαιστιναῖον εὐαγγέλιον Μάρκου, ὡς ἔχει ἡ ἀλήθεια, συντεθείκαμεν καὶ τὴν ἐν αὐτῷ ἐπιφερομένην δεσποτικὴν ἀνάστασιν. Now this is none other than an extract from Victor of Antioch's [v] commentary on St. Mark, which they all annex in full to the sacred text, and which is expressly assigned to that Father in Codd. 12, 37, 41. Yet these very twenty-four manuscripts have been cited by critical editors as adverse to the authenticity of a paragraph which their scribes never dreamt of calling into question, but had simply copied Victor's decided judgement in its favour. His appeal to the famous Palestine codices which had belonged to Origen and Pamphilus (*see* p. 55 and note), is found in twenty-one of them, possibly these documents are akin to the Jerusalem copies mentioned in Codd. Evan. Λ, 20, 164, 262, 300, &c.

All other codices, e. g. ACD (which is defective from ver. 15, *primâ manu*) EF^{w}GH (begins ver. 14) KMSUVXΓΔΠ, 33, 69, the Peshitto, Jerusalem and Curetonian Syriac (which last, by a singular happiness, contains vv. 17–20, though no other part of St. Mark), the Harkleian text, the Sahidic (only ver. 20 is preserved), the Bohairic and Ethiopic (with the exceptions already named), the Gothic (to ver. 12), the Vulgate, all extant Old Latins except *k* (though *a primâ manu* and *b* are defective), the Georgian, the printed Armenian, its later manuscripts, and all the lesser versions (Arabic, &c.), agree in maintaining the paragraph. It is cited, possibly by Papias, unquestionably by Irenaeus (both in Greek and Latin), by Tertullian, and by Justin Martyr [1] as early as the second

from which Griesbach had drawn inferences which Burgon (Last Twelve Verses, &c., Postscript, pp. 319–23) has shown to be unwarranted by the circumstances of the case.

[1] Dr. C. Taylor, Master of St. John's College, Cambridge, in *The Expositor* for July, 1893, quotes more evidence from Justin Martyr—hinting that some also remains behind—proving that that Father was familiar with these verses. Also he cites several passages from the Epistle of Barnabas in which traces of them occur, and from the Quartodeciman controversy, and from Clement of Rome. The value of the evidence which Dr. Taylor's acute vision has discovered consists chiefly in its cumulative force. From familiarity with the passage numerous traces of it arose; or as Dr. Taylor takes the case reversely, from the fact of the

century; by Hippolytus (*see* Tregelles, An Account of the Printed Text, p. 252), by Vincentius at the seventh Council of Carthage, by the Acta Pilati, the Apostolic Constitutions, and apparently by Celsus in the third; by Aphraates (in a Syriac Homily dated A. D. 337), the Syriac Table of Canons, Eusebius, Macarius Magnes, Didymus, the Syriac Acts of the Apostles, Leontius, Ps.-Ephraem. Jerome, Cyril of Jerusalem[1], Epiphanius, Ambrose, Augustine, Chrysostom, in the fourth; by Leo, Nestorius, Cyril of Alexandria, Victor of Antioch, Patricius, Marius Mercator, in the fifth; by Hesychius, Gregentius, Prosper, John, abp. of Thessalonica, and Modestus, in the fifth and sixth[2]. Add to this, what has been so forcibly stated by Burgon (*ubi supra*, p. 205), that in the Calendar of Greek Church lessons, which existed certainly in the fourth century, very probably much earlier, the disputed verses were honoured by being read as a special matins service for Ascension Day (*see* p. 81), and as the Gospel for St. Mary Magdalene's Day, July 22 (p. 89); as well as by forming the third of the eleven εὐαγγέλια ἀναστάσιμα ἑωθινά, the preceding part of the chapter forming the second (p. 85): so little were they suspected as of even doubtful authenticity[3].

The earliest objector to vers. 9–20 we know of was Eusebius (Quaest. ad Marin.), who tells that they were not ἐν ἅπασι τοῖς ἀντιγράφοις, but after ἐφοβοῦντο γάρ that τὰ ἑξῆς are found σπανίως ἔν τισιν, yet not in τὰ ἀκριβῆ: language which Jerome *twice* echoes and almost exaggerates by saying 'in raris fertur Evangeliis, omnibus Graeciae libris paene hoc capitulum fine non habenti-

occurrence of numerous traces evident to a close observer, it is manifest that there pre-existed in the minds of the writers a familiarity with the language of the verses in question.

[1] It is surprising that Dr. Hort, who lays very undue stress upon the silence of certain early Christian writers that had no occasion for quoting the twelve verses in their extant works, should say of Cyril of Jerusalem, who lived about A.D. 349, that his 'negative evidence is peculiarly cogent' (Notes, p. 37). To our mind it is not at all negative. Preaching on a Sunday, he reminds his hearers of a sermon he had delivered the day before, and which he would have them keep in their thoughts. One of the topics he briefly recalls is the article of the Creed τὸν καθίσαντα ἐκ δεξιῶν τοῦ πατρός. He must inevitably have used Mark xvi. 19 in his Saturday's discourse.

[2] Several of these references are derived from 'The Revision Revised,' p. 423.

[3] Nor were these verses used in the Greek Church only. Vers. 9–20 comprised the Gospel for Easter Monday in the old Spanish or Mozarabic Liturgy, for Easter Tuesday among the Syrian Jacobites, for Ascension Day among the Armenians. Vers. 12–20 was the Gospel for Ascension Day in the Coptic Liturgy (Malan, Original Documents, iv. p. 63): vers. 16–20 in the old Latin *Comes*.

bus.' A second cause with Eusebius for rejecting them is *μάλιστα εἴπερ ἔχοιεν ἀντιλογίαν τῇ τῶν λοιπῶν εὐαγγελιστῶν μαρτυρίᾳ*[1]. The language of Eusebius has been minutely examined by Dean Burgon, who proves to demonstration that all the subsequent evidence which has been alleged against the passage, whether of Severus, or Hesychius, or any other writer down to Euthymius Zigabenus in the twelfth century, is a mere echo of the doubts and difficulties of Eusebius, if indeed he is not retailing to us at second-hand one of the fanciful Biblical speculations of Origen. Jerome's recklessness in statement has been already noticed (Vol. II. p. 269); besides that, he is a witness on the other side, both in his own quotations of the passage and in the Vulgate, for how could he have inserted the verses there, if he had judged them to be spurious?

With regard to the argument against these twelve verses arising from their alleged difference in style from the rest of the Gospel, I must say that the same process might be applied—and has been applied—to prove that St. Paul was not the writer of the Pastoral Epistles (to say nothing of that to the Hebrews), St. John of the Apocalypse, Isaiah and Zechariah of portions of those prophecies that bear their names. Every one used to literary composition may detect, if he will, such minute variations as have been made so much of in this case[2], either in his own writings, or in those of the authors he is most familiar with.

Persons who, like Eusebius, devoted themselves to the pious

[1] To get rid of one apparent *ἀντιφωνία*, that arising from the expression *πρωῒ τῇ μιᾷ τοῦ σαββάτου* (*sic*), ver. 9, compared with *ὀψὲ σαββάτων* Matt. xxviii. 1, Eusebius proposes the plan of setting a stop between *Ἀναστὰς δέ* and *πρωΐ*, so little was he satisfied with rudely expunging the whole clause. Hence Cod. E puts a red cross after *δέ*: Codd. 20, 22, 34, 72, 193, 196, 199, 271, 345, 405, 411, 456, have a colon: Codd. 332, 339, 340, 439, a comma (Burgon, *Guardian*, Aug. 20, 1873).

[2] The following peculiarities have been noticed in these verses: *ἐκεῖνος* used absolutely, vers. 10, 11, 13; *πορεύομαι* vers. 10, 12, 15; *τοῖς μετ᾽ αὐτοῦ γενομένοις* ver. 10; *θεάομαι* vers. 11, 14; *ἀπιστέω* vers. 11, 16; *μετὰ ταῦτα* ver. 12; *ἕτερας* ver. 12; *παρακολουθέω* ver. 17; *ἐν τῷ ὀνόματι* ver. 17; *κύριος* for the Saviour, vers. 19, 20; *πανταχοῦ*, *συνεργοῦντος*, *βεβαιόω*, *ἐπακολουθέω* ver. 20, all of them as not found elsewhere in St. Mark. A very able and really conclusive plea for the genuineness of the paragraph, as coming from that Evangelist's pen, appeared in the *Baptist Quarterly*, Philadelphia, July, 1869, bearing the signature of Professor J. A. Broadus, of South Carolina. Unfortunately, from the nature of the case, it does not admit of abridgement. Burgon's ninth chapter (pp. 136–190) enters into full details, and amply justifies his conclusion that the supposed adverse argument from phraseology 'breaks down hopelessly under severe analysis.'

task of constructing harmonies of the Gospels, would soon perceive the difficulty of adjusting the events recorded in vers. 9–20 to the narratives of the other Evangelists. Alford regards this inconsistency (more apparent than real, we believe) as 'a valuable testimony to the antiquity of the fragment' (N. T. *ad loc.*): we would go further, and claim for the harder reading the benefit of any critical doubt as to its genuineness (Canon I. Vol. II. p. 247). The difficulty was both felt and avowed by Eusebius, and was recited after him by Severus of Antioch or whoever wrote the scholion attributed to him. Whatever Jerome and the rest may have done, these assigned the ἀντιλογία, the ἐναντίωσις they thought they perceived, as a reason (not the first, nor perhaps the chief, but still as a reason) for supposing that the Gospel ended with ἐφοβοῦντο γάρ. Yet in the balance of probabilities, can anything be more unlikely than that St. Mark broke off so abruptly as this hypothesis would imply, while no ancient writer has noticed or seemed conscious of any such abruptness[1]? This fact has driven those who reject the concluding verses to the strangest fancies;—namely, that, like Thucydides, the Evangelist was cut off before his work was completed, or even that the last leaf of the original Gospel was torn away.

We emphatically deny that such wild surmises[2] are called

[1] 'Can any one, who knows the character of the Lord and of His ministry, conceive for an instant that we should be left with nothing but a message baulked through the alarm of women' (Kelly, Lectures Introductory to the Gospels, p. 258). Even Dr. Hort can say 'It is incredible that the Evangelist deliberately concluded either a paragraph with ἐφοβοῦντο γάρ, or the Gospel with a petty detail of a secondary event, leaving his narrative hanging in the air' (Notes, p. 46).

[2] When Burgon ventures upon a surmise, one which is probability itself by the side of those we have been speaking of, Professor Abbot (*ubi supra*, p. 197) remarks upon it that 'With Mr. Burgon a conjecture seems to be a demonstration.' We will not be deterred by dread of any such reproach from mentioning his method of accounting for the absence of those verses from some very early copies, commending it to the reader for what it may seem worth. After a learned and exhaustive proof that the Church lessons, as we now have them, existed from very early times (Twelve Verses, pp. 191–211), and noting that an important lesson ended with Mark xvi. 8 (*see* Calendar of Lessons); he supposes that τέλος, which would stand at the end of such a lesson, misled some scribe who had before him an *exemplar* of the Gospels whose last leaf (containing Mark xvi. 9–20, or according to Codd. 20, 215, 300 only vers. 16–20) was lost, as it might easily be in those older manuscripts wherein St. Mark stood last.

for by the state of the evidence in this case. All opposition to the authenticity of the paragraph resolves itself into the allegations of Eusebius and the testimony of ℵB. Let us accord to these the weight which is their due: but against their verdict we can appeal to a vast body of ecclesiastical evidence reaching back to the earlier part of the second century[1]; to nearly all the versions; and to all extant manuscripts excepting two, of which one is doubtful. So powerfully is it vouched for, that many of those who are reluctant to recognize St. Mark as its author, are content to regard it notwithstanding as an integral portion of the inspired record originally delivered to the Church[2].

12. Luke ii. 14. If there be one case more prominent than another in the criticism of the New Testament, wherein solid reason and pure taste revolt against the iron yoke of ancient authorities, it is that of the Angelic Hymn sung at the Nativity. In the common text all is transparently clear:

ΔΟΞΑ ΕΝ ΥΨΙϹΤΟΙϹ ΘΕΩ,	Glory to God in the highest,
ΚΑΙ ΕΠΙ ΓΗϹ ΕΙΡΗΝΗ·	And on earth peace:
ΕΝ ΑΝΘΡΩΠΟΙϹ ΕΥΔΟΚΙΑ.	Good will amongst men.

The blessed words are distributed, after the Hebrew fashion, into a stanza consisting of three members. In the first and second lines heaven and earth are contrasted; the third refers to both those preceding, and alleges the efficient cause which has brought God glory and earth peace. By the addition of a single letter to the end of the last line, by merely reading *εὐδοκίας* for *εὐδοκία*, the rhythmical arrangement is utterly marred[3], and the simple shepherds are sent away with a message, the diction of

[1] The Codex lately discovered by Mrs. Lewis is said to omit the verses. But what is that against a host of other codices? And when the other MS. of the Curetonian includes the verses? Positive testimony is worth more than negative.

[2] Dr. Hort, however, while he admits the possibility of the leaf containing vers. 9–20 having been lost in some very early copy, which thus would become the parent of transcripts having a mutilated text (Notes, p. 49), rather inconsistently arrives at the conclusion that the passage in question 'manifestly cannot claim any apostolic authority; but it is doubtless founded on some tradition of the apostolic age' (*ibid.* p. 51).

[3] Dr. Hort will hardly find many friends for his division (Notes, p. 56),

Δόξα ἐν ὑψίστοις θεῷ καὶ ἐπὶ γῆς,
Εἰρήνη ἐν ἀνθρώποις εὐδοκίας.

which no scholar has yet construed to his own mind[1]. Yet such is the conclusion of Lachmann, Tischendorf, Tregelles, Westcott and Hort, although Tregelles and the Cambridge fellow-workers allow εὐδοκία a place in their margins. Of the five great uncials C is unfortunately defective, but ℵ*AB*D, and no other Greek manuscript whatever, read εὐδοκίας: yet A is so inconstant in this matter that in the primitive 14th or Morning Hymn, a cento of Scripture texts, annexed to the Book of Psalms, its reading is εὐδοκεία (Baber, Cod. Alex., p. 569), and such was no doubt the form used in Divine service, as appears from the great Zürich Psalter O[d]. The rest of the uncials extant (ℵ[c]B[3]EGHKLMPSUVΓΔΛΞ, &c.), and all the cursives follow the common text, which is upheld by the Bohairic, by the three extant Syriac (the Peshitto most emphatically, the Jerusalem, and the Harkleian both in the text and Greek margin), by the Armenian and Ethiopic versions. The Vulgate, as is well known, renders 'in hominibus bonae voluntatis,' and thus did all the forms of the Old Latin, and after it the Gothic. Hence it follows, as a matter of course, that the Latin Fathers, such as Hilary and Augustine, and the Latin interpreters of Irenaeus (who seems really to have omitted ἐν, as do D and a few cursives) and of the false Athanasius, adopted the reading of their own Bibles. Origen also, in a passage not now extant in the Greek, is made in Jerome's translation of it manifestly to choose the same form. We can only say that in so doing he is the only Greek who favours εὐδοκίας, and his own text has εὐδοκία in three several places, though no special stress is laid by him upon it. But here comes in the evidence of the Greek Fathers—their virtually unanimous evidence—with an authority from which there is, or ought to be, no appeal. Dean Burgon (The Revision Revised, pp. 42–46) affords us a list of forty-seven, all speaking in a manner too plain for doubt, most of them several times over, twenty-two of them having flourished before the end of the

[1] I am loth to sully with a semblance of unseasonable levity a page which is devoted to the vindication of the true form of the Angelic Hymn, and must ask the student to refer for himself to the 470th number of the *Spectator*, where what we will venture to call a precisely parallel case exercises the delicate humour of Addison. 'So many ancient manuscripts,' he tells us, concur in this last reading, 'that I am very much in doubt whether it ought not to take place. There are but two reasons which incline me to the reading as I have published it: first, because the rhyme, and secondly, because the sense, is preserved by it.'

fifth century, and who must have used codices at least as old and pure as א or B. They are Irenaeus, of the second century; the Apostolical Constitutions and Origen three times in the third; Eusebius, Aphraates the Persian, Titus of Bostra, Didymus, Gregory Nazianzen, Cyril of Jerusalem (who has been quoted in error on the wrong side), Epiphanius, Gregory of Nyssa four times, Ephraem Syrus, Philo of Carpasus, a nameless preacher at Antioch, and Chrysostom (nine times over, interpreting also *εὐδοκία* by *καταλλαγή*) in the fourth; Cyril of Alexandria on fourteen occasions, Theodoret on four, Theodotus of Ancyra, the Patriarch Proclus, Paulus of Emesa, the Eastern Bishops at Ephesus in 431, and Basil of Seleucia in the fifth; Cosmas Indicopleustes, Anastasius Sinaita, and Eulogius of Alexandria in the sixth; Andreas of Crete in the seventh; with Cosmas of Maiuma, John Damascene, and Germanus, Archbishop of Constantinople, in the eighth [1]. Such testimony, supported by all later manuscripts, together with the Bohairic and Syriac versions, cannot but overpower the transcriptional blunder of some early scribe, who cannot, however, have lived later than the second century.

To those with whom the evidence of אBD and of the Latins united appears too mighty to resist, we would fain prefer one request, that in their efforts to extract some tolerable sense out of *εὐδοκίας*, they will not allow themselves to be driven to renderings which the Greek language will not endure. To spoil the metrical arrangement by forcing the second and third members of the stanza into one, is in itself a sore injury to the poetical symmetry of the passage, but from their point of view it cannot be helped. When they shall come to translate, it will be their endeavour to be faithful, if grammatical faithfulness be possible in a case so desperate. 'Peace on earth for those that will have it,' as Dean Alford truly says, is untenable in Greek, as well as in theology: 'among men of good pleasure' is unintelligible to most minds. Professor Milligan (Words of the New Testament, p. 194) praises as an interesting form 'among men of his good pleasure,' which, not at all unnecessarily, he expounds to signify 'among men whom He hath loved.' Again, 'among men in whom He is well pleased' (compare chap. iii. 22) can

[1] This torrent of testimony includes ninety-two places, of which 'Tischendorf knew of only eleven, Tregelles adduces only six' (R. R., p. 45, note).

be arrived at only through some process which would make any phrase bear almost any meaning the translator might like to put upon it. The construction adopted by Origen as rendered by Jerome, *pax enim quam non dat Dominus non est pax bonae voluntatis*, εὐδοκίας being joined with εἰρήνη, is regarded by Dr. Hort 'to deserve serious attention, if no better interpretation were available' and for the trajection he compares ch. xix. 38; Heb. xii. 11 (Notes, p. 56). Dr. Westcott holds that since 'ἀνθρώποις εὐδοκίας is undoubtedly a difficult phrase, and the antithesis of γῆς and ἀνθρώποις agrees with Rom. viii. 22, εὐδοκία claims a place in the margin' (*ibid.*): no very great concession, when the general state of the evidence is borne in mind[1].

13. Luke vi. 1. Ἐγένετο δὲ ἐν σαββάτῳ δευτεροπρώτῳ. Here again Codd. ℵB coincide in a reading which cannot be approved, omitting δευτεροπρώτῳ by way of getting rid of a difficulty, as do both of them in Mark xvi. 9–20, and ℵ in Matt. xxiii. 35. The very obscurity of the expression, which does not occur in the parallel Gospels or elsewhere, attests strongly to its genuineness, if there be any truth at all in canons of internal evidence[2]: not to mention that the expression ἐν ἑτέρῳ σαββάτῳ ver. 6 favours the notion that the previous sabbath

[1] Every word uttered by such a scholar as Dr. Field (d. 1885) is so valuable that no apology can be needed for citing the following critique from his charming 'Otium Norvicense,' Part iii. p. 36, on the reading εὐδοκίας and the rendering 'among men in whom he is well pleased.' 'To which it may be briefly objected (1) *that it ruins the stichometry*; (2) that it separates ἐν from εὐδοκία, the word with which it is normally construed; (3) that "men of good pleasure" (אַנְשֵׁי רָצוֹן) would be, according to Graeco-biblical usage, not ἄνθρωποι εὐδοκίας, but ἄνδρες εὐδοκίας; (4) that the turn of the sentence, ἐν ἀνθρώποις εὐδοκία, very much resembles the second clause of Prov. xiv. 9: וּבֵין יְשָׁרִים רָצוֹן, rendered by Symmachus καὶ ἀναμέσον εὐθέων εὐδοκία.' But this is almost slaying the slain.

[2] Κυριακὴ δευτεροπρώτη is cited by Sophocles in his Lexicon from 'Eustr. 2381 B' in the sense of *low Sunday* (McClellan, N. T., p. 690). Canon Cook conjectures that it may mean the first sabbath in the second month (*Iyar*), precisely the time when wheat would be fully ripe (Revised Version, p. 69). [More probably it is 'the first sabbath after the second day of the Passover.'] On the other hand, 'If the word be a reality and originally in the text, its meaning, since in that case it must have been borrowed from something in the Jewish calendar, would have been traditionally known from the first.' (Green, Course of Developed Criticism, p. 56.) But why would it? The fancy that δευτεροπρώτῳ had its origin in numerals of reference (B A) set in the margin will most commend itself to such scholars as are under the self-imposed necessity of upholding Codd. ℵB united against all other evidence, of whatever kind.

had been definitely indicated. Besides ℵB, δευτεροπρώτῳ is absent from L, 1, 22, 33, 69 (where it is inserted in the margin by W. Chark, and should not be noticed, *see* above), 118, 157, 209. A few (RΓ, 13, 117, 124 *primâ manu*, 235) prefer δευτέρω πρώτω, which, as the student will perceive, differs from the common reading only by a familiar itacism. As this verse commences a Church lesson (that for the seventh day or Sabbath of the third week of the new year, *see* Calendar), Evangelistaria *leave out*, as usual, *the notes of time;* in Evst. 150, 222, 234, 257, 259 (and no doubt in other such books, certainly in the Jerusalem Syriac), the section thus begins, Ἐπορεύετο ὁ Ἰησοῦς τοῖς σάββασιν: this however is not, properly speaking, a various reading at all. Nor ought we to wonder if versions pass over altogether what their translators could not understand [1], so that we may easily account for the silence of the Peshitto Syriac, Bohairic, and Ethiopic, of the Old Latin *b c l q f* (*secundâ manu*) *q*, and (if they were worth notice) of the Persic and the Polyglott Arabic, though both the Roman and Erpenius' Arabic have δευτέρῳ, and so too the Ethiopic according to Scholz; *e* 'sabbato mane,' *f* 'sabbato a primo:' the Harkleian Syriac, which renders the word, notes in the margin its absence from some copies. Against this list of authorities, few in number, and doubtful as many of them are, we have to place the Old Latin *a* f^{*} ff^{2} $g^{1.2}$, all copies of the Vulgate, its ally the Armenian, the Gothic and Harkleian Syriac translations, the uncial codices ACDEHKMRSUVXΓΔΛΠ, all cursives except the seven cited above, and the Fathers or scholiasts who have tried, with whatever success, to explain the term: viz. Epiphanius, Chrysostom, Isidore of Pelusium, Pseudo-Caesarius, Gregory of Nazianzus, Jerome [2], Ambrose (all very expressly, as may be seen in Tischendorf's note, and in Dean Burgon's 'The Revision Revised,' pp. 73–4), Clement of Alexandria probably, and later writers. Lachmann and Alford

[1] Just as Jerome, speaking of the latter part of 1 Cor. vii. 35, says, 'In Lat. Codd. OB TRANSLATIONIS DIFFICULTATEM hoc penitus non invenitur.' (Vallars. ii. 261, as Burgon points out.)

[2] Dr. Hort and the *Quarterly Reviewer* (October, 1881, p. 348) almost simultaneously called attention to the question put by Jerome to his teacher Gregory of Nazianzus as to the meaning of this word. 'Docebo te super hac re in ecclesia' was the only reply he obtained; on which Jerome's comment is, *Eleganter lusit* (Hier. *ad Nepotianum*, Ep. 52). Neither of these great Fathers could explain a term which neither doubted to be written by the Evangelist.

place δευτεροπρώτῳ within brackets, Tregelles rejects it, as does Tischendorf in his earlier editions, but restores it in his seventh and eighth, in the latter contrary to Cod. ℵ. Westcott and Hort banish it to the margin, intimating (if I understand their notation aright) that it seems to contain distinctive and fresh matter, without deserving a place in the text even as well as Ἰησοῦ in Matt. i. 18. On reviewing the whole mass of evidence, internal and external, we submit the present as a clear instance in which the two oldest copies conspire in a false or highly improbable reading, and of a signal exemplification of the Canon, *Proclivi orationi praestat ardua.*

14. LUKE x. 41, 42. Ἑνὸς δέ ἐστι χρεία. This solemn speech of our Divine Master has shaken many a pulpit, and sanctified many a life. We might be almost content to estimate Cod. B's claim to paramount consideration as a primary authority by the treatment this passage receives from the hand of its scribe, at least if the judgement were to rest with those who are willing to admit that a small minority, whereof B happens to form one of the members, is not necessarily in the right. Westcott and Hort in the margin of their published edition (1881) reduce the whole sentence between Μάρθα ver. 41 and Μαρία ver. 42 to the single word θορυβάζῃ, the truer reading in the place of τυρβάζῃ: in their privately circulated issue dated ten years earlier they had gone further, placing within double brackets μεριμνᾷς καί and from περὶ πολλά downwards. They could hardly do less on the principles they have adopted, while yet they feel constrained to concede that, though not belonging to the original Gospel, the excluded words do not, on the other hand, read like the invention of a paraphrast. They do not indeed: and it is when abstract theories such as modern critics have devised are subjected to so violent a strain, that we can best discern their intrinsic weakness, of which indeed these editors have here shown their consciousness by a change of mind not at all usual with them. For the grave omission indicated above we have but one class of authorities, that of the D, *a b e ff*[2] *i l*, and Ambrose, the Latins omitting θορυβάζῃ too: while ἑνὸς δέ ἐστι χρεία is not found in *c* also, and does not appear in Clement. The succeeding γάρ or δέ is of course left out by all these, and by 262, the Vulgate, Curetonian Syriac, Armenian,

and Jerome. This testimony, almost purely Western, is confirmed or weakened as the case may be, by the systematic omissions of clauses towards the end of the Gospel in the same books, of which we spoke in Chap. X (*see* p. 299, note).

We confess that we had rather see this grand passage expunged altogether from the pages of the Gospel than diluted after the wretched fashion adopted by ℵ and B: *ὀλίγων δὲ χρεία ἐστιν ἢ ἑνός*· the first hand of ℵ omitting *χρεία* in its usual blundering way. This travestie of a speech which seems to have shocked the timorous by its uncompromising exclusiveness, much as we saw in the case of Matt. v. 22, is further supported (with some variation in the order) by L, by the very ancient second hand of C, by 1, 33, the Bohairic, Ethiopic, the margin of the Harkleian, by Basil, Jerome, Cyril of Alexandria in the Syriac translation of his commentary [1], and by Origen as cited in a catena: *ὀλίγων δέ ἐστι χρεία* is found in 38, the Jerusalem Syriac, and in the Armenian (*ὧδε* being inserted before *ἐστιν*). This latter reading is less incredible than that of ℵBL, notwithstanding the ingenuity of Basil's comment, *ὀλίγων μὲν δηλονότι τῶν πρὸς παρασκευήν, ἑνὸς δὲ τοῦ σκοποῦ*. In this instance, as in some others, the force of internal evidence suffices to convince the unprejudiced reader (it has almost convinced Drs. Westcott and Hort, who have no note on the passage), that the Received text should here remain unchanged, vouched for as it is by AC*EFGHKMPSUVΓΔΛΠ (X and Ξ being defective), by every cursive except three, by the Peshitto and Cureton's Syriac (the latter so often met with in the company of D), by the Harkleian text, by *f* g^1 g^2 *q* of the Old Latin, and by the Vulgate. Chrysostom, Augustine (twice), John Damascene and one or two others complete the list: even Basil so cites the passage once, so that his comment may not be intended for anything more than a gloss. No nobler sermon was ever preached on this fertile text than that of Augustine, De verbis Domini, in Evan. Luc. xxvii. His Old Latin copies, at any rate, contained the words 'Circa multa es occupata: porro unum est necessarium. Jam hoc sibi Maria legit.' 'Transit labor multitudinis, et remanet caritas unitatis' is his emphatic comment.

[1] Cyril applies the whole passage to enforce the duty of exercising with frugality the Christian duty of entertaining strangers: 'And this He did for our benefit, that He might fix a limit to hospitality' (Dean Payne Smith's Translation, pp. 317–20).

15. Luke xxii. 17–20. This passage has been made the subject of a most instructive discussion by Dean Blakesley[1] (d. 1885), whose notion respecting it deserves more consideration than it would seem to have received, though it must no doubt be ultimately set aside through the overpowering weight of hostile authority. He is perplexed by two difficulties lying on the surface, the fact that the Lord twice took a cup, before and after the breaking of the bread; and the close resemblance borne by vv. 19 and 20 to the parallel passage of St. Paul, 1 Cor. xi. 24, 25. The common mode of accounting for the latter phenomenon seems very reasonable, namely, that the Evangelist, Paul's almost constant companion in travel, copied into his Gospel the very language of the Apostle, so far as it suited his design. In speaking of the two cups St. Luke stands alone, and much trouble has been taken to illustrate the use of the Paschal cup from Maimonides [d. 1206] and other Jewish doctors, all too modern to be implicitly depended on. Dean Alford indeed (N.T. *ad loc.*) hails 'this most important addition to our narrative,' which 'amounts, I believe, to a solemn declaration of the fulfilment of the Passover rite, in both its usual divisions—the eating of the lamb, and drinking the cup of thanksgiving.' Thus regarded, the old rite would be concluded and abrogated in vv. 17, 18; the new rite instituted in vv. 19, 20. To Dean Blakesley all this appears wholly unsatisfactory, and he resorts for help to our critical authorities. He first gets rid of the words of ver. 19 after σῶμά μου, and of all ver. 20, and so far his course is sanctioned by Westcott and Hort, who place the whole passage within their double brackets, and pronounce it a perverse interpolation from 1 Cor. xi. 24, 25. This much accomplished, the cup is now mentioned but once, but with this awkward peculiarity, that it precedes the bread in the order of taking and blessing, which is a downright contradiction of St. Matthew (xxvi. 26–29) and of St. Mark (xiv. 22–25), as well as of St. Paul. Here Westcott and Hort refuse to be carried further, and thus leave the remedy worse than the disease[2], if indeed

[1] Praelectio in Scholis Cantabrigiensibus habita Februarii die decimo quarto, MDCCCL, quâ . . . Lucae pericopam (xxii. 17–20) multis ante saeculis conturbatam vetustissimorum ope codicum in pristinam formam restituebat, Cathedram Theologicam ambiens, J. W. Blakesley, S. T. B., Coll. SS. Trinitatis nuper Socius (Cambridge, 1850).

[2] 'Intrinsically both readings are difficult, but in unequal degrees. The

there be any disease to remedy. Dean Blakesley boldly places Luke xxii. 19 (ending at *σῶμά μου*) before ver. 17, and his work is done: the paragraph thus remodelled is self-consistent, but it is robbed of everything which has hitherto made it a distinctive narrative, supplementing as well as confirming those of the other two Evangelists.

Now for the last step in Dean Blakesley's process of emendation, the transposition of ver. 19 before ver. 17, there is no other authority save *b e* of the Old Latin and Cureton's Syriac, the last with this grave objection in his eyes, that it exhibits the whole of ver. 19, including that *τοῦτο ποιεῖτε εἰς τὴν ἐμὴν ἀνάμνησιν* which he would regard as specially belonging of right, and as most suitable for, St. Paul's narrative (Praelectio, p. 16), although Justin Martyr cites the expression with the prelude *οἱ γὰρ ἀπόστολοι ἐν τοῖς γενομένοις ὑπ' αὐτῶν ἀπομνημονεύμασιν, ἃ καλεῖται εὐαγγέλια.* The later portion of ver. 19 and the whole of ver. 20, as included in the double brackets of Westcott and Hort, are absent from Cod. D, and of the Latins from *a b e ff i l*, as is ver. 20 from the Curetonian Syriac also: authorities for the most part the same as we had to deal with in our Chap. X. p. 299, note. Another, and yet more violent remedy, to provide against the double mention of the cup, is found in the utter omission of vers. 17, 18 in Evst. 32 and the *editio princeps* of the Peshitto Syriac, countenanced by many manuscripts of the same [1]. Thus both the chief Syriac translations found a difficulty here, though they remedied it in different ways [2].

The scheme of Dean Blakesley is put forth with rare ingenuity [3], and maintained with a boldness which is best engendered

difficulty of the shorter reading [that of pure omission in vers. 19, 20] consists exclusively in the change of order, as to the Bread and the Cup, which is illustrated by many phenomena of the relation between the narratives of the third and of the first two Gospels, and which finds an exact parallel in the change of order in St. Luke's account of the Temptation' (iv. 5–8; 9–12). Hort, Notes, p. 64.

[1] Adler says 'in omnibus codicibus,' and *guelph. heidelb.* Dawkins iii and xvii in Jones, and cod. Rich are specified. Lee sets the verses in a parenthesis. But the Curetonian has them after ver. 19 in words but little differing from his or Schaaf's.

[2] 'Si fides habenda A. F. Gorio "in Conspectu Quattuor Codicum Evangeliorum Syriacorum mirae aetatis" apud Blanchini Evangelium Quadruplex p. DXL, et hi quattuor Codices cum Veronensi [*b*] faciunt.' Blakesley, *Schema* facing *Praelectio*, p. 20.

[3] Especially mark his mode of dealing with *ἐκχυννόμενον* ver. 20, which by

and nourished by closing the eyes to the strength of the adverse case. We have carefully enumerated the authorities of every kind which make for him, a slender roll indeed. When it is stated that the Received text (with only slight and ordinary variations) is upheld by Codd. ℵABCEFGHKLM (*hiant* PR) SUXVΓΔΛΠ, by all cursives and versions, except those already accounted for, it will be seen that his view of the passage can never pass beyond the region of speculation, until the whole system of Biblical Criticism is revolutionized by means of new discoveries which it seems at present vain to look for.

16. Luke xxii. 43, 44. *ὤφθη δὲ αὐτῷ ἄγγελος ἀπ' οὐρανοῦ ἐνισχύων αὐτόν. καὶ γενόμενος ἐν ἀγωνίᾳ, ἐκτενέστερον προσηύχετο· ἐγένετο δὲ ὁ ἱδρὼς αὐτοῦ ὡσεὶ θρόμβοι αἵματος καταβαίνοντες ἐπὶ τὴν γῆν.* It is a positive relief to know that any lingering doubt which may have hung over the authenticity of these verses, whose sacred words the devout reader of Scripture could so ill spare, is completely dissipated by their being contained in Cod. ℵ[1]. The two verses are omitted in ABRT, 124, 561 (in 13 only *ὤφθη δέ* is *primâ manu*), in *f* of the Old Latin, in at least ten manuscripts of the Bohairic[2], with some Sahidic and Armenian codices. A, however, whose inconsistency we had to note when considering ch. ii. 14, affixes to the latter part of ver. 42 (*πλήν*), 'to

a little violence (not quite unprecedented) is made to refer to *ποτήριον* instead of to *αἵματι*: 'Ex Matthaeo vel Marco accessit clausula ista *τὸ ὑπὲρ ὑμῶν ἐκχυννόμενον*, fraude tamen ita piâ accessit, ut potius grammaticis legibus vim facere, quam vel literulam demutare maluerit interpolator. Ita fit ut vel hodie male assutus pannus centonem prodat. Postulat enim sermonis ratio, ut cuivis patet, *τῷ ὑπὲρ ὑμῶν ἐκχυνομένῳ*, non *τὸ ὑπὲρ ὑμῶν ἐκχυνόμενον*, quod tamen in Matthaeo Marcoque optime Graece dicebatur, cum subjectum de quo praedicabatur non *ἡ διαθήκη* verum *τὸ αἷμα* esset' (*Praelectio*, p. 22).

[1] Very undue stress has been laid on Tischendorf's statement, 'Hos versus A corrector uncis inclusit, partim etiam punctis notavit; C vero puncta et uncos delevit,' and ℵ[a] has sometimes been spoken of as only a little less weighty than ℵ itself. I had the satisfaction, through Dean Burgon's kindness, of showing some of our critics, Dr. Hort included, a fine photograph of the whole page. The points are nearly, if not quite, invisible, the unci are rude slight curves at the beginning and end of the passage only, looking as likely to have been scrawled fifty years since as fourteen hundred. Yet even now Dr. Hort maintains that Tischendorf's decision is probably right, strangely adding, 'but the point is of little consequence' (Notes, p. 65).

[2] Bp. Lightfoot's Codd. 2, 4, 8, 9, 16, 17, 19, 22, 26 omit them altogether: they are in the margin of 1, 20. They stand in the text of 3, 14, 21, and so in 18 *primâ manu*, but in smaller characters.

which they cannot belong' (Tregelles), the proper Ammonian and Eusebian numerals for vv. 43–4 $\left(\frac{\sigma\pi\gamma}{\iota}\right)$, and thus shows that its scribe was acquainted with the passage[1]: some Armenian codices leave out only ver. 44, as apparently does Evan. 559. In Codd. Γ, 123, 344, 512, 569, (440 *secundâ manu* in ver. 43) the verses are obelized, and are marked by asterisks in ESVΔΠ, 24, 36, 161, 166, 274, 408: these, however, may very well be, and in some copies doubtless are, lesson-marks for the guidance of such as read the divine service (*cf. sequent.*). A scholion in Cod. 34 [xi] speaks of its absence from some copies[2]. In all known Evangelistaria and in their cognate Cod. 69* and its three fellows, the two verses, omitted in this place, follow Matt. xxvi. 39, as a regular part of the lesson for the Thursday in Holy Week: in the same place the margin of C (*tertiâ manu*) contains the passage, C being defective in Luke xxii from ver. 19. In Cod. 547 the two verses stand (in redder ink, with a scholion) not only after Matt. xxvi. 39, but also in their proper place in St. Luke[3]. Thus too Cod. 346, and the margin of Cod. 13. Codd. LQ place the Ammonian sections and the number of the Eusebian canons differently from the rest (but this kind of irregularity very often occurs in manuscripts), and the Philoxenian margin in one of Adler's manuscripts (Assem. 2) states that it is not found '*in Evangeliis apud Alexandrinos*, proptereaque [non ?] posuit eam S. Cyrillus in homilia . . .:' the fact being that the verses are not found in Cyril's 'Homilies on Luke,' published in Syriac at Oxford by Dean Payne Smith,

[1] Yet Dr. Hort contends that 'The testimony of A is not affected by the presence of Eusebian numerals, of necessity misplaced, which manifestly presuppose the inclusion of vv. 43, 44: the discrepance merely shows that the Biblical text and the Eusebian notation were taken by the scribe from different sources, as they doubtless were throughout' (Notes, p. 65). It is just this readiness to devise expedients to meet emergencies as they arise which is at once the strength and the weakness of Dr. Hort's position as a textual critic. These sections and canons illustrate the criticism of the text in some other places: e.g. Matt. xvi. 2, 3; xvii. 21; ch. xxiii. 34; hardly in Luke xxiv. 12.

[2] Ἰστέον ὅτι τὰ περὶ τῶν θρόμβων τινὰ τῶν ἀντιγράφων οὐκ ἔχουσιν: adding that the clause is cited by Dionysius the Areopagite, Gennadius, Epiphanius, and other holy Fathers.

[3] Thus in Evst. 253 we find John xiii. 3–17 inserted *uno tenore* between Matt. xxvi. 20 and 21, as also Luke xxii. 43, 44 between vers. 39 and 40, with no break whatever. So again in the same manuscript with the mixed lessons for Good Friday.

nor does Athanasius ever allude to them. They are read, however, in Codd. ℵDFGHKLMQUXΛ, 1, and all other known cursives, without any marks of suspicion, in the Peshitto, Curetonian (omitting ἀπ' οὐρανοῦ), Harkleian and Jerusalem Syriac (this last obelized in the margin), the Ethiopic, in some Sahidic, Bohairic, and Armenian manuscripts and editions, in the Old Latin *a b c e ff*^{2} *g*$^{1.2}$ *i l q*, and the Vulgate. The effect of this great preponderance is enhanced by the early and express testimony of Fathers. Justin Martyr (Trypho, 103) cites ἱδρὼς ὡσεὶ θρόμβοι as contained ἐν τοῖς ἀπομνημονεύμασιν ἅ φημι ὑπὸ τῶν ἀποστόλων αὐτοῦ καὶ τῶν ἐκείνοις παρακολουθησάντων (see Luke i. 3, Alford) συντετάχθαι. Irenaeus (iii. 222) declares that the Lord ἵδρωσε θρόμβους αἵματος in the second century. In the third, Hippolytus twice, Dionysius of Alexandria, and Pseudo-Tatian; in the fourth, Arius, Eusebius, Athanasius, Ephraem Syrus, Didymus, Gregory of Nazianzen, Epiphanius, Chrysostom, Pseudo-Dionysius Areopagita; in the fifth, Julian the heretic, Theodore of Mopsuestia, Nestorius, Cyril of Alexandria, Paulus of Emesa, Gennadius, Theodoret, Bishops at Ephesus in 431; and later writers such as Pseudo-Caesarius, Theodosius of Alexandria, John Damascene, Maximus, Theodore the heretic, Leontius of Byzantium, Anastasius Sinaita, Photius, as well as Hilary, Jerome, Augustine, Cassian, Paulinus, Facundus [1]. Hilary, on the other hand, declares that the passage is not found 'in Graecis et in Latinis codicibus compluribus' (p. 1062 a, Benedictine edition, 1693), a statement which Jerome, who leans much on others in such matters, repeats to the echo. Epiphanius, however, in a passage we have before alluded to (p. 270, note), charges 'the orthodox' with removing ἔκλαυσε in ch. xix. 41, though Irenaeus had used it against the Docetae, φοβηθέντες καὶ μὴ νοήσαντες αὐτοῦ τὸ τέλος καὶ τὸ ἰσχυρότατον, καὶ γενόμενος ἐν ἀγωνίᾳ ἵδρωσε, καὶ ἐγένετο ὁ ἱδρὼς αὐτοῦ ὡς θρόμβοι αἵματος, καὶ ὤφθη ἄγγελος ἐνισχύων αὐτόν: Epiphan. Ancor. xxxi [2]. Davidson states

[1] 'Upwards of forty famous personages from every part of ancient Christendom recognize these verses as part of the Gospel; fourteen of them being as old, some of them being a great deal older, than our oldest manuscripts' (The Revision Revised, p. 81).

[2] The reader will see that I have understood this passage, with Grotius, as applying to an orthodox tampering with Luke xix. 41, not with xxii. 43, 44. As the text of Epiphanius stands I cannot well do otherwise, since Mill's mode of punctuation (N. T., Proleg. § 797), which wholly separates καὶ γενόμενος from the

that 'the Syrians are censured by Photius, the Armenians by Nicon [x], Isaac the Catholic, and others, for expunging the passage' (Bibl. Critic. ii. p. 438).

Of all recent editors, before Westcott and Hort set them within their double brackets, Lachmann alone had doubted the authenticity of the verses, and enclosed them within brackets: but for the accidental presence of the fragment Cod. Q his hard rule —'*mathematica recensendi ratio*,' as Tischendorf terms it—would have forced him to expunge them, unless indeed he judged (which is probably true) that Cod. A makes as much in their favour as against them. So far as the language of Epiphanius is concerned, it does not appear that this passage was rejected by the orthodox as repugnant to their notions of the Lord's Divine character, and such may not have been at all the origin of the variation. We have far more just cause for tracing the removal of the paragraph from its proper place in St. Luke to the practice of the Lectionaries, whose principal lessons (such as those of the Holy Week would be) were certainly settled in the Greek Church as early as the fourth century (*see* above, Vol. I. pp. 74–7, and notes). I remark with lively thankfulness that my friend Professor Milligan does not disturb these precious verses in his 'Words of the New Testament:' and Mr. Hammond concludes that 'on the whole there is no reasonable doubt upon the passage.' Thus Canon Cook is surely justified in his strong asseveration that 'supporting the whole passage we have an array of authorities which, whether we regard their antiquity or their character for sound judgement, veracity, and accuracy, are scarcely paralleled on any occasion' (Revised Version, p. 103).

17. Luke xxiii. 34. We soon light upon another passage wherein the Procrustean laws of certain eminent editors are irreconcileably at variance with their own Christian feeling and critical instinct. No holy passage has been brought into disrepute on much slighter grounds than this speech of the Lord upon the cross: the words from Ὁ δὲ Ἰησοῦς down to ποιοῦσιν are set within brackets by Lachmann, within double brackets by Westcott and Hort. They are omitted by only BD*, 38, 435,

words immediately preceding, cannot be endured, and leaves καὶ τὸ ἰσχυρότατον unaccounted for. Yet I confess that there is no trace of any meddling with ἔκλαυσε by any one, and I know not where Irenaeus cites it.

among the manuscripts: by E they are marked with an asterisk (comp. Matt. xvi. 2, 3; ch. xxii. 43, 44); of ℵ Tischendorf speaks more cautiously than in the case of ch. xxii. 43, 44, 'A [a reviser] (ut videtur) uncos apposuit, sed rursus deleti sunt,' and we saw there how little cause there was for assigning the previous omission to ℵ[a]. In D the clause is inserted, with the proper (Ammonian) section (τκ or 320), in a hand which cannot be earlier than the ninth century (*see* Scrivener's Codex Bezae, facsimile 11, and Introd. p. xxvii). To this scanty list of authorities for the omission we can only add *a b* of the Old Latin, the Latin of Cod. D, the Sahidic version, two copies of the Bohairic[1], and a passage in Arethas of the sixth century. Eusebius assigned the section to his tenth table or canon, as it has no parallel in the other three Gospels. The passage is contained without a vestige of suspicion in ℵACFGHK (even L) M (*hiat* P) QSUVΓΔΛΠ, all other cursives (including 1, 33, 69), *c e f ff*² *l*, the Vulgate, all four Syriac versions, all Bohairic codices except the aforenamed two, the Armenian and Ethiopic. The Patristic authorities for it are (as might be anticipated) express, varied, and numerous:—such as Irenaeus and Origen in their Latin versions, the dying words of St. James the Just as cited in Eusebius, Eccl. Hist., lib. ii. cap. 23, after Hegesippus, ἐπὶ τῆς πρώτης τῶν ἀποστόλων γενόμενος διαδοχῆς (Eus.), Hippolytus, the Apostolic Constitutions twice, the Clementine Homilies, Ps.-Tatian, Archelaus with Manes, Eusebius, Athanasius, Gregory of Nyssa, Theodorus of Heraclea, Basil, Ephraem Syrus, Ps.-Ephraem, Ps.-Dionysius Areopagita, Acta Pilati, Syriac Acts of the Apostles, Ps.-Ignatius, Ps.-Justin, Cyril of Alexandria, Eutherius, Anastasius Sinaita, Hesychius, Antiochus Monachus, Andreas of Crete, Ps.-Chrysostom, Ps.-Amphilochius, Opus Imperfectum, Chrysostom often (sometimes loosely enough *more suo*), Hilary, Ambrose eleven times, Jerome twelve times, Augustine more than sixty times, Theodoret, and John Damascene. Tischendorf adds—*valeant quantum*—(but only a fraction of this evidence was known to Tischendorf), the apocryphal Acta Pilati[2]. It is almost incredible

[1] Lightfoot's Codd. 22, 26. The clause stands in the margin of 1, 20, in the text of 2, 3, 8, 9, 14, 16, 17, 19, 21, 23.

[2] Dean Burgon (Revision Revised, p. 83), who refers to upwards of forty Fathers and more than 150 passages (*see* also Miller's Textual Guide, App. II), burns with indignation as he sums up his results: 'And *what* (we ask the question with sincere simplicity), *what* amount of evidence is calculated to

that acute and learned men should be able to set aside such a *silva* of witness of every kind, chiefly because D is considered especially weighty in its omissions, and B has to be held up, in practice if not in profession, as virtually almost impeccable. Vain indeed is the apology, 'Few verses of the Gospels bear in themselves a surer witness to the truth of what they record than this first of the Words from the Cross; but it need not therefore have belonged originally to the book in which it is now included. We cannot doubt that it comes from an extraneous source' (Hort, Notes, p. 68. Nor can we on our part doubt that the system which entails such consequences is hopelessly self-condemned.

18. JOHN i. 18. ὁ μονογενὴς υἱός, ὁ ὢν εἰς τὸν κόλπον τοῦ πατρός ... This passage exhibits in a few ancient documents of high consideration the remarkable variation θεός for υἱός, which however, according to the form of writing universal in the oldest codices (*see* Vol. I. pp. 15, 50), would require but the change of a single letter, $\overline{\text{ΤC}}$ or $\overline{\text{ΘC}}$. In behalf of $\overline{\text{ΘC}}$ stand Codd. ℵBC *primâ manu*, and L (all wanting the article before μονογενής, and ℵ omitting the ὁ ὢν that follows), 33 alone among cursive manuscripts (but prefixing ὁ to μονογενής, as does a later hand of ℵ), of the versions the Peshitto (not often found in such company), and the margin of the Harkleian (whose affinity with Cod. L is very decided), the Ethiopic, and a host of Fathers, some expressly (e.g. Clement of Alexandria, Didymus 'de Trinitate,' Epiphanius, Cyril of Alexandria, &c.), others by apparent reference (e.g. Gregory of Nyssa). The Egyptian versions may have read either θεός or θεοῦ, more probably the latter, as Prebendary Malan translates for the Bohairic[1], the

inspire undoubted confidence in any given reading, if not such a concurrence of authorities as this? We forbear to insist upon the probabilities of the case. The Divine power and sweetness of the incident shall not be enlarged upon. We introduce no considerations resulting from internal evidence. Let this verse of Scripture stand or fall as it meets with sufficient external testimony, or is clearly forsaken thereby.'

[1] 'Gospel according to St. John from eleven versions,' 1872, p. 8. Dr. Malan also translates in the same way the Peshitto 'the only Son of God' and its satellite the Persic of the Polyglott as 'the only one of God.' With much deference to a profound scholar, I do not see how such a rendering is possible in the Peshitto: it is precisely that which he gives in ch. iii. 18, where the Syriac inserts ܒܪܗ ܕ. Bp. Lightfoot judges θεός the more likely rendering of the Bohairic, though θεοῦ is possible.

Sahidic being here lost. Their testimonies are elaborately set forth by Tregelles, who strenuously maintains θεός as the true reading, and thinks it much that Arius, though 'opposed to the dogma taught,' upholds μονογενὴς θεός. It may be that the term suits that heretic's system better than it does the Catholic doctrine: it certainly does not confute it. For the received reading υἱός we can allege AC (*tertiâ manu*) EFGHKMSUVXΔΛΠ (D and the other uncials being defective), every cursive manuscript except 33 (including Tregelles' allies 1, 69), all the Latin versions, the Curetonian, Harkleian, and Jerusalem Syriac, the Georgian and Slavonic, the Armenian and Platt's Ethiopic, the Anglo-Saxon and Arabic. The array of Fathers is less imposing, but includes Athanasius (often), Chrysostom, and the Latin writers down from Tertullian. Origen, Eusebius, and some others have both readings. Cyril of Jerusalem quotes without υἱός or θεός,—ὃν ἀνθρώπων μὲν οὐδεὶς ἑώρακεν· ὁ μονογενὴς δὲ μόνος ἐξηγήσατο. C. 7, l. 27, p. 107, ed. Oxon., Pereira.

Tregelles, who seldom notices internal probabilities in his critical notes, here pleads that an ἅπαξ λεγόμενον like μονογενὴς θεός [1] might easily be changed by copyists into the more familiar ὁ μονογενὴς υἱός from John iii. 16; 18; 1 John iv. 9, and he would therefore apply Bengel's Canon (I. *see* p. 247). Alford's remark, however, is very sound: 'We should be introducing great harshness into the sentence, and a new and [to us moderns] strange term into Scripture, by adopting θεός: a consequence which ought to have no weight whatever where authority is overpowering, but may fairly be weighed where this is not so. The "praestat procliviori ardua" finds in this case a legitimate limit' (N. T., note on John i. 18). Every one indeed must feel θεός to be untrue, even though for the sake of consistency he may be forced to uphold it. Westcott and Hort set μονογενὴς θεός in the text, but concede to ὁ μονογενὴς υἱός a place in their margin.

Those who will resort to 'ancient evidence exclusively' for the recension of the text may well be perplexed in dealing with this passage. The oldest manuscripts, versions, and writers are hopelessly divided, so that we can well understand how some critics (not very unreasonably, perhaps, yet without a shadow of authority worth notice) have come to suspect both θεός and

[1] We are not likely to adopt Tischendorf's latest reading and punctuation in Col. ii. 2, τοῦ Θεοῦ, Χριστοῦ.

υἱός to be *accretions* or spurious additions to μονογενής. If the principles advocated in Vol. II. Ch. X be true, the present is just such a case as calls for the interposition of the more recent uncial and cursive codices; and when we find that they all, with the single exception of Cod. 33, defend the reading ὁ μονογενὴς υἱός, we feel safe in concluding that for once Codd. אBC and the Peshitto do not approach the autograph of St. John so nearly as Cod. A, the Harkleian Syriac, and Old Latin versions[1].

19. JOHN iii. 13. Westcott and Hort remove from the text to the margin the weighty and doubtless difficult, but on that account only the more certainly genuine, words ὁ ὢν ἐν τῷ οὐρανῷ. Tischendorf rejected them (as indeed does Professor Milligan) in his 'Synopsis Evangelica,' 1864, but afterwards repented of his decision. The authorities for omission are אBL (which read μονογενὴς θεός in ch. i. 18) T^b [vi], 33 alone among manuscripts. CDF are defective here: but the clause is contained in AEGHKMSUVΓΔΛΠ, and in all cursives save one, A* and one Evangelistarium (44) omitting ὤν. No versions can be cited against the clause except one manuscript of the Bohairic: it appears in every one else, including the Latin, the four Syriac, the Ethiopic, the Georgian, and the Armenian. There is really no Patristic evidence to set up against it, for it amounts to nothing that the words are not found in the Armenian versions of Ephraem's Exposition of Tatian's Harmony (*see* Vol. I. p. 59, note 2); that Eusebius might have cited them twice and did not; that Cyril of Alexandria, who alleges them once, passed over them once; that Origen also (in the Latin translation) neglected them once, inasmuch as he quotes them twice, once very expressly. Hippolytus [220] is the prime witness in their behalf, for he draws the theological inference from the passage (ἀποσταλεὶς ἵνα δείξῃ αὐτὸν ἐπὶ γῆς ὄντα εἶναι καὶ ἐν οὐρανῷ), wherein he is followed in two places by Hilary and by Epiphanius. To these add Dionysius of Alexandria [iii], Novatian [iii], Aphraates the Persian, Didymus, Lucifer, Athanasius, Basil,

[1] Hence we cannot think with Prebendary Sadler (Lost Gospel, p. 48) that μονογενὴς θεός is very probably the original reading, and must even take leave to doubt its orthodoxy. The received reading ὁ μονογενὴς υἱός is upheld by Dr. Ezra Abbot in papers contributed to the American *Bibliotheca Sacra*, Oct. 1861, and to the *Unitarian Review*, June, 1875; it is attacked with characteristic vigour and fullness of research by Dr. Hort in the first of his 'Two Dissertations' (pp. 1–72) written in 1876 as exercises for Theological degrees at Cambridge.

besides Ambrose, Jerome, Augustine, and by John Damascene (thrice), by Cyril of Alexandria, Chrysostom, and Theodoret each four times,—indeed, as Dean Burgon has shown[1], more than fifty passages from thirty-eight ecclesiastical writers; and we then have a *consensus* of versions and ecclesiastical writers from every part of the Christian world, joining Cod. A and the later manuscripts in convicting ℵBL, &c., or the common sources from which they were derived, of the deliberate suppression of one of the most mysterious, yet one of the most glorious, glimpses afforded to us in Scripture of the nature of the Saviour, on the side of His Proper Divinity.

20. John v. 3, 4. *ἐκδεχομένων τὴν τοῦ ὕδατος κίνησιν. ἄγγελος γὰρ κατὰ καιρὸν κατέβαινεν ἐν τῇ κολυμβήθρᾳ, καὶ ἐτάρασσε τὸ ὕδωρ· ὁ οὖν πρῶτος ἐμβὰς μετὰ τὴν ταραχὴν τοῦ ὕδατος, ὑγιὴς ἐγίνετο, ᾧ δήποτε κατείχετο νοσήματι.* This passage is expunged by Tischendorf, Tregelles, Alford, Westcott and Hort, obelized (=) by Griesbach, but retained by Scholz and Lachmann. The evidence against it is certainly very considerable: Codd. ℵBC*D, 33, 157, 314, but D, 33 contain *ἐκδεχομένων . . . κίνησιν*, which *alone* A*L, 18 omit. It may be observed that in this part of St. John A and L are much together against ℵ, and against B yet more. The words from *ἄγγελος γάρ* to *νοσήματι* are noted with asterisks or obeli (employed without much discrimination) in SΛ, 8, 11?, 14 (*ἄγγελος . . . ὕδωρ* being left out), 21, 24, 32, 36, 145, 161, 166, 230, 262, 269, 299, 348, 408, 507, 512, 575, 606, and Armenian manuscripts. The Harkleian margin marks from *ἄγγελος* to *ὕδωρ* with an asterisk, the remainder of the verse with obeli. The whole passage is given, although with that extreme variation in the reading which so often indicates grounds for suspicion[2], in EFGHIKMUVΓΔΠ (with an asterisk throughout), and all known cursives not enumerated above[3]: of these

[1] The Revision Revised, p. 133. Also Miller's 'Textual Guide,' App. VI.

[2] To give but a very small part of the variations in ver. 4: *δέ* (*pro γάρ*) L, *a b c ff*, Vulg. —*γάρ* Evst. 51, Boh. + *κυρίου* (*post γὰρ*) AKLΔ, 12, 13, 69, 507, 509, 511, 512, 570 and fifteen others: at *τοῦ θεοῦ* 152, Evst. 53, 54. —*κατὰ καιρὸν a b ff* *ἐλούετο* (*pro κατέβαινεν*) A (K), 42, 507. Ethiop. —*ἐν τῇ κολυμβήθρᾳ a b ff*. *ἐταράσσετο τὸ ὕδωρ* C³GHIMUVΛ*, 440, 509, 510, 512, 513, 515, 543, 570, 575, Evst. 150, 257, many others. + in piscinam (*post ἐμβάς*) *c*, Clementine Vulg. *ἐγένετο* FL, 69, at least fifteen others.

[3] Either Dean Burgon or I have recently found the passage in Codd. 518, 524, 541, 560, 561, 573, 582, 594, 598, 599, 600, 602, 604, 622.

Cod. I [vi] is of the greatest weight. Cod. A contains the whole passage, but down to *κίνησιν secundâ manu*; Cod. C also the whole, *tertiâ manu*. Of the versions, Cureton's Syriac, the Sahidic, Schwartze's Bohairic [1], some Armenian manuscripts, *f l q* of the Old Latin, *san. harl.** and two others of the Vulgate (*vid.* Griesbach) are for omission; the Roman edition of the Ethiopic leaves out what the Harkleian margin obelizes, but the Peshitto and Jerusalem Syriac, all Latin copies not aforenamed, Wilkins' Bohairic, and Armenian editions are for retaining the disputed words. Tertullian clearly recognizes them ('piscinam Bethsaidam angelus interveniens commovebat,' *de Baptismo*, 5), as do Didymus, Chrysostom, Cyril, Ambrose (twice), Theophylact, and Euthymius. Nonnus [v] does not touch it in his metrical paraphrase.

The first clause (*ἐκδεχ . . . . . . κίνησιν*) can hardly stand in Dr. Scrivener's opinion, in spite of the versions which support it, as DI are the oldest manuscript witnesses in its favour, and it bears much of the appearance of a gloss brought in from the margin. The succeeding verse is harder to deal with [2]; but for the countenance of the versions and the testimony of Tertullian, Cod. A could never resist the joint authority of ℵBCD, illustrated as they are by the marks of suspicion set in so many later copies. Yet if ver. 4 be indeed but an '*insertion to complete that implied in the narrative with reference to the popular belief*' (Alford, *ad loc.*), it is much more in the manner of Cod. D and the Curetonian Syriac, than of Cod. A and the Latin versions; and since these last two are not very often found in unison, and together with the Peshitto, opposed to the other primary documents, it is not very rash to say that when such a conjunction does occur, it proves that the reading was early, widely diffused, and extensively received. Yet, after all, if the passage as it stands in our common text can be maintained as genuine at all, it must be, we apprehend, on the principle suggested above, Vol. I. Chap. I. § 11, p. 18. The chief difficulty, of course, consists

[1] Of Lightfoot's list of manuscripts, the passage is omitted in Codd. 2, 4, 5, 7, 8, 16, 17, 18, 19, 21, 23, 25, 26. It stands in the text of 3, 9, 14, in the margin only of 1, 20.

[2] 'Both elements, the clause ἐκδεχομένων τὴν τῶν ὑδάτων (*sic*) κίνησιν, and the scholium or explanatory note respecting the angel, are unquestionably very ancient: but no good Greek document contains both, while each of them separately is condemned by decisive evidence' (Hort, Introd., p. 301).

in the fact that so many copies are still without the addition, if assumed to be made by the Evangelist himself: nor will this supposition very well account for the wide variations subsisting between the manuscripts which do contain the supplement, both here and in chh. vii. 53—viii. 11[1].

21. JOHN vii. 8. This passage has provoked the 'bark' of Porphyry the philosopher, by common consent the most acute and formidable adversary our faith encountered in ancient times [d. 304]. 'Iturum se negavit,' as Jerome represents Porphyry's objection, 'et fecit quod prius negaverat: latrat Porphyrius, inconstantiae et mutationis accusat.' Yet in the common text, which Lachmann, Westcott and Hort, apparently with Professor Milligan, join in approving, ἐγὼ οὔπω ἀναβαίνω εἰς τὴν ἑορτὴν ταύτην, there is no vestige of levity of purpose on the Lord's part, but rather a gentle intimation that what He would not do then, He would do hereafter. It is plain therefore that Porphyry the foe, and Jerome the defender of the faith, both found in their copies οὐκ, not οὔπω, and this is the reading of Tischendorf and Tregelles: Hort and Westcott set it in their margin. Thus too Epiphanius and Chrysostom in the fourth century, Cyril in the fifth, each of them feeling the difficulty of the passage, and meeting it in his own way. For οὐκ we have the support of ℵ (AC *hiant*) DKMΠ, 17 *secundâ manu*, 389: add 507, 570, being Scrivener's pw (two excellent cursives, often found together in vouching for good readings), 558, Evst. 234, the Latin *a b c e ff*[2] *l secundâ manu*, Cureton's Syriac, the Bohairic, Armenian, and Ethiopic versions[2], a minority of the whole doubtless, yet a goodly band, gathered from east and west alike. In this case no hesitation would have been felt in adopting a reading, not only the harder in itself, but the only one that will explain the history of the passage, had not the palpable and wilful emendation οὔπω been upheld by B: *ignoscitur isti*, even when it resorts to a subterfuge which in any other manuscript would be put

[1] Dean Burgon has left a long vindication of the whole passage amongst his papers not yet published.

[2] Add from Dr. Malan (*ubi supra*, p. 97), the Georgian, Slavonic (text, not margin), Anglo-Saxon, and Persic. His Arabic (that of Erpenius) agrees with the Peshitto Syriac. The Armenian version of Ephraem's Tatian also reads *non*.

aside with scorn. The change, however, from the end of the third century downwards, was very generally and widely diffused. Besides B and its faithful allies LT, οὔπω is read in EFGHSUVXΓΔΛ, in all cursives not cited above, in *fgq*, in some Vulgate codices (but in none of the best), the Sahidic, Gothic, and three other Syriac versions, the Harkleian also in its Greek margin. Basil is alleged for the same reading, doubtless not expressly, like the Fathers named above. It is seldom that we can trace so clearly the date and origin of an important corruption which could not be accidental, and it is well to know that no extant authorities, however venerable, are quite exempt from the influence of dishonest zeal.

22. JOHN vii. 53—viii. 11. On no other grounds than those just intimated when discussing ch. v. 3, 4 can this celebrated and important paragraph, the *pericope adulterae* as it is called, be regarded as a portion of St. John's Gospel. It is absent from too many excellent copies not to have been wanting in some of the very earliest; while the arguments in its favour, internal even more than external, are so powerful, that we can scarcely be brought to think it an unauthorized appendage to the writings of one, who in another of his inspired books deprecated so solemnly the adding to or taking away from the blessed testimony he was commissioned to bear (Apoc. xxii. 18, 19). If ch. xx. 30, 31 show signs of having been the original end of this Gospel, and ch. xxi be a later supplement by the Apostle's own hand, which I think with Dean Alford is evidently the case, why should not St. John have inserted in this second edition both the amplification in ch. v. 3, 4, and this most edifying and eminently Christian narrative? The appended chapter (xxi) would thus be added at once to all copies of the Gospels then in circulation, though a portion of them might well overlook the minuter change in ch. v. 3, 4, or, from obvious though mistaken motives, might hesitate to receive for general use or public reading the history of the woman taken in adultery.

It must be in this way, if at all, that we can assign to the Evangelist chh. vii. 53—viii. 11; on all intelligent principles of mere criticism the passage must needs be abandoned: and such is the conclusion arrived at by all the critical editors. It is entirely omitted (ch. viii. 12 following continuously to ch. vii. 52) in the uncial Codd. ℵA[1]BC[1]T (all very old authorities) LX[2]Δ, but LΔ leave a void space (like B's in Mark xvi. 9–20) too small to contain the verses (though any space would suffice to intimate the consciousness of some omission), before which Δ* began to write ch. viii. 12 after ch. vii. 52.

Add to these, as omitting the paragraph, the cursives 3, 12, 21, 22, 33, 36, 44, 49, 63 (*teste* Abbott), 72, 87, 95, 96, 97, 106, 108, 123, 131, 134, 139, 143, 149, 157, 168, 169, 181, 186, 194, 195, 210, 213, 228, 249, 250, 253, 255, 261, 269, 314, 331, 388, 392, 401, 416, 453, 473 (with an explanatory note), 486, 510, 550, 559, 561, 582 (in ver. 12 *πάλαι* for *πάλιν*): it is absent in the first, added by a second hand in 9, 15, 105, 179, 232, 284, 353, 509, 625: while ch. viii. 3–11 is wanting in 77, 242, 324 (sixty-two cursive copies). The passage is noted by an asterisk or obelus or other mark in Codd. MS, 4, 8, 14, 18, 24, 34 (with an explanatory note), 35, 83, 109, 125, 141, 148 (*secundâ manu*), 156, 161, 166, 167, 178, 179, 189, 196, 198, 201, 202, 219, 226, 230, 231 (*secundâ manu*), 241, 246, 271, 274, 277, 284?, 285, 338, 348, 360, 361, 363, 376, 391 (*secundâ manu*), 394, 407, 408, 413 (a row of commas), 422, 436, 518 (*secundâ manu*), 534, 542, 549, 568, 575, 600. There are thus noted vers. 2–11 in E, 606: vers. 3–11 in Π (*hiat* ver. 6), 128, 137, 147: vers. 4–11 in 212 (with unique rubrical directions) and 355: with explanatory scholia appended in 164, 215, 262[3] (sixty-one cursives). Speaking generally, copies which contain a commentary omit the paragraph, but Codd. 59–66, 503, 526, 536 are exceptions to this practice. Scholz, who has taken unusual pains in the examination of this

[1] Codd. AC are defective in this place, but by measuring the space we have shown (p. 99, note 2) that A does not contain the twelve verses, and the same method applies to C. The reckoning, as McClellan remarks (N. T., p. 723), 'does not preclude the possibility of small gaps having existed in A and C to mark the *place* of the Section, as in L and Δ.'

[2] Yet Burgon's caution should be attended to. 'It is to mislead—rather it is to misrepresent the facts of the case—to say (with the critics) that Codex X leaves out the "pericope de adulterâ." This Codex is nothing else but *a commentary on the Gospel, as the Gospel used to be read in public.* Of necessity, therefore, it leaves out those parts of the Gospel which are observed *not* to have been publicly read' (*Guardian*, Sept. 10, 1873).

[3] The kindred copies Codd. Λ, 215 (20 has an asterisk only against the place), 262, &c., have the following scholium at ch. vii. 53: *τὰ ὠβελισμένα ἔν τισιν ἀντιγράφοις οὐ κεῖται, οὐδὲ Ἀπολ[λ]ιναρίῳ· ἐν δὲ τοῖς ἀρχαίοις ὅλα κεῖ[ν]ται· μνημονεύουσιν τῆς περικοπῆς ταύτης καὶ οἱ ἀπόστολοι, ἐν αἷς ἐξέθεντο διατάξεσιν εἰς οἰκοδομὴν τῆς ἐκκλησίας.* The reference is to the Apostolic Constitutions (ii. 24. 4), as Tischendorf perceives.

question, enumerates 290 cursives, others since his time forty-one more, which contain the paragraph with no trace of suspicion, as do the uncials DF (*partly defective*) GHKUΓ (with a hiatus after στήσαντες αὐτήν ver. 3): to which add Cod. 736 (*see addenda*) and the recovered Cod. 64, for which Mill on ver. 2 cited Cod. 63 in error. Cod. 145 has it only *secundâ manu*, with a note that from ch. viii. 3 τοῦτο τὸ κεφάλαιον ἐν πολλοῖς ἀντιγράφοις οὐ κεῖται. The obelized Cod. 422 at the same place has in the margin by a more recent hand ἐν τῆσιν ἀντιγράφης οὕτως. Codd. 1, 19, 20, 129, 135, 207 [1], 215, 301, 347, 478, 604, 629, Evst. 86 contain the whole *pericope* at the end of the Gospel. Of these, Cod. 1 in a scholium pleads its absence ὡς ἐν τοῖς πλείοσιν ἀντιγράφοις, and from the commentaries of Chrysostom, Cyril of Alexandria, and Theodore of Mopsuestia; while 135, 301 confess they found it ἐν ἀρχαίοις ἀντιγράφοις: Codd. 20, 215, 559 are obelized at the end of the section, and have a scholium which runs in the text τὰ ὠβελισμένα, κείμενα δὲ εἰς τὸ τέλος, ἐκ τῶνδε ὧδε τὴν ἀκολουθίαν ἔχει, and on the back of the last leaf of both copies τὸ ὑπέρβατον τὸ ὄπισθεν ζητούμενον. In Codd. 37, 102, 105, ch. viii. 3–11 alone is put at the end of the Gospel, which is all that 259 supplies, though its omission in the text begins at ch. vii. 53. Cod. 237, on the contrary, omits only from ch. viii. 3, but at the end inserts the whole passage from ch. vii. 53: in Cod. 478, ch. vii. 53—viii. 2 stands *primâ manu* with an asterisk, the rest later. Cod. 225 sets chh. vii. 53—viii. 11 after ch. vii. 36; in Cod. 115, ch. viii. 12 is inserted between ch. vii. 52 and 53, and repeated again in its proper place. Finally, Codd. 13, 69, 124, 346 (being Abbott's group), and 556 give the whole passage at the end of Luke xxi, the order being apparently suggested from comparing Luke xxi. 37 with John viii. 1; and ὤρθριζε Luke xxi. 38 with ὄρθρου John viii. 2 [2]. In the Lectionaries, as we have had occasion to state before (Vol. I. p. 81, note), this section was never read as a part

[1] Yet so that the first hand of Cod. 207 recognizes it in the text, setting in the margin τὸ δὲ λοιπὸν ζήτει εἰς τὸ τέλος τοῦ βιβλίου (Burgon, *Guardian*, Oct. 1, 1873).

[2] A learned friend suggests that, supposing the true place for this supplemental history to be yet in doubt, there would be this reason for the narrative to be set after Luke xxi, that a reader of the Synoptic Gospels would be aware of no other occasion when the Lord had to lodge outside the city: whereas with St. John's narrative before him, he would see that this was probably the usual lot of a *late* comer at the Feast of Tabernacles (ch. vii. 14). Mr. J. Rendel Harris

of the lesson for Pentecost (John vii. 37—viii. 12), but was reserved for the festivals of such saints as Theodora Sept. 18, or Pelagia Oct. 8 (*see* Vol. I. p. 87, notes 2 and 3), as also in Codd. 547, 604, and in many Service-books, whose Menology was not very full (e.g. 150, 189, 257, 259), it would thus be omitted altogether. Accordingly, in that remarkable Lectionary, the Jerusalem Syriac, the lesson for Pentecost ends at ch. viii. 2, the other verses (3–11) being assigned to St. Euphemia's day (Sept. 16).

Of the other versions, the paragraph is entirely omitted in the true Peshitto (being however inserted in printed books with the circumstances before stated under that version), in Cureton's Syriac, and in the Harkleian; though it appears in the Codex Barsalibaei, from which White appended it to the end of St. John: a Syriac note in this copy states that it does not belong to the Philoxenian, but was translated in A. D. 622 by Maras, Bishop of Amida. Maras, however, lived about A.D. 520, and a fragment of a very different version of the section, bearing his name, is cited by Assemani (Biblioth. Orient. ii. 53) from the *writings* of Barsalibi himself (Cod. Clem.-Vat. Syr. 16). Ridley's text bears much resemblance to that of de Dieu, as does a fourth version of ch. vii. 53—viii. 11 found by Adler (N. T. Version. Syr., p. 57) in a Paris codex, with the marginal annotation that this 'σύνταξις' is not in all the copies, but was interpreted into Syriac by the Abbot Mar Paulus. Of the other versions it is not found in the Sahidic, or in some of Wilkins' and all Schwartze's Bohairic copies[1], in the Gothic, Zohrab's Armenian from six ancient codices (but five very recent ones and Uscan's edition contain it), or in *a f l* (text) *q* of the Old Latin. In *b* the whole text from ch. vii. 44 to viii. 12 has been wilfully erased, but the passage is found in *c e* (we have given them at large, pp. 362–3), *ff*[2] *g j l* (margin), the Vulgate (even *am. fuld. for. san.*), Ethiopic, Slavonic, Anglo-Saxon, Persic (but in a Vatican codex placed in ch. x), and Arabic.

thinks that the true place for the *pericope* is between ch. v and ch. vi, as for other reasons which we cannot depend upon, so from our illustrating the mention of the Mosaic Law in ch. viii. 5 by ch. v. 45, 46.

[1] Yet on the whole this paragraph is found in more of Bp. Lightfoot's copies than would have been anticipated: viz. in the text of 3, 8, 14, 16, 17, 18, 23, 24, in the margin of 1, and on a later leaf of 20. It is wanting in 2, 4, 5, 7, 9, 19, 21, 25, 26.

Of the Fathers, Euthymius [xii], the first among the Greeks to mention the paragraph in its proper place, declares that *παρὰ τοῖς ἀκριβέσιν ἀντιγράφοις ἢ οὐχ εὕρηται ἢ ὠβέλισται· διὸ φαίνονται παρέγγραπτα καὶ προσθήκη*. The Apostolic Constitutions [iii or iv] had plainly alluded to it, and Eusebius (Hist. Eccl. iii. 39 *fin.*) had described from Papias, and as contained in the Gospel of the Hebrews, the story of a woman *ἐπὶ πολλαῖς ἁμαρτίαις διαβληθείσης ἐπὶ τοῦ κυρίου*, but did not at all regard it as Scripture. Codd. KM too are the earliest which raise the number of *τίτλοι* or larger *κεφάλαια* in St. John from 18 to 19, by interpolating *κεφ. ι′ περὶ τῆς μοιχαλίδος*, which soon found admittance into the mass of copies: e.g. Evan. 482.

Among the Latins, as being in their old version, the narrative was more generally received for St. John's. Jerome testifies that it was found in his time 'in multis et Graecis et Latinis codicibus;' Ambrose cites it, and Augustine (de adult. conjugiis, lib. ii. c. 7) complains that 'nonnulli modicae fidei, vel potius inimici verae fidei,' removed it from their codices, '*credo metuentes peccandi impunitatem dari mulieribus suis*[1].'

When to all these sources of doubt, and to so many hostile authorities, is added the fact that in no portion of the N. T. do the variations of manuscripts (of D beyond all the rest) and of other documents bear any sort of proportion, whether in number or extent, to those in these twelve verses (of which statement full evidence may be seen in any collection of various readings)[2], we cannot help admitting that if this section be indeed the composition of St. John, it has been transmitted to us under circumstances widely different from those connected with any other genuine passage of Scripture whatever[3].

Second Series. Acts.

23. Acts viii. 37. Εἶπε δὲ ὁ Φίλιππος, Εἰ πιστεύεις ἐξ ὅλης

[1] 'Similiter Nicon ejectam esse vult narrationem ab Armenis, *βλαβερὰν εἶναι τοῖς πολλοῖς τὴν τοιαύτην ἀκρόασιν* dicentibus.' Tischendorf *ad loc.* Nicon lived in or about the tenth century, but Theophylact in the eleventh does not use the paragraph.

[2] Notice especially the reading of 48, 64, 604, 736 (*primâ manu*) in ver. 8 *ἔγραφεν εἰς τὴν γῆν ἑνὸς ἑκάστου αὐτῶν τὰς ἁμαρτίας.*

[3] We are not surprised in this instance at Dr. Hort's verdict (Introd. p. 299): 'No interpolation is more clearly Western, though it is not Western of the earliest type.' Dean Burgon has left amongst his papers an elaborate vindication of this passage, from which however the Editor cannot quote.

τῆς καρδίας, ἔξεστιν. Ἀποκριθεὶς δὲ εἶπε, Πιστεύω τὸν υἱὸν τοῦ Θεοῦ εἶναι τὸν Ἰησοῦν Χριστόν [1]. We cannot safely question the spuriousness of this verse, which all the critical editors condemn, and which seems to have been received from the margin, where the formula Πιστεύω κ.τ.λ. had been placed, extracted from some Church Ordinal: yet this is just the portion cited by Irenaeus, both in Greek [2] and Latin; so early had the words found a place in the sacred text. It is contained in no manuscripts except E (D, which might perhaps be expected to favour it, being here defective), 4 (*secundâ manu*), 13, 15, 18?, 27, 29, 36, 60, 69, 97, 100, 105, 106, 107, 163, 227, Apost. 5, 13 once; and in the margin, 14, 25 &c., in Cod. 186 alone out of Scrivener's thirteen: manuscripts of good character, but quite inadequate to prove the authenticity of the verse, even though they did not differ considerably in the actual readings they exhibit, which is always in itself a ground of reasonable suspicion (*see* pp. 361, 368, 374) [3]. Here again, as in Matt. xxvii. 35, Gutbier and Schaaf interpolated in their Peshitto texts the passage as translated into Syriac and placed within brackets by Elias Hutter: the Harkleian also exhibits it, but marked with an asterisk. It is found in the Old Latin *g* and *m* although in an abridged form, in the Vulgate (both printed and *demid. tol.*, but not in *am.* primâ manu, *fuld.* &c.), and in the satellites of the Vulgate, the Armenian, Polyglott Arabic, and Slavonic. Bede, however, who used Cod. E, knew *Latin* copies in which the verse was wanting: yet it was known to Cyprian, Jerome, Augustine, Pacian, &c. among the Latins, to Œcumenius and Theophylact (twice quoted) among the Greeks. Erasmus seems to have inserted the verse by a comparison of the later hand of Cod. 4 with the Vulgate [4]; it is not in the Com-

[1] The form τὸν Ἰησοῦν Χριστόν, objected to by Michaelis, is vindicated by Matt. i. 18, the reading of which cannot rightly be impugned. *See* above. Compare also ver. 12.

[2] ὡς αὐτὸς ὁ εὐνοῦχος πεισθεὶς καὶ παραυτίκα ἀξιῶν βαπτισθῆναι, ἔλεγε, Πιστεύω τὸν υἱὸν τοῦ θεοῦ εἶναι Ἰησοῦν Χριστόν. Harvey, vol. ii. p. 62.

[3] Such are αὐτῷ with or without ὁ Φίλιππος in E, 100, 105, 163, 186, 221, the Harkleian with an asterisk: σου added after καρδίας in E, 100, 105, 163, 186, *tol.*, the Harkleian with an asterisk, the Armenian, Cyprian; but *ex toto corde* the margin of *am.* and the Clementine Vulgate: τόν omitted before Ἰησοῦν in 186, 221 and others.

[4] 'Non reperi in graeco codice, quanquam arbitror omissum librariorum incuria. Nam et haec in quodam codice graeco asscripta reperi, sed in margine.' Erasmus, N. T., 1516.

plutensian edition. This passage affords us a curious instance of an *addition* well received in the Western Church from the second century downwards (*see* p. 164), and afterwards making some way among the later Greek codices and writers.

24. Acts xi. 20. We are here in a manner forced by the sense to adopt, with Griesbach, Bp. Chr. Wordsworth, Lachmann, Tischendorf, and Tregelles, the reading Ἕλληνας in the room of Ἑλληνιστάς of the Received text, retained by Westcott and Hort[1]. Immediately after the call of the Gentiles to the privileges of the Gospel was acknowledged and acquiesced in at Jerusalem (ver. 18), we read that some of those who had been scattered abroad years ago went about preaching the word to Jews only (ver. 19). In this there was nothing new: there had been Ἑλληνισταί 'Greek-speaking Jews' among the brethren long since (ch. vi. 1), and to say that they were again preached to was not at all strange: the marvel is contained in ver. 20. 'But there were some of them, men of Cyprus and Cyrene, which, when they came to Antioch, spake unto the Greeks also' (καὶ πρὸς τοὺς Ἕλληνας: καί intimating the additional information), and that with such success in converting these heathen Greeks, that Gentile Christians first obtained at Antioch the name, no longer of Nazarenes (ch. xxiv. 5), but of Christians (ver. 26). The meaning being thus evident, we look to the authorities which uphold it, and these are few, confessedly insufficient if the sense left us any choice, but recommended to us, as the matter stands, by their intrinsic excellence: they are AD* (the latter without καί, which is, however, otherwise abundantly attested to) Cod. 184, one of the best of the cursives, but not its kindred 221, the Peshitto Syriac, the Armenian, perhaps the Ethiopic. The Vulgate, Bohairic, Sahidic, and Harkleian Syriac draw no distinction between Ἕλληνες and Ἑλληνισταί: the Peshitto unquestionably does, since it renders 'Greek disciples' in ch. vi. 1, 'those Jews who knew Greek' (an excellent definition) in ch. ix. 29, but 'Greeks' here. Eusebius clearly reads Ἕλληνας,

[1] They plead, besides the confessed preponderance of manuscript evidence for Ἑλληνιστάς, that 'A familiar word standing in an obvious antithesis was not likely to be exchanged for a word so rare that it is no longer extant, except in a totally different sense, anywhere but in the Acts and two or three late Greek interpretations of the Acts; more especially when the change introduced an apparent difficulty' (Hort, Notes, p. 93). *Judicet lector.*

as does Chrysostom in his exposition (not in his text), all the more surely because he is perplexed how to expound it: his words are echoed by Œcumenius and in both commentaries of Theophylact, only that they substitute Ἑλληνιστάς for Ἕλληνας in repeating his words *διὰ τὸ μὴ εἰδέναι ἑβραϊστί, Ἕλληνας ἐκάλουν*: they both have Ἑλληνιστάς in the text. Thus for once B is associated with E, with a later hand of D (of the seventh or eighth century), with the later uncials HLP and all cursives except one, in maintaining a variation demonstrably false. C is defective here, and the first hand of א, which presents us with the wonderful *εὐαγγελιστάς*, makes so far in favour of B; but א[c] corrects that error into Ἕλληνας.

25. Acts xiii. 18. We have here as nice a balance between conflicting readings (differing only by a single letter) as we find anywhere in the N. T. The case is stated in the margin to our Authorized version of the Bible, more minutely than is its wont, though modern printers have unwarrantably left out the reference to 2 Macc. vii. 27 in copies not containing the Apocrypha[1]. For *ἐτροποφόρησεν* 'suffered he their manners' of Tregelles, of Westcott and Hort, are cited אB, the very ancient second hand of C, D (in the Greek), HLP, 61 with almost all other cursives and the catenas: for the alternative *ἐτροφοφόρησεν* 'fed them like a nurse' of Lachmann and Tischendorf (Tregelles placing it in his margin) we find ACE, 13, 24* (not 24** with Tischendorf), 68, 78* (margin), 93, 100, 105, 142, *d* against its own Greek and the Vulgate jointly. Versions are in such a case of special weight, but unfortunately they too are somewhat divided. For *π* we find the Vulgate and a Greek note set in the Harkleian margin, for *φ* the Peshitto and Harkleian Syriac, both Egyptian, the Armenian, and both Ethiopic, with Erpenius' Arabic: the Arabic of the Polyglott gives both renderings. Thus the majority of the versions incline one way, the oldest and most numerous manuscripts the other. It is useless to cite Greek writers, except they show from the context which word they favour. The form with *φ* was doubtless read in the Apostolic Constitutions, and twice in Cyril of Alexandria, and that word is supported as well by 2 Macc. vii. 27, as by the other text cited in the margin of the Authorized English Bible,

[1] Cambridge Paragraph Bible, Introduction, pp. lvi and lxxxii.

Deut. i. 31, to which the Apostle's reference is so manifest, that we cannot but regard it as nearly decisive which expression he used. Although in Deuteronomy also Greek copies vary a little between π and φ, yet both A and B[1] read the latter, indeed the Hebrew (נָשָׂא), *pace Hortii*, would admit of nothing else. For π Origen is express, both in his Greek commentary (not his text) and Latin version, but then he seems to employ it even in Deut. i. 31, where it cannot be correct. Chrysostom and Theophylact give no certain sound. Wetstein seasonably illustrates ἐτροπ. from Rom. ix. 22. Internal evidence certainly points to ἐτροφοφόρησεν, which on the whole may be deemed preferable. The Apostle is anxious to please his Jewish hearers by enumerating the mercies their nation had received from the Divine favour.[1] God had chosen them, exalted them in Egypt, brought them out with a high hand, fed them in the wilderness, and given them the land of Promise. It would hardly have suited his purpose to have interposed, by way of parenthesis, in the midst of his detail of benefits received, the unwelcome suggestion of their obstinate ingratitude and of God's long forbearance.

26. ACTS xiii. 32. Here for τοῖς τέκνοις αὐτῶν ἡμῖν Lachmann, Tischendorf, Tregelles, Westcott and Hort read τοῖς τέκνοις ἡμῶν. As well from the fact that it is much the harder form (*see* Canon I), as from the state of the external evidence, they could not act otherwise. In defence of ἡμῶν we have ℵABC*D, but apparently no cursives, the Vulgate version, Hilary, Ambrose, Bede (with the variant ὑμῶν in *tol.* and elsewhere), and both Ethiopic. We cannot resist the five great uncials when for once they are in harmony. The Received text is supported by the third hand of C, by EHLP, by all the cursives, by the two Syriac and Armenian versions, the catenae, Chrysostom and Theophylact. The Sahidic omits ἡμῖν, the Bohairic both pronouns. To take up ἡμῖν without αὐτῶν, the reading of a solitary cursive of the eleventh century, Cod. 76, would approach the limits of mere conjecture, yet every one can see how well it would account for all other variations. 'The text, which alone has any adequate authority, and of which all

[1] But with the same lack of accuracy which so often deforms this great copy: ως ετροφοφορησεν σε κ̅ς̅ ο θ̅ς̅ σου ως ει τις τροποφορησει *primâ manu* (Vercellone).

or nearly all the readings are manifest corrections, gives only an improbable sense. It can hardly be doubted that ἡμῶν is a primitive corruption of ἡμῖν, τοὺς πατέρας and τοῖς τέκνοις being alike absolute. The suggestion is due to Bornemann, who cites x. 41 in illustration' (Hort, Notes, p. 95). *Optimè.*

27. ACTS xiii. 33. The variation πρώτῳ for δευτέρῳ of the Received text commended itself to Griesbach, Lachmann, Tischendorf, and Tregelles, merely from its apparent difficulty; yet there is no manuscript authority for it except D, *g*, and 'quidam codices' known to Bede. Origen and Hilary indeed mention the variation, but they explain at the same time the cause, as do Eusebius and others. Tertullian and Cyprian also quote the words as from the first Psalm, and the arrangement of the two Psalms sometimes together, sometimes separate, is as old as Justin Martyr's time. Under these circumstances Westcott and Hort are surely fully justified in abiding by the common reading, against which there is no other evidence than what has been named above.

28. ACTS xv. 34. ἔδοξε δὲ τῷ Σίλᾳ ἐπιμεῖναι αὐτοῦ. This verse is omitted by ℵABEGHP, and of the cursives by 31, 61 of the first rank, by 24, 91, 184, 185, 188, 189, 221, and full fifty others. Erasmus inserted it in his editions from the margin of Cod. 4. It is wanting in the Peshitto (only that Tremellius and Gutbier between them thrust their own version into the text), in the Bohairic, Polyglott Arabic, Slavonic, the best manuscripts of the Latin Vulgate (*am. fuld. demid.*, &c.), and by Chrysostom and Theophylact in at least one copy. In C it runs εδοξεν δε τω σιλα επιμειναι αυτους, which is followed by many cursives: some of which, however, have αὐτοῦ, two αὐτοῖς, 42, 57, 69, 182, 186, 187, 219 αὐτόθι, with the Complutensian Polyglott. The common text is found in the Sahidic, Tremellius' Syriac, in the Harkleian with an asterisk, also in Erpenius' Arabic, Theophylact, and Œcumenius. In D we read εδοξε δε τω σειλεα επιμειναι [προς *secundâ manu*] αυτους (sustinere eos *d*) μονος δε ιουδας επορευθη, which Lachmann cites in Latin as extant *in this form* only in one Vienna Codex (for which see his N.T., Proleg. vol. i. p. xxix): thus too *tol.*, the Armenian (not that of Venice), and the printed Slavonic. The common Vulgate, Cassiodorus

and Hutter's Syriac add 'Jerusalem,' so that the Clementine Latin stands thus: 'Visum est autem Silae ibi remanere; Judas autem solus abiit Jerusalem.' The Ethiopic is rendered 'Et perseveravit Paulus manens,' to which Platt's copies add 'ibi.'

No doubt this verse is an unauthorized addition, self-condemned indeed by its numerous variations (*see* p. 361). One can almost trace its growth, and in the shape presented by the Received text it must have been (as Mill conjectures) a marginal gloss, designed to explain how (notwithstanding the terms of ver. 33) Silas was at hand in ver. 40, conveniently for St. Paul to choose him as a companion in travel.

29. Acts xvi. 7. After πνεῦμα at the end of this verse Lachmann, Tischendorf, Tregelles, Westcott and Hort most rightly add Ἰησοῦ. The evidence in its favour is overwhelming, and it is not easy to conjecture how it ever fell out of the text: compare Rom. viii. 9. It is wanting only in HLP and the mass of the cursives, even in Codd. 184, 221: Codd. 182, 219 omit the whole clause from καὶ οὐκ εἴασεν, nor does Ἰησοῦ appear in the Sahidic version, or in three Armenian manuscripts, nor is it recognized by Chrysostom or Theophylact. Ἰησοῦ is read by ℵABC**DE, 13, 15, 31, 33, 36, 61 (*primâ manu*), 73, Apost. 40: but Cod. 105 and a few others have τοῦ Ἰησοῦ. The versions are all but unanimous for the addition, being all the known Latin except *demid.*, the Bohairic, both Syriac, both Ethiopic, and three manuscripts of the Armenian: two more of its codices with one edition read χριστου, six (with Epiphanius) τὸ ἅγιον in its room, while *demid.* has κυρίου with the first hand of C. The catenae exhibit Ἰησοῦ in spite of Chrysostom, as do Didymus, Cyril of Alexandria, and the false Athanasius both in Greek and Latin.

30. Acts xx. 28. τὴν ἐκκλησίαν τοῦ θεοῦ, ἣν περιεποιήσατο διὰ τοῦ ἰδίου αἵματος. This reading of the Received text, though different from that of the majority of copies, is pretty sure to be correct: it has been adopted by Alford (who once rejected θεοῦ for κυρίου), and by Westcott and Hort: Tregelles places it in his margin, though, with Lachmann and Tischendorf, he has κυρίου in the text. ΘΥ̅ is upheld by ℵB (the latter now for certain),

4, 22, 23, 25, 37, 46, 65, 66* (?), 68, 84, 89, 154, 162, Apost. 12, and *ex silentio*, on which one can lay but little stress, by Codd. 7, 12, 16, 39, 56, 64, together with 184 and 186, codices not now in England. 'Dei' is read by all known manuscripts and editions of the Vulgate except the Complutensian, which was probably altered to suit the parallel Greek. From the Vulgate this form was taken by Erasmus, and after him by Tyndale's and later English versions. Lee's edition of the Peshitto has θεου, from three codices (the Travancore, a Vatican Lectionary of Adler [xi], and one at the Bodleian), and so has the Harkleian text. Τοῦ κυρίου (differing but by one letter, *see* our Plates v. No. 13; x. No. 25) is in AC*DE (and therefore in *d, e*), 13, 15, 18, 36 (*text*), 40, 69, 73, 81, 95*, 130, 156, 163, 180, 182, 219, Apost. 58, some catenae, the Harkleian *margin*, the Sahidic, Bohairic, Armenian, and possibly also the Roman Ethiopic, though there the same word is said to represent both $\overline{\theta\upsilon}$ and $\overline{\kappa\upsilon}$. Platt's Ethiopic, all editions of the Peshitto except Lee's, and Erpenius' Arabic, have τοῦ χριστοῦ, with Origen once, Theodoret twice, and four copies of Athanasius: the Old Latin *m* reads 'Jesu Christi.' Other variations, too weakly supported to be worth further notice, are τοῦ κυρίου θεοῦ 3, 95**, the Polyglott Arabic; τοῦ θεοῦ καὶ κυρίου 47; and the Georgian τοῦ κυρίου τοῦ θεοῦ. The great mass of later manuscripts give τοῦ κυρίου καὶ θεοῦ, viz. C (*tertiâ manu*), HLP, 24, 31, 111, 183, 185, 187, 188, 189, 221, 224, and more than one hundred other cursives, including probably every one not particularized above. This is the reading of the Complutensian editors, both in the Greek and Latin, and of some modern critics who would fain take a safe and middle course; but is countenanced by the reading of no version except the Slavonic, and by no ecclesiastical writer before Theophylact. It is plainly but a device for reconciling the two principal readings; yet from the non-repetition of the article and from the general turn of the sentence it asserts the Divinity of the Saviour almost as unequivocally as θεοῦ could do alone. Our choice evidently lies between κυρίου and θεοῦ, which are pretty equally supported by manuscripts and versions: Patristic testimony, however, may slightly incline to the latter. Foremost comes that bold expression of Ignatius [A. D. 107] ἀναζωπυρήσαντες ἐν αἵματι θεοῦ (ad Ephes. i), which the old Latin version renders 'Christi Dei,' and the later interpolator softens into χριστοῦ: so again (ad

Roman. vi), τοῦ πάθους τοῦ θεοῦ μου. It may be true that Ignatius 'does not adopt it [the first passage] as a quotation' (Davidson *ad loc.*), yet nothing short of Scriptural authority could have given such early vogue to a term so startling as αἷμα θεοῦ, which is also employed by Tertullian (ad uxorem, ii. 3) and Clement of Alexandria (Quis dives, 34). The elder Basil, Epiphanius (*twice*), Cyril of Alexandria (*twice*), Ibas (in the Greek only), Ambrose, Caelestine, Fulgentius, Primasius, Cassiodorus, &c., not to mention writers so recent as Œcumenius and Theophylact, expressly support the same word. Manuscripts of Athanasius vary between θεοῦ, κυρίου, and χριστοῦ, but his evidence would be regarded as hostile to the Received text, inasmuch as he states (as alleged by Wetstein) that οὐδαμοῦ δὲ αἷμα θεοῦ καθ' ἡμᾶς παραδεδώκασιν αἱ γραφαί· 'Αρειανῶν τὰ τοιαῦτα τολμήματα (contra Apollinar.): only that for καθ' ἡμᾶς (*which even Tischendorf cites in his seventh edition*), the correct reading is δίχα σαρκός or διὰ σαρκός, a citation fatal to any such inference. In Chrysostom too the readings fluctuate, and some (e.g. Tregelles) have questioned whether the Homilies on the Acts, wherein he has θεοῦ, are of his composition. In behalf of κυρίου are cited the Latin version of Irenaeus, Lucifer of Cagliari, Augustine, Jerome, Ammonius, Eusebius, Didymus, Chrysostom (whence Theophylact), possibly Theodoret, and the Apostolic Constitutions, while the exact expression *sanguis Dei* was censured by Origen and others. It has been urged, however, and not without some show of reason (Nolan, Integrity of Greek Vulgate, p. 517, note 135), that the course of Irenaeus' argument proves that θεοῦ was used in his lost Greek text. After all, internal evidence—subjective feeling if it must be so called—will decide the critic's choice where authorities are so much divided as here. It seems reasonable to say that the whole mass of witnesses for τοῦ κυρίου καὶ θεοῦ vouches for the existence of θεοῦ in the earliest codices, the commonplace κυρίου being the rather received from other quarters, as it tends to point more distinctly to the Divine Person indicated in the passage. If this view be accepted, the preponderance in favour of θεοῦ, *undoubtedly the harder form*, is very marked, and when the consideration suggested above from Dean Alford is added, there will remain little room for hesitation. It has been pleaded on both sides of the question, and appears little relevant to the case of either, that St. Paul employs in ten places the expression ἐκκλησία τοῦ θεοῦ, but never once ἐκκλησία τοῦ κυρίου or τοῦ χριστοῦ.

It is right to mention that, in the place of τοῦ ἰδίου αἵματος, the more emphatic form τοῦ αἵματος τοῦ ἰδίου ought to be adopted from ℵA (*see* Plate v. No. 13) BCDE, 31, 182, 184 (Sanderson), with some twenty other cursives, Didymus, &c.; while τοῦ ἰδίου αἵματος is only in HLP, the majority of cursives, Athanasius, Chrysostom, &c. We must, however, protest strongly against the interpretation put upon τοῦ αἵματος τοῦ ἰδίου by Mr. Darby in his 'New Translation,' 'the blood of his own,' 'le sang de son propre [fils],' as being no less unwarrantable, though more reverential, than that of Wakefield, which Bp. Middleton (Doctrine of the Greek Article, pp. 293–5) condemns so justly. Nor can we do less than repudiate unreservedly Dr. Hort's expedient (Notes, p. 99), who would render 'through the blood that was His own,' i. e. as being His Son's. Indeed he has so little faith in it that he is constrained to say 'It is however true that this general sense, if indicated, is not sufficiently expressed in the text as it stands.'

31. Acts xxvii. 16. Καῦδα, the form which Erasmus noted as that of Cod. B, is adopted by Lachmann, Tregelles, Westcott and Hort, in preference to Κλαῦδα of Tischendorf and the Received text. Putting *Kura* of the Peshitto, *Keda* of Pell Platt's Ethiopic, out of the question, we note that ℵ^c, the Vulgate and Latins (Jerome has *Cauden*, Cassiodorus *Gaudem*), followed by the Roman edition of the Ethiopic, alone omit the λ. In the first century Pomponius Mela wrote *Cauda*, the other Pliny *Gaudos*, and Suidas speaks of *Caudo* as an island near Crete: it is now called Gozo, and is not to be confounded with the island of Gaulus near Malta, now bearing the same name. The λ is inserted by Ptolemy, the celebrated geographer of the second century, and by later writers: it is found in ℵ*AHLP, in all known cursives (with a like variation in the termination as in the other form), the Bohairic, the later Syriac both in its text and in Greek letters in its margin, the Armenian, and Erpenius', or the only trustworthy form of the Arabic. Chrysostom and Bede have the same reading, which must surely be retained unless the union of Cod. B with the Latins is to prevail against all other evidence put together.

32. Acts xxvii. 37. In the place of διακόσιαι ἑβδομήκοντα ἕξ Westcott and Hort have received into their text ὡς ἑβδομήκοντα ἕξ, placing the common reading in the margin. Their form is supported by Cod. B and the Sahidic version only, and was plainly resorted to by those who were slow to believe that a corn ship, presumably heavily laden (vers. 6, 18), would contain so many souls. There is a slight variation in the other authorities, as is usual where numbers are concerned, from the ancient practice of representing them by letters, whereof many traces are yet remaining throughout Codex Sarravianus of the Septuagint, dating from the end of the fourth century, and in our present copies (Cod. D in Acts xiii. 18; 20; xix. 9) of the New Testament: even in this place Cod. 61 has coς. Hence A reads πέντε for ἕξ, 31 omits ἕξ entirely, one Bohairic copy has the incredible number of 876 (ωοϛ), another 176 (ροϛ). The Ethiopic is reported by Tregelles to read ὡς διακόσιαι ἕξ, but that in the Polyglott favours the common text; Epiphanius comes nearest to B (ὡς ἑβδομήκοντα), 'libere' adds Tischendorf. For the more specific number assigned by B ὡς is not so well suited.

In ordinary cases the common reading would be abided by without hesitation, upheld as it is by ℵCHLP, by all cursives, virtually by A, 31, completely by the Latin, both Syriac, the Armenian, and most copies of the Bohairic. It is obvious also that the writer wishes to impress upon us the fact that out of so large a party all were saved, and seventy-six would be a small number indeed. Josephus was wrecked in the Adriatic with 600 on board (Josephus' Life, c. 3: see Whiston's note)[1]. It is right, however, to point out that, on the possible supposition that numeral letters, not words, were employed in St. Luke's autograph, the difference between B and the Received text would consist of the insertion or the contrary of the letter ω: whether in fact it be assumed that the Evangelist wrote ωcoϛ or coϛ, 'about 76' or '276.' Surely it is more likely that ω was inserted than omitted.

In ver. 39 the first hand of B, this time favoured by C, and supported by the Bohairic, Armenian, and (in Tregelles) the

[1] Witness too Lucian's ὑπερμεγέθη ναῦν καὶ πέρα τοῦ μέτρου, μίαν τῶν ἀπ' Αἰγύπτου εἰς Ἰταλίαν σιταγωγῶν (Navig. seu Vota, c. 1) which was driven out of its course to the Piraeus. Mr. Smith, of Jordan Hill, cannot bring its dimensions under 1,300 tons.

Ethiopic versions, has another curious variation, also promoted into the text by Westcott and Hort, ἐκσῶσαι for the common ἐξῶσαι, which they banish into the margin. This change also is very minute, being simply the resolution of *xi* into the two consonants for which it stands, and the reading very ingenious, unless indeed it be regarded as a mistake made *ex ore dictantis* (*see* p. 10), which with Madvig as cited by Mr. Hammond (Outlines of Textual Criticism, first edition, p. 13, note) we regard as a slovenly plan, such as one would be loth to impute hastily to the scribes of so noble a copy as Cod. B. Here, however, as ever, internal evidence being equiponderant, we must decide by the weight of documentary proof, and adopt ἐξῶσαι with אAHLP, all cursives (including 61), the Latin and Syriac versions.

Third Series. St. Paul.

33. Rom. v. 1. Δικαιωθέντες οὖν ἐκ πίστεως εἰρήνην ἔχομεν πρὸς τὸν Θεόν. Here, as in 2 Cor. iii. 3, we find the chief uncials supporting a reading which is manifestly unsuitable to the context, although, since it does not absolutely destroy the sense, it does not (nor indeed does that other passage) lack strenuous defenders. Codd. אB for ἔχομεν have *primâ manu* ἔχωμεν, and though some doubt has been thrown on the primitive reading of B, yet Mai and Tregelles (An Account of the Printed Text, p. 156) are eyewitnesses to the fact, which is now settled: Tischendorf in 1866 referred ἔχομεν to the third hand of B, Codd. ACDEKL, not less than thirty cursives, including 104, 244? 257 and the remarkable copies 17, 37, also read ἔχωμεν, as do *d e f g*, the Vulgate ('habeamus'), the Peshitto Syriac (ܢܗܘܐ ܠܢ ܫܝܢܐ), Bohairic, Ethiopic (in both forms), and Arabic. Chrysostom too supports this view, and so apparently Tertullian ('monet justificatos ex fide Christi . . . pacem ad Deum habere'). The case for ἔχομεν is much weaker in itself: Codd. א^{a}B^{3}FG (in spite of the contrary testimony of *f g*, their respective Latin versions) P, perhaps the majority of the cursive manuscripts (29, 30, 47, 221, 260, 265, &c.), Didymus, Epiphanius, Cyril (once), and the Slavonic. The later Syriac might seem to combine both readings (ܗܘܐ ܐܝܬ ܠܢ ܠܘܬ ܐܠܗܐ ܫܝܢܐ): White translates 'habemus,' but has no note on the passage[1]. Had the scales

[1] Dr. Field, however, says that 'this is a mistake.' The Syriac is ἔχωμεν

been equally poised, no one would hesitate to prefer ἔχομεν, for the closer the context is examined the clearer it will appear that *inference* not *exhortation* is the Apostle's purpose: hence those who most regard 'ancient evidence' (Tischendorf and Tregelles, Westcott and Hort; Lachmann could not make up his mind) have struggled long before they would admit ἔχωμεν into the text. The 'Five Clergymen' who in or about 1858 benefited the English Church by revising its Authorized version of this Epistle, even though they render '*let us have peace with God*,' are constrained to say, 'An overwhelming weight of authority has necessitated a change, which at the first sight seems to impair the logical force of the Apostle's argument. No consideration, however, of this kind can be allowed to interfere with the faithful exhibition of the true text, as far as it can be ascertained; and no doubt the real Word of God, thus faithfully exhibited, will vindicate its own meaning, and need no help from man's shortsighted preference' (Preface, p. vii). Every one must honour the reverential temper in which these eminent men approached their delicate task; yet, if their sentiments be true, where is the place for internal evidence at all? A more 'overwhelming weight' of manuscript authority upholds καρδίαις in 2 Cor. iii. 3: shall we place it in the text, 'leaving the real Word of God to vindicate its own meaning'? Ought we to assume that the reading found in the few most ancient codices—not, in the case of Rom. v. 1, in the majority of the whole collection—must *of necessity* be the 'real Word of God, faithfully exhibited'? I see no cause to reply in the affirmative, nor do Meyer and Dr. Field[1].

We conclude, therefore, that this is a case for the application of the *paradiplomatical* canon (VII): that the itacism ω for ο, so familiar to all collators of Greek manuscripts[2], crept into

and nothing else. For ἔχομεν this version (and all others) would put ܐܝܬ ܠܢ: but 'when the word is in the subjunctive mood, since ܐܝܬ is indeclinable, it is a peculiarity of the Harkleian to prefix the corresponding mood of ܗܘܐ, here ܢܗܘܐ' (Otium Norvicense, iii. p. 93). For this strange phrase he cites Rom. i. 13; 2 Cor. v. 12, and to such an authority I have but *dare manus*.

[1] It is simply impossible to translate with Jos. Agar Beet, in the [Wesleyan] *London Quarterly*, April, 1878, either 'Let us then, justified by faith, have peace with God,' or 'Let us then be justified by faith and have peace with God.' Acts xv. 36 will help him little: the other places he cites (Matt. ii. 13, &c.) not at all.

[2] Dr. Vaughan (Epistle to the Romans) has ἔχωμεν in his text, and compares

some very early copy, from which it was propagated among our most venerable codices, even those from which the earliest versions were made:—that this is one out of a small number of well-ascertained cases in which the united testimonies of the best authorities conspire in giving a worse reading than that preserved by later and, on the whole, quite inferior copies.

34. I Cor. xi. 24. I am as unwilling as Mr. C. Forster could have been to strike out from the Received text 'a word which (if genuine) THE LORD GOD HAD SPOKEN!' (A new Plea for the Three Heavenly Witnesses, Preface, p. xvii), but I cannot censure Lachmann, Tischendorf, Tregelles, or Westcott and Hort, or Dean Blakesley for deciding on the state of the evidence, as now generally taken, that it is not genuine. Yet it is with great satisfaction that I find Bp. Chr. Wordsworth able to retain *κλώμενον*, and to save the solemn clause *τὸ ὑπὲρ ὑμῶν* from being 'bald and impressive without the participle.' Mr. Forster's argument in behalf of *κλώμενον*, that it refers to ch. x. 16, *τὸν ἄρτον ὃν κλῶμεν*, has a double edge, and might be employed to indicate the source from which the word crept in here. It is more to the purpose to urge with Bp. Wordsworth that early scribes were offended by the apparent inconsistency of the term with John xix. 36, and because there is nothing like it in the narratives of the three earlier Evangelists. If we decide to retain *κλώμενον*, it must be in opposition to the four chief manuscripts ℵABC, though ℵC insert it by the third hand of each. Cod. D, like its namesake of the Gospels and Acts, is

Heb. xii. 28, *ἔχωμεν χάριν*, 'where there is the same variety of reading.' B is lost in this last place, but *ἔχομεν*, which is quite inadmissible, is found in Codd. ℵKP, the Latin of D, 31 and many other cursives, the printed Vulgate, and its best manuscripts. In Rom. xiv. 19 even Dr. Hort is driven by the versions and the sense to adopt in his *text* *διώκωμεν* of CD and the mass of cursives, rather than *διώκομεν* with ℵABFGLP, &c. The like confusion between *ο* and *ω* appears in the text we shall examine next but one (1 Cor. xiii. 3) and in the subjoined note (p. 384). See also *φορέσομεν* and *φορέσωμεν*, 1 Cor. xv. 49. We must confess, however, that in some of our oldest extant MSS. the interchange of *ο* and *ω* is but rare. In Cod. Sarravianus it is found in but twenty-three places out of 1224 in which itacisms occur, 830 of them being the mutation of *ει* and *ι*. On the other hand, *ο* stands for *ω* and *vice versâ* very frequently in that papyrus fragment of the Psalms in the British Museum which Tischendorf, perhaps a little hastily, judged to be older than any existing writing on vellum.

somewhat inclined to paraphrases, and has *θρυπτόμενον*[1] by the first hand, *κλώμενον* by the second. Only two cursives here side with the great uncials (17, and the valuable second hand of 67), as do Zohrab's Armenian, Cyril of Alexandria and Fulgentius in the fifth century, and Theodoret's report of Athanasius. The word *κλώμενον* is found in EFGKLP, all other cursives, the Latin versions of DE (*quod frangitur*), with Ambrosiaster: G and the interlinear Latin of F, which, as has been already shown under that MS., is taken from G, prefer *quod frangetur*, with both Syriac, the Gothic, and the Armenian of Uscan. The Latin Vulgate has *tradetur* (but *traditur* in *harl.*[2], even in the parallel column of F and against its Greek, and so Cyprian: the Bohairic renders *traditur;* but the Sahidic and Ethiopic *datur*, after the *διδόμενον* of Zacagni's Euthalius, derived from Luke xxii. 19. Theodoret himself knew of both forms. The main strength of *κλώμενον* rests on Patristic evidence. Mr. Forster has added to our previous store the 'conclusive testimony' of Basil (Forster, p. xxvi) and of Athanasius himself (*ibid.* p. xvii), which is better than Theodoret's report at second hand; and thus too Chrysostom in three places, one manuscript of Euthalius, John Damascene, the Patriarch Germanus (A. D. 715, *ibid.* p. xix), Œcumenius and Theophylact. Mr. Forster is perfectly justified also in pressing the evidence of the Primitive Liturgies, in all of which *κλώμενον* occurs in the most sacred words of Institution (*ibid.* pp. xx, xxi). Whatsoever change these services have received in the course of ages, they have probably been little altered since the fourth century, and very well established must the word have then been to have found a place in them all. On the whole, therefore, we submit this important text as a proof that the united readings of ℵABC are sometimes at variance, not only with the more modern codices united, but with the text of the oldest versions and most illustrious Fathers. We confess, however, that in ver. 29 *ἀναξίως* (compare ver. 27) and *τοῦ κ͞υ* look too much like glosses to be maintained confidently against the evidence of ℵ*ABC*, 17, (67**) and some manuscripts of the Ethiopic.

35. I Cor. xiii. 3. *ἐὰν παραδῶ τὸ σῶμά μου ἵνα καυθήσωμαι,*

[1] Dr. Hort (Notes, p. 116) observes that *διαθρύπτω* is specially used in the Septuagint (Lev. ii. 6; Isa. lviii. 7) for the breaking of bread.

'though I give my body to be burned.' Here we find the undoubtedly false reading καυχήσωμαι in the three chief codices ℵAB and in 17, adopted by Drs. Westcott and Hort[1], and it is said to have been favoured by Lachmann in 1831, by Tregelles in 1873 (A. W. Tyler, Bibl. Sacra, 1873, p. 502). Jerome testifies that in his time 'apud Graecos ipsos ipsa exemplaria esse diversa,' and preferred καυχήσωμαι (though all copies of the Latin have *ut ardeam* or *ut ardeat*), which is said to be countenanced by the Roman Ethiopic: the case of the Bohairic is stated by Bp. Lightfoot (Chap. IV)[2]. Tischendorf cites Ephraem (ii. 112) for καυχήσομαι. This variation, which involves the change of but one letter, is worth notice, as showing that the best uncial MSS. are not always to be depended upon, and sometimes are blemished with errors' (Wordsworth, N. T., *ad loc.*). As a parallel use, Theodotion's version of Dan. iii. 8 (παρέδωκαν τὰ σώματα αὐτῶν εἰς πῦρ) is very pertinent: and for the punishment of burning alive, as practised in those times, consult (if it be thought needful) Joseph., Antiq. xvii. 6, 4 (Hort). Καυχήσωμαι may have obtained the more credit, inasmuch as each of the other principal readings, namely Tischendorf's καυθήσομαι (DEFGL, 44, 47, 71, 80, 104, 113**, 253**, 254, 255, 257, 260, 265, with nine of Matthaei's, and some others: καθήσομαι 244) and καυθήσωμαι (CK, 29, 37, and many others, Chrysostom, Theodoret, &c.) of Lachmann and Tregelles, are anomalous, the former in respect to mood, the latter to tense. The important cursive 73 has καυθήσεται with some Latin copies: Codd. 1, 108*, Basil (perhaps Cyprian) adopt καυθῇ: the Syriac (ܢܐܩܕ), and I suppose the Arabic, will suit either of these last. Evidence seems to preponderate on the side of καυθήσομαι, but in the case of these itacisms manuscripts are very fallacious we know. Such a subjunctive future as καυθήσωμαι, however, I should have been disposed to question, had it not passed muster with much better scholars than I am: but to illustrate it, as Tregelles does (An Account of the Printed Text,

[1] Few things are too hard for Dr. Hort, yet one is almost surprised to be told that 'The text gives an excellent sense, for, as ver. 2 refers to a faith towards God which is unaccompanied by love, so ver. 3 refers to acts which seem by their very nature to be acts of love to men, but are really done in ostentation. First the dissolving of the goods in almsgiving is mentioned, then, as a climax, the yielding up of the very body; both alike being done for the sake of glorying, and unaccompanied by love' (Notes, p. 117).

[2] Tyler compares *shoushou* also in 2 Cor. vii. 5, 9; Ps. v. 11 (12).

p. 117, note), from ἵνα δώσῃ Apoc. viii. 3, is to accomplish little, since δώσει is the reading of ℵAC, 1 (although Erasmus has δώσῃ with BP, 6, 7, 91, 98, and the Complutensian), 13, 28, 29, 30, 37, 40, 48, 68, 87, 94, 95, 96 (δωσι 8, 26, 27: δω 14), together with the best copies of Andreas, and is justly approved by Lachmann and Tischendorf, nay even by Tregelles himself in his second revision (1872). It seems most likely that in both places ἵνα, the particle of design, is followed by the *indicative* future, as (with Meyer and Bp. Ellicott) I think to be clearly the case in Eph. vi. 3. In John xvii. 3 even Tregelles adopts ἵνα γινώσκουσιν [1].

36. I COR. xv. 51. We have now come to a passage which has perplexed Biblical students from St. Jerome's time, and has exercised the keen judgement of Bp. Pearson in his Exposition of the seventh article of the Apostles' Creed. There is but little doubt that the Received text, as rendered in our English versions,

[1] Neither Winer nor his careful translator, Professor Moulton, seems disposed to yield to Lachmann's authority in this matter. 'In the better class of writers,' says Winer, 'such forms are probably due to the transcribers (Lobeck on Phrynichus, p. 721), but in later authors, especially the Scholiasts (as on Thucydides iii. 11 and 54), they cannot be set aside. In the N. T., however, there is very little in favour of these conjunctives' (Moulton's 'Winer,' p. 89 and note 4, p. 361 and note 1). Yet Tregelles thinks 'there would be no difficulty about the case, had not one been made by grammatical critics' (An Account of the Printed Text, p. 211, note †). But in his own example, John xvii. 2, ἵνα . . . δώσῃ is read by ℵᶜACGKMSX, 33, 511, 546, and (so far as I can find) by no other manuscript whatever. On the other hand δώσει (read by Westcott and Hort; *see* Introd., Notes, p. 172) is supported by BEHUYΓΔΛΠ (ℵ has δωσω, D εχῃ, L δως), and (as it would seem) by every other codex extant: δώσῃ came into the common text from the second edition of Erasmus. Out of the twenty-five collated by myself for this chapter, δώσει is found in twenty-four (now including Wake 12 or Cod. 492 and Cod. 622), and the following others have been expressly cited for it: 1, 10, 11, 15, 22, 42, 45, 48, 53, 54, 55, 60, 61 (Dobbin), 63, 65, 66, 106, 118, 124, 127, 131, 142, 145, 157, 250, 262, Evst. 3, 22, 24, 36, and at least fifty others, indeed one might say all that have been collated with any degree of minuteness: so too the Complutensian and first edition of Erasmus. The constant confusion of ει and η at the period when the uncials were written abundantly accounts for the reading of the few, though AC are among them. In later times such itacisms were far more rare in careful transcription, and the mediaeval copyists knew their native language too well to fall into the habit in this passage. In Pet. iii. I ἵνα κερδηθήσονται is read by all the uncials (ℵABCKLP), nearly all cursives, and the Complutensian edition, in the place of -σωνται of Erasmus and the Received text; just as we have ἵνα γινώσκομεν in ℵAB*LP, 98, 99, 101, 180, 184, 188, 190 in I John v. 20. The case for ἀρκεσθησόμεθα I Tim. vi. 8 is but a shade less feeble.

is the true reading: (a) Πάντες μὲν οὐ κοιμηθησόμεθα, πάντες δὲ ἀλλαγησόμεθα. Some of the leading authorities omit μέν, a few put δέ or γάρ in its place, but, with this trifling exception, the clause stands thus in B, the third hand of D, and consequently in EKLP, 37, 47, 265, and indeed nearly all the cursives, as in some manuscripts known to Jerome, and has the support of Theodore of Heraclea and Apollinarius: and so the two Syriac, the Bohairic (the Sahidic not being extant), the Gothic, and one edition of the Ethiopic version. For the same form may be cited Ephraem the Syrian, Caesarius, Gregory of Nyssa, and Chrysostom (often) in the fourth century; Theodoret and Euthalius in the fifth century; Andreas of Caesarea in the sixth; John Damascene in the eighth. A modification of this main and true reading (b) Οὐ πάντες κοιμησόμεθα, πάντες δὲ ἀλλαγησόμεθα is supported only by Origen and some copies known to Jerome: it is only a clearer way of bringing out the foregoing sense. The next form also hardly enters into competition, (c) Πάντες [μὲν] ἀναστησόμεθα, οὐ πάντες δὲ ἀλλαγήσομεθα: it is supported by the first hand of D, by the Vulgate (whose manuscripts vary between *resurgimus* and *resurgemus*, while *m* omits the negative), by Tertullian and Hilary. Even the Latin versions of EF maintain it against their own Greek, while Jerome and Augustine note it as a point wherein the Latin copies diverge from the Greek. A fourth variation is due to Cod. A alone, (d) Οἱ πάντες μὲν κοιμησόμεθα, οἱ πάντες δὲ ἀλλαγησόμεθα, the second οι being altered by the first hand, and ου by the same or a very early hand superadded after οἱ πάντες δέ: but this is only a correction of transcriptional error. The real variation consists in the transfer of the negative from the first clause to the second, (e) Πάντες [μὲν] κοιμηθησόμεθα, οὐ πάντες δὲ ἀλλαγησόμεθα of ℵC(F)G, 17, and apparently of A also by intention. This last is discussed by Jerome, who alleges in its favour Didymus and Acacius of Caesarea; it appears also in Origen, Cyril of Alexandria, and in copies known to Pelagius and Maximus, but their testimony fluctuates. In its favour are quoted the Armenian and one form of the Ethiopic, but all the Latin prefer (c) except the interlinear version of G, and the rendering set above the Vulgate text of F, which is assimilated to the latter. The Complutensian margin in a special note chronicles one other change, Πάντες μὲν οὖν κοιμηθησόμεθα, ἀλλ' οὐ πάντες ἀλλαγησόμεθα, but this is bye-work.

'The objection made in ancient times to the Received reading was, that the *wicked* would not be changed, namely, glorified; but St. Paul is here speaking only of the resurrection of the Just' (Bp. Chr. Wordsworth): compare 1 Thess. iv. 14–17. Thus Cod. B and the cursives for once unite to convict of falsehood a change which men were pleased to devise in order to evade a difficulty of their own making.

37. EPH. v. 14. It is instructive to observe how a reading, pretty widely diffused in the fourth century, though not obtaining much acceptance even at that period, has almost entirely disappeared from extant codices. In the place of *ἐπιφαύσει σοι ὁ χριστός* the first hand of D, followed of course by E (Sangermanensis) and the Latin versions of both, exhibits an interesting variant *ἐπιψαύσεις τοῦ χριστοῦ*, *continges Christum*. Jerome had heard of it in the form *ἐπιψαύσει*, id est *continget te Christus*, but refused to vouch for it, as do Chrysostom and Theodoret, though they treat it with somewhat more consideration. The Latin interpreter of Origen (against his own Greek twice, and the Latin once), with Victorinus and the writer cited as Ambrosiaster, adopt it as genuine. Augustine (on Psalm iii) has *et continget te* once, but once elsewhere the common reading. Theodore of Mopsuestia, in the Latin version of his Commentary on St. Paul's Epistles, recently edited by Dr. Swete from two manuscripts, one at Amiens (Cod. 68) brought from Corbey [x], a second from Cuza, now Harleian. 3063 [ix], after translating *inluminabit tibi Christus*, goes on to say 'alii *continget te Christus* legerunt; habet autem nullam sequentiam' (Swete, vol. i. p. 180). The variation of D* is surely too curious to be lost sight of altogether. 'The two imperatives [*ἔγειρε* and *ἀνάστα*] doubtless suggested that the following future would be in the second person, the required *σ* stood next after *ἐπιφαύσει*, easily read as *ἐπιψαύσει*, and then the rest would follow accordingly.' Hort, Notes, p. 125. Such are the harmless recreations of a critical genius.

38. PHIL. ii. 1. *εἴ τις κοινωνία πνεύματος, εἴ τινα σπλάγχνα.* For *τινα*, to the critic's great perplexity, *τις* is found in ℵABCD EFGKLP, that is, in *all* the uncials extant at this place. As regards the cursives nearly the same must be said. Of the seventeen collated by Scrivener, eleven read *τις* (29, 30, 252, 254, 255,

257, 258, 260, 265, 266, 277), and six τι (31, 104, 221, 244, 253, 256). Mill enumerates sixteen others that give τις, one (40) that has τι: Griesbach reckons forty-five in favour of τις, eight (including Cod. 4) for τι, to which Scholz adds a few more (18, 46, 72, 74). Thus *am. fuld. tol.* of the Vulgate render *si quid viscera*, for the more usual *si qua viscera*. One cursive (109) and a manuscript of Theodoret have τε. Basil, Chrysostom (in manuscript) and others read τις, as do the Complutensian, the Aldine (1518), Erasmus' first four, and R. Stephen's first two editions. In fact it may be stated that no manuscript whatever has been cited for τινα, which is not therefore likely to be found in many. Theodore of Mopsuestia alone, in his Latin version published by Dr. Swete (vol. i. p. 214), has *si qua et viscera* against the Vulgate. In spite of what was said above with regard to far weaker cases, it is impossible to blame editors for putting τις into the text here before σπλάγχνα: to have acted otherwise (as Tischendorf fairly observes) would have been '*grammatici quam editoris partes agere*.' Yet we may believe the reading to be as false as it is intolerable, and to afford us another proof of the early and (as the cursives show) the well-nigh universal corruption of our copies in some minute particulars. Of course Clement and later Fathers give τινα, indeed it is surprising that any cite otherwise; but, *in the absence of definite documentary proof*, this can hardly be regarded as genuine. Probably St. Paul wrote τι (the reading of about nineteen cursives), which would readily be corrupted into τις, by reason of the σ following (ΤΙϹΠΛΑΓΧΝΑ), and the τις which had just preceded. See also Moulton's 'Winer,' p. 661, and note 3.

39. Col. ii. 2. τοῦ μυστηρίου τοῦ Θεοῦ καὶ πατρὸς καὶ τοῦ χριστοῦ, 'of the mystery of God the Father, and of Christ.' The reading of B (approved by Lachmann, by Tischendorf in his eighth edition, by Tregelles, Westcott and Hort, Bp. Chr. Wordsworth, and Bp. Ellicott), τοῦ μυστηρίου τοῦ θεοῦ χριστοῦ ('ita cod. nihil interponens inter θεοῦ et χριστοῦ,' *Mai*, 2nd ed.[1]), has 'every

[1] Tischendorf, however, boldly interposes a comma between the words (*see* p. 359, note), and is followed by Westcott and Hort and by Bp. Lightfoot, whose note on the passage (Coloss. p. 318) is very elaborate. This mode of punctuation would set χριστοῦ in apposition to μυστηρίου, in support of which construction ch. i. 27 (ὅ); 1 Tim. iii. 16 (ὅς) are alleged. This, however, is not the sense favoured by Hilary (in agnitionem *sacramenti dei Christi*, and again *Deus Christus*

appearance of being the original reading, and that from which the many perplexing variations have arisen' (Canon II). At present it stands in great need of confirmation, since Hilary (de Trin. ix) alone supports it (but *καὶ χριστοῦ* Cyril), though the Scriptural character of the expression is upheld by the language of ch. i. 27 just preceding, and by the Received text in 1 Tim. iii. 16. Some, who feel a difficulty in understanding how *χριστοῦ* was removed from the text, if it ever had a place there, conceive that the verse should end with *θεοῦ*, all additions, including *χριστοῦ* the simplest, being *accretions* to the genuine passage. These alleged accretions are *τοῦ θεοῦ ὅ ἐστι χριστός*, manifestly an expansion of *χριστοῦ* and derived from ch. i. 27; *τοῦ θεοῦ πατρὸς τοῦ χριστοῦ* : *τοῦ θεοῦ καὶ πατρὸς καὶ τοῦ χριστοῦ*, the final form of the Received text. Now, of these four readings, *τοῦ θεοῦ* the shortest, and, according to Griesbach, Scholz, Tischendorf in his seventh edition, Alford, and Dr. Green, the true one, is found only in the late uncial P, and in a few, though confessedly good, cursives : 37, 71, 80*, 116 (*καὶ θεοῦ* 23), and the important second hand of 67; witnesses too few and feeble, unless we consent to put our third Canon of internal evidence to a rather violent use. Of the longer readings, *ὅ ἐστιν χριστός* is favoured by D (though obelized by the second hand, which thus would read only *τοῦ θεοῦ*), *d e* (whose parallel Greek speaks differently), by Augustine and Vigilius of Thapsus, but apparently by no cursives. The form best vouched for appears to be that of ℵ*AC, 4, of the Sahidic according to one of the readings of Griesbach, and of an Arabic codex of Tischendorf, *τοῦ θεοῦ πατρὸς τοῦ* (ℵ* omits *τοῦ*) *χριστοῦ*. To these words '*ihu*' is simply added by *f* (FG, *g* are unfortunately lost here) and by other manuscripts of the Vulgate (*am. fuld.*, &c.), though the Clementine edition has 'Dei patris et Christi Jesu,' the Complutensian in the Latin 'dei et patris et C. J.' With the Clementine Vulgate agree the Bohairic, and (omitting *ἰησοῦ*) the Peshitto Syriac, Arabic, 47, 73, Chrysostom; while 41, 115, 213, 221, 253* (*τοῦ θ. καὶ π. τοῦ χ.*), so far strengthen the case of ℵAC. The Received text is found in (apparently) the great mass of cursives, in D (*tertiâ manu*), EKL, the Harkleian Syriac (but the *καί* after *πατρός* marked with one of Harkel's asterisks, Theodoret, John Damascene and others. The minor

sacramentum est), and would almost call for the article before *χριστοῦ*. In meaning it would be equivalent to D*, &c., *ὅ ἐστιν χσ*.

variations, τοῦ θεοῦ ἐν χριστῷ of Clement and Ambrosiaster, τοῦ θεοῦ τοῦ ἐν χριστῷ of 17, uphold D*, as may the Ethiopic ('domini quod de Christo'): to the reading of Cod. 17 Zohrab's or the Venice Armenian (A. D. 1789) simply adds 'Jesu.' We also find 'dei Christi Jesu patris et domini' in *tol.*, 'dei patris et domini nostri Christi' in *demid.*, 'dei patris in Christo Jesu' in Uscan's Armenian; but these deserve not attention. Theodore of Mopsuestia (Swete, vol. i. p. 283), has *mysterii Dei Patris et Christi*, which need not imply the omission of καί before πατρός.

On reviewing the whole mass of conflicting evidence, we may unhesitatingly reject the shortest form τοῦ θεοῦ, some of whose maintainers do not usually found their text on cursive manuscripts almost exclusively. We would gladly adopt τοῦ θεοῦ χριστοῦ, so powerfully do internal considerations plead in its favour, were it but a little better supported: the important doctrine which it declares, Scriptural and Catholic as that is, will naturally make us only the more cautious in receiving it unreservedly. Yet the more we think over this reading, the more it grows upon us, as the source from which all the rest are derived. At present, perhaps, τοῦ θεοῦ πατρὸς τοῦ χριστοῦ may be looked upon as the most strongly attested, but in the presence of so many opposing probabilities, a very small weight might suffice to turn the critical scale.

40. I THESS. ii. 7. We have here a various reading, consisting of the prefix of a single letter, which seems to introduce into a simple verse what is little short of an absurdity. Instead of ἤπιοι of the Received text, of Tischendorf and Tregelles, we find νήπιοι adopted by Lachmann as a consequence of his own stringent rules, and by Westcott and Hort of their own free will, unless indeed it be said that they also are working in chains of their own forging. How St. Paul can compare himself to a babe in one clause of the verse and to its nurse in the other would be quite unintelligible if Origen, who read νήπιοι, had not instructed us that the nurse is playing at baby for the babe's amusement (ἐγένετο νήπιος καὶ παραπλήσιος τροφῷ θαλπούσῃ τὸ ἑαυτῆς παιδίον καὶ λαλούσῃ λόγους ὡς παιδίον διὰ τὸ παιδίον, iii. 662). It needs but the exercise of common sense to brush away such a fancy as this, and the state of the evidence will show us how the best authorities are sometimes hopelessly in the wrong; for νήπιοι is the

form favoured by ℵ*BC*D*FG, 5, 23, 26, 31*, 37, 39**, 74, 87, 109**, 114, 115, 137, 219*, 252, and is easily accounted for by the accidental reduplication of the letter after N in ΗΜЄΝΗΠΙΟΙ (*see* p. 10). The Vulgate and the Latin versions accompanying DEFG (*e* testifying against its own Greek) have *parvuli*, and so the Bohairic, Ethiopic, Clement of Alexandria (ἤπιος οὖν ὁ νήπιος), Ambrosiaster, Jerome, and Augustine very expressly. On the other hand ἤπιος is vouched for by ℵ**AC**D**EKLP, 17, 47, 61, 260, and by all cursives not named above, by both Syriac versions, by the Sahidic and by its follower the Bashmuric, by the Armenian, by Clement and Origen elsewhere (but their inconsistency means nothing but carelessness), Basil, Chrysostom, Theodore of Mopsuestia[1], Theodoret, Euthalius, Œcumenius, John Damascene and the catenae. Theophylact knew of and expounds both readings. It is almost pathetic to mark Dr. Hort's brave struggle to maintain a cause which in this instance is simply hopeless. 'The second ν might be inserted or omitted with equal facility; but the change from the bold image to the tame and facile adjective is characteristic of the difference between St. Paul and the Syrian revisers (cf. 1 Cor. iii. 1, 2; ix. 20, &c.). It is not of harshness that St. Paul here declares himself innocent, but of flattery and the rhetorical arts by which gain or repute is procured, his adversaries having doubtless put this malicious interpretation upon his language among the Thessalonians' (Notes, p. 128). For his alleged Syrian revision, *see* above, p. 287.

41. 1 Tim. iii. 16. Θεὸς ἐφανερώθη ἐν σαρκί. This text has proved the *crux criticorum*. The Vatican has now failed us, but all manuscripts (D *tertiâ manu*, KLP, 300 cursives) read Θεός with the common text, except ℵ*A*? C*? FG, 17, 73, which have ὅς, D* which (after the Latin versions) has ὅ: the Leicester codex, 37, gives ὁ θς̄ (*see* facsimile No. 40, l. 1), as if to combine two of the variations[2]. In the abridged form of writing usual in all manuscripts, even the oldest, the difference between ΟC and ΘC̄ consists only in the presence or absence of

[1] In Dr. Swete's edition, vol. ii. p. 11, Theodore expounds thus in the old Latin version: *sed facti sumus quieti in medio vestro*, hoc est, 'omni mediocritate et humilitate sumus abusi, nolentes graves aliquibus videri.'

[2] A like combination is seen in Cod. 37 in 1 Tim. vi. 19 τῆς αἰωνίου ὄντως ζωῆς.

two horizontal strokes; hence it is rather to be regretted than wondered at that the true reading of each of the uncial authorities for the former is more or less open to question. Respecting Cod. א we have the statement of Tischendorf, a most consummate judge in such matters: '*corrector aliquis, qui omnium ultimus textum attigit, saeculi ferè duodecimi,* [*pro* ος *primae manûs*] *reposuit* θεος, *sed hoc tam cautè ut antiquissimam scripturam intactam relinqueret*' (Notitia Cod. Sinait. p. 20), which is unequivocal enough: *see* facsimile No. 13 in Scrivener's 'Collation of Cod. Sin.,' and Introd., p. xxv: also Plate iv, facsimile No. 11 c of this volume, wherein the twelfth century θε above the line, the new accent over OC, and the triple points to denote insertion, are very conspicuous. Nor is there any real doubt respecting the kindred codices FG. From the photographed title-page of the published 'Cod. Augiensis' (F) l. 9, and Matthaei's facsimile of G (N. T., vol. i. p. 4)[1], it will be seen that while there is not the least trace of the horizontal line within the circle of omicron, the line above the circle in *both* ($\overline{\text{OC}}$) is not horizontal, but rises a little towards the right: such a line not unfrequently in F, oftener in G, is used (as here) to indicate the rough breathing: it sometimes stands even for the *lenis* (e. g. ἴδιον 1 Cor. vi. 18; vii. 4; 37; ἴσσα Phil. ii. 6). Those who never saw Cod. C must depend on Tischendorf's Excursus (Cod. Ephraemi, pp. 39–42) and his facsimile, imitated in our Plate x. No. 24. His decision is that the primitive reading was OC, but he was *the first to discern a cross line within* O (facsimile, l. 3, eighth letter); which, however, from the colour ('*subnigra*') he judges to belong to the second or third hand, rising upwards (a tendency rather exaggerated than otherwise in our Plate); while the coarse line above, and the musical notes (denoting a word of two syllables) below, are plainly of the third hand. This verdict, especially delivered by such a man, we know not how to gainsay, and merely point to the fact that the cross line in Θ, the ninth letter further on, which is certainly *primâ manu*, also ascends towards the right. Cod. A, however, I have examined at least twenty times within as many years, and yet am not quite able to assent to the conclusion of Mr. Cowper when he says 'we hope that no one will think it possible,

[1] Dean Burgon has just presented me with the photographed page in Cod. G, respecting whose evidence there can be no remaining doubt.

either with or without a lens, to ascertain the truth of the matter by any inspection of the Codex' (Cod. Alex., Introd. p. xviii). On the contrary, seeing (as every one must see for himself) with my own eyes, I have always felt convinced with Berriman and the earlier collators that Cod. A read $\overline{\Theta C}$, and, so far as I am shaken in my conviction at all, it is less by the adverse opinion even of Bp. Ellicott[1], than by the more recently discovered fact that OC (which is adopted by Griesbach, Lachmann, Tischendorf, Davidson, Tregelles, Alford, Ellicott, Wordsworth, Hort and Westcott), was read in ℵ as early as the fourth century.

The secondary witnesses, versions, and certain of the Fathers, also powerfully incline this way, and they deserve peculiar attention in a case like the present. The Peshitto (ܕ) and Harkleian (text and ܗܘ in margin) Syriac have a relative (whether ὅς or ὅ); so have the Armenian, the Roman Ethiopic, and Erpenius' Arabic. The Gothic supports ὅς; the Sahidic, Bohairic, and Platt's Ethiopic favour ὅς or ὅ: all Latin versions

[1] The true reading of the Codex Alexandrinus in 1 Tim. iii. 16 has long been an interesting puzzle with Biblical students. The manuscript, and especially the leaf containing this verse (fol. 145), now very thin and falling into holes, must have been in a widely different condition from the present when it first came to England. At that period Young, Huish, and the rest who collated or referred to it, believed that $\overline{\Theta C}$ was written by the first hand. Mill (N. T. *ad loc.*) declares that he had first supposed the primitive reading to be $\overline{OC}$, seeing clearly that the line *over* the letters had not been entirely made, but only thickened, by a later hand, probably the same that traced the coarse, rude, recent, horizontal diameter now running through the circle. On looking more closely, however, he detected 'ductus quosdam et vestigia satis certa . . . praesertim ad partem sinistram, qua peripheriam literae pertingit,' evidently belonging to an earlier diameter, which the thicker and later one had almost defaced. This old line was afterwards seen by John Berriman and four other persons with him (Gloucester Ridley, Gibson, Hewett, and Pilkington) by means of a glass in the bright sunshine, when he was preparing his Lady Moyer's Lecture for 1737–8 (Critical Dissertation on 1 Tim. iii. 16, p. 156). Wetstein admitted the existence of such a transverse line, but referred it to the tongue or *sagitta* of Є on the reverse of the leaf, an explanation rejected by Woide, but admitted by Tregelles, who states in opposition to Woide that 'Part of the Є on the other side of the leaf *does* intersect the O, as we have seen again and again, and which others with us have seen also' (Horne, iv. p. 156). This last assertion may be received as quite true, and yet not relevant to the point at issue. In an Excursus appended to 1 Timothy in his edition of 'The Pastoral Epistles' (p. 100, 1856), Bp. Ellicott declares, as the result of 'minute personal inspection,' that the original reading was 'indisputably' OC. But the fact is, that the page is much too far gone to admit of any present judgement which would weigh against past judgements, as any one who examines the passage can see for himself. Woide could see the line in 1765, but not in 1785.

(even *fg* whose Greek is ΟͨC) read 'quod,' while *θεός* appears only in the Slavonic (which usually resembles KL and the later copies) and the Polyglott Arabic. Of ecclesiastical writers the best witness for the Received text is Ignatius, *Θεοῦ ἀνθρωπίνως φανερουμένου* ('Ephes.' 19), both in the Greek and Old Latin, although the Syriac abbreviator seems to have *τοῦ υἱοῦ*: the later interpolator expanded the clause thus: *θεοῦ ὡς ἀνθρώπου φαινομένου, καὶ ἀνθρώπου ὡς θεοῦ ἐνεργοῦντος.* Hippolytus (Adv. Not. 17: fl. 220) makes a 'free reference' to it in the words *Οὗτος προελθὼν εἰς κόσμον, θεὸς ἐν σώματι ἐφανερώθη,* and elsewhere with *ὁ* before *προελθών.* The testimony of Dionysius of Alexandria (265) can no longer be upheld (Tregelles, Horne, iv. p. 339), that of Chrysostom to the same effect is by some deemed precarious, since his manuscripts fluctuate, and Cramer's catena on 1 Tim. p. 31 is adverse[1]. The evidence borne for *θεός* by Didymus (de Trin.) and Gregory Nyssen[2] is beyond all doubt; that of later writers, Theodoret, John Damascene, Theophylact, Œcumenius (as might be looked for) is clear and express. The chief Latins, Hilary, Jerome, Augustine, &c., exhibit either *qui* or *quod*: Cyril of Alexandria (for so we must conclude both from manuscripts and his context)[3], Epiphanius (*twice*), Theodore of Mopsuestia (in Latin)[4], and others of less weight, or whose language is less

[1] Yet how can it be *precarious* in the face of such testimony as the following (*Quarterly Review*, Oct. 1881, p. 363)? *Τὸ δὲ θεὸν ὄντα ἄνθρωπον θελῆσαι γενέσθαι καὶ ἀνασχέσθαι καταβῆναι τοσοῦτον . . . τοῦτό ἐστι τὸ ἐκπλήξεως γέμον. Ὃ δὴ καὶ Παῦλος θαυμάζων ἔλεγε· καὶ ὁμολογουμένως μέγα ἐστὶ τὸ τῆς εὐσεβείας μυστήριον· ποῖον μέγα; θεὸς ἐφανερώθη ἐν σαρκί· καὶ πάλιν ἀλλαχοῦ· οὐ γὰρ ἀγγέλων ἐπιλαμβάνεται ὁ θεός* (Chrysostom, i. 497). It is necessary to study the context well before we can understand the strength or weakness of Patristic evidence.

[2] Twenty-three times in all, as Ward (*see* p. 394, note) observes, adding that 'nothing can be more express and unquestionable than his reading.' The *Quarterly Reviewer* speaks very well (*ubi supra*), 'A single quotation is better than many references. Among a multitude of proofs that Christ is God, Gregory says: *Τιμοθέῳ δὲ διαρρήδην βοᾷ ὅτι ὁ θεὸς ἐφανερώθη ἐν σαρκί, ἐδικαιώθη ἐν πνεύματι*' (ii. 693).

[3] Bentleii Critica Sacra, p. 67, '*Σχόλια* Photii MSS. (Bib. Pub. Cant.) *ad loc. ὁ ἐν ἁγίοις Κύριλλος ἐν τῷ ιβ κεφαλαίῳ τῶν σχολίων φησίν, ὃς ἐφανερώθη ἐν σαρκί.*' Photius also quoted Gregory Thaumaturgus (or Apollinarius) for *θεός*.

[4] Dr. Swete, in his masterly edition of the Latin translation of Theodore's commentary on St. Paul's Epistles, after citing the Latin text as *qui manifestatus est in carne*, adds 'Both our MSS. read *qui*, here and [15 lines] below and use the masculine consistently throughout the context. . . . Thus the present translation goes to confirm the inference already drawn from the Greek fragment of Theodore, de Incarn. xiii (Migne, P. G. 66, 987), that he read *ὃς ἐφανερώθη*'

direct, are cited in critical editions of the N. T. in support of a relative; add to which that θεός is not quoted by Fathers (e.g. Cyprian, p. 35; Bentleii Critica Sacra, p. 67) in many places where it might fairly be looked for; though this argument must not be pushed too far. The idle tale, propagated by Liberatus the Deacon of Carthage, and from him repeated by Hincmar and Victor, that Macedonius Patriarch of Constantinople (A. D. 506) was expelled by the Emperor Anastasius for corrupting O or OC into ΘC, although lightly credited by Dr. Tregelles (An Account of the Printed Text, p. 229) and even by Dr. Hort (Notes, p. 133), is sufficiently refuted by Bp. Pearson (On the Creed, Art. ii. p. 128, 3rd edition).

On a review of the whole mass of external proof, bearing in mind too that OC (from which ὅ of D* is an evident corruption) is grammatically much the *harder* reading after μυστήριον (Canon I), and that it might easily pass into ΘC, we must consider it probable (indeed, if we were sure of the testimony of the first-rate uncials, we might regard it as certain) that the second of our rules of Comparative Criticism must here be applied, and θεός of the more recent many yield place to ὅς of the ancient few [2]. Yet even then the force of the Patristic testimony remains untouched. Were we to concede to Dr. Hort's unproved hypothesis that Didymus, de Trinitate, abounds in what he calls Syrian readings, and that they are not rare with Gregory Nyssen (Notes, p. 133), the clear references of Ignatius and

(vol. ii. p. 135 n.): pertinently observing that if Theodore used ὅς, he was in harmony with the Syriac versions.

[1] The *Quarterly Reviewer* (Oct. 1881, p. 365), in his trenchant style, goes a good way beyond this: '"Ος is in truth so grossly improbable—rather, so *impossible*—a reading, that under any circumstances we must have anxiously inquired whether no escape from it was discoverable: whether there exists no other way of explaining *how* so patent an absurdity as this may have arisen? . . . We shall be landed in a bathos indeed if we allow *gross improbability* to become a constraining motive with us in revising the sacred Text.'

[2] 'Conspectum lectionis hujus loci optime dedit in sermone vernaculo William H. Ward, V. D. M. in Bibliothecâ Sacrâ Americanâ, anni 1865,' Tregelles N.T. *ad loc.* For a copy of this work I am indebted to the kindness of A. W. Tyler of New York. Mr. Ward wonders that neither Tregelles nor I have noticed a certain pinhole in Cod. A, which was pointed out to Sir F. Madden by J. Scott Porter, made by some person at the extremity of the sagitta of the Є on the opposite page, and falling exactly on the supposed transverse line of the Θ. I cannot perceive the pinhole, but the vellum is fast crumbling away from the effects of time, certainly through no lack of care on the part of those who keep the manuscript.

Hippolytus are not thus to be disposed of. I dare not pronounce θεός a corruption.

This decision of Dr. Scrivener would probably have been considerably strengthened in favour of θεός, if the above passage had been written after, instead of before, the composition and appearance of Dean Burgon's elaborate and patient examination of all the evidence, which occupies seventy-seven pages in his 'Revision Revised' (pp. 424–501). Dean Burgon shows at length that after about 1770 the passage in A became so worn that it has been since that time increasingly difficult to see it; he casts much doubt upon the witness of C for ὅς, which Mr. Hoskier (Cod. 604, Appendix J), after a long examination of the MS., not only confirms, but actually removes in the opposite direction by claiming C as a witness for θεός; he maintains with reason that the transverse line in F and G is the sign of contraction; he exhibits the consentient testimony of the cursives; he claims upon the testimony of the scholar who was editing the Harkleian that version, as also the Georgian and Slavonic; and he adds to the Fathers enumerated above, besides doubtful testimonies, Gregory of Nazianzus, Cyril of Alexandria, Severus of Antioch, Diodorus of Tarsus, Euthalius, Macedonius, Epiphanius of Catana, Theodorus Studita, Euthymius, some scholia, the author of Περὶ θείας σαρκώσεως, and an anonymous author,—making some fifty testimonies in all.

42. I TIM. vi. 7. By omitting δῆλον of the Received text, Lachmann, Tischendorf, Tregelles, Westcott and Hort, produce a Greek sentence as inconsequential as the most thorough votaries of the 'harder reading' can wish for: 'For we brought nothing into the world, because neither can we carry anything out.' Dr. Hort sees, of course, that St. Paul could not reason in this fashion, and says that 'The text [i.e. *his* text, without δῆλον] is manifestly the parent of all the other readings, which are futile attempts to smooth away its difficulty. A primitive corruption must lurk somewhere,'—and then ventures on the awkward suggestion that OTI arose from the transcriptional repetition of the last syllable of κοσμου (ON being read as OTI), a guess which we observe that Dr. Westcott does not care to vouch for (Notes, p. 134). But why create a difficulty at all? Cod. B, which ends in Heb. ix. 14, is now lost to us, and of the rest δῆλον is omitted in ℵ*AFG and

its Latin version *g* with copies of the Vulgate referred to by Lachmann, the Bohairic (καί for ὅτι), Sahidic; the Armenian and both Ethiopic varying with the Bohairic. Instead of δῆλον D*, *m*, *fuld.*, Cyprian and the Gothic have ἀληθές, and the printed Vulgate with its codices (even *f*) and Ambrosiaster *haud dubium*, which will suit δῆλον well enough, as will ܘܝܕܝܥܐ (*et notum est*) of the Syriac versions. For δῆλον itself stand ℵ**D** (*hiat* E) KLP, all the cursives save one, and of the Fathers Basil, Macarius, Chrysostom, Euthalius, Theodoret, and John Damascene, evidence which we should have liked to see a little stronger.

43. PHILEM. 12. For ὃν ἀνέπεμψα· σὺ δὲ αὐτόν, τουτέστι τὰ ἐμὰ σπλάγχνα, προσλαβοῦ of the Received text, the critics, Lachmann, Tischendorf, Tregelles (but not his margin), Bp. Lightfoot, Westcott and Hort read ὃν ἀνέπεμψά σοι, αὐτόν, τουτέστι τὰ ἐμὰ σπλάγχνα, omitting προσλαβοῦ, which they judge to have been interpolated from ver. 17. Tregelles and Bp. Lightfoot, moreover, put a full stop after σοι, so that αὐτόν is regarded as an 'accusative suspended; the sentence changes its form and loses itself in a number of dependent clauses; and the main point is not resumed till ver. 17 προσλαβοῦ αὐτὸν ὡς ἐμέ, the grammar having been meanwhile dislocated.' So Lightfoot, who vindicates the emphatic place he has assigned to αὐτόν by the not very close parallels John ix. 21, 23; Eph. i. 22. Manuscripts, of course, will not help us much in punctuation, but Codd. ℵ*A, 17 are very good witnesses for σοι in the room of σὺ δέ and for the omission of προσλαβοῦ, a simple, although somewhat rude, construction well worthy of attention. For σοι, with or without σὺ δέ following, we have the additional support of C*DE, *d e* and *g* against its own Greek, the Clementine Vulgate and such Vulgate codices as *demid. harl.*[2]**, the Peshitto Syriac, Bohairic, Armenian, Ethiopic, &c. For the omission of προσλαβοῦ, which is of course the chief variation, besides ℵ*A, 17 are cited F and G in the Greek but not in their Latin versions, 37 and others setting it before αὐτόν. It is found in all the rest, D**E**KLP, all other cursives, and (as might have been anticipated) the versions, as well Latin as Syriac, Bohairic (which reads as Cod. 37), Gothic, and Ethiopic: *g*, the Armenian and Theodoret put it after αὐτόν.

Fourth Series. Catholic Epistles.

44. JAMES iv. 4. Μοιχοὶ καί should be omitted before μοιχαλίδες on the testimony of ℵ*AB, 13. The Peshitto, Bohairic, Latin, Armenian, and both Ethiopic versions have 'adulterers' (*fornicatores ff*) only, but since no Greek copy thus reads, we must suppose that their translators were startled by the bold imagery so familiar to the Hebrew prophets (Isa. liv. 5; Jer. ii. 2; Ezek. xvi. 32 are cited from a host of similar passages by Wordsworth) and endeavoured to dilute it in this way. Tischendorf would join μοιχαλίδες with δαπανήσητε ver. 3, alleging the point or stop placed after it in Cod. B: but this point is not found in Vercellone's edition, although he leaves a small space before οὐκ. The full form Μοιχοὶ καὶ μοιχαλίδες of ℵ^c KLP, the later Syriac, and all other known copies, is evidently a correction of early scribes.

45. JAMES iv. 5. The variation between κατῴκισεν and κατῴκησεν is plainly to be attributed to a mere itacism, whichsoever is to be regarded as the true form. We find ι in ℵAB, 101, 104 only, nor is it quite accurate to say with Tischendorf that collators are apt to overlook such points. In KLP, and apparently in all other manuscripts of every class, η is read, and so the catenas, with Theophylact and Œcumenius, understand this difficult passage. That all the versions (Latin, Syriac, Egyptian, &c.) thus render seems decisive in favour of η. The combination of ℵAB, however strong, has repeatedly been seen not to be irresistible; and while it must be confessed that in our existing Greek copies the interchange of ι and η (though found in Cod. A) is not an itacism of the very oldest type (p. 10), yet here the testimony of the versions refers it back to the second century. Lachmann, Tischendorf, Tregelles, Westcott and Hort, combine in reading κατῴκισεν.

46. I PET. i. 23. Here we have a remarkable example to illustrate what we saw in the cases of Rom. viii. 20; 2 Cor. iii. 3, Phil. ii. 1, that the chief uncials sometimes conspire in readings which are unquestionably false, and can hardly have arisen independently of each other. For σπορᾶς φθαρτῆς Codd. ℵAC have φθορᾶς φθαρτῆς, the scribe's eye wandering in writing

σπορᾶς to the beginning of the next word: Cod. B is free from this vile corruption. When Mill records the variation for Cod. A, he adds (as well he might), 'dormitante scribâ:' but that the same gross error should be found in three out of the four oldest codices, *and in no other*, is very suggestive, and not a little perplexing to false theorists.

47. 1 PET. iii. 15. *Κύριον δὲ τὸν θεὸν ἁγιάσατε ἐν ταῖς καρδίαις ὑμῶν.* For *θεόν* we find *χριστόν* (a change of considerable doctrinal importance)[1] in ℵABC, 7, 8 (Stephen's *ια'*), 13, 33 (*margin*), 69, 137, 182, 184 (but not 221: *see* p. 310, note 2), Apost. 1 (*ιν̅ χν̅ ἡμῶν*) with its Arabic translation. Thus too read both Syriac versions, the Sahidic, Bohairic, Armenian (*τὸν αὐτὸν καὶ χριστόν*), Erpenius' Arabic, the Vulgate, Clement of Alexandria, Fulgentius, and Bede. Jerome has 'Jesum Christum:' the Ethiopic and one other (Auctor de promiss., fourth century) omit both words. Against this very strong case we can set up for the common text only the more recent uncials KLP (not more than seven uncials contain this Epistle), the mass of later cursives (ten out of Scrivener's twelve, also Wake 12, or Cod. 193), the Polyglott Arabic, Slavonic, Theophylact, and Œcumenius, authorities of the ninth century and downwards. It is a real pleasure to me in this instance to express my cordial agreement with Tregelles (and so read Lachmann, Tischendorf, Westcott and Hort), when he says, 'Thus the reading *χριστόν* may be relied on *confidently*' (An Account of the Printed Text, p. 285). I would further allege this text as one out of many proofs that the great uncials seldom or never conspire in exhibiting a really valuable departure from the later codices, unless supported by some of the best of the cursives themselves. See, however, Acts xiii. 32.

48. 2 PET. ii. 13. The resemblance between the second epistle of St. Peter and that of St. Jude is too close to be unobserved by the most careless reader, and the supposition that the elder

[1] 'As the Apostle here applies to *Christ* language which in the Old Testament is made use of with reference to Jehovah (*see* Isa. viii. 13), he clearly suggests the supreme godhead of our Redeemer,' as Dr. Roberts puts the matter (Words of the New Testament, p. 170). Not, of course, that our critical judgement should be swayed one way or the other by individual prepossessions; but that those who in the course of these researches have sacrificed to truth much that they have hitherto held dear, need not suppress their satisfaction when truth is gain.

Apostle's letter was in Jude's hands when he wrote his own is that which best meets the circumstances of the case. The σπῖλοι of the present verse, for example, looks like the origin of σπιλάδες in Jude 12, where the latter word is employed in a signification almost unprecedented in classical Greek, though the Orphic poems have been cited for its bearing the sense of 'spots,' which all the ancient versions rightly agree with our Authorized Bible in attributing to it. Bearing in mind the same verse of St. Jude, it seems plain that *ἀπάταις* of the Received text cannot be accepted as true, as well because it affords so poor a meaning in connexion with *ἐντρυφῶντες* and *συνευωχούμενοι*, as because the later writer must have seen *ἀγάπαις* in his model, when he paraphrased it by *οἱ ἐν ταῖς ἀγάπαις ὑμῶν σπιλάδες συνευωχούμενοι*. For this change of two letters we have the support of Cod. A (as corrected by the first hand) and B alone of the manuscripts, but of the versions, the Latin Speculum *m* which in these later epistles is strangely loose, yet cannot be misunderstood in the present place, the Vulgate, the Sahidic version, the Ethiopic, the Syriac printed with the Peshitto [1], and the margin of the Harkleian version. Add to these Ephraem and the Latin author of the tract 'de singularitate clericorum,' both of the fourth century. The little group of cursives 27, 29, and the second hand of 66 read *ἀγνοίαις*; but *ἀπάταις, nescio quo sensu* [2], still

[1] This translation of 2 Peter, 2, 3 John, and Jude, printed by Pococke from Bodl. Orient. 119, well deserves careful study, being totally different in style and character both from the Peshitto and the Harkleian, somewhat free and periphrastic, yet, in our paucity of good authorities just here, of great interest and full of valuable readings. Thus, in this very verse it reads *ἀδικούμενοι* ('being wronged as the hire of their wrong-doing') with ℵ*BP and the Armenian, difficult as it may seem to receive that word as genuine: in ver. 17 it omits *εἰς τὸν αἰῶνα* with ℵB and some other versions: in ch. iii. 10 it sides with the Sahidic alone in receiving *οὐχ εὑρεθήσεται* (apparently correctly) instead of *εὑρεθήσεται* of ℵBKP, of the excellent cursives 27, 29, 66 *secundâ manu*, of the Armenian and Harkleian margin, where the Received text follows the obvious *κατακαήσεται* of AL and the rest, and C hits upon *ἀφανισθήσονται* in pure despair.

[2] Bp. Chr. Wordsworth speaks as though there were a *paronomasia*, a play on the words *ἀγάπη* and *ἀπάτη*, comparing (after Windischmann) 2 Thess. ii. 10. 'The false teachers called their meetings *ἀγάπαι*, *love feasts*, but they were mere *ἀπάται*, *deceits*. Their *table* was a *snare*' (Ps. lxix. 22). This view might be tenable if St. Peter, with whom the *paronomasia* must have taken its rise, were not the earlier writer of the two, as the Bishop of Lincoln believes he was, as firmly as we do. Perhaps Dr. Westcott's notion that 2 Peter is a translation, not an original, at least in ch. ii, will best account for the textual variations between it and St. Jude.

cleaves to the text of Tischendorf and of Westcott and Hort, and to the margin of Tregelles, who in the text prefers ἀγάπαις with Lachmann and Westcott and Hort's margin. Codd. ℵA (in its original form) CKLP, all other cursives, the catenas (Cod. 36, &c.), the Bohairic, Armenian, and Harkleian versions also have ἀπάταις, and so Theophylact and Œcumenius, but hardly Jerome as cited by Tischendorf.

49. I JOHN ii. 23. The English reader will have observed that the latter clause of this verse, '*but he that acknowledgeth the Son hath the Father also*,' is printed in italics in our Authorized version, this being the only instance in the New Testament wherein variety of reading is thus denoted by the translators, who derived both the words and this method of indicating their doubtful authenticity from the 'Great Bible' of 1539 [1]. The corresponding Greek ὁ ὁμολογῶν τὸν υἱὸν καὶ τὸν πατέρα ἔχει (which appears to have been lost out of some copies by Homoeoteleuton), was first inserted in Beza's Greek Testament in 1582 [2], it is approved by all modern editors (Griesbach, Scholz, Lachmann, Tischendorf, Tregelles, Westcott and Hort), and, though still absent from the *textus receptus*, is unquestionably genuine. This is just such a point as versions are best capable of attesting. The 'Great Bible' had no doubt taken the clause from the Latin Vulgate, in whose printed editions and chief manuscripts it is found (e. g. in *am. fuld. demid. tol. harl.*), as also in both Syriac, both Egyptian (the Sahidic not for certain), the Armenian, Ethiopic, and Erpenius' (not the Polyglott) Arabic version. Of manuscripts the great uncials ℵABC (with P) contain the clause, the later KL omit it. Of the cursives only two of Scrivener's (182, 225) have it, and another (183) *secundâ manu:* from twelve or more of them it is absent, as also from seven of Matthaei's: but of the other cursives it is present in at least thirty, whereof 3, 5, 13, 66** (*marg.*), 68, 69, 98 are valuable. It is also acknowledged by Clement, Origen (*thrice*), Eusebius, both Cyrils, Theophylact, and the Western Fathers. The younger Cyril, possibly Euthalius, and one or

[1] See the Cambridge Paragraph Bible, Introduction, pp. xxxv, xxxvii.

[2] 'Restitui in Grecis hoc membrum ex quatuor manuscr. codicum, veteris Latini et Syri interpretis auctoritate. sic etiam assueto Johanne istis oppositionibus contrariorum uti quam saepissimè.' Beza, N. T., 1582.

two others have ὁμολογεῖ for the final ἔχει: the Old Latin *m*, Cyprian, and Hilary repeat τὸν υἱὸν καί before τὸν πατέρα ἔχει. The critical skill of Beza must not be estimated very highly, yet in this instance he might well have been imitated by the Elzevir editors.

50. I JOHN v. 7, 8. *Ὅτι τρεῖς εἰσιν οἱ μαρτυροῦντες [ἐν τῷ οὐρανῷ, ὁ Πατήρ, ὁ Λόγος, καὶ τὸ Ἅγιον Πνεῦμα· καὶ οὗτοι οἱ τρεῖς ἕν εἰσι. καὶ τρεῖς εἰσιν οἱ μαρτυροῦντες ἐν τῇ γῇ], τὸ πνεῦμα, καὶ τὸ ὕδωρ, καὶ τὸ αἷμα· καὶ οἱ τρεῖς εἰς τὸ ἕν εἰσιν.*

The authenticity of the words within brackets will, perhaps, no longer be maintained by any one whose judgement ought to have weight; but this result has been arrived at after a long and memorable controversy, which helped to keep alive, especially in England, some interest in Biblical studies, and led to investigations into collateral points of the highest importance, such as the sources of the Received text, the manuscripts employed by R. Stephen, the origin and value of the Velesian readings, and other points. A critical *résumé* of the whole discussion might be profitably undertaken by some competent scholar; we can at present touch only upon the chief heads of this great debate[1].

The two verses appear in the early editions, with the following notable variations from the common text, C standing for the Complutensian, Er. for one or more of Erasmus' five editions. Ver. 7. —ἐν τῷ οὐρανῷ *usque ad* τῇ γῇ ver. 8, Er. 1, 2. —ὁ *prim. et*

[1] Horne (Introduction, vol. ii. pt. ii. ch. iii. sect. 4), and after his example Tregelles (Horne, iv. pp. 384–8), give a curious list of more than fifty volumes, pamphlets, or critical notices on this question. The following are the most worthy of perusal: Letters to Edward Gibbon, Esq., by G. Travis, Archdeacon of Chester, 1785, 2nd edit.; Letters to Mr. Archdeacon Travis, &c., by Richard Porson, 1790; Letters to Mr. Archdeacon Travis, &c., by Herbert Marsh [afterwards Bp. of Peterborough], 1795; A Vindication of the Literary Character of Professor Porson, by Crito Cantabrigiensis [Thomas Turton, afterwards Bp. of Ely], 1827; Two Letters on some parts of the Controversy concerning I John v. 7, by Nicolas Wiseman, 1835, for which *see* Index. For Dr. Adam Clarke's 'Observations,' &c., 1805, *see* Evan. 61. Add F. A. Knittel on I John v. 7. Professor Ezra Abbot's edition of 'Orme's Memoir of the Controversy on I John v. 7,' New York, 1866, has not fallen in my way. As elaborate works, on the verses are 'A new plea for the authenticity of the Text of the Three Heavenly Witnesses, or Porson's Letters to Travis eclectically examined,' Cambridge, 1867, being the performance of a literary veteran, the late Rev. Charles Forster, whose arguments in vindication of the Pauline origin of the Epistle to the Hebrews, published in 1838, modern Biblical writers have found it easier to pass by than to refute; and 'The Three Witnesses, the disputed text in St. John, considerations new and old,' by the Rev. H. T. Armfield, Bagster, 1883.

secund. Er. 3. [*non* C. Er. 4, 5]. + και (*post* πατήρ) C. — τό Er. 3. πνεῦμα ἅγιον Er. 3, 4, 5. — οὗτοι C. + εις το (*ante* εν) C. Ver. 8, επί της γης C. — τὸ *ter* Er. 3, 4, 5 [*habent* C. Er. 1, 2]. — καὶ οἱ τρεῖς *ad fin. vers.* C. They are found, including the clause from ἐν τῷ οὐρανῷ to ἐν τῇ γῇ in no more than three Greek manuscripts, and those of very late date, one of them (Cod. Ravianus, Evan. 110) being a mere worthless copy from printed books; and in the margin of a fourth, in a hand as late as the sixteenth century. The real witnesses are the Codex Montfortianus, Evan. 61, Act. 34, whose history was described above, p. 187[1]; Cod. Vat.-Ottob. 298 (Act. 162), and, for the margin, a Naples manuscript (Act. ~~83 or~~ 173, q. v.). On comparing these slight and scanty authorities with the Received text we find that they present the following variations: ver. 7. ἀπὸ τοῦ οὐρανοῦ (*pro* ἐν τῷ οὐρανῷ) 162. — ὁ *prim. et secund.* 34, 162. — τό 34, 162. π̄ν̄ᾱ ἅγιον 34, 162. — οὗτοι 162. + εἰς τό (*ante* ἕν) 162. Ver. 8. εἰσί 73 *marg.* ἐπὶ τῆς γῆς 162. — τό *ter* 34. — καί (*post* π̄ν̄ᾱ) 34, 162. — καὶ οἱ τρεῖς *ad fin. vers.* 34, 162, *fin.* εἰσι 173. No printed edition, therefore, is found to agree with either 34 or 162 (173, whose margin is so very recent, only differs from the common text by dropping ν ἐφελκυστικόν), though on the whole 162 best suits the Complutensian: but the omission of the article in ver. 7, while it stands in ver. 8 in 162, proves that the disputed clause was interpolated (probably from its parallel Latin) by one who was very ill acquainted with Greek.

The controverted words are not met with in any of the extant uncials (ℵABKLP) or in any cursives besides those named above[2]: the cursives that omit them were found by the careful calculation of the Rev. A. W. Grafton, Dean Alford's secretary

[1] That the Codex Montfortianus was influenced by the Vulgate is probably true, though it is a little hasty to infer the fact at once from a single instance, namely, the substitution of χριστός after that version and Uscan's Armenian for the second πνεῦμα in verse 6: 'quae lectio Latina Graece in codicem 34 Dublinensem illum Montfortianum recepta luculenter testatur versionem vulgatam ad cum conficiendum valuisse' (Tischendorf *ad loc.*).

[2] It is really surprising how loosely persons who cannot help being scholars, at least in some degree, will talk about codices containing this clause. Dr. Edward Tatham, Rector of Lincoln College, Oxford (1792–1834), writing in 1827, speaks of a manuscript in his College Library which exhibited it, but is now missing, as having been once seen by him and Dr. Parsons, Bishop of Peterborough (Crito Cantabrigiensis, p. 334, note). Yet there can be no question that he meant Act. 33, which does not give the verse, but has long been known to have some connexion with the Codex Montfortianus, which does (*see* Act. 33).

(N.T. *ad. loc.*), to amount to 188 in all (to which we may now add Codd. 190, 193, 219–221), besides some sixty Lectionaries. The aspect of things is not materially altered when we consult the versions. The disputed clause is not in any manuscript of the Peshitto, nor in the best editions (e.g. Lee's): the Harkleian, Sahidic, Bohairic, Ethiopic, Arabic do not contain it in any shape: scarcely any Armenian codex exhibits it, and only a few recent Slavonic copies, the margin of a Moscow edition of 1663 being the first to represent it. The Latin versions, therefore, alone lend it any support, and even these are much divided. The chief and oldest authority in its favour is Wiseman's Speculum *m* and *r* of the earlier translation; it is found in the printed Latin Vulgate, and in perhaps forty-nine out of every fifty of its manuscripts, but not in the best, such as *am. fuld. harl.*[3]; nor in Alcuin's reputed copies at Rome (*primâ manu*) and London (Brit. Mus. Add. 10,546), nor in the book of Armagh and full fifty others. In one of the most ancient which contain it, *cav.*, ver. 8 precedes ver. 7 (as appears also in *m. tol. demid.* and a codex at Wolfenbüttel, *Wizanburg.* 99 [viii] cited by Lachmann), while in the margin is written '*audiat hoc Arius et ceteri*,' as if its authenticity was unquestioned[1]. In general there is very considerable variety of reading (always a suspicious circumstance, as has been already explained), and often the doubtful words stand only in the margin: the last clause of ver. 8 (*et hi tres unum sunt*), especially, is frequently left out when the 'Heavenly Witnesses' are retained. It is to defend *this* omission by the opinion of Thomas Aquinas, not to account for the reception of the doubtful words, that the Complutensian editors wrote a note, the longest and indeed almost the only one in their New Testament. We conclude, therefore, that the passage from ἐν τῷ οὐρανῷ to ἐν τῇ γῇ had no place in ancient Greek manuscripts, but came into some of the Latin at least as early as the sixth century.

[1] Of the two Spanish MSS. one *leon.*[2] contains the passage only in the margin, the other *leon.*[1] adds at the end of ver. 8, *in xpo ihu.* Canon Westcott cites a manuscript in the British Museum (Add. 11,852), of the ninth century, to the same effect, observing that, like *m* and *cav.*, it contains the Epistle to the Laodiceans. This MS. runs 'quia tres sunt qui testimonium dant sps et aqua et sanguis, et tres unum sunt. Sicut in caelo tres sunt pater verbum et sps et tres unum sunt.' Westcott's manuscript is, in fact, *ulm.*, and had already been used by Porson (Letters, &c., p. 148).

The Patristic testimony in its favour, though quite insufficient to establish the genuineness of the clause, is entitled to more consideration. Of the Greek Fathers it has been said that no one has cited it, even when it might be supposed to be most required by his argument, or though he quotes consecutively the verses going immediately before and after it[1]: [but a passage occurs in the Greek Synopsis of Holy Scripture of uncertain date (fourth or fifth century), which appears to refer to it, and another from the Disputation with Arius (Ps.-Athanasius)]. The same must be said of the great Latins, Hilary, Lucifer, Ambrose, Jerome[2], and Augustine, with others of less note. On the other hand the *African* writers, Vigilius of Thapsus, at the end of the fifth century, and Fulgentius of Ruspe (fl. 508) in two places, expressly appeal to the 'three Heavenly Witnesses' as a genuine portion of St. John's Epistle; nor is there much reason to doubt the testimony of Victor Vitensis, who records that the passage was insisted on in a confession of faith drawn up by Eugenius Bishop of Carthage and 460 bishops in 484, and presented to the Arian Hunneric, king of the Vandals [or of Cassiodorus, an Italian, in the sixth century]. From that period the clause became well known in other regions of the West, and was in time generally accepted throughout the Latin Church.

But a stand has been made by the maintainers of this passage on the evidence of two African Fathers of a very different stamp from those hitherto named, Tertullian and Cyprian. If it could be proved that these writers cited or alluded to the passage, it would result—*not by any means that it is authentic*—but that like Acts viii. 37 and a few other like interpolations, it was known and received in some places, as early as the second or third century. Now as regards the language of Tertullian

[1] Mr. Forster (*ubi supra*, pp. 200–209) believed that he had discovered *Greek* authority of the fourth century for this passage, in an isolated Homily by an unknown author, in the Benedictine edition of Chrysostom (Tom. xii. pp. 416–21), whose date Montfaucon easily fixes by internal evidence at A. D. 381. As this discovery, if real, is of the utmost importance in the controversy, it seems only right to subjoin the words alleged by this learned divine, leaving them to make their own way with the reader: (1) εἶς κέκληται ὁ Πατὴρ καὶ ὁ Υἱὸς καὶ τὸ Πνεῦμα τὸ Ἅγιον: (2) δεῖ γὰρ τῇ ἀποστολικῇ χορείᾳ παραχωρῆσαι τὴν Ἁγίαν Τριάδα, ἣν ὁ Πατὴρ καταγγέλλει. Τριὰς Ἀποστόλων, μάρτυς τῆς οὐρανίου Τριάδος.

[2] The 'Prologus Galeatus in vii Epistolas *Canonicas*,' in which the author complains of the omission of ver. 7, 'ab infidelibus translatoribus,' is certainly not Jerome's, and begins to appear in codices of about the ninth century.

(which will be found in Tischendorf's and the other critical editions of the N. T.; advers. Prax. 25; de Pudic. 21), it must be admitted that Bp. Kaye's view is the most reasonable, that 'far from containing an allusion to 1 John v. 7, it furnishes most decisive proof that he knew nothing of the verse' (Writings of Tertullian, p. 550, second edition); but I cannot thus dispose of his junior Cyprian (d. 258). One must say with Tischendorf (who, however, manages to explain away his testimony) '*gravissimus est* Cyprianus *de eccles. unitate* 5.' His words run, 'Dicit dominus, *Ego et pater unum sumus* (John x. 30), et iterum de Patre, et Filio, et Spiritu Sancto scriptum est, *Et tres unum sunt.*' And yet further, in his Epistle to Jubaianus (73) on heretical baptism: 'Si baptizari quis apud haereticos potuit, utique et remissam peccatorum consequi potuit,—si peccatorum remissam consecutus est, et sanctificatus est, et templum Dei factus est, quaero cujus Dei? Si Creatoris, non potuit, qui in eum non credidit; si Christi, nec hujus fieri potuit templum, qui negat Deum Christum; si Spiritus Sancti, cum tres unum sunt, quomodo Spiritus Sanctus placatus esse ei potest, qui aut Patris aut Filii inimicus est?' If these two passages be taken together (the first is manifestly much the stronger [1]), it is surely safer and more candid to admit that Cyprian read ver. 7 in his copies, than to resort to the explanation of Facundus [vi], that the holy Bishop was merely putting on ver. 8 a spiritual meaning; although we must acknowledge that it was in this way ver. 7 obtained a place, first in the margin, then in the text of the Latin copies, and though we have clear examples of the like mystical interpretation in Eucherius (fl. 440) and Augustine (contra Maximin. 22), who only knew of ver. 8.

Stunica, the chief Complutensian editor, by declaring, in controversy with Erasmus, with reference to this very passage, 'Sciendum est, Graecorum codices esse corruptos, nostros [i.e. Latinos] verò ipsam veritatem continere,' virtually admits that ver. 7 was translated in that edition from the Latin, not derived from Greek sources. The versions (for such we must call them) in Codd. 34, 162 had no doubt the same origin, but

[1] The writer of a manuscript note in the British Museum copy of Travis' 'Letters to Gibbon,' 1785, p. 49, very well observes on the second citation from Cyprian: 'That three are one might be taken from the eighth verse, as that was certainly understood of Father, Son, and Holy Ghost, *especially when Baptism was the subject in hand*' [Matt. xxviii. 19].

were somewhat worse rendered: the margin of 173 seems to be taken from a printed book. Erasmus, after excluding the passage from his first two editions, inserted it in his third under circumstances we have before mentioned; and notwithstanding the discrepancy of reading in ver. 8, there can be little or no doubt of the identity of his 'Codex Britannicus' with Montfort's[1]. We have detailed the steps by which the text was brought into its present shape, wherein it long remained, unchallenged by all save a few such bold spirits as Bentley, defended even by Mill, implicitly trusted in by those who had no knowledge of Biblical criticism. It was questioned in fair argument by Wetstein, assailed by Gibbon in 1781 with his usual weapons, sarcasm and insinuation (Decline and Fall, chap. xxxvii). Archdeacon Travis, who came to the rescue, a person 'of some talent and attainments' (Crito Cantab., p. 335, note), burdened as he was with a weak cause and undue confidence in its goodness, would have been at any rate—*impar congressus Achilli*—no match at all for the exact learning, the acumen, the wit, the overbearing scorn of Porson[2]. The

[1] It will be seen upon examination of our collations on p. 402 that the points of difference between Codex Montfortianus (34) and Erasmus' printed text are two, viz. that 34 omits καί after πνεῦμα in ver. 8, and with the Complutensian leaves out its last clause altogether; while, on the other hand, Erasmus and Cod. 34 agree against the Complutensian in their barbarous neglect of the Greek article in both verses. As regards the omission in Cod. 34 of the last clause of ver. 8 (καὶ οἱ τρεῖς εἰς τὸ ἕν εἰσιν), it is obvious to conjecture that the person, whosoever he was, that sent the transcript of the passage to Erasmus, who never saw the MS. for himself, might have broken off after copying the disputed words, and neglected to note down the further variation that immediately followed them. After the foregoing explanation we must leave the matter as it stands, for there is no known mode of accounting for the discrepancy, whereof Mr. Forster makes the very utmost in the following note, which, as a specimen of his book, is annexed entire: 'Bishop Marsh labours hard to identify the Codex Britannicus used by Erasmus, with the Codex Montfortianus. Erasmus's own description of the Codex Britannicus completely nullifies the attempt: "Postremo: Quod Britannicum etiam in terrae testimonio addebat, καὶ οἱ τρεῖς εἰς τὸ ἕν εἰσι, quod non addebatur hic duntaxat in editione Hispaniensi." Now as this clause is also omitted in the Montfort Codex, it cannot possibly be the same with the Codex Britannicus. In this as yet undiscovered MS., therefore, we have a second and independent Gr. MS. witness to the seventh verse. The zeal of the adversaries to evade this fact only betrays their sense of its importance' (p. 126). Alas! *Hi motus animorum.*

[2] I side with Porson against Travis on every important point at issue between them, and yet I must say that if the former lost a legacy (as has been reported) by publishing his 'Letters,' he was entitled to but slender sympathy. The prejudices of good men (especially when a passage is concerned which they have

'Letters' of that prince of scholars, and the contemporaneous researches of Herbert Marsh, have completely decided the contest. Bp. Burgess alone, while yet among us [d. 1837], and after him Mr. Charles Forster [d. 1871], clung obstinately to a few scattered outposts after the main field of battle had been lost beyond recovery [1].

On the whole, therefore, we need not hesitate to declare our conviction that the disputed words were not written by St. John: that they were originally brought into Latin copies in Africa from the margin, where they had been placed as a pious and orthodox gloss on ver. 8: that from the Latin they crept into two or three late Greek codices, and thence into the printed Greek text, a place to which they had no rightful claim. We will close this slight review with the terse and measured judgement of Griesbach on the subject: 'Si tam pauci, dubii, suspecti, recentes testes, et argumenta tam levia, sufficerent ad demonstrandam lectionis cujusdam *γνησιότητα*, licet obstent tam multa tamque gravia, et testimonia et argumenta: nullum prorsus superesset in re criticâ veri falsique criterium, et *textus Novi Testamenti universus planè incertus esset atque dubius*' (N. T., *ad locum*, vol. ii. p. 709).

51. I JOHN v. 18. In this verse, according to the Received text, we have the perfect *γεγεννημένος* of continued effects and the aorist *γεννηθεὶς* of completed action used for the same person, although elsewhere in the same Epistle the man begotten of God is invariably *γεγεννημένος* (ch. ii. 29; iii. 9 *bis*; iv. 7; v. 1, 4).

long held to be a genuine portion of Scripture, clearly teaching pure and right doctrine) should be dealt with gently: not that the truth should be dissembled or withheld, but when told it ought to be in a spirit of tenderness and love. Now take one example out of fifty of the tone and temper of Porson. The immediate question was a very subordinate one in the controversy, namely, the evidence borne by the Acts of the Lateran Council, A.D. 1215. 'Though this,' rejoins Porson, 'proves nothing in favour of the verse, it proves two other points. That the clergy then exercised dominion over the rights of mankind, and that able tithe-lawyers often make sorry critics. *Which I desire some certain gentlemen of my acquaintance to lay up in their hearts as a very seasonable innuendo*' (Letters, p. 361, quoted from 'A Tale of a Tub' p. 151). As if it were a disgrace for an Archdeacon to know a little about the laws which affect the clergy.

[1] Gaussen (Theopneustia, pp. 115–7) has still spirit remaining to press the masculine forms *οἱ μαρτυροῦντες* ver. 7 and *οἱ τρεῖς* ver. 8 as making in favour of the intervening clause: 'Remove it, and the grammar becomes incoherent:' a reason truly, but one not strong enough to carry his point.

Hence the special importance of the various reading *αὐτόν* for *ἑαυτόν* after *τηρεῖ*, since, if this were to be accepted, *ὁ γεννηθεὶς* could be none other than the Only-begotten Son who keepeth the human sons of God, agreeably to His own declaration in John xvii. 12[1]. In behalf of *αὐτόν* we can allege only AB, 105 (a cursive collated by Matthaei), and the Vulgate (*conservat eum*), the testimony of A, always so powerful when sanctioned by B, being nothing weakened by the fact that it is corrected into *ἑαυτόν* by the original [?] scribe[2], who in copying had faithfully followed his *exemplar*, and on second thoughts supposed he had gone wrong. *All* other authorities, including copies, versions, and Fathers, ℵ and the rest (C being lost here), have *ἑαυτόν*, the Peshitto very expressly [and Origen thrice, Didymus four times, Ephraem Syrus and Severus twice each, besides Theophylact and Œcumenius [3]]. We venture to commend this variation as one of a class Dean Vaughan speaks of, which, seeming violently improbable at first sight, grows upon the student as he becomes familiar with it. It must be confessed, however, that St. Paul makes but slight distinction between the two tenses in Gal. iv. 23, 29, and that we have no other example in Scripture or ecclesiastical writers of *ὁ γεννηθεὶς* being used absolutely for the Divine Son, though the contrast here suggested is somewhat countenanced by that between *ὁ ἁγιάζων* and *οἱ ἁγιαζόμενοι* in Heb. ii. 11. [So that Dr. Scrivener's view demands considerable sacrifice for its acceptance.]

[1] We are compelled to draw a sharp distinction between *γεγεννημένος* and *γεννηθεὶς* in the same context, and, with all deference to the *Quarterly Reviewer* (April, 1882, p. 366), we do not think his view of the matter more natural than that given in the text: 'St. John,' he suggests, 'is distinguishing between the mere recipient of the new birth (*ὁ γεννηθεὶς ἐκ τοῦ Θεοῦ*),—and the man who retains the sanctifying influences of the Holy Spirit which he received when he became regenerate (*ὁ γεγεννημένος ἐκ τοῦ Θεοῦ*).' [The distinction given between the perfect and aorist, as I have altered it in the text, is perfectly just, and explains the passage. The effects of regeneration if continued are indefectible, but the mere fact of regeneration entails constant watchfulness.]

[2] So it certainly seems to me after careful inspection of Cod. A, although it may be too bold to say, as some have, that there are in it no corrections by later hands. Above in ver. 10 *ἐν αὐτῷ* is supported by ABKLP and a shower of cursives in the room of *ἐν ἑαυτῷ* of ℵ and the Received text, but here there is no difference of sense between the two forms. Dr. Hort (Introd., Notes, p. 144) has an exhaustive and cautious note on the breathing of *αυτου, αυτῳ*, &c., and ultimately declines to exclude the aspirate from the N.T.

[3] The Revision Revised, pp. 247–8.

52. Jude 5. Here we have a variation, vouched for by AB united, which it is hard to think true, however interesting the doctrinal inference would be. Instead of ὁ κύριος λαὸν ἐκ γῆς Αἰγύπτου σώσας, the article is omitted by ℵAB, and perhaps by C*, so that it must at any rate resign its place; while for ΚC of ℵ (apparently of C*) and the mass of copies, with the Harkleian, we find IC in AB, 6, 7, 13, 29, 66 (*secundâ manu*), the Vulgate, Sahidic, Bohairic, and both Ethiopic versions. The Bodleian Syriac has yet another variation, ὁ Θεός, in support of which we have the important second hand of C, 5, 8, 68, *tol.* of the Vulgate, the Armenian (with ισ in the margin), the Arabic of Erpenius, Clement of Alexandria, and Lucifer. The Greek of Didymus has κσ ισ, but his Latin translation ισ, which Jerome also recognized, although he wrongly supposed that Joshua was meant. While we acknowledge that the Person who saved Israel out of Egypt was indeed the Saviour of the world, we should rather expect that He would be called the Christ (1 Cor. x. 4) than Jesus. There is a similar variation between χν, κν, and θν in the parallel passage 1 Cor. x. 9.

Lachmann alone reads Ἰησοῦς here, though Tregelles gives it a place in his margin. Westcott and Hort would be acting on their general principle if they received it, but, while setting Κύριος in the text and Ἰησοῦς in the margin, they brand the passage as corrupt, and would be inclined to believe that the original words were ὁ . . . σώσας, without either of the nouns. Dr. Hort (Notes, p. 106) points out how slight the change would be from OTIO to OTIC (one I being dropped) in the simple uncials of early times.

Fifth Series. Apocalypse.

53. Apoc. xiii. 10. Εἴ τις αἰχμαλωσίαν συνάγει, εἰς αἰχμαλωσίαν ὑπάγει. This reading of the Received text is perfectly clear; indeed, when compared with what is found in the best manuscripts, it is too simple to be true (Canon I, Chap. VIII). We read in Codd. ℵBC: ει (C) τις εις αιχμαλωσιαν υπαγει (ὑπάγῃ B), the reading also of those excellent cursives 28, 38, 79, 95, and of a manuscript of Andreas: εἰς is further omitted in 14 (*sic*), and in 92 its echo, in 32, 47, the Bohairic (?), Arabic (Polyglott), and a Slavonic manuscript: and so Tregelles in 1872. The sense of this reading, if admissible at all, is very harsh and elliptical:

that of the only remaining uncial A, though apparently unsupported except by a Slavonic manuscript and the best copies of the Vulgate (*am. fuld.* and another known to Lachmann), looks more probable: *εἴ τις εἰς αἰχμαλωσίαν, εἰς αἰχμαλωσίαν ὑπάγει*: 'if any one *is* for captivity, into captivity he goeth' (Tregelles, Kelly: the latter compares Jer. xv. 2, LXX): the second *εἰς αἰχμαλωσίαν* being omitted by Homoeoteleuton in the above-mentioned codices. Tregelles (in 1844), Lachmann, Tischendorf, Kelly, Westcott and Hort follow Cod. A, and it would seem rightly.

All other variations were devised for the purpose of supplying the ellipsis left in the uncials. For *συνάγει* of the common text (now that it is known not to be found in C) no Greek authority is expressly cited except Reuchlin's Cod. 1, after Andreas (whence it came into the text of Erasmus) and the *recent* margin of 94. The favourite form of the cursives is that printed in the Complutensian Polyglott: *εἴ τις ἔχει αἰχμαλωσίαν, ὑπάγει*, after P, 2, 6, 8, 13, 26, 27, 29, 30, 31, 37, 40, 41, 42, 48, 49, 50, 89, 90, 91, 93, 94*, 96, 97, 98, perhaps some six others, a Slavonic manuscript, Andreas in the edition of 1596. The Vulgate, the Latin version printed with the Peshitto Syriac, and Primasius in substance, read 'Qui in captivitatem duxerit, in captivitatem vadet,' but (as we stated above) *am. fuld.* (not *demid.*) and the best codices omit 'duxerit' and have 'vadit' (Syr. ܐܙܠ ... ܡܘܒܠ), *which brings the clause into accordance with Cod. A.* The Greek corresponding with the *printed* Vulgate is *εἴ τις εἰς* (33 omits *εἰς*) *αἰχμαλωσίαν* (*ὑπάγει* 87), *εἰς* (*ἐς* 87) *αἰχμαλωσίαν ὑπάγει*, 33, 35, 87. Other modes of expression (e. g. *εἴ τις αἰχμαλωτίζει εἰς αἰχμαλωσίαν ὑπάγει*, 7; *εἴ τις αἰχμαλωτιεῖ, αἰχμαλωτισθήσεται*, 18; *εἴ τις αἰχμαλωτησεῖ, εἰς αἰχ. ὑπ.* 36, &c.) resemble those already given, in their attempt to enlarge and soften what was originally abrupt and perhaps obscure.

We submit the two following as a pair of readings which, originating in the pure error of transcribers, have been adopted by eminent critics in their unreasonable and almost unreasoning admiration for Bengel's canon, 'Proclivi orationi praestat ardua.'

54. Apoc. xv. 6. In the transparently clear clause *ἐνδεδυμένοι λίνον καθαρόν* Lachmann, Tregelles in his text, Westcott and Hort,

present the variation λίθον for λίνον 'arrayed with stone,' i.e. precious stone, for which καθαρόν 'clean' would be no appropriate epithet. Dr. Hort (Notes, p. 139) justifies what he rightly calls 'the bold image expressed by this well-attested reading' by Ezek. xxviii. 13 πάντα λίθον χρηστὸν ἐνδέδεσαι (or ἐνδέδυσαι), σάρδιον καὶ τοπάζιον κ.τ.λ., but that was said of a king of Tyre, not of the angelic host. The manifestly false λίθον is only too 'well-attested' for the reputation of its advocate, AC, 38 in the margin, 48, 90, the best manuscripts of the Vulgate (*am. fuld. demid. tol. lips.*[4.5.6], &c.), though not the printed editions. Andreas knew of the variation without adopting it: Haymo and Bede also mention both readings. Cod. ℵ reads καθαροὺς λίνους with the Bohairic, and so helped to keep Tischendorf right: Tregelles sets this form in his margin. For λίνον or λινοῦν or λην- we have all the other manuscripts and other authorities, including BP, that excellent cursive Cod. 95, Primasius. Between the two forms with ν we should probably choose λινοῦν of B, [7], 14, 18, 92, 97, as λίνον seems to belong to the raw material in a rough state. The later Syriac has ܟܬܘܢܐ (χιτῶνα), which admits of no ambiguity.

55. Apoc. xviii. 3. For πέπωκε of the Received text, or πέπωκαν of Lachmann and Tischendorf, Tregelles (whose margin has πεπτώκασιν), Westcott and Hort in their text (not margin) have πέπτωκαν. Dr. Hort has no note on this place, but treats it in his index of 'Quotations from the Old Testament' as a reference to Isa. li. 17, 22 (ἡ πιοῦσα τὸ ποτήριον τῆς πτώσεως) and to Jer. xxv. 27 (πίετε καὶ μεθύσθητε ... καὶ πεσεῖσθε), with the notion of stumbling through drink. What is required to complete the parallel in some passage in the Septuagint wherein πέπτωκαν stands alone, whether τοῦ οἴνου be in the text or not, and, in the absence of such parallel, πέπτωκαν must be regarded as incredible on any evidence. Yet πέπτωκαν or the virtually identical πεπτώκασιν is found in ℵAC, in B, 7, 8, 14, 25, 27, 29, 91, 92, 94, 95 (πέπτωσι *primâ manu*), the Bohairic and Ethiopic. The alternative reading πέπωκαν or πεπώκασιν (πέπωκε 96) occurs in P, 1, 18, 31, 32, 36, 37, 38, 39, 47, 48, 49, 50, 79, 87, 90, 93, 97, 98, the Latin and later Syriac. Thus the very versions are divided in a case where the omission of a single letter produces so great a change in the sense.

56. Apoc. xxi. 6. Καὶ εἶπέ μοι, Γέγονε. ἐγώ εἰμι τὸ Α καὶ τὸ Ω. Here the true reading Γέγοναν 'They are done' (adopted, with or without εἰμι after ἐγώ, by Lachmann, Tischendorf, Tregelles, Kelly, Archdeacon Lee in the 'Speaker's Commentary,' Westcott and Hort) is preserved by Cod. A, whose excellency is very conspicuous in the Apocalypse: its compeer C is defective here. The very valuable Apoc. 38 confirms it (γεγόνασιν), as did ℵ[c], but the whole word was afterwards erased: the interpreter of Irenaeus renders *facta sunt*, and this is all the support A has. The first hand of ℵ with BP, 1, 7, 8, 11, 12, 13, 26, 27, 31, 32, 33, 35, 47, 48, 79, 87, 89, 91, 92 (*hiat* 14), 93, 96, 97, 98, the Armenian, Origen (*quod mireris*), Andreas, Arethas, with the Complutensian, read γέγονα, most of them omitting either the ἐγώ or the ἐγώ εἰμι which follows. Erasmus was too good a scholar to adopt from Apoc. 1 a meaning for γίγνομαι which it cannot possibly bear, and seems to have got his own reading Γέγονε (though he recognizes that of Apoc. 1 in his Annotations) from the Vulgate *factum est*, which is confirmed by Primasius: it probably has no Greek authority whatsoever. The Syriac printed with the Peshitto (commonly assigned to the sixth century) appears, like the hand which followed ℵ[c], to omit γέγονα, as do the Bohairic and Ethiopic versions, with *lux.* of the Vulgate. Those which read γέγονα yet retain the following ἐγώ (ℵBP, 7 and some others) obviously differ from the true reading γέγοναν by the single stroke which in uncial manuscripts was set over a letter to represent *nu*, especially at the end of a line, and so avoid the monstrous rendering necessarily implied in 1, 8, 93, 96, 97, 98, 'I have *become* alpha and omega, the first and the last.' P accordingly puts the proper stop after γέγονα.

God grant that if these studies shall have made any of us better instructed in the letter of His Holy Word, we may find grace to grow, in like measure, in that knowledge which tendeth to salvation, through faith in His mercy by Christ Jesus.

APPENDIX A.

ON SYRIAC LECTIONARIES.

A VERY interesting group of Syriac manuscripts is found in the collections of Syriac MS. Lectionaries which have descended to us. That the number of them is large may be inferred from the fact that thirty-five may be found in the British Museum alone (Catalogue, i. pp. 146–203).

Syriac Lectionaries are of two classes, (i) those according to the Greek Use, and (ii) those according to the native Syriac Use. The former, or *Malkite* Lectionaries, may be dismissed from the present enquiry. They are only Greek works in a Syriac dress, and their value is historical rather than critical [1].

The true Syriac Lectionaries, whether Jacobite or Nestorian, follow as to their main features the Greek Lectionaries which have been described in our first volume, coming under two main classes, Evangelistaries and Apostolos [2]. But they present one important contrast. In both families of Syriac descent, the Ecclesiastical year begins with Advent, and not, as in Greek Lectionaries, with Easter; and in general the arrangement is similar in both, so that the system must at least be of considerably greater antiquity than the days of the schism. In some of the Jacobite copies the text of the Harkleian revision has been substituted for the ancient Peshitto. Some include Lessons from the Old Testament. Some contain a Menology. In a few instances the Lessons for special festivals form a separate volume.

The majority of the Syriac MS. Lectionaries are comparatively late, but others possess an antiquity which, in the case of some MSS., would be considered remarkable. The British Museum copies, Add. 14,485 and 14,486, are each dated A. GR. 1135=A.D. 824. Others must be referred to the same century. Add. 14,528, foll. 152–228 (an Index), and the leaf in Add. 17,217, appear to be three centuries older. Another sixth century MS., Add. 14,455 (the Four Gospels), contains many Rubrics, a pr. m. in the text, besides those in the margins by later hands, such as occur in MSS. of all ages. When to these facts we add the consideration already mentioned, that the same system was in use in

[1] For a very full and clear account of a MS. of this class, the reader may consult an article by Prof. Isaac H. Hall in the 'Journal of the American Oriental Society,' vol. xi, No. 2, 1885.

[2] It is not meant that these terms occur as titles. *Apostolos* (ܫܠܝܚܐ) as applied to a book means the fourteen Epp. of St. Paul. *Evangeliom*, in the sense of *Evangelistary* in a title, is quoted in 'Thesaurus Syriacus.'

But many liturgical terms were borrowed from the Greeks, especially by the Maronites. For a succinct account of Greek and Latin Service Books, *see* Pelliccia's 'Polity' (tr. Bellett, 1883), pp. 183–8: for the Syriac system, *see* Etheridge's 'Syrian Churches,' pp. 112-6.

both branches of the Syrian Church, we see the importance of the testimony of works of this class. They are very ancient ecclesiastical records from the unchangeable East. Like Greek Lectionaries, they are difficult to use, because of their arrangement of Lessons in the succession ordered by the calendar: they are of course public documents, and in consequence possess an importance above that of copies which were in many cases the property of private persons, and may have been carelessly and cheaply prepared. Yet it would not be right to claim for copies of a version a position quite as important as that held by the Greek service-books, since the evidence of versions, as well as of quotations in ancient writers, is only subsidiary. Nevertheless, in the fact that the number of ancient Greek copies of the New Testament is relatively small as compared with the early copies of the Peshitto version, we are warned not to underrate Syriac Lectionaries, though they are of less value for the Syriac, on account of the large number of very ancient and well-written copies which have come down to us, such as those which have been enumerated in our account of the materials for ascertaining the text of the Peshitto.

APPENDIX B.

ADDITIONAL BOHAIRIC MANUSCRIPTS IN EGYPT (1893).

CAIRO 1 [1184] attributed and possible date, fol., *chart.*, ff. 290, 27 × 18·6 (23), κεφ., Copt. Gr., *Am.*, *Eus.*, *pict.* Evann., Copt., restored under patronage of Athanasius, Bp. of Abutij, 1794, whose statement gives date 900 of the martyrs. Dedication to monastery of St. Antony in the eastern desert; now in the library of the Patriarch in Cairo, numbered 12 and 14.

Ancient writing begins St. Matt. v. 25,
" continues to St. Luke x. 2.
" begins St. Luke x. 27,
" continues to St. Luke xxii. 52.
" begins St. Luke xxii. 66,
" continues to St. Luke xxiv. 53.
" begins St. John i. 31,
" continues to St. John xix. 24.

Cairo 2 [1291], fol., *chart.*, ff. 409, 26·9 × 18 (24, 25), κεφ., Copt. Gr., *Am.*, *Eus.*, *pict.* (pictures of SS. Mark, Luke, and John). Evann. Copt. Arab. Written by Deacon Barsuma, mended by Michael of Akhmîm, monk of monastery of Siryani (Nitrian), under patronage of Cyril, 112th Patriarch, 1878. Dedication to monastery of St. Barsuma, called Al Shahrân, 1329; now in the library of the Patriarch in Cairo, numbered

Cairo 3 [xviii], fol., *chart.*, ff. 342, 22·8 × 13 (29), *Carp.* and *Eus. t.* at end of St. Mark, *proll.*, κεφ. *t.*, κεφ., Copt. Gr., *Am.*, *Eus.*, *pict.* Evann. Copt. Arab. Written by Michael Pilatos, who gives his name in the duplicate book at Alexandria, and who wrote the Epistles and Acts below in 1714. In the library of the Patriarch in Cairo. Text same as Curzon 126.

Cairo 4 [1327], fol., *chart.*, ff. 395, 27·5 × 17·8 (27), κεφ., Copt., *Am.*, *Eus.*, *pict.* Evann. Copt. Written by Thomas. Dedication to the Church of St. Mercurius in old Cairo, where it now rests. Text of St. Matt. is same as Brit. Mus. 3381.

Cairo 5 [1257], fol., *chart.*, ff. 382, 26·4 × 19 (25), *prol.* St. Luke, Capp. Copt. *Am.*, *Eus.*, *pict.*, *mut.* Evann. Copt. Arab. *Mut.* St. Matt. i—iv. 5, St. Mark i. 1–7, St. John i. 1–21; a few leaves restored. Written by monk and priest Gabriel, who wrote in the house of Ibn 'Assâl; now in the Church of Al Moallaqah in old Cairo. Text similar to manuscript of Göttingen.

Cairo 6 [1272], fol., *chart.*, ff. 328, 24·9 × 17 and 25·7 × 18. Epilogue to St. Matt. Κεφ., Copt., *Am.*, *Eus.*, *pict.*, *mut.* Evann. Copt. St. Matt. by more recent writer. SS. Mark, Luke, and John written by original scribe, Simon Ibn Abu Nasr. Text of St. Matt. similar to Bodl. vii. In the Patriarchal Library in Cairo.

Cairo 7 [xiv], 4to, St. Luke, restored under Bp. Athanasius of Abutij. Text unimportant.

Besides several which are too late to have any critical importance.

APOCALYPSE.

1. [xix], folio.

ALEXANDRIA 1 [xviii], fol., paper, duplicate of Cairo 3, by same writer. Evann.

2. [xix], SS. Matt. and Mark.

3. [1861], St. John, Copt.

DAYR AL MOHARRAQ, nr. Manfalût on the Nile (station and telegraph Nasâli Gânûb).

1. [1345], fol., *chart.*, 22·5 × 14·2 (27), *Carp.* at end. *Mut.*, but fairly perfect, *pict.*, and richly glossed. Text unimportant. Evann. Copt. Arab.

ST. PAUL, CATH., ACTS.

1. [xii ?], probably of same date as Evann., Cairo 1, fol., *chart.*, ff. 432, 25·6 × 18·2 (24), κεφ., Copt. Gr. Thess., Heb., Tim., *pict.*, Copt.: restored Rom. and 1 Cor. i—xvi. 12, copious glosses in Arabic.

2. [xiv], fol., *chart.*, 26 × 18·5 (25), κεφ., Copt. Gr., *pict.* Philemon, Hebr., Copt.

INDEX I.

TEXTS OF THE NEW TESTAMENT ILLUSTRATED IN THIS TREATISE.

(Where the page is given alone, the reference is to the first volume. *n* indicates *note.*)

INDEX II.

OF SUBJECTS.

(N.B.—For Greek manuscripts of the N.T. consult Vol. I. Index I. For separate Fathers, see Vol. II. pp. 172–4, and for present owners of MSS., Vol. I. Index I. *n* indicates *note*.)

END OF VOL. II.

You may also enjoy ...

Wandering Between Two Worlds: Essays on Faith and Art
Anita Mathias
Benediction Books, 2007
152 pages
ISBN: 0955373700

Available from www.amazon.com, www.amazon.co.uk
www.wanderingbetweentwoworlds.com

In these wide-ranging lyrical essays, Anita Mathias writes, in lush, lovely prose, of her naughty Catholic childhood in Jamshedpur, India; her large, eccentric family in Mangalore, a sea-coast town converted by the Portuguese in the sixteenth century; her rebellion and atheism as a teenager in her Himalayan boarding school, run by German missionary nuns, St. Mary's Convent, Nainital; and her abrupt religious conversion after which she entered Mother Teresa's convent in Calcutta as a novice. Later rich, elegant essays explore the dualities of her life as a writer, mother, and Christian in the United States--Domesticity and Art, Writing and Prayer, and the experience of being "an alien and stranger" as an immigrant in America, sensing the need for roots.

About the Author

Anita Mathias was born in India, has a B.A. and M.A. in English from Somerville College, Oxford University and an M.A. in Creative Writing from the Ohio State University. Her essays have been published in The Washington Post, The London Magazine, The Virginia Quarterly Review, Commonweal, Notre Dame Magazine, America, The Christian Century, Religion Online, The Southwest Review, Contemporary Literary Criticism, New Letters, The Journal, and two of HarperSanFrancisco's The Best Spiritual Writing anthologies. Her non-fiction has won fellowships from The National Endowment for the Arts; The Minnesota State Arts Board; The Jerome Foundation, The Vermont Studio Center; The Virginia Centre for the Creative Arts, and the First Prize for the Best General Interest Article from the Catholic Press Association of the United States and Canada. Anita has taught Creative Writing at the College of William and Mary, and now lives and writes in Oxford, England.
Website: www.anitamathias.com/
Blog: wanderingbetweentwoworlds.blogspot.com/

www.ingramcontent.com/pod-product-compliance
Lightning Source LLC
Chambersburg PA
CBHW032100230426
43662CB00034B/65